NEW ZEALAND HANDBOOK

NEW ZEALAND HANDBOOK

JANE KING

Please send all comments, corrections, additions, amendments, and critiques to:

JANE KING
c/o MOON PUBLICATIONS
722 WALL STREET
CHICO, CA 95928 USA

NEW ZEALAND HANDBOOK
Second Edition

Published by
Moon Publications Inc.
722 Wall Street
Chico, California 95928 USA
tel. (916) 345-5473

Printed by
Colorcraft Ltd., Hong Kong

PRINTING HISTORY
First edition
May 1987
Reprinted
October 1987
Second Edition
March 1990

Library of Congress Cataloging in Publication Data

King, Jane, 1956-
The New Zealand Handbook / Jane King. — 2nd ed.
p. 536 cm.

Includes bibliographical references. (p. 537)
ISBN 0-918373-34-4 : $14.95
1. New Zealand—Description and travel—1981- —Guide-books.
I. Title
DU405.5.K56 1989 89-13245
919.304'37—dc20 CIP

Printed in Hong Kong

Cover art: Courtesy of New Zealand Tourist and Publicity Travel Office.

ACKNOWLEDGEMENTS

A heartfelt thank-you goes out to all the people who helped create the second edition of *New Zealand Handbook,* to the friendly New Zealanders who made each of my visits so pleasurable, and to the many readers who took time to send travel tips, suggestions, and corrections. Thank you to family and friends who continue to provide support and encouragement—and Mum, your love, concern, and those weeks we spent together during a difficult time are treasures we (including "TBB") will never forget.

Special thanks goes to my editor, Christa Jorgensen. Your patience ("I'll bring you a chapter tomorrow"), tolerance ("Urr Christa, looks like I'll be in next week"), buffering abilities ("Why was **that** removed?"), sense of humor and friendly smile, as well as editing skills were all truly appreciated! Also thanks to the entire Moon team: Magnus Bartlett, Chairman; Bill Dalton, Publisher; Mark Morris, Managing Editor; Donna Galassi, Marketing Director; Cindy Fahey, Business Manager; Dave Hurst, Production Manager/Creative Director; Bob Race, Cartographer; Asha Johnson, Computer Department/"Traffic" Manager; Rick Johnson, Royalty Management/Shipping Department; Nancy Kennedy, Format and Layout; Virginia Michaels, Publicity Manager; Beth Rhudy, Editorial Assistant; Todd Clark, Production Assistant; Lucinda Stram, Bookkeeper; Bette Wells, Sales and Promotions Coordinator; the rest of the Moon Units who directly or indirectly influenced *New Zealand Handbook 2.*

Thanks also to Carolyn Tolley, Lousie Foote, and Diana Lasich Harper for illustrations; Wayne Pease and Ellen Ramsey for photographs; Michelle Bonzey for wading through corrections. Thanks to the New Zealand Tourist and Publicity Dept. Travel Office staff throughout New Zealand and North America; the Dept. of Conservation staff of each national park for proofreading and correcting all national park chapters; and the PRO and information center staff throughout New Zealand.

Finally, a special thank you and an extra big hug for Bruce, my husband, friend, supporter, and ally, and Rachael, our "packable" and most tolerant baby daughter. May the three of us discover new horizons, follow the ends of rainbows, gaze at the stars, stop to smell the flowers, soar with the winds to new destinations and exciting adventures, and savor the great beauty of this planet—together.

ILLUSTRATION AND PHOTO CREDITS

front cover: Mount Cook and sheep; courtesy of New Zealand Tourist and Publicity Travel Office, San Francisco. **illustrations:** Louise Foote—pages 1, 5, 6, 7, 8, 13, 21, 25, 29, 31, 57, 116, 118, 119, 123, 130, 134, 136, 137, 150, 155, 174, 214, 246, 254, 273, 278, 281, 282, 284, 288, 294, 295, 299, 300, 301, 311, 315, 350, 369, 379, 393, 400, 403, 423, 430, 441, 445, 456, 461, 464, 466, 470, 478, 488, 510, 513, 519, 520, 524, 536; Carolyn Tolley—border on title page, and pages 24, 55, 175, 247, 321; Diana Lasich Harper—pages 89, 195, 215, 240, 315, 380, 407, 446, 468, 521. **black and white photos:** Bruce King—pages 11, 27, 40, 44, 59, 62, 74, 79, 92, 93, 107, 109, 110, 121, 129, 133, 147, 171, 177, 179, 183, 190, 192, 199, 201, 203, 204, 212, 217, 220, 227, 234, 237, 264, 269, 290, 292, 309, 318, 320, 347, 351, 355, 357, 360, 362, 363, 374, 377, 382, 384, 411, 414, 416, 419, 420, 422, 424, 425, 426, 437, 438, 442, 448, 450, 463, 482, 483, 485, 489, 496, 501, 505, 517, 523, 526, 527, 529, 532, 535; Jane King—pages 15, 72, 95, 97, 100, 108, 132, 141, 143, 148, 173, 181, 182, 187, 197, 210, 228, 251, 253, 259, 313, 340, 345, 353, 358, 373, 386, 418, 429, 473, 492; Ellen Ramsey—page 502; Paul Scaife, Harris Mts. Heli-Skiing, Wanaka—page 472; Ted Sturt—page 495.

IS THIS BOOK OUT OF DATE?

We have strived to produce the most well-researched and up-to-date travel guide to New Zealand available. But! Accommodations and restaurants come and go, others change hands, new attractions spring up out of nowhere, prices go up, taxes increase (12½% added to all goods and services in 1989)—and your concerned travel writer loses considerable sleep over it all! You can help. If you discover some wonderful off-the-beaten-track attractions, new places to stay and eat, have info you'd like to share, find inaccuracies or map errors, please scribble your comments into your copy of *New Zealand Handbook* and send us a synopsis when you get home. If you can improve a map, add a map of your own, or have artwork, good-quality color slides, or black-and-white prints that you'd like to see in the next edition, send them too. We need your input. All information will be checked, and if we use your artwork or photos, Moon Publications will own the publication rights but you'll be mentioned in the credits and receive a free copy of the book. Moon Publications is not responsible for unsolicited manuscripts, photos, or artwork, and unless you send return postage, cannot undertake to return them—so please keep copies. All your comments or ideas on how to make *New Zealand Handbook* better are welcomed, so grab this opportunity to get something off your chest and write to:

Jane King
c/o Moon Publications
722 Wall Street Chico
CA 95928 USA

ALL PRICES IN THIS BOOK ARE QUOTED IN NEW ZEALAND DOLLARS UNLESS OTHERWISE NOTED.

TELEPHONE NUMBERS ARE CHANGING THROUGHOUT NEW ZEALAND AT PRESENT. IF YOU GET A BUSY TONE, CALL LOCAL INFORMATION FOR POSSIBLE NEW NUMBER.

CONTENTS

SOUTH ISLAND . . 333

LIST OF MAPS

THE NORTH ISLAND

THE SOUTH ISLAND

LIST OF TABLES AND CHARTS

ABBREVIATIONS

a/c—air conditioned
B&B—bed & breakfast
C—centigrade
C.—century
D—dinner
d—double occupancy
E—east
ha—hectare
I.—island
km—kilometer
L—left
m—meter
min.—minute
N—north
OW—one way
pd—per day
pn—per night
pp—per person
R—right
RT—round trip
s—single occupancy
S—south
t—triple occupancy
tel.—telephone number
W—west

MAP LEGEND

MAIN HIGHWAYS
SECONDARY ROADS
UNPAVED ROADS
FOOT TRACKS
5 HIGHWAY NUMBER
BRIDGE
TUNNEL
STEPS
PARK
PARK BOUNDARY
NATIONAL PARK BOUNDARY
TOWNS & VILLAGES
LARGER CITIES OR TOWNS
POINT OF INTEREST
TOURIST ATTRACTION
ACCOMMODATIONS
Y.H. YOUTH HOSTEL
SKI AREA
MOUNTAIN
WATER

All maps are oriented with North at the top of the map unless otherwise noted.

INTRODUCTION

NEW ZEALAND HANDBOOK CHAPTER HEADINGS

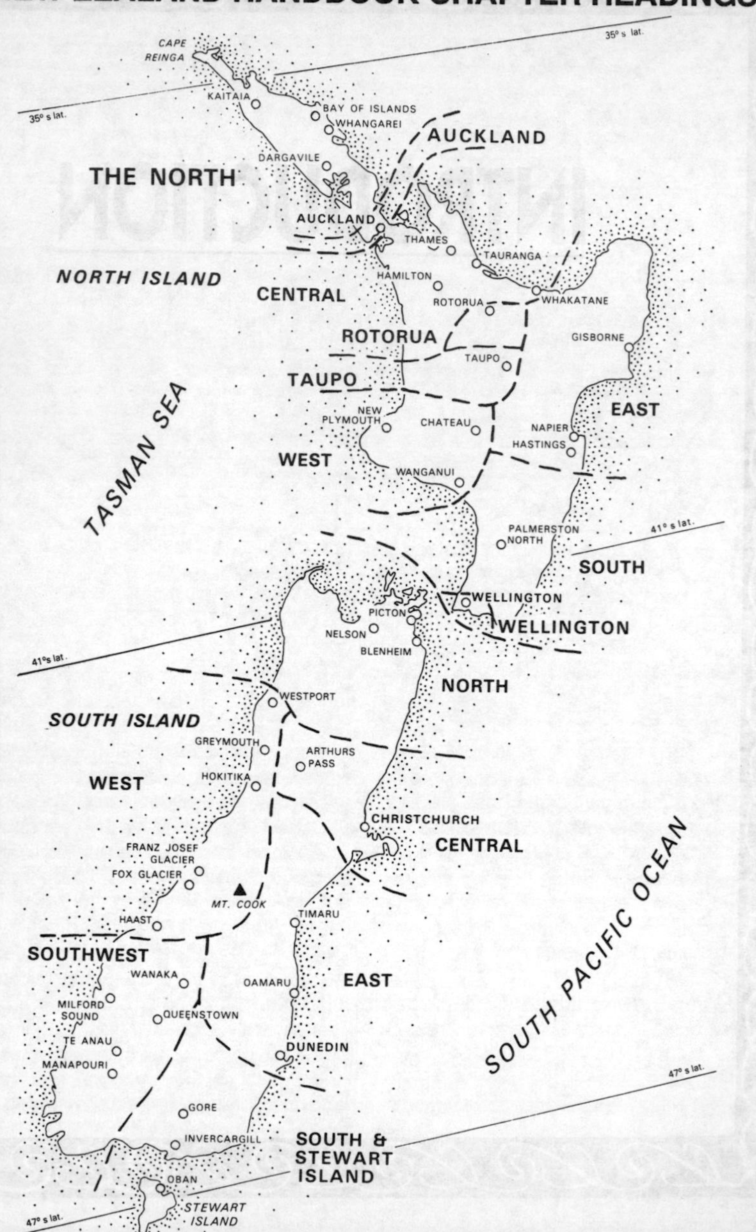

INTRODUCTION

New Zealand lies between 34 and 47 degrees south latitude and is composed of two long, narrow main islands, **North Island** (114,500 square km) and **South Island** (150,700 square km). North Island, with its golden beaches, ancient kauri forests, lakes, volcanos, thermal areas, and large cities (including Wellington, the capital), is the more densely populated. South Island, with its snowcapped mountains, glaciers, lush native bush, and fiords, is the larger of the two, proudly called "the mainland" by residents (though North Islanders are quick to disagree!). Tiny **Stewart Island** (1,750 square km), an unspoiled, bird-filled bush and beach paradise at the foot of the South Island, is the closest most people ever get to the Antarctic. Also within New Zealand's territorial jurisdiction lie several small island groups including the Chatham, Kermadec, and Tokelau Islands, Campbell I., Auckland, Antipodes, Snares, Solander, and Bounty Islands, and Ross Dependency, Antarctica.

Surrounded by South Pacific Ocean on the east and Tasman Sea on the west, New Zealand appears to be a mere speck on the globe, and yet it's about 1,770 km from top to bottom—similar in size to the British Isles or Japan. Australia, 2,092 km northwest, is New Zealand's closest neighbor, and due to this relative proximity the two countries are often mistakenly believed to be one. But beware! To innocently suggest this to "Kiwis" (as New Zealanders like to call themselves) is to risk running afoul of their good natures! New Zealand is an independent self-governing nation.

THE LAND

An Ancient Country

Around 150 million years ago New Zealand was just a small part of the supercontinent called Gondwanaland, consisting of present-day Australia, Antarctica, India, Africa, and South America. About 70 million years ago, New Zealand separated from Australia and Antarctica. Geographically isolated and uninhabited by humans until A.D. 700 (at the earliest), New Zealand reveals its unique natural history in its unusual animals and plants which have long since disappeared elsewhere.

The Pacific and Indian-Australian tectonic plates meet along a line of collision that runs through present-day New Zealand, causing the Taupo Volcanic Zone in the North Island and Alpine Fault in the South Island. Recently, a deep-sea survey revealed that a new continent is gradually being created on New Zealand's east coast. As the Pacific Ocean crust plunges under the eastern North Island, thick slabs of sea sand and mud are scraped off in huge wedges and slowly pasted to the offshore edge, forming a series of ridges along the coast between East Cape and Kaikoura.

PACIFIC & INDIAN-AUSTRALIAN PLATES

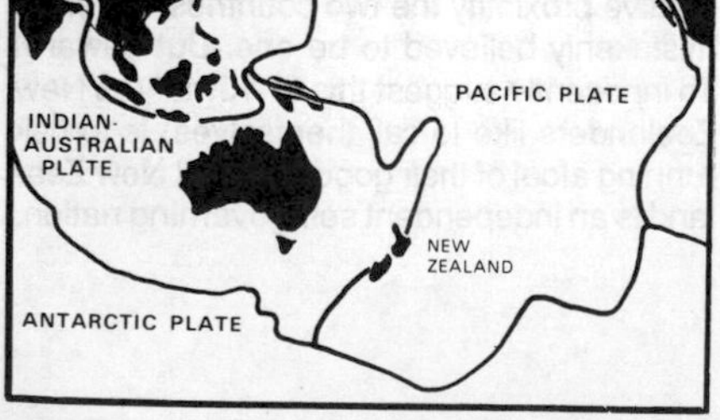

Volcanos

The North Island produces enough boiling water and steam to fill all the jacuzzis and saunas in the galaxy—or at least Los Angeles! Volcanic and geothermal areas smolder along the Taupo Volcanic Zone from the Bay of Plenty to the central North Island. Three volcanos dominate this area: **Mt. Ruapehu** and **Mt. Ngauruhoe,** both active, and dormant **Mt. Tongariro.** About 50 km offshore from Whakatane in the Bay of Plenty lies **White I.,** an active volcano often obscured by clouds of steam. Discovered and named by Capt. Cook in 1769, White I. erupts ash intermittently to this day. On the west coast the dormant cone of **Mt. Egmont** towers over the Taranaki Volcanic Zone, and farther north, both Auckland and the Bay of Islands are classified as separate volcanic zones. The waters of **Lake Taupo** lie in an enormous deep crater in the center of the North Island—the area has a violent history of volcanic eruptions, though the last one was 1,861 years ago. No volcanos active within the last 2,000 years are found on the South Island, but you can see remains of the colossal twin volcanos that formed Banks Peninsula, south of Christchurch.

Mountains, Glaciers, And Lakes

Although the North Island has impressive volcanos and mighty Lake Taupo, the South Island is really the place to go for snow-capped mountain scenery and picture-perfect lakes. Most of New Zealand is at least 200 meters above sea level, but the tallest peak, **Mt. Cook** (3,764 meters), is found amongst the magnificent **Southern Alps,** spine of the South Island. Spectacular glaciers are scattered throughout the landscape—the mighty **Fox** and **Franz Josef** are still easily accessible from the main route down the West Coast. In other areas of the South Island are U-shaped valleys, moraines, and deep lakes left behind by glaciers of earlier ice ages. New Zealand's numerous lakes vary greatly in size and depth, many of the largest concentrated in the South Island, fed by glaciers and snow packs of the Southern Alps. Many fast-flowing rivers and meandering streams follow the contours of the land. Extensive flat plains of rich alluvial soil deposited by these rivers provide plenty of valuable agricultural land; vast gravel plains, such as those found in the South Canterbury region of the South Island, are predominantly used as sheep country.

The Coastline

New Zealand's coastline offers a bit of everything. In some areas sand stretches as far as the eye can see, such as **Ninety Mile Beach** at the tip of the North Island; in other areas, deep coves and sheltered bays dotted with tiny islands fringe the coast, such as those found in the **Bay of Islands** in the northeast of the North Island, and **Marlborough Sounds** at the South Island's northern tip. The west coast of the South Island is lined with rocky cliffs, blowholes, caves, and rugged surf beaches where seals haul themselves ashore; in the far southwest corner, 14 magnificent fiords deeply indent the coastline, and along a small section of the east coast, several sandy beaches are strewn with large, unique, perfectly circular boulders. For sandy beaches and warm, aquamarine waters, stay in the north; for rugged surf-swept beaches, intriguing rock formations, and deep, mirror-surfaced fiords, head south.

Parks

Covering more than 2.1 million hectares of the country, 12 of New Zealand's most beautiful areas have been set aside for total preservation in their natural state and designated national parks. They offer vast areas of untouched wilderness where hikers, mountaineers, anglers, hunters, and flora and fauna enthusiasts are in their element. In the North Island lie **Urewera, Tongariro, Egmont,** and **Whanganui national parks;** in the South Island, **Abel Tasman, Nelson Lakes, Arthur's Pass, Westland, Paparoa, Mount Cook, Mount Aspiring,** and **Fiordland national parks.** Three maritime parks, **Bay of Islands** and **Hauraki Gulf maritime parks** in the North Island and **Marlborough Sounds Maritime Park** in the South Island preserve some of the most spectacular and accessible coastal scenery, and 19 forest parks, used for conservation, recreation, and timber production, contain some of the best bush scenery in the country.

All the national parks, reserves, forest parks, and state forests are under the jurisdiction of the Department of Conservation, created on 1 April 1987 by the Conservation Act. The department manages the land and wildlife for conservation purposes, promotes the conservation of natural and historic resources, produces educational and promotional material, and fosters recreation and tourism in conjunction with conservation. For more info write to the Information Officer, Dept. of Conservation, Central Office, P.O. Box 10-420, Wellington, or call (04) 710-726.

CLIMATE

New Zealand has an oceanic, temperate climate; although it varies from subtropical in the north to almost subarctic in the mountainous areas of the south, overall it's relatively mild. Seasonal variations are not pronounced: summers never get uncomfortably hot; winters are mild, with snow usually confined to the high country and southern lowlands. Rainfall levels vary throughout New Zealand; winter tends to be the wettest season—but not so wet that it should be avoided. If you're coming from the Northern Hemisphere, keep in mind that the seasons are opposite—spring is Sept. through Nov., summer Dec. through Feb., autumn March through May, and winter June through August.

North Island

The North Island tends to be warmer and drier than the South Island, though the highest mountain peaks often have snow yearround. It has an average rainfall of 130 cm and prevailing westerly winds. **Auckland** (where most visitors enter New Zealand) averages a summer temperature of 23 degrees C and a winter temperature of 14 degrees. **Wellington,** perched on the edge of Cook Strait, generally receives slightly colder weather with temperatures ranging from 26 degrees C in summer to 2 degrees C in winter. The capital also has a reputation for windy weather, at times making the ferry trip between the two main islands unforgettably rough!

South Island

The differences in temperature and weather in each area are more pronounced in the South Island. The pressure systems travel west to east (the Southern Alps have a noticeable "wet" and "dry" side), the lows dumping considerable rain and cold temperatures on the west side of the mountains; snow is a permanent fixture on the highest peaks. On the east side of the Southern Alps the rainfall can be as low as 30 cm and temperatures are a good deal warmer. On the east coast, **Christchurch** averages temperatures in the low 20s C in summer and low teens in winter. **Dunedin,** farther south, averages 19 degrees C in summer and 10 degrees C in winter, and **Invercargill,** New Zealand's southernmost city, experiences slightly colder temperatures. Snow is relatively common in the southern lowlands as well as the higher hills, and is occasionally seen even at sea level.

Mountain Weather

As the mountains generally run north-south and the pressure systems move west-east, the worst weather hits the highest barrier—the Southern Alps. Rivers and streams can flood rapidly from snow melt and rain, avalanche risks increase dramatically, and temperatures drop quickly. Watch for an increase in wind strength and the formation of large sheets of cloud. Also watch for clouds gathering over the lee side of the ranges—and expect rain. Gale-force winds, snow, or bliz-

AVERAGE DAILY TEMPERATURES (MAX) AND ANNUAL RAINFALL

Locality	Midsummer	Midwinter	Rainfall (mm)
NORTH ISLAND			
Bay of Islands	25 C	15 C	1648
Auckland	23 C	14 C	1268
Rotorua	23 C	12 C	1511
Napier	24 C	13 C	780
Wellington	20 C	11 C	1271
SOUTH ISLAND			
Nelson	22 C	12 C	999
Christchurch	22 C	12 C	658
Queenstown	22 C	8 C	849
Dunedin	19 C	10 C	772
Invercargill	18 C	9 C	1042

zards can come with these storms at *any time of year* in the mountains. The N.Z. Mountain Safety Council suggests three important rules to follow: be aware of approaching bad weather (expect it in the mountains), be adequately prepared with warm, wind- and waterproof clothing, and don't cross flooded rivers—wait until they subside (generally as quickly as they flood). For detailed weather forecasts, check the newspaper or tune in to local radio or TV stations. If you're in a national park, park HQ usually has the latest local weather forecast.

Clothing To Suit The Climate

If you're traveling clear around the country you're sure to bump into most types of weather—and even if you're staying in one area, the weather still changes rapidly. The safest policy is to be equipped for everything, no matter the season. Wear layers of clothing (shirt, sweater, and windproof jacket) to strip off and replace as needed. Wet-weather gear, a warm windproof jacket, wool sweater or cardigan, bathing suit, and comfortable footwear (hiking boots if you're venturing off the beaten track) are essentials at all times of year. (For more clothing tips, see "What To Take," p. 39.)

FLORA

The Bush

New Zealand's long isolation from other continents is responsible for some unique developments in both plant and animal life. Prior to the arrival of mankind, much of the country was covered in dense tangled forests and heavy undergrowth alive with native birds, many flightless. With the introduction of grazing animals, much of the undergrowth was thinned out, the forests were felled by early settlers, and introduced predators chased many unique birds into extinction. Today, the remaining native forests are lush wonderlands of subtropical appearance. Ferns, mosses, and lichens carpet the floor, tree ferns grow up to 10 meters high, and twining creepers, nikau palms, palm lilies, tree ferns, and many species of native trees intermingle to form a dense green canopy overhead—called "the bush" by New Zealanders. For fern lovers (one of the country's national emblems), New Zealand is a delight. They seem to grow everywhere—on trees, along rivers and streams, on hillsides, and in open areas, and the more than 150 species range in size from filmy two-cm ferns to impressive 15-meter tree ferns.

tree fern

Trees

Altogether 112 native tree species can be found in New Zealand amongst the dense undergrowth and large areas of scrub (mainly *manuka* or tea-tree). A few ancient kauri pine *(Agathis australis)* forests can still be appreciated on the North Island, growing naturally only north of latitude 39 degrees south. These magnificent trees grow up to 53 meters high, losing their lower branches to become long bare cylinders of intricate design with large bushy tops. They were the favorites of the forest for Maori war canoes—a vast canoe could be chiseled out of one tree trunk. Unfortunately, they were also the favorites of early shipbuilders and settlers who rapidly depleted the forests without much thought to the future—the kauri takes about 800 years to mature. Nowadays, these impressive trees can be seen in relatively few areas, towering above the other trees in small groves or randomly in the bush. Two areas in Northland, northwest of Dargaville, are worth a special visit just to see these giants—**Waipoua Forest Park,** with two very famous trees (one is estimated to be at least 2,000 years old), and the small but beautiful **Trounson Kauri Park.**

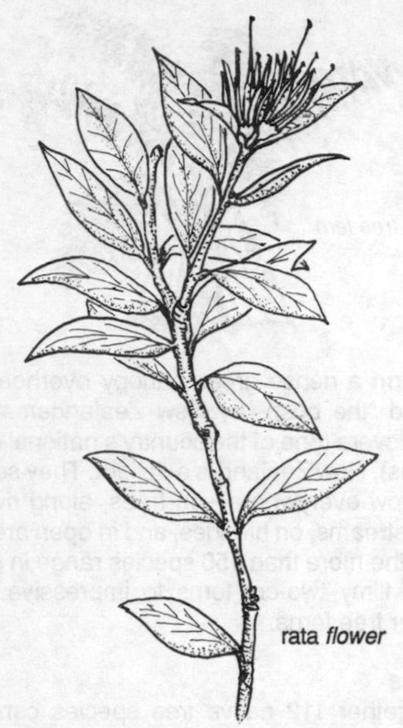
rata *flower*

Most of New Zealand's flowers are white or cream. However, native flowering trees and shrubs add red and yellow highlights to the evergreen flora of New Zealand. A few of the most spectacular flowering trees are the *pohutukawa, rata,* and *kowhai*. The striking *pohutukawa (Metrosideros tomentosa),* or New Zealand Christmas tree, is a mass of scarlet flowers in December. The *rata (Metrosideros robusta),* another vividly colored tree also covered in red blossoms, is initially a parasitic vine, growing up a host tree (often strangling it) until it has grown roots and become a tree in its own right. The bright yellow hanging blossoms of the *kowhai (Sophora tetraphera)* can be seen in all their glory during spring. Large beech *(Nothofagus)* forests with little undergrowth cover upland areas, and vast areas of land throughout New Zealand have been planted with exotic trees for timber purposes, thus saving the remaining indigenous trees. The most common non-native tree is the radiata pine. It flourishes here, growing to complete maturity within 35 years—a popular tree with the timber industry.

Flowers

At least three-quarters of New Zealand's flowering plants are endemic. Orchids are abundant, adding multihued splashes of color to the landscape. About 60 different species thrive in the lowland forests and countless beautiful parks and gardens. The alpine flowers are vastly different from those of other countries, with about 500 species of flowering plants found only in New Zealand's alpine areas. Large, white mountain daisies (Genus *Celmisia*) are the most common; the beautiful Mount Cook Lily (*Ranunculus lyallii*) is the largest of the buttercups. A rather strange growth called vegetable sheep (*Raoulia eximia*), a large, low-to-the-ground, cushion-like plant covered in white hairs, grows only in the South Island and is easily mistaken for a sheep from a distance! Apart from the abundance of native wildflowers, New Zealanders also take great pride in their gardens. If you're a flower fancier, take a stroll through any of the city suburbs (particularly Hamilton, Cambridge, New Plymouth, Napier, and Christchurch) to see a great variety of both indigenous and exotic plantlife, tended with obvious TLC (most New Zealanders are born with green thumbs!). Botanical gardens, reserves, and beautiful parks (called "domains") are found in most cities, and are highly recommended as part of any walking tour.

FAUNA

Birds

Until humans arrived these islands had no native land animals, except for two species of bat discovered by early settlers. However, the country was alive with birds, no less than 250 species. A perfect balance of nature existed between vegetation and birdlife, but when humans set foot on the islands they brought rats, cats, and introduced mammals and birds. Many native birds, unable to adapt to the foreign predators, became extinct. Native birds in the forest today include the *tui* (with its beautiful song), bellbird (its crystal-clear call is like the ping-pong of a door bell), fantail, *kea, kaka, pukeko, morepork,* and wood pigeon. The *kaka* is a shy, brown and

BIRDS OF NEW ZEALAND

western weka

kingfisher

whitehead

kiwi

kaka

morepork

bellbird

silvereye

green parrot. The *kea,* a dull brownish-green parrot with red underwings and a hooked beak, lives in the high country and is commonly seen in the Southern Alps where it scavenges around campsites. Cheeky and daring, it can cause a lot of damage to tents, boots, bicycle seats, or anything it can tear with its strong beak, and has the reputation for sliding down the iron roofs of alpine huts in the wee hours of the morning!

The *takahe,* a rare bird unique to New Zealand, is found mainly in Southern Fiordland. Large, flightless, blue and green with red feet and bill, it was thought to be extinct until a small colony was rediscovered in 1948. Since then, 120 *takahes* have been found and are now protected in a restricted area in the Murchison Mountains. Probably the best-known creature of New Zealand is the nocturnal kiwi, a flightless bird found nowhere else in the world—the national emblem of New Zealand. It has a round body covered in dense, stiff feathers (looks like shaggy fur from a distance), strong legs (kicks out when frightened), no tail, tiny invisible wings, a long beak, and a piercing call—"ki-wi." It's not easy to find a kiwi in the bush, but in the many excellent nocturnal houses throughout the country they can be seen in a simulated natural environment.

sika deer

The *weka,* another flightless bird, is as bold as the *kea* but not as common. Found in the west coast forests of the South Island and the Gisborne area of the North Island, it also helps itself to the food and property of campers. Introduced birds include the blackbird, thrush, magpie, chaffinch, sparrow, skylark, myna, white-eye, and goldfinch.

Fish, Insects, And Reptiles

Known for its excellent fishing (fly and lure), angling enthusiasts come from around the world to dangle their lines in the lakes and rivers of New Zealand, where fish grow to a healthy size and braggable weight, and put up an admirable fight. Brown and rainbow trout, salmon, and char are the best-known freshwater fish. Brown trout are widespread and common; rainbow are more common in North Island lakes, but also occur in many upland lakes of the South Island. Deep-sea fishing for marlin, sharks, and tuna is a popular sport in the Bay of Islands.

Of all the numerous forms of insect life found throughout the country, one of the most audible is the cicada. Twenty or so species of cicada exist in New Zealand, mostly above the timberline. Often mistaken for crickets, their song in the summer heat is an incredibly loud, raspy, clicking noise—one that seems to intensify in the evening hours—a distinct part of the summer atmosphere in New Zealand. The *tuatara,* a lizard-like reptile, is only found on about 30 islands off the country's coast (see a live one in the Southland Centennial Museum Tuatarium in Invercargill). It is believed to live at least 100 years, has a distinctly prehistoric appearance, and is often referred to as a "living fossil."

Animals

The *wild* animals in New Zealand are descended from pigs, goats, opossums, rabbits, weasels, ferrets, and deer released by European settlers. Some of these—especially deer, rabbits, goats, and opossums—

adapted to their new environment so well that they rapidly became an environmental problem and had to be drastically hunted to control their populations. Many domestic animals also adapted well to New Zealand, and play a large part in the success of the country's economy. Sheep (more than 68 million of which dot the countryside—roughly 20 sheep for every resident), cattle, and poultry are of prime importance.

Out of eight species of deer, the red deer is the most common and widespread. When first released they had an abundant food supply (rapidly destroying the native forest undergrowth) and no predators, and their numbers increased rapidly. Commercial hunting from helicopters began in the 1960s, followed by profitable heli-hunting with live capture for deer farms. Hunting is still encouraged, but in recent years controlled deer farming for antler velvet, meat, and breeding stock has become a valuable part of the economy. The largest alpine mammals are tahr and chamois, distantly related to the goat. Excellent rock climbers, they are hunted for trophies.

HISTORY

The Moa-hunters

Exactly when the first Polynesians arrived in New Zealand is still unknown. Maori legends claim the Polynesian navigator Kupe first sighted New Zealand in the 10th C., naming it Aotearoa, "Land of the Long White Cloud" (one of many translations), but archaeological evidence suggests that an archaic Maori population originating in Polynesia may have been established in New Zealand as early as A.D. 700. The first arrivals were hunters—stalking flightless birds, predominantly the large emu-like moa (now extinct)—gatherers, and excellent fishermen. No evidence suggests that the moa-hunters were a warrior society. Their camps were originally concentrated in the South Island, but by the 12th C. they also inhabited the North Island.

Classic Maori Society

By the 13th and 14th centuries, a new kind of Polynesian culture began to replace moa-hunter society. Dwindling moa caused an increasing dependence on other fowl and fish. Legends speak of the arrival at this time of East Polynesians and the "Great Migration" of the 14th century. They came from the Society Island Group (Hawaiiki of Maori legends) where over-population, food shortages, and war had been a part of everyday life. Crossing the Pacific in many large canoes, it is from these legendary canoe voyagers that most present-day Maori claim their descent. With the new arrivals came a change in lifestyle. About 40 tribes developed, each a territorially based social unit; subtribes were based on kinship and ancestral descent. Cultivation of the fleshy *kumara* (sweet potato) became important; since the kumara needed warmth and sunshine to flourish, the Maori spread to the north of the North Island.

The new Polynesian culture placed great emphasis on a strict warrior code. The Maori took pride in being fierce warriors. *Pa* (fortified villages) were skillfully built on top of hills or ridges, with at least one side blocked by a natural barrier such as a river or the sea; fences and trenches further protected the thatched cottages within from enemy attack. *Mana* (prestige) and *utu* (retribution) were important qualities. If one Maori insulted another, the offended family would demand *utu*, eventually leading to war.

The focus of community life was the *marae* (central square) in front of the large, intricately carved meeting house (today the term also covers the meeting house itself and any auxiliary buildings). Maori leaders were usually hereditary chiefs or priests. The people were governed by strong family loyalties, and religious beliefs and traditions. *Tapu* (sacred) was a positive force from the gods—certain places, acts, and people were *tapu*. Noa was the opposing negative or evil force; together these elements regulated every area of Maori life.

To the Maori, all nature was alive and had magic or supernatural powers; the people lived in harmony with the land, respecting it as property of the gods. They had many gods; different gods looked after such things as the sea, forests, and crops. With no written language, their tribal history was passed on through song and dance, story-telling, and arts and crafts. They were (and still are) excellent craftsmen, expressing great symbolism in their intricate, decorative carvings. Rituals were another important part of life. Some, such as offering the first fish of a catch to Tangaroa and first bird to Tanemahuta, have been continued, and those associated with traditional arts such as weaving and carving, and Maori ceremonial gatherings, are strictly maintained and an integral part of society today.

European Discovery

The Dutch navigator, Abel Tasman, is believed to have been the first European to discover "Aotearoa" in 1642. Searching for a great unknown continent in the South Pacific for trade purposes, he stumbled across the west coast of the South Island. He named the new land "Staten Landt" to honor the States-General of the United Netherlands, and because he thought it could be connected with Staten Landt, an island off the tip of South America. Tasman's theory was disproved within the year, and the name was changed to "Nieuw Zeeland"—no doubt after the Dutch island province of Zeeland. In one encounter with the Maori, several of his men were killed, and Tasman sailed away disillusioned by the lack of friendly trading prospects.

Captain James Cook—from a 1784 engraving of the portait by Nathaniel Dance

In 1769 the British navigator, Capt. James Cook, landed on the east coast of the North Island. He was also in search of the vast unknown continent, but for scientific purposes. On arrival at Gisborne, Cook also had misunderstandings with the natives which led to bloodshed, but he persevered, circumnavigating both islands, charting the coastline in great detail, and concluding that most Maori were helpful and friendly. Cook took possession of "New Zealand" for Britain, and New Zealand became known to the world. Many French explorers followed Cook, some for scientific reasons, some for trade.

Whalers And Sealers

Within 30 years of Cook's discovery, other Europeans were sailing to New Zealand shores, and a period of great exploitation began. Whaling stations sprang up around the coast, sealers slaughtered the colonies along the southern shores (almost to extinction), and the magnificent kauri trees were drastically logged for ship-building purposes. Trade in whale oil, seal skins, timber, and flax began with New South Wales in Australia. In the late 1820s, Kororareka (now called Russell) in the Bay of Islands became the first European settlement—a refuge for whalers, sealers, adventurers, and escaped Australian convicts, it earned the name "Hell-hole of the Pacific." With the traders came disease, alcohol, and muskets, all of which had devastating impact on the Maori.

Intertribal Wars

The musket was of great interest to Maori warriors, and quickly became a coveted wea-

The Treaty House at Waitangi

pon. They welcomed the traders and their muskets and Maori society was irrevocably changed. Hongi Hika, chief of the Northland Ngapuhi tribe, was the first to recognize the weapon's potential. He, followed by other great chiefs, slaughtered many rival tribes throughout the North Island with its aid. As the wars spread to the south, many tribes began trading for muskets, eventually equalizing the balance of power. With the realization in the 1830s that the weapon was annihilating the Maori race, the intertribal wars gradually ended.

Colonization

Missionaries of many denominations spent the early 1800s establishing missions. Many recognized the exploitation of the Maori by the Pakeha (white man) and tried to protect them. They also taught the Maori the latest European agricultural techniques. Until 1832 there had been no law and order in New Zealand. James Busby, a New South Wales civil servant, was the first to be sent over from Australia as "British Resident" to protect the Maori from further exploitation and establish some order. Busby had an impossible task and no police; he became known as "a man-of-war without guns." When he proved ineffective, Capt. William Hobson was sent over from Britain in 1840 to be Lieutenant-Governor, to unite the Maori chiefs with Britain by extending British sovereignty to New Zealand. On 6 February 1840, Hobson, representatives of the Crown, and a number of leading Maori chiefs signed "The Treaty of Waitangi." New Zealand became a British colony. Though this made land available for European settlement, it also specified that all property belonged to the Maori and guaranteed that it could not be taken without their consent and/or payment. It gave them the "rights and privileges of British subjects." Though meant to protect the Maori, it later became obvious that they had not fully understood the treaty they had signed. Colonists began flooding into the new country.

The Land Wars

The early Europeans found the concept of Maori land use and ownership hard to comprehend. The *kumara* fields and burial grounds made sense, but *tapu* areas, and land specifically designated for fishing and hunting, were considered a waste of good agricultural land. The land belonged to entire tribal groups and consent for a change in ownership had to be agreed by all—new occupation had previously occurred only by conquest. At first the Maori were eager to "sell" their land (they thought they were selling the "shadow of the land" like a lease) for money and alcohol. However, the growing number of colonists demanding land put increasing pressure on the Maori, and the ideals of the Waitangi Treaty were soon overlooked. As the European population grew and the Maori became increasingly reluctant to sell land, antagonism also grew. Fighting broke out in 1843, and continued sporadically as more settlements were established. Between 1860 and the early 1880s, war raged between the Maori tribal chiefs and government troops over land purchase (even the Maori were divided—some tribes joined the government side to even old scores with rival tribes), and the fighting spread across the central regions of the North Island.

The Maori lacked any kind of unifying nationalism, and tradition forced them to prove they were the best fighters; against artillery, they had no chance. Ancestral land was confiscated from "rebel tribes" and given as a reward to "friendly tribes" (further destroying unity) and to military settlers who fought for the government, or sold to recoup some of the cost of the wars. In 1862, Land Courts forced the Maori to name 10 owners, and then only one owner of each block of land—this destroyed any remaining unity and made it relatively easy for crooked land agents to buy the land for less than its worth with money or alcohol. Traders deliberately let the Maori run into debt, forcing them to sell or go to jail. By 1982 only 4.5 million hectares of land remained under Maori ownership—some of it leased to settlers, the rest too rugged to be useful.

Wool And Gold

While the North was at war, the South Island forged ahead. The small Maori population was still eager to sell land. Settlement spread rapidly and many large sheep runs were established on the vast areas of tussockland. Thousands of sheep, predominantly merino for their fine wool, were shipped from Australia. Between 1850 and 1880, many Australian squatters came over to lease large areas of tussockland for their flocks. This became known as the "wool period." However, sheep scab came with the Australian flocks, causing the death of thousands of sheep, and in the 1860s, a plague of rabbits forced many runholders into abandonment and bankruptcy. Some turned to rabbiting as the export in rabbit skins soared.

In 1861, gold was discovered in the South Island's Otago district. The rush lasted for less than a decade, but for those years the Shotover River became "the richest river in the world," soon followed by the Arrow River. The discovery attracted thousands of miners from the goldfields of California and Australia, further stimulating growth and establishing the south as a commercial and industrial center. Railways and roads were built. After the rush in Otago, miners moved to the west coast where Hokitika temporarily became a busy port.

Administration

Auckland had been chosen as the capital in 1840, and Wellington, New Plymouth, Nelson, Dunedin, and Christchurch were founded over the next 10 years. In 1852 direct rule from Britain ended, marking the beginning of "self-government." New Zealand's central government was made up of a Governor appointed by London, a Legislative Council appointed by the Governor, and a House of Representatives elected by the people. The country was divided into six provinces—Auckland, New Plymouth, Wellington, Nelson, Canterbury, and Otago, each with its own government. In 1865, Wellington replaced Auckland as capital of New Zealand, and by 1873, four more provinces had been added—Hawke's Bay, Marlborough, Westland, and Southland.

Trade

In 1882 refrigeration was introduced, causing a major change in farming. Many of the big wool runs were abandoned as farmers recognized new export possibilities. Many turned to meat and dairy production. The high country became the merino area for wool production, the hill country became lamb breeding land, and fat-lamb farms were developed to breed lambs specifically for export. With the introduction of refrigerated cargo ships, Britain and Europe became eager consumers of the meat, and New Zealand entered the overseas market as a major food producer.

Twentieth Century

The 20th C. became the era of advanced social legislation. Two major political groups, the Liberal and Labour parties, emerged in 1890. The Liberal Party held power until 1912, introducing many changes in social legislation. Their first landmark legislation was the introduction of the Old Age Pension. New Zealand was the first country in the world to give women the vote (1893). In 1894 the world's first form of compulsory state arbitration for industrial disputes was introduced. The Liberals successfully combined capitalism with socialism, and New Zealand became a country of progressive social policies. With the interruption of WW I and the following Depression, it was not until the first Labour government in 1935 that New Zealand again took up the social welfare banner. The Social Security Act was introduced, guaranteeing free health care, education, and welfare benefits for all. Sickness pensions, low-cost housing, and a 40-hour work week were introduced over the years, and in 1972, the Accident Compensation Act was passed, insuring all people against accidental injury. These were the foundations of New Zealand's modern welfare state.

World Wars

During WW I, New Zealand sent 100,000 troops to support Britain—16,000 were killed, 45,000 wounded in action. After WW I, New Zealand became a member of the League of Nations. In WW II, 150,000 New Zealanders joined the Allied War effort; more than 11,000 were killed and 17,000 wounded. After WW II, ties with "the mother country" weakened. New Zealand claimed full independence in 1947. For most of the years between 1949 and 1978, the National Party held power. National and Labour have been the two major parties in recent years.

Modern Maori

The Maori population grew rapidly with improved health opportunities and social education, but the adjustment to urban life further weakened Maori culture. By 1962 the Maori annual growth rate was more than twice the Pakeha rate—and one of the highest in the world. Pakeha had to adjust to an increasingly assertive, fast-growing Maori and Polynesian population. For years New Zealand has been promoted as a country of racial harmony, though there's considerable unrest and ongoing land disputes between some Maori and Pakeha—problems that date back to the Treaty of Waitangi. Today New Zealanders are showing a renewed interest in *Maoritanga*—the Maori way of life. The language, arts and crafts, and song and dance are being taught in schools all over the land, and many Maori are looking back to the ways of their ancestors, searching for their identity and regaining a culture till recently submerged in the ways of the Pakeha.

Maori carving

GOVERNMENT

New Zealand is a sovereign independent state, its government based on the British parliamentary system. The Head of State, Queen Elizabeth II of Britain, is represented in New Zealand by a resident **Governor General.** Appointed for five years, he's advised by the Ministers of Cabinet.

Since 1950, the New Zealand Parliament has had only one chamber, the **House of Representatives.** Made up of 92 members, this number includes four Maori members elected by the Maori population. The House of Representatives is primarily responsible for keeping the government in check; no tax or expenditure can be made until the proposed bill has been read, debated, and authorized. The final authorization is made by the Governor General, and if approved by all these channels, the bill becomes law. The **National (Conservative), Labour,** and **Social Credit Political League** are the three political parties in the House of Representatives. Elections occur every three years, but a government may request an earlier election to vote on a topic of national importance. The party that wins the most seats becomes government; its leader automatically becomes **Prime Minister.** The leader of the other major party is called the Leader of the Opposition. At present the Labour Party is in its second term of office. The **cabinet** is made up of the Prime Minister and selected ministers of his party; they form policy, promote legislation, and become the heads of the **Departments of State.** Cabinet ministers and other government members are together called the **Caucus.**

The 40 or so government departments are staffed by members of the **Public Service** who retain their jobs despite government changes. The departments provide services for the country: mail, telephone, media, transportation, education, finance, health, housing, etc. **Local government** consists of county, borough, and district councils, special-purpose bodies, and regional government. The **High Court** deals with major crimes, important claims, and appeals, **Lower** or **District Courts** deal with all minor offenses, and **Family Courts** deal with most family matters and divorce proceedings.

The voting age is eighteen. In 1893 New Zealand became the first country in the world to give women the right to vote. Registration to vote became compulsory in 1924—though not obliged to actually vote, more than 80% usually do.

ECONOMY

New Zealand's major source of income comes from agriculture. Advanced techniques have been developed to utilize the country's rugged land, including specially designed aircraft to replace land machinery. Many areas are highly mechanized. About 50% of total export income comes from meat, dairy products, and wool; the land supports some 68 million sheep and 4.6 million beef cattle. New Zealand is one of the world's largest exporters of lamb and mutton, has a growing beef industry (about 75% of which is produced in the North Island), and supplies about 90 countries with meat (the major markets are the U.K., Iran, Russia, Japan, U.S., and Canada). New Zealand is also one of the largest and most efficient exporters of dairy products. The combination of a good growing climate, stable rainfall, and lush grass year-round has produced an average herd of about 120 cows; most of the 3.3 million dairy cows in the country are jerseys (that's one cow per person!). Butter and cheddar cheese are the major dairy exports, but casein and skim-milk powder are also in demand. New Zealand's rich and creamy dairy products are among the best in the world—one taste and you'll be convinced!

Sheep

Sheep are a predominant part of the landscape throughout the whole of New Zealand—in fact, it's almost impossible to take a landscape photo without getting some sheep in it! New Zealand is the third largest producer and second largest exporter of wool in the world, with an average flock of about 1,800 sheep. In North Island hill country, sheep are farmed for their wool; the fertile lowland farms (up to 25 sheep per hectare) specialize in lamb and mutton production. Teams of sheepshearers travel around the country from woolshed to woolshed, many shearing more than 200 sheep each a day (don't miss any opportunity to watch shearers in action—their speed and dexterity are really something!). Most of the medium-to-coarse crossbred wool used for carpetmaking and knitting yarn comes from romney sheep; the fine wool used for soft fabrics and high-quality yarn comes from merino sheep. High-quality sheepskins are a popular tourist purchase.

Crops And Fruit

Most of the crops—wheat, barley, maize, oats, vegetables, berry fruit, and tobacco—are grown for the local market. However, malting barley, herbage seeds, some herbs, and oilseed rape have become export crops. The citrus export industry is growing in leaps and bounds as kiwifruit, tamarillos, feijoas, and passionfruit are becoming more popular worldwide; apples and pears are also important exports. Orchards in the North produce apples, apricots, peaches, plums, cherries, nectarines, berryfruit, cherries, lemons, and oranges, mostly for local consumption, but increasingly for export. Hops and tobacco leaf (plus orchard fruit) are grown for the local market in the warm, sunny Nelson area of the South Island.

Timber

After agriculture, forestry is New Zealand's next important industry—with about 1.1 million hectares of production plantation forest in the country. Native trees (very slow growing) are used for less than one-quarter of New Zealand's timber needs—the planted forests of exotic radiata pine are the major suppliers. Radiata grows rapidly here, producing a high amount of usable wood per tree. Forest export products consist of timber, wood pulp and chips, paper, building boards, plywood, veneers, and various oils. Australia and Japan are N.Z.'s largest customers of forest product exports.

Industry

Many basic industries, such as textiles and leather goods, tobacco, rubber and plastics, fruit and vegetables, building supplies, and furniture, are flourishing in New Zealand. Light manufacturing provides an increasing range of both consumer and industrial goods. Aircraft manufacture, motor vehicle assembly, and the textiles and garment industry all provide employment. Two steel companies in New Zealand make heavy equipment from imported steel. In electronics many advancements have been made in highly specialized equipment for agricultural, medical, and veterinary areas.

sheepshearer in action

Energy

New Zealand does not have large mineral deposits and so relies heavily on imported raw materials to manufacture chemicals. Imported petroleum supplies almost 50% of New Zealand's energy needs, the rest supplied by hydroelectricity, natural coal and gas, solar energy, and geothermal steam. Nuclear power is not foreseeable in New Zealand's future (hooray!), the objective being to harness the country's own natural power resources. New ventures include oil refining, aluminium smelting, and ironsand deposit mining, processing New Zealand's own offshore oil and gas condensates, and processing associated with steel and glass production. At Lake Grassmere in Marlborough, the first solar salt works converts seawater from the mudflats into household and industrial salt through evaporation. Schemes to change natural gas into synthetic petrol are promoted and encouraged by the government, and solar units to heat household water are increasing in popularity—an alternative to electricity.

Tourism

Tourism has become a major part of the New Zealand economy. In fact, it is the top earner of foreign exchange. The **New Zealand Tourist and Publicity Travel Department** has done an excellent job of developing facilities while maintaining the natural and cultural aspects of the country; the department also promotes New Zealand overseas. The majority of visitors flock across from Australia (more than 230,000 in 1985); however, more and more visitors from North America, the U.K., and Europe are discovering New Zealand.

PEOPLE

THE NEW ZEALANDERS

New Zealand has a population of 3.3 million. Kiwis (as New Zealanders like to call themselves) are good-humored, relaxed, easy to get along with, and hospitable. They take the time to talk to one another—and to visitors. Don't be surprised if you're frequently asked to their homes for "tea" or a cold beer. Of the total population, about 280,000 are native Maori (403,000 claim Maori descent), 250,000 are Pacific Islanders, the rest are mainly of British descent. The Maori population has increased dramatically in the last 30 years as a result of their growing awareness of the importance of good health, nutrition, and education, which lowered a previously high infant-mortality rate.

New Zealanders enjoy a high standard of living. Comprehensive health services and subsidized medicines are available to all citizens. They have high-quality housing, plentiful food, a five-day, 40-hour work week, and both sexes claim equal rights and opportunities. Churches of all major denominations can be found throughout New Zealand, and minor religious sects are found mainly in the larger cities. (For info regarding services, check the daily newspapers, or ask at the local N.Z. Tourist and Publicity Travel Office, Public Relations Office, or Visitor Centre.)

Demographics

The population is unevenly distributed. Historically the South Island has always had a smaller population than the North Island (except for during the gold rush era), but recent times have seen a *steady* drift from south to north. In the 1960s New Zealanders began to migrate in large numbers from the rural areas to cities in search of better opportunities. Today over 70% of the people live in the North Island, 55% in urban areas.

Races

After a colorful history of racial resentment and resulting land wars, today the Pakeha (white man), Maori, and Pacific Islander live in relative harmony, though there's been increasing unrest over land disputes in the last few years—disputes that originated in the 1840s with the signing of the Treaty of Waitangi. Intermarriage has increased dramatically in the last 30 years, leaving very few full-blooded Maori in New Zealand. It's estimated that one out of 12 New Zealanders is at least half-Maori in origin, and many more are part Maori. No longer do you find the modern Maori wearing ceremonial costume, cooking in boiling pools, and living as they are depicted on postcards. Only those involved in the tourist industry continue to give this picture of Maori life—mainly in Rotorua, where visitors enjoy authentic performances of the fierce *haka* (war dance) of Maori men, the graceful *poi* dance and beautiful singing of the women, traditional arts, crafts, and carving.

It is estimated that about 57% of the Maori population live in main urban centers. The Maori had difficulties adjusting to urban life and Pakeha ways, and a break in their culture and tradition occurred. With the recognition of these problems by the government and Maori themselves, programs to ease the situation were introduced. Out of these programs came a growing Maori nationalism, and an eventual upsurge of interest by Pakeha in *Maoritanga,* the Maori way of life. Today the Maori language, traditions, arts and crafts, music and dance are taught in schools throughout New Zealand, and there is an increasing national interest in preserving the once fading Maori culture.

LANGUAGE

The common language of New Zealand is English. The Maori also have their own melodic language, mainly heard in songs and chants and on ceremonial occasions. However, some Maori phrases such as *"Haere mai"* meaning "Welcome" and *"Haere ra"* meaning "Farewell" have been adopted by Pakaha and integrated into general use. With the renewed interest in Maori culture, the Maori language was made an official language of New Zealand in 1974.

Beautifully descriptive Maori place names are scattered throughout New Zealand. Places were often named after particular events, such as *Taumatawhakatangihangakoauauotamateapokaiwhenuakitanatahu*—"the place where Tamatea, the man with the big knees, who slid, climbed and swallowed mountains, known as 'landeater,' played his flute to his loved one." (There's also a longer version, claimed to be the world's longest place name!) The Maori language was entirely verbal until the early missionaries recorded it in a written

continued on page 21

COMMON MAORI WORDS AND PHRASES

ao: cloud
aotearoa: Land of the Long White Cloud (one of several translations)
atua: god
awa: river, valley
haere mai: welcome
haera ra: farewell
haka: a war dance and chants performed by the men
hangi: a Maori feast where the food is cooked/steamed in an earth oven
hau: wind
Hawaiiki: legendary homeland of the Maori
kia ora: good luck
kumara: sweet potato
makomako: bellbird
mana: prestige
manu: bird
maunga: mountain
moana: sea or lake
moko: tattoo
motu: island, or anything that is isolated
pa: fortified village
pakeha: foreign, white man, European
po: night
puna: spring of water
rangi: sky
roto: lake
rua: two; e.g. Rotorua: two lakes
tapu: sacred
utu: retribution
wai: water
whanga: bay, stretch of water, inlet
whare: house
whenua: land

COMMON ENGLISH WORDS AND PHRASES

Aussie: Australia, or an Australian

bastard: sometimes meant as an endearment, but more often used as an insult

bathroom: literally the room with bath and basin—the toilet is usually separate

beaut: beautiful

beehive: the main government building in Wellington

big smoke: city

bike or **motorbike:** motorcycle

billion: one million millions in New Zealand

biscuits: cookies. (Scones are similar to American biscuits.)

bloke: a guy or man

bludger: someone who "borrows" something but does not necessarily give it back; e.g. "May I bludge a cigarette?"

bonkers: a bit crazy

bonnet: the hood of a car

boot: the trunk of a car, or footwear

Boxing Day: Dec. 26—a national holiday

brolly: umbrella

bush: the wild untouched areas of native forest and woodland

caravan: a small mobile house-trailer generally used for vacations

car park: parking lot for autos

cheesed off: mad at something or someone

chemist: pharmacy or drug store

choppers: teeth—e.g."Sink your choppers into this, mate!"

ciggies: cigarettes

cloakroom: toilet

clothes pegs: clothespins

coach: long-distance bus, making only a few stops

"Come again!": "Repeat what you just said, please."

cordial: a bottle of concentrated fruit-flavored juice which is reconstituted into a drink by adding water

crook: ill, not feeling well

cuppa: usually refers to a cup of hot tea

dairy: small shop selling dairy products, snack foods, a small selection of canned foods, and newspapers. Often open when everything else is closed in the area, but usually more expensive

date: Note that in New Zealand, the day comes before the month, followed by the year—e.g. Sept. 11, 1956, is written 11/09/56

deli: delicatessen, a more expensive version of a dairy

(on the) **dole:** unemployment benefits

domain: a well-tended public park with lots of flowers and trees

dressing gown: bathrobe

dustbin: garbage can

dustmen: garbage collectors (also call themselves "garbologists!")

eiderdown: a warm quilt, most often filled with feathers

entree: a small appetizer *before* the main course of a meal

"Fair dinkum": either means "Honestly, it's true," or asked in a questioning tone means "Is that true?"

"Fair go": "Give me a chance."

fortnight: two weeks or fourteen nights

fridge: refrigerator

flat: apartment

flicks: the movies or cinema

footie/football: soccer. American football is called "gridiron"

gallon: the N.Z. imperial gallon is bigger than an American gallon

"Giday": a greeting meaning good day, or hi! The Australian version sounds more like "geday."

go for a burn: go for a fast ride in the car

"Good on yer, mate": "Good for you, pal."

greengrocer: fruit and vegetable (vegie) shop

gumboots: everyone has a pair of these rubber boots for rainy days

hotel: a public bar; accommodation is a secondary income source

jumper/jersey: sweater

kiwi: a flightless bird, the national symbol of New Zealand. Many New Zealanders also like to call themselves "Kiwis."

late-night shopping: Due to the 40-hour week, most shops are usually open weekdays 0900-1700 and Sat. 0900-1200, closed on Sun., but on one night a week in each shopping area most of the shops stay open till 2100.

laundrette: laundromat or laundry

left luggage: an area in a railway station, airport, etc., where you can safely leave your baggage, usually for a small fee

letter box: mailbox

lift: elevator

loo: toilet, usually in a room on its own

(continued)

COMMON ENGLISH WORDS AND PHRASES (CONT.)

mate: friendly way of addressing someone, be they friend or stranger; e.g. "Giday mate, how ya goin'?"

metal surface: the road surface is gravel, not paved

milk bar: a shop selling dairy products, hot snack foods, some canned food, sweets and candy bars; open longer hours than most shops and on weekends

motor camp: a safe clean place to stay inexpensively, with tent and caravan sites, cabins and tourist flats, and communal bathroom, kitchen, and laundry facilities

motorway: freeway/highway/autobahn.

mozzies: mosquitos (their bite is not as bad as sandflies)

muckin' around/muckin' about: fooling around

nappies: baby diapers/napkins

ocker: a derogatory way of describing a person from Australia

paddock: a field

pavement: sidewalk

peckish: a bit hungry

petrol: fuel/gas

petrol station: gas station

"Piss off!": "Get lost!" ("I'm pissed off": "I'm angry.")

postman/postie: mailman

prang: car or bike accident

pushbike: bicycle

return ticket: a RT ticket, to destination and back

rubber: an eraser

rubbish: garbage

rubbish bins: garbage cans

sandfly: a tiny biting insect (the bite leaves an itchy welt that when persistently scratched leaves a small scar) that can drive you bonkers (not literally!) unless you're armed with strong insect repellent

sandshoes: tennis shoes/gymshoes/sneakers

school: primary and secondary school, or junior and senior high, but does not apply to college or university education

sealed road: a paved road

"She'll be right": often heard, means everything will be OK

stirrer: a troublemaker or person who likes to joke around

takeaway: food to go, to take home

tea: has various meanings—can be a cup of tea, a light evening meal, or dinner, depending on the context (it's always best to confirm the exact meaning before you show up at someone's place!)

telly: television

toll call: a long-distance telephone call

torch: flashlight

tramp/tramper/tramping: hike/hiker/hiking

trundler: shopping cart

tucker: food

uni: university

wee: small

winge: complain; e.g. "He's a bit of a winger."

woolies: usually means long underwear or outer winter wear

Yank: an American

Yank tank: slang for a large American-made car

z: In New Zealand (and Britain and Australia), the letter Z is pronounced "zed."

form. The sounds broke down into eight consonants: h, k, m, n, p, r, t, w; five vowels: a, e, i, o, u; and two combinations: wh, and ng. "Wh" is pronounced as f, "Ng" is a nasal sound, as in siNG. All words end in a vowel, and each syllable has equal stress. Many words are Maori pronunciations of English words, but they look Maori, such as motaka—motor car. The easiest way to say Maori words is to pronounce each syllable phonetically.

ARTS AND CRAFTS

Fantastic scenery, an appreciation of beauty, and pride in their country seem to inspire many New Zealanders to become artists. Art comes in many media—painting, pottery, sculpture, glassware, spinning, weaving, and woodcarving. Music, theater, ballet, modern dance, literature, filmmaking, and architecture are also well represented. Drama is alive and well; the two most recognized theaters for professional live drama are the **Mercury Theatre** in Auckland and the **Downstage Theatre** in Wellington. Music flourishes through the internationally known National Symphony Orchestra and Brass Band. Government-funded support for the arts is provided by the Queen Elizabeth II Arts Council, which also trains promising dancers and musicians. Regional and community arts councils provide assistance to amateur groups and individuals, and promote the arts throughout New Zealand. Since 1960 the visual arts have particularly flourished. Pottery, rapidly becoming an in-demand export, is the favorite, and woolcraft is also popular—as you'd expect from a country with more than 68 million sheep.

Display museums are found throughout New Zealand—many specialize in Maori arts and crafts, history, and culture. The **Dominion Museum** in Wellington has Maori and Pacific exhibits; the **Auckland War Memorial Museum** features zoology, botany, ethnology, and Maori exhibits; the **Canterbury Museum** in Christchurch displays New Zealand birds, a diorama of a historic Christchurch setting, and a planetarium; the **Otago Museum** in Dunedin features ethnology, pottery and sculpture, marinelife and skeletons, and local history. New Zealand architecture generally reflects European and American influences of the appropriate time; however, many well-preserved pre-European Maori buildings are still extant, particularly in the north of the North Island. Some of New Zealand's most beautiful historic homes and buildings, restored and maintained by the New Zealand Historic Places Trust, are open to the public year-round; small admission charge.

Maori Art

The most important and sacred Maori art was sculpture, predominantly wood but also jade, ivory, and whalebone. Trained in the art from an early age, the best carvers of early Maori society became men of high rank. Only men could become carvers—women, regarded as inferior, were not even allowed to watch the carvers at work. The canoe *(waka)*, meeting house *(whare whakairo)*, and food store-

house *(pataka)* were the main vehicles for Maori relief sculpture. Enormous pieces of indigenous timber were deeply carved into highly decorative spiritual designs, both on the interior and exterior. Well-preserved wood-carvings, decorative interior panels of woven reed, and painted rafters are best seen in *marae* or meeting grounds throughout the country, and all the major museums feature Maori art. All useful items of the Maori were covered in abstract designs, inspired by plants (a fern design is fairly common) or symbols, and inset with abalone shell. The human body, in particular the sacred head, was the major figurative element. Profiles with birdlike heads were *manaia* or evil beings.

The Maori also decorated their bodies—which the earliest European visitors found particularly intriguing. Apart from wearing flax cloaks and kilts decorated with woven borders, tufts of colorful feathers, or dog hair, they adorned themselves with beautiful greenstone pendants, ear pendants, and combs; the men painfully carved intricate symmetrical designs *(moku)* into their faces and thighs with tiny chisels filled with paint, and the women tattooed their lower lips and chins. Nowadays you see few authentic tattoos (only on the very elderly), but they're still effectively painted on for ceremonial occasions.

The *tiki,* a spiritual carving of human form representing the Maori conception of the beginning of life, was worn as a good luck pendant—it has been mass-produced in all mediums for tourists. Unfortunately, a lot of Maori art is now machine-made and you have to search for hand-carved original pieces. One of the best places to see hand-carved works is the New Zealand Maori Arts and Crafts Institute at Whakarewarewa, Rotorua, the home of Maori culture. Other areas where you can find carvers in action are the far north and the east coast of the North Island, and in the town of Hokitika on the west coast of the South Island.

A cultural concert of Maori songs, chants, games, and graceful dances is a colorful spectacle that shouldn't be missed, especially when combined with a *hangi* (Maori feast). Men perform fierce war chants *(haka)* and women sing and perform graceful flowing dances, twirling *poi.* Rotorua is the best place to go to appreciate Maori culture in all its forms, past and present.

FESTIVALS AND EVENTS

New Zealand seems to have some festival or event going on somewhere almost every day of the year. Sporting events of all kinds are very popular, as are the multitude of excellent agricultural shows that draw large crowds of locals and visitors alike. Drama, ballet, and musical events are also highly recommended. Head for the nearest N.Z. Tourist and Publicity Travel Office or Public Relations Office for the latest info on current festivals and events. The NZTP annually publishes a pamphlet, *New Zealand What's On,* which is chock-a-block with activities. Agricultural and pastoral shows are held throughout the year. Events include animal handling, sheepdog trials, horse jumping, local crafts, and fruit and vegetable displays and competitions. These shows have a distinctly local atmosphere and typical "New Zealand feeling."

Horse racing is another part of life in New Zealand. Thoroughbred horses, bred to race, compete internationally. The trots (harness-racing) is also very popular throughout the year, as is greyhound racing; meetings are generally held in the evenings under flood-lights, gather an enthusiastic crowd, and are lots of fun!

Major Nationwide And Local Holidays

On major nationwide holidays (see chart) a newcomer can quickly feel stranded as New Zealand appears to close down! Try not to travel to a new place on a holiday, don't count on attractions and restaurants being open, and stock up on neccessities the day before! Also many regions, individual cities, and towns celebrate their anniversary days by taking a holiday (see chart). If the holiday falls

NATIONWIDE HOLIDAYS

New Year's Day
Waitangi Day: 6 February
Good Friday and Easter Monday: April
Anzac Day: 25 April
Queen's Birthday: first Mon. of June
Labour Day: fourth Mon. of October
Christmas Day
Boxing Day: 26 December

LOCAL HOLIDAYS

Wellington: 22 January
Aukland: 29 January
Northland: 29 January
Nelson: 1 February
Taranaki: 8 March
Otago: 23 March
Southland: 23 March
Hawke's Bay: 17 October
Marlborough: 1 November
Westland: 1 December
Canterbury: 16 December

on a Tues. through Thurs., it's celebrated on the previous Monday. If it falls on a Fri. through Sun., it's celebrated on the following Monday. Almost all the shops close except for milkbars, usually on the outskirts of town; plan accordingly.

Annual Major Events

January: The **Trentham Thoroughbred Sales** take place in Wellington; in Auckland is the **Annual Yachting Regatta**—a spectacular event in the harbor of a city known for its water sports. Also in Auckland, both the **New Zealand Open Tennis Tournament** and the **New Zealand International Grand Prix** are held.

February: the **Treaty of Waitangi Celebrations** are held in the Bay of Islands area to commemorate the signing of the Treaty on 6 Feb. 1840. This national holiday's events are televised throughout New Zealand. In Wellington, the **Auckland Cup Harness Racing Meeting** is held.

March: The **Ngaruawahia River Regatta,** the only Maori canoe regatta, is held mid-March near Hamilton. Events also include horse swimming, rowing, and speedboat racing, tribal dance competitions, and much more. **The Golden Shears Sheep Shearing Contest** is held in Masterton, and up in the Bay of Islands, the exciting **International Bill-Fish Tournament.** If you're lucky enough to meet some of the competitors, you may be invited aboard one of the deep-sea fishing boats participating in the tournament (if you suffer from seasickness, stock up on Dramamine—it can get pretty rough out there!).

April: The **New Zealand Easter Show** and **Auckland Festival** are both held in Auckland; the **Hastings Highland Games** are held during Easter. There is a real Scottish atmosphere at these games; expect haggis, hurling, caber tossing, Highland dancing, and bagpipe bands.

June: Agricultural Field Days are held at Mystery Creek, near Hamilton, offering everything a modern farmer would like to see. The **Great Northern Hurdles and Steeplechase Meeting** is held in Auckland.

July: International Ski Racing is held at the Mt. Hutt ski field. In Wellington, the **Wellington Hurdles and Steeplechase Meeting** is held.

November and December: The **Canterbury Show** week is held in Christchurch during Nov., and in Nov. and Dec. the **International Trout Fishing Contest** is held in Rotorua. These are but a few of a multitude of events held throughout the year; some large festivals are only held once every couple of years.

THE GREAT OUTDOORS

A multitude of exciting activities awaits you in the great New Zealand outdoors. Spectacular scenery lies around every bend, and action-packed adventures are more than likely to lure you off the beaten track into some of the most beautiful countryside you're ever likely to see. Whether you want to run wild white-water rapids, ski the slopes of a smoldering volcano, skim the shallows in a high-speed jetboat, cast a fly-rod in an icy stream, or settle back to watch cricket, lawn bowls, or have a bet on "the trots," New Zealand offers it all!

TRAMPING

A National Walkway Network

Also known as hiking, trekking, and back-packing, tramping is one of the favorite out-door pursuits of New Zealanders and visitors alike. The small population, vast areas of wilderness (some still unexplored), diverse landscapes, and wide variety of terrain guarantee a good walking experience. Tramping is most popular Nov. through April when the weather is best.

A great way to really see New Zealand is through the use of the National Walkway Network. The idea of a national walkway was passed as an Act of Parliament in 1975, with the aim of providing a network of tracks eventually linking the farthest point north to the farthest point south. So far, more than 65 walkways have been created, passing through public and private property to points of scenic or historic interest. Most tracks can generally be done within a day, and are classified as one of three types: *walk*—well-formed track suitable for the average family; *track*—well-defined track suitable for people of good average physical fitness; or *route*—lightly marked route for use only by well-equipped experienced trampers. Details on individual walks can be found in each chapter, but be sure to pick up a copy of the *New Zealand's Walkways* booklet from any Dept. of Conservation office for the rundown on every walking track available. For info on tramping clubs, write to the Secretary, Federated Mountain Clubs of New Zealand Inc., P.O. Box 1604, Wellington.

Major Hiking Tracks

Many major tracks throughout New Zealand are famous for outstanding scenery; each takes several days to complete. They all require a knowledge of bushcraft, tramping experience, and appropriate equipment. In the North Island, the **Waikaremoana Track** wanders around Lake Waikaremoana in Urewera National Park, the **Round The Mountains Track** encircles the volcanos of Tongariro National Park, and the **Round The Mountain Track** encircles Mt. Egmont in Egmont National Park. The **Heaphy Track** in North West Nelson State Forest Park and the **Abel Tasman Coastal Track** meander across the northern tip of the South Island, and the **Hollyford Valley Walk, Milford Track** (through Fiordland National Park), **Routeburn Track** (through Fiordland and Mount Aspiring national parks), and **Caples and Greenstone tracks** are all found in the southwest corner of the South Island. **Stewart Island** has a multitude of short bush walks and a seven- to 10-day track that meanders along the coast and in and out of lush native forest.

All tracks are extremely popular during the summer; huts are located at regular intervals (approximately a six-hour walk between each) but in peak periods, especially Jan., they can become overcrowded and you need to carry your own tent and stove. The Milford

Track is the most well known, and due to its popularity, an advance booking (up to one year ahead) is required by the THC Te Anau Hotel; it can also be done as part of a guided group (expensive) Nov. through March. Get all the facts and options (most can be done independently or with a guiding company) well in advance to avoid disappointment (more details in the appropriate chapters).

Commercial Operators
Many commercially operated trekking tours cover both North and South islands. These can be booked through travel agencies or any N.Z. Tourist and Publicity Travel office. They offer straight hiking trips, or hiking combined with mountain climbing, canoeing, jetboating, or river rafting. Overnight or several-day trips generally include a combination of activities, camping gear or cabin accommodations, all meals, equipment, and transportation. Most are offered only during the summer; at least one experienced guide takes each tour. The prices vary but you can expect to pay at least $250 per adult, slightly less per child 10 to 14 years old.

Parks
In the 12 beautiful national parks and many forest parks scattered throughout New Zealand you can find everything from a short gentle stroll to a hard, adventurous, several-day hike, with huts ($8-14 pp per night) provided along the tracks for overnight stays. The park rangers have all the info on what to see and do, including hiking track and hut info, and detailed maps can be purchased for a relatively small price. (See individual chapters.)

MOUNTAINEERING

Of many first-class climbing areas, the main ones are **Mt. Egmont** (2,517 meters) and **Mt. Ruapehu** (2,796 meters) in the North Island, and a multitude of climbs in the skyscraper peaks of the **Southern Alps** in the South Island. Eight out of the 12 national parks are mountainous, providing reasonably good access and well-equipped huts. All park HQS have climbing and tramping info, and weather

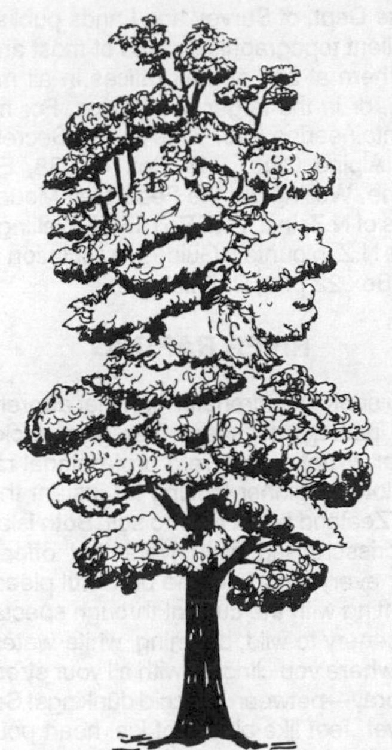

Exclusive to New Zealand, totara *timber is favored for Maori carvings and canoes.*

forecasts. **Mt. Cook** (3,764 meters), **Mt. Tasman** (3,497 meters), **La Perouse** (3,078 meters), and **Mt. Sefton** (3,157 meters) in Mt. Cook and Westland national parks are very popular with experienced climbers—but only when weather conditions are just right. Many routes are long and difficult, demanding experience and appropriate equipment, and most of the mountains have glaciers, demanding ice- and rock-climbing ability. There are few solid rock climbs in New Zealand—the best is found on the firm granite of the **Darran Mountains** in Fiordland National Park.

The climbing season is Nov. to April, but more and more winter climbing is attempted each year and new routes are always being discovered. Several guiding companies offer climbs, walks, and various levels of instruction. Bring your own equipment to New Zealand, it's expensive to buy; however, the latest equipment is available should you need it. The Dept. of Survey and Lands publishes excellent topographical maps of most areas; buy them at any of their offices in all major cities, or in the larger bookshops. For more mountaineering info, write to the Secretary, N.Z. Alpine Club, P.O. Box 41-038, Eastbourne, Wellington; the Federated Mountain Clubs of N.Z. Inc., P.O. Box 1604, Wellington; or the N.Z. Mountain Guides Association Inc., P.O. Box 22-590, Christchurch.

RIVER RAFTING

If you seek the adrenalin high that apprehension, panic, and sheer fear give, look no further. Whether you're a professional rafter or a total beginner looking for instant thrills, New Zealand has a river to suit. Both islands are crisscrossed with rivers that offer the rafter everything from the peaceful pleasure of drifting with the current through spectacular scenery to wild, churning, white-water rapids where you cling on with all your strength and pray—between icy-cold dunkings! Soaking wet, feet like blocks of ice, heart pounding, poised at the top of a fearsome rapid, you may wonder for a moment why you're doing this—but when it's all over, you know you'll be back for more!

The Rivers

The **Wairoa,** a rapid-filled river meandering down from the Kaimai Ranges to meet the ocean near Tauranga, provides both quiet water and short bursts of raging, grade 3-5 rapids. The highlights are aptly named "Waterfall" and "Rollercoaster." The nearby **Rangitaiki River** (not as wild) comes down from the Ahimanawa Ranges to meet the ocean just north of Whakatane. The **Motu River** provides quiet-water stretches through breathtaking scenery and several exciting rapids as it winds through the Raukumara Range (East Cape) to come out at Haupoto. Hydro-development has sadly tamed much of the **Tongariro River** but a few sections still offer exciting rafting action. The **Mohaka** (near Gisborne), **Ngaruroro** (between Napier and Hastings), and **Rangitikei rivers** (south of Wanganui) offer combinations of quiet water and rugged scenery, and wild, heart-stopping rapids that can raise the hair on the neck of even the experienced rafter. In the South Island, the most popular rafting is on the **Kawarau** and **Shotover rivers** near Queenstown (large choice of companies offering grade 3-5 rapids), the **Rakaia River** near Christchurch, and the wild **Landsborough River.** Generally the best months for rafting are Oct. through Jan., though most operators run the rivers till April, depending on water levels and weather conditions. The high-water levels on all rivers are usually Oct. through Dec. and sometimes January. The low water levels are Feb. and March.

Equipment

Low-grade rivers (3 and below) introduce you to rafting, let you employ basic rafting techniques, and at the same time, give you a few thrills. Advanced rafters head for grade 4 and 5 rivers. Life jackets are mandatory, and on some trips, crash hats are also provided. Keep in mind that it's always possible to find yourself unexpectedly body-surfing the rapids. Before you start out, you're taught basic paddling skills, how to stay afloat and ride the rapids if you're ejected, and how to get back to the raft or shore. A minimum age is often set depending on the kind of river being run.

Wear a bathing suit, shirt, shorts, wool sweater, waterproof jacket, thick wool socks, and tennis shoes or sneakers (essential)—take a change of clothes for later. Leave your camera behind unless you're doing a float trip or one of the mildest grade rivers (or have a waterproof camera that you can firmly attach to yourself)—you generally don't have much time between rapids to take photos.

Commercial Operators

Many commercial river-rafting companies operate in both the North and South islands (more in the south), and more spring up each rafting season. They offer trips varying from a couple of hours to 12 days including tent or hut accommodations, meals, and transportation. Trips generally go between Oct. and April, dependent on water levels and weather, and most companies hire full- or part-length wetsuits, and provide the mandatory life jackets; before you save pennies, remember that the rivers are icy cold! Choose a good and safe operator—avoid trips that have a reputation for fooling around, falling into the rapids for fun, etc.—they usually employ the least experienced guides. Ask around about safety records; check with the local info center, and make sure the company is a member of the N.Z. Professional Rafting Association (P.O. Box 26, Nelson). In the **North Island:** tours operate out of Rotorua rafting the Rangitaiki River, and out of Taupo and Turangi rafting the Tongariro, Mohaka, and Rangitikei rivers. In the **South Island:** tours operate out of Christchurch rafting the Waimakariri River, and out of Queenstown (lots of companies) rafting the Shotover, Dart, Waiatoto, and Kawarau rivers. If you want to learn how to raft, improve your white-water skills, or become a professional boatman, rafting schools are available between Nov. and March. These vary from two-day introductory courses to intensive seven-day courses; for more info, write to Danes Back Country, P.O. Box 230, Queenstown; tel. 1144.

JETBOATING

The world-famous Hamilton jetboats were invented in New Zealand and are very popular. Commercial jetboat companies operate tours throughout both islands, providing trips of varying lengths through spectacular scenery. Jetboating is particularly popular on the Shotover River in the Queenstown area. Experienced boatmen operate the jetboats and provide thrilling rides ranging from a short ride skimming the shallows to combination trips including jetboating, white-water rafting, and a helicopter ride. Jetboating tends to be expensive, but if you like whizzing across rapids only centimeters deep, twisting and churning to just miss overhanging branches and the occasional bridge pylon, whirling 180 degrees on the spot at high speed, this activity is a must! The scenery is always spectacular—on the Shotover River you see abandoned gold mines and equipment along the way. Expect to get wet, particularly if you're

selected to sit in the back seat! Take your camera in a waterproof container and firmly attach it to yourself. Mandatory life jackets are supplied, and some operators also provide light waterproof jackets.

CANOEING AND KAYAKING

Several tour companies offer canoe or kayak trips; canoes can also be hired without guides for a few hours or for an entire river camping trip. In the North Island, canoe tours operate out of Palmerston North using the **Wanganui River** or **Lake Tarawera.** In the South Island, you can canoe the **Kawarau River;** tours operate out of Queenstown. Because of the nature of the rivers, life jackets, crash helmets, and wetsuits are essential; most equipment can be hired. For more remote areas, helicopter services are available to fly you in to the rivers. For more info, write to the N.Z. Canoeing Association, P.O. Box 5125, Auckland, or P.O. Box 3768, Wellington. They have nine detailed guidebooks that cover about 1,500 rivers. Written for the canoe or kayak enthusiast, they sell for $3 each plus postage and handling. Kayak clinics are also offered during the summer for both introductory and advanced levels; for more info, write to Danes Back Country, P.O. Box 230, Queenstown; tel. 1144.

RIVER AND LAKE FISHING

Often called a fisherman's paradise, New Zealand fishing is world famous. Some of the friendliest New Zealanders are found congregating around rivermouths and lakeshores, fishing rods in hand, hats covered in assorted flies and lures. Originally, brown trout ova from the U.K. via Tasmania (Australia) and rainbow trout ova from the Russian River in California were introduced to New Zealand waters in the late 1860s. Streams and rivers providing both fast- and slow-flowing water, crystal-clear lakes, and an abundant supply of food all helped the fish thrive in their new environment, and modern hatcheries and good conservation methods ensure that New Zealand's good fishing continues.

Fishy Locations

In general the north is known for large rainbow trout, the south for large brown trout, and Quinnat salmon run in many of the rivers of the North Island's lower west coast and the South Island's east coast. **North Island:** all the lakes, particularly **Lake Taupo** (New Zealand's largest) and **Lake Tarawera,** are well stocked with rainbow trout, but the rivers seem to attract the larger rainbows and browns. The finest fishing is naturally found at off-the-beaten-track locations; boats are often necessary to get to the best stream mouths. Fly-fishing is at its best in rivers and streams that flow into lakes during April through June when the fish swim upstream to spawn, and in Nov. and Dec. when they return to the lake. Use a wet lure fly and fast-sinking line downstream, and a weighted nymph on floating line upstream.

South Island: most lakes are stocked with brown trout, some with rainbow trout and land-locked salmon. Good fishing is found at times similar to the North Island lakes, but a dry fly and floating line are used. Spinning is popular from the shore, as is trolling with weighted lines from a boat. Brown trout are mainly caught in the rivers using dry flies (or lures), and in some eastern rivers, Pacific salmon are caught. In South Westland, brown trout come in from the sea in late summer and are caught on both wet and dry fly and spinners. For fishing info and beautiful photography, pick up a copy of the N.Z. magazine, *Flyfisher*. If you're going to N.Z. mainly for the fishing, write to Club Pacific, 790 27th Ave., San Francisco, CA 94121, for details on their unique, personal, "Angler-To-Angler Holidays"; tel. (415) 752-0192.

Equipment

Bringing your own fishing gear into New Zealand is permitted but it may be fumigated. Renting fishing tackle and waders is difficult—it's better to bring your own. Thigh waders are suggested for South Island fishing, chest waders for North Island. For all types of trout fishing, the experts suggest you have one reel with five replaceable spools and the following lines: a floating line of 5-7 weight, A.H.D. fast-sink line of 8-10, a shooting head line (preferably number 10), a floating line with sink tip for nymphing, and a medium sinking line of 8-9. Dry flies and nymphs such as the Red Tipped Governor, Royal Wulff, Adams, Blue Dun, Hare, and Copper all work well in New Zealand. Streamer or lure flies representing smelt are best bought locally. Imported ready-made trout flies can be brought into the country without fumigation, but certain fly-tying materials such as loose feathers have to be fumigated.

Regulations

Most anglers fly-fish or troll. Spinning or lure fishing is fairly uncommon—most of the best fishing areas are designated for fly-fishing only. Each local district has its own fishing rules, and fishing seasons vary area by area. You can get copies of all the regulations from the Government Printer in Wellington or from any Dept. of Internal Affairs wildlife offices in major cities, and all the fishing info you need from the local sporting goods store. Or write to the Hunting and Fishing Officer, NZTP Travel Office, 67 Fenton St., Rotorua.

Licenses

Each district requires a fishing license; from around $6 per day or $16 per week. If you're planning on fishing throughout the country, you can buy a special tourist license before you start out—valid for one month anywhere in the country except the Maori Lakes, and Rotoaira and Green lakes. At $55 per adult, $11 per junior under 16 years, unless you're fishing in a different area every day of the month, it's cheaper to buy district licenses as you need them. A fishing license allows a 20-meter public right-of-way along the banks of fishing rivers and lake shores; however, permission is required from the owner if you need to cross private land to reach the water.

Limits
These vary according to each district, ranging anywhere from four to 50 per day! In the Rotorua and Taupo districts in the North Island the limit is usually eight a day; in the South Island the limit ranges from four to 20 per day and there are extra limitations on salmon.

rainbow trout

Size
The sizes of New Zealand trout vary from district to district depending on environment, food available, climate, and angling pressure. In most areas the trout must be at least 356 mm long to keep, in a few districts at least 304 mm.

BIG-GAME FISHING

Big-game fishing is a very popular (and expensive) sport concentrated along 500 km of the northeast coast of the North Island from **Cape Runaway** to **North Cape.** The season is generally Jan. through April, attracting flocks of overseas visitors eager to haul in a trophy from the sea. A fishing license is not required. Broadbill, striped, black, and blue marlin, hammerhead, mako, and thresher shark, yellowtail, kingfish, and tuna are the main game fish species; the best months in the Bay of Islands are usually Feb. and March. The most prolific, fighting, big-game fish is the striped marlin—the most successful months are Dec. to June; catch sharks from Nov. to May and tuna from Dec. to March. Big-game fishing clubs abound from Whangarei to the Bay of Islands, competition is tough, and international tournaments are held each year. To try your luck, head up to the Bay of Islands via the coastal route, comparing charter prices at the deep-sea fishing resorts as you head north. If you join the prestigious **Bay of Islands Swordfish Club** in Russell ($5 plus GST per day) and catch something worthwhile, the fish is officially weighed in, you're issued a certificate, and become eligible for most club trophies. Charter boats (gear provided) and experienced crews are always available, but at $660 per day, unless you have a large budget, you need to find several other people willing to share costs.

SCUBA DIVING

Coral reefs, caves, multicolored sponges, various large brown kelps, friendly fish, and a large number of shipwrecks lure the scuba diver and underwater photographer to New Zealand shores. When the weather is suitable, underwater visibility is about nine to 12 meters along the coast, but around the offshore islands it's usually 18-24 meters and on good days exceeds 45 meters. The **Bay of Islands, Hauraki Gulf, Coromandel Peninsula,** and **Cook Strait** all offer good diving. **The Poor Knights Islands,** a small island group off the northeast coast of the North Island, are "a diver's dream," offering turn-of-the-century sunken ships as an added feature. Water temperatures vary from 14-22 degrees C, lower in the far south; locals recommend wetsuits. Summer usually provides the calmest weather; diving conditions are at their best from Jan. to April. Some years a plankton bloom occurs in spring and early summer, clouding the coastal waters. No underwater flora or fauna are dangerous to divers apart from sharks—and they're rarely seen. Gear can be hired with at least a CMAS One-Star Diver's Certificate or equivalent; no permits needed. For more info, write to the N.Z. Underwater Association, A.A. Mutual Building, O'Connell and Chancery sts. (Box 875), Auckland, or call 895-456.

SAILING

New Zealanders are water people—if they're not *in* the water, they're on it! Most people seem to have a yacht or boat of some sort (Auckland is "The City of Sails"), and all kinds and sizes are available for hire—however, you need a substantial budget or several people to share costs. Charter yachts are very popular Nov. to May (the yachting season), and you have the choice of hiring a crew or sailing it yourself (previous sailing experience is necessary). Some companies also offer crews that give instruction; most supply all the necessary equipment minus bedding and food. Premier sailing locations are liberally dotted around the country's coastline; the major operators in the North Island are found in the **Bay of Islands, Auckland, Paihia, Taupo,** and **Wellington,** and in the South Island at **Picton.** Prices are not cheap, around $100-350 per day (the more expensive sleep up to six people), but special rates are offered for longer hire periods. N.Z. Tourist and Publicity Travel offices have all the details and arrange sailing and yacht charters. For more info, write to the N.Z. Yacht Charter Association, P.O., Opua, Bay of Islands.

SURFING

Surf can be found throughout the year along the entire New Zealand coastline. The most popular North Island areas are **Northland,** the **west coast, New Plymouth, Bay of Plenty, Gisborne,** and **Wellington.** The favorite surf beach is **Raglan** on the west coast, 56 km from Hamilton—considered New Zealand's premier point break, with three left-breaking points in a row. It's rarely flat and has powerful and often large waves typical of the North Island's rugged west coast. In the South Island, surfing beaches are most accessible on the **east coast.** A large variety of beach breaks, river bars, and reef points lie along the coastline; however, quality surf over three to four meters is fairly hard to find. Wetsuits are necessary from autumn through spring. Surfboards can be hired at some of the most popular beaches during summer. For more detailed info, contact the N.Z. Surfriders Association, P.O. Box 1026, Gisborne.

CYCLING

New Zealand is an ideal place for a bicycling vacation if you're reasonably fit. Temperate climate, excellent roads, low-density traffic, and a wide variety of terrain and scenery appeal to those with enough time to see the country at a slower pace. However, a beginner cyclist may find the terrain too steep and demanding to be pleasurable, particularly in the mountainous South Island, and the traffic rather frightening on narrow roads. Talk to experienced cyclists before you commit yourself to a cycling tour of the country. One way of dealing with carrying your gear is to pack up everything you don't need for a few days in cardboard boxes, then mail them to your next destination a few days down the road. This way you always have clean clothes and other basic necessities to look forward to as a reward at the end of a few days' hard work! Or take a tour. The **Bicycle Touring Company** in Wellington offers a wide variety of tours on both North and South islands ranging from seven to 24 days. The tours include a leader, chef, accommodation (from hostels to first-class hotels depending on prearranged price), use of a touring cycle, and an accompanying "sag wagon" for equipment, luggage, even weary bicyclists!

If you haven't cycled before, a reasonably priced tour is a good way to start. If you're taking your own bicycle over to New Zealand, buy a bike box and wash the tires well—New Zealand is strict on pest control and your entire bike will be washed if there's a speck of foreign dirt on the tires (same goes for tents and hiking boots). Touring maps are available from overseas NZTP Travel offices, and from Dept. of Survey and Lands offices in all New Zealand's large cities. When in New Zealand, be sure to pick up the *Healing Guide to Cycle Touring in the North Island* and *South Island* by J.B. Ringer, published by Southern Cyclist magazine. *Cycle Touring in the South Island* (third edition) by Helen Crabb, published by the Canterbury Cyclists' Association (P.O. Box 2547, Christchurch), is also recommended. For more info, write to the Bicycle Association of New Zealand, P.O. Box 1454, Wellington.

SKIING

New Zealand skifields provide some of the best skiing in the world. International ski teams and skiing fanatics of all standards are lured from the Northern Hemisphere for excellent skiing on uncrowded treeless slopes from June to Oct. (sometimes Nov. in the North Island). There's always plenty of good snow *somewhere* in New Zealand, even during a mild winter. Reputable ski schools, fine weather, magnificent scenery, and reasonable costs (by international standards) complete the picture. Facilities range from simple rope tows in club-operated fields to a full range of chairlifts, T-bars, and pomas, and heli-skiing is available or can be arranged. Most fields have cafeterias or snack bars, and ski equipment is available for hire on-field or at sports stores in nearby urban centers.

Apart from numerous conventional skifields, you can fly up to the mountain tops for an exhilarating heli-skiing, glacier skiing (skiplane), or ski-touring adventure in virgin powder. Heli-skiing is particularly good in the Harris Mountains near Wanaka (South Island), offering more than 60 different runs (600-1,200 vertical meters) on 35 mountains. Although New Zealand slopes never seem to get crowded, the best time to ski is still midweek; most New Zealanders are weekend skiers, but Aug. is usually busy all month when families with school-age children take their skiing vacations.

The Skifields

Of the more than 20 recognized skiing areas in the country, most are in the Southern Alps—many are club skifields with limited facilities and a friendly atmosphere. In the North Island the two major commercial skifields, **Whakapapa** and **Turoa,** are both situated on the volcanic slopes of Mt. Ruapehu in Tongariro National Park. Several other fields are operated by ski clubs in both Tongariro and Egmont national parks. In the South Island the major commercial skifields are **Coronet Peak** at Queenstown, and **Mt. Hutt** at Methven. Smaller commercial skifields, with a variety of lifts, cafeterias, ski equipment rental, but limited adjacent accommodation, are found at **Rainbow** near St. Arnaud, **Porter Heights** near Christchurch, **Erewhon, Mt. Dobson** and **Fox Peak** in central South Island, **Tekapo** and **Lake Ohau** near Mt. Cook, and **Treble Cone, Cardrona,** and **Harris Mountains** near Wanaka. Most larger fields offer varying ski packages—NZTP Travel offices throughout the country have all the details and can arrange complete ski vacations. Many private fields operated by ski clubs (day visitors are welcome at cost) are conveniently situated near major cities. The Southern Alps also provide plenty of scope for heli-skiing, ski-touring, and ski-mountaineering. For more info, write to the N.Z. Ski Association, P.O. Box 2213, Wellington.

HUNTING

Several species of deer—**red, white-tail, fallow, wapiti, sika, sambur,** and **rusa**—are well established in New Zealand. Red deer are the most widespread in both North and South islands, fallow are also found in both islands, white-tail in restricted areas of the South I. and Stewart I., wapiti in Fiordland National Park (restricted to seasonal hunting), and sika, sambur, and rusa are found only in the North Island; deer-stalking is the

wild pig

most popular form of hunting. All deer (other than wapiti), chamois, tahr, pigs, and goats may be killed at any time of the year with no restrictions, and no limits, licenses, fees, or "male only" laws; these animals are considered "pests" in New Zealand. Chamois and Himalayan tahr inhabit the tussock country of the Southern Alps above 915 meters, and wild pigs, goats, wallabies, hares, rabbits, and opossums live in both islands; all can be hunted without a license. Native birds are protected at all times, but there is limited hunting for ducks, Canada geese, swans, pheasants, and quail; the season (and limits) vary, but generally opens in May; licenses (from sporting stores) are required.

Big-game hunting in New Zealand is not easy for the overseas visitor; the extremely rugged terrain requires a high degree of physical fitness, and competition with local hunters who know the conditions, hunting techniques, and animal habits is tough. Professional hunting guides are available for hunting in the wilds or on their own protected lands; the rates vary widely (generally expensive). The Dept. of Conservation is in charge of the recreational hunting areas; permits are required in national parks. Fully automatic firearms and pistols are illegal—.030, .270, and 30.06 calibers are adequate for general shooting. Firearms and ammunition are readily available in sports stores; if you bring your own gun into New Zealand, you must obtain an import license from N.Z. police. For more hunting info, write to the Hunting and Fishing Officer, NZTP Travel Office, Private Bag, Rotorua; N.Z. Deerstalkers Association, P.O. Box 6514, Te Aro, Wellington; N.Z. Big Game Hunters Association, Box 46, Tuakau; N.Z. Bowhunters Society, 17 Berkley Ave., Hillcrest, Hamilton.

BUNGY JUMPING

This is the latest way to get an adrenalin rush in New Zealand. Imagine standing on a high bridge spanning a river-filled canyon, your ankles securely tied together with a towel and bungy cord, the river far below. And then, in front of a large audience who enthusiastically do a "countdown," you dive off for a long, long free-fall! At the end of the fall, just before you hit the water or after you are momentarily submerged to your waist (you choose between a wet or dry fall), the elastic rope rebounds and you're flying upward toward the bridge again. This continues until you run out of momentum, and then you're rescued by boat and taken to shore. To experience this you have to cough up $75, but those who have taken the plunge proudly swagger around the countryside in a specially designed bungy-jumping T-shirt—and you have to *do* it to get the shirt. If this sounds like something you'd like to try, head for Queenstown, where the operators are the most experienced in the country—they started it all!

FLYING

One of the most visually exciting ways to experience New Zealand is from the air. If you have your private pilot's license and want to fly in New Zealand, you must get it validated before taking to the air—that is if you plan on being behind the controls. To do this have your current license, medical certificate, radio operator's license, and log book with you. Then get your hands on a copy of the N.Z. *Visual Flight Guide* (borrow it if you can—it costs $80!) and learn the Flight Rules and Regulations section. All applicants must pass a multiple-choice exam—Part 1 is on flight rules, Part 2 is an open-book VFG test; one hour and 10 minutes is allowed—in Auckland, Wellington, or Christchurch. Then, *voilà,* your license is validated indefinitely.

Make an appointment to take the test by contacting the Dept. of Transportation (in Wellington call 600-400). Each time you return to N.Z. your license must be revalidated, but you don't need to re-take the exam. Before hiring an airplane you'll be asked to take a flight check with an instructor. Prove you're safe and the sky's the limit!

PRACTICALITIES

GETTING THERE

The only practical way to get to New Zealand is by air. In today's crazy competitive world, airlines come and go, buy each other out, swap routes, and raise and lower prices on what seems like a daily basis! One way to keep up with what's happening is to find yourself a reputable travel agent willing to do the ground work required to suit your desires and budget. If you can't find one, or are a do-it-yourselfer, call the airlines direct: compare air fares, ask if they're offering any special promotions (such as a two-for-one ticket), advance-purchase fares, student discounts, or standby flights. Before you buy your ticket, check the prices on special passes for internal transportation within New Zealand—some passes are only valid if purchased overseas (see "Getting Around" below).

All the airlines offer a variety of fares—economy, business, and first-class, advance-purchase excursions (APEX) which require ticketing and payment 14 days before departure date, and special promotional fares (often the cheapest way to go) which have catchy names and are usually plastered across newspapers or advertised on TV. The cheaper fares generally require a minimum of six days and a maximum of six months in New Zealand, and include penalties (25% of the ticket price is non-refundable, for example, if you cancel within 14 days of departure). Some tickets allow you to change the date of return within a certain time limit, others don't—always check the limitations and penalties in the fine print before you buy a special-rate ticket. The other major thing to consider before purchasing your ticket is the time of year; low season (also called "off peak" or "basic") in the Northern Hemisphere is high season in the Southern. To benefit from departing at low-season prices, you must leave the Northern Hemisphere between 1 April and 30 November. If you head for N.Z. between 1 Dec. and 31 March, you pay high season (also called "peak") prices, generally considerably higher. However, high, shoulder, and low-season fares are not standardized throughout all airlines—call them and find out their seasons! If you're a student, check with a student-oriented travel agent; they can generally offer much better prices than anyone else (see below).

International Carriers From North America

Air New Zealand, United Airlines, Qantas, UTA French Airlines, Continental Airlines, and Hawaiian all fly from the U.S. to Auckland via a variety of routes. The prices below are the least expensive quoted for travel from the West Coast (San Francisco or Los Angeles) to Auckland (flights to Wellington or Christchurch are generally more expensive). In the U.S., the farther you live from the West Coast, the more expensive the fare will be. Keep in mind that the names of promotional flights change, as do the prices—use this info only as a guide!

United Airlines offers flights to Auckland via Honolulu for $1140 RT off peak and $1400 RT peak, with a free stopover in Honolulu. Air New Zealand offers a low-season APEX fare for $970 RT, high season $1413 RT (currently called the "Kiwi Smile Fare"); it includes free stopovers in Honolulu and Fiji. Continental's standard fare is $970 RT low season, $1355 RT high season, with no advance purchase necessary and a free stopover in Honolulu. UTA French Airlines flies from the West Coast via Tahiti; their APEX fare runs $970 RT low season and $1170 RT high season, with one free stopover in Tahiti. Qantas (Australia's airline) flies to Auckland via Australia; their APEX fare is $970 RT low season, $1400 RT high season, with free stopovers in Hawaii, Fiji, and Australia.

If you're a student, contact one of the **Council Travel Services** offices for their lower prices. They offer an $849 OW fare or a $1129 RT fare from L.A. to Auckand with free stopovers in Honolulu and Fiji. To qualify for

COUNCIL TRAVEL SERVICES

IN THE UNITED STATES

Amherst: 79 South Pleasant St.
Amherst, MA 02116
tel. (413) 256-1261

Austin: 1904 Guadalupe St., Suite 6
Austin, TX 78705
tel. (512) 472-4931

Berkeley: 2511 Channing Way
Berkeley, CA 94704
tel. (415) 848-8604

Boston: 729 Boylston St., Suite 201
Boston, MA 02116
tel. (617) 266-1926

La Jolla: UCSD Student Center B-023
La Jolla, CA 92093
tel. (619) 452-0630

Long Beach: 5500 Atherton St., Suite 212
Long Beach, CA 90815
tel. (213) 598-3338.

Los Angeles: 1093 Broxton Ave.
L.A., CA 90024
tel. (213) 208-3551

New York: 205 E. 42nd St.
New York, NY 10017
tel. (212) 661-1450; or

New York Student Center
356 West 34th St.
New York, NY 10001
tel. (212) 661-1450

Portland: 715 S.W. Morrison, Suite 600
Portland, OR 97205
tel. (503) 228-1900.

Providence: 171 Angell St. (at Thayer),
Suite 212,
Providence, RI 02906
tel. (401) 331-5810

San Diego: 4429 Class St.
San Diego, CA 92109
tel. (619) 270-6401

San Francisco: 312 Sutter St.
S.F., CA 94108
tel. (415) 421-3473; or

919 Sutter St.
S.F., CA 94108
tel. (415) 421-3473.; or

919 Irving St., Suite 102
S.F. 94122
tel. (415) 566-6222

Seattle: 1314 Northeast 43rd St.
Suite 210, Seattle, WA 98105
tel. (206) 632-2448

IN EUROPE:

Bonn: Thomas Mann Strasse 33
5300 Bonn 1
West Germany

Bordeaux: 9 Place Charles Gruet
Bordeaux 33000, France
tel. (56) 44-68-73

Nice: 10 rue de Belgique
Nice 06000, France
tel. (93) 87-34-96

Paris: 31 rue St. Augustin
Paris 75002, France
tel. 42-66-34-73; or

51 rue Dauphine
Paris 75006, France
tel. 43-26-79-65; or

16 rue de Vaugirard
Paris 75006, France
tel. 46-34-02-90

IN JAPAN:

Tokyo: Sanno Grand Building, Room 102,
14-2 Nagata-Cho, 2-Chome, Chiyoda-ku,
Tokyo 100, Japan
tel. (03) 581-7581

these prices, you have to prove you're a "degree-seeking student." You need an International Student I.D. card ($10 from CTS), a valid student I.D., and a letter from the registrar or a list of classes (at least eight units). Once in N.Z., your international student I.D. gets you discounts on all sorts of things—check with your CTS office before departure. CTS also offers non-students the same fare—$849 RT low season or $1129 high season from S.F. or L.A. (the student fares may have more stops or fewer restrictions); same restrictions and penalties for all APEX tickets apply. For a list of CTS offices, see p.34.

STA also provides good deals for students. No advance purchase necessary, flights include free stopovers in Honolulu, Fiji, and the Cook Is., for low season $1035 RT, high season $1375. You need an International Student I.D. card ($10 from STA), proof of attendance at a school or a list of classes (at least eight units), proof of birthdate, and a passport photo. Once in N.Z., you can get student standby fares on almost all domestic airlines, fare concessions on Auckland bus transportation, discount accommodations (only at certain places), discount prices at galleries, concerts, community theaters and independently operated cinemas in Wellington, Christchurch, and Dunedin, and discounts at a range of shops. Once in N.Z., pick up a copy of the discount listings at any STA office: in Auckland at 10 High St., tel. (09) 399-995; in Wellington at 207 Cuba St., tel. (09) 850-561; in Christchurch at 223 High St., tel. 799-098; in Dunedin at 32 Albany St., tel. 740-146. For a list of overseas STA offices, see p. 36.

International Carriers From The Rest Of The World

From Canada: Cathay Pacific Airways and Air New Zealand are the major international air carriers to New Zealand. **From South America:** Aerolineas Argentinas and Lan Chile. **From Australia:** Air New Zealand, British Airways, Continental, Qantas, and United. **From Asia** (with connections from Australia): Air India, Air New Zealand (direct services from Singapore, Hong Kong, and Tokyo), Alitalia, All Nippon Airways, British Airways, Cathay Pacific Airways, Garuda Indonesian Airways, Japan Airlines (direct from Tokyo), KLM Royal Dutch Airlines, Lufthansa, Malaysian Airline System, Philippine Airlines, Singapore Airlines (direct from Singapore), Thai International, United Airlines, and UTA French Airlines. **From Britain and Europe** (direct): Air New Zealand, British Airways, Canadian Pacific Air, Cathay Pacific, Qantas, Singapore Airlines, United Airlines, and UTA; **from Britain and Europe** (with connections in Australia): Air India, Alitalia, Garuda Indonesia, KLM, Lufthansa, Malaysian, Scandinavian Airlines, Singapore Airlines, and Thai International. Contact a reputable travel agent or call the airlines direct for more flight information, current fares, and bookings.

GETTING AROUND

New Zealand is one of the easiest countries in the world to get around—good roads and an excellent public transportation system get you anywhere you want to go. The friendly people enjoy meeting overseas visitors. It's still relatively safe to hitchhike (compared with other parts of the world), though it's a good idea for women to hitch only during the day and with at least one other person. For all your internal transportation info, stop by either a NZTP Travel Office in any of the major cities or any Public Relations Office (PRO) or Visitor Centre throughout New Zealand—they have all the latest info on the various forms of transportation, routes, fares, and special passes; PROs and info centers are listed under "Information" in each chapter. Also see the "Transportation" section at the end of each chapter.

By Coach And Train

The InterCity network covers most of the country by coach, train, and ferry. Their five-, eight-, or 22-day **Travelpass** allows great travel flexibility at an unbeatable price. The high-season pass (Dec. and Jan.) and the low-season eight-day pass (Feb. to Dec.) *must be purchased overseas.* But the 15- and 22-day low-season passes can be bought in New

STA OFFICES

IN NORTH AMERICA:

Dallas: 6609 Hillcrest Ave.
Dallas, TX 75205
tel. (214) 360-0097

Honolulu: 1831 S. King St., Suite 202
Honolulu, HI 96826
tel. (808) 942-7755

Los Angeles: 2500 Wilshire Blvd., Suite 507
L.A., CA 90057
tel. (213) 380-2184

West Hollywood: 7204 Melrose Ave.
W. Hollywood, CA 90046
tel. (213) 934-8722

Northridge: 8949 Reseda Blvd., Suite 201
Northridge, CA 91324
tel. (818) 886-0804

San Diego: 6447 El Cajon Blvd.
San Diego, CA 92115
tel. (619) 286-1322

San Francisco: 166 Geary St., Suite 702
S.F., CA 94108
tel. (415) 391-8407

IN EUROPE AND ASIA:

ARTU
Hardenbergstrasse 9
Berlin 12
West Germany

CTS
Via Genova 16
Rome
Italy

DIS
Skindergade 28
Copenhagen K
Denmark

HKSTB
130-2 Des Voeux Rd.
Hong Kong

NBBS
Dam 17
Dam Sq.
Amsterdam
Netherlands

NFUCA
Sanshin-Hokusei Bldg., 2-4-9-Yoyogi
Shibuya-ku
Tokyo
Japan

SFS-RESOR
Drottninggatan 89
Stockholm
Sweden

SSR
3 Rue Vignier
1205 Geneva
Switzerland

SSR
Leonhardstrasse 10
Zurich
Switzerland

STA
74 Old Brompton Rd.
South Kensington S.W.7
London
United Kingdom

STA
Ming Hotel Court
Singapore

USIT
7 Anglesea St.
Dublin 2
Republic of Ireland

USIT
6 Rue de Vaugirard
Paris
France

Zealand; Travelpasses start at $299 for five days, low season, or $344 for five days, high season. A seven-, 10-, 15-, or 25- day **Kiwi Coach Pass** allows unlimited coach travel at very reasonable prices on scheduled services of InterCity, Mount Cook Line, and Newmans Coachlines (the three main operators). A seven-day pass starts at around $235.

By Air

Three major airlines, Air New Zealand, Mount Cook Airlines, and Ansett New Zealand, plus a myriad of smaller scheduled airlines, make up New Zealand's internal air services between all major cities, resorts, and large provincial towns. Air New Zealand offers a "Visit New Zealand Pass" for four or six flight sectors on domestic flights, valid for 60 days, but it *must be purchased overseas*. The four-flight pass is adult $370, child $250; six flights adult $495, child $340. Another alternative to consider is the "Kiwi Air Pass," valid for 30 days, which allows travel on any Mount Cook Airline scheduled services; $799 pp. Again this *must be purchased overseas* (only available in Australia, USA, Canada, UK, Singapore, and Pacific Islands), and issued by an Air New Zealand office.

Inter-island Ferries

The least expensive and most enjoyable way to travel between the North and South islands is by ferry. The ferries offer daily services, take passengers and vehicles, and have cafeteria and bar facilities on board; the trip across from Wellington to Picton takes about 3½ hours. Basic fare starts around adult $30, child $15; the InterCity Travel Pass is valid on the ferry crossing. If you're renting a car on either island, arrange to pick up another on the other side. If you have your own car, transporting it to the other island starts from around $104-134 depending on the vehicle's overall length. More details in the "Wellington" and "Picton" chapters.

By Car

Car rental is expensive, as is petrol (around 95 cents per litre!). All the major international car rental companies usually offer both car and campervan rentals, along with many other small rental outfits throughout the country. To hire a car you must be at least 21 years old, have a current international driver's license (or a domestic permit from Australia, Austria, Canada, Fiji, German Federal Republic, Nambia, The Netherlands, South Africa, Switzerland, UK, or USA), and have comprehensive automobile insurance (arranged by the rental companies).

They rent by the day plus charge for each km, or charge on unlimited mileage; cars average $62.50 per day plus 27 cents each kilometer, or $97 per day unlimited kilometers (3-7 days). *You drive on the left-hand side of the road in New Zealand* (as in the U.K. and Australia). The **Automobile Association** is invaluable if you're a member. On proof of any overseas AA membership, pick up their excellent maps covering every area of New Zealand in detail, invaluable accommodation guides covering everything from tentsites to first-class hotels, and touring information. Offices are located in just about every large town. At main ports of entry, the offices are located in: **Auckland** at 33 Wyndham St.; in **Wellington** at 342 Lambton Quay; in **Christchurch** at 210 Hereford Street.

ENTRY REQUIREMENTS

Rules and regulations come and go. The best way to find out exactly what you need is to visit a reputable travel agent; you can also visit (or write to) the nearest NZTP Travel Office (see "More Information" below).

Immigration

The basic entry requirements for visitors staying up to six months on non-working visas are: a fully paid onward or RT ticket (and firm bookings on special-rate air fares), sufficient funds ($1000 per month, or at least $400 per month if you're staying with a N.Z. citizen, or prepaid accommodation), a valid temporary permit or visa, and passport (valid for at least three months beyond the date of departure from New Zealand). Australian passport holders and Australian residents with current resident return visas do not need a permit or another visa.

Temporary Permits (like visas but easier to get) are required for tourist visits or business trips of up to **six months** by British citizens, provided they hold passports which give them the right of permanent residence in the UK; for visits up to **three months** by citizens of Austria, Belgium, Canada, Denmark, Finland, France (if normally resident in continental France), the Federal Republic of Germany, Greece, Iceland, Indonesia, Ireland, Italy, Japan, Liechtenstein, Luxembourg, Malaysia, Malta, Monaco, The Netherlands, Norway, Portugal (only if the visitor has the right to enter Portugal for permanent residence), Singapore, Spain, Sweden, Switzerland, Thailand, Tuvalu, and the USA (not applicable to American Samoans or any other U.S. nationals); for visits up to **30 days** by citizens of France (normally resident in French Polynesia or New Caledonia). Note that Australian citizens or those from Commonwealth countries who are now permanently residing in Australia can enter New Zealand without prior permission (re-confirm this regulation with your travel agent); however, Australian citizens require passports to re-enter Australia.

If you wish to stay longer than the above entry permits allow (Australian citizens and citizens of Commonwealth countries and Ireland who live in Australia are exempt), you must get prior permission in the form of a visa. It is illegal to work, make financial gains, study, obtain medical treatment, overstay the period indicated on your entry permit, or settle in New Zealand without special permission prior to entering the country.

Visas: Citizens of all other countries than those listed above require visas to enter New Zealand. Travel agents usually arrange all necessary visas and other documentation—but allow plenty of time (at least several weeks), especially if you haven't a passport. Another source of info on vacation and work visas is your nearest New Zealand Embassy or Consulate.

Customs

If you're over 17 years old, you can bring duty-free items into New Zealand worth up to NZ$250, plus 200 cigarettes or 50 cigars or 250 grams of tobacco, 4.5 liters of wine or beer (six 750 ml bottles), and 1,125 ml of spirits (hard liquor). Contact your own country's customs office to find out what you may bring back duty-free.

New Zealand is understandably strict on agricultural requirements. Prior to landing in N.Z. you're required to fill in a declaration form stating whether you have been on a farm within the last 30 days, and what foods, plants, or animal products you are carrying. The *N.Z.—A Growing Land—Passenger Arrival Information* brochure is available from any N.Z. Embassy or Consulate. If you've been on a farm, your boots or shoes may be examined for dirt, and camping equipment such as tents and sleeping bags, and bicycles may also be checked for soil particles, insects, etc. Attempting to bring in drugs (other than prescription) is asking for big trouble, as is a dishonest declaration on any official documents—don't risk it.

More Information

For more detailed information, write to your nearest overseas N.Z. Government Tourist Bureau office (see list below). When you're in New Zealand, contact New Zealand Tourist and Publicity Travel offices (NZTP) in Auckland, Rotorua, Wellington, Christchurch, Queenstown, and Dunedin.

In the U.S.A.—**San Francisco:** Suite 810, 1 Sansome St., S.F., CA 94104; tel. (415) 788-7404. **Los Angeles:** Suite 1530, 10960 Wilshire Blvd., L.A., CA 90024; tel. (213) 477-8241. **New York:** Suite 530, 630 Fifth Ave., N.Y., NY 10111; tel. (212) 698- 4680.

In Canada—**Vancouver:** Suite 1260 IBM Tower, 701 West Georgia St., Vancouver, B.C. V7Y 1B6; tel. (210) 684-2117.

In Australia—**Sydney:** 84 Pitt St., Sydney, N.S.W. 2000; tel. (02) 233-6633. Or GPO 614, Sydney, N.S.W. 2001.

In the U.K.—**London:** N.Z. House, Haymarket, London SW1Y 4TQ; tel. (01) 930-8422.

In Germany—**Frankfurt:** N.Z. Tourist and Publicity Office, Kaiserhofstrasse 7, D6000 Frankfurt am Maine, West Germany; tel. (069) 288-189.

In Japan—**Tokyo:** N.Z. Embassy Annex, Toho Twin Tower Building 2F 1-5-2 Yurakucho Chiyoda-ku 100, Tokyo; tel. (03) 508-9981.

In **Singapore:** N.Z. Tourist Office, 13 Nassim Rd., Singapore 1025; tel. 235-9966.

WHAT TO TAKE

Clothing

Most New Zealanders are casual dressers (by day and night), attending to comfort and suiting the occasion. However, dressing up is the norm for fine restaurants, nightclubs, and discos in the resorts and major cities—a few places still require a jacket and tie or smart attire, and restrict jeans, T-shirts, and thongs. New Zealand's weather is unpredictable, especially in mountainous areas; it's best to be prepared for everything no matter which season you arrive—and keep in mind that the seasons are opposite to those of the Northern Hemisphere. If you're an outdoor type, in summer take shorts, jeans, shirts, and a good pair of slacks or a dressy dress for evenings on the town, a bathing suit, warm sweater, windproof jacket, raincoat or poncho (great for covering you *and* your backpack), at least one pair of thick wool socks, hiking boots, tennis or sandshoes and dressier sandals, plus your basic necessities. Don't forget sunscreen, and a small bottle of vinegar—for dabbing on sandfly bites! In winter you need all of the above, but add thermal underwear, flannel shirts or lightweight sweaters, another wool sweater or two, more wool socks, an extra warm jacket (down is great) or coat, a long raincoat, and substitute shoes for sandals. If you're going to hit all the resorts, take some dressier clothes and appropriate footwear to be on the safe side.

Buying clothes in N.Z. can be expensive, but wool products, in particular sweaters, bush shirts, and sheepskin coats, are of high quality and you can pick up a bargain if you're willing to shop around. Leave your electric razor or hairdryer at home, or buy an adaptor—N.Z. is on 230 volts AC, 50 hertz, and sockets accept three-pin flat plugs; hotels and motels often provide 110-volt AC sockets for razors only.

One last tip: If you're backpacking, take less than you think you'll really need—you'll invariably discard some of your "essentials." The occasional sheepskin rug, woodcarving, and other paraphernalia collected along the way soon add up and make life miserable. Eliminate all but the essentials—you'll be glad you did!

Photo Equipment

New Zealand is a photographer's paradise—great light, spectacular scenery, and friendly people everywhere you go. Take a 35mm camera, several lenses, and plenty of film. Film is widely available in chemists' shops (pharmacies) and at photographic dealers in New Zealand, but it's expensive to buy and develop. If you're coming from the U.S., it's cheaper to stock up on film at home and take it back with you (in your main luggage) for developing; if you're worried about the X-ray machines at the airport spoiling undeveloped film in your camera, request that the camera be hand-searched—it's better to be safe than sorry!

Special Hobby Equipment

If you're an angler, it's best to bring your own fly rod, fishing pole, and waders with you—they're hard to hire. Flies and lures are readily available in sporting stores. Big-game fishing equipment is generally included in the cost of hiring a boat and guide. Hunters can bring their own guns into the country but need to get permits from N.Z. police (for details, see hunting, p. 31). Scuba diving and skiing equipment are both easy to hire. If you're a mountaineer, you may want to bring your own equipment to ensure your safety, but most of it can also be hired (bring your own rope).

ACCOMMODATIONS

Forest huts, free campsites, inexpensive motor camps, hostels, cozy bed and breakfast guesthouses, farmstays, first-class motels,

Travel with a tent and sleeping bag and you'll find perfect camping spots wherever you go!

hotels, and luxury lodges—New Zealand provides accommodations of international standards with a wide price range to suit all budgets. Use the prices throughout this book as an approximate guide. At present, prices in general are increasing at a rapid rate, and the goods and services tax (GST) of 12½% has added to the confusion! Save yourself time and money by letting your fingers do the walking—telephone ahead to compare and confirm current rates, and always ask if any off-peak concessions are available.

Free

If you enjoy camping out and have a tent and stove, New Zealand is a camper's paradise. You can put up a tent pretty much anywhere off the beaten track—but avoid camping close to tramping tracks and areas designated as "reserves." "No Camping" signs are only too obvious in areas where you're not permitted to camp—those who camp there anyway may be asked to move on, or fined. In remote but popular areas (such as along the road to Milford), campsites with limited facilities and a source of drinking water have been provided, some free, some at minimal charge. **Forest Service huts** are scattered throughout the forests of New Zealand; Dept. of Conservation staff have first option, but if they're not full you can stay in the huts for free or for a few dollars. Some have stoves, others open fireplaces—some have no cooking facilities. The maximum stay is three nights and you can't book ahead; in peak periods they fill up rapidly—take camping and cooking gear just in case.

National Park Huts

All the national parks provide comfortable huts along major hiking tracks and climbing routes. Backcountry huts are classed according to the facilities provided. Payment is through a ticket system; buy the tickets ($4 each) in advance from Dept. of Conservation offices, visitor centers, outdoor recreation clubs, or places displaying the "Backcountry Huts Tickets Sold Here" sign. Ask for Dept. of Conservation's very handy *Accommodation and Camping Guide* at any Conservation office; it lists all the national, maritime, forest park, and scenic reserve huts throughout the country, their locations and facilities. Date the ticket when you reach the hut, deposit one section of each ticket there, and display the other section the following day (to prove you've paid your fee). Buy 15 tickets or more and you get a 10% discount.

All huts have bunks with mattresses or sleeping platforms. Category 1 (fully serviced) huts have stoves, fuel, toilet facilities, and a water supply. They may also have lighting, heating, radio communications, drying facilities, and a hut warden; $12 a night (three tickets). Category 2 (intermediate) huts have toilet facilities and a water supply. They may also have cooking and heating facilities; $8 a night. Category 3 (basic) huts have toilets and a water supply; $4 a night. Category 4 shelters are free. If you camp beside a category one or two hut, your campsite costs $4 a night. Like the forest huts, you can only stay in each for a couple of nights, and you can't book ahead; take a tent and stove in peak periods as the huts are more than likely to be crowded.

Motor Camps

Motor camps are one of New Zealand's best accommodation values, and great places to meet fellow travelers—particularly vacationing New Zealanders. They provide tentsites (from $6 pp) and caravan sites (from $8 pp) or have on-site caravans for hire (from $18 d), sparsely furnished cabins (from $20 d, provide your own sleeping bag or linen), and tourist flats with or without private facilities (from $30 d, provide your own linen). Usually containing bunk beds, pillows, table and chairs, and heater, the cabins and flats vary in price according to the number sharing and the facilities provided; for the price they're very reasonable—and especially appreciated when you're tired of camping out or when it's raining cats and dogs and all your belongings are wet! All motor camps provide communal bathroom, kitchen, and laundry facilities, and some have a TV and/or game room, pool, sauna, and playground facilities for the kids. Many of the kitchen blocks also provide boiling water on tap and a refrigerator for communal use, but you need to provide your own crockery, utensils, pots and pans. In the resorts during peak periods and school holidays, cabins and tourist flats may be booked out, but you can usually find a bed at motor camps on the outskirts of town; finding tent and caravan sites is usually no problem.

If you're an Automobile Association member, stop by any AA office in New Zealand and collect their invaluable *AA North Island Outdoor Guide* and *South Island Guide* (free to members). Also pick up the *New Zealand Camp, Cabin and Caravan Accommodation Guide,* the directory of the Camp & Cabin Association, available free from PROs and tourist info offices.

Finally, pick up a handy *New Zealand Accommodation Guide* booklet, free from any NZTP Travel Office.

YHA Hostels

Youth hostels are situated throughout the country, offering inexpensive comfortable lodging and plenty of good company. Many of the hostels, ranging from cozy little farmhouses to wonders of modern architecture, are located in prime locations—often not far from the luxury hotels, and they're great places to meet Kiwis and overseas travelers. Sleeping in bunk beds in single-sex dorms (a few hostels have "family rooms"), members share communal bathroom, kitchen, living room, and laundry facilities; from $8-14 pp per night depending on the facilities provided. You have to be a Youth Hostel Association member, and it's a good idea to have your own pillowcase and sleeping bag, crockery, and cooking utensils. You can also hire bed linen for a small fee.

You don't need to be a "youth" to stay in a YH—members of all ages over five are welcome! Membership can be obtained overseas (it's less expensive to join in your home country), or bought in New Zealand from any YH or YHA office (New Zealanders can also join at any Westpac Bank); $20 for a senior membership (over 18) plus an initial $10 joining fee, $10 for a junior membership with no joining fee, valid internationally. Once you're in N.Z., you can buy a **discount card**—the 20/200 card giving you 20 nights for $200; the 9/99 card giving you nine nights for $99; or a "Go as you please" card where you collect 12 hostel stamps and get the 13th night for free—from YHA offices in Christchurch, Auckland, and Wellington, or hostel managers. If you join in New Zealand, the handy YHA *Come Hostelling Handbook* is issued free with membership; it tells you where all the hostels are, what each hostel is like, and lists local activities and attractions. If you're traveling light, ask for *The Good Bed Guide* pamphlet instead.

Most of the hostels are closed during the day (1000-1700) unless the weather is really bad, and there is a 2230 curfew at night (later in major resorts and cities). Maximum stay is three nights, and you're expected to help with the clean-up each morning. Hostels fill up rapidly during vacation periods and school holidays, but you can book ahead—a good idea if the hostel is in a popular tourist resort or major city. Write to the individual hostel warden, or to the YHA National Reservations Centre, P.O. Box 1687, Auckland, including a money order or bank draft for the first night and an International Reply coupon. The organization's main office is at 28 Worcester St., Christchurch, tel. 799-970, and there's another in Auckland at Australis House, 36 Customs St. East. Other benefits come with membership—discount car rental, discounts on rail and ferry rides and some attraction admissions, special package holidays (ski packages), and discounts on some commercially operated activities (rafting). The organization also offers many reasonably priced Hostelling Holidays (package tours), including all scheduled land or air transportation within N.Z., accommodation at YHA hostels, sightseeing, and the YHANZ Handbook—book through any YHA travel office.

Backpacker Lodges

Budget lodges can be found in most of the major cities and resorts throughout the country. These lodges, primarily catering to backpackers and those traveling on a small budget, provide bunk-bed dorms (some have private single and double rooms), shared bathroom, kitchen, and laundry facilities, a common room, and a laid-back atmosphere where it's usually a breeze to make new friends. Some of the best have extra facilities, such as a shop selling all the basics, BBQ area, bicycle and outdoor recreational equipment hire, transportation service, and more. And some motor camps make dorm rooms or shared cabins available at backpacker prices if you're willing to share a room with others. In general you can expect to pay from $12-17.50 pp per night.

Pick up the latest *New Zealand Budget and Backpackers Accommodation* brochure (free) at visitor info centers; it lists many of the best lodges, along with their addresses, facilities, and the price per night, and the brochure is paper-light (handy for cyclists). Also refer to the *New Zealand Backpackers Bible* booklet, which advertises lodges throughout New Zealand and Australia.

YMCAs And YWCAs

These are generally found in the larger towns and cities. Usually full of students and temporary workers, they're considerably less packed than YHs during peak vacation periods and are a little more private. From around $20 pp, they offer similar accommodations to YHs but you have a private room or share with only one other person, linen is provided, and breakfast and dinner are usually provided as part of the overnight rate. Some Ys serve three meals a day.

Bed And Breakfast Guesthouses And Private Budget Hotels

B&Bs, most very comfortable and full of character, run about $20-40 pp per night depending on the locality and facilities provided, and the breakfasts are usually hearty enough to last you till dinner! They're yet another good way to meet New Zealanders and are very popular, especially in the larger cities—if you have some idea of where you want to stay and you'll be there during a vacation period, book ahead. Some budget hotels provide breakfast, some don't. If the budget hotel you choose is full, most managers will tell you where to find similarly priced accommodations, and some have lists of all the budget hotels around the country available for the asking.

Motels

For the most part, New Zealand motels are very different from the usual motels of other countries. There are two types: motel flats and serviced motels. **Motel flats** are complete apartments—great value for the price! For about $40-80 d, you get several rooms—

often two bedrooms with two single beds or a double bed in each, a living room with TV, a fully equipped kitchen including utensils, pots and pans, toaster (occasionally even a blender!), a bathroom with shower, and sometimes even your own laundry facilities. They usually also provide a swimming pool, spa, playground, and/or other facilities. Many motels are part of a major chain but privately run, and the owners are friendly and eager to suggest places to see, things to do, and good local restaurants. **Best Western Motels, Hotels, and Motor Inns** are always good-value; book by calling the Central Reservations Office in Auckland at tel. 792-854 (they accept all major credit cards) or through any travel agent. **Serviced motels** are like standard motels, offering a sparsely furnished room (linen provided) with a private bathroom, kettle or hot water jug, coffee and tea bags, and usually a bottle of milk. The prices are a little less or comparable to motel flats, but not as good-value.

Before you leave home, have your travel agent check for special package deals; some (such as Best Western) occasionally offer a package containing both accommodation and car rental vouchers for a very reasonable price. To get the savings, the package must be purchased overseas. The drawback is that you have to specify a date to start the deal and use the vouchers up consecutively every night. The vouchers cover accommodation in motel flats and top-class hotels all around New Zealand—you usually get the least fancy rooms they have but they're still very comfortable. A list of applicable motels comes with the vouchers, and booking ahead is not absolutely necessary—unless you're traveling around the country during peak vacation periods.

Farm Holidays

Many farm properties throughout New Zealand offer you the opportunity to either join in with farm activities or just stay there and do your own thing. Most offer extras like a pool, tennis court, horseback riding, golf, hunting, and fishing. Some accommodation is in the family home, sharing facilities; some may be in separate houses. A stay can range from one night with breakfast to several weeks full board, and prices vary accordingly from about $70-150 d per night, depending on the activities offered.

Many organizations offer a large range of farms to choose from: Farmhouse Holidays, 83 Kitchener Rd., Milford, Auckland 9, tel. 492-171, sponsors go-as-you-please farm holidays with no set itinerary and very reasonable full-board rates. The Friendly Kiwi Home Hosting Service, P.O. Box 5049, Port Nelson (tel. 85-575), provides farm stays specializing in outdoor activities. Farmstay Limited, P.O. Box 630, Rotorua, tel. 24-895 or 83-536, offers farm accommodation which includes all meals, and transfers by private car. NZ Home Hospitality Ltd., P.O. Box 309, Nelson, tel. 82-424, has B&B, farm holidays, and self-drive tours. Farm Holidays Ltd., P.O. Box 1436, Wellington, tel. 723-216, provides accommodation at working farms in homesteads or in separate farmhouses; kitchen utensils provided, you provide linen and food. Rural Tours, P.O. Box 228, Cambridge, features homestead holidays in the Cambridge area of the North Island. For more details on any of the above, a larger selection, or bookings, contact any NZTP Travel Office in N.Z. or any N.Z. Tourist office overseas.

Host Family Accommodations

Several organizations offer accommodation with families throughout New Zealand—an excellent chance to meet Kiwis and make everlasting friends! Both city and country locations are offered, and prices vary accordingly. Rates start at around $40 s or $70 d B&B; most places also provide dinner or full board at extra cost.

New Zealand Home Hospitality Ltd., P.O. Box 309, Nelson, provides homes throughout both islands and all meals; reservations and pre-payment required. Homes are also available through New Zealand Travel Hosts, 279 Williams St., Kaiapoi, Canterbury, tel. 27-6340. The Friendly Kiwi Home Hospitality Box 5049, Port Nelson, tel. 83-130, is only for Nelson City and district, pre-booking not necessary but desirable. Homestay Limited, Rotorua, P.O. Box 630, Rotorua, tel. 24-895,

For a delicious traditional hangi, *geyser views, and a Maori cultural concert, go to Geyserland Hotel in Rotorua.*

offers homes throughout the North Island only, all meals, and transfers to and from the city.

Luxury Accommodations
New Zealand has plenty of first-class hotels (more are blossoming everywhere due to the rapidly growing tourist industry), widely recognized international hotel chains (such as Best Western, Flag Inns, Hyatt Kingsgate, Regency, Regent, Sheraton, and Travelodge), and private lodges catering to sportsmen of all kinds. Many of the most ritzy lodges specifically cater to fishing and hunting enthusiasts, and provide all kinds of facilities and experienced guides at extra cost; prices vary greatly but you can expect to pay anything from $95-400 pp per night for full board. The Tourist Hotel Corporation of New Zealand (THC) operates a string of first-class hotels throughout the country. Most of their buildings are located in the most beautiful areas, have the best views, and are often the center of activities in remote areas. Even if you're camping down the road, you'll probably visit a THC during your trip—to purchase tour tickets, eat (some have reasonable cafes as well as first-class restaurants), be entertained, or just admire the architecture (e.g. the THC Tongariro); prices start at around $90 d and go all the way up! For more info on THCs, contact the Tourist Hotel Corporation of New Zealand, 35 Albert St., Auckland, tel. 773-689.

FOOD

New Zealand is a land of plenty. Rich, creamy, dairy products, lamb "fed on lush meadow grass and mother's milk," and the brown furry kiwifruit (brought over from central China about 80 years ago, it was called a Chinese gooseberry and renamed for export), are just a few of the many delicious items New Zealand produces. Most of the food should be familiar to visitors; New Zealand boasts French, Greek, Chinese, Mexican, Japanese, Italian, Indian, American, Vietnamese, and vegetarian, as well as traditional New Zealand and Polynesian restaurants. A Maori *hangi* (feast), featuring Maori specialties steamed to perfection in an underground oven, is an eating experience that shouldn't be missed (see "Food" under "Rotorua," p. 189).

Meats
Lamb is naturally one of the most popular traditional dishes. Often cooked as a juicy roast with garlic and rosemary and served slightly pink with a tangy mint sauce, lamb is generally on the menu of almost every restau-

rant in the country. Hogget, or one-year-old lamb, is more tasty than younger lamb but not as strong as mutton. Beef is excellent and reasonably priced in restaurants—and nothing beats sizzling, thick juicy steaks and sausages, crisp salads, chilled wine or beer, good company, and cicadas singing from the trees at a traditional New Zealand "barby." Chicken or "chook" is another favorite; sausages or "bangers" come in all shapes and sizes and are most frequently served battered and deep fried at takeaways. New Zealanders are also partial to farm-raised or "home-grown" venison (expensive unless bought patty-form in a venison burger), veal, duck and pheasant (some of the sporting lodge restaurants specialize in game), and wild pork. If you like experimenting with different tastes, try muttonbird—it's a Maori delicacy that tastes like fish-flavored chicken!

Hot meat pies loaded with lamb or beef and gravy enclosed in flaky pastry, commonly served warm (from takeaways) with potato chips or pub-style with mashed potatoes, peas, and gravy, are virtually a national dish. If you're a pie fancier, try the many kinds of savory pies—egg and bacon, pork, and mincemeat; they make a quick and filling, inexpensive lunch. When you're in the mood for potato chips, try salt and vinegar flavor.

Seafood

New Zealand's bountiful variety of shellfish ranges from *toheroa, tuatua, pipi, paua,* cockles, and oysters (several varieties), to lobsters, scallops (great in Marlborough, season Aug. to Feb.), and crayfish (also called spiny lobster or rock lobster). *Toheroa,* found along the northwest beaches of the North Island, make one of the best shellfish soups in the world, but unfortunately it's seldom available fresh due to strict conservation measures—if you get the chance, take it (otherwise find it canned in supermarkets). Other seafood, such as cod, flounder, *hapuka,* kingfish, John Dory, snapper, squid, and *terekihi,* are all good tasting and widely available. Bluff oysters (try them fresh during the winter months in the south of the South Island) and marinated mussels are very popular with connoisseurs—if you can't get fresh, look for them canned in the supermarket. Freshwater fish lovers can easily find salmon (fresh and smoked), whitebait (tiny transparent fish fried in batter or cooked in fritters—another N.Z. delicacy), and eels. To sample a rainbow or brown trout fresh from a crystal-clear stream is a real treat—both are superb. Trout are not sold commercially, but if you catch one yourself (it's not too difficult!), most restaurants will prepare it for you on request. Fish and chips, wrapped in paper and newspaper, from the local takeaway or fish and chip shop is one of the best and least expensive ways to sample a wide variety of New Zealand seafood.

Fruit And Vegies

Fresh fruit and vegetables are abundant throughout the year. Try some of the more exotic ones if you have the chance. A few you may not recognize are aubergines (eggplants), beetroot (red beets), bilberries (blueberries), courgettes (small zucchinis), *feijoas* (an exotic-tasting fruit available April and May), Chinese gooseberries or kiwifruit (high in vitamin C, best from May to Dec.), *kumara* (a root vegetable similar to a sweet potato), rock melon (a small sweet melon), and *tamarilloes* or tree tomatoes—red jelly-like fruit found May to December. Strawberries, raspberries, boysenberries, and loganberries are best in Jan. and Feb., melons and avocados after Christmas, passion fruit in March and April, and asparagus in September.

Desserts

Every tearoom in the country offers a variety of cakes filled with fresh cream, custard- or fruit-filled tarts, and cream buns. The famous and traditional dessert, pavlova, is made of meringue, crunchy on the outside and gooey inside, filled with whipped cream and fresh fruit—traditionally strawberries and kiwifruit, dribbled with passionfruit. Both New Zealand and Australia take pride in the invention of this dessert (natives of each argue over where it was first created) in honor of dancer Anna Pavlova, who visited New Zealand in the 1920s. Feeling peckish yet?!

Dairy Foods

New Zealand's rich dairy foods are lethal to the waistline but oh-so-good! Ice cream, especially the fruit-flavored ice creams loaded with chunks of real fruit, takes top place for any sweet tooth. Creamy milk is still delivered in glass bottles (New Zealanders generally prefer glass to cartons, though both are available), and a wide variety of tasty cheeses, including local Camembert, feta, Gouda, Romano, Gruyère, N.Z. blue vein, Brie, and Cheddar, are readily available.

Breakfast

One of the things N.Z. lacks is chain-type restaurants serving cheap breakfasts at breakfast-time and all hours. The best breakfasts are provided by bed and breakfast guesthouses, usually either Continental—O.J., rolls or croissants, and coffee, or cooked breakfasts ("a grill")—eggs, bacon or sausages, grilled tomatoes, toast and marmalade . A cooked breakfast usually lasts you till dinner! Vegemite or Marmite, salty spreads made from yeast extract, are almost always provided for serious toast spreading, as well as jam or jelly—New Zealander, Australian, and British children grow up on Vegemite or Marmite sandwiches and seem to experience DTs if deprived for some length of time! An alternative is to have a reasonably priced brunch (from about 1000) in one of the many tearooms scattered across the land.

Lunch

The least expensive and most delicious way to have lunch is to stop at a deli and buy a loaf of bread, butter, and a variety of cheeses, fresh fruit, etc. Hot pies are also tasty and cheap, and numerous takeaways sell fish and chips, sausages, pies, battered and deep-fried goods, and of course hamburgers. Another alternative is the tearoom. Tearooms are found in just about every town in New Zealand. They start with morning teas at about 1000-1100, progress to lunch, followed by afternoon teas—but eating in a tearoom can often end up costing you more because you can't resist trying something new! They sell all sorts of hot pies, sandwiches, and filled rolls (typically meat and salad, just salad, or egg salad and cheese), and other intriguing morsels such as baked beans and melted cheese on toast and fat sausages filled with mashed potato and cheese! Beetroot (red beets) is slapped in almost everything, including all hamburgers, so if you don't like it be sure to specify "no beetroot." All sorts of desserts are also available. Tipping is not required nor expected.

Dinner

Dinner is often called "tea" by New Zealanders. Cooking your own dinner is the least expensive method, but reasonably priced takeaways are everywhere—Chinese is one of the most popular. Pubs offer good deals on dinners, and some chain restaurants (such as Cobb & Co., attached to pubs) offer substantial meals at a fairly reasonable price. Many restaurants have a special BYO (bring your own) license that lets you carry your own wine in. This means they don't need a liquor or wine license so the food is generally less expensive; it also lets you buy wine within your budget. Some of the fanciest restaurants have a strict dress code requiring men to wear jacket and tie (almost phased-out) and women to be "smartly dressed"; all restaurants require decent attire and entry is not permitted without a shirt and shoes. If you think you want to splurge on a meal or entertainment sometime during your stay, take a good jacket, dressy dress, and appropriate shoes, in case—old battered tennis shoes and jeans are somewhat frowned upon! Tipping is not required nor expected, but is appreciated if extra good service is given.

Drinks

New Zealand has excellent public water supplies and tap (faucet) water is safe to drink throughout the country. All the usual fruit juices, mineral waters, and soft drinks are available—try "Lemon and Paeroa," lemon-flavored mineral water from Paeroa in the

North Island. A wide range of beer and wine, both local and imported, is available from licensed hotels or pubs, bottle shops (often attached to the hotel), or discount bottle stores. Licensed hotels serve alcohol from 1100-2200 Mon. through Fri., till 2300 on Sat. nights, and are closed on Sundays. Licensed restaurants can serve alcohol with meals any hour. The best deals and choices are found at the discount bottle store, and then taken to a BYO restaurant; a small corkage fee is generally charged for opening the bottle. Discount bottle stores offer alcohol at bargain prices but you have to buy at least two gallons!

Commonly Misunderstood Words

If you like "ketchup" with your fries, ask for tomato sauce (ketchup also exists but it's completely different from American-style). "French fries" are called hot chips, potato chips are just called chips. "Tea" can mean a cup of hot tea, or a complete dinner—confirm the exact meaning before you accept an invitation! "Napkins" are called serviettes.

MONEY

New Zealand has been on the decimal currency system based on dollars and cents since 1966; 1-, 2-, 5-, 10-, 20-, and 50-dollar notes, and 1-, 2-, 5-, 10-, 20-, and 50-cent coins are used. Banks and other financial organizations offer a variety of services. Trading banks are open Mon. to Fri. from 0900-1600, closed weekends and public holidays; however, banking facilities at airport terminals provide foreign exchange services for all international arrivals and departures (occasionally closed for late-night departures).

The easiest and safest way to carry your money is in the form of travelers cheques—either foreign-dollar travelers cheques (the best deal) which you need to exchange at a trading bank (or hotels, restaurants, and large stores where the exchange rate is not as good), or N.Z. dollar travelers cheques which can be cashed anywhere. If you're likely to be hiking off the beaten track, it may be wise to carry cheques of both currencies so that you don't have to worry about reaching a bank before weekends or holidays. Be sure to jot down the number of each cheque and the place where you cashed it, and keep the records separate from the actual cheques. This will greatly speed up a refund if you should lose them; some companies won't refund without your transaction records.

Another way to access money is to open a bank account on arrival in New Zealand and have your bank at home wire money over. Of

course the exchange rate will be non-fluctuating (often an advantage), but you'll be making interest while you travel. New Zealand post offices are also handy institutions for getting money; open up a p.o. savings account anywhere and you can withdraw from any p.o. in the country, Mon. to Friday. Major credit cards such as American Express, Visa, MasterCard, Diners Club, and Carte Blanche are generally accepted throughout New Zealand.

When you first enter New Zealand, you may be asked to prove that you have enough money with you to cover your intended length of stay—$1000 per month, or at least $400 per month if you have a guarantee of accommodation from a N.Z. resident, or evidence of pre-paid accommodation, or an American Express, Bankcard, Diners Club, MasterCard, or Visa credit card. This seems to happen with regularity to those expecting to stay in the country for at least a couple of months without a work visa (permission to work and a work visa must be obtained prior to entry). There's no restriction on the amount of foreign or N.Z. currency brought in or out of the country, but be sure to exchange most of it prior to your departure to benefit from current exchange rates.

HEALTH

New Zealand is a "healthy" country. Vaccinations are not required to enter. The drinking water is good tasting and safe to drink from the tap throughout the country. There are no dangerous wild animals or poisonous snakes to worry about; the only poisonous spider is the *katipo* but it's very rarely seen. If you enjoy soaking in natural hot springs or thermal pools (public or private), keep your head above water at all times and don't let the water enter your nose or ears—there's always the possibility of getting amoebic meningitis (inflammation of the brain) in hot pools.

Public and private hospitals and medical treatments are of high standards, but it's wise to have health insurance as medical and hospital treatments due to illness are not free. Accident compensation (covering personal injuries occurring while in N.Z.) is free; it includes compensation for medical and hospital expenses or permanent incapacity directly due to the accident, no matter whose fault it is. (The insurance does not cover a loss of earning ability.)

If you take a prescription drug of any kind, take adequate supplies with you, and the prescription in case you run out. Chemists (pharmacies) are open normal shopping hours, and they usually have after-hours chemists listed on the door. Also, if you wear eyeglasses or contact lenses, take your prescription or a spare pair. If you should need an ambulance, dial 111 in major centers; the telephone number is also listed inside public telephone booths and in the front section of all telephone directories.

Tips To Prevent Jet Lag

A long-distance flight causes your body's natural time-clock to go haywire, and the air conditioning causes dehydration. Try to get plenty of sleep the night before flying, wear loose, comfortable clothing and footwear during the flight, walk around the plane regularly (about once an hour) to reduce swollen feet and ankles, and drink plenty of water, fruit juices, or soft drinks (and no alcohol) throughout the flight. If you still arrive tired and grumpy with swollen feet, check into a hotel the first night and sleep as long as you can—then your vacation will get off on the right foot!

PRACTICAL INFORMATION

Electrical Appliances

New Zealand runs on 230 volts AC, 50 hertz, and most power sockets only accept three-pin flat plugs. If you're taking an electric appliance such as razor or hairdryer, buy a voltage transformer and suitable plug adaptor from a hardware store, or an appliance that can switch to the appropriate voltage.

Telephone Services
Local calls from a public telephone box (or booth) are generally 20 cents—instructions are found inside the box or in the front section of the telephone directory. Calls can also be made using a plastic phone card—buy a $5, $10, $20, or $50 card at a dairy, service station, or Telecom Centre. Trunk or long-distance calls have to be placed through the long-distance operator, and costs are based on the duration of the call. National and international toll calls can be dialed direct or placed through the operator (more expensive). Phone numbers throughout New Zealand are being/have been changed recently. If you get a busy signal, call directory assistance and check the number.

Shopping
Most shops and stores are open Mon. to Thurs. from 0900-1730, on Fri. from 0900-2100 for "late-night shopping" (in major cities, each suburb has its own late shopping night which is not necessarily Fri.), on Sat. from 0900-1200, and closed Sunday. The only shops open on Sun. are milkbars or dairies (selling groceries, dairy products, fruit, and snacks), newsagents (usually open only for a short period to sell the Sun. paper), and tourist shops in the major cities and resorts.

Some New Zealand Embassies And Consulates

Athens: The N.Z. Embassy
An. Tsoha 15-17, Ambelokipi
Athens 115 21
tel. (01) 641-0311/2/3/4/5

Bonn: The N.Z. Embassy
Bonn-Centre H.I. 902,
Bundeskanzlerplatz
5300 Bonn
tel. (0228) 21-40-21/22/23

Brisbane: The N.Z. Consulate-General
GPO Box 62, Brisbane
QLD 4001
tel. (07) 221-9933

Canberra: The N.Z. High Commission
Commonwealth Ave.
Canberra, A.C.T. 2600
tel. (062) 73-3611

Jakarta: The N.Z. Embassy
P.O. Box 2439 JKT
Jakarta
tel. (021) 330-552/620/622/680/696

London: The N.Z. High Commission
New Zealand House
The Haymarket
London SW1Y 4TQ
tel. (01) 930-8422

Los Angeles: The N.Z. Consulate-General
Suite 1530 15th Floor
Tishman Building
10960 Wilshire Blvd.
L.A., CA 90024
tel. (213) 477-8241

Melbourne: The N.Z. Consulate-General
GPO Box 2136T
Melbourne, Vic. 3001
tel. (03) 670-8111

New York: The N.Z. Consulate-General
Suite 530, 630 Fifth Ave.
Rockerfeller Centre
N.Y., NY 10111
tel. (212) 698-4650

Ottawa: The N.Z. High Commission
Metropolitan House, Suite 801
99 Bank St., Ottawa
Ont. K1P 6G3
tel. (613) 238-5991

Paris: The N.Z. Embassy
7 ter, rue Leonard de Vinci
75116 Paris
tel. (01) 4500-2411

Perth: The N.Z. Consulate
GPO Box X2277
Perth, W.A. 6001
tel. (09) 325-7877

Rome: The N.Z. Embassy
Via Zara, 28
Rome 00198
tel. (06) 851-225

San Francisco: The N.Z. Trade Commission and Tourist Publicity Office
Suite 810, 1 Sansome St.
S.F., CA 94104
tel. (415) 788-7444

Sydney: The N.Z. Consulate-General
GPO Box 365
Sydney, N.S.W. 2001
tel. (02) 233-8388

Tokyo: The N.Z. Embassy
20-40 Kamiyama-cho
Shibuya-ku, Tokyo 150
tel. (03) 467-2271/5

Washington: The N.Z. Embassy
37 Observatory Circle N.W.
Washington, D.C. 20008
tel. (202) 328-4800

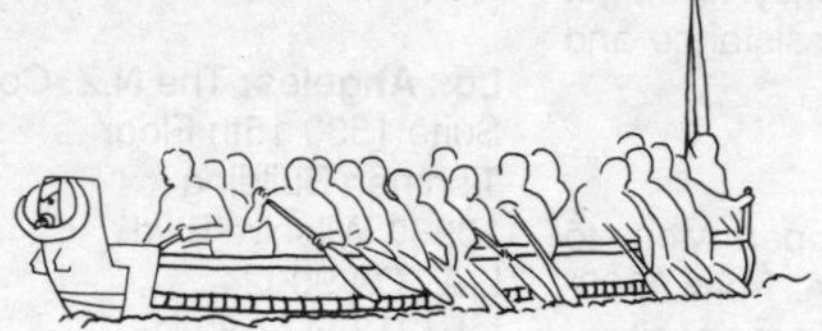

NORTH ISLAND

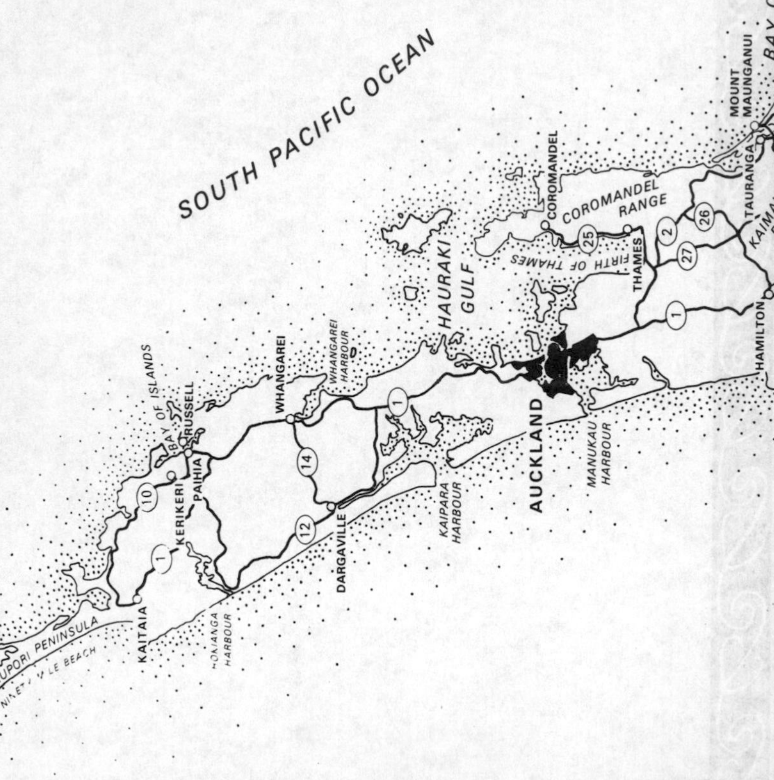
THE NORTH ISLAND
SOUTH PACIFIC OCEAN
CAPE REINGA
AUPORI PENINSULA
KAITAIA
KERIKERI
PAIHIA
RUSSELL
BAY OF ISLANDS
WHANGAREI
WHANGAREI HARBOUR
DARGAVILLE
KAIPARA HARBOUR
AUCKLAND
MANUKAU HARBOUR
HAURAKI GULF
COROMANDEL
COROMANDEL RANGE
FIRTH OF THAMES
THAMES
HAMILTON
TAURANGA
MOUNT MAUNGANUI
BAY OF PLENTY
1
10
12
14
25
2
26
27

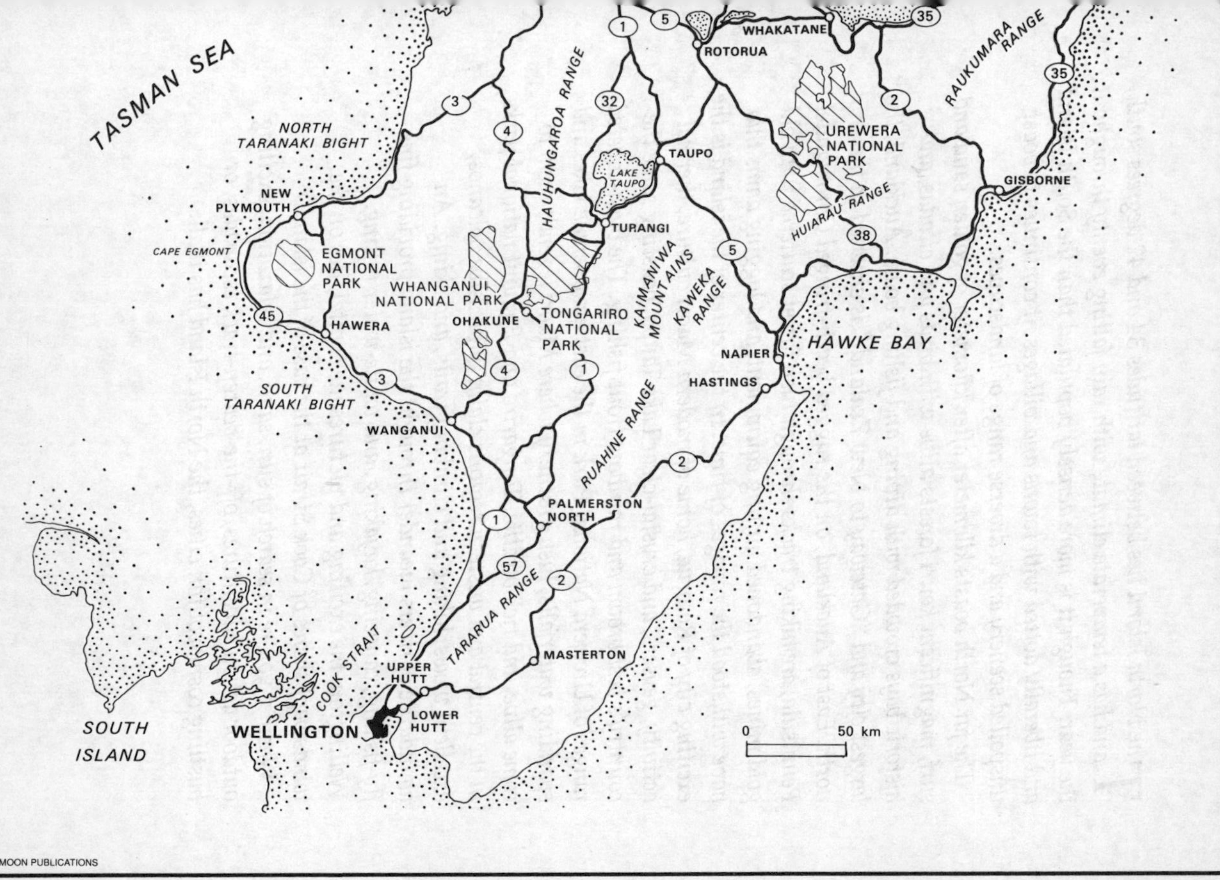
TASMAN SEA
NORTH TARANAKI BIGHT
NEW PLYMOUTH
CAPE EGMONT
EGMONT NATIONAL PARK
WHANGANUI NATIONAL PARK
HAWERA
OHAKUNE
TONGARIRO NATIONAL PARK
SOUTH TARANAKI BIGHT
WANGANUI
HAUHUNGAROA RANGE
LAKE TAUPO
TAUPO
TURANGI
ROTORUA
WHAKATANE
UREWERA NATIONAL PARK
HUIARAU RANGE
RAUKUMARA RANGE
GISBORNE
KAIMANAWA MOUNTAINS
KAWEKA RANGE
HAWKE BAY
NAPIER
HASTINGS
RUAHINE RANGE
PALMERSTON NORTH
TARARUA RANGE
MASTERTON
UPPER HUTT
LOWER HUTT
COOK STRAIT
WELLINGTON
SOUTH ISLAND
0
50 km
1
2
3
4
5
32
35
38
45
57

The North Island lies between latitudes 34 and 42 degrees south, and has a temperate climate with rain falling evenly throughout the year. Though it is more densely populated than the South Island and liberally dotted with towns and villages, it continues to boast unspoiled scenery and a diverse range of landscapes.

The far North boasts kilometer after kilometer of golden sand and surf, magnificent kauri forests alive with birds and cicadas, and historic bays crowded with diving and fishing boats. Auckland, the largest city and "Gateway to New Zealand," is situated in the north. East of Auckland, on the rugged beach-fringed Coromandel Peninsula, are hiking tracks through lush forest scattered with old gold mines, abandoned mining equipment, and logging dams that have withstood the ravages of time. In the center of the island is the exciting city of Rotorua, home of modern Maori culture, thermal activity, geysers, and crystal-clear Lake Taupo, boasting some the country's best brown and rainbow trout fishing. The bush-covered ranges of Urewera National Park in the east have serene lakes and sparkling waterfalls, lush greenery where Maori legends seem to come alive, and rich birdlife. Tongariro and Egmont national parks in the central and western regions claim impressive volcanos, excellent views, hiking and climbing trails, and skiing. An abundance of rivers meander throught the island providing fine fly-fishing, canoeing, kayaking, and white-water rafting. Wellington, the exciting and picturesque capital, lies on the windswept shores of Cook Strait at the base of the island.

Whether you're in search of sun, sand, and relaxation, exciting outdoor action adventures, off-the-beaten-track escapades, or bustling cosmopolitan cities, the North Island has it all.

AUCKLAND

INTRODUCTION

Auckland, a vibrant, exciting city, has attractions to suit both outdoor enthusiasts and those who thrive in a bustling, concrete-and-glass metropolis. Most of the country's overseas visitors first arrive here, so it's often referred to as "the Gateway to New Zealand." Largest city in the country, almost one-quarter of the population (over 829,000) lives within its sprawling urban area; it's also home to one of the world's largest Polynesian populations (140,000).

Straddling a narrow piece of land between magnificent Waitemata and Manukau harbours, Auckland is flanked by the South Pacific Ocean to the east and the Tasman Sea to the west—a sailor's paradise. All year 'round Waitemata Harbour is dotted with boats of all kinds, the water a sparkling backdrop to many colorful sails. Home to thousands of sailing vessels, it's easy to see why Auckland has been affectionately nicknamed the "City of Sails."

Auckland is also known for its many fine beaches, beautiful parks and gardens, and a great variety of restaurants and nightlife. The city's eastern shoreline offers calm water and protected beaches, while the western shores boast wild waves, good surfing, and desolate windswept beaches. The urban area is wrapped around a number of extinct volcanic peaks which host vantage points with great views. From these scattered lookouts, you can see how Auckland has also been developed around parks and gardens—packed on weekends with walkers, joggers, cricketers, kite enthusiasts, and families enjoying the year-round pleasant climate. Twenty-three degrees C is the average temperature in summer (Dec. to March), 14 degrees C in winter (June to Aug.); rainshowers can be expected any time of year (Auckland's mean annual rainfall is 1,268 mm). Take time to explore the many different features of this stimulating city, particularly from the water. A ferry ride, harbor cruise, or trip to one of the many volcanic islands that riddle the harbor are a good way to experience the true maritime aspect of Auckland.

When To Arrive

Auckland is an enjoyable city any time of the year, and the downtown area is a busy cosmopolitan center. However, it's best seen for the first time on a weekday or Saturday morning when it bustles with businesspeople, shoppers, and tourists—on a Saturday afternoon or a Sunday it could be mistaken for a ghost town! On weekends, Aucklanders depart in droves for beaches/and ocean, or nearby parks and gardens. On Saturday most shops close around 1230 (only central tourist shops remain open), and on the whole, cafes and restaurants close after lunch and re-open for dinner. On Sunday *everything* appears to be closed unless you know your way around, which can be disconcerting to see from the airport bus after a 17-hour plane ride. Try to avoid arriving in Auckland on a Sunday, but if you do, follow the local tradition and take the day off! The best places to head to thenare the museums, art galleries, parks, and markets, which stay open on weekends. Otherwise take this opportunity to meet other new and disoriented tourists who will also be found walking the inner city streets in search of signs of life and places to eat!

SIGHTS

ON FOOT

Walks

The Auckland City Council Parks and Recreation Dept. (on Wellesley St.) offers a handy "Parks Pack" which contains 11 pieces of literature and maps covering short and longer self-conducted walks focusing on the city environment, history, and waterfront. In summer pick up their *Auckland City Summer Guide* to find out about the three free summer programs, People in Parks, guided Auckland Walkabouts, and the Band Concert Series; it's available at the Auckland Visitors Centre (tel. 366- 6888), libraries, and Citizens Advice bureaux. For pre-recorded info on local activities, phone the "Recreation Hotline" at 377-603.

Queen Street

The city's main drag, Queen St., stretches from the waterfront as far as the suburb of Newton, with regular bus service. It's lined with shops and arcades, cafes and restaurants, and two main sources of visitor information, the New Zealand Tourist and Publicity Travel Office (NZTP) at no. 99 and Auckland Visitors Centre at no. 299. At the waterfront end, you find the Chief Post Office, Duty Free Shop, Downtown Airline Terminal, and Downtown Shopping Centre. The Ferry Building Terminal is on Quay St. (pronounced "key"), from where many harbor cruises and ferries depart. Also on Queen St. are the two main squares, Queen Elizabeth Square with its Japanese wind tree sculpture, and Aotea Square farther up, next to the imposing Auckland Town Hall. For a great view from the highest building in Auckland, take a rapid ride up to the **BNZ Tower Observation Deck** (BNZ Building access from Queen St.) for $2 adult, $1 child; it's open 0900-1700 Mon. to Thurs. and 0900-2000 Friday. Toward the upper end, Queen St. crosses Karangahape Rd., nicknamed "K Road." This area has a bustling Polynesian atmosphere and a variety of foreign nationalities represented in the shops, restaurants, and takeaway food stands (see p. 80).

Ponsonby

A fashionable suburb within walking distance from K Rd., many of the old homes and shops have been beautifully restored. Entirely preserved Renall St. depicts a slice of 19th C.

Auckland Town Hall

Auckland. It's narrow, steep, and the houses are close together, each with a view of the harbor over the rooftops. Ponsonby is also known for its gourmet restaurants, intriguing shops, and trendy people. Buses run there from Queen Elizabeth Square past Victoria Park and College Hill. Get off at the Three Lamps stop; Renall St. is a block away.

Parnell

Parnell is another trend-setting suburb with chic shops and historic buildings; little cafes in shady arcades, and Italian restaurants by the handful (often residents call it "Parnelli" with a chuckle) lure locals and visitors alike. Attractive **Ewelme Cottage** at 14 Ayr St. (off Parnell Rd., tel. 790- 202) is made of kauri, New Zealand's native timber. It's one of Parnell's many buildings preserved by the New Zealand Historic Places Trust (brochures on all the city's historic buildings are available from the Visitors Centre at Aotea Square); open 1030-1200 and 1300-1630 every day, admission $1.75 adult, 50 cents child. **Kinder House,** built from Rangitoto Island volcanic stone and completed in 1857, contains Georgian furniture, family heirlooms, and a collection of Rev. John Kinder's pioneer photographs taken between 1860 and 1888; at 2 Ayr St. (corner of Parnell Rd.) it's open 1030-1600 daily, admission adult $1; Devonshire teas are available for an extra $3. Another local attraction is the spectacular **Parnell Rose Gardens**, which contain more than 4,000 roses. The Rose Garden of Parnell Restauraunt here serves smorgasbord lunches 1100-1400 Sun. to Fri. and public holidays, tel. 370-136; at the northeast end of the gardens there's access to Judges Bay, a popular swimming beach. Parnell is a gentle uphill hike from the city center—walk along Customs St. East (at the harbor end of Queen St.), curve left onto Beach Rd., pass the railway station and make a left on Parnell Rise, which becomes Parnell Road. It can also be reached by buses 635, 645, and 655 from Platform 3 at the Downtown Bus Terminal, behind the main post office. (For more info, see p. 80.)

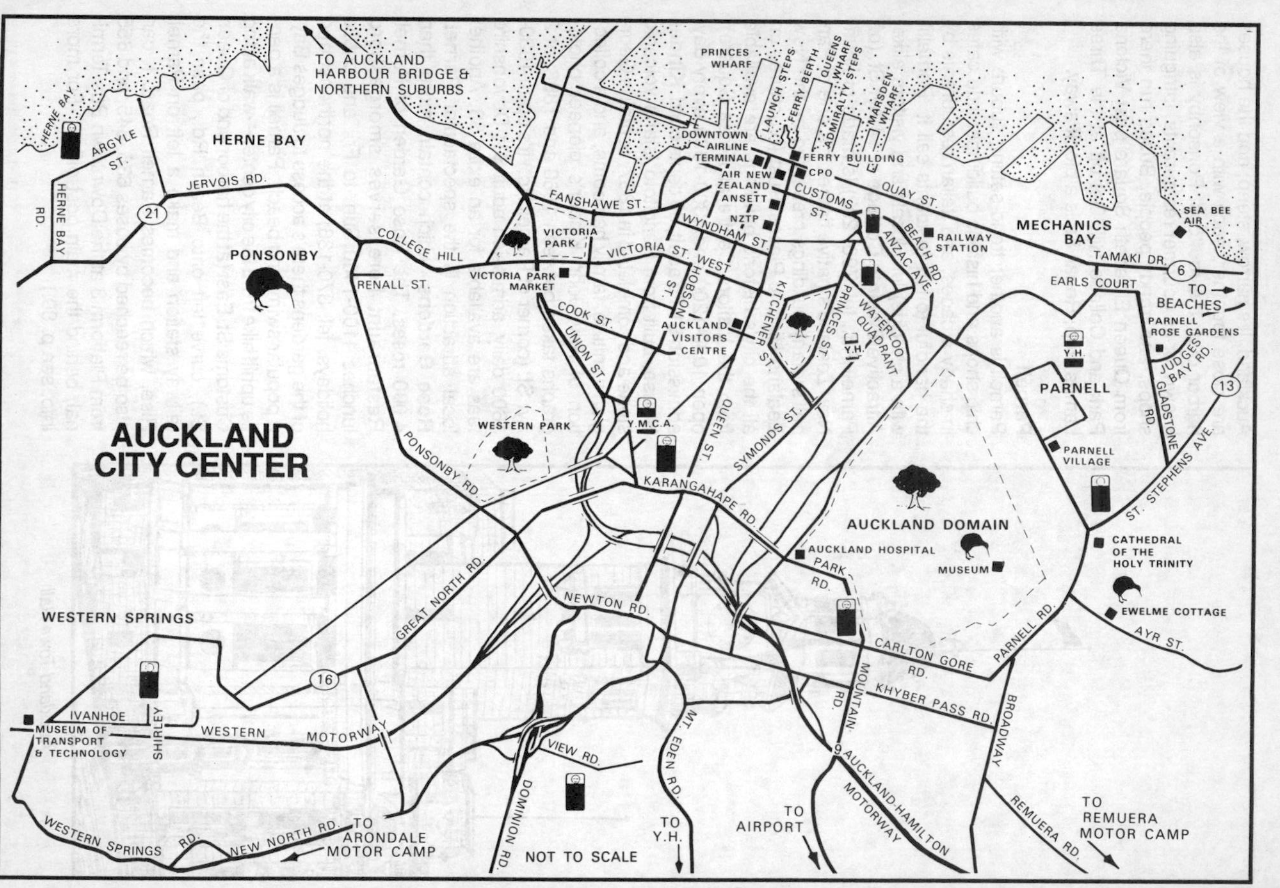

AUCKLAND CITY CENTER
NOT TO SCALE
TO AUCKLAND HARBOUR BRIDGE & NORTHERN SUBURBS
HERNE BAY
HERNE BAY
ARGYLE ST.
HERNE BAY RD.
JERVOIS RD.
PONSONBY
COLLEGE HILL
RENALL ST.
PONSONBY RD.
VICTORIA PARK
VICTORIA PARK MARKET
WESTERN PARK
FANSHAWE ST.
PRINCES WHARF
LAUNCH STEPS
FERRY BERTH
QUEENS WHARF
ADMIRALTY STEPS
MARSDEN WHARF
DOWNTOWN AIRLINE TERMINAL
FERRY BUILDING
CPO
AIR NEW ZEALAND
ANSETT
NZTP
CUSTOMS ST.
QUAY ST.
WYNDHAM ST.
VICTORIA ST. WEST
HOBSON ST.
COOK ST.
UNION ST.
AUCKLAND VISITORS CENTRE
KITCHENER ST.
PRINCES ST.
WATERLOO QUADRANT
Y.H.
ANZAC AVE.
BEACH RD.
RAILWAY STATION
MECHANICS BAY
SEA BEE AIR
TAMAKI DR.
EARLS COURT
TO BEACHES
PARNELL ROSE GARDENS
JUDGES BAY RD.
Y.H.
PARNELL
GLADSTONE RD.
PARNELL VILLAGE
ST. STEPHENS AVE.
Y.M.C.A.
QUEEN ST.
SYMONDS ST.
KARANGAHAPE RD.
AUCKLAND DOMAIN
AUCKLAND HOSPITAL
PARK RD.
MUSEUM
CATHEDRAL OF THE HOLY TRINITY
EWELME COTTAGE
AYR ST.
PARNELL RD.
CARLTON GORE RD.
KHYBER PASS RD.
BROADWAY
MOUNTAIN RD.
NEWTON RD.
GREAT NORTH RD.
WESTERN SPRINGS
IVANHOE
MUSEUM OF TRANSPORT & TECHNOLOGY
SHIRLEY
WESTERN MOTORWAY
VIEW RD.
DOMINION RD.
MT. EDEN RD.
TO Y.H.
TO AIRPORT
AUCKLAND-HAMILTON MOTORWAY
REMUERA RD.
TO REMUERA MOTOR CAMP
WESTERN SPRINGS RD.
NEW NORTH RD.
TO ARONDALE MOTOR CAMP

THE DOMAIN

Auckland Domain is a large, lush, shady park within walking distance from both the city center and Parnell area. Covering more than 80 hectares, the park offers the War Memorial Museum, Wintergardens, Fern Glen, Planetarium and Herb Garden, a kiosk selling drinks and ice cream, and a restaurant that's a favorite spot for wedding receptions. On the hillsides, particularly outside the museum, kite-flying is popular—on a bright summer day the sky is alive with color and movement. Though the Domain's likely to be busy on weekends, it's still a good time to visit since many other Auckland attractions are closed.

The Auckland War Memorial Museum

Built on the highest point of the Domain, the museum boasts terrific views of Waitemata Harbour, Rangitoto I., and the North Shore from the steps leading up to the its impressive entrance. Inside is one of the best collections of Maori art and artifacts. Several floors feature a large variety of both permanent and changing exhibitions: the Hall of Pacific Art contains art and objects from islands throughout the Pacific; in another area Auckland's fascinating volcanic history is explored, complete with sound effects and audio-visuals; other halls feature New Zealand's natural history, its birdlife, ceramics, English furniture, military and maritime history, and Asian arts. You can lose complete track of time here—a good spot to keep in mind for a Sunday, when many attractions are closed, or a rainy day. There's also a small coffee lounge and a good selection of Maori carvings, jewelry, books on New Zealand, and souvenirs available at average Auckland prices in the museum shop. Half-hour walk from downtown, open 1000-1700 Mon. to Sun., tel. 773-932; admission free. For an introduction to Maori culture, attend one of the short tours of the Maori foyer with a traditional greeting, then a Maori Concert Party performance in the small auditorium at either 1030 or 1345 (double-check times at tel. 390-443) for $5 pp.

Wintergardens

The beautiful Wintergardens (free) are a short stroll from the museum. Flower gardens, several greenhouses with amazing hothouse plants, lily pond, and shady courtyards with statue-lined footpaths make this a relaxing spot to hang out. A small lake is home to a flock of greedy ducks—a popular place with small, bread-toting children!

City Art Gallery

Located on Kitchener St. next to Albert Park, a pleasant green spot within the inner city area, this is the oldest and largest gallery in New Zealand. It contains an extensive historic and contemporary New Zealand art collection, as well as British and old master

one of the many statues in the Wintergardens

paintings, and a drawing and print collection. Open 1000-1630 Mon. to Sun., with guided tours available at 1200 weekdays or 1400 Saturdays, tel. 792-020, ext. 7704; admission free except to specified exhibitions. The gallery coffee shop on the first floor is open 1000-1600 Mon. to Fri., 1300-1630 weekends, the prices are reasonable, and there's also a small bookshop.

VOLCANIC VANTAGE POINTS

Mount Eden

Head to the top of this extinct volcano, highest point in Auckland at 196 meters, for a 360-degree view of the city. Walking tracks lead around and into the large egg-shaped depression at the top where the crater used to be. Used as an ancient Maori fortress by the Waiohua people, their storage pits and defense terraces can still be seen around the outside. The inner crater area shows no signs of occupation, as it was considered sacred to Matuaho, God of Volcanos. From downtown you can walk to Mount Eden in about 1½ hours (follow the Coast to Coast Walkway signs), or catch a bus from the Downtown Bus Terminal for Mt. Eden Rd. and Khyber Pass Road. Mountain Rd. takes you to the summit, and you can also drive to the top.

One Tree Hill

Amongst the 60-odd volcanic cones that dominate Auckland's skyline, this is another prominent extinct volcano (182 meters) offering spectacular views over Auckland. Once the home of the largest prehistoric Maori settlement in the region, it was originally called Te Totara-i-ahua after the solitary *totara* tree that was planted on the summit in 1640. The name has remained, although sadly the tree was destroyed by vandals. Nowadays a solitary pine tops the summit along with a monument dedicated to Maori-European friendship. Walk or drive to the top through the sheep-filled terraced fields and shady trees of this little inner-city oasis. One Tree Hill is the central landmark of Cornwall Park, a popular place for joggers and walkers. It's also on the Coast to Coast Walkway (see below), about a 3½-hour walk from downtown, 1½ hours from Mount Eden. It takes approximately 50 minutes to walk from the base to the summit of One Tree Hill and back down. Also in the One Tree Hill "Domain" (commonly used New Zealand word for park) near the Manakau Rd. entrance is **Auckland Observatory**. Lectures, films, and slide shows are shown on Tues. nights at 1830 for children (30 minutes) and 1930 for adults (one hour); double-check times at tel. 656-945, donations welcomed. View the Southern Cross and other Southern Hemisphere stars, weather permitting.

Manmade Vantage Point

For excellent views of Auckland from the city center, take the elevator up the BNZ Tower (the BNZ Building is on Queen St., downtown) to the observation deck. It's the highest building in Auckland. Open 0800-1700 Mon. to Thurs., 0900-2000 Fri.; $2 adult, $1 senior or child.

LONGER HIKES

The Coast To Coast Walkway

This well-marked urban walkway crosses the nine km of land that separates the Pacific Ocean on the east from the Tasman Sea on the west. On this remarkable track you get tremendous views of the city and the main harbors, climb two volcanic peaks, saunter through parks, gardens, and woods, and listen to native birds. It's a great way to appreciate the old and new, the land and water that make up Auckland today. The walk starts from the Ferry Building downtown and it takes about four hours to cover the entire 13 km at an easy pace. Or you can use the bus service to cover one area at a time—bus routes are within close range, as are public toilets and refreshments. It finishes at Onehunga, a Manakau Harbour-side suburb. The Auckland City Council publishes a descriptive pamphlet which contains a fairly detailed map of the route, distances and average walking times, places of interest, viewing points, parks and gardens, refreshments, and other walks in the area. Pick it up at the various visitor info centers.

The Point England Walk
It takes about three hours to do this 8.7-km, well-marked walk which starts on Tamaki Drive above St. Heliers Bay and meanders through parks, paddocks, and two nature reserves. Catch tremendous views of the city from St. Johns Ridge before finishing on St. John's Road. If you want to walk around the **Tahuna-Torea Nature Reserve** ("Gathering Place of the Oyster-Catcher") along the way, add about 1½ hours, including time-out for bird-watching. A City Council pamphlet with a map of this walk is available from Auckland Visitors Centre, Aotea Square.

BEACHES

Close To Town
Beaches are found on all sides of Auckland, some surprisingly close to city center, ranging from sheltered sandy coves on the east to pounding surf and black sand on the west. Tamaki Drive leads south out of downtown along the waterfront toward Mission Bay, Kohimaramara Beach, and St. Heliers Bay. The many sheltered beaches along the Tamaki waterfront are popular, offering good safe swimming and calm water. The first, **Judges Bay,** is only minutes from the city center, accessible from Parnell Rose Gardens. Farther along is **Mission Bay,** known for an attractive fountain that dances at the push of a button. Here you can hire bicycles, catamarans, and windsurfers; in summer it's usually packed. Beyond **St. Heliers Beach** is access to **Lady's** and **Gentleman's bays**, Auckland's two nude beaches. All along Tamaki Drive are boat anchorages, boat-launching and clothes-changing facilities, and cafes; buses leave from the Downtown Bus Terminal.

North Shore Beaches
Over Auckland Harbour Bridge to the North Shore are many more beaches to choose from. **Takapuna Beach** is one of the best known and probably most crowded, but nine others are accessible by ARA buses which leave from Victoria St. West or Lower Albert St. in the city. Ferries are another way to cross to the northern beach suburbs of **Devonport, Cheltenham,** and **Narrow Neck.** They leave from the Ferry Building on Quay St., and bus service links with the ferries.

West Coast Beaches
On the west coast are kilometers of wind- and surf-swept beaches, many quite isolated. They're beautiful but can also be dangerous, known for large unpredictable swells and strong rips. (Safest to swim at the beaches with lifesaving club patrol.) **Piha** is a popular surf beach, patrolled in summer, as are North Piha, Karekare, Te Henga and Muriwai beaches. **Karekare Beach** is known for large pounding surf. **Muriwai Beach Domain** is about 45 km from Auckland along the northwestern motorway. Known for good surf, black sands, and magnificent sand dunes, Muriwai also has a motor camp, campground, and shop. A track leads to nearby **Maori Bay,** where there are unusual geological formations known as "pillow lavas," plus excellent coastal bush walks, long deserted stretches of black sandy beach, and good surf fishing. The west coast meets Manakau Harbour along the sandy shores of desolate **Whatipu Beach,** only accessible by walking tracks but with large sand dunes and good surfing. See the brochure on walking tracks in the Waitakere Ranges, available from Auckland Visitors Centre.

Park Beaches
Another attractive sandy beach among *pohutukawa* and *kowhai* trees can be found in **Wenderholm Regional Park**, 48 km north of Auckland on the eastern coastline. Tracks take you through native bush onto the headland for spectacular views of Hauraki Gulf, lots of birdlife, and safe swimming. Many regional parks on both coasts boast some beautiful and fairly remote beaches, and tracks that range from an hour-or-so stroll to a week-long tramp. For more info visit the

Regional Parks Office, corner of Nelson and Wellesley streets, (tel. 794-420); open weekdays 0815-1630.

COMMERCIAL ATTRACTIONS

Auckland's many commercial attractions are widely advertised in the free tourist and daily newspapers, and in brochures at the various info centers. Here are some of the best-value places.

Kelly Tarlton's Underwater World

This is a unique, particularly intriguing aquarium on Tamaki Drive, Orakei. Travel on a moving walkway through a crystal-clear acrylic tunnel, and step off at any point onto the footpath that runs alongside. Other than the walkway beneath your feet you're surrounded by water—all sorts of indigenous New Zealand sea creatures skim the tunnel around you, eels and crayfish peek out of rock crevices. The lighting, dark-blue carpeting, and sound effects add to the submarine atmosphere. The tunnel becomes darker as you enter the deep-sea area, where sharks and other exotic creatures glide above and around you. In the small theater to the left of the main entrance room, an excellent audiovisual slide show features underwater photography; it's 10 minutes long, shown every 15. Displays of shells and sea urchins and other objects of marine interest, a souvenir shop, and lots of articles about sharks complete this Auckland attraction (call ahead to find out shark feeding times). Open 0900-2100 daily, admission is $9 adult, $4.50 child. Best visited between 1700-2000 when it's quieter; call 580-603 to see if there's a bus tour or school group to avoid!

Museum Of Transport And Technology

On Great North Rd., Western Springs, this museum is commonly referred to by its acronym, "MOTAT." Next to the attractive Western Springs Park, MOTAT gives a glimpse into New Zealand's past with exhibitions of early agricultural machinery, airplanes, vintage cars, fire and steam engines, and a pioneer village. The aviation building is a flying buff's delight, with an extensive historic display featuring Richard Pearse, New Zealand's answer to the Wright Brothers. His first aircraft made several flights in 1902. His last aircraft is on display, and many of the revolutionary features Pearse used on it have been incorporated into modern aircraft. Nearby Keith Park Memorial Airfield houses the largest vintage aircraft collection in the Southern Hemisphere; it's connected to MOTAT by a double-decker bus and an electric tram service. MOTAT is open 0900-1700 weekdays, 1000-1700 weekends and holidays; admission $9.70 adult, $5 child. An electric tram runs regularly between the museum and Auckland Zoo. Take bus 045 (Pt. Chevalier) from Customs St. to Western Springs. Call MOTAT (tel. 860-199) for more information.

Auckland Zoo

Also located in the Western Springs area on Motions Rd., the zoo contains a large collection of exotic and indigenous animals living in as near to a natural state as possible. One of the highlights is the nocturnal house where the curious kiwi (native bird and a national symbol) can be seen doing his thing during the daytime (most active in the morning—fed at 0930). A souvenir shop and restaurant overlook the park. Open daily 0930-1730, last admission 1615 (feeding times for many of the animals is 1500-1600), tel. 764-785; admission $8 adult, $4.50 senior citizen, child $4. The zoo is connected to MOTAT by tram. Take bus 045 from Customs St., or call 797-119 for more bus information.

New Zealand Heritage Park

This large theme park on Harrison Rd., Mt. Wellington, has three main areas—Natureworld, Agriworld, and Cultureworld. Go on nature walks, take in audio-visuals, arts and crafts, and Maori song and dance demonstrations as you wander throughout the complex. You can also take in a Maori Concert Party and *Hangi* (feast cooked in an earth oven) for $20 adult, $12 child (including admission), but early reservations are essential. For visi-

view from Devonport ferry

tor info call (09) 590-424. Open 0930-1730 daily in summer (end of Oct. to end of April), reduced winter hours; admission $10 adult, $5 child, special family concessions. For bus info to the park call 797-119.

Tours

If you're unfortunately on a restricted time schedule, you may want to consider taking one of the many tours available—be it a city sights tour or a several-day trip to more distant locations. Call in at the Auckland Visitors Centre on Queen St. or Touriststop Tourist Services in the Downtown Airline Terminal (see "Information") to see all that's currently available, and make bookings.

Bush & Beach offers a number of small-group nature tours—to Waitakere rainforest and west coast beaches, a gannet colony, east coast beaches, a sheep farm and kauri park, an orchard, or you can go forest trekking on horseback; trips range from $35-55 pp. For more info tel. 378-209. **Gray Line** runs a **Morning Highlight Tour** for $30 adult, $15 child, a **Lunchtime Supercruise** for $20 adult, $10 child, and an **Afternoon Highlight Tour** for $28 adult, $14 child. For more info and bookings call 395-395; tickets can be bought at tourist offices, the Downtown Airline Terminal, Mount Cook Line Travel, Fullers Captain Cook Cruises, or the Ferry Kiosk. **That Other Tour** also offers morning, afternoon, and evening tours in a minibus ranging from $35-60 adult. For more info and bookings call 366- 3523.

If you're looking for a several-day active adventure at a reasonable cost—white-water rafting, canoeing, horse trekking, climbing a mountain, or a tramping trip with experienced guides—give **Making Tracks Ltd.** at Browns Bay a call at 478-9712/3962. Each trip is three days, requires a minimum of five people and a maximum of 10, includes meals and accommodation (provide your own sleeping bag or linen), has self-drive options, and the cost ranges from $200-280 per person.

HARBOR CRUISING

There are so many ways to cruise the harbor that your first stop should be the attractive renovated Ferry Building on Quay Street. On the ground floor several companies offering everything from ferry transportation to crewing a sailing boat in a race have info booths and booking offices here. Find out all the options, current prices (add GST to all prices below), times of departure, and best ways to see the harbor and the islands to suit your desires, or more importantly, your budget, before you make a reservation.

Ahoy North Shore

One of the most enjoyable and inexpensive ways to view Auckland from the water is via the **Seabus** to Devonport, a North Shore suburb, for only $5 adult, child $2.50 RT (about 10 minutes OW). The ferry departs every hour, on the hour, Sun. to Friday. The Devonport Ticket Sales office at the Ferry Building is open daily from 0630-2300. From the ferry you can appreciate inner-city architecture, Auckland Harbour Bridge, and Devonport, an attractive shoreside town with a sheltered beach facing the city. Once you get to Devonport, be sure to take the 15-minute walk up **North Head,** a historic reserve which was an important base for Army operations toward the end of the 19th century. Walking tracks lead to many underground tunnels and chambers, gun emplacements and batteries, and a good viewing point. Nearby **Mt. Victoria,** an extinct volcanic cone rising 85 meters, offers panoramic views of the harbor; a walking track leads to the top. If time is a problem, buy a ferry and coach tour combo ticket for adult $19, child $9.50 (tickets can also be bought from the tour driver at the Devonport Ferry Terminal); Old Devonport Tourist Co. Ltd. vans meet the ferries that depart the city on the hour between 1000 and 1500, seven days a week.

Devonport is also known for its large number of artists' studios, arts and crafts shops, and trendy boutiques. If you're hot and thirsty and awaiting the ferry, The Esplanade Hotel on the waterfront is a good place to drop in for a cool drink, and a number of delis, bakeries, cafes, restaurants, and historic pubs are all within easy walking distance of the ferry.

A really enjoyable way to see the harbor by night is to hop on one of the old Devonport ferries, the **MV *Kestrel.*** Built in 1905, it's been beautifully refurbished, with a bar and bistro onboard. Now it runs to Devonport and back on Fri. and Sat. nights from 1900-2200 and features a live jazz band—cruise back and forth all night for only $9 adult, or get on and off whenever you want. For more info call 3033-319.

The Auckland Harbour Cruise Company

This company offers a unique opportunity to sail an 18.2-meter ocean-cruising catamaran, ***Pride Of Auckland,*** weather permitting—join in the sailing activities or just sit back and relax. Morning and afternoon coffee cruises are $28 pp, the luncheon cruise (1230-1430) is $28 pp without lunch or $40 with, and their "Dinner Afloat" cruise, which includes a formal three-course menu, is $66 pp. If you've always fancied yourself as a bit of a boatie, or want to try your hand at sailing under expert direction, try some exciting Americas Cup-style racing in one of their four 15-meter Harbour Challenge yachts (the ones with the blue-and white-striped sails). They race against each other every day, weather permitting (the staff say wet days are just as enjoyable as fine), between 1500-1700 for $35 pp—expect to actively participate in the sailing. Lunch or dinner cruises are also available on the yachts for $40 or $66 pp. All depart from Launch Steps on Quay Street. Bookings (as far in advance as possible in summer) are advisable at tel. 734-557, or drop by the office on the corner of Quay and Albert streets.

Fullers Captain Cook Cruises

Fullers operates a variety of cruises, the Northcote/Birkenhead ferries (adult $4, child $2 RT) and Devonport ferry (see above), and a number of Island Hopper Ferry Services (to Rangitoto, Motutapu, Motuihe, Rakino, Waiheke, and Pakatoa islands—see "The Islands" below). The **Rangitoto Lunch Time Cruise** to Rangitoto I. departs daily at 1215, returns at 1400, and costs $24 adult, child free, lunch $15. The **Coffee Cruise** departs daily at 1430, returns at 1600, and includes afternoon tea for $19 adult, child free. The **Great Barrier Day Trip** only runs on Sundays and you can cruise the island's coastline and take an optional bus trip from Port Fitzroy to Tryphena. The cruise departs at 1000, returns at 1800, costs $52 per adult, $26 per child (snacks available on board); the island coach tour costs an extra $19 adult, $10 child. In summer they also offer Saturday fishing trips leaving at 0800 and returning at 1630 for $35 pp. For the entire rundown visit the Cruise Centre at the back of the Ferry Building, or call 774-074 or 394-901.

Sea Flight Cruises

At the Sea Flight Cruises booking office in the Ferry Building you can buy tickets for one of several cruises. The **Kawau Island Day Trip** leaves at 1000 on Wed., Fri., and Sun. and returns at 1600, allowing plenty of time to explore this beautiful island, visit the Mansion House, or just relax on the beach; adult $38, child $19, optional lunch $15 pp. The **Great Barrier Island Day Trip** (88 km from the mainland) departs daily at 0930 and returns at 1630; adult $52, child $26, optional lunch $15 pp, and for an additional $19 adult, $10 child you can take the two-hour bus trip to the sandy eastern beaches. They also run a direct service to the island on Fridays and Sundays for $52 adult OW or $104 RT, $26 child OW or $52 RT. Another popular cruise is the **Night Flight,** which allows you to savor an Auckland sunset and city night lights while you sip a glass of wine (the first is complimentary), enjoy dinner, and then dance the evening away to a live band. It departs on Tues., Thurs., and Sat. at 1900, returns at 2300; $60 pp includes dinner. For more info on any of the cruises and bookings (essential), call 366-1421.

By Steam Tug

On Sundays from Oct. to June, cruise the harbor in one of the only two remaining steam tugs in New Zealand. Passage on the 1930s steam tug ***William C. Daldy*** is a genuine trip back in time. The crew encourages visits to the engine room to see the triple expansion engine in action and the boiler room—and if you have an overwhelming urge to shovel coal they won't stand in your way! The ½-hour cruise departs Sundays at 1100 and 1400 from Marsden Wharf on Quay Street. For more info and current ticket price call 266-9038.

THE ISLANDS

Hauraki Gulf Maritime Park

The park is made up of 47 islands spread over more than 13,600 square km of Pacific Ocean. The closest and most accessible islands, Rangitoto, Motutapu, and Motuihe, are wonderful places to hike, swim, picnic, and explore, and the less accessible have become important botanical and wildlife refuges. Many outer islands, particularly **The Poor Knights,** are a diver's paradise. Warm currents teeming with tropical fish, colorful coral beds, dramatic cliffs, rock arches and caves add to their allure, and all flora and fauna are protected. (See "Whangarei," p. 89.) **Fullers Captain Cook Cruises** (tel. 774-074 or 394-901) runs a daily service to Rangitoto, a five-times-a-week service to Motutapu, Motuihe, and Rakino Islands, a Motuihe Express service on weekends, daily service to Waiheke, and weekday service to Pakatoa, all departing from Launchman's Steps (opposite the Downtown Air Terminal on Quay Street). Check seasonal time changes, the current timetable, and prices before you set out.

Rangitoto Island

This island dominates the harbor's horizon, easily recognized by its elongated shape. It last erupted only 200 years ago, spreading jagged lava flows out from the peak for a 2.5-km radius. Rangitoto has no soil or fresh running water, yet it supports an astonishing array of native and introduced plant species, small colonies of wallaby, deer, and many birds. On the island you can climb to the 259-meter summit for fabulous views, following the walking track from Rangitoto Wharf. If you're walking up (the view is worth the effort!) wear sturdy footwear and take suntan lotion and sunglasses as the glare can be intense. Several other walking tracks are on the island; see the free pamphlet put out by the Hauraki Gulf Maritime Park Board which has a good map showing all the walking tracks. One of the tracks follows the coast and finishes up at Islington Bay, where you can catch the ferry from Islington Wharf to the city instead of backtracking to Rangitoto Wharf. Fullers Captain Cook Cruises provides daily ferry service to Rangitoto, departing at 0930 weekdays, 1230 weekends, for $15 adult, $8 child.

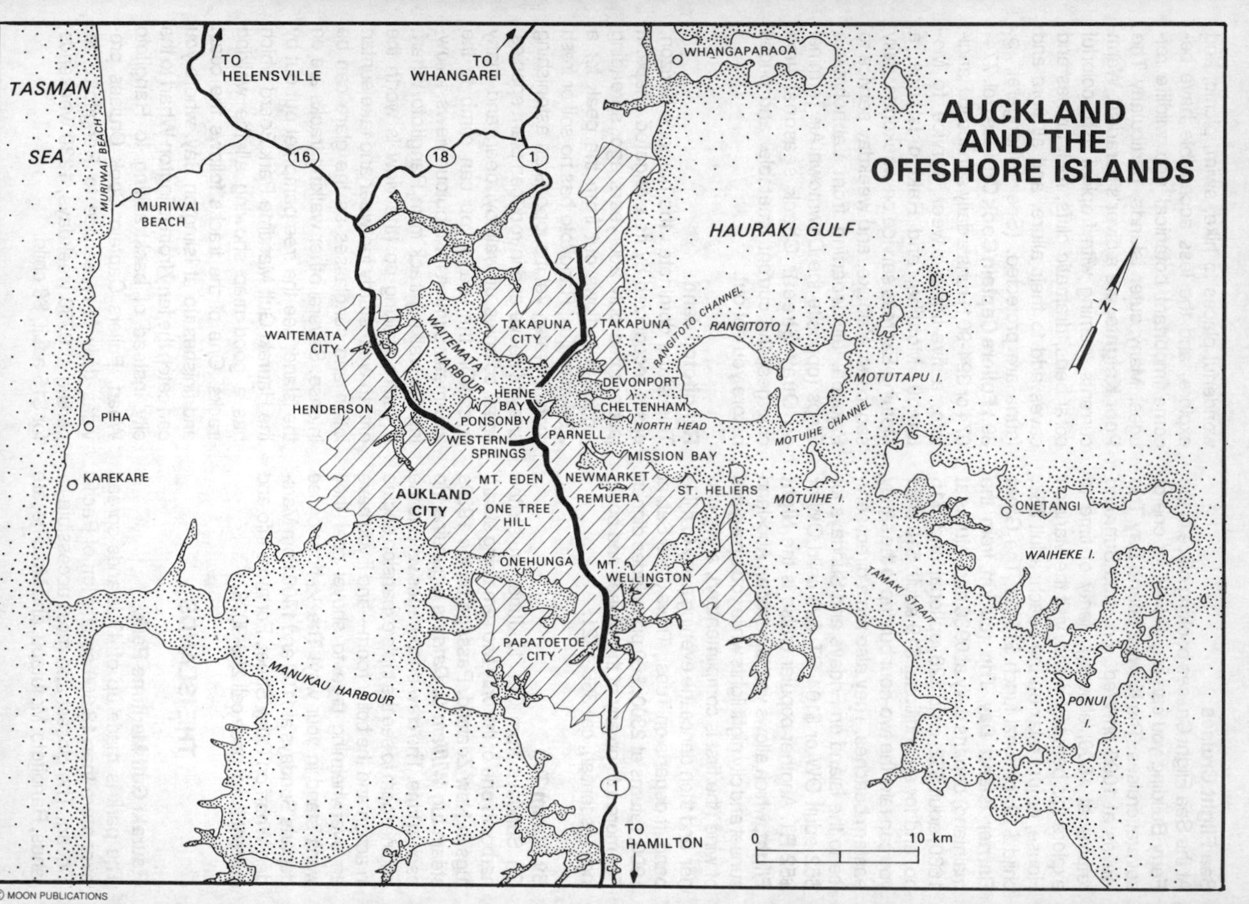
AUCKLAND AND THE OFFSHORE ISLANDS
TASMAN
SEA
MURIWAI BEACH
TO HELENSVILLE
TO WHANGAREI
16
18
1
MURIWAI BEACH
WHANGAPARAOA
HAURAKI GULF
N
RANGITOTO CHANNEL
RANGITOTO I.
TAKAPUNA
TAKAPUNA CITY
WAITEMATA CITY
WAITEMATA HARBOUR
HERNE BAY
DEVONPORT
CHELTENHAM
MOTUTAPU I.
HENDERSON
PONSONBY
NORTH HEAD
PIHA
WESTERN SPRINGS
PARNELL
MOTUIHE CHANNEL
MISSION BAY
KAREKARE
MT. EDEN
NEWMARKET
REMUERA
ST. HELIERS
MOTUIHE I.
AUKLAND CITY
ONE TREE HILL
ONETANGI
WAIHEKE I.
ONEHUNGA
MT. WELLINGTON
TAMAKI STRAIT
PAPATOETOE CITY
MANUKAU HARBOUR
PONUI I.
1
TO HAMILTON
0
10 km
© MOON PUBLICATIONS

Motutapu Island
Motutapu I. is connected to Rangitoto I. by a natural causeway, yet the islands' vegetation are in complete contrast to one another. Motutapu is run as a farm park by the Park Board. A walking track (three hours RT) meanders through lush paddocks where sheep and cattle roam, with spectacular views along the way. The track starts at Islington Bay (look for white wooden posts that mark the track) and ends at Home Bay—a lovely beach with a campground (tents only) is nearby. To stay in the campground there's a small nightly fee—call the Senior Ranger (tel. 727-674) to ensure a campsite. Toilets and water provided; bring cooking equipment and a stove as no open fires are permitted. Catch the return ferry from Home Bay Wharf. Fullers Captain Cook Cruises provides ferry service to Motutapu I. daily except Tues. and Thurs., departing at 0930, for $15 adult, $8 child.

Motuihe Island
Motuihe is one of the most popular islands in the park with its two long white-sand beaches on either side of a narrow isthmus, separated by a band of sand dunes and tall Norfolk pines. One side or the other is always protected from the wind, making it attractive for sailing enthusiasts, beach lovers, and picnickers. Around the coastline lie extensive mudstone reefs, and at low tide the rock pools teem with life. Tracks take advantage of the numerous natural vantage points to offer the most spectacular views. Fullers Captain Cook Cruises provides ferry service to Motuihe I. daily except Tues. and Thurs., departing at 0930, for $15 adult, $8 child. They also run the Motuihe Express service on weekends, departing at 1000 for the same price.

Waiheke Island
Waiheke I. is not part of Hauraki Gulf Maritime Park but is the largest island in the gulf. Its permanent population of 6,000 swells by up to 20 thousand in summer as city-slickers swarm over to relax on the beautiful white-sand beaches or walk through rolling farmland and native bush. Walking, fishing, diving, and horseriding on farm, bush, and beach trails (call Shepherds Point Riding Centre at tel. 8104) are the most popular activities. Fullers Captain Cook Cruises' ***Quick Cat*** departs daily at 1000 and 1400 from the Ferry Building, Quay Street. The trip takes just 35 minutes, $18 adult, $9 child. Buses meet all ferry arrivals for other destinations on the island, such as to Onetangi, where there's a YH (tel. 09-600-174) on Seaview Rd. ($11 pp per night). Check with the Auckland YHs before you go over—sometimes a special ferry and hostel accommodation package is available for YH members. Car rentals are also available (tel. 8635) on the island, as are minibus sightseeing day tours from $20 pp through **Tour Waiheke;** for more info and bookings call 7151 on the island or 72-7151 from Auckland.

Great Barrier Island
About 35 minutes by plane from Auckland, with only a few hundred permanent residents (mainly farmers, fishermen, and artists), this island attracts those who appreciate solitude and isolated beauty. Lonely beaches, quiet inlets, and bush are the main sources of enjoyment. A free campground with water and toilets is at Harataonga Bay; take your own cooking equipment and a stove. (See below for flight info to the island.) A day trip to the island with Fullers Captain Cook Cruises is $52 adult, $16 child, departing every Sun. at 1000 and returning by 1800, with an optional coach tour from Port Fitzroy to Tryphena for $19 adult, $10 child. A day trip with Sea Flight Cruises departs daily at 0930, returns at 1630; adult $52, child $26. Alternatively you can take the Great Barrier Commuter Express on Fridays or Sundays for $89 adult, $45 child. For the latest info on car ferry transportation (takes approximately six hours and costs from $352 RT for a car plus passenger fare) to the island, call in at the Auckland Visitors Centre.

Flightseeing
A fun way to see the islands is with **Sea Bee Air Ltd.**, which flies out of Mechanics Bay in Auckland. (Buses run along the Tamaki Drive

waterfront to Mechanics Bay.) The company's two large amphibious planes, *The Widgeon* and *The Goose,* provide daily chartered service to Waiheke I., on demand to Great Barrier I. and many other islands. The planes take off and land on water, and drive up onto land, making the start and end of the flight quite the novelty! Depending on the destination, the fare starts at $84 OW, $148 RT to Great Barrier Island. Scenic and joyride flights start at $33 pp for 10 minutes; for more info, call 774-406. For a bird's-eye view, several other airlines connect the islands with the mainland and offer flightseeing and charter flights—best to shop around. **Great Barrier Airlines Ltd.** (tel. 275-9120) flies out of Auckland Domestic Terminal and runs daily RT flights to Great Barrier I. for $84 OW or $148 RT. **New Zealand Air Charter** (tel. 299-8590), based at Ardmore Airfield, offers scenic flights—from $129 for 30 minutes (minimum three), $236.50 for one hour (minimum three). **The Helicopter Line** has a large number of set scenic flights available, ranging in price from a short $55 Harbour Views flight to a $920 North Island Extravaganza flight (seven hours). Many other options are also available. The helicopter departs from the heliport at the Sea Bee Air Terminal, Mechanics Bay. For info and reservations call 774-406.

CENTENNIAL MEMORIAL REGIONAL PARK

This scenic park lies west of Auckland and covers some wild west coast scenery and much of the Waitakere Ranges. It offers spectacular views and an enormous range of bush hikes and walking tracks. Formed by volcanic action about 17 million years ago, the Waitakere Ranges are made up of a steep eastern face and rugged valleys, rivers, streams, and waterfalls. A network of about 135 marked tracks covers a distance of more than 185 km, with about 40 tracks suitable for easy walks in dry weather. High rainfall can cause problems for the inexperienced; park rangers suggest you plan routes carefully and leave your intentions at the park info center (see below).

Park Information

The **Arataki Information Centre** on Scenic Drive is five km beyond Titirangi; get maps and track guides here. Ask if the excellent pamphlet, *A Walking and Tramping Guide to the Waitakere Ranges*, is still available —it gives a good overall idea of the various walks. It contains a map, track descriptions and times, and park regulations. (You may also find it at Auckland Visitors Centre in Aotea Square.) Park rangers will discuss your planned route and warn you of any hazards. Camping in the park requires a permit from the info center as only a limited number of primitive sites are available. For guided walks, call the Auckland Regional Authority (tel. 817-7137) for info, and Buz-a-Bus (tel. 797-119) for bus timetables and routes to the park. The Information Centre is open weekdays 1300-1630, weekends and public holidays 1000-1700, tel. 817-7134.

HUNUA RANGES

The bush-clad Hunua Ranges, about 50 km southeast of Auckland, are the focal point of one of the Auckland Regional Authority coach tours. The tour also visits **Waharau Regional Park**, which commands spectacular views of the Coromandel Range and the Firth of Thames. Costs $34.50 pp, $19 child, including morning tea and a BBQ lunch. The tour leaves from the Downtown Bus Terminal at 0930 and returns at 1630. Call Sightseer Tours at 770-886 for more info and bookings.

ACCOMMODATION

Auckland offers a full range of accommodations and prices, but in general, the places listed here will appeal to the budget traveler. (All prices are approximate and quoted in New Zealand dollars.) Budget accommodations are crowded at any time of year, but during vacation periods you'll save energy and money by tracking down your bed for the night by phone. To experience genuine New Zealand hospitality, try one of the many bed and breakfast guesthouses, ranging from reasonable ($45 d) to luxury class, including a Continental or cooked breakfast. They have far more New Zealand charm than a bland generic hotel room, and are a good way to meet fellow travelers. The best-value or most appealing are listed in the B&B section, and the rest can be easily located through N.Z. Tourist And Publicity (NZTP) Travel Offices or any of the info centers. To meet New Zealanders, try one of the farmstay or homestay programs in which families throughout the North and South islands offer family-style accommodations; for more details ask at any NZTP Travel Office.

HOSTELS

YHA Hostels

Parnell Hostel is on a quiet street, a 15-minute walk from the city center but close to bustling Parnell Village, Auckland Domain, and the museum. It's a relatively new hostel with attractive comfortable rooms, communal bathroom, cooking, laundry, and pack storage facilities—even city views. Open all day. Costs $14 per night; bookings advisable between Dec. and March. At 2 Churton St., Parnell, tel. 790-258.

About three km from the city center at the foot of Mt. Eden, the **Mount Eden Hostel** is harder to get to, but it's in a quiet area. Provide your own sleeping bag; there are communal bathroom, cooking, and laundry facilities, and a covered bicycle shed; $12 pp per night. The hostel is at 5A Oaklands Rd., Mt. Eden, tel. 603-975. By bus from the city, board on Customs St. East near the YHA office, get off at the Three Kings stop, walk along Mount Eden Rd. toward the city and turn right onto Oaklands Road. On foot, walk up Queen St. to the end (it crosses the motorway and becomes Upper Queen St.), make a left on Newton Rd., right on Dundonald St., left on Basque, straight ahead onto Mt Eden Rd. (continue quite a way) and left on Oaklands Road. If you have a heavy pack, be warned, it's a long walk uphill. This route is not recommended after dark for a woman walking on her own—take the bus!

Auckland YMCA And YWCA Hostels

The **YMCA** offers accommodation in single or shared rooms, no couples—sexes on separate floors. Usually full during university semesters (Feb. to Nov.), occasionally they have a few spare rooms. They accept written bookings depending on room availability, but you need to write a few weeks in advance. In Dec. and Jan. it's fairly easy to get a room without advance booking, but call and check first. From $29.70 pp the first night, then $22 per night which includes dinner, bed and breakfast; linen is provided. Generally you pay for meals whether you have them or not, but if you have a confirmed room and don't want dinner on the first night, arrive after 1800 and you'll only be charged $26.40 pp B&B. A cut lunch (sandwiches) on weekdays, and a cooked lunch on weekends are available as optional extras. There are no bed-only rates, and the accommodation costs don't include the use of Y sports facilities.

The Y is located on the corner of Pitt St. and Greys Ave. (tel. 32-068). Office hours are 0800-2100 Mon. to Fri., 0900-2100 weekends (ask for one of the Y brochures which has a handy map of the main city streets). It's fairly central but still quite a walk from downtown, especially with a heavy pack. From the airport, take the Airporter Shuttle bus. By bus from the city, go up Queen St., get off at Karangahape Rd. and walk right (west), then right on Pitt Street. From the railway station, take the blue and white bus to K Road.

The **YWCA** has rooms (linen provided) in the main hostel for women only, with shared bathroom facilities, a fully equipped kitchen, and dining and TV rooms for $15 pp. However, at the rear of the hostel are backpacker dorms for both men and women (bunks in twin, triple, or dorm rooms—need own sleeping bag) with a fully equipped kitchen; $11 pp per night. The hostel is at 10 Carlton Gore Rd., a 15-minute walk from the Downtown Bus Terminal, tel. 794-912. The Airporter Shuttle bus will deliver you to the door for $8.

PRIVATE HOSTELS

Georgia Travellers, Backpackers and Hikers Hostel

This hostel is a converted old mansion—the original character and style can still be appreciated in the stained-glass windows, antique fireplaces, and large spacious rooms. There are dorms and individual rooms, shared bathroom and laundry facilities, a kitchen, and breakfast supplies are sold in the shop. Costs from $15 pp per night for a dorm bed, from $16.50 pp d or twin; you need your own sleeping bag and pillow (pillowcase and sheet provided), and blankets can be hired. The hostel is fairly central (about a two-km walk from downtown), opposite Auckland Domain, at 189 Park Rd. and the corner of Carlton Gore Rd., Grafton (tel. 399-560). From the airport, take the airport bus to the Sheraton Hotel, then walk one km along Grafton Bridge Rd., pass Auckland Hospital on Park Rd. to the intersection of Carlton Gore Road. By bus, take no. 283 ("Hospitals") from Platform 2 at the Downtown Bus Terminal to Oxtons Garage on the corner of Mountain and Park rds.—the hostel is opposite. For hitchhikers, the hostel is about 250 meters from the Motorway South, and about two km to the Motorway North.

Ivanhoe Travellers Lodge

This is good, hassle-free accommodation for the price. Run by a friendly young guy who puts a lot of work into the place, the dorms can get a little crowded ("It's hard to turn anyone away," says Mark), but the individual rooms are clean, bright, and simply furnished. The bathroom, kitchen, and laundry facilities are communal, and there's a small dining room with a TV, a large sundeck, spa and games room, and outdoor patio and BBQ. Shops, banks, and a post office are within a five-minute walk, and if you like pizza, ask for directions to the local Nakhle Pizza Parlour (see p. 76). From $12 pp for a dorm bed, $18 s, and $30 d or twin; you provide your own sleeping bag or linen. In the separate overflow dorm, a bed is only $12 pp per night. Pay for six nights, get the seventh free. Located at 14 Shirley Rd., Western Springs (tel. 862-800), it's rather far from city center but easily accessible by bus, and very close to MOTAT and the zoo. From the airport, take the Johnson's Airporter bus to the lodge for $8, or if you come in on a UTA flight look out for the Ivanhoe courtesy van. By bus from the city, take no. 045 from Customs St. to Grey Lynn P.O., walk down Turangi Rd., and follow the sign to the lodge. If you get stuck somewhere after the buses have stopped, or come in on a late flight or coach, call and someone may be able to collect you.

Eden Lodge

This is upmarket budget accommodation in an old homestead with spacious grounds in a quiet residential area. Everything is spotlessly clean (you have to leave your shoes in a rack by the door so the carpets aren't ruined), the rooms are large, bright, and clean, the kitchen is fully equipped, and there's a dining area, TV room, and plenty of space for off-road parking. Dorm beds are $13 pp, singles are $16, doubles are $30 (need your own sleeping bag, or you can hire linen). It's a popular place so it's wise to call ahead and reserve a bed. At 22 View Rd. (off Mt. Eden Rd.), Mt. Eden, tel. 600-174. To get there by bus hop on no. 255, 256, 257, 258,

265, or 267 from St. James Theatre on Queen St. and get off at the second or third stop at View Road.

International Network Traveller's Hostels And Cotels
IN Hostels and Cotels provide budget accommodation (dorms, shared bathrooms, kitchen) in a very relaxed laid-back atmosphere. If you're looking for somewhere to party, these are popular places to go. Free luggage storage. Airport shuttle bus to doors. At 6 Constitution Hill, downtown (tel. 34-768), from $18-24 pp; 2 Franklin Rd., Ponsonby (tel. 780-168), $14 pp in a dorm (has a double bunk room for couples); and 25 St. Georges Bay Rd., Parnell (tel. 770-832), $14 pp in a dorm.

BED AND BREAKFASTS

Aspen Lodge Bed And Breakfast Tourist Hotel
This small, friendly hotel has simply furnished rooms (linen provided), an attractive guest lounge, and a dining room with TV. Shared bathroom and laundry facilities, but no kitchen use. The Continental breakfast is help-yourself style all- you-can-eat, and tea- and coffee-making facilities are available the rest of the day. From $41 s B&B, $56 d or twin B&B. Centrally located at 62 Emily Pl. in the inner city (tel. 796-698), it's only a short walk from downtown, but a little difficult to find with a poor street map. From the airport, take the airport bus and tell the driver you want Aspen Lodge—it's on the route. From the train station and long-distance bus terminal, it's only a five-minute walk—cross Beach Rd. and take the zigzag path up, turn right on Anzac Ave., left on Parliament St., right on Eden Cres., right onto Emily Place. From the Downtown Airline Terminal, walk up Queen St., left on Customs St., right on Emily Place, follow it up until it bends in both directions and take the left branch.

Heathmaur Lodge
This lovely three-story mansion is a private hotel overlooking Herne Bay, surrounded by old revamped houses. The attractive area is great for walking with its quiet bay beaches and water views. The hotel's rooms are delightfully spacious and sunny, and the attic rooms have bay views. The bathroom facilities are communal but each room has its own handbasin. Cheerful dining and living rooms, polished wood floors, stained-glass windows, and rambling narrow corridors add to the unique atmosphere. There's also a TV lounge, pool table, sun room, and tea- and coffee-making facilities. Many people staying at the lodge are semi-permanent students so it's often quite full. Call first and see if there's room; from $30 s, $45 d or twin in the main lodge, or $40 s, $55 d per night for a separate self-contained flatette, linen provided. The help-yourself breakfast is $4.50 Continental or $6.50 cooked. A two-course dinner is also available for $12 pp. The lodge is at 75 Argyle St., Herne Bay, tel. 763-527 or 786-204. From the airport, take the airport bus downtown. From the downtown bus terminal, take the ARA yellow bus to Herne Bay via Ponsonby, get off at the last stop at Jervois Rd., walk down Herne Bay Rd. toward the bay, and turn right on Argyle Street.

Ascot Parnell
This charming B&B, a completely restored historic home on a quiet street off busy Parnell Rd., is within walking distance from the city and Parnell Village shopping center. Numerous restaurants and cafes are a short walk away. Heidi Hassencamp, the friendly owner, makes you feel quite at home, and the elegantly furnished rooms are bright, spacious, and paneled in kauri, New Zealand's native timber (no smoking in the rooms). Breakfast is a filling affair with anything you want, Continental or cooked. From $58 s B&B, $79 d or twin plus GST, with shared bathroom facilities (no arrivals after 2200 or before 0700); 36 St. Stephens Ave., Parnell, tel. 399-012. It's on the Super Shuttle and Airporter Express bus services from the airport.

Devonport Villa
This Victorian guest house in a quiet North Shore suburb boasts a large patio and swim-

Devonport Villa

ming pool, and it's only one block from Cheltenham Beach. Devonport is known for its bustling waterfront parade, park, beach, intriguing shops, artists' studios, and good cafes and restaurants. The three bright spacious rooms with shared bathrooms have all the finishing touches you'd expect at a good B&B—a hospitable and friendly owner, fresh flowers from the garden in every room, teddy bears—even resident cocker spaniels that are as cuddly as they look. Homebaked muffins and breads are provided for breakfast along with muesli (granola), fruit juice, eggs, and coffee. Rates are $70 s, $95 d. At 21 Cheltenham Rd., Devonport (tel. 452-529), it's easily reached from city center by Devonport ferry (courtesy car from ferry or airport if arranged in advance). By car, cross the Harbour Bridge, take the Takapuna exit east, turn right on Lake Rd., and follow it into Devonport. Continue through the shopping area and down to the harbor. Go left at the waterfront and continue all the way to the end to Cheltenham Rd. The house is one block from the beach.

HOTELS

The **Railton Travel Hotel,** one of the most reasonable hotels in Auckland, has excellent friendly staff, off-street parking, and it's in the city center. Comfortable rooms with private facilities, TV, and telephone start at $55 s, $78 d or twin, $113 triple, and include juice, fruit, cereal, and a full cooked breakfast—a bargain. Rooms with tea- and coffee-making facilities, laundry, and a morning paper are $60 s, $84 d, $124 triple. Fully equipped suites with cooking facilities are $112. If you're looking for something more basic, ask for one of their standard rooms—there's a handbasin in each room but shared bathroom facilities; $40 s, $60 d, includes breakfast. Also within the hotel is a small shop selling snacks, soft drinks, and personal essentials (open daily 0600-2200), and **The Palace Carvery** restaurant, open daily from 1700-2000, which serves a good and substantial smorgasbord dinner for only $18 pp. The Railton is at 411 Queen St., tel. 796-487.

Another of the more reasonable hotels is the **Smart Budget Hotel** on the corner of City Rd. (off Queen St.) and Liverpool St., tel. 392-801. It's relatively new, modern, centrally located, has small comfy rooms with tea- and coffee-making facilities, city and harbor views, but shared bathrooms for each floor (separate for men and women); from $48 s, $77 d (breakfast not included). Also within the hotel is **Bytes Cafe**, serving meals from 0700 daily (blackboard menu, changes daily), and picnic boxes are available. From the airport take the Airporter bus and get off at the

Sheraton Hotel stop. For more of an upmarket version of the Smart Budget, consider staying at **The Park Towers Hotel** at 3 Scotia Place, tel. 392-800. Rooms start at $66 s or d, $115 s or d with private facilities. Another recommendation by locals is the **Albion Hotel** on Hobson St., tel. 794-900. Rooms with renovated Victorian-style decor start at $75 s or d, $85 twin.

Auckland, like any international city, has plenty of first-class hotels—from old-fashioned comfortable mansions to ultra-modern gleaming architectural masterpieces. For a full listing, call in at the Auckland Visitors Centre in Aotea Square, 299 Queen St., and ask what's available. They also have a helpful handout that lists many of the hotels with their locations and current rates.

MOTOR CAMPS

New Zealand "motor camps" are an ingenious form of budget accommodation, and one of *the* places to meet vacationing New Zealanders. All provide the traveler with a safe place to put up a tent, park a caravan or motor home, or stay in a rustic cabin or comfortable flat (not all have these). Facilities include communal toilet and shower blocks, kitchen block with stoves and a refrigerator, and a laundry room with coin-operated washers and dryers. Many also provide TV and/or game rooms, a swimming pool, spa, playground for the kids, shop, and other facilities. For a list of motor camps, their addresses, and current rates, ask at the Auckland Visitors Centre for their "Accommodation List Camping Grounds," or refer to the AA Accommodation book.

North Shore Caravan Park

This motor camp on the north shore of the city caters to caravanners and campervanners with plenty of grassy sites and some tentsites. However, there's also a dorm block for $15 pp, small bunk rooms (each containing two single bunk beds, heater, table and stools, sink, crockery, cutlery, and hot water jug) for $25 s, $35 d, budget cabins (with fridge) for $25 s, $35 d, and roomier cabins (with fridge and TV) for $35 s or $45 d. All have the use of the large communal bathroom and kitchen blocks, and laundry facilities (large washers and dryers), but you need to provide your own sleeping bag or linen. Motel units have their own private showers, and linen is provided; $60 s, $70 d. Next to the motor camp is a Pizza Hut Restaurant and a gas station where you can also buy basics—milk, butter, newspapers, etc. The motor camp is at 52 Northcote Rd., Takapuna, tel. 419-1320. To get there from city center, cross the Harbour Bridge in the Whangarei lane. Four kilometers north take the Northcote Rd. exit (not the Northcote-Birkenhead exit) and turn left. In less than one kilometer, look for the sign and driveway down the right side of the Pizza Hut Restaurant.

Remuera Motor Lodge And Camping Ground

The closest camping area to town is surrounded by trees, and has a large swimming pool and a landscaped camping area. There are relatively few flat grassy spots for tents ($7 pp), but lots of space for caravans (from $8 pp). Tourist units start at $48 d, you provide your own linen and blankets; motel units from $68 d. The motor camp is located at 16A Minto Rd., Remuera, tel. 545-126. From the Downtown Bus Terminal, take the ARA yellow bus going to Meadowbank or call Buz-a-Bus for more information. By car, take the southern motorway out of the city to the Green Lane turnoff onto Remuera Rd., and turn right on Minto Road.

Avondale Motor Park

Tent sites in the large grassy area are $8 pp and caravan sites start at around $9 pp (minimum $12 per night). On-site caravans can be hired for $26 s, $33 d (supply your own linen), cooking facilities are provided. Tourist cabins are $30 s, $40 d. Tourist flats are $40 s, $50 d with private facilities. Located at 46 Bollard Ave., Avondale, tel. 887-228; call Buz-a-Bus for bus information.

FOOD

Auckland's hundreds of cafes and restaurants have prices from cheap to mind-boggling! Least expensive is to buy food from the markets and cook your own. However, while the exchange rate remains favorable, you may be surprised to find you're able to eat out fairly often without adversely affecting your budget. Pick up a copy of the free Auckländer Dining Guide (put out twice a year), which contains a good number of restaurants, cafes, taverns, and nightclubs. It can be found at NZTP Travel Offices and the Auckland Visitors Centre, along with the other free tourist papers.

BUDGET

University Students Union Restaurant

This student hangout offers a good meal at a cheap price, and has a BYO license. The Students Union Complex is on the corner of Princes and Alfred streets. Open 1700-2000 Feb. to Nov., and from 1630-1945 during university vacations. Free parking in the university carpark after 1730.

Victoria Park Market

This is a good place to go when you're really hungry and in the mood for exotic takeaways. Apart from Rick's Cafe Americain (see below), many foodstalls throughout the market sell a wide range of regular and ethnic food: everything from pies and hot dogs to falafels and pasta dishes, a wide range of salads, and pastries, donuts, and ice cream. Sit and eat indoors or out, and for coffee afterward go to Rick's Cafe. From Thurs. to Sun. nights, outdoor movies are often screened at dusk. Located on Victoria St. W., across from Victoria Park. Open Mon. to Sat. 0900-1900 (later on Fri.) and Sun. 1000-1900.

Food Halls

Food halls are springing up all over the place and they're popular because you can choose from a wide selection of dishes to take away and not have to pay an arm and a leg to satisfy your hunger. At the **BNZ Tower International Food Hall,** lower floor of the building (access from Queen St.), you'll find deluxe filled croissants, seafood, Chinese meals, a salad bar, roasts, Mexican or Turkish delicacies, fish and chips, and more—and everything is very reasonable in cost. Tables and chairs are provided, though at lunchtime and dinner it's hard to find a spare seat. The hall is open Mon. to Thurs. 0900-1730, Fri. 0900-2100, and Sat. 0900-1300. Choose from another really good selection of tasty dishes at the **Chase Plaza Food Hall,** off Queen St. (near Victoria).

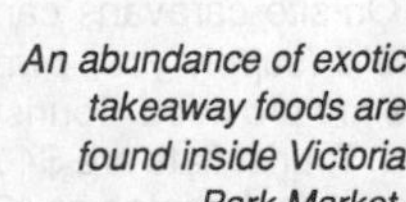
An abundance of exotic takeaway foods are found inside Victoria Park Market.

CAFES

There are cafes on almost every street downtown; all generally have a good selection of sandwiches, filled rolls, savory pastries, pies, cream cakes, and desserts. For a satisfying light lunch with coffee or a soft drink, expect to pay around $5-8 per person. **The Ploy Cafe** on High St. has a large variety of healthy filling sandwiches and good coffee. Expect to pay about $8 for two at lunch.

For something a little different try the aptly named **Hard To Find Cafe**, which serves tasty Mexican food. Deliciously crunchy nachos are $5-7, small meals are $10, main course combinations are $13-15, delicious desserts $6. BYO license. If you like your coffee to pack a wallop try the "Hard to find your way home coffee" with amaretto and whiskey, or the "Absolutely impossible to find your way home coffee" with tequila and kahlua! Background music, and quick friendly service. Located at 47 High St., tel. 734-681. Open weekdays for lunch (1200-1430), and every night 1800-2200 (later on weekends). Finding it: From Queen St. turn into Shortland Street. Turn right onto High St. and look for a small neon sign—it's up a little corridor and to the back.

RESTAURANTS

Vegetarian

Simple Cottage serves delectable vegetarian and natural foods at reasonable prices—most main courses (cooked) at lunch are under $7—and there's a good salad bar. Live entertainment some nights; located at 50 High St., tel. 303-4599. Open Mon. to Sat. 0900-2100, Sun. 1500-2100. **Gopals Vegetarian Restaurant** is run by the local Hare Krishna group. Sit at regular tables, or on floor cushions around low tables, in a large sunny room and enjoy a vegetarian lunch for around $5. If you have a sweet tooth, don't miss their sweet apple crumble and yogurt. On Sun. they put on a feast at 1700, and on Thurs., Fri., and Sat. between 1700-2030 it's all you can eat for $6.50. There's a small separate viewing area for Hare Krishna movies. At 291 Queen St. near Wellesley St. W., look for the sign on the street—the restaurant is up a narrow flight of stairs on the first floor (not far from the Auckland Visitors Centre).

Salad Bar Heaven

Queen Street Brasserie on Customs St. W. at the waterfront end of Queen St. has one of the best salad bars in town ($10 if you have it as a meal but you can go back as many times as you want), and prices for all the other standard dishes are reasonable too. Expect to pay $9.50-12.50 pp for lunch, $15-18 pp for dinner (main course). It's open daily from 0630-2300 (tel. 778-920), popular at any time of day (go early or late to avoid mealtime crowds when you may have to wait for a table), and the creative desserts (pricey but oh so good!) and cappuccinos draw the after-movie crowds.

Tastes Of Asia

To sample a variety of tastes from Vietnam, Malaysia, Indonesia, and a number of other Asian countries, large portions at reasonable prices ($9.50-15), and an unusual tropical decor, go straight to **Bananas** in Parnell Village. Try the three spring rolls with salad, but if you want some extra pizzazz, ask for a bowl of their hot spicy sauce; $9.50. Wash it down with their refreshing, chilled, pink drink (rose-hip syrup and condensed milk); $2.50. Open 1200-1430 and 1845-2400 (last order at 2230). Upstairs at 317 Parnell Village (upper end of Parnell Rd.), tel. 799-360.

American-style

For a lively night on the town, try **Rick's Cafe Americain** in Victoria Park Market. Snacks are $4-8, though a cheese board for two is $14. Main meals (huge burgers, sandwiches, fresh baby salmon) range from $10-16, but be warned—a tempting cocktail, delectable dessert, or one of their exotic coffee drinks can easily double it! Happy hour is weekdays 1700-1900 with half-priced drinks and $12 meals. Live or taped music every night, attractive casual surroundings, and friendly people make this a popular spot with the locals. Located on Victoria St. West (tel. 399-074), they're open every day from 1130. On Mon. to Thurs. they close at 2100, but on Fri. and Sat. nights stay open till everyone leaves. On weekends only, they serve breakfast from 0900-1200.

Chinese

The Golden Phoenix Chinese Restaurant is mainly set up for takeaway orders, but they have a few tables where you can sit and eat. Main dishes range from $6-12, but at lunchtime they offer fast smorgasbord lunches and specials for $4.90-5. The seafood special with nuts on rice is tasty and enough for two average appetites. Located at 193 Parnell Rd., Parnell, tel. 794-006. Open Mon. to Wed. 1200-2100, Thurs. to Sat. 1200-2030, Sun. 1600-2100. The **New Orient Restaurant** offers a 10-course Chinese buffet lunch on weekdays 1200-1430 for $14 pp, and a Hong Kong-Style Yum Char lunch on Sun. from 1200-1430. It's also open every night from 1800 but the dinners can be fairly expensive. This restaurant was recommended by locals for good food at reasonable prices, and it's fully licensed. In the Strand Arcade, off Queen St., tel. 797-793/794.

Smorgasbord

The **Railton Hotel,** at 411 Queen St. (tel. 796-487), puts on a good smorgasbord meal daily between 1700-2000 for $18 pp. Expect soup, salad bar, a choice of several hot main meat dishes with vegetables, a carved roast, dessert, tea or coffee. It's mainly for hotel guests, but everyone is welcome—buy your ticket at reception.

Steak And Seafood

When you want steak and seafood, locals say **Oceans**—you get a sea and tree view from the inside or outside deck as an added bonus. Aside from the fresh seafood, you'll find steak, chicken, lamb, spaghetti, and other dishes on the menu. Appetizers start at $5.50 (for $4 extra, light eaters can combine an appetizer with a salad and fries to make a small meal), mains range from $16-20, and good-value specials are offered every day. Open Mon. to Fri. 1200-1400, Mon. to Sun. 1730-2200, it's upstairs in the North City Plaza, at 159 Hurstmere Rd., Takapuna (North Shore), tel. 462-206; car parking in the basement.

Pizza

If you're visiting the Museum of Transport and Technology, don't miss **Nakhle Pizza Parlour (Michele's)** just across the street. Medium pizzas are $7-9, large combination pizzas (just right for two) run about $11-16, and vegetarian pizzas are $8-15; soup, garlic bread, and lasagne are also on the menu. MOTAT is on a main bus route so the restaurant is easily reached, but if it's late you may need to plan on alternate transport back into town—check with Buz-a-Bus. At 794 Great North Rd., Western Springs, tel. 860-963; open Mon. and Tues. 1700-2100, Wed. 1700-2200, Thurs. 1700-2300, Fri. and Sat. 1700-2400, and Sun. 1600-2100. (Very convenient for those staying at Ivanhoe Lodge.) **Pizza Hut** is also open seven days a week (on weekends from 1130 to late), below the Strand Arcade off Queen Street.

Dining By The Water

Cin Cin On Quay Brasserie and Bar has great water views—it's on the ground floor at the back of the Ferry Building on Quay St.—and it seems to be a very popular meeting spot in all kinds of weather. On the expensive side, mains are $12-15, and salads, fries, vegies, bread, etc., are extra. Open 1000-0200. Upstairs in the Ferry Building the more elaborate **Harbourside Seafood Bar and Grill** also has good water views and an outdoor balcony. It's known for serving good food, but take your credit cards. Entrees range from $8.50-15, salads from $13-16, mains (pasta, seafood, meat and poultry dishes) from $16-25, but you have to pay extra for accompanying vegetables, salads, etc.

Parnell Favorites

Many of Aucklanders' favorite restaurants are found in the Parnell area. Some local suggestions include **Valerios** in Parnell Village, open

Mon. to Sat. 1200-1430 and 1830-2000. It has an appealing outside courtyard, a blackboard menu with a variety of Italian specials ranging from $8.50-14.50, and it's a BYO. Another local favorite, **La Trattoria,** at 259 Parnell Rd. (at the back of a narrow alleyway; tel. 795-398), is open for lunch and dinner. Italian specialties—pasta, lasagne, fettucine, spaghetti—start at $10. Open seven days 1100-1500 and 1800-2300. Fully licensed. The upstairs **Veranda Bar And Grill** also in Parnell is open seven days from 1200-2400; 279 Parnell Rd., tel. 396-289. Chicken, salads, fish and chips, lamb cutlets, and grills are $11.50-17.50. Their supper menu, from 2230-2400, ranges from $11.50-13. **Toncis Terrace Eatery** between York and Churton streets on Parnell Rd. (tel. 771-745) has a BYO license. It's open for lunch from 1200-1430 and dinner Mon. to Sat. from 1800-2200—another often-mentioned local hangout.

LATE-NIGHT MUNCHIES

Night owls can satisfy those late-night hunger pangs at **Just Desserts Cafe** with vegetarian meals at reasonable prices. People into alternative lifestyles seem to be drawn here, and it's a good meeting place. Soups, cakes, biscuits, and homemade ice cream are the specialties. At 32 Lorne St., tel. 799-897; open every day till at least 2400. **The Middle East Cafe** is another good place for cheap tasty lunches and dinners. Falafels, salads, cakes, and coffee for under $6. At 23A Wellesley St., tel. 794-843, it also stays open till midnight.

ENTERTAINMENT AND EVENTS

Current information and show times for music, opera, cabarets, theater, dance, and exhibitions are listed in *The Great Time Guide To Auckland,* available free from various info centers around town. For musical events the *Saturday Herald* gives good coverage of what and where, and Auckland Visitors Centre on Queen St. also has lots of info on Auckland entertainment.

Music, Theater, And Movies

Aotea Centre is Auckland's most modern entertainment center. Go here for excellent concerts, musical recitals, arts and crafts exhibits—all sorts of events. It's on Queen St., next to the tourist office, tel. 375-050.The **Kenneth Maidment Arts Centre** in the Students Union Complex puts on films, concerts, and a large variety of musical and theatrical events throughout the year. Programs are available at the Centre and from public libraries. Free parking in university carpark after 1730. The complex is on the corner of Princes and Alfred streets, tel. 793-474. The **Mercury Theatre,** largest professional theater company in New Zealand, puts on programs ranging from modern New Zealand works to international hits (expect to pay about $20 adult, $17 senior or student, $10 student standby). At 9 France St. (off K Rd.), Newton. The box office is open Mon. to Fri. 0900-2000 and Sat. 1000-2000; for enquiries and bookings tel. 303-3869.

Movie theaters can naturally be found throughout the city; for listings refer to the daily newspapers. For a choice of eight movies, head for the **Movie Centre** on Queen St. (same block but opposite side of the street from the Visitors Centre).

Folk, Jazz, And Blues

The **Poles Apart Folk, Jazz, and Blues Club** meets for music and poetry recitals. Generally folk and blues sessions are held on Fri. and Sat. nights, jazz on Wed. and Thurs. nights; small cover charge, visitors welcome. At 424 Khyber Pass Rd., Newmarket, tel. 542-401. The **Devonport Folk Music Club** meets at the Bunker at Mt. Victoria, Devonport (top of the steps by the bend in the mountain road) on Mon. evenings, starting about 2000. Take a ferry across to Devonport on the North Shore from the Ferry Building on Quay St. (and be sure to check return times so you don't get stranded). All kinds of traditional folk music, bluegrass, and American blues are enjoyed; small cover charge, visitors welcome. Call ahead to find out what's on at tel. 452-435.

Bands And Concerts

For live music, *The Auckland Star* contains a "Gig Guide" in Wed. to Sat. editions. **The Globe Tavern** at 82 Wakefield St. has rock, jazz, or blues bands playing nightly Wed. to Saturday; cover charge. For more info call 735-125. The **University** often puts on big-name rock concerts—they're advertised in the local papers. **Windsor Castle** at 144 Parnell Rd., Parnell, lets new local bands take the stage Mon. to Wed. nights, established bands Thurs. to Sat. nights; cover charge. Many other clubs and taverns have rock music; see entertainment guides for the "in" places to go.

Floatation

For something entirely different, or a new way to end a stressful day in the big city, you may want to visit **Equilibrium Floatation** for a one-hour session in their float tank. The tank is 2.4 meters long, 1.2 meters wide, and 1.2 meters high, containing Epsom salt-saturated water 250-300 mm deep. You can float in a dark and sound-free environment, or listen to music coming from the underwater stereo system. One one-hour visit is $25. The Centre is open Mon. to Sat. 1000-2200, closed Mondays. It's at 48 Bellevue Rd., Mt. Eden, tel. 606-337. Who knows—you may come out a whole new person!

Another Kind Of Plunge

The Teps—Auckland Tepid Baths are open Mon. to Fri. 0600-2200, weekends and public holidays from 0800-1900. Enjoy the 25-meter and 18-meter pools, gym, aquarobics, spa, sauna, steam bath, a massage, then replace some energy in Champions Cafe, which features nutritious food. For more info call 794-794. The Teps is on the corner of Customs St. W. and Lower Hobson St., downtown. Parking is available on Customs St. W. at the metered Pay and Display machine or in the ACC Downtown Parking Building diagonally opposite The Teps.

EVENTS

New Year's Eve

New Year's Eve festivities (usually involving heavy-duty drinking) run rampant throughout the city, but Aotea Square by the Town Hall is the center of celebration some years. On New Year's Day, **Auckland Cup Day,** the big event in horseracing, takes place at Ellerslie Racecourse.

Anniversary Day Regatta

This is one of the most looked-forward-to sailing events, held on the Monday nearest to 29 January. The harbor is chock-a-block with sailing boats of all kinds, and people flock to all the high points around the harbor for the best views.

March Happenings

If you're fortunate enough to be in Auckland in March you may notice some crazy happenings—such as a Mr. Dusty Beauty Contest (featuring the garbagemen, of course!), Garbage Collectors Derby (where teams of garbagemen pit their speed and strength against each other in various events), a Waiters' Race, and all sorts of frivolous competitions, parades, and hilarious events which can occur during **Auckland Fiesta.** Musicians, entertainers, clowns, and comics stroll amongst lunchtime crowds, and cafes offer their goodies from streetside stands. Also in March is the annual **Round the Bays Run,** a 10.5-km race that starts at Victoria Park and finishes at St. Heliers.

PiPS

Throughout the summer the PiPS (People in Parks) program is run by Auckland City Council, providing free entertainment all over the city in the form of cultural and artistic activities. Lunchtime concerts in Aotea and Queen Elizabeth squares are two of the regular events. Look in the free tourist papers for details and locations.

Auckland International Film Festival
This annual event takes place in July. Here's your chance to see many major films representing countries from all over the world.

Guy Fawkes Night
Celebrated on 5 Nov. each year by real kids and grown-up kids, this holiday, originated in England in 1605, commemorates the foiling of a conspiracy by Guy Fawkes and his men to blow up London's Parliament buildings and all its occupants, including King James I, on opening day of Parliament. (They were rebelling against the severity of penal laws against the Catholic religion, but the plot and the 38 barrels of gunpowder were discovered before the fireworks began.) Nowadays large bonfires, bonfire feasts, spectacular fireworks, and general merriment are the order of the day. Watch the Auckland sky light up; for the best viewing position head to the top of Mt. Eden.

OTHER PRACTICALITIES

SHOPPING

Shopping Hours
Weekdays 0900-1730, Sat. 0900-1300 (not all shops), most closed Sunday. The late-night shopping night varies suburb to suburb: Fri. nights until 2130 in the central city, Newmarket, and St. Heliers areas; Thurs. nights in Remuera, Takapuna, along K Rd., St. Lukes, Meadowbank, and Milford. In the fashionable areas of Parnell, Ponsonby, and Herne Bay, many shops stay open all day Saturday. On Sun. most shops are closed except for bakeries and newsagents (open a few hours in the morning), and dairies (many of which stay open all day). Victoria Street Market is open on weekends. Be aware of public holidays (see "Introduction," p. 22-23) when most places close—often catching the unwary visitor by surprise.

Markets
Colorful markets are fun to browse around at leisure—and they bring out the Aucklanders by droves on sunny weekends when many other places are closed. Directly across from Victoria Park, **Victoria Park Market** takes up a whole city block. Once Auckland's rubbish destructor facility, its 38-meter chimney can be seen from quite a distance. The cobbled courtyard area is alive with activity as people crowd around colorful vendor carts. The interior of the former stable buildings has been converted into shops which sell art and handcrafts, clothes and jewelry, posters, records, and all sorts of curious knick-knacks. On the upper floor you can talk to local artisans and pick up bargains in woven articles, wall hangings, rugs, wool sweaters, pottery, glassware, and leatherwork. The lower floor offers a large variety of ethnic foods in the food hall;

Mass-produced for tourists, the tiki *is found in almost every souvenir shop.*

foodstalls are also found throughout the market place. The festive atmosphere is enhanced by daytime entertainment provided by buskers (street musicians or actors); Thurs. to Sun. nights outdoor movies are shown at dusk. The market is a 10-minute walk from Queen St., or on weekdays you can catch bus no. 005 from outside the Great Northern Arcade, corner of Queen and Customs sts., and get off at the market entrance. Located on Victoria St. W., the market is open seven days a week; Mon. and Tues. 0900-1900, Wed. to Sat. 0900-2100, and Sun. 1000-1900.

Multicultural Karangahape Road
Locally referred to as "K Road," this is one of Auckland's oldest established shopping areas. A large variety of cosmopolitan stores and restaurants, a range of shops stocked with Polynesian and Eastern foods, and many of the city theaters are found in this bustling area. On Thurs. nights, shop till 2100. On Sun. at 1200, a small but very popular market takes place on the corner of K Rd. and Ponsonby Road. Walk from Queen St. W along K Rd., crossing the motorway— the market is farther along on the right. (K Road crosses the top end of Queen St., a main bus route.)

Parnell Village
Parnell is a fun place to browse and buy, but don't forget your travelers cheques—it ain't cheap! The Village has a large variety of specialty shops, boutiques, and courtyard cafes. The cobblestone courtyards, wooden and wrought-iron lace work, steps up and down here, there, and everywhere, and intriguing alleyways leading to equally intriguing shops lure droves of shoppers. Most shops in the Village are open Mon. to Fri. 0930-1700, and many are also open on Sat. until 1600.

Takapuna Village
Takapuna Village is similar to Parnell Village but located on the North Shore in the center of Takapuna City (buses run from city center to Takapuna). Cobbled paths, covered verandas, and little alleyways separate a host of specialty shops. Open Mon. to Fri. regular hours and Sat. mornings; late-night shopping is on Thurs. until 2100.

Downtown Shopping Centre
For two floors of shops, specialty stores, coffee lounges, and lunch bars in the city center, visit the Downtown Shopping Centre at Queen Elizabeth Square and Custom Street. The center is open Mon. to Thurs. 0900-1730, Fri. 0900-2100, and Sat. 0930-1230.

Seven-day Shopping
In general, shops close on Sat. at 1230 and don't reopen till Monday. However, seven-day shopping *is* available in several inner-city shopping areas, two of which are within a block of each other. The **Downtown Airline Terminal** on Quay St. offers a few gift shops, a sheepskin shop (good prices), the Touristop shop (a good place for general Auckland info), and the Downtown Air and Coach Terminal. If you're interested in taking home some tasty reminders of New Zealand, check out the Farm Produce Shop. It offers New Zealand meat, game, seafood, and fruit packed in insulated containers, complete with the necessary documentation. They need 24-hours' notice before your departure; American, Australian, and Japanese currency are accepted (change given only in NZ$). For enquiries or telephone orders, call 798-503. There's also a branch at Auckland International Airport, tel. 275-0789, ext. 846. In the attractive building that houses the **Old Customhouse Shopping Centre,** 22 Customs St. W. at the corner of Albert St., there are shops, a restaurant and tavern, and a movie theater. The Old Customhouse is open regular shopping hours Mon. to Sat., Fri. until 2100, and on Sun. 1200-1700. Numerous other shopping arcades with regular shopping hours branch off Queen Street. Victoria Park Market is also open on weekends (see "Markets" above).

Ewelme Cottage, Parnell

INFORMATION

Print Media

Pick up the free newspapers *Tourist Times* (put out every week) and *The Great Time Guide* (every month). These are found in the tourist info centers and contain all the latest attractions, eating-out and entertainment info, and usually a good inner-city street map.

Information Centers

The **Travellers Information Centre** is in the International Terminal at Auckland International Airport, tel. 275-7467/6467. Run by a non-profit private organization, it's open Mon. to Sun. 0630-2300. They offer free advice and brochures, and book accommodations for a small booking fee. The Centre also runs a left luggage service, and for a small fee you can take a shower and rent a towel.

Once you're downtown, stop in and see Otto and Joan Spinka, the always-helpful friendly couple who own **Touristop Tourist Services Ltd.** in the Downtown Airline Terminal on Quay Street. They offer all kinds of tourist services for *free,* booking accommodations (according to your budget), airline and bus tickets, tours—you name it! Touristop is also a good starting point if you're considering renting a car; they keep up on current "specials," the cheapest rates, and deal with both big name and lesser-known car rental companies. Open all week from 0800-1730; tel. 775-783.

The **N.Z. Tourist And Publicity Travel Office,** 99 Queen St. (tel. 798-180 or 275-9597), is open weekdays 0830-1645, Sat. 0930-1200. If you need advice and/or tour or accommodation bookings for anywhere in New Zealand, the staff will get you organized—for a fee (check how much before you book). **Auckland Visitors Centre,** 299 Queen St. (Aotea Square), tel. 366-6888, is open weekdays 0830-1730 and weekends 0900-1600. The helpful staff provide free information and advice, mostly free brochures, time-tables, newspapers, and maps, and a comfortable place to sit and absorb all the information or watch the video on Auckland's highlights. They also sell detailed maps, cycling guides, and pictorial guides on New Zealand.

The Automobile Association is located at 99 Albert St., tel. 774-660; open Mon. to Thurs. 0830-1700, Fri. 0830-2100. On proof of any worldwide AA membership, this helpful association provides free maps, info, and advice on request. Be sure to ask for the current *Accommodation Directory* and *Outdoor Guide* for both North and South islands, free to members.

The Government Bookshop, 25 Rutland St. (tel. 303-2919), behind the public library, is a good source for info on any aspect concerning New Zealand, as well as topographical maps of the entire country. **The Central Public Library** (tel. 770-209) on Lorne St. is open Mon. to Thurs. 0930-2000, until 2100 on Fridays. It has a newspaper reading room in the basement with current papers from all over New Zealand, as well as some British, Australian, Canadian, and U.S. papers; generally open regular library hours plus Sat. 0930-1700 and Sun. 1300-1700—these change slightly season to season.

Maps

The **Dept. of Survey and Lands** sells a series of detailed topographical maps of New Zealand (from around $7). If you plan to hike, particularly in any of the national parks, get these excellent maps first. Located in the State Insurance Building on Wakefield St., (tel. 771-899), they're open weekdays 0900-1700. Also visit the **Government Bookshop** and the **Automobile Association** for more maps (see above).

SERVICES

Banks

Open weekdays 1000-1600, closed weekends and public holidays, the banks are the best place to exchange travelers cheques. Most large hotels and stores will cash cheques but the exchange rate will be considerably in their favor (particularly in the tourist shops). **Money exchange:** You can also exchange foreign money at Thomas Cook on the corner of Queen and Customs St. E., tel. 79-3924 (open Sat. 0900-1200, closed Sun.), and at American Express at 95 Queen St., tel. 79-8243 (open Sat. 0900-1230, closed Sunday).

Post Offices

Most are open weekdays 0900-1700; however, the **Chief P.O.** in Queen Elizabeth Square on Lower Queen St. is open Mon. to Thurs. 0800-1730, Fri. 0800-2030. On weekends it's closed but the telegraph office on the first floor is open for telegrams, cables, and international toll calls. The post office at the airport is open on Sat. from 0900-1900, closed Sunday. Local calls can be made from any call box—there's a battery of phone boxes outside the main post office. A Philatelic Bureau can be found opposite the p.o in the Downtown Shopping Complex.

Laundromats

Look in the Yellow Pages for the one nearest you. Some have self-serve facilities, others wash, dry, and fold your clothes for you. Parnell Laundry, 409 Parnell Rd., Parnell has washers, dryers, and dry-cleaning services, and is open Mon. to Fri. regular hours (closed for lunch 1230-1330), open Sat 0900-1500.

Left Luggage Services

Many places listed in the "Accommodation" section will look after luggage for a limited amount of time, often for a small fee. Otherwise the main left luggage facilities are: the Travellers Information Centre in the International Terminal at the airport; the main Railway Station on Beach Rd.; and Johnston's Airporter Service office in the Downtown Airline Terminal on Quay St.; a backpack or suitcase is $1.50 for a couple of hours, $2 a day, or $2.50 a night.

Auckland Hospitality

If you'd like to spend a few hours with an Auckland family, take advantage of the city's hospitality service which enables visitors to get to know some New Zealanders with the same hobby or profession. This is *not* for accommodation. Call Mrs. Ring, tel. 556-655, for more details.

Handy Telephone Numbers

Police, Fire, or Ambulance: tel. 111, free call.

Auckland Hospital: tel. 797-440. All public hospitals operate 24-hour emergency departments.

Emergency Medical Or Dental Services: After 1800 call St. John's Ambulance for a referral to a doctor or dentist on call, tel 599-099 (medical or dental) or tel. 591-015 (dental).

Urgent Chemist: tel. 732-497 (at 153 Newton Rd. and corner of Symonds Street).
Downtown Airline Terminal: tel. 796-056.
Railway Station: tel. 792-500.
Buz-a-Bus Information Centre: tel. 797-119.
Youth Hostel: tel. 603-975.
N.Z. Tourist And Publicity Travel Office: tel. 798-180.
Harbor Ferry Terminal: tel. 790-092.
Airport Bus Shuttle: tel. 796-055.
Taxi: tel. 32-899/ 792-792.
Weather Forecasts: tel. 792-800 (Auckland district weather); tel. 799-611 (marine); and tel. 275-4197 (aviation).

Consulates
For a full list see yellow pages in the phone directory.
Australian Consulate: 32-38 Quay St., tel. 303-2429 (visas/immigration tel. 303-3473).
British Consulate: Norwich Union Bldg., corner of Queen and Durham streets, tel. 303-2971.
German Federal Republic Consulate: 17 Albert St., tel. 773-460.
Japanese Consulate: National Mutual Bldg., Shortland St., tel. 303- 4106/4279.
U.S. Consulate: General Bldg., corner of Shortland and O'Connell Sts., tel. 390-992.

TRANSPORTATION

Auckland has an excellent transportation network and you can get almost anywhere by bus, rail, or ferry. The city roads are good, and hitchhiking around town is fairly easy if you look clean and decently clad.

AIRLINES

Companies

All internal air service arrives at the Domestic Terminal of Auckland International Airport, connected to the International Terminal by shuttle bus. **Air New Zealand** is the primary domestic carrier, **Mount Cook Airlines** covers major cities and resorts, and **Ansett** flies to Wellington, Christchurch, Dunedin, and Queenstown. Air New Zealand offers discount prices for pre-booked flights, students, and senior citizens, specially priced "air passes" with proof of international air tickets and ID (an excellent deal if you're short on time), and fairly regular "special" fares. Ask about the specials at the Air New Zealand office, 1 Queen St., tel. 797-515. Standby flights are also available for full-time New Zealand university students. Call for seat availability; if spare seats are likely, it's safest to wait at the airport to make sure you get one, and pay when your seat is confirmed. For info on Mount Cook Airline flights, call in at one of the two Travel Centres at 105 Queen St. or the Downtown Coach Terminal on Quay St. (reach both at tel. 778-389). For info on Ansett flights, visit the downtown office at 75 Queen St., tel. 390-061 or 376-950 (reservations). Many smaller companies also operate scheduled flights throughout the country.

At The Airport

Airport services include tourist information, bank, post office, rental car agencies, giftshops, luggage lockers; showers can be found in the International Terminal building.

Bus Service Between The Airport And City Center

Johnston's Airporter Bus Shuttle leaves from outside the International Airport Terminal Mon. to Sun. from 0630-2200, from the Downtown Airline Terminal (tel. 796-056) in city center from 0530-2100, and runs every half-hour in each direction. It goes to the Domestic Terminal, Airport Travelodge, and Sheraton Hotel, finishes at the Downtown Airline Terminal on Quay St., and takes about 40-45 minutes; adult $8 OW, $14 RT, child (5-14) $3 OW, $6 RT. Buy your ticket on the bus, at the terminal, or from a travel agent. The Downtown Airline Terminal office is open Mon. to Fri. 0600-2100, Sat. 0600-1900, and Sun. 0800-2100. For more luxurious mini-coach door-to-door service, call 275-1234 an hour before you need transportation for the **Airporter Express.** This service, in conjunction with the scheduled coach service, takes about 35 minutes from city center to the airport and costs $12 pp or $9 pp for two people.

The other way to get from the airport to city center or vice versa is with **Super Shuttle,** which offers door to door service and costs $12 pp or $9 pp two passengers. For more info and reservations, tel. 375-210. (A taxi between the airport and city center is approximately $25 OW.)

TRAINS

Long Distance

From the impressive red-brick Central Railway Station with its palm tree-lined entrance (it's being considered as a possible venue for New Zealand's first casino) on Beach Rd., **InterCity** operates passenger rail services to many destinations. Call at the **InterCity Auckland Travel Centre** in the station for long-distance train and coach routes, info, timetables, and bookings; open Mon. to Thurs. 0745-1730, Fri. 0745-1800, Sat. 0800-1430, and Sun. 0800-1730, tel. 792-500. Daily trains run to Wellington—*The Silver Fern* departs Mon. to Fri, at 0830 (book at least one day ahead); $79 OW to Wellington. *The Northerner* departs daily at 2115; $69 OW (no sleeping cars or diner, but refreshments available). InterCity long-distance coach services also depart from the Central Railway Station. For long-distance services it's best to book a seat in advance through an InterCity depot or travel agent. Bicycles are carried on the *Northerner* ($14; pre-booking necessary) but not on *The Silver Fern*. Cancel at least 30 minutes before departure for a refund (10% penalty).

If you're going to be covering the country by public transportation (train, coach, *and* ferry), the best deal is the **Travelpass** for 8, 15, or 22 days for use over 14, 22, or 31 days. Passes start at $275, $355, or $440, but cost more during the summer high season. When you want to start using your Travelpass, validate it at InterCity Travel Centres in Auckland, Wellington, or Christchurch. Other coach companies also offer special passes, but the InterCity pass covers all land transportation modes, and can also be used on linking Delta and Newman coach services if an InterCity coach isn't going where you want to go. A taxi stand is located at the front of the station—if there isn't one waiting, call 792-792.

Suburban

Cityline, the suburban service, runs on weekdays only, and not in the evenings. Their office is open Mon. to Fri. 0700-1830. Cityline routes run from the city west to Waitakere via Newmarket, south to Papakura via Newmarket and Penrose, and south to Papakura via Panmure and the eastern suburbs; one stage is 90 cents adult, 50 cents child, 10 stages $6 adult, $3 child. You can get routes and timetables from the stations and from the staff on the trains. Get a Cityline special discount such as the **Ten Trip Ticket** saving you about 20%, or a monthly season ticket of train and bus travel which saves up to 50 percent. There's also the **Day Rover Ticket** which allows unlimited travel for one day on services leaving after 0900 for around $6.60 adult, $3.30 child, family concessions available. For more info, call 794-600.

Railway Station Services

A left luggage service in the station building is open Mon. to Fri. 0800-1730. Also within the station there's a paper and sweet shop, and cafeteria—open weekdays only. InterCity long-distance coach services and buses leave from outside the station, and a taxi stand is by the entrance. **InterCity Auckland Travel Centre** in the station is open Mon. to Thurs. 0745-1730, Fri. 0745-1800, Sat. 0800-1430, and Sun. 0800-1730; go here for all InterCity info, bookings, and tickets.

LONG-DISTANCE BUSES

Downtown Airline Terminal Departures

Located on Quay St., this is both the **Mount Cook Landliner Coach Terminal** (tel. 778-389) and the **airport bus terminal.** The Mount Cook office is open Mon. to Fri. 0600-

2100, Sat. 0730-1430, and Sun. 0730-1430 and 1830-2100. A daily Landliner coach runs to Wellington via Taupo (pre-book), departing at 0830, taking 11 hours, with three meal stops en route; $74 OW. A Landliner coach departs at 0830 for Hawkes Bay (Napier and Hastings); eight hours with two meal stops. Mount Cook also services Rotorua, departing at 0815 daily from Auckland, taking three hours (a good day trip); $32 OW. Make reservations at Freefone tel. 395-395, or call in at one of the two Travel Centres at 105 Queen St., or the Downtown Coach Terminal, Quay St. (open seven days), both reached at tel. 778-389. **Newmans Coach Lines'** long-distance coaches (main office at 205 Hobson St.) also arrive and depart from the Downtown Airline Terminal. Newmans runs north to Whangarei, or south to Hamilton and New Plymouth, with connections to other destinations; bookings and ticketing at the Touristop shop, or call 399-738.

Johnston's Airporter Express coach service and left luggage service is also based here. Friendly staff are more than willing to assist unfamiliar visitors with transportation info, and they provide an inexpensive left luggage service; a backpack from $1.50 for a couple of hours, $2 a day, or $2.50 overnight. A coach ticket to the International Airport is $8 OW. Also within the Downtown Airline Terminal is the Touristop Shop, a cafe, a few tourist shops, public toilets, and telephones.

United Airlines Explorer bus service also starts at the Downtown Airline Terminal—explore five of Auckland's commercial attractions (Victoria Market, Mission Bay, Kelly Tarlton's Underwater World, Rose Park Gardens (request stop), War Memorial Museum, and Parnell Village) in one day for $5 adult (attraction admissions extra). The bus leaves the terminal daily on the hour from 1000-1600.

Railway Station Bus Departures

InterCity long-distance coaches (all non-smoking services) leave from the Railway Station. Call at the InterCity Auckland Travel Centre in the station for long-distance train and coach routes, info, timetables, and bookings; open Mon. to Thurs. 0745-1730, Fri. 0745-1800, Sat. 0800-1430, and Sun. 0800-1730, tel. 792-500. If you make a booking three days ahead of departure your seat is guaranteed. To take a bicyle on board you need to pre-book, and it costs $14. One-way fare from Auckland to Rotorua is $32, to Paihia $35, to Wellington $69, to Bombay (first stop after the motorway and therefore a good spot to hitchhike south) $9.

LOCAL BUSES

Downtown Bus Centre

The main city bus depot is located behind the Chief P.O., taking up the city block. **Auckland Regional Authority** (ARA) operates an efficient local bus service covering the entire urban area (except when they're on strike). Their bright yellow-and-white buses also cover the western and southern suburbs, North Shore, and Hibiscus Coast. Bus fares start at 90 cents per stage and go up to $5 for 8 stages. Day tickets for unlimited travel are $5.50 adult, $2.75 child, and must be used after 0900 until the last bus. The Downtown Bus Centre is the main ARA terminal (ticket kiosk open Mon. to Sat. 0700-2130, and Sun. 0900-1700), but there are also two suburban centers, in New Lynn and Otahuhu, each with an information kiosk.

Collect a timetable, brochures, concession tickets, or Senior Citizen Fare permits from these kiosks, or from The Bus Place, Victoria St. West (the North Shore terminus) outside the Bank of New Zealand, open Mon. to Fri. 0815-1630. Ask for the map showing downtown bus departure points. They offer 10-trip concession tickets, and family passes allowing unlimited travel for one day for around $7; purchase from the driver. Busabout Day Passes are a great way to sightsee cheaply: unlimited travel for one day is $5.50 adult, $2.75 child; purchase from the driver. The only restriction on special fares is that they must be used after 0900 on weekdays (anytime on weekends and public holidays). The Bus Place also runs an excellent telephone info service (tel. 797-119) called **Buz-a- Bus**. Call Mon. to Sat. between 0600-2300, tell them where you want to go and they figure out the rest!

United Airlines Explorer Bus
This is an efficient way to get to some of Auckland's main commercial attractions in one day, starting at the Downtown Airline Terminal; all-day fare is $5—get off and on when you want throughout the day (see "Downtown Airline Terminal" above). For more info call 866-335.

FERRIES

Head for the **Ferry Building** on Quay St. for harbor information and timetables. Keep in mind when buying tickets that the normal RT ticket is usually cheaper than two singles. The **Devonport Ferry** crosses to Devonport on the North Shore seven days a week ($5 adult, $2.50 child RT) and connects with bus services to Stanley Bay, Cheltenham, Narrow Neck, and Takapuna. Ferry service also crosses to Stanley Bay weekdays only. The ferries depart from Queens Wharf, Quay Street. Bicycle transportation on ferries usually costs the equivalent of a child's fare. Concession tickets and combined bus-ferry tickets can be bought at the ticket office in the Ferry Building. Call Mon. to Sat. between 0630-2300, or Sun. between 0700-2200.

Waiheke Shipping Company connects Waiheke I. with the city through daily ferry services departing from the Ferry Berth (around $18 adult RT, $9 child, bicycle $5), but these don't run late in the evening. Timetables, discount return tickets, bicycle fares, 10-trip tickets, and combined bus-ferry tickets are all available from the Ferry Building ticket office. For further info, call 790-092 between 0830-1730 weekdays, 0900-1700 weekends.

Fullers Captain Cook Cruises runs a ferry service between the North Shore and the city, a large variety of cruises, and daily launch services from the city to Rangitoto I., Motutapu I., Motuihe I., and Rakino I. (see "Harbor Cruising," p. 63). Their boats depart from the Ferry Building, Quay Street. Bicycles welcome. For current timetables and more info, visit the Fullers Captain Cook Cruises office in the Ferry Building.

PEDAL POWER

Transporting Your Bicycle
Cyclists are not allowed to ride on motorways or cross the Auckland Harbour Bridge. The easiest way to cross the harbor with your bike is on the Devonport Ferry service, which operates seven days a week. Bicycles are usually carried for a child's fare (see ferry section), and New Zealand Railways carries bicycles in the luggage compartment on Cityline services. Waiheke Shipping Company also carries bicycles across to Waiheke I. (a bike is a great way to get around the island). To take your bike to and from the airport via the airporter bus, if it's not in a box or bag, you're required to remove the pedals, drop the seat, turn the handlebars parallel to the front wheel, and wrap any part that may leak oil onto other baggage. These requirements also apply to all Air New Zealand flights.

Cycle Touring
For info on enjoyable local rides contact the Auckland Bicycle Association or the Auckland Cycle Touring Association. They organize rides most weekends, listed in *Southern Cyclist* Magazine, or contact the ARA Transporation Planning Dept. (tel. 794-420). A very good bike route around Auckland covers about 50 km and takes at least three hours. If you ride at a leisurely pace over a full day you'll have the opportunity to visit many city attractions along the route. A map is available from the Auckland Visitors Centre, Aotea Square.

Cycle Hiring
Many bicycle shops hire out bikes and equipment (see Yellow Pages), and on weekends bike rentals are available at many public places around town; The Domain, Mission Bay, Okahu Bay, various places along the

waterfront, and on the North Shore at Devonport. Scotties Rentals, tel. 602-625, also rents bicycles.

Bicycles For Sale

Youth hostel info boards are good places to check if you're interested in buying or selling a bike. Many overseas visitors bring their bikes with them or buy one in New Zealand, and on leaving the country want to make a quick sale, often at a bargain price for the buyer. Leave a note saying what you'd like and the price you're willing to pay. These notice boards are also good for leaving messages to friends.

Commercial Touring

New Zealand Pedaltours based in Auckland offer a variety of bicycle adventure tours ranging from 6-18 days in length and $654-2695 in price. Accommodation is in small country inns, motels or hotels, a farmstay; three meals a day, enthusiastic tour guides, and a sag wagon are provided. All you need to bring is your bike (they can be rented for $12 a day), helmet, and casual gear (sleeping bag not necessary). For more info call 674-605, or write to NZ Pedaltours, Box 49-039, Auckland 4. Another company offering guided tours is **Bicycle Tour Services.** For more info write to Box 11-296, Auckland 5, or tel. 591-961.

TRAVELING BY CAR

To find out where all the parking lots are in Auckland, pick up the handy *Parking In Central Auckland* brochure put out by Auckland City Council, available at info centers. It has a map showing their locations and descriptions of each lot and the hours open. Street parking in the central city is otherwise generally metered.

Rentals

Many car rental companies operate in and around Auckland. All the major companies—Budget, Avis, Hertz, Letz—are represented, but their rates are all high. The small, lesser-known companies are more reasonable, but beware of the cheapest ones. Some fly-by-night companies have been known to rent unreliable cars and are reluctant to return your money even when you've been stranded. These are quickly exposed on places such as YH info boards! Also watch out for those that offer a great deal but require drop-off only in certain cities—you'll invariably not want to finish up in those places!

Tips

Get reliable free info at the Touristop shop in the Downtown Airline Terminal on Quay Street. Or check the YH bulletin boards where special deals are often written up. Otherwise, you're likely to spend a lot of coins in the telephone box tracking down the best deals.

Regulations

All rental car companies must offer comprehensive insurance. You must also have third-party personal insurance (arranged by the rental co.), be over 21 years of age, and have a current driver's license to be eligible. An international license is required for overseas visitors.

Rates

On the whole, the cheapest way to hire a car is on the unlimited kilometer system, paying a flat daily rate. The less expensive car rental companies offer small economy cars such as Toyotas, Hondas, Mitsubishis, and Nissans, starting at about $22 per day plus around 19 cents a kilometer for rent-a-wrecks, or $45 per day with unlimited kilometers. If you only want a car for a day or so and are not traveling far, the day rate plus so many cents per km is a cheaper way to go. Petrol is expensive; it's the same high price throughout the country. Be sure to ask about special weekend rates. **Maui Rentals,** Richard Pease Dr. (in the Newmans Rentals building by the Airport Travelodge), tel. 793-277, generally offers reasonable rates and reliable service, as does **Henderson Rental Cars Ltd.** at 9 Dora St., Henderson, tel. 836-8089. Other companies offering less expensive rates (at the moment—they come and go) are Russell's

Rentals (tel. 836-3309), Ace (tel. 767-353), and Scotties (10% off for YHA members; tel. 602-625).

Rental Vans And Motorcycles

Some of the small companies also offer vans equipped for sleeping. This can save you money if you're not equipped to camp, but generally it's still a lot cheaper to hire a small car and camp out. Also, many companies offer campervans and fully equipped motor homes, usually on an unlimited kilometer rate only and for a minimum number of days. Most have low-season rates between May and Sept., but in summer, reservations need to be made well in advance. You can rent a motorcycle at Graeme Crosby Motorsports, 299 Great North Rd., tel. 763-320 or 762-711.

Used Cars

If you plan to be in New Zealand for several months, one of the cheapest ways to travel is to buy a used car as soon as you arrive, then sell it when you leave. Used-car dealers are required by law to provide a warrant of fitness valid for six months on all cars sold. This allows you to buy something fairly cheaply that must run for at least six months. However, expect to pay at least $2000 for a used car that still has some life in it. You hear stories of those who have bought a good used car from a dealer, traveled around New Zealand for almost six months, and then resold it for more than they originally paid!

The Wed. and Sat. editions of the *Herald* and the *Saturday Star* newspapers advertise a large selection of used cars. If you belong to an automobile association, you can have the car inspected before you buy at the Vehicle Inspection Service Centre, 162 Victoria St. West—a very wise idea. Advance bookings are necessary, tel. 799-200.

A **Car Fair,** or auction, is held every Sat. morning at the Newmarket Carpark on Broadway, in the Auckland suburb of Newmarket. If you want to buy a car for under $3000, be there between 0800 and 0930 when the older cheaper cars are sold. As the day progresses the price increases (0930-1100 $3000-5000, after 1100 $5000-10,000), and the most expensive cars are sold last. You'll be surprised how many Aucklanders attend this car fair—it's almost a social gathering! If you want to sell your car there, you have to pay an entrance fee and be there at least 20 minutes before the selling session, then sit with the car and wait for prospective buyers. For more info, call 669-775. Takapuna Car Fair is held in the Takapuna Carpark on Sat. from 1300 (tel. 480-5612), and another car fair is held in the Manakau City Carpark on Sun. from 0900-1200 (tel. 542-182). Another place to advertise for buying or selling a car is on the YH info board. Often you'll find someone who is looking for a traveling partner to share wheels and expenses.

Guaranteed Buy-back

If you're going to be in New Zealand for several weeks or several months, and don't have the time to shop for a car or sell the car when you leave, **New Zealand Guaranteed Buy-back Vehicle Associates Ltd.** at 825 Dominion Rd., Mt. Roskill, Auckland, may suit your needs. They're open Mon. to Sat., tel. 696-587. You buy a car from them for $2000-4000 cash depending on how long you need the car (check the car out thoroughly first—you may get a great car, or you may not—it depends on what comes in when you need it). The car will cost you $700 the first month, $600 the second, $500 the third, etc., plus GST and insurance. Any repairs you have to make are repaid by the company on proof of receipts; however, tires, punctures, lubrications, shattered windscreens, and any damage not covered by insurance are not included. All this is deducted from the original deposit and you get the rest back when you return the car. This works out a lot cheaper than car rental if you get a good car that doesn't need any repairs; however you must return the car to Auckland, and if you have problems with the car, you may be out extra money (temporarily) and time while it's fixed. Be sure to ask in advance what arrangements will be made if the car breaks down, say, in the South Island, as you must return the car to Auckland. Find out any drawbacks before you sign the contract and drive off!

THE NORTH

SUN, SAND, SEA, AND SAILS

Above Auckland lies a spectacular region that particularly appeals to sun worshippers, island hoppers, sailors, nature enthusiasts, and history buffs. Northern residents claim they "have it all!" Apart from a mild climate and plenty of sunshine, the north has great beauty and variation. The Bay of Islands, where nature and history blend in an unbeatable combination, attracts the largest number of the region's visitors. The irregular 800-km coastline is fringed with soft sandy beaches and sheltered coves; the bay, formed by a drowned river system, is dotted with some 150 islands. Diving thrills and sensational underwater photography await in the crystal-clear, submarine world of coral reefs and shoals of brightly colored fish, and for excitement, you can't beat a day of deep-sea fishing for the magnificent gamefish that cruise the Bay of Islands in abundance. This tropical paradise also lures both overseas and New Zealand sailors, who congregate in the bay taking on supplies, getting repairs, and soaking up the atmosphere, much as the traders and whalers did at the end of the 18th century.

A great deal of New Zealand's early history occurred in the north, and throughout the region (particularly in the Bay of Islands) are many well-preserved, historic buildings, and remains of Maori *pas* (fortified towns). Magnificent Ninety Mile Beach stretches as far as you can see, and if you follow the road to the end, you come to Cape Reinga, one of the northernmost tips of New Zealand. See the clashing waves where the Pacific Ocean and Tasman Sea merge. At the southern end of Ninety Mile Beach still stand several mighty *kauri* forests. The north is small enough to be covered in a few days by car, but to spend time in the many special places it deserves at least a week, especially if your interests include hiking, deep-sea fishing, or diving. Here's hoping you have the time!

GETTING OUT OF AUCKLAND

By Car

The most direct route north is State Hwy. 1, crossing the Waitemata Harbour via Auckland Harbour Bridge. The alternate route out of Auckland is Hwy. 16 to Helensville where the road branches off to Parakai (a popular thermal resort built around hot springs), and up along Kaipara Harbour. It joins Hwy. 1 at Wellsford but takes an extra 45-minutes driving time. If time is short, take Hwy. 1—there's so much more to see!

By Bus

InterCity runs several coaches a day from Auckland to Whangarei (refreshment stop), Kawakawa (transfer point), Paihia, Kerikeri, Kaikohe, and all the way up to Kaitaia. Book at least 72 hours in advance to assure a seat. Expect to pay around $35 OW Auckland to Paihia. Get timetables and the latest fares (ask if they're offering day-excursion tickets) at the Auckland Travel Centre in the railway station on Beach Rd., or tel. 792-500. The Centre is open Mon. to Thurs. 0745-1730, Fri. 0745-1800, Sat. 0800-1430, and Sun. 0800-1730. **Newmans Coach Lines,** 205 Hobson St., also departs Auckland daily (except Sat.) for Whangarei. **Clarks Coachline** runs their Northliner Express Coach Service to Whangarei ($24 OW), Paihia ($38 OW), and Kerikeri (with connections at Kawakawa to Russel and Kaikohe), departing from the Downtown Airline Terminal (tel. 375-873) daily Sun. to Fri.—on the Mon. to Fri. service you can enjoy on-board videos.

By Air

Mount Cook Airlines has several flights a day Mon. to Fri., two on Sat., and two on Sun. from Auckland to Kerikeri. **Eagle Air** flies daily to Whangarei and Kaitaia, and **Great Barrier Airlines** (tel. 275-9120) flies from Auckland to Paihia, landing at Haruru Falls. **Sea Bee Air** also offers regular amphibious flights to Paihia departing from Mechanic's Bay, Auckland.

By Thumb

For a good spot to hitch north out of Auckland on a weekday, take bus no. 895 to Waiwera, no. 893 to Orewa, or no. 899 to Silverdale from the city bus station and get off at Albany. On weekends take bus no. 895.

THE HIBISCUS COAST

Traveling up Hwy. 1 you quickly leave the suburbs behind, and get a first taste of rural New Zealand: rich agricultural land, lush green fields, grazing sheep and cows. Greenhouses and nurseries line the roads in some areas, and roadside stalls sell fresh fruit and vegetables at good prices. The town of Silverdale, only 40 km from Auckland, marks the beginning of The Hibiscus Coast, which includes Whangaparaoa ("Bay of Whales") Peninsula, and stretches as far north as Hatfields Beach.

Shakespear Regional Park

At the eastern tip of the Whangaparaoa Peninsula, the park offers good bush and farm walks, and three sandy beaches safe for swimming. If you're in the area on a windy day, head for the steep cliffs near Army Bay and check out the hang-glider action. Another popular activity is shellfishing, good at low tide; place the shellfish on a BBQ and cook them until they open.

Red Beach

If you're an early riser, head for this beach before it gets light—it's spectacular at sunrise. The wet orange shells left by the receding tide reflect the sun rays, and the entire beach takes on a red glow. Also adding to the beauty are the native flax flowers, and *pohutukawa* trees (covered in bright scarlet flowers at Christmas) at the southern end. The beach offers safe swimming, surf suitable for beginners, lifeguard patrol on weekends and holidays, and short rock walks at

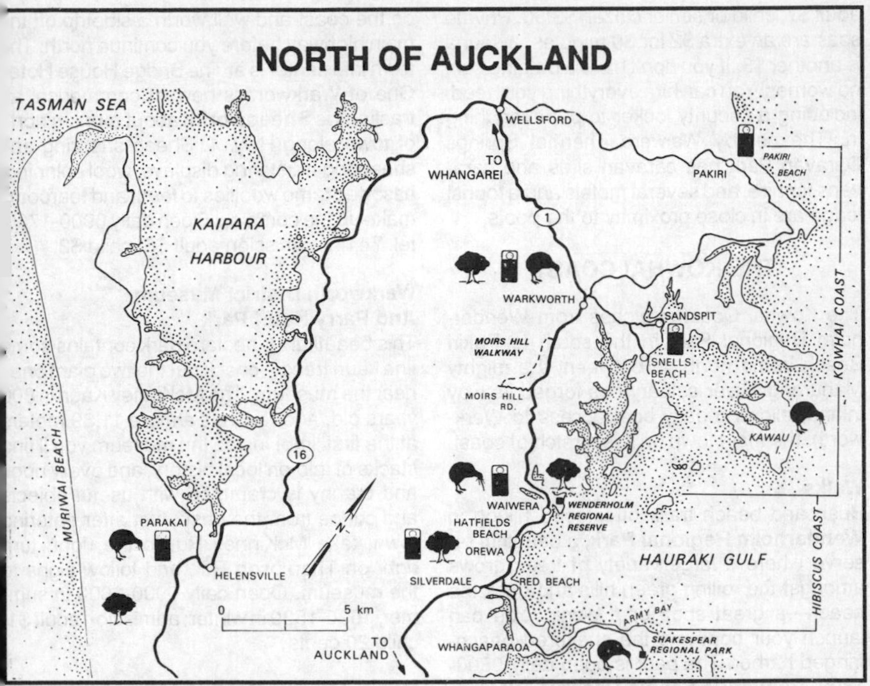

either end. If you like good, savory pies, try the Red Beach Store on the beachfront.

Orewa Beach

This beach's long stretch of sand is popular, but beware of the strong rip where the Orewa River meets the sea; on weekends and holidays it's patrolled by local surf club members. At the northern end you can see the remains of an ancient Maori *pa* site on the hilltop above Orewa House, and at the extreme north, over Grut's Bridge and sharply to the left, is the entrance to **Eaves Bush.** This small reserve contains some impressive kauri trees and lots of native ferns. A 15-minute walk brings you to a stream at the back of Puriri Park Camp and Caravan Grounds. The other campground, Orewa Reserve Camping Ground, which fronts both the river and the beach, is very large and busy. Many motels, fast-food takeaways, and restaurants are nearby.

Orewa is very popular for beginner **windsurfing,** but also attracts advanced windsurfers in easterly winds. Boards, wetsuits, and instructors can be hired in summer, as can diving gear, catamarans, canoes, and fishing tackle, etc. (watch for signs advertising rentals along the main road). A windsurfing school is held on Waiwera Beach during summer. If you're looking for a quick tasty bite (filled rolls, sandwiches, pies, pastries), try the **Windsor Cafe** in the main shopping center (past the post office).

Waiwera

Waiwera is a thermal resort and busy tourist area. If hot pools and lots of people are your thing, follow the signs to Waiwera Hot Pools from the main road. The pools vary in temperature from 33-40 degrees C, and there are private spas, water slides, picnic areas, and a food kiosk. Open daily 0930-2200 (private pools and "choobs" 1030-2130); admission adult $7, child or senior citizen $3.50. Private spas are an extra $2 for 30 minutes, a sauna is another $3. If you don't have a bathing suit, no worries! You can hire everything you need, including a security locker to put everything in. The nearby Waiwera Thermal Springs Caravan Park has caravan sites and caravans for hire, and several motels and a tourist lodge are in close proximity to the pools.

THE KOWHAI COAST

The Kowhai Coast stretches from Wenderholm Regional Park in the south to Pakiri Beach in the north. In between, the mighty Mahurangi River estuary has forged its way inland, allowing easy boat access to Warkworth, the main town on this stretch of coast.

Walks

Bush and beach trails offer good hiking in **Wenderholm Regional Park,** a beautiful reserve where a large variety of trees grows amongst the rolling green hills and back the beach—a great spot for a picnic. You can launch your boat into the sheltered beach-fringed harbor. The park is open daily 0800-1800. **Pohuehue Scenic Reserve,** off Hwy. 1, is another enjoyable place for hiking. Well-signposted walkways lead through a spectacular variety of native trees, ferns, and exotic plantations. **Moir Hill Walkway** also starts on Hwy. 1, six km south of Warkworth, and takes 3½ hours to walk the six km (five to six hours RT). The path climbs up through the trees, drops down to a stream and waterfall, and again climbs to Moir Hill lookout; great views of Hauraki Gulf. As an alternate return route, the track meanders back through Pohuehue Scenic Reserve.

WARKWORTH

There are many small family orchards to the south of this charming fishing village (at roadside stalls the fruit is freshly picked and cheaper than in town) with its colonial-style architecture, numerous cafes and restaurants, along the upper tidal reaches of the Mahurangi River. Warkworth is the main town on the coast and well worth a sidetrip off the main highway before you continue north. The town info center is at The Bridge House Hotel. One of Warkworth's newest commerical attractions is **Sheepworld,** about four km north of town along Hwy. 1. Sheep shearing and sheepdog mustering displays, wool spinning, assorted tame woollies to feed, and tearooms make up the complex. Open daily 0900-1700, tel. 7444; admission adult $5, child $3.

Warkworth District Museum And Parry Kauri Park

This beautiful ½-hectare park contains some fine kauri trees—check out the two giant ones near the museum. The McKinney Kauri is 800 years old, and reaches a mere 11.89 meters at the first limb! Inside the museum you'll find stacks of info on local history, and every nook and cranny is crammed with useful objects and curios from the past. Just after entering town, take McKinney Rd. to the right, turn right on Thompson Rd., and follow signs to the museum. Open daily 0900-1600 in summer, 1030-1530 in winter; admission adult $1, child 20 cents.

Cement Works Ruins

Between the 1860s and the 1880s, Nathaniel Wilson and his sons began to manufacture here the first "Portland Cement" made in New Zealand. The ruins are not far from Warkworth Museum, along Wilson Rd., and are open all hours. When no one is manning the entrance, there's an honesty box for the $3 admission fee. Before leaving the ruins, head

Warkworth Museum

the old "Portland Cement" works, Warkworth

down to the river below; several good swimming holes offer welcome relief on a hot day. Also near the old cement works is the 80-year-old Wilson house, lovingly restored to an elegant home by its present occupants. Not open to the public.

Pakiri Beach

This long white sandy beach is particularly known for good surfing, surfcasting, and excellent coastal views. A campground is nearby, and there are several campgrounds and many motels in Warkworth. To get to Pakiri Beach from Warkworth, take the road to the coast and head north.

Kawau Island

Sandspit Wharf, only 6.5 km from Warkworth, is the place to catch ferries and cruise boats to Kawau I. and a number of other lesser-known islands. The road to Sandspit is a short but worthwhile scenic drive. Kawau I. was the home of Sir George Grey, governor of New Zealand from 1845-1853 and 1861-1867. His elegant mansion has been renovated to its former glory, and is open to the public; admission $3. You can also walk around the island—stroll across the lush farmland, discover small sheltered bays, and take in all the wildlife—or refresh yourself at the tea kiosk (lunches available in summer). Four species of wallaby introduced by Sir Grey around 1870 continue to dominate the animal life, along with many bird species. **Fullers Kawau Island Ferries** depart from Sandspit daily at 0745, 1030, and 1400 (more often during summer), leaving Mansion House at 1315 and 1600, taking 50 minutes OW; adult $20, child $10 RT. On Mon., Wed., and Fri. the mail and supply ferry makes a daily trip, departing Sandspit at 1030; adult $30, child $15 RT. The ticket office is open daily from 0730-1700. For more information tel. (0846) 8006 between 0900-1600, after hours 28-877.

Want to camp overnight before island hopping? Try **Sandspit Motor Camp** (tel. 8610) on a great grassy bank along a pebble and sand beach, next to the deep-water anchorage at Sandspit.

B&B Detour

As an alternative to camping out or staying in motels, one great way to get to know the locals is to stay at a home providing bed and breakfast. In this area, take the road to Snells Beach from Warkworth and you'll eventually come to the appealing whitewashed homestead, **Aurelia Farm Bed And Breakfast,** at 416 Mahurangi East Rd. (about 11 km from Warkworth, tel. (846) 55-465—call ahead). Perched on the top of a small hill with a sweeping veranda, great views of the surrounding lush countryside and distant ocean beaches (10 good ones in the area) are at your command! For $30 s or $50 d per night you get one of the three attractive upstairs guest rooms (shared bathroom), the "run of the house," and a choice of a Continental or cooked breakfast. Hospitable owners, Jim and June Simons, also offer one-day tours to local attractions ($15-25 pp depending on where you want to go). If you don't have transportation, take a Gubbs Motors bus from Warkworth to Snells Beach—ask to be dropped off at Aurelia Farm (it's on the main road)—or call ahead and see if you can get a ride.

Dome Forest Walk

This track, signposted on Hwy. 1 between Warkworth and Wellsford, climbs up through Dome Forest to The Dome, a flat-topped mountain, at 336 meters one of the highest peaks in the area, with great views of Hauraki Gulf. The path to the summit takes an hour;

on to Waiwhiu Kauri Grove takes another 30 minutes. The path is well marked (white markings on the tree trunks). Steps have been cut in the steepest sections, but the track itself is quite steep, and it gets pretty slippery when wet. If you do it in winter, wear sturdy hiking boots. Same route back down.

WELLSFORD TO WHANGAREI

On entering Wellsford from the south, look out for the friendly Wellsford Inn—a good spot to meet locals over a cold beer. About 28 km north of Wellsford is the junction of Hwys. 1 and 12, and a sign to Matakohe Museum. This is an excellent museum (don't miss it!), but if you're continuing north, it's more convenient to stop on the return trip down the western side—the main route south goes right through the town of Matakohe. (See p. 130.) This **Otamatea Kauri and Pioneer Museum** houses the largest collection of kauri gum in the world, kauri furniture, timber and gum-digging equipment, and a souvenir shop crammed with well-made kauri products (open daily 0900-1700; admission adult $3.50, child $1). Down the street from the museum there's the Gumdigger's Tearooms, serving goodies made on the premises. Sit inside and watch them baking while you sample the most recent batch, or take in a rural view from the veranda out back.

The Coast

Waipu is a popular surf beach and sea-fishing resort, and the surf is particularly good eight km southeast of town. Not far north of Ruakaka is the turnoff to **Marsden Point Refinery**, New Zealand's only oil refinery which opened in 1964. No visitors are allowed inside the refinery because of the inflammable nature of its product, but you can clearly see the flare coming from the refinery from the top of Pilbrow's Hill (to the south of Waipu). However, at the **Marsden Visitors Centre** adjacent to the main entrance (on Marsden Point Rd., Ruakaka, tel. 28-194 eight km from the State Hwy. 1 turnoff) you can see an intricate model of the refinery, and videos on the half hour; admission is free. Next to the Centre is Cafe North, open for light snacks and meals. As you get closer to Whangarei, the road passes through a vineyard area, and quite a few places offer wine tasting.

WHANGAREI

Whangarei, "City of Trees," is the only city in the far north. Founded on the edge of an extremely deep and sheltered harbor, it quickly became a thriving port. Today the harbor is also a mecca for recreational water activities, particularly yachting—many of the brochures describe the city as the "International Yachting Centre of the North Island". Whangarei's mild climate boasts about 2,000 sunshine hours a year, 1,600 mm of rain, and temperatures ranging from 6 to 28 degrees C throughout the year—the average temperature is 19 degrees C.

SIGHTS

Clapham's Clock Collection

This unusual attraction contains an intriguing assortment of nearly 1,000 clocks and watches contributed by Mr. A. Clapham, many of which he made himself. It's on Water St., next to the rose garden and Cafler Park, tel. 483-993, after hours tel. 71-384. Open Mon. to Fri. 1000-1600, weekends and public holidays 1015-1500; admission $3 adult, $1 child.

Northland Regional Museum
Visit historic Clarke Homestead and Exhibition Centre which make up the museum. Situated on a beautiful 25-ha property, the museum grounds also offer good bush walks to a stream and various waterfalls, and during the summer months the staff put on free open days (usually around the middle of the month) when you can also see a steam engine operating. Located on Hwy. 14 on the west outskirts of the city—follow signs out of town to Dargaville or the Base Hospital; tel. 489-630. Clarke Homestead is open Tues. to Sat. 1230-1530, Sun. 1000-1600 and the Exhibition Centre is open Sun. to Fri. 1000-1600, Sat. 1230-1530; admission adult $2.50, child 50 cents.

Whangarei Falls
These falls are a photographer's dream. They drop 25 m into a deep green pool surrounded by bush, and numerous walkways allow views from above and below. On a hot summer day, the upper swimming hole, directly above the falls, is a hive of activity. Local children swing out on tree ropes, or dive from the top limbs of a tree into one of the deep holes, entertaining (or terrifying!) tourists with their audacity. With little prompting, the smaller kids enthusiastically tell tales of the local Maori boy they call "the big fella," who thrills his audience by diving off the top of the falls! The falls are on the outskirts of Whangarei in the suburb of Tikipunga, next to Ngunguru Rd. (buses run from downtown to Tikipunga).

Scenic Reserves
Several scenic reserves are found in the Whangarei area. **Parahaki Scenic Reserve** contains Parahaki Mountain, with good bush walks and great views of Whangarei from its 241-meter summit. Two of the clearly marked walks leave from Mair Park, at the western foot of Parahaki, the third from Dundas Rd. at the southern foot. All converge at the summit where the tall column of the Parahaki War Memorial stands. Ross Track features a goldmine near the summit and a waterfall near the base. About a 10-minute walk from Dundas Rd. (close to the YH), it takes about 1.3 hours uphill, one hour downhill. Drummond Track takes only 40 minutes downhill to cover the 1.6-km route—it's pretty steep, and features a giant kauri tree along a short sidetrack, one-third the way down. Dobbie's Track starts at Dobbie's Park, and takes about one hour to the summit, featuring many varied views of Whangarei.

On all the walks, Maori pits and old gum-digging workings can be clearly seen. Regenerating kauri trees and a variety of ferns (from the tiny crepe and kidney ferns to the large tree ferns) are also found in abundance along the tracks. Pick up the free *Footprints* pamphlet—a guide to Scenic Reserves and Walkways in the Whangarei District, available from the PRO in Forum North. **A.H. Reed Memorial Kauri Park,** in the suburb of Tikipunga about five km from downtown next to Whareora Rd., is an appealing little park with a good variety of trees and a choice of several paths; see the surviving remnant of a kauri forest, Wai Koromiko Stream, and a waterfall.

Whangarei Falls

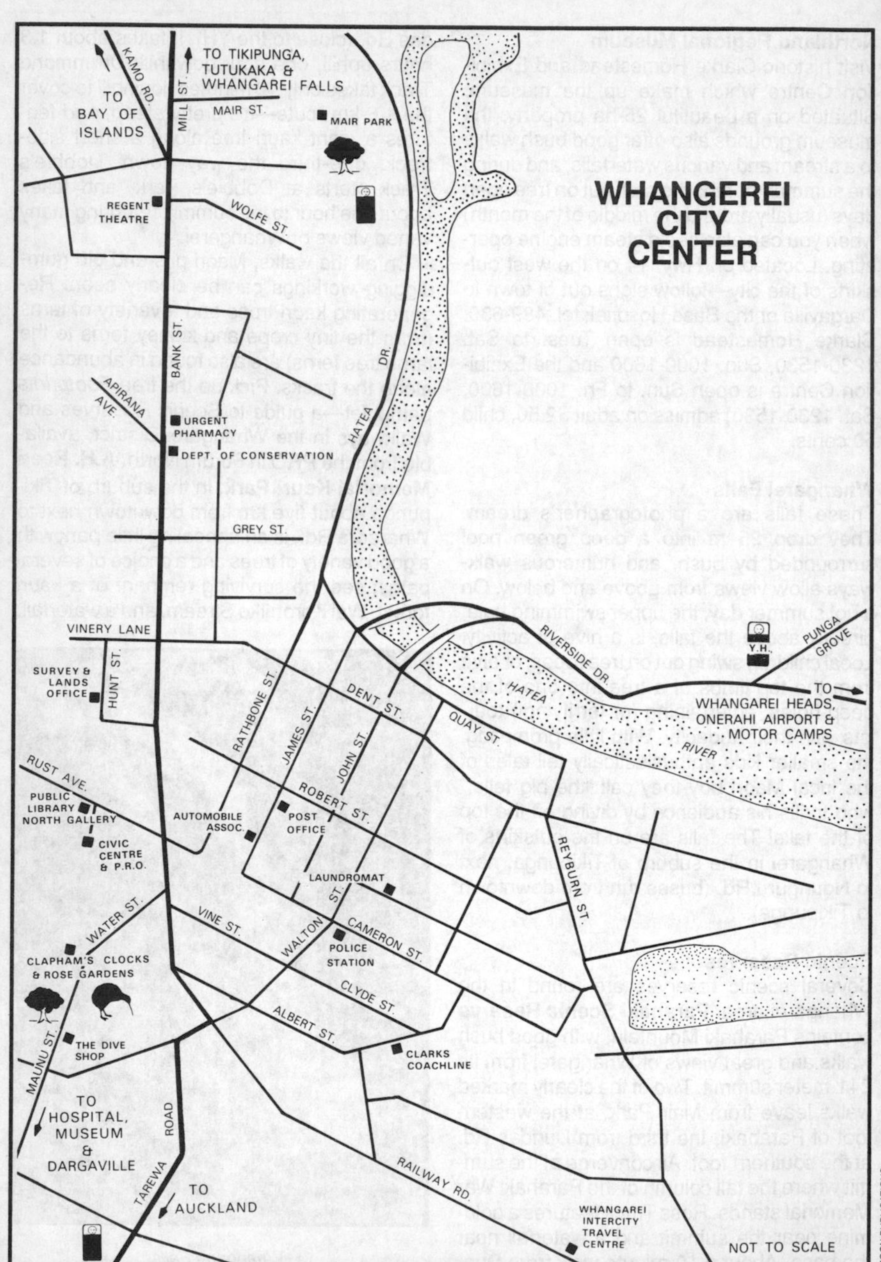
WHANGEREI
CITY
CENTER
TO TIKIPUNGA,
TUTUKAKA &
WHANGAREI FALLS
KAMO RD.
MILL ST.
TO
BAY OF
ISLANDS
MAIR ST.
MAIR PARK
REGENT
THEATRE
WOLFE ST.
BANK ST.
APIRANA
AVE.
HATEA
DR.
URGENT
PHARMACY
DEPT. OF CONSERVATION
GREY ST.
VINERY LANE
RIVERSIDE DR.
PUNGA
GROVE
Y.H.
TO
WHANGAREI HEADS,
ONERAHI AIRPORT &
MOTOR CAMPS
HATEA
RIVER
SURVEY &
LANDS
OFFICE
HUNT ST.
RATHBONE ST.
DENT ST.
JAMES ST.
JOHN ST.
QUAY ST.
RUST AVE.
PUBLIC
LIBRARY
NORTH GALLERY
AUTOMOBILE
ASSOC.
POST
OFFICE
ROBERT ST.
CIVIC
CENTRE
& P.R.O.
LAUNDROMAT
REYBURN ST.
WATER ST.
VINE ST.
WALTON
ST.
CAMERON ST.
POLICE
STATION
CLAPHAM'S CLOCKS
& ROSE GARDENS
CLYDE ST.
ALBERT ST.
THE DIVE
SHOP
CLARKS
COACHLINE
MAUNU ST.
TO
HOSPITAL,
MUSEUM
&
DARGAVILLE
TAREWA
ROAD
RAILWAY RD.
TO
AUCKLAND
WHANGAREI
INTERCITY
TRAVEL
CENTRE
NOT TO SCALE

Riding Treks
To see some of Whangarei's natural bush and reservoir scenery by horseback, call **Valley Riding and Treking Centre** at 437-1729. They provide good horses (not the can't-wait-to-race-home variety of four-legged critters) to suit anyone from beginner to advanced rider for $12 an hour, or you can go on a trek for $14 an hour pp, $20 for two hours. They're on Whau Valley Rd. (west side of town), or arrange your trek through Brian at Whangarei Falls Motor Camp (see below).

Boating Adventures
Take to the water! Deep-sea fishing (from $100 pp), line fishing with bait supplied (from $50 pp), diving off the Poor Knights, Hen and Chickens, and Mokihenau's islands (call for rates), water-skiing (from $66 per hour), water taxi service, or sightseeing tours (from $25 pp) are all offered by **Eziway Holidays** in Whangarei. For more info and bookings, call Jan and Peter Rosoman at (089) 21-751. If you're staying at Whangarei Falls Motor Camp, ask Brian to arrange a dive charter or deep-sea fishing trip from Tutukaka—chances are he'll be more than willing to come diving too! Gear can be hired at both **The Dive Shop** (PADI) on Water St. (how appropriate!) and **Sub-Aqua Dive** (NAUI) on Clyde Street.

ACCOMMODATION

Hostels
Whangarei Youth Hostel is small, and centrally located on a hill overlooking the Whangarei River; $12 pp. Diving off the Poor Knights Islands and other nautical activities can be arranged. At 52 Punga Grove Ave., tel. 488-954. The Whangarei **YWCA** has limited accommodation; call first. It's on Rust Ave., off Bank St. downtown, tel. 482-664/926. Backpackers are also made welcome at **Whangarei Falls Motor Camp** (see below) where dorm beds are $13 pp and other budget accommodation is also available.

"Go on, dive from the top!" Upper hole, Whangarei Falls.

Motor Camps
Alpha Caravan Park is the most central motor camp. It has few tent sites (adult $6 pp, child $3) but many caravan sites (adult $7 pp, child $3.50). They also offer units starting at $35 s or d, and self-contained units starting at $45 d. It's located at 34 Tarewa Rd., 800 meters south of the p.o. on the main road into town, tel. 489-867. **William Jones Park,** next to Mair Park at the western foot of Parahaki, is about 2.5 km from the p.o., tel. 487-846. Tentsites $5 pp, child $2.50 pp; caravan sites $5.50 pp, child $2.75; heated cabins from $20 s or d (GST included). This motor camp can get very busy in summer—book ahead by phone.

Whangarei Falls Caravan Park is on the Whangarei-Tutukaka Rd. at Whangarei Falls, about five km northeast of town, tel. 437-0609. Tent and caravan sites $6.80 pp, child $3.50 pp. Heated cabins from $21 s, $28 d (GST included); linen hire available. There's also a bunk room (dormitory-style, provide your own sleeping bag) with 10 bunks; $13 pp. Enjoy the spa or pool, participate in the rip-roaring BBQs held on Wed. and Sat. nights throughout summer ($5 pp), or join in one of the parties put on at the drop of a hat (ask to see the photo album of Christmas and New Year's Eve activities!). Brian and his family particularly enjoy the company of backpackers, and they offer free pick-up from the city and delivery to your departure point when you leave. Brian is also a diving enthusiast and will happily arrange dive charters (two dives average $45; gear hire $60) and drive you out to Tutukaka for free.

If you want to stay out along Whangarei Harbour, several first-class motor camps offer beach- or waterside camping (busy in summer) at Whangarei Heads. Cross the Hatea River onto Riverside Rd., then follow Whangarei Heads Rd. out to the Heads. The motor camps are located along this road.

Motels

At the many motels in the area, expect to pay around $45-70 s, from $60 d. For extensive listings, refer to the *AA Accommodation Directory North Island* or call in at the PRO for a copy of their *Accommodation In Whangarei* booklet (rates not included). One motel with less expensive rates is the **Hibiscus Motel** at 2 Deveron St. (NW of downtown), tel. 488-312; $46 s, $58 d or twin, $10 each extra person.

Homestays And Farmstays

To find out who's currently offering homestays and farmstays, call in at the PRO. The staff can give you all the details, then organize the accommodation of your choice (usually bed and breakfast, often full board).

FOOD

Lunch

Many coffee lounges offering good lunches and snacks at any time of the day can be found throughout the city. **Davy Jones Coffee Lounge,** on Rathbone St. next to the chief p.o., is open Mon. to Fri. from 0700-1600. They offer a delicious Family Night Smorgasbord at reasonable prices on Fri. nights only from 1600-1930. **Kendells Coffee Lounge,** 31 Bank St., serves homemade food and Chinese cuisine (and roast dinners between 1630 and 1830 on Fri. nights). **Something Else** in the Civic Arcade specializes in croissants and quiches; open Mon. to Thurs. 0800-1630, Fri. till late. **The Log Cabin,** 6 James St. (upstairs), is open Mon. to Fri. from 0630-1600, to 1900 on Thurs. nights, and on Sat. from 0900-1200—budget roasts from $8. Bistro lunches at reasonable prices are available at the **Forum Tavern and Restaurant** (Forum North Complex) Mon. to Fri. 1200-1400. For outstanding stuffed potatoes, head for **Taste Spud** on Water St., under the railway bridge. They're open seven days, and once you've sampled one of their potatoes (a nutritious meal in itself for around $3.50) you'll know why they're always busy. The **Flying Dragon Chinese Restaurant** at 214 Bank St. (opposite the Regent Theatre) whips up several-course lunches for $8-9 Tues. to Sat. 1130-1430.

Dinner

The **Cobb & Co. Restaurant** has the same menu here as in all its restaurants throughout New Zealand. Starting around $9 pp for a Cobb salad (smoked chicken with help-yourself salad bar) to a large variety of main dishes from $9-15 and desserts for $5, they serve a good meal for the price in a relaxed atmosphere. It's usually busy, expect a wait on weekends, and casual dress is fine; in the Kamo Hotel at 567 Kamo Rd., Kamo (a few km north of city center)—tel. 50-011 for reservations, though it's not necessary. The **Forum Tavern and Restaurant** has two eating sections. Reasonably priced bistro meals are served Mon. to Sat. 1100-2200 in the tavern, and a more expensive a la carte menu is offered in the restaurant, Mon. to Sun. 1800-2200; it's part of the Forum North Complex, tel. 481-737. **Davy Jones Coffee Lounge** serves a smorgasbord on Fri. nights 1600-1930 (see "Lunch" above).

The Carvery is in the Whangarei Hotel on Cameron Street. Prices start at about $10 for a large serving (roasts, steaks, etc.), less for a light meal, and it's good food. Open for breakfast, lunch, and dinner from 1730-2100, tel. 483-739. The more expensive **Brasserie** is another place to try a variety of dishes. Lunches range from $5.50-15.50, dinners from $14.50-19, and they have a BYO license. It's on Water St., open Tues. to Sun. 1800-2200 (lunch Wed. to Fri. 1200-1400). **Shaolin Viet Restaurant,** 2 Clyde St., tel. 483-061, serves unique Vietnamese and Chinese food, and has a BYO license; open Mon. to Sat. from 1800.

Cafe Monet at 144 Bank St. is open for dinner Tues. to Sat. nights from 1830-2400. This cafe, decorated with appropriate Monet prints and posters, serves a large variety of deliciously different meals (locals rave about it), but expect to pay $8-10 for an appetizer and $16.50-21 for a main course. If you're in the mood for a pizza ($16-20 for two), try **Revas Pizza Parlour** on the corner of Dent and James sts. (next to the King Pin Bowling Centre). They also have soups, lasagne, spaghetti, etc., on the menu; open Tues. to Thurs. 1200-2100, Fri. 1200-2200, Sun. 1200-2030. **Flying Dragon Chinese Restaurant and Takeaway** serves Cantonese food prepared by Hong Kong chefs. At 214 Bank St., tel. 487-921; open Tues. to Sat. for lunch, Mon. to Sat. from 1630, and Sun. from 1600 for dinner. Dishes range from $5.80-13.50; a special dinner for two is $20.50, for three $26.80.

Taste Spud specializes in stuffed potatoes—and delicious potatoes they are! This is the place to come if you just want a quick but filling meal at a cheap price without the waiting time or formality of a restaurant. Their potatoes, filled with chili or all kinds of select-your-own combinations, range from $3.50-3.80. They also serve curries, tacos, and great-looking desserts. On Water St., tel. 481-164, they're under the railway bridge and open every day from 1130-1900 (later some nights). At **Pizza Hut** meals start at $12 pp; at 116 Bank St., tel. 489-546. **McDonald's Family Restaurant** is on the corner of Bank St. and Apirana Ave., tel. 484-950; open Mon. to Wed. 1000-2100, Thurs. 1000-2200, Fri. and Sat. 1000-2330, Sun. 1000-2100.

Natural Food

For health food supplies **Price's Health Food Centre Ltd.** has everything you need; at 11 Water St. (opposite entrance to Claphams Clock Museum), tel. 487-594. Open Mon. to Thurs. 0830-1700, Fri. 0830-1900, and Sat. 0930-1200.

ENTERTAINMENT

Dive Charters

The Poor Knights Is. and Hen and Chickens Is. are the main charter-boat destinations from Tutukaka, weather permitting. If you have your own transportation, take the scenic drive out to Tutukaka to consider for yourself all the dive and deep-sea fishing options available and get the complete rundown. A dive charter (two dives) starts at around $45 per diver, $25 per non-diver, and all your gear can be hired in Whangarei (from $60 for all you need). Also see "Whangarei To The Bay Of Islands" (pages 102-104) for more in-, on-, and under-the-water details. If you're staying at Whangarei Falls Motor Camp, ask Brian (the owner) about dive charters—he's an enthusiastic diver and can probably get you a good deal. Otherwise, get more info at Whangarei PRO where the staff can also make bookings.

Live And Lively Entertainment

The Grand Establishment Lounge Bar on Vine St. has good bands Wed. to Sat. nights 1930-2400, tel. 484-279. Live bands, meals, and full bar facilities are found at **Oscars** on Vine Street. **Pips,** also on Vine St., is another local favorite (admission to both nightclubs depends on the entertainment). **Onerahi Hotel** puts on good New Zealand bands some nights in the Portland Lounge (it's rather far out of town but can be reached by local bus), and **Foxy's** at Whangarei Hotel also puts on live music.

If your idea of live entertainment is more energetic, don't miss a visit to **King Pin Bowl-**

ing Centre on the corner of Dent and Rathbone streets. The **Ted Eliott Memorial Pool** is open to the public Mon. to Sat. from 0630-2000 and Sun. 0800-2000; admission adult $2.50, senior, child, or spectator $1.50, and use of the spa (from 0630-1900) is $2.50 pp.

Movies

The **Odeon Theatre** is on Cameron St., tel. 488-104, and the **Regent Theatre** is on Upper Bank St., tel. 484-523. For current features and times see the local newspapers.

SERVICES AND INFORMATION

Urgent

Ambulance, police, or **fire:** tel. 111.
Emergency doctor: tel. 480-900 for 24-hour answering service.
Hospital: Northland Base off Hospital Rd., tel. 482-079.
Urgent Pharmacy: 160 Bank St., tel. 484-685. Hours Mon. to Wed. 1900-2100, Sat. 1300-1630 and 1900-2100, Sun. 1000-1230, 1400-1630, and 1900-2100. Prescription charge is $1, however if you need to call the after-hours number, tel. 481-530, a $19.50 "opening fee" will be added to the cost of the prescription.
Police station: Lower Cameron St., tel. 487-339.

sculpture outside Forum North, Whangarei

Regular

Most **banks** are open Mon. to Fri. between 0900-1600 (some 0830-1630); however, Auckland Savings Bank at 8 Rathbone St. extends its hours on Fri. to 2000, and will cash travelers cheques. (The P.O. Savings Bank also stays open till 2000 on Fridays.) Country Wide Bank, 36 Cameron St. in the mall, provides foreign exchange services. The **central p.o.** on Rathbone St., tel. 488-699, is open Mon. to Thurs. 0830-1730, Fri. 0830-1900. The Savings Bank section of the p.o. is open Mon. to Thurs. 0830-1600, Fri. 0900-2000.

Shopping hours are generally Mon. to Fri. 0900-1700, Sat. 0900-1200. Almost everything is closed on Sun. so make sure you've bought your food supplies and necessities by 1200 on Saturday! The **Automobile Association** is at 7 James St., tel. 487-079, 0830-1700. For breakdown service tel. 484-848. For repair and tow service call Parahaki Motors Ltd., tel. 488-599. A **laundromat** is at 19 Hannah St., tel. 487-155; open Mon. to Fri. 0700-1730 and Sat. 0800-1230.

Information

The main **Whangarei PRO** is in the Forum North Centre on Rust Ave., downtown, tel. 481-079. The staff can provide info on Whangarei and Northland in general, and make bookings as required; open Mon. to Fri. 0830-1700. If they're closed when you need info, use the 24-hour electronics marketing unit (EMU) on the outside wall to the right of the Forum North Centre entrance. The **Information Centre** on Otaika Rd., just as you enter town from the south, stays open all week in summer. Pick up a map (80 cents) with suggested scenic route and major attractions, and literature on Whangarei. The **Depart-**

ment of Conservation Whangarei District Office is at 154 Bank St. (across the road from McDonalds), tel. 480-299—go here for maps, charts, and books. The **public library** on Rust Ave., tel. 482-780/489-833, is open Mon. to Thurs. 0900-1900, Fri. 0900-2000, Sat. 1000-1200. The Kamo Library is on Kamo Rd., tel. 50-375. The *Northern Advocate* and *Whangarei Report* are the two main local newspapers.

TRANSPORTATION

By Bus

Whangarei Bus Service covers local transportation (the terminal is on Rose St. by the Grand Hotel). It operates the blue and white buses from Porowini Ave., tel. 483-104; office hours weekdays 0700-1630. **InterCity** operates long-distance coach services leaving Whangarei several times a day for Kaitaia ($30 OW), Waitangi, Paihia ($12 OW), Rawene, Opononi, Kaikohe ($16 OW), Kawakawa, Dargaville ($13 OW), and Auckland ($26 OW); these link with other local services. Reservations are necessary, and your seat is guaranteed if it's booked 72 hours in advance. The Whangarei Travel Centre is on Railway Rd., tel. 482-653. Office hours are Mon. to Fri. 0800-1700, Sat. 0800-1300, but if closed you can buy tickets at the station tearooms; InterCity timetables are also available at the PRO.

Newmans Coachlines offers luxury charter coach service to Auckland; on Port Rd., tel. 487-142. **Clarks Coachlines** runs a daily Northliner service (except Sat.) to Auckland ($24 OW) and the Bay of Islands (to Paihia $11 OW, to Kaikohe $14 OW) via the main route north. The office is on Albert St., tel. 483-206; open weekdays 0900-1700. Access to Rawhiti (on the Bay of Islands coast) is by scenic gravel road, offering the off-the-beaten-track explorer good surf beaches, forest walks, and excellent campsites. Bobbie Ingham runs a private van along this route on Mon., Tues., Thurs., and Fri., year-round, for $12 OW, $24 RT. For more info tel. (36) 800.

By Air

Local flightseeing tours are run by **Northland District Aero Club,** Onerahi Aerodrome, tel. 60-890. On weekdays **Northern Commuter Airlines** flies four times a day between Whangarei and Auckland. **Eagle Air** also operates flights from Whangarei to Auckland, and farther south. Bookings for both can be made at Small World Travel on Rathbone St., tel. 482-939.

By Car

Pay and Display Parking is available at the Forum North Carpark; buy a ticket (from 20 cents for 30 minutes to $4.80 for nine hours; change available at the PRO inside the center) from one of the three dispensers and place ticket on car dashboard. Local taxis are operated by **Kiwi Cabs** from 31 Porowini Ave., tel. 482-299. The main rank is on Rathbone St., and they also arrange sightseeing tours. **Marsden Taxis** can be reached at tel. 27-582. The main rental car agencies in Whangarei are **Avis Rent-A-Car,** tel. 482-929/487-023; **Budget Rent-A-Car,** tel. 487-292; **Hertz Rent-A-Car,** tel. 489-790/70-535/70-588; **Letz Rent-A-Car,** tel. 487-499; and **Thrifty Car Rental** at tel. 487-837. For tours contact Don or Cheryl Young of **Whangarei Tourist Services,** 50 Kokich Crescent, tel. 61-438.

WHANGAREI TO THE BAY OF ISLANDS

A SCENIC ROUTE

Public transportation runs up Hwy. 1 to Paihia; however, if you're hitching (allow plenty of time) or traveling by car, the scenic road to Tutukaka (29 km from Whangarei) is an enjoyable sidetrack on your way north. The road emerges at a beautiful stretch of the northern coastline, and as it's also a loop road, eventually rejoins Hwy. 1 at Hikurangi—no backtracking is necessary. It adds about 80 km of driving but the coastal scenery makes it worthwhile. Heading north through downtown Whangarei, pass through the main business area then turn right at the Regent Theatre Shopping Centre on Mill Rd. to Tutukaka (don't take the main road north). This road also leads to Whangarei Falls. Ngunguru, the first town along the route, is situated on the edge of the Ngunguru River. A sandy beach, lots of swimming and boating action, and many holiday homes give Ngunguru its vacation atmosphere.

WHANGAREI AREA

SANDY BAY
WOOLLEY BAY
WHALE BAY
TO PAIHIA & KAIKOHE
1
WOOLLEY BAY LOOKOUT
MATAPOURI
MARUA
MARUA RD.
MATAPOURI RD.
MATAPOURI BAY
HIKURANGI
TUTUKAKA
TUTUKAKA HEAD
TUTUKAKA HARBOUR
NGUNGURU
WHANGAREI FALLS
WHANGAREI
14
PORTLAND RD.
WHANGAREI HARBOUR
CEMENT WORKS
PORTLAND
MARSDEN PT.
OIL REFINERY
BREAM BAY
1
0 5 km
TO WARKWORTH & AUCKLAND
RUAKAKA

Tutukaka

This coastal town and base for deep-sea fishing and diving proclaims the title "Gateway to the Poor Knights Islands." The booking office of the Whangarei Deep Sea Anglers Club at Tutukaka Marina has all the info on local fishing, diving, cruising, and chartering boats (see below). For spectacular views of the coastline with its irresistible bays, colorful sailing boats, and shell-studded beaches, follow Tutukaka Block Rd. up to Tutukaka Heads.

Matapouri

The holiday town of Matapouri has a long white sandy beach, calm water (perfect for swimming and snorkeling), and several other small, more private beaches—reached by wading around the rocks at the northern end. At the back of the third small beach is a trail (take shoes or sandals) which passes through a rock tunnel to emerge at a beautiful cove—good snorkeling. Sometimes in summer, the waters off Matapouri Beach become thick with plankton; this doesn't seem to put the local swimmers off, but it's a rare and unforgettable sensation to swim unexpectedly into the thick, jelly-like substance when the water appears to be clear!

Whale Bay Reserve

Continuing along the road toward Sandy Bay, keep your eyes peeled for the lookout at Whale Bay Reserve—great views. An easily followed, cliffside trail leads from the lookout to the right. Passing through some exotic natural bush and groves of *pohutukawa* trees, the trail leads down the cliffs and emerges at beautiful Whale Bay Beach. The walk from the carpark to this fairly isolated beach takes about 20 minutes, but if you suffer from hayfever-type allergies, this walk can be miserable in summer! After passing Sandy Bay (known for good surfing—it usually boasts large waves when none of the other beaches do), the road swoops back inland toward Hikurangi where it re-joins Hwy. 1.

ACCOMMODATION

Camping Out

The biggest problem on the Tutukaka route is the lack of free camping areas. Many perfect camping spots are strung along the road, but almost all are "reserves" with no toilet facilities or water, and an abundance of NO CAMPING signs. Quite a few people camp at Matapouri Beach despite the signs, and no visible signs prohibit camping on the tiny beaches farther north, reached only by wading around the rocks at low tide. At Whale Beach Reserve only NO DOGS signs are on the beach. Many motor camps along the route offer tentsites, caravan sites, and cabins, and there are also quite a few motels. Note that no *legal* places to just pull off and put up a tent are found between Ngunguru and Hikurangi.

Motor Camps

Tutukaka Coast Motor Camp can be pretty crowded in summer. Expect to pay around $7.50 pp for tentsites, slightly more for caravan sites, and from $28 d for cabins; communal bathroom, kitchen, and laundry facilities. Opposite the boat ramp in Ngunguru, 400 meters south of the p.o.; tel. 33-700. The other motor camp is **Ngunguru Bay Holiday Park** on the main road through town, tel. 33-851. A tent or caravan site is around $16 d; on-site caravans start at $28 d. Cabins and tourist flats range from $27-35 d. Communal bathroom, kitchen, and laundry facilities.

Motel With A View

If you feel like a splurge and fancy a self-contained unit with either a fantastic ocean or harbor view, and use of a pool, spa, and private beach, head for **Pacific Rendezvous Motel.** Stay in one of the "Harbour View Units" which sleep four to seven, an "Ocean View Unit," or one of their "Ocean View Executive Suites" (have your gold credit card handy!). The Harbour View units start at $75 twin or double. A minimum unit charge is levied during Christmas, Jan., holiday weekends and school holidays (the price per night goes up quite a bit), and at these times it's almost impossible to get a unit without prior booking. Book as far in advance as possible and confirm with a deposit; in winter, just turn up and try your luck. In the off-season (usually starting in April) you can get less expensive rates for stays of three nights or longer. It's located on Motel Rd., Tutukaka; tel. 33-847. From the south, go two km beyond Ngunguru, take the Tutukaka Block Rd., then turn onto Motel Rd. and follow it to the end.

IN, ON, AND UNDER THE WATER

Deep-sea Fishing

The season is usually from mid-Jan. through April, no license required, for catching marlin, shark, or yellowtail tuna. The **Whangarei Deep Sea Anglers Club** at the Tutukaka Marina charters boats for deep-sea fishing starting from $460 a day. If you're by yourself, they try to hook you up with a group of at least three other people at a minimum cost of $90 pp per day. Line fishing, as part of a group, costs $30 pp per day. **Vane and Waimana Charters** provides all fishing gear and bait for gamefishing; tel. 33-823 for bookings. **Tutukaka Coast Charter Boat Association** has many fully equipped boats ready for gamefishing charters; tel. 33-755 for more information. **Tutukaka Charters' *Masada,*** a luxury launch, charters for game and line fishing and coastal cruises; tel. 33-671.

The Poor Knights Islands

A marine reserve known for its stone archways and underwater caves and tunnels teeming with colorful marinelife, the Poor Knights lie only 22 km off the main coast. The two islands were named by Capt. Cook in 1769, their shape reminding him of two knights (from the game of chess) lying on their sides. The Poor Knights and nearby Hen and Chickens Is. are two of New Zealand's most important wildlife sanctuaries, administered by the Department of Conservation. Some of the plants and birds surviving on the Poor Knights have not been found elsewhere, and the islands are the only breeding ground in the world for the Buller's Shearwater. Landing is prohibited without a special permit, but limited fishing (spearfishing and stray-line fishing) and scuba diving are permitted.

The best time to scuba dive around the Poor Knights Is. is Jan. through May, when visibility is regularly 30 meters, and can range up to 45 meters on a good day. The visibility is poor Oct. through Dec. when the water turns a milky green from plankton bloom. Known for their enormous variety of tropical and temperate indigenous marinelife, the Islands attract scuba divers from all over the world. In some parts, the towering island cliffs seen above the waterline plunge down almost vertically under the surface. With over more than 100 charted dive sites, just ask the local divers for the best locations.

To charter a boat, head down to the Tutukaka marina where many charter companies are ready and willing to swoop you out to sea. If you book a dive charter with the Whangarei Deep Sea Anglers Club, do so at least two days in advance so they can get a group together; groups pay from $45 pp for a two-bottle dive on the express boat, from $35 pp on the slow boat (which leaves very early in the day and comes back late). All the fishing charter companies listed in the fishing section above specialize in deep-sea fishing and diving charters, and you can hire all you need from the Tutukaka Dive Shop, open 0730-1930. They hire a full set of diving gear and two tanks, or individual pieces of equipment: tanks, regulators, backpacks, suits, weight-belts, fins, mask and snorkel, and a buoyancy compensator. Locally recommended divers Bryan and Eve Bell take charter diving, fishing, and sightseeing groups out to the Poor Knights in their large luxurious catamaran Pacific Hideaway. They also offer BBQ lunch charters—price negotiable. For current rates phone 33-675.

HIKURANGI TO PAIHIA

Waiomio Caves

On Hwy. 1 between Towai and Kawakawa, look out for the small sign to Waiomio Caves on the right. These limestone caves, on private land belonging to a Maori family, have been kept in a totally natural state. When enough visitors turn up to make a small group (the caves are closed in wet weather), a member of the family collects a small admission fee (several dollars pp, less for children). You can go through the lower cave only, or on an extended tour through an upper cave and come out at the top of the hill. The guide gives an informative and amusing commentary throughout the tour, with frequent stops to try your hand at playing the musical stalactites and stalagmites, or to admire glowworms (and hear their macabre lifecycle), and to look for, and hear tales of, the horrific widow spider. Keep your mouth closed when looking up! It's a worthwhile, out-of-the-ordinary glowworm tour.

Decision Time

After bypassing the town of Kawakawa, Hwy. 1 continues up to Paihia. If you're traveling by car, it's best to decide whether to stay in Paihia or Russell before the turnoff to Opua. It's less hassle and cheaper to leave the car in Paihia, and the passenger ferry service across to Russell is short, enjoyable, and frequent. Many of the attractions in Russell are within walking distance from the ferry. However, if you want to explore Russell by car, the only car ferry service leaves from Opua (south of Paihia), and crosses the Veronica Channel to Okiato (south of Russell). It costs about $5 OW, and the last ferry back from Okiato departs at 2045 most nights, 2145 on Fri. nights. It's also possible to drive all the way from Hwy. 1 to Russell avoiding the ferry altogether, but on the unsealed road, be warned, it takes forever!

BAY OF ISLANDS

The Bay of Islands is one of New Zealand's most beautiful and historic areas. Situated 257 km north of Auckland, its irregular coastline and 144 islands are lapped by warm, aquamarine waters and bathed in sunshine year-round. The mild climate of the "Winterless North" and the calm waters have made the area a sailor's paradise ever since its discovery by Capt. James Cook in the 18th century. Quiet coves, soft sandy beaches, sparkling waters, and island groves of *pohutukawa* trees abound. For excitement there's the challenge of deep-sea fishing for a magnificent marlin or shark, or the chance to dive into a colorful submarine habitat. The three main centers of interest, the towns of **Paihia, Waitangi,** and **Russell** are close to each other, and easily reached by public transportation. **Kerikeri,** a citrus center and home to many artists and craftspeople, is a short drive from Paihia.

HISTORY

First Contacts

Captain Cook named the Bay of Islands in 1769. At that time, it was inhabited by a large Maori population, whose *pas* (fortified dwellings) studded the bay. Capt. Cook's ship, the *Endeavour,* was met by a small fleet of canoes, manned by fearless warriors who came to gaze in astonishment at the huge "winged canoe." The first meeting between European and Maori was friendly; however, this changed three years later when a series of blunders by the French explorer, Marion Du Fresne, led to his murder by the local tribe, and in retaliation some 250 Maori were slain.

Trade Center

By the end of the 18th C. the Bay of Islands had become a thriving trade center, with the whalers, timber-seekers, and traders calling in at Kororareka (present-day Russell) for supplies, as well as the proverbial wine, women, and song. The migratory path of whales, unfortunately close to the northern coastline, contributed to their plunder. The tall, straight kauri trees that fringed the bay and lowlands were quickly depleted for ship masts or export to Sydney. Traders also brought predators, disease, and massive exploitation to New Zealand. In the early 19th C. many missionaries arrived, and their Christian influence helped end Maori warfare.

Treaty Of Waitangi

There was considerable foreign interest in New Zealand by 1831 and, in fear of takeover, a group of local Maori chiefs asked Britain for protection. In Feb. 1840, with the ceremonial signing of The Treaty of Waitangi, New Zealand became a British colony. Within the next year, New Zealand's "capital" was set up at Okiato and named Russell, but it was soon decided that the capital should be moved to the more desirable site of Auckland. The name Russell was then transferred to the town of Kororareka, in the hope that the new name would give the "Hellhole of the Pacific" a new image.

PAIHIA SIGHTS

When you first enter Paihia you go by a mass of motels and hotels, many competing with one another and advertising their rates along the beachfront. Continue around the point and along the beach to the wharf and main shopping area.

Paihia Wharf

The wharf is a great place to soak up the Bay of Islands' vacation atmosphere, meet people, and swap fishing stories! Whenever a shark or striped marlin is caught in local waters, the news spreads like wildfire around town, and Paihia wharf is the place to be for the official "weigh-in." If you notice a large crowd gathering at the wharf, you'll probably see at least one of the magnificent gamefish

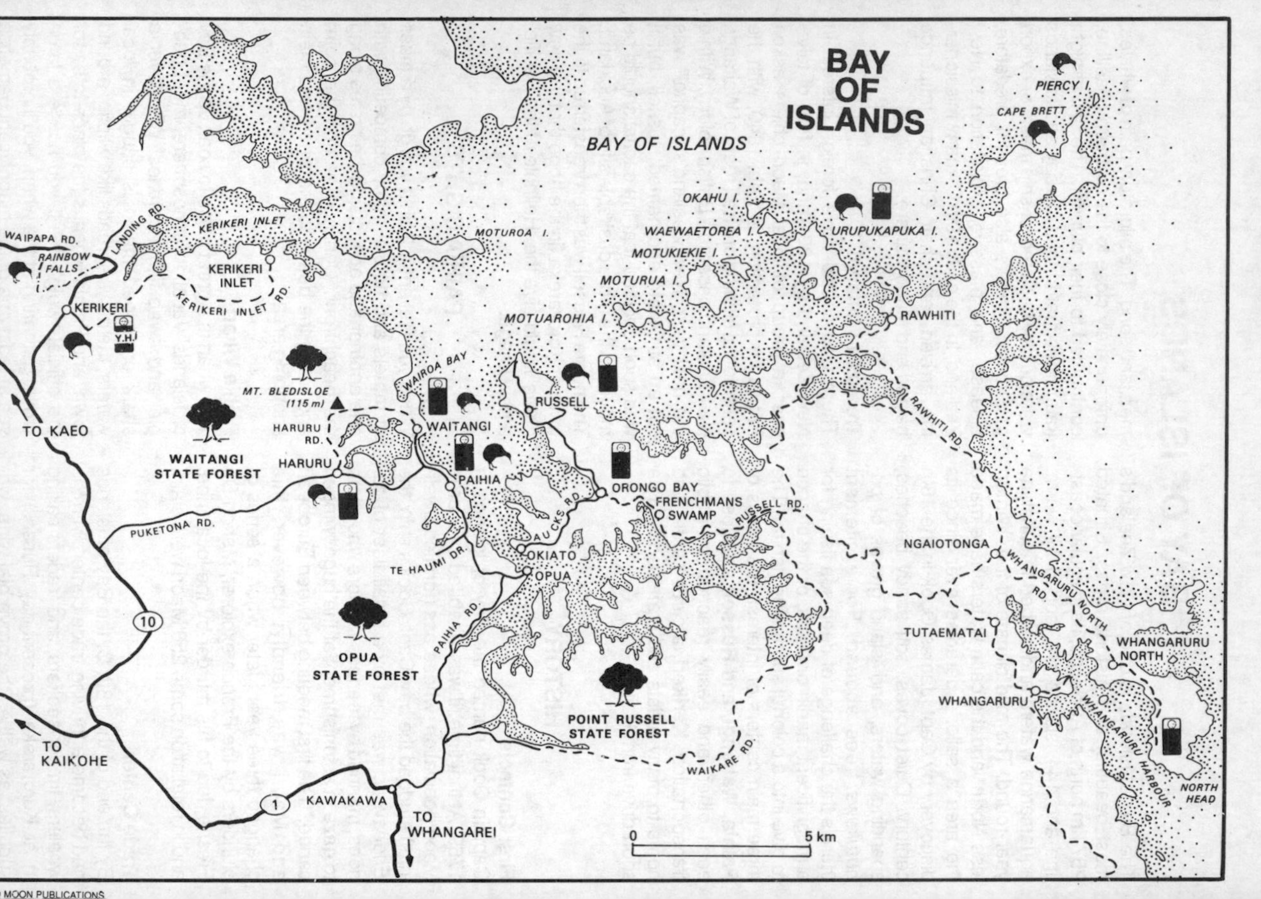
BAY OF ISLANDS
BAY OF ISLANDS
PIERCY I.
CAPE BRETT
OKAHU I.
WAEWAETOREA I.
URUPUKAPUKA I.
MOTUKIEKIE I.
MOTURUA I.
MOTUROA I.
MOTUAROHIA I.
RAWHITI
RAWHITI RD
WAIPAPA RD.
LANDING RD.
KERIKERI INLET
RAINBOW FALLS
KERIKERI INLET
KERIKERI INLET RD.
KERIKERI
Y.H.
MT. BLEDISLOE (115 m)
WAIROA BAY
RUSSELL
TO KAEO
HARURU RD.
WAITANGI
WAITANGI STATE FOREST
HARURU
PAIHIA
ORONGO BAY
FRENCHMANS SWAMP
RUSSELL RD.
PUKETONA RD.
AUCKS RD.
OKIATO
TE HAUMI DR.
OPUA
NGAIOTONGA
WHANGARURU NORTH RD.
10
OPUA STATE FOREST
PAIHIA RD.
TUTAEMATAI
WHANGARURU NORTH
WHANGARURU
POINT RUSSELL STATE FOREST
WHANGARURU HARBOUR
WAIKARE RD.
NORTH HEAD
TO KAIKOHE
1
KAWAKAWA
TO WHANGAREI
0
5 km

close up. At the Paihia waterfront you can charter game-fishing and diving boats, go for a scenic launch ride, waterski, take an exhilarating jet-boat ride, or hop on a high-speed water taxi to many of the islands.

Haruru Falls
These mighty falls on the Waitangi River are only two km inland from Paihia and Waitangi, easily reached by the track through Waitangi National Reserve, or by car along the main highway west out of Paihia. They're particularly amazing after a good rain, and are flood-lit at night.

Flightseeing
Another fun way to appreciate the beauty of the Bay of Islands is to go for the bird's-eye view. **Great Barrier Airlines** operates from Paihia Airfield on Puketona Rd., four km west of Paihia, one km west of Haruru Falls. They offer scenic flights starting at a 10-minute local flight for around adult $20; before you head out there, contact the Fullers office at Paihia wharf or call 27-421 for more info—scenic flights need to be arranged ahead of time—or try the airfield at tel. 27-887.

WAITANGI SIGHTS
From Paihia, continue north along the waterfront to the first intersection and go straight ahead toward Waitangi (if you turn left here you'll come to Haruru Falls). This road will take you to all the sights.

Shipwreck Museum
Aboard the barque *Tui,* this floating museum contains a fascinating collection of relics and treasures from over 1,800 New Zealand shipwrecks. The collection was put together by diver Kelly Tarlton, and a film with special sound effects gives insight into some of his salvage expeditions. The *Tui* is moored beside Waitangi Bridge (on the main road from Paihia to Waitangi), open 0900-1730 daily, extended hours during holidays, admission adult $4, child $2; tel. 27-018 for more information.

weighing the trophies

Waitangi National Reserve
This is the place to absorb some New Zealand history, and to witness the birthplace of the nation as we know it today. In The Treaty House on Feb. 6, 1840, the Treaty of Waitangi was signed, whereby the Maori surrendered the government of their country to Queen Victoria of Britain, in return for protection and "the rights and privileges of British subjects." On first entering this historic park, don't miss the excellent audiovisual in the Visitor Center, then stroll through the beautifully kept grounds to **Waitangi House.** Originally designed as a home for James Busby, British Resident (1832-1840) and drafter of the Treaty, Waitangi House stands in its original condition, and is open to the public. Near The Treaty House is the intricately carved and highly decorated *Whare Runanga* (Maori Meeting House), where the local Maori discussed issues, entertained neighboring tribes, and gathered for instruction, storytelling, or games. The war canoe building, just

war canoe Ngatokimatawhaorua

a short walk from the meeting house, houses the war canoe *Ngatokimatawhaorua* ("The Adzes Which Shaped It Twice"), adorned with carvings, shells, and feathers. An amazing 35 meters in length, carved from three mighty kauri trees, it has the capacity to carry a crew of 80, plus passengers! If you're planning a visit to this area early in Feb., check out the annual local celebrations commemorating the signing of the treaty; the canoe is regularly launched on these occasions.

For an enjoyable hike, consider the Haruru Falls-Treaty Grounds Track. Starting near the Visitors Centre, it crosses Hutia Creek via Mangrove Forest Boardwalk, and finishes at spectacular Haruru Falls. A map of the track is available in the Visitors Centre. Waitangi National Reserve grounds, buildings and Visitors Centre (tel. 27-308) are open daily from 0900-1700; admission adult $3.50, child free.

Mount Bledisloe

This mountain marks the northwest boundary of Waitangi National Reserve and is an excellent vantage point. The summit lookout (115 meters), a short walk from the carpark, gives one of the best panoramic views of the Bay of Islands. Follow the road for 3.2 km beyond The Treaty House (passing the 18-hole Waitangi Golf Club on the way). For an alternate route back to Paihia and Waitangi, turn left on Haruru Falls Rd. to Haruru Falls, left again at the main road (Puketona Rd.) which takes you back to Paihia.

KERIKERI SIGHTS

Savor The Flavor

This historic town, 23 km from Paihia, is well worth a visit. Once the home of Chief Hongi Hika and the Ngapuhi warriors, who conquered much of the North Island in the late 18th and early 19th centuries, it was also site of one of the earliest missions. Kerikeri boasts impressive buildings and trees, lush agricultural land, and the attractive Kerikeri River and Rainbow Falls. It's a citrus center (the signs proclaim it's "The Fruitbowl of the North"), quite obvious by the great number of orchards that line the roads between Paihia and Kerikeri, and from the delicious oranges, mandarins, and tangelos available June to January. It's also rapidly becoming an important kiwi cultivating center. (If you're looking for accommodations in the Kerikeri area and want to meet the locals, see "Meet The People" on p. 115.)

Arts And Crafts

Kerikeri has a distinct appeal for arts and crafts collectors, and music lovers. The town supports a large community of artists; spinning and weaving, ceramics, and stained-glass art are most popular (the shopping center is off the main road to the right just before Cobham Road). Don't miss a stop at **Origin Art & Craft Co-Operative** on the main highway (Hwy. 10). Inside you'll discover pottery, knitwear, weaving, stained glass, leatherwork, woodwork, furniture—it's a shopper's delight—and they except major credit cards just to remove any last doubts you may have in buying up the entire shop! Open daily 1000-1700, tel. 79-065. In Jan., the Kerikeri

Arts Centre celebrates opera and dance at its Festival of Music. Stop first at the information booth on the left side of the main street (entering town from the south), and pick up a free map. The main Tourist Information Centre is at Trixie Newton Travel, Village Mall on Kerikeri Rd., the main street downtown (tel. 79-437).

Historic Buildings

New Zealand's oldest stone building, the **Stone Store** on Kerikeri Inlet Rd., is just one of many attractive buildings that give Kerikeri its unique charm. Built by the Church Missionary Society in 1832, the Stone Store was an inpenetrable place of refuge in troubled times, and a storehouse. Still used as a storehouse, you can also see nicknacks from the past and buy groceries and souvenirs. The upper floor has been developed into a museum displaying articles that belonged to early settlers, open daily 0900-1700; admission adult $1, child 50 cents. Across the road is a grassy knoll (pleasant spot for a picnic) that overlooks Kerikeri Basin. The knoll is the remains of **Kororipo Pa,** a fishing base built by Hongi Hika and other Ngapuhi chiefs, where many historic meetings took place. **Kemp House,** just behind the Stone Store, was built in 1821, and lays claim to being the oldest wooden building in the country. It has been preserved by the Historic Society in much the same state as when the early missionaries lived there, and the surrounding gardens are beautiful despite the damage caused by severe flooding in 1981. Kemp House is open daily from 1030-1230 and 1330-1630; adult $3, child 50 cents.

For a delicious tea break or dinner with lots of historic atmosphere and a picture-perfect view, try the **Stone Store Tearooms** across the road from the Stone Store (see "Food" below).

Rainbow Falls Scenic Reserve

Spectacular Rainbow Falls can be easily reached by car to the top, or by foot to the bottom. The water plummets 27 meters over easily eroded soft lava columns, and there are several viewing points. To get to the bottom of the falls, take the one-hour track which starts at the Ranger Station (BOI Historic and Maritime Park) on Landing Road. The track follows Kerikeri River, passes Fairy Pools, and comes out at the bottom of the falls. Fairy Pools can also be easily reached along a road just south of the YH. To view Rainbow Falls from the top, enter the reserve off Waipapa Rd. about two km from the Stone Store. The road to the falls is well signposted and there's a large carpark; a short stroll through natural bush brings you to the vari-

the Stone Store, Kerikeri

Russell from Flagstaff Hill

ous lookouts. From the second lookout at the top, on a sunny day, you can see how the falls got their name.

RUSSELL SIGHTS

Captain Cook Memorial Museum

Allow lots of time here! The museum contains all sorts of relics from early Kororareka (Russell's original name), and gives an insight into the people and the history of this colorful town. The highlight and pride of the museum is the seven-meter replica of Captain Cook's ship the *Endeavour,* accurately reproduced down to the finest detail. Located on York St., tel. Russell 37-701, the museum is open daily 1000-1600; admission adult $1.50, child 25 cents.

Historic Buildings

Walk around Russell to discover many historic buildings scattered throughout. The impressive **Pompallier House** is on the Strand, which runs along the waterfront. Historic relics are displayed within this stately house, named after one of its early owners, Bishop Pompallier. It's open daily 1000-1230 and 1330-1630, tel. 37-861; admission to house and grounds adult $2.50, child 50 cents. Toward the other end of the Strand stands the **police station.** Built in 1870, it has been a customs house, courthouse, jail, and continues to be the Russell police station today. It's also the local policeman's home (there's only one!) and is therefore not open to the public. Check out the fantastic Morton Bay Fig Tree *(Ficus macrophyllia)* with its intricately gnarled and patterned trunk, growing between the police station and **The Duke of Marlborough Hotel.** This old hotel is the proud holder of the first liquor license issued in New Zealand and was amongst the many "grog shops" of Kororareka's rowdy past. **Christ Church,** a couple of blocks back from the Strand, was built in 1835 and is the oldest standing church in New Zealand. It still bears cannonball and musket holes from the days of the Maori Wars, and the gravestones (and the stories they tell) in the cemetery are intriguing.

Bay Of Islands Maritime And Historic Park Headquarters

This is another not-to-be-missed place, particularly for those interested in hiking, camping, and other outdoor activities in the park. It's an info center on the Bay of Islands, in general, and the park islands that can be visited (see "Camping Out" below). Check out the informative displays and excellent audiovisual on the early history of New Zealand; there's always a park ranger around ready to help or issue camping permits. Pick up the pamphlets on camping and fishing info at the front desk; a good number of books and pamphlets on the area are also available at varying prices. On the Strand, tel. 37-685; open daily 0830-1700.

Maiki Hill

Also known as Flagstaff Hill, this historic landmark offers outstanding views of Russell and the Bay of Islands—great for getting oriented and watching all the boats that cruise the bay.

In the early 1840s at the top of Maiki Hill the British raised a flagstaff in order to fly the British flag. Hone Heke, Chief of the Ngapuhi, saw the flagstaff as a symbol of British authority (for which he had little respect), and he and his warriors spent much of their time over the years chopping down the hated flagstaff, despite many British attempts to keep the flag flying. Chopped down for the fourth time in 1845, it wasn't until 1857 that a permanent reconciliation formed. At the top of the hill is a monument to these historic events. A good 30-minute track up the hill begins at the boat-ramp end of the Strand, follows the beach around to Watering Bay, and then heads up through native bush to the flagstaff. At high tide, take Wellington St. up instead of the track. By car, take Queen St. out of town, and follow signs to the top.

An Organized Tour

Russell Mini Tours operates a one-hour tour of the local area taking in the main historic and scenic attractions, and it's particularly good for those on a short time schedule. The minibus departs Russell Wharf daily at 1100, 1245, 1400, and 1530 (less often during low season); adult $8, child $4. For reservations in Russell call Dot at tel. 37-891 or Fullers at tel. 37-866, in Paihia call Fullers at tel. 27-421.

THE BAY BY BOAT

Cream Trip

One of the best ways to get a true taste of the Bay of Islands is from the water, and one of the most popular cruises (deservedly) is the Cream Trip. Operated by Fullers Cruises, it departs Paihia daily at 1000, Russell at 1015, and leisurely cruises around many of the beautiful islands in the bay, the captain's commentary keeping passengers informed and amused. On Mon., Wed., and Fri. the boat makes a short stop at many of the islands to deliver mail and groceries free of charge to the farmers and island-caretakers scattered around the bay. The cruise is $39 adult, $15 child, including a one-hour stop for

lunch at picturesque Otehei Bay on Urupukapuka Island. Lunch itself is extra, with a choice of a picnic snack (a small salad) for around $8 or a delicious BBQ steak and salad (good value) for $12. (It's easiest to buy the lunch ticket along with the cruise ticket, otherwise line up and buy one when you reach the island.) After lunch there's time for a quick swim or a walk up the hill for good views. The four-hour Cream Trip is very good value, and during summer and on public holidays be sure to book at least several days ahead. Call Fullers Cruises, tel. Paihia 27-421 or Russell 37-866 for bookings.

Other Cruises

Fullers also has other cruises around the Bay of Islands. The most well-known and popular one is the **Cape Brett, Hole In the Rock Cruise,** which departs Paihia daily at 0900 and 1230, Russell 0910 and 1220, returning around 1200 and 1630 (in summer there's also an afternoon cruise). It visits Cape Brett, Motukokako Island, and Cathedral Cave, and weather permitting, the boat passes through the famous "Hole in the Rock." It also stops at Otehei Bay for lunch (not included); like the Cream Trip, the fare is $39 adult, $15 child. They operate a reduced schedule during June, July, and August. For reservations tel. Paihia 27-421. (Also see "Entertainment" on p. 117 for evening cruises.)

Kirky's Cruises offers their Super-cruise—a half-hour cruise taking in the inner islands of the bay, Cape Brett, Cathedral Cave, and a half-hour island stopover. Call at their booking office by the info center, Paihia wharf, for current departure times and fares, or tel. 27-221.

Take To The Water In Style

The most unique and stylish way to tour the bay is onboard the stunning ***R. Tucker Thompson,*** a gaff-rigged square topsail schooner that has circumnavigated the world, taken part in Australia's Bicentenary as one of the tall ships re-enacting the Australian First Fleet voyage, and has starred in the TV series "Adventurer." Take part in the sailing activities or just relax, stop at an island (time for swimming allowed), and savor a Devon tea, wine with lunch (provide your own food), and then afternoon tea. The six- to seven-hour trip is only $55.80 pp adult, $28 child under 15 years old—take a swimsuit, towel, sun block, warm jacket, and lunch. Make bookings at the Paihia Wharf office, open seven days from 0800-1700, tel. 28-430 (after hours tel. 37-380).

Yacht Charters

So many yacht outfits (commercial and private) do charters that it's best to stop by the info center at Paihia wharf to pick up all the current brochures, then call around for yourself. **Freedom Yacht Charters Limited** lures you out to sea in a skippered yacht for "day sailing," departing Russell wharf at 0900, returning at 1600, and costs $45 pp (minimum of three) which includes a light lunch. The company also hires out sail-yourself yachts (from $155 to $607 per day depending on the boat and the season), and they'll teach you how to sail if you want (or need!) lessons. For more info call Russell 37-781; bookings are essential. **A Place In The Sun Yacht Charters** cruises only from Oct. to April. You can take sailing lessons, island hop, swim, snorkel around the reefs, or just relax on a luxury ketch; departing daily from Russell wharf at 1300 and returning at 1630, it costs around $27 pp including lunch. Overnight cruises (two days and one night), all meals included, start from around $250 pp, and extended cruising rates are available (from $150 pp per day). Bookings are essential, tel. Russell 37-615.

The ***Carino*** is another charter sailing boa[t] to consider. Go day sailing for $45 pp (minimum two) which includes morning and afternoon tea, fishing and snorkeling gear, sailing tuition if required, and an island stop; departs daily from Russell at 0930 and Paihia at 1000 returning around 1700. Half-day sailing from 0830-1230 or 1300-1600 is $35 pp (minimum four). Other alternatives include an evening BBQ cruise for $45 pp which includes the meal ashore, or an overnight cruise (minimum six) for $360 (bring own food and drinks). For more info and bookings call Russell 37-230. If fighting a feisty fish is most likely to be the highlight of your cruising experience, step aboard the ***Ginger Nut*** charter boat from Paihia and reel 'em in from 0800-1430. They specialize in six types of fishing and you get to keep whatever you catch; from $55 pp. Call 27-035 for the complete rundown.

ACCOMMODATIONS

Camping Out

Two camping areas lie within the Bay of Islands Maritime and Historic Park—Urupukapuka Island and Whangaruru North Head. You can camp anywhere on **Urupukapuka Island** except Indico, Paradise, and Otehe bays. Largest in the bay, to camp on this recreational reserve you need to be totally self-sufficient with tent, stove, fuel, and food but fresh water is available at Urupukapuka and Kapurarahurahu (Cable) bays; camp fee is $4 pp per night. Open fires are not allowed. Check the tourist agencies and info centers in Russell and Paihia for the latest info on boat services, and possible grocery deliveries to the various island reserves.

At Puriri Bay in **Whangaruru North Head Reserve,** there are 60 tent or caravan sites (no power), fresh water, and toilets. Fees are $6 per site per night, and it's very busy during the peak summer season (first come, first served; closed from July 1 to Sept. 30). Puriri Bay can be reached by car along an unsealed road but it's a long way. Go to Orongo Bay south of Russell, take Russell Rd. toward Frenchmans Swamp and Tutaematai. Before reaching Tutaematai, turn left on Rawhiti Rd. to Ngaiotonga. Turn right on Whangaruru North Rd. and follow it to the end. Puriri Bay can also be reached by boat, and has anchorage in the bay and several nice beaches. Ask for the "Bay of Islands Maritime and Historic Park," "Huts and Camping," and "Urupukapuka Island Campers" brochures at the Park HQ and Visitors Centre in Russell.

Park Huts

Within the BOI Maritime Park are three reserves providing basic hut accommodation starting at $4 pp per night (children half price). Take your sleeping bag, food, stove, and cooking equipment for all the huts, and book at Park HQ in Russell (tel. 37-685), or the Kerikeri Ranger Station (tel. 78-474). Impressive **Ranfurly Bay Reserve** at the entrance to Whangaroa Harbour is known for rugged volcanic rock formations. The Ranfurly Bay hut has 12 bunks, toilet facilities and water, and deep-water anchorage in the bay. Three well-marked tracks can be hiked from the bay, each providing outstanding harbor views; however, the reserve can only be reached by boat. Many Whangaroa tourist launches cruise to this bay, or make anchor—try to arrange transportation with them. Water taxis are also available, but expensive.

Motukawanui (Big Cavalli Island) is a large island reserve, known for its scenic track (1½ hours) which covers the length of the island. The island hut has eight bunks, toilet facilities, and fresh water.

Cape Brett (Rakaumangamanga) scenic reserve was named by Capt. Cook. A track, starting at Oke Bay on Rawhiti Rd., takes eight to nine hours. Classified as a hard tramp, it's only recommended for those with above-average fitness and experience (sea access is possible in calm conditions). The old lighthouse on the point was built in 1909, and the lighthouse keeper's cottage has been converted into a hut that can sleep 12, with toilet facilities and water; $4 adult, $1.50 child. For info on the walks in each reserve, ask for the *Walking in the Bay of Islands Maritime and Historic Park* pamphlet from Park HQ (tel. 37-685).

Hostels

There is no YH in Paihia or Russell, but there are several private hostels. Ask at the PRO in Paihia for the most recent additions to the listings.

In Paihia: Mayfair Lodge offers bunk-bed, dormitory-style accommodation from $13 pp, and the use of the spa pool, table tennis and billiard facilities. They also do bookings for bus tours, horse riding, etc. At 7 Puketona Rd., Paihia, tel. 27-471. **Centabay Travellers Hostel** is behind the shops on Selwyn Rd., Paihia (tel. 27-466), and costs from $12 per night, hostel-style. Twins and doubles are also available. You can hire bicycles here, or head out for some reasonably priced sailing activities on a charter yacht. The hosts also do bookings for all local activities. **Lodge Eleven Travellers Hostel** is another good place to go for budget accommodation, dorm rooms, private facilities with each unit, TV and game room, fully-equipped kitchen and dining area, and off-street parking. Call for courtesy coach to and from the bus terminal. Rates start at $13 pp. It's on the corner of McMurray and Kings roads, tel. 27-487.

In Russell: Near Russell, **Orongo Bay Holiday Park** is an associate YH providing 50 beds in four-berth rooms for $32 per room per night (discount for YH members). There's a large, equipped kitchen and dining room, comfy TV lounge, communal showers and toilets, and a shop. Supply your own sleeping bag or linen, or hire linen. Double rooms are $27 d, $7.50 each extra adult. On the Opua car ferry road, three km from Russell, tel. 37-704 (also see "Motor Camps In Russell" below).

In Kerikeri: Kerikeri YHA hostel is on Main Rd. not far from the Stone Store, on the outskirts of town, tel. 79-391; $12 pp. The InterCity bus from the north passes the hostel door, and the bus from the south stops at the post office 800 meters away. **Puriri Park's** friendly owners provide budget accommodation in a delightful garden and orchard setting; from $10 pp. Work in their kiwifruit orchards is also available in season. It's signposted on the main road to Kerikeri (Hwy. 10) from Paihia. **Hideaway Lodge** also offers budget accommodation from $11-15 pp a night for share, twin, or double rooms, tent sites from $7 pp. Kitchen and laundry facilities, pool, TV and game room. On Wiroa Rd., tel. 79-773 (free transportation to and from Kerikeri bus depot at 1030 and 1615). Seasonal work is also available.

Motor Camps In Paihia

Of the several motor camps in the Paihia area, none are downtown. **Twin Pines Tourist Park** got our vote as the most friendly and easy going. It's just three km out along Puketona Rd. (the main road west out of Paihia) on the banks of the Waitangi River, adjacent to spectacular Haruru Falls (floodlit at night, and heard clearly throughout the camp). Gordon, Mamie, and John Putt, owners/managers, are always thinking up something to make your stay more enjoyable—whether it's harnassing Gordon's creative genius, cooking up a storm on the BBQ in summer for anyone who wants to participate, or handing out free pieces of smoked fish which they caught in the river below. The Putts will recommend and book local activities free of charge—if you like exciting water action, ask them if the "Mud Run" is on! Fishing gear is also available—ask at the office. Many scenic walks are close to the camp (don't miss the steep three-minute bamboo trail that Gordon constructed from the camp down to the river with its built-in loveseat, view of the falls, and water access), a grocery store is down the road, and the popular Twin Pines Tavern and Restaurant is also on the premises (see "Food" below). Tent and caravan sites start at $7 pp (add GST to all prices) and budget accommodation is available at $11 pp in the Lodge, also part of the tourist park; communal showers, toilets, kitchen, and laundry; you provide linen, cooking equipment, etc. Attractive A-frame cabins are available from $12 pp per night, but there's a nightly minimum per unit between 1 Dec. and 25 April. Each cabin sleeps up to six and has a refrigerator; you supply linen, cooking equipment and crockery, and have the use of the communal kitchen facilities. Tourist flats sleep up to four anc are fully self-contained; you supply linen; $3 per night for two people (minimum nightl rate), $12 each extra adult; tel. Paihia 27-322

Panorama Motor Lodge and Carava Park is along the road from Twin Pines, alsc on the banks of the Waitangi River, and ha a great view of Haruru Falls from farthe down-river. Guests can use the private jetty boat ramp, pool, and spa (charge), and hir dinghies and canoes; restaurant on the prem ises. Camp and caravan charges start at $1 d per night, accommodation in the lodg starts at $50 d; tel. 27-525. **Smiths Holida Camp** is 2.5 km from Paihia, on the roa toward Opua (and the car ferry to Russell). I has its own private bay, camp store, anc games room, boat ramp and boats for hire and the usual communal facilities. Tent anc caravan sites from $7.50 pp, cabins from $3 d; you supply linen and blankets; tel. 27-678

Motor Camps In Russell

Head three km from Russell on the road fron the Opua car ferry for lush green **Orong Bay Holiday Park.** Aside from the usua shower and toilet blocks, there's a fully equipped kitchen and dining area, comf game and TV room with fireplace, swimmin pool, and a shop in the office. Tentsites ar $6 pp, $3 child, and caravan sites are $7 pp $4 child; tel. 37-704. In the lodge, dorm-styl rooms are only $27 d. **Russell Holiday Par** is on Long Beach Rd., tel. 37-826. TV anc dining room, communal facilities (metere showers); tent and caravan sites from $7 pp $4 per child. They also have cabins equippe with crockery and cutlery that range fron $28-30 d per night; you supply linen an blankets. **Arcadia Lodge** on Florence Ave (access from Brind Rd. or Florence Ave.) ha well-equipped units from $38-53 per night d you supply linen or hire available; tel. 37-756

Motels

You'll see an enormous number of motels i the Bay of Islands area, most of which ar more expensive than other resort areas. Th prices also go up during the summer and o public and school holidays. Refer to the *AA Accommodation Directory* for all the details and current rates. In Paihia, **A 1 Motel** charges from $37 s, $40-50 twin or d (higher rates during holidays), and they also offer reduced off-season rates and group reductions; on Davis Crescent, Paihia, tel. 27-684. **Dolphin Motel** at 69 Williams Rd. (opposite Paihia wharf), tel. 28-170, has rooms from $50-55 d, and special weekly rates. One of the most recommended motels in Paihia is the attractive flower-decked **Swiss Chalet Lodge Motel** at 3 Bayview Rd., tel. 27-615. Facilities include appealing rooms with private balconies, a kitchen with microwave ovens, breakfast room service, parking, and all sorts of little "comforts of home." Rates from $50-60 s, $55-90 d (minimum $83 per night during peak holiday periods but off-season rates also available). Bookings advisable—this motel is understandably popular! For a list of reasonably priced motels, stop in at the Bay of Islands Information Centre, Maritime Building, Paihia, or the info center at Russell wharf.

Meet The People

Kerikeri has two particularly relaxing places to stay—both bed and breakfasts. The friendly owners of **Puriri Park** provide two comfortable rooms (shared facilities) in a lovely home surrounded by beautifully kept gardens, kiwifruit and orange orchards (drink as much freshly squeezed OJ as you can handle!). Rates are $28 s, $40 d, with breakfast $40 s, $60 d, or stay in the bright clean budget rooms in a separate building (shared facilities) with cooking and laundry facilities for only $10 pp (plus GST)—a steal! If you're looking for a tent or campervan site, they can put you up for $5-7 pp. Dinner is also available for $20 pp. It's well signposted on Bulls Rd. (Hwy. 10—main road from Paihia), tel. 79-818.

Wilsons House is another comfortable place to stay, at 25 Kemp Rd., tel. 78-217 (call ahead to see if a room is available). Hospitable and artistic Mrs. Wilson provides one unit (two single beds with private facilities) off a veranda with stunning Stone Basin and garden views, and healthy breakfasts. It's also within walking distance of the Stone Store, a Maori village and *pa,* Rainbow Falls Reserve, and town via a walking track over the hill. Rates are only $30 s, $50 d B & B.

Homestay Limited has two country houses in Kerikeri on the books where you can stay in the homes of friendly New Zealand families. However, you need to book in advance, and the organization requests pre-payment. It's a splurge at $70 pp but includes a 24-hour stay, all meals, the opportunity to make friends, and a lift (if needed) to and from the nearest bus stop. Write to Homestay Limited, P.O. Box 630, Rotorua, tel. 24-895/83-536.

FOOD

Light Meals And Snacks

The Blue Marlin cafe and takeaway on the waterfront at Paihia has substantial cooked breakfasts, served all day, for $7. **The Pantry Coffee Lounge** is known for good home cooking. In the off-season, it's open Mon. to Fri. 0800-1600, Sat. 0800-1330, and in summer, Mon. to Sun. 0800-1700; on Selwyn Rd., Paihia (tel. 27-185). **Waltons Carvery** in the Paihia mall is a great place to head for lunch or dinner to go. Choose from three roast meats, carved to order, in a roll with salad for $3.80-4, or complete roast meals from 1700-2000 for only $8.50. It's open weekdays to 1900. **Bistro 40** in the Bayswater Inn at 40 Marsden Rd. (next to the Stone Church on the waterfront), Paihia (tel. 27-444), has great lunches and sea views from its courtyard by the bay. It's open daily from 1200- 1400; expect to pay $9-15 pp. **Paihia Refreshment Bar** is open seven days, 0700-2100, for breakfasts, teas, and light meals. Dairy and grocery items are also available; on Marsden Rd., Paihia (tel. 27-590).

Two good cafes to try in Russell are **The Traders Cafe** across from the Captain Cook Museum, and **Verandah Cafe** (nice outside deck) just a little farther along, both on the main road as you enter town. For delicious home-baked food, historic atmosphere (one of the oldest buildings in Kerikeri), and delightful water views from inside or on the outside veranda, drive out to the **Stone Store Tearooms** in Kerikeri for a light meal, morning or afternoon tea, or dinner (1800-2100, mains $10-17; bistro on Fri., Sat., and Sun. nights for $10 pp); at Kerikeri Basin (just across from the Stone Store).

Restaurants

For budget roast meals with vegies and salad bar (mini-meals from $4, buffet from $8), try **Maree's Backpackers and Licensed Restaurant** in the Paihia mall. **Goffes Restaurant,** on the upper floor of Twin Pines Tavern at Haruru Falls is an elegant place to eat. Full a la carte menu and daily blackboard specials, but expect to fork out at least $15-19 for a main course, $30 pp for a meal including wine. However, downstairs in the Dewdrop Bar, you can get light lunches and family-style bistro meals starting at about $10 pp. On pleasant summer evenings, a filling BBQ meal is served in the Garden Bar for around $8-10 pp, and enjoyed in the outside courtyard. Twin Pines Tavern is on Puketona Rd. at Haruru Falls, tel. Paihia 27-195.

Anchorage Grill in the THC Waitangi Hotel at Waitangi whips up grills, salads, and daily specials, with main courses averaging $12. Open Mon. to Sat. 1200-1400 and 1800-2100, closed Sun.; tel. 27-411. If you're in a more dressy mood, head for the **Poolside Restaurant,** also in the hotel; an average main course starts at $15. If you're driving out to Kerikeri, try dinner at the **Stone Store Tearooms** from 1800-2100—great bistro meals on Fri., Sat., and Sun. nights for $10 pp. See "Light Meals And Snacks" above.

The Ferryman's Licensed Restaurant (tel. 27-515) at Opua (where the car ferry crosses to Russell) is a local favorite for nautical atmosphere and seafood so fresh it may just swim off your plate. Aside from the restaurant section (dinner served 1800-2100), there's also a more casual bistro bar with a BYO license (open 1200-1430). Steak or seafood lunches range from $9-15, dinners from $12-20, but daily specials are more reasonable. In the General Store Building, on the waterfront at Opua, tel. 27-515. If you're just waiting for the ferry and want a tasty seafood snack or burger to go, try the takeaway next door. The **Reef Bar Bistro** in the Russell Duke of Marlborough Tavern offers fresh fish and steaks at family prices—main courses are usually around $15. It's open for lunch from 1200-1400 and dinner from 1730-2100, in the Duke Tavern Family and Garden Bar, tel. Russell 37-831. **Quarterdeck Restaurant** next to Fullers Cruises on The Strand, Russell, serves all sorts of delectable dishes with mains averaging $11-15, and all come with vegies and salad bar. Their sea-

Twin Pines Tavern

food platter for $22 is large enough for two, and they don't mind you sharing. Desserts average $5. Savor your seafood and sea view in the appropriately nautical atmosphere; it's open daily for dinner from 1800-2030, tel. 37-761 or 37-645. The **Swordfish Club Restaurant** on The Strand at Russell is another popular local spot, but you need to be a member of the club, an affiliated or kindred member of an overseas club, or brought by a member to eat here. The food is excellent, the prices reasonable (mains $14-18), and it's open July to Nov. on Wed. to Sat. from 1900, and in summer seven days a week.

ENTERTAINMENT

There's not a lot of wild nightlife in the Bay of Islands—it's more of a wind-down-and-relax kind of place. However, Fullers Cruises does evening **disco cruises** during the summer months for $20 pp, departing from Paihia at 2030. The THC Waitangi Resort Hotel in Waitangi puts on a **Maori Pageant and Feast** on Sun. evenings at 1900. It's a good way to hear a bit of history, eat a traditional meal, and have a good time. Reservations are essential. Call Paihia 27-411 for current costs and bookings. The hotel also has several bars. The **Duke of Marlborough Hotel** on the corner of York and Chapel streets, Russell, is a popular watering hole where you can enjoy a drink and soak up some of the history that permeates the surroundings. It holds the first license issued in New Zealand—on 14 July, 1840.

If you get your kicks from running, the annual **Tall Ships Fun Run** is usually held early in January. This 10-km undulating tar-sealed course gives the runners (if they have the energy to notice!) spectacular views of the Bay of Islands along the route. Starts at Okiato Point (the ferry landing) and finishes at Russell waterfront; small registration fee (you can enter on the day). For more info, write to Tall Ships Fun Run, Box 36, Russell. The annual **Tall Ships Race** (a sailing event of some magnitude, usually run in Jan.) starts in Russell and attracts a good crowd of fun-loving people out to appreciate all the ships (they have to be over 30 feet tall and have two masts to enter), the sea, and the sunshine.

GAME FISHING

The Fish

The Bay of Islands is New Zealand's most popular game-fishing grounds, and fishing is a year-round activity. They say the best game-fishing is in Feb. and March, but keep in mind that plenty of "big ones" are also caught in Jan., April, and May (the average is three fish a day). Striped, blue, and black marlin, mako, thresher, blue and hammerhead sharks, yellowfin tuna, and yellowtail (or kingfish) cruise the waters in abundance. The most prolific big-game fish is the striped marlin; the best months are Dec. to June. For sharks, the best time is Nov. to May, and for tuna, it's Dec. to March. Yellowtail are caught year-round but are mainly fished during June and July.

Charters

Paihia wharf is a hub of deep-sea fishing activity; for info check the Maritime Building on the wharf. Paihia is home base to most of the local game-fishing boats, and the many companies that offer diving expeditions, sailing trips, sightseeing cruises, and dine-and-dance trips. The Game Fishing Charter Association, based in Paihia Maritime Building, offers single, shared, or live-aboard charters (minimum two days, maximum four people), and all boats are fully equipped with gear and tackle to suit beginners to experts. The boats collect their passengers at Paihia, Russell, or Waitangi at around 0800, and return at 1730. A solo game-fishing charter starts at $660 per day, a share charter (maximum four people) starts at $180 pp per day, but note that a discount is often given on daily rates during Nov. and December. Non-angling passengers can also go along to watch the action for $55 pp per day. If you're into light tackle fishing, you're in luck; the charters are much cheaper, but get a firm price when you book.

Call the 24-hour info line, tel. Paihia 27-311. In arrangement with the Northland Charter Boat Association based in Russell, they take bookings for all types of fishing—from deep-sea to light tackle. They also cater to divers, and run various cruises around the bay.

Bay Of Islands Swordfish Club
This prestigious club, located at both the Russell and Paihia waterfronts, is the base for many of the big-game fishing tournaments. Many different tournaments are held from Tutukaka to the Bay of Islands from Jan. through June. Club officials perform the weigh-ins and record the vitals whenever a game fish is brought in. Day membership can be bought for $5 (plus GST) prior to going fishing, which includes an official weigh-in and certificate, and eligibility for most club trophies. Look for a crowd gathering around either Russell or Paihia wharfs as it's likely to mean they're bringing in a magnificent game fish for a weigh-in. Records of these weigh-ins are written on blackboards by 1615 daily, and displayed at both wharves. There's also a good licensed restaurant at the Russell club for members, affiliated and kindred members from an overseas club, or guests of members.

INFORMATION

The **Bay of Islands Information Centre** is in the Maritime Building on the Paihia waterfront, open from 0800-1700 daily, tel. 27-426. During holiday periods Freedom Yacht Charters Ltd. on the wharf acts as the **Russell Information Centre,** tel. 38-011; open daily 0800-1730. The **Kerikeri PRO** is at the entrance to town, open 0830-1730, tel. 79-702. **Park HQ** is on The Strand, Russell (open daily 0830-1700, tel. 37-685), and the other info center is the **Kerikeri Ranger Station** on Landing Road. **Kerikeri Tourist Information Centre** is at Trixie Newton Travel, in the Village Mall, tel. 79-437.

Fullers Cruises offices: Williams Rd., Paihia, tel. 27-631 on the 24-hour line, the marine office at Paihia Wharf, tel. 27-099, and at Russell wharf. All book Fullers cruises, passenger and car ferries, and InterCity coach travel.

TRANSPORTATION

On Foot

The best way to see Russell, Paihia, and Waitangi is on foot. The towns are small, connected by an excellent ferry service, and most sights are within walking distance from one another. Otherwise take minibus tours to the main attractions, or taxis (in Paihia tel. 27-506, in Russell contact Birke Lovett or see Bay of Islands Swordfish Club).

By Water

A **passenger ferry** connects Paihia and Russell, seven days a week, starting at 0800 from Russell and ending at 1730 from Paihia (extended evening services in the peak summer months). The ferry crosses about once an hour or so and takes about 15 minutes; see the current timetable for exact times. Costs around $4.40 adult RT, child $2.50. Waitangi and Russell are also connected by ferry, but the crossings are much less frequent. Be sure to check the schedule or you may find yourself stranded on the wrong side of the water when night falls! If this happens, don't panic. **Think Pink Water Taxi Service** operates a 24-hour service, tel. 27-161 or 27-426, and **Island Water Taxi** can be reached at tel. 37-123.

A **car ferry** runs continuously between Opua (south of Paihia) and Okiato Point (south of Russell) between 0700-2100, seven days a week (2200 on Fri. nights). Fare for car and driver is $6 OW plus $1 each extra passenger (double for the RT), campervans $9 OW, motorcycle $2.50 OW, adult passenger $1 OW. Buy your ticket on board. Next to the dock is The Ferryman's Licensed Restaurant (restaurant and bistro bar; see "Food" above), and next door the takeaway serves quick tasty seafood snacks and burgers.

CONTINUING NORTH

By Coach

Unless you're hitching or have a car, the next best way to see the far north is to take one of two outstanding coach tours. On the **Cape Reinga Bus Tour,** the driver's narration introduces you to the north's history while you travel in comfort to the northern-most tip; the return route includes a thrilling ride on the sands of Ninety Mile Beach (see below). The coaches depart daily from Paihia and Kerikeri at 0730, return 1800; depart Mangonui and Coopers Beach 0815, return 1645; and depart Kaitaia at 0930, return 1630. Adult fare is $47 pp from Paihia, $37 from Kaitaia.

The exciting **Tu Tu Fun Bus Tour** is aboard the 40-seat, six-wheel dune buggy "Tu Tu" ("Play About" in Maori), designed to travel over the mighty sand dunes, rocks, and beaches of the north with ease. This exhilarating ride departs from Fullers South Rd. depot daily at 1000, returning at 1400; $37 adult, $17 child. A 20% discount is available to YHA members, a 10% "Twin Tour discount" to those who take both tours. Book ahead and call for current prices, tel. Kaitaia 81-500. Reservations can also be made with the Kaitaia YH warden, tel. 81-840.

By Bus

InterCity runs regular coach services from Waitangi to Kaitaia (or south to Whangarei and Auckland). If you don't have time to see the far north you can catch a bus from Waitangi to Kawakawa, change buses, and continue across the northern region to Kaikohe, Rawene, Opononi, and down to Dargaville. Reservations are necessary; if you buy your ticket 72 hours in advance your seat is guaranteed. Book at the Fullers offices in Paihia and at most travel agents.

By Car

From either Paihia or Kerikeri the most obvious route north is State Hwy. 10. The alternate route, State Hwy. 1, is the central and more major highway, but you have to backtrack from the Bay of Islands to get to it. To avoid seeing the same bit of road twice, enjoy the wonderful coastal views along Hwy. 10 going north, and feast your eyes on the lush forest greenery and skyscraper trees that border Hwy. 1 returning south.

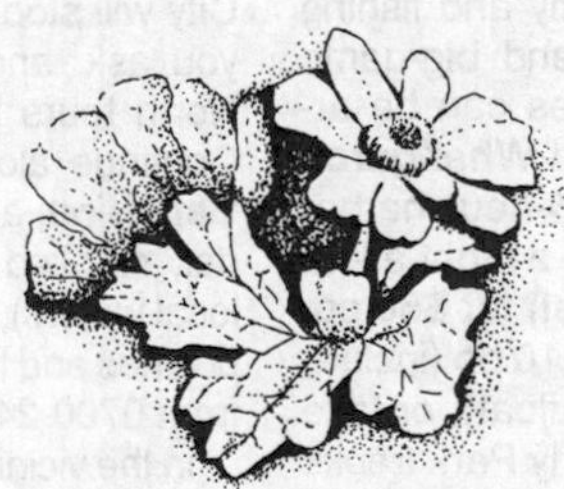

NORTHLAND

FROM THE BAY TO THE CAPE

The Coastal Route

Highway 10 to Awanui gives the traveler-in-a-hurry the opportunity to absorb beautiful coastal scenery while driving, yet lures the hiker and nature enthusiast into frequent stops to smell the flowers! Scenic reserves intermingled with fir tree plantations line the north's major highways, soft white-sand beaches lead you to the ocean, and in summer the roads are bordered with wildflowers. In some areas endless rows of pine trees follow the contours of the land—planted as a windbreak, these magnificent hedges separate the rolling hills and fields into giant patchworks of color.

Coastal Culture

The several small towns along the route share a relaxed atmosphere. Fishing boats, small private beaches, cottage arts and crafts, and tempting tearooms may delay your venture north. Like being on the water? Take a sidetrack to **Whangaroa,** six km north of Kaeo, and stay at the YHA Associate Hostel. **Sunseeker Lodge,** Old Hospital Rd., on the shores of Whangaroa Harbour, is known for its friendly service. A dinghy and fishing gear are available for hire, and big-game fishing trips and harbor cruises can be arranged. Locally recommended **Whangaroa Harbour Cruises** offers a 1½-hour harbor cruise for $22 adult, $11 child, a night afloat (including dinner and breakfast) for $50 pp, weekends on the harbor for $110 pp (including all meals and two nights afloat), or take the harbor cruise to the Ranfurly Park tracks and hike around the bay, staying overnight at either Kingfish Lodge ($30 per night, meals extra) or Lane Cove Cottage (a Park Board hut, $5 per night; advance bookings required with the Kerikeri Ranger, Dept. of Conservation, at tel. 78-474), then return by ferry ($22).

Roughly 30 km northwest, the small waterfront town of **Mangonui** on Doubtless Bay estuary was originally a busy whaling base and trading station. Nowadays the main undertaking is commercial fishing and boat hire for local game fishing (from $10 an hour with an outboard)—though you can catch snapper, John Dory, and kingfish from the wharf on an incoming tide. While you're there, don't pass up the **Saltwater Aquarium** (open daily 1000-1700, tel. 60-500; admission adult $2, child $1.10), and the **Mangonui Fish Shop** (deliciously fresh seafood). If you're looking for somewhere to stay, try **The Old Oak Inn** on the main road, a stone's throw from the water. You can't miss it—made of pit-sawn kauri and established in 1861, the white-washed homestead lures you in for a delicious Devonshire tea ($2.50) or a light meal in summer (dinners $12-14), and a visit to the craft shop chock-a-block full of well-made kauri products. Wayne Hunter, the friendly owner, provides budget accommodation in clean bright twin or double rooms (the front ones have alluring water views with access to the veranda) for only $12 pp. Facilities include a fully-equipped kitchen, a big living room, and shared bathrooms, and you can hire mountain bikes, canoes, dinghies, etc. Inter-City will stop at the door on its route north if you ask, and Fullers also operates its Far North tours from Mangonui (from $30 pp). Continue along the road and you come to **Cafe Nina,** a local favorite for seafood chowder, smoked fish pie (using fresh fish from local waters), huge addictive bacon rolls, cappucinos and freshly brewed coffee; open daily from 0700-2400, with prices from $2.50-6.

In the vicinity, **Coopers Beach, Cable Bay,** and **Taipa** are all known for their white-sand beaches and handsome groves of *pohutukawa* trees. Coopers Beach has a campground and motor camp. Though Cable Bay's small beach is attractive to campers, it's a reserve, so camping is not permitted. After crossing the Taipa River you enter the town of Taipa with another fairly large motor camp. Get great views of the Tokerau Beach peninsula and Cape Karikari from the Taipa area.

THE FAR NORTH—LAND OF SAND AND LEGENDS

Aupori Peninsula

Both the main road from Awanui to Te Kao (sealed) and the minor road that reaches Cape Reinga (unsealed) are easy driving. As you continue north, the landscape progressively gets drier. The colorful fields become scrubland (watch out for the odd suicidal sheep or cow on the road), and exotic pine plantations are the only evidence of man-made change to this desert-like landscape. Huge rolling sand dunes can be seen in all directions, and the large saltwater marshes are loaded with birdlife. In March, on the mighty dunes of the north, the *kuaka* or Eastern bar-tailed godwit gather in great numbers before their annual migration to breeding grounds on the Alaskan and Siberian tundra. Much of the far north has been made into a government reserve, **Te Paki Farm Park,** thus protecting it from development and other intrusion. The last motor camp on the way up is in **Pukenui,** but campsites are available at the end of Rarawa Beach Access Rd., north of **Ngataki,** and a beautiful camping area is located at **Taputupotu Bay,** not far south of Cape Reinga (see "Camping Out" below).

Just south of Pukenui, Houhora Heads Rd. branches off the main road to the east. **Houhora Heads** has campsites, and is the home of the well-known **Wagener Museum** (tel. Houhora 850) which contains extensive natural history exhibits, Maori and whaling artifacts, a kauri gum collection, shells, firearms, butterflies, and insects. Open daily 0900-1700; admission $2.75. If you're driving to Cape Reinga, be sure to check your gas before you leave **Te Kao** (last village at the end of the sealed road), and if you plan on camping it's a good idea to pick up final food supplies, sunscreen (a must!), and stove fuel. A store and tearooms are found farther north at **Waitiki Landing,** but since this is the very last place you can get any supplies, it's best not to count on it—there's more variety in Te Kao.

Cape Reinga

Since it's the most accessible northern point by car or bus, Cape Reinga is often thought to be the northernmost tip of New Zealand, but this honor really goes to **Kerr Point,** just north of North Cape. From Cape Reinga's rocky promontory you get tremendous views in all directions. Looking back to the east you can see **North Cape** and the **Surville Cliffs,** the northernmost seashore of the North Island. To the west lies **Cape Maria Van Deimen,** and on the northern horizon, 57 km off Cape Reinga, are the **Three Kings Islands.** This nature reserve made up of 40 islands and rocks is only clearly seen from the Cape in fine weather. Also to the north and not far offshore is **Columbia Bank,** the point at which the Tasman Sea and the Pacific Ocean converge. Look for turbulent water and large clashing waves—in stormy weather they can

view from Cape Reinga

reach up to 10 meters high! If you walk to the very tip of the Cape you'll see the famed *pohutukawa* tree, the roots of which are the legendary path for Maori spirits of the dead (see below). Cape Reinga has no facilities, just the well-known, white-washed Cape Reinga lighthouse—New Zealand's northernmost manned lighthouse.

Walking Tracks

The northern section of the New Zealand Walkway starts at Cape Reinga. Don't attempt any of the tracks without a map, and be adequately prepared for beach camping—there are no overnight huts. If you plan on doing all the tracks, start at the Eastern end of Spirits Bay. A 28-km track runs from Spirits

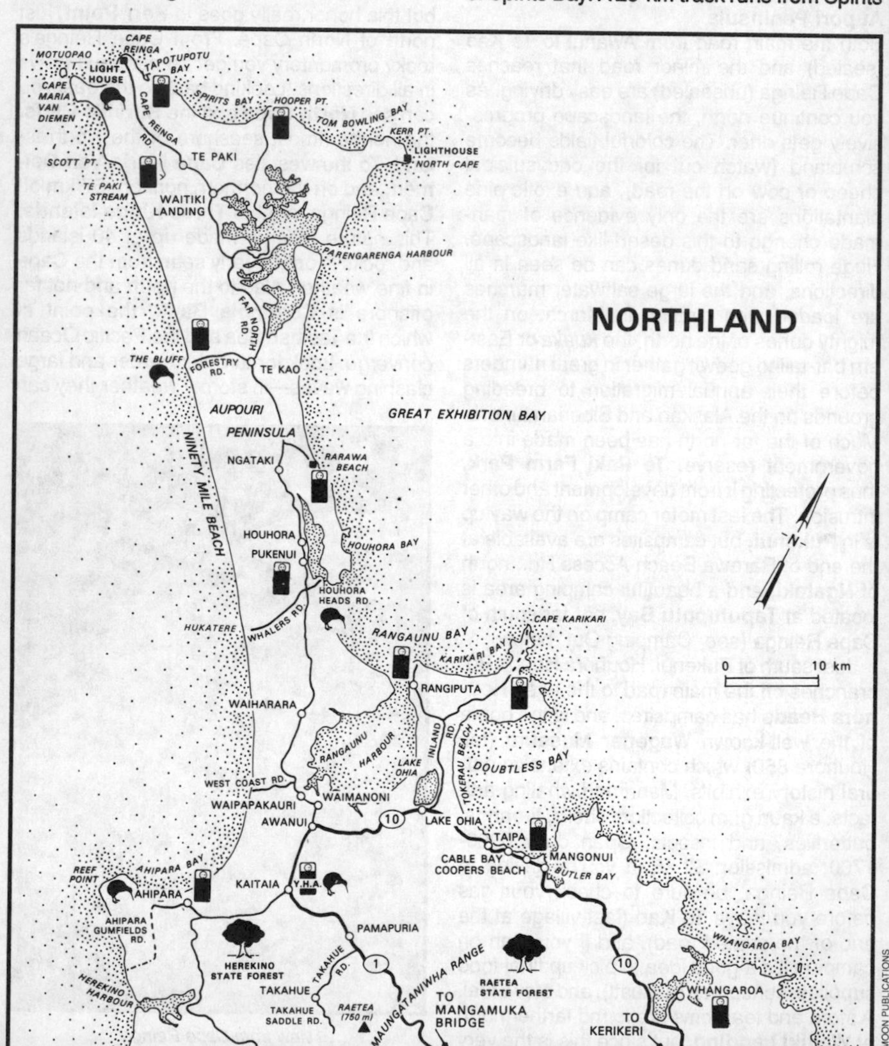

Bay to Cape Reinga, involves some steep sections toward the end, and takes about 11½ hours. From Cape Reinga a 22-km cliff-and-beach track heads south to Te Paki Stream (look out for treacherous quicksands in this area), taking about seven hours. The next track starts at Te Paki Stream and follows Ninety Mile Beach all the way down to Ahipara, at the south end of the beach. It takes a good two to three days to hike the entire 83 km to Ahipara, but you can leave the track and get back onto the main road at The Bluff (19 km), Hukatere (51 km), or Waipapakauri (69 km). Many other walking tracks in Te Paki Farm Park lead to points of historic or archaeological interest and scenic lookouts—pick and choose from a short 30-minute walk to a several-day hike.

Expect to cover beaches, sand dunes, swamps, and pastureland during the various hikes, and be sure to take plenty of water, energy food, suntan lotion, and insect repellent. A large map with lengths, times, and descriptions of the various tracks is located in Cape Reinga's parking area. For more info and maps see the ranger at Waitiki Landing (on the main road to the Cape) or call in at the Information Centre on South Rd. in Kaitaia. For fairly detailed maps and track descriptions pick up the free booklet *New Zealand Walkway—Walks in the Northland District* or the *New Zealand Walkway—Far North* brochure.

Camping Out

If you don't mind roughing it for a night or two, you can camp at several nice places in the far north. Most have fresh water, some have toilets, some have no facilities at all. Try the campground at **Tapotupotu Bay.** Three km from the main road and well signposted, it's down the last road to the east before reaching Cape Reinga. The camping area is at the back of a beautiful surf beach, and a park ranger supervises it over peak holiday periods from one of the resident caravans. Open all year, it operates on an honesty-box system when the ranger isn't there. Campsites are around $6 per vehicle per night for two adults, $3 per extra adult, $1 per child, and there's water, toilets, and showers. A stream (considerably warmer than the ocean) runs by the campground and out to sea, and the beach is a long stretch of golden sand with rock formations at the south end and big surf. Be aware of the strong rip where the stream meets the sea.

The campground at **Spirits Bay** also has water, toilets, and showers; $6 per vehicle per night. Take Te Hapua Rd., then Spirits Bay Rd. to Hooper Point. The camping area is a long way from the main road but very handy for hikers doing the Spirits Bay to Cape Reinga Track. Another campground is at **The Bluff.** Take Te Ahu Rd. from the main road; it passes through a lush forest before emerging at the beach. The campground, part of a

Cape Reinga lighthouse

Maori Reserve, is in the dune area directly behind the beach; $6 per site. The Bluff is an excellent area to view Ninety Mile Beach in both directions, the surf is good, and the hard white sand is covered with shells. Offshore lies Wakatehaua Island.

At Pukenui, a YHA Associate Hostel is next to Houhora Harbour Wharf—hire fishing boats and gear from the warden. **Pukenui Lodge** is on the corner of Main and Wharf rds., Pukenui, tel. 837. For a good selection of motor camps, motels, and hotels, head down to Kaitaia.

NINETY MILE BEACH

Abel Tasman called these northwestern shores "the desert coast." The etymology of "Ninety Mile Beach" remains unknown, although one could easily be forgiven for estimating this unbroken stretch of sand at 90 miles! The beach is actually 56 miles in length or almost exactly 90 km—the name giver must have been an early advocate of the metric system! Huge white sand dunes reaching 143 meters high and six km wide fringe the beach, kept in place by mass plantings of marram grass and pine trees. The main access roads to the beach are at Ahipara, West Coast Rd., Hukatere, and the Bluff.

Driving

The sand below high-water mark is concrete hard, at times solid enough to support motor vehicles. During low spring tides a belt of around 250 meters of sand is considered safe under normal conditions for motoring. The Automobile Association recommends not to drive on it for at least three hours before and after high tide. The sand is safe to *drive* on, but don't leave the car standing on wet sand for even a short time: the wheels can sink in very rapidly. Some car rental firms specify no driving on Ninety Mile Beach; check the contract before taking the risk. Another area of the beach which locals sometimes use as a road is Te Paki Creek, but it's very hazardous for those who don't know it. Some areas around Te Paki Stream are closed because of lethal quicksands.

Fishing

Anglers fishing off the beach beware: every now and again an unexpected roller will come way up the beach or rocks, submerging previously safe areas; keep way back from the water's edge. Every January, reels scream and large gamefish dance in the shallows off Ninety Mile Beach as hordes of anglers compete for big-money prizes in one of the world's largest surf-fishing contests. Apart from being a shell-collector's paradise, this amazing beach is well known for good surfing conditions, particularly at Ahipara and Wreck Bay (walk around the rocks from the Ahipara access).

A Seafood Delicacy

Ninety Mile Beach is also famous for the shellfish that live deep within its sands. The *toheroa (Amphidesma ventricosum)* is like a clam, can grow up to 152 mm (six inches) long, has been a prized delicacy since an-

LEGEND

The main legend of the North concerns the final trip of ancient Maori spirits of the dead. After death, the spirit padded up Te-Oneroa-A-Tohe (the Maori version of Ninety Mile Beach, not a direct translation) with a token of home in hand. The spirit left the token at Te Arai Bluff, then continued to Scott Point where it climbed the highest hill and took a last look back at the land of the living. After quenching its thirst in Re-Wai-O-Raio-Po, the stream of the underworld, it trudged on to Cape Reinga. At the northern tip of this rocky promontory you can see the famed *Pohutukawa* tree with its exposed root, which the spirit slid down, and gently dropped into the sea. The kelp parted, and it swam to the Three Kings Island. After surfacing for a last look at New Zealand, the spirit took up the trail to Hawaiiki, its Polynesian homeland. Legend also states that the spirits of the sick sometimes got as far as Te-Oneroa-A-Tohe, but if they didn't quench their thirst at the stream the spirits returned to their bodies.

cient Maori times, and is considered New Zealand's finest seafood. The *toheroa* prefers to burrow deep in the sand along beaches backed by sand dunes, thus it's most common along Ninety Mile Beach. (It can also be found on beaches near Dargaville, Levin, and along Foveaux Strait.) The great popularity has depleted supplies of *toheroa,* and digging is now prohibited. The *toheroa* is eaten raw, made into a famous soup, minced for fritters, or baked in the shell. The delicious fritters are generally available in season at local takeaway shops, and the soup can be sampled in good restaurants or found canned in the supermarket. Another similar shellfish that lives in the sand and is often mistaken for *toheroa* is the *tuatua.* It's smaller and sweeter, lives in the same conditions as the *toheroa,* but is considered less of a delicacy.

KAITAIA

Kaitaia (population 5,000) is the main business and commercial center of the far north. It's also a good base for exploring Aupouri Peninsula to the north and the forests and harbors south. Shopping centers, lots of motels, motor camps, and several engaging attractions within the area make it a worthwhile stop. Boosted by tourist interest in the north, the town has also become a center for bus and coach trips up the peninsula. If your interests include arts and crafts, stop at the Far North PRO and Information Centre (by Jaycee Park) on South Rd. for a *Craft Trails of the Far North* brochure; there are plenty of places to visit—and buy!

SIGHTS

Far North Regional Museum

This excellent museum is a fund of information on the historical aspects of the northern region. Displays focus on ancient Maori lifestyles, including agricultural, fishing, and hunting methods and equipment, intricate feather capes and articles of clothing, and a comprehensive display of Maori carving styles and art forms. Other highlights include a display of New Zealand birds, an ancient anchor and various shipwreck articles, and a 1909-1936 photograph collection featuring kauri gum digging activities. Don't miss the info board at the entrance where descriptions and prices of all the latest tours up the cape are advertised. The museum is at 6 South Rd., tel. 408-1403; open 1000-1700 weekdays, 1300-1700 weekends, admission adult $2, child 50 cents.

Sullivan's Nocturnal Park

Don't miss this Kaitaia attraction! It's an excellent place to see glowworms and kiwis in their natural environment. Brendon Sullivan, a delightful New Zealander with a great sense of humor and an extensive knowledge of indigenous flora and fauna, and his wife Liz own and operate the park. The best time to go is early evening (take your dinner and enjoy it in the outside picnic/BBQ area). After dark, check-in at the office for your guide. A gently sloping boardwalk path (wheelchair accessible) with lighted handrail (tiny lights that blend in with the glowworms) leads you up along an old fault line where a river now gurgles down—magical in the dark. This natural rock- and bush-filled canyon is home to thousands of tiny glowworms (the farther you go, the more you see). Strolling along the path, your guide relates the fascinating lifecycle of this glowing creature, and in some areas, with the aid of a flashlight, you can get close enough to the glowworms to see the threads that hang below each one for food-catching purposes (don't touch the worm—it'll die). Cameras (and tripods) and video cameras are encouraged.

At the end of the walk is the nocturnal house, one of the best in the country, where you can get an outstanding view of kiwis in action through one-way glass, along with other indigenous creatures and plants. Ask your guide to do a kiwi call and see what happens! Admission is a worthwhile $6 adult, $3 child. The park is at Fairburn, open daily 1200-2400 (the nocturnal house is open to 2200), tel. 408-4100. To get there head south out of Kaitaia on Hwy. 1 for about eight km and turn left at the Fairburn sign. Continue for another nine km along a rough semi-paved road (go slowly in the dark) following the signs (fluorescent at night)—the drive takes about 15 minutes from town.

Pukeroa Park

This farm zoo has all kinds of tame animals for petting—hens, ducks, sheep, goats, peacocks, pigeons, rabbits, guinea pigs, Captain Cooker pigs (tamed wild pigs), cows, donkeys, even a working team of bullocks—and there's a BBQ area and toilets by the river. Take the family out there for picnics; donkey, horse, bullock, and pony (and cart) rides are an extra 50 cents to $1. It's a kid's delight; admission $2 adult, $1 child. The park is one km south of Kaitaia on Hwy. 1, tel. 408-0158.

Ahipara Gum Fields

Just above Ahipara is a stark, barren plateau which used to be home to hundreds of Yugoslav gum diggers in the 1890s. Vast forests of kauri trees once covered the north, but most of these forests were quickly decimated by the colonial timber-cutters of the early 1800s. Sadly, no thought was given to conserving the slow-growing giants of the forest. Kauri resin, which hardens into gum on contact with air, dribbled down the trees, collected around the bases, and petrified under forest debris. When the timber rush finished, the gum rush began. The ground where mighty trees once stood was dug up, denuded of its gum, and made barren. By the 1890s the fossilized gum, used as a base for slow-drying hard varnishes and for making linoleum, had become one of New Zealand's major exports. (The Maori first utilized the gum for fuel, tattooing, and chewing gum.) Most of the gum fields of the north have been ploughed and fertilized into agricultural land, but the Ahipara Plateau has been preserved by the Historic Places Trust as a reminder of the past, and hopefully to prevent such desecration from ever happening again.

Kaitaia Track

This nine-km track, part of the New Zealand Walkway, lets you enjoy great views of the Northland Peninsula, Okahu Falls, and Diggers and Takahue valleys. A sidetrack heads up to Puketutu summit (420 meters) for even better views. From Kaitaia, take Hwy. 1 south for about three km and turn right into Larmers Rd., go past the quarry and continue along the metal track to the parking area where the main track starts. The track finishes on Diggers Valley Road; classified as a walk, it takes about three hours each way. Wear sturdy footwear, particularly in wet weather.

Northward Ho—By Bus

Kaitaia is a main base for many tour companies that daily explore the far northern tip of the country. Drop in at the info center for current brochures detailing each trip, then call around and compare prices—though they all offer similar trips at similar prices. **Fullers** operates both a **Cape Reinga** trip (departs 0930; adult $45, child $20) and **Tu Tu Fun Bus** trip (departs 1000; adult $45, child $20); book at the Fullers office on South Rd., across from the Far North Regional Museum, or tel. 408-1500. **Mike's Cape Reinga Tours** operates a friendly relaxed day up the cape with time to swim, visit museums, and collect shellfish, leaving Kaitaia at 0900 for $30 adult, $18 child. Book at the Commerce St. office or tel. 408-2826. **Cuzzie Tours** do their version of the Cape Reinga trip via Ninety Mile Beach, with a stop at the Wagener Museum, Ninety Mile Beach, Cape Reinga, Tapotupotu Bay, and a lunch stop at Waitiki Landing, departing Kaitaia at 0900. Book at their office or make reservations through Mike's Tours. **Sand Safaris** also do the same route with small groups in a 12-seater 4WD mini-bus (light lunch and recreational gear provided) for adult $36, child $18. Departing at 0845 the trip takes about eight hours. Book at 27 South Rd., through the PRO or your accommodation, or tel. 408-1778.

ACCOMMODATION

Hostel

The YHA hostel is the northernmost hostel in New Zealand. It has plenty of twin and family rooms, a day room, and a garden for relaxing; $12 pp. It's at 160 Commerce St. (the main road through Kaitaia), tel. 408-1840.

Main Street Hostel is an excellent private hostel. Hospitable owners Peter and Kerry Kitchen not only arrange horse trekking, fishing trips, glowworm and marae visits, and recommend and book tours to the north, they also throw authentic *hangis* (Maori feasts) every month (everyone is encouraged to participate and the food costs about $7 pp), and have frequent sheep-on-a-spit nights or BBQs where all guests are invited to join in. Very casual, laid-back, kiwi-style atmosphere. They also dive for seafood, and if you want to join in on these diving trips, you're welcome. From $12 (if you pay in advance for two nights it's only $11, for three nights $10) for bunk room accommodation to $14 pp for family or private rooms (in summer it gets pretty busy and bunk rooms may be all that's available). Facilities include powerful hot showers (aaahhh!), a fully equipped kitchen, bright sunny dining room, lounge, laundry, bicycles, and a courtesy car (let the owners know ahead of time if you need a ride). At 235 Commerce St., tel. (09) 408-1275 (call ahead if you can and book your bunk).

Motor Camps

Dyers Motel And Motor Camp has tentsites for $7 pp and caravan sites for $7 pp plus $1 per site; tourist flats with private facilities are $40 d. (They also have motel units, see below.) Communal bathroom, kitchen, laundry facilities, TV and game room, swimming pool, and next door is a dairy (shop selling dairy products and other essentials) and takeaway. At the southern end of town at 69 South Rd., tel. 408-0333. **Ninety Mile Beach Camp** is a few km north of Kaitaia at Waipapakauri Ramp, just north of Awanui (on the main Cape Reinga bus route), tel. 77-298. Communal bathroom, kitchen, and laundry facilities, game room, BBQ, and store. Tent and caravan sites are $7 pp per night, $3.50 child; cabins range from $24-33 d.

Pine Tree Lodge Motor Camp is at Ahipara, 18 km west of Kaitaia, tel. 864. Tentsites are $7.20 pp per night, $3.50 child, and caravan sites are the same as tentsites plus $1 per site. Communal facilities, swimming pool, and BBQ. On Takahe St., by the golf course, Ahipara, tel. 864. **Karikari Motor Camp** is 21 km off South Hwy. 10, 36 km from Awanui at Karikari Bay, tel. 408-7501. It has five km of beach frontage, boats for hire, and a smokehouse (for the big one that didn't get away!). Communal facilities, shop, and dairy. Camp charges are around $9 d per night, the two cabins (sleep four) are $25 per night, and the cottage (sleeps five) is $40 per night.

Motels

Many motels are located in and around the Kaitaia area, but expect to pay from $36 s, $45 d at most of them; ask at the PRO in Kaitaia for the latest listings. Here are a few reasonable ones. The **Northern Queen Motel** has rooms for $35 s, $55 d or twin, at Ahipara Beach, tel. 759. **Dyers Motel Flats** has two-bed units for $40 s, $50 d or twin, and larger units sleeping two to five for $40 d or twin; at 69 South Rd., tel. 80-333. **Orana Motor Inn** on North Rd. (Hwy. 1), tel. 82-800, has a heated swimming pool, billiards room, and rooms with all the mod cons for $55 s, $68.20 d or twin (reduced rates in low season).

Reef Lodge, on the beachfront at Rangiputa, is the place to go if you want to get off the beaten track. It has units that sleep up to five with private bathroom and kitchen facilities. Spa pool, dinghies, and horseriding, as well as BBQ, fish-cleaning house, smokehouse, and freezer shop. Call first for current rates and reservations at tel. 522 Waiharara—and buy food supplies before heading out there. To get there from Kaitaia, head north up Hwy. 1 to Awanui, turn east onto Hwy. 10. Just beyond Lake Ohia turn left onto Inland Rd. and continue to the end. Turn left onto Rangiputa Rd. and when you reach Rangiputa, ask for directions to Davelle Estate.

FOOD AND ENTERTAINMENT

Kaitaia has several restaurants and a large number of takeaways offering a variety of food—most located along Commerce St. (the main drag)—but not much in the way of evening entertainment.

For lunch try one of the many takeaways along Commerce St. or one of the supermarkets (most provide salad bars and/or delis). **108 Sandwich Bar** specializes in filling sandwiches—with pick-your-own fillings. **Kurry Kai Fast Food And Takeaways** specializes in Chinese, Indian, and European food—a little different from the norm, and very good. Try one of the curries (made as hot or as mild as you want) with rice and vegies; $11 for two (substantial portions) but half-portions are produced if you ask. **Time Out** has good lunches, a salad bar, mains for $13-16, and takeaways. Another popular takeaway is **Steve's Snapper Bar,** also on Commerce Street. **Mills Coffee Lounge** features baked goodies made on the premises, open 0700-1600, opposite the DECA store.

At most of the restaurants you're looking at about $10-15 pp for a filling lunch, and up to $30 pp for a complete dinner. The **Beachcomber Restaurant** in Kaitaia Plaza on Commerce St. serves seafood, steak, and chicken (mains $11-17 plus daily specials) with an excellent salad bar, and has a BYO license; open for lunch, dinner from 1700-2030, and takeaways (weekdays 1200-1430 and 1700-2030, Sat. 1730-2030). **Kauri Arms Tavern** has a very good bistro with reasonable prices, and the **Kaitaia Hotel** has an old-fashioned menu with inexpensive carvery meals and a choice of hot vegies or cool salads. **Orana Motor Inn** offers breakfast from 0730-0900, lunch from 1200-1330, and dinner (expensive) from 1830-2100, seven days a week; on Commerce Street. At the **Collard Tavern,** a couple of km north of Kaitaia, you can feast on generous servings of good food in the bistro. For late-night munchies, try the **White Lady Pie Cart** on Bank St. for burgers, toasted sandwiches, meals, and Irish coffee—all highly recommended by locals. It's open Thurs. 1630-2400, Fri. to 0200, and Sat. to 0300. **Time Out Cafe** on Commerce St. is also open till late, serving tasty alternative and vegetarian food in appealing surroundings.

For entertainment try the various hotels—the **Kauri Arms Tavern, Kaitaia Hotel, Collard Tavern**—or motor inn bars. The Collard Tavern has live bands on Thurs., Fri., and Sat. nights, and in peak summer months provides a free bus ride from town. The other options are the **Kaitaia Cinema,** or the public **swimming baths** on Bank Street. Check in at the PRO to see what else is going on.

INFORMATION AND SERVICES

The Far North PRO and Information Centre is by Jaycee Park on South Rd., just along the road from the museum, tel. 408-0879; open Mon. to Fri. 0900-1630. The main street downtown is Commerce St. on which you'll find just about everything you need. To find the **InterCity depot,** continue north along Commerce St. from the p.o. and turn left on Taffe St., tel. 408-1333. The **hospital** (tel. 408-0011) and **police station** (tel. 408-1111) are both on Redan Rd., off Commerce St. heading toward Ahipara. Looking for a **laundromat?** You'll find one in Kaitaia Plaza on Commerce Street.

TRANSPORTATION

Tours To The Far North

Kaitaia has become a center for coach and four-wheel drive tours to the far north. See "By Coach" under "Continuing North," p. 119, and "Northward-Ho By Bus" above. Contact

rural scene along Hwy. 12

Fullers at tel. 408-1501; Mike's Tours at tel. 408-2826; and Sand Safaris at tel. 408-1778. For moped hire, contact the Princess Theatre on Commerce Street.

HEADING SOUTH

By Bus

InterCity provides coach service from Kaitaia's downtown depot to Waitangi, Whangarei, and Auckland. You have a choice of two routes to Auckland: either down the main road via Kaikohe, Kawakawa, and Whangarei taking just under seven hours, or via the east coast, Bay of Islands, and Whangarei taking just under eight hours. Both routes are serviced several times a day, every day. Book at the InterCity depot or at any travel agent.

By Air

Kaitaia Airport is about nine km north of town. Haines Haulage provides bus service to the airport from Kaitaia Travel Bureau on Redan Rd., tel. 408-0540 or after hours 408-1145. It leaves for the airport 50 minutes prior to each departure, and 15 minutes after each arrival for the return trip to Kaitaia; several dollars pp OW. Air New Zealand flies from Kaitaia to most major centers in the North Island and several in the South.

By Car

The main route south out of Kaitaia and quickest to Auckland is Hwy. 1, but you've got several choices on the way down. If you haven't been over to Ahipara to see the gum fields (see "Sights" above), you may want to head in that direction first, and then south. To sightsee or hike in the magnificent kauri forests of the west, try this shortcut: take Hwy. 1 to Mangamuka Bridge, branch off onto the more minor road to the west, then south on Mohuiti Narrows Rd. to Kohukohu and the Rawene car ferry. The alternate route is Hwy. 1 to Ohaeawai, followed by Hwy. 12 to Kaikohe and Opononi, then south—a considerably longer and less scenic route. Either way, if you have time, don't miss the kauris.

THE NORTHWEST COAST

SOUTH OF KAITAIA

Mangamuka Gorge And Walkway

Mangamuka Gorge is a gorgeous drive, particularly on a sunny day when you'll probably find yourself leaping in and out of the car at regular intervals, camera in hand, to capture giant tree ferns and assorted flora and fauna. Allow plenty of time to meander through all this lushness (chances are you won't have any other choice if you come up behind a large truck!). Mangamuka Gorge Walkway starts 26 km southeast of Kaitaia and crosses a part of Maungataniwha Range. The route winds through the beautiful Raetea State Forest and Mangamuka Gorge Scenic Reserve, emerging at Hwy. 1 north of Mangamuka township. During the hike expect to traverse open farmland, dense forests, and lush native bush with its wonderland of ferns, mosses, and lichens. Climb to the radio mast atop Raetea summit (751 meters) for spectacular panoramic views of North Cape and Karikari Peninsula to the north, Hokianga Harbour to the south, Bay of Islands to the east, and Reef Point and Ahipara to the west. At the summit, the main track doubles back and continues east—don't head south along the minor track toward Broadwood unless it's familiar; this track fizzles out in places and it's easy to get lost in the dense bush. Keep on the main marked track at all times.

The 19-km full-day trail (OW) is steep, muddy, and hard going. It's recommended for experienced hikers only, and it's best to have transportation awaiting you at the end. Wear sturdy hiking boots, and carry rain gear and a change of warm clothes (the weather can turn bad quickly), food, and water—no streams along the ridge. To get to the western entrance take Hwy. 1 south of Pamapuria, turn west onto Takahue Valley Rd., then left on Takahue Saddle Road.

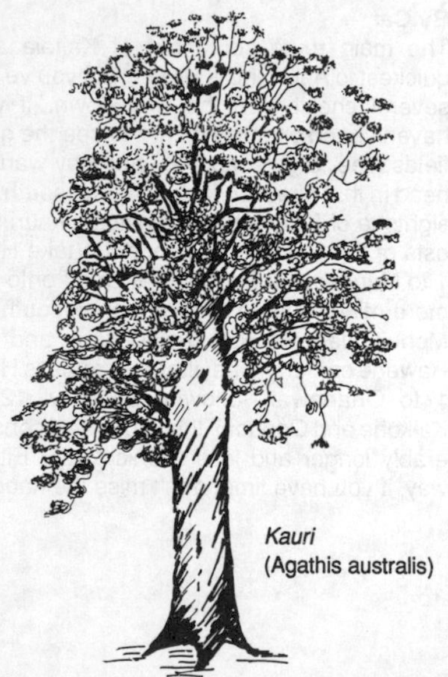

Kauri
(Agathis australis)

Hokianga Harbour

Stretching inland for more than 50 km, Hokianga Harbour has forged a deep channel almost halfway across to the Bay of Islands! In the early 19th C., this fiord-like harbor was lined with kauri forests, and bustled with marine activity. Droves of ships sailed over from Sydney, defying the treacherous sandbars and large surf at the harbor mouth in order to keep up with demand for kauri timber. Once the shores had been stripped of their slow-growing forests, the timber mills closed and the ships left. Nowadays the harbor lies relatively undisturbed, slowly reverting to its original wildness and desolation. Few roads lead to the tangled mangrove forests, mighty sand dunes, and green valleys that line its shores. The peaceful beauty and quiet has attracted quite a community of artists and people into alternative lifestyles; watch for out-of-the-ordinary houses, and roadside arts and crafts stands where you can often pick up real bargains.

The best way to appreciate the harbor is by boat, and willing operators can be found in Rawene, Opononi, and Omapere. Continuing south, Hwy. 1 detours east around this mighty harbor toward Okaihau, and the Hwy. 12 junction to Kaikohe. Alternately, the shorter and more scenic route is to cross the harbor at the "Narrows" via car ferry, and continue south down Hwy. 12. To get to the ferry, pass through Mangamuka Scenic Reserve, turn right at Mangamuka Bridge, go through Kohukohu and on to the Narrows.

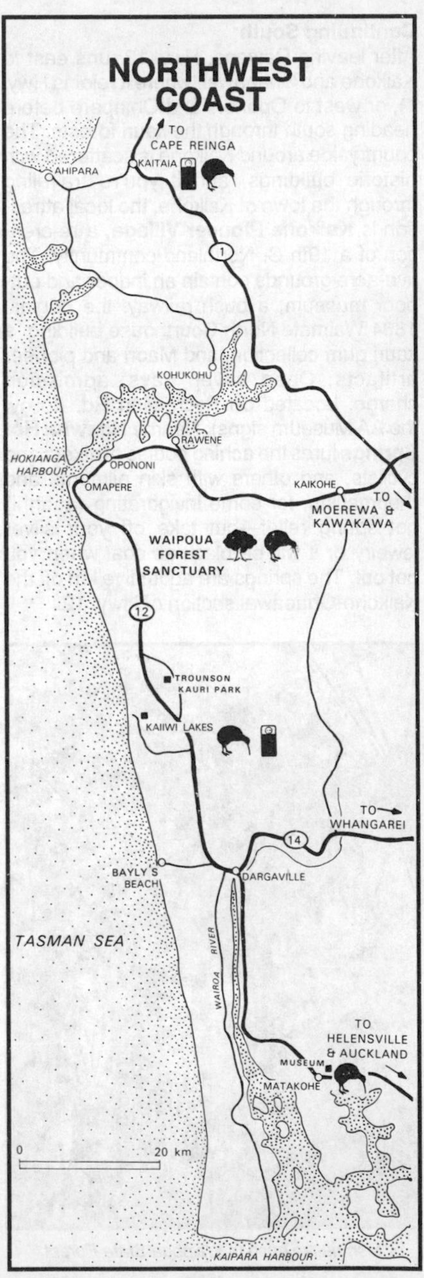

Hokianga Vehicular Ferry

The ***Kohu-Ra*** operates daily between The Narrows and Rawene. In summer it departs The Narrows every hour (on the hour) from 0800-1800, and Rawene every hour from 0745-1745. In winter it departs The Narrows every hour from 0845-1715, Rawene from 0830-1700. Try to time it so you arrive about 10-15 minutes before the crossing—there's nothing to do while you wait (and no facilities) but you need to get in the line-up. The crossing takes about 15 minutes and costs around $8 per car and driver plus $1 per passenger OW, or $12 plus $2 per passenger RT; from $16 for a car and caravan (depending on length) plus $1 pp OW; $2 for a motor bike OW; $1 for passengers on foot OW.

Rawene

Getting off the ferry at Rawene, third oldest settlement in New Zealand, is like taking a step back in time. On your way through don't miss **Clendon House,** a historic building preserved by the Historic Places Trust. Built in 1860 by James Clendon, ship owner, trader, and first United States Consul in New Zealand, it contains many of the owner's possessions, and period furnishings. Located on the foreshore, the house is open daily 0900-1500; small admission charge. The **Masonic Hotel,** built in 1875, is Rawene's local watering hole. You'll also find a small supermarket, a smattering of shops, takeaways, gas station, post office, and public toilets (up the main street, on the right).

Continuing South

After leaving Rawene, Hwy. 12 runs east to Kaikohe and Ohaeawai (where it rejoins Hwy. 1), or west to Opononi and Omapere before heading south through the kauri forests. The countryside around Kaikohe is scattered with historic buildings, and if you're traveling through the town of Kaikohe, the local attraction is **Kaikohe Pioneer Village,** a re-creation of a 19th C. Northland community. The five-acre grounds contain an indoor and outdoor museum, a bush railway, the original 1864 Waimate North Courthouse building, a kauri gum collection, and Maori and pioneer artifacts. Open seven days; admission charge. Located on Recreation Rd. (follow the AA Museum signs). Nearby **Ngawha Hot Springs** lures the aching bodies of hikers and cyclists, and others with skin ailments and rheumatism, for some invigorating (aaahh!) hot spring relief—but take off your silver jewelry or it will be black as coal when you get out. The springs are about five km off the Kaikohe-Ohaeawai section of Hwy. 12.

lush native bush in Waipoua State Forest

Situated at the mouth of Hokianga Harbour, the twin towns of Opononi and Omapere boast golden beaches and beautiful views up the harbor and out to sea. At Omapere you can appreciate the harbor best by cruise boat—get the details at the info center. For the best views turn off Hwy. 12 just south of Omapere and take the road out to South Head. Opononi became quite notorious in the summer of 1955 when a friendly dolphin the locals named "Opo" came to play with swimmers every day—a memorial statue to the dolphin stands on the seafront. Both towns have motor camps and a large number of motels, there's a hostel near Opononi (Old School, Pakanae, tel. 792; $8 pp), and the area is also known for great seafood (try the Blue Dolphin Cafe and Takeaways for seafood and sea views). For the rundown on the area, stop at the **Hokianga Visitor Information Centre** on the main road.

THE KAURI FORESTS

The Trees

The northland forests provide the nature lover with a wide range of native plant and bird life, and the chance to appreciate many tree varieties. These include *rimu, rata, towai, kahikatea,* and *tawa,* though all are dwarfed by the magnificent kauri. The kauri *(Agathis australis)* is a conifer, grouped botanically with pines and firs that grow north of 38 degree south latitude. The kauri is New Zealand's native giant—similar but less majestic trees of the same family can be found in Australia, Malaysia, the Philippines, Fiji, and other Pacific islands. The kauri is easily recognized by its tall columnar trunk (it self-sheds the lower branches), massive, heavily branched crown, and thick, leathery leaves. The highly decorative bark is silver-gray in color and covered in irregular, circular patterns. Another characteristic of the older kauri trees is the large mound of *pukahu* or humus at the base of the trunk. This mound is made up of bark, shed over several hundred years, and root systems. Note that the kauri is dependent on its surface root network for essential nutrients, and survival depends to a large degree on not having its vital roots trampled—keep on the tracks to ensure these magnificent trees' future.

Some of the trees have been estimated at well over a thousand years old. Their rate of growth is very slow, taking 80 to 100 years to reach millable size. A young kauri is called a "ricker." The timber is straight grained, easily worked, durable, and very popular with carpenters and craftsmen. In the early 1800s the kauri dominated forest vegetation and covered about three million hectares from the North Cape to Waikato. By the end of the century only one quarter of the kauri forests remained; the trees had been cut down for ship-building, leached for gum, or burned when the land was cleared for agricultural purposes. Nowadays the policy is to preserve the remaining ancient forests such as Waipoua State Sanctuary, and newly planted kauri forests are regenerating in the Waitakere Ranges, Coromandel Ranges, Great Barrier Island, and around the Russell area.

Tane Mahuta—*"Lord of the Forest"*

Waipoua State Forest

Beginning about 30 km south of Opononi, Hwy. 12 runs 16 km through the cool lush greenery of Waipoua State Forest, a place where time seems to stand still. The Waipoua Forest Sanctuary, oldest and largest remnant of New Zealand's once extensive kauri forests, covers an area of more than 9,000 hectares and contains five known giant trees, each estimated to be at least 1,000 years old. Apart from these giants there are 300 other species of trees, palms, ferns, and mosses, and although it's possible to enjoy the forest from the road, the best way to appreciate the grandeur is to get on some of the tracks. The forest is criss-crossed with trails; great picnic spots abound. The well-marked tracks range from short 10-minute walks to particular kauri giants, or longer hikes that offer a far richer assortment in sights and sounds of the forest.

A short track, a couple of minutes from the road, leads to the 1,200-year-old *Tane Mahuta* (Lord of the Forest). Standing nearly 52 meters high and with a girth of 13 meters, it's believed to be the largest kauri in the country. Farther along the highway, a particularly beautiful 15-minute track leads to *Te Matua Ngahere* (Father of the Forest) which reaches 30 meters high and 15 meters wide. Its exact age is unknown but it may be nearly 2,000 years old. If you have the time, sit opposite the tree for a while and soak up the surroundings. The tranquil beauty of the bush and splendor of the "Father," cheerful bird songs, and buzzing cicadas create a natural high! Another good trail is the 15-minute Kauri Rickers Track which starts north of Forest HQ and passes through a stand of young kauri. About two km in from the southern park boundary there's a lookout point with extensive views of the sanctuary, Waipoua Forest, and Tasman Sea.

The Waipoua Forestry HQ (tel. Donnelly's Crossing 605) is located off Hwy. 12 in the southern section of the forest, to the right after crossing Waipoua River. Go there for info on forest management, local legends, and walking tracks, and see the cottage museum where the lifestyle of a kauri bushman is on display; open daily.

Camper's Delight

If you want to stay the night somewhere along this forest-clad area of the country (32 km north of Dargaville), keep your eyes peeled for signs advertising **Kauri Coast Motor Camp** and Trounson Kauri Park, then turn off. Continue for about three km (seven to the park). Friendly Mary and Vaughn Darby own and operate this motor camp in a superb setting at Kaihu (tel. 36-521). Imagine camping on emerald-green grassy lawns, under shady trees, beside a river that has both rainbow and brown trout to keep the angler happy and three superb swimming holes to keep everyone happy on a hot day. Another good reason to stay here is to take Vaughn up on his offer (every other night) of a 45-minute guided evening walk in Trounson Kauri Park to look for kiwis, giant *wetas,* and kauri snails. It's free ($5 pp for non-guests), and although you may not always be lucky enough to find a kiwi, you'll still learn all kinds of interesting things about the forest and see plenty of other nocturnal creatures. Tent and powered sites are $7 (open fires permitted, wood provided), bunk room beds are $10 pp, and the self-contained cabin for two costs $24 pp. Communal toilet and shower blocks with facilities for handicapped persons, fully equipped kitchen, and laundry are provided.

Trounson Kauri Park

This small but superb stand of kauri is located about 15 km south of Waipoua State Forest. Turn left off Hwy. 12 onto Trounson Park Road. A track through the park takes about half an hour RT, and the highlight is The Four Sisters tree—actually two kauri trees, each with twin trunks that have grown together as one. At one point the track runs under a fallen kauri for a close-up view, and farther along, the root system of a large, 600-year-old fallen kauri can be appreciated from a viewing platform. An attractive campground with limited campsites is located within the park near the ranger's residence, maximum stay two nights; tentsites are around $5 per night, caravan sites with power points are $6 per night, and toilet and shower facilities are provided.

SOUTH TO AUCKLAND

Kai-Iwi Lakes And Taharoa Domain Campground

If you plan on camping out before continuing back down to Auckland, this is another scenic location. The three brilliantly blue, freshwater lakes, Kai-Iwi, Taharoa, and Waikere, offer swimming, fishing, sailing, and waterskiing. In addition, soft white-sand beaches, good sheltered bays for swimming and snorkeling, rolling farmland, and lots of pine trees make this an even more attractive place. Lake Taharoa is stocked with trout and offers shoreside camping; on the banks of Lake Waikere is a waterski club—a hive of activity on summer weekends. Two walks, to **Sandy Bay** (one hour), and to **Maunganui Bluff** (half an hour to the coast, then one hour along the beach, closed Aug. to Sept.), start on Kai-Iwi Lakes Road. They're part of the New Zealand Walkway network,

To get to the lakes take Hwy. 12 to Maropiu and turn west on Omamari Road. At the end turn right onto Kai-Iwi Lakes Rd. then right on Domain Road. Follow it to the end to Taharoa Domain—a campground at Pine Beach on the edge of Taharoa Lake (bookings tel. 7059 Dargaville). Tent or caravan sites are several dollars pp per night; drinking water, toilet and shower facilities. For more private swimming, follow the dirt track beyond the camping area to the next beach at Sandy Bay. The other campground is at Promenade Point, farther along Kai-Iwi Lakes Rd., and has drinking water and toilet facilities only; small pp nightly fee. Continue along the road and you come to Kai-Iwi Lakes Water Ski Club at Lake Waikere.

Dargaville

Located at the northern end of Wairoa River, Dargaville was originally a busy kauri timber and gum-trading center. Nowadays it's the commercial center for the surrounding dairy districts. The info center is on the main street. The hilltop **Northern Wairoa Museum** in Harding Park (tel. 7555) displays items of local seafaring interest, Maori artifacts, pioneer relics, and an ancient Maori *pa;* open daily 0900-1600, admission $2 adult, 50 cents child. **Lighthouse Restaurant** attached to the museum is open seven days for morning tea and lunch, and on Wed. to Sun. evenings for dinner, serving mains (pork, steak, ham, fish, lamb, with salad bar) from $7.50-10 (for small servings) to $10-15 ("normal" servings). Some nights they put on entertainment (dinner and show $18 pp). Great views from the park. To get there turn right on River Rd., then right on Mahuta Rd. and follow the signs. Dargaville also has a YH at 13 Portland St. (corner of Gordon St.), tel. 6342; $11 pp. Another place that comes highly recommended by fellow travelers is **Awakino Point Lodge** just outside Dargaville (tel. 884-7870). Bed and breakfast (private facilities) is $60 d, and the hosts, Wally and June Birch, really make you feel at home. Call ahead for directions and to see if they've room.

To the west of Dargaville, about 13 km along Bayly's Coast Rd., lies **Bayly's Beach.** It's a popular surf beach in summer and *toheroa* source in winter, with a motor camp next to it. If you want to see this area in more detail call **Kauri Coaster Tours,** tel. 8339. Their two landrover trips each take about six hours: a "North Trip" to Kai-Iwi Lakes, Waipoua Forest, Trounson Park, Maunganui Bluff, and West Coast Beach; a "South Trip" to West Coast, Pouto Lighthouse, Kaipara Heads, and Kelly's Bay. Call for current prices and make reservations in advance if possible.

Matakohe

Continuing south, Hwy. 12 runs through the small village of Matakohe. The highlight is the **Otamatea Kauri and Pioneer Museum** (tel. 37-417) which contains almost everything you'd want to know about the kauri. There's timber, an outstanding gum collection, furniture, wood flowers, old photos of lumberjacks, kauri-processing equipment, and a reproduction of a colonial cottage done entirely in kauri. Another room is panelled in all the different types of timber available in New Zealand, and at the souvenir shop you can pick up beautifully crafted kauri products at reasonable prices. Don't miss it! It's open daily from 0900-1700; admission $3.50 adult, $1 child.

To find it, look out for the windmill between Ruawai and Paparoa and turn up the hill to the right for 500 meters. **The Gumdiggers Tearoom** is farther along the road from the museum. Sample assorted baked goodies made on the premises, and tearoom-type snacks at reasonable prices.

Helensville

Highways 12 and 1 intersect at Brynderwyn, where Hwy. 1 continues south to Wellsford and on down to Auckland. An alternate scenic route south, Hwy. 16 via Helensville, branches off at Wellsford. The Helensville area, less than an hour's drive north of Auckland, boasts gentle countryside, many poultry and deer farms, and orchards and vineyards; in summer the highways are lined with wildflowers.

If you like hot pools and masses of people, head northwest out of Helensville along South Head Rd. to the town of **Parakai,** where you'll find the Parakai **Aquatic Park.** The pools are naturally heated by thermal mineral springs, so the temperatures vary a little each day—generally the outdoor pool is around 29 degrees C, the indoor a sizzling 36 degrees. On winter weekday evenings, you can slowly bake in the therapeutic indoor pool while taking in video movies on the giant screen! Bathing suits, security lockers, and property bags can be hired. Located at the corner of Parkhurst and Spring streets the park is open daily 1000-2200 (tel. 8998 Parakai); admission charge, but free if you're staying in the adjacent campground (see below). If you fancy whizzing down the "Hydro Slide," or screaming down the 25-meter almost vertical "Rampage" slide, you have to fork out an extra few dollars or so on top of admission (concessions for campers).

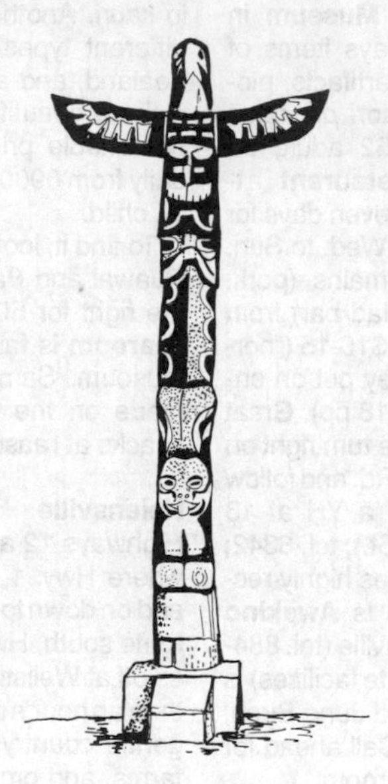

Camping Out

Next to Aquatic Park in Parakai is the fully equipped **Aquatic Park Holiday Camp;** very busy during holiday periods (tel. 8884). Tent and caravan sites are $7 pp, $3.50 child; reduced rates for seven nights or more. Stay here and admission to the hot pools is free, with Hydro Slide and Rampage concessions. Many motels and hotels offering private hot pools are also located close to Aquatic Park, but they're not cheap (from $40 s per night).

CENTRAL

COROMANDEL PENINSULA

INTRODUCTION

Less than a two-hour drive (about 115 km) through Auckland's suburbs and to the southeast lies the Coromandel Peninsula, a place that no hiker or outdoor enthusiast should miss. This finger of land stretches northward, separating the Hauraki Gulf and Firth of Thames on the west from the South Pacific Ocean on the east. Like vertebrae, the rugged mountains of the Coromandel Range snake down the center of the Peninsula, supporting the 72,000 hectares of wilderness and bush that make up Coromandel State Forest Park. The Peninsula is an area of contrasts: along the western shores steep rocky cliffs terminate abruptly at the sea, while the eastern shores offer sandy beaches and private sheltered coves. The rugged bush-clad ranges with their ancient volcanic plugs and dense remnants of kauri forest look down on deep valley gorges and fertile farmland. Wherever you travel here the scenery is worthwhile, but for some of the best, hike to the upper peaks of the park or head for the more isolated beaches around the northern tip.

History

The Coromandel Peninsula has survived the same land exploitation as the far north. It has seen both poverty and prosperity, and a dramatically fluctuating population over the last 200 years. In the early 1800s it was ravaged for kauri timber. Vast areas were stripped, and only a few of the more inaccessible forest remnants survived. The timber seekers were followed by the gum diggers. In the mid-1800s the land was further exploited after gold was discovered in 1852 (the township of Coromandel was the first place in New Zealand to boast discovery of the precious metal), and permanently scarred with deep shafts and mines.

Today the Coromandel Peninsula is again a quiet and peaceful place, recognized for its great beauty and value as a wilderness area. The small permanent population is scattered mainly along the coastline. Although a few of the most easily reached towns (mostly along the east coast) are rapidly becoming tourist attractions, don't let the tricky gravel roads and steepness of the terrain prevent you from discovering the more beautiful, wild side of the Coromandel. Start your discovery at the CPRP office at 529 Pollen St. in Thames (tel. 86-970).

Getting There

Departing Auckland, InterCity buses operate a daily service east to Thames (gateway to the Peninsula) via Maramarua taking about two hours. A daily service runs Mon. to Fri. from Thames to Coromandel taking 45 minutes, and northeast to Whitianga taking 2½ hours. A service departs several times daily from Auckland to Paeroa (about 2½ hours), Waihi (about three hours), and on down to Tauranga.

If you're driving, take Hwy. 1 south through the suburbs of Auckland, then turn east onto Hwy. 2. At the intersection of hwys. 25 and 27, take the left fork onto 25 and continue east to Thames. Highway 25 is a scenic and colorful route. It passes through green rolling hills dotted with sheep, lush agricultural land, field after field of corn, and a large number of deer farms. In the distance lie the beckoning dark-blue mountains of the Coromandel Range.

Exploring By Car

If you plan on seeing the entire Peninsula by car, keep in mind that many of its roads are loose gravel, slow going, and tricky if you're not used to them, so allow plenty of time. Regular rental cars manage just fine—the roads aren't bad enough to need 4WD. The mainly coastal Hwy. 25 circumnavigates the Peninsula. It runs as far north as the towns of Coromandel and Kuaotunu, down the east coast, then returns inland to rejoin Hwy. 26 at Paeroa. Alternately, four main roads go over the Coromandel Range to the east coast;

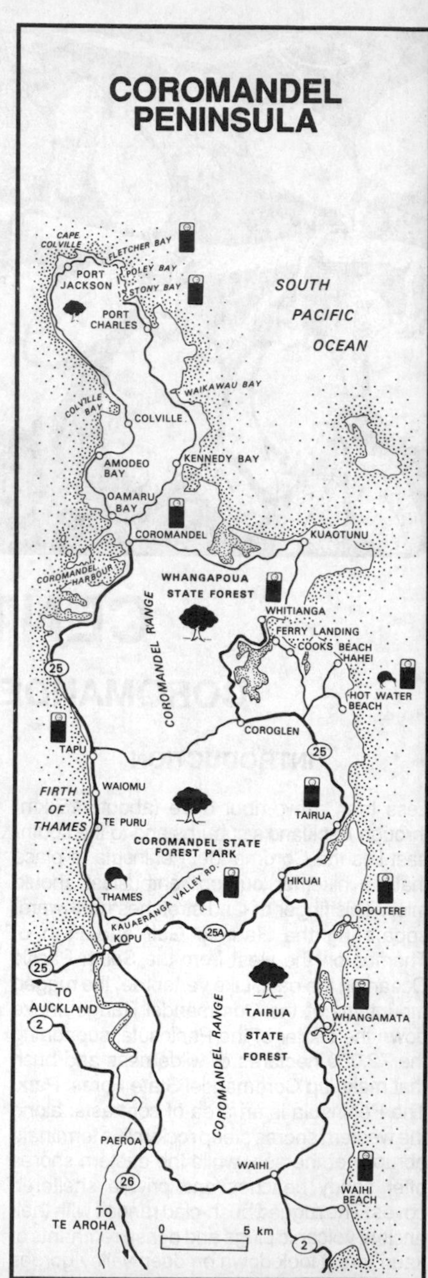

Hwy. 25A from Kopu to Hikuai, the most recently constructed, carries the most traffic.

Accommodation

Five free campgrounds are located at various bays around the northern tip of Coromandel Peninsula, as are basic mountain huts in the high backcountry of Coromandel State Forest Park. The Peninsula's YH is located at Opoutere on the east coast. Motor camps and motels are abundant, particularly between Thames and Amodeo Bay on the west coast, and in all the resort towns down the east coast. You'll have no difficulty finding them—most are well signposted from the main road (see each section for details).

THAMES

After crossing Waihou River, Hwy. 25 swings north to Thames, the gateway to the Coromandel Peninsula. Sitting at the foot of the Coromandel Range, it's the ideal base for hiking in Coromandel State Forest Park wilderness. In 1852 gold was first found farther north in the area of the present town of Coromandel. It wasn't till 1867 that the Thames district was officially opened up for gold prospecting. In the next three years Thames became a booming gold town. The rush continued until 1924, and many of the old-style buildings around town are reminders of this colorful past. Today Thames is a commercial center for surrounding farmlands, and is rapidly becoming more of a tourist attraction with its gold-rush history and close proximity to Coromandel Forest Park.

SIGHTS

The first place to go is the **Thames Information and PR Centre** on Queen St. (tel. 87-284) where you can pick up all the info you need on Thames and the entire Peninsula; open seven days in summer from 0900-1600, shorter hours the rest of the year.

Mining

If you're into rocks, check out the **School of Mines and Mineralogical Museum** which features an extensive collection of local and overseas mineral samples, and a working model of a stamper battery (used on quartz claims to pound quartz into powder). On the corner of Brown and Cochrane sts., open seven days in summer 1100-1600 (check at info center for low-season hours), admission is $2 adult, $1 child. Most mining attractions in Thames are well signposted from the main roads, but for the exact location of old gold mines, mine dumps, shafts, and abandoned mining machinery around the local area, pick up the free pamphlet *Explore Thames of Yesterday* from the info center. If you plan on venturing into any of the old mines, approach with caution. Don't go alone, tell someone else your plans, and before going underground check the entrance and supporting timber struts. Also watch out for holes in the floor, and be sure to take a candle to indicate the presence of gas (gas puts out the flame).

Historic

The **Thames Historical Museum** is inside the Methodist Church. The building itself is more than 100 years old, and the museum features turn-of-the-century printing and photographic equipment, and 19th C. clothing. Located on the corner of Mackay and Sealey sts.; open in summer daily 1100-1600 (check at info center for low-season hours), admission adult $1, child 20 cents. **Thames Port** used to be the Peninsula's link with the rest of New Zealand, and was frequented by large river boats and cutters. Today the port is very quiet, and caters to a small fishing fleet and many recreational boats.

Scenic

For good views of Thames, Hauraki Plains, and Hauraki Gulf, head for **Monument Hill.** The 1914-1918 Peace Monument stands at the northern intersection of Pollen and Queen sts. (Hwy. 25), and the walk (or drive) to the prominent lookout is worthwhile (the largest building you can see is Thames Hospital). For an enjoyable **scenic drive** through the native bush of Coromandel Forest Park and many opportunities to hike short tracks, head for the **Kauaeranga Valley** to the southeast of Thames. Information on all the walks (and free campsites) is available in a brochure from the info office in Thames, or the Park Information Centre on Kauaeranga Valley Road.

Wine Tasting

South of Thames you can visit **Totara Valley Vineyards** for a bit of award-winning wine tasting, and a sample of their delicious kiwifruit liqueur. Located about five km south of Thames on R.D. 1, Totara, tel. 86-798.

ACCOMMODATION

Hostel

There's no YHA hostel, but a private hostel is located in Thames—and many good motor camps lie just north of town. A fair amount of traffic travels up Hwy. 25 as far as Coromandel so hitching shouldn't be a problem. The other alternative is to stay in one of the reasonable hotels in Thames.

Sunkist Lodge at 506 Brown St. (tel. 88-808) is one of Thames' appealing historic buildings left behind from gold-mining days, with a spacious upstairs veranda. Choose from dorms or single, twin, double, or triple rooms, with the use of communal bathrooms, a fully-equipped kitchen, dining room, TV lounge, pool table, and laundry; from $12-15 pp. It's a popular place at any time of year, but there's usually plenty of room.

Motor Camps

Closest to town is the excellent **Dickson Holiday Park,** three kilometers north, just off the main highway, with a lush park-like camping area in a natural bush setting—a great spot to get away from it all and unwind. Jack and Anne will be happy to provide you with info on local short walks (several start at the campground), peninsula hiking tracks (baggage storage available), and commercial attractions. Facilities include communal bathroom blocks (the metered showers require 10-cent pieces but the water stays piping hot), kitchen and laundry facilities, swimming pool, trampolines, and a camp office selling basics from 0800-1800. Tentsites are $6 pp, caravan sites $7 pp, bunk room accommodation is $9 pp (supply own linen), cabins (with fridge and cooking hot plate) and on-site vans range from $22-27 d, and comfy tourist flats (private bathroom, kitchen facilities, TV, and radio) are $45 d. Located on Victoria St. (take the right branch at the sign), Tararu, tel. 87-308.

Boomerang Motor Camp is 11 km north of Thames. Communal bathroom (metered showers), kitchen and laundry facilities, TV and game room. Tentsites are $6.50 pp, caravan sites $8 pp, cabins are $22-25 d, converted trams and on-site vans are $20 d. Located at Te Puru, tel. 78-879.

Waiomu Motor Camp is also along Hwy 25, 13.5 km north of Thames. It has a swimming pool, spa (extra charge), TV and game room, tennis courts, trampoline, and camp store. Communal bathroom, kitchen, and laundry facilities. Tentsites are $6 pp, caravan sites $8 pp, an on-site caravan and cabins with cooking facilities are $25 d, and a self-contained tourist flat is $40 d. A self-contained motel unit is $50 twin or double. Located on Hwy. 25 at Waiomu, tel. Te Puru 78-777.

Tapu Motor Camp, 18 km north of Thames, tel. 74-837, has tentsites $5.50 pp, caravan sites for $7.50 pp, cabins from $18 d, and self-contained caravans for $23.50 double.

Hotels

Brian Boru Hotel, an eye-pleasing colonial hotel built in 1868 on Pollen and Richmond sts., tel. 86-523, has a wide range of rooms (small and cozy, large and spacious, some with shared bathroom facilities, some with private) at prices from $35-50 s, $57.50-75 d or twin, plus an attractive old-fashioned licensed dining room (all meals available)

Brian Boru Hotel

comfy lounge and bar, and plenty of old-time atmosphere. Specials for budget backpackers are also available, depending on the season and availability (call ahead for prices). The owner (an active overseas promoter of the Coromandel Peninsula), Barbara Doyle, also puts on "Mystery, Intrigue & Murder Weekends" for would-be sleuths at the hotel (the perfect setting)—pretend you're Agatha Christie and join 30 guests and eight actors spending a weekend solving a murder (from $300 pp, reservations necessary)! At 204 Richmond St., adjoining the Brian Boru Hotel's courtyard, are modern luxury units with queen-sized beds, private bathrooms, fridge, tea- and coffee-making facilities, and TV, from $66 s or $88 d.

Salutation Hotel has rooms from $23 s, $40 d, and meals (optional and extra) are available; at 400 Mary St., tel. 86-488. **Imperial Hotel's** rooms are $30-45 s, $45-55 d or twin, and meals (optional and extra) are available in the bistro (carvery on Sun. nights); located on Pollen St., tel. 86-200. **Junction Hotel** has rooms from $33 s, $44 d or twin, and meals (optional and extra) are available; on the corner of Pollen and Pahau sts., tel. 86-008.

Motels

Of the many motels in and around Thames (refer to your *AA Accommodation Directory* for complete listings and prices), the most reasonable is **Motel Rendezvous.** Located on the main highway (25 S) at Kopu, it's about five km south of Thames, tel. 88-536. Self-contained units sleeping two to six people are $48 s, $55 d or twin, $11 each extra adult; Continental or cooked breakfast extra.

OTHER PRACTICALITIES

Food And Entertainment

The usual tearooms, takeaways, and cafes are found throughout Thames, most on mile-long Pollen St., the main shopping street downtown. There's not much in the way of evening entertainment. Your best bet is to try the public bars and hotel lounges; the occasional restaurant has dining and dancing. Also find out what's happening at the info center.

The Country Touch on Pollen St. has a good range of sandwiches and typical tearoom fare. For cheap counter meals try the public bar at the **Hotel Imperial** between 1200 and 1400. The **Pan & Handle Lounge and Bistro Bar** puts on reasonably priced steak and seafood meals and a salad bar from 1200-1400 and 1800-2000. The Imperial also has a good carvery on Sundays between 1800 and 2000, and a fancier meal at fancier prices in the Regency Room Restaurant where an a la carte menu is served from 1830. The Imperial Hotel is at 476 Pollen St., tel. 86-200. **Pizza Cabin** is open Mon. to Sun. from 1700-2100; located at 702 Pollen Street. For a substantial Chinese meal at a very reasonable price, try the **Golden Dragon** also on Pollen Street. It's open Tues. to Sun., has a BYO license, and mains (big enough for a very healthy appetite) will only set you back about $7-12 pp. Next door you can get Chinese meals to go.

Information

The **Thames Information and PR Centre** is in Porrit Park on Queen St., tel. 87-284. **Coromandel State Forest Park Information Centre** is on Kauaeranga Valley Rd. (about 15 km from Thames); open 0800-1600 (call ahead to check if it's open), tel. 86-381, after hours tel. 86-380. The **Automobile Association Breakdown Service** is at Valley Panelbeaters, tel. 86-801. **The InterCity bus depot** is at the northern end of Pollen Street. **Thames Hospital,** tel. 86-550. **Medical Centre,** tel. 89-444. **Police station,** tel. 86-040; if no answer call Hamilton 80-989 collect. **Ambulance, fire,** or **police emergency,** tel. 111. **Thames Laundromat** is located at 742 Pollen St. (opposite the bus depot), tel. 87-170; open seven days, from 0700-1900 weekdays and 0900-1700 on weekends and holidays. Other **information centers** for the Peninsula are located at Paeroa, Whangamata, Pauanui, Tairua, and Whitianga.

Transportation

Regular bus service runs west to Auckland, the Hauraki Plains, and Hamilton, and on the Peninsula to Coromandel, Whitianga, Paeroa, and Waihi. The **InterCity depot** at the northern end of Pollen St. is open Mon. to Fri. 0830-1215 and 1330-1700, tel. 86-074. To see a good chunk of the Peninsula, take the RT bus from Thames to Coromandel to Whitianga and back which departs Thames Mon. to Fri. at 1030 for only $32 ($16 OW to Whitianga), or $24 if you travel off-peak on Tues., Wed., Thurs., or Saturday. Book one day ahead. To give you an idea of distances on the Coromandel, Tapu is a 30-minute drive, Coromandel one hour, Colville 1¾ hours, Port Jackson 3½ hours, Kennedy's Bay 1¾ hours, Whitianga 1½ hours, Tairua one hour, Pauanui one hour, and Whangamata 1½ hours. A **taxi** can be reached at tel. 86-543.

THE WEST COAST

Thames Coast

The 32-km Thames Coast borders the Firth of Thames from Thames to Wilsons Bay. This coastal road, perhaps most beautiful in summer when the bordering *pohutukawa* trees are ablaze with red flowers, passes by rocky outcrops, picture-perfect bays, and small beaches. The towns and villages along the route, backed by the Coromandel Range, provide a wide choice in motor camps and stores, and activities ranging from bush walking and mineral fossicking to swimming and boating.

Tapu

About 16 km from Thames, Tapu is located at the Thames-Coromandel-Whitianga junction. If time is precious and you want to see a more isolated part of the Peninsula, continue north. If you're looking for action and lots of people, head across to Whitianga and down the east coast.

Tapu is known for its long stretch of sandy beach, shallow water, and safe swimming. The local commercial attraction is **Rapaura Watergardens** in Rapaura Falls Park—beautiful gardens that blend with the natural surroundings; take a picnic lunch. Open daily 1000-1700 between 1 Oct. and 30 April, small admission charge. Tapu has a motor camp, general store, hotel, and restaurant.

Tapu Motor Camp is located on the beach opposite the hotel at the main road junction, tel. 74-837. Communal bathroom, kitchen (metered), and laundry facilities. Tentsites $5.50 pp; caravan sites are $7.50 pp; on-site

Luxuriant greenery edges all the interior highways of the Coromandel.

caravans start at $23.50 d; a cabin is $26 d. **Birdwood Cabins** have private cooking facilities for $19 s and $23 d per night; communal bathroom facilities. Located on Main Rd. adjoining Tapu Hotel, tel. Tapu 74-737 or 74-804.

Coromandel

A quiet fishing and crafts village about an hour's drive from Thames, Coromandel is particularly appealing. Despite its small size, it's the business center of the far north, offering quite a variety of services—and it's the last place (other than one store at Colville) to stock up on supplies before continuing north. There's also the **Coromandel School of Mines Museum** containing historical displays of early goldmining and colonial era artifacts (on Rings Rd., tel. 58-825, open in summer from 1000-1200 and 1400-1600; admission adult $1, child free), and the **Coromandel Stamper Battery** on Rings Rd. where you can see ore-crushing demos for gold extraction, pan amalgamation, and plate amalgamation. A half-hour tour costs $3 pp; to see the static display only it's $2. Open summer 1300-1500, winter by arrangement (tel. 58-765).

Coromandel also has quite a choice of accommodation. **Tui Lodge,** surrounded by grassy paddocks and citrus and macadamia orchards (guests can help themselves), provides budget accommodation (single beds; provide own sleeping bag or linen), toilet and shower, and cooking facilities (cold water only) for $12-14 pp, or you can stay in the comfortable self-contained flat (private facilities and everything you need) for $44 d (linen provided). It's at Whangapoua Rd. (Hwy. 25); if you need a ride out there (several kilometers from Coromandel), give the owners a call at tel. 58-237 and they'll collect you. For cheap overnight camping with communal bathrooms (metered) and cooking and laundry facilities, try beachfront **Long Bay Domain Camp,** three km west of the village, tel. 58-720. Tentsites are $5.50 pp, caravan sites are $8 pp. Row boats are also available for hire. **Coromandel Motel and Caravan Park** has communal bathroom, kitchen, and laundry facilities, a pool, recreation room, trampolines, BBQ, etc. Tentsites $8 pp, $3.50 child; caravan sites are the same as tentsites plus $2.50 per night for power; cabins are $20 s, $30 d, but off-season rates are available from May to October. Located on Rings Rd., tel. 58-830. The licensed **Coromandel Hotel** has rooms for $25 s, $50 d per night, tel. 58-760.

The hotel bistro has good meals for around $10 pp from 1800-2000, and the hotel dining room is open Mon. to Sat. 1800-1900. For delicious freshly baked bread, pastries (your thighs will never forgive you!), pies, and great pizza, check out the **Bakehouse** on Wharf Rd., tel. 58-554. It's open seven days a week from 0730-1700, in summer till 2100. For excellent inexpensive fresh seafood takeaways, try **D.J.'s** on Kapanga St. (main street). **Coro Foodbar,** another restaurant and takeaway, is on Wharf Rd., tel. 58-206, open every day. For more info on the village and areas to the north, call in at the **Coro-**

mandel Information Centre on the main road (next to the surgery and a small park); open Mon. to Fri. 1000-1500, 0900-1600 in summer. Ask for handouts on Coromandel's history, walking tracks, and craft trails.

Colville

At the end of the sealed road, this small settlement has only one store, a restaurant, and a p.o., and is the very *last* place to get supplies and petrol before heading on to the northern tip. The Colville General Store is open seven days a week and sells fresh fruit and vegies, dairy products, groceries, camping needs, and petrol. **The Colville Restaurant,** serving seafood, steak, and vegetarian meals, is open seven days through summer; call for winter hours at tel. 805.

To The Top

If heading to Port Jackson is what you have in mind, expect to ford several streams (generally not too deep except after heavy rain) along this coast-hugging gravel road. You'll pass some stretches of beautiful coastline with enchanting bays and excellent camping spots, and wind up at the open white sands of Port Jackson beach—lots more perfect camping spots beside crystal-clear streams, plenty of driftwood for campfires, and relatively few fellow explorers. What more could you ask for?! The rocky coastline near Port Jackson holds great appeal for anglers; the Gulf water is deep, clear, and abounds with large snapper. The road leads around the top of the Peninsula and ends at Fletcher Bay, and at this point the only way to continue south is on foot via the Coromandel Track.

THE EAST COAST

The Coromandel Track

This seven-km track, part of the New Zealand Walkway network, crosses Cape Colville Farm Park in the far northern tip of the Peninsula, from Fletcher Bay to Stony Bay. It takes about 2½ hours OW, three hours on the return trip. On this rather isolated track you traverse beach, open farm land, and bush, and are rewarded with some fabulous coastal scenery. The track follows an easy grade for the most part, with only one short steep section (marked with red disks) near the center. The small sandy beach at Poley Bay (where a stream runs out to sea) may tempt you in for a swim, but resist the urge! Many submerged rocks are dangerously close to the surface, and safer swimming is found at the end of the track. Also avoid drinking from this particular stream—the water is bad.

Farther along, the track wanders through scrub, with the Moehau Range dominating the skyline to the west. The small streams in this area are drinkable. At the back of Stony Bay beach, Stony Bay and Doctors creeks merge to form a large lagoon—a good swimming hole if the sea is rough. Aseparate track leads from Stony Bay to the summit of Moehau (892 meters). The views are worth the long hard climb, and if you're lucky you may see one of the "fairies" that Maori legends claim inhabit this area. Campsites and freshwater streams are located at both ends of the track, and Fletcher Bay has toilet facilities. Wear sturdy shoes or hiking boots, carry food and water, and a stove if you plan on camping overnight at either end before returning.

Camping Out

The Dept. of Conservation administers five camping areas at the far north of the Coromandel Peninsula—Fantail Bay, Port Jackson, Fletcher Bay, Stony Bay, and Waikawau Bay. All have freshwater streams, but Fletcher Bay is the only camping area with toilet facilities; $10 per site per night (up to 10 people)—give fee to ranger or leave in the honesty box. No shops in the vicinity so be sure to take food and other supplies (don't forget matches!) before heading for the campgrounds, and take a stove and cooking equipment.

COASTAL RESORTS

The soft sandy beaches that line the entire east coast of the Peninsula attract hordes of holidaymakers in Dec. and January. The larger towns with their apartment blocks, flats, and countless holiday homes are populated by a fairly large retirement community; in summer they're inundated with families on vacation. The smaller coastal towns in the north are also fairly crowded in summer, but can be best appreciated during the quiet off season. Wherever you go on the east coast you'll find beautiful beaches. If you also want peace and quiet, and maybe your own private bush-fringed cove, stay in the north! For lots of people and the bustle of a coastal resort, head for the large towns at the southern end of the Peninsula.

Inland Routes West Coast To East Coast

The road between Coromandel, Kuaotunu, and Whitianga is unsealed (patches of sealed) and slow going. The main sealed road from the south to Whitianga is Hwy. 25A from Kopu which passes through Hikuai, Tairua, and Coroglen. However, if you don't mind driving the winding unsealed Tapu Hill route from Tapu to Coroglen, you're well rewarded with views of lush valleys, clear streams, giant tree ferns, and near the top of the range, the 2,500-year-old "Square Kauri."

On the unsealed "309 Road" between Coromandel and just south of Whitianga (allow at least 40 minutes to an hour depending on your familiarity with curvy gravel roads) take plenty of film to capture natural bush panoramas. Stop at **309 Honey Cottage,** a real retreat about 15 minutes from Whitianga, for delicious honey, crafts, animal petting (lots of tame critters), or to stay in an old kauri cottage in a river and bush setting for only $10 pp. The cottage has showers, a fully-equipped kitchen, lounge with log fire, and washing machine—campers ($5 pp) can also use the cottage facilities. On the farm are endless possibilities for bush walks, gem collecting in the river, and cooling off in natural swimming holes—it's a gorgeous place! The owners are also willing to trade a few hours labor for accommodation if you can stay a week or more. For more info call George or Diana Lancaster at tel. 65-151.

Whitianga Highlights

Whitianga, with its sheltered harbor and long sandy Buffalo Beach, is a popular holiday resort. It's also a base for big-game fishing and scuba diving in Mercury Bay, and is now on the world map for being the home base of the small Mercury Bay Boating Club which Michael Fay used when he challenged the Americas Cup in 1988. The operations base and starting "hut" for the club is a turquoise 1956 Ford Zephyr—the trunk stores the flags and transit poles for racing events, the glove locker the protest forms and instructions! Local promoters call the area "Cup Challenge Country" and claim that Whitianga *will* be the future home of "the auld mug," the Americas Cup trophy!

A passenger ferry runs across "The Narrows" (0730-1200 and 1300-1830; adult $1.40 RT, child 70 cents, bikes 25 cents) to tranquil **Ferry Landing,** original site of Whitianga, several scenic reserves featuring ocean views and sandy beaches, and the town of Cooks Beach. At Whitianga you can visit the small local museum (see Mercury Bay when the pioneer settlers arrived; open daily in summer), explore historic goldmines, or meander through a number of excellent craft shops, go fishing or diving, mini-bus sightseeing, river rafting or jet boating, experience a 4WD adventure, go pony trekking, play a round of golf, hire a wind surfer or canoe, or get a bird's-eye view on a scenic flight. A full range of shopping facilities (open seven days during the summer vacation) are found in Whitianga, and the many motor camps, lodges, and motels provide quite a choice in accommodation (see below). (For less of a crowd, check out the motor camps farther south at Hahei and Hot Water Beach.)

Whitianga Practicalities

The most centrally situated motor camp in Whitianga is **Buffalo Beach Tourist Park,** on Eyre St. next to beautiful Buffalo Beach (northeast end of town), a short walk from downtown (tel. 65-854). Friendly hosts, Alan and Trudi Hopping, provide spotlessly clean communal bathroom (metered showers), kitchen, and laundry facilities, TV and pool room amongst four hectares of landscaped grass and trees, only a few strides from the beach. Tentsites (all rates include GST) $8.50 pp; caravan sites same as tentsites plus $2.50 per night for power. A three-bed bunkroom is available in the off season for $13 pp, supply own linen. On-site caravans or a trailer home are $17.50 s, $34 d, supply own linen. Ask about their reduced tariffs in the off season.

If you're looking for excellent backpacking accommodation (dorm beds from $13 pp, $28 d, shared bathrooms, kitchen, comfy lounge) and plenty of fellow backpackers for company, continue along waterfront Buffalo Beach Rd. to number 46 (corner of Bruce St.)—**Coromandel Backpackers Lodge.** The Spanish-style building faces a large reserve, the beach, and the bay, and the enthusiastic owners offer guests the free use of kayaks and surf or body boards, and have catamarans for hire. Ask about their unique do-it-yourself landrover trips to local highlights (from $15 pp) or two-day trips to the top of the peninsula (from $45 pp), and their three-hour cruises around Mercury Bay ($20 pp). For more info tel. 65-380.

For bed and breakfast accommodation in a unique home designed to make any cat fancier smile, head for **Cosy Cat Cottage** on the main road (41 South Hwy., tel. 64-488). You'll see cats just about everywhere you look—cat ornaments (inside and out), wall hangings, prints, photos, calendars, cats on the shower curtains, on the bedspreads, homemade cat-shaped cookies, and a couple of resident cats (live ones!) who share their backyard with vacationing friends' and neighbors' cats in the purrfectly designed cattery; for $35 s, $30 pp d (shared bathroom), the friendly owners include a Continental or cooked breakfast, and a home-cooked dinner is also available for $15 pp if required. The waterfront **Marlin Motel** at 13 Buffalo Beach Rd. (tel. 65-860) has good off-season rates. In the high season fully equipped units start at $44-50 s, $50-61 d (higher rates from 24 Dec. to 28 Feb. and at Easter).

Whitianga also has a large variety of restaurants and a few cafes. For tearoom-type fare, try **Wildflower Cafe,** across Albert St. from the info center. **The Kingfisher Restaurant** next to Trusteebank Waikato, Albert St., tel. 65-114, has family-priced meals. For excellent seafood, locally recommended **Snapper Jacks,** also on Albert St. (corner of Monk St.), is open for lunch and dinner. **Whitianga Information Centre** is at 35 Alberts St., tel. 65-555; generally open weekdays 0900-1600 and weekends 0900-1230, but hours fluctuate according to the number of visitors in town!

Hahei

Hahei is best known for its sheltered, soft pink beach (caused by crushed shells mixed in with the sand), and dramatic headlands with two *pa* sites at the southern end. Beyond the *pas* lie two blowholes, magnificent at high tide in stormy weather. At the northern end of Hahei Beach, a one-hour walk OW leads to **Cathedral Cove Reserve** where at low tide you can walk through a huge sea cavern. **Hahei Tourist Park** has tentsites for $6.75 pp; caravan sites $7.75 pp; cabins $27 d (less in the off season); tourist flats $35 d ($40 for a one-night stay and between 25 Dec. and 31 Jan.).

Hot Water Beach

If you enjoy soaking in natural hot pools this place shouldn't be missed! Hot springs seep up through the sand near the mouth of the Tauwaiwe Stream; flooded at high tide, this area is accessible about three hours either side of low water when a large number of people usually take baths in the sand. Dig a hole between the cliff and the large rock just offshore and *voilá,* your own private hot pool! (The deeper you dig, the hotter the water

Dig your own hot pool at Hot Water Beach!

becomes.) Follow this with an exhilarating swim in the surf and you'll feel brand new. Stay at **Hot Water Beach Motor Camp** right beside the beach (camp closed in June and July); communal facilities and four private mineral plunge pools. A store selling all the basics is part of the motor camp, tel. Whenuakite 735. Tentsites $7 pp; caravan sites are same as tentsites plus $2 per night for power.

On the way back from Hot Water Beach look out for a sign to the left marking **Kauri Grove Walk.** This walk leads down through exotic tree ferns and native bush to a small stream, then parallels the stream which descends in a series of small waterfalls. Birdsongs, the buzz of cicadas, and the whistling stream add to the all-around beauty. The track eventually crosses the stream and climbs up into a young kauri forest. The first loop takes about 1½ hours RT, the track that leads to the coast is 2½ hours OW, and the one to the coast and on to Sailor's Bay is 3½ hours OW.

Tairua

Popular with holidaymakers, particularly in summer, Tairua offers great coastal views and lots of motor camps. Just north of Tairua, keep your eyes peeled for **Twin Kauri Scenic Reserve**—two stunning kauri trees standing side by side right next to the road (easily missed if you're coming from the north—look for the small pullout). Attention arts and crafts fanciers and collectors! "Easterly—The Cottage Craft Shop" on Ocean Beach Rd. (off the main road to the east at the north end of town, marked "Scenic Drive" from the highway) in Tairua displays and sells high-quality pottery, screen-printing, basketry, painting, leather craft, weaving, and jewelry. And don't miss a stroll along the path through their spectacular garden. If you're interested in **diving,** contact Dive Tairua for info on *Supercat* and *Almarco* dive charters at tel. 48-426 or 48-868. Or call Bernie Bliss at tel. 47-190 and ask if any diving trips are going on. An inexpensive passenger ferry operates from Tairua to **Pauanui Beach,** a rapidly growing resort, from 0730-1900 and 2200-2300.

A popular place to stay is **Paku Lodge and Caravan Park,** situated on Paku Headland to the northeast of Tairua, tel. 48-557. Tent and caravan sites are regularly $8.30 pp, but jump to $20 minimum per site at Christmastime. A tourist flat is $44 d; a unit using camp facilities is $33 d. Motel units are also available but expensive, particularly during the Christmas season. After crossing Tairua River just south of Tairua, get tremendous views of The Pinnacles (794 meters).

Owharoa Falls, between Waihi and Paeroa

Opoutere
Continue down Hwy. 25 south of Hikuai to the turnoff to Opoutere, at Keenan's Corner. The **Opoutere YH,** four km down Opoutere Rd., is ideally situated for hiking and beachcombing. Backed by native bush and on the edge of a tidal estuary, it has the added bonus of being within a few minutes' walk of Opoutere Beach. The nearest p.o. and shop are four km but the hostel shop sells a wide range of supplies including vegetarian and health foods; $11 pp per night; tel. Whangamata 59-072.

Whangamata
Climbing up Hwy. 25 between the road junction with Hwy. 25A and Whangamata, look back for spectacular views of Coromandel State Forest Park. Whangamata has become a popular holiday resort and retirement community, crowded during vacation periods. Its great surf is popular with both serious surfers and swimmers who enjoy large waves. Whangamata also boasts good surf-fishing. The Whangamata **Information Centre** is on the main street next to the District Council office building; open seven days a week in holiday periods, shorter hours in the off season. **Ocean Beach,** reached via Ocean Rd. from the highway, is a long stretch of golden sand with off-shore bush-covered islands—worth a drive out there whether you're going to catch it on film, work on your tan, or plunge into the Pacific.

Pinefield Motor Camp is only 800 meters from the beach and close to the local golf course. Communal facilities, TV and recreation room, spa pool. Tentsites $7 pp; caravan sites $15 d; cabins from $30 d; tourist flats are $40 d, $10 each extra adult, reduced in the off season. Located on Port Rd., tel. 58-791.

Waihi And Waihi Beach
These two towns are also crowded with vacationers and tourists in summer. If you're into water lilies, check out **Waihi Water-Lily Gardens** on Pukekauri Rd., tel. 8267. The several acres of gardens have over 80 varieties; open seven days from 1000-1600 during 1 Nov. to 30 April, small admission charge. Other local attractions include the **Goldfields Vintage Railway** (signposted off the highway), **Waihi Gold Company Gold Mine** (open for tours on weekdays; for more info tel. 8192 ext. 841), and an **Art Centre.** For the complete rundown, call in at the local info center (look for the sign on the highway).

Waihi Beach is considered one of the safest beaches along the coast—it's patrolled in summer and on holidays by local lifesaving club members. **Waihi Beach Holiday Motor Camp** is adjacent to both Ocean and Waihi beaches, 11 km from Waihi, tel.

5-5044. Communal facilities, TV and game rooms, and camp store. Tent and caravan sites are $7.70 pp; equipped cabins start at $27-33 d a night in the holiday season (reduced in the low season).

Waihi To Paeroa

The stretch of road between Waihi and Paeroa is quite enjoyable (get your camera ready), particularly toward the Paeroa end where the highway parallels Karangahake Gorge (part of the Ohinemuri Goldfield, opened in 1875) and River, edged by large pampas grass and luscious tree ferns. Stop at **Karangahake Reserve** to stroll the 4.5-km **Karangahake Gorge Historic Walkway** (allow 1½ to two hours OW; pre-arrange transportation at the other end or be prepared to take the same route back). It meanders along the river passing old bridges, abandoned mining equipment and relics, and mining shafts (stay on the track)—a walk back in time. The walkway is signposted from the highway at either end—at the Waihi end, pull off to take a short amble down through another small, incredibly lush, scenic reserve to impressive **Owharoa Falls.** Several craft shops are also signposted off the highway.

Paeroa

Located at the junction of hwys. 25 and 26, Paeroa's claim to fame is the nationally renowned soft drink "Lemon and Paeroa," which originated here. The mineral water was pumped from a deep Paeroa well and mixed with lemon to make the popular light-tasting drink (an L & P bottle, large enough to satisfy King Kong's thirst, at the southern end of town is probably one of the most-photographed local features). Another popular attraction is the **Maritime Museum** (small admission fee); for more info on the local area call in at the Paeroa **PRO,** Railway Reserve, at the eastern end of Belmont Road.

COROMANDEL STATE FOREST PARK

This park (73,000 hectares) offers extensive hiking tracks that range from short walks to mining or kauri-logging sites, to rugged several-day hikes in the mountainous backcountry. Apart from recreational purposes the park is used for timber production, plant and animal conservation, and as a source for domestic water supplies. The most easily reached section of the park is from the Kauaeranga Valley. From Thames heading south, turn left on Banks St. before you cross the Kauaeranga River, then turn right on Parawi Rd. which becomes Kauaeranga Valley Road. This road winds through the beautiful Kauaeranga Valley, passing the Park Information Centre, several good camping areas, and four short tracks, before terminating at the starting point of some of the more difficult hiking tracks.

Park Information Centre

Call in here for track and hut info, hunting and mining permits, and maps. A detailed map of the park is available for around $7, a worthwhile purchase. If you plan on hunting or want to try your hand at mining, you must obtain a permit from a Dept. of Conservation office before setting out. A "rock-hounding" permit is valid for two days; only geological hammers can be used, no digging or explosives, and the daily limit is 2.2 kg (five pounds) of rock pp. The hunting permit, valid for 30 days, allows hunting wild pigs or goats. You'll be assigned to a particular area which, for safety purposes, is generally a good distance from hiking tracks and recreational areas.

Be sure to check the latest track and hut info and weather forecasts with the ranger as flooding and landslides can occur quite quickly. If you're hiking in the backcountry the rangers recommend filling out an intention sheet. The Park Information Centre is located on Kauaeranga Valley Rd., tel. 86-381, after hours tel. 86-380; open daily in summer from 0750-1600, in winter on weekdays only from 0800-1600. During the summer, rangers give free guided walks to areas of interest throughout the park.

logging dam, a short walk from Park HQ

Short Walks

Four short walks lead off Kauaeranga Rd. beyond the info center. About 30 minutes or less, each is classified as suitable for light footwear in dry weather. They wander through various types of native bush and give great views of the Kauaeranga River and Valley.

Hiking Tracks

Thirty-three marked tracks criss-cross the rugged Coromandel Forest Park. For details on each track pick up the *Hut and Track Information* pamphlet from the park info center. Keep to the marked tracks on all the hikes; many deep mining shafts overgrown by bush are scattered throughout the Peninsula and have claimed the lives of unwary explorers.

Camping Out

A number of campgrounds, huts, and an emergency shelter are located within the park. Camp fees are $10 per site per night (but only $2 pp for backpackers). Buy a back-country hut ticket at the info center before heading out into the wilderness. The three closest huts to the info center are the Moss Creek Hut, Pinnacles Hut, and Waiwawa Hut. Because of the steep surrounding terrain it takes a person in very good shape about 2½ hours to get up to the huts, about 1½ hours to come down. Moss Creek and Pinnacles huts have kitchen and dining areas, and are serviced by the Park with cooking gas and firewood (take your own candles, matches, and first-aid gear). The unserviced Waiwawa Hut necessitates your own stove and cooking equipment, etc. All huts have fresh-water streams nearby. Get a hut update from the info center before you set off!

The Wires Recreation Area

Located in the Maratoto Block of Coromandel Forest Park 28 km southeast of Thames, this area is known as "the Wires" because the Auckland-to-Wellington telegraph line was once diverted through here during the Waikato Land Wars. You can still see some of the original posts from the Wires Track. The regenerating bush and scrub is intermingled with isolated remnants of virgin forest. Hunting goats and pigs is encouraged in this area by the Dept. of Conservation, but permits must be obtained from the Park Information Centre. To get to the area take Hwy. 26 south from Thames. Two km south of Hikutaia turn east onto Maratoto Rd. and continue for six km to the signposted gravel road on the left. This leads to a gate and carpark, and the beginning of an off-road vehicular track.

The **Wires Walking Track** starts 500 meters before the carpark from the bottom of a paddock, takes 2½ hours, and joins the Whangamata vehicle track at the Wires Plateau. The **Wentworth Track** is most easily reached from Whangamata by driving half-way up the Wentworth Valley. The sign-posted track runs up to the vehicular Loop Track, taking about two hours. Enjoy spectacular Wentworth Falls from the track. For more info, call in at the Park Information Centre on Kauaeranga Valley Road.

HAMILTON

INTRODUCTION

Hamilton, "The Fountain City" and center of the Waikato region, is often missed in the rush to get down to Rotorua or back to Auckland. It's located on Hwy. 1 less than 130 km south of Auckland and on all public transportation routes. Though the city itself offers the visitor few attractions, Hamilton is an ideal base for exploring the area's several forest park reserves, and the western surf beaches. The Waikato River, originally the main shipping route between Hamilton and Auckland, meanders through the inner city, and along its banks are numerous parks and gardens. The east and west banks are connected by five city bridges, and footpaths run along the river on both sides.

The lush green fields dotted with dairy cows that stretch away from Hamilton in all directions are part of the Waikato Plains, one of the most productive dairying and agricultural districts in New Zealand. The city started out as a fairly small Maori village, Kirikiriroa, on the west bank of the Waikato. The first European settlement was a military camp established in 1864, and the resulting town was named after a navy officer killed in the Battle of Gate Pa at Tauranga the same year. Hamilton has grown rapidly over the years and is now the fifth largest population center (102,000) in the country.

SIGHTS

Inner-city Walks

Three circular walking routes have been identified: ask for a city map and accompanying brochures at the Tourism Waikato Information Centre (at Centerplace on Ward St.). The **Short Historic and Scenic Walk** starts at the Tourism Waikato office, then leads

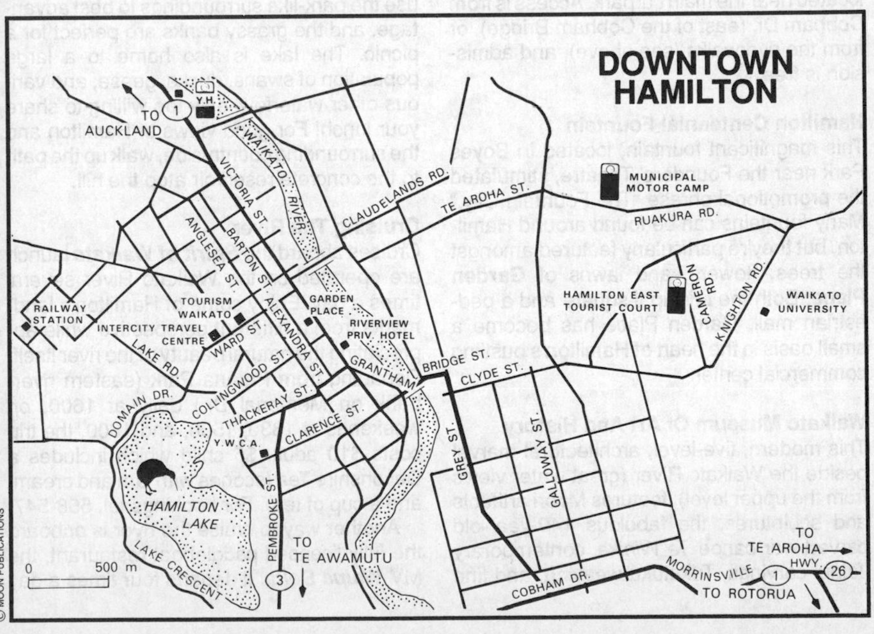

along Victoria St. (Hamilton's main shopping drag) and over Victoria Bridge. Returning along the River Walk route, the entire trip takes about 1½ hours. The scenic three- to four-hour **River Walk,** also known as Five Bridges Walk, runs along the banks of the Waikato River. It starts from beyond Fairfield Bridge in the north and runs to beyond Cobham Bridge in the south, links all five city bridges, and takes in several parks and some of the older residential streets. **The One-day Scenic Walk** covers much of the River Walk route but also includes several more parks and the delightful grounds around Hamilton Lake, taking five to eight hours to complete.

Hamilton Gardens

Masses of roses, chrysanthemums, daffodils, camellias, magnolias, rhododendrons, vegetable gardens, a perfume garden, trees that burst into brilliant color in autumn, and display houses sheltering tropical plants, cacti, succulents, bromeliades, and insectiverous plants can all be found in Hamilton Gardens. Start your discovery at the map located near the main carpark. Access is from Cobham Dr. (east of the Cobham Bridge), or from the riverwalks (see above), and admission is free.

Hamilton Centennial Fountain

This magnificent fountain, located in Boyes Park near the Founders' Theatre, stimulated the promotional phrase "The Fountain City." Many fountains can be found around Hamilton, but they're particularly featured amongst the trees, flowers, and lawns of **Garden Place.** Both the principal square and a pedestrian mall, Garden Place has become a small oasis in the heart of Hamilton's bustling commercial center.

Waikato Museum Of Art And History

This modern, five-level, architectural marvel beside the Waikato River (great water views from the upper level), features Maori artifacts and sculptures, the fabulous 140-year-old carved war canoe *Te Winika,* contemporary Tainui carvings, Tukutuku weaving, and fine art exhibits, along with changing exhibitions. Don't miss the aerial sculpture, "Ripples," which hangs between the trees outside (best viewed from the River Gallery inside). It accurately represents a pebble dropping in water—a suspended moment in time. In the museum shop pick up some high-quality arts and crafts, posters, prints, books, and artcards. Adjoining the museum is a restaurant/cafe open for light snacks and lunches during museum hours, dinner from 1800 (tel. 383-172). The museum is open seven days a week from 1000-1630; admission is free (donation box) but there may be an admission charge for special exhibitions. Located at 1 Grantham St. (corner of Victoria St.), tel. 386-533.

Hamilton Lake

Also known as Lake Rotoroa, this is a great place to escape the bustle of the city on weekdays. On weekends and holidays it's very popular with local residents for swimming, sailing, and sunbathing. Footpaths enable walkers, joggers, and rollerskaters to use the park-like surroundings to best advantage, and the grassy banks are perfect for a picnic. The lake is also home to a large population of swans, ducks, geese, and various other waterfowl only too willing to share your lunch! For good views of Hamilton and the surrounding countryside, walk up the path to the concrete reservoir atop the hill.

Cruising The River

Cruises aboard the ***Spirit of Waikato*** launch are operated on the Waikato River several times a day. Enjoy some of Hamilton's landmarks from a different perspective while appreciating the natural beauty of the river itself. Departing from Parana Park (eastern riverbank on Memorial Dr.) daily at 1600, on weekends at 1330, 1500, and 1600, the trip costs $10 adult, $5 child which includes a Devonshire Tea (scones with jam and cream, and a cup of tea). For bookings tel. 558-547.

Another way to cruise the river is onboard the fully licensed paddleboat restaurant, the MV ***Waipa Delta.*** It departs four times a day from Woodcocks Wharf, Memorial Park on Memorial Drive. Morning or afternoon tea cruises depart at 1030 and 1500, last 1½ hours, and cost $15 pp; the smorgasbord lunch cruise departs at 1230, lasts 1½ hours, and costs $28 pp; the four-hour Moonlight Dinner Cruise (buffet dinner and dancing) departs at 1900 and costs $65 pp. For more info and reservations (a good idea), tel. 394-419.

Canoeing

Another way to enjoy the river is to take a group canoe trip with **Waikato Canoes.** Their professionally guided river trips are available on weekends and evenings for groups of 10 or more, with all equipment provided and no experience necessary. The "Fun Trip" covers 10 km, takes about 1½ hours, and costs $15 pp. Meet at Malcolm St., finish at Days Park,

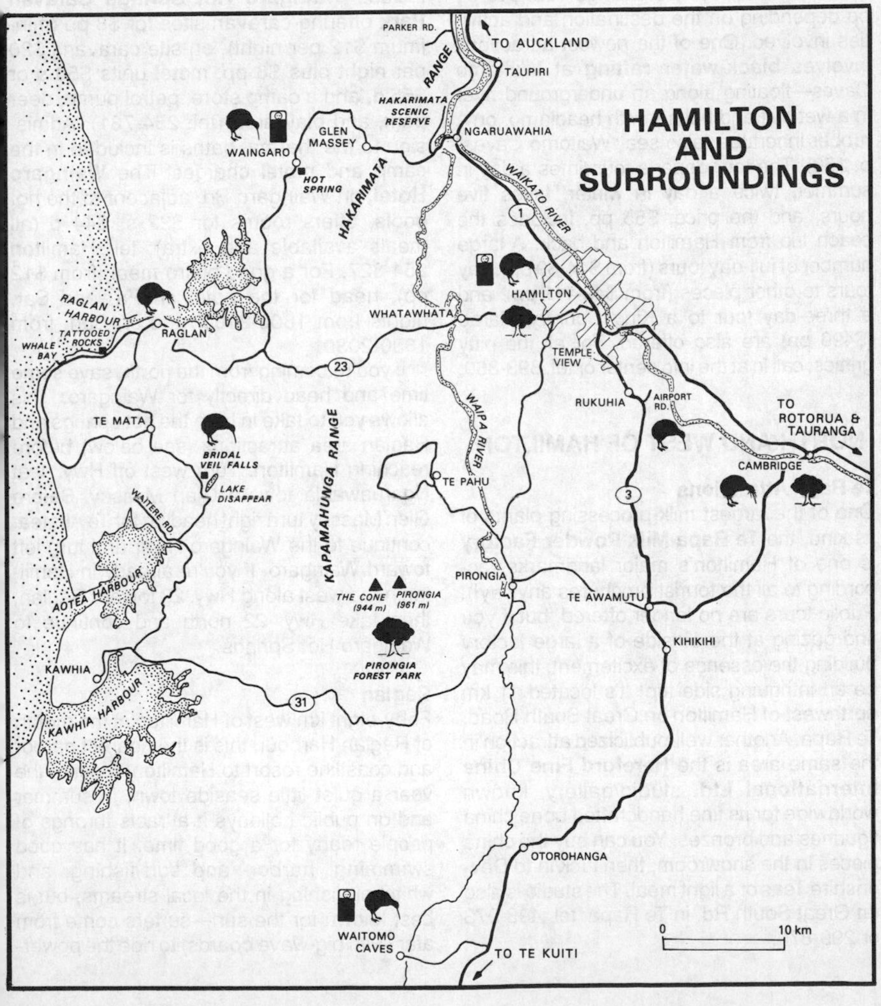

and take a change of clothing. For all the details call Kevin or Glenis, tel. 557-833.

Short On Time

If you don't have time or private transportation, the quickest way to see Hamilton's sights is to take one of the half-day **sightseeing coach tours** departing from the Waikato Visitor Information Centre, Centreplace, Ward Street. These tours range from $19-81 pp depending on the destination and activities involved. One of the newest attractions involves **black-water rafting** at Waitomo Caves—floating along an underground river in a wet suit and helmet with headlamp, on a rubber innertube (also see "Waitomo Caves" p. 156). The tour departs four times a day in summer, twice a day in winter, takes five hours, and the price, $55 pp, includes the coach trip from Hamilton and back. A large number of full-day tours (from $44-89 pp), day tours to other places (from $49-111 pp), and a three-day tour to a King Country Marae ($499 pp) are also offered. For all the nitty gritties, call in at the info center or tel. 393-360.

NORTH AND WEST OF HAMILTON

Te Rapa Attractions

One of the largest milk-processing plants of its kind, the **Te Rapa Milk Powder Factory** is one of Hamilton's major landmarks (according to all the tourist brochures anyway!). Public tours are no longer offered, but if you find gazing at the outside of a large factory building the essence of excitement, this may be an intriguing side trip! It's located 11 km northwest of Hamilton on Great South Road, Te Rapa. Another well-publicized attraction in the same area is the **Hereford Fine China International Ltd.** studio/gallery, known worldwide for its fine handcrafted bone china figurines and bronzes. You can buy the china pieces in the showroom, then tuck in to Devonshire Teas or a light meal. The studio is also on Great South Rd. in Te Rapa, tel. 493-973 or 299-870.

Waingaro Hot Springs

Located 42 km northwest of Hamilton, the sulphur-free bubbling waters of this thermal spring have been diverted into three concrete pools. The temperatures range from 30-42 degrees C. Open daily from 0900-2200, tel. (071) 254-761; admission $4 adult, $2 child, but hydroslides are an extra $2.50 per half hour. The resort grounds also include **Waingaro Hot Springs Caravan Park** offering caravan sites for $8 pp (minimum $12 per night), on-site caravans $20 per night plus $8 pp, motel units $50 s or $55 d, and a camp store, petrol pump, deer park, and play area (tel. 254-761). Admission to the thermal baths is included in the camp and motel charges. The **Waingaro Hotel,** on Waingaro Rd. adjacent to the hot pools, offers rooms for $22 s, $44 d (all meals available and extra); tel. Hamilton 254-827. For a good bistro meal (from $12 pp), head for the hotel on Fri. and Sat. nights from 1800-2100, and on Sun. from 1630-2030.

If you're coming from the north, save some time and head directly for Waingaro. This allows you to take in both the hot springs and Raglan area attractions (see below) before reaching Hamilton. Turn west off Hwy. 1 at Ngaruawahia toward Glen Massey. Before Glen Massey turn right heading for Te Akatea, continue to the Waingaro River and turn left toward Waingaro. If you're already in Hamilton head west along Hwy. 23 toward Raglan, then take Hwy. 22 north and continue to Waingaro Hot Springs.

Raglan

Forty-eight km west of Hamilton at the mouth of Raglan Harbour, this is the nearest harbor and coastline resort to Hamilton. Most of the year a quiet little seaside town, in summer and on public holidays it attracts throngs of people ready for a good time. It has good swimming, harbor- and surf-fishing, and whitebait fishing in the local streams, but is best known for the surf—surfers come from afar (with big-wave boards) to ride the powerful swells off Raglan shores, the reef-point break at **Whale Bay** (just south of Raglan), and seldom-calm **Manu Bay** around the corner. Buses run daily from Hamilton to Raglan.

Whale Bay has spectacular views to the north. Easiest access to Whale Bay cove is through Tasman Heights Picnic Park. Just north of Whale Bay look out for the signpost to **Tattooed Rocks,** intricate Maori rock carvings, their artist unknown. If continuing south along the inland roads, pass through Te Mata to reach the spectacular **Bridal Veil Falls** near Lake Disappear, 21 km southeast of Raglan off the main road to Kawhia. Walk about 10 minutes along a bush trail to emerge at a thundering torrent of water plummeting 60 meters down a lava rock face into a deep pool, a popular swimming hole in summer. For an even more dramatic view continue for another 10 minutes down the steep track to the base of the falls.

SOUTH OF HAMILTON

Mormon Temple

This magnificent temple, located at **Temple View** about eight km southwest of Hamilton, gives panoramic views of the Waikato from its grounds. It was the first Mormon temple built in the Southern Hemisphere, and although only a few select people of the Mormon faith are allowed to actually enter the temple, a Visitors Centre (complete with guides) welcomes the rest of humanity with open arms! The pride and joy of the Visitors Centre is a towering statue of Christ, "the Christus." The work of Italian sculptor Aldo Rebechi, it's a replica of the original Christus created by the "famous" 19th C. Bertel Thorvaldsen of Denmark! The Centre is open daily from 0900-2100, admission free. Temple View is linked with Hamilton city by a regular bus service; call the Visitors Centre (tel. 78-601) for more information.

Animal Appeal

If you want to learn more about New Zealand's agricultural scene, **Farmworld** will be right up your alley. Wander through the various farm, tree, dairy, and Clydesdale muse-

Clydesdale

ums, then take in one of the two stage show presentations (1030 and 1430) in the Big Dome. Here you'll view all kinds of live farm animals, cows being milked on an automated rotary platform, then a multi-image widescreen presentation on the story of agriculture. The Clydesdale Museum was originally established as a tribute to New Zealand's pioneering past. Displays still focus on agricultural equipment, but the main attraction is the magnificent Clydesdale horses. The horses are bred, worked, and put through their paces here. Devonshire teas or light lunches are available in the tearooms, and the craft shop has a variety of locally made crafts. Farmworld is open daily from 0900-1630; admission $5.70 adult, $4.50 senior, or $2.50 child. Located between hwys. 1 and 3 at Mystery Creek, 16 km south of Hamilton. Look for the airport—the museum is one km southeast, off Airport Rd., tel. 437-990.

Another place to appreciate a wide variety of animals is **Hilldale Zoo Park**. The main theme is conservation, and rare birds and animals are held here to establish breeding colonies. It's open daily from 0900-1700 (admission charge) on Brymer Rd. (by Horseshoe Lake), north of the city, tel. 386-720.

Cambridge

If you've been to England, Cambridge, "Town of Trees," will bring back memories of tree-lined avenues, immaculate flower-filled gardens, old buildings, and the traditional village green. The jade-green Waikato River runs through this scenic town, and the streets are bordered by abundant varieties of trees which meet overhead in a lush colorful archway (spectacular in late April and May when they take on brilliant autumnal colors). Between Hamilton and Cambridge you'll see field after field of racehorses intermingled with stud stables, which cater to an international yearling market. Cambridge is located 20 km southeast of Hamilton on Hwy. 1. The **Cambridge Public Relations Office** is adjoined to the library on the main street (access from inside the library foyer).

While you're in Cambridge, don't miss a stop at the **Craft New Zealand Centre** (you can't miss the two-story orange-red wood building) at 92 Victoria St. (tel. 8715). Here you can either shop for high quality artwork, pottery, woodwork, silk scarves, jewelry, and woven clothing and wall hangings, or eat breakfast or a light meal in the **All Saints Cafe** upstairs (the specialty is orange cheesecake—dee-licious!). The center is open daily from 0900-1800, the cafe from 0900-1700.

Waitomo Caves

These magnificent limestone caves are 74 km south of Hamilton, 19 km northwest of Te Kuiti. A vast network of caverns, many still unexplored, are found in the Waitomo area. One of the most spectacular, Waitomo Cave, has been opened to the public and is one of New Zealand's major tourist attractions. It's definitely worth a visit but expect hordes of people, bus tours, school groups, etc. The main attraction within this cave, also known as Glowworm Cave, is the magical glowworm grotto. Quietly glide through the grotto in a guided boat, gazing upward at the vast ceiling of twinkling lights. Tours through the Glowworm Cave are run daily, generally every hour on the hour from 0900-1600, with extra tours at 1630 and 1730 in peak periods; admission $10 adult, half fare child. Buy your ticket at the entrance to the cave or at the Waitomo Hotel.

For camp and caravan sites or cabin accommodations try **Waitomo Caves Camp and Caravan Park** (tel. 87-639) next to the Hotel, but again expect heaps of people (and maybe no vacancies) during vacation periods. At the **THC Waitomo Hotel** (tel. 88-228) rooms with private facilities start at $99 twin, $275 a suite. To get to Waitomo take Hwy. 3 southwest out of Hamilton to Otorohanga. To the south of Otorohanga turn off to the west to Waitomo Caves.

A new, exciting, two- to three-hour adventure being offered at Waitomo is **black-water rafting.** This involves plunging into the Huhunui stream (wetsuits, helmets with headlamps, and tubes provided) and drifting along an underground river. In some places you need to get off and scramble, and in Ruakuri Cave, jump down a waterfall! Glowworms put on a magical display along Okohua stream. Afterward a hot shower and a snack are provided. All you need to take is a swimsuit (wear it), towel, socks, tennis or running shoes, and a camera (preferably waterproof!) with flash. The tour departs daily at 0900, 1200, and 1500 (depending on water flow) and costs $35 pp. For more info contact the Museum of Caves, Waitomo Caves, at (0813) 87-640.

WALKING TRACKS

For info on local hikes in the Hamilton area and track maps, call in at the Tourism Waikato office in Hamilton (see below), or for general info write to Hamilton Tramping Club, Box 766, Hamilton, or Waikato Tramping Club, Box 685, Hamilton. For great area maps, stop by the Department of Conservation on London Street.

Hakarimata Walkway

This 15-km walk runs along the top of the Hakarimata Range behind Ngaruawahia (19 km north of Hamilton), with great views and two large kauris toward the end. It starts at the Ngaruawahia-Waingaro Rd., four km west of the Waipa River Bridge, and ends about 12 km north of Ngaruawahia on Parker Rd. (off Huntley West Road). Classified as a track, you need to be fit, and have hiking boots, warm clothes, and water. It takes about seven hours to complete, and it's wise to pre-arrange transportation at the far end. You can also join the track at Hakarimata Trig

(374 meters); cross the Waipa River bridge at Ngaruawahia and follow the Waterworks Track up Mangarata Stream (steep toward the end).

The Karamu Walkway
Another good track for panoramic views of Hamilton, Mt. Pirongia (961 meters), Kakepuku, and Raglan. The northern end of the track starts at the eastern corner of the Four Brothers Scenic Reserve, almost at the top of the Kapamahunga Range. Take the Hamilton-Raglan Rd. (Hwy. 23) to the reserve. The track finishes 10 km south of Whatawhata on Limeworks Rd., Karamu, and takes about four hours; as a shorter alternative, the section between Four Brothers Scenic Reserve and Old Mountain Rd. can be done in an hour. In good weather it's easy walking in tennis shoes or sneakers, but take warm clothes for the exposed ridge sections, and carry water.

Pirongia Forest Park
The small town of Pirongia, 31 km southwest of Hamilton, sits at the foot of the impressive Pirongia mountain range where two extinct volcanic peaks, Mt. Pirongia (962 meters) and The Cone (945 meters), dominate the landscape. Nearly 1,300-hectare Pirongia Forest Park carpets the rugged slopes and offers the hiker, angler, hunter, and photographer an extensive network of trails, ranging from easy walks around the lower peaks to strenuous backcountry hikes in the high ones. For track info, check at the PRO in Te Awamutu or Otorohanga (both towns are south of Hamilton along Hwy. 3), or the Tourism Waikato office or Department of Conservation office in Hamilton.

On the lower northeastern slopes of Pirongia Forest Park lies a beautiful campground and picnic spot at the end of a 30-minute track. The camping area is amongst native bush beside Kaniwhaniwha Stream, and the immediate area offers several short tracks, delightful swimming holes, and swing bridges over numerous streams. Access to the track is from the Pirongia road to Te Pahu, 40 km from Hamilton. (It's hard to find on a map; locate Kaniwhaniwha Stream, then Te Pahu.) At Te Pahu take the Te Pahu (gravel) side-road for about six km to a concrete bridge over the Kaniwhaniwha Stream; the track entrance is over a stile. To get to the camp area follow the track over the first swing bridge. Don't cross the second swing bridge which leads to a picnic area; continue along Track 12 to the track branch and follow the red markers to the campground.

ACCOMMODATION

Hostels
The modern **Helen Heywood YH** has a great location on the bank of the Waikato River at the north end of Hamilton. Within easy walking distance from downtown, it's 300 meters from the nearest dairy, 1.5 km from the bus depot in Ward St., and two km from the train station on Queens Avenue. Open 0800-1000 and 1700-2200, $12 pp per night; at 1190 Victoria St. (Hwy. 1), Hamilton, tel. 80-009. The **YWCA** is within walking distance of downtown and Hamilton Lake, but the students from Waikato University keep it pretty full most of the year. Best to check late in the afternoon or early evening when they know for sure if they have a spare bed. In vacation periods however, getting a bed for the night (or week) is no problem. Even when it's full, if you absolutely can't find room anywhere else in Hamilton, they'll give you a mattress on the floor for $10 pp. Bathroom, kitchen, and laundry facilities are communal. A room costs $20 pp. Weekly rate is $75 s, $70 pp d. Located at 28 Pembroke St. and corner of Clarence St., tel. 82-218.

Motor Camps
Two motor camps in Hamilton are in the eastern section of town, and another is 11 km south. **Hamilton East Tourist Court,** three km from downtown, is adjacent to Hamilton East P.O. and a few shops, within easy walking distance of Waikato University. Communal facilities. Tent and caravan sites are $10 s, $15 d; comfy standard cabins are $15 pp, and the tourist cabins with kitchen facilities

are $37 s or d. Tourist flats are $45 d. Located on Cameron Rd., Hamilton East, tel. 66-220. To get there go to the south end of Victoria St. and cross the river via Bridge Street. Turn right on Grey St., left at the Riverina Hotel onto Clyde St., and left onto Cameron Rd. (just before the Knighton Rd. intersection). By bus, take the Peachgrove bus from outside DEKA on Victoria St. (usually says "University" or "Peachgrove" or both). They depart every 20 minutes in peak periods, half-hourly and hourly in off-peak. Ask the driver for the nearest stop.

The **Municipal Camp** in the same area has tent and caravan sites but no cabins. Communal facilities. Tentsites $9 s, $12 d; caravan sites $12 s, $15 d. Located on Ruakura Rd., Hamilton East, tel. 558-225 after midday. To get there cross the central downtown bridge at Claudelands Rd., turn right on Grey St., left on Te Aroha Street. At the Peachgrove Rd. intersection continue straight ahead onto Ruakura Road. By bus, take the same bus as for above motor camp and ask the driver.

Narrows Park Christian Camp is 11 km south of Hamilton near Hamilton Airport. Communal facilities, and a swimming pool. Tent and caravan sites $6.50 pp; cabins $22 d. Located next to Narrows Golf Club on R.D. 3, tel. 436-862. (For caravan sites and cabins northwest of Hamilton, see "Waingaro Hot Springs," p. 154.)

Private Hotels

Hamilton has several private hotels with lodging and breakfast at reasonable prices. The best value is at **Riverview Private Hotel,** $22 pp B & B; the Continental breakfast is served in your room. Communal bathroom facilities with handbasin in each room; no guest kitchen, but tea- and coffee-making facilities; TV lounge. Located at 60 Victoria St. (almost opposite the intersection of Knox and Victoria sts.), tel. 393-986. The other private hotels include **Parklands Travel Hotel,** tel. 82-461, **Grand Central Hotel,** tel. 81-619, and **New Empire Hotel,** tel. 75-467. Hamilton's many motels have rooms from $50 s, $60 d—get listings from the *AA Accommodation Directory* or at the Tourism Waikato office. One of the newest is the **Grosvenor Motor Inn** at 165 Ulster St., tel. 383-399. Rooms with all the little luxuries you'd expect start at $110 s, $121 d or twin, and good but pricey meals are also available in the licensed restaurant.

FOOD

For Breakfast Or Lunch

Try one of the many tearooms, coffee bars, and cafes for good snacks and light meals at reasonable prices. Victoria St. has a good selection. Many taverns (bars) also serve cheap yet filling lunches and dinners. Try the **D.B. Frankton Hotel** for homestyle and seafood dishes where a four-course meal costs about $15 pp. Open 1200-1330 and 1800-2000; located at the corner of Commerce and High sts., Frankton, tel. 75-065. **The Governors Restaurant** serves a bistro-type meal from $15 pp and an a la carte menu from $16 pp between 1200-1400 Mon. to Fri., and from 1800 Mon. to Saturday. Located at 2 Bryce St., tel. 82-209.

For Dinner

Hamilton's large number of restaurants provide a wide range in both tastes and prices, and the Tourism Waikato office downtown is a good source of info if you're looking for a particular type of food. Ask for the *Dining Out in the Waikato* brochure for suggestions and prices. The following restaurants are recommended for filling meals worth the price. **The Red Rooster** serves various roasts with french fries and vegies from $12, steaks from $15, and has an excellent salad bar. Comfortable surroundings, BYO license, but note that a surcharge of 10% is added on weekends and public holidays. Open Mon. to Thurs. 0900-2100, Fri. and Sat. 0900-2200, and Sun. 1700-2100. Located at 589 Victoria St., tel. 395-969.

The Old Flame Restaurant is a great place to go when you're really hungry and don't mind a bit of a splurge to quiet the rumbling stomach. It offers deliciously prepared smorgasbord-style food in elegant yet comfortable surroundings. Pick from a huge selection of salads, seafood, and cold dishes, and steaks (only in the evening) grilled to order. An entree, main course, dessert, fruit juice, and coffee will set you back $12-15 pp at lunch, $22-26 pp at dinner (sometimes specials for adult $20, child $10), but you're encouraged to eat as much as you want. BYO license with small corkage fee. Open seven days from 1200-1400 and 1800-2100. Located upstairs in the Aorangi Building at 571 Victoria St., tel. 80-641; it's not easy to spot unless you're looking up at the second floor level, but it's above Devon Art and not far from The Red Rooster Restaurant.

Another good place for a four-course smorgasbord—eat as much as you desire—and a salad bar is **Wilsons Carvery** in the Southern Cross Motor Inn at 222 Ulster St., tel. 383-299. It's open seven days from 0700-2200 (no lunch on Sat.); lunches cost $10-12 pp, dinners $19-21. **No. 8 Restaurant** at 8 Alma St. serves innovative Italian food with mains in the $12-16.50 range. It's open Mon. to Sat. from 1800, tel. 80-631. For spicy Mexican food and very-Spanish decor, try **Eldorados,** also on Alma St., tel. 81-013. Mains range from $13.50-17. Open seven days from 1800-2200.

Cobb & Co. Restaurant, adjacent to the Commercial Establishment Hotel, has the standard menu of steaks, seafoods, and salads served throughout the Cobb & Co. chain—good food for the price. Meals start at about $9-15 pp. Open seven days from 0700-2200. Located on Victoria St. at the corner of Collingwood St., tel. 391-226. For a splurge, try the excellent a la carte menu at the **Grosvenor Motor Inn** at 165 Ulster St., tel. 383-399. Expect to pay from $15-25 pp for lunch, $18-25 for dinner (major credit cards accepted). It's open seven days from 0700-1000, 1200-1400, and 1830-2300.

Fast Food

All the usual fast-food restaurants and takeaways can be found in Hamilton. **McDonald's** is on Victoria St., tel. 80-247, and **Kentucky Fried Chicken** is on Ulster St., tel. 395-228. **Wimpy Bar** on Victoria St. serves sandwiches, light snacks, and ice-cream sundaes, Mon. to Thurs. 1100-1930, Fri. 1100-2100, Sat. and Sun. 1100-2000; in Historic House, 161 Victoria St., tel. 80-763.

ENTERTAINMENT

Music

Many taverns and hotels around Hamilton have live bands Wed. through Sat. nights, but for the best bands on Fri. and Sat. nights there's usually an admission charge. The **D.B. Frankton Hotel** has live piano entertainment in the evenings. Located on the corner of Commerce and High sts., Frankton, tel. 75-065. On Thurs. nights the local **folk club** meets at Hamilton YH, 1190 Victoria Street. If lunch or dinner, dancing, and cruising grabs your fancy, chug up the Waikato River on the **MV *Waipa Delta*** while you sample the smorgasbord menu. It runs seven days a week, from 1230-1400 and 1900-2300, departing from Memorial Park on River Rd.; lunch $28 pp, dinner (includes wine or beer) $65 pp. Bookings essential at tel. 394-419.

Theater

Several theaters offer plays and other forms of live entertainment, including the **Founders Theatre** in Boyes Park, the **Drury Lane Theatre** on Clarence St., tel. 393-082, and **Riverlea Theatres and Arts Centre** on Riverlea Road (southeast Hamilton). Ask what's playing at the Tourism Waikato office in Hamilton, or call the theaters.

Active

For some cheap and healthy entertainment try **Hamilton City Centennial Pools.** Open Mon. to Thurs. from 0600-2100, Fri., Sat., and Sun. from 0900-2100, the center includes indoor and outdoor heated pools, a heated diving pool, and waterslides. Admission $1.70 adult, $1 child or senior citizen, $1 spectator, hydroslide $3 for half an hour. Located on Garnett Ave., tel. 494-389. **Mini Golf** is open only on weekends and public holidays between 1000 and dusk, on Richmond St., tel. 390-447. If you're into maxi golf a large number of clubs are in the local area; **Hamilton Golf Club** is at St. Andrews, tel. 492-069.

SERVICES AND INFORMATION

Emergency: for general emergencies call 111.
Ambulance: tel. 82-644.
Police: on Bridge St., tel. 80-989.
Waikato Hospital: on Pembroke St., tel. 398-899.
Emergency doctor or dentist: call St. John Ambulance at tel. 82-644.
Urgent pharmacy: tel. 393-999; located on the corner of Victoria and Rostrevor streets.

The main **post office** is on Victoria St., open 0800-1630, tel. 80-979.

Information

The **Tourism Waikato Information Centre** in Centreplace on Ward St., tel. 393-360, is a great place to start for any info on Hamilton. The helpful personnel take time to get you anything you need. It's open Mon. to Fri. 0900-1630 and Sat. 0900-1200, in summer open seven days a week. The **Automobile Association,** a good source of maps and general info, is on Anglesea St. (near London St.), tel. 391-397. For general info on New Zealand head for the **Government Bookshop** at 33 King St., tel. 70-639, and for detailed maps, visit the local **Department of Conservation Office** on London Street. **Hamilton Public Library** is on Barton St., tel. 80-106; open Mon. to Fri. 0930-2030, and Sat. 0930-1230. The library has a newspaper room, open library hours. The local **newspapers** are the *N.Z. Herald,* the morning daily; the *Waikato Times,* the evening daily; *Hamilton Press,* weekly on Wed.; and the *Weekender,* weekly on Friday.

TRANSPORTATION

By Car

Hamilton is a merging point for several main highways. Central State Hwy. 1 runs north-south through Hamilton, north to Auckland and south to Taupo. Hwy. 26 branches east toward Paeroa and the Coromandel Peninsula, and Hwy. 3 branches west toward New Plymouth and Egmont National Park. Call in at the Automobile Association (see above) for good road maps and travel information, free with proof of any AA membership.

By Bus

Local buses run weekdays only. The **City Bus Terminal** and **taxi stand** are on Victoria St., and the city bus office is on the corner of Seddon Rd. and Somerset St., tel. 76-119. Go to the **InterCity Travel Centre,** corner of Ward and Anglesea sts. (tel. 81-979), for all on-going bus information; open Mon. to Thurs. 0700-1730, Fri. 0700-1930, Sat. 0700-1330, and Sun. 0930-1730 (closed for lunch). Taxis are available outside the center. **InterCity** provides regular coach service in all directions; from Hamilton north to Auckland ($18 OW), east to Tauranga ($17 OW), or south to Rotorua ($17 OW), Wellington ($54 OW), Wanganui ($42 OW), and New Plymouth. **Newmans Coach Lines** also operates out of the InterCity Travel Centre and departs for Auckland, Hawera, New Plymouth, Otorohanga, Palmerston North, Te Awamutu, Te Kuiti, Waitara, Waitomo turn-off, Wanganui, and Whangarei. **Mount Cook Landline** coaches depart from outside Focus Travel on Victoria St., north for Auckland, Taupo, Napier, Hastings, and Wellington.

By Rail

Hamilton Railway Station is on Queens Ave., not far from Hamilton Lake. The InterCity Northerner departs Hamilton daily for Wellington ($54 OW) in the early evening, and daily in the early morning for Auckland ($18 OW). The InterCity Silver Fern Railcar departs Hamilton in the evening Mon. to Fri. for Auckland ($23 OW), and in the morning Mon. to Fri. for Wellington ($64 OW). Book at the InterCity Travel Centre, corner of Ward and Anglesea streets.

By Air

Hamilton Airport is about 16 km south of the city. Take Hwy. 3 south to Rukuhia and continue about one km. Airport Rd. branches off the highway to the east just before Mystery Creek, and eventuallly joins up with Hwy. 1.

Air New Zealand services Wellington in the North Island, and Blenheim, Christchurch, Dunedin, Hokitika, Invercargill, Nelson, Oamaru, Timaru, and Westport in the South Island. The Air New Zealand ticket sales and reservations office is at 33-35 Ward St., downtown Hamilton, tel. 399-800 (reservations) or 399-835 (Travel Centre). **Eagle Airways** also services the North Island, with departures to Auckland, Gisborne, Napier, New Plymouth, Palmerston North, Wanganui, and Wellington.

To get to the airport catch the **Airport Transport Ltd.** bus from the City Mini Bus Terminal on Ward St., opposite InterCity. The bus service departs for the airport 45 minutes prior to each Air New Zealand departure, and returns to the city 10 minutes after each arrival; fare $4.50 adult, $2 child OW.

BAY OF PLENTY

INTRODUCTION

If you're hankering for a few lazy days where the only work you do is on your tan, or want to try your hand at various watersports (sailing and fishing are popular), this narrow coastline has plenty to offer! However, if you're short on time and crave tourist attractions, evening action, and tons of people, you may be happier heading directly for the visitors' mecca of Rotorua.

Facing due north, the magnificent crescent-shaped Bay of Plenty stretches from the Coromandel Peninsula in the west to Cape Runaway in the east. It includes several small islands, and is backed by the Kaimai and Raukumara Ranges to the south. Captain

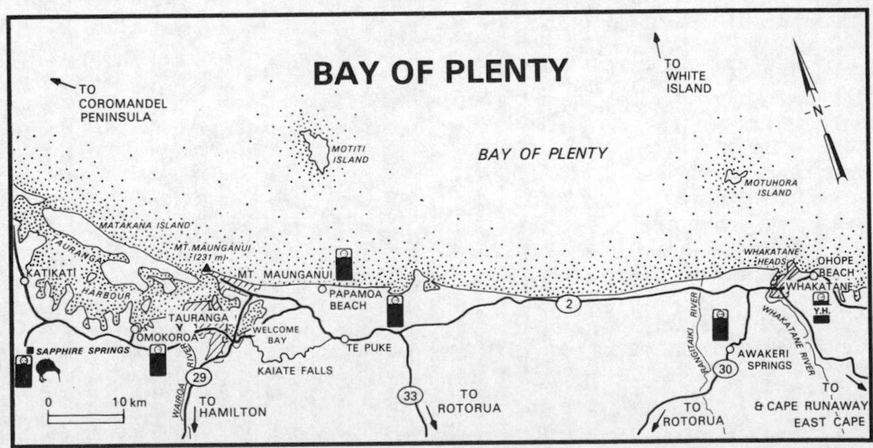

Cook first sailed its shores in 1769; on finding several friendly and prosperous Maori villages along the coast he was able to restock some badly needed provisions, prompting him to name the area the Bay of Plenty. But the Bay's history long predates Cook. According to Maori legends, nine of the original 22 emigrant canoes from Hawaiiki landed in this area, and it became home for some of the strongest and most powerful Maori tribes. The remains of many *pa* can still be viewed along its shores.

Today this aptly named Bay with its mild climate, broad sweeps of golden sand, and crystal-clear waters attracts thousands of vacationing New Zealanders during the summer months and reverts to a relaxingly quiet resort area in winter. The fertile land produces a large variety of sub-tropical fruit—kiwifruit, feijoas, and tamarillos; the area is also well known for its citrus orchards, supplying a quarter of the country's total fruit crop. You can't miss the many signs that welcome visitors to the self-proclaimed "Kiwi Coast" or "Orchard Coast." The three main towns—Tauranga, Mount Maunganui, and Whakatane—are situated along the coast, interconnected by Hwy. 2 (which continues southeast to Gisborne). Tauranga and Mount Maunganui are also inter-connected by impressive Tauranga Harbour Bridge (toll $1).

History

In the early 19th C., the Tauranga area was the scene of many inter-tribal battles between the powerful Ngapuhi tribe of Northland and the local Ngaiterangi tribe. During the 1830s the first European missionary settlement was established on the Te Papa Peninsula, and by 1839 the entire Peninsula had been bought from the Ngaiterangi by Reverend Brown, on behalf of the Church Missionary Society. A mission house, now called The Elms, was completed in 1847; this historic building, one of the oldest in New Zealand, can still be viewed today (see "Sights" below).

Many battles, both inter-tribal and Maori versus Pakeha (white man), were fought over land ownership. The **Battle of Gate Pa** in 1864 between British government troops and the local tribe was one of the fiercest and best-known battles in the area. Heavy fighting and great loss of life affected both sides, but the better-armed British troops eventually stamped out most resistance and confiscated the Maori land they desired. The military settlement they built on it was the beginning of modern-day Tauranga. Today, many of the local sights are memorials to these early battles, and the *pas*, redoubts, military settlements, and missions found throughout the area are the remains of a colorful (and gory!) past.

TAURANGA

SIGHTS

The city and port of Tauranga ("Sheltered Anchorage") is 88 km north of Rotorua. Largest coastal city in the Bay of Plenty area, it lies along a section of the large and sprawling Tauranga Harbour. Tauranga is a good place to go when you're tired of being on the road. Lots of beautiful parks and no major attractions give you the excuse to lie back and do nothing! However, if you're planning on doing some white-water rafting sometime during your stay in the North Island, Tauranga is home base to several rafting companies. Unrivaled excitement on some of the North Island's most exhilarating rivers awaits the adventurous spirit, and Tauranga is a good place to do some investigating into the great variety of trips and prices available (see "Rafting" below, and "River Rafting," p. 26).

Walking Downtown

The main shopping drag in Tauranga is **The Strand,** but you can escape the hustle and bustle of the commercial center by strolling through the **Strand Gardens** on the eastern side of the street. For an enjoyable one-hour walk back a hundred years, continue to the northern end of The Strand where the intricately carved Maori war canoe *Te Awanui* is on display, then follow the path up to the complex earthworks of **Monmouth Redoubt.** This area, commonly called "The Camp," was the site of the original military settlement that overlooked the Bay. The well-kept **Robbins Park,** on the knoll between the Redoubt and the cemetery, has a Begonia House (open daily) and rose gardens within its grounds. For fairly graphic descriptions of Tauranga's past, check out the gravestones in the **Military Cemetery** on Cliff Rd.—some have quite a story to tell! **The Elms** on Mission St. (off Cliff Rd.) was the original mission house built between 1838 and 1847 by the missionary Reverend Brown. The Elms is privately owned, but the grounds are open to the public from 0900-1700 Mon. to Saturday. Tours of the house are generally conducted daily at 1400, but check with the Information Centre on The Strand (tel. 788-103) for the latest tour times.

Tauranga Historic Village

This 14-acre "living" museum renders a part of Tauranga's history through many working exhibits. The architecture, tools, machinery, clothing, and artifacts of previous times are displayed in an authentic, old-world village. A visit is like stepping through a time machine to see the lifestyles of early New Zealanders accurately portrayed. Open daily 1000-1600, tel. 781-302, admission is $5.20 adult, $2.10 child, with a discount for YHA members; located on 17th Ave. West, off Cameron Road.

Hot Pools

There are five hot pools to choose from in the local area. The 840-foot bores at Tauranga are the source for internationally known Fernland Sparkling Mineral Water, but if you'd rather immerse yourself in it than drink it, head for **Fernland Mineral Hot Pools** in the Tauranga suburb of Te Reti. The water (38-40 degrees C) is pumped daily from 200 meters underground into the main public pool and eight large private pools. Open daily 1000-2200; located at 250 Cambridge Rd. near the Rose Gardens, tel. 783-081 for current admission charges. From downtown (about six km from the p.o.) follow Cameron St. to 11th Ave. and turn right; 11th becomes Waihi Rd., continue, then turn left onto Cambridge Road.

Winery

A fun (and free) way to get some of your daily vitamin C requirement is to sample the award-winning kiwifruit wines and liqueur at **Durham Light Kiwi Fruit Winery.** The winery is open Mon. to Sat. 1000-1700, tel. 785-043; the tour and tasting are free. Buy the wines (from $8) and liqueur (from $15) there, or at any large bottle shop throughout New Zealand—they make most appreciated gifts! To get there from town you need a car. Follow Cameron St. almost out of town; before you reach Hwy. 2, turn left onto Chadwick Road. Turn right onto Oropi Rd. and right on Glen Lyon Place—the winery is at the end. Another good local winery at which to wet your whistle is **Prestons Kiwifruit Winery** on Belk Rd., tel. 401-926—free tastings, kiwifruit products, winery tours, and wholesale prices (wine from $7, liquer $22) . From Tauranga take Cameron Rd. to Hwy. 29 and turn right toward Hamilton. Continue for about 7.5 km, then turn left on Belk Rd. for another three km.

Te Rerekawau Falls

At the bottom of a fairly steep track through native bush you'll find three beautiful waterfalls (they used to be called Kaiate Falls), the third plummeting into a very deep, bush-fringed pool and popular (icy cold!) swimming hole. It's a great place for photographers into slow-speed water shots. You'll also need a car to get to these falls, but keep all valuables locked out of sight or with you—or leave a pit bull in your car! Take Hwy. 2 out of Tauranga toward Mount Maunganui but turn right toward Welcome Bay before crossing the harbor. Continue along Welcome Bay Rd. and just after the bay turn right on Waitao Rd.—the falls are signposted from here.

Bird's-eye View

An exhilarating way to get high in this area is to head for Tauranga Airport! It's directly across the harbor from downtown Tauranga on the Mount Maunganui peninsula (see "Transportation" below). **Tauranga Aero Club** operates scenic flights of varying lengths starting at $15 pp, Mon. to Sun., tel. 753-104, and if you're lucky, you'll have the chance to watch some great skydiving action. **Tauranga Gliding Club** will take you silently soaring on an introductory flight (lasting about 10-15 minutes, weather permitting) for $25 pp, weekends only. This worthwhile experience is a wonderful way to appreciate the beauty of the Bay of Plenty, to get oriented, and, be warned, may addict you to the sport of gliding!

Mayor Island

If you're looking for some excellent game fishing or diving action, Mayor Island is the place to go (about 42 km due north off Tauranga). The game-fishing season starts late in Dec. and runs well into April, when marlin, sharks, tuna, and yellowtail kingfish cruise the Bay of Plenty. The island also offers abundant marinelife in the crystal-clear waters, and great bush walks through *pohutukawa* forests to two colorful crater lakes (in ancient times the island was a center of intense thermal activity). There's a large variety of birdlife (listen for the distinct bell bird) and great swimming at Opo Bay at the southern end of the island. Take food and drink with you.

In summer, catch a trip to the island aboard the ***Te Kuia,*** departing Tauranga Marina at 0700, Salisbury Wharf at Mount Maunganui at 0730, returning at 1830 and 1900; adult $30 RT same day, child $15. You can also stay overnight (see below) on the island; a stopover RT ticket is adult $45, child $25. Get tickets at Coronation Pier, or Drum Tackle And Sports on Maunganui Rd., Mt. Maunganui. For current schedules call 789-685 (day), 779-235 (night). Another way to take to the water is via one of the **Reef Fishing Trips** (need your own fishing gear, bait, knife, bag for fish, lunch and drinks) which depart on Tues. and Thurs.; adult $25, senior $20, child $15. The **MV *Manutere*** also operates out of Tauranga and Mount Maunganui for **Family Reef Fishing Trips** on Wed. and Fri., departing Tauranga at 0800 and Mount Maunganui at 0830; adult $25, senior $20, child $15. Book at Tauranga Information Centre Salisbury Wharf, or call 754-165, after hours 443-072. You can also buy a ticket on the boat. The rest of the year, weather permitting you can get to the island via one of the many charter boat operators, but expect much higher prices.

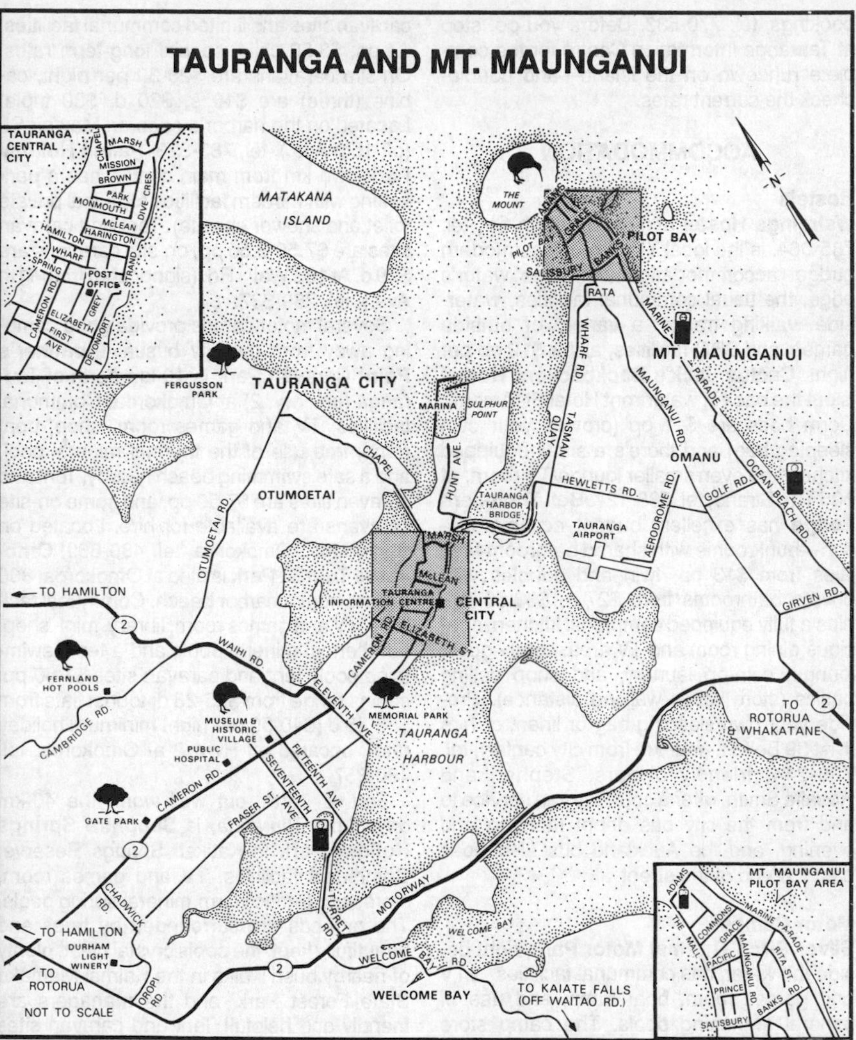

Tauranga Game Fishing Club has its headquarters on Mayor Island. They permit visitors to become Associate Members for $12 pp per day which includes use of club facilities, cabins, and the dining room at **Mayor Island Lodge.** Once you're a member, the OB (own sleeping bag) cabins are $18 s, $29 d; the VIP cabins (linen provided) are $30 s, $42 d. Most of the cabins have private bathrooms but no cooking facilities other than a community under-cover fireplace and BBQ; breakfast in the club dining room is $6-8, lunch $8, dinner $11-12.50 pp. Tentsites are only $3 pp. For accommodation and meal bookings, tel. 770-533. Before you go, stop at Tauranga Information Centre for the complete rundown on the island—and double-check the current rates.

ACCOMMODATION

Hostels

Waireinga Hostel at 171 Elizabeth St., tel. 785-064, is the local YH. It provides modern budget accommodation along the water's edge, the usual communal facilities, waterside walking tracks, a variety of outside games, and BBQ facilities, all for $12 pp per night. **Cactus Jack's Backpackers Hostel** is out the back of waterfront Hotel St. Amand. Dorm beds are $11 pp (provide your own sleeping bag) and there's a small equipped kitchen and even smaller lounge/TV room. At 105 The Strand, tel. 788-127. **Bell Travellers Lodge** has excellent budget accommodation—bunkrooms with shared bathroom facilities from $13 pp, twin and doubles with private bathrooms from $27 s, $33.50 d—plus a fully equipped communal kitchen, spacious dining room and TV area, comfy guest lounge, coin-op laundry, and shop selling basics (store within walking distance). Provide your own sleeping bag or linen, or hire it. At 39 Bell St. (four km from city center), tel. 786-344; friendly owners, Stephen and Rosalie Smith, offer a courtesy van service to and from the city bus depot morning and evening, and the Auckland bus also goes past the end of the street.

Motor Camps

Silver Birch Thermal Motor Park, right beside the water, has communal facilities, a TV and games room, boat ramp, and use of mineral swimming pools. The camp store stocks all the basic necessities; open in summer 0700-2100, in winter to 1900. Tent and caravan sites are $9 pp; cabins $28 s, $35 d; tourist flats with private facilities from $35 s $48 d; motel flats are $48 s, $55 d. Located at 101 Turret Rd. (extension of 15th Ave.) by Hairini Bridge, tel. 784-603. **Mayfair Caravan Park,** in the same area, offers tent and caravan sites and limited communal facilities; $7 pp, $3.50 child, special long-term rates. On-site caravans are $20-30 per night, cabins (three) are $10 s, $20 d, $30 triple. Located on the harbor's edge on Mayfair St. (off 15th Ave.), tel. 783-323. **Palms Holiday Park,** two km from main center, has a park setting with modern facilities (optional private toilet and shower ensuite). Tent and caravan sites are $7.50-8.50 pp, on-site caravans are $29 d. At 162 Waihi Rd. (signposted from 11th Ave.), tel. 789-337.

Several motor camps provide good camping away from the city bustle. **Plummer's Point Caravan Park** is 19 km north of Tauranga (up Hwy. 2) at Omokoroa. Communal facilities, TV and games room, shop, boat ramp, free use of the thermal mineral pool, and a safe swimming beach nearby. Tent and caravan sites are $7.50 pp, and some on-site caravans are available for hire. Located on Station Rd., Omokoroa, tel. 480-669. **Omokoroa Tourist Park** is also at Omokoroa, 800 meters from a harbor beach. Communal facilities, TV and games room, library, mini- shop, hot thermal mineral pools and a tepid swimming pool. Tent and caravan sites $7.50 pp; cabins range from $25-28 d; tourist flats from $35-45 d ($40-50 per night minimum holiday rate). Located off Hwy. 2 at Omokoroa, tel. 480-857.

Farther north, but well worth the 40-km drive from Tauranga, is **Sapphire Springs Holiday Park** in Katikati Springs Reserve. Communal facilities, TV and games room, store, and terrific warm mineral spring pools. The grounds are surrounded by trees and beautifully kept, the pools crystal clear, plenty of nearby bush walks in the Kaimai Mamaku State Forest Park, and the managers are friendly and helpful! Tent and caravan sites $8 pp; dorm beds $10 pp, cabins $25 d; on-site caravans $30 d. Located on Hot Springs Rd. at Katikati Springs Reserve, three km south of Katikati, tel. 490-768.

Hotels

Tauranga has its share of pricey hotels and motels which mainly cater to the influx of holidaymakers each summer. Refer to the *AA Accommodation Directory* for complete listings and rates. Two of the most reasonable and central hotels are the Hotel St. Amand and Tauranga Hotel. The pink and turquoise waterfront **Hotel St. Amand** has old-fashioned rooms with private bath or shower and tea- and coffee-making facilities (no TV or phone) for $35 s, $50 d; good meals are available in the hotel's Cooks Cove family restaurant. Located on The Strand, tel. 788-127. **Tauranga Hotel** has rooms from $33 s, $48 d; meals extra. Located on the corner of Harrington St. and The Strand, tel. 788-059.

FOOD AND ENTERTAINMENT

Coffee Shops

The Coffee Lounge is open 0800-1630 Mon. to Thurs. and 0800-2000 on Fri.; located in the BSB Arcade on Devonport Rd., tel. 787-895. **Cafe 100** is open 0930-1630 Mon. to Thurs., to 2100 on Thurs., and from 1100-1500 on Saturday; located on the lower level of Baycourt, downtown. **Sea Front Coffee Lounge** serves sandwiches and takeaways. Open Mon. to Sat., located on the corner of The Strand and Wharf Street. **Monterey Coffee Shop and Dairy** has a good selection of hot foods for lunch and afternoon tea, but breakfast is their specialty. Open weekdays from 0600 to late; located just past the 11th Ave. intersection, tel. 786-919.

Health Food

For a great sit-down meal or food to go, try **The Sunrise Natural Foods Restaurant:** hot dishes and salads, combination sandwiches, healthy cakes and desserts, and a large variety of teas. Open Mon. to Thurs. 0930-1630, Fri. 0930-1700; located at 10 Wharf St., tel. 789-302. **Healthworld** is a health food shop where you can buy ready-made summer salads, wholemeal scones, yogurt shakes, and freshly squeezed fruit juices to go, along with regular bulk health food supplies; located at 61 Devonport Rd., tel. 781-824.

Restaurants

Just Browsing Cafe Bar attached to the Hotel St. Amand on The Strand has a tempting variety of tasty Spanish tapas—seafood, savory meatballs, pasta, etc. Choose from a wide range of $3, $4, or $5 dishes. It's open Mon. to Thurs. 1100-2200, Fri. and Sat. 1100-2300. **Chimbleys Restaurant** is a reasonably priced steak bar with a BYO license; mains $10-14. Open from 1730 Tues. to Sat. nights; located on the corner of 10th St. and Cameron Road. Reservations recommended at tel. 785-627. **Hatter's** offers meals to eat in—but is mainly a take-out; family prices. Open Mon. to Sun. from 1100; located at 91 Devonport Rd., tel. 788-491.

Pub Meals

The local **Cobb & Co.** is at the Greerton Motor Inn. This popular restaurant (mains $10-15, good salad bar) and bar has live entertainment most nights, and even holds a children's talent quest on Sun. nights. Open seven days a week from 0730-2200; located on Cameron Rd., Greerton (southern Tauranga), tel. 788-164. The Hotel St. Amand operates **Cook's Cove,** an attractive family restaurant and bar (access from hotel lobby) with a comfortable atmosphere. Expect to pay $11-15 for a main course. Open seven days for lunch and dinner; located on The Strand, tel. 788-127. The Otumoetai Trust Hotel in western Tauranga operates a family-style restaurant, open Tues. to Sun. from 1600; located on Bureta Rd. in Otumoetai, tel. 62-221. **Te Puna Tavern** puts on an excellent bistro at a good price ($10-14), Mon. to Sat. 1200-1400 and 1800-2000, and features country singers on weekends; on Waihi Rd., Te Puna, tel. 25-705.

Takeaways

For good seafood and other tasty delicacies made fresh on the premises, head for **Brookfield Fish and Takeaways** in the Brookfield Shopping Centre. Open Tues. to Fri. 1000-1930, Sat. and Sun. 1630-1930, tel. 763-353. **Kentucky Fried Chicken** is on Cameron Rd., tel. 782-042. **McDonald's** is on the corner of 11th Ave. and Cameron. **Pizza Hut** is on Cameron, near Kentucky Fried.

Evening Entertainment

There's not much in the way of entertainment in Tauranga other than live bands playing in the local pubs on Fri. and Sat. nights. Some restaurants put on live entertainment cabaret style, but in general these places are expensive and have pain-in-the-neck dress codes. Always-lively **Cactus Jack's Saloon,** a "disco-free zone" in the Hotel St. Amand, has live music Mon. to Sat. nights, and plenty of Mexican influence—both in the decor and drinks. They specialize in tequila drinks, margaritas by the carafe, "Headless Mexicans" (Corona, tequila, and kahlua!), "Cactus Juice" (secret recipe), and Coronas. Other local recommendations include **Mid City Tavern** on the corner of Spring and Devonport for pub meals, and live music or a DJ (fussy dress standard); **Alexander's Nightclub** for music, dancing, and a rage on the town (another fussy dress standard) at 132 Devonport Rd., and **Harringtons** for pubbing and dancing (younger crowd) at 10 Harrington Street. **Te Puna Tavern** on Waihi Rd. hosts live country music every weekend; the **Otumoetai Trust Hotel** on Bureta Rd. has an "entertainment lounge bar"; and **The Greerton Motor Inn** on Cameron Rd. has live entertainment most weeknights. Find out what's on in the local newspaper or tourist papers, or drop in at the Information Centre.

Outdoor Entertainment

If you enjoy kicking back while taking in some local windsurfing and sailing action, head for the western harbor-side parks. **Kulim Park,** off Bureta Park in Otumoetai, or **Fergusson Park,** off Levers Rd. at Matua, are both popular windsurfer launch points. For some on-the-water action of your own, head for Tauranga Marina at **Sulphur Point.** There's also a swimming pool, skating rink, and a **Mini-Putt** golf course in Memorial Park (open 1000-2100; adult $2.50, child $1.75), or the **Greerton Indoor Swimming Pool** on Kiteroa St., open seven days.

Rafting

Two rafting operators are based in Tauranga. **Woodrow Rafting Expeditions** range from a 90-minute trip on the Wairoa for $48 to a three-day trip on the Motu for around $465 pp. Wetsuits, lifejackets, and helmets are provided. They also raft the Mohaka, Rangitaiki, Rangitikei, and Ngaruroro rivers—and just about anything can be arranged; tel. 762-628. **Wet And Wild Rafting Company Ltd.** also offers a variety of rafting experiences and white-water action—half-day trips for $48-65, day trips for $65-108, weekend combinations for $108-165, and two- to five-day overnighters for $249-495. For the complete rundown, tel. 784-093.

INFORMATION

The first place to head to for info on Tauranga and Mount Maunganui is the **Tauranga Information Centre** (the PRO) on The Strand, tel. 788-103; open Mon. to Fri. 0900-1700, and in peak summer period weekends from 1000-1400. They have brochures and tourist newspapers, and also give out info and take bookings for the boat ride to Mayor Island on the MV *Manutere.* For track and backcountry route info on the Kaimai Mamaku State Forest Park, call the Officer in Charge, Department of Conservation, Tauranga, tel. 787-677. **Tauranga Hospital** on Cameron Rd. can be reached at tel. 784-192. The **post office** is on the corner of Grey and Spring sts., tel. 782-999.

TRANSPORTATION

Getting There

If you're driving down the coast from the Coromandel Peninsula, take Hwy. 2 south from Waihi to Tauranga. The other highways that feed the towns along the Bay are Hwy. 1, followed by 29 from Hamilton to Tauranga, 33 from Rotorua to Mount Maunganui, 30 from Rotorua to Whakatane, and Hwy. 2 from the south. **InterCity** coaches connect Tauranga with Auckland, Thames, Hamilton, Rotorua, Whakatane, Opotiki, Gisborne, and just about anywhere you want to go. The **InterCity Travel Centre** is on the corner of Hamilton and Durham streets. (two blocks back from The Strand), tel. 782-839; open weekdays 0730-1745, Sat. 0730-1030 and 1130-1345, and Sun. 1515-1945.

If you're short of time but long on coin, **Air New Zealand** flies into Tauranga from Kaitaia, Whangarei, Auckland, Rotorua, Gisborne, and Wellington in the North Island; or from Blenheim, Nelson, Westport, Hokitika, Oamaru, Timaru, Christchurch, Dunedin, and Invercargill in the South Island.

Getting Around

By bus: The local bus companies are the **Bayline Company** located at 2 Sherson St., tel. 783-113, and **Black and White Buses,** also based on Sherson St., tel. 788-205. Call for schedules and fares. **By car:** The **AA Centre** is on the corner of Hamilton and Cameron roads. For regular taxi rides or sightseeing tours, **Tauranga Taxis** offers a 24-hour service. They're based on The Strand next to the Information Centre, tel. 786-086. **Budget** is at 55 Second Ave., tel. 785-156 or 786-766; **Hertz** is on Spring St., tel. 789-143; **Avis** is on the corner of First Ave. and Cameron Rd., tel. 784-204 or 783-911; **Rent-A-Dent** can be reached at tel. 781-772.

By air: Tauranga Airport is much nearer to Mount Maunganui than Tauranga. The only way to get there is to hitchhike or take a taxi; a taxi to the airport is about $12 OW. The **Air New Zealand office** is on the corner of Devonport Rd. and Elizabeth St., tel. 784-124.

MOUNT MAUNGANUI

SIGHTS

Mount Maunganui ("Big Hill"), at the mouth of Tauranga Harbor, is the rapidly developing port for the central North Island timber industry. It's just across the water from Tauranga via Tauranga Harbour Bridge (toll $1 per car). The 232-meter cone-shaped mountain (The Mount) that overshadows the town was originally an island, and the narrow sandbar that built up between the island and the mainland became the site of modern-day Mount Maunganui. The locals often affectionately call their city "The Mount," or just "Mount." Known for its wonderful surf beach and mellow vacation atmosphere, the town in winter becomes a city in summer when it attracts thousands of domestic vacationers to its sunny shores.

The Mount

Just by looking at its shape and position you can see how The Mount made an impressive Maori *pa* (fortified stronghold) in the 18th and 19th centuries. The old fortifications can still be seen, particularly on the southeastern side. Several tracks lead to the top of this volcanic peak, and the climb (about 1½ hours RT) rewards your effort with a magnificent, 360-degree, panoramic view. Other tracks run around the base of the mountain and up at several points; it takes about an hour to complete the circular route. A race to the top is held annually on New Year's Day and the record is about 20 minutes!

Beaches

The most popular beach in this area is Ocean Beach. The golden sands and sparkling surf stretch for about 15 km and can be reached from Marine Parade on the eastern side of Mount Maunganui, and from Papamoa Beach. Additionally, some small sheltered harbor beaches run along Pilot Bay, finishing at Salisbury Wharf on the western side of town.

Hot Saltwater Pools

Unique hot saltwater pools are found at the foot of The Mount, the only ones of their kind in the Southern Hemisphere. The saltwater comes from a 40-meter-deep bore, and when the water is first brought up from underground it's a sizzling 45 degrees C! Cooled to a still-hot 39 degrees before being pumped into the large main pool and several smaller pools, it's a great place to soothe aching muscles and tired feet! You can rent bathing suits and towels at the complex, and it's open daily from 0800-2200. Admission adult $2.50, child $1.50, private pools adult $3.50, child $2.50 for 30 minutes. Located off Adams Ave., tel. 55-880.

Flightseeing

For flightseeing over volcanic White Island (see "White Island," p. 172), Rotorua Lakes and Mt. Tarawera, and Bay of Plenty scenic trips, contact the Tauranga Aero Club at the Airport, Mount Maunganui. For current prices tel. 53-104, or after hours tel. 55-782.

ACCOMMODATION

Motor Camps

The two **Mount Maunganui Domain Motor Camps** have a terrific location surrounding the hot water pools at the base of The Mount (1 Adams Ave., tel. 54-471), and lie on both ocean and harbor beaches. Communal facilities, metered showers. Tent and caravan sites are $12-14 d; on-site caravans from $28-34 d.

Cosy Corner offers communal facilities, pool table and swimming pool, and is adjacent to the beach at Omanu, four km from The Mount Post Office. Tent and caravan sites are $8 pp; on-site caravans are $32 d. Located at 40 Ocean Beach Rd., Omanu, tel. 55-899 Tauranga. **Papamoa Beach Holiday Park** is situated farther away from the tourist bustle, 13 km southeast of town. Communal facilities, camp store, TV and game rooms, spa pools (extra charge). Tent and caravan sites are $8 pp ($16 minimum per night for caravan sites from the end of Dec. to the end of Jan.). Located adjacent to Papamoa Beach at 535 Papamoa Beach Rd., tel. 420-816 Tauranga.

Hotels And Motels

Anchor Inn offers rooms from $22 s, $40 twin with private facilities. Meals are also available. Located on the corner of Maunganui Rd. and Rata St., tel. 53-135 Tauranga. **Hotel Mount Maunganui** on Girven Rd., tel. 55-089, has rooms with private facilities, TV, phone, fridge, tea- and coffee-making facilities, from $88 s or twin. There's also a swimming pool and a restaurant. The **Blue Haven Motel** at 10 Tweed St., tel. 56-508 or 54-817, is always popular. Located only a short walk from the beach, each unit has full cooking facilities, telephones, video machines, and the rates start at $50 s, $60 d; summer rates from $60-71.

FOOD AND ENTERTAINMENT

The usual coffee shops and lounges are scattered throughout downtown but if you're looking for a health food shop, call in at **Harvest Health Foods**—they make great muesli (or granola) fresh daily. For homemade baking enjoyed inside or outside in the sunshine, try **The Old Cottage**. It's open every day and specializes in breakfast. Located at 373 Maunganui Rd., The Mount. The **Quality Inn** puts on a la carte meals and inexpensive bistro meals 1200-1400 and 1830-2200; located on Girven Rd., The Mount, tel. 55-089. **Lady Di's** offers a la carte dining, and a good Sunday smorgasbord. It's fully licensed and also has dining and dancing—the local raging spot; located at 317 Maunganui Rd., check current prices at tel. 55-567. The predominantly green **Palms BYO Restaurant** has interesting creole and Thai dishes along with its regular menu, with entrees starting at $7, mains ranging from $17-19, desserts from $7-9. It's on the corner of Maunganui Rd. and Pacific (at the roundabout), tel. 52-539; open Tues. to Sat. from 1800.

Perhaps the most enjoyable restaurants are those along Marine Parade, but be forewarned, you pay for the great beach views! If you feel like a splurge try **Oceanside** on Marine Parade at the base of Mount Maunganui for seafood; open for lunch between

1200-1400 and dinner from 1800. Sierra Bianca is also on Marine Parade (terrific views), open Mon. to Fri. 1200-1400 and Mon. to Sat. from 1800. On Sat. nights dining and dancing is the entertainment, tel. 54-897. Local pubs have the usual live bands on weekends, but for good-value entertainment and an active nightlife head for Rotorua!

More Information

The **Mount Maunganui Information Bureau** on Salisbury Rd. by the old ferry wharf, tel. 55-099, is run by enthusiastic volunteers who staff the center "for the love of The Mount." In summer it's open Mon. to Fri. 1000-1500, Sat. 1000-1200, the rest of the year on weekdays from 1000-1300, Sat. 1000-1200.

For the **police,** tel. 53-143; the **Mount Medical Centre** can be reached at tel. 53-073. **Girven Road Chemist** is reached at tel. 52-777. For emergencies check the window of the info bureau—all pertinent info is usually posted. The local **post office** is at the back of an arcade, one shop from the BNZ Bank on the main street before you reach The Mount.

WHAKATANE

The main reason to go to Whakatane is to enjoy the sunshine and beaches, to go rafting on the Rangitaiki River (see "Rafting," p. 26), or flightseeing over White Island (see "White Island," p. 172), an active volcano. It's also the closest large town north of Urewera National Park (see p. 215). A good quiet place in winter to rest up after strenuous hiking in the park (as an alternative to year-round crowded Rotorua), but in summer Whakatane also tends to become crowded with sun-seeking vacationers. The town is not a particularly notable place for dining or evening entertainment—again, in Rotorua you'll find plenty of everything.

Sights And Local Action

When you're downtown, don't miss the impressive **Wairere Waterfall** behind the Commercial Hotel, Mataatua Street. **Whakatane Museum** contains displays of Maori artifacts, the lifestyle of early Maori and European

Soar over The Mount and get hands-on experience in a glider from Tauranga Airport.

settlers, a history of the district through black-and-white photos, and a New Zealand book collection. Open Mon. to Fri. 1000-1600, weekends 1330-1600, admission adult 50 cents, child 20 cents; located on Boon St., tel. 85-498. **Gardiner Gallery** is another interesting place to spend some time viewing and/or buying Maori artifacts, crafts, collectibles, and out-of-print and rare books; it's at 12 Domain Rd., open six days, admission free, tel. 70-613. Whakatane is also known for its cardboard manufacturing mills. **Whakatane Board Mills** is across the river off Hwy. 2 north (cross Mill Bridge); free tours start at 1030, Mon. to Friday. Call them direct at tel. 71-899 for more info.

The best-known surf beach, **Ohope Beach,** only six km from Whakatane, attracts surfers and fishermen year-round, holiday-makers by the hordes in summer, and hikers in search of great coastal views. The harbor at the end of Ohope Beach has safe swimming, good windsurfing, fishing, and locals claim it's particularly noted for shell fishing. If you're looking for some on-the-water action, call in at the info center to find out who is currently offering fishing trips (usually starting at $20 pp). Or go for an exciting jet boating trip on the Matahina Dam and the Rangitaiki River ($45 adult, $28 child) with **Aniwhenua Jets,** 6 Kohai St., tel. 85-414, or a white-water rafting trip with **Whakatane Raft Tours** on the Wairoa, Rangitaiki, Whirinaki, or Moto rivers (from $58 pp to $495 pp for a four-day trip), tel. 87-760. Another way to take to the water is by kayak—book a scenic three-hour trip through the Information Bureau, or call 70-569.

White Island

White Island lies about 50 km north of Whakatane, at the northern end of the Taupo-Rotorua volcanic faultline. This is an excellent active volcano because of its intense thermal activity. Originally named by Capt. Cook in 1769 because of the shroud of steam that surrounded the island, today it continues to belch steam, noxious gases, and toxic fumes into the atmosphere. Occasional eruptions send up huge clouds of ash that can be seen from the mainland, weather permitting. Geysers, fumaroles, holes of sulphuric acid, and boiling water pools lie within the crater, best enjoyed from a safe distance—like from the sky!

Sulphur used to be mined on the island until an explosive landslide in 1914 killed all the miners and wiped out the mining settlement. Several other mining attempts were made, but due to the unpredictable and violent nature of the island, all were abandoned. Despite the lack of fresh water and toxic fumes, parts of the island are covered by *pohutukawa* trees and inhabited by quite a variety of birdlife. Gannets, red-billed gulls, and petrels seem to thrive in this strange environment and have made their breeding grounds on the island. Now a private scenic reserve, no regular boat trips go out to White I., but it's possible (though expensive) to charter boats from Whakatane, Tauranga, or Mount Maungaui. The *Island Cat* cruises from Whakatane and Tauranga and includes White I. on the itinerary; from $55 adult, $30 child, which includes a BBQ lunch. For flight-seeing over White I. contact Pegasus Aviation at Tauranga Airport; tel. 53-104, after hours tel. 55-782. You can also land on the island by helicopter, or fly over by Bel-Air plane—get more info at the Whakatane Information Bureau.

Accommodation

Whakatane Family Motor Camp has the usual communal facilities, TV lounge and games room, swimming pool, and hot spa pool (charge). Grassy tent and caravan sites are $6.75 pp; cabins from $20-23 d. It's on McGarvey Rd., tel. 88-694.

There are several good motor camps at Ohope Beach, but if you're going on toward Rotorua you may enjoy staying at **Awakeri Hot Springs.** About 16 km from Whakatane on the main highway to Rotorua (tel. 49-117), it has the usual motor camp facilities but the added plus of warm mineral swim baths and hot mineral spa pools (extra charge). Tent and caravan sites are $7 pp; cabins with cooking facilities are $30 d; tourist flats are

local waterfowl

$40 d, but note the minimum charge during holiday periods.

The **Commercial Hotel** provides reasonable rooms for $25 or $35 s, $40 twin, $50 or $55 d; some have showers, all have handbasins. Located on The Strand, tel. 87-399. The **Bay Private Hotel** provides B&B for $35 and $40 depending on the room, and there's a TV lounge. Dinner is available by arrangement. Located at 90 McAllister St., tel. 86-788. If you're looking for a nice motel with good dining facilities, try **Chatswood Manor** at 34 Domain Rd. (by McAllister St.), tel. 70-600. Units are $71.50, $82.50, or $104.50 s, d, or twin. Facilities include a swimming pool, two spa pools (some of the units have their own spa), sauna, and BBQ.

Food, Entertainment, And Information

For the best dining at reasonable prices, or for a large variety in evening entertainment, save your money and head straight for Rotorua—it's only 90 km away and it's all there! In Whakatane **Marshalls Coffee Shop** is an excellent place for breakfast, morning or afternoon tea, and lunch. They have a great selection of tearoom-type fare, a salad bar, and a daily special blackboard menu; breakfast is $4-9, light meals are $7-13. On the corner of Boon St. and The Strand, tel. 87-315. **The Wedgewood,** middle of The Strand, has inexpensive good-value family-style meals (lunch $4-7, dinner $10-13). Other local recommendations include **Heidi** on The Strand (great spot for lunch), and for more expensive dining out, **The Buccaneer** on The Strand, and **The Reef** at the Heads. Depending on weather conditions, you can also go out on the ***Island Cat*** BBQ dine and dance cruise from 1800-2230 for $38 pp. Make reservations at tel. 24-236 or through the Information Bureau.

For more info on Whakatane, including what's on, call in at the **Whakatane Information Bureau** on Boon St. (signposted off The Strand), tel. 86-058. The **Department of Conservation office** is on Commerce St., as is the **public library.**

Transportation

InterCity connects Whakatane with Tauranga ($18 OW), Gisborne ($36 OW), Rotorua ($17 OW), Auckland ($43 OW), Napier ($54 OW), and Wellington ($72 OW). You can make coach reservations with any accredited travel agent but you need to buy a ticket 72 hours in advance to guarantee a seat. **Whakatane Travel Centre** is at 209 Pyne St., tel. 88-208, open Mon. to Fri. 0730-1730 and Sat. 0800-1200.

Whakatane Airport (intriguing architecture!) is on Aerodrome Rd. about 10 km north of town; the only way to get there is to hitch or take a taxi (about $11 OW). **Air New Zealand** flies to Auckland, with connections to Whangarei, Wanganui, and Wellington on the North Island and all major centers on the South Island. The **Air New Zealand** office is at Budget Travel on The Strand, tel. 88-399; open at the airport when a flight is leaving or arriving. **Bell-Air Aviation** operates scheduled air services direct to Auckland twice a day Mon. to Fri. ($105 OW), and scenic flights from $18-85 pp depending on the length of the flight. For more info, call 86-656. **Hertz Rent-A-Car** is at 105 Commerce St., tel. 86-155. **Budget** can be reached between 0600 and 2200 at tel. 86-399.

ROTORUA

This resort city is alive with thermal activity. All sorts of natural attractions abound throughout the region, but the best-known features are spectacular geysers, steaming cliffs, hot springs spurting from the ground, bubbling pools of boiling mud, and soothing mineral hot pools. Steam seems to waft out of every drain, crack in the pavement, and hole in the ground, and the ever-present but soon-unnoticed smell of rotten-egg gas (hydrogen sulphide) permeates the atmosphere for many kilometers in all directions. (You often hear people calling this area "Rotten-rua," but this isn't wise when locals are within earshot!) Rotorua is an ideal base for exploring both the immediate thermal wonders and the surrounding area with its contrasting natural features: magnificent bush-fringed lakes, icy-cold springs, crystal-clear trout streams, and mighty forests.

History

The Rotorua region has been inhabited by Maori since the 14th century. Originally a wild and swampy wasteland dotted with steaming pools and mud holes, the Maori had been using the healing properties of the mineral hot pools for 500 years before their benefits were recognized by Europeans in the late 1870s. Fifty acres of land containing the "healing springs" were given as a gift to British government representatives by the original Maori landowners, on which the early township of Rotorua was built. The Government Garden Reserve was developed into a fashionable spa resort and sanitarium, where victims of the mighty Mt. Tarawera eruption of 1886 were treated. In addition to the area's healing qualities, its recreational value prompted rapid development into a tourist attraction.

Go, Go, Go!

The Rotorua region is also a center of Maori culture, with a great deal of New Zealand native art, architecture, song and dance, and colorful evening entertainment to offer. Tourism is Rotorua's principal industry; this makes the city expensive if you plan on visiting all the major attractions. However, some of the natural attractions are still free and, despite the year-round crowds, the unpredictable and volatile atmosphere that seems to seep up from beneath your feet sets Rotorua apart—it's one of the unique areas of New Zealand that shouldn't be missed!

SIGHTS

THERMAL

Rotorua is situated about midway along a volcanic faultline that runs from White Island in the Bay of Plenty to Mount Ruapehu in Tongariro National Park. The most active thermal areas have been developed in the name of tourism, and these are safe as long as you stay on the well-defined footpaths (hold on to the kids at all times!). More commercial thermal areas other than those listed below are found south of Rotorua on the main road to Taupo, and north off Hwy. 30 to Whakatane. Only a couple of the less spectacular hot spots around town have not been commercialized and are still free—in Government Gardens near Polynesian Pools, and at Ohinemutu along the shores of Lake Rotorua. Some of Rotorua's natural thermal energy has been tapped through artesian-type bores and other methods for central and hot-water heating by local hotels, motels, and some homes. The Maori continue to use it for

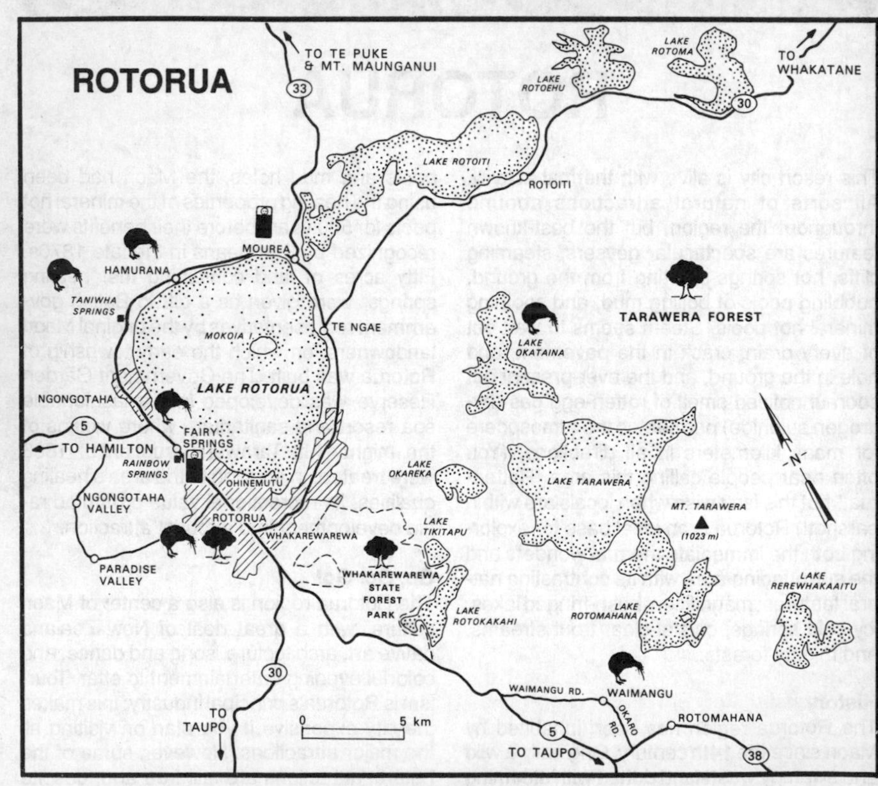

cooking and heating as they have done for centuries, and you can see some of their methods at Whakarewarewa (see below).

Polynesian Pools

Polynesian Pools are on the site of the first public bath house built in Government Gardens (see "Around Town" below) in the 1880s. They enclosed the spring Te Pupunitanga, and used the soft waters of Whangapipiro Cauldron, later renamed the Rachel Pool. You can still see Rachel Spring boiling away at 100 degrees C along with several other steaming holes in the ground between Polynesian Pools and Tudor Towers—not walled off in any way, still free, fascinating viewing! The original baths were replaced by the Ward Baths in 1933 and the Aix Wing was added, offering hot air massage. The baths were completely renovated in 1972 and turned into the present-day Polynesian Pools. The complex continues to boast several hot mineral spring pools, private pools, public pool (live poolside jazz on Sun. nights 1930-2130), and Aix Massage. Admission (plus GST) is $5 adult, $2.50 child; a sauna is $5.50, massage $30 by appointment; costumes and towels can be hired for a small fee. Open 1000-2300 daily. Located on Hinemoa St. by Government Gardens, tel. 481-328.

Whakarewarewa

The best-known and closest thermal resort to the city, only three km south, even the locals who can pronounce the word just affectionately call it "Whaka." Unfortunately, admission costs continue to increase each year, but it's such an intriguing place that it earns a position on the "must-see-at-least-once list." The literal translation of Whakarewarewa is "to rise up," "soar," or "float." Originally the meanings referred to the uprising of a war party from Wahiao, but today it's still appropriate in reference to the area's thermal activity.

The main entrance to Whaka is through the **New Zealand Maori Arts and Crafts Institute,** where young Maori are taught the techniques of their ancestors; their works of art are on display seven days a week, but the carvers can only be seen at work on weekdays. Entrance to the Institute (only) is free. Once inside the thermal area (admission charge, see below) you'll see amazing geysers gushing skyward, hot-water springs, eerie boiling mud pools, and steaming silica terraces. Pohutu Geyser is particularly impressive but showtimes are totally unpredictable. After seeing the thermal attractions you can wander past the accurate replica of a *pa,* watch Maori women demonstrate their methods of utilizing natural steam for cooking, and take in a 45-minute lunchtime Maori Cultural Concert (daily at 1215). Guided tours leave every hour on the hour from 0900 to 1600, but you can also cruise around the place on your own; allow about an hour.

one of the many geysers in the region

Admission to the thermal area and model *pa* is $7.50 adult, $4 child; the lunchtime Maori Cultural Concert is $8 adult, $2.20 child, family concessions available. Open daily 0830-1700 (last tour at 1600). The main entrance to Whakarewarewa is located on Hemo Road. Follow Fenton St. south out of the city onto Hemo Rd., from which it's well signposted. The local bus service runs past the entrance, and many of the guided tours around Rotorua include Whaka. If admission is beyond your budget, head for Geyserland Resort Hotel on Fenton St. for a drink in the hotel bar. For the price of a beer you get a tremendous view of the geysers from a distance—the bar and terrace overlook Whaka, and on summer evenings after the thermal area is closed to the public, you can watch Maori kids dive from Whaka's steaming white terraces into the hot pools far below. (See "Food and Entertainment" for more cheap ideas.)

Waimangu

Waimangu Thermal Valley is another large and exciting active thermal spot. It's located at the southern end of the huge area devastated by the 1886 Mt. Tarawera Eruption, about 26 km southeast of Rotorua. Take the Valley Walk (about three km) down through beautiful bushland where thousands of deafening cicadas crowd the trees in summer while you view Southern Crater, Emerald Pools, and the steaming blue-green lake of Waimangu Cauldron. The lake occupies the crater of the 1917 explosion (the last minor eruption was in 1973), and although its temperature averages 50 degrees C, it's claimed to be the "world's largest boiling lake." Surrounded by smoldering rocks, steaming bush, and disguised by the mysterious patterns created by surface steam, the large cauldron is at the same time majestic and eerie.

Farther along you'll view Cathedral Rock and the colorful orange, yellow, and red decomposing cliffs, and cross Hot Water Creek where the water temperature varies from 47-65 degrees C! A worthwhile 59-step sidetrack leads up to the pale blue-gray steaming waters of Inferno Lake and Ruaumoko's Throat. Backed by tall smoldering cliffs, the water gurgles out of rock crevices around the lake, and steam cushions the surface. The main trail continues past the slimy yellow Iodine Pool with its hissing steam vents, Lake Rotomohana with the Mt. Tarawera crater in the distance, and the colorful silica formations of Warbrick Terrace. At the end of the Valley Walk, a bush trail (alive with native birds) leads down to Lake Rotomohana (1.8 km—largest of the 1886 craters) where you can catch a launch cruise (extra price) to the western shores, passing the famous Pink and White Terrace sites destroyed in the big eruption. Alternately, a minibus or truck cruises the entire track fairly regularly, giving free rides back up the hill to the tearooms.

Even with average fitness it takes a couple of hours to see everything. Benches have been strategically placed at lookouts and at regular intervals, and if you get tired you can always catch the minibus back. Admission (plus GST) for the Waimangu Valley Walk alone is $6 adult, $3 child; for the walk plus launch trip it's $13.50 adult, $6.75 child, family tickets available; pay in the tearooms (tel. 489-137) at the main entrance. To get there by car take Hwy. 5 south out of Rotorua, turn left onto Waimangu Rd., and follow the signs.

Gray Line does a half-day tour to Waimangu including transportation to and from Rotorua, a guided tour of the valley, and the first launch cruise for $37 adult, $18.50 child, family tickets available; book at tel. 460-640. The coach departs from the Mount Cook Travel Centre on Amohau Street.

Hell's Gate

Aside from 10 hectares of ferocious and uncanny volcanic activity (can be seen in about 30-45 minutes), Hell's Gate has unique hot Kakahi Falls, which at 38 degrees C plummets down steaming and hissing through lush natural bush—an unforgettable sight. Open daily 0900-1700, admission is $6 adult, $2 child, and guidesheets are available in seven languages. It's located 16 km from Rotorua at Tikitere, on Hwy. 30 to Whakatane, tel. 453-151.

Waiotapu

Waiotapu (tel. 485-637) is perhaps the most colorful of all the thermal areas, but also the farthest away from Rotorua—about 30 km

Tudor Towers, Government Gardens

along the highway toward Taupo. Follow the tracks past stunning Lady Knox geyser which shoots water and steam up to 21 meters into the sky at 1015 every day, Bridal Veil Falls where water cascades down white, red, yellow, and green silica terraces, the lacy Pink and White Terraces, boiling mud pools, craters, hot and cold pools, steaming fumaroles, the orange-edged Champagne Pool, and cliffs of sulphur stalactites, just to mention some of the best-known highlights! It costs $5.50 adult, $2.25 child to wander through the park, $6 adult, $3 child to also see the geyser do its stuff (add GST). Get your ticket at the reception, tearooms, and souvenir shop building. To get there take the highway south to Taupo as far as the Waiotapu Hotel. Turn left opposite the hotel and continue for about one km on the loop road.

TOWN SIGHTS

Government Gardens

If you enjoy walking, head for Government Gardens on the eastern side of town, where many attractions lie within a relatively small area. Enter through the big arches to see steaming thermal hot spots set incongruously amongst orderly flower gardens and lawns, plus a fantastic orchid house, the Rotorua Croquet Club, and the huge sports center, **The Sportsdrome,** behind the Tudor Towers Building (see below). Don't miss **The Orchid Gardens** building where hundreds of beautiful multi-colored orchids are displayed in landscaped surroundings (the floodlit night tour is spectacular), along with a captivating water organ (fountains of colored water that dance to music) and Microworld, a gift shop, and the Greenhouse Teagarden (see "Food"); open daily 1000-2030, admission is $6.60 adult, $2.20 child (plus GST).

Rotorua Museum And Art Gallery

The Bath House is the original Tudor Bath House building where people with joint afflictions and skin diseases came for various treatments using the soothing local volcanic mud and mineral water. Today it houses the Rotorua Museum and Art Gallery, the licensed Tudor Restaurant and Top of the Towers Cabaret (see "Food and Entertainment"), and in the basement there's a fascinating display of equipment that was used in conjunction with mud bath therapy in this building between 1906 and 1966.

To know more about the Volcanic Plateau, the mighty eruption of Mount Tarawera in 1886, and the Pink and White Terraces—a famous tourist attraction of the 19th C. destroyed in the eruption—Rotorua Museum is the place to go. Don't miss the fascinating historical photo collection. The Maori section has some intricately carved greenstone (New Zealand jade) ornaments that "have no equal in all of Polynesia," along with some beautiful feather cloaks and many other objects from the past. You can also see a large display of mounted native New Zealand birds, and upstairs, a replica of a settler's cottage furnished with a variety of appropriate colonial objects. The art gallery features New Zealand art and sculpture, and special exhibitions. All sections are open daily, Mon. to Fri. 1000-1600, Sat. and Sun. 1300-1630, and holiday weekends 1000-1600. Minimal admission charge, child or Rotorua resident free.

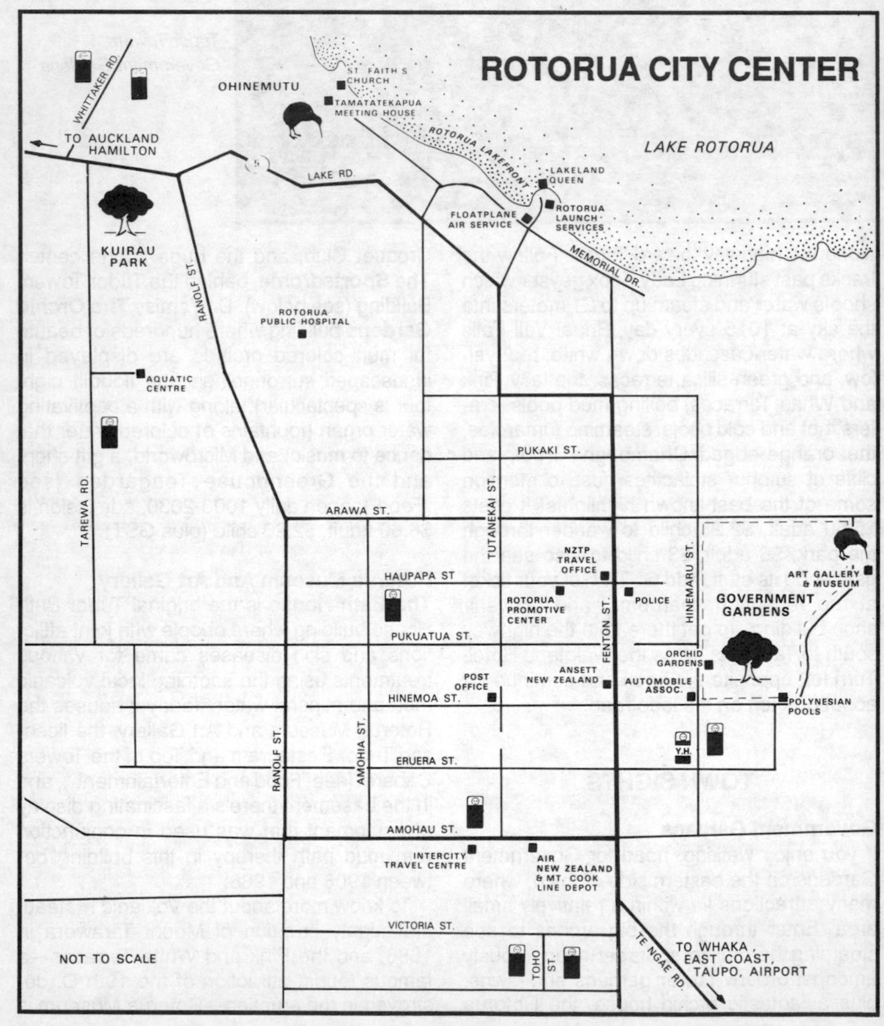

The Lakefront

This is a good place to head to for on-the-water activities and fishing guide info—check out the Lake Facilities Guide Board at the lake front, or for more detailed fishing info, make a call on the free "fish phone." If you want to see the lake at your own speed you can also hire two- or four-seater speed boats from **Lakefront Boat Hire. Rotorua Lakes Self Drive Budget Boat Hire** says it all! Hire an aluminium boat (fishing gear available) for a day or an overnight camping trip; for more info call 461-249 or A.H. 461-613. For a scenic cruise over to the legendary Mokoia I. in the middle of Lake Rotorua, see **Rotorua Launch Services.** Their scenic cruise is offered daily between 1000-1200 and 1400-1600, their day-excursion cruise 1000-1600. Take your swimsuit, food, and drink. Buy tickets onboard or book at tel. 479-852. In peak holiday times they run special lunch, BBQ, and moonlight cruises. Also up the street from the lake front you can hire single and tandem bicycles.

Cruise the lake in old-fashioned steamer style on the ***Lakeland Queen.*** Departing from the lakefront, this luxurious paddle steamer does several cruises a day (year-round but on demand in winter)—the morning tea cruise from 1000-1130 or afternoon tea cruise from 1430-1600 for $15 pp, the lunch cruise from 1230-1330 for $25 pp, and a dinner cruise from 1900-2230 for $35 pp. Phone for reservations at 486-634 or 471-766. Tickets are available at the on-site ticket office at the lake.

Flightseeing

Sightseeing by float or land plane is always a blast. If you can afford it, it'll really add a third dimension to this fascinating thermal area. **Floatplane Air Services** operates a large variety of scenic flights from the lakefront. The most reasonably priced are the 10-minute "Town and Around" flight from $30 adult, $20 child, and the 30-minute "Mt. Tarawera, the Sleeping Giant" flight from $75 adult, $50 child. However, you can also fly to Orakei Korako, Taupo, over active volcanic White I., or combine floatplane/jetboat adventures or floatplane/Lake Rotorua fishing adventures; for more info, call 484-069, after hours call 478-172. **Geyserland Airways** also has a range of flights to suit all, starting at $35.50 adult for a 15-minute flight over Rotorua, Whaka, Blue Lake, and Green Lake; office at Rotorua Airport, tel. 456-749, or book through the NZTP Travel office.

St. Faith's Church, Ohinemutu

For a spectacular flight you'll never forget, not to mention picture-perfect views, go for a flight in one of **White Island Airways'** open-cockpit, brightly colored, antique Tiger Moths. You'll be appropriately attired in a flying jacket or suit, helmet, and goggles, then it's off into the wild blue yonder. For an exhilarating flight over the city it's $75, over the city and Blue and Green lakes $88 pp, an aerobatic flight $99 pp (go on, take the challenge!), around the lakes $110 pp, Mount Tarawera crater (with an optional loop and role) $135 pp, or the ultimate—the one-hour Grand Tiger Tour for $295 pp (if you want to do aerobatics, ask before you set off!). Colin,

Tamatekapua Maori Meeting House, Ohinemutu

the owner/pilot, also has a twin-engine De Havilland Dove available for longer flights to White I. and Ruapehu. For more info call Colin or Christine at tel. 459-832, after hours 455-493, or drop by their office at Rotorua Airport.

The Helicopter Line, operating from the the heliport on Te Ngae Rd. (one km from city center), serves up a variety of heli-seeing flights starting at $56 pp for a quick flight over the city. The sky's the limit on the kind of flights (and costs!) available. Another alternative way to get a bird's-eye view is to take an early morning balloon flight with **Balloon Safaris,** floating off just after dawn for approximately one hour in the air (depending on wind and weather) and landing for the traditional champagne and croissants. Allow four hours total time; from $165 pp. Book through the NZTP Travel Office.

Ohinemutu

The Maori village of Ohinemutu is at the northern end of town along the shores of Lake Rotorua, an easy walk from the lakefront. Here you'll find steaming holes in the ground, pipes sticking out of house foundations that belch steam away from the house, and the awesome sound of boiling water coming from deep below (a free thermal spot!). On the shorefront stands the beautiful Maori Anglican **St. Faith's Church.** Completely decorated with Maori art, woven wall panels, and intricate carvings, it features a particularly effective etched-glass window at the far end. Services are held at 1000 and 1900 on Sun., and Holy Communion at 1000 on Wednesdays. A stone's throw from the church is the **Tamatekepua Meeting House,** another good place to admire the beauty of Maori carvings inlaid with *paua* shell. If it's open, admission is free; if closed, be sure to take a peak in through the windows. A Maori concert is held here nightly at 2000 (tel. 82-269 or 86-456 for current prices and reservations), and concert tickets can be bought at the door from 1930. To get there by car, take Lake Road north, turn right on Ariariterangi Rd., then right at the lakefront, following the shoreline to the village.

Scenic View

If you have a car (or enjoy long torturous bicycle rides to build up stamina), you can head up Mount Ngongotaha for great views. This 760-meter mountain overshadows Rotorua and has a lookout at the top—but too many trees block the view. The best 180-degree views are from the lookout at Aorangi Peak Restaurant (see "Food"), which is on

:he way up, almost at the top. To get there 'rom town, take Lake Rd. to the Fairy Springs Rd. intersection and continue straight ahead onto Clayton Road. Continue along Clayton Rd. (past Edmund Rd. and Thomas Crescent) and turn right into Mountain Rd. which winds slowly and steadily up the mountain to the summit. The alternate way to score a great view is to take a ride up the mountain (from Fairy Springs Rd.) on the **chairlift** for $1.50 pp, or take the chairlift and exciting one-km high-speed **luge** down; one ride $3.50. The other rapid way to get down is via the popular 600-meter Skyline ride, hanging from a wire by a harness!

Hillside Herbs

These fascinating gardens grow a large variety of herbs, aromatic shrubs, and perfumed roses. Talented herbalist Lorraine Nowland started her herb business many years ago in a caravan. Now it's grown into a several-acre garden. Browse through the gardens, or take in a demonstration or two—the friendly salespeople show how to cook with herbs (and you can sample the finished works of art), how to make potpourri, and how to use healing herbs. Guided tours happen every half-hour. In the large shop (where inhaling is a joyful experience), you can buy dried herbs, fragrant soaps, potpourri, live plants, and a large assortment of great- smelling gifts at reasonable prices. Admission $4 adult; open seven days a week from 0830-1700, tel. 479-535. Located at 166 Fairy Springs Rd., the main road north out of Rotorua.

Agrodome

Anyone interested in sheep, sheepshearing, or just having a good laugh should head for one of the shows at the Agrodome. Inside the large auditorium are fine woolly representatives of all the different breeds of New Zealand sheep, tied up along the sides for petting, admiring, or making funny faces at. During the show, each well-trained sheep runs in turn up the stairs and onto the platform while its breed and characteristics are described. When they're all gathered center stage, a talented sheepdog is put through his paces. Vocal and whistle commands have the dog barking with delight as he scampers from sheep back to sheep back (much to the obvious disgust of the woolly stars of the show), and then a sheep from offstage is sheared by a professional sheepshearer. After the indoor show the audience moves outside for a more realistic sheepdog demonstration. Showtimes are 0915, 1100, and 1430 daily; admission adult $6, child $2.75.

stars of the Agrodome show

To top off this amusing show, try the Agrodome Tearooms where delicious savory and sweet treats—steak and kidney pies and cream-filled desserts at average to slightly high prices (but worth it)— are available from 0900-1600, and the "special of the day" is served from 1130-1400. The Agrodome shop sells high-quality wool and sheepskin products—often quite a bit cheaper than city prices. You can catch a bus out but it leaves the Travel Centre only once a day at 1000. Several of the scenic tours include the Agrodome as one of the attractions. The Agrodome is located at Riverdale Park on Western Rd., tel. 474-350 Ngongotaha; from town take Fairy Springs Rd. (Hwy. 5) toward Hamilton, turn right on Western Rd. (after Ngongotaha Stream) and follow the yellow AA signs.

Get Lost!

Looking for fun and frustration? Trying to lose someone? Head for **Te Ngae Park 3D Maze** on Te Ngae Rd. (heading toward the Whakatane Hwy., it's several kilometers beyond the airport, about a 10-minute drive from town), tel. 55-275. This carefully constructed three-dimensional maze has 1.7 km of paths to get lost on, and drinks and ice cream available—that is if you ever get out! It's open seven days a week; admission adult $3, child $1.50.

Tours

If you don't have your own transportation, no worries! You can see many of Rotorua's main attractions, and some of the lesser-known sights, on one of the many tours available. Call in at the NZTP Travel office, peruse all the current brochures, and compare prices. Four of the more unique tours designed for small groups of the young and the young-at-heart are: **Carey's Caper's Volcanic Tour** to all the thermal highlights (take a swimsuit and towel, sneakers, camera, and lunch; $45 pp includes admissions with a 10% discount for Travelpass, Kiwi Coach Pass, or Travelcard if paid by cash to driver); **Nomad Treks** to on- and off-the-beaten-track scenic highlights with several hours of walking in native bush (take warm clothes, rain gear, sturdy footwear, and lunch; $35 pp, tel. 459-375); **Doug's,** an unforgettable 4WD tour including swimming in a hot thermal river with waterfall, and "skiing" in Mt. Tarawera crater ($40 pp); lots-of-fun half-day 4WD safaris (small groups) to **Mount Tarawera** with Murray Thompson ($38 pp, and highly recommended by a reader) and two-day safaris to the **East Cape** (book through the NZ Outdoor Adventure Centre, tel. 480-623).

InterCity operates morning tours to city highlights for $33 pp, afternoon tours for $21 pp, and full-day tours for $45 pp. For more info contact the InterCity travel Centre at tel. 481-039. **Great Sights** runs daily guided tours to Whaka, Rainbow Springs, and the Agrodome from $21 pp (book at the NZTP Travel office, tel. 485-179). **Gray Line** has a Historic Tour for $19, a Thermal Valley Adventure tour for $37, and their Rotorua Spectacular for $39. You can also go white-water rafting with **The Rafting Company** (starting at $58 pp for the shortest trip on the Wairoa; tel. 480-233 for info and bookings); trout fishing with Bryan Colman (tel. 487-766); cruising to Mokoia I. on the MV *Ngaroto* (tel. 479-852); and horse riding (by the hour or day) through prime farmland and lush native bush at **The Farmhouse** (Sunnex Rd., tel. 423-771). Are we having fun yet?!

TROUT SPRINGS

Rainbow Springs, Fairy Springs, And Rainbow Farm

If you'd like to see just how large a rainbow or brown trout can grow, this is the place! Amongst a wide range of beautiful native ferns and natural bush, a trail leads to many pools where the trout are segregated by age and size. Here you can observe fish (and duck) frenzy by throwing in "trout food" (sold in the souvenir shop). Fairy Springs Walk continues through the bush past numerous waterfalls to Fairy Springs, where 24 million liters of crystal-clear water gush out of the ground per day! Apart from all the pools teeming with trout are underwater viewing ponds, aviaries, deer and wild pig enclosures, a kiwi house, tearooms, and shop (good prices on some of the tourist paraphernalia) within the grounds. Admission is $7.50 adult, $3 child. Rainbow and Fairy springs are open 0800-1700 daily; located four km north of Rotorua on Hwy. 5, tel. 481-887. Many of the guided tours from town include these springs in the Rotorua itinerary. Also near Rainbow Springs is the cobblestone walkway leading under the main highway to **Rainbow Farm.** Here you can walk through the farm and take in a show (with plenty of audience participation) featuring past and present farming methods, animals, sheep mustering and shearing; shows at 0900, 1030, 1300 (by arrangement only), 1430, and 1600.

Hamurana Springs

These are Rotorua's largest springs, located along the northern shores of Lake Rotorua. The 30-minute track follows Hamurana Stream through beautiful grounds, passing all kinds of native waterfowl, peacocks, and both white and black swans. Crossing the stream by swing bridge, the trail passes through a stand of California redwoods, and on to the spring itself where an amazing 4.5 million liters of incredibly clear water pours out per hour! At the main entrance is a nine-hole golf course, souvenir shop, and tearooms. Admission $4 adult, $2 child. Located 19 km from downtown; take Hwy. 5 north out of town and follow the road around Lake Rotorua, passing Rainbow, Fairy, and Taniwha springs along the way. (If you're into fly-fishing, there's an excellent spot across the road, at the point where Hamurana Stream enters Lake Rotorua. Many of the "big ones" are caught here. It's also a good place to meet local anglers who'll divulge the latest hot fishing tips.)

WHAKAREWAREWA STATE FOREST PARK

Exotic Greenery

This 3,830-hectare park lies southeast of Rotorua. Adjoining Whaka thermal reserve, it includes most of the older part of Whakarewarewa Forest, one of New Zealand's first exotic forests. Tree planting was begun right after the eruption of Mt. Tarewera in 1886 to renew the attractiveness of the Rotorua region, and to regain tourism that was lost when the main local tourist attraction—the Pink and White Terraces—was destroyed. Many species of trees were tried, but the most successful species were European larch, Corsican pine, Douglas fir, and eucalyptus species, and the easiest to grow was the Radiata pine from California. In parts of the forest you'll also come across small areas of other surviving species such as California redwoods, and the two main areas of native forest are found adjoining Lake Tikitapu and north of Kakapiko. Planting was completed in 1916. Today the plantation is mainly managed for timber production, but the many tracks through lush native ferns and stately trees, lake views, and attractive picnic spots have successfully put the forest on the map as a great recreational area. There's little thermal activity within the forest park boundaries—just one boiling mud pool on the southern side of Pohaturoa.

Trails

Eight well-marked walks are available in the park. They range from short one- to two-km trails at rest areas and picnic spots to the 33-km "Around the Forest Park Walk" which takes about eight hours. You'll find the most people at Redwood Memorial Grove (where a map shows the main tracks and features of the park), Long Mile area (and info center), Blue and Green lakes lookout, and Green Lake picnic area—these areas are accessible by car. The more natural parts are reached only on foot via the internal tracks and roads. Before setting off on any of the longer hikes, drop by the **Park Information Centre** on Long Mile Rd. for valuable info, and free maps and trail guides. Access to the park is available from Hwy. 5 (Rotorua-Taupo Rd.), Tarawera Rd., and Long Mile Rd. behind the Forest Research Institute. For more info, call the Forest HQ, tel. 481-165.

OKATAINA WALKWAYS

Eastern Walkway

Lake Okataina ("Lake of Laughter" from Maori legends) is one of the most beautiful, unspoiled lakes in the area—a paradise for outdoor enthusiasts. Deep blue and lined with sandy beaches and sheltered coves, it's backed by native bush, tropical-looking tree ferns, *pohutukawa* trees, and magnificent fuchsia flowers. It's also well stocked with trout!

The eight-km Eastern Walkway is the most popular as it weaves in and out of and up and down (steep and tricky in some places) the rocky shores of the lake, allowing fairly constant access to the water. To get to the start of the track at Tauranganui Bay (toilet facilities and picnic area) at the northern end of Lake Okataina, take Hwy. 30 toward Whakatane, turn right at Ruato onto lush Okataina Road. You can catch an InterCity bus from Rotorua to Ruato but there's no public transportation down Okataina Road. The track finishes at Humphries Bay on Lake Tarawera. Taking about three hours OW and returning along the same route, the track is for those with average fitness and can be done in sandshoes or tennis shoes in dry weather, hiking boots in wet weather. Take food, water (don't rely on streams), warm clothing, and stay on the main track.

Western Walkway

The Western Walkway doesn't follow the lakeshore but provides magnificent views of the Bay of Plenty, Coromandel Range to the north, and some offshore islands from the 758-meter Whakapoungakau Trig. This track climbs steadily, is steep and rugged in places, and suits the more experienced tramper. Old logging roads branch off the main track so you need to concentrate on following the markers. The 22.5-km track starts at Ruato on Hwy. 30 and finishes at Miller Rd. at Lake Okareka (toilet facilities), taking up to eight hours OW. Cut off about 4.5 km by starting at the Education and Recreation Centre (toilet facilities) off Okataina Road. Take food and water, warm clothing, and wear sturdy shoes in dry weather, boots in wet. Prearrange transportation from the end of the track.

ACCOMMODATION

HOSTELS

YHA Hostel

The large **Colonial Inn** hostel has bright sunny rooms, thermal heating in winter, and even a luxurious thermal plunge pool! It's a cheerful place to hang your hat or stow your pack for a few days, and the hostel's central location makes it easy to walk to many of the city attractions; $14 pp. Located on the corner of Eruera and Hinemaru sts., across from the Hyatt Kingsgate Hotel, tel. 476-810.

Budget

The friendly managers of **Ivanhoe Lodge** offer no-frills accommodation in individual rooms or cabins at budget rates. Communal facilities, huge kitchen and living area, and a TV lounge, games room, in-house video, and hot pool. Open 24 hours a day, come and go as you please. It's a good place to meet fellow travelers in a relaxed atmosphere, and it's popular—many stay on for days, and spare beds go fast. Cabins are $12.50-17.50 pp, supply own linen; rooms with linen provided are $17.50-20.50 pp (including GST). They also rent bicycles by the day. Located at 54 Huapapa St., tel. 486-985.

Popular **Thermal Lodge** at 60 Tarewa Rd. (northwest side of town, tel. 470-931), virtually backs on to the Aquatic Centre. Choose from two- or four-bed thermally heated bunk rooms (single $16.50, shared twin $13 pp), or grassy tent and caravan sites ($6 pp), with the usual communal bathroom, kitchen (they loan you a set of dishes and cutlery), and laundry facilities, a TV/recreation room, and

a feathered friend at Ohau Channel Lodge

office store (handy one-meal quantities). Linen hire available for $4.50 pp; mountain bikes for $12 a day, bicycles $6.

CITY MOTOR CAMPS

Many motor camps are located around the shores of Lake Rotorua, but only a few are central to the city. A couple of the closest are caravan parks with a limited number of tentsites or none at all, but reasonably priced cabin accommodation is an alternative. If you definitely want to camp out, head out of Rotorua along Hwy. 30 or Hwy. 5 and follow the lake. Most of the motor camps around Lake Rotorua have tentsites, and hitching shouldn't be too much of a problem as the roads get plenty of traffic.

Rotorua Thermal Motor Camp
This motor camp is a bit of a hike with a heavy pack from downtown (or a five-minute bus ride), but only a short walk from one of the main attractions, Whakarewarewa Thermal Reserve. Communal facilities, game room, camp store, heated swimming pool, and thermal plunge pools. Tent and caravan sites are $7.50 pp. Bunk room beds (supply own sleeping bag) are $9 pp. Standard cabins are $24-32 d, tourist cabins from $30 d. Located at the south end of Old Taupo Rd. opposite the golf course, tel. 463-140.

Cosy Cottage Motor Camp
On the northwestern side of town, a short stroll from the lake, excellent Cosy Cottage Motor Camp has communal bathroom (piping hot showers!), kitchen (fully equipped) and laundry facilities, large TV and game room, a hot soothing mineral pool, camp store, and plenty of tent- and caravan sites and cabins. Sites are $15 d; backpacker cabins are $22 s, $24 d; thermally heated cabins with cooking facilities and fridge from $29 d; tourist flats (two bedrooms and private bathroom, kitchen, and lounge) from $45 d. Located on Whittaker Rd., off Lake Rd., tel. 483-793.

Lakeside Motor Camp
This camp, by the lake as the name implies, has tent and caravan sites, reasonably priced cabins, and tourist flats, plus the usual facilities, a camp store, and a large indoor mineral pool (extra charge). Tentsites are $7 pp, caravan sites are $16 d; cabins with cooking facilities and TV start at $32 s or d; tourist flats (private bathroom and cooking facilities) start at $42 d; completely self-contained beachfront chalets are $46. Located on Whittaker Rd., tel. 481-693.

A LITTLE FARTHER AFIELD

Ohau Channel Lodge And Tourist Cabins
If you're into fly-fishing, or just nature for that matter, head for this first-class motor camp on Hwy. 30, about 17.5 km from Rotorua. It's at the northern end of the lake, on the narrow strip of land that separates Lake Rotorua from Lake Rotoiti. The camping area lies along the shores of both Ohau Channel and Lake Rotorua. It's a great spot for trout fishing, attracts hordes of New Zealand anglers in summer, and is the kind of place where you're likely to find entire duck and black swan families nonchalantly sunning themselves on your tent flap! It's very relaxed, a good place to meet people, and gets some of the best views of Rotorua sparkling across the lake at sunset. Hot private spa pools cost extra; buy your fishing license, supplies, and equipment at the camp store, and if you don't

know how to angle properly, they also operate fly-fishing schools. Tentsites from $5.50 pp; caravan sites $7.50 pp; cabins range from $28-44 (one to four persons), $38-44 (one to six persons), and tourist flats from $36-48 d (add GST to all prices). Located on Hamurana Rd., tel. Okere Falls 761 or 730.

BED AND BREAKFAST

Eaton Hall Guest House
If you feel like a bit of pampering and want a central location Eaton Hall is the place to go. Grace Dorset, the friendly owner, not only supplies comfy beds and a delicious breakfast, she also makes you feel right at home. Each room has a handbasin, and tea- and coffee-making facilities. Communal facilities and TV room. A two-course dinner with fresh vegies and fruit from the garden, homemade jams, etc., is also available for $12 if previously arranged. Bed and Continental or cooked breakfast is $34 s, $55 d or twin. Non-guests can also drop in for breakfast ($5-7) between 0730-0930—handy for hungry hostelers next door. Located at 39 Hinemaru St., opposite the Hyatt Kingsgate Hotel, tel. 470- 366.

Trescoe International Guest House
This guest house, run by Leon and Doreen Maitland, has a comfortable homey atmosphere. Each thermally heated room (d, twin, or triple) has its own handbasin and tea- and coffee-making facilities. You'll also find a washer and thermal drying room, TV lounge, and hot mineral pool. Rates are $36 s, $55 d or twin, $66 triple which includes a Continental or cooked breakfast. Sightseeing tours can be arranged. Located at 3 Toko St., tel. 489-611 (courtesy car from bus depot or airport if requested).

Morihana Guest House,
Kerry Lee will also make you feel at home at 20 Toko St. (tel. 488-511). Use of a hot mineral pool, comfy TV lounge, communal bathrooms, tea- and coffee-making facilities, and off-street parking, a bed (lots of singles, all rooms with handbasins) and Continental breakfast is $34 s, $52 d, $66 t—$5 pp extra for a "damn good cooked breakfast!"

Spa Tourist Hotel
Good budget accommodation in individual rooms with handbasins and own tea- and coffee-making facilities are offered at this private hotel; B&B is $22 pp, cabins are $12 pp. Located at 69 Amohau St., opposite the Travel Centre, tel. 483-486.

PRIVATE HOTELS

Many private hotels and plenty of motels are scattered around the city (get listings from the NZTP Travel Office). Deluxe hotels (all the major chains—**Hyatt Kingsgate, THC Rotorua International Hotel, the Rotorua Travelodge, Geyserland Resort Hotel, Princes Gate Hotel**) are also well represented in Rotorua. Refer to the *AA Accommodation Directory* for full listings and current rates. Those listed below are the most reasonable small private hotels.

Australia Inn
This cozy hotel provides rooms with private bathroom facilities, tea and coffee-making facilities, color TV, and the use of two thermal mineral pools; $38.50 s, $55 d (plus GST). All meals are available. Located at 15 Hinemoa St., tel. 488-516.

Ngongotaha Motor Inn
You can find this locally recommended hotel in the small town of Ngongotaha, eight km from Rotorua on the western side of the lake. Communal TV lounge, guest tea and coffee kitchen, breakfast and dinner also available in the family restaurant. All rooms have private facilities for $27.50 s, $55 d; tel. 474-195.

The Personal Touch
If you prefer to stay in a private home, meeting some of Rotorua's most hospitable residents, call **Home Stay, New Zealand** at tel. 55-978. Maureen Steen can answer all of your questions and make bookings for your

stay in a local home. She can arrange for meals, full bar facilities, billiard room, spa pool, laundry service, transportation, accompanied sightseeing tours, and hunting and fishing trips. A private bedroom (s or d) with ensuite, rural and lake views from your own balcony, and all meals, starts at around $100 pp. However, you can just stay for bed and breakfast for $40 pp, or dinner, bed, and breakfast for $60 pp.

FOOD AND ENTERTAINMENT

EATING OUT

Tearooms

Greenhouse Tearooms adjacent to the Orchid Gardens in Government Gardens serves snacks, Devonshire teas, and light meals from $7.50-10.50 in a lush plant-filled environment—a good place to go for lunch after oohing and aahing over all those spectacular orchids. **The Agrodome's Farmhouse Tearooms** have tasty savories, light lunches, and a variety of cream-filled pastries and desserts, at average to slightly expensive prices. Open daily from 0900-1600; the "special of the day" is available from 1130-1400 and goes fast. In the evenings it becomes a steak house restaurant. On Western Road, Ngongotaha (see "Sights" for directions). **Polynesian Pools Tearooms** is in the Polynesian Pools complex by Government Gardens. Open daily from 1100-2200, serving coffee and morning and afternoon teas. **Dianne Dairy and Deli** has a selection of filled rolls and pastries, along with the usual deli products. Open every day from 0630-2300; on the corner of Arawa and Tutanekai streets. **Picnic Coffee Lounge** serves breakfasts weekdays from 0700, at 36A Eruera Street.

Pub Meals

The **Cobb & Co. Restaurant** has satisfying main courses for around $9-15, and it's fully licensed. Open seven days a week from 0730-2200. Located in the Grand Establishment, Hinemoa St., tel. 482-089. **Fenton's Tavern** whips out bistro-style meals for $13.50, Mon. to Sat. between 1200-1515 and 1800-2115. At the corner of Fenton and Amohau streets., tel. 477-056.

The Westbrook Tavern is recommended for roasts and grills with an average main course costing around $14; open Mon. to Sat. 1200-1400, Mon. to Wed. 1800-2030, Thurs. to Sat. 1800-2100, on Malfroy Rd., tel. 470-687. **Lake Tavern** overlooks Ohinemutu Village and the lake, and a main course costs about $10-12. Open Mon. to Fri. 1200-1400, Mon. to Sat. 1800-2100. **The Homestead** has light meals and grills, with an average main course around $12-15. Open Mon. to Sat. 1200-1400, Mon. to Thurs. 1800-2100, Fri. and Sat. 1800-2130. Entertainment by a local band on Thurs., Fri., and Sat. nights. Located on Fairy Springs Rd., tel. 480-665.

Good Food, Good Prices

The Cabbage Tree Cafe is open seven days from 1000-1400 and 1800-2200 (tel. 463-121), offering an intriguingly different menu (especially tasty vegetarian, spicy Mexican, and assorted Asian dishes). Nothing is over $10 and it has a BYO license. Ask locals for eating-out suggestions and trendy **Floyd's Cafe** is almost always mentioned. Open Mon. to Fri. for lunch from 1100, for dinner Mon. to Sat. from 1800, main courses (chicken, spaghetti, steak, lamb, seafood, and homemade desserts) range from $12-17 pp and it has a BYO license. It's on Haupapa St., tel. 470-024.

The Bushman's Hut specializes in seafood and wild game, is fully licensed, and has dancing on Sat. nights. A main course averages $10.50-18 pp, with many dishes around $12. Open Mon. to Sat. from 1800. Located at 167 Tutanekai St., tel. 483-285. For good Chinese food at around $15 a main course, head for the **Hoo Wah Chinese Restaurant.** Open from 1800; at 82 Eruera St., call for reservations, tel. 485-025 or 486-366. **Pizza Hut** has quite a choice of other dishes too, from around $10 pp. A jumbo pizza is $20. Open and licensed seven days a week from 1130; at the corner of Lake Rd. and Tutanekai St., tel. 486- 926.

Fast Food And Takeaways

Baker Boy's four shops sell delicious hot bread, meat pies, rolls, and pizzas to go. On Tutanekai St., Pererika St., Fairy Springs Rd., and at the Te Ngae Shopping Centre. **Kentucky Fried Chicken** sit-down section, drive-through, or takeaway, is open every day; at 20 Amohau St., tel. 482-877. **Ohinemutu Fish and Chips** also has hamburgers, chicken, oysters, and scallops to go. Open daily until 2000. At 47 Lake Rd., tel. 479-331. Another good place for takeaway fish is **Ollies Fish** on Fenton Street. **McDonald's** is on the corner of Amohau and Fenton sts., tel. 479-541; open Sun. to Wed. 1000-2200, Thurs. 1000-2230, Fri. and Sat. 1000-2400.

Splurge

For Continental flare, try **Gazebo** at 45 Pukuatua St., tel. 481-911—pricey, but popular with locals out for a bit of a splurge. Open Tues. to Fri. 1200-1400, Mon. to Sat. from 1800. Expect to pay at least $10-21 for a main course (veal, beef, chicken, pork, lamb, baby salmon). Another restaurant that gets good local support is **Lewishams** at 115 Tutanekai St., tel. 481-786. It's open for lunch on Mon., Wed., Thurs., and Fri., for dinner every night but Tuesday. For a really first-class evening (throw your traveler's cheques to the wind!), delicious food, and excellent service, **Laura's** at the Hyatt Hotel is another local rave. **Geyserland Hotel** at Whakarewarewa has a great family-priced smorgasbord on Sundays between 1800-2100 from $26 pp adult, $13 child, and a la carte or buffet dinners Mon. to Fri. 1800-2100. Enjoy Whaka's thermal attractions while you eat.

Aorangi Peak Restaurant is aptly described as "Rotorua's restaurant complex in the sky." Fantastic views of the city and Lake Rotorua from Mt. Ngongotaha—and you pay for them! The Tarawera Room serves snacks and drinks from 1000-1600, light lunches (small salad or sandwich) from 1200-1400. If you just want a drink and the view, head for Ihenga's Look-Out Lounge and Cocktail Bar after 1730. The elegant Mokoia Room Restaurant does lunch from 1200-1400, dinner from 1830; expect to pay from around $16 just for a main course from the a la carte lunch menu, and at least $36 pp from the dinner menu (not including wine)—allow more than $100 for dinner for two. Reservations are necessary in the evenings, and most people dress for the occasion. Located on Mountain Rd., tel. 470-045.

the start of the hangi: *opening the steam oven at Geyserland Motor Hotel*

The Colonel's Retreat, in Little Village at Whakarewarewa, features an international dinner menu, fully licensed. A main course is around $14. Dressy. Call for reservations at tel. 481-519. Another good place for an expensive but worthwhile evening is **The Landmark.** This fully licensed restaurant specializing in New Zealand lamb, seafood, and steaks is located in a lovingly restored Edwardian-style house. Live background music. Expect to pay around $25 pp for a main course only. Open for lunch Mon. to Fri. from 1200-1400, and dinner daily from 1800. Dress up for this one too. Located on Meade St., at the Whaka end of Fenton St.; reservations are essential, tel. 489-376.

PAINTING THE TOWN RED!

The Maori *Hangi*

Rotorua is the best place in New Zealand to enjoy a traditional Maori *hangi* or feast, together with a Maori concert. This particular Rotorua event shouldn't be missed. The traditional *hangi* uses an earth oven. A fire built from native timber heats a layer of stones. Onto the hot stones goes a layer of leaves, then the food, then more leaves (nowadays muslin cloth replaces this second layer). Water is thrown on just prior to the food, the oven is closed with a layer of soil, and the steam, flavored from the wood below, cooks the food. The boxes around natural steam vents in Whaka village are used by the Maori villagers to cook all their food in this manner. They've been successfully using this unique method for well over a hundred years, and no ill effects are caused by cooking in the sometimes sulphurous water and steam. The several large hotels in Rotorua that put on a *hangi* are better able to control the steam in their ovens, and can open them up to put delicate foods in later so that everything is cooked to perfection. The traditional lamb and pork take about three hours to cook, seafood 30 minutes, vegetables *(kumara* or sweet potato, a basic food of the Maori people, pumpkin, and various others) 30 minutes, and traditional steamed pudding about an hour in the controlled steam ovens.

Quite a few of the large hotels in Rotorua put on a *hangi* and Maori concert several times a week throughout the year. Most *hangis* (including the concert) range from $30-39 pp. Concerts alone are in the $9-15 pp range. In summer, you can always find one somewhere. **Geyserland Motor Hotel** puts on a good *hangi* and Cultural Concert Party on Mon., Wed., and Fri. nights from Aug. to May, more often during the peak summer holiday period; $30. The hotel overlooks Whaka thermal reserve, so you get the added bonus of an active and steamy view while you tuck in to some of the best food New Zealand has to offer. Afterward a group of talented Maori singers and dancers present a traditional Maori concert, which includes the fierce war dances of the men, the soft fluent *poi* dances of the women, and some beautiful singing. The *hangi* starts at 1745. The concert alone starts at 1915. Geyserland Hotel is on Fenton St. overlooking Whaka; reservations necessary, tel. 482-039.

The **THC Rotorua International Hotel** on Tyron St. puts one on every evening Oct. to March, only on Sun. evenings April to September. The feast starts at 1830, the concert at 2030, $33 pp for both or $12.50 for concert, tel. 481-189 for reservations. **The Rotorua Travelodge** has daily feasts and concerts starting at 1930 for $33 pp; call 481-174 for day, current price, and reservations. **The Hyatt Kingsgate** *hangi* is $36.50 pp; at **the Sheraton** it's also $39 pp, concert only is $25 pp.

Maori Cultural Concerts

These feature local Maori groups in traditional costume, singing and dancing. In addition to the hotels (usually $9-15 pp), in summer you can attend a Maori concert at 1900 at the **Municipal Concert Chamber** on the corner of Haupapa and Fenton sts. or alternative venues; call 485-912 or 486-591 for current info. Very entertaining cultural concerts are also held in the **Tamatekepua Meeting House** in the Maori village of Ohinemutu, along the shores of Lake Rotorua. Concerts start at 2000, tickets can be bought at the door from 1930; call 483-492 or 486-456 for the current price.

Maori cultural group in concert at Geyserland Motor Hotel

Cabaret

Club Tudor Towers presents a cabaret in the evening with live music and entertainment between 2145-0300 (cover charge); light meals also available. Located in Government Gardens off Hinemaru St., call 485-833 for more information.

Live Music

Many of the pubs, taverns, and hotel bars around town sponsor live bands on Thurs., Fri., and Sat., nights, usually with a small cover charge. To find out who's on and where, pick up one of the free tourist papers or ask at the NZTP Travel Office (see "Information" below).

OTHER PRACTICALITIES

SERVICES

Help!

For a **police, fire, or ambulance emergency** phone the operator, tel. 111. For a **doctor** or **dentist** call St. John Ambulance, tel. 486-226. The **Urgent Pharmacy** is at the lake end of Tutanekai St., tel. 484-385. The **Police Station** is on Fenton St., tel. 480-009.

Disabled Services

For free wheelchair service in the central city, drop by the depots at Odeon Pharmacy at the lake end of Tutanekai St., or the David Meek Pharmacy, City Plaza. Call for more info at tel. 489-777 or 484-417. Or call in at the Red Cross on Rangiuru Street.

Business

All **trading banks** are open Mon. to Fri. from 1030-1600, and traveler's cheques and travel facilities are available. Some banks are open 0930-1630 Mon. to Thurs. and have extended hours on Fri. nights. **Shopping hours** are generally 0830-1700 Mon. to Thurs., till 2100 for "late-night shopping" on Fri., and from 0900-1200 on Sat. mornings. The central **post office** is on the corner of Tutanekai and Hinemoa sts., tel. 473-899. Open Mon. to Thurs. 0830-1730, Fri. 0830-2000. **Public telephones** take one 20-cent coin, and for toll calls you need a handful of coins and operator advice. A **24-hour petrol station** is at the junction of Lake and Old Taupo roads; however, you can find several scattered around the city.

Good Buys

Looking for good-quality original souvenir sweatshirts and T-shirts at reasonable prices? **Kiwi Klothes,** at 308 Tutanekai St. (tel. 485-930), downtown, is *the* place to go. Say "Hi" to Brian and Kaye, the friendly owners, unofficial New Zealand ambassadors who genuinely enjoy chatting with visitors. Another must-stop is **Pauline Mossman's shop.** Here you'll find stunning hand-knitted wool and mohair sweaters with unique designs and textures, and locally produced quality greenstone jewelry all at much better prices than you'll find elsewhere. Delightful owners too! It's at the corner of Te Ngae Rd., Margeurita, and White sts. (from downtown, take Fenton St. onto Te Ngae Rd. then continue to the first street on the right—the shop is next to Farmlands, across the road from a mini race track), tel. 479-697; open Mon. to Fri. 0900-1700, Sat. 0900-1300, and after hours by appointment.

Laundromats

At the **Wash House** you can do your laundry yourself or have it done for you, including camping and tramping gear. Open seven days 0700-1900 at 89 Fenton St., opposite the police station. Self- service **Laundrette** is open Mon. to Fri. 0900-1630, Sat. and Sun. 1000-1400. Located on the corner of Amohau and Amohia sts., opposite the InterCity Travel Centre.

INFORMATION

The NZTP Travel Office is the best place in town for information—on Rotorua and the entire country. The friendly staff can advise you on everything; open daily from 0830-1700, located on the corner of Fenton and Haupapa sts. opposite the Civic Theatre, tel. 485-179. Ask for the latest *Rotorua Gateway To Geyserland* sightseeing map which has all kinds of useful info on the back. The **Visitors Information Centre** at the Rotorua Travel Centre on Amohau St., tel. 481-039 (AH 481-036), is also open seven days. Lots of brochures and free information for the asking.

The **Automobile Association** is another good place for travel info and maps (free for members). Open Mon. to Fri. 0830-1700; on the corner of Hinemoa and Hinemaru streets. Call for the 24-hour breakdown service, tel. 483-069. **Rotorua Public Library** is at the north end of Fenton Street. The local newspaper is *The Daily Post,* and the free tourist paper, the *Thermalair,* is available from the NZTP Travel Office, info centers, and hotels and motels. **Church services** are listed in the Sat. edition of the *Daily Post.*

Whakarewarewa State Forest Park Information and Visitor Centre is open daily from 1000-1600, located off Long Mile Rd., tel. 483-839. The **Department of Conservation office** sells detailed topographical maps (from around $7); on the corner of Tutanakei and Pukaki streets.

TRANSPORTATION

Getting There

The two main roads into Rotorua are Hwy. 5 which runs north to Auckland and south toward Taupo, and Hwy. 30 which runs east toward Whakatane and Tauranga. The highways converge on Fenton St., one of the main city streets. You can either fly or take a bus in from anywhere in New Zealand. The **InterCity Travel Centre and Depot** on Amohau St. is the depot for InterCity and local bus service; tel. 481-309. **Mount Cook Line** operates from the Air New Zealand building, also on Amohau Street. Rotorua Airport is located nine km northeast of town off Hwy. 30 (see "Air" below).

Bicycle

In summer you can find bicycle hire outside the NZTP Travel Office on Fenton St., or go for a ride in a comfy bike-wagon with someone else doing all the work! The **Youth Hostel,** on the corner of Eruera and Hinemaru sts., hires out standard, three-speed, or 10-speed bicycles with tour maps to scenic attractions supplied—see the warden for more info or call 476-810 or 476-506. **Ivanhoe Lodge** hires out bicycles by the day for $11 for guests and non-guests. **Thermal Lodge** also hires out ordinary bicycles for $6 and mountain bikes for $12. **Lady Jane's Ice Cream Parlour** hires bikes, tandems, 10-speeds, and mopeds at the lake end of Tutanekai St. tel. 479-340.

Car

Avis is at 116 Fenton St., tel. 488-184; **Hertz** is at 77 Amohau St., tel. 484-081; **Budget Rent-A-Car** is at 215-217 Fenton St., tel.

485-767 or 488-127. For a **taxi** call Rotorua Taxis, tel. 485-079.

Bus

InterCity Travel Centre and Depot, on Amohau St., tel. 481-039, is the place to go for both local and ongoing bus info and timetables, and general information. Open Mon. to Sat. 0800-1730, Sun. 0800-0930 and 1230-1730. Local buses service the western suburbs of Western Heights, Kawaha Point, and along the lake to Ngongotaha (ask for bus timetable no. 1; fare $2 peak, $1.60 off-peak 0900-1500); to the southwestern suburbs of Fordlands and Mill Hostel (timetable no. 2); to the south to Whakarewarewa ($1.50 OW peak, $1 off-peak), and to the east to Otaramarae, Okere, and Owhata (timetable no. 3). By Platform 8 is a taxi stand. From Rotorua you can catch an InterCity coach to Auckland ($32 OW), Waitomo Caves ($50 OW), Gisborne ($49 OW), Wairakei, Taupo ($17 OW), Napier ($37 OW), Hastings, Tauranga, Wellington ($55 OW), Hamilton ($17 OW), Whakatane ($17 OW), Wairoa, Opotiki ($28 OW), Waikaremoana ($21 OW), Taihape, Palmerston North and Wanganui (connecting service). InterCity also does half- and full-day sightseeing tours, with a 25% discount for all Travelpass holders.

Mount Cook Line Depot is in the Air New Zealand building on Amohau St., tel. 477-451. The company has direct coach service south to Taupo (connecting coach north to Auckland), Turangi, and on down to Wellington (eight hours).

Air

Rotorua Airport is nine km northeast of town along Hwy. 30; connections are provided by Rotorua Taxis (tel. 485-079) from the City Mini-Bus Terminal, Air New Zealand office at 38-42 Amohau Street. A shuttle bus leaves the city 55 minutes prior to each departure, the airport 10 minutes after each arrival, taking approximately 35 minutes as it stops at most city hotels; $8 pp adult OW, $4 child, tel. 462-386. At the airport you'll find offices for **Avis, Hertz, Budget,** and **Thrifty** car rentals, a cafeteria, a souvenir shop, and a free phone for local calls. Outside is a taxi stand; $12 into city center.

Air New Zealand flies from Rotorua to Auckland, Tauranga, and Wellington in the North Island, and Blenheim, Christchurch, Dunedin, Hokitika, Invercargill, Nelson, Oamaru, Timaru, and Westport in the South Island. Book flights at the **Air New Zealand office** at 38-42 Amohau St., tel. 87-159. **Ansett New Zealand** also flies out of Rotorua for Wellington, Christchurch, Dunedin, Glentanner, Queenstown, Te Anau, and Wanaka. The Ansett office is at 113 Fenton St., tel. 470-599, toll free (09) 376-950.

Several companies operate **scenic flights** out of Rotorua Airport, and most provide courtesy transportation to and from the flights if requested. For more flightseeing info, call **White Island Airways,** tel. 459-832 or (AH) 455-493, **Geyserland Airways,** tel. 456-749; **Volcanic Wunderflites,** tel. 456-079; or **The Helicopter Line,** tel. 476-086. Also see "Flightseeing" under "Sights."

Guided Tours

InterCity does a large variety of guided tours around Rotorua, and to the thermal or scenic attractions in the surrounding area. They range from morning tours for adult $33 pp, child $16, and afternoon tours for adult $21, child $10, to full-day tours for adult $45, child $22 (add GST to all fares). All tours depart from the InterCity Travel Centre on Amohau St. at 0845; call 481-039 for more info, or pick up a brochure from The Travel Centre or NZTP Travel Office. **Gray Line** also has a wide variety of tours to suit all tastes and budgets, departing from the NZTP Travel Office (also hotel/motel pickups by arrangement); for more info and 24-hour bookings, tel. 460-640. (Also see "Tours" under "Sights.")

TAUPO

THE LAKE

Lake Taupo, also known as Taupo Moana ("Sea of Taupo"), is the largest lake in New Zealand. Located exactly in the middle of the North Island, the crystal-clear, bright blue waters of this inland sea cover a 616-square- km area—about 42 km long and 27 km wide. White pumice beaches and sheltered rocky coves line its shores, vast pine forests cover much of the surrounding plains and ranges, and at the southern end are the rugged Kaimanawa Mountains and the impressive volcanic peaks of mounts Tongariro, Ngauruhoe, and snowcapped Ruapehu (see "Tongariro National Park," p. 247).

Lying along the same faultline as Rotorua, the Taupo region is also geothermally active. The lake itself is a volcano, its base and surroundings involved in several gigantic eruptions 330,000, 20,000, and 1,850 years ago. During those explosions, pumice, ash, and rock debris were hurled high into the atmosphere, pyroclastic flows charred and devastated vast areas of the landscape, and the resulting crater eventually filled with water to become Lake Taupo. It's a great chance to swim or sail in a volcano! The remains of volcanic activity can still be seen in the pumice beaches, coves of "floating rocks" around the lake, and the colorful steep cliffs along Western Bay that were part of the ancient volcano.

At the northeastern end of the lake lies the town of Taupo. Though not a fancy resort, Taupo still attracts large numbers of vacationers year-round to take advantage of its excellent lake fishing for rainbow and brown trout, sailing and watersports, spectacular lake views, and local geothermal attractions. At the southern end of the lake is the town of Turangi, originally built to accommodate the workers on the Tongariro Power Development scheme. Don't judge the town itself on

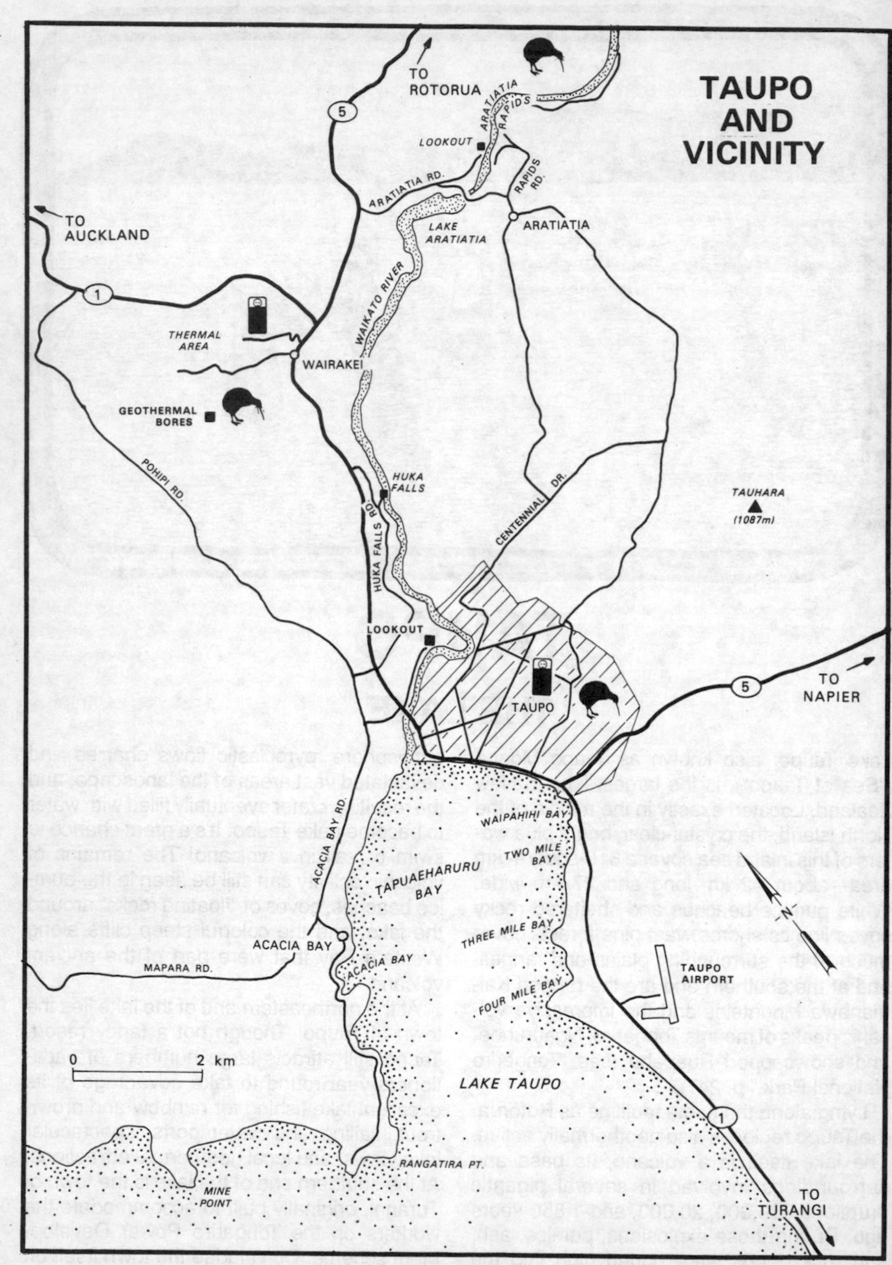
TAUPO AND VICINITY
TO ROTORUA
5
ARATIATIA RAPIDS
LOOKOUT
ARATIATIA RD.
RAPIDS RD.
ARATIATIA
LAKE ARATIATIA
TO AUCKLAND
1
WAIKATO RIVER
THERMAL AREA
WAIRAKEI
GEOTHERMAL BORES
POHIPI RD.
HUKA FALLS
HUKA FALLS RD.
CENTENNIAL DR.
TAUHARA
(1087m)
LOOKOUT
TAUPO
TO NAPIER
5
ACACIA BAY RD.
WAIPAHIHI BAY
TWO MILE BAY
TAPUAEHARURU BAY
THREE MILE BAY
ACACIA BAY
ACACIA BAY
MAPARA RD.
TAUPO AIRPORT
FOUR MILE BAY
N
0
2 km
LAKE TAUPO
1
RANGATIRA PT.
MINE POINT
TO TURANGI

first impressions: if you're into heavy-duty fly-fishing in trout-laden rivers, white-water rafting, or hiking or skiing in Tongariro National Park, Turangi, self-proclaimed "Trout Capital of the World," is an excellent and relatively inexpensive base. Neither town offers much after dark in the way of sex, drugs, or rock 'n' roll—but at the end of an action-packed outdoorsy type of day, a good meal, a soak in a hot pool, and a comfortable place to lay your head are likely to be quite enough.

Highway 1 follows the eastern shore of Lake Taupo, connecting Taupo and Turangi with a good (but winding) 51 km of sealed road. Allow extra time, as the road follows the shoreline much of the way, and the clear blue water and lush grassy reserves may lure you into frequent swimming and tanning stops! You can also circumnavigate the lake by taking Hwy. 41 from Turangi northwest to Kuratau Junction, then Hwy. 32 north up the western side; however, the main road is a good distance from the lake, the shores are pretty inaccessible, and you only get glimpses of the lake every now and again.

THE TOWN

SIGHTS

Thermal

Highway 5 from Rotorua and Hwy. 1 from Hamilton merge just north of the geothermally active Wairakei area, eight km north of Taupo. Before continuing into town, don't miss several of the area's thermal attractions. **Wairakei Natural Thermal Valley** is located adjacent to the Wairakei Hotel and the Geothermal Power Project; the entrance is 50 meters from the Wairakei Steam Pipe bridge (on the right if you're heading south). Drive to the end of the road, passing all sorts of tame birds and a large caged area of guinea pigs, and enter through the Barn Tearoom and ticket office where you may also meet two large, woolly pet sheep that hang out here trying to sneak inside! The main features of this natural thermal spot are the steaming pools of boiling pink, gray, and brown mud, colorful rock formations, and the surprisingly cold Wairakei Stream that flows through this hot steamy area. Allow at least an hour to see everything. Admission $4 adult, 75 cents child. The friendly owners also operate the tearoom, serving reasonably priced sandwiches, cakes, coffee, and tea from 0730-1700 daily, plus a small motor camp amongst attractive grounds (see "Accommodation" below), tel. 48-004. Guest campers are admitted to the Valley for half price.

Just down the road you'll find the huge and highly developed **Wairakei Geothermal Power Station.** A vast underground water system, naturally heated by very hot, perhaps molten, rocks, has been tapped. Bores release the high pressure of the water far below, which causes it to reach boiling point and produce the desired steam. At present, 57 bores supply commercial quantities of steam. For heaps of info and a good 15-minute audio-visual, drop by the **Geothermal Bore Field Information Centre** on Wairakei Rd. (tel. 48-216), at the turnoff beside the 24-hour B.P. Gas Station and Restaurant. Open daily

Wairakei Natural Thermal Valley

0900-1200 and 1300-1630, someone is always on hand to answer questions, and admission is free.

Another natural thermal area that shouldn't be missed is **Craters of the Moon,** just three km north of Taupo off Hwy. 1. Apart from manmade paths through the thermal area, everything has been left untouched. Steaming, bubbling areas lie amongst bush-covered hills and valleys, steam-filled craters give brief glimpses of boiling mud below, and small holes on the hillsides forcefully belch out torrents of steam. Follow the trail up the steps to the top of the hill for a great view of the thermal valley and Taupo in the distance, and continue down through the bush back to the carpark. Allow about an hour to see the whole thermal area. The sign to Craters of the Moon is very small, so keep your eyes peeled for a gravel road and small rest area as you get closer to town—a right turn when heading south. Follow the gravel road onto Q Line Rd. and continue to the parking area. Keep all valuables locked in the trunk or out of sight, or leave someone with your vehicle—theft from parked cars has reportedly occurred on many occasions, and the police are, according to one visitor, "relatively unsympathetic." If the area is particularly active, thermally speaking, you may find the gate closed for safety purposes; otherwise it's generally open dawn to dusk, and admission is free.

The Waikato River And Taupo Walkway

The magnificent Waikato, longest river in New Zealand, runs northward 425 km from its source on the slopes of Mt. Ruapehu in Tongariro National Park (this stretch is called the Tongariro River), through Lake Taupo, to finally meet the Tasman Sea southwest of Auckland. The river pours out of the lake at Taupo, and about four km downstream hurtles with tremendous force through a narrow rock chasm and down the well-known **Huka Falls.** This massive volume of water falling in a raging torrent to a frothy churning pool below is really something to see; particularly spectacular at night under floodlights. A footbridge and path provide access to various viewpoints overlooking the falls (this is another spot where valuables have been stolen from vehicles—keep them out of sight, locked in the trunk, or with you). You can walk to Huka Falls from town by taking the one-hour (OW) **Taupo Walkway** along the eastern banks of the river, starting at Spa Thermal Park (off Spa Rd.) in Taupo. If you have wheels, take Hwy. 1 out of town to Huka Falls Rd. and turn right. Pass Huka Village (see below) and continue along this scenic road (note the good camping areas) to the various lookouts; the road eventually rejoins the main highway. Some of the local guided bus tours include Huka Falls; check with Taupo PRO.

Taupo Walkway continues from Huka Falls along the eastern bank to the impressive **Aratiatia Rapids,** 11 km north of town. The Aratiatia Powerhouse control gates (part of the hydroelectric scheme) are released at 1000 and 1430 daily (check these times with Taupo Information Centre before you walk there) which causes spectacular flooding of the river valley below within a matter of minutes. (If you don't take photos, no one will believe you!) The trail takes about two hours OW, but you can follow the road back across the river to Hwy. 5 where it's relatively easy to hitch a ride back to town. The rapids can also be reached by car; take Hwy. 1 out of Taupo, then Hwy. 5, turn right onto Aratiatia Road.

Commercial Attractions

One of the most popular activities in the area is a **day cruise** on the ***Taupo Cat.*** Jump on the spacious, 25-meter, white and blue catamaran to leisurely explore the Western Bay wilderness and Waihi and Motutaiko islands. You'll enjoy both morning and afternoon tea *and* a tasty smorgasbord lunch in air-conditioned comfort before whizzing back along the eastern bays to Taupo. It departs daily from Pier 87, Taupo Boat Harbour (head to-ward Acacia Bay and look out for the sign to the left), at 1000, returns at 1530; adult $68.50, child $25. Alternatively there's a shorter **dinner cruise** which departs at 1900, returns around 2200, has full bar facilities on board, and includes a smorgasbord dinner; adult $54, child $20. For more info, contact Troutline of New Zealand at Pier 87, or tel. 86-052.

Huka Falls

Huka Village on Huka Falls Rd. (two km from Taupo, on the road to Huka Falls) is a working reconstruction of a New Zealand pioneer village. Check out the period buildings, furniture, handcrafts of the past (and souvenirs of the present!), while you imagine what Taupo was like a hundred years ago. **Huka Homestead Restaurant** within the village serves mouth-watering morning and afternoon Devonshire teas and a smorgasbord lunch daily, and dinner on Fri., Sat., and Sun. evenings by reservation only (see "Food," p. 206). The village is open daily from 0900-1700; admission $3.50 adult, child free, restaurant meals extra; tel. 85-326. If you don't have your own transportation, ask at the info center if the free Huka-looka bus is running—usually daily at 1030, 1200, and 1330.

Cherry Island lies in the middle of the Waikato River. Watch the fat Taupo trout cruise by the underwater viewing windows, take a walk around the park-like island grounds viewing all kinds of birds and baby animals, or check out the upstairs gallery, which features New Zealand artists. You can sit inside, or outside on the sundeck, while you enjoy food and drinks from the island tearoom. Open daily from 0900-1700, tel. 89-427; admission $6.80 adult, $4 students, $2 child. To get there take Spa Rd., turn left on Motutahae St., then right on Waikata Street.

If you're interested in deer farming, ask at the Taupo Information Centre if any of the local farmers are willing to show you around. Otherwise take a guided tour that includes one of the large deer farms where the deer virtually run free in large paddocks (arrange through the Info Centre; expect to pay an admission fee).

Relax after a hectic day of sightseeing at the **A.C. Thermal Pools,** open Sun. to Thurs. 0800-2000, late on weekends and holidays. Lake Taupo water heated up to 37 degree C supplies the swimming pools; private 40-degree C thermal mineral pools, a hot-water slide, and sauna are set amongst flower gardens and lawns. Admission $4 adult, $2 senior or child, $3 for 20 minutes in a private hot pool. Keep your head above the water in the hot pools—amoebic meningitis can develop if you let water enter your nose when swimming or diving. Also keep in mind that dizziness or faintness can occur if you stay in the hot water for more than 20 minutes. Located on A.C. (Armed Constabulary) Baths Avenue. Another place to relax in thermal hot pools is at **De Bretts Thermal Pools** off Hwy. 5 south to Napier, tel. 88-559; adult $3.50, child $1.50, private pools $4.

Cheap Ways To Enjoy The Lake

The clear, refreshingly cold water of Lake Taupo is a joy for swimming, boating, or catching an elusive rainbow or brown trout for dinner. Many agreeable swimming spots wait to be discovered along the waterfront beaches, especially at the lake edge about two km from town along Lake Terrace (almost opposite Taharepa Rd.). Here Waipahihi Hot Springs bubble up into the lake, noticeably warming the water when the lake is at a suitable height. One of the best places for swimming, boating, or fishing is six km west of Taupo at **Acacia Bay.** Lie on the sandy public beach and make some fine feathered friends with the large local duck population, swim leisurely out to the pontoon, or hire one of the row boats, canoes, or motorboats from the friendly owners of Acacia Bay Lodge (see "Accommodation," p. 204) across the road.

There's no better or cheaper way to see the lake or catch a fish than from a boat. A single canoe ranges from around $8 per hour to $24 for three hours, a double canoe or rowboat from $10 per hour to $26 for three hours, and a motor boat from $20 per hour to $150 per day (daylight to dusk). You can also hire fishing gear with the boat, or alone if you want to try your luck from one of the rocky promontories farther along the lake. To get to Acacia Bay, drive or walk out of town along Hwy. 1 and take the first street to the left after crossing the river—it's signposted to Acacia Bay. Turn left on Acacia Bay Rd., continue for about five km and you'll end up at this attractive part of Lake Taupo. It's fairly easy to catch a ride along here, or you can take a taxi for about $11.

Once you're paddling or zooming around the lake, head west of the bay beyond several of the points, keeping fairly close to the shoreline (you don't want to be caught out by sudden weather changes and end up in Turangi a few days later!) and you'll see one of the lake highlights—the intricate and fabulous Maori rock carvings on the point at Mine Bay. It takes about an hour to row to the carvings.

For a good several-kilometer walk, continue along Acacia Bay Rd. to eventually reach a

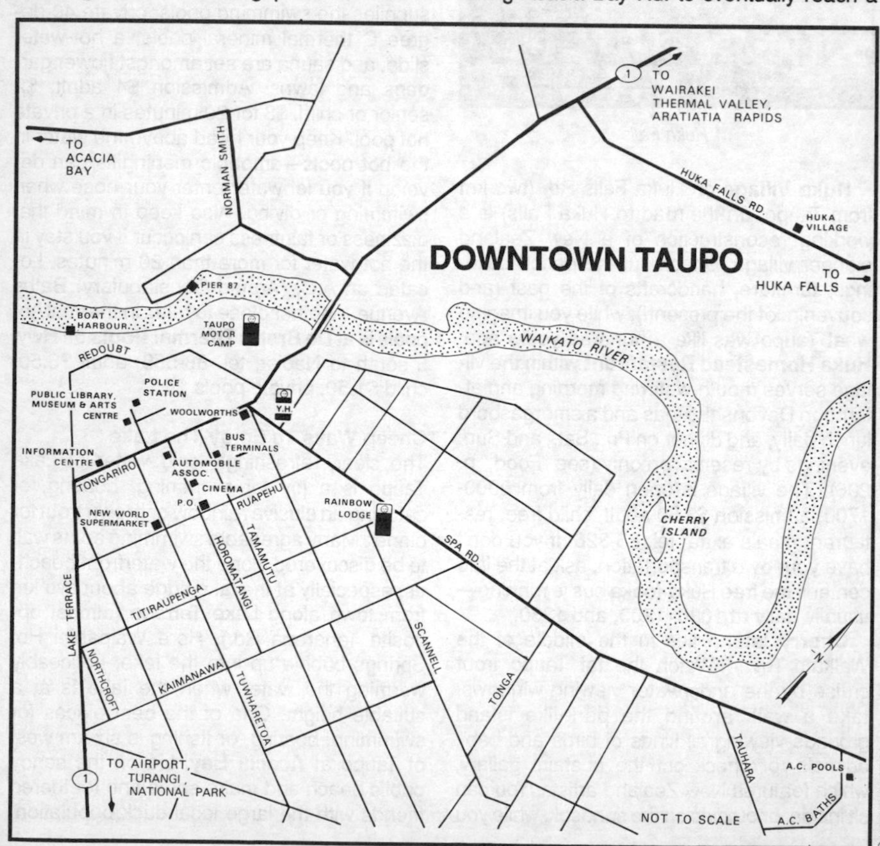

Maori rock carvings at Mine Bay

good track leading down through the bush to a rocky point, and good fishing. Keep in mind that the road eventually dead-ends at private property—not much traffic apart from the occasional angling enthusiast or land developer.

GUIDED TOURS

By Road

If you want to see Taupo's highlights in one fell swoop, call **Paradise Tours** at tel. 89-955 before 0900 or after 1600, or inquire at the Taupo Information Centre, tel. 89-002. See Taupo's Boat Harbour, Huka Falls, Wairakei Geothermal area, Aratiatia Rapids or Wairakei Thermal Valley (extra admission charge) in 2½ hours, for $22 adult or $12.50 child. They also do a **Taupo Cat Shuttle** from town for $4 pp OW or $6 pp RT.

By Water

Taupo's marina, **Boat Harbour,** is located at the mouth of the Waikato River. Here you can hop on a boat for lake sightseeing, assist in sailing a fabulous yacht, or charter one of many fishing boats and/or trout guides. One of the best ways to get to know the lake, past and present, is to take a two-hour cruise onboard the attractive old steamer **MV *Ernest Kemp.*** The captain gives a fascinating historical commentary while you enjoy the lakefront, Hot Water Beach, Two, Three, and Four Mile bays, Mine Bay and the intricate Maori rock carvings, and the serene beauty of Acacia Bay. It departs from the Boat Harbour's main wharf at 1030 and 1400 during summer, and only once a day at 1400 during winter; a very worthwhile two hours at $16 adult, $9 child (bookings essential). Get your ticket at the Wharf office and Information Centre, tel. 83-218. Another great way to take to water (and one of the best sightseeing deals in Taupo) is on the 40-foot ketch ***The Barbary,*** once owned by Errol Flynn, now by Bill and Maggie Dawson. This friendly couple encourages you to take part in the sailing activities, or you can just sit back, relax, and work on a Taupo tan. A fantastic 3½ hours of sailing bliss costs only $15 per adult, $10 per child, and the yacht leaves from Taupo Wharf, Taupo Boat Harbour (bookings advisable). You can also catch a dinner cruise in summer, taking in one of Taupo's spectacular sunsets; $15 adult plus dinner $12 (order dinner before 1400 at the office, and take a warm jacket). For bookings call 85-230.

To pick and choose according to your budget among a variety of fishing boats and guides, stroll along the marina and check out all the boats, or call in at the Info Centre to pick up the current brochures. Launch charters starting at around $40 per hour (depending on the size of the launch and the number of passengers) can be arranged through the center. **Taupo Commercial Launchmen's** fishing boats and experienced guides run from $44-88 per hour, depending on the size of boat. For more info call 85-230. On the 33-foot launch **MV *Bonita,*** fishing will cost you $65 per hour, but if you (or they) can find two other interested anglers it's only $110 for up to three hours (max. three people). If you only want a boat to tootle around the lake for a joyride, see **Taupo Lakeside Services,** who hire self-drive runabouts from $26 per hour. They also offer charter launch fishing ($55-65 pp), scenic cruises, and water-skiing rides (from $35 per half-hour); tel. 85-596. In summer you can hire small boats or kayaks for reasonable prices from the lakefront.

Flightseeing

A great way to see the Taupo area is by air, especially if you don't have a lot of spare cash to fritter away on commercial attractions. Although it costs almost $100 to charter a seaplane for an hour, **Ark Aviation** down at the lakefront gives several short and exciting scenic flights, ranging from a 10-minute flight over the geothermal power station, Huka Falls, Taupo, and the Boat Harbour for $20 adult, $10 child, to a one-hour 10,000-foot cruise south beyond Lake Taupo over the snow-capped volcanos of Tongariro National Park for $96 adult, $48 child. If you want to do the latter, book as soon as possible (tel. 87-500 or 89-441) so that weather conditions can be evaluated and a suitable time arranged. The calmest flights, particularly in summer, are those early in the day when it's still cool; overcast skies are generally the best weather conditions for smooth flightseeing.

Several aviation services based out at Taupo Airport operate everything from short scenic flights to regular charter and safari flights, and a fly-in service to the Kaimanawa Mountains (southeast of Taupo) for excellent bush hiking, trout fishing, and hunting in some wild and beautiful backcountry. The **Taupo Air Services** office at the airport is open from 0700-1700 on Mon., Wed., and Fri., from 0800-1700 on Tues., Thurs., Sat., and Sun., tel. 85-325. Scenic flights range from $25 pp for their local "Buzzaround" flight to $100 pp for an excursion over the volcanos of Tongariro National Park. Charters are also available. The Kaimanawa Forest Park trips fly in to **Boyd Lodge** in the Recreational Reserve area near the Ngaruroro River. The Lodge is a fairly luxurious forest hut with bunk rooms and a kitchen, 20 minutes by air from Taupo; you provide your own sleeping bag, food, and cooking utensils. You can fly in and walk out, or walk in and fly out, or fly in and fly out, or walk in and walk out! If you plan an extended trip they'll fly supplies in on pre-arranged dates. The area is accessible year-round but you need to be equipped for snow conditions in winter, and you need to buy hunting permits from the Dept. of Conservation in Turangi (tel. 7724), and/or a fishing license from any NZTP Travel Office or fishing tackle shop before you go. Get more info and brochures from the office (tel. 85-325/326), and get the detailed map of Kaimanawa Forest Park (which shows walking tracks, huts, and recreational activities) for $7.30 from Taupo PRO.

The **Air Charter Taupo** office is also at the airport. Open daily from 0800-1700, tel. 85-467 or after hours tel. 88-163. Their six scenic flights range from a 10-minute local buzz for $20 pp to a one-hour flight over Tongariro National Park for $95 pp. The fly-in plane service to both private and forest park land in the Kaimanawa and Kawkeka ranges costs $130-150 pp RT from Taupo, plus landing fee. Helicopter service is also available, but costs a lot more. Permits for forest land must be bought from the Dept. of Conservation in Turangi but permits for private land can be bought directly from Air Charter Taupo. They also operate guided hunting safaris using helicopter access and all the necessary gear can be hired—but expect to cash a bundle of traveler's cheques for these!

Guided Rafting And Outdoor Recreation Trips

Several rafting and outdoor adventure companies operate out of Taupo. One very good local company is **Kaimanawa Tours,** covering white-water rafting, fishing, and game

Acacia Bay beach, a stone's throw from Acacia Bay Lodge

hunting trips, with camping gear and food provided on the extended trips. Their guided rafting trips (excellent safety record) are run on demand year-round, depending on which river is run. One-day "thrills and spills" trips start at around $65 pp per day; three-day trips, including fishing, hunting, and camping (all gear and food supplied) start at around $350 pp. They also do five-day trips starting at around $450 pp, and all their "adventures" operate throughout the year. Call 87-902 for current trips, prices, and bookings.

ACCOMMODATION

Free Camping

For some excellent camping spots right on the Waikato River, walk or drive along Huka Falls Rd., north of town. Several flat grassy areas are surrounded by trees and separated from the road by native bush. Look for a small dirt road (no sign) off to the right when heading toward the falls. No facilities other than long-drop toilets, so take your cooking equipment (and TP) with you. However, if you can't sleep with the constant "whoosh" of rushing water, camp somewhere else!

YHA Hostel

The Taupo YH is a seasonal hostel, open only during Dec. and Jan., in the Taupo Nui-a Tia College "Home Science" block on Spa Rd.; $11 pp. You can use the college tennis courts (small donation for tennis racket hire). The warden operates a shop, has discount vouchers available for the A.C. Baths, and organizes reasonably priced sightseeing bus trips around Taupo for hostellers only.

Private Lodges

Hospitable and enthusiastic Mark and Susan Dumble opened **Rainbow Lodge** in '85, thus providing Taupo with excellent budget accommodation in a central location. The atmosphere is comfortable and relaxed, and it's a great place to stay. Heated dorms and individual double and twin rooms, communal facilities, large fully equipped kitchen and living area with pool table and wood stove, a coin-operated sauna, and luggage storage are just some of the facilities. Guests can rent all sorts of recreational gear, at a minimal rate: 3-, 10-, and 14-speed bicycles, mountain bikes, bicycle gear and panniers, tents, backpacks, a canoe, tennis rackets, golf clubs, and fishing equipment. Wilderness horse treks, white-water rafting, fishing trips, skiing, hunting, local sightseeing tours—anything can be arranged. Check out the excellent info board to find out more, or ask the owners. A courtesy bus will drop off hitchhikers at the end of town (and collect you from the bus station if you need a ride). Bunk beds in dorms are $13 pp; a twin or double is $15 pp, child half rate ($10 key deposit). Provide your own sleeping bag, or hire linen at a small cost. Located 500 meters from town and the bus station, at 99 Titiraupenga St., tel. 85-754. To get there from the bus station, continue up Tamamutu for two blocks to Titiraupenga and turn left, then continue for another two blocks.

Sunset Lodge is another popular budget hostel, close to the lake and beach but a good hike from downtown (free pick-up). Fully equipped kitchen, comfy TV lounge, laundry facilities, linen and blankets for hire, free bikes, daily rides to Huka Falls and Craters of the Moon. Dorms from $12 pp, $28 d or twin. The hostel is at 5 Tremain Ave., tel. 85-962.

Cabins

Taupo Cabins have both standard cabins and tourist flats, communal kitchen (ask at the office for crockery and cutlery) and dining area with TV, and the usual communal facilities. Cabins range from $18-30, and tourist flats are $41 d plus $8.80 each extra adult. Book well ahead if you know you want a cabin in Dec. or January. Located one km from downtown at 50 Tonga St., tel. 84-346.

Acacia Bay Lodge is *the* place to stay if you want to be right on the lake, with a picturesque sandy beach directly in front, a variety of rowboats and powerboats for hire, and good fishing and hiking in the immediate area. The laid-back atmosphere seems to attract amiable people, and the fishing attracts anglers, year after year. The store sells all the basics seven days a week, and you can hire or buy a full range of fishing tackle and licenses. Fish-cleaning facilities and freezer space keep the successful angler beaming, and a tree-shaded BBQ area overlooks the lake. The two shady tent or campervan sites are $12-15 d (no kitchen but there is a BBQ at the tentsites), and the comfortable cabins and chalets range from $35-72 d, $45-94 during Christmas and public holidays. Located at 868 Acacia Bay Rd., tel. 86-830; it's six km out of town around the west side of the lake, but don't let that put you off. If you don't have wheels, hitching out there is still quite easy—there's quite a community of easy going locals living in the area, and everyone knows the congenial manager, Bo Liebergreen, and the location of Acacia Bay Lodge. It's at 868 Acacia Bay Rd., tel. 86-830. A taxi ride out (tel. 85-100) costs about $11 OW.

Motor Camps

The most central is the tree-shaded **Taupo Motor Camp** along the banks of the Waikato River. Communal facilities, TV lounge, and a shop. Tentsites are $6.50 pp, caravan sites $7.50 pp, cabins start at $24 d. It's very busy during holiday periods—book ahead. Ask for a discount ticket for the A.C. Baths, usually available at the office, which is open 24 hours a day. Located on Redoubt St., tel. 86-600.

To get to **Acacia Holiday Park** you need your own transportation (it's on the road to Acacia Bay), but the friendly welcome you'll get from Davie and Martha Hylands is worth

Acacia Holiday Park

it! Lots of grassy well-kept grounds for tent and caravan sites from $7.50 pp, standard cabins from $24 d ($32 during holidays), on-site vans from $33 d ($42.50 during holidays), and self-contained units from $42 d (holiday minimum $54). Provide your own linen and cooking gear, or hire linen for $5 pp. Spotlessly clean bathroom, kitchen, and laundry facilities, and a TV/dining room. It's on Acacia Bay Rd., tel. 85-159.

Wairakei Natural Valley is primarily a thermal attraction, but a small, attractive motor camp is within the secluded grounds. Communal facilities, and tearooms open daily from 0730-1700. Tentsites from $5 pp, caravan sites from $6 pp, on-site caravans and two cabins from $10 pp (minimum $20 per night). If you arrive after the tearooms close, pay at the main house. Drive or hitch up Hwy. 1 to Wairakei (about eight km); the entrance is along the road to the left just past the Steam Pipe Bridge (signposted to Thermal Valley). Continue for about one km to the end. For more info, call 48-004.

Bed And Breakfast

Call in at the Info Centre to see who is currently offering B&B. One local B&B highly recommended by fellow B&B operators is **Koha Lodge** at 50 Koha Rd., tel. 87-647. Stay in this large private home with lake views, relax on the sundeck, in the TV lounge, billiard room with bar, thermal plunge pool, or landscaped gardens, and savor the wild game and gourmet New Zealand foods that the lodge specializes in. Your hosts can arrange guides and activities if desired, and a courtesy car service is available. Bed and breakfast is $80 s, $100 d or twin, $150 suite. Lunch (or hamper) is $15, and a four-course dinner with drinks and wine is $35 pp.

Motels And Private Hotels

Taupo has an ever-expanding number of motels—more spring up along the lakeshore every year, along with timeshare after timeshare. Expect to pay from $50 s, $65 d at the least expensive end, up to $500 s, $374 pp d at the exclusive **Huka Lodge**, where you can hob-nob with the rich and famous! For full listings and current prices, refer to the *AA Accommodation Directory.*

If you're looking for a modern, very comfortable room with full kitchen facilities, TV, phone, and private spa pool, head for the **Spa Hotel** on Spa Rd., tel. 84-120. These luxurious chalets are only $50 s, $68 d, each extra adult $12, child $10, and on the premises, a short stroll away, are a public bar and bistro, liquor mart, fully licensed restaurant, and heated outdoor and thermal indoor pools. A hot stream runs through the landscaped grounds, and Tiki Te Tamamutu, the only privately owned "Meeting House" in New Zealand (carved between 1800 and 1810) stands within the grounds. Budget accommodation is also offered in the hotel's original wing; these older, more basic rooms start at $31 s B&B, $50 d B&B, and have tea- and coffee-making facilities. One double suite has its own kitchen, TV, and phone for $55 d B&B.

Bradshaw's Private Hotel has rooms with handbasins, private or communal facilities, TV lounge, and breakfast from $30 s B&B ($35 private bath), $50 d B&B ($55 with private bath), and dinner is available from $12 in the hotel dining room. Located at 130 Heu Heu St., tel. 88-288. **The Lake Establishment Hotel** has rooms with handbasins (communal facilities), or rooms with own bath or shower, from $39 s B&B, $65 d B&B; the very good **Cobb and Co.** restaurant is also on the premises. Located on the corner of Tongariro and Tuwharetoa sts., tel. 86-165.

FOOD AND ENTERTAINMENT

Brunch

The best tearoom for morning or afternoon tea or lunch is the **Pioneer Cafe** near the bus depots. In the old-fashioned decor help yourself to all kinds of fresh sandwiches, salad rolls, prepared salads, hot foods, cream-filled cakes and pastries for around $3-7 pp for a filling lunch. The **El Toreador Coffee Lounge** has tasty tearoom-type snacks and light meals, and a wide range of coffee drinks. Reasonable prices—lunch costs around $4-7 pp. Open Mon. to Fri., and Sat. mornings, located on Horomatangi Street. Across the street is the **Alpine Coffee Lounge** with similar food and prices; both cafes are busy during lunch hour. Two other good spots for lunch are **the Red Barrel** and **Echo Cliff,** both near the waterfront. The Echo Cliff is upstairs at the lake end of Tongariro St., lunch $5-10, closed Tuesday. For quick bistro-type meals try any of the pubs around town—many serve cheap main courses for less than $10 a plate.

If you get the urge to sink your gnashers into scones and pikelets (small sweet pancakes) loaded with strawberry jam and whipped cream (a.k.a. Devonshire tea), you can fulfill your most fattening desires for $6 pp. Or perhaps a filling "Farmhouse Smorgasbord" lunch for around $10-12 pp is more to your liking. Either way, waste no time heading out to **Huka Homestead Restaurant** in historic Huka Village (if you just want to eat there, ask for the tea or lunch ticket alone—saves you the village admission fee). Teas are served daily from 1000-1600, lunch from 1200-1400. Located on Huka Falls Rd. (off Hwy. 1 north), tel. 82-245 or 85-286.

Another good place for lunch, particularly if you're out doing a bit of thermal sightseeing, is at the rather grand **THC Wairakei Hotel.** The fairly casual family lounge bar around the side is open daily for bistro meals from 1130-1400, but if you're a "gang member wearing or possessing gang type uniforms or emblems," the sign at the entrance proclaims, you'll have to eat somewhere else! Main courses average $15 pp, and the "special menu of the week" is usually a good deal. The delicious smorgasbord lunch at the fancier main restaurant is more like $23 pp from 1200-1345 daily, but "acceptable dress" is required for entrance. Located on Hwy. 1 at Wairakei, tel. 48-021.

Dinner

Margarita's serves a large variety of delicious, spicy, Mexican dishes from 1700 till late in a warm, cozy atmosphere—a little bit of Mexico right in downtown Taupo! Mains (large portions with salad or beans and rice) range from around $10-17, happy hour (fully licensed, but you can BYO bottled wine) from 1700-1900 gathers quite a crowd, and on Fri. nights from 2200-0100 there's a live band and plenty of young people out for a raging good time. It's upstairs in the Knowles Real Estate Building at 63 Heu Heu St., tel. 89-909.

Cobb & Co. Restaurant at the Lake Establishment Hotel serves the usual good meals from $10-15 a main course. It's fully licensed, very popular with Taupo-ites, and particularly busy on weekends. Open seven days a week from 0730-2200; located on Tuwharetoa Street. Or try the good meals at fairly cheap prices offered by many of the other hotels around Taupo—look for signs saying "Bistro Bar" or "Family Restaurant" which usually indicate reasonable prices. **Craig's Cafe Restaurant** is another busy place farther up Tuwharetoa St. specializing in grills. Open for lunch and dinner; lunch from $9, a main dinner course from $18-20 and up. **Italian Connection** ("Lakeside Cafe" during the day) at the lake end of Tongariro is often recommended by locals, tel. 86-894. It's open Mon. to Sat. from 1800, has a BYO license, and "great Italian food" for $11-16.

Another good place for dinner is the **Huka Homestead Restaurant,** but they only serve dinner on Fri., Sat., and Sun. nights from 1830, by reservation only. A main course in these historic surroundings will set you back about $20-25, desserts from $7 (the Sunday buffet from 1830 is the best value). The food is made on the premises and worth the price. Check that they're open before you make the treck out there, and make a reservation at tel. 82-245; located within Huka Village on Huka Falls Road. A popular place with the locals is the fully licensed **Gulliver's Restaurant** at the Suncourt Motor Hotel. Main courses start at around $15, desserts from $6, and the $13 smorgasbord lunches are reportedly good value. Located on Northcroft St., tel. 88-265.

For a dressy splurge, try the main restaurant at the **THC Wairakei Hotel.** Dinner is served from 1830-2100, and main courses start around $33 pp. On Hwy. 1 at Wairakei; make reservations at tel. 48-021. For a gourmet meal (at a gourmet price) head for the dressy **Huka Lodge** licensed restaurant.

Food connoisseurs and wine lovers travel from afar to eat here—from $150 pp including pre-dinner drinks! Dress to suit the occasion.

Fast Food, Takeaways, And All-nighters

Taupo has a large variety of late-night dairies and takeaways. Most are located on the main drag, Tongariro St., and around the corner on Lake Terrace or Roberts Street. **Maxi's Restaurant and Dairy** serves light meals, hamburgers and hotdogs, milk, etc., 24 hours a day. Sit there or order food to go; on Roberts Street. **Potato Palace** specializes in hot potatoes smothered in a large variety of fillings for $2.40-4; on the lakefront, open Tues. to Sat. from 1100. **Kentucky Fried Chicken Restaurant** is also on Roberts Street. For pizza, go to **Pizza Hut,** off Lake Terrace at 24 Roberts St., tel. 82-42—be prepared for a wait as it's always busy. For excellent Chinese food to go (and hamburgers, fish and chips, curry dishes, chicken, grills, etc.), try **Grasshopper Chip Bar** in the Hilltop Shopping Centre, tel. 87-533. Most Chinese dishes are in the $7-8.50 range. Add a container of steamed rice for $2.35 and you have a meal for two and a snack for one for the next day! However, expect a wait if you haven't pre-ordered—it's always doing a booming business.

Entertainment

Find a friend and make your own! Nightlife in Taupo seems to focus around drinking in the public bars weeknights, drinking to a live band weekends, or drinking in the park opposite the takeaways! For **live music**, check out the main drag downtown (Tongariro St.) on Fri. and Sat. nights and follow your ears—expect a minimal cover charge at the hotels on weekends. Or try **Margaritas** (see "Food"), where admission is free if you're having a meal, $5 if you just turn up for the music (live band on Fri. nights). Some of the fancier restaurants also provide live bands toward the end of the week. The local **cinema** is on Horomatangi St., off Tongariro, tel. 87-515. The two local papers list current entertainment in the back pages.

Probably the most entertaining thing to do is to head for the **A.C. Baths** (see "Sights" above) and soak the old bod. They stay open late on weekends and public holidays, and if you're continuing south, you won't find many more thermal mineral hot pools (apart from a few at Tokaanu and Tongariro National Park), so be good to yourself while you can! Follow this with a moonlight stroll down to the lakefront and around to the marina.

In summer, some local boat owners offer an assortment of twilight or **dinner cruises**—ask what's happening at the Boat Harbour. One of the best is the dinner sunset cruise on the 13-meter yacht ***The Barbary*** for $15 pp plus $12 pp for dinner (summer only). It departs from Taupo Wharf; call Bill or Maggie Dawson, tel. 85-230, for times and bookings. Or try the "Taupo Nightlights Experience" onboard the ***Taupo Cat***—a dinner cruise on weekends for $53 adult, $20 child, bookings essential.

Two local summer events attract large crowds annually. The very popular **Great Taupo Weekender Bathtub Regatta** happens around the end of Feb., and the **Lake Taupo Promotional Association Fishing Tournament,** a serious fishing event attracting local, national, and overseas anglers, is usually held around mid-April. Contact the Information Centre for more details, and rules and regulations.

SERVICES

Urgent

Ambulance: emergency tel. 111, otherwise call St. John's Ambulance at tel. 82-777. **Taupo Public Hospital** is on Kotare St., tel. 88-100. The **Urgent Pharmacy** is at 21 Tongariro St., tel. 84-949; open Mon. to Fri. 1900-2100, Sat. 1400-1700 and 1900-2100, Sun. 1000-1400 and 1800-2100, public holidays from 1000-2100; **Taupo Police Station** is at the lake end of Tongariro St. on Story Place, tel. 86-060.

Regular

Taupo's main shopping area lies east of Tongariro St., and the shopping hours are 0900-1700 Mon. to Thurs., late night to 2100 on Fri., and Sat. mornings from 0900-1200. Some delis and takeaway food bars open early and stay open late. The main **post office** is on Horomatangi St., tel. 89-090; open Mon. to Fri. 0900-1700 and Sat. 0900-1145. The **Public Library and Museum and Arts Centre** is on Story Place (off Tongariro), tel. 87-554. **Public toilets** are located on Tongariro St., almost opposite Tamamutu Street.

INFORMATION

For free info and maps of Taupo, the lake, and the surrounding area, and souvenirs and postage stamps, visit the amiable people at the **Taupo Information Centre** toward the lake end of the main drag, Tongariro St. (next to the traffic lights), tel. 89-002/003; open daily 0830-1700. The **Flightseeing Centre** is on the lakefront; around the corner, where the lake flows out into the Waikato River, you'll find charter boats and yachts, lake sightseeing cruises, and fishing guide info at the offices along **Boat Harbour.** The **Automobile Association** office on Tamamutu St. (in the Suncourt Shopping Centre) is a good source of road info and maps, tel. 86-000; open Mon. to Fri. 0900-1700. If you'd like to know more about local geothermal activity, in particular the Wairakei Power Station, call in at the **Geothermal Bore Field Information Centre** on Wairakei Rd., Wairakei. Taupo's local newspaper, the *Taupo Times,* is printed four times a week, and the free *Taupo Weekender* comes out once a week on Fri., a good source of local happenings and current entertainment.

TRANSPORTATION

Two main highways pass through Taupo: Hwy. 1 runs north to Auckland and south to Turangi, and Hwy. 5 runs northeast to Rotorua and southeast to Napier and Hawkes Bay.

Hitching

Hitching in and out of Taupo is *fairly* easy as long as you walk to the outskirts of town in each direction—it's almost impossible to catch a ride when you're still near the shopping area. The locals are great when it comes to giving rides, though it helps if you have an attention-grabbing sign, or perhaps an enormous cardboard thumb—be original!

Bus

Mount Cook Landlines and InterCity depots are side by side on Gascoigne St. (off Tamamutu). The Taupo Information Centre is the booking agent for both when the depots are closed. Local sightseeing and scheduled coach service to other main centers is provided by **Mount Cook Landlines.** The office is on the corner of Gascoigne and Paroahape sts., tel. 89-030; open Mon. to Fri. 0830-1700, weekends 0900-1130 and 1300-1530. They run several services a day from Taupo to Auckland ($33 OW), Rotorua, Hastings ($25 OW), Napier ($22 OW), Hamilton, and Wellington ($45.50 OW), with discounts available to YH and ISAC card holders. **InterCity** coaches come through Taupo on the way north from Wellington, servicing Auckland ($33 OW), Napier ($23 OW), Hastings ($25 OW), Rotorua ($17 OW), Tauranga ($32 OW), and Wellington ($45 OW). Ask about off-peak saver fares (25% off on certain days of the week if you buy your ticket a day in advance), the InterCity office is on Gascoigne St., tel. 89-032 or 89-055; open Mon. to Fri. 0800-1700, Sat. 0800-1245, and Sun. 1415-1530.

Air

Taupo Airport is about six km south of town, off Hwy. 1 to Turangi. A **taxi** stand is located on Heu Heu St., tel. 85-100 (it's about $12 OW to the airport). **Air New Zealand** connects Taupo with Auckland, Wanganui, and Wellington ($111 OW) in the North Island, and most major centers in the South Island. For more info and bookings, call James Travel Service on Horomatangi St., tel. 87-065. **Mount Cook Airline** flies to Rotorua, Auckland ($125), Wellington, and Christchurch ($209 OW), but "specials" are also available.

Book at the Mount Cook Landlines depot (they're also an agent for Air New Zealand) or through a local travel agent. **Taupo Air Services** flies direct to Auckland on Mon., Wed., and Fridays. **Lakeland Aviation** and **Float Plane Air Services** operate a variety of sightseeing services (see "Flightseeing," p. 202).

TURANGI

The town of Turangi, located at the southern end of Lake Taupo on the banks of the Tongariro River, used to be a very small village famous for its fishing prior to the opening of the Tongariro Development Project. It was built up and developed into a town in 1964 to accommodate hydroelectric construction workers, but since then, it's been recognized (though little publicized) as an excellent resort area for anglers, hikers, white-water rafters, skiers, and lovers of the great outdoors. The locals, proud of their self-proclaimed title "Heart of the Great New Zealand Outdoors," are eager to assist you in discovering their neck of the woods.

If you want a large choice in gourmet restaurants and exciting after-dark action, save your time and continue south to Wellington. Turangi is a real discovery only if you like to get away from the madding crowd, explore beautiful untouched backcountry, or dabble in an exciting outdoor adventure or two.

SIGHTS

Around Town

The first place to go is the **Turangi Information Centre** on Ohuanga St. near the shopping center; open seven days a week from 0900-1700, tel. Turangi 8999. Apart from the amicable people running the center, a fund of info on the town and surrounding area is free for the asking. An audio-visual on the local area is screened on request, and lots of displays focus on fishing and forestry. Models of the Tongariro Power Development, the major contributing factor in the town's development, fill the museum area, and if you're suddenly overwhelmed by an urge to see the Scheme in person, the center does free conducted tours.

Another place that shouldn't be missed by any angling enthusiast is the **Tongariro National Trout Centre.** It's located a few km south of town on Hwy. 1—the entrance is hard to see, look out for a dip in the road and a small sign. The attractive building houses a small museum full of assorted fishing tackle used over the last hundred years, mounted trophy trout, and displays depicting the life cycle of a trout stream. Downstairs is a fasci-

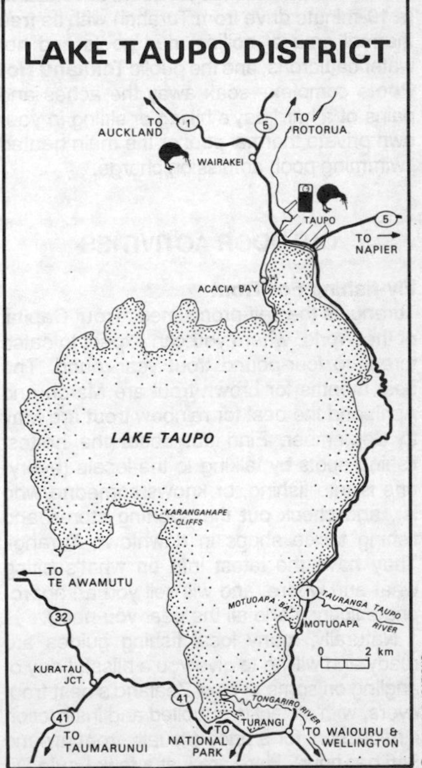

nating underwater viewing chamber of the Hatchery Stream, where in winter you can watch the spawning process, and the rest of the year watch trout of all sizes observing *you* through the window! Open from 0900-1600, admission is free. Trout eggs are hatched and young fish reared in the other Hatchery buildings—feeding times are 0930 and 1530 daily, and there's also an outdoor fishing pool full of tiny trout (opened six days a year for children to try their hand at the art of fly-fishing). The grounds around the Hatchery are quite superb, especially in the summer when the *kowhai* trees are in bloom. A short walk brings you out on the sandy beach along Birch Pool, a popular fishing hole in the Tongariro River.

If you're driving around Lake Taupo, don't miss the small historic settlement of **Tokaanu** (a 10-minute drive from Turangi) with its free thermal area of boiling mud pools and hot water cauldrons, and the public **Tokaanu Hot Pools** complex—soak away the aches and pains of a hard day's hiking or skiing in your own private thermal pool or the main heated swimming pool; admission charge.

OUTDOOR ACTIVITIES

Fly-fishing For Trout

Turangi is the self-proclaimed "Trout Capital of the World" where you can expect to catch three- to four-pound trout year-round. The best months for brown trout are March and April, and the best for rainbow trout are May to September. Find out about the hottest fishing spots by talking to the locals (everyone is into fishing, or knows someone who is), and check out the sporting stores and fishing tackle shops in downtown Turangi. They have the latest info on what's biting what and where, and will sell you an appropriate license and all the gear you need.

Naturally, many local fishing guides are ready and willing to give you a blissful day of angling on some of New Zealand's best trout rivers, with all tackle supplied and instruction if necessary for a price (usually from around $45 per hour). Here are just a few: Louie De Nolfo (locally known as "Louie the Fish!") at tel. 7953—river fishing from $45 an hour (minimum two hours), lake fishing $45 an hour (minimum three hours), half day $150, full day including license and lunch $275; Frank Harwood, tel. 7929; Tony Hayes, tel. 7946; Don Campbell, tel. 7409 or 8597; Tim McCarthy, tel. 8996 or 8207. You can hire a small boat from the Marina at Motuoapa Bay on Lake Taupo—book at tel. 5331. Spectrum Charters charges $55 an hour (one to five people), tel. 7333 or 5331.

White-water Rafting

Rafting the Tongariro River at the foot of the Kaimanawa Ranges is one of the most exhilarating, heart-pumping activities around, and if you're looking for this kind of action the Turangi area is a good place to try it out.

For angling excitement and mouth-watering taste, nothing beats a Taupo rainbow trout.

Mount Cook (Bruce King)

1

2

3

1. lawn bowlers in Government Gardens, Rotorua (Wayne Pease)
2. horseback riders in the Southern Lakes District (Bruce King)
3. windsurfers swooshing across Otago Harbour (Bruce King)

1

2

3

1. boats moored on the Hatea River, Whangarei (Jane King)
2. rafters on the Shotover River (Bruce King)
3. a trotter on Carters Beach, Westport (Bruce King)

1. West Coast greenery on the way to Franz Josef Glacier (Jane King)
2. tree ferns in Urewera National Park (Bruce King)
3. Kaiate Falls (Jane King) 4. one of the many waterfalls in Urewera National Park (Bruce King)

Some of the Tongariro has been harnessed for hydroelectric generation, but the most scenic and untouched stretches still provide plenty of white-water thrills. A couple of rafting operators run the river. Try Garth Oakden, owner/operater of **Turangi White Water Rafting,** tel. 8856. He offers a 1½-hour trip safe enough for children from $20 pp from Nov. to March, and a 4½-hour trip (2½ on the river) for $55 pp. Also available is Wilderness Trout Fishing with a professional fishing guide from Dec. to the end of May, call for current price. The company supplies excellent quality, *full-length* wetsuits (an unusual bonus and one you'll appreciate), helmet, and lifejacket; you supply your own sand or tennis shoes (a necessity), wool socks, wool sweater, and waterproof windbreaker (and wear a swimsuit). Leave your camera at home unless it's totally waterproof and firmly secured to your body.

After arriving at the river, a thorough safety talk covers mastering the paddle, paddling techniques, how to stay in the raft, and what to do if you fall out. They supply paddles and expect you to use them! A few quick practice strokes in the calm water and you're off with no turning back. Tongariro rapids with horrifying names are interspersed with short, beautiful calm stretches. Fat trout cruise the water, birdlife tweets from the trees, and you quickly become a mere speck on the river between the tall cliffs. By the time you've survived (and mastered) Snooker Hole, Devil's Elbow, and other appropriately named rapids, Garth will have you feeling a little more confident, maybe even ready for "your next white-water river." For more info, call Turangi 8856.

River Rats Rafting Company also offers a number of exciting white-water rafting adventures, ranging from two hours on the Wairoa River for $65 pp to four days on the Motu River for $595 pp. The company provides guides, wetsuits, life jackets, safety helmets, a hot drink and snack after the trip, hot showers, courtesy pickup (from Turangi motels) if required, and return transportation to your vehicle. For more info call tel. 393-389.

Hiking

There are so many places to hike in the Turangi area that the best thing to do is to call in at Turangi Information Centre and get the entire run-down. Their free brochures cover everything from short local walks to extended wilderness backpacking. Or call in at the Department of Conservation at Turanga Place, tel. 8520 or 8607; open Mon. to Fri. 0800-1700. Perhaps the two best places for off-the-beaten-track hiking in beautiful backcountry are the rugged **Kaimanawa State Forest Park,** directly south of Turangi, and the volcanic **Tongariro National Park** to the southwest (see p. 247). Apart from hiking in Kaimanawa, you can also fish for trout in the virgin water of four main rivers, hunt for sika and red deer (need a permit), and discover idyllic camping spots. The five forest huts can also be used for free overnight stays but forest workers have priority use. Be prepared for the harsh climate—the park experiences hot, dry weather in summer, snow and heavy frosts in winter, and conditions can change quickly at any time. Hunting permits are available from the Department of Conservation in Turangi, and a Taupo fishing license can be bought from local sporting goods stores. Before you set off into the wilds be sure to get a hold of the detailed "Guide to Kaimanawa State Forest Park" map ($5.50) and the pamphlet "Kaimanawa State Forest Park General Information" from Turangi or Taupo Information Centres, Department of Conservation offices, or map outlets. If you want to get right into the heart of the park quickly, fly in to one of the forest hut airstrips (see below).

Flightseeing

Turangi Scenic Flights flies hikers, fishermen, and hunters into the Kaimanawa Ranges (apply for current prices), as do several flying outfits based at Taupo. You also have a large choice of scenic flights and joy rides, ranging from a 10-minute local flight for $26 pp to a 90-minute flight over the volcanic peaks of Tongariro National Park for $145 pp. Get more info at Grace Road Airfield (tel. 7870), north of town off Hwy. 1.

the finish: Turangi Raft Race

Skiing

The best skiing is in Tongariro National Park between June and Oct. when the volcanic peaks that attract hikers in summer turn into a snow-covered winter wonderland (see p. 253). Turangi is a good base for skiers—accommodation up the mountain can get really expensive, and is booked far in advance for the peak ski season. Turangi, however, has plenty of accommodation, and buses provide regular service (about a 35-minute trip) to the skifields throughout winter.

ACCOMMODATION

Budget

Originally built to house construction workers, **Tongariro Accommodation Centre** is now good budget accommodation. They offer reduced rates for groups, and special package deals including daily outdoor adventure activities such as skiing in winter, white-water rafting in summer, and guided rock climbing, caving, and abseiling. Singles, doubles, and family rooms have handbasins, each block has communal bathroom and laundry facilities, and the main building has a comfy recreation room with TV and large open fireplace. Backpacker rooms (two-, three-, or four-bed rooms) are $13 pp, a single is $30 pp, a double or twin is $18 pp. All meals are available in the on-the-premises Clouds Restaurant; Continental breakfast $7 (daily but on request, let them know the day before), cooked breakfast $12 (weekends only), and dinner $19. Located on Ohuanga Rd., opposite the fire station, within easy walking distance of downtown, tel. 7492. The center guide can arrange any kind of outdoor activity you desire—rafting, fishing, horse trekking, etc., and **Alpine Scenic Tours** (see "Transportation") offers van pickup service from the center to Ketatahi hot springs, Mangtepopo, Whakapapa, and Taupo.

Motor Camps

Turangi Holiday Park, with the usual communal facilities and a TV/recreation room, is within walking distance of the downtown shops. Tent and caravan sites are $7.30 pp; cabins from $14 pp. Located on Ohuanga Rd., off Hwy. 41 south, tel. 8754.

Motuoapa Domain Camp has an excellent location on Lake Taupo. Tent and caravan sites are $5 pp. Located at Motuoapa, eight km north of Turangi, tel. 5333. **Tauranga-Taupo Lodge and Caravan Park** provides communal facilities alongside the Tauranga-Taupo River. Tentsites $6.60 pp, caravan sites $7.40 pp, cabins $27.50 s, $33 d, and motel rooms are from $55 s, $66 d. Located 11 km north of Turangi on Hwy. 1 south, tel. 8385/8356.

Fishing Lodge

Creel Lodge has an excellent bushland location on the banks of the Tongariro River: spacious private grounds, a tepid swimming pool, and smokehouse; you can hire fishing tackle and buy licenses. The luxurious units are quite reasonable at $44 s, $58 d, each additional person $12, and a Continental breakfast is available. Located on Taupehi Rd., tel. 8081.

Motels
For a comprehensive listing of all the local motels within a 20-km radius of Turangi, stop in at the Turangi Information Centre and ask for their free *Visitor Information Accommodation Guide.* It has all the addresses, grades (budget, motel, hotel, private home), and a handy map showing the location of each. Otherwise, refer to the *AA Accommodation Directory.*

FOOD

There's not much in the way of restaurants or entertainment; ask some cooperative locals for their recommendations. The main shopping center has two good tearooms/coffee lounges, **Kosy Kettle Coffee Lounge** and **Coffee Time.** For good food to go, try the **takeaway** next to the Shell gas station on the main road into town, just before the turnoff to the info center. Great oyster burgers (when in season)! Open seven days a week.

The **Turangi Motor Hotel** has a restaurant serving up a la carte family meals, smorgasbord lunches on Sun., and "Video Disco nights" Fri. and Sat. in the Rainbow Bar from 1900. Also in the shopping center is the fully licensed **Gamekeepers Loft.** In the splurge category in the evenings, it's open Mon. to Sat. from 1800. A main course at dinner is $18-21. The menu includes pheasant and wild pork, and they'll cook a trout you've caught yourself by prior arrangement (they're not allowed to serve trout unless an angler brings it in—to protect New Zealand sport fishing).

If you don't mind a 35-minute drive to Tokaanu and feel like indulging for dinner, try the main restaurant in the **THC Tokaanu Resort Hotel.** Prices start at $15 for a main course, desserts average $7, but they allow half portions for half price. On Sundays, smorgasbord lunches are $12 adult, $7 child, dinners $16 adult, $10 child. Then follow your meal with a sauna and swim in the Tokaanu Thermal Domain's private or public thermal pools. What a great way to finish the day!

INFORMATION AND SERVICES

The main source of info is the **Turangi Information Centre** off State Hwy. 1 on your way into town, tel. 8999; open seven days a week from 0900-1700. For **Kaimanawa Forest Park** info and hunting permits, call the Dept. of Conservation at tel. 8607/8520, or Taupo tel. 89-210. For info on **Tongariro National Park** check in at the Dept. of Conservation Office on Turanga Place, Turangi, tel. 8520, or Park HQ at Whakapapa.

Services
In a **medical emergency,** call Dr. Liaw at tel. 8898, or Dr. Guthrie at tel. 8049, or an ambulance at tel. 111. In the main shopping center you'll find the **Turangi P.O. and Savings Bank.** The postal section is open Mon. to Fri. 0830-1700, and Thurs. evening from 1830-2000, and the savings bank is open from Mon. to Fri. 0830-1630, later on Wednesday. **Shopping hours** are generally Mon. to Fri. from 0900-1700, and Sat. from 0900-1200 (the supermarket till 1600), closed Sun., but dairies usually have extended hours. Late-night shopping in Turangi is Thurs. night when everything stays open till around 2000. The **banks** are generally open from 0900-1630. The **AA agent** is also located in the shopping center in the Turangi Chronicle Building, tel. 8335, and there's a good **public library,** open Mon. to Fri. 1030-1630 and Sat. 1000-1200. **Colleen's Laundry Laundromat** has self-service facilities, or the staff will do your laundry for a small charge, same-day service. It's at Turanga Place (near the Holiday Park), tel. 8564; open Mon. to Fri. 0900-1700 and weekends 0900-1400.

Unique Gifts
For a truly superb, hand-carved pendant or sculpture, see "Louie the Fish," a local artist. He transforms bone and ivory into miniature marlin, sharks, trout, dolphins, and other marine creatures; the pendants range from $48-90 apiece, the much larger "living" sculptures

are in the hundreds of dollars. Call Louie De Nolfo, tel. 7953, to make an appointment to see his fabulous work.

TRANSPORTATION

Road

The main **InterCity Bus Station,** just past the shopping center on the left, takes reservations for all bus and rail-ferry travel, and freight inquiries. Open Mon. to Fri. 0715-1145 and 1315-1700, on Sat. from 0745-1145, closed Sun., tel. 8918. You can reach Turangi by bus from Taumaranui, Hamilton, Rotorua, Taupo, Wellington, Palmerston North, Taihape, and Gisborne. Buses leave from Turangi for Napier, Auckland, Te Kuiti, Bulls, and Tauranga, as well as the above, and in many places there is a connecting bus service to other destinations. On Tues., Thurs., and Sun. InterCity runs coach service to Ketetahi and Rangipo, Chateau, National Park, and Ohakune. Call 8918 for current schedule and fares.

Alpine Scenic Tours runs budget transportation to Ketetahi ($7.50 pp OW), Mangatepopo ($13.50 pp OW), Chateau and Whakapapa ($13.50 pp OW), and Taupo ($7.50 pp OW). If you want to go somewhere else off the beaten track, call for a quote (cheaper if several are traveling together) at tel. 8392, or book through the info center. For a taxi call Turangi Taxis at tel. 7700/ 7816/7441.

Air

The small local airstrip is off Grace Rd., a couple of km north of Turangi off Hwy. 1. Local aviation companies give scenic flights and joy rides, and fly hikers, anglers, and hunters into remote areas of Kaimanawa State Forest Park.

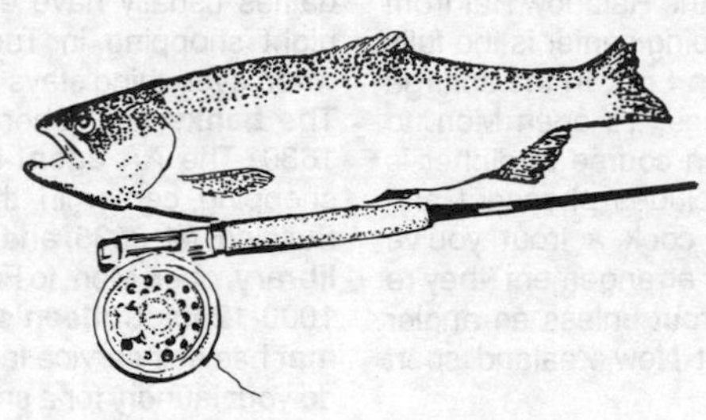

EAST

UREWERA NATIONAL PARK

Introduction

Third largest in New Zealand (214,000 hectares), Urewera National Park boasts rugged ranges, almost continuous green forest, serene lakes, rivers, and dazzling waterfalls—a vast, untamed wilderness where the sounds of running water and melodic birds are ever-present. In the early morning and late evening dense fog blankets the high forest peaks, and mist creeps mysteriously across the lakes to swirl upward through the trees. Flapping wings and sharp notes pierce the silence, giving away the presence of a variety of birds, hard to spot amongst the dense, vibrant greenery. You can feel the silence, and lose yourself in the beauty.

The Park preserves the hauntingly beautiful land of the Tuhoe Tribe or "Children of the Mist," where legendary fairies and goblins play deep in the forest, where every tree has its own spirit, and every rock, lake, and waterfall has a symbolic "presence." For hikers and photographers, Urewera abounds with mysterious and unspoiled splendor, a place to let your imagination run free while you get back to nature.

The Land

The Huiarau Range runs across the middle of the Park dividing the north from the south. In the northern sector the Waimana and Whakatane rivers run northward and empty into the Bay of Plenty, and the Whirinaki River passes through the western edge of the Park; in the southern sector the catchment waters of lakes Waikaremoana and Waikareiti run southeast through several hydroelectric power stations and out to sea at Hawke Bay. Most of the other forest-clad ranges run north-south, all cut by many faults—a main structural feature when seen from a high viewpoint (such as Huiarau Summit) or from the air. The 54-sq-km Lake Waikaremoana or "Sea of Rippling Waters" (585 meters deep), one of the Park's focal points, offers good swimming, boating, fishing, and walks. The impressive Panekiri Bluff, regularly obscured by a dense blanket of fog that appears to pour off the end and down to the water below, rises 600 meters above lake level to dominate the southern shores. The other much smaller lake, almost 300 meters higher than Lake Waikaremoana, is the secluded Lake Waikareiti ("Little Rippling Waters"), reached only by track. Both lakes can be very cold even in mid summer—take adequate clothing. Waterfalls are dominant features throughout the Park. Some of the most magnificent are close to the main road, or at the end of short tracks through lush forest (see "Waterfalls" below).

The Park is divided into three main sections for easy administration and reference, each with its own ranger station and info center. Taneatua, the northern sector, has a Ranger Station and Information Centre at Taneatua (outside the Park boundary), and a Ranger Base at Orouamananui. Murupara is the western sector; the Ranger Station and Visitor Centre is located two km south of Murupara, close to the Park boundary. Waikaremoana is the southern and most popular sector of the park, and Park HQ and the main Visitor Centre are located at Aniwaniwa on the eastern arm of Lake Waikaremoana.

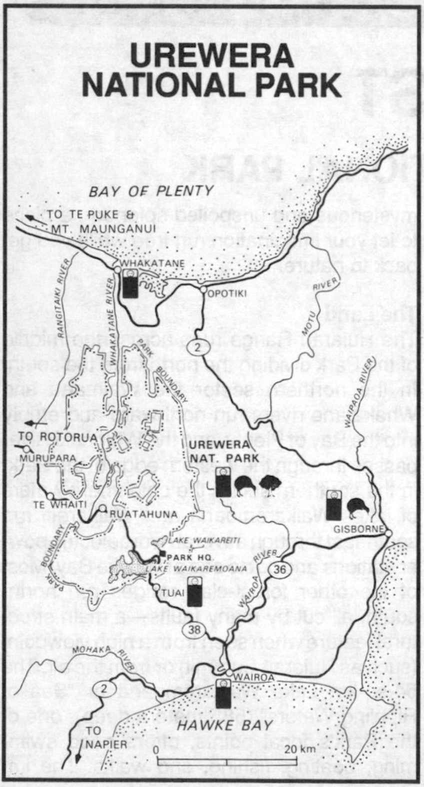

Climate

The ubiquitous lush greenery, wide rivers, and cascading waterfalls are evidence of Urewera's high precipitation—daily rainfall of over 100 mm is not uncommon. The Lake area receives the most rain (the average rainfall is 2,500-3,000 mm per year), the western area is generally much drier. In Feb., the warmest month, daily temperatures range from around 12-21 degrees C. The coldest month is generally July when the temperatures range from 3-9 degrees C, and snow covers the upper forest peaks. Fog and mist, integral parts of the Urewera landscape, form throughout the year but are most common in winter and spring, and high winds can also be expected at any time of year. If you want to be comfortable when hiking in the park, be adequately prepared for all kinds of weather in any season!

Flora And Fauna

Urewera National Park is the largest remaining area of native forest in the North Island, and due to the range in altitude (about 150-1,400 meters) contains quite an astonishing array of vegetation. The lower altitudes grow *rimu, northern rata,* and *tawa* forest, and *toe toe* grass (largest endemic grass found in New Zealand, similar to pampas grass) is rampant (if you suffer from allergies, come to Urewera prepared!). At around 800 meters is beech and *rimu* forest, and at 900 meters the *rimu* disappears and beech dominates the higher ranges, along with *Hall's totara* and *tawari.* To the northwest of Lake Waikareiti lie the open tundra regions where woody scrub, mosses, and subalpine plants have adapted to the very wet conditions.

Bats, lizards, and introduced animals such as deer, pigs, cats, hares, weasels, and opossums live in the Park, but the bush is so dense you're unlikely to spot them unless particularly hunting them down. The large variety of birds is also hard to see, yet you hear them all around you. The most easily seen (and heard) bird is the plump, white-breasted *kereru,* New Zealand's only native pigeon, which makes a loud and heavy flapping noise when it flies. Other birds you're more likely to hear than see are the nocturnal kiwi with its shrill whistle "keee-weee," and three species of parrot—*kaka, morepork* and red-crowned and yellow-crowned parakeet.

Legends

Urewera's past is an intriguing mixture of mysterious legends and historic facts. The original people of Urewera, the Tuhoe, claim descent from the symbolic union of Te Maunga, the Mountain, and Hine-Pukohu-Rangi, the Mist-Maiden. This seems quite appropriate once you've spent any time in this legendary "Land of Mist." The Maori name "Urewera" means "burnt penis." This came about when an old helpless man, Mura-kareke, was lying by a fire and his privates were accidentally roasted. Urewera became the designated name of the area after this incident, and Mura-kareke's descendants traditionally acquired the tribal name "Te Urewera." The Maori word is definitely more appealing than its direct English translation in reference to this beautiful park!

Lake Waikaremoana was formed over 2,000 years ago by a giant landslip that blocked off a narrow river gorge, but local legend explains its formation with much more magic and imagination. The great chief Maahu was angered by his daughter, Hau-mapuhia, and in his rage he tried to drown her. To help her escape, the gods turned her into a *taniwha* (monster) so that she could free herself from her father and burrow through to the sea before daylight (rays of the sun turn a *taniwha* to stone). In her frantic struggle she gouged out a deep area that became the "Sea of Dashing Waters." The sun came up and the *taniwha* was captured in stone to lie forever at the mouth of the Waikaretaheke River, just below Kaitawa. Sometimes jets of water shot high into the air above the rock of Hau-mapuhia and the sounds of wailing were heard—a signal to the ancient Maori that a great storm was on its way. In recent times the waters of the Waikaretaheke River were diverted for hydro-electric power, and the hillside slip that resulted completely buried the rock that was Hau-mapuhia.

SIGHTS

Waterfalls

Waterfalls can be found along all the rivers that dissect this magnificent Park. Here are some of the most accessible: Near the north-west entrance to Urewera, Hwy. 38 passes 20-meter-high **Totarapapa Stream and Falls** before entering some typically rugged Urewera scenery—look on the right side of the road. The beautiful **Hopuruahine Cascades and Falls** can only be seen by going

Mokau Falls

down Hopuruahine Landing road and walking back up and in the river. A huge waterfall that even the least adventurous will be able to view without getting out of the car is the fabulous 34-meter **Mokau Falls**—the highway runs in a loop toward, over, and away from them, 11 km north of Park HQ.

Continue along the highway to Park HQ and the Visitor Centre at Aniwaniwa, where a wide variety of hikes leads to waterfalls, lakes, and deep into the bush. **Hinerau's Track** starts and finishes at HQ, is only a half-hour walk, and gives great views of the three spectacular **Aniwaniwa ("Rainbow") Waterfalls**—Momahaki and Bridal Veil Falls (15 meters), and Te Tangi O Te Hinerau (11 meters). **Aniwaniwa Valley Walk** also starts at HQ and follows the Old Gisborne Rd. for two km (this route continues to Ward's Hut) and turns off down a two-minute bush track to emerge at the bottom of dazzling 20-meter **Papakorito Falls.** Another small track allows access to the top of these falls, but at the bottom a great swimming hole (pleasant temperature in summer) is surrounded by enormous boulders, tree ferns, and heaps of *toe toe*—a super-secluded spot for soaking up some sun!

Launch Trip On Lake Waikaremoana

This is the way to experience sheltered quiet bays, rugged shoreside scenery, splendid waterfalls, and the historic sites of Lake Waikaremoana, to catch a trout fresh from the sea of rippling waters, or to get to and from either end of the Lake Track. The launch *Huiarau* operates from Home Bay (Waikaremoana Motor Camp) regularly during summer, and by arrangement with the launchmaster for fishing trips (gear supplied), water

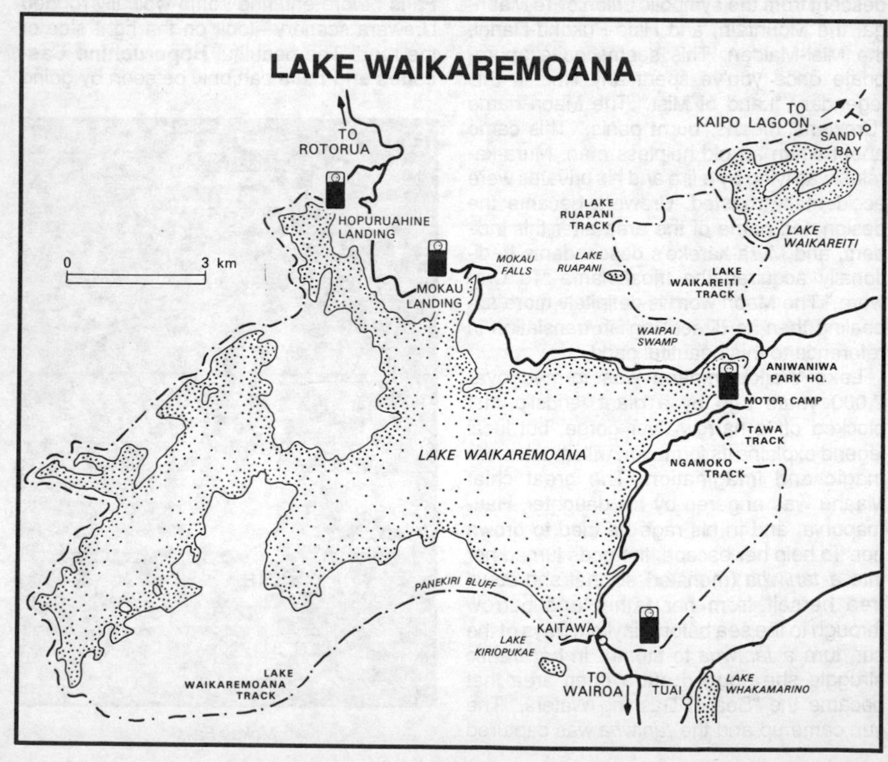

taxi service, and charters. The two-hour, 42-km cruise with commentary usually runs in the afternoon, $22 adult, $10 child; another cruise explores waterfalls and *pa* sites—usually run in the morning, it takes just over an hour and costs $15 adult, $7 child. Two-hour fishing trips start at around $30 pp. See the notice board at the motor camp store for current trips and times. More details are available in the store, or call launchmaster Dave Rothschild, tel. Tuai 871. (The motor camp also has rowboats for hire.)

HIKES

Short Walks

Apart from short walks to the most accessible waterfalls, literally hundreds of kilometers of track riddle the Park. Call in at the Visitor Centre at Aniwaniwa for brochures, track guides, and maps, or buy the Park handbook *Land of the Mist* ($8.75) which contains all the short walks and a fairly detailed map.

The enjoyable **Lake Waikareiti Track** leads about 3.5 km through dense beech forest, exotic fuchsia gullies, and sunny fern-filled glades alive with songbirds, up to a small sheltered lake (878 meters) popular with hikers, anglers (an average rainbow trout is one kg), and swimmers who enjoy an icy dunking! It takes about an hour to hike up to Lake Waikareiti, less coming down, and toilets and a day shelter (no overnight stays) are located at the lake. The lake is dotted with six small islands, one of which, Rahui, contains a small lake of its own called Tamaiti-O-Waikaremoana—unique because of its total isolation from man or browsing animals. Rowboats for this lake are available from Park HQ at $2 per hour plus an $8 overnight fee, with a $30 deposit—get your key, rowlocks, and directions from HQ before you set off. You can also hike farther around the west shores to the sandy beach at Tawari Bay (20 minutes OW) or continue to the northern end and stay at the Sandy Bay Hut (another three hours OW). To get to the start of the Lake Waikareiti Track, cross the bridge from HQ and follow the highway for about 200 meters to the signpost.

Another good one-hour track starts at the same place as the Waikareiti Track and leads past a series of small silted lakes to **Waipai Swamp,** known for its unique swamp plants, sundews, and orchids. The **Lake Ruapani Track** passes through Red and Silver beech forests with mixed stands of *rimu, miro, kahikatea, kamahi,* and *tawari,* on the way to the swamp, and the mysterious quiet of these green and serene groves is disturbed only by birdsong and fluttering wings. You can continue past the swamp for another hour and come out at the grassy verges and groves of beech trees that edge small Lake Ruapani, or continue another three hours to join the Waikareiti Track (see above).

Long Hikes

Many extensive tracks lead to fabulous waterfalls, rapids, spectacular scenic views, or good fishing and hunting areas. Get a complete run-down at Park HQ or the ranger stations; before starting out on any trip, get the latest info on river conditions and weather forecasts, track descriptions, maps, and hut availability. The rangers suggest you leave details of your intentions—you'll be venturing out into some rugged ranges and wild backcountry, days away from help should you need it. Be equipped for all kinds of weather, and take a tent, cooking equipment, and energy food. Water is drinkable throughout the Park.

Perhaps the most popular is the well-defined 50-km **Lake Waikaremoana Track** which starts at Onepoto off Hwy. 38 at the southern end of the lake, crosses the spectacular Panekiri Range (great views), and then closely skirts the west shores all the way north to Hopuruahine Landing on the main highway. It takes about three to four days to cover, with five huts along the route. Best done in summer but as it's most popular at that time, it's wise to take your own tent and cooking equipment as the huts may be full. For a long hike with stops to appreciate magnificent scenery, and some of the best fishing and hunting in the Park, ask for info on the **Waiau Valley-Lake Waikaremoana Track.** It takes about five to six days to cover and

Papakorito Falls, Urewera

starts at Mimiha Bridge on Hwy. 38, seven km northwest of Rutahuna. Seven huts are along the route for overnight stays. The track joins the southwest end of the Lake Waikaremoana Track at Marauiti Hut, and finishes at Hopuruahine Bridge on the main highway. Another popular tramp along the scenic and historic Whakatane Valley is the four- to five-day **Whakatane River Track** which starts at the end of Mataatua Rd., Ruatahuna.

FISHING AND HUNTING

Fishing Season

Anglers can expect excellent fishing for rainbow trout (and some brown trout) in the lakes and rivers throughout the Park. The lake fishing season runs from 1 Oct. to 30 June; river fishing season from 1 Dec. to 30 June; a valid Rotorua trout-fishing District License is required for any location in the Park—on sale at Waikaremoana Motor Camp, in the store at Ruatahuna, and at sports shops in the towns closest to the Park. Don't bring homemade trout flies made from bird feathers or skins into the Park unless they, and all fly-tying equipment, have been fumigated: at present the Park is free of some of the worst bird diseases—and they want it to stay that way. Ready-made imported trout flies are OK, and appropriate flies made locally can be bought in any of the sports stores near the Park.

Lakes

Lakes Waikaremoana and Waikareiti provide the easiest access for anglers, with both fly- and spoon-fishing permitted. The average rainbow trout is 1.3 kg, the average brown trout 2.3 kg in Lake Waikaremoana; in Lake Waikareiti you'll only catch rainbows which average one kg. The main trout spawning streams for Lake Waikaremoana are the Waiotukupuna, Hopuruahine, and Mokau. If you want to get out on Lake Waikaremoana, hire a rowboat from the motor camp or charter a fishing trip on a motor camp launch. If you prefer fishing Lake Waikareiti from on top, HQ hires rowboats and dinghies.

Rivers

The lakes may have easier access, but the backcountry rivers often provide better fishing. The Waimana, Whakatane, Waiau, Whirinaki, and Ruakituri rivers offer kilometer after kilometer of angling heaven. The upper reaches of the Ruakituri and Waiau rivers and tributaries have produced some monsters in recent years—up to six-kg rainbow trout (no browns) have been reported by gleeful anglers! The Whakatane, Waimana, and Whirinaki Rivers and tributaries (except for Horomanga and Wheao) are also fished with fly or spoon, but many of the other rivers permit fly only, under strict seasonal regulations. Check with HQ or ranger stations before you set out.

Hunting

Considered one of the best hunting areas in the North Island, in Urewera's wild and remote areas even inexperienced hunters may find a deer or pig. Red deer and wild pigs are widespread, Javan rusa deer are unique to the Park, and opossum trapping is operated on a block system. As all of these introduced animals cause considerable damage to the natural flora, hunting is encouraged; permits are available from HQ, ranger stations at Murupara and Taneatua, and Conservation Department offices at Opotiki, Rotorua, and Gisborne. Hunting the catchment areas of Lakes Waikaremoana and Waikareiti is prohibited from 25 Dec. to 31 Jan. each year.

ACCOMMODATION

Northern Sector—Taneatua

You can put up your tent anywhere within Urewera National Park boundaries, but due to the odd shape of the Park you cover private land along some of the tracks where the owner's permission is needed to camp. The Waimana Valley is a popular camping area in summer. Rustic huts (4-18 bunks) are located along all the main tracks, but in summer the huts fill up quickly, so it's best to carry a tent. None of the huts have cooking or eating utensils. The rangers suggest hikers carry a portable gas stove and fuel as there's a severe shortage of dead firewood all through the Park. Wood-burning stoves provided in each hut are for heating purposes only (use sparingly). The overnight hut fee is $4 pp. Hut use should be pre-paid at Park HQ or ranger stations and evidence of payment carried, or leave the fee in the honesty box at each hut (but you may face a surcharge for hut collection).

The closest commercial campgrounds/motor camps to the northern sector of the Park are on the Bay of Plenty coast at Whakatane and Ohope Beach (see "Bay of Plenty," p. 172). Taneatua, a little closer to the Park, has hotel accommodation only. In the **Taneatua Hotel,** rooms, breakfast and dinner are available; on Hwy. 2, 13.5 km south of Whakatane, tel. 29-227. Call ahead for rates and room availability.

Central Sector—Murupara

Highway 38, running through the Murupara sector of the Park, has quite a variation in accommodation. Camping is free in the Roadside Camping Area at Te Whaiti on the bank of the Whirinaki River, and it has toilet facilities. You can put up your tent anywhere you choose, but some established camping areas with minimal facilities are located at Ngaputahi, Mangapae Bridge, and Mimiha Bridge. All the main hiking routes have huts (see above).

Ruatahuna on the main highway has the only motel accommodation in this sector. The **Ruatahuna Motel's** four units (with cooking facilities) each sleep four from $38.50 s, $44 d; adjoining tearooms, store, and petrol station. It's on Hwy. 38, tel. 65-393. The **Murupara Hotel** at Murupara on the western outskirts of the Park (about 50 km west of Ruatahuna) has rooms for $25 s, $33 twin, meals available, TV lounge; on Pine Dr., tel. 65-871. The **Murupara Motel** has units with cooking facilities for $34 s, $42 d, breakfast available, tel. 65-583.

Southern Sector—Waikaremoana

This sector has beautiful secluded camping spots on the edge of the lake or up in the forest, and plenty to see and do. Camping areas with toilets and easy access from Hwy. 38 are found (north to south) at **Orangihikoia, Te Taita a Makoro, Hopuruahine Landing, Mokau Landing, Aniwaniwa,** and **Rosie Bay. Mokau Landing,** down a two-km road from the main highway, is a great place to crash—put your tent wherever you like on the large grassy area backed by tree-covered hills, right on the edge of the lake. A small beach, crystal-clear water, and a boat ramp attract a relaxed crowd of anglers, boaters, and windsurfers in summer. Another favorite and private spot, **Te Maraateatua Point** ("Garden of the Gods"), is not marked as a camping area—the signpost on the main road, between Mokau Landing and HQ, says

"Access To Lake 5 Minutes." However, if you have the energy to drag all your camping gear down the very steep five-minute bush trail, you emerge at a rock- and boulder-strewn beach and a good fishing point. Walk around to the right (facing the lake) over the boulders for another 10 minutes and you'll find a beautiful sheltered cove. Small sandy areas amongst the rocks are suitable (and more comfortable than they look) for putting up a tent. Though, if you suffer from hayfever-type allergies from grasses, go prepared!

All the main tracks have huts at regular intervals. The Lake Track has five huts along the route, and there's a hut at the northern end of Lake Waikareiti, but keep in mind that all of the huts are popular in summer. The fully equipped **Waikaremoana Motor Camp** at Home Bay, tel. 826 Tuai, is also located within this sector on the eastern arm of Lake Waikaremoana. Surrounded by tree-covered hills and located right on the lakeshore, it's run by the Park, but don't count on staying here in summer or Easter vacation if you haven't booked up to six months ahead! From the motor camp many well-marked trails lead off in all directions, ranging from 15-minute walks to two-hour hikes. The motor camp shop sells basic grocery supplies, fishing gear and licenses, and petrol, and has rowboats for hire; community kitchen and hot showers available. Tentsites are $5 pp, caravan sites are $6 pp, cabins are $24 d, motel units and chalets are $44-50 d. Linen and blankets can be hired.

There's also a campground at Kokako near Tuai (outside the Park boundary) but the closest town of any size is Wairoa, about 54 km from Urewera's eastern boundary. **Riverside Motor Camp** on the banks of the Wairoa River, tel. 6301, has communal bathroom (metered showers), kitchen, and laundry facilities. Tentsites $5 s, $8.50 d, caravan sites $7 s, $11 d, cabins $22 d the first night ($20 for each additional night). **Clyde Hotel** has rooms for $27.50 s, $49.50 d or twin, meals available in the restaurant; on Marine Parade, tel. 7139. The **Ferry Hotel Motel** has rooms for $20-35 s, $30-45 d, meals available in the hotel dining room; on Carroll St., tel. 8229. The **Motel Vista Del Rio** has rooms for $52-55 s, $63-66 d, all meals available; on the highway (north end of the bridge), tel. 8279.

FOOD AND INFORMATION

Take Your Own

There's not much in the way of stores (and no restaurants) once you enter Urewera National Park—take as much food and supplies as you can carry. Coming from the northwest, Murupara is the last town where you can buy produce and basics at an average price. There's a small store and tearooms at Ruatahuna on Hwy. 38, but the only places you can really restock once you're in the Park (the higher prices reflect the cost of transporting goods to this off-the-beaten-track location) are the Waikaremoana Motor Camp Store or the store at Tuai. You can also buy fishing gear and licenses, petrol, and hire boats here. If you enter the Park from the southeast, get all your supplies in Wairoa, the last town of any size, 54 km south of the Park.

Urewera National Park HQ And Visitor Centre, the main source of info, is in the heart of the Park at Aniwaniwa on Hwy. 38. (The Chief Ranger can be contacted at tel. Tuai 803.) The Visitor Centre has vivid displays, plentiful reading on Urewera legends and local history, and detailed info on the Park flora and fauna. Ask the ranger to put on the excellent audio-visual—it really gets you in the mood for further exploration! The friendly rangers can assist you in planning hiking trips, fishing and hunting expeditions, and will let you in on the fine, lesser-known camping spots and the hottest fishing areas if you ask; open seven days a week from 0800-1700 all year.

Before undertaking any of the longer tracks, check out the local weather forecast and river conditions (many of the tracks ford or run along rivers), and leave details of your intentions with the ranger on duty. A detailed map of the Park ($5.50) and equally detailed map of Lake Waikaremoana ($5.50) are available. For more info, write to the Chief Ranger, c/o Urewera National Park HQ, Private Bag 213, Wairoa.

Ranger Stations
The **Taneatua Ranger Station** on Morrison St., Taneatua, tel. 29-260, and the **Murupara Ranger Station** on Main Rd., Murupara, tel. 65-641, are open Mon. to Fri. from 0800-1700, closed weekends. Pick the rangers' brains before you delve deeper into the "Land of Mist."

TRANSPORTATION

Cars
To get the most out of the Park you need a reliable form of transportation (preferably a car), two able and willing feet, and a decent length of time. If you like to see everything from behind a windshield and only have a day or two, don't bother to drive through Urewera. Only two roads lead into the Park; the rest is unexplored except for a few hiking tracks. The minor unsealed Matahi Rd. in the Waimana Valley enters the northern sector and runs down as far as Ngutuoha via a narrow winding track (not recommended for caravans or trailers). The more popular and scenic Hwy. 38 is a winding, loose gravel road most of the way, extremely dusty in summer. It runs for about 100 km through the southern central section of the Park, skirting the beautiful Lake Waikaremoana, and passing HQ at Aniwaniwa.

Hitching And Cycling
Hitching is not easy—relatively little traffic most of the year. In summer, cars full of families on vacation are unlikely to stop. If you do get a ride, but not as far as you planned, the main road is an unpleasant place to find yourself unexpectedly stranded in what seems to be the middle of nowhere when darkness falls. No towns, lots of mist, unfamiliar eerie sounds—not recommended! The same bad news goes for bicycle touring on the steep loose gravel hills—only recommended for confirmed masochists.

Buses
Buses run along Hwy. 38 through the Park three times a week, each way, connecting Rotorua with Wairoa—get schedule, prices, and book tickets at the InterCity Travel Centre on Amohau St., Rotorua, tel. 481-039, or call Park HQ for current bus schedules at tel. Tuai 803. Get off the bus at Park HQ and Visitor Centre at Aniwaniwa (Rotorua is 160 km and Wairoa is 64 km from here) where you can camp out, stay in the nearby motor camp (but don't count on it in summer—see "Accommodation" above), and choose from a variety of short walks or a long hike around the lake. Before getting on the bus for Urewera, buy all your food and supplies, and take a tent, stove, fuel, and cooking equipment with you—there's a store at the motor camp but the prices aren't cheap!

THE EAST CAPE

The East Cape is a splendid and relatively remote area of the North Island. Here you'll find golden beaches interspersed with rocky points, and a coastal road that's lined with ancient *pohutukawa* trees and backed by rugged mountains. Major rivers challenge the most suicidal white-water rafting or canoeing enthusiast, and a smattering of historic landmarks scattered along the coast commemorate the discovery of New Zealand by Capt. Cook. Add sunshine year-round and not too many other visitors and you get the picture. You can also revel in the knowledge that, due to its close proximity to the International Date Line, "the sun rises on the East Cape before anywhere else in the British Commonwealth" and, according to local residents, it "rises on Gisborne before any other city in the world!"

The East Cape is the easternmost tip of New Zealand, a rounded piece of land jutting far out into the Pacific Ocean. Running down the center in a northeast-southwest direction is the formidable Raukumara Range with its highest non-volcanic peak, Mt. Hikurangi, standing 1,754 meters tall. Riddled with small rivers and streams the range also gives rise to three major rivers—the Waiapu, Waipaoa, and remote Motu, popular with commercial white-water rafting outfits.

Most of the Cape is inaccessible by car and relatively unexplored by foot. Two main roads service the region: one hugs the coast all the way around the Cape from Opotiki to Gisborne; the other cuts off the whole peninsula to connect the two. Due to its relative isolation, the East Cape has a large Maori population: over half the rural population and more than a third of the people of Gisborne. Neither of the two main routes lays claim to any major tourist attractions—leisurely venture the coastal wilderness of the East Cape if you've plenty of time, or if you just want to escape the commercial rat race for a few more days.

THE INLAND ROUTE

Highway 2 is the 148-km route (about two to three hours by car non-stop) which connects Opotiki on the Bay of Plenty to Gisborne on the far east coast. It passes through fern-lined gorges with riverbank rest areas and waterfall views, and contrasting dairy farms, orchards, and vineyards that neatly patchwork the land as you approach Gisborne. The 30-km **Waioeka Scenic Highway,** part of Hwy. 2 at the Opotiki end, is a particularly magical stretch for lovers of ferns and native forest. The **Motu Gorge,** a sidetrack which runs from Matawai to Toatoa, has wild and rugged scenery. To get in there take Motu Rd. which closely follows the untamed Motu River, but take note: although it looks like an hour's drive on the map, it really takes about half a day—pretty hairy driving at that, not recommended for the fainthearted. If you take this sidetrack, don't miss splendid **Motu Falls,** five km downstream from Motu.

Another waterfall, a large variety of non-native trees, and an abundance of flowers can also be appreciated on your way to Gisborne if you don't mind a 48-km sidetrack (35 km from Gisborne). At the town of Makaraka turn right onto the main highway south (instead of going into Gisborne) and continue through Makaraka to the Waipaoa River Bridge. Don't go into Patutahi township but keep on the road to Ngatapa. As you near Ngatapa follow the AA signs to Eastwoodhill, continuing past Ngatapa village and onto Wharekopai Rd. toward Rere. At the junction of Rere and Hihiroroa roads the **Eastwoodhill Arboretum** is well worth a stop. It's a huge collection of trees, shrubs, and climbers not native to New Zealand—most of them are from the Northern Hemisphere. If you're there in spring and bulbs turn you (or your camera)

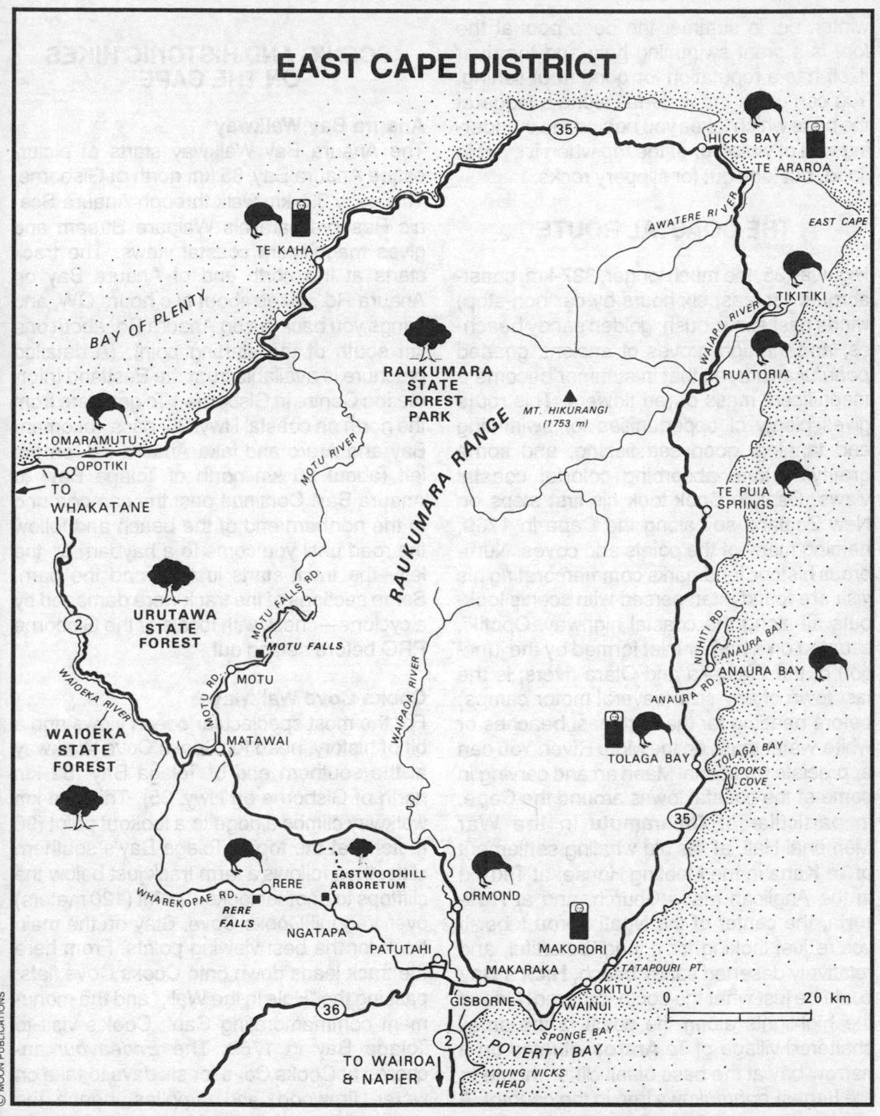

on, the daffodil patch is a flower spectacular that shouldn't be missed. The gardens are open year-round except June and July, on weekends and holidays from 1000-1600; admission $4. After visiting the Arboretum, continue along Wharekopai Rd. to **Rere Falls.** The falls and picnic area are within a two-hectare reserve along the banks of the Wharekopai River. The 24-meter-high, 45-meter-wide falls are perhaps most impressive in winter, but in summer the deep pool at the foot is a great swimming hole and the river itself has a reputation for good trout fishing. You can cross the waterfall along a ledge at the base which takes you behind the thundering wall of water, or at the top when it's not in flood, but look out for slippery rocks.

THE COASTAL ROUTE

Highway 35, the much longer, 327-km, coastal route (at least six hours by car non-stop) winds past exotic bush, golden sandy beaches, and through groves of ancient, gnarled *pohutukawa* trees that in summer become a magnificent mass of red flowers. This route gives plenty of opportunities for swimming and tanning, good sea fishing, and some gratifying time absorbing colorful coastal views. Captain Cook took his first steps on New Zealand soil along the Cape in 1769, naming many of the points and coves. Numerous historic landmarks commemorating his visit are found interspersed with scenic lookouts all along the coastal highway. Opotiki, situated on a harbor inlet formed by the junction of the Waioeka and Otara rivers, is the last town of any size (several motor camps) before heading for the northeast beaches or white-water thrills on the Motu River. You can appreciate traditional Maori art and carving in some of the coastal towns around the Cape, in particular at **Omaramutu** in the War Memorial Hall, at the old whaling settlement of **Te Kaha** in the Meeting House, at **Tikitiki** in the Anglican Maori Church, and at **Ruatoria,** the center of the Ngati Porou tribe. If you're just looking for a long, beautiful, and relatively deserted sandy beach, **Hick's Bay** could be just what the doctor ordered! One of the highlights along the coast is the small sheltered village of **Te Araroa** situated on a narrow bay at the base of tall cliffs—home to the largest *pohutukawa* tree in the country. A passenger courier service runs from Gisborne to Hick's Bay and back Mon. to Fri. for $36 OW (tel. Te Aroa 711). For accommodation around the Cape see "East Cape Motor Camps," p. 231, and for bus transportation see "Long-Distance Buses," p. 233.

SCENIC AND HISTORIC HIKES ON THE CAPE

Anaura Bay Walkway

The Anaura Bay Walkway starts at picturesque Anaura Bay, 85 km north of Gisborne. This easy 3.5-km walk through Anaura Scenic Reserve parallels Waipare Stream and gives magnificent coastal views. The track starts at the north end of Anaura Bay on Anaura Rd., takes about two hours OW, and brings you back out on Anaura Rd. about one km south of the starting point. (A detailed brochure is available from the Eastland Information Centre in Gisborne.) To get there from the north on coastal Hwy. 35, pass Tokomaru Bay and Arero and take Anaura Rd. on the left (about 20 km north of Tolaga Bay) to Anaura Bay. Continue past the campground to the northern end of the beach and follow the road until you come to a haybarn on the left—the track starts just beyond the barn. Some sections of the track were damaged by a cyclone—check with locals or the Gisborne PRO before setting out.

Cooks Cove Walkway

For the most spectacular ocean views and a bit of history, head for Cooks Cove Walkway at the southern end of Tolaga Bay (52 km north of Gisborne on Hwy. 35). This five-km walkway climbs a ridge to a lookout point (90 meters) at the top of Tolaga Bay's southern cliffs, then follows a farm track just below the clifftops to another lookout point (120 meters) over tranquil Cooks Cove. Stay on the main track for the best viewing points. From here the track leads down onto Cooks Cove flats, passing the "Hole in the Wall," and the monument commemorating Capt. Cook's visit to Tolaga Bay in 1769. The *Endeavour* anchored at Cooks Cove for six days to take on water, firewood, and supplies, hence the name. This easy track takes just over an hour OW. Take a windbreaker and something to drink—there's no fresh water—and wear sturdy shoes. Toilets are located at the wharf near the beginning of the track, and there's a motor camp nearby (see "Accommodation,"

p. 231). A detailed brochure on the walkway is available from the Eastland Information Centre in Gisborne. To get there from the north follow Hwy. 35 to Tolaga Bay and about two km after the township turn left on Wharf Road. At the end turn left and continue to the first carpark—the track starts across the road.

GISBORNE

A CITY WITH A TALE TO TELL

Gisborne is one of New Zealand's most historic cities. **Young Nick's Head** at the southern end of **Poverty Bay** was the first New Zealand promontory sighted by Capt. Cook and his crew on 6 Oct. 1769, named after the *Endeavour* cabin boy who first sighted it. The crew landed at **Kaiti Beach** where Capt. Cook took formal possession of the new country in the name of His Majesty King George III. On attempting to make friends with the local Maori and restock supplies, Cook found the natives more than a little hostile, and the crew lifted anchor and left with nothing but a small amount of firewood. Over the next five months they circumnavigated the new land that became known as New Zealand. As they had not been welcomed with open arms, Cook named the bay on which Gisborne now stands Poverty Bay—a name that the locals have humorously retained despite the obvious agricultural wealth of the fertile alluvial Poverty Bay flats, busy fishing fleet, and abundant natural attractions that the area presents to the explorers of today.

SIGHTS

Historic Sights On Foot

The first place to go is the Eastland Information Centre (see "Information," p. 233) off the main shopping street downtown. The staff gladly hands out brochures (if you like to fish, ask for their info-packed "Guide to Trout Fishing in the Gisborne Area" brochure) and maps, and can suggest more things to see and do than you can possibly handle! Also pick up the free "Gisborne District" brochure—a good way to become oriented with Gisborne and the surrounding lay of the land. Next to the info center is small **Alfred Cox Park,** dominated by the unusual sight of a large totem pole, a gift from Canada to celebrate the bicentenary of Capt. Cook's first landing in 1769.

From Grey St. turn right onto Gladstone Rd. and continue over the bridge. Veer right under the railway embankment and follow the harbor past the freezing works and overseas wharf. You can take Kaiti Beach Rd. all the way to the Yacht Club (the beach is not good for swimming) or, at the impressive **Capt. James Cook Monument** which marks the

downtown Gisborne from Captain James Cook Memorial Park

spot where Capt. Cook first landed, take the short track across the road that leads up Kaiti Hill to **Captain James Cook Memorial Park.** Revel in history here and take in a fantastic 180-degree view of the city, harbor, meeting of the Taruheru, Waimata, and Turanganui rivers, and magnificent Poverty Bay. Check out the amazingly clear blue water that appears to surround Gisborne! The white cliff headland to the south is **Young Nick's Head.**

At the foot of Kaiti Hill where Queens Dr. and Ranfurly St. meet, the road passes the **Te Poho-o-rawiri Meeting House,** one of the largest decorative meeting halls in New Zealand. A small Maori church also lies above. The hall is usually open to the public (enter via the side door); the intricate Maori carving and *tukutuku* reed work (done in Rotorua) are worth seeing. If it's closed, ask the caretaker who lives next door for permission to enter.

Museums And Art Gallery

The fascinating **Gisborne Museum** standing along the Taruheru River features east coast, Maori, and colonial artifacts, and natural history; Wyllie Cottage, originally built in 1872 and the oldest house in Gisborne, stands within the museum grounds. The art gallery (open Tues. to Sun.) has changing exhibitions, and local art and crafts on display are for sale. Light lunches and snacks are available at The Deck Restaurant, open weekdays only. The center is open Tues. to Fri. from 1000-1600, weekends and public holidays from 1400-1630, admission $2 adult, student or child 50 cents. Located on Stout St. by the Peel St. Bridge (tel. 83-832), on the other side of the Taruheru River from downtown.

The *Star of Canada* was shipwrecked on Kaiti Beach in 1912. The ship's bridge, deck, Captain's cabin and chartroom were salvaged and turned into a house, and then moved to their present location overlooking the river and opened as a museum! Inside you can follow the mariners' impressive contribution to the development of Gisborne through a number of whaling, shipping, and water transportation displays, and view hundreds of photographs with a decidedly maritime theme. Open Tues. to Fri. 1000-1600, weekends and public holidays 1400-1630, tel. 83-832. Admission is adult $3, child $1—get your admission token at the reception desk of the Gisborne Museum first.

Botanical Gardens

These tranquil gardens, sandwiched between Aberdeen Rd. and the banks of the Taruheru River, feature a free-flight aviary amongst the flowers, trees, and lawns. It's a peaceful green place to take your lunch and catch up on postcard writing. Walk along Gladstone Rd. away from downtown, turn right on Carnarvon St. and left on Aberdeen Road.

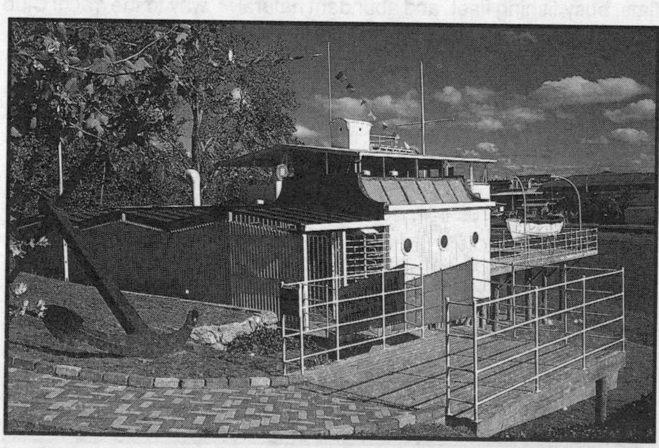

Star of Canada Maritime Museum, Gisborne

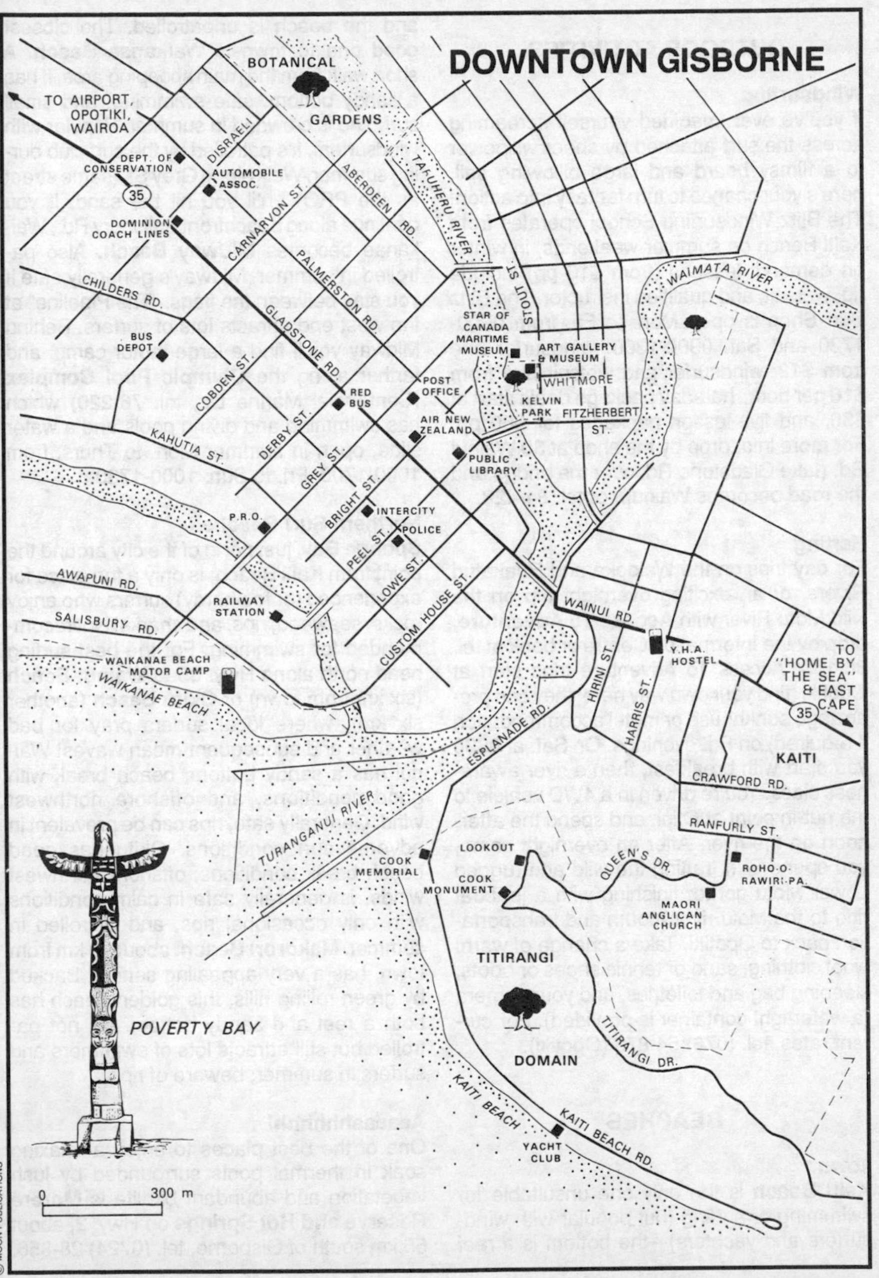
DOWNTOWN GISBORNE
TO AIRPORT, OPOTIKI, WAIROA
BOTANICAL GARDENS
DISRAELI
DEPT. OF CONSERVATION
AUTOMOBILE ASSOC.
35
DOMINION COACH LINES
CARNARVON ST.
ABERDEEN RD.
TARUHERU RIVER
PALMERSTON RD.
CHILDERS RD.
GLADSTONE RD.
BUS DEPOT
COBDEN ST.
STOUT ST.
WAIMATA RIVER
STAR OF CANADA MARITIME MUSEUM
ART GALLERY & MUSEUM
WHITMORE
KELVIN PARK
FITZHERBERT ST.
POST OFFICE
RED BUS
AIR NEW ZEALAND
DERBY ST.
KAHUTIA ST.
GREY ST.
PUBLIC LIBRARY
BRIGHT ST.
INTERCITY
POLICE
P.R.O.
PEEL ST.
LOWE ST.
CUSTOM HOUSE ST.
AWAPUNI RD.
SALISBURY RD.
RAILWAY STATION
WAINUI RD.
Y.H.A. HOSTEL
TO "HOME BY THE SEA" & EAST CAPE
35
HIRINI ST.
HARRIS ST.
WAIKANAE BEACH MOTOR CAMP
WAIKANAE BEACH
ESPLANADE RD.
KAITI
CRAWFORD RD.
TURANGANUI RIVER
RANFURLY ST.
LOOKOUT
QUEEN'S DR.
COOK MEMORIAL
ROHO-O-RAWIRI-PA.
COOK MONUMENT
MAORI ANGLICAN CHURCH
TITIRANGI
POVERTY BAY
DOMAIN
TITIRANGI DR.
KAITI BEACH
KAITI BEACH RD.
YACHT CLUB
0
300 m
© MOON PUBLICATIONS

OUTDOOR ACTIVITIES

Windsurfing

If you've ever imagined yourself screaming across the surf attached by sheer willpower to a flimsy board and large billowing sail, here's your chance to turn fantasy into action! The Blitz Windsurfing School operates from Kaiti Beach on summer weekends, in winter on demand; lessons (from $15 pp) include rig, wetsuit, and qualified instructor. The Blitz Surf Shop is open Mon. to Fri. from 0900-1730 and Sat. 0900-1300: windsurfer hire from $12; windsurfer and wetsuit hire from $16 per hour, half-day package deals start at $36, and five-lesson packages for $60 pp. For more info, drop by the shop at 30 Wainui Rd. (take Gladstone Rd. over the bridge and the road becomes Wainui), or tel. 84-428.

Rafting

For day trips on the Waioeka and Ruakaturi Rivers, or an exciting overnight trip on the wild Motu River with **Access To Adventure,** drop by the Information Centre or book at tel. 86-139. Access To Adventure trips start at Opotiki (find your own way here; they can prearrange bunkhouse or motel accommodation if required) on Fri. evenings. On Sat. at 0830 you start with breakfast, then a river awareness class. You're driven in a 4WD vehicle to the put-in point at Otipi, and spend the afternoon on the river. After an overnight camp, you spend Sun. rafting the wild and rugged Lower Motu gorge, finishing with a jet-boat ride to the Motu river mouth and transportation back to Opotiki. Take a change of warm wool clothing, sand or tennis shoes or boots, sleeping bag and toiletries, and your camera (a watertight container is provided). For current rates, tel. (076) 54-873 (Opotiki).

BEACHES

Town

Kaiti Beach is the only one unsuitable for swimming or surfing (but popular with windsurfers and yachters)—the bottom is a reef and the beach is unpatrolled. The closest good one to town is **Waikanae Beach.** A short walk from the main shopping area, it has a sandy bottom, safe swimming, and small surf, and is crowded in summer. Popular with windsurfers, it's patrolled by the surf club during summer. Walk along Grey St. (same street as the PRO) until you hit the sand. If you continue along beachfront Salisbury Rd., Waikanae becomes **Midway Beach.** Also patrolled in summer, Midway's generally safe if you stay between the flags. "The Pipeline" at the west end attracts lots of surfers. Behind Midway you'll find a large motor camp, and farther along the **Olympic Pool Complex** (Centennial Marine Dr., tel. 76-220) which has swimming and diving pools and a water slide, open in summer Mon. to Thurs. from 1000-1700, Fri. to Sun. 1000-1730.

Northern Surf Beaches

Sponge Bay, just north of the city around the point from Kaiti Beach, is only a fun place for experienced (or foolhardy) surfers who enjoy rocks, seaweed, rips, and sharks! Not recommended for swimming. For the best surfing head north along Hwy. 35 to **Wainui Beach** (six km from town) or **Okitu Beach** (another six km), where local surfers pray for bad weather and subsequent mean waves! Wainui has a sandy bottom, beach break with good conditions, and offshore northwest wind. Generally safe, rips can be prevalent in adverse surf conditions. Okitu has good beach break conditions, offshore northwest winds, is generally safe in calm conditions with only occasional rips, and patrolled in summer. **Makorori Beach,** about 10 km from town, has a very appealing setting. Backed by green rolling hills, this golden beach has both a reef and sandy bottom. It's not patrolled but still attracts lots of swimmers and surfers in summer; beware of rips.

Aaaaaahhhhhh!

One of the best places to enjoy a relaxing soak in thermal pools surrounded by lush vegetation and abundant birdlife is **Morere Reserve and Hot Springs** on Hwy. 2, about 55 km south of Gisborne, tel. (0724) 28-856.

Soak in the Nikau Pools (two hot pools, cold plunge pool, hot foot pool, changing facilities, showers, and toilets), in the private hot pools, in the hot indoor pool, or the cold freshwater outdoor pool—with a choice like that, how can you go wrong! Everything is beautifully landscaped to blend in with the forest environment. Or go for a woodland walk (the tracks range from 10 minutes to 5½ hours) to appreciate all the tweeting from the trees, have a picnic, or take advantage of the nextdoor tavern and restaurant. Open weekdays 1000-1700, weekends and public holidays 1000-1900/2000; admission adult $2.50, child $1.50, private pools adult $3.50, child $1.75.

ACCOMMODATION

Budget

The **Gisborne YHA Hostel** is in a rambling house with a rambling atmosphere, and the Gisborne YHA actively organizes frequent hikes and outings—a good source of info on what to see and do in the great local outdoors; $11 pp. Located at 32 Harris St. on the east side of town, tel. 83-269. From Gladstone St. (the main street), cross the bridge and turn right at the traffic lights. The hostel is in the second block beyond the bridge.

A Home By The Sea is just that! For only $12 pp you can stay in a beachside house with dorm-style accommodation (one room has double bunks), communal bathroom and cooking facilities, a laid-back holiday atmosphere, and impressive stereo system! Walk out the back door and you're *on* a gorgeous surf beach. Bicycles can be hired from the manager. It's only open during summer (usually from 1 Oct. to April)—in winter the waves batter the back door! At 11 Wairere Rd., Wainui Beach (about five km north of Gisborne), tel. 78-058 (call and see if it's open before you go out there, or ask for a pickup).

City Motor Camps

Waikanae Beach Holiday Park is adjacent to sandy Waikanae Beach, only 800 meters from downtown—a great spot for walking and swimming. Along with the usual community facilities (spotlessly clean) there's a cool room with lockers, tennis courts (racket hire $4 for two), and at the office you can rent bicycles, surfboards, boogie boards, etc. Tentsites $10 d; caravan sites $12 d; ranchhouse cabins $20 s or d, tourist cabins (with private bathroom and cooking facilities, but you supply bedding) are $43 d. Located on Grey St., tel. 75-634.

The Showgrounds Motor Camp is a long walk from the center of town on the west side, and not available as a motor camp when it's being used as a showground (usually October). However, if you're into golf you'll probably enjoy staying here—it's next to the ninehole Park Golf Course. Communal facilities. Tentsites are $5.50 d, caravan sites $7.50 d, cabins $11.50-15.50 d. Located in The Showgrounds, tel. 74-101. From downtown follow Gladstone Rd. to the west end—it becomes Hwy. 35. When you see the golf course to the left start looking for the motor camp—it's just down the road, also on the left.

East Cape Motor Camps

Tolaga Bay Motor Camp is 65 km north of Gisborne up Hwy. 35, the route that follows the Cape coastline. The camp has an excellent location next to a sandy beach, near a long pier popular with fishermen, with several good hikes in the area. Communal facilities (metered showers). Tentsites are $11 d, caravan sites $13.50 d, cabins $20-22 d, on-site caravans $22 d. Located one km from the main road at Tolaga Bay beach, near the wharf, tel. 716.

Te Araroa Holiday Park is only a four-minute walk from a safe sandy beach, has a freshwater stream running through the camp, and horses available for hire in Dec. and January. Communal facilities, recreation and TV room, store, BBQ, and fish smoker. Tentsites are $5.50 pp, caravan sites $6.50 pp, dormitory bunks $7.50 pp, cabins $26 d, tourist flats $38.50 d. Located 6½ km north of Te Araroa on Hwy. 35, midway between Hick's Bay and Te Araroa, tel. 873.

Te Kaha Holiday Park has a swimming pool, BBQ, trampoline, game and TV room, and camp store. Tent and caravan sites are $7.70 pp, cabin $26 d, tourist flats $45 d.

Located three km north of Te Kaha on Hwy. 35, tel. 894.

Private Hotels

Gisborne has many private hotels and oodles of motels (refer to your *AA Accommodation Directory* for complete listings). Two of the most reasonable private hotels are: the **Royal** with rooms from $25.50 s, $38 d, meals available, located on Gladstone Rd., tel. 89-184; and the **Albion Club** also on Gladstone Rd., tel. 79-639, $22 s, $28 d, breakfast and dinner available.

FOOD

Light Snacks And Takeaways

For a quick lunch on your way to Kaiti Hill try **Ocean Garden Lunch Bar** on The Esplanade by the wharf. Sit outside under the umbrella and people-watch while you munch on a crayfish roll (a local specialty), homemade pie, or fish 'n chips, or buy some fresh fish to go. Another place to head in the evening or wee hours is **Kaiti Takeaways,** half a km east of the Gladstone St. Bridge at 108 Wainui Rd., tel. 83-673; open Mon. to Thurs. from 1630-2400, Fri. and Sat. 1630-0300. If you're planning on taking a lunch to any of the local beauty spots, feast your eyes on and give the old tastebuds a treat with food from the **Wheat Sheaf Delicatessen** at 73 Gladstone Road. They have cold meats, pâté, hot chicken, crispy salads, french bread, croissants, pastries, and homemade gateaux and carrot cake that'll make burning off the calories a necessity the rest of the day! **Eddie Moore's Coffee Lounge** at 273 Gladstone Rd. (tel. 75-640) serves breakfast and takeaways from 0700, hot meals and salads all day, and the specialties are tacos, delicious filled rolls, and burgers.

Looking for the usual takeaway choices? **Kentucky Fried Chicken** is next to Pizza Hut on Grey Street. **McDonald's** is on Bright Street.

Meals

For a good selection of tasty salads try **Captain Morgan's** at 285 Grey St. across from the motor camp—a stroll from the beachfront. Aside from the salad bar (small $3.50, large $6), a variety of tearoom fare, and specialty ice creams, they also serve light lunches, and steak and seafood dinners (mains $11-13.50, desserts $3.50) to 2000. Eat inside, or out on the sunny deck. At dinner it pays to book ahead at tel. 87-821.

For reasonable prices and a self-serve BBQ and salad bar, try **Long John's Barbeque and Bar** in the Sandale Park Motor Hotel. Open from 1100-2000 Mon. to Sat., it also has an outdoor beer garden, and entertainment five nights a week. Another hotel with main courses from $9-15 is the **Royal** in the Cooks Gallery restaurant. The **Lyric Cafe** at 24 Gladstone Rd. between Peel and Bright sts. specializes in seafood (from $10) and tasty grills ($8-10), and is one of the relatively few places open for breakfast (around $6 pp). They also whip up fresh fish takeaways—call in your order to go at tel. 74-134. The **Pizza Hut Restaurant** on Grey St. (and the corner of Kahutia St.) serves up the usual (and good) pizza and salads. Expect to pay around $25 for two for pizza, salad, and coffee. Another place to try for a quick grilled meal or takeaway is **Woolworth's Family Restaurant,** on the corner of Gladstone Rd. and Bright Street.

For Continental cuisine and a dressy splurge, **Petes On The Beach** opposite the Olympic Pool at Midway Beach will satisfy your appetite for both. Mains are $12.50-20. Open seven days for lunch and dinner, tel. 75-861. Another expensive and dressy place is **The Marina** at River Junction, Marina Park; mains start around $14. It's open for lunch and dinner, tel. 85-919.

ENTERTAINMENT

Pubs

The main source of evening entertainment radiates around chugging a few in the pubs and hotel bars and taking in a good live band. The following hotels or clubs usually have something happening weeknights, and regular live entertainment on weekends—call for what's on. The **D.B. Gisborne Hotel** (tel.

84-109) attracts big-name acts from around New Zealand as well as local groups. The **Albion River Bar** (tel. 83-568) also features good live bands on Fri. and Sat. nights. Also try the **Sandown Park Hotel** (tel. 84-134), the **Chalet Rendezvous** (tel. 75-419), **Peaches Nightclub** above The Kiln restaurant on Derby St. (tel. 83-111), or **Crossroads Nightclub** (tel. 81-006).

Movies

For movies, check out the **Odeon Theatre** (tel. 83-339). The current movies playing are advertised in the local paper, the *Gisborne Herald.*

SERVICES AND INFORMATION

Urgent

For **emergency** help (ambulance, police, fire, pharmacy) dial 111. The **police station** is on the corner of Peel St. and Childers Road. **St. Johns Ambulance** on the corner of Palmerston Rd. and Bright St. is the place to go to find out the local on-duty emergency doctor, dentist, or urgent pharmacist. **Gisborne Hospital** is on Ormond Rd., tel. 79-099. The **Urgent Pharmacy** is at 245 Gladstone Rd., tel. 78-108; hours Mon. to Thurs. 1830-2000, Sat. 1200-1400 and 1730-2000, Sun. and holidays 1100-1300 and 1830-2000.

General

For all the info you need on Gisborne and a large amount of printed material on the whole country, see the helpful people at the **Eastland Information Centre,** 209 Grey St., tel. 86-139. Ask for the free "Gisborne District" brochure which covers annual events, history and culture, eating and entertainment spots, accommodation, outdoor activities, walking tours and scenic places, arts, crafts, galleries, museums, and wineries, services and maps. For info on N.Z. Walkway tracks, call in at the **Department of Conservation** at 430 Palmerston Rd.; open weekdays 0800-1630. The central **p.o.** is on Grey St. between Gladstone and Palmerston roads, and the **public library** is on Peel St., tel. 76-709; open Mon. to Fri. 1000-1700, Sat. 1000-1200.

TRANSPORTATION

Getting There

The main road in and out of Gisborne, Hwy. 2, runs south from Opotiki (Bay of Plenty), and north from Wairoa (Hawke Bay). Opotiki and Gisborne are also connected by the much longer coastal route, Hwy. 35, which winds through the fairly isolated villages and quiet beach settlements of the East Cape. Gisborne is easily reached by bus from Whakatane and Opotiki (by hwys. 2 or 35), from Rotorua via Waikaremoana and Wairoa, and from Taupo via Napier and Wairoa. It's also serviced by a national airport. Hitching is hard from Urewera National Park because of the sparse traffic, but relatively easy from Napier, or Wairoa via Hwy. 2. Unless you have all the time in the world don't try hitching around the East Cape.

Local Buses

Gisborne's several bus companies service the local area. **Gisborne City Council Bus Services,** suburban transport, is located on Childers Rd., tel. 82-049. **Red Bus Service** covers the rural areas of Bartletts, Whatatutu, Te Karaka, and Muriwai, and both north and south main highways. They also do one-day sightseeing trips to Morere, and Waikaremoana in Urewera National Park; on Derby St., tel. 87-423. **Hindmarsh Bus Service** operates a rural schedule between Patutahi and Gisborne; tel. 648, Patutahi.

Long-distance Buses

You can easily get to Gisborne from Opotiki by **InterCity,** either direct by Hwy. 2 south or through Te Kaha, Hick's Bay, Te Araroa, Ruatoria, and Tolaga Bay (coastal route). The Opotiki depot is on Elliot St., tel. 56-146. From Gisborne, InterCity operates to Opotiki ($32 OW), Whakatane ($18 OW), Rotorua ($24.50 OW), Hamilton ($27 OW), and Auckland ($32.50 OW), and to Tauranga (via separate bus route; $54 OW). One way to see the East Coast is to take the InterCity Day Excursion trip from Gisborne to Hick's Bay, Opotiki, Whakatane, and back to Gisborne, Sun. to

Ornate verandas are a common feature in older New Zealand homes. Travel by road to see some of the best.

Fri., departing Gisborne at 0830 and returning at 1845. Get more info and the current excursion fare from the Gisborne Travel Centre at Childers Rd. and Bright St., tel. 86-195/196; open Mon. to Fri. 0730-1715, Sat. and Sun. 0730-1015. **Dominion Coachlines** services Napier ($25 OW), Hastings, and return, with connections at Napier (through Newmans) for destinations south and east—Palmerston North, New Plymouth, and Wellington ($64 OW); Gisborne, Palmerston North, Wanganui ($60 OW; overnight $50); and services north (through Mt. Cook) to Rotorua ($60 OW), Hamilton ($64 OW), and Auckland ($80 OW). The quickest, least expensive way to Wellington is on the Dominion overnight service for $56 OW. The depot is at 393 Gladstone Rd. and the corner of Disraeli St., tel. 89-083; open Mon. to Fri. 0630-1715, Sat. 0630-0900.

Cars

The Automobile Association office is a great place for road maps and travel info. It's located on the corner of Palmerston Rd. and Disraeli St., about four blocks west of downtown. For **AA Breakdown Service** call Gisborne Panelbeaters all hours at tel. 76-729. **Dominion Budget Rentals** is at 397 Childers Rd., tel. 79-794. **Avis** is on Grey St., tel. 89-084. **Hertz** is at 346 Gladstone Rd., tel. 79-348. **Rent-A-Wreck** has rental cars, scooters, and vans "cheaper than cheap." On the corner of Grey St. and Awapuni Rd., tel. 78-164. For taxi service or sightseeing tours call **Gisborne Taxis,** 209 Palmerston Rd., tel. 76-869, or visit the Derby St. depot. The **Midway Service Station** is open 24 hours, located on the corner of Gladstone Rd. and Cobden St., tel. 85-082.

Air

Gisborne **Airport** is on the west side of the city. Get there via taxi (about $7.50 pp OW; tel. 76-869) or the **Airport Shuttle Service** for about $5 pp OW (tel. 74-765 or 89-785). The easiest route by car is to take Gladstone Rd. west out of town and just before the golf course make a left on Chalmers Road. Continue almost to the end and turn right on Aerodrome Road. **Air New Zealand** flies regularly to all major centers in both North and South islands. The Air New Zealand office is at 37 Bright St., tel. 84-079. **Eagle Air** serves Auckland, Whangarei, Kaitaia, Hamilton, Napier, Palmerston North, Tauranga, and Wellington (via Air New Zealand). For schedules and fares phone the Eagle Air office at the airport, tel. 81-608. **Cookson Air Services** connects Gisborne with Wairoa, Napier, and Auckland; tel. 84-075. For sightseeing or charter flights, drop by the airport and see **Air Gisborne,** or tel. 74-684.

NAPIER

A SEASIDE CITY

Napier is another place to enjoy sea breezes whipping through your hair and bright sun on your face, but its distinct seaside-town atmosphere and earthquake history set it apart from the other towns along the east coast. Sauntering along stately, Norfolk pine-lined Marine Parade, it's hard to believe that this elegant city was completely rebuilt after total destruction in the Hawke's Bay earthquake of 1931. During the earthquake the city, at that time a busy trading post, was lifted six to eight feet, and the salt marshes, swamps, and inner harbor were completely drained. Although there was great loss of life and almost

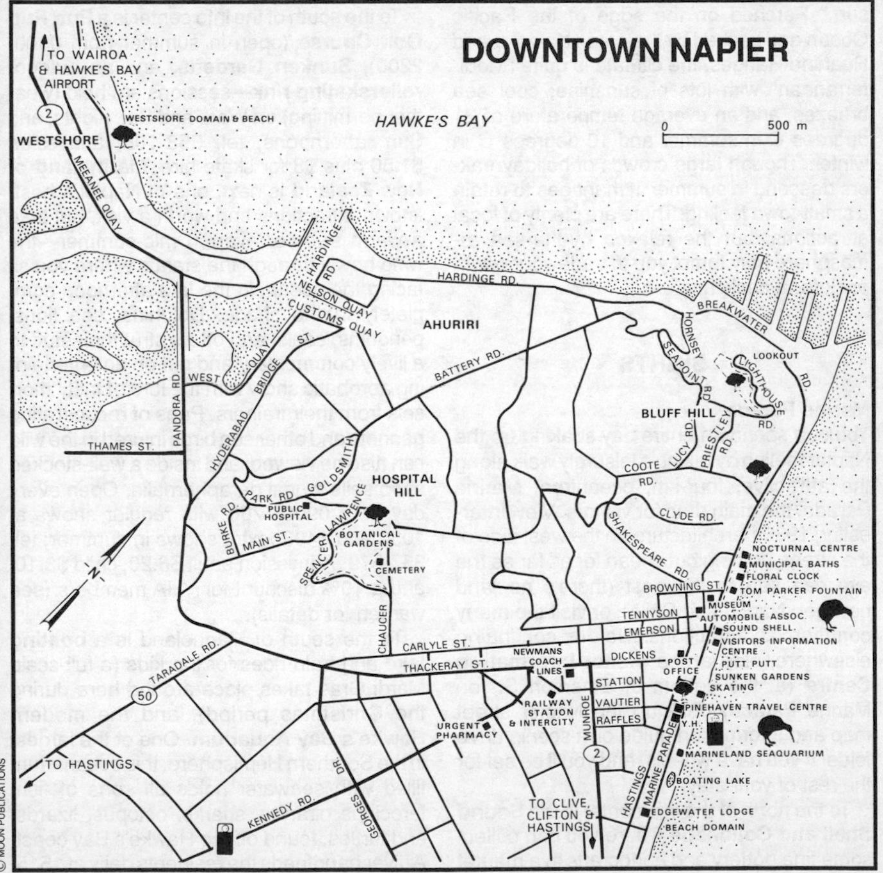

all the brick buildings of the city collapsed, the earthquake gave the survivors an extra 10,000 acres of land, and now the airport and a large section of Napier stand on what used to be the sea floor. The wreckage from the earthquake lies buried beneath Marine Parade. Today the port is the third largest exporter in the country. It has an active fishing fleet, and Hawke's Bay attracts large numbers of yachtsmen and boat enthusiasts to sail along this scenic coastline.

Along with all New Zealand cities, Napier has its nicknames—"Capital of the Sunrise Coast" and "the city where the turf meets the surf." Perched on the edge of the Pacific Ocean and backed by the green Kaweka and Ruahine Ranges, the climate is quite "Mediterranean" with lots of sunshine, cool sea breezes, and an average temperature of 21 degrees C in summer and 10 degrees C in winter. Though large crowds of holidaymakers descend in summer, it manages to retain a small-town feeling. There are plenty of local attractions, but the relaxed by-the-sea atmosphere may tempt you to trade your backpack for a deckchair.

SIGHTS

Marine Parade

You can spend an entire day soaking up the Napier feeling by taking a leisurely walk along the attractive, four-km, oceanfront Marine Parade, the main drag for visitors. View interesting 1930s' architecture on the west side of the street, nothing but ocean for as far as the eye can see to the east (there's no land between Napier and Chile), or visit the many commercial attractions. Before continuing elsewhere, stop at the **Visitor Information Centre** (at the bottom of Emerson St. on Marine Parade). Pick up the Napier street map and information guide or a scenic drive folder if you have wheels, and you'll be set for the rest of your stay.

To the north of the info center is the **Sound Shell and Collonade** where you can collect some fine pottery and handcrafts in a market setting on Saturdays, and the **Tom Parker Fountain, Floral Clock,** and **Marine Parade Baths,** open only in summer from 1000-1730 (70 cents pp), tel. 58-633. Farther along you'll find the intriguing **Kiwi House,** open daily from 1000-1600 but most entertaining around 1430 when the animals are fed. Get a close-up view of the nocturnal antics of the kiwi, native frog, *weta,* opossum, glowworms, and other creatures of the night. During holiday periods special shows are held at 1100 and 1300; admission adult $2.60, child $1, 10% discount on admission for YHA members (see hostel warden), tel. 357-553.

To the south of the info center is a **Putt Putt Golf Course** (open in summer from 0900-2200), **Sunken Gardens,** and an outdoor **rollerskating rink**—sessions are held (weather permitting) on Wed. and Sat. nights, and Sun. afternoons, tel. 358-188; admission $1.50 plus $3 for skate hire. **Marineland of New Zealand** is next, one of Napier's best-known attractions and worth a visit, but take a warm sweater even in mid-summer—the wind howls through the stands where you sit facing the ocean, in the late afternoon completely in the shade. Dolphins, sea lions, penguins, seals, and otters strut their stuff to a lively commentary and put on an entertaining aerobatic show with the lure of tasty morsels from their trainers. Pens of recuperating gannets and other sea birds injured in the wild can also be viewed, and inside a well-stocked shop sells tourist paraphernalia. Open every day from 0900-1700 with regular shows at 1030 and 1400, extra shows in summer; tel. 357-579. Admission adult $6.20, child $3.10, and a 10% discount for YHA members (see warden for details).

To the south of Marineland is a **boating lake** and train rides for the kids (a full-scale Mardi Gras takes place around here during the Christmas period), and the modern **Hawke's Bay Aquarium.** One of the largest in the Southern Hemisphere, this oceanarium filled with seawater holds all sorts of fish, ferocious piranha, sharks, octopus, lizards, and turtles, found off the Hawke's Bay coast. A diver handfeeds the residents daily at 1515.

Open seven days a week from 0900-1700, from 0900-2100 in summer, admission adult $6, child $3, tel. 358-493.

Scenic Lookouts

Just past the wildlife center at the northern end of Marine Parade, Coote Rd. branches off to the left, passing attractive **Centennial Gardens** where an artificial waterfall splashes down a 100-meter cliff face into ponds and rock pools amongst flowerbeds and lawns. Coote Rd. continues up Bluff Hill to the **Bluff Hill Lookout** for great ocean views. (Turn right off Coote Rd. onto Thompson Rd., then right on Lighthouse Rd. and follow it to the end.) If you don't have a city map it's quite easy to get lost up here even when you're trying your best to follow the blue and yellow scenic drive signs. If you don't mind stumbling around in a maze of one-way streets and fascinating architecture, fancy homes, and the odd glimpse of city or sea, try finding your way to **City View Outlook** while you're in the mood. It's a great spot at night to view the city lights. Take Coote Rd. (off Marine Parade) to the top, turn left, then immediately left again onto Clyde Rd. passing the Girls High School, and you *should* end up at the viewing point. (Temporarily ignore the scenic drive arrows if you're following the above directions.)

Hawke's Bay Art Gallery And Museum

For an excellent collection of Maori art, historic presentations of early Hawke's Bay, 18th and 19th C. European antiques, and an extensive art collection, stop by Hawke's Bay Museum for a few hours. Art and film presentations are also regularly shown in the Century Theatre. Perhaps the most remarkable feature is the audiovisual presentation of the 1931 earthquake—if you get there and find it already playing, explore the rest of the museum and come back to get the full impact of the film from the beginning. The museum and shop are open from 1000-1630 weekdays, from 1400-1700 weekends and public holidays, admission adult $2, child free. The adjoining museum of natural history is only open on weekends and public holidays from 1400-1600. Located on Herschell St., off the Marine Parade end of Tennyson St., tel. 357-781.

The Stables Museum, Waxworks, And Earthquake

Here's your chance to experience a simulated (but very real) earthquake (feel it and pray!) and view a historic film on Napier's great catastrophe. Also check out the several historic old buildings with wax and action figures in realistic colonial trade and commerce situations. It's at 60 Marine Parade (opposite Marineland), tel. 351-937. Open daily 0900-1700 (shorter hours in winter), admission to the museum and waxworks is adult $2.50, child $1.50, to the Earthquake '31 exhibition adult $2.50, child $1.50, or to both adult $4, child $2.

Art Deco Napier

To appreciate all the intriguing Art Deco and Spanish Mission styles of architecture (built at lightning speed during the depression after

skeleton of a moa in Hawke's Bay Art Gallery and Museum

the earthquake in 1931), pick up the free "Take A Walk" brochure from the Visitor Information Centre—or better still, take a guided walk with an expert from the Hawke's Bay Art Gallery and Museum for added insight and color. The tour starts in the museum foyer at 1400 every Sun. with a short slide presentation explaining the Art Deco style, then you walk around Napier, watch another film, and finish things off with a cup of tea or coffee; adult $3, child free (guide maps are also on sale at the museum).

Botanical Gardens

Napier residents are understandably proud of their Botanical Gardens. Perfect lawns give way to beds of flowers and blooming shrubs, and paths lead through shady groves of assorted trees in this small inner-city oasis. A stream flows through the gardens and trickles down in tiny waterfalls; here and there miniature ornamental bridges or stepping stones allow passage back and forth. The main feature is a spacious aviary. The Botanical Gardens are located in the Hospital Hill area, a couple of km west of downtown between Napier Terrace, Spencer Rd., and Chaucer Rd. South. To get there from the info center cross Marine Parade and take Emerson St. past Clive Square (it becomes Carlyle St.). Continue down Carlyle, turn right on Chaucer Rd. South, turn left on Napier Terrace. Next to the gardens is an old tree-shaded graveyard where some of the older gravestones date back to the 19th C. and lie abandoned or broken amongst grass and wildflowers.

Free Tours

If you've ever wondered what goes on in a sheepskin factory, head for **Classic Decor Tannery** on Thames St., or call for the free courtesy car Mon. to Fri. at tel. 359-662. Free tours are held daily at 1100 and 1400 during which the entire tanning and manufacturing process is seen, but the tour naturally ends in the factory shop where suckers for sheepskin products can kiss their money goodbye. The shop is open Mon. to Fri. from 0730-1700, and Sat. 0900-1600. From the city center take Emerson St. (away from the ocean) which becomes Carlyle St., and continue onto Hyderabad Road. Continue round the corner (following Hwy. 2 north signs) and branch off over the railway line onto Pandora Road. The first street to the left is Thames Street.

Another free tour is provided by **Ahuriri Woolen Mills,** West Quay, Ahuriri. To see a wool craft studio display featuring visiting arts and crafts people, and to experience 20 years of know-how in carding wool for hand spinners, visit **Kane Carding Hawke's Bay** at Old Napier Woollen Mills, 32 Main St., tel. 354-322.

If Time Is Short

A guided tour may be just what you need if you're short on time. Contact **Bay Tours** at 102 Harold Holt Ave., tel. 436-953, for wine tours, factory warehouse tours, Hawke's Bay highlights, mystery tours, tours to the gannet colony at Cape Kidnappers and to scenic gardens, day trips to Taupo, Rotorua—or wherever you desire. Prices start at around $19-39 pp for the shorter tours; the costs for day trips are based on the number of kilometers covered. Call for a quote.

Vineyards

If you enjoy a bit of wine tasting and have your own transportation, you can get more than your fill of the drink of the gods in the Hawke's Bay Wine Region. Before heading out, collect a free "Tread The Wine Trail" brochure from the info center. It features most of the wineries in the local region, and gives good road directions so you can easily find them on your map (important after a few stops!), or collect a "Taste Our Tradition" brochure which also has a list of wineries, their facilities, and a map. Most of the vineyards are open for tasting and buying Mon. to Sat. from 0900-1700 (some longer). **Hastings,** "The Fruit Bowl of New Zealand" and Napier's twin city in the center of the vineyard region, is known for its Mediterranean climate, fertile soil, and

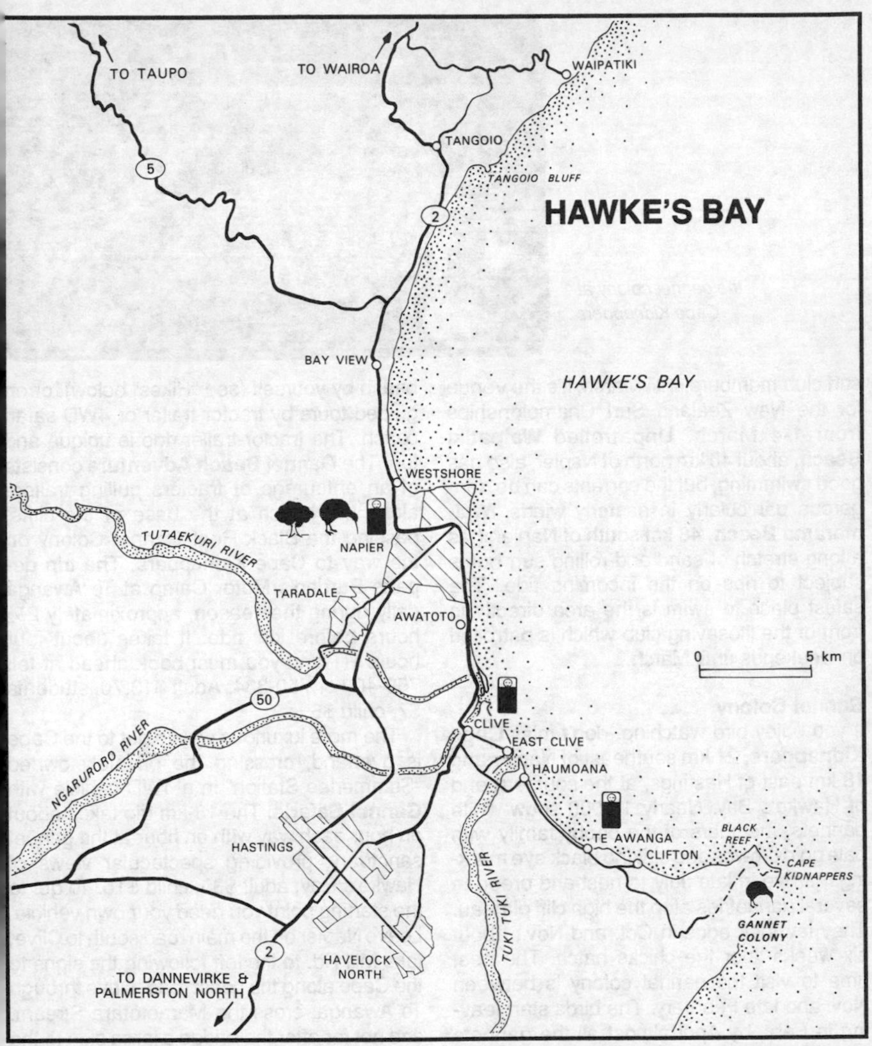

artesian water, and is particularly worth a visit in spring when all the colorful magnolia trees are in bloom.

Beaches

The long stretch of shingle beach directly in front of **Marine Parade** is better for walking than swimming. It's safe when calm, but easterly winds quickly whip up coastal breakers and rough conditions. It's patrolled on weekends until March—during the week look out for red-flag warnings on the lifesaving clubhouse. The closest sandy beach with safe swimming and a light surf is **Westshore** (about two km north of city center) on the northern side of Bluff Hill. Patrolled by local

the gannet colony at Cape Kidnappers

surf club members until March, it's the venue for the New Zealand Surf Championships from 1-4 March. Unpatrolled **Waipatiki Beach,** about 40 km north of Napier, also has good swimming, but the currents can be dangerous particularly in easterly winds. **Waimarama Beach,** 48 km south of Napier, has a long stretch of sand and rolling surf but is subject to rips on the incoming tide. The safest place to swim is the area directly in front of the lifesaving club which is patrolled on weekends until March.

Gannet Colony

If you enjoy bird watching, don't miss **Cape Kidnappers,** 21 km southeast of Napier and 18 km east of Hastings, at the southern end of Hawke's Bay. Nearly 15,000 snow-white gannets, members of the booby family with pale gold crowns and striking black eye markings, arrive in late July to nest and breed in several gannetries atop the high cliff plateau. They lay their eggs in Oct. and Nov.; about six weeks later the chicks hatch. The best time to visit the gannet colony is between Nov. and late February. The birds start leaving in Feb., by April almost all the gannets have gone; the colony is closed to the public from 1 July to mid-Oct. so that the birds aren't disturbed in their early nesting phase. Easily visited Cape Kidnappers is the only known mainland nesting place of gannets in the world.

You can reach the colony on foot along the beach by yourself (see "Hikes" below), or on guided tours by tractor trailer or 4WD safari coach. The tractor-trailer ride is unique and fun. The **Gannet Beach Adventure** consists of an entourage of tractors pulling trailers along the beach at the base of the cliffs, passing the Black Reef Gannet Colony on the way to Cape Kidnappers. The trip departs Burden's Motor Camp at Te Awanga daily during the season, approximately 2½ hours before low tide. It takes about four hours RT and you must book ahead at tel. 750-400 or 750-334. Adult $13.70, students $7, child $6.

The more luxurious way to get to the Cape is overland, crossing the privately owned "Summerlee Station" in a 4WD vehicle with **Gannet Safaris.** The 18-km trip takes about an hour each way with an hour at the gannet sanctuary, providing spectacular views of Hawke's Bay; adult $30, child $15. To get to the starting point you need your own vehicle. Leave Napier on the main road south to Clive, take Mill Rd. to the left following the signs to the Cape along the coast road. Drive through Te Awanga, cross the Maraetotara Stream, and not far after the bridge a large sign to the right says "Summerlee Station." For bookings and current price call Hastings, tel. 750-511.

Arts And Crafts

The Hawke's Bay region has more than its share of talented artists and craftspeople—many opening their studios to visitors at regular hours, others by arrangement. Ask for the handy "A Guide To Arts And Crafts In Hawkes Bay" brochure, available free from the Visitor Information Centre. It covers studios in the Havelock North, Hastings, Napier and Districts areas.

HIKES

Beach Hike To Cape Kidnappers

This enjoyable, eight-km hike along a beautiful sandy beach starts at Clifton Domain and takes about two hours to walk OW at low tide. Note that the farmland between the domain and the Cape is privately owned (no camping), and the high cliffs between Clifton and Black Reef are unstable—look out for rock slides and avoid sheltering directly under the cliffs. In addition, you can only take the beach route at low tide; the safest time to leave Clifton is no sooner than three hours after high tide. Leave the Cape no later than 1½ hours after low tide. For current tide times call the Dept. of Conservation in Napier at tel. 357-369, or ask at the info center in Napier or Hastings. The track follows the beach past Black Reef gannet colony, climbs up the cliff, and about one km beyond the reef is a rest area with water and toilets. The formed track continues up to the plateau where the gannets can be seen close up (but keep your distance so as not to disturb them). A ranger stationed at the reserve from Nov. to Feb. is only too happy to answer any questions you may have about the birds or the reserve. Don't forget your camera and plenty of film, suntan lotion, hat if you burn easily, and windbreaker.

New Zealand Walkways

Several walkways are located in the Hawke's Bay region. **Tangoio Walkway,** 25 km north of Napier on the main highway to Wairoa, is the closest to the city. It winds for six km through the native forest and pine plantations of scenic Tangoio Valley, providing a panoramic view of the Bay and many waterfalls along the route. The nine-km **Tutira Walkway,** 45 km north of Napier, runs to and along the eastern shore of Lake Tutira, providing rugged hill-country views and (on a fine day) a view of Hawke's Bay from the Ruahine Range all the way to Urewera National Park. You need sturdy boots for this track, and it's wise to take along a windproof jacket, food, and drink. **Boundary Stream Walkway,** 60 km north of Napier, passes through Boundary Stream Scenic Reserve; the highlight of this 12-km hike is the spectacular **Shine's Falls.** Starting on Pohokura Rd., it takes up to four hours to reach Heays Access Rd., then another hour to the falls. (You can also start on Heays Access Rd. if you just want to do the four-km walk to the falls.) This track also demands strong boots, a windproof jacket and warm sweater (the weather can be quite unpredictable), food, and drink.

Two walkways are south of Napier. The 2.2-km **Te Mata Peak Walkway** starts six km south of Havelock North on Te Mata Peak and provides magnificent views of Hawke's Bay. The steep track runs downhill (about 45 minutes) to Waimarama Rd. where it's a good idea to have transportation awaiting you. Wear sturdy boots and take a jacket. Two-km **Monckton Walkway,** 12 km northwest of Takapau, passes through a steep gorge in Monckton Scenic Reserve and crosses the beautiful Tanarewai Stream with its good swimming holes. It takes about 1½ hours RT; wear strong shoes. For more detailed info on any of the above tracks, pick up the individual track brochures (free at the info center).

ACCOMMODATION

Hostels

The **Napier YHA** is spacious, and quite luxurious as hostels go, with small dorms giving more privacy than the norm, twin or family rooms, and a large kitchen, dining room, and common rooms. It also has an excellent central location on oceanfront Marine Parade across from Marineland; $12 pp. At 47 Marine Parade, tel. 357-039.

Criterion Backpackers Inn is a rather unique hostel. In the old, rather grand, spacious Criterion Hotel, this budget inn provides large, bright, roomy dorms at $13 pp, equally as bright twin rooms for $14 pp or doubles for $15 pp (own key, $10 deposit), plus a roomy living room with TV and pool table, and a fully equipped kitchen. Linen hire is also available. Downstairs the bar serves excellent bistro meals from $4 during the day, and evening meals on Thurs., Fri., and Sat. nights from $6 pp. The inn is on Emerson St., tel. 352-059 or 357-162. If you're heading north, consider staying at **Glenview Farm Hostel** where you can join in on hill country sheep station activities, go horse riding or on scenic walks, or just relax; beds from $11 pp. It's 31 km north of town on Aropaoaunui Rd., two km off State Hwy. 2 (look for the AA sign on the main road at the top of the hill), tel. 266-232/234.

Budget Hotel

Just down the street from the YH, **Waterfront Lodge** has excellent accommodation at budget prices, and it's often full no matter what the season. From outside appearances you'd never guess that there are 14 attractively furnished rooms, community bathrooms, a TV lounge, communal kitchen, and laundry beyond the front entrance! Single rooms are $22 s, $38 d, which include breakfast, and you can make your own dinner at night. Ask the friendly hostess for a free visitors guide. Located at 36 Marine Parade; call ahead and reserve a room as far ahead as possible at tel. 353-429.

Motor Camps

The most central motor camp is in the Napier suburb of Marewa, about 2.5 km from downtown. **Kennedy Park Camp's** attractive grounds are adjacent to beautiful Kennedy Rose Gardens. Communal facilities, TV lounge, pool table, trampolines, general store, breakfast and dinner are available. Tentsites are $6.70 pp, caravan sites $11 s, $14.50 d, bunk-bed huts $28 d, cabins $34 d, tourist flats $47.20 s, $53.25 d. Located off Kennedy Rd., tel. 439-126. The next closest camp is **Westshore Holiday Camp,** four km from downtown but with a great location 140 meters from Westshore Beach (safe swimming and good surf). Communal facilities, indoor spa pool (extra charge), TV room, and adjacent store. Tentsites are $6.50 pp, caravan sites $7 pp, cabins start at $17 d, tourist flats start at $35 d. Located on Main Rd., Westshore, tel. 359-456.

Two motor camps south of Napier are near enough for a visit to Cape Kidnappers Gannet Colony (see above) if you have your own transportation. **Clive Motor Camp,** one km north of Clive P.O., has the usual; tentsites are $9.50 d, caravan sites $10 d. Located on Farndon Rd., Clive, tel. 700-609. **Burden's Motor Camp** is 17 km southeast of Hastings but only 12 km from Cape Kidnappers; the owners operate the popular guided tour "Gannet Adventures" via tractor trailer departing from the motor camp grounds. The camp is on a sandy beach next to a boating stream—good swimming, surfing, and fishing. Communal facilities, spa pool, and store. Tentsites $10 per night, caravan sites $11 per night, and cabins from $17 d. Located on the beach at Te Awanga, tel. 750-334.

Hotels

Many small hotels (varying rates) are scattered along Marine Parade and around town—ask for listings at the info center. Two of the best local recommendations include **Pinehaven Travel Hotel** at 259 Marine Parade, tel. 355-575, and the fancy **Edgewater Motor Lodge**, tel. 351-148. Pinehaven has a hospitable hostess who makes you feel right at home, a comfy TV lounge, tea- and coffee-making facilities, and a no-smoking policy; rooms, all with handbasins and some with great waterfront views, are $36 s, $48 d or twin (including 12.5% GST), with Continental or cooked breakfast available. The Edgewater, also on the Marine Parade

1

2

1. woolly scene between Kerikeri and Kaeo (Jane King)
2. the Stone Store and Kemp House, Keri Keri (Jane King)

1. South Island farmland (Bruce King) 2. Lake Manapouri (Jane King)
3. Milford Sound (Bruce King) 4. Raukawa Falls on the Mangawhero River (Bruce King)

1. Mount Ruapehu (Jane King) 2. California poppies, Wanaka (Jane King)
3. lupines in Mt. Cook National Park (Wayne Pease)

sunset on The Strand, Russell (Jane King)

beachfront, has a saltwater plunge pool, game room, laundry facilities, and comfortable units ranging from $70-110 s, d, or twin.

FOOD

Snacks And Light Meals

The **Sound Shell Tea Rooms** also on Marine Parade opposite the Putt Putt serves tea, coffee, and light meals seven days a week. The **Courtyard Cafe** is a good spot for breakfast, lunch, and light meals, and reasonable prices. It's on Hastings and the corner of Dickens; open for lunch Tues. to Sat., and dinner Mon. to Saturday.

The **Tri-Pot Coffee Lounge** has tasty goodies to eat there or take away, located in the Ahuriri Shopping Centre, Bridge St., northwest of downtown. If you don't mind a bit of a drive to the western suburb of Taradale, the **Carthew's Deli and Eatery** is a great place for lunch. You can whip up a combination of deli goodies, mix and match from the salad bar, or get good food to go; at 215 Gloucester St., Taradale, tel. 449-729. Another good place to eat in Taradale is **Poppies Coffee Lounge** on Gloucester St. next to Taradale Post Office. Devon Cream Teas (mmm!), homemade pies, savories, and cakes are available seven days a week, tel. 446-595.

Pub Meals

You can rely on pubs and hotels for good food at budget prices. The **Cobb & Co. Restaurant and Bar,** part of the Masonic Establishment, serves the usual; $8-14. Open daily, on Marine Parade, tel. 358-689. Another pub with a blackboard menu is the **Ahuriri Tavern** at Westshore. Popular **Parrot Cafe** has good pub meals and salad bar for $4.50-6 daily from 1200; on Hastings between Tennyson and Emerson. The **Doods Roundhouse Restaurant** is open for lunches Mon. to Sat. 1200-1330, and dinner 1800-2100. Located at West Quay, Westshore (four km north of downtown), tel. 359-654. The **Marineland Motel Restaurant** has a reasonably priced blackboard menu Tues. to Sat. nights, family roasts Sun. and Mon. nights, and more pricey a la carte dining. Located at Meeanee Quay, Westshore, tel. 352-147.

Reasonable Restaurants

Harston's Cafe has a blackboard menu for lunch ($5.50-7 pp), tasty main courses at dinner ($11-13), big helpings, always something spicy on the menu, and an interesting, old-fashioned, early-Americana interior. Try their delicious taco and artfully arranged salad for $5.50 at lunch. For an excellent smorgasbord (from around $15 pp, but worth it) try **The Old Flame Restaurant** on Tennyson St., city center. If you're more in the mood for a splurge, dressing up, and sea views, try **Bayswater On The Beach** on Hardinge Rd. (north end of town), just before Bridge St., tel. 358-517. It's open seven days for lunch and dinner. Expect to pay $14-17 for a main course, $7.50-8.50 for dessert.

Takeaways

Kentucky Fried Chicken is on Carlyle St., **Pizza Hut** on Marine Parade, **McDonald's** on Dickens Street. Numerous other takeaway shops are found around the downtown area—try **Fair Winds,** or **China Light** on Tennyson St., or **Henry's Kitchen** in Clive Square off Dickens Street. At Henry's you can get good weekday lunch specials from $6 pp; open seven days.

ENTERTAINMENT

Pub Scene

Most hotels and taverns are open for serious drinking Mon. to Sat. from 1100-2000 (some open earlier). The following Napier establishments generally provide a live band or videos Thurs. through Sat. nights: **Masonic Hotel** on Marine Parade, **Westshore Hotel** on Main Road, Westshore, **Ahuriri Tavern** at Ahuriri, **Shakespeare Inn** on Shakespeare Rd., **Criterion Hotel** on Emerson St. (weekend entertainment only), and **D.B. Onekawa** on Taradale Road.

Night Clubs

For a splurge on the town or disco-ing with a DJ, try one of Napier's two nightclubs, **Egos Nite Spot** on Hastings St. or **Club Oddessey** on Ocean Blvd. and Arcade off Dickens Street. Call the nightclubs to find out what's on, current admission price (which changes with the entertainment), and specific dress code (you can pretty much expect one!).

Movies

The **State Theatre** and **Kerridge Odeon** are Napier's movie houses, and the current movies are advertised in the local newspaper. If the current movie doesn't grab your fancy, try the **State Theatre** or **Westend Theatre** in nearby Hastings (a 20-km drive).

Something Different

Laser Strike! If you've always wanted to shoot someone with a ray gun, you may want to have a go at this. You're introduced to the rules of the game, fitted with chest computer and backpack computer, given instructions, and then put on a team and let loose in an imaginary world of tunnels, mirrors, fog, and booby traps to score hits with your ray gun on your opponents' sensors. It's open Wed. and Thurs. 1600-2000, Fri. 1600-2200, Sat. 1400-2200, and Sun. 1400-2000 on Dickens St., tel. 351-585; adult $5, child $4.

SERVICES AND INFORMATION

Shopping hours are generally Mon. to Fri. 0830-1700, and Sat. 0900-1200. Late-night shopping until 2030 is in central Napier (and Hastings) on Fri. nights, and on Thurs. nights in the suburbs of Maraenui, Marewa, Onekawa, and Pirimai.

If you want to do your laundry *or* have it done for you, the **Balmoral Automatic Laundrette** in the Balmoral Shopping Centre is open seven days a week, corner of Kennedy and Wellesley rds., tel. 354-323. Indoor **Harbour Market** is held every Sat. and Sun. from 1000-1630 next to Iron Pot in Ahuriri, and admission is free—plenty of clothing, arts and crafts, toys, food, and ice cream.

Urgent

For **ambulance, police, or fire,** call 111. The local **urgent pharmacy** is on Kennedy Rd., tel. 355-867. For an **emergency doctor or hospital** call 354-969. Napier's **Public Hospital** is located on Hospital Terrace, west of the Botanical Gardens. The **police station** is on Station St., downtown.

General Information

The **Visitors Information Centre** is on Marine Parade—the first place to go for general and accommodation info, free brochures, and a city map. Open Mon. to Fri. 0830-1700, weekends and public holidays 0900-1700, tel. 357-182 or 354-949. **Hastings Public Relations Office** is on Russell St. North, a stone's throw from the p.o., tel. 60-205, or 775-532 after hours; open weekdays 0830-1700. The **Main P.O.** is on Hastings St., open regular hours and late Fridays. Public telephones are also located there; to make a toll call dial the operator on 0, to send a telegram dial 14. The **public library** is on Station St., tel. 357-579. For sightseeing or hunting info in local and regional forests, call the **Dept. of Conservation** office. The **Youth Hostel Association** can be reached at tel. 357-039. Napier **AA Centre** is on Dickens Street.

TRANSPORTATION

Getting There

The main road in and out of Napier is Hwy. 2. Highway 5 from Taupo joins Hwy. 2 from Wairoa just north of Napier. Highway 2 continues south out of Napier along the coastal route to Hastings, and on down to Dannevirke. The alternate inland route is Hwy. 50 southwest out of Napier through Maraekakaho (bypassing Hastings) and eventually rejoining Hwy. 2 near Takapau.

Hitching in and out of Napier is not too bad as long as you head out to the city boundary before hanging out your finger. As the major roads branch off in several directions (giving the drivers an excuse to ignore you), the easiest way to get a ride is to write your destination on a large piece of white cardboard—you'd be surprised how many more lifts you get this way. (The odd plea, i.e. "Desperate To Get There Today" is also an effective car stopper—be creative!). Napier is easily reached by public transportation: by bus from all major centers, by train (it's on the main Gisborne to Wellington route), and Hawke's Bay Airport is located a few km north of the city.

Buses

The **Mount Cook Line Terminal** is at 20 Station Street. For schedules and current prices for city, suburban, Hastings, and general sightseeing services, call at the terminal or tel. 435-919. For info on services to Hastings via the coastal route call 353-199. Mount Cook Line doesn't run a service directly south from Napier, but **Newmans Coachlines** goes daily to Palmerston North, Wanganui, New Plymouth, Petone, and Wellington. The reservation office is on Thackeray St., tel. 352-009. The **InterCity** office is at the railway station on Station St.; open Mon. to Fri. 0800-1730. InterCity operates coach services from Napier and Hastings to Auckland ($53 OW), Hamilton ($40 OW), Rotorua ($37 OW), Taupo ($23 OW), Tauranga ($52 OW), Gisborne ($24 OW), Palmerston North ($25 OW), New Plymouth ($53 OW), Wanganui ($33 OW), and Wellington ($38 OW). **Dominion Coachlines** has an inter-city express coach service between Napier and Gisborne, twice a day Mon. to Fri. and once a day weekends. For more info contact Mount Cook Line or a local travel agent.

Commercial Tours

Bay Tours operates several interesting tours (see "Sights"). **Direct Tours** offers taxi rides to Cape Kidnappers (from $35 per car; up to five adults), Trelinnoe Scenic Gardens (from $20 pp; minimum two people), and Taupo or Rotorua (from $350 per car); call for the latest fares at tel. 439-241, 354-133, 357-103, or 85-910.

Trains

The **railway station** is on Station Street. A daily train runs south to Wellington and takes about six hours, departing Napier in the early afternoon and arriving in Wellington in the evening; about $39 OW. For current schedules, prices, and ticket reservations call 353-199 or drop by the station.

Cars

For **rental car information** call **Avis** at tel. 351-828, **Budget** at tel. 355-166, or **Hertz** at tel. 356-169. For **Automobile Association** info and maps, call in at the office on Dickens St.; for AA breakdown service and road conditions call 356-889. **Public Carparks** are on the corner of Tennyson and Dalton streets. A **taxi stand** is on Lower Emerson St. near Clive Square; tel. 357-777 for regular taxi service or to arrange city sightseeing by taxi (if you have plenty of spare cash to fritter away).

Air

Hawke's Bay Airport is a couple of km north of Napier. Take main Hwy. 2 north to Westshore and turn left onto Watchman Road. There's no scheduled coach service to the airport—taking a taxi there costs about $8 OW. **Air New Zealand** connects Hawke's Bay with Kaitaia, Whangarei, Auckland, Gisborne, and Wellington in the North Island and all major centers in the South Island. The Air New Zealand office is in the Housing Corporation Building on the corner of Hastings and Station sts., tel. 351-171. For ticket reservations call 353-288. **Eagle Air** services Gisborne, Hamilton, New Plymouth, Palmerston North, Rotorua, and Wellington. For current prices and reservations call 355-599, or Air New Zealand. Scenic flights are offered by **Napier Aero Club,** starting at around $30 pp for a 15-minute "Napier Buzzaround." For all the details call 356-192.

Bicycle Hire
Napier Cycle World is the place to hire a three- or 10-speed bicycle; from $8 for three hours, half day $10, full day $12, week $35. They also stock a good supply of freeze-dried foods, all kinds of camping equipment and supplies, and local and New Zealand Walkway info, and sell the invaluable Dept. of Survey and Lands topographical maps. Located at 104 Carlyle St., tel. 359-528, or 448-270 after hours; open Mon. to Fri. 0800-1730 and Sat. 0900-1200. Mopeds can be hired at the **Dive Centre** on Hardinge Rd. from $12 per hour (with a $40 refundable bond), but you must be over 18 years old and have a current driver's license.

WEST

TONGARIRO NATIONAL PARK

Tongariro National Park, New Zealand's original national park, is dramatic, spectacular, and beautiful—a restless land of contrasting elements and continuous change: rolling hills carpeted in purple heather, and green and yellow tussocklands dotted with *toe toe;* dense *rimu* forest sheltering an abundance of birdlife; a desolate desert area and a lunar landscape scattered with sharp chunks of black volcanic rock; icy cold waterfalls and bubbling hot springs; and three magnificent volcanoes that dominate the surrounding landscape—these are the images of Tongariro in summer. In winter a thick blanket of snow turns the park into a white wonderland. Backcountry explorers and ice climbers joyfully head out into the frigid elements, skiers ride gravity down the steep volcanic slopes, and the small year-round settlement of Whakapapa Village and the two nearest towns, National Park and Ohakune, come alive with the full-blown bustle and activity of winter ski resorts. This ancient land shouldn't be missed by any lover of the great outdoors.

The Land

Lying at the southern end of the Volcanic Plateau, the park's geological features and volcanic activity are directly due to the Indian-Australian Plate overriding the Pacific Plate. Three major volcanoes tower above the surrounding landscape, dominating the horizon from all directions. Snow-capped **Mount Ruapehu,** the highest mountain in the North Island (2,797 meters), consists of vents, lava flows, and many mud flows that have occurred over thousands of years. Eruptions (the last in 1975) have repeatedly ejected sulphurous water and ash from the 17-hectare crater onto the upper slopes of the mountain. In the past, this caused mud flows *(lahars)* to run far out onto the surrounding land creating a distinct ring plain around the mountains, valleys, and ash-covered desertscapes. Rounded hummocks or small hills in the area around the junction of hwys. 47 and 48 are the final pile-ups of these lahars. The seemingly calm but suspiciously warm and highly acidic water of **Crater Lake** continues to hide the violent nature of this volcano that smolders not far below the surface—but this doesn't seem to deter the thousands who ski Ruapehu in winter or hike up it throughout the year.

The composite andesite volcano of **Mount Ngauruhoe** is the most easily recognized with its perfectly symmetrical cone and 32-degree slopes. It's 2,291 meters high, rising 650 meters above the southern slopes of Tongariro, and is New Zealand's most continuously active volcano. Steam wafts eerily from its crater. **Mount Tongariro,** a truncated multiple volcano, stands 1,968 meters high and contains a number of small craters. **Red Crater** and **Te Maari Craters** are the most recently active, and emit steam, gas, and hot air. Volcanic activity can be enjoyed bodily at **Ketetahi Hot Springs** (see p. 252) on the north side of Mount Tongariro.

On the eastern side of the volcanic peaks lies the **Rangipo Desert,** a desolate windswept landscape where few living things survive the temperature extremes. On the contrasting western side of the Park the hills and valleys are covered in dense bush and beech forest, home to myriad insects, birds, and small animals. Two areas of Tongariro National Park are designated as "wilderness areas" (totally undeveloped)—**Hauhungatahi,** which stretches from the western slopes of Mt. Ruapehu to Erua on Hwy. 4, and **Te Tatau-Pounamu,** which lies northeast of Mt. Tongariro between Central Crater and the Desert Road.

Climate

The main climatic factor affecting Tongariro National Park is wind, which assaults the volcanic peaks from all directions. The prevailing moist westerlies drop almost all of their moisture on the west side of the mountains—by the time they reach the east side they're pretty dry. Although the winds from the west to northwest bring most of the rain, they carry only light snowfalls; southerly winds are generally colder and can bring snow at any time of year. The rainfall around Whakapapa Visitors Centre is about 2,200 mm and evenly distributed throughout the year. At Ohakune on the south side, about 1,250 mm of rain falls per year. No particular month is considered "the wettest"—most months are wet! Frosts can occur year-round, and snow heavily blankets the peaks most winters. Average daily temperature is 13 degrees C with a maximum of 25 and a minimum of one degree C (in mid-winter the average is down to a frosty three degrees C). Pamphlets on weather and daily mountain forecasts are available at Whakapapa Visitors Centre and ranger stations.

If you're backcountry hiking, keep in mind that the air temperature drops at the rate of around six degrees C per 1,000-meter gain in altitude; be adequately prepared at any time of year for all kinds of weather—conditions can change rapidly.

Flora And Fauna

Ranging in altitude from 500-2,700 meters above sea level, five distinct vegetation types are found within Park boundaries—mixed rainforest, beech forest, tussock grasslands, wetlands, and alpine desert. In the lower areas you find the large podocarp trees, broadleafs, vines, orchids, and ferns that make up the mixed rainforest—a lush and tropical home for an abundance of native birds. Birds such as the **native pigeon** which literally stuffs itself on berry fruits, the nectar-sipping ***tui*** and **bellbird,** and the insect-eating **robin, fantail,** and **tomtit** are the most easily seen birds in the rainforest, along with the **whitehead** and nocturnal **kiwi.** A large variety of insects is found in the trees and amongst the debris on the forest floor, and the noisy **cicadas** can be quite deafening in summer. A good place to experience this kind of exotic greenery is the Ohakune area in the southwest sector of the Park.

Climb up to the 1,000-meter level and the rainforest gives way to mountain beech and cedar forest where the tiny green **rifleman** (one of New Zealand's smallest birds), **silver**

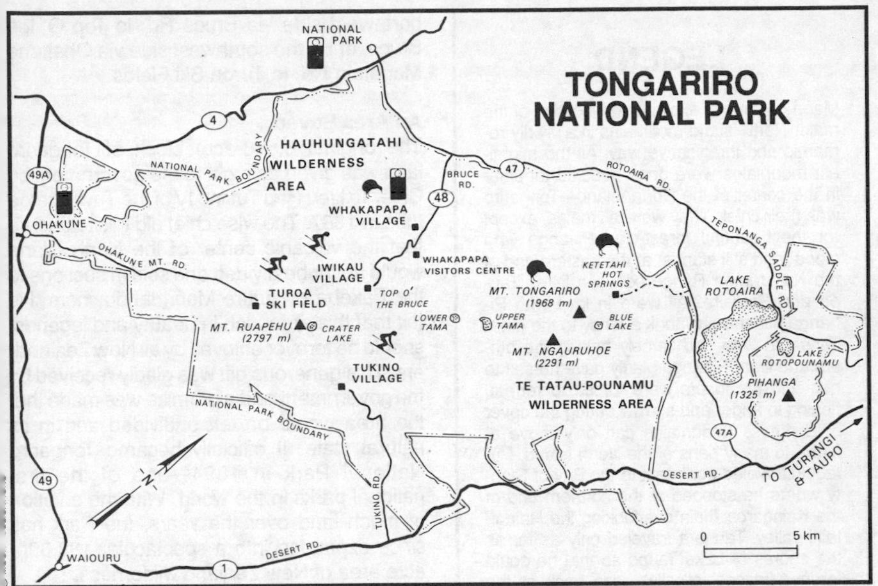

eye, and occasional **parakeet** are seen. Continuing upward, the forest opens out into attractive tussock shrublands where alpine plants, tussock, and heather are the dominant species. Here the **native falcon** can be seen searching for small birds and animals, the sounds of the **pipit** and secretive **fernbird** can be heard, and mice and hares scurry in the dense shrubbery.

The wetlands environment is found along the bogs, pond edges, stream banks, and waterfalls within the Park. **Ourisia,** a delicate plant with white flowers, buttercups, daisies, and sundews live along the water's edge with fresh-water crayfish and a large variety of aquatic insects. Check out the extensive bogs and intriguing plantlife on the western slopes of Mt. Ruapehu, near Mt. Hauhungatahi. The **blue duck** (or *whio* to the Maori) has become an endangered species but can still be seen in the Park in areas around fast-flowing streams.

The desertlands on the park's east side are mainly barren, an amazing contrast after seeing the western side of the park. This is not only due to a lack of rain but is also caused by the harsh dry winds blowing from the northwest over Mt. Ruapehu. The soil is sandy gravel, the wind and temperature extremes attract little in the way of flora or fauna, and fairly frequent flashfloods further desecrate the surface. The highest level of the park is an alpine environment where low-to-the-ground plants suited to harsh winds, snow, frost, and dust storms survive in their extreme but natural habitat. The **woolly mountain daisy, mountain snowberry,** and **whipcord hebe** are several of the most recognizable alpine flora. Most of the Park flowers are white, apart from an occasional purple or mauve orchid, and the region is quite spectacular in Dec. and Jan. when everything is beginning to bloom. Tussockland birds are also seen in this area, along with the odd rabbit or hare.

The boundaries of each vegetation type aren't really obvious when you're leisurely hiking (unless you go straight up at a high rate of speed!)—they gently merge into one another. The best way to appreciate the changes in both landscape and flora is from Mount Ruapehu. Hike to the top, or drive up the

LEGEND

Maori mythology explains the location of the major North Island mountains in a vividly romantic and imaginative way. All the mightiest mountains were once huddled together in the center of the North Island—Tongariro was their chief. They were all males, except for the beautiful forest-clad Pihanga who stood (and still stands) at the eastern end of the Kakaramea Range between lakes Taupo and Rotoaira. All were in love with Pihanga but she only took a fancy to the great Tongariro who had fiercely battled the others and won. Pihanga gladly gave herself to him and the losers were forced to retreat, fleeing in anger and sorrow during the cover of darkness (mountains can only move at night) to many parts of the North Island. Putauaki traveled northeast to the Bay of Plenty where he stopped at the northern end of the Kaingaroa Plain overlooking the Raingitaiki valley. Tauhara traveled only as far as the shores of Lake Taupo so that he could forever (masochistically) gaze back at the lovely Pihanga. Taranaki (also known as Mt. Egmont) angrily fled with great speed to the west coast where he stopped when he reached the sea.

Many centuries passed before the mountains "came alive with fire." A great priest, Ngatoro-i-rangi, climbed Ngauruhoe to view the surrounding terrain. On reaching the top he was suddenly trapped in a terrible snowstorm, and in his fear (snow was a new and unpleasant experience) he called out for help to his priestess sisters in the north, begging them to send him fire so that he wouldn't freeze to death. Hearing his pleas they got the fire-demons to send volcanic heat via White Island and Rotorua, the fire bursting up through the ground in many places before finally reaching the summit of Ngauruhoe. The priest sacrificed a female slave, Auruhoe, to add impact to his pleas, and when the fire burst forth he ceremoniously hurled her body into the bubbling crater, and the volcano became known as "Ngauruhoe" after this gruesome incident. Tongariro was also named during this event from tonga meaning "south wind" (mentioned in the priest's prayers) and rio which means "seized."

northwest side via Bruce Rd. to Top O' the Bruce, or up the southwest side via Ohakune Mountain Rd. to Turoa Ski Fields.

An Area Saved

The original 6,518-acre block of Tongariro land was given as a gift to the government by Chief Te Heu Heu Tukino IV of the Tuwharetoa tribe in 1887. The wise chief did this to ensure that the volcanic center of the North Island would never be divided and sold in sections to the Pakeha by future Maori landowners. He felt that this area, rich in beauty and legends, should be forever enjoyed by all New Zealanders. This generous gift was gladly received by the government and a promise was made that the area would be left undivided and in its natural state. It officially became Tongariro National Park in 1894—one of the first national parks in the world. With the addition of much land over the years, the Park has since expanded into a spectacular 188,000-acre area of New Zealand wilderness.

MOUNTAIN SCENERY

Viewpoints

If you have a car or can catch a ride, the best and quickest way to get oriented to this magnificent volcanic area is by taking both main roads up Mount Ruapehu as far as you can go. (A third road only suitable for 4WD vehicles heads up the eastern side of the mountain to Tukino Village, a ski area.) Each gives a different aspect of the Park and is worth checking out if you can afford the time and gas. (You can also hike to the top, but again you need plenty of time and energy!) In summer Ruapehu Alpine Lifts operates two chairlifts from Top O' the Bruce to 2,000 meters above sea level where you can enjoy panoramic views, and lunch from the veranda of the Knoll Ridge Cafeteria. The lifts operate 0900-1700, weather permitting, from the end of Dec. through Jan. and at Easter; adult $10, child $5, family $25. Take a warm windproof jacket, sturdy footwear, sunglasses, and suntan lotion.

If you're coming to Tongariro from the north, turn left off Hwy. 47 onto Hwy. 48 which takes you up to Whakapapa Village, past the Visitors Centre, and on up the steep tarsealed Bruce Rd. to Top O' the Bruce and Whakapapa Skifields—from here you get spectacular views of the volcanoes and northern sector of the Park. In winter the upper section of the road can become quite treacherous—you need chains. Luckily, buses service the skifields at this icy time of year. All sorts of tracks of varying lengths lead off Bruce Rd. (see below).

If you're coming to Tongariro from the south, take Hwy. 49 (or Hwy. 4 then 49 from Wanganui) to the town of Ohakune, then follow Ohakune Mountain Rd. past the Ohakune Ranger Station up through the subalpine forest that carpets the western side of the mountains. This road gives great views of Mount Ruapehu and its glaciers above as you climb, passes a couple of tracks to magnificent waterfalls, and terminates at Turoa Skifield where you get equally fabulous views of the Park stretched out far below (this road also requires chains in winter).

The third way to grasp and admire the contrasting and varied scenery of this area is to circumnavigate the Park via hwys. 1, 49, 49A, 4, and 47. Highway 1, the Desert Rd., is the most direct route south. If you don't have time to get into Tongarlro, this is the route to take. It passes through the amazingly desolate landscape (great for dramatic photographs) found on the dry, windswept, eastern side of the volcanoes, and presents some interesting mountain views. To reach the most popular park attractions, head for the western side of the Park. Drive clear around (just over three hours without stops or one day to include stops at the main attractions) and you can see it all! A hiker worth his salt won't be able to resist staying at least a few days.

HIKES

The many tracks provide a wide variety of scenery and terrain and range from short 15-minute walks suitable for anyone to a strenuous six-day hike around the mountains only recommended for very fit people. If your route involves leaving the marked track, you need to be an expert map reader and compass navigator; the park experiences "whiteout" conditions every now and again that can be both frightening and hazardous if you're not adequately prepared. If you're hiking across snow, take sunglasses, sunscreen, and something to drink. First stop should be either Whakapapa Visitors Centre or one of the two ranger stations (see "Information," p. 260). The Park handbook *The Restless Land* also has a section on hiking (and recreation in general) and describes the shorter walks to the most popular attractions. Tramping huts are situated along the walking tracks at regular intervals—five or six hours between huts. They accommodate up to 22 people (bunk-bed style) and are supplied with firewood—carry your own stove, fuel, and utensils or you may have to settle for dried fruit and nuts for dinner! The hut fee is $8 pp, $4 child—buy tickets in advance at the Whakapapa Visitors Centre or ranger station.

on the way up Mt. Ruapehu

Short Walks
There are so many short walks along well-graded tracks here that the best thing to do is to drop in at the Visitors Centre or ranger station and tell them the kind of terrain you'd like to see—you'll get plenty of suggestions and can load up with relevant brochures and maps. Several pamphlets on short walks are also available for 30 cents each. Some of the most easily accessible shorter walks are located around Whakapapa Village and Ohakune.

The shortest walk (40 minutes RT) in the Whakapapa Village area is along **Ridge Track,** starting 150 meters above the Visitors Centre, leading to a lookout point above treeline. The six-km (two-hour RT) **Whakapapanui Walk** starts 300 meters above the Visitors Centre at the Whakapapa Motor Camp, follows the Whakapapanui Stream through some beautiful beech forest and native bush, and ends on Hwy. 48, three km below the center. The enjoyable six-km (three-hour RT) track to colorful **Silica Springs and Rapids** starts just above the motor camp, follows the Waikare Stream to the white rapids and on to the spring source, and back to Bruce Road. The 15-minute (RT) **Mounds Nature Walk** which leads to the remnants of several huge mud flows starts on Hwy. 48, five km below Whakapapa Visitors Centre. **Tawhai Falls** splashes down over the lip of a lava flow near the Whakapapanui Stream and is worth the short walk (30 minutes RT); the track starts on Hwy. 48, four km below the Visitors Centre. Beautiful **Taranaki Falls**, plummeting 20 meters down a major lava flow, is reached by a track starting from Chateau Tongariro or Skotel in Whakapapa Village. It takes about one hour to get to the falls, up to 2½ hours RT, and the return route follows the banks of the Wairere Stream.

Take Ohakune Mountain Rd. up the southwest side of Mt. Ruapehu for several more tracks of varying distances. **Waitonga Falls Walk** takes about 40 minutes OW, and the spectacular **Mangawhero Falls** lookout, to the right farther up the road, is only a couple of minutes' walk from the main road—well worth a stop and click of the camera. **Mangawhero Forest Walk** starts opposite the Ohakune Ranger Station and takes you for a 1½-hour RT walk through podocarp forest. The 20-meter **Rimu Track** also starts opposite the Ohakune Ranger Station. Another short walk, but in the northern sector, is along the track to the small and serene **Lake Rotopounamu** that lies sheltered in a forested crater on the northwest side of Mt. Pihanga. Access is from Te Ponanga Saddle Rd. (Hwy. 47) between Turangi and Lake Rotoaira; the walk takes about 20 minutes OW to the lake, or 1½ hours around the lake.

Longer Hikes
The park offers an extensive network of well-graded tracks that suit everyone from the first-timer to the serious and experienced hiker, with comfortable park huts. One of the most popular tracks leads to **Ketetahi Springs** on the northern side of north crater (where the legendary fire sent by the fire demons spurted from the ground on its way to Mt. Ngauruhoe). Here you'll find boiling mud, blowholes, fumaroles, small geysers, hot springs, and some great bathing spots in the warm "health-giving" stream below the thermal area. It has been left in a totally natural state—no concrete pools, dressing sheds, or toilets here! The 2½-hour (OW) track starts at the Ketetahi Carpark on Hwy. 47A and climbs to this exciting hot spot. Wear sturdy boots and don't forget your swimming gear (have it on underneath if you're shy). Keep on the marked track at all times when you're in the thermal area—if the steam gets too concentrated to see, wait until it clears before you progress along the track—or you may find out first-hand how a lobster feels when he's plunged into boiling water! The track continues uphill to Ketetahi Hut, eventually arriving at the active craters of Mt. Tongariro.

The **Round The Mountain Track** is also popular, but you need to be in pretty good shape, and able to carry at least six days' worth of food, supplies, and warm clothing on your back. Huts are located five or six hours

Sharp chunks of volcanic rock litter lower Mt. Ruapehu.

apart along the various tracks, which all link to form a roughly circular trail around the three main volcanoes. Other tracks lead off to various attractions such as hot springs and splendid waterfalls, or cross the rugged and eerily desolate tops of the volcanoes. Before you set off on any of the longer hikes, leave your intentions with the rangers in case you get stranded or lost in bad weather.

SKIING

The Season

Thousands flock to the beautiful skifields of Mount Ruapehu each year. Apart from the excellent snow conditions, variety of trails, and long ski season—from late June to early Nov,—you can't beat the views of snow-covered mountains and steaming craters! The best time for skiing the volcanic slopes of Tongariro National Park is Sept. to Nov. when the snow is deep and the weather fair. As far as skiing conditions go, Turoa on the southern slopes generally receives drier snow and colder temperatures than Whakapapa on the western slopes. For more skifield info and a calendar of events, see the operators of Ruapehu Alpine Lifts at Whakapapa Skifield or Turoa. Info is also posted in public areas, at local shops, and at most accommodation establishments. Adult day passes at Whakapapa start at $38, child $15 (discounts on midweek packages, and season passes are available).

Whakapapa Skifield

The tops of Whakapapa's groomed western slopes are reached by chairlift and T-bar, and rope tows and platter lifts let first-timers try their skill on gentle beginners slopes. A variety of ski trails ranging from easy to "impossible" criss-cross the mountain slopes, all patrolled. A ski school operated by Ruapehu Alpine Lifts caters to private and group lessons for beginners through experts. The school HQ is at Schusshaus on Hut Flat, but bookings can be made at the Ski School office at Top O' the Bruce (tel. Mt. Ruapehu 738) or the Ski School desk in the Chateau. Fast-food service is available at Top O' the Bruce, at the Schusshaus on Hut Flat, the top of the Waterfall chair lift, and the National Down Hill. Public shelters are located at the top of the Waterfall chair lift and Top O' the Bruce—the many private lodges on the field are for members only. All your skiing equipment can be hired on the field, along with ski repairs and a ski shop at Top O' the Bruce. The main lift ticket kiosk is also at Top O' the Bruce and is open daily from 0800, but you can buy tickets at the Schusshaus Canteen at Hut Flat at the top of the first double-chair lift. You can drive directly to the carparks, or take the shuttle service which runs several times a day from the carpark below the Whakapapa Tavern to the Iwikau Public Shelter on the skifield—get your ticket at the carpark kiosk. For current road conditions use the Snow Phone, tel. 833, or call in at

Whakapapa Visitors Centre or the Chateau at Whakapapa Village.

Turoa Skifield

Located on the southwest slopes above Ohakune, Turoa's variety of lifts provides easy access to open and diverse terrain interspersed with small valleys and wide open, unobstructed slopes (all patrolled) where you can experience runs up to four km long. The base of the skifield is 1,600 meters, the top is at 2,320 meters, the vertical rise is 720 meters, and there are runs to suit all levels of skiers. Turoa provides three cafeterias at the main lift terminals, public shelters, creche for kids, and a ski school. The lift ticket office is in the base facilities area on the mountain. Casual lessons for all skill levels are held on weekends only, mid-week "Introduction to Skiing" classes are held at the Valley Rope Tow, and week-long "ski academies" are available for all levels. They also offer private lessons but you need to book ahead for these. Hire your skiing equipment at the Turoa Skifields Hire Shop on Clyde St. in Ohakune before heading up the mountain; open Mon. to Sun. 0800-1800, Sat. 0730-1800 during the ski season. (Limited ski hire is also available in the Alpine Lodge complex next to the Mountain Ticket Office, but don't count on getting everything you need.) The Skifields Information Centre is on Clyde St. at the north end of Ohakune; if you don't have transportation, catch a ride on the regular 4WD bus that runs up the 17 km from the info center to the skifield each day. For weather, snow, and conditions 24 hours a day call the Turoa

Skifield Information Centre at tel. 58-456, or after 1700 tel. 58-255 for a weather and snow report, or call in at the info center during regular hours.

Tukino Skifield

On the eastern side of Mt. Ruapehu lies the more remote and wild Tukino Skifield at the end of a rough 12-km road. Access in winter for the last six km is only possible with 4WD vehicles; the skifield is operated by three ski clubs with limited facilities and two rope tows. The slopes are patrolled by ski club members, and ski hire is not available on the field. If you like the less commercial things in life, less people, and can bring your own equipment, this skifield will probably hold more appeal.

OTHER PARK ACTIVITIES

Climbing

The three volcanoes afford some exciting climbing over a variety of terrain, and good practice climbs if you plan on attempting the difficult peaks of the South Island's Southern Alps. Within the park you'll find intriguing peaks, walls, towers, buttresses, and couloirs, and you can expect hard snow and icy rocks on all exposed ridges. Both ice and rock climbing are popular activities throughout the year.

Climb up to the mysterious, steel-gray **Crater Lake** at the top of Mt. Ruapehu, or to Tahurangi, at 2,797 meters the Park's highest peak. The steep slopes of **Mt. Ngauruhoe** offer quite a challenge in summer when loose stones frequently threaten from upper slopes, and the knowledge that the volcano could erupt at any time provides quite an adrenalin rush. Winter conditions require more specialized equipment—ice axes, ropes, and crampons, and a competent knowledge of ice climbing. Many other peaks in the park provide a wide range of climbs that satisfy the beginner right through to the most experienced.

Check at Whakapapa Visitors Centre or the ranger stations and find out if you're properly equipped for the Tongariro climbing experience and local weather conditions. If possible, climb in a group. If you want to learn how to snow and ice climb or improve your skills, **Plateau Guides** give one- to five-day courses—the cost of each includes equipment, food, and transportation. For more info and current costs write to P.O. Box 29, National Park, or call National Park 740.

Fishing And Hunting

Fish are not abundant in Tongariro rivers but the best places are the Mangawhero, Whakapapanui, and upper tributaries of the Wanganui. You'll probably need a fair bit of patience and considerable skill to catch anything worth keeping! The closest good fishing is at Lake Rotoaira to the north, and even farther north at the world-renowned Lake Taupo and the Tongariro River.

Hunting for deer (throughout the Park) or pigs (in the northern area) is still fairly good in Tongariro, but you must get a permit from one of the ranger stations before you set off. The best hunting is found in the valleys on the southern and western sides of Mt. Ruapehu.

Rafting

Several rafting operators in the towns bordering Tongariro National Park (and several in Turangi—see p. 210) provide both white-water thrills and tranquil floats along the wild and beautiful rivers of this region. The two main operators are **Plateau Guides** in National Park (tel. 740), and **Ruapehu Outback Experiences** in Ohakune (tel. 58-733). Tongariro Outdoor Centre in Turangi also offers white-water rafting trips (tel. 7492).

Flightseeing

One of the best ways to appreciate all the natural beauty that abounds in this area is to take a scenic flight with **Mountain Air.** Choose from one of their three regular trips—over the Chateau and Tama lakes for $30 pp, over the Chateau, Ketetahi Springs, Mt. Tongariro, and Mt. Ngauruhoe for $50 pp, or over the entire park for breathtaking views of Mt. Ruapehu for $70 pp—or all sorts of charters can be arranged. Get more info at the office by the airport on Hwy. 47 (eight km from National Park) almost opposite the Hwy. 48 intersection, or call National Park 812.

PRACTICALITIES

ACCOMMODATION

Camping Out

Beautiful **Mahuia Campground** is located by the Mangahuia Stream, six km from National Park on Hwy. 47. Free tent and caravan sites, toilets, and fireplaces are provided. Another free camping area, **Mangawhero,** same facilities, is located above Ohakune on Ohakune Mountain Rd. which leads up to Turoa Skifields.

Mountain Huts

Get hut info at Whakapapa Visitors Centre or Ohakune or Turangi Ranger Stations. Nine park huts (adult $8, child $4; tentsite using hut facilities $4) are located along the main tracks—**Mangaehuehu Hut,** three km east of Mangaehuehu Stream; **Mangatepopo Hut,** on the western side of Mt. Ngauruhoe; **Oturere Hut,** below Oturere Crater; **Rangipo Hut,** on the poled route south of Tukino Rd.; **Waihohonu Hut,** near the old hut of the same name; **Whakapapaiti Hut,** in the Whakapapaiti Valley; **Blyth Hut,** on the southern slopes of Mt. Ruapehu, two hours from Waitonga Falls carpark on Ohakune Mountain Rd.; **Ketetahi Hut,** a 30-minute hike above Ketetahi Hot Springs; and **Mangaturuturu Hut** in Mangaturuturu Valley, 1½ hours north of Ohakune Mountain Road.

Youth Hostel

Modern **Ohakune YH,** on the western boundary of the Park, is in a perfect location for the outdoor enthusiast, but be sure to book way in advance if you plan on staying here during ski season (July to Oct.). Close to public transportation, a shuttle bus leaves daily from across the road for the skifields in winter. If the weather is bad the common room is left open during the day. Twin or family rooms available (own key); $12 pp. Located at the west end of town on Clyde St., 100 meters past the p.o. and opposite the Turoa Information Centre, tel. 58-724.

Motor Camps

The most central motor camp is **Whakapapa Camp,** located in Whakapapa Village. It's sheltered by native bush, has the usual communal facilities, and a store stocked with foods and essential items—open every day from 0800-1800. Rates are $6 pp a night for tentsites (limited number of sites), $8 pp for caravan sites plus $3 per night for power, dorm beds in the lodge for $10 pp (not available during the Christmas holidays or ski season when groups book the lodge), from $9-12 pp (minimum $28-38 per night) for cabins, $15 pp (minimum $46 per night) for the self-contained cabin. Provide your own bedding, crockery, and utensils. June, Oct., Dec., and Jan. are the busiest—book ahead! It's located 250 meters above the Chateau, on the main road, tel. 23-897. Several short walks start in the immediate area.

Tongariro Motor Camp is about 17 km northeast of the Chateau turnoff on Hwy. 47. It has communal facilities, a shop, petrol, ski hire, and meals available in the dining room and restaurant. Tent- or caravan sites start at $8.50 pp ($12 per night minimum). Located next to Eivins Lodge, Tongariro, tel. Turangi 8062.

Ohakune Borough Camp provides communal facilities (the showers and electric cooking rings are coin-operated), a limited number of tentsites but plenty of caravan sites. Centrally located, the motor camp is next to an attractive scenic reserve—and Turoa Skifields, only 18 km away, are easily reached by bus in season. Tentsites are $7.70 pp; some are usually available any time of year. Caravan sites with power are $15.40-17.60 (depending on the season) but usually fully booked way in advance during ski season. No cabins or on-site caravans available. Located at 5 Moore St., Ohakune, tel. 58-561. (For more motor camps see "Turangi Accommodation," p. 212.)

Lodges And Chalets

Marshal Gebbie is the entertaining owner of **Buttercup Alpine Resort** in the town of National Park, nine km northwest of the Chateau turnoff into Tongariro National Park. A limited number of beds (from $55 dinner, B&B), communal facilities (no kitchen), a cozy recreation lounge, and meals in the Butternut Farmhouse Restaurant are available. Located at National Park, junction of hwys. 4 and 47, tel. 702. **Howard's Lodge** on Carroll St. (tel. 827) and **Macrocarpa Lodge** on the main highway (tel. 878), both in National Park, offer good budget backpackers' accommodation from $12 pp per night.

Ruapehu Skotel is a great place to stay, no matter what time of year it is. It's particularly appealing for the budget-conscious in the off-season (summer)—rates are lower yet the park is just as beautiful. Located in Whakapapa Village (excellent location), outstanding mountain and valley views can be enjoyed from its veranda. Aptly described as the place "for all seasons," the Skotel has a gymnasium, TV room, bar, Pinnacles Restaurant, indoor and outdoor saunas and spas, dining room and equipped kitchen (provide your own crockery and utensils or buy a plastic set for $2). There's nothing quite like soaking in the hot bubbling water of the spa at the end of a hard day's hiking or skiing—outside and separate from the main building but glass enclosed, it's a very appealing spot to kick back and gaze at mountains or stars while the swirling water brings your body back to life. In winter the Skotel also has a ski shop for rentals (guests only).

In summer rooms range from $34-47 s or twin, $56-72 d, and a limited number of budget rooms (you may have to share), each with its own handbasin and heater, are always available from $17 pp. The standard rooms (provide your own linen) share bathroom and drying room facilities; the deluxe rooms have private bathrooms, and the super deluxe rooms also have radio, TV, video, tape music, and their own patios. Chalets with fully

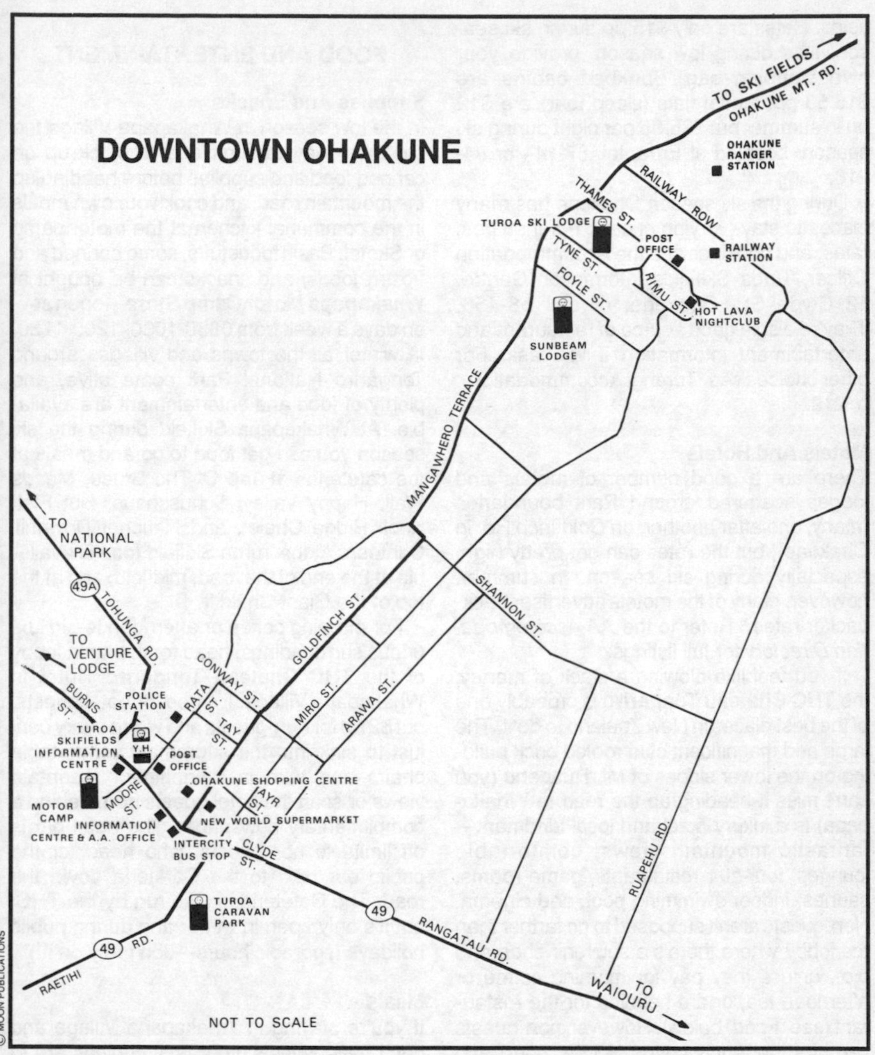

equipped kitchens, TVs, and carports start at $72 d. In winter the rates are almost double, but ask if they're offering any "specials." Winter "packages" include accommodation and breakfast. The large kitchen/dining area is an easy place to meet fellow travelers. The Skotel is off Hwy. 48, Whakapapa Village, tel. Mt. Ruapehu 819. Be sure to pick up the 13 excellent scenic guide brochures produced by the Skotel—they're free at the reception desk.

Another reasonable place to stay is **Erua Ski Lodge** at Erua, six km south of National Park on Hwy. 4. Communal facilities, recreation room, and in winter it has ski hire, a ski shop, and provides transportation to the skifields. Rates are only $15 pp during ski season, less during low season, provide your own sleeping bag. Bunkbed cabins are $16.50 pp, tourist flats (sleep four) are $12 pp in summer but $85-95 per night during ski season. Located at Erua, tel. 87-144 or 84-216.

During the ski season Ohakune has many places to stay (varying prices). For inquiries, rates, and bookings see the Accommodation Officer, Turoa Skifields Information Centre, 12 Clyde St., Ohakune, or call 58-456. They're also a good source of restaurant and entertainment information if you ask. For other choices see "Turangi Accommodation," p. 212.

Motels And Hotels

There are a good number of motels and lodges scattered around Park boundaries (many, one after another, on Goldfinch Rd. in Ohakune), but the rates can get pretty high, especially during ski season. In summer, however, many of the motels advertise "backpacker rates." Refer to the *AA Accommodation Directory* for full listings.

If you feel like blowing a stack of money, the **THC Chateau Tongariro** is probably one of the best places in New Zealand to do it. The large and magnificent blue roofed brick building on the lower slopes of Mt. Ruapehu (you can't miss it heading up the road to Whakapapa) is a luxury hotel and local landmark—fantastic mountain views, comfortable lounges, four-star restaurants, game rooms, saunas, indoor swimming pool, and cinema. Non-guests aren't supposed to go farther than the lobby where there's a souvenir shop and p.o., unless they pay for morning coffee or afternoon tea, or are heading for the restaurant (see "Food" below). However, non-guests can hire the tennis courts ($3 per hour) and equipment (another $5.50 per hour), or play a round of golf ($5.50—equipment hire another $5.50) on the THC golf course in front—pay in the hotel lobby. "Economy" rooms (add GST to all rates) start at $82 s, $115.50 d in summer, $135 s, $190 d in winter, more for premium rooms and suites. Located on Hwy. 48 at Whakapapa Village, tel. Mt. Ruapehu 809.

FOOD AND ENTERTAINMENT

Supplies And Snacks

In the low season in Whakapapa Village the cheapest way to survive is to stock up on canned food and supplies before heading up the mountain road, and cook your own meals in the communal kitchen at the motor camp or Skotel. Basic foodstuffs, some canned and frozen foods, and snacks can be bought at **Whakapapa Motor Camp Store**—open seven days a week from 0830-1030, 1200-1730. In winter all the towns and villages around Tongariro National Park come alive, and plenty of food and entertainment are available. At Whakapapa Skifield during the ski season you can get food to go and meals at the cafeterias at Top O' The Bruce, Meads Wall, Happy Valley, Schusshaus, Hut Flat, Knoll Ridge Chalet, and National Downhill Canteen. At the Turoa Skifield food is available at the end of the road, midfield, and at the top of the Giant Chairlift.

For morning coffee or afternoon tea in luxurious surroundings, head for the main lobby of the **THC Chateau Tongariro Hotel** in Whakapapa Village. It's free for hotel guests, but $2 pp for non-guests and worth every cent just to sink into the supremely comfortable chairs and take in magnificent mountain views or scan the hotel guests from behind a complimentary newspaper. The hotel bar is off limits to non-guests, who head for the public bar next to the Cafeteria down the road. The Cafeteria is also run by the THC, but it's only open in winter and during public holidays (sporadic hours—don't rely on it!).

Meals

If you're staying in Whakapapa Village and don't have wheels, your only choices are to cook your own, eat at the Cafeteria or the excellent Skotel restaurant, or splurge on a meal at the THC Hotel (see "Splurge" below). The **Skotel's Pinnacles Restaurant** is open year-round for breakfast from 0800-0900, lunch 1200-1400, and dinner 1800-2100; casuals welcome. Enjoy one of the bistro and salad meals in summer (from $13-17.50 for

THC Chateau Tongariro Hotel

a main course at dinner), salad bar and hot vegies with all meals in winter. Otherwise, head for Ohakune on the west side of the Park where you'll find a range of restaurants, cafes, and takeaways. **Girdlestone Restaurant** in the Ohakune Hotel offers reasonably priced meals in cozy surroundings, Mon. to Sat. for breakfast, lunch, and dinner—a popular hangout for skiers after the lifts close. Lunches average $7.50, dinners $14-15. Located on Clyde St., tel. 58-268.

For good tearoom fare, burgers, fish, salads, pizza to go, and light meals ($3-7.50), try the **Cafe Stutz** on Clyde St., tel. 58-563; open six days a week. Another popular place for pizza, pasta, capuccino, and hot chocolate is **La Pizzeria** on Thames St., Ohakune Junction. **The Pipers' Kings Court** on Tyne St. has two fully licensed restaurants (wide range in meal prices), cocktail bar, and apres-ski bar. The least expensive section is the Bistro and Cabaret—for prices and bookings call Ohakune 58-648. **Raetihi Hotel** on Seddon St. at Raetihi (11 km west of Ohakune) offers moderate bistro lunches from 1200-1330 and more pricey a la carte dinners from 1800-2100. Fully licensed, tel. 54-016.

Several of the local ski lodges open their restaurants to casual guests but most recommend calling to make reservations. On Foyle St. in Ohakune, **Sunbeam Ski Lodge** offers pricey meals and a Sun. night smorgasbord from 1800-1930. BYO license, bookings advisable, tel. 58-470. **Venture Lodge,** 1.5 km along Burn St. in Ohakune, is primarily a ski lodge but the restaurant also caters to casuals; tel. 58-322. In National Park try the **Butternut Farmhouse Restaurant** on the main highway.

Takeaway

Cafe Stutz on Clyde St. in Ohakune has both takeaways and sit-down meals. Open Mon. to Sat., and late nights on Mon. and Fri., tel. 58-563.

Splurge

Ruapehu Restaurant, part of the THC Chateau Tongariro at Whakapapa Village, is open to the public. Breakfast, from 0730-0900, starts at around $9 Continental or $14 for a cooked meal. A delicious buffet-style lunch, from 1230-1330 every day of the year, is about $20 pp. On Sun. a sumptuous smorgasbord is put on for $19 pp. Dinner is a more formal affair, served from 1830-2100—expect to pay from $18-30 for a main course alone, and note that a "high standard of dress" is required (no jeans, tennis or sandshoes, or shorts), reservations essential. In winter the more casual **Carvery,** also part of the THC complex, is open to the public and appeals to the non-budget-conscious starving skier. Bistro dinners will set you back at least $19 pp.

Entertainment

Being a national park area, the main entertainment around here occurs during the day—by evening you're too tuckered out to attempt much more than climbing into the sack. If you have any energy left over after a full day and a filling meal, you can always soak in a hot spa pool. Otherwise, the communal kitchen and dining room at both the Skotel and Whakapapa Motor Camp are good places to meet people, and after all, when you throw a bunch of people from all over the world together, who needs more in the way of entertainment?

Otherwise, head for the public bar next to the Cafeteria in Whakapapa Village or one of the many hotels in Ohakune—some put on live entertainment during the ski season, though not much goes on during low season (when the town recovers from the hectic ski season and goes into summertime hibernation). The Ohakune Hotel has a disco on Sat. nights from 1945-2300 for a small cover charge. The **Hot Lava Nightclub** is another "hot spot" in Ohakune on weekends; on Thames Street. For Chateau Tongariro guests and the public, a movie is shown on Thurs. and Sun. nights in the hotel cinema; or head for either the Ohakune Kings Theatre or the Raetihi Royal Theatre. Pick up the local newspaper to see what's on, or make friends with the locals—they'll tell you what's happening and where.

INFORMATION AND SERVICES

Sources

The main source of Park info is **Whakapapa Visitors Centre** in Whakapapa Village, Mt. Ruapehu, tel. 23-729. Open daily from 0800-1700, the center has many interesting displays featuring local geology, volcanism, earthquakes, flora and fauna, as well as track descriptions and hut info, brochures on hiking trails, short walks, special attractions, and skiing information. In summer the Park runs day trips that let you get the most out of it in a short time. If you'd like to see the technicolor spectacle of a volcanic eruption complete with awesome stereo effects, ask one of the personnel to put on the Tongariro National Park audio-visual in the theater—it's really something!

Pick up a detailed Dept. of Survey and Lands topographical map of the park before you set out into the wilds, and get the latest mountain weather forecast—essential for backcountry hiking. The Park handbook *The Restless Land* is also a worthwhile purchase. During the ski season you can call for road info at tel. Mt. Ruapehu 23-729. A public phone lies just inside the Visitors Centre's main entrance.

The **Ohakune Ranger Station and Park Information Centre** is at the start of Ohakune Mountain Rd. (the road up to Turoa Skifields) on the west side of the Park, tel. 58-578, open from 0800-1700 in winter. You can get maps, free brochures and pamphlets on the short walks, hiking trails, and huts, and hunting permits, weather forecasts, and skifield and road information. The **Ruapehu Information Centre** is another source of local info; at 54 Clyde St., tel. 58-151. The other more distant place to get park info is the **Turangi Ranger Station** in Turangi, tel. 8607.

Emergency

Skiing Emergency: at Whakapapa call the Visitors Centre, tel. 23-729 (24 hours), or at Turoa call Ohakune Ranger Station, tel. 58-578, 58-604, 59-043, or 58-170. **Police:** National Park tel. 869, Taumarunui tel. 8119, Ohakune tel. 58-551, Raetihi tel. (5) 4002, Wanganui tel. (54) 488, or Turangi tel. 7709. **Ambulance or hospital:** tel. Raetihi 4616. **Doctor:** tel. Ohakune 58-356 or Raetihi 54-211.

Skiing Information

For specialized skiing info and the latest weather forecast visit the **Iwikau Public Shelter** on Whakapapa Skifield, open 0800-1700, or call Mt. Ruapehu at tel. 23-738 (skifield operator) or tel. 833 (ansaphone). A Skifield Information Sign on Whakapapa Skifield shows the current facilities operating, snow and weather conditions, a location map, and avalanche information. **Turoa Skifields Information Centre,** 12 Clyde St. (north end of Ohakune) is open 0800-1700, or call 58-456. For the most up-to-date info on weather, snow and ski conditions at Turoa (24 hours a day), tel. Ohakune 58-255.

General

Whakapapa: Whakapapa postal agency (no banking) is in the souvenir shop inside the main entrance of the THC Chateau Tongariro Hotel, open Mon. to Fri. from 0800-1230 and 1330-1700; mail is collected from the mailbox outside the shop daily at 0815.

Ohakune: The **p.o.** on Clyde St. is open Mon. to Thurs. from 0900-1700 and Fri. 0900-1800, and you can make toll calls, local calls, and send telegrams from the public phone boxes outside.

TRANSPORTATION

Getting There

Tongariro National Park is easy to get to if you have your own transportation—but a bit of a hassle by bus (unless you're there during the ski season when a snow bus departs Ohakune several times each morning, returning in the afternoon—buy your ticket on board) or train. Hitchhikers can expect quite a wait (get those creative desperate plea signs out again!). Highway 1 runs down the entire eastern boundary of the park, but if you're coming from the north and plan on visiting Whakapapa Visitors Centre you need to get onto Hwy. 47 which runs along the northern boundary. You can either turn off at Turangi onto Hwy. 41, then take Te Ponanga Saddle Road (great views) to Hwy. 47, or continue down Hwy. 1 south of Turangi and take the more major turnoff onto Hwy. 47A. If you're coming from the south, head for Ohakune (Hwy. 49A) on the western side where there's another access road (Ohakune Mountain Rd.) into the Park.

The main north-south rail line runs through Ohakune on the western side, and InterCity coaches also service the town. In the ski season several companies provide 4WD services up the mountains to the two main skifields. For a **taxi** call Ohakune 58-573.

Bus

InterCity coaches connect **Ohakune** with Rotorua, Taihape, Palmerston North, Wanganui, and Wellington ($36 OW), as well as **National Park,** Taumarunui, Hamilton, and Auckland ($44 OW). The Ohakune bus stop is on Clyde St., next to the AA office and info center. From National Park to Whakapapa Village the bus costs $4 OW, from Ohakune (and the YH) $10 OW, from Taupo $18 OW. On Tues., Thurs., and Sun. Intercity runs a coach from Rotorua to **Chateau, National Park,** and **Ohakune.** Another way to reach Whakapapa Village or track entrances in the park is via **Alpine Scenic Tours** from Turangi. They meet InterCity and Mount Cook Line buses in Turangi, run up into the park, then collect people in the Village for the return trip back to Turangi. For a current schedule and fares, call Turangi 8392. **Rivercity Tracks** operates daily service from Ohakune to Wanganui and return; for more info call 58-395.

Train

Ohakune railway station is on Railway Row (off Ohakune Mountain Rd. which leads to the skifields), Ohakune Junction; for train timetables and current ticket prices call Ohakune 58-426 or drop by the station. The daily *Northerner Express* and *Silver Fern Railcar* stop at Ohakune, connecting the outskirts of Tongariro National Park with Auckland ($54 OW) to the north and Wellington ($46 OW) to the south.

WANGANUI

If you don't have much time and are doing the old one-day-here one-day-there routine, the west coast city of Wanganui is a great base for exploring the river and bush scenery of Whanganui National Park to the north, and the volcanic wonders of Tongariro National Park to the northeast and Egmont National Park to the northwest. Situated on the shores of South Taranaki Bight at the mouth of the Wanganui River, about midway between the cities of New Plymouth to the north and Wellington to the south, Wanganui has river attractions, good surfing beaches, beautiful parks, and many hospitable locals eager to proudly show you their hometown. If you're looking for the bustle, comforts, and attractions a city has to offer or want to explore the inland beauty of the wild upper stretches of the Wanganui River, take a few days to appreciate life in Wanganui, "The Friendly River City."

SIGHTS

Scenic Walks

The best way to get the feel of the city is on foot, and the **Information Wanganui** office on Guyton St. (see "Information" below) is a good place to start. Collect a Wanganui city map and the handy brochure "Scenic Walks in and around Wanganui." The info center offers a free personalized tour to overseas visitors (with one-day advance notice)—a local person asks your interests and takes you to the city sights you'd probably find the most fascinating. Take advantage of this excellent service.

Wanganui Cultural And Civic Centre

Within Queens Park are the impressive architectural buildings of the **Regional Museum** (see below), **Sarjeant Art Galley** (open Mon. to Fri. 1030-1600, Sat. 1030-1200 and 1330-1600, Sun. 1330-1600; admission free), and **Davis Public Library** (the public reading room has newpapers from cities around New Zealand; open Mon. to Fri. 1000-2000, Sat. 0900-1200).

Wanganui Regional Museum, largest regional museum in New Zealand, is also one of the best in the country. A vast display room features Maori architecture, carving, art, greenstone weapons, feather cloaks, intriguing displays on tattooing, and the incredible 25-meter Te Mata-O-Hoturoa War Canoe that carried a crew of 70! Throughout the rest of the museum there's a reconstruction of a colonial cottage and an entire Wanganui street from times gone by, a spectacular and comprehensive collection of mounted birds (see the display of *moa*—a huge flightless bird native to N.Z. that's been extinct for centuries), parrots of the world, mounted fish, whales, and animals, a shell collection, and a room full of fluorescent butterflies and moths! The museum is open Mon. to Fri. 1000-1600, weekends and holidays from 1300-1630 (allow plenty of time), and well worth the small admission cost of $2 adult, 65 cents child. Just outside the museum is the **Carillon** which automatically plays delightful music every quarter hour between 1200-1400—don't miss it! The civic center is located one block east of Victoria Ave., at the top end of Maria Place, and the museum is on Watt St., tel. 57-443.

Durie Hill Elevator And War Memorial Tower

Head here for great views of the city, its three major bridges, and the Wanganui River winding out to the coast. Admission to the tower is free, open till 1800 every night. To get there on foot from downtown, cross the river via Wanganui City Bridge (the main bridge) and take the unique 72-meter elevator through the hill to the summit. To get there by car, cross the bridge, turn left, and follow the signs to "Scenic Drive View Point." At the summit is a 34-meter Memorial Tower built entirely out of fossilized seashell rock (indicating that the river must have been a large inlet at one time for the builders to find seashells so far up the banks). For another aspect and views of the rolling hills behind the city, head for the **Water**

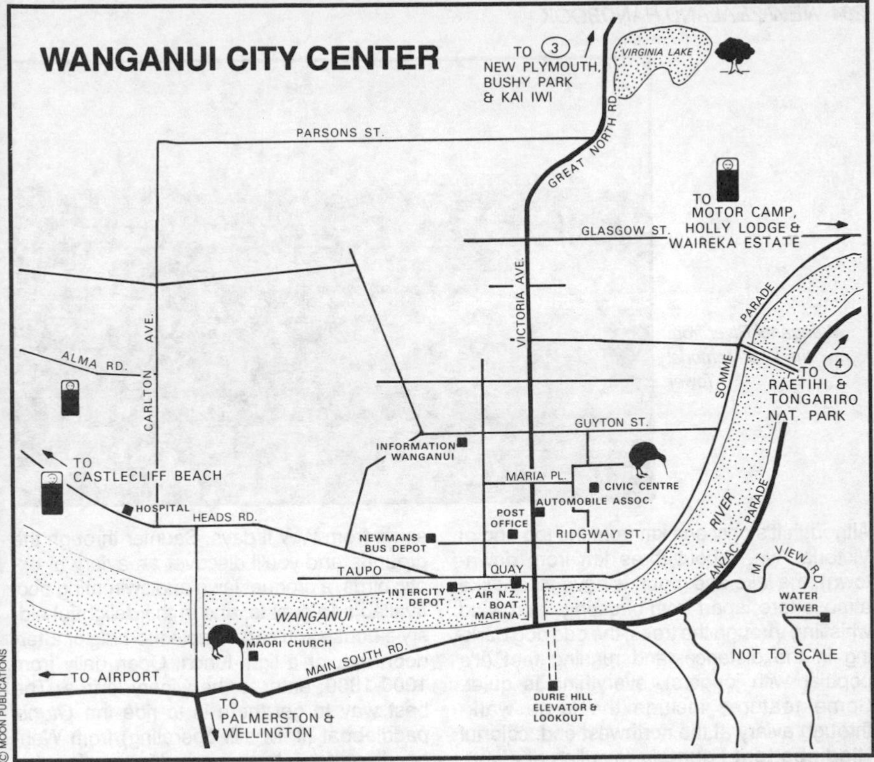

Tower on the same side of the river as the Memorial Tower but a couple of km north. To get there, go back down to the river (but don't cross it), turn right on the main road, Anzac Parade. Just after the start of **Kowhai Park** (a child's paradise) on the left, turn right on Mountain View Rd. which twists and turns up Bastia Hill. Turn left on Bastia Ave. and you'll end up at the tower—climb it for great views.

Maori Church

Another "must see" on the eastern side of the river is the small beautiful St. Paul's Memorial Church at Putiki. This is not just another church. The entire interior is magnificently decorated with Maori carvings, *tuku tuku* (woven reeds) wall panels, and stained- and etched-glass windows. Brightly colored designs on the wooden beams are rich with spiritual meaning (ask someone to point out the "Stairway to Heaven") patterned on things found in nature—look for the fern fronds designs. As it's a place of worship, treat it accordingly (sadly there have been reports of vandalism)—if it's locked, ask for the key next door; admission is free but a donation is requested. For more Maori art, peek in the Meeting Hall next to the church. If you're in luck you may catch a free concert—on certain early evenings the local Maori women practice their traditional songs and dances. The church and hall are located on Anaua Street. To get there from the Memorial Tower head south along Putiki Dr. (by the river) and just before the motorway turn right on Anaua Street. To get there from town cross the river via Cobham Bridge; Anaua St. is immediately off to the left.

Virginia Lake Reserve

Tranquil Virginia Lake is nestled between woods, lawns, and beds of bright flowers.

Wanganui River from the War Memorial Tower

Although it's only one km from the top end of Victoria Ave. (about three km from downtown), the lake and grounds have a park-like atmosphere; apart from birdsongs and wind whistling through the trees, the odd dog barking in the distance, and running feet (it's popular with joggers), everything is quiet. Some features include the large walk-through aviary at the northwest end, colorful **Higginbottom Fountain** (startling at night), and the tropical flower- and fern-filled **Winter Gardens** (open Mon. to Sat. 1000-1600, Sun. 1000-1700; admission free). Some delightful tracks weave through the trees and around the lake—if you have time, follow the trail around the left side of the lake (from the road) to the small statue of *Tainui*—the romantic legend of the lake is inscribed below. To get to the lake from downtown follow Victoria Ave. away from the river. At the top end turn right onto Great North Rd. and follow its curves until you reach the lake on your right. If you're driving, park on Babbage Pl. just beyond the park at the aviary end.

Holly Lodge Estate Winery

At the Holly Lodge Estate you can see grape vines (surprise, surprise!), production processes, Barrel House, Wine Shop, and get lips-on experience at the tasting bar. The complex also features a memorabilia museum from WW II days. Saunter through the grounds and you'll discover an aviary of exotic birds, a croquet lawn and swimming pool available to guests, and in the delightful old-style house you can sample morning or afternoon tea, or a light lunch. Open daily from 1000-1800; entry to the winery is free. The best way to get there is to ride the *Otunui* paddleboat (if it's still operating) from Wanganui, or if you have a car, drive north out of the city along Somme Parade which follows the river. Continue onto Papaiti Rd. (Upper Aramaho); call 39-344 for bookings. They also operate jet boat rides that run up-river from the winery (see "On The River" below).

Waireka Estate Museum

One km beyond Holly Lodge Winery, this unique museum is contained inside a beautiful old riverside homestead and its contents are bound to fascinate all ages! The collection features all kinds of things—very lifelike animals and birds (some of which are extinct) taxidermied by the original owner's son, *moa* and bird skeletons, a butterfly and moth collection, Nazi war helmets, spears, snakes in jars, Maori artifacts, fishing gear found after river floods, wood carvings, guns, shoes, cannonballs, a "wife-beating stick," even a handbag made out of an armadillo. A guide gives a fascinating explanation of all the objects in the room, including how they were obtained. It's open in summer and over Easter (the rest of the year for pre-arranged tour groups, but if you just turn up and the guide is available, you may be able to get in), and Devonshire teas are available in summer; admission is a worthwhile $4 pp (extra for tea). Afterward, don't miss the sunken garden which was "rediscovered," the two cannons on the front lawn which are still fired on special occasions, the miniature train and donkey rides for the kids, and all the hand-carved fairies and goblins and other creatures that peek out of every garden nook and cranny. The scenic riverside drive out to the museum is also worthwhile; from town take Somme Parade east along the river, pass Holly Lodge Winery, and continue for another km until you come to the museum on your left.

Beaches And Bush
The most popular city beach is **Castlecliff** where the Wanganui River flows out to sea. Eight km west of the city center, it has a "Marine Parade," and is known for good beach-break surf (dangerous currents at the river mouth). To get there from downtown, catch the regular local bus to Castlecliff (get a schedule and list of stops at the info center) or follow Taupo Quay along the riverfront onto Heads Road. Continue onto Bryce St. and at the end turn right onto Cornfoot St. then left on Manua St.—you'll end up at Castlecliff Beach Domain.

Mowhanau Beach (also called Kai Iwi Beach) is another good place for surfing and swimming, eight km farther north—take Hwy. 3 north, then turn off just south of the town of Kai Iwi onto Kai Iwi Valley Rd. which ends at the beach. Another great spot and a nature-lovers' paradise in the Kai Iwi area is **Bushy Park Scenic Reserve,** where you can walk through 214 acres of native bush and see and hear plenty of birds in this natural sanctuary; open seven days 1000-1700 (late in summer), and public and school holidays. You can also stay in the old colonial homestead (see "Accommodation" below). Day entry adult $2 , child $1. It's located at the end of Bushy Park Rd. off Hwy. 3 north, just north of Kai Iwi. Thirty km south of Wanganui is the popular **Turakina Beach**—take Hwy. 3 south and turn off just north of Turakina onto Turakina Beach Road.

Scenic Drive
If you have a car and plenty of time, the 79-km scenic drive north along the Wanganui River to the picturesque village of **Pipiriki** is worthwhile. It's the gateway to the "wilderness" reaches of the Wanganui River (only jet boats can continue upriver) and Whanganui National Park (see p. 274), and a meeting place for hikers, campers, canoeists, rafters, and jet boaters. A large Maori population used to live across the river from the present-day village. Then, in the early 1900s, steamboats that could only cruise the river as far as Pipiriki brought great numbers of tourists to what quickly became a booming tourist resort. Today it's again a quiet little village attracting those who wish to explore the river, or hike the well-known **Matemateaonga Track** (see "A Wilderness Hike," p. 269) and other tracks. A **Ranger Station** and **Colonial House Information Centre and Museum** are the other main sights. For jet boat info call **Pipiriki Jet Boat Tours** at tel. Raetihi 54-733. At Pipiriki, the road turns sharply east away from the river toward Raetihi where it rejoins Hwy. 4 (it's about 180 km RT from Wanganui).

WANGANUI RIVER

The magnificent Wanganui River, often called "the Rhine of New Zealand," is the second longest river and the longest navigable waterway in the country. Starting on the slopes of Mt. Tongariro, the river runs a 315-km course north to Taumarunui then south toward Wanganui, the last 32 km as a wide tidal estuary before flowing into the Tasman Sea. It's navigable as far as Taumarunui (only by jet boat above Pipiriki), contains 239 rapids, and the upper and middle stretches are exhilarating. The quieter but equally scenic lower stretch by the city treats boaters to romantic reflection shots, native bush-covered banks, and a different aspect of Wanganui's bridges and city sights. The river also offers a large range of outdoor recreation activities, including hiking and hunting along its banks and scenic reserves, canoeing and jet boating the many rapids, and several already have been preserved as "Whanganui River National Park." Each year on Waitangi Day (Feb. 6) Wanganui hosts a colorful river regatta, and the celebrations and events involve historic Maori canoes.

Legend And History

The river has legendary beginnings and a colorful history. When Mt. Tongariro won the heart of Mt. Pihanga, the rival suitor Mt. Taranaki was forced to flee. He tore through the hills, bush, and forest to the coast and then headed north to his permanent resting place (where he still stands today as Mt. Egmont/ Taranaki), leaving behind him a deep ravine that became the Wanganui River. For centuries Maori people lived in villages along the shores of the Wanganui; today's modern city used to be a thriving Maori center prior to the arrival of the first white settlers (1830s). The river was an important Maori canoe route to the center of the North Island; with the Europeans came the first steam boats to puff upriver. Today most of the original villages lie abandoned, but priceless Maori artifacts found along the banks have been preserved and are on display at various riverside settlements. The remains of many Maori *pa* can still be viewed from the river. In 1870, Town Bridge was erected over the river, which considerably opened up the district and was the beginning of a connection with Wellington in the south. The original bridge stood for almost 100 years before it was replaced with the modern Wanganui City Bridge. Today three city bridges and a railway bridge span the mighty river.

Wanganui River Reserves

Many of the most scenic or historic areas along the Wanganui River have been protected and classified as reserves by the Dept. of Conservation. In fact, about 150 separate reserves adjacent to the river have good tracks to waterfalls, historic sites, ancient Maori villages, and scenic lookouts. Most easily reached from the water by jet boat (based at Wanganui, Pipiriki, and Taumarunui), you can also follow the river as far as Pipiriki (79 km from Wanganui) by road. For more info call the Senior Ranger, tel. Raetihi 54-631, or the Reserves Assistant, tel. Taumarunui 8201; brochures on many of the walks are available at the info center in Wanganui. Also see "Whanganui National Park," p. 274.

ON THE RIVER

Stop by the Information Wanganui office (see "Information" below) where you'll be inundated with brochures on exploring the scenic beauty of the Wanganui River and its historic places by jet boat, raft, historic paddle steamer, on foot, etc.—the great variety allows you to pick the best one to suit your budget and fancy.

The Wine Trip

One of the most pleasurable trips along the lower stretch is onboard the old paddlewheel steam boat *Otunui,* which operates from Wanganui to Holly Lodge Estate Winery and back. Built in London, England, and shipped over, it was put to work on the river in 1908. The captain narrates the river's historic and scenic aspects while you watch the paddlewheel churn and the beautiful scenery float by, or sit inside in the old-fashioned red-and-gold interior. Sailing under three city bridges and past several city attractions, a striking sandstone-colored cliff full of holes which the locals call Sparrows Rock, and ancient Maori fortifications along the way, your final destination is Holly Lodge Estate Winery (see above). The three-hour trip departs Mon. to Fri. at 1000 from the City Marina (bottom end of Victoria Ave.), weekends at 1000 and 1400 from the estate for a two-hour trip upstream; adult $11 pp RT, child $7. To get to the winery by road take Somme Parade north out of town following the river and continue onto Papaiti Road. Bookings are preferred but not necessary, tel. 39-344.

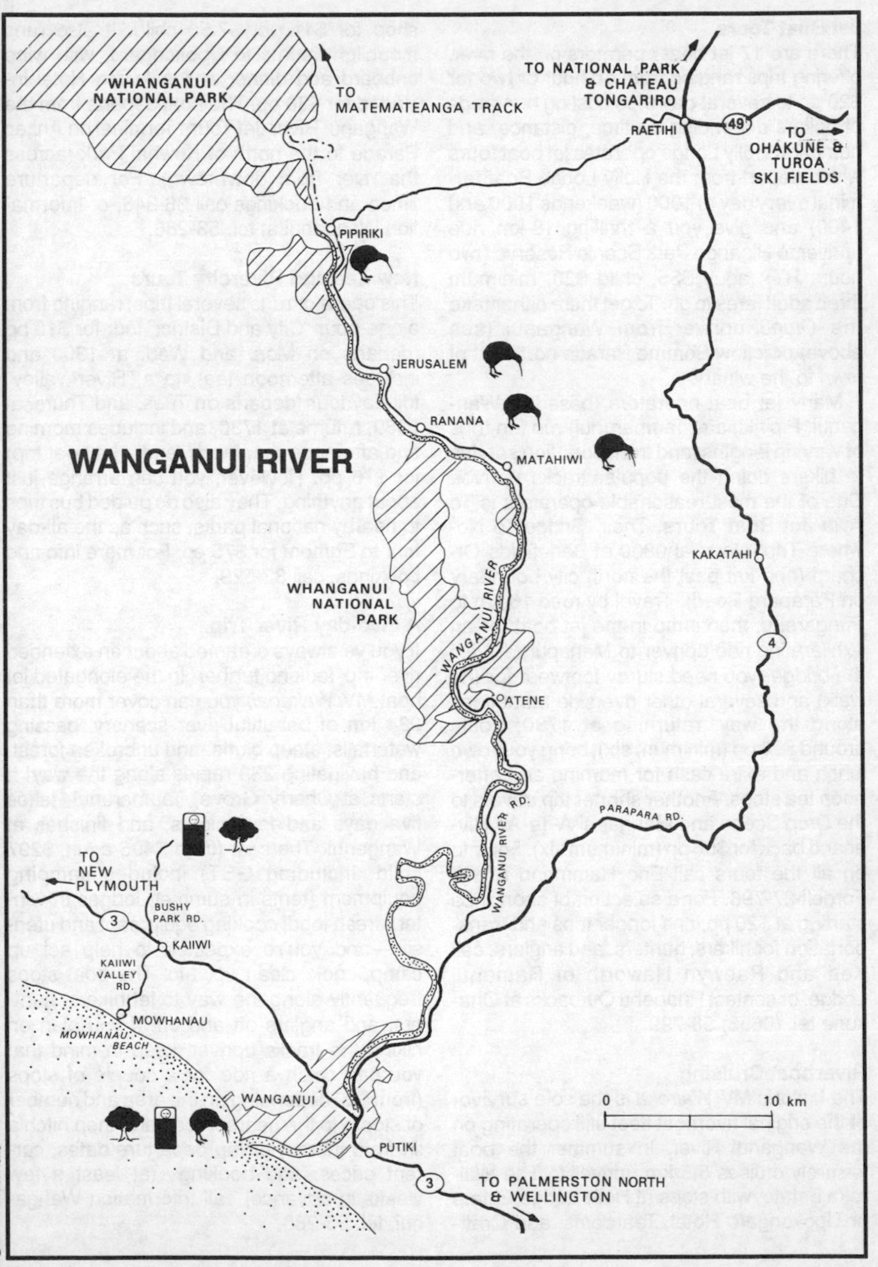
WHANGANUI
NATIONAL PARK
TO
MATEMATEANGA TRACK
TO NATIONAL PARK
& CHATEAU
TONGARIRO
RAETIHI
49
TO
OHAKUNE &
TUROA
SKI FIELDS
PIPIRIKI
JERUSALEM
RANANA
MATAHIWI
WANGANUI RIVER
WHANGANUI
NATIONAL
PARK
KAKATAHI
WANGANUI RIVER
4
OATENE
WANGANUI RIVER RD.
PARAPARA RD.
TO
NEW
PLYMOUTH
3
BUSHY
PARK RD.
KAIIWI
KAIIWI
VALLEY
RD.
MOWHANAU
MOWHANAU
BEACH
WANGANUI
0
10 km
PUTIKI
3
TO PALMERSTON NORTH
& WELLINGTON

Jet Boat Tours

There are 17 jet boat operators on the river, offering trips ranging from an hour or two for $20 pp to several-day trips costing hundreds of dollars depending on time, distance, and numbers. Holly Lodge operates jet boat tours which depart from the Holly Lodge Boat terminal every day at 1000 (weekends 1000 and 1400) and give you a thrilling 18-km ride upriver to Hipango Park Scenic Reserve (two hours RT); adult $35, child $28, minimum three adult fares to go. To get there either take the *Otunui* upriver from Wanganui (see above) or follow Somme Parade north out of town to the winery.

Many jet boat operators (based in Wanganui, Pipiriki, and Taumarunui) run fun trips of varying lengths, and transportation service to hikers doing the popular tracks upriver. One of the most reasonable operators is **Te Awa Jet Boat Tours.** Their "Bridge To Nowhere Trip" starts at 0800 at Benefields Orchard (one km past the north city boundary on Parapara Road). Travel by road 16 km to Pungarehu, then jump in the jet boat for an exhilarating ride upriver to Manapurua. Visit the bridge (you need sturdy footwear for the walk) and several other riverside attractions along the way, returning at 1730; costs around $90 pp (minimum six), bring your own lunch and extra cash for morning and afternoon tea stops. Another shorter trip travels to the Drop Scene and Manganui-A-Te-Ao River and back for $66 pp (minimum six). For info on all the tours call Eric Hammond at tel. Fordell 27-796. For a selection of short trips starting at $20 pp, and longer trips and transportation for hikers, hunters, and anglers, call Ken and Raewyn Haworth of Ramanui Lodge, or contact Ruapehu Outbacks at Ohakune tel. (0658) 58-799.

Riverboat Cruising

The historic MV *Waireka* is the sole survivor of the original riverboat fleet still operating on the Wanganui River. In summer the boat leisurely cruises 5.5 km upriver to The Waireka Estate, with stops at Holly Lodge Estate or Upokongaro Hotel, Tearooms, and Craftshop for $11 pp, $7.50 child. It also runs moonlight jaunts to Upokongaro, with wine onboard and dinner at the Avoca Hotel included for $30 pp. The boat departs from the Wanganui River Jet Tours Terminal on Anzac Parade to the north of Kowhai Park (across the river from downtown). For departure times and bookings call 36-346, or Information Wanganui at tel. 53-286.

New Zealand Rivercity Tours

This operator runs several trips, ranging from a one-hour "City and District" tour for $10 pp (departs on Mon. and Wed. at 1300 and includes afternoon tea), to a "River Valley" full-day tour (departs on Tues. and Thurs. at 0830, returns at 1730, and includes morning and afternoon tea, lunch, and a jet boat trip) for $76 pp. However, you can arrange just about anything. They also do guided bus trips to nearby national parks, such as the all-day tour to Egmont for $75 pp. For more info and bookings, call 32-529.

A Five-day River Trip

If you've always dreamed about an extended river trip, look no further! In the elongated jet boat MV *Wakapai,* you can cover more than 234 km of beautiful river scenery, passing waterfalls, steep bluffs, and unbroken forest, and navigating 239 rapids along the way! It starts at Cherry Grove, Taumarunui, takes five days and four nights, and finishes at Wanganui. The cost (from $495 adult, $297 child, including GST) includes camping equipment (tents in summer, lodges in winter), fresh food, cooking equipment and utensils—and you're expected to help set up camp, cook, clean up, etc. The boat stops frequently along the way to let hikers, hunters, and anglers off and on. If you plan on hiking the tracks upriver, keep in mind that you can catch a ride for a couple of stops (from $20 depending on the area and number of stops) to the nearest road and then hitch a lift from there. For trip departure dates, current prices, and bookings (at least a few weeks in advance) call Information Wanganui, tel. 53-286.

Senior citizens enjoy a day outing to Holly Lodge Estate.

Canoeing

A number of canoe tour operators present a selection of canoe and camp tours from points upstream to Wanganui; others hire out canoes and equipment so that you can do your own thing. For more info call in at the Information Wanganui office on the corner of Guyton and St. Hill sts., or tel. 53-286. **Rivercity Tours** offer one- to two-day trips or four- to five-day trips canoeing the Wanganui River, with guide, food, and transport included, and no experience necessary (from $88 pp per day). Contact them at tel. 32-529 for all the details.

A WILDERNESS HIKE

The Matemateaonga Walkway

This wild 42-km bush walk along the top of the Matemateaonga Range and through Mt. Humphries State Forest takes about four days. You can walk it either direction. If you travel west to east you need to pre-arrange jet boat pickup at Ramanui on the Wanganui River (about 25 km upstream from Pipiriki), and carry enough food to last you at least six days (in case you miss your jet boat rendezvous and have to walk back). If you go east to west you need to get to the beginning by jet boat and pre-arrange transportation at the other end—no public transportation is available. Three huts located along the track have wood stoves and rainwater tanks ($12.50 pp in honesty boxes at each hut). Take a compass, a detailed map (NZMS 1 sheet N120 for sale at any Dept. of Conservation office), sturdy boots, warm and waterproof clothing (if it's raining in the Taranaki area it'll be pouring cats and dogs on you!), tent and portable stove in case the huts are full. The track starts on Mangaehu Rd. (unsealed) inland from Makahu (48 km east of Stratford) and finishes at Ramanui on the Wanganui River. For jet boat info call **Pipiriki Jet Boat Tours** at tel. Raetihi 54-633 or Ramanui Lodge for the ride between Pipiriki and Ramanui. They'll also arrange minicoach transportation from Wanganui to Pipirihi (extra) if desired. You can also arrange inexpensive transportation with **Rivercity Tours,** but you need to allow at least a couple of days organizing the details; tel. 32-529.

ACCOMMODATION

Hostel

Comfortable **Wanganui YH** is centrally located at 43 Campbell St., near several fastfood outlets, tel. 56-780. Family and twin rooms available; $12 pp per night.

Motor Camps

There's quite a choice. Two are located in the beach suburb of Castlecliff (about eight km west of the city center), the Gonville Caravan Park (no tentsites but on-site caravans for hire) is between Castlecliff and downtown, and another motor camp lies at the other end of the city (6.5 km east) on the banks of the Wanganui River.

Aramoho Park Camp is a great place to stay if you want to surround yourself with greenery, get a bit of rest, and don't mind sharing your food with numerous noisy families of the waterfowl variety. (Check under your car in the morning for hitchhiking ducks!) Situated in lush park-like surroundings with lots of trees, the river is a few steps away. Communal facilities (non-campers can get a shower here for $1.50 pp), TV and game room, BBQs, adjacent dairy and general store open seven days a week. Tentsites are $8 d, caravan sites $15 d, bunkhouse accommodation $10 pp. Cabins start at $22.50 s or d; tourist flats start at $40 s or $45 d. Located on Somme Parade in Upper Aramoho on the city-side bank of the Wanganui River (10 km from Dublin St. Bridge), tel. 38-402. To get there from town follow Somme Parade east along the river, or ask at the info center for local bus schedules.

Gonville Caravan Park has communal facilities, hot spa pools, recreation and TV room, pool table, and camp store. Caravan sites and on-site caravans are $11 s or d. Located in Gonville, three km from downtown, at 86 Bignell St., tel. 42-012. To get there by road take Taupo Quay (along the riverfront) west onto Heads Rd., continue for about two km, turn right on Kings Ave., then left on Bignell Street.

Avro Motel and Caravan Court is at 36 Alma Rd., tel. 55-279 or 58-462. Facilities include a large swimming pool, private spa pools, playground, guest laundry, and unique self-contained shower, washroom, toilet, and dressing room for each caravan site; $14 s, $18 d. Motel units each have a fully equipped kitchen, TV, video, telephone, radio, and heating; from $58 s, $66 d or twin.

Castlecliff Camp, adjacent to the beach and eight km from the main p.o., has communal facilities, a TV and game room, and adjacent store. Tentsites are $6 pp; caravan sites $8 s, $13 d; on-site caravans $16 s, $21 d, one cabin $11 s, $18 d. Located on the corner of Karaka and Rangiora sts., Castlecliff, tel. 42-227. **Alwyn Motor Court** is a carbon copy of the above, with a swimming pool. Cabins are $13 s, $26 d, tourist flats are $25 s, $35 d; weekly and off-season rates available. Located at 65 Karaka St. (off Rangiora St.), Castlecliff, tel. 44-500. To get out to Castlecliff Beach, follow Taupo Quay west onto Heads Rd., continue onto Bryce St., at the end turn right on Cornfoot St., then left on Rangiora Street. Regular local bus service runs Mon. to Sat. from downtown to Castlecliff Beach.

Private Hotels

The attractive **Riverside Inn,** built in 1895, is centrally located, has a TV lounge, and cooked or Continental breakfasts are available (as are cut lunches for $7.70, and dinners on request for around $11.25 pp). Comfortable rooms with shared bath are $32.70 s, $44.50 d or twin; large cooked breakfast included; rooms with private facilities are also available (extra cost). Located at 2 Plymouth St., tel. 32-529. The bright attractive **Cairnbrae Private Hotel,** built in 1900, is directly across the road from the river. Facilities include a TV lounge, and tea- and coffee-making necessities; from $31 s for a cheerful room and a substantial, cooked, English-style breakfast, or $44 d, B&B (discounts for longer stays). A bed in one of the four cabins with shared facilities, linen provided, is $12 per night (doesn't include breakfast). Dinner is available for $11.25 pp. The owners also operate tours to local and distant highlights (ask for their Rivercity Tours brochure); a five-day package including accommodation, meals, and tours is $300 pp. Located at 24 Somme Parade, tel. 57-918.

Bushy Park Historic Homestead

If you have your own transportation and don't mind the 24-km drive north to Kai Iwi, stay at the beautiful **Bushy Park Scenic Reserve.**

Communal kitchen with all crockery, cutlery, and cooking utensils supplied, and Continental breakfast available; $40 s, $45 d. For more info and bookings tel. Kai Iwi 29-879. Located on Rangitatau Rd., off Hwy. 3 eight km north of Kai Iwi.

FOOD AND ENTERTAINMENT

Cafes

For an enjoyable outdoor-indoor feeling, head to the end of the Tudor Court arcade on Victoria Ave. (near Maria Place) and try **Dr. Johnson's Coffee Lounge.** The "outdoor" tables are actually inside the arcade, but the trickling fountain, background music, skylight, and next-door plant shop turn morning or afternoon tea or a light lunch into a rejuvenating experience. It's open Mon. to Fri. from 0800-1630 and Sat. mornings. **Kiplings** on Wicksteed St. (off Guyton St.) is a popular local hang-out; open for breakfast from 0730-0930, for morning and afternoon teas and lunches to 1600—enjoy your meal outside on the patio. Another locally recommended coffee lounge is **Capers** in the Victoria Mall. **Expresso Coffee House** has good coffee and regular tearoom fare at regular prices. Located at 142A Victoria Avenue. **Shangri-La Restaurant,** overlooking beautiful Virginia Lake, serves morning and afternoon tea, and lunch seven days a week. It has a BYO license; located on Great North Road. **The Cellars** adjacent to the Riverside Tavern on Somme Parade not only provides a large variety of wine, beer, liquor, deli foods, and snacks, but also a large assortment of unusual goodies to go. It's the perfect place to pack an impromptu gourmet picnic on your way upriver, or collect the makings for a delicious gorge back at your campsite!

Restaurants

Two local favorites include **The Green House Restaurant** at the upper end of Victoria Ave. just beyond Woolworths Superstore, and **Cameron House** on the corner of Dublin and Wicksteed. The Green House whips up good-value steak and seafood dishes (mains average $10-15, large servings) seven nights a week, but it's particularly busy on Thurs. and Fri. "Fish Nights." For $8.50 you can tuck in, and in, and in to as much fish as you can manage with chips and coleslaw, or choose from the regular menu; bookings advisable at tel. 58-037 unless you're willing to eat early, and takeaways are also available. It's open Mon. and Wed. from 1700, Thurs. and Fri. 1130-1400 and 1700 on, and weekends from 1700. The Cameron House is more suitable for a fancier occasion, with mains averaging $20. **Bibi's Wine and Coffee Bar** (part of the Bryvern Motor Inn) has snacks and smorgasbord meals available every day from 0730-2100. It's licensed to sell beer and wine, located at 321 Victoria Ave., tel. 58-408.

Head for **The Strand Bistro** in Hurley's Grand Hotel (the Best Western) for a quick snack or full roast meal at the fast-food bar. Located at 99 Guyton St., tel. 50-955. The **Chamomile Vegetarian Health Restaurant** serves healthy meals and takeaways Mon. to Sat. at 18 Maria Mall. The licensed **Palm Lounge,** open weekdays only, offers excellent smorgasbord meals (soup, bread, meats, vegies, dessert, and coffee) for $11 pp; at 2 Campbell St., tel. 57-282. At **The Oriental** you can get inexpensive Chinese from $8 for a main course, a special banquet from $14 pp; at 5 Maria Place (off Victoria), tel. 57-472. **Colonial Rooms Restaurant** on Alma Rd. is another local recommendation for good food and fancier surroundings; expect to pay from $15 for a main course.

Takeaways

Try **The Chef's Bar** family restaurant on Guyton St., tel. 55-080. **Kentucky Fried Chicken** is at 265 Victoria Ave., tel. 54-741. **McDonald's, Pizza Hut,** and **Big M.C.** (fish and chips, New Zealand's fast-food chain) are all located along Victoria Avenue.

Entertainment

Probably the most unique entertainment in Wanganui is a **Moonlight Cruise** on the Wanganui River in the historic riverboat MV *Waireka* (see p. 268). The hotels and public bars do a booming business—just follow your ears to the most popular watering spots in town. For the rest of your evening entertainment, call in at the info center to find out what's on or pick up a local paper.

SERVICES

Emergency

Ambulance: tel. 53-909, or dial 111 and ask for an ambulance. **Hospital** or **weekend doctor on duty:** tel. 53-909. The public hospital is located on Heads Road. The **police station** is on Bell St., tel. 54-488 or dial 111. **Fire:** tel. 58-505. **Urgent Pharmacy:** tel. 53-851, at 264A Victoria Avenue.

General

The main **p.o.** is located on Ridgway St., tel. 58-349. The postal section is open weekdays 0830-1730 and Fri. 0830-2000. The telegraph branch is open weekdays 0830-1700, Sat. 0830-1130, for 24-hour service dial 14. **Trusteebank Wanganui** at Central City and Mid-Avenue is open Mon. to Thurs. from 0900-1630, Fri. 0900-2000. A number of money machines are located along Victoria Ave.; see the map at the Information Wanganui office for precise locations. **Late-night shopping** in downtown Wanganui is on Fri. nights till 2000. The **Automobile Association** office is on Victoria Ave. between Maria Place and Ridgway Street.

INFORMATION

There's only one place to go in Wanganui for city info—the aptly named **Information Wanganui** on the corner of Guyton and St. Hill sts., tel. 53-286 or 58-529; open Mon. to Fri. 0930-1700, weekends 1000-1400. The people running it ensure a most enjoyable experience in Wanganui. Don't forget to ask about their free personalized tours for overseas visitors (they need a day's notice). They have accommodation and dining guides for the asking, heaps of info on the Wanganui River, its reserves and many boat operators, and will make bookings for any trip or accommodation you desire. These guys love their city and it shows—don't go anywhere else first!

For the complete rundown on Whanganui National Park, visit the **Dept. of Conservation office** at 299 Victoria Ave. (tel. 52-402) where you can buy all sorts of brochures covering basic info, short nature walks, many hiking tracks, and a map. You can also quiz one of the on-duty rangers! It's open Mon. to Fri. 0800-1630.

TRANSPORTATION

Getting There

Getting to Wanganui is easy by thumb, car, or bus. If you approach from the north or the south, Hwy. 3 runs through the center of Wanganui. From the east, Hwy. 4 comes from Tongariro National Park via the town of Raetihi. The main public transportation to the city is by long-distance coach. From Ohakune and Raetihi near Tongariro you can catch a **Hammond's Services** bus direct to Wanganui, or from New Plymouth in the north or Wellington in the south catch an **InterCity** coach. Although railway tracks come through Wanganui, no passenger service is available. Wanganui has an airport serviced by two airlines (see below).

Buses

Local bus service is provided by **Greyhound** at 160 Ridgway St. (between Victoria Ave. and St. Hill St.), tel. 57-100. They run east to Aramoho (motor camp), west to Carlton, Gonville (caravan park), and Castlecliff (the beach and motor camps), northwest to Springvale and St. John's Hill, and southeast to Wanganui East on the other side of the river. Note that the service is frequent Mon. through Fri., less often on Sat., and non-existent on Sundays. Stop at the Information Wanganui office and collect a "Greyhound Bus Guide" for Wanganui City which has current schedules and stops listed.

Newmans Coachlines operates regular service to Bulls, Dannevirke, Hastings, Marton, Napier, Palmerston North, Waiouru, Waipukurau, and Woodville, departing from the terminal at 156 Ridgway St., tel. 55-566. Regular **InterCity** coaches depart for Auckland, Hamilton, Rotorua, New Plymouth, and Wellngton. Get current schedules and prices at Taupo Quay opposite Trafalgar Place, or call 54-439. Hammond's Services runs up Hwy. 4 to Raetihi and Ohakune and the depot is at 156 Ridgway St., tel. 55-566. **Dominion Coachlines'** depot is at 16 Wilson St., tel. 57-343.

Air

Wanganui Airport is a couple of km west of the city center on the south side of the river; by taxi it costs about $8 OW. The **taxi depot** is at Dominion Coachlines opposite Newmans on Ridgway St., tel. 54-444. To get to the airport by car, cross the river at Cobham Bridge, turn right on Wikitoria Rd. which becomes Airport Rd. and continue to the end. The **Air New Zealand** office is at 57 Taupo Quay (corner of Victoria Ave.), tel. 54-089, reservations tel. 55-518. Providing two northbound and two southbound flights a day, Air New Zealand flies to Auckland, Taupo, Wellington, Whakatane, and Whangarei in the North Island, and all major centers in the South Island. **Air Wanganui** flies to Auckland on Tues. and Thurs. at 0730, returning at 1730; tel. 58-999. For an exciting bird's-eye view of the city from a bright-yellow vintage tiger moth, call **Wanganui Aero Work** at tel. 53-994 to arrange a 20-minute flight for $70 pp. Goggles are provided, and at the end of the flight you get a certificate with a photo as a souvenir of an unforgettable experience—fun, fun, fun!

statue of Tainui in Virginia Lake Reserve

WHANGANUI NATIONAL PARK

Established in 1987, 74,231-hectare, remote, and relatively isolated Whanganui National Park is one of the two newest national parks in the country. Divided into three major sections, most of the park lies within the catchment of the mighty Wanganui River, longest navigable river in New Zealand. However, although the river is without a doubt a major feature and the main accessway into and through the park, the riverbed itself is not included in park land.

The Maori have lived in villages along the Wanganui for many centuries, evidenced by the many archaeological sites found in the park, and the river and adjoining forests still have important spiritual and traditional values to the Whanganui Maori people. Starting in the 1840s, European pioneers, explorers, missionaries, traders, and farmers also set up homes along the river. The worst hazards they faced (and modern-day explorers still face) were landslides and flooding—the entire park lies within the most active seismic zone in New Zealand!

Today, visitors to the park can choose from a variety of energetic recreational activities—hiking, canoeing, jet boating, hunting, and fishing. But if sightseeing is more what you have in mind, drive the scenic Wanganui River Rd. from Wanganui to Pipiriki to see picturesque villages, a colonial house and museum, several historic sites, a swing bridge, and captivating waterfalls, and perhaps stroll along some of the short trails. You'll get a taste of the park without wandering too far off the beaten track.

The Land

Whanganui National Park covers several separate areas of land, linked to one another by the Wanganui River. At the north end, starting 17 km downstream from Taumarunui at Te Maire, a series of small riverside blocks of land extend south to Whakahoro. The large, rugged, central core of the park begins at Whakahoro, and extends 92 km south—downstream from Pipiriki. Farther south, the third main section lies between Ranana and Atene. Much of the park is dense lowland forest lying along the Wanganui River—the park's focal point. Third longest in the country, this magnificent 290-km river meanders for 170 km through the park. The Whakapapa, Ongarue, Ohura, Tangarakau, Retaruke, Whangamomona, and the Manganui o te ao are major tributaries. With its gentle gradient, large volume of water, and 234 km of navigable water, the Wanganui has always been a major transport route. Today it's extensively used by canoeists, to a lesser extent by jet boaters, and is the main accessway into the wilderness sections of the park.

The Wanganui basin is an uplifted mass of young Tertiary marine sediments—soft sandstone and mudstone deposit—deeply incised by erosion. The main geological features you're likely to see as you explore the park are steep sharp ridges, papa cliffs (some bare, some covered in vegetation), deep, narrow, winding gorges, and river valleys with small areas of flat terraced land. Add to this a dense blanket of broadleaf podocarp forest, grasslands, regenerating native bush, river tributaries, and inspirational waterfalls and you can understand why the park attracts people in search of a scenic wilderness experience. Almost half of this lowland park is less than 300 meters above sea level, the rest between 300-600 meters, with a few higher peaks. The most dominant feature northwest of Pipiriki is the Matemateaonga Range.

History

Due to the Wanganui River's easy navigability, the area has a long and varied Maori and European history. The river has always been an access to the North Island interior, and the Maori, finding an abundance of fish, birds, and berries along the river and in the forest, lived in villages along its banks. You can still see the evidence of earthworks and regenerating stands of native forest where villages once stood. Today's Maori generally live along the lower reaches of the river.

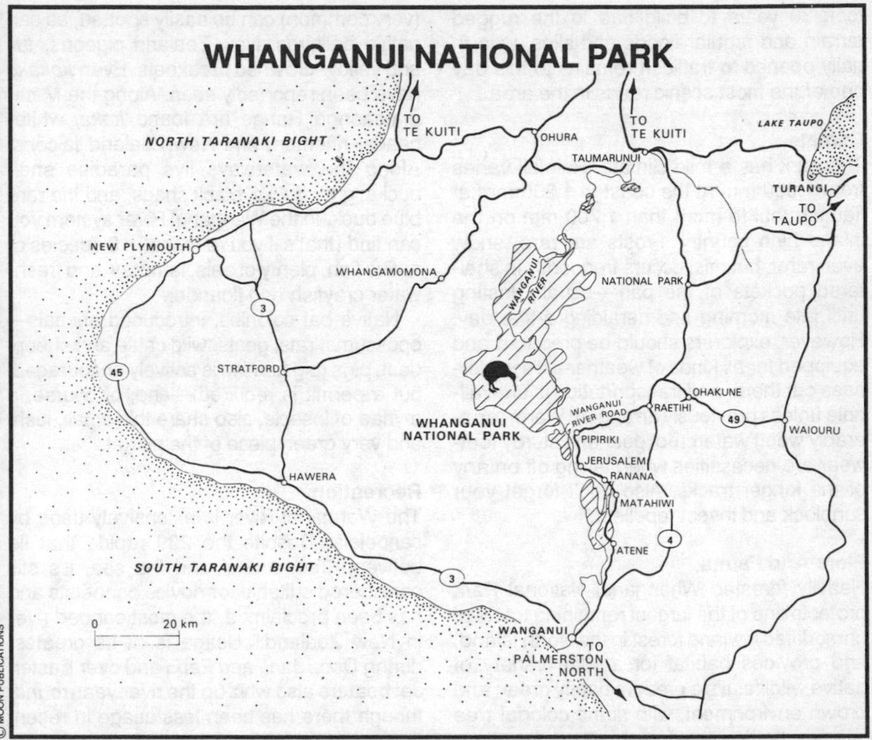

In the 1840s the first European missionaries arrived. Villages were located on land suitable for farming, and wheat was planted along the river. Flour mills were established in the 1850s, and in the 1860s, when the river's scenic attractions were recognized, tourism began in a big way. The Hatrick & Co. Riverboat Service introduced a steamer service which, by the turn of the century, had a fleet of 12 vessels carrying passengers to the Pipiriki House Hotel and the Houseboat—a fancy floating hotel moored in the upper reaches of the river. The boats also serviced villagers and farmers right up to the depression years of the 1930s.

In the early 1900s development in the form of roads and farming settlements was planned, but the densely forested countryside, the isolation, erosion, and decreasing soil fertility collectively proved to be just too big a barrier to overcome. Today you can still stumble across signs of previous settlement—clearings in the bush, regenerating forest, homestead ruins, fences, old roads and bridges—now being reclaimed by the forest. In 1934 Wanganui River Road which

LEGEND

When the majestic mountains Tongariro and Taranaki fought over the beautiful mountain Pihanga, Taranaki lost. In his anger and grief he fled north, tearing a deep wound in the earth as he traveled. Soon a clear spring spurted from Tongariro's side and the water filled and healed the wound in the earth. Lush green forests filled with birds sprang up along the newly formed river. Today that river is called the Wanganui.

took 30 years to build due to the rugged terrain and regular floods and slips, was finally opened to traffic. It remains to this day one of the most scenic roads in the area.

Climate

The park has a mild climate. Rainfall varies from 1,000 mm at the coast to 1,250 mm at Taumarunui to more than 1,700 mm on the inland high country. Frosts are rare, snow even rarer, but mist occurs frequently in sheltered pockets of the park—usually lasting until late morning and heralding a fine day. However, explorers should be prepared and equipped for all kinds of weather—it's wilderness out there, and transportation is unavailable unless previously arranged. Warm (preferably wool) waterproof gear and sturdy footwear are necessities when taking off on any of the longer tracks. Also don't forget your sunblock and insect repellent.

Flora And Fauna

Heavily forested Whanganui National Park protects one of the largest remaining tracts of unmodified lowland forest in the North Island, and provides habitat for a wide variety of native wildlife. It's a predominantly green and brown environment, with some colorful tree species dotting the forest with red, yellow, and white, and impressive towering tree ferns that always make great photographic subjects. *Kamahi, tawa, miro, rimu, totara, kahikatea, matai,* northern *rata,* and black, silver, and hard beech are all represented in the park's central core. Native vegetation, *totara, nikau, akeake, ngaio,* and *karaka,* blanket the areas closest to the coast. You'll also find grasslands (about 6,000 hectares altogether) and areas of regenerating bush within park boundaries, and pastureland (now regenerating) and introduced plants (some of which are considered a problem and will be controlled) along the riverbanks and in areas where the land used to be farmed.

Birds abound in this forested habitat, particularly in the more isolated central areas of the river valley. Brown kiwi (one of the largest populations in the country), fantails, greywarblers, silvereyes, tits, and North Island robins (very common) can be easily spotted, as can native bellbirds, New Zealand pigeons, *tui,* and yellow-crowned parakeets. Even *kokako* have been reportedly seen. Along the Matemateaonga Range are found *kaka,* whiteheads, riflemen, and New Zealand falcons. Along the waterways live paradise shelducks, grey ducks, black shags, and the rare blue duck. In the Wanganui River system you can find (that's if you're trying!) 18 species of native fish, plenty of eels, lamprey, and freshwater crayfish and flounder.

Native bat colonies, introduced animals—opossums, rats, goats, wild cattle and sheep, deer, pigs (pig hunting is actively encouraged, but a permit is required)—and, of course, a myriad of insects, also share this small, lush, and very green piece of the planet.

Recreation

The Wanganui River is extensively used by canoeists. Despite the 239 rapids that lie between Taumaranui and the sea, it's still considered suitable for novice canoeists and has been proclaimed "the most canoed river in New Zealand." Usage is at its greatest during Dec., Jan., and Feb., and over Easter. Jet boaters also whiz up the river year-round, though there has been less usage in recent times due to high boat and fuel costs. Hikers and hunters use the jet boat services as a quick and convenient way to get to trailheads; several commercial companies provide transportation services: from Wanganui (contact River City Tours at tel. 44-194 or 32-529), Pipiriki wharf (contact Pipiriki Jet Boat Tours at tel. 54-733), Raetihi (contact Ken and Raewyn Haworth at Ramanui Lodge, tel. 58-799), or Taumarunui (contact Pioneer Jet Boat Tours, tel. Taumarunui 8074).

The river also attracts a number of rafters, and some of the more enthusiastic anglers. Brown and rainbow trout can be caught (the farther upstream you go, the better the fishing gets) but not in great numbers. Outside the park the fishing is generally more productive—anglers in the lower stretches of the river may have to be very persistent, or hungry! Get rules and permits at any of the info centers.

Hiking in the park is very popular. The three main tracks are the **Matemateaonga** (runs west-east in the south central section of the park taking three to four days), **Mangapurua/Kaiwhakauka** (runs north-south through the north central section taking three to four days), and **Atene Skyline** (in the southern section of the park taking one day). Maps and brochures with all the details on the major tracks can be bought at any of the info centers. Shorter walks are also available at Te Maire, Maraekowhai, and Atene. To get to the Matemateaonga Track (the most well known) by bus, consider **John Hammond** delivery van service (tel. 54-635) from Wanganui to Pipiriki, or **Midhirst Motors** (tel. 772 Midhirst) from Stratford to the Kohi Saddle. To get to the track by jet boat, consider **Pioneer Jet Boat Tours** (tel. 8074) from Taumarunui, **River City Tours** (tel. 44-194 or 32-529) from Wanganui, **Pipiriki Jet Boat Tours** (tel. 54-733) from Pipiriki, or **Ramanui Lodge and Jet Boat Service** (tel. 58-799 Raetihi) from Ramanui Lodge.

If you'd like to experience the park via a guided tramping, camping, or canoeing trip, call **Camp 'N Canoe** at tel. (0663-26) 738 Kaponga. This company operates four-day tramping holidays along the Matemateaonga Walkway once a week or on demand from Dec. to March (from $128 pp; accommodation and food extra), and five-day wilderness camping and canoeing or kayaking holidays in the park Dec. to March (from $318 pp kayak, $590 pp canoe).

Hunting for pigs, deer, and goats is also encouraged as a means of animal control, but keep in mind that the most remote and undeveloped areas of the park attract only experienced hunters (and hikers). Hunting permits are required. Find out the current rules and regulations at any of the info centers.

PRACTICALITIES

Accommodations

Five **park huts (Omaru, Pouri, Puketotara, Humphries,** and **Otaraheke**) are located along the Matemateaonga Track. They're steadily used by hikers over the summer months, by hunters in winter. In the Mangapurua Valley there are no huts, but plenty of good campsites with access to water.

Toilets and water are being supplied at serviced riverside campsites near **Kirikiriroa, John Coull Hut** (gas stove provided), **Mangawaiiti Stream, Mangapurua Landing, Tieke, Ngaporor,** and **Te Maire/Owairua.** Pack out all your rubbish when you leave the park. **Otumaire** campsite at **Atene** has tentsites, toilets, and water. At **Pipiriki** you can camp on the former Pipiriki House site or by the riverside picnic area, or stay in the public shelter which has hot water, toilets, and a fireplace. At **Ohinepa** there's a camping area with tentsites, water, toilets, and a boat ramp, and at **Whakahoro,** a hut and camping area are also available.

If you're looking for more comfort, stay at **Ramanui Lodge** along the banks of the Wanganui River, 21 km above Pipiriki within Whanganui National Park. Hosts Ken and Raewyn Haworth provide bunkrooms, hot showers, home-cooked meals, and plenty of good old hospitality from $35 pp for dinner and B&B (provide your own sleeping bag or linen) or $42 (linen supplied). Lunches are $6, a packed lunch is only $5. They also operate a shuttle jet boat service for hikers heading to the Matemateaonga Walkway, offer a two-day heli-jet rafting experience, hunting trips by arrangement, and have canoes available for lodge guests. For details and bookings, tel. (0658) 58-799.

For a good selection of hotel/motel/B&B accommodation, restaurants, and more park info, the city of Wanganui (see p. 262-273) is only 35 km south of the southernmost section of the park. Otherwise hotels, motels, and campgrounds can be found at Raetihi, Taumarunui, and Stratford.

Information

The **Whanganui District Office,** main administration center for the park, is at 299 Victoria Ave. in Wanganui (tel. 52-402; see p. 272); open Mon. to Fri. 0800-1630. See static displays and info boards, collect resource material, speak to a ranger to get more info on all the recreational possibilities, and purchase brochures, maps, and relevant park publications here. Other park info centers are located at **Cherry Grove** in Taumarunui (tel. 0812-8201) and **The Colonial House Information Centre and Museum** in Pipiriki (tel. 54-631), or stop by any Department of Conservation office.

Transportation
The main way into and through the park, to hiking tracks and hunting grounds, is by canoe or jet boat up the Wanganui River; water transportation can be most easily arranged in the city of Wanganui (see p. 266-269) and at Pipiriki wharf. There are four main road access routes to park boundaries. No roads run through the park. On the west side: from Hwy. 43, take Brewer or Mangaehu roads, then Upper Mangaehu Rd. to the Kohi Saddle. On the north side: from Hwy. 4, take either the road from Owhango or Raurimu to Whakahoro. On the east: from Hwy. 4, take the road to Ruatiti, then continue to the road-end. From the south: follow the scenic Wanganui River Rd. from Wanganui to Atene and Pipiriki. Bus services run along both highways 43 (Taumarunui/Stratford via New Plymouth) and 4 (Taumarunui/Wanganui), and a local mail service provides public transportation from Wanganui to Pipiriki. Get current timetables and fares at Wanganui or New Plymouth.

EGMONT NATIONAL PARK

Snow-capped Mount Egmont (Taranaki to the Maoris), a solitary 2,518-meter peak, is the kind of mountain that begs to be climbed or hiked just because it's there. Standing loftily on Cape Egmont where the western coastline juts into the Tasman Sea, its remote location, height, and harsh climate have produced some interesting flora and fauna; good hiking, rock-, snow-, and ice-climbing on an extensive 300-km network of tracks, and skiing have made it one of the most visited mountains in New Zealand. Access to the upper slopes is easy if you have your own transportation, and the energetic are amply rewarded with fabulous views from the summit—Taranaki and Tongariro National Park to the east, New Plymouth to the north, the Tasman Sea to the west, and to the south (on a clear day) the faint outline of the South Island mountains.

Mount Egmont is the dormant volcanic centerpiece of the Taranaki region and the most dominant feature of Egmont National Park. The Park covers 33,537 hectares within a 9.6-km radius of the mountain summit, and includes Pouakai and coastal Kaitake Ranges. Completely encircling the Park but at a distance is a sealed 180-km "Around-The-Mountain" route dotted with small towns that cater to Park visitors. Highway 3 runs down the east side from New Plymouth (the main city in the area) to Hawera, and coastal Hwy. 45 completes the circle on the west side. If you plan on exploring the Park on foot, drive straight up the access roads. If you're not so much into outdoor activities but enjoy scenic views, take the slightly longer coastal route on your way north or south (about two hours non-stop) for great views of Mt. Egmont from various angles—and if you like flowers, don't miss **Pukeiti Rhododendron Trust Gardens** on Carrington Rd. (see p. 294). If you can time it, travel the coastal road on a clear evening—the snow-capped peak tinged in pink and regularly wreathed in wispy clouds makes a striking picture you won't quickly forget.

The Land

Egmont National Park's dominant features are the volcanic cone of dormant **Mt. Egmont** and the two older volcanoes, **Kaitake,** 15 km southwest of New Plymouth, and **Pouakai,** 10 km southwest of Kaitake. Mount Egmont is believed to have formed over 70,000 years ago, becoming active as the other two volcanoes became extinct. It formed two peaks (the northern peak collapsed 23,000 years ago) and thousands of small rounded hills on the mountain's west side through repeated *lahars* or mudflows (the Pungarehu *lahar* mounds); elsewhere on the ring plain the *lahars* progressed as a flood and no mounds were created. More recently, geologically speaking, lava regularly spilled down the mountain sides to form a series of lava cliffs and gorges; volcanic ash, the basis of Taranaki's rich topsoil, repeatedly blanketed the surrounding land giving rise to the agriculturally affluent Taranaki region. The last volcanic eruption was in 1755 (a minor affair) when ash alone was ejected onto the upper slopes. In the last 400 years, most damage to the Park has been caused by "debris flows" due to severe storms—the torrential rain runs down the bare unstable upper slopes causing destructive landslides.

All that remains of the extinct Kaitake volcano, active about 500,000 years ago, is the eroded 683-meter-high Kaitake Range; extinct Pouakai, active 250,000 years ago, has also been eroded from its original height of possibly 2,000 meters to its present height of 1,399 meters. Water is another powerful and artistic element seen in all its forms throughout Egmont National Park. Ice and snow permanently cover the upper slopes and peak, splendid waterfalls roar over jagged lava flows to drop into deep, dark pools far below, and rivers sing over the smooth, pol-

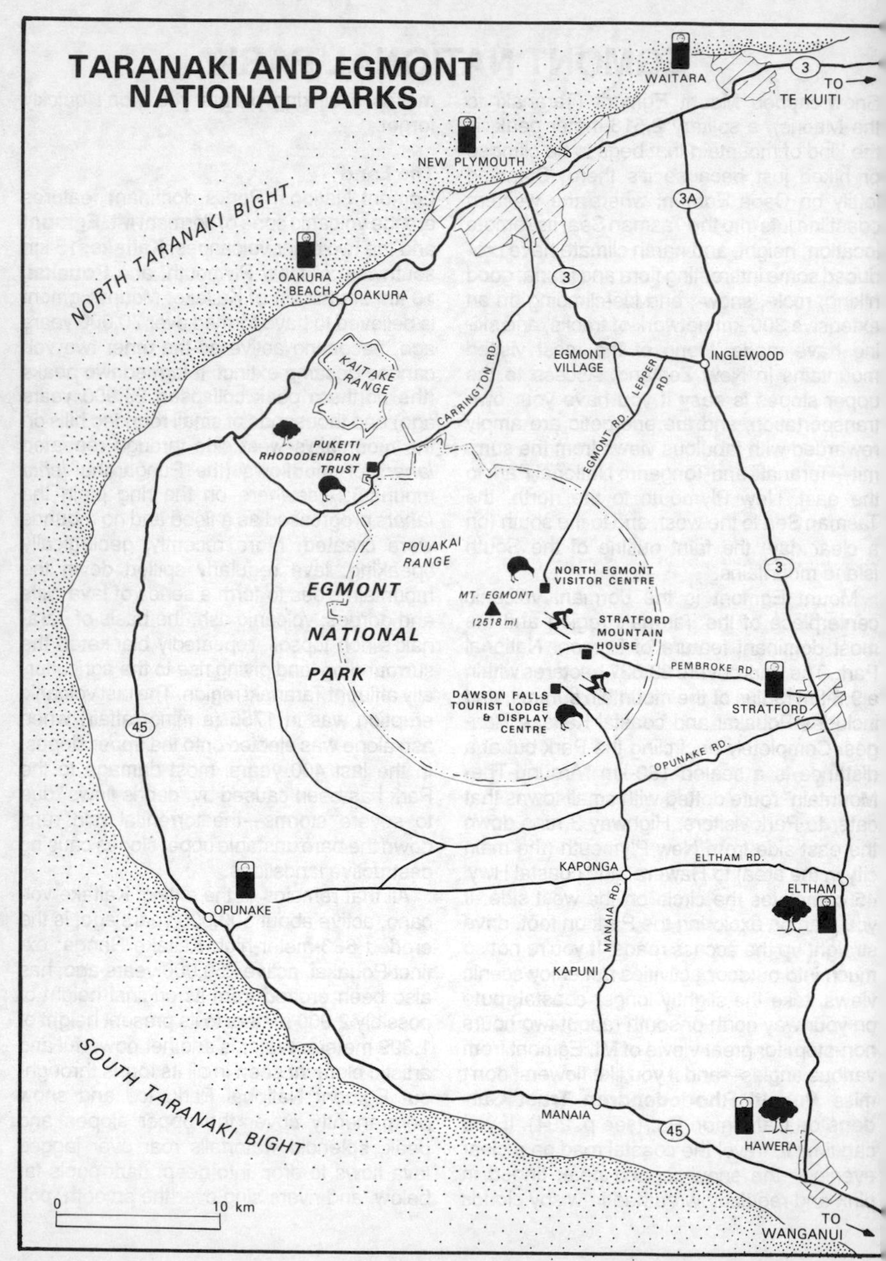
TARANAKI AND EGMONT NATIONAL PARKS
WAITARA
3
TO TE KUITI
NEW PLYMOUTH
3A
NORTH TARANAKI BIGHT
OAKURA BEACH
OAKURA
3
KAITAKE RANGE
CARRINGTON RD.
EGMONT VILLAGE
LEPPER RD
INGLEWOOD
EGMONT RD.
PUKEITI RHODODENDRON TRUST
POUAKAI RANGE
EGMONT NATIONAL PARK
NORTH EGMONT VISITOR CENTRE
MT. EGMONT (2518 m)
STRATFORD MOUNTAIN HOUSE
3
PEMBROKE RD.
STRATFORD
DAWSON FALLS TOURIST LODGE & DISPLAY CENTRE
45
OPUNAKE RD
ELTHAM RD.
KAPONGA
ELTHAM
MANAIA RD
OPUNAKE
KAPUNI
SOUTH TARANAKI BIGHT
MANAIA
45
HAWERA
0
10 km
TO WANGANUI

ished rocks and dance down to the lower altitudes in a series of waterfalls.

Climate

Ask the locals in any of the towns around the base of Mt. Egmont for a personal weather forecast and you're likely to hear something like—"if you can't see the mountain, it's raining up there. If you can see the mountain, it's going to rain!" Coastal position, a wide range in elevation (100-2,500 meters), continually changing winds, and frequent alternation between fine and stormy weather are the main climatic features affecting Egmont National Park. Long periods of fine settled weather are common in summer; winter brings the intense, long-lasting depressions that result in nasty storms. The coldest month is usually July, the warmest Feb., with most of the high annual rainfall experienced May to Oct.—the northwestern slopes of the mountains generally receive the most rain. Expect wet weather when a low pressure system is forecast and you have northerly winds and mild temperatures.

The weather affecting Egmont National Park should be seriously considered before venturing up the mountain—detailed weather forecasts are available at the ranger station (see "Information"). The Park is notorious for rapidly changing weather (usually for the worse) and although it's generally OK in summer, it can cause some hazardous situations in winter. Freezing temperatures have been recorded in all months of the year (except January). Low clouds or fog can disorient even the most experienced outdoorsperson, and the frequent combination of rain, rapid drop in temperature, and strong wind can quickly turn a pleasurable hike into a life-threatening situation due to exposure and hypothermia. The rangers strongly suggest that if you're climbing or hiking in the Park leave your intentions and estimated time of return at the ranger station or with someone reliable, and turn back at the first sign of bad weather. Be adequately prepared, get a weather forecast, take warm clothing, food and drink, observe cloud and temperature changes particularly when venturing up to the higher altitudes, and resist trying to make the summit when the weather is obviously deteriorating.

Flora

The combination of a wet mountain climate and periods of dry hot weather promotes a luxurious growth of vegetation, and the variations in altitude on Mt. Egmont give rise to several distinct vegetation zones—large forest trees, small shrubs, tussocks and herbs, mosses and lichens—easily seen from any of the three main access roads. The lower slopes (about 500-900 meters) are covered by the broadleaf-podocarp rainforest where many varieties of native trees are found—*rimu,* northern *rata, kamahi, mahoe, broadleaf* and tree fuchsia. Beneath the tree canopy the undergrowth is prolific—creepers grow in profusion garlanding the smaller trees, and lush ferns, mosses, and lichens carpet the forest floor. The Kaitake Range, oldest and most eroded, has forest to the top, and the semi-coastal forest on the lower slopes is dominated by *puriri, karaka, kohekohe, pukatea,* and *nikau* palm trees. The higher Pouakai Range has several zones: forest (dominated by *montane kamahi),* shrub, tussock, and herbfield. On Mt. Egmont at the 900-1,100-meter level, the *totara* and *kaikawaka* (mountain cedar) trees become dominant, and above lies a dense belt of leatherwood scrub followed by a broad tussock grass zone.

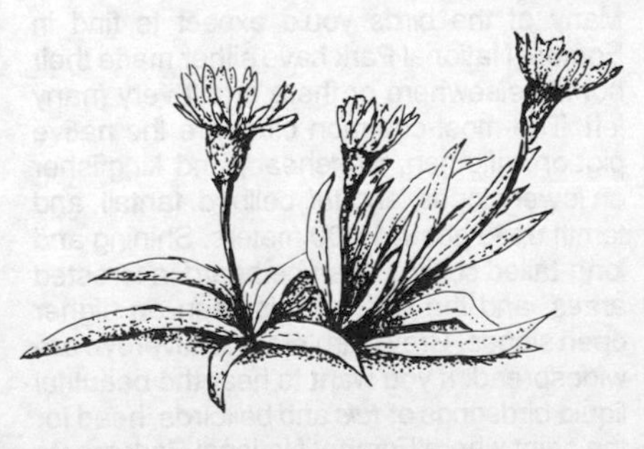

mountain daisy

Above 1,400 meters you find many plants unique to Mt. Egmont, and other alpine species that you'd expect to find (like mountain beech) are conspicuously absent—the long history of volcanic disturbance and relative isolation from seed sources caused this mountain region to evolve differently from other alpine habitats. A variety of small (some unique) herbaceous plants, ferns (the rare *Polystichum cystostegia* flourishes only on Mt. Egmont), and mountain daisies (two species are slightly different from those found elsewhere in N.Z.) cover the slopes just below the permanent snow line (for more detailed info refer to the *Park Handbook*). Other Mt. Egmont plants that are slightly different from their relatives elsewhere are the large-leaved ourisia, tussock grass, harebell, broom, and *koromiko.*

tui

Fauna

Many of the birds you'd expect to find in Egmont National Park have either made their homes elsewhere or there aren't very many left. The most common birds are the native pigeon, rifleman, whitehead, and kingfisher on lower slopes, and *tui,* bellbird, fantail, and tomtit up to about 1,300 meters. Shining and long-tailed cuckoos can be heard in forested areas, and the N.Z. *pipit* is seen on higher open slopes. Grey warblers and silvereye are widespread. If you want to hear the beautiful liquid birdsongs of *tuis* and bellbirds, head for the point where Egmont National Park meets the entrance to Pukeiti Rhododendron Trust on Carrington Rd.—the birds tune up their voices early in the morning, so grab a cup of coffee and a filled roll to go, and start your day with a magnificent after-dawn chorus.

A great number and variety of insects are found in the Park, some endemic to Mt. Egmont. Several moths are only found on the mountain—*Tortrix antichroa, Graphania averilla, Leucania harti,* and *Leucania paraxysta,* but Egmont is poor in butterfly species. The isolation and volcanic activity also caused the mountain to miss out on some alpine insects found commonly elsewhere at similar altitudes, such as certain grasshoppers, cicadas, and common butterflies.

The Park is free of deer—they were never liberated in the Egmont region (except for one male red deer deliberately introduced in the late 1800s!), but goats, stoats, opossums, rats, mice, hares, and rabbits are all common wildlife, considered "pests." Goats and opossums do the most damage to the vegetation and are actively hunted, trapped, or poisoned.

Hiking Information

Mount Egmont lures hikers and climbers year-round. Walking and climbing routes criss-cross the Park's mountains, ranging from short easy walks to difficult several-day hikes to poled climbing routes. Tracks lead up to the summit, around Mt. Egmont via the popular **Round-The-Mountain Track,** through all the various vegetation zones, to dramatic waterfalls or quiet streams, and to scenic lookouts. When the the snow melts off the main slopes in summer, the scoria slopes are fairly easy to negotiate in fine weather and many reach the summit. Above the bushline (1,500 meters) from Nov. to Jan. the alpine flowers in bloom make the climb worth the effort. In bad weather the scoria slopes can become treacherous as they are entirely unmarked—it's easy to get lost if thick clouds or fog suddenly descend on you, and some of the slopes and gullies end in sheer bluffs! To reach the summit of Mt. Egmont in winter climbers need crampons, ice-axes, rope, companions, and experience.

On the longer marked tracks, huts with facilities are available for overnight stays—

take your own sleeping bag, cooking equipment, and supplies. Before you venture off the beaten track, head for the Ranger Station, Park Display Centre, or accommodation houses on the mountain (see "Information," p. 289), or info offices in New Plymouth, Stratford, or Hawera. Pick up a detailed Survey and Lands topographical map and the walk brochures with individual track maps and descriptions. If you're heading for the higher altitudes or one of the long hikes, get a detailed weather forecast from the ranger station and ask if you're properly equipped—lives have been lost (45 since 1891) due to rapid deterioration in weather followed by disorientation, exposure, and hypothermia.

LEGEND

According to legend, Taranaki (or Mt. Egmont) was forced to flee from his original location in the center of the North Island when he lost a battle to Mt. Tongariro over his love, Mt. Pihanga. As he angrily fled through the cover of darkness toward the west coast he gouged out the mighty Wanganui River, and on reaching the sea he traveled north to the Pouakai ranges on Cape Egmont. A spur was thrown out to anchor him and Taranaki was forced to settle there forever. The Maori originally called the mountain "Taranaki" (many New Zealanders rightfully feel it should still be called Taranaki—you may see it written as Egmont/Taranaki). They had great respect for the impressive volcano, worshipping the mountain as a god and recognizing its great influence on the weather of the local region. The upper slopes were tapu and they believed that the stones were part of the skull of the mountain and the shrubs were its hair. So strong was this belief that when some early European climbers brought stones and shrubs down to study, the Maori quickly replaced them on the mountain so as not to anger the spirits. The only times the Maori climbed the mountain were when they needed red ochre, or to ceremoniously bury their chiefs in secret places.

NORTH EGMONT

Facilities

To get into the northern area of the Park take Hwy. 3 to Egmont Village (5.5 km west of Inglewood), then the 16-km Egmont Rd., following signs to Kaimiro and the Park. The alternate route is via Lepper Rd. off Hwy. 3 just west of Inglewood which joins Egmont Rd. at Kaimiro. Along the road within the Park lie picnic areas, lookouts, the start of several tracks, and toward the end, the **North Egmont Visitor Centre** and carpark, a cafeteria, public shelter and toilets, the **Camphouse** (see p. 287), and upper carpark. The Visitor Centre, open daily from 0900-1730 most of the year (to save yourself a trip, call ahead to check if it's open at Egmont Village tel. 710), has exhibits, comprehensive displays on its natural history, a track orientation map, displays of local walks, and regular films and talks. Guided walks with a ranger are also offered in summer and by arrangement. Four local walks of varying difficulty, suitable for most people, start from both the upper carpark and visitor center carpark—they're marked with color-coded tags so you can't get lost.

Short Walks

The easiest **Short Nature Walk** (color-coded red) takes only 15 minutes. It starts at the southern end of the Visitor Centre carpark, passes through a *totara* and *kamahi* forest, gives great views over the Ngatoro Valley, and leads up to a ridge overlooking the Ngatoro Stream. The walk comes out on Translator Rd.—turn right, and you'll end up at the upper carpark. **The Ngatoro Walk** (blue) takes approx. 30 minutes, starting at the bottom eastern corner of the Visitor Centre carpark below the Camphouse. After taking the first turn-off to the right, you descend and cross the Ngatoro Stream bed, then climb up through beautiful mountain cedar trees to Translator Road. Follow the road to the right for five minutes to the upper carpark. **The Connett Walk** (orange, 30 minutes) starts on the same track as the Ngatoro Walk, but you descend farther down the ridge before branching off at the first turn to the left. The track crosses the slope of the mountain and joins the Ngatoro Track before you turn right and climb gradually uphill to the carpark.

Longest of the short walks in this area is **The Veronica Walk** (yellow, 1½ hours-plus). The track starts at the western corner of the upper carpark, crosses the slope of the mountain through *totara* and *kamahi* forest (don't take the **Veronica Track** on the right—continue straight ahead), passes an old reservoir, and takes you up the mountain for great views of the Ram Stream and Pouakai Range. Near the highest point the track joins up with an old track to the summit; turn left and head down the well-beaten track to the Ambury Memorial and finish at the upper carpark below the camphouse.

Hike to Wilkies Pools via the track starting at The Plateau.

Several of the long hiking tracks also start from Egmont Rd. and the two main carparks. For details, track descriptions, maps, and weather forecasts, call in at the North Egmont Visitor Centre and leave your intended route and time of return in the trampers' book.

Ice And Snow Climbing

In winter the local climbing clubs and other enthusiastic madmen head for the higher slopes with their ice- and snow-climbing equipment. Several popular routes lead to the summit from the northern slopes. Contact one of the local climbing clubs for details—you may also be lucky and find a willing and experienced climbing partner to show you the best way up. In New Plymouth contact New Plymouth Tramping Club, N.Z. Alpine Club, or Taranaki Alpine Club; in Stratford contact Stratford Mountain Club; in Hawera contact Mount Egmont Alpine Club. The Park rangers have more information and can also tell you who to call, and the *Park Handbook* has a small section on mountaineering and lists the most popular ice and snow routes to the summit.

EAST EGMONT

Facilities

To get into the eastern area of the Park, take Hwy. 3 to Stratford, then turn off onto Pembroke Road. This 15-km road takes you past the **East Egmont Ranger Station** soon after leaving Stratford (just past Barclay Rd.), by picnic areas and the start of several walking tracks, and leads up to **Stratford Mountain House** where you'll find a public shelter, toilets, motel, restaurant, tearooms, and a souvenir shop; ski and tramping gear is available for hire. The Ranger Station is open daily from 0800-1630. Pembroke Rd. continues past Stratford Mountain House for another three km, passing lookouts to end up at **The Plateau.** From the lookout at the Plateau, highest point on the mountain you can reach by car, begin many tracks of varying difficulty. Above the Plateau, within walking distance of the carpark, lies the well-known **Manganui Skifield.**

Short Walks

The intriguing 30-minute **Kamahi Walk** starts at the right end of the Stratford Mountain House at the direction sign (red), and winds through a magical moss-clad forest of *kamahi* trees and dense undergrowth—just the kind of place you'd expect to find elves and goblins frolicking in the greenery! The one-hour **Patea Walk** (yellow) takes you through more lush forest. It starts at Stratford Mountain House, follows the Waingongoro Track for a distance, then turns sharply right to parallel the Patea River. It comes out on Pembroke Rd. which you walk back down.

A bit longer is the 1½-hour **Enchanted Walk** just below Stratford Mountain House. It crosses the Patea River and its tributaries, and the Waingongoro River tributaries, passes the junction with the lower track to Dawson Falls, and climbs a long ridge to the Trig at Jackson's Lookout for fabulous views. Connecting with the Round-The-Mountain Track, it's then only a short walk back to the Plateau. The longer and more difficult **Curtis Falls Track** (orange, 1½ hours OW) starts near Stratford Mountain House and crosses some typically rugged volcanic land to descend into the Manganui Gorge to two spectacular waterfalls plunging down over ancient lava flows. From the Plateau you can take various tracks to **Twin Falls, Wilkies Pools, Bubbling Springs,** and over to **Dawson Falls.** For more detailed info on the longer walks and track maps, call in at the East Egmont Ranger Station.

Skiing

Mount Egmont offers some exciting volcano skiing with its club-operated **Manganui Skifield,** one of the most challenging ski areas in the country. The main features are the 30-degree (average) gradient slopes, consistently good spring snow, and two rope tows, beginners tow, and a T-Bar. A normal ski season at Egmont runs from June to September. When the slopes of the Top Tow are icy, the ski area attracts big-name Taranaki racers, and when the snow conditions are good, scores of recreational skiers scream down the upper slopes. The lower ski ground is more suitable for beginners or cautious intermediates, and private ski instruction and group classes are offered, along with specialized training programs for racers. Daredevil mountaineers can also climb to the summit and ski down one of the best runs on the mountain; contact the local ski clubs for detailed info—and you might even find an equally crazy partner! At the end of the season the annual **Crater Race** is held. Starting on the Summit Dome, the racers whoosh down the south entrance and south face to Rangitoto Flat (between the main peak and Fanthams Peak) with the average gradient of the run over 30 degrees.

Manganui Skifield is only a 1.5-km walk through Manganui Gorge from the end of the sealed road at the Plateau. Ski equipment can be hired from Stratford Mountain House. Ski reports and snow conditions are given between 0800-0830 during ski season on Radio Taranaki, the local radio staion. The closest accommodation (expensive) and facilities to the skifields are located at Stratford Mountain House. For more reasonable prices head back down to the town of Stratford, or farther afield (see p. 287).

SOUTH EGMONT

Facilities

To get to Dawson Falls resort on the southern slopes of the Park, take Hwy. 3 to the town of Eltham then 15-km Eltham Rd. to Kaponga. At Kaponga, turn north up Manaia Road. This 15-km stretch of sealed road winds steeply up the mountainside through fantastic lush greenery and shady green tunnels where the trees meet overhead, passing lookouts, track starting points, and magnificent waterfalls (at the end of short walks), and terminates at **Dawson Falls Display Centre, Konini** (budget accommodation), and **Dawson Falls Tourist Lodge.** The Display Centre (open daily from 0900-1800) features Park flora and fauna, and volcanic and human history displays. A large model highlights all the volcanic features. In the immediate vicinity you'll find picnic areas, public shelter, toilets, lookout, and starting points of numerous tracks leading to crystal-clear streams, bubbling springs, and waterfalls.

If you're in Stratford and want to take a shortcut over to Dawson Falls, take Opunake Rd. west out of Stratford toward the villages of Cardiff and Mahoe, and continue straight until you meet Manaia Rd. (not far after crossing Kapuni Stream). Turn right toward the mountain.

Short Walks

Before setting off anywhere, call in at the **Dawson Falls Display Centre** and check out a detailed display showing the comprehensive track system that radiates from Dawson Falls. **Kapuni Walk** is probably one of the easiest walks and leads to a "must-see" local attraction. Starting at the sign on the road just below Dawson Falls Lodge, the track (pink, one hour) follows the forested banks of Kapuni Stream to a view of magnificent **Dawson Falls** dropping an impressive 18 meters down an ancient lava flow—you can also get down to the base by taking the steep track farther along. For great mountain views, take the short sidetrack before the falls that crosses the stream and leads to a lookout; the main track returns to the road and carpark through some mature rainforest. The circular **Konini Dell Walk** (blue, one hour) starts above Dawson Falls Tourist Lodge, runs along a ridge top and through a *totara* and *kamahi* forest (a favorite spot in spring for the melodic bellbirds and *tuis)* to a lookout. The nearby popular **Wilkies Pool Walk** (red, one hour) starts at the Display Centre. It's an easy walk upriver along Kapuni Stream to Kapuni Gorge, where the water has carved an intricate channel through an old lava flow to form a series of spectacularly polished rockpools. A sidetrack leads to **Victoria Falls,** and many other interesting tracks can also be easily reached from this walk.

Hasties Hill Track is longer and more difficult (orange, at least 2½ hours RT) but the unobstructed views of Mt. Egmont, plains, and Tourist Lodge are worth the climb. It starts above the Display Centre and follows a section of the Summit Track. At the second junction turn left onto the track leading to the Round Trip and Hasties Hill. At the next junction turn right onto Hasties Hill Track. It goes down to cross the middle branch of Kaupokonui Stream, then climbs to the top of 996-meter Hasties Hill for fabulous views of South Taranaki and ancient lava domes called the Beehives. The return route backtracks to the stream and the junction of the Round Trip Track—for an alternate return route, turn right toward Lower Kaupokonui Falls on the East Branch of Kaupokonui Stream.

Ice Climbing

The most popular ice and snow route from the southern slopes to the summit is Dawson Falls via Fanthams Peak. For detailed info or a mountain guide, contact the Mt. Egmont Alpine Club, or inquire at Dawson Falls Tourist Lodge, the Display Centre, or the PRO in New Plymouth (see p. 298). **Mountain and Ski Guides** provide experienced private guides for summer climbs (Nov. to April) up the North Ridge, the Surrey Rd. route, and the E. Ridge route, summit climbs, and winter climbing and skiing (May to Oct.); C. Prudden, tel. 88-261 New Plymouth, or J. Jordan, tel. 752 Tariki.

HUNTING AND FISHING

Hunters are encouraged in Egmont National Park but permits must first be obtained from the Ranger Station. Wild goat hunting is the most popular and strenuous sport; there are no deer in the Park and they want to keep it that way; opossums are trapped or poisoned. All Park birds are protected. Some rivers and streams cascading down Mt. Egmont in all directions offer angling possibilities. Trout fishing can be found in the large number of streams in the Dawson Falls area. Call at the

Ranger Station or Display Centres or ask at the various mountain houses for hot fishing tips.

ACCOMMODATION

Within The Park

About 10 **Park huts** are situated along the main tracks; always open, first-there, first-bedded situation; $8 pp. Take your own sleeping bag, cooking equipment, and food supplies. Purchase your hut pass at the Ranger Station, Visitor Centre, or lodges on the mountain before you explore.

All three mountain resorts have limited accommodation ranging from cheap to expensive. At **North Egmont** the Park operates the 32-bed **Camphouse:** basic bunkhouse accommodation with a large common room, heating stoves, cooking facilities, and showers for the reasonable nightly rate of adult $8, child $4. Take your own sleeping bag, cooking equipment, and food. For more details, contact the manager at the North Egmont Visitor Centre at tel. 710 Egmont Village, or the Dept. of Conservation at tel. 80-433 New Plymouth.

At **East Egmont,** the privately owned **Stratford Mountain House and Motel** has rooms starting at $65 s, $70 d; licensed bar and restaurant, cafeteria, souvenir shop, ski and tramping gear for hire. Located 14.5 km from Stratford on Pembroke Rd., tel. 6100 Stratford. Some of the privately owned ski lodges provide accommodation in winter, subject to availability. Call the **Stratford Mountain Club Lodge** on Manganui Skifield direct at tel. 5493, or tel. 7277 for availability, current prices, and bookings (if they don't have space, they may know other clubs that do).

At the end of Manaia Rd. at **South Egmont** you'll find the cheap and comfortable Park-operated **Konini:** basic bunkbed accommodation, a large common room, woodstove heating, cooking facilities, and showers; adult $12, child $6. Take your own sleeping bag, cooking equipment, and food. Accommodating up to 38 people, it attracts large school groups, so if you plan on staying here, call Dawson Falls Tourist Lodge (see below) first to see if it's fully booked before heading up the mountain—pay at the Tourist Lodge. The luxurious **Dawson Falls Tourist Lodge** also at South Egmont has Swiss chalet-style rooms and breakfast starting at $72.50 s, $95 d, and a four-course dinner is available in the licensed restaurant (walk-ins must book) for around $28 pp. The Alpine Inn Coffee Lounge in the Lodge serves morning and afternoon tea and lunch (walk-ins must book), and packed lunches are available for guests on request. For more info and bookings call the manager at tel. 5457 Stratford.

Outside The Park

The closest YH is found at New Plymouth, about 23 km away from the northern Park boundary (see p. 295), along with a YWCA, a few reasonably priced guest houses, private hotels, and motor camps. The closest motor camps to the main access roads into the Park are located in several towns along Hwy. 3 on the eastern side, with a few motor camps along coastal Hwy. 45 on the western side. For those looking for camping or budget accommodation, the motor camps below are your best bet, or head for New Plymouth.

Motor Camps

At Stratford, 14.5 km from Egmont Plateau on Hwy. 3, **Stratford Holiday Park** is adjacent to a quiet park with native bush walks, river swimming, and municipal swimming baths nearby. Communal facilities. Tent- and caravan sites from $5.50 pp; cabins $17 d, tourist cabins $23 d. Located on Page St., 800 meters from the p.o., Stratford, tel. 6440.

At Eltham on Bridger Place (off Collingwood St.) you'll find **Presbyterian Camp,** tel. 8201. It has sites for camping and the usual facilities. Tentsites are $5 pp, and bunkroom beds (provide your own linen) are also $5 pp.

At the junction of hwys. 3 and 45 to the south of the Park is the fairly large town of Hawera—a good place to stock up on supplies before heading into "the sticks" if you're coming from the south. **King Edward Park** is situated in a sheltered domain with attractive

gardens and the adjacent municipal heated Olympic swimming pool complex (charge). Communal facilities (scalding hot showers!). Tentsites and caravan sites are $6.60 s, $13.20 d; cabins from $20 d (minimum per night). Located on Waihi Rd., tel. 88-544.

On The West Side

One place to stay on the north side of the mountain is at Oakura, 13 km southwest of New Plymouth on coastal Hwy. 45. **Oakura Beach Camp's** hedge-sheltered grounds are situated on the beach, tel. 861 Oakura. Communal facilities (metered showers). Tentsites are $10 s or d, caravan sites are $12 s or double.

FOOD AND ENTERTAINMENT

In The Park

The cheapest way to visit the Park is to take enough food to last your stay and cook it yourself. The Park huts, Konini, and the Camphouse have cooking facilities, but you need all your own equipment. No food shops are within the Park, only cafeterias at the North and East Egmont resorts, and licensed restaurants (expensive) and bars at both the east and south resorts. Entertainment is provided by your own two feet during the day, and comes in an exhausted form of sweet dreams in the evening!

Outside The Park

When you're in Egmont Village don't miss **Village Crafts and Tearooms,** on the corner of Egmont Rd. and Hwy. 3 near the petrol station. Open every day, 0900-1700, they serve the usual fare and great homemade cakes at regular prices (get there early for the best selection)—but be warned, if you're easily tempted by beautifully made crocheted, woven, or knitted wool products, you may lose some of your daily budget on your way through the crafts shop back to the tearooms.

If you're in **Stratford** and want quick tearoom treats, walk down bustling Broadway (everything you need is on the main street) and try **Taranaki Farmers** (upstairs; tel. 6199) the **Hob Nob Coffee Lounge** (tel. 6534), or **Berties Bakery and Tearooms** (tel. 7688). For delicious takeaways, health foods, salads, and cold meats, go to the deli (tel. 6487). For full meals head for **Continental Tea Rooms** (tel. 6855), or **Radich Restaurant** (tel. 5123). **Wong's Restaurant and Takeaways** (tel. 6435) has everything from takeaways to light meals to four-course feasts, closed Mondays.

In **Eltham,** tearoom fare can be found upstairs on High St. at the **Attic Coffee Lounge,** tel. 8774. For full meals head for **Eltham Restaurant,** tel. 7161, or the BYO-licensed **High Street Restaurant,** tel. 8610, serving takeaways, light snacks, or full meals, all week.

Egmont National Park and surrounding area is not the place to come for a wild nightlife or exciting evening entertainment. If you're hankering for a bit of action, your best bet will be to head for the city of New Plymouth (but even there it's pretty sparce unless you befriend some locals). There's always a pub or local bar in every town (follow your nose!).

SERVICES

Emergency

For emergency numbers, look in the Taranaki phone directory under the "Stratford" section. On-duty emergency doctors and pharmacies are listed in the Wed. Issue of the *Stratford Press* newspaper. **Stratford Public Hospital** is on Miranda Street. The **Stratford Police Station** is on Broadway, and **Eltham Police Station** is on Bridge Street.

General

The central Taranaki office of the **Automobile Association** is located on Broadway North in Stratford, tel. 7331. One **chemist** with after-hours telephone numbers is located in Stratford—**Moss, Rocard, and Smith** at 256 Broadway, tel. 6566, after-hours tel. 5733 or 6361. In Kaponga, **L.A. Nisbet** is located at 31 Victoria St., tel. 886, after-hours tel. 757 KPO. **Stratford P.O.** is on Miranda St., **Eltham P.O.** is on the corner of High South and Bridge Street.

INFORMATION

Sources In The Park

The main sources are: **North Egmont Visitor Centre** at the end of Egmont Rd. at North Egmont (publications available); the **Ranger Station** on Pembroke Rd., 10 km from Stratford (the road is on the north side of town), tel. 5144 (where you can buy a detailed map of the Park, and get specific info on hiking tracks, climbing routes, and weather forecasts); and the **Dawson Falls Display Centre** at the end of Manaia Rd., South Egmont. The accommodation houses and lodges at each resort are also good sources of info, brochures, maps, and ski reports.

Central Taranaki Information Centres

In Stratford call in at **The Pioneer Village**, or tel. 5399. In Eltham visit **Eltham Book Centre** and pick up the handy *Central Taranaki Visitor Guide* or tel. 7036 ELT, after-hours tel. 8816, 8607, or 8162. In Kaponga try the **Town Library Office** on Victoria St., tel. 869 KPO, after-hours tel. 706.

TRANSPORTATION

Getting There

Getting to New Plymouth is easy by public transportation, but getting up and into Egmont National Park is a challenge unless you have your own wheels. **InterCity** runs daily service from the north and south to New Plymouth, and connects the city with New Plymouth Airport. To get to Egmont National Park from New Plymouth or from Wellington, take the bus either to Stratford Depot on Regan St. (the taxi office), tel. 6029, or to Eltham Depot at Stark's Shop, Eltham, tel. 8605—then hitchhike in, or ask the locals for advice.

Getting Around

Getting into the Park and up to the resorts or higher slopes and walking tracks is mainly up to you. The three resorts are located at the end of their individual access roads, and public transportation is not available. The easiest way is by car or bike (if you're fit!); hitching is not too difficult as long as the weather is fine—in wet miserable weather settle down for some serious letter writing in a cozy tearoom, or head somewhere else! If you don't have your own transportation and want to travel up all the access roads, you might consider renting a car for a day or two. All the major rental car firms are represented in New Plymouth. **Jamieson Motors** on Pembroke Rd., Stratford, offers passenger charter work to any destination, tel. 5843 for prices. **Taranaki Service Station** also may have rental cars available; tel. 5831. Tour buses run to the Park resorts from New Plymouth as well, but you don't get the chance and the time to do your own exploring (see p. 299).

NEW PLYMOUTH

On the northwest coast of Cape Egmont, this city is the metropolitan and cultural center for the lush agricultural Taranaki region. Known for its beautiful parks and reserves (one-fifth of the urban area is green), the tourist brochures have aptly named it "The Garden City." Sandwiched between popular surf beaches along North. Taranaki Bight and dominated by majestic snow-capped Mount Egmont to the south, the city is also recognized for its scenic beauty. Rich on- and offshore oil and natural gas fields have led to increasing affluence and development and the title "Energy Centre of New Zealand." Apart from local city attractions, New Plymouth is an ideal base for exploring Egmont National Park, the "Round-The-Mountain" route (see p. 282), and the gently rolling hedge-divided countryside of the surrounding Taranaki dairylands.

SIGHTS

On Foot

Head directly for the PRO on Liardet St. and collect the current "City Walks" brochure. The brochure covers inner-city parks, domains (see "Barrett Domain" below), historic sites, Maori *pa,* fine swimming beaches, and general places of interest. Also pick up the latest "What's On" which has plenty of handy local info, and the "New Plymouth City Map" which suggests the best scenic routes.

Parks And Reserves

If you enjoy beautiful parks, take a 10-minute walk from the city center to the 21-hectare **Pukekura Park**—a lush urban oasis that shouldn't be missed. Paths lead through native bush and flowers, an abundance of tree ferns, exotic flowers, and along streams and lakes that provide the photographer with good scenery shots and Mt. Egmont reflections. An illuminated fountain (very colorful at night) plays at the drop of a coin, and for another coin you can enjoy an 11-meter illuminated waterfall bordered by lush ferns cascading down several falls. The park is open daily; the fabulous Fernery and Begonia Display Houses, interconnected by moss-festooned tunnels, are open daily Christmas to Easter from 0900-1200 and 1300-1630, the rest of the year weekdays 0900-1200 and 1300-1630. The Tea House is open daily except Tuesdays. The main entrance is past the sportsground on Liardet St., a couple of blocks south of the downtown PRO; admission free.

Adjoining **Brooklands Park** is quite a contrast with its sweeping perfect lawns and formal plantations of both introduced deciduous and native trees. Beside the main path through the center of the reserve (just beyond

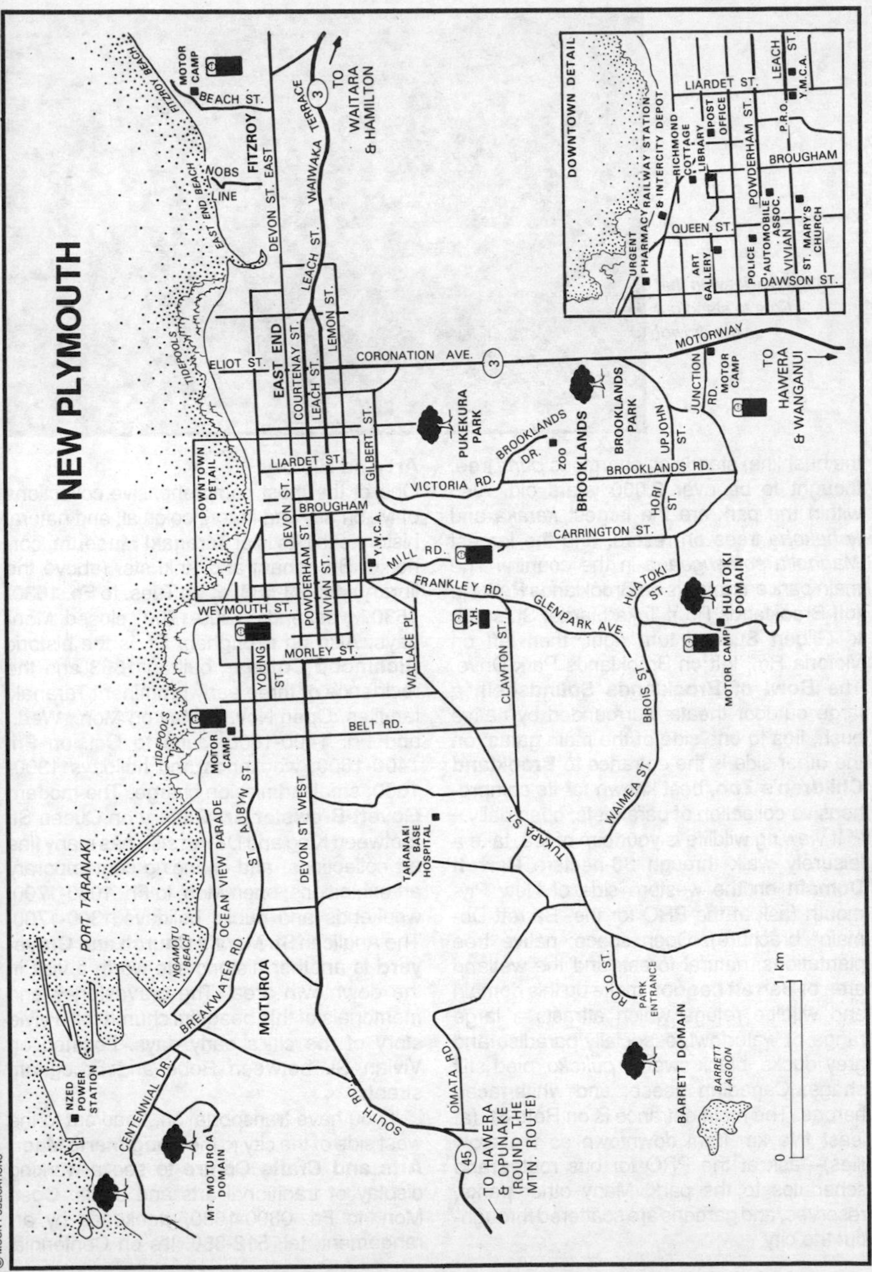
NEW PLYMOUTH
DOWNTOWN DETAIL
URGENT PHARMACY
RAILWAY STATION
& INTERCITY DEPOT
RICHMOND COTTAGE
LIBRARY
POST OFFICE
LIARDET ST.
LEACH ST.
Y.M.C.A.
P.R.O.
POWDERHAM ST.
BROUGHAM
AUTOMOBILE ASSOC.
ST. MARY'S CHURCH
VIVIAN
QUEEN ST.
ART GALLERY
POLICE
DAWSON ST.
MOTORWAY
TO HAWERA & WANGANUI
JUNCTION RD.
MOTOR CAMP
BROOKLANDS PARK
UPJOHN ST.
BROOKLANDS
HORI ST.
BROOKLANDS DR.
ZOO
BROOKLANDS RD.
PUKEKURA PARK
CORONATION AVE.
3
TO WAITARA & HAMILTON
WAIWAKA TERRACE
DEVON ST. EAST
FITZROY
BEACH ST.
MOTOR CAMP
FITZROY BEACH
EAST END BEACH
NOBS LINE
LEACH ST.
LEMON ST.
EAST END
COURTENAY ST.
ELIOT ST.
TIDEPOOLS
GILBERT ST.
LIARDET ST.
DEVON ST.
VICTORIA RD.
BROUGHAM
Y.W.C.A.
MILL RD.
CARRINGTON ST.
FRANKLEY RD.
GLENPARK AVE.
HUATOKI ST.
HUATOKI DOMAIN
MOTOR CAMP
WEYMOUTH ST.
YOUNG ST.
POWDERHAM ST.
VIVIAN ST.
MORLEY ST.
WALLACE PL.
Y.H.
CLAWTON ST.
BELT RD.
MOTOR CAMP
TIDEPOOLS
ST. AUBYN ST.
WAIMEA ST.
BROIS ST.
TUKAPA ST.
TARANAKI BASE HOSPITAL
DEVON ST. WEST
OCEAN VIEW PARADE
PORT TARANAKI
NGAMOTU BEACH
BREAKWATER RD.
MOTUROA
ROTO ST.
PARK ENTRANCE
BARRETT DOMAIN
BARRETT LAGOON
0
1 km
OMATA RD.
SOUTH RD.
45
TO HAWERA & OPUNAKE (ROUND THE MTN. ROUTE)
NZED POWER STATION
CENTENNIAL DR.
MT. MOTUROA DOMAIN
© MOON PUBLICATIONS

One black swan that likes to stand out in the crowd!

the bushline) stands an enormous *puriri* tree, thought to be over 2,000 years old. Also within the park are the largest *karaka* and *kohekohe* trees on record, and the largest *Magnolia soulangeana* in the country. The main park entrance is on Brooklands Park Dr. (off Brooklands Rd.). Take Liardet St. south to Gilbert St. and turn right, then left on Victoria Rd., left on Brooklands Park Drive. The **Bowl of Brooklands Soundshell,** a large outdoor theater surrounded by native bush, lies to one side of the main gates; on the other side is the entrance to **Brookland Children's Zoo,** best known for its comprehensive collection of parakeets; open daily.

If viewing wildlife is your cup of tea, take a leisurely walk through 36-hectare **Barrett Domain** on the western side of New Plymouth (ask at the PRO for the "Barrett Domain" brochure). Open space, native tree plantations, natural forest, and the wetland area of **Barrett Lagoon** make up this domain and wildlife refuge which attracts a large range of waterfowl, especially paradise and grey ducks, black swans, *pukeko,* pied stilt shags, Canadian geese, and white-faced herons. The main entrance is on Roto St. (at least five km from downtown as the crow flies)—ask at the PRO for bus routes and schedules to the park. Many other parks, reserves, and gardens are scattered throughout the city.

Art And History

One of the most comprehensive collections of Maori art, and Maori, colonial, and natural history exhibits is at **Taranaki Museum,** corner of Brougham and Ariki sts. (above the library), tel. 89-583; open Tues. to Fri. 1030-1630, weekends 1300-1700, closed Mondays. Also on Brougham St. is the historic **Richmond Cottage,** built in 1853 and the residence of three early prominent Taranaki families. Open Nov. to May on Mon., Wed., and Fri. 1400-1600, June to Oct. on Fri. 1400-1600, weekends and holidays 1300-1600; small admission charge. The modern **Govett-Brewster Art Gallery** on Queen St. (between King and Devon sts.) has many fine art collections, and changing contemporary art exhibitions; open Mon. to Fri. 1030-1700, weekends and public holidays 1300-1700. The Anglican **St. Mary's Church and Graveyard** is another historic site worth a visit in the downtown area. The gravestones and memorials of this beautiful church tell a vivid story of the city's early days. Located on Vivian St. between Robe and Brougham streets.

If you have transportation, head out to the west side of the city to the **Rangimarie Maori Arts and Crafts Centre** to see a working display of traditional arts and crafts. Open Mon. to Fri. 0800-1630, weekends by arrangement, tel. 512-880. It's on Centennial

Dr., beyond the thriving, man-made **Port Taranaki.** While you're in this neck of the woods, don't miss the **Moturoa Lookout** which provides good views of Mt. Egmont/Taranaki to the south, and on a clear day, Mt. Ruapehu to the east of Mt. Egmont/Taranaki.

Energy Sites

The economic boom of the Taranaki region is mainly due to the discovery of natural gas and oil throughout the region and offshore. The one closest to the city is the gas-operated **New Plymouth Power Station.** If you're interested, two-hour tours depart on Wed. at 1000 and Sun. at 1400 (double-check with the PRO) from the security gates on Breakwater Road. To get there take St. Aubyn St. (at the west end of town) which leads directly to Port Taranaki on Breakwater Road.

A **Gas-To-Gasoline Plant** at Motonui on the North. Taranaki coast (20 km northeast) has an info center, open seven days from 1000-1700. Enter at the main gates; tel. Waitara 6480. A **Chemical Methonal Plant** in the Waitara Valley (15 km northeast) offers visitors a view of the Plant from the "lookout" situated on Matarikoriko Rd., just off Mamaku Rd. at the rear of the plant. **Petrocorps Exploration's McKee No. 2 Well,** located on Otaroa Rd., Waitara (13 km southeast of Waitara), has an observation platform only. The **Maui Production Station** located at Oao-nui (52 km southwest of New Plymouth), tel. 87-609, has an info center at the plant, open daily. The **Maui LPG Extraction Plant** in the same area has no tours but energy buffs can visit the model room. The **Maui A Platform** where gas was first discovered in

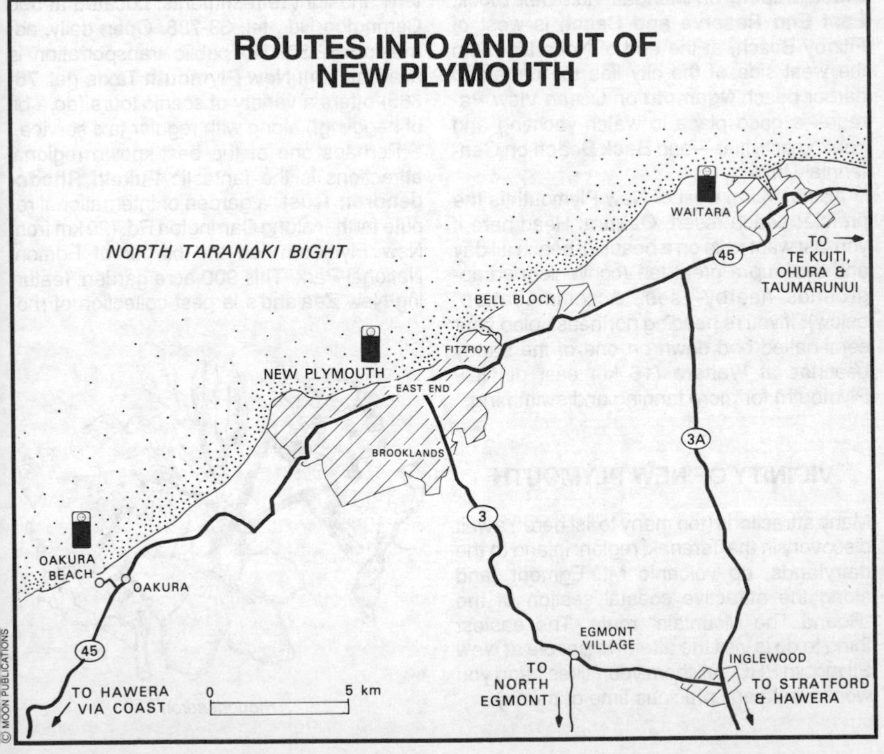

1969 is situated about 35 km offshore Oaonui. No tours, but you can see it from most road ends. The **Gas Treatment Plant** at Okaiawa (southeast of Mt. Egmont) was the first large-scale natural gas plant, and opposite is the **Ammonia Urea Plant.** No tours are available at these sites, but you can drive past them via Palmer Rd., Kapuni.

Beaches

New Plymouth's city beaches stretch along the curved sandy seafront in both directions, but the best surfing beaches are at the eastern end of town. Most popular **Fitzroy Beach** is known for its excellent surf, and together with **Strandon Beach,** they form a continuous 1.6-km sweep of luxurious sand; access from Beach St., about three km from city center. Farther east, about seven km from downtown (heading for the airport), is **Bell Block Beach,** on Mangati Rd., Bell Block. **East End Reserve and Beach** is west of Fitzroy Beach, at the end of Nobs Line. On the west side of the city lies the protected harbor beach **Ngamotu** on Ocean View Parade—a good place to watch yachting and boating activities—and **Back Beach** on Centennial Drive.

About 14 km west of New Plymouth is the premier beach resort, **Oakura.** Head here if you just want to lie on a beautiful beach all day and soak up a great tan (convenient campgrounds nearby—see "Accommodation" below). If you're heading northeast, plop your semi-naked bod down on one of the sandy beaches at **Waitara** (16 km east of New Plymouth) for more tanning and swimming.

VICINITY OF NEW PLYMOUTH

Many attractions (too many to list here!) await discovery in the Taranaki region: inland to the dairylands, up volcanic Mt. Egmont, and along the attractive coastal section of the "Round The Mountain" route. The easiest thing to do is visit the attentive people at New Plymouth PRO, tell them your "likes," and you won't waste any precious time or money.

Carrington Road

If you have your own transportation, a trip along Carrington Rd. is a worthwhile jaunt from downtown New Plymouth to view two local attractions, and if you're continuing south, the road rejoins the main coastal highway without the need for any backtracking. From the PRO take Liardet St. south (away from town), turn right on Gilbert St., and left on Victoria Road. Turn left on Brooklands St. and continue to the end where it becomes Carrington Road.

Pouakai Wildlife Reserve offers bushwalks past lakes where you can view waterfowl, foreign birds, ornamental ducks (not of the garden gnome variety!), and peacocks, saunter through the interior of a large aviary, and view deer, cattle, several kinds of goats, "uncommon" sheep, ponies, and opossums. A souvenir shop sells local handcrafts, pottery, and light refreshments. Located at 590 Carrington Rd., tel. 33-788. Open daily, admission $2.50. No public transportation is available, but **New Plymouth Taxis** (tel. 75-665) offers a variety of scenic tours (do a bit of haggling!) along with regular taxi service.

Perhaps one of the best-known regional attractions is the fantastic **Pukeiti Rhododendron Trust,** a garden of international repute farther along Carrington Rd. (20 km from New Plymouth) on the border of Egmont National Park. This 900-acre garden, featuring New Zealand's largest collection of rho-

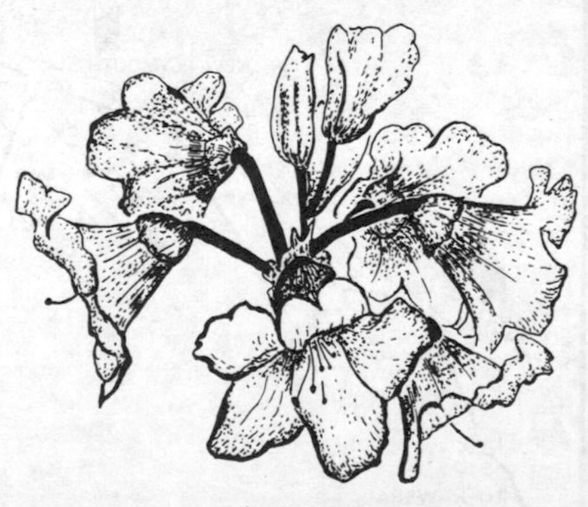

rhododendron

dodendrons and azaleas, trees, shrubs, and perennials, is colorful at all times of the year, but the peak flowering of rhododendrons is generally Sept. through Nov. (and a sight for sore eyes). Bushwalks lead through spectacular gardens dominated by native forest, all kinds of birds twitter in the trees (particularly *tuis* and bellbirds in the early morning and evening), and you can get outstanding views of the surrounding countryside from the summit of **Pukeiti Hill.** The gardens are open seven days a week during daylight hours; admission $5. Refreshments, maps, brochures, postcards, slides, and plants are for sale at the Gatehouse. No public transportation is available, but **Neuman's Sightseeing Tours** (tel. 84-622) in New Plymouth includes Pukeiti on their various tour itineraries; call for their current schedule and price.

Commercial Tours

Neuman's Sightseeing Tours provides a range of excursions from half-day to full-day trips from New Plymouth. Pick up one of their pamphlets at the PRO, or make direct contact at tel. 84-622 or after hours tel. 512-611. Another operator, **Smith Scenic Farm Tours** also offers various tours throughout the Taranaki region. Contact them at tel. 89-960 or 21-536.

ACCOMMODATION

Hostels

New Plymouth YH is a modern suburban hostel, a couple of km south of city center; $11 pp; 12 Clawton St., tel. 35-720. The **New Plymouth YWCA Hostel** is usually full of students (male and female), but if they have a spare bed in one of the shared rooms, they take in extras; $10 pp (provide your own sleeping bag) or $12 pp (linen included). It has a fairly central location several blocks south of the city center, at 15 Bulteel St. (no YWCA sign on the street), tel. 86-014. From the PRO head west along Leach St. straight ahead onto Vivian St., then turn left down Robe Street. Bulteel is the second on the right. Clean, bright, comfortable **Hostel 69** is a backpackers hostel located at 69 Mill Rd., a few blocks south of the city center. Large kitchen/living area. Pickup is available at tel. 87-153 (you can phone from the PRO). Shared rooms are $13 pp, a double room is $14 pp.

Motor Camps

Fitzroy Seaside Park Motor Camp, closest motor camp to the city center (about three km), boasts an excellent surf beach, recrea-

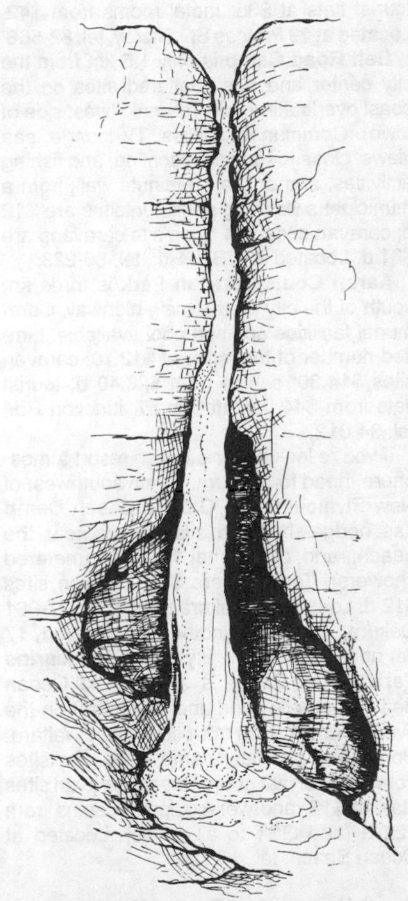

81.5-meter Mt. Damper Falls, one of the highest waterfalls in New Zealand, is a Taranaki attraction. Find out how to get there at the New Plymouth PRO.

tion and TV hall, and the usual facilities. Tentsites are $6.50 pp, caravan sites $14 d (additional persons $7.50); at Beach St. next to the beach, tel. 82-870. Another camp in the Fitzroy area about one km from the beach and 3.5 km from city center is **Princes Tourist Court.** Communal facilities, tepid swimming pool and hot spa, TV and recreation room, and camp store. Tentsites $6 s, $11 d, caravan sites $13 s or d; cabins start at $23, tourist flats at $35, motel rooms from $42. Located at 29 Princes St., Fitzroy, tel. 82-566.

Belt Road Camp is only 1.5 km from the city center and has sheltered sites on the coast overlooking Port Taranaki (west side of town). Communal facilities, TV lounge, sea views, close to boating, yachting, and fishing activities, and only a 10-minute walk from a municipal swimming pool. Tentsites are $12 d; caravan sites $14 d; on-site caravans are $31 d. Located at 2 Belt Rd., tel. 80-228.

Aaron Court Caravan Park is three km south of the city on the main highway. Communal facilities and spa pool available. Limited number of tent sites at $12.10; caravan sites $14.30; cabins from $26.40 d; tourist flats from $44. Located at 57 Junction Rd., tel. 34-012.

If you're looking for a beach resort atmosphere, head for Oakura, 13 km southwest of New Plymouth. The **Oakura Beach Camp** has hedge-sheltered sites on or near the beach, and communal facilities (metered showers). Tentsites are $10, caravan sites $12 d. Located at Oakura Beach, tel. 27-861 Oakura. Waitara is another beach resort, 17 km northeast of New Plymouth. The **Marine Park Motor Camp** is adjacent to Ocean Beach (gravelly sand and small surf) on the river mouth, 1.5 km from downtown Waitara. Communal facilities, camp store. Tentsites from $5 pp on flat grassy areas, caravan sites start at $12, and well-equipped cabins from $22 d (add GST to all prices). Located at Ocean Beach, tel. 4-7121.

Guest Houses And Private Hotels

Aotea Private Hotel is an attractive old-style yellow-washed building with a cozy atmosphere. Nicely furnished rooms with handbasins, electric blankets, and tea- and coffee-making facilities, shared bathrooms, comfy TV lounge, and dining room with huge wooden fireplace add to its overall appeal; from $27.50 s B&B, $36 d B&B, $37 s dinner, B&B, and $66 d dinner, B&B. They also offer a family-style dinner for $10 pp available to casual guests who book by lunchtime. Located at 26 Weymouth St. on the corner of Young St., a couple of blocks northwest of city center, tel. 82-438.

The **Tasman** offers rooms with handbasins, communal facilities, and a TV lounge. All meals are available and extra. Rooms are $20 s, $31 d (two nights or more). Centrally located on St. Aubyn St., tel. 86-129. The **White Hart** is similar—$18 s, $20 d. All meals available. Centrally located on the corner of Queen and Devon sts., tel. 75-442.

Motels

New Plymouth has a large number of three- and four-star motels scattered throughout the city. Refer to the *AA Accommodation Directory* for an extensive listing (several pages!) of all the motels, yet relatively few hotels.

FOOD

Light Lunches

If you like healthy natural food, head straight for **The Steps Restaurant** at 37 Gover St., tel. 83-393. Friendly waitresses serve good cheap food made on the premises (a huge slab of broccoli and feta pie with two types of salad start at a meager $4). Most main courses range from $3-5, desserts from $2.60, freshly squeezed fruit juices $1.50. Also open for breakfast, it's mainly a lunch and take-away restaurant, and very popular with locals—eat there early for the best selection. Open Mon. to Thurs. 0730-1600, Fri. 0730-2100, closed weekends; BYO license, tel. 83-393. For a light lunch (1200-1400 daily except Tues.), or morning or afternoon teas (1000-1600 daily except Tues.) in beautiful park surroundings, head for **Pukekura Park Kiosk** on Liardet St. in Pukekura Park, tel. 84-927. At the **Centre City Shopping Com-**

plex on Gill St. is **Tastings Foodcourt** with six over-the-counter boutiques featuring Chinese, Italian, and seafood meals, natural foods, sandwiches, and desserts.

Main Meals

The fully licensed **Cobb & Co. Restaurant** on the corner of Gover and Devon sts. (tel. 85-373) serves standard good meals for $10-20; open daily from 0700-1000 for breakfast, and from 1000-2200 for continuous meals. **Piccadily Restaurant** boasts "seafood experiences" at reasonable prices. Open Mon. to Thurs. 1100-2030, Fri. 1100-2130, weekends 1700-2000. Located at 108 Devon St. West, tel. 84-652. **Pizza Hut's** prices start at around $10 pp. Open daily from 1130; located on the corner of Clemow Rd. and Sackville St., Fitzroy, tel. 82-811.

The **Plymouth Sun Hotel** has an a la carte three-course menu, reasonably priced from $20 pp. An excellent Sat. and Sun. buffet dinner (from $19 pp), and a buffet lunch Mon. to Fri. are also available. Located on the corner of Courtenay, Leach, and Hobson sts., tel. 80-589. **Bellissimo Cafe** (upstairs overlooking the Mall) specializes in Italian, vegetarian, steak, and roast meals, at 38 Currie St., tel. 80-398; open daily except Tues. from 1700. **The Egmont Steam Flour Mill** is open for lunch from 1130-2000 and dinner from 1700 onward, on Powderham St., tel. 81-935. **Golden Phoenix Chinese Restaurant** offers blackboard menu lunches weekdays 1130-1430, dinners Mon. to Sun. from 1800, and a good Sun. night smorgasbord recommended by locals. For authentic Indonesian food at reasonable prices try **The Black Olive** on the corner of Devon and Egmont sts., tel. 88-561; open Wed. to Sun. from 1700.

The Dancing Bear BYO Restaurant is a local favorite for delicious steaks, seafood, and salads. It's upstairs on Egmont St., tel. 89-703. At the **Centre City Shopping Complex** on Gill St. is **Tastings Foodcourt** with six over- the-counter food boutiques. Go here for quick Chinese, Italian, or seafood meals, natural foods, sandwiches, or desserts. Another local hot spot is **Portofino,** a very popular, casual, BYO Italian restaurant on Gill St., opposite the main entrance to Centre City, tel. 78-686. At dinner expect to pay $13-16 for a main course, from $9.50 for a tasty pizza. Takeaways are also available.

Takeaways

Kentucky Fried Chicken is on the corner of Courtenay and Gover sts.; open daily. **California Takeaways** is open seven days for lunch and dinner; located at 201a Coronation Ave., tel. 80-052. **Lotus Chinese Takeaways** specializes in—you guessed it; open seven days a week serving lunch and dinner, at 63 Devon St. East, tel. 83-856. **McDonald's** is on the corner of Eliot and Leach sts.; open daily.

ENTERTAINMENT

Movies

The best sources for current entertainment are the local newspapers and the PRO. For movies try the **Mayfair Theatre** (Pacer Kerridge) on Devon St. Central, tel. 84-918, or the **State Theatre** (Amalgamated/Hoyts) on Devon St. East, tel. 82-255.

Theatre And Opera

The **Bowl of Brooklands,** a magnificent outdoor theater surrounded by native bush, seats hundreds; it's located beside the entrance gates to Brooklands Park—call the PRO for performance info and current ticket prices. The **Opera House** on Devon St. Central also puts on regular live shows; tel. 84-947 for more information.

Pubs And Clubs

Many of the local pubs and hotels provide good entertainment a few nights a week—live bands, discos, talented local groups, etc. Look in the daily newspapers. **Westown Motor Hotel** on Maratahu St. is open for entertainment on Thurs. to Sat. nights. Also in the same hotel is the more uptown **Gazebo**—a restaurant and cocktail bar (dressy, take your credit card!); bookings essential at tel. 87-697. **The Egmont Steam Flour Mill** on Powderham St. (tel. 81-935) has nightclub entertainment and dancing, Wed. to Sat. 2030-0300. **Ziggy's Nite Club** is located at 51 Gill St., tel. 87-006, and is open 1730-0300 daily; $3 admission. The **Duke of Devon** located on the hill in city center has reasonably priced pub food, and live entertainment Thurs. to Sat. nights; open Mon. to Thurs. 1100-2200, Fri. and Sat. from 1100-2300, tel. 81-971.

Energetic

For those in the throes of rollerskate DTs, rent skates and attend a regular public session at the **East End Reserve** on Nobs Line, Fitzroy. For session times and prices call the New Plymouth Amateur Roller Skating Club at tel. 86-233. Bowling fanatics can also get their fix at**Ten Pin Bowling** on Centennial Drive, tel. 512-037; open weekdays 1900-2200, weekends 1230-2200.

A game of squash (an accurately named game of speed and skill similar to American raquetball) can be played on weekdays from 0900-2100, Sat. 0900-1700, and Sun. 1300-1700 at the **Y Community Centre.** Racquets are available but you have to buy a ball; located on Liardet St., tel. 83-666 for squash court bookings (up to three days in advance), and if you fancy finishing yourself off in a sauna, bookings are essential. If you're in the New Plymouth area in Feb., check out the exact date of the annual running race, **The Mountain To The Surf Marathon,** which finishes at Waitara Beach, about 17 km northeast of the city—watching all those sweaty bodies stagger over the finish line is quite a spectacle.

Flower Power

If you're lucky enough to be in New Plymouth in early Nov., your eyes are in for one heck of a flowery spectacle. The annual **Rhododendron Festival** lasts ten days, usually starting at the beginning of Nov., and features flowers, flowers, and more flowers! Attend all sorts of flower-oriented events, competitions, and horticultural lectures, and visit many of the private homes in the area that have spectacular rhododendron gardens.

SERVICES

Urgent

For any emergency, dial 111 and ask the operator for the service required. For an **ambulance** or **hospital** tel. 36-139; **police** tel. 75-449; **fire** tel. 75-505. For an **emergency doctor** call the DCS answering service at tel. 85-683 or the hospital. The **urgent pharmacy** is at 124 St. Aubyn St., tel. 84-492. **Taranaki Base Hospital** is on David St., tel. 36-139. The New Plymouth **police station** is on Powderham St., tel. 75-449. Problems or just need someone to talk to? Call **Lifeline** at tel. 86-333.

General

Normal shopping hours in the city are Mon. to Fri. 0830-1700, late-night shopping is on Fri. nights until 2030, and Sat. morning shopping is from around 0900-1200. **Centre City Shopping Complex** on Gill St. is open Mon. to Thurs. 0900-1730, Fri. 0900-2100, Sat. 0900-1630, tel. 84-688. The **Central P.O.** is on Currie St., tel. 80-999; open Mon. to Fri. from 0830-1700. The **public library** is located on Lower Brougham St., tel. 84-544 or 75-910. For a **laundrette** head for the corner of Devon and Elliot sts.; open Mon. to Fri. from 0800-1730.

INFORMATION

The main source of city info is the **New Plymouth Public Relations Office** at 81 Liardet St., tel. 86-086. Open Mon. to Fri. 0830-1700, public holidays 0900-1300 (if the office is closed read the info boards at the main entrance). Ask the helpful personnel for their "Dining-Out Guide," recommended sightseeing tours, local bus routes and schedules, and the free tourist newspapers. They also have info on Egmont National Park and descriptions of hiking trails and walks along the coastal highway south, and sell scenic postcards and detailed pamphlets on some of the local attractions.

TRANSPORTATION

Getting There

The main road running north-south through New Plymouth is Hwy. 3. Highway 45 starts at New Plymouth, runs southwest along the coast giving a western aspect of Mt. Egmont/Taranaki, and rejoins Hwy. 3 at Hawera. The city is serviced by coach through **Inter-City** and **Newmans,** and by air through **Air New Zealand.** No passenger train service runs through the city. Hitchhiking is generally fairly easy from Wellington and Wanganui in the south, but can get very frustrating from the north (slow roads, no major towns, less traffic).

Buses

The local **New Plymouth City Transport** covers all the places you'd want to go throughout the city, and more! Pick up the detailed *NPCT Bus Time Tables* handbook from the PRO, or from the bus depot on the corner of Egmont and Rangi streets. It answers most questions. Alternatively, for advice on the best bus routes to specific places, call 82-799 Mon. through Fri. between 0830-1700. After hours or on weekends, tel. 88-099—it's a great service for the visitor-in-a-hurry.

For long-distance coach service out of New Plymouth, go to the **InterCity New Plymouth Travel Centre** on St. Aubyn St. (tel. 87-729, after hours tel. 82-759) which runs regular services south to Wanganui and Wellington, or north to Hamilton and Auckland. **Newmans Coach Lines** at 32 Queen St. (tel. 75-482), runs north daily, stopping at Te Kuiti, Waitomo Caves, Hamilton, and Auckland, and south along the coastal highway to Okato, Opunake, Manaia, and Hawera on weekdays and Sat., connecting with other operators.

Sightseeing By Bus

Neuman's Sightseeing Tours at 76 Devon St. East offers tours around the city, to the various resorts up Mt. Egmont/Taranaki, to various attractions around the mountain, and to the Taranaki energy complexes. They need at least three people for the half-day tours and five for the full-day tours; tours from $10-50 pp. You can get free motel/hotel pick-up service; for more info and current prices, tel. 84-622.

Cars

The **Automobile Association** office is at 49-55 Powderham St., tel. 75-646. Office hours are Mon. to Fri. 0830-1700, breakdown service available from 0800-2300 all week. The **BP Powderham Petrol Station** at 71 Powderham St. offers 24-hour service, tel. 84-171. For a **taxi** call 75-665 (they also offer sightseeing tours). All the regular car rental agencies are located in New Plymouth. **Avis** is at 25 Liardet St., tel. 75-736 (24-hour service). **Budget** is at 71 Powderham St., tel. 88-039. **Hertz** is at 187 Devon St. West, tel. 88-189 (24-hour service). **National** is located on Gill St., tel. 78-255. **Cross Country Rentals** is also on Gill St., tel. 84-468 (anytime), for cars, vans, trucks, minibuses, and 4WD utilities.

Air

New Plymouth Airport is about 12 km north of town (take Hwy. 3 north and it's signposted off to the left before you reach Waitara), but easily reached by bus. **With-A-Truck Rentals** provides service from Egmont St. to the airport, stopping at any bus stop along Devon

St. East, and Plymouth Sun Hotel, The Devon, and Bell Block township; $6 pp OW from city center, $9 pp from the outer suburbs. For coach times tel. 511-777 or after hours 512-328. Coaches depart from the airport 10 minutes after each Air New Zealand arrival.

Air New Zealand connects New Plymouth with Auckland, Kaitaia, Whangarei, and Wellington in the North Island and all major centers in the South Island. The main office is on Devon St. Central; for domestic reservations call 87-674, international call 79-057; the office at the airport is reached at tel. 70-701.

Flightseeing

For exciting scenic flights ranging from a short "City Roundabout Flight" to flights over the north coast, over Mt. Egmont's summit, and the Taranaki energy projects, call **Air New Plymouth** at tel. 70-500.

SOUTH

Three main roads funnel traffic from the north into the Manawatu district, converging near Palmerston North, the area's major city. Highway 3 on the west coast is the main route south from New Plymouth, Egmont National Park, and Wanganui (about a 3½-hour drive to Wellington); central Hwy. 1 connects Taupo and Tongariro National Park (5½ hours to Wellington) with the south; and Hwy. 2 connects the east coast cities of Gisborne and Napier (about six hours to Wellington) with the south. The attractive city of Palmerston North is a good place to break up a long day's drive or relieve the numb bum bus syndrome on your way to Wellington. Two main routes continue south from Palmerston North toward the capital: Hwy. 1 (the most direct route) runs down the attractive Kapiti Coast; and Hwy. 2 meanders inland to Masterton, then passes Lake Wairarapa and the "dormitory" cities of Upper Hutt and Lower Hutt before entering Wellington.

Whichever route you choose has things to see and do—but keep in mind there's a lot *more* to do in the elegant capital of New Zealand before you catch the ferry to the South Island. If time is relatively precious, head straight down the coast to Wellington, and content yourself with good beach stops along the way. If time is relatively unimportant and you want to get off the beaten track, take the inland route south which passes through scenic hilly countryside scattered with sheep, trout-filled streams, and lakes, and sleepy little villages where excitement is a new face in town. The southeast area of the North Island is wild, remote, untouched (in direct contrast with the highly populated urban southwest), and well worth checking out if transportation and time are your own.

PALMERSTON NORTH

SIGHTS

Civic Centre

To see what New Zealand artists are doing in the world of painting, ceramics, and sculpture, head for **Manawatu Art Gallery** beside the Convention Centre on Main St. West (opp. Andrew Young St.), tel. 88-188; open Tues. to Fri. 1000-1630, weekends 1300-1700. The interesting **Manawatu Museum** is also worth a visit, featuring the history of the

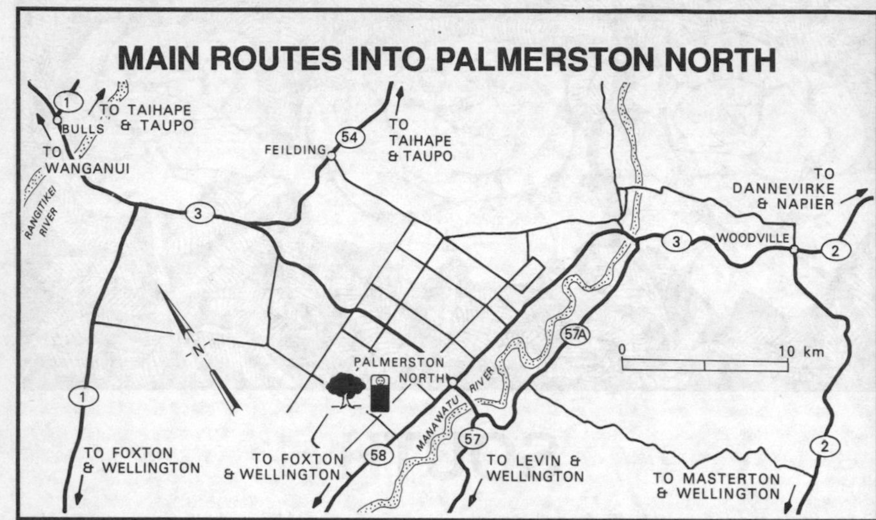

district from Maori to European settlements, and the beginning of the local dairy industry. On Church St. at the south end of The Square, tel. 83-951; open Tues. to Fri. 1000-1600, weekends 1400-1600, closed Mondays. For an excellent view of The Square, the city, and surrounding hills, whiz up to the **Lookout** at the top of the Civic Centre building; open 1000-1500.

If you're still in a museum mood, the **Rugby Museum** is a must for anyone interested in the sport (or the differences between rugby and other ball games). Photographs, badges, jerseys, caps, all sorts of rugby paraphernalia from around the world occupy this *different* museum! Located on the corner of Grey and Carroll sts., tel. 86-947; open daily 1330-1600. And while you're doing the local museums, don't miss **Tokomaru Steam Engine Museum** on the main highway, tel. 298-867. For more cultural and scenic suggestions, pick up the excellent *Heartland Manawatu Your Personal Guide* (55 cents) and *Tour Guide Heartland Manawatu* pamphlets (they contain everything you need to know about Palmerston North!), and a variety of other brochures from the Information Centre in The Square.

Parks

Palmerston North is an attractively laid-out city where the emphasis has been given to shady parks and flower-filled gardens. **The Square,** a six-hectare park in the middle of the city, provides some welcome green relief to the busy commercial center. Saunter past perfect lawns, beds of shrubs and flowers, and all sorts of trees, and don't miss the sunken gardens, floral clock, ornamental ponds and fountains, and chiming clocktower. In summer, large numbers of Palmerstonians head for The Square for lunch or afternoon tea, and throughout the year **The Soundshell** and **Open-Air Ampitheatre** host musical performances and public speaking events. (**Palmerston North Information Centre** is located on the western side of The Square.)

One of the most popular city parks, **The Esplanade** (a couple of blocks south of The Square—walk down Fitzherbert Ave.) covers 25 hectares of bush and gardens along the banks of the Manawatu River and appeals to all your senses. It features the **Lido Swimming Centre** (indoor pool open daily from 0600-2100 Easter through Oct., the outdoor pool open from Oct. to April), an aviary of native and exotic birds, rose gardens, tropical plant conservatory, riverside nature trails, and (give your nose a treat) special scented gardens. Drive through the park by entering at Park Road. Within a short walk of The Esplanade (heading east, cross Fitzherbert Ave. onto Centennial Dr.) is **Centennial Lake,** home to a large percentage of the Palmerston duck population, and a good place for a few hours' suntanning in a canoe or paddle boat (available for hire on weekends). For more parks and reserves, walkway, beach, and river suggestions, ask for the *Heartland Manawatu Guide to Outdoor Activities* brochure at the Information Centre.

South Of The River

For terrific views of Palmerston North, the surrounding countryside, and (on a clear day) Mt. Ruapehu to the north and Mt. Egmont to the northwest, take a short drive to **Anzac Park** (about four km south of the city along the southern banks of the river) where there's a lookout and observatory; cross the river at Fitzherbert Bridge and turn left on Cliff Rd. just before the university turnoff. **Massey University,** five km south, is the city's main educational facility. The 35-hectare campus consists of an intriguing blend of historic old homesteads and ultra-modern architecture set in superb surroundings; from city center take Fitzherbert St. south, cross the river, turn right on Tennent Drive. **Bledisloe Park,** on the northern campus boundary, is a quiet place to catch up on a bit of reading or swim in a small woodland stream; off Tennent Dr. just before the university entrance.

ACCOMMODATION

Camping And Cabins

There's no youth hostel in this area, but Dec. through Feb. a centrally located **summer hostel** opens at 10 Linton St., a three-minute walk from The Square, tel. 64-347; $11 pp. The **Municipal Camp,** two km from city center, provides good budget accommodation in peaceful park surroundings. It's adjacent to The Esplanade Park, Manawatu River, and Lido public swimming pool complex (open year-round), and provides the usual facilities and TV lounge. A snack kiosk opens up next to the camp in summer. Tentsites $6.60 pp, caravan sites $7.15 pp (minimum $10 per night), cabins range from $18.70-30.25 per night, tourist flats from $30.25-44 per night.

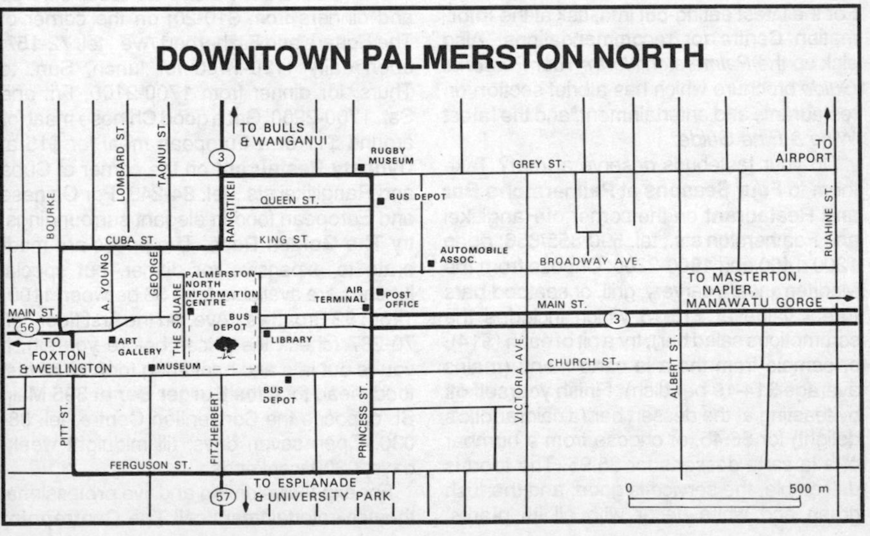

Located on Dittmer Dr., off Ruha St. and Park Rd., tel. 80-349.

Hotels And Motels

Many hotels (from $100 d), motels (average $40-70 d per night), and motor inns (from $100 s or d) are found in and around the city—the closer to Wellington, the higher the prices. Ask for listings and the *Heartland Manawatu Accommodator* guide (it has a handy map showing motel locations) at the Information Centre. **Chaytor House,** two blocks south of city center, offers B&B for $35.20 s, $59 d or twin. Each room has a handbasin, the bathrooms are communal (three rooms have private facilities). There's a TV lounge, tea-making facilities, and dinner is an available extra; located at 18 Chaytor St. (off Fitzherbert Ave.), tel. 86-878. The **Majestic Hotel,** a good hotel with less expensive rates, is on Fitzherbert Ave., tel. 80-079. Rooms start around $42 d, $65 d, shared facilities, or $55 with private bathroom. Centrally located **Central Motel** at 26 Linton St. (a stroll from The Square), tel. 72-133, has comfortable rooms from $44 s, $55 d.

FOOD AND ENTERTAINMENT

For the latest eating-out info, ask at the Information Centre for recommendations. Also pick up the *Palmerston North: Your Personal Guide* brochure which has a brief section on restaurants and entertainment, and the latest *Wine & Dine Guide.*

Do your tastebuds deserve a treat? Take them to **Four Seasons** at **Palmerstons Bar and Restaurant** on the corner of Rangitikei and Featherston sts., tel. 590-855/856; open 1200-1400 and 1800-2200. Choose from the Mediterranean, carvery, grill, or seafood bars (great value at $13-15 which includes the scrumptious salad bar), try a bit of each ($14), or sample from the a la carte menu (mains average $14-19 per dish). Finish yourself off by feasting at the dessert bar (a caloraholic's delight) for $6.45, or choose from a number of a la carte desserts for $5.95. The food is delectable, the service is good, and the lush green and white decor with all its plants, skylights, and picture-windows is relaxing. What more can I say?! To get there take Rangitikei St. (Hwy. 3 to Bulls and Wanganui) north from Cuba St. for a couple of blocks to the Featherston St. intersection. You can't miss it.

The **Cobb & Co. Family Restaurant and Bar,** part of the Empire Establishment, is always a safe bet ($10-15 average main course at dinner). Open seven days a week from 0730-2200; located at 526 Main St. (corner of Princess St.), tel. 78-002. **Hatters Family Restaurant** is also open all week. At 196 The Square, tel. 67-497; open for lunch and dinner, a main course averages $8-9. The **Brittania Restaurant and Family Lounge Bar** in the Hotel Majestic is less formal than it sounds, serving meals ($10-15 main course) seven days a week from 1200-1400 and 1700-2130; located at 45 Fitzherbert Ave., tel. 80-079. **Pizza Piazza,** near the Convention Centre on the D.I.C. side of The Square, creates yummy pizzas and doughnuts, has a BYO license, and is open seven days from 1100-2100 (later on Fri. and Sat. nights), tel. 87-424. A large pizza is around $18-20. Eat in or take away.

Fishermans Table Restaurant & Bar offers a good brunch menu for around $8 pp and dinners from $10-20; on the corner of The Square and Fitzherbert Ave., tel. 72-157, open daily 1130-1400 for lunch, Sun. to Thurs. for dinner from 1700-2100, Fri. and Sat. 1700-2200. Get a good Chinese meal for around $11 or a European meal for $15 at **Dynasty Restaurant** on the corner of Cuba and Rangitikei sts., tel. 84-243. For Chinese and European food in elegant surroundings, try **The Golden Rose.** The prices are moderate to expensive for dinner, but special lunches are available from $6 between 1100-1430; 82 Broadway Ave. on the first floor, tel. 70-287 (check the prices before you sit). If you're out late and hankering for a bit of fast food, head for **Gibs Burger Bar** at 395 Main St. opposite the Convention Centre, tel. 88-030. Open seven days, till midnight weekdays, 0300 weekends.

For expensive dining and live professional theater entertainment call **The Centrepoint**

Theatre at tel. 86-983 or 89-329 (dinner starts and bar opens at 1845, show at 1945) to see what's playing. A show and coffee costs $18 pp weeknights, $20 weekends, show and a meal $38 pp weeknights, $42 on weekends; located on the corner of Pitt and Church streets. For theater entertainment head for the downtown complex on Broadway Avenue. Go to **The Abbey Theatre Restaurant** for more live theater and licensed dining facilities, and the **Opera House** for opera. **The New Globe Theatre** houses a local amateur theater group.

The three city cinemas are **The Regent, The Odeon,** and **The State**—see local newspapers for current films and screening times. For **live music,** check out the many bars and hotels around town—many feature good bands on the weekends for a small cover charge, and a **nightclub** catering to night owls offers live entertainment Thurs. to Sun. nights till 0300 on the corner of Pitt and Cuba streets. If you're in the mood for a bit of horse racing and gambling, call the **Awapuni Racecourse** for information.

SERVICES AND INFORMATION

Urgent

For **emergency police, fire, or ambulance,** tel. 111. The **Public Hospital** is on Ruahine St., tel. 69-169—call for the on-duty **doctor or dentist.** An **urgent pharmacy** is located on the corner of Main and Ruahine sts., tel. 88-287; open Mon. to Wed. 1830-2130, Sat. 1300-1700 and 1900-2100, Sun. 1000-1230, 1300-1700, and 1900-2100, public holidays 0930-1230, 1400-1700, and 1900-2100. The main **police station** is on Church St., tel. 70-859.

General

The **Chief P.O.** is on Princess St., tel. 85-188; open weekdays 0800-1730, Fri. to 2000, and Sat. 0900-1130. **Palmerston North Public Library** is on The Square and Main St., tel. 83-076. The main **city shopping areas** are located on all sides of The Square, and suburban shopping centers are found at Hokowhitu, Highbury, Terrace End, Awapuni, and Milson. Most city shops are open Mon. to Thurs. 0830-1730, Fri. 0830-2100, and Sat. 0900-1200. Large shopping complexes and department stores generally stay open on Sat. till 1600. For specialty arts and crafts, head for the **Manawatu Community Arts Centre** at the Square Edge Complex on Church St. (next to the All Saints Church). **Agitator Launderette** at 44 Victoria Ave. (tel. 71-303) is open seven days a week; do your own or have it done for you, and a same-day dry-cleaning service is also available.

Information

The source of all the Palmerston North info you need is the excellent **Palmerston North Information Centre** in The Square, opposite the main entrance of the Civic Centre, tel. 85-003; open Mon. to Thurs. 0830-1730, Fri. 0830-1800, and Sat. 0930-1300. Pick up a city map, tourist pamphlets and papers, and the handy *Palmerston North Your Personal Guide* (55 cents) which has lots of handy info and a good city map. Other main sources of maps are the **Dept. of Survey and Lands,** and the **Automobile Association** (see below).

TRANSPORTATION

Getting There

Getting to Palmerston North is easy. All the main roads from the north converge just north and east of the city (good hitchhiking), and continuing south to Wellington is also a snap as there's plenty of traffic (you can often catch a ride all the way to the ferry terminal). Palmerston North is also on the main north-south railway line (Auckland to Wellington), and the eastern Wellington to Napier/Gisborne line. Both **InterCity** and **Newmans Coach Lines** connect the city with main destinations throughout the North Island, and **Air New Zealand** services Palmerston North airport.

Trains

The **railway station** is off Tremaine Ave., tel. 81-169; take Rangitikei St. north from The Square, turn left on Tremaine Ave., pass Coronation Park on the right and turn right at the next street. The *Northerner* and *Silver Fern Railcar* run north to Auckland and south to Wellington daily; a service runs east to Napier and Gisborne; and on weekdays only, a direct rail service connects Palmerston North with Woodville, Masterton, and Wellington.

Buses

For all **InterCity** info and current prices, stop by the office on Church St., outside the city bus depot and opposite the police station. They operate direct service from Palmerston North to Auckland, Rotorua, Napier, and Hastings, with connecting services. The city bus terminal is on Church Street. **Newmans Coach Lines** office and terminal is at 15-17 Princess St., tel. 77-079, and they provide regular service to Bulls (no bull!) and Wanganui, Hastings and Napier, Levin, Lower Hutt, Wellington, and the Wellington Ferry Terminal. For info on **city and suburban buses,** timetables, and current ticket rates, call **Palmerston North City Bus,** tel. 70-903.

Cars Or Bikes

The **Automobile Association** office is on Broadway Ave., a couple of blocks east of The Square. **Dominion Budget** hires cars at 193 Rangitikei St., tel. 81-575. **Avis** and **Hertz** also have offices in Palmerston North. For a **taxi** contact Palmerston North Taxis, 56 Bennett St., at tel. 76-076. For **bicycle rental** info and rates, call 85-003.

Air

Palmerston North's Milson Airport is about five km north of the city center—the only way to get out there other than by car is by taxi, about $8 OW. By car, from The Square take Main St. east, turn left at Ruahine St., then right on McGregor Street. **Air New Zealand** flies to Auckland, Kaitaia, Whangarei, Hamilton, and Wellington in the North Island, and Blenheim, Christchurch, Dunedin, Hokitika, Nelson, Oamaru, Timaru, Westport, and Invercargill in the South Island. The city office is on the corner of Princess and Main sts., tel. 77-149. **Eagle Air** flies to Auckland, Gisborne, Hamilton, Kaitaia, Tauranga, and Whangarei; book through Air New Zealand. **Air Nelson** services Wellington, Christchurch, Hokitika, Motueka, Nelson, Takaka, Timaru, and Westport. For reservations tel. 82-028.

TO WELLINGTON BY CAR OR BIKE

Two main routes south connect Palmerston North to Wellington, with public transportation on both. If you have your own wheels, many spots along each route await further exploration. The most direct route is via Hwy. 1 through Levin and along the scenic Kapiti Coast (see p. 311). However, if you have time and want to get off the beaten track to explore the relatively undeveloped southeast area, take the inland route via Hwy. 2.

THE INLAND ROUTE

Mount Bruce National Wildlife Centre

About 30 km south of Palmerston North on Hwy. 2 is a native bird reserve on the outskirts of beautiful **Mount Bruce State Forest.** Walk through the forest past gigantic cages cleverly constructed around trees and shrubs, and if you look hard and long enough, you'll spot all kinds of native birds, including some of New Zealand's rare and endangered birds (each cage has identifying pictures and characteristics of the birds inside). If you enjoy birdsongs your ears will be in seventh heaven! The purpose of the sanctuary is to protect the rare, study and breed the endangered, heal the sick, and liberate those that have been successfully bred into appropriate habitats in the wild. Entrance is free, donations welcome. Pick up a free pamphlet showing the layout of the sanctuary on your way in. The complex also features a large visitors center, nocturnal house, craft shop, and tearooms.

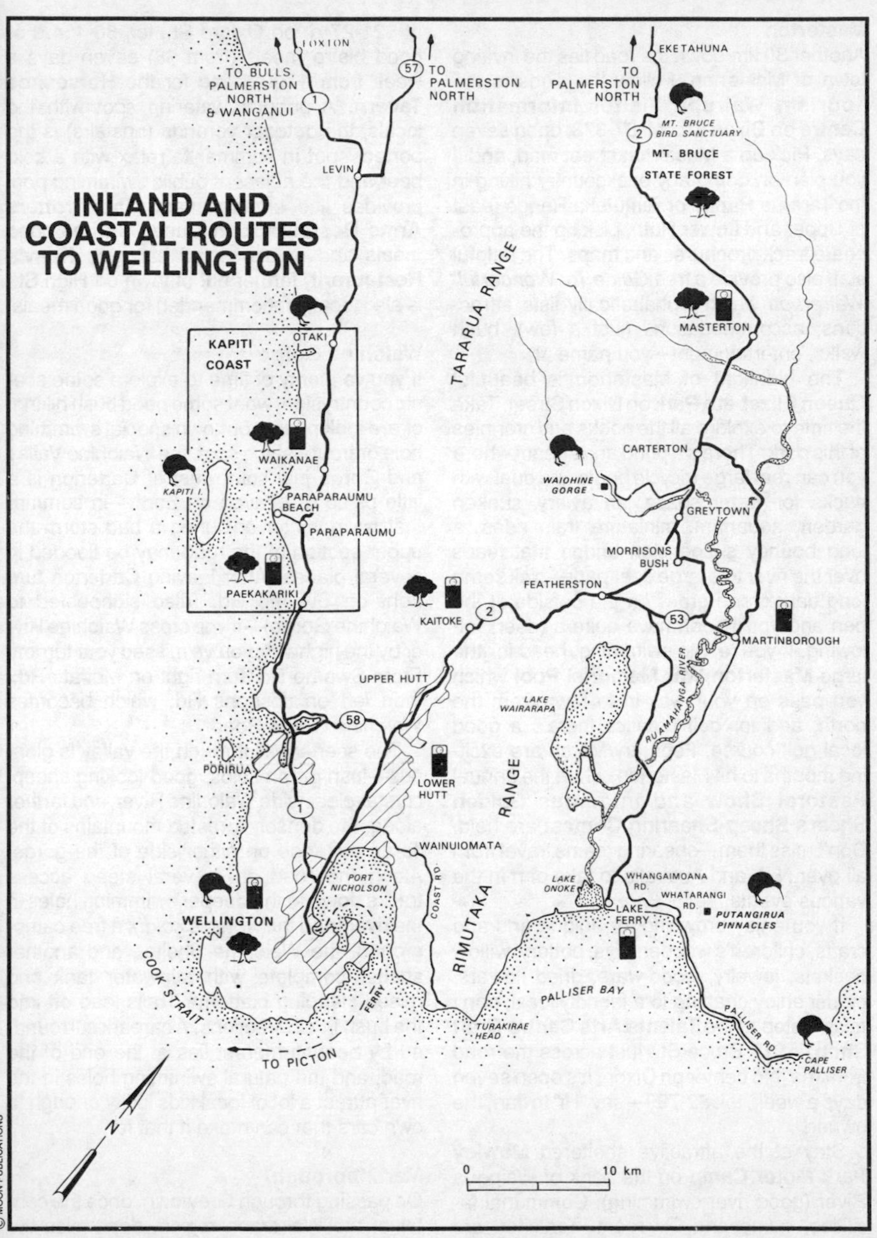
INLAND AND
COASTAL ROUTES
TO WELLINGTON
FOXTON
TO BULLS,
PALMERSTON
NORTH
& WANGANUI
1
57
TO
PALMERSTON
NORTH
EKETAHUNA
TO
PALMERSTON
NORTH
MT. BRUCE
BIRD SANCTUARY
2
MT. BRUCE
STATE FOREST
LEVIN
TARARUA RANGE
MASTERTON
OTAKI
KAPITI
COAST
WAIKANAE
KAPITI I.
PARAPARAUMU
BEACH
PARAPARAUMU
CARTERTON
WAIOHINE
GORGE
GREYTOWN
MORRISONS
BUSH
PAEKAKARIKI
FEATHERSTON
KAITOKE
2
53
MARTINBOROUGH
UPPER HUTT
LAKE
WAIRARAPA
RUAMAHANGA RIVER
58
PORIRUA
LOWER
HUTT
1
RIMUTAKA
RANGE
WAINUIOMATA
COAST RD.
PORT
NICHOLSON
WELLINGTON
LAKE
ONOKE
WHANGAIMOANA
RD.
WHATARANGI
RD.
LAKE
FERRY
PUTANGIRUA
PINNACLES
COOK STRAIT
FERRY
PALLISER BAY
TURAKIRAE
HEAD
PALLISER RD
CAPE
PALLISER
TO PICTON
N
0
10 km

Masterton

Another 30 km down the road lies the inviting town of Masterton. Follow the signs to the **Tourism Wairapa Visitor Information Centre** on Dixon St., tel. 87-373; open seven days. Pick up a Masterton street map, and if you plan on doing any backcountry hiking in the Tararua Range or Rimutaka Range (east of Upper and Lower Hutt), pick up the appropriate track brochures and maps. The helpful staff also provide a free *Guide To "Wonderful" Wairarapa* which alphabetically lists attractions, accommodations (just a few), bush walks, entertainment—you name it!

The highlight of Masterton is beautiful **Queen Elizabeth Park** on Dixon Street. Take the time to explore all the nooks and crannies of this park. There's a pond and stream where you can rent large tricycle boats and duel with ducks for water space, an aviary, sunken garden, aquarium, miniature train rides, a long bouncy suspension bridge that leads over the river to a large deer park—pick some long dark-green grass on the outside of the pen and you'll soon have quite a (deer) following. If you're into swimming, head for the large **Masterton War Memorial Pool** which you pass on your way in to town from the north, and for golf fanatics there's a good local golf course. February/March are exciting months to hit Masterton, when the annual **Pastoral Show** and infamous **Golden Shears Sheep-Shearing Contest** are held. Don't miss them—shearing teams travel from all over N.Z. and Australia to take part in the various events.

If you enjoy browsing for unique arts and crafts, children's wooden toys, pottery, willow baskets, jewelry, wood-ware, dried flowers, or just enjoy chatting to a friendly local, don't miss a stop at the **Talents Arts Centre Craft Shop.** At 12 Bruce St., just across the road from the info center on Dixon, it's open seven days a week, tel. 82-799—say "Hi" to Jan, the owner!

Stay at the attractive sheltered **Mawley Park Motor Camp** on the bank of Waipoua River (good river swimming). Communal facilities, game and TV room. Tentsites are $10.50 d, caravan sites $12.50 d, cabins start at $21-27 d; on Oxford St., tel. 86-454. For good bistro meals (from $8) seven days a week from 1700, head for the **Horseshoe Tavern.** A popular watering spot with the locals, the outdoor veranda (upstairs) is the perfect spot in summer to relax with a cold beer and the adjacent public swimming pool provides live entertainment! **The Crofters Arms Restaurant** on Queen St. has good meals and deluxe salad bar, and **Rosy's Restaurant,** farther out of town on High St., is also locally recommended for good meals.

Waiohine Gorge

If you've plenty of time to explore some scenic countryside, want some good bush hiking, or are looking for your own special swimming hole or trout-fishing spot, the Waiohine Valley and Gorge just southwest of Carterton is a little piece of heaven on Earth—in summer that is; in winter or during a bad storm the upper section of the road may be flooded in several places. After leaving Carterton turn right on Swamp Rd. (also signposted to Waiohine Gorge)—if you cross Waiohine River by the highway, you've missed your turnoff. From Swamp Rd. turn right on Moffats Rd., then left on Josephs Rd. which becomes Waiohine Gorge Road.

The scenery all through the valley is glorious—lush green fields, good-looking sheep, crystal-clear wide Waiohine River, and farther along, the densely forested mountains of the Tararua Range on either side of the gorge. Along the road are several steep access tracks down to the deeper swimming holes in the river (and the water is *cold!),* a free campground, the Waiohine Shelter, and another shelter complete with rainwater tank and raised sleeping platform. Trails lead off into the bush in all directions. A carpark surrounded by beautiful forest lies at the end of the road, and the natural swimming holes in the river attract a lot of local kids lucky enough to own cars that can make it that far.

Martinborough

On passing through Greytown, once the center of the Wairarapa region, don't miss the **Cobblestone Museum** on the main road.

Camp at Martinborough Council Camp and you get the public swimming pool all to yourself after hours.

This early settlers museum, once the site where Cobb & Co. coaches used to wait, has all sorts of ancient agricultural machinery and coach equipment outside, and a well-deserved reputation for being the most interesting museum in "these 'ere parts"; open daily 0900-1600, admission adult $2, child 50 cents, family $5. For another scenic ramble off the main highway, take the road just south of Greytown to Morrisons Bush, then follow the signs to the quaint town of Martinborough (but don't try this detour without a detailed map!). The scenery all along the route is flat farmland (a rainbow of color in the late afternoon and early evening), and the road crosses the meandering Ruamahanga River just before entering the wide veranda-lined street of Martinborough.

The downtown **Colonial Museum** is open 1400-1600. Martinborough also has a number of vineyards, all producing award-winning red and white wines. Stay at **Martinborough Council Camp** on the corner of Princess and Dublin sts., tel. 69-801, after hours 69-720. It's adjacent to the large **Martinborough Public Swimming Pool;** the best part of staying in the shady grass area at the back in summer is free use of the pool after closing hours. The pool (floodlit at night) has stadium-type benches along it (fantastic suntanning), an old wooden diving board, and a BBQ area; the camp has the usual communal facilities. Tentsites are $8 per night, powered caravan sites are $10. The gate into the campground is locked at around 2230 each night "to keep the local hoons out!" Finding the motor camp can be hard as there are no signs—from the central roundabout take the road with the Waiko Butchery on it, and ask anyone you see where the public pool is located.

The Lakes

Perched on the eastern shore of **Lake Onoke** where the waters of the Tauherenikau River and shallow **Lake Wairarapa** (known for good fishing and boating) run out into **Palliser Bay,** the seaside resort of **Lake Ferry** (about 60 km south of Martinborough at the end of the road) attracts quite a crowd in summer. Lake Ferry motor camp is situated on the shores of Lake Onoke. The ocean beach drops off steeply and dangerous rips make the rugged shores of Palliser Bay an unappealing place to swim, but the swampy shores and mudflats of Lake Onoke are a bird-watcher's paradise, and good surfcasting from the beach keeps anglers happy.

Inland from Palliser Bay on the way to Lake Ferry (about 17 km before the resort) lie the fantastic gray vertical rock pillars and intriguingly shaped cliffs of **Putangirua Pinnacles.**

To get there (you need a good map with the Pinnacles marked on) take the road to Lake Ferry, turn left onto Whangaimoana Rd., then left onto Whatarangi Rd. which becomes Cape Palliser Road. The eroded rock formations are less than an hour's walk from the head of the Putangirua Stream. After returning to the road, continue the drive around the bay (this road can be treacherous after heavy rains—the rivers are not bridged) to the end of Cape Palliser Rd., and you'll come to the **lighthouse** and a fairly large **seal colony.** An **underwater wreck** also attracts divers to these waters.

Kaitoke

After rejoining Hwy. 2 at Featherston and before continuing south, stop at the **Fell Museum** in the center of Kaitoke. It houses the last remaining Fell steam engine in the world, beautifully restored by a group of enthusiasts—the engines were used to haul passenger trains over the rugged and steep Rimutaka Range to Wellington. The last place for a bit of bush hiking in **Kaitoke Regional Park** or **Tararua Forest Park** before becoming submerged in the sprawl of suburbia is also found around the small town of Kaitoke. **Kaitoke Youth Hostel** (oldest YH in the North Island) is the last one before reaching Wellington. For info on hiking, tubing in the nearby Pakuratahi River, and gliding (the nearby gliding club operates on weekends), see the hostel info board or ask the warden; $8 pp—get the key from the p.o. or adjoining cottage (until 2100). The hostel is on Marchant Rd., 100 meters from the intersection with Hwy. 2, tel. 267-251; get off the bus at Kaitoke p.o.; the nearest train station (eight km) is Maymorn.

THE HUTT VALLEY

The Hutt River valley lies hemmed in by the **Kapiti** and **Porirua** coasts to the west and the impressive **Rimutaka Range** to the east, the **Tararua Range** to the north and the bay of **Port Nicholson** (Wellington Harbour) to the south. Although often referred to as the dormitory suburbs of Wellington, **Upper Hutt,** 32 km north of Wellington, and **Lower Hutt,** 14 km north, are cities in their own right, with a large percentage of the population engaged in either in-town manufacturing industries (biscuits, leather goods, motor vehicles, glass, plastics, electronics, to name but a few) or research work (large units of the Dept. of Scientific and Industrial Research are based here, along with a soil bureau, and a nuclear reactor). They *were* originally spillover residential areas for Wellington, but have now grown into important industrial and commercial cities of their own.

Attractively laid out and abloom with summer flowers, and flowering trees and shrubs, it's obvious that the residents take pride in the appearance of their inner cities. If you're passing through Lower Hutt, feed your soul at the beautiful **Tutukiwi Orchid and Fern House** downtown (corner of Laings Rd. and Myrtle St., by the fountain). Open weekdays 1000-1600, weekends and public holidays 1300-1600; free admission.

For more info see the people at **Lower Hutt Public Relations and Information Centre** in The Pavilion (across from Town Hall) on Laings Rd., tel. 697-428, open Mon. to Fri. 0830-1500 and Sat. 0930-1230; or visit the **Citizen's Advice Bureau,** 34 Knights Rd., tel. 666-039, open Mon. to Fri. 0900-1600.

If you'd rather stay in the Hutt Valley than battle your way into Wellington, the excellent **Hutt Park Holiday Village** at 95 Hutt Park Rd., Moera (call 685-913 for road directions), is the last motor camp (three km from Lower Hutt P.O., 13 km from Wellington Ferry Terminal) before entering the capital city. The office is open daily from 0800-2000—pick up all the handy free info on Lower and Upper Hutt, including the several-page Lower Hutt restaurant guide and a guide to recreational facilities. All the usual facilities (everything spotlessly clean), immaculate grounds—even ducks to feed in the morning! Tentsites are $12-16 d, caravan sites $18 d; cabins start at $22 d, tourist cabins $30-33 d, tourist flats from $42. Provide your own linen.

For a good meal, try **Fishermans Table** restaurant on The Esplanade at Petone. Aside from fabulous views of the harbor and distant Wellington, you'll enjoy fish or steak specialties for around $7-10 an appetizer, $14-18 a main course, $6 dessert, and daily blackboard specials in an attractive wood, fishing net, and fishy decor.

The main north-south railway line runs through both Upper and Lower Hutt, and both are well serviced by bus companies. Pick up the *Cityline Hutt Valley Times & Routes* guide, map, and timetables from the PRO, or from Hutt Park Holiday Village.

Rimutaka Forest Park

If you're not quite ready to enter Wellington, take a sidetrack from Lower Hutt up over the hill (great views of the Hutt Valley, Wellington, and the harbor) to **Wainuiomata,** a suburb of Lower Hutt. Continue along Coast Rd. to scenic **Catchpool Valley,** part of Rimutaka Forest Park, where many short walks range from 30 minutes to two hours, there's safe swimming in the surrounding streams, and a campground. Stop at the info center on Catchpool Rd. (off Coast Rd.) about nine km from Wainuiomata, and pick up some park brochures. Longer hikes also go to **Mt. Matthews** (940 meters), and along the **Orongorongo River** (about two hours OW)—track brochures and maps are also available at the info center.

Turakirae Head

Got to see what's at the end of the road? Continue toward Turakirae Head and the **Turakirae Head Scientific Reserve**—the road ends at a carpark. From here it's a three-km walk along a private road which crosses the Orongorongo River bridge and runs along the shores of Cook Strait to the reserve. Earthquakes over the last 7,000 years (the last in 1855) raised a sequence of five beaches; platforms of large boulders separate the ridges. Amongst the dense scrub, swamp vegetation, and on the beaches grow all sorts of unusual flora (for the region) such as wild spaniards, a native viola, eyebright, and bamboo orchids. On the beach terraces one km farther along the cape lies a remnant of the *karaka* forest which once covered the area. The cape is particularly interesting in winter when up to 500 New Zealand fur seals colonize the point, getting into shape for the summer breeding season when they leave for the south of the South Island. You'll also see various kinds of lizards, black-backed gulls, gannets, spur-winged plovers, swallows, yellowhammers, chaffinches, and starlings in the reserve.

THE COASTAL ROUTE TO WELLINGTON

The most direct route south from Palmerston North is Hwy. 57 west to Levin, then Hwy. 1 down the gently curved sandy beaches of the Kapiti Coast to the harborside suburb of Porirua, and on into Wellington.

Levin

This town sits on the fertile **Horowhenua Plain** stretching from the foothills of the rugged **Tararua Ranges** to the Tasman Sea. The lush scenic area is the second largest vegetable producer in the country, but is best known for its kiwifruit, berries, apples, and cut flowers. The roads at the south end of town are lined with stands selling fruit and vegies

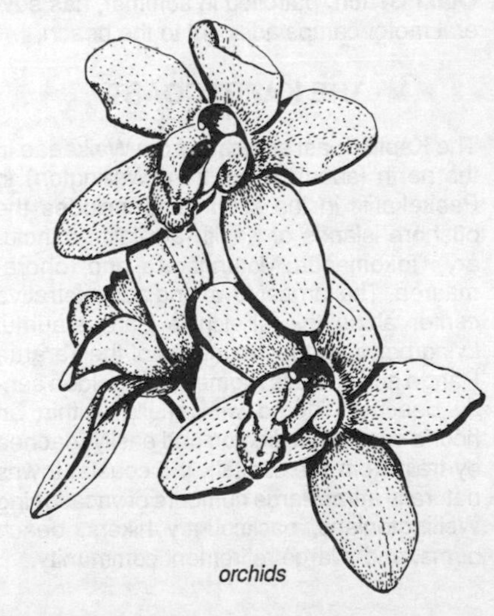

orchids

in season; quite a few of the gardens and orchards have pick-your-own specials—fun, delicious, and economical.

Otaki
A well-populated Maori area prior to European settlement in 1840, Otaki has a Maori church that shouldn't be missed. The **Rangiatea Maori Church** on Te Rauparaha St. was built in 1849. Plainer than most on the outside, its interior is beautifully decorated with red *totara* slabs and intricately designed *tukutuku* panels; open daily from 0800 till sunset. Farther along the street is **Otaki Maori Mission** with a church and buildings from the early 19th C., and memorials and graves of early missionaries. The **Otaki Museum** on Hwy. 1 contains Maori artifacts and relics from the pioneering days; open daily from 1000-1600 in the old BNZ building. Get info on the Otaki area and Kapiti Coast at the **Otaki Information Centre** on the main highway, tel. 45-073. Access to marked **hiking trails** in the Tararua Ranges is easy from Otaki if you have your own transportation. Head south out of town crossing the Otaki River and turn left onto Otaki Gorge Rd., following it to the end. The seaside resort of **Otaki Beach,** patrolled in summer, has several motor camps adjacent to the beach.

THE KAPITI COAST

The Kapiti Coast stretches from Waikanae in the north (about 58 km from Wellington) to Paekakariki in the south, and includes the offshore islands of Kapiti (a wildlife sanctuary), Tokomapua, Motungarara, and Tohoramaurea. The largest town and administrative center along this stretch is Paraparaumu. Lying between the mountains of the Tararua Range and endless kilometers of golden sandy beaches littered with shells (within an hour's drive of Wellington and easily reached by train from the capital), the coastal towns naturally attract large numbers of vacationing Wellingtonians, backcountry hikers, beach bums, and a large retirement community.

Waikanae Beach
This long flat beach is backed by sand dunes and sheltered by offshore Kapiti Island. At the northern end of Waikanae Beach lies the wreck of the fishing trawler *Phyllis,* and if you continue north you'll come to **Peka Peka Beach** with good surfcasting and a refreshing lack of commercial development. The **Waikanae River Estuary** (a reserve attracting more bird species than anywhere else on the Wellington coast), **Waimanu Marina,** and **Waimanu Lagoon** are located at the southern end of Waikanae Beach.

The **Waikanae Christian Holiday Park** on Kauri St. off Te Moana Rd., three km from the main road (tel. 36-287), has a swimming pool, tennis courts, camp store, and the usual facilities. Tentsites are $8 d, caravan sites $10 d; cabins from $18 d, tourist flats from $33 d. Waikanae also has plenty of coffee shops and restaurants to choose from.

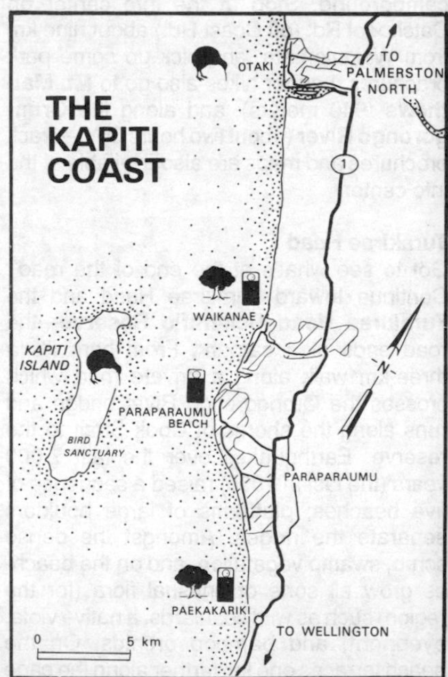

bird habitat in Queen Elizabeth Park

Wildlife Reserves And Bush Walks

Nga Manu Bird Sanctuary hosts over 50 species of native birds in 10 hectares of native bush and swamp, but the main interest is breeding the once-common red-crowned parakeet. Take a short bird-spotting walk through the bush, passing the aviaries, ponds, and through the fernery, arboretum, and gardens. Open Tues. to Fri. 1000-1630, weekends 1000-1730, tel. 4131 Waikanae; small admission charge. From the main highway at Waikanae, turn right on Te Moana Rd. just past the shopping center, then right on Ngarara Rd. (passing Waikanae Pool, cemetery, and riding school), then right again on the access road to the sanctuary. For a longer bush walk or hike through a beautiful bird-filled *kohekohe* forest with great views of Kapiti and the west coast, head east of Waikanae (a short walk from Waikanae shopping center) to the **Hemi Matenga Memorial Park Scenic Reserve** on the foothills of the Tararuas. The "walk" takes 30 minutes RT and the "track" takes three hours RT.

Mangaone Track

Part of the New Zealand Walkway network, the Mangaone Track is a fern-lover's delight (over 50 species have been identified along the route). It runs along the western foothills of the Tararua Range east of Waikanae, fords several streams along the way (expect to get wet feet), and runs through **Kaitawa Scenic Reserve.** Start at either the end of Mangaone South Rd. (eight km east of Waikanae via Reikorangi, signposted from the main road), or the end of Mangaone North Rd. (six km east of Te Horo); it's three hours OW—arrange transportation at the far end or retrace the track.

Paraparaumu

Paraparaumu is the main center on the Kapiti Coast: several motor camps, plenty of coffee lounges, takeaways, and restaurants, and a main shopping center. If you plan on staying any length of time, your first stop should be the **Kapiti Information Centre** in the Coastlands Shopping Centre Carpark (watch out for "trundlers"—a.k.a. shopping carts), tel. 88-195; open Mon. to Sat. from 0930-1530. Pick up maps of all the coastal towns, brochures on what to see and do, walking track brochures and maps, and restaurant and entertainment guides.

One of the pleasurable things to do here is a day visit to **Kapiti Island** bird sanctuary and nature reserve, but you need to write in advance for a permit (to the Dept. of Conservation, Box 5086, Wellington), or stop in at the office on Stout St., Wellington, and pick one up before setting out for the island—no permit, no landing. Originally a stronghold of Maori chief Te Rauparaha, the island became a whaling base, then an official bird sanctuary. With your permit, check at the Kapiti Information Centre for the current boat operators and their rates, tel. 88-195. Anyone interested in vintage cars should stop at the **Southwards Car Museum** on Otaihanga Rd. (off Hwy. 1) at Paraparaumu and check out the 250-car collection; open daily from 0900-1700, tel. 71-221.

Paekakariki

Paekakariki ("Hill of the Parakeet"), affectionately shortened to Paekak (sounds like Piecok) by the locals, has a good sandy beach patrolled in summer—a treasure strip for avid shell collectors—and safe swimming. The other main attractions are the attractive 638-hectare **Queen Elizabeth Park** (yes, *another* QE Park) which runs along the coast, two Maori *pas,* a **Tramway Museum** providing vintage tram rides from the Memorial Gates at McKays Crossing to the beach on weekends and public holidays 1100-1700, some old campsites of American marine camps from WW II, and the government-run **Whareroa Sheep Farm** open to the public, admission free.

For extensive views of the Kapiti Coast, Kapiti Island, and the South Island on a clear day, head up Paekakariki Hill Rd. (left off Hwy. 1 heading south) to **Summit Viewpoint.** Traveling between Wellington and Paekakariki is a snap by train—a main line ends at Paekakariki and a ticket only costs a few dollars OW. Hitching is also relatively easy due to the high amount of traffic.

Paekakariki provides budget accommodation at **Batchelors Holiday Park** adjacent to the beach at the north end of town, and very reasonable hostel accommodation at the **Barn Owl's Loft Private Hostel.** Run by Ruth Buchanan, one of New Zealand's friendliest unofficial ambassadors, the Barn Owl's Loft is a perfect base to relax or to set out for the special nooks and crannies of the Kapiti Coast with the welcome advice of your knowledgeable hostess—Ruth is a keen birdwatcher, and knows plenty about the Maoris. The hostel is small—just turn up and see if there's a spare bed. The rooms are comfortable, the kitchen fully equipped, but shared bathroom facilities; $8 pp, provide your own sleeping bag or linen. Located at 52 Tilley Rd., tel. 28-081 or 28-498; a short walk from shops and the railway station—walk south from the station to Robertston St., then right on Tilley Road. From the main highway, turn right on Beach Rd., right on Wellington, right on Cecil, then left on Tilley. If you're not in the mood to cook, try **Paekakariki Tearooms** or **Hotel Paekakariki** both on Beach Road. A couple of more expensive licensed restaurants are also in Paekakariki.

Colonial Knob Walk

Another New Zealand Walkway, Colonial Knob Walk climbs the bush- and farmland-covered hills along the coast west of Porirua and Tawa, through two scenic reserves containing some of the last remaining native forest in this area, and up to the summit of Colonial Knob (468 meters) for one of the most spectacular views of the offshore islands, Wellington peninsula, Cook Strait, and the South Island. The 7.5-km track is pretty steep in places and the upper section is exposed to the wind; it takes five to six hours RT. Start at either the Broken Hill entrance to Colonial Knob Scenic Reserve, or Elsdon Youth Camp, Raiha St., Porirua. Porirua town is mainly a suburb of Wellington—continue on down to the big city!

WELLINGTON

Wonderful windy Wellington, scenic capital of New Zealand and "City of a Thousand Views," lies perched on the edge of Cook Strait in the southwest corner of the North Island. Hemmed in by the Tararua Ranges to the north and the Rimutaka Ranges to the east, the city spills up and down bush-covered hills around the large sparkling bay of Port Nicholson. Colorful, cosmopolitan, exciting—Wellington is fun to explore whether you thrive in the great outdoors or in cozy little seaside cafes. Soft sandy beaches, sheltered coves, rocky outcrops, and boat-filled marinas line Wellington Harbour where the water is always a bright, bright blue dotted with multicolored sails. Imposing Parliament buildings, old and new, and modern skyscrapers dominate Wellington's center, in contrast with historic pioneer homes and elegant mansions that line the steep and narrow streets of the older suburbs. Scattered throughout the city are flower-filled gardens and shady parks that provide a quiet escape from the continuous hum and bustle of the busy commercial center.

According to the Maori, Wellington Harbour was first discovered in ancient times by the Polynesian navigators, Kupe and Ngahue, and it wasn't until the early 19th C. that Europeans first sailed all the way into the magnificent harbor (Capt. Cook missed the harbor entrance on his 1770 expedition but sailed through the heads in 1773). In 1826 Capt. James Herd entered in his barque *Rosanna,* landed, and officially named the harbor Port Nicholson—the name by which it's still known today. The New Zealand Company bought the land that was to become Wellington City from the Maori in 1839, and the first settlers arrived on 22 Jan. 1840—nowadays celebrated as a holiday throughout the region. In 1865, after much argument with Aucklanders, Wellington was chosen as New Zealand's official capital due to its central location, natural harbor, and population growth—the city became the seat of government, the harbor flourished, and banks, insurance companies, traders, and stock and land agents moved to the capital. Today, Wellington is the second largest city in New Zealand with an urban area population of 320,000.

Tell anyone you're going to Wellington and you're more than likely to hear horror stories about the weather—non-Wellingtonians seem to enjoy the capital city's bad reputation, rubbing it in any chance they get! Wellington's weather could best be described as...changeable. On just about any day of the year you can get bright sunshine, a sudden downpour, fog, and almost always wind. The wind, which howls in through Cook Strait, batters the city with everything from sea

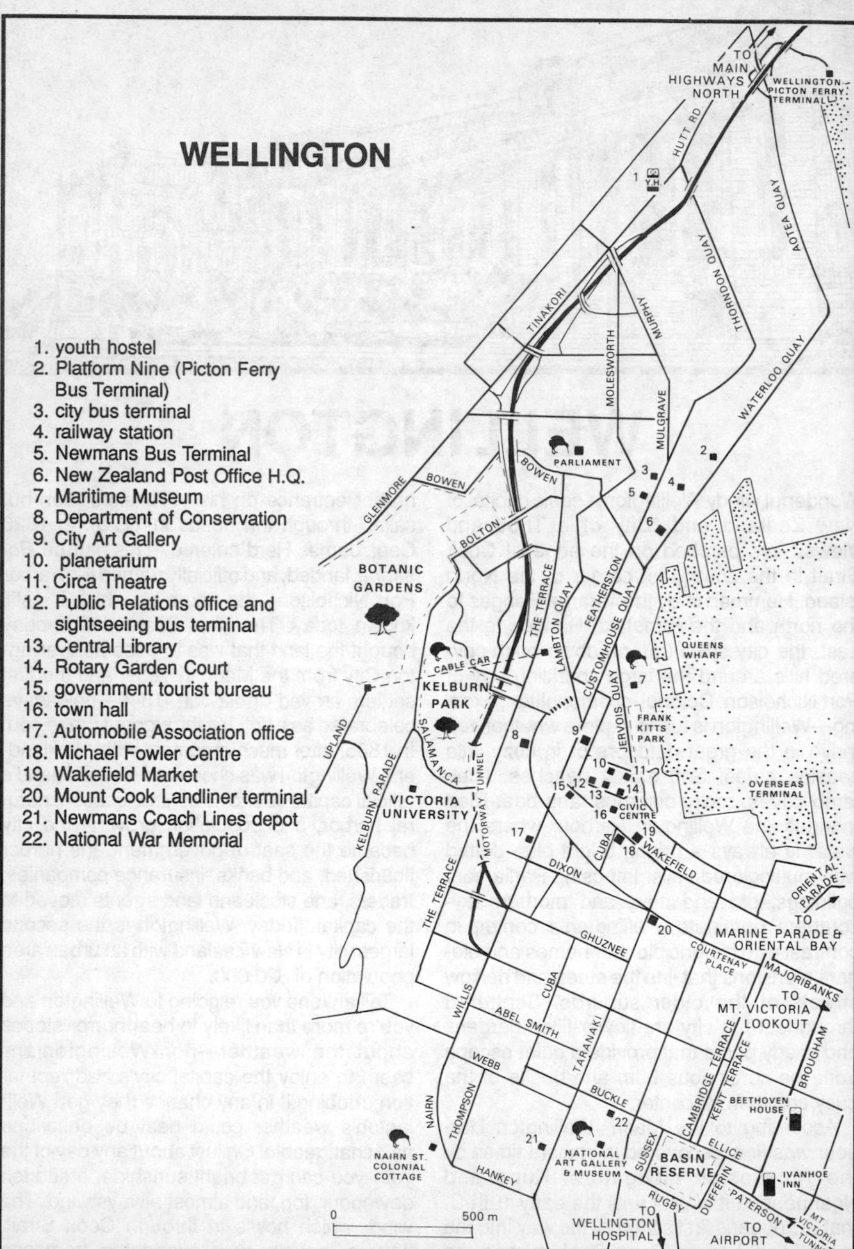
WELLINGTON
1. youth hostel
2. Platform Nine (Picton Ferry Bus Terminal)
3. city bus terminal
4. railway station
5. Newmans Bus Terminal
6. New Zealand Post Office H.Q.
7. Maritime Museum
8. Department of Conservation
9. City Art Gallery
10. planetarium
11. Circa Theatre
12. Public Relations office and sightseeing bus terminal
13. Central Library
14. Rotary Garden Court
15. government tourist bureau
16. town hall
17. Automobile Association office
18. Michael Fowler Centre
19. Wakefield Market
20. Mount Cook Landliner terminal
21. Newmans Coach Lines depot
22. National War Memorial
TO MAIN HIGHWAYS NORTH
WELLINGTON-PICTON FERRY TERMINAL
HUTT RD.
Y.H.
AOTEA QUAY
THORNDON QUAY
TINAKORI
MURPHY
MOLESWORTH
MULGRAVE
WATERLOO QUAY
PARLIAMENT
BOWEN
GLENMORE
BOLTON
THE TERRACE
LAMBTON QUAY
FEATHERSTON
CUSTOMHOUSE QUAY
QUEENS WHARF
BOTANIC GARDENS
CABLE CAR
KELBURN PARK
JERVOIS QUAY
FRANK KITTS PARK
UPLAND
SALAMANCA
MOTORWAY TUNNEL
KELBURN PARADE
VICTORIA UNIVERSITY
OVERSEAS TERMINAL
CIVIC CENTRE
CUBA
WAKEFIELD
DIXON
ORIENTAL PARADE
TO MARINE PARADE & ORIENTAL BAY
GHUZNEE
COURTENAY PLACE
MAJORIBANKS
TO MT. VICTORIA LOOKOUT
WILLIS
ABEL SMITH
TARANAKI
CAMBRIDGE TERRACE
KENT TERRACE
BROUGHAM
WEBB
THOMPSON
BUCKLE
BEETHOVEN HOUSE
NAIRN
SUSSEX
ELLICE
NAIRN ST. COLONIAL COTTAGE
NATIONAL ART GALLERY & MUSEUM
BASIN RESERVE
IVANHOE INN
HANKEY
RUGBY
DUFFERIN
PATERSON
MT. VICTORIA TUNNEL
0
500 m
TO WELLINGTON HOSPITAL
TO AIRPORT
© MOON PUBLICATIONS

breezes (most days) to Antarctic gales (not too often), but no matter the weather, there's always a scenic viewpoint, sandy beach, exotic restaurant, or snug reading nook to be found. Take a windbreaker, raincoat, and umbrella *(everyone* in Wellington has an umbrella) and you'll be ready to tackle Wellington's sights *and* elements!

SIGHTS

Civic Centre

After visiting the excellent **PRO** in the Town Hall on Wakefield St., go to the small city block that makes up the Civic Centre for sightseeing information and several inner city attractions. The **NZTP Travel Office, Central Library, Rotary Garden Court** (see below) and modern **Michael Fowler Centre** (conducted tours for $2.20 pp are available—ask at the PRO for current tour schedule) are all located on Mercer St. (off Victoria St.). Walk around the corner to Harris St. where you'll find the **Circa Theatre** (see p. 326) and **Golden Bay Planetarium,** with shows every Sun. at 1330, 1430, 1530; admission adult $4, child $2. Completing the block, walk back to Victoria St. and into the **City Art Gallery.** With a distinct character of its own, this small gallery features all sorts of fascinating modern art exhibitions; open daily 1000-1800, Wed. to 2000, it's on the other side of the road from the **Newspaper Reading Room** (open weekdays 0930-2030, Sat. 0930-1700, and Sun. 1300-1700 from May to Oct.).

Get brochures and a good city street map from the NZTP, then walk east along Mercer St. toward the waterfront. **Rotary Garden Court's** fountain and small covered tropical garden is a quiet place to study your map and get your bearings, or continue along Mercer St. to Jervois Quay and cross the road into **Frank Kitts Park**—a peaceful retreat with good harbor views and in summer on some Sundays, the site of an outdoors artists' market.

The Maritime Museum

Ahoy me hearties! If model ships (in the most intricate detail), ships' instruments, old relics from wrecks, ancient maps, sea journals, and diving gear grab your fancy, check out this small but intriguing museum. Run by the Wellington Harbour Board, it's open Mon. to Fri. 0900-1630, weekends 1300-1630, tel. 728-899; admission (shiver me timbers!) is free. Located on the waterfront—from Jervois Quay turn off at Queens Wharf and look for museum signposts.

The Kelburn Cable Car

An excellent way to get acquainted with (and fall for) the city is by taking the cable car from Cable Car Lane (off Lambton Quay) up the super-steep track to Kelburn Terminal. Three stops (a six-minute journey) along the way allow you to discover Clifton Terrace, Talavera Terrace, and Salamanca Rd., but the view from the top is by far the most spectacular. From here you can stroll through the adjacent Botanical Gardens (see below). The cable car operates Mon. to Fri. 0700-2200 (every 10 minutes), Sat. and public holidays 0920-1800, Sun. 1030-1800; $1.10 adult ($2 RT), 40 cents child OW ("Day Rover" one-day tickets also cover the cable car ride—see "Transportation," p. 330).

Botanical Gardens

Wellington's Botanical Gardens stretch for more than 26 hectares over several ridges just west above the city center. Formal rose gardens contrast with wild indigenous areas and exotic tree, flower, and shrub plantations—it's a colorful "tiptoe through the tulips" while enjoying city views. Don't miss the fabulous **Lady Norwood Rose Garden** (open daily 0930-1600) at the northern end where thousands of perfumed roses bloom from early Nov. through April (quite intoxicating on a warm summer evening), and in spring, masses of bulbs burst into a spectacular floral display. Wander through the gardens and discover a waterfall, the Begonia House (open 0930-1600), Tea House (open 0930-1600), Camellia Garden, Sunken Gardens,

Interpretive Centre in The Dell (open Mon. to Fri. 0830-1600, weekends 0930-1600, tel. 757-084), and many lookouts over the city. Get there from downtown by cable car (to Kelburn Terminal), or by a no. 12 bus to the main gates on Glenmore Street. If you're staying at the YH, it's a level walk southwest along Tinakori Street.

Victoria University

Situated high on a hill above the city, not far south of the Botanical Gardens, Victoria University's Campus commands great city views. Stroll around the well-kept grounds, past attractive old ivy-covered buildings, and if you're a rockhound, check out the **Alexander McKay Geological Museum** with its comprehensive N.Z. rock, mineral, and fossil display. It's open weekdays 0900-1600, but closed from 23 Dec. to 5 Jan.; located in the Cottan Building (the lecture block at the top of Kelburn Parade), tel. 721-000 ext. 2831.

The Beehive and War Memorial

The University's a heavy-breather hike uphill from downtown (only attempt it with a map!), but easily reached by cable car. Get off at the Salamanca Rd. stop and walk south toward Kelburn Parade and the main entrance.

Houses Of Parliament And The Beehive

Three totally different styles of architecture add interest to the Parliament buildings on Molesworth St. (north of the Civic Centre). The oldest of the three is a gothic-style stone building housing the General Assembly Library; the middle building—brick, granite, and marble—houses the House of Representatives; the most modern, an 11-story circular building aptly called "The Beehive," houses the Ministers, their staff, and the Cabinet room. Free tours are conducted several times on weekdays from the main reception desk at 0900, 1000, and 1100, and when Parliament is not in session, on Mon. through Thurs. at 1330, 1430, and 1530. If you're visiting in the afternoon and a session is on, go up to the Gallery of the Debating Chamber and see what's happening. Tours are also offered on weekends but the times change according to what's on the agenda—double check session and tour times with the PRO before you go, or tel. 749-199 ext. 8608 or 735-063.

National Museum

This excellent museum and research center (at the south end of town) consists of a **Maori Hall** focusing on the Maori lifestyle, a **Pacific Gallery** with colorful displays of art, crafts, jewelry, clothing, masks, and useful objects from Polynesia, Melanesia, Micronesia, the Philippines, Indonesia, and Australia, a **Colonial History Gallery** covering New Zealand history from 1769 to the mid-19th C., and a **Bird Gallery** featuring sea and shore birds, native and introduced waterfowl, forest and inland birds, and *wattle* birds (those with histories of more than 10 million years). This must-see Wellington attraction is a good place to visit on a Sun. or public holiday (except Christmas Day and Good Fri.) when many other attractions are closed. Open every day 1000-1645; admission free. The Museum Coffee House is open 1000-1600. Located on Buckle St., tel. 859-609. The museum doesn't look too far from the center of town on the map, but it's quite a walk if you've already been tramping the concrete for a couple of hours. The easiest way to get there is by taking a no. 3 bus to Basin Reserve, or a no. 11 bus to Buckle St. (which also goes to the Zoo).

In front of the museum is the impressive **National War Memorial** building with its Hall of Memories and Carillon; open weekdays from 1030-1215 and 1245-1730, Sun. 1300-1700, weekends and public holidays 1030-1700, admission free.

National Art Gallery

Wellington's main art gallery, above the Museum, houses fine collections of national, international, old, modern, and decorative arts, plus sculpture, and photography. It's also open daily from 1000-1645, and is another place to keep in mind for Sundays and public holidays. The main entrance is on Buckle St., tel. 859-703; get there by the museum bus.

Historic Buildings

Nairn Street Colonial Cottage, an attractive two-story house on a steep hill, is quite a hike south from city center but not far from the Art Gallery and Museum. Built in 1858 and being slowly restored, the typically small rooms, steep staircase, and fine handcraftmanship throughout this pioneer cottage give an insight into life in Wellington's colonial days. The cottage is open Wed. to Fri. from 1000-1600, on weekends and public holidays from 1300-1630; admission adult $2.30, child 50 cents. Located at 68 Nairn St. in one of the older suburbs, Te Aro, tel. 894-122; from the Museum walk west along Buckle St. to Taranaki St. and turn left. Turn right on Webb St., left on Thompson, right on Hankey and immediately right on Nairn. The cottage is on the left side. Notice the mixture of assorted architectural styles in this hilly area.

Antrim House is the headquarters of the New Zealand Historic Places Trust; go there for info if you'd like to visit any of the many historic homes and buildings scattered around Wellington. The mansion itself is one of the best preserved large townhouses of the Edwardian period, with its elegant exterior and kauri-panelled interior; the grounds and a section of the house are open to the public on weekdays during regular office hours. Located at 63 Boulcott St., just south of the Civic Centre, tel. 724-341; open weekdays 1000-1630.

Mount Victoria

The best place for orienting yourself to the lay-out of Wellington is from the top of Mt. Victoria (194 meters), southeast of the city center. The summit lookout provides a 360-degree panorama and one of the best city-scapes of Wellington (unreal at night), and it's easy to get there by bus (a 15-minute ride from downtown, weekdays only) or car (get a map first!), or via the scenic bus tour that leaves from the PRO (see "Tours" below). Catch a no. 20 bus at the railway station (every hour Mon. to Fri.), or on Lambton Quay, Willis St., Cuba St., Manners St., or Courtenay Place; $1.90 OW to the summit. If you'd rather walk back down, several paths take at least 20 minutes through the forested town belt and suburb of Mount Victoria, one of the oldest city suburbs (many colonial-style homes), to Courtenay Place where you can catch the bus back. If you're driving or cycling (guaranteed to get your old heart a-pumpin') from city center, take Jervois Quay south to Wakefield St. and turn left, then right on Kent Terrace and left on Majoribanks Street. Turn left on Hawker St. and follow the signs to the lookout. It's also visited every day by scenic bus tours—ask at the PRO for details.

Marine Drive

Thirty-km Marine Drive, "one of the world's best coastal drives" and a route anyone with wheels and a camera shouldn't miss, runs from **Oriental Bay** (southeast of the city center) along the inner harbor and outer shoreline to **Owhiro Bay.** The route takes you past at least 20 small bays and most of Welling-

Wellington from the top of Mt. Victoria

ton's sheltered sandy **beaches,** past built-up areas where striking homes perch on precarious sites high above the road, and through surprisingly wild areas that seem quite uninhabited. The views along the route are stunning on a bright sunny day, but the locals claim that the drive is most spectacular during a southerly storm (preferably a gale!). Start at Oriental Bay, an area of coffee shops, fashionable restaurants, and a strip of sandy beach where the younger set, look-at-me's, and people-watchers in general gather in large numbers (particularly in summer) to check each other out—it's a good place to find out the current Wellington trends in fashion, hairstyles, music, and flirting!

From Oriental Bay, Marine Drive is signposted here and there, but it really helps if you have a good, detailed map of the city center and outer suburbs to Cook Strait (and a compass, tent, two days' food ration, water, and flare...!). The return route to the city sounds simple enough but has the potential to become a nightmare without a map—from Owhiro Bay take the road through Happy Valley to the suburb of Brooklyn (about 28 km), turn right on Brooklyn Rd., go down the hill and straight ahead onto Upper Willis St. (passing the YWCA on the right) and continue straight into the city center.

Tours And Cruises

If you're short of time and want a crash course on Wellington, take the worthwhile **City Transport Scenic Bus Tour,** one of the "red buses" operated by Wellington City Council. The 2½-hour tour includes many of Wellington's main attractions and a commentary on local landmarks and history; adult $17.20, child $8.60, family of four $42, departing daily at 1400 from the PRO on Mercer St. (also at 1000 in summer). Several other operators do similar tours of the city (and farther afield) starting around $16.50 pp—pick up the brochures at the PRO or NZTP Travel Office.

A **harbor cruise** with **Bluefin Launches** is a great way to appreciate the oceanside aspect of Wellington. Cruises of varying duration are offered day and evening throughout the summer, departing from Harbour Gallery off Customhouse Quay (opposite the end of Whitmore St., a block south of the train station). For more info ask at the PRO or tel. 698-203. **Harbour City Cruises** operates harbor sightseeing trips ($20 pp) twice a day throughout the summer on the MV ***Glenroyal***, departing from Greta Point, tel. 852-466. Or choose from their other cruises—BBQ ($38 pp), Buffet ($38 pp), or Finger Food ($26 pp). For more info contact the office at 124 Oriental Parade, or tel. 852-466.

Another fun and inexpensive way to appreciate Wellington's harbor aspect is to catch the Days Bay-Eastbourne ferry (adult $5 OW, senior $4, child $2.50) from Queen's wharf (between Jervois and Customhouse quays) to Days Bay. At Days Bay visit Williams Park and the beach (favorite summertime hangouts for Wellingtonians toting BBQs and picnic lunches), local shops and galleries, eat at the restaurant, or go for nearby bush walks; buy your ticket from one of the Government Printing Office bookshops at 25-27 Mercer St. or on Mulgrave Street. For more info tel. 737-505.

WELLINGTON WALKS

City

Several city walkway routes, devised by the Parks and Recreation Dept., encourage walking through some of the most attractive areas of the "Harbour City." Pick up your free city street map, the various free brochures *(Northern Walkway, Southern Walkway,* etc.) containing route descriptions and maps, a *Walking Around Wellington* pamphlet, and a *Discover Wellington* brochure which contains scenic driving and walking routes; all are available at the PRO. Another very handy brochure, *Bus & Walk,* is put out by Wellington City Transport and Parks & Recreation department of Wellington City Council. It lists many of the most popular local walkways, how to get to them by bus, what to see, where the walks finish, and how to get back.

The **Otari Open-Air Native Plant Museum** is a must-walk attraction, less than 20 minutes by bus northwest of the city center. Several walkways, graded and color-coded according to length and difficulty, run through this unique sanctuary "devoted solely to the cultivation and preservation of indigenous New Zealand plants." Eighty hectares of native bush and two hectares of cultivated garden contain more than 1,200 plant species, and the area is alive with native birds. Natural forest and cultivated gardens, rock garden and fishpond, fernery, alpine garden, and numerous picnic spots are just some of the features along the various trails; native wood pigeons, fantails, silver eyes, and kingfishers can often be spotted, along with introduced magpies, thrushes, goldfinches, and starlings; the beautiful native songbird, the *tui,* is often heard but rarely seen. To get there take a no. 14 Wilton bus from the city to the main entrance at the junction of Wilton Rd. and Gloucester St.; open daily from dawn to dusk—to get the best out of your visit, take a picnic lunch.

Regional

The six-km (RT) **Makara Track,** part of the New Zealand Walkways network, starts and finishes at Makara Beach (16 km northwest of Wellington). This popular walk lets hikers experience some remote and rugged coastal scenery, fabulous views, hilly farmland, and good swimming at sheltered beaches. The "track" requires good fitness and takes about four hours RT; note that the inner section is closed during Aug. and Sept. for lambing. Wear good boots, and take warm clothing (you'll be exposed to the wind, and quite possibly blown along the track in places!), and water—nothing drinkable along the route. It's also another good place to take a picnic. To get there from Wellington you need your own transportation and a detailed map (the PRO provides a free brochure); head for Karori Rd. in the western suburb of Karori West. Take Makara Rd. west and continue to Makara Beach where the walkway is clearly signposted.

ACCOMMODATION

BUDGET

Wellington Youth Hostel

The centrally located YH is fun and convenient. A short walk downhill takes you to the Houses of Parliament (the railway station is not much farther), and the Botanical Gardens and cable car are also within walking distance. For $14 pp the old, rambling, two-story building with large kitchen/dining area and separate living room (open all day) provides plenty of elbow room and an easy-going atmosphere—getting to know fellow travelers or finding a traveling companion is particularly easy. An overflow building is not far away. Buy your milk, eggs, bread, frozen meat, and fruit juices at reasonable prices at the hostel office.

The YH is located at 40 Tinakori Rd., tel. 736-271. To get there by bus or train from the railway station, head up Molesworth St. (passing The Beehive) and cross the motorway, turn right at the traffic lights onto Tinakori Rd.; from the ferry terminal by bike or car, follow the signs to the city, turn right at the second set of traffic lights onto Molesworth St., cross the motorway and at the traffic lights turn right on Tinakori Rd.; from the ferry terminal on foot, turn left out of the terminal, walk about 100 meters and cross the road bridge over the railway tracks to the right, turn left at Hutt Rd. and take the steps up to Tinakori Rd.—about a 10-minute walk.

Maple Lodge

Located in the southeast suburb of Mount Victoria (within walking distance of the Museum and Art Gallery), these laid-back accommodations have a range of rates to suit everyone. Prices depend on the room's location in the building, number of beds per room, and whether you're willing to share a room, and provide your own linen: from $14 pp for dormitory rooms (provide your own sleeping bag), $22 s, $29 d (linen provided). Communal facilities, kitchen and dining room, TV lounge, washer and dryer ($2.50 a load), and private parking at the back. Non-smoking building. The hotel's locked annex is a real bonus—store your excess luggage for free until you return (very handy if you're going down to the South Island and don't know how long you'll be gone). A small store up the street sells all the basics; takeaway places and several bars are within walking distance.

Located at 52 Ellice St., Mt. Victoria, tel. 853-771, this area is safe by day but not recommended for women on their own at night—get there by bus before dark, by taxi after. Reservations accepted. The easiest approach is by bus from the railway station bus terminal to Basin Reserve (many bus routes pass Basin Reserve—ask at the terminal), then walk up Ellice St. (one of the main streets off the square). By car from city center, head south along the harborfront Jervois Quay, turn left onto Wakefield St. and continue to the end. At the traffic lights turn right onto Kent Terrace and at the square (notorious for rowdy cricket matches in summer), turn left onto Ellice Street.

Beethoven House

Beethoven House is usually crowded, and crammed with bodies spilling out into the overflow building during peak visitor periods; it's also one of the few places that will accept late arrivals from the South Island ferry. Smokers are not made welcome (signs on the door make this quite clear!). Dormitory rooms (provide your own sleeping bag), communal bathroom facilities, good kitchen but no laundry facilities, guest lounge and music room. Courtyard and tea-house are out back, "beer garden" in front. Dorms $13 pp which includes breakfast. No reservations taken.

Located on the southern side of the city at 89 Brougham St. (not far from Ivanhoe Inn), Mount Victoria, tel. 842-226. To get there take city bus no. 2 to Miramar or Kilburnie which runs along Brougham St.; by car follow Jervois Quay along the waterfront then left onto Wakefield Street. Turn right at the traffic lights on Kent Terrace, left on Majoribanks St., then right onto Brougham Street.

Camping Out

The closest motor camp, **Hutt Park Holiday Village,** is about 13 km north of Wellington in the adjacent city of Lower Hutt (see p. 310)—well worth the 15-minute drive; take the Petone exit off the motorway along The Esplanade and Waione St., following signs to Wainuiomata (not Petone). Cross the river, at the roundabout turn right on Seaview Rd. toward Eastbourne, then left on Parkside Rd. to the motorcamp. It's a good idea to phone ahead at tel. 685-913 to reserve a cabin/tourist flat (plenty of campsites) if you're arriving late. The camp facilities include spotlessly clean bathroom blocks, kitchen, coin-operated commercial-size washers and dryers, a TV room, and a playground that would keep any energetic rugrat happy! Tentsites from $12 s, $16 d, caravan site $18, cabins $22-33 (you supply linen), tourist flats $42. Some cabins have their own cooking facilities. If you're heading north via the coastal route to Palmerston North or Wanganui, you'll find many motor camps beside the attractive sandy beaches of the Kapiti Coast (see p. 312).

PRIVATE HOTELS AND GUESTHOUSES

Most of the more reasonable hotels and guesthouses are located on the south side of the city and provide communal bath (most with sinks in each room) and guest TV lounge. **Rowena Budget Hotel** offers rooms for $20 s, $38.50 d (triples and dorm also available), several lounges, Continental or cooked breakfast from $3 pp, and off-street parking at 115 Brougham St., tel. 857-872. Next door **Richmond Guest House** provides B&B for $30 pp and cooking facilities (takeaways close by); 116 Brougham St., tel. 858-529.

Hampshire House has breakfast available and rooms with shared facilities from $40 s, $55 twin, $58 d, and self-contained units from $66-75 d, on the corner of The Terrace and Ghuznee St., tel. 843-051. **Terrace Travel Hotel** provides a TV lounge, rooms with tea- and coffee-making facilities from $35 s, $45 d or twin, Back Pack Cabins from $17 pp, and Continental or cooked breakfast available, at 291 The Terrace, tel. 829-506.

Tinakori Lodge is a locally recommended B&B at 182 Tinakori Rd. (opposite the Hawkestone St. ramp over the motorway), tel. 733-478. All rooms have handbasins, tea- and coffee-making facilities, TV, from $55 s, $66 d or twin, $88 triple. Laundry facilities also available.

Motels And Hotels

Wellington has an enormous number of average-to-expensive motels and hotels scattered throughout the city, and its share of top-of-the-line hotels in the city center. If these are your preference (or you feel like a splurge), head for the NZTP Travel Office (they have complete listings of Wellington accommodations and make bookings) in the Civic Centre or the PRO (listings but no bookings) on Wakefield St. (see "Information," p. 328).

Trekkers Hotel Motel has plenty of rooms, each with its own handbasin, a TV lounge on the ground floor, spa and sauna, house bar, and all meals available in the cafe or licensed restaurant. Rates from $25 pp (bunkrooms), $47.20 s (shared bathroom), $74.60 d or twin (rooms with private facilities also available); on Dunlop Terrace (off Vivian St. or Upper Cuba St.), tel. 852-153. If you want to stay in one of the many first-class hotels in Wellington (rooms from $150-248 s), try the **West Plaza** at 110 Wakefield St. (tel. 731-440), the **James Cook Hotel** on The Terrace (tel. 725-865), the **Parkroyal Hotel Wellington** at 360 Oriental Parade (tel. 859-949), **Plimmer Towers Hotel** on the corner of Boulcott St. and Gilmer Terrace (tel. 733-750), or the most recently constructed, concrete and glass, downtown **Plaza International Hotel** at 148-176 Wakefield St. (tel. 733-900), next to the Michael Fowler Centre.

FOOD AND ENTERTAINMENT

Good cafes and restaurants are found almost everywhere you look in Wellington. For a fairly large selection of cafes, BYO and fully licensed restaurants, and the average prices you can expect in each place, pick up the handy dining guide at the PRO. The tourist paper *Capital Times* is another good source of dining-out and entertainment info. Although no city in N.Z. is particularly known for its exciting nightlife and swinging entertainment, Wellington has more than anywhere else (except Auckland)—so put on your dancing shoes, get out your credit cards, and live it up now while you still have the chance!

CAFES

Greenock Coffee Lounge is at 110 Lambton Quay at the back of a small arcade (signposted "Masons Lane, Steps To The Terrace" with a branch of the ANZ Bank at the arcade entrance). A takeaway section with all sorts of delicious sandwiches is downstairs, and upstairs in the sit-down restaurant you can feast on mouth-watering meat and vegie pies (made on the premises daily), vegetarian dishes, and all sorts of salads, sandwiches, desserts, and good coffee. The prices are reasonable, the service quick and friendly, and they're open Mon. to Fri. from 0730-1600.

The Great New Zealand Soup Kitchen offers breakfast, brunch, lunch (average $4.50-8), and takeaways in attractive woodsy surroundings. The house specialties are soups, salads, muffins, and sandwiches; open Mon. to Thurs. 0730-1500 and Fri. 0730-1930. Located at 32 Waring Taylor St. (between Lambton and Customhouse quays), around the corner from a park with an impressively large and ever-trickling water sculpture. Green-and-white **Glossops Eaterie** at 149 Willis St. (in the section between Dixon and Manners sts.) serves soups, sandwiches, salads, main dishes, and desserts. Expect to pay from $5-11 for lunch, from $5.50-13 for dinner. Open seven days 1130-1430 and 1830-2130.

The upstairs **San Souci Lounge** on Manners St. (near Taranaki St.) is open Mon. to Thurs. 0630-1630, Fri. 0630-2000, Sat. 0700-1300, offering a really good selection of tearoom fare—soups, sandwiches, salad bar, sweet treats—and on Fri. nights a smorgasbord dinner for only $8 pp. **The Victoria Cafe** at 59 Brougham St. (south of city center on the same street as Beethoven House) is open Tues. to Sat. from 1100-1400 for lunch (average main $8.50) and from 1800-2200 for dinner. Nutritious three-course dinners, such as soup, quiche and salad, dessert, and coffee can be bought for under $20 pp if you choose carefully. The cafe features healthy food at reasonable prices, has a BYO license, and there's live entertainment every Fri. and Sat. night.

The Brasserie in the Michael Fowler Centre on Wakefield St. has excellent cafe fare. Sample one of the crisp salads or tasty sandwiches, pick from an assortment of "tearoom-type" goodies, go for the special hot meal of the day (always good value at around $4-6.50), and waddle out after a delectable dessert and a good cappucino! Another bonus—it's open during the day on weekends.

Lunch On The Run

The popular **Jaco's Health Food** takeaway shop, located in Cablecar Arcade (off Lambton Quay), offers all sorts of fresh salads, smoothies, and juices. Put some pep in your day with their delicious "energy tub"—yogurt, muesli (granola), nuts, dried apricots, coconut, and honey, for several dollars a serving. **Rainbow Health Food** in the Grand Arcade is another good place to go for an assortment of colorful $3-4 salads, fruit, and yogurt. It's mainly a takeaway shop but you can also eat at the small lunch bar. Open Mon. to Fri. 0700-1730.

On Fri., Sat., and Sun. you can choose from a wide assortment of takeaway foods at **Wakefield Market,** the brightly painted, several-story building on the corner of Jervois Quay and Taranaki Street. Many of Wellington's young and trendy hang out here on weekends, particularly on Sun. afternoon—shopping for clothes, jewelry, the latest haircuts, and nicknacks—along with hamburgers, hot dogs, sandwiches, ice cream, you name it!

PUB MEALS

Pub meals are usually filling and good value, with the added bonus of a bar and entertainment of some sort (usually big-screen movies or rock videos weeknights, disco or live music Fri. and Sat. nights). **The Southern Cross Tavern** on Abel Smith St. (south of city center) serves lunches from 1200-1400 and dinners from 1800-2000—and the food is great! Try one of their pepper, garlic, or BBQ steaks with french fries and unlimited salad bar for around $8 pp. They also serve lamb chops, ham steaks, and various seafood specials starting at $5.50 pp. From downtown take Willis St. south to Abel Smith Street.

The Beef and Brew Restaurant is above the Clarendon Hotel Tavern at 45 Taranaki St. and the corner of Courtenay Place (a couple of blocks southeast of the Civic Centre). Beef and Yorkshire pudding (the specialty), open beef sandwiches, chicken and chips, fish, and ham steaks range from $4-8 at lunch (1200-1400); dinner is slightly more expensive but not more than $12 a main course (1800-2030). On Thurs., Fri., and Sat. nights the pub rocks to live entertainment.

The familiar **Cobb & Co. Restaurant** on Willis St., tel. 739-139, provides the usual good family-style meals at reasonable prices (lunch from $8, a main course at dinner averages $10-15). Breakfast is available from 0700-1000, and the a la carte menu is served from 1000-2200 seven days a week.

RESTAURANTS

That's Natural caters to vegetarians, and people on special diets or with allergies—serving macrobiotic, vegetarian, raw foods, seafood, and poultry. Lunch ranges from $3-6, dinner from $7-11; located at 88 Manners St. Mall.

Chevys on Dixon St., open seven days a week, has all sorts of dishes ranging from budget to moderate ($4.50-15), and it's extremely popular. Look for the gigantic neon cowboy marking the entrance. Walk along Willis St. and you'll discover a number of good restaurants. The **Bengal Tiger** on Willis is the place to go if you're hankering for a spicy Indian meal. They can make their dishes mild or spicy to suit your fancy; prices range from $10.50-14.50 for a main course. It's open Mon. to Fri. for lunch, Mon. to Sat. for dinner, tel. 829-195.

In more of the splurge category, **The Settlement Restaurant** is open Mon. to Fri. 0900-1700 for coffee, 1200-1400 for lunch, and Mon. to Sat. from 1800 for dinner, at 155 Willis St., tel. 858-920. Enjoy a variety of dishes amongst the stunning all-wood and stained-glass interior furnished with antiques, and decorated with plants and dried flowers. Dress up for dinner. Just along the road is **Glossops Eaterie** (see "Cafes" above). And then there's the brick, wood, and poster-decorated **Armadillos,** another popular spot with locals (good music). Try their oyster entrees for $12, venison steaks for $20, or deliver some pizzazz to your mouth with their spicy Mexican dishes.

For peaceful water views, seafood cuisine (most of the fish is caught fresh daily by the restaurant-operated trawler), and somewhat of a splurge, head for **The Shorebird Restaurant** at Greta Point (southeast of the city around the harbor). Gorge yourself on their seafood platter in a half clam shell, house specialty, in rustic kauri wood and brass surroundings. An average main course is around $17. Open every day but Sat. for lunch from 1200-1400, daily for dinner from 1800, reservations not required; located at 301 Evans Bay Parade, Greta Point, tel. 862-017.

Another good place to part with extra cash is the **Grain Of Salt Restaurant.** Fashionably located at 232 Oriental Parade, French cuisine (mains from $27; expect to pay $150 for dinner and wine for two) and excellent harbor views are the order of the day. Open Tues. to Fri. for lunch from 1200, every night for dinner from 1800. Reservations recommended at tel. 848-642; put on your best dress, mama!

If you're heading out to Hutt Park Holiday Village (see "Accommodation") you may want to sample the fishy fare or steaks (mains $14-18 plus blackboard specials) at **Fishermans Table.** The bar and restaurant are fully licensed (the combo of several drinks and the decidedly fishy decor may have you believing you're inside a boat!), and if you're lucky enough to nab one of the window tables, the view of Wellington sparkling across the harbor is quite magnificent on a bright sunny day. It's on The Esplanade at Petone; open daily from 1100 for lunch and dinner.

Fast Food

Whether it be chicken, pizza, or hamburgers you desire, you'll find **Kentucky Fried Chicken, Pizza Hut,** and **McDonald's** all on Manners St. (between Willis and Victoria sts.). This area hums on Sat. nights.

ENTERTAINMENT

Sources

If you're in the mood for some action, pick up the free tourist paper *Capital Times*. The daily newspapers list all the current movies, and the **PRO** on Wakefield St. advertises current entertainment on the notice boards inside, and has an electronic marketing unit which provides 24-hour info (handy when the office is closed); ask the staff what they suggest in the way of entertainment—the most reliable and up-to-date source of info around. To find out what annual events and public holiday happenings are going on, pick up the free *Greater Wellington Region Calendar of Events.* It also lists museums and galleries (and their hours), sightseeing suggestions by boat and airplane, and contains a veritable fund of other info within its colorful cover.

Major Events

Every other March (1990, 1992, etc.) Wellington celebrates **New Zealand International Festival of the Arts; Nissan Mobil 500 waterfront street race** is held every year in early Dec; you'll find **Summer City Festival** in Wellington's city parks and gardens every Jan., and the **Wellington Cup** and associated festival in late January. Get all the nitty gritties at the PRO.

Theater And Dance

The **Circa Theatre** at 1 Harris St. (next to the Planetarium in the Civic Centre) puts on performances Tues. through Sat. nights at 2000 and Sun. at 1600, tel. 728-778. Book through the State Opera House Agency at tel. 850-832, or buy your ticket at the door Tues. through Sat. nights 1830-2000 or on Sun. afternoon 1430-1600. Other performance venues to check out are: the **Downstage Theatre** on the corner of Cambridge Terrace and Courtenay Place, tel. 849-639; the **Repertory** at 13 Dixon St., tel. 850-832; **Shoestring Theatre** at Victoria University, Kelburn Parade; the **Depot** at 12A Alpha St., tel. 844-531; **Bats** on Kent Terrace, tel. 894-507; **St. James,** Courtenay Place, tel. 849-767; and the **Michael Fowler Centre** on Wakefield St. in the Civic Centre (there's a Bass booking center inside where you can book for all sorts of venues throughout Wellington and the entire country), tel. 723-088. Expect to pay $5-20 for a theater ticket. Dance performances are frequently held at the **State Opera House** off Manners St., tel. 850-832.

Music

Bands come and go, as do venues, but some places have live music on a regular basis (good bands fetch a small cover charge). Check out **Clarendon Tavern** on the corner of Taranaki St. and Courtenay Place, tel. 842-864 (Thurs. through Sat. nights); **The Folk Centre** at 10 Holland St. (off Tory St.), tel. 850-617; **The Pulse** upstairs bar in the Clyde Quay Tavern at 5860 Oriental Parade, tel. 845-498; the **Terminus Tavern** on the corner of Courtenay Place and Taranaki St., tel. 845-689; and the **Upstage Cafe,** in the Willis St. Village (upstairs), 142-148 Willis St., tel. 842-589. The easiest way to find bands on the weekends is to follow your ears!

Movie Theaters
Embassy, Kent Terrace, tel. 847-657; **Mid-City Cinemas One, Two, and Three,** Manners St., tel. 843-567; **Kings,** 17 Dixon St., tel. 847-099; **Paramount International,** 29 Courtenay Place, tel. 843-553; **Penthouse,** 205 Ohiro Rd., tel. 843-157; **Regent Theatres one, two, and three,** Manners Mall, tel. 725-182; and the university theater at **Victoria University.**

Summer City
December through Feb., Wellington comes alive with its annual festival, **Summer City.** To find out what's happening where, pick up a brochure from the PRO, check out the ads in the local newspapers, listen to the local radio stations, or call Summer City at tel. 851-929/853-603. Lunchtime activities take place in the inner city parks and malls, special day and evening entertainment (live concerts, jazz bands, dancing, country hoedowns, crazy competitions, entertainment for the kids, and much much more) happens at The Dell (next to the Rose Gardens) in the Botanical Gardens, and just before Christmas, Carols by Candlelight sessions spontaneously combust at several locations around town—an enjoyable event on a warm summer's eve.

Local Holiday
January 22 is the provincial anniversary and annual holiday for the entire Wellington area including Lower and Upper Hutt. On this day you'll be hard pressed to find *anything* open, so stock up on food, drinks, and essentials on Jan. 21 or thereabouts. (When the holiday falls Fri. through Sun. it's usually observed on the following Mon.—if it falls Tues. through Thurs. it's observed on the preceding Monday.) No particular events take place—everyone just takes the day off! If you don't need a shop or service, it's a good time to explore Wellington's non-commercial attractions—all the locals seem to take this opportunity to leave town, but you're likely to find fellow travelers wandering vacantly around the inner city area (hungry and thirsty) trying to figure out why it's closed!

The American Super Bowl
If you're interested in seeing the Super Bowl live from the States (last Sun. in Jan.), head for the **Prince of Wales Tavern** on Ellice St., Mt. Victoria (an easy walk from Ivanhoe Inn). In one of the public bars they have a big-screen TV hooked up to a satellite dish, and you'll find the bar packed from opening to closing time with *all* the American football enthusiasts in Wellington, and a surprisingly large number of interested New Zealanders (women are outnumbered by men approximately 20 to one!). Get there early for a seat.

SERVICES AND INFORMATION

Urgent
In an **emergency,** tel. 111 for ambulance, police, or fire. For a **doctor,** ask the manager of your lodgings, or call the Free Ambulance at tel. 722-999 for the nearest on-duty doctor. **Wellington Hospital** is on Riddiford St., Newton, tel. 855-999. For emergency **dental** services, tel. 727-072. The **urgent pharmacy** is located at 59 Cambridge Terrace (southeast of the city center), tel. 858-810; hours Mon. to Thurs. 0600-2300, Fri. and Sat. 0900-2300, Sun. and holidays 1000-2300. For urgent pharmacies in other areas look in the telephone book.

Regular
N.Z. Post Office HQ is on Customhouse Quay; the postal section is open Mon. to Thurs. 0800-1730, Fri. 0800-2030, and Sat. 0830-1130; telegraph, telex, and toll-call telephone booths are open Mon. to Fri. 0800-1730 (at other times go to the fifth floor of the Courtenay Place P.O.). If you're a stamp collector, don't miss a visit to the **philatelic**

sales section of the p.o. at 58-66 Willis St. where you can buy some really stunning old and new editions. The impressive building that houses **Wellington Central Library** is on Mercer St.; open Mon. to Thurs. 0930-2030, Fri. till 2100, and Sat. till 1700.

The **WCC Victoria Street Ladies' Rest Rooms** provides a few handy facilities apart from the obvious, including a lounge, use of a shower or washrooms and towel for $2, use of an iron for 15 minutes for 70 cents, and a parcel-minding service during the day for $1 a parcel! Located on Mercer St. next to the PRO; open Mon. to Thurs. 0800-1800, Fri. 0800-2100, closed weekends. The **Mens' Rest Rooms** are behind the PRO on Mercer Street.

Shopping

Regular shopping hours are Mon. to Thurs. from 0900-1700, Fri. till 2000, and Sat. 0900-1200. Tourist shops, milkbars, and takeaways stay open longer hours and are generally open throughout the weekend. **Government Bookshops,** good sources of all sorts of info on New Zealand, are found by the NZTP office on Mercer St. and on Mulgrave St., tel. 737-320; open Mon. to Fri. 0900-1700, till 2000 on Fri. nights. The **Duty-Free Shop** next to the Air New Zealand building on Grey St. sells the usual jewelry, watches, perfume, cameras, radios, clothing, etc., and typical N.Z. products, but the prices aren't particularly cheap—if you shop around you may find better. It's open Mon. to Fri. from 0830-1730. The Duty-Free Shop at the airport is open for last-minute grabs on all overseas departures.

For equipment, supplies, books, the latest magazines, and general info on all outdoor sports throughout N.Z., head for the **Living Simply** shop in the Phoenix Centre, Lambton Quay, tel. 728-459. They also sell the excellent topographical maps put out by the Survey and Lands Dept. (from $7 apiece)—a must if you're heading for any of the National Parks.

INFORMATION

Wellington Public Relations Office

This main source of city and regional info is in the Town Hall on Wakefield St., tel. 735-063. Open every day 0900-1700, including public holidays, the knowledgeable staff dispense free brochures and pamphlets on attractions, walks, and accommodation, their dining-out booklet, all the latest entertainment and transportation info, and a city street map. Sightseeing bus tours covering many of Wellington's main attractions with guided commentary also leave from outside the PRO daily. If the office is closed, use the electronic marketing unit which provides 24-hour info service. What more could you ask?

NZTP Travel Office

Another excellent source of info on Wellington *and* the entire country, the staff books for everything from local accommodation (small fee) and entertainment to white-water rafting trips or guided tours in the South Island; they're located on Mercer St., open Mon. to Thurs. 0830-1700, Fri. 0830-2000, and Sat. 0930-1230, tel. 739-269.

Airport Information

The info center in the Domestic Terminal is open Mon. to Fri. 0730-2000, Sat. 0800-1900, and Sun. 0900-2000. The exuberant staff will load you up with info on everything you need to know (and more!). If the office is closed when you arrive, check out the useful notice boards nearby. Store excess baggage in the airport luggage lockers (20-50 cents) near the info center.

Sunday Afternoons And Public Holidays

If you arrive in Wellington on a Sun. afternoon or public holiday and everything seems closed, ask for directions to the PRO on Wakefield Street. If the PRO's closed, use the Electronic Marketing Unit (EMU) outside where push-button tourist info is always available.

International Advisory Service
Anyone who doesn't speak English too well can call the International Advisory Service, tel. 856-438, or see them at 314 Upper Willis Street. Staffed by multilingual volunteers, this service provides assistance to visitors and migrants to New Zealand. Ask them if they still hold monthly **International Coffee Time** sessions in the first floor Conference Room of the Friendship Centre at 52-56 Boulcott Street. At these you can hear guest speakers, see films or slides, and participate in discussions—the idea is for New Zealanders and other nationalities to meet and get to know a little about each other; small admission charge to cover refreshments.

Maps And Other Sources
The **Dept. of Conservation** is on Boulcott Street. The **Survey And Lands Dept.** map center is at 274 Wakefield St., tel. 735-022, but if you want to buy some of the vast range of topographical New Zealand maps, go to the Charles Fergusson Building on Bowen St., tel. 735-022. Another source of maps and road info is the **Automobile Association** on Willis near Dixon. **The Newspaper Reading Room** is on Victoria St. and open Mon. to Fri. from 0930-2030, Sat. 0930-1700, Sun. 1300-1700 May to October.

TRANSPORTATION

GETTING THERE

Wellington is, not surprisingly, one of the easiest places in New Zealand to get to by public transportation. It has an international airport, local bus and long-distance coach depots, railway station, overseas cruiseliner terminal, ferry terminal, a fast motorway leading in and out of the city, all the major car rental companies, and taxis. **Air New Zealand** flies into Wellington from all the main centers in the country; **Ansett New Zealand** flies in from other major cities. **Air Nelson** provides daily service to Palmerston North, Blenheim, Nelson, Motueka, and Westport; **Safe Air** links Christchurch and the Chatham Islands with Wellington; and **Skyferry** links Wellington with Blenheim and Picton. **Mount Cook Landliner, InterCity,** and **Newmans** all provide coach service into the capital. **InterCity** runs train service to Wellington from Auckland via Chateau and Palmerston North, from Auckland via Waitomo and Hamilton, and from Gisborne and Napier via Palmerston North. Regular suburban train services run from Paraparaumu (on the northwest coast) and the Hutt Valley (central north) to Wellington. Ferries (up to four sailings a day subject to weather and sea conditions) come across Cook Strait from the South Island and dock at the Aotea Quay Terminal.

Once you're in Wellington, it's just as easy to get around by local transportation—bus service is excellent and numerous special fares encourage further exploration by bus. The best bonus of all is the large number of places where you can get all the transportation info you need, quickly and easily. See the people at the PRO first—on the off chance that they can't answer your question, they'll tell you who can and where. Also collect the very handy *Bus & Walk* brochure which lists many of the local walkways, how to get to them, what to see, where the walk ends, and how to get back, along with bus routes to swimming pools, beaches, major sporting parks, and Wellington Zoo; the brochure is free!

GETTING AROUND

Buses And Trains
The Wellington City Transport Dept. has come up with some special deals to encourage you to use local public transportation. Each time you get on a bus you pay for one section—approximately 80 cents, but **The**

Downtowner ticket costs only $2.20 for five trips within the city section (between the railway station and the other end of the city), and it can also be used on the cable car. Valid weekdays between 0900-1500, purchase it from any bus driver and hold on to it until you've had your five rides! The **Day Tripper** ticket allows you to travel anywhere in Wellington by bus or cable car (best value) for $5.50 per day but it can only be used after 0900 on weekdays, all day (till 2400) on weekends. The **Day Rover** ticket is the best deal if you want to travel around as much of the Wellington region as you can in one day.

For around $13 pp per day you can use the Red Buses, cable car, InterCity suburban buses, and Cityline suburban trains between 0900-1600, after 1800 Mon. to Fri., and 1200-2400 weekends and holidays. It's not valid for Eastbourne buses, ferries, or sightseeing buses. Buy the Day Tripper or Day Rover tickets a day in advance or on the day of travel at Transport terminals or at the Railway Station. **Cityline** suburban trains service the Hutt Valley, Johnsonville, and Paraparaumu.

For all your bus transportation info, drop by the **City Bus Information Centre** on the corner of Bunny, Lambton Quay, and Molesworth; it's open Mon. to Fri. from 0730-1630. Pick up the free *Wellington City Bus Route Guide* here or from the PRO. For advice and timetable info by phone, call the Bus Line at tel. 856-579.

Cable Car

The cable car runs from Cable Car Lane (off Lambton Quay) in the city center up the steep track to Kelburn with three stops along the route, taking about six minutes to the top. It's a very handy connection between the city center and Botanical Gardens and Victoria University. Cars depart both terminals Mon. to Fri. at 0700, running at about 10-minute intervals until 2200. On Sat. they start at 0920 and run till 1800, and on Sun. 1030-1800; adult $1.10, child 40 cents OW, to the top. If you take the cable car up, get off at the Kelburn Terminal and walk through the adjacent Botanical Gardens to the other side, you'll come out on Glenmore St.—if you want an alternate route down to the city, catch a no. 12 bus from here which runs down Bowen St. onto Lambton Quay.

Cars, Taxis, Or Bicycles

All the major car rental companies (and many minor ones—check the phone book) have offices in Wellington, and a couple have outlets at the Ferry Terminal. **Dominion Budget** has two offices in Wellington—at the airport, tel. 887-659, and at 81 Ghuznee St., tel. 859-085. **Avis** is at 25 Dixon St., tel. 850-266. **Letz** is in the Roadmaster Building, corner of Wakefield and Taranaki sts., tel. 842-745; and **Hertz** is at 166 Taranaki St., tel. 843-809; **The Automobile Association** office is on Willis near Dixon.

For a taxi, call **Black, White and Grey Cabs** at tel. 859-900, **Capital City Cabs** at tel. 893-023, or **Wellington Co-Op Taxis** at tel. 859-888. Authorized taxi stands are found at Wellington Railway Station, on Whitmore St. (between Lambton Quay and Featherston St.), outside the James Smith on Lambton Quay, on the Bond St. corner (off Willis St.), outside the Woolworths Store on Dixon St., at the Willis and Aro sts. intersection, and opposite the p.o. on Cambridge Terrace.

If you want to rent a bicycle, head for **Bicycle Village** at 39-41 Ghuznee St., tel. 847-512. They rent them by the hour, day, weekend, and week—call for current rates.

FROM WELLINGTON

Coach

The **InterCity Terminal** (and Picton Ferry Bus Terminal) is located at Platform 9 at the Railway Station, on the Waterloo Quay side. InterCity runs from Wellington to Auckland, Hamilton, Rotorua, Tauranga, Palmerston North, New Plymouth, Wanganui—in fact, just about everywhere you want to go—with connections everywhere else. For current schedules and prices, call the **Railway Station Travel Centre** on Bunny St., tel. 725-399; open Mon. to Sat. 0700-2045, and Sun. 0800-2045.

The **Mount Cook Landliner Terminal** is at 101-103 Courtenay Place (corner of Taranaki

St.), tel. 854-136; open weekdays 0830-1700. Their airport office is also open on Sat. 0800-1200. Coaches run to Auckland ($74 OW), Rotorua ($59 OW), Taupo ($45 OW), Napier ($55 OW), Hastings ($56.50), and other destinations, with connections. The **Newmans Coach Lines Depot** is at 260 Taranaki St. (at the southern end near the Art Gallery and Museum), tel. 851-149; open Mon. to Fri. 0800-1730, and weekends 0800-1130 and 1330-1730. Service is provided from Wellington to Levin ($13 OW), Hastings ($37 OW), Napier ($39 OW), Palmerston North ($20 OW), Wanganui ($23 OW), New Plymouth ($42 OW), and Auckland via New Plymouth ($91 OW). **Newmans Bus Pick-up Depot** is on Stout St. by the railway station.

Trains

Wellington Railway Station's main entrance is off Bunny St. (between Featherston and Waterloo Quay), north of the Civic Centre. Inside the station is the **InterCity Information Centre** which has local and long-distance train info, InterCity bus info, and makes bookings for both. The center is open Mon. to Sat. from 0700-1800, Sun. 0800-1800, tel. 725-599; reservations can be made for train and rail-ferry travel Mon. to Sat. from 0700-1800, Sun. 0800-1600. A handy **left luggage** area, beside Platform 9 behind the fruit stand, will look after your luggage for free up to seven days by showing a railway ticket, an InterCity bus ticket, or rail-ferry ticket. After seven days you're charged 50 cents per piece per day.

The long-distance trains run north to Auckland via Palmerston North, National Park, and Hamilton (*The Northerner* leaves daily in the evening, the *Silver Fern Railcar* leaves Mon. to Fri. in the mornings, and the *Northerner Express* leaves in the evenings on weekends only); north to Palmerston North via Masterton and Woodville; and northeast to Gisborne via Palmerston North, Hastings, and Napier. Suburban trains depart from Wellington Railway Station for the northern suburbs of Ngaio, Khandallah, and Johnsonville; the western coastal towns as far north as Paraparaumu; and to the northern cities of Lower and Upper Hutt. "Day Rover" tickets can be used on all suburban train lines—see "By Buses and Trains" above.

Cook Strait Rail-Ferries

Wellington-Picton Ferries cross Cook Strait up to four times a day, every day of the year, departing from the Aotea Quay Terminal. To get to the terminal, catch the Picton Ferry bus from Platform 9 at the Railway Station, departing 35 minutes before each sailing, $1.50 OW. Be sure to make reservations well in advance if you're taking a vehicle over, or be prepared to go stand-by and expect a wait in summer (stand-bys need to line up by 0600 to have a chance of getting on!). These large ferries (the new ones are quite luxurious) carry passengers, vehicles, and boxcars; each has a cafeteria, gift shop, and newsstand. The crossing usually takes around 3½ hours.

If you don't already have a rail-ferry or bus-ferry ticket, head down to the terminal and buy your ticket well ahead of departure time (leave luggage in the left luggage area for a small fee); depending on the season, fares start at adult $24-30 pp OW, pushbikes $12.50 year-round, motorcycles $24-30, canoes $15 year-round, small cars $75-100 and large cars $100-130 (depending on length). If you're renting a car, arrange to drop it off at Wellington and pick up another in Picton to save the ferry fare. Check out the weather condition board where you buy tickets—if you see the word "rough," stock up on Dramamine! If you're dreading a rough crossing, try to time it so you travel on the newest ferry—it's much quieter and you don't feel the swell as much. Put your large luggage on the yellow luggage carts just before you board. You can also fly from Wellington to Picton (see "Air Services" below), though you'll miss out on a splendid approach (keep your camera and plenty of film on hand) to the South Island.

Wellington International Airport

The airport, on the south side of the city, is easily reached by the 30-minute shuttle service provided by **Vickers Airport Shuttle,** tel.

872-018. The buses depart from Bunny St. (outside Rutherford House) in front of the railway station every 20 minutes from 0600-2120 Mon. to Friday. On Sat. buses depart every 30 minutes from 0700-1930, and on Sun. every 30 minutes from 0700-2130. Buses leave the airport every 20 minutes from 0630-2150 on weekdays, every 30 minutes from 0730-2000 on Sat., and every 30 minutes from 0730-2200 on Sunday. The bus stops en route to the airport if pre-arranged at Midland Park on Lambton Quay (at the corner of Waring Taylor St.), Featherston St. at the Air New Zealand Travel Centre, at Willis St. and Chews Lane, at Manners St. outside Ruby Restaurant, and on Kent Terrace (south of the Embassy Theatre). Adult fare $4.50, child $2.25 OW. To check current schedule and fare and arrange pickup, tel. 872-018.

The **International Terminal** is quite dead unless a flight is arriving or departing. The duty-free store is open for all international departures, the bank is open for all incoming and departing flights, and there are shops for gifts, books, and coffee, an observation deck and bar, and a covered walkway through to the Domestic Terminal.

The **Domestic Terminal** teems with life at all times of the day and night—head here for general info and all your regular airport services. The **Information Centre** is open Mon. to Fri. from 0730-2030, Sat. 0800-1900, and Sun. 0900-2030, and you can leave luggage here for long-term storage for around 50 cents per piece per day (they also sell stamps). The friendly staff will book InterCity rail-ferry reservations, Newmans reservations, and accommodations. For short-term **luggage storage** (up to 14 days) get one of the lockers around the corner from the info center for 20-50 cents. If luggage is left beyond 14 days, it's removed and put under the charge of the Airport Manager's office and you have to pay a daily 25-cent surcharge to get it back.

Also in the Domestic Terminal is a branch of the **ANZ Bank,** open regular weekday hours and before and after each international arrival and departure (ATM machines in both domestic and international); **Mount Cook Line Travel Centre** (coach tours, sightseeing, accommodations, and domestic travel arrangements); a **cafeteria,** open from around 0600-1900 each day; **book and souvenir shops**; and Avis, Budget, and Hertz **rental car** branches. You can also contact Thrifty and Southern Cross car rentals through the info center.

Air Services

Air New Zealand is the primary domestic carrier, flying to most local airports in the country. The **Air New Zealand Regional Office and Travel Centre** is at 139 Vivian St., tel. 859-911. The other Travel Centre is located on the corner of Featherston and Grey sts., tel. 859-911. For reservations, call 859-922; for flight arrivals and departures, call 889-900. **Ansett New Zealand** services Auckland, Christchurch, Dunedin, and Queenstown from Wellington. The main reservation office is on the corner of Featherston St. and Lambton Quay, tel. 711-044.

The **Mount Cook Airlines** office is on the corner of Taranaki St. and Courtenay Place, tel. 844-136. **Air Nelson** flies daily to Palmerston North, Blenheim, Nelson, Motueka, and Westport. Make bookings at the info center or at Air New Zealand in the terminal, or tel. 726-034. **Safe Air** connects Christchurch and the Chatham Islands with Wellington; book through Air New Zealand.

Skyferry provides a 25-minute Cook Strait crossing to Picton several times a day, weather permitting. From Wellington, check in at least 15 minutes before departure at the Domestic Air Terminal Information Centre; fare adult $39, child $20.50 OW (to Blenheim adult $49, child $25 OW). Fifteen kg of baggage is free, excess baggage may be carried on a space-available basis at an extra charge per kilo. For schedule, bookings, and current fare, call 888-380.

SOUTH ISLAND

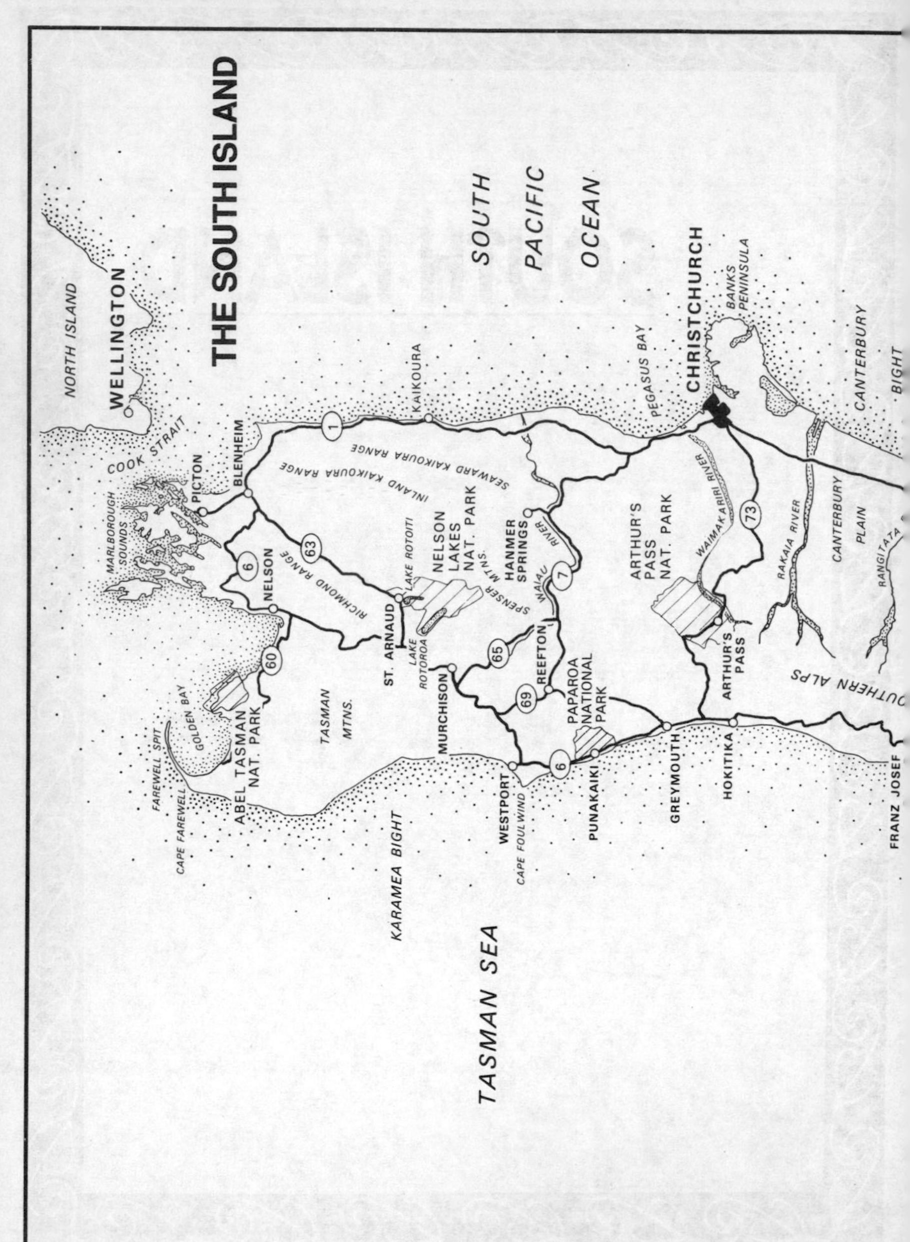
THE SOUTH ISLAND
NORTH ISLAND
WELLINGTON
COOK STRAIT
MARLBOROUGH SOUNDS
PICTON
BLENHEIM
NELSON
FAREWELL SPIT
CAPE FAREWELL
GOLDEN BAY
ABEL TASMAN NAT. PARK
TASMAN MTNS.
KARAMEA BIGHT
TASMAN SEA
WESTPORT
CAPE FOULWIND
PUNAKAIKI
PAPAROA NATIONAL PARK
GREYMOUTH
HOKITIKA
FRANZ JOSEF
MURCHISON
ST. ARNAUD
LAKE ROTOROA
LAKE ROTOITI
RICHMOND RANGE
NELSON LAKES NAT. PARK
SPENSER MTNS.
REEFTON
HANMER SPRINGS
WAIAU RIVER
INLAND KAIKOURA RANGE
SEAWARD KAIKOURA RANGE
KAIKOURA
SOUTH PACIFIC OCEAN
PEGASUS BAY
CHRISTCHURCH
BANKS PENINSULA
ARTHUR'S PASS NAT. PARK
ARTHUR'S PASS
WAIMAKARIRI RIVER
RAKAIA RIVER
CANTERBURY PLAIN
RANGITATA
CANTERBURY BIGHT
SOUTHERN ALPS
1
6
7
60
63
65
69
73

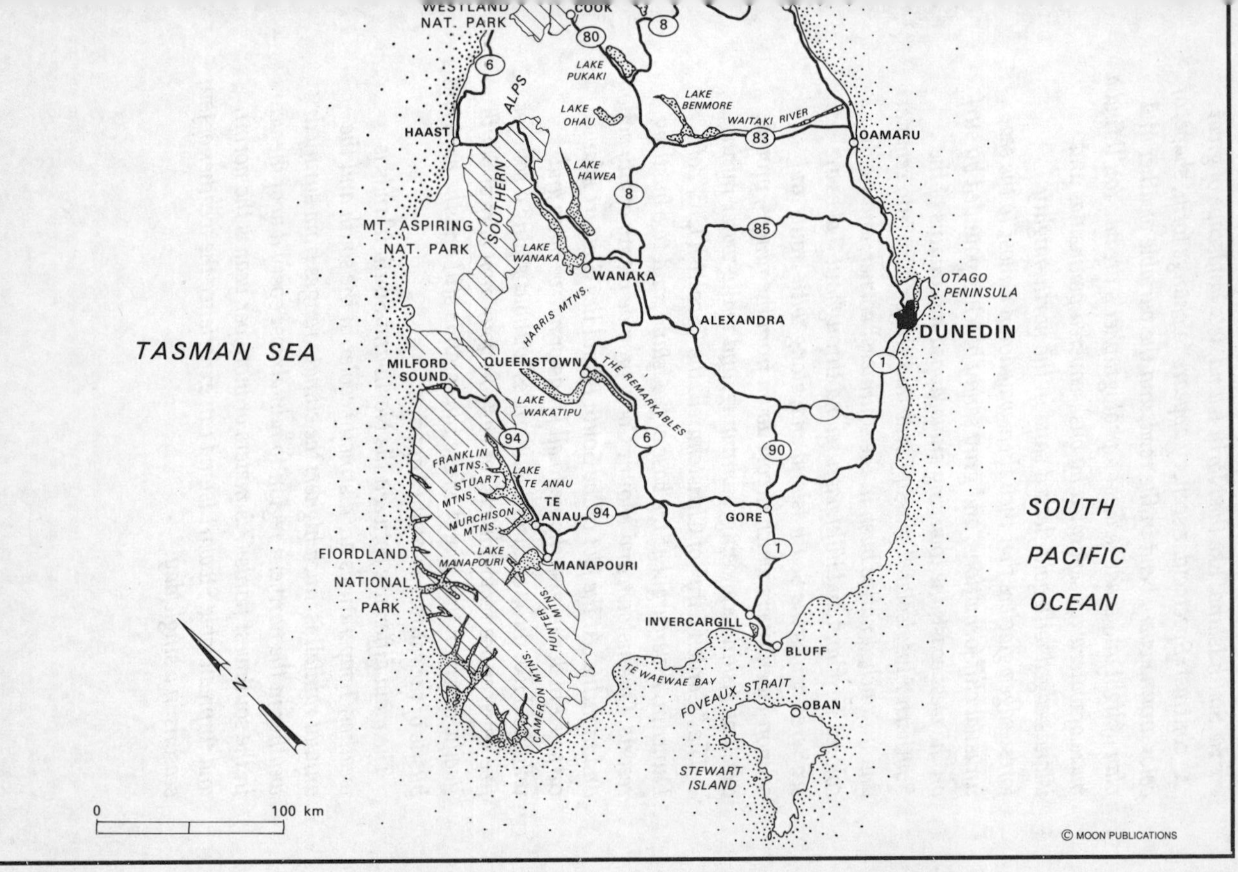
WESTLAND NAT. PARK
COOK
8
80
6
LAKE PUKAKI
ALPS
LAKE BENMORE
LAKE OHAU
WAITAKI RIVER
HAAST
83
OAMARU
LAKE HAWEA
SOUTHERN
8
85
MT. ASPIRING NAT. PARK
LAKE WANAKA
WANAKA
OTAGO PENINSULA
HARRIS MTNS.
ALEXANDRA
DUNEDIN
TASMAN SEA
MILFORD SOUND
QUEENSTOWN
THE REMARKABLES
1
LAKE WAKATIPU
94
6
90
FRANKLIN MTNS.
STUART MTNS.
LAKE TE ANAU
TE ANAU
94
MURCHISON MTNS.
GORE
SOUTH PACIFIC OCEAN
LAKE MANAPOURI
FIORDLAND NATIONAL PARK
MANAPOURI
1
HUNTER MTNS.
INVERCARGILL
CAMERON MTNS.
BLUFF
TE WAEWAE BAY
FOVEAUX STRAIT
OBAN
N
STEWART ISLAND
0
100 km
© MOON PUBLICATIONS

The South Island, like the North Island, is a landscape of great contrast. Spectacular scenery appears to change form, shape, or color around every bend in the road, and the variable weather and play of light and shade make it a photographer's dream. You'll find a maze of waterways separated by bush-covered peninsulas and islands edged with gold-flecked sand in the north; mighty forest-edged glaciers that inch their way down almost to the sea, unusual cliff formations, and gray sandy beaches pounded by surf on the west coast; the towering snowcapped mountains of the Southern Alps; isolated glassy fiords that finger deep into remote and untouched native bush in the southwest corner; and richly colored farmland and hilly pastureland throughout. Lakes are scattered across the South Island and, along with trout- and salmon-laden rivers which cavort down from the ranges, provide excellent fishing, canoeing, swimming, and white-water rafting.

The "Garden City" of Christchurch, the "Scottish City" of Dunedin, Invercargill at the base of the island, and two bustling resorts, Queenstown and Mount Cook, provide plenty of city action and nightlife. At the foot of the South Island lies Stewart Island, carpeted in dense bush, home to all kinds of native birds and wildlife. Hike through virgin wilderness without seeing a soul for five days, cruise remote inlets, or bask on your own perfect South Pacific beach on this island where time stands still and the hum and bustle of the rat race is easily forgotten.

The main difference between the North and South islands is weather. Temperatures are distinctly cooler in the south and the annual rainfall is much higher; the climate ranges from sunny dry weather in the northern region to rain almost every day of the year in the southwest fiords (7.5 meters or more per year is the norm), and unpredictable Stewart Island can experience the weather of four seasons in a single day!

California House, Nelson

NORTH

PICTON

After a spectacular ride across Cook Strait (especially beautiful on a bright day), the ferry cruises up colorful Queen Charlotte Sound, one of the two major inlets of Marlborough Sounds Maritime Park (see below). Your final destination is the small town of Picton, a main port of entry to the South Island and a popular seaside resort. If you enjoy magnificent seascapes, cruising up sounds, island hopping, hiking, fishing, sea kayaking, diving, or beach camping, the Picton area has a lot to offer. Due to the complexity of the landscape, however, you need a fair bit of cash and several companions to share costs of a boat or rental car, or you need to be fit, energetic, and have plenty of time to explore it by thumb and foot.

When Capt. Cook sailed up Queen Charlotte Sound in 1770 he found about 400 Maori living in huts along the shores—the remains of their pits and middens can still be clearly seen today. Ship Cove at the northwest side of Queen Charlotte Sound was the first anchoring spot in Marlborough Sounds for the crew of the HMS *Endeavour*. After European discovery, Marlborough Sounds became famous for productive whaling stations (the last closed in 1964), gold mining in the 1860s, timber milling from the 1860s to 1915, farming in the 1920s, and from then on for exotic tree plantations—check them out from the ferry.

On Arrival

Once disembarked, collect your luggage from the yellow ferry carts. If you're trying to decide whether to push on south or stay in Picton a few days, leave your backpack, luggage, etc., in lockers at the terminal building in the **left luggage area** while you look around town. The lockers are opened and closed by employees and it's best to agree on a set rate before you go (usually about 30 cents an hour). The town, only a short walk

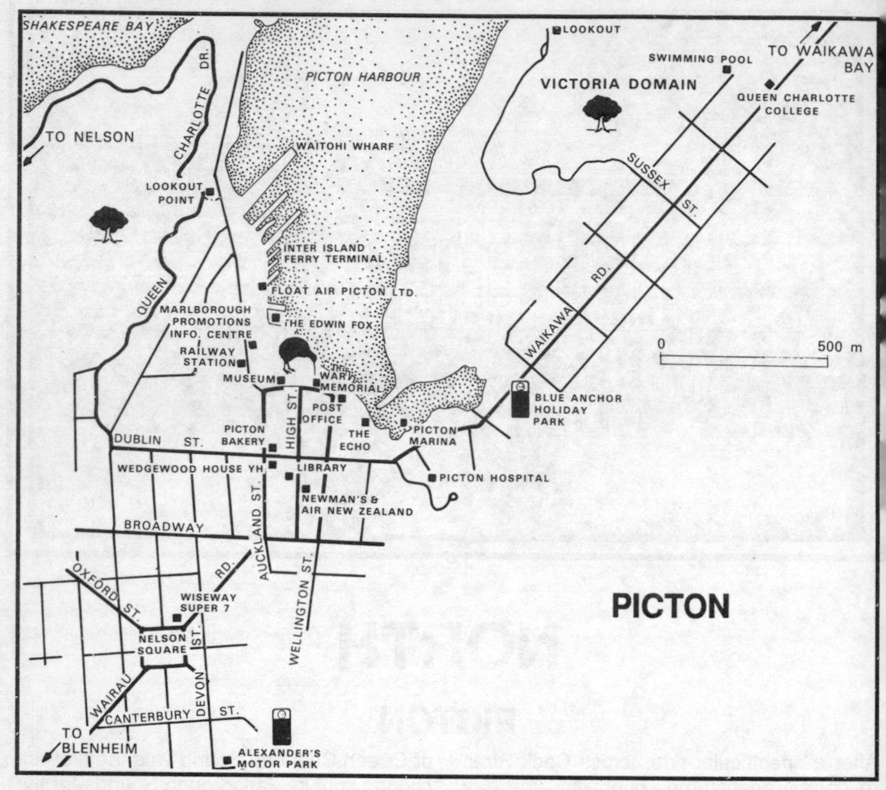

away, is a couple of dollars by taxi. It's also easy (but expensive) to rent a car—the major car rental company offices beside the terminal open for all ferry arrivals and departures. If you arrive in town on a weekday between 0900-2000 in summer, 0900-1600 in winter, or 1000-1500 weekends, the first place to go is the **Marlborough Promotions Information Centre** on Auckland St., tel. 37-513 (see "Information" below).

TOWN SIGHTS

The Harborfront

Between the ferry terminal and downtown Picton is Dunbar Wharf where the *Edwin Fox,* a grand old sailing ship built in 1853, is moored. Over the years it has put in duty as a tea trader, troop, merchant, then immigrant ship, a freezer vessel, and a coal hulk. Today it's being restored to original condition to house a floating maritime museum. Open daily, admission and a historical tour is adult $2, child $1, family $5. As you continue into town you pass powerboat, runabout, and cabin cruiser rentals (tel. 36-531), the **Float Air Flying Dolphin Service** office (daily flights to Wellington from $49 pp; tel. 36-433), a number of car rental company offices, and the Float Air Picton office (scenic flights from $30 pp for 15 minutes in a Beaver). Coin-operated public showers (50-cent pieces—take two) and laundry facilities are available in the building beside the marina (enter from the marina side).

Walk down the memorial steps at the harbor end of High St. into the attractive flower-filled park that lines the bay, and turn left. Just past the public restrooms you'll find **Picton Museum** featuring the town's colorful colonial past. It's crammed to the rafters with all sorts of intriguing objects, Maori clothing, carvings, ancient clocks, a fantastic shell collection, old photographs, even the 1902 Picton doctor's bicycle. One room is entirely devoted to relics from local whaling history, and another features the lifestyle of early Maori settlers. If you're interested in traditional Maori carving, sculpture, and jewelry, don't miss the case displaying the intricate work of top N.Z. artist Norman Clark (his studio is on Main Rd., Rai Valley, between Havelock and Nelson—call ahead to check if there's someone there at tel. 26-257, Nelson). The friendly curator, Mrs. Foley, is a fund of local information. She's also a good person to see if you plan on staying in Picton awhile and want part-time work at a local vineyard or health farm in return for full lodging, or if you hit town in a peak holiday period and you're having trouble finding a bed. Picton Museum is open seven days 1000-1600; admission adult $2, child 50 cents. Located on London Quay.

Continue east along the waterfront (away from the ferry terminal) until you come to *The Echo,* an 80-year-old cargo boat with kauri-frame timbers that played an important part in Marlborough's transport industry between Blenheim and Wellington for more than 40 years. Beached on Picton Harbour, she's now the converted home of the Marlborough Cruising Club and a local attraction. You can't go onboard unless invited, but if you're interested in sailing and hang around for awhile, with luck you'll be asked up for a drink—an offer any sailing enthusiast shouldn't refuse!

Go to **Picton Marina** to soak up some of the nautical vacation atmosphere for which Picton is famous; it's also a departure point for commercial launch rides, fishing charters, and water taxis to the outer islands (see "Marlborough Sounds" below). If you have your own transportation, cruise out to **Waikawa Bay Marina** (a 10-minute drive east of town along Beach Rd.) to see hundreds of boats clinking and twinkling in the sun. **Waikawa Bay** is also worth a visit—to sit in the sun and take in the bay view, watch local children taking sailing lessons, and have a snack on the deck of the Waikawa Bay Food Market and Tearooms.

The New Zealand Experience

The best reason to visit this Picton attraction is the excellent, 20-minute, multiple-projector movie and slide show with wrap-around sound and other have-to-be-seen-to-be-appreciated special effects. It's a stimulating way to see what the rest of New Zealand has in store for you—or what you'll miss if you don't travel right around the country! Aside from the movie, the $6 admission fee takes you through an "Infinity Tunnel," into a hall of very realistic laser-produced holograms, and through a playroom where both kids and adults can romp with gay abandon. On London Quay, tel. 36-690; open in summer 0900-1700, in winter from 0930.

Victoria Domain

This area of unspoiled bush along the headlands east of the harbor has spectacular views of Picton Ferry Terminal, the sound, and Waikawa Bay—take your camera. To get there from town take Dublin St. east, pass Picton Hospital onto Waikawa Rd. and go about 800 meters. Turn left at Sussex St. and follow the steep road to the lookout.

Queen Charlotte Drive

A **lookout** and picnic spot lies up on Queen Charlotte Dr. (which leads west out of Picton toward Havelock and Nelson). It can be reached by car (take Dublin St. west and turn right at Queen Charlotte Dr.), or on foot via **Beatty's Track** which starts near the base of Waitohi Wharf and leads up to the lookout. If you have wheels, continue along the twisty bushclad Queen Charlotte Dr. for some of the best waterscapes in the South Island—the views of the next couple of sounds are well worth the drive. However, the road is steep and tortuous, and not recommended for unreliable cars (or unreliable drivers) or cars towing long caravans. Hitchhiking along here is tedious!

For ooh-and-aah scenery along the entire route, take Queen Charlotte Dr. from Picton all the way to Nelson, passing through the

view from Queen Charlotte Drive

quiet settlements of **Momorangi Bay, The Grove,** and **Linkwater.** At Linkwater, consider stopping for tea, a light meal ($10-16), dinner (from $32 pp; by advance reservation only), or stay overnight in one of the three spacious guest rooms (from $25 s, $40 d, breakfast $6.50-10 extra) at attractive **Linkwater Lodge** (on the main road, tel. 42-507 Havelock), built in 1925. If you don't have a vehicle, reach it on a Greenline bus, or catch a ride out with one of the rural delivery trucks.

Adventurers shouldn't miss a chat with the owners of the **Marlborough Sounds Adventure Company** between Linkwater and Havelock (look for their sign on the main road). They offer a variety of **sea kayaking** trips to suit all standards and most budgets. Rent one of the kayaks and set off on your own (from $30 a day for a single, $45 a day for a double, less per day for three days or more), take a single or double kayak trip with the owner as your guide (from $190 for two days, $290 three days), get some instruction (from $50 per half-day), or sharpen your skills at one of their workshops (from $150 pp per weekend, provide your own food and accommodation). Discounts for resident YH members. According to kayakers, *this* is the only way to really appreciate the beauty of the sounds.

At **Havelock**, where many outdoor activities await discovery—walking and hiking tracks, cruising the sounds, mail boat adventures, fishing, and glowworm viewing, to name but a few—stay at the excellent **Rutherford YHA Hostel,** originally a historical school house. A large comfy living room, well-equipped kitchen and shop, spotlessly clean bathrooms, notice board packed with useful info on the local area and farther afield, and bicycle hire are just some of the reasons to stay here. Ask hospitable manager Bill Gourley about the discounts available for local attractions. The hostel is at 46 Main Rd., tel. 42-104; $11 per night. Between Pelorus and Rai Valley, **Flat Creek Gallery and Norman Clark Studios,** tel. 26-257, is a good place to go for quality carvings, sculpture, ethnic art, and jewelry.

MARLBOROUGH SOUNDS

Marlborough Sounds Maritime Park

If you have a tent, cooking equipment, food, and some cash for a boat ride, this maze of bright blue waterways, 900 km of foreshore reserves separated by high peninsulas, islands with soft sandy beaches, and fine camping spots is a place that should be seriously explored for at least a couple of days. Within the Park boundary lie innumerable reserves, the two major inlets of Queen Charlotte and Pelorus sounds, D'Urville Island, and Croisilles Harbour, altogether covering about 2,914 sq km of coastline and islands. If your car is reliable, you can reach many areas of the middle and outer sounds by road (some of it paved, some gravel); the more remote areas can only be reached by boat, but commercial cruises and the mail boat make regular trips everywhere, or you can hire one. All the commercial operators (in Picton or Havelock) are willing to drop you off and pick you up at prearranged points and times (agree on a price beforehand), allowing one-day island exploration or a several-day hike (see "Cruising" below). For more info and maps of the Park, contact the Conservation Department in the Mariners Mall on High St., tel. 37-582.

Free camping is permitted on any reserve in the Park other than in designated picnic areas, nature or scientific reserves, or where the shore fronts private property. Other areas set aside especially for camping have been designated: "campsites" (no services but water nearby), "camping areas" (toilets and a fresh water supply), or "campgrounds" (showers, kitchens, power, a resident caretaker, small fee per night). See "Camping Out" below. Load all your supplies, suntan lotion, sunglasses, hat, fishing rod, and a friend onto a boat, and head out for the wilds of Marlborough Sounds—it's guaranteed to drop your blood pressure and give you one heck of a suntan.

Cruising

Many commercial launch operators cruise Queen Charlotte Sound (from Picton) and Pelorus Sound (from Havelock). The easiest way to find out what's available is to head for Picton Town Wharves, Picton Marina, Waikawa Bay Marina, or Marlborough Promotions Information Centre. **Beachcomber Cruises** slip through Queen Charlotte Sound's Grove Arm every day at 1015 and 1415. The two-hour cruise costs $24 pp; buy your ticket at the office on London Quay by the post office. Their **Magic Mail Run** sails from Picton Town Wharf on Mon. and Thurs. at 1115, returning mid to late afternoon, and Tues. and Fri. (different route) for $35 pp. Take your own lunch; tea and coffee provided.

Glenmore Cruises' mail launch takes passengers on several different routes depending on the day of the week (Tues., Wed., and Thurs.) starting from Havelock. Cover an extensive area of Queen Charlotte Sound, appreciating beautiful secluded bays, isolated homesteads, old whaling stations, historic landmarks, perfect beaches, and lots of birdlife. Take a picnic lunch—tea-making facilities are on board; adult $40, child $20, 50% discount for YH members. On the Tuesday. Western Run you can get off at Wilson Bay and stay at a backpacker's cottage for only $20 a day, which includes a bed and three meals; arrange through Glenmore Cruises (tel. 42-276 Havelock) or Havelock YH.

Canoes (from $5 per hour), dinghies, small runabouts (from $35 per day, fuel extra), powerboats, small diesel launches, even skipper-yourself motor sailers can all be hired in Picton—just stroll along the waterfront from the ferry terminal to the marina to see all the ways you can take to the water. **Pelorus Sound mail launch** leaves from Havelock Mon., Tues., Thurs., and Fri. for a route to remote outlying farms and guesthouses; it also drops off anglers at excellent fishing points and collects them on the return trip.

Fishing And Skindiving

Snapper is the best fighting and perhaps most delicious local fish, averaging 4.5 kg. The most popular places for fishing for snapper are Pelorus and Kenepuru sounds; for blue cod try Queen Charlotte Sound, the head of the Sounds, and Tory Channel. Surf fishing is best anywhere along the east coast from the Sounds to Kaikoura (particularly well known), and you're likely to catch snapper, moki, kahawai (an exciting fighter but not so good in the taste department), red cod, and dogfish. Any of the local fishermen, launch operators, and sports dealers are good sources of info on what's being caught, how, and where. Expect to pay from $25 pp for a half-day trip with all the necessary equipment supplied. For info on river fishing for trout (the Rai River, which enters the Sounds, is one of the hot spots) and

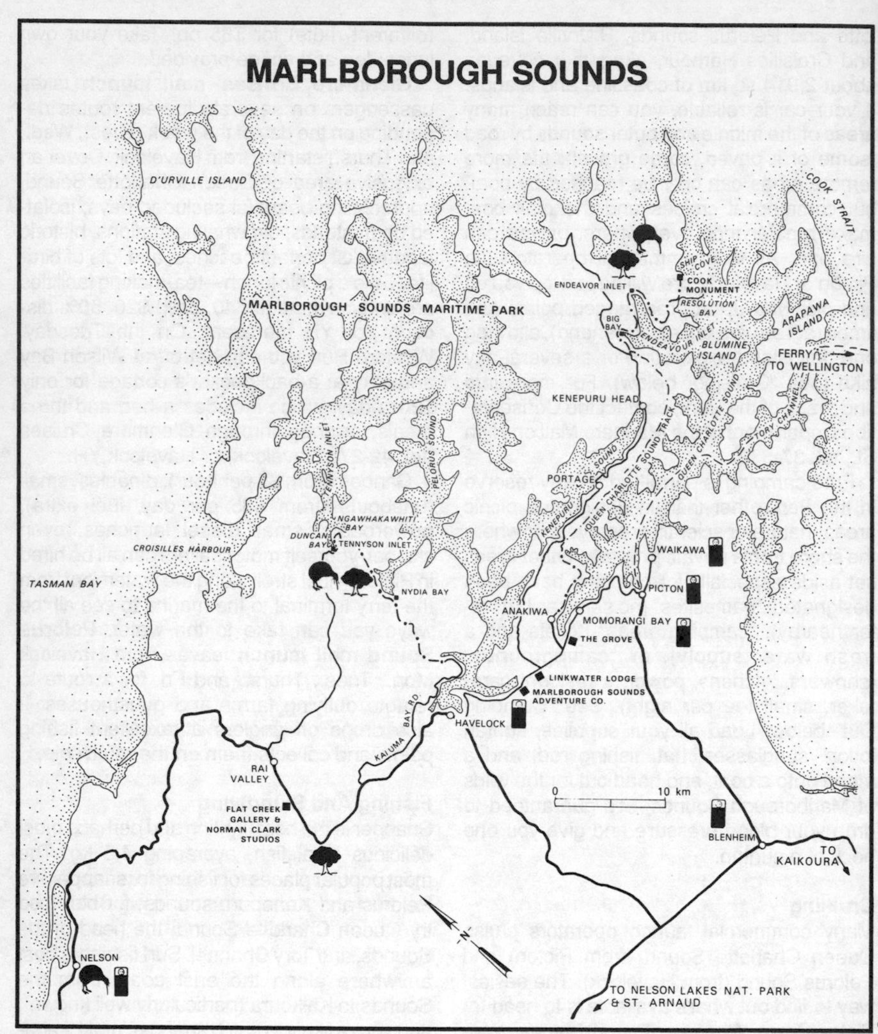

a fishing license, see the people at the local sports shop, and ask for the leaflet "A Guide to Marlborough's Trout Fishing" at the info center. Fishing gear can be hired from Picton Sports Centre on High Street.

Skindivers will find underwater shipwrecks (including a Russian cruise ship), rich and colorful marinelife, and plenty of crayfish and scallops in Marlborough Sounds. You can get tanks filled, and hire all equipment and a charter boat especially equipped for divers to take you out to the best spots. For more info call **Picton Underwater Centre** at 41 Wellington St., tel. 37-323.

Flightseeing

If you're short on time (or enjoy a bird's-eye view), one of the most exciting ways to appreciate the spectacular beauty of Marlborough Sounds is from the air. **Float Air Picton** does short scenic flights from $30 pp for 15 minutes to $60 for 30 minutes in its six-seater float plane. The office, open seven days year-round, is at the ferry terminal—walk out of the terminal toward town and you can't miss the sign on the left, or call 36-433 for current prices and all the possible destinations. The company also offers their "Flying Dolphin" service from Picton to Wellington ($49 pp direct) via Kenepuru Sound ($68 pp) and Endeavour Inlet lodges and resorts ($78 pp).

HIKES

Short Walks Close To Town

From town, a track follows the harbor edge east for one km and comes out at sheltered **Bob's Bay**—pleasant picnicking and safe swimming. From here you can climb up the bush track to the headland, Victoria Domain, and a lookout for spectacular views of Queen Charlotte Sound and Picton. **Essons Valley** is another enjoyable short walk (45 minutes OW)—particularly good in the dark when glowworms strut their stuff along the track. It starts at Garden Terrace at the south end of Picton and leads to **Humphrey's Dam.**

Walking Tracks

A track network, ranging from 15-minute walks to several-day hikes, has been established throughout Marlborough Sounds Maritime Park, but access for many is by boat. For track info and maps visit the Department of Conservation in Mariners Mall on High St., or call the Secretary of the Park Board in Blenheim at tel. 86-079 or the Ranger at Mahakipawa Rd., Havelock, tel. 42-159.

Anakiwa Walk (19 km) takes about 6½ hours to walk from the starting point just beyond the Outward Bound School at Anakiwa (at the head of Queen Charlotte Sound) to the finish at Portage. The track follows the coastline to Davies Bay (safe swimming and campsites), climbs up through dense native bush with great views, and emerges at Mistletoe Bay (3½ hours). A camping area and guest house are located at Te Mahia. Several steep climbs are encountered between Mistletoe Bay and the finish at Portage (three hours), where you'll find the Portage Hotel and a public camping area at Cowshed Bay, half a km west of the hotel. Either end of the track can be reached by car.

Endeavour Walk, perhaps one of the most interesting hikes in the Sounds, rewards the energetic with tremendous coastal views, awesome reflections of Kenepuru Sound, native bush alive with birds, and historic sights at Ship Cove. The 11-km track starts at Kenepuru Saddle, directly above Camp Bay on the west coast of Queen Charlotte Sound. Reachable by car, it's far easier to get there by boat from Picton. A four-hour hike follows the coast through pastoral land and bush around the head of Endeavour Inlet. Not far after the swing bridge the track passes the N.Z. Working Men's Union Holiday Camp (cabins for hire and a shop). The track continues past Furneaux Lodge (tourist hotel with chalets and campsites—a good place to break up the track and stay the night), then it's three hours to Resolution Bay (no facilities), and another two hours to peaceful and historic Ship Cove, reserve, and monument to Capt. Cook (no camping permitted, only picnic sites).

One of the most popular and well-defined walking tracks, 49-km **Queen Charlotte Sound Track,** runs along Queen Charlotte Sound from **Anakiwa** to **Ship Cove** and takes a hiker of average fitness about five days to comfortably cover. Road access is at Anakiwa, Te Mahia, Portage, and Kenepuru Saddle; sea access at Anakiwa, Mistletoe Bay, Torea Bay, Camp Bay, Endeavour Inlet, Resolution Bay, and Ship Cove—get more info from local boat operators. Camping areas, cottages, motels, or hotels are located along the track at Davies, Mistletoe, and Onahau bays, Te Mahia, Portage, Cowshed Bay, Punga Cove, Camp Bay, Endeavour Inlet, and Resolution Bay. The closest YH is the excellent Rutherford Hostel at Havelock. For detailed track info contact the Secretary of Marlborough Sounds Maritime Park, Box 445, Blenheim, and pick up brochures and a map at the Marlborough Promotions Information Centre in Picton.

Nydia Walk starts at Kaiuma Bay, 1.5 km east of Havelock. On this 22-km hike you pass through farmland, climb up through lush native forest to the Kaiuma Saddle, and drop back down into beautiful Nydia Bay (four hours), where there are good places to camp. It then follows the western shore of the bay, climbs through beech forest to a great lookout, drops down to Ngawhakawhiti Bay (four hours), and finishes at Duncan Bay (one hour) on the shores of Tennyson Inlet. Total track time is at least eight hours, with road access to both ends—prearrange transportation. Another walk in this area, about three hours OW, is the **Archer Track** which starts at Penzance Bay (follow the road around from Duncan Bay). This easy walk (no climbing) follows the coastline through forest, along a pine plantation, and finishes at Elaine Bay where there are campsites; Elaine Bay can be reached by car—prearrange transportation.

ACCOMMODATION

Camping Out

Within Marlborough Sounds Maritime Park are a large number of coastal reserve campgrounds. The following "campsites" in Queen Charlotte Sound have no facilities and are accessible only by boat: Bottle Bay, Torea Bay, Wharehunga Bay, Ngaruru Bay (Arapawa I.), Blumine I., and Cannibal Cove. "Camping areas" with toilets and access by sea or road in Queen Charlotte Sound are located at Whatamongo Bay, Aussie Bay, Davies Bay, Kaipakirikiri Bay, Ratimera Bay, and Camp Bay (Endeavour Inlet, access by sea only). The only "campground" in Queen Charlotte Sound is at Momorangi Bay (access by sea or road), with showers, toilets, caretaker, shop, and small charge. For a full list of camping possibilities in Pelorus Sound, Tennyson Inlet, Kenepuru Sound, and outer sounds, contact the Department of Conservation in Mariners Mall, High St., or call in at the info center (see "Information" below).

Motor Camps

Blue Anchor Holiday Park is only 400 meters from Picton P.O. and provides the usual facilities, TV and recreation room, and a swimming pool. Tent and caravan sites from $12 s, $16 d, cabins from $24-36 d, tourist flats $50 d, motel unit with private bathroom, kitchen, and laundry facilities $60 d, $12 each extra adult. Rates higher between Dec. and 26 January. Located on Waikawa Bay Rd. at the eastern end of town, tel. 37-212. **Alexander's Motor Park** is one km from the p.o. (an easy 10-minute walk) in the quiet southern area of town. Waitohi Stream rushes through the attractive grounds. The managers are friendly and helpful. Communal facilities, TV lounge, a kitchen where it's easy to meet fellow travelers, and an office where you can pick up useful info on the local area, buy basic foodstuffs, postcards, etc., and rent tandem bikes for $2 an hour, $5 half a day, and $10 a day. Tent and caravan sites are $7 pp, on-site caravans are $17 d; cabins from $23-31 d. Located on Canterbury St., tel. 36-378. From town, cross the railway tracks and follow Wairau Rd. (sign says Hwy. 1 south) to Devon St. and turn left. At Canterbury St. turn left following motor camp signs.

The next closest motor camp to Picton, **Parklands Marina Holiday Village,** is three km east at **Waikawa Bay** on the corner of Beach Rd. and Mara Place, tel. 36-343. Communal facilities, TV and game room, boat park and wash. Tent and caravan sites $16 d; on-site caravans and cabins from $32 d; tourist flat $39 d. **Waikawa Bay Caravan Park** at 302 Waikawa Bay Rd., tel. 37-434, has a grassy camping area and on-site caravans and cabins, a short drive from a food market and the bay beach. Tentsites start at $10 d, cabins at $25 d.

Momorangi Bay Motor Camp has an excellent location on the shores of Queen Charlotte Sound; on Queen Charlotte Dr., tel. 37-865. Communal facilities, store (open seven days), and dinghies for hire ($7 per hour—great for transient anglers). Tentsites $5 s, $10 d, caravan sites $14 d. Campsites at Aussie Bay are only $3 pp. Take Queen Charlotte Dr. out of Picton heading for Havelock, about 15 km to Momorangi Bay.

Hostels

Wedgewood House, a converted older-style guest house turned into an associate youth hostel, has small homely rooms (two with ensuite facilities), the usual communal facilities, and a day room that's open all day; $12 pp (you don't have to be a member to stay here). At 10 Dublin St., tel. 37-797. **Picton Backpackers Hostel** is an attractive old house with bright, comfortable rooms (dorms, singles, and doubles) and friendly people, at 34 Auckland St., tel. 36-598; from $15 pp for a dorm bed (blanket hire available). Continental eat-as-much-as-you-want breakfast is an extra $5.

Private Hotels And Guest Houses

Of the many motels and hotels in the Picton area, the most reasonable is **Admirals Lodge** at 22 Waikawa Rd., tel. 36-590. TV lounge, tea-making facilities; from $33 s, $48.40 d (breakfast tray extra), off-season rates available. Another good place to try is **Brannans** at 11 Dorset St. (off Buller St.), tel. 37-177. The owners provide one comfortable self-contained flat with private bathroom, kitchen, and balcony from $21 s, $35 d (self catering), $30 s, $45 d (bed and Continental breakfast), $45 s, $75 d (dinner, B&B), but it's often booked ahead. Call to see if it's available and to get road directions— it's about 1.5 km from downtown. **Marineland Private Hotel and Motel** at 26-28 Waikawa Rd., tel. 36-429, has self-contained motel units (from $66 s or d), hotel single and double rooms ($38-55), and features a "shark-free swimming pool!" For more info on all the guest lodges scattered around the Sounds (some very reasonable but access mainly by boat or float plane), collect brochures at the info center.

FOOD AND ENTERTAINMENT

Picton has a number of small supermarkets, specialty shops, cafes, and restaurants. Everything is open Mon. to Fri. 0900-1700 and Sat. 0900-1200, but on Sat. afternoons the town goes comatose, and on Sun. (apart from the odd tourist shop), Picton appears to be dead! The only places that stay open on weekends are the hotel restaurants and bars. For a cheap quick breakfast or lunch, try one of the many tearooms and cafes, or **Picton Bakery** which is open seven days a week. Looking for a hamburger ($2.50-4) or Chinese takeaway meal ($5-9.50)? **Wiseway Super 7** at 2 Nelson Square has a large variety of takeaway foods. Open Tues. to

Oxleys Hotel, Picton

Sun. 1630-2000, tel. 36-189. For a more substantial meal, try the **Federal Hotel,** open seven days a week; bar lunches start at $5, restaurant lunches from $10, served from 1200-1400. **Oxley's Hotel Tavern Restaurant** at 1 Wellington St. serves reasonably priced bistro meals—local seafood, steaks, chicken dishes, and roasts from $13-16 a main course and daily specials for under $10. **The Crow Tavern** serves fresh seafood at Nelson Square.

The casual **Tides Inn BYO Restaurant** on High St. whips up tasty steaks, grills, and fish at average prices (from $10.50-14.50 a main course)—or they'll deliver to your door (or tent flap if requested!), tel. 37-091. For more of a splurge (and delicious seafood—the *only* thing to eat when you're in Picton), try the fully licensed, fancy **Ship Cove** in the Strand Arcade at 33 High St., tel. 37-304. Enjoy fish or beef (from $15-36 a main course) in historic surroundings—Capt. Cook spent 100 days at Ship's Cove; open seven days from 1800. For another splurge, good food, and magnificent harbor views, try the **Moby Dick Restaurant** at Whalers Inn, 27 Waikawa Road.

For evening entertainment, head for the larger hotels and buy a local a drink! Picton's a laid-back, make-your-own-entertainment type of a place. Another fun thing to do is to hire a boat for your own sunset cruise—it's not too expensive if you have enough people. To find out what's happening around town, check at the info center, or call Radio Marlborough, the news and entertainment station. In summer the community pocl at Queen Charlotte College is open weekdays from 1545-1745 and weekends from 1400-1700. Roller skating to music happens on the foreshore on weekends, holidays, and summer months (small admission charge)—see times on the gate—and roller skate rental is available.

SERVICES

Urgent

For an **ambulance,** tel. 36-207; the **hospital** is on Seaview Crescent (off Waikawa Bay Rd.), tel. 36-402; for a non-life-threatening emergency call 36-405 or 36-092 (local GP); emergency **pharmacies** are McGuires on High St. (open 1200-1215, 1800-1815), Webb's on High St. (open Mon. to Thurs. 0900-1730, Fri. 0900-2100, and Sat. 0930-1230), or Queen Charlotte Pharmacy in Mariners Mall; the **police station** is at the top end of High St., tel. 36-439, or call Blenheim collect at 85-279.

General

Late-night shopping in Picton is on Fri. until 2000. Keep in mind that most shops are closed on Sat. afternoons and all day Sunday. **Picton p.o.** is on the corner of Wellington St. and London Quay. **Canterbury Savings Bank** is at 19 High Street. **Bank of New Zealand** is at 56 High Street. **Picton Public Library** is at 67 High St. in the Picton Borough Council Building. The town **laundrette** is at Picton Villas, Wellington Street. **Public toilets** are located on the harborfront—go down Memorial Steps and turn left. There's also a ladies' restroom in the Plunket Rooms on Lower Wellington St., and toilets in the Red Cross Rooms on Auckland Street.

INFORMATION

For all the info on Picton, Marlborough Sounds, and the local region, stop first at the **Marlborough Promotions Information Centre** just along from the ferry terminal, tel. 37-513; open daily 0900-1700 and 1900-2000 in summer, 0900-1600 in winter, weekends 1000-1500. Apart from a large selection of free brochures, pamphlets, and maps, the helpful staff can advise you and make bookings for current accommodations, entertainment, and everything else. A display room shows the main routes in and out of Picton, the local parks and reserves, and all the available recreational activities. It's also a valuable place to go for onward travel info when you're heading out of town.

The local **Automobile Association** agent is found at Marlin Motel, 33 Devon St., tel. 36-784. For **Marlborough Sounds Maritime Park information,** contact the Department of Conservation upstairs in the Mariners Mall on

High St., tel. 37-582 (open Mon. to Fri. 0900-1700), or the Ranger, Mahakipawa Rd., Havelock, tel. 159, or the Park Secretary, Blenheim, tel. 86-079.

TRANSPORTATION

Getting There

Getting to Picton is easy by rail-ferry from Wellington on the North Island (see p. 330-332), or via train, bus, or thumb from anywhere in the South Island. Bus and train service connects with at least one ferry arrival or departure per day—if you're going on from either Picton or Wellington, check which ferry crossing to catch to make the onward connection. The nearest national airport to Picton is at Blenheim, 28 km south. For ongoing road, rail, and ferry bookings, call in at the **Picton Travel Centre** just across the road from the Marlborough Promotions Information Centre; open Mon. to Fri. 0900-1700, weekends 1130-1430.

Ferries

Picton's ferry terminal at London Quay is the main port of entry to and exit from the South Island. Up to four ferry crossings are made daily (five in peak periods) across Cook Strait from Picton to Wellington and back. Check current schedule at any InterCity ticket office, Rail Travel Agency, NZTP Travel Office, or the Marlborough Promotions Information Centre in Picton. If you're taking a vehicle across (expensive) you need to book ahead, particularly during holidays. Otherwise expect to end up in a long stand-by line and miss several ferries before you get on. Prices start at $75-100 (depending on the season) for a car, more if you're taking a stationwagon, caravan, motorhome, etc. (ticket price varies according to the length of the vehicle). Passengers can usually buy their tickets (adult $24-30, child $12-15 OW) just before departure and walk right on, but it's wise to be at the terminal early to get your luggage onto the yellow ferry carts (make sure they're the carts going on the next crossing!). Ask about the latest "saver fares"—usually have to be purchased in advance. You can leave luggage in the lockers in the left luggage area for around 30 cents an hour or have your baggage through-checked at the railway station or ferry terminal.

Pick up the detailed *Cook Strait Cruise Guide* at the ferry terminal to find out the latest info on connecting train and bus services to the rest of the South Island. An express train from Christchurch connects with the 1420 ferry for Wellington; the same train leaves Picton for Christchurch at 1410 (double-check times). Buses to and from Blenheim, Nelson, and Christchurch connect with

Picton Ferry Terminal from Queen Charlotte Drive

some rail-ferry arrivals and departures—pick up current timetables at the Picton Rail-Ferry Terminal (and see "Buses" below). If you're in a hurry or can't face the ferry crossing, see "Air" below.

Trains

The **railway station** is just around the corner from London Quay on the way to the ferry terminal. **InterCity** trains depart from Picton daily for Blenheim, Kaikoura, and Christchurch, arriving at Christchurch about six hours later; $43 OW. Get your timetable and book tickets at the railway station. The reservations and ticketing office (tel. 36-880, ext. 673) is open Mon. to Fri. 0900-1700 and weekends 1100-1400 for bus, train, ferry, and Delta Coachlines reservations.

Buses

InterCity also connects Picton with Christchurch, departing Picton Tues. through Sat. at 0700. For current schedules and fares, call in at the railway station. Local bus services connect the 28 km between Blenheim and Picton, departing London Quay and the ferry terminal; pick up a timetable from London Quay Souvenirs. The **Mount Cook Landline Starliner booking office** is in the ferry terminal, providing coach services to Christchurch, Invercargill, and Dunedin. **Newmans Coach Lines** has an office on High St., and one at the ferry terminal, tel. 36-687. Coaches connect with all ferry arrivals and run south to Blenheim, then down the east coast to Christchurch, and west to Nelson (and on north to Takaka) and over to Westport and Greymouth on the west coast.

Delta Greenline offers bus services from Picton to Blenheim, and along Queen Charlotte Dr. to Nelson, departing from the Beachcomber office on London Quay, tel. 36-175. The buses connect with **Skyline Travel** coach service to Motueka and Abel Tasman National Park from Dec. to the end of March, providing handy tramper transportation to the tracks (10% discount for YH members). For more info call Skyline Travel at tel. 80-285 Nelson or 88-850 Motueka. **Connections** also run an efficient and reasonable bus service between Picton and Nelson, and an accommodations booking service; tel. (054) 68-650.

Cars Or Bike Hire

All the major car rental agencies have offices at the ferry terminal building (they open for each ferry arrival and departure) and in town. Hire a small scooter from **Waterfront Kiwi Road Runner** just down from the p. o., for $12 an hour. For bicycle and tandem bike hire, visit **Sounds Service Station** for current rates. For a taxi call **Picton Taxi,** tel. 36-207; they also offer one- and three-hour scenic tours (up to five adults per vehicle).

Water Taxis

For water transportation in Queen Charlotte Sound and Tory Channel areas, call **Beachcomber Cruises** at tel. 36-844. Or try **Leisure Launch Charters** at tel. 37-925 for fast catamaran taxi service. They also offer all-day and extended charters, and fishing and diving charters.

Scenic Tours

Marlborough Scenic Tours operates mail car and bus tours of Picton and the Marlborough Sounds area. For more info, schedules, and prices, call 36-262. Also call in at the Marlborough Promotions Information Centre.

By Air

The nearest national airport to Picton is at Blenheim (28 km south); however, if you'd rather soar than sail, you can cross Cook Strait by air (25 minutes) via **Outdoor Aviation's Skyferry** from Picton's Koromiko Airfield, five km south of town. Several flights a day; adult $39 OW, child $20. Fly from Blenheim to Wellington for $49 OW. Take up to 15 kilos of baggage free, and if there's enough room, excess baggage (friends and relations don't count!) costs around 40 cents a kilo.

A transfer vehicle departs from the Picton Ferry Newmans Terminal (look for the Skyferry stand) for the airfield daily at 0740, 1040, 1310, and 1625. Newmans buses also stop at the airport if pre-booked. For more info and the current schedule, call Outdoor Aviation in Wellington at tel. (04) 888-380, Picton/Blenheim at tel. 37-888, Picton Taxis, or the local travel agent.

Outdoor Aviation also offers scenic flights to remote and exclusive airfields throughout Marlborough Sounds, and to both ends of the **Heaphy** and **Whangapeka Tracks;** call for current fares. **Float Air Picton** based at the ferry terminal also offers a "Flying Dolphin" twice-daily service from Picton to Wellington (Porirua Harbour; $49 pp direct) via Kenepuru Sound ($68 pp) and Endeavour Inlet lodges and resorts ($78 pp), and a variety of scenic flights starting at $30 pp for the 15-minute flight.

DECISIONS, DECISIONS!

If you're relatively short of time to spend on the South Island, take an invaluable moment to decide what kind of scenery and activities you're looking for. If you're not in a hurry, Nelson and the northwest are definitely worth exploring, but for those with a limited schedule, the glaciers and mountains of the West Coast shouldn't be missed; city lovers will appreciate the east coast and Christchurch, the most picturesque city in the South Island. If you're finding the decision a tough one to make, don't worry—wherever you go something special awaits you!

Northwest

If you've become understandably addicted to sunshine, beach life, and outstanding water views from Picton and the Marlborough Sounds, you may want to stay a little longer in "the sun belt of the South Island"—turn off Hwy. 1 at Blenheim onto Hwy. 6 and head west for the relaxed resort town of **Nelson** (for a more scenic route, see p. 358). For those of you with plenty of time, the deliciously laid-back atmosphere of Nelson, home to many of New Zealand's best potters, weavers, and arts and craftspersons, is well worth a visit, and it's the kind of place where you're likely to meet other relaxed fellow travelers. Continue farther northwest around Tasman Bay to the isolated and ruggedly beautiful **Abel Tasman National Park** for outstanding hiking and scenery, and on to **Golden Bay** which stretches round to the far northern tip of the South Island and has secluded sandy beaches, not many people, lots of birdlife, and scenery ranging from water panoramas to rugged mountains. (The access road to the well-known Heaphy Hiking Track is from Collingwood in the far north.)

West Coast

For rugged coastal scenery, impressive rock formations, untamed native bush, and the mighty Franz Josef and Fox glaciers farther south (a helicopter ride over the glaciers is an expensive but unforgettable highlight!), either take the most direct route to the West Coast via Hwy. 63 west (turn off Hwy. 1 at Blenheim) or continue there from Nelson via Hwy. 6. (See "The West Coast," p. 408.)

East Coast To Christchurch

The beautiful "Garden City" of **Christchurch** with its manicured flower gardens, striking cathedral, English atmosphere, and canoeing on the tree-lined Avon River will grab anyone's fancy—from Picton go straight down Hwy. 1, a beautiful stretch of road which winds along the gray sandy beaches, rocky shores, and aquamarine waters of the scenic east coast (see "Christchurch," p. 382). On the way down don't miss a stop for fresh crayfish at one of the many roadside stands, and if you want to break the journey, pull off at **Kaikoura.** Sandwiched between the rugged Kaikoura Ranges and the sea, this attractive coastal town is known for its good surf fishing, extensive pebble beaches, and nearby fur seal colony (great views from the lighthouse)—a good place to stay over if you like to catch fish or just eat it freshly caught. Stay at **Kaikoura Holiday Camp** on Beach Rd. next to the railway station for campsites, onsite caravans, motel units, and a hospitable manager who gets up to answer the bell with a smile, even in the wee hours of the morning. Or try the modern **YH** (on the Esplanade) which has incredible mountain and sea views. Another intriguing place to stay is the **Staging Post** farm, 18 km north of Cheviot (look for the sign on the main highway) where you can expect a friendly welcome, stay in rustic handmade cottages and cabins with shared facilities or set up camp amongst rolling hills and fields, and savor home-cooked meals in the large old-fashioned farm kitchen.

NELSON

The Nelson region, according to proud residents, is no less than the center of, well, everything. Not only is it recognized as the geographical center of New Zealand, but it's also the center of apple-, hops-, and tobacco-growing areas. In addition, locals claim Nelson as the "sunshine" center, the "arts and crafts" center, and even the "conference" center of the country! Hyperbole not-withstanding, the city of Nelson *is* a lively base from which to head out for hiking trips in Abel Tasman National Park in the northwest, Nelson Lakes National Park in the south, or the well-known Heaphy Hiking Track on the northwest coast. Add plenty of sunshine, sea, and sand, and you have the local equation for perfection. The people are creative, relaxed, and make you feel right at home. Partly due to this atmosphere the town attracts a mellow crowd—even in mid-summer when New Zealanders flock to the region for R & R, a deep suntan, and bargain hunting from a wide array of locally produced crafts. Finally, Nelson is also the main commercial center for the northwest (Motueka to the west is busy but smaller—less variety), and it's a good idea to stock up on camping equipment and hiking supplies here before continuing to the national parks or walking tracks.

Christ Church Cathedral

SIGHTS

Where To Start

The large **PRO,** corner of Trafalgar and Halifax sts., is the first place to go; if you're exploring Nelson on foot, pick up handy *City Walks* pamphlets (also available from the City Council Office at the other end of Trafalgar St.). Ask if there's anything going on in the local parks—regular "park days" with bright carnival atmosphere and various festivities are put on to promote the use of the many parks. Two other brochures worth pursuing are the *Nelson Potters Guide* and the *Wine Trail.* Before you leave the PRO, be sure to check the outside notice boards: useful info on local tours, launch trips, guided walks, arts and crafts outlets, and transportation to and from the two main hiking tracks (Heaphy and Wangapeka) in the Nelson region.

Christ Church Cathedral

Walk south from the PRO along Trafalgar St. to Nelson's impressive Christ Church Cathedral, on small Church Hill at the south end of

Pounding silver into a piece of art in Jen Hansen's Gold and Silversmiths studio.

the main shopping street. This Anglican cathedral was built in 1925, much of the building is of Takaka marble (from Takaka Hill, about 70 km west of Nelson), and its landmark 35-meter tower dominates the inner city area. Open daily from 0800-1600 as well as regular service times, volunteer guides (on hand during the busy summer period) point out the many memorials and historic links with early Nelson housed inside the cathedral.

Regional Architecture; Arts And Crafts

To view some of Nelson's attractive older buildings, take Nile St. West (off Church St. on the west side of the cathedral), then turn left on South Street. Both streets are lined with many old cottages—some dating back to the 1800s. **South Street Gallery,** at 10 Nile St. opposite the Quality Inn, is definitely worth a stop to view its rustic interior while appreciating the works of 23 regional artists, and maybe picking out a superb piece of local pottery for which the gallery is renowned. It's open Mon. to Fri. 1000-1700 (later on Fri.), weekends 1000-1600, tel. 88-117.

Intriguing little shops selling everything from fine silver jewelry and paintings to fantastic handmade wool sweaters (from $80 and worth it!) and other woolen products are located along Nile Street. (The meter maids around here are ferocious!) For silver art, return to the cathedral and head for **Jen Hansen's Gold and Silversmiths** workshop at 320 Trafalgar Square (tel. 80-640). In the front room fine silver jewelry is displayed; in the back room talented silversmiths pound, solder, and shape beauty out of hunks and strands of the precious metals—and they don't seem to mind the odd curious visitor watching over their shoulders. While you're in this area don't miss another historic home at the top end of Trafalgar Street. Situated amongst several acres of beautiful trees, the home has been restored and is used as a community center; open daily from 1000-1800.

For fine crafts from around New Zealand (and delicious morning and afternoon teas and light lunches), visit **Landmark Gallery** at 279-281 Hardy St., tel. 87-579; open seven days 1000-1630. If you're continuing west, the **Craft Habitat** on the corner of Salisbury Rd. and Richmond Deviation has an excellent selection of pottery, weaving, handblown glass, wood and metal products, carved bone, handcrafted baskets, fabric art, and handblown glass, and you can watch many of the craftsmen actually creating their works of art; open seven days, tel. Richmond 45-657. Save a few dollars for a refreshing

Devonshire tea or light lunch in the Habitat Coffee House!

Collingwood Street Attractions
From Trafalgar St. turn onto Nile St. East, then Collingwood St. where you'll find handspun wool and handwoven articles made on the premises of **Seven Weavers** at no. 36; open weekdays 1000-1600, the staff will gladly ship your purchases overseas. Continue along Collingwood St. to no. 29 to view another of Nelson's beautifully restored **colonial homes.** Built in 1893 in one of Nelson's quieter residential areas, it has been transformed into a charming bed and breakfast guesthouse known for its spacious, comfortable rooms, 24 original stained-glass windows, and fantastic breakfasts—*the* place to pamper yourself! (See p. 356.)

Suter Art Gallery
Described as "the most lively and central art gallery in New Zealand," this one shouldn't be missed by any true art lover. Along with the large permanent art collection are varied exhibitions, films, and recitals; at the excellent craft shop you can buy top-quality pieces of local pottery, weaving, and prints. A restaurant overlooks adjacent **Queen's Gardens,** one of Nelson's most attractive reserves containing many rare tree specimens (all named), a fernery, flowering bushes, and ornamental pond swarming with ducks—don't miss it! The gallery and restaurant are open daily from 1030-1630; admission adult $1, child 20 cents, family $2.20. On Bridge St.; from Collingwood St. turn east onto Bridge Street.

Historic Houses In Western Nelson
Broadgreen, built around 1855, is a magnificent, two-story, mid-Victorian "cob" house made from mud and clay mixed with straw, horse hair, and other reinforcing materials. The house is set amongst perfect lawns and rambling rose gardens, and the interior period furnishings are an antique buff's delight. Located on Nayland Rd., Stoke, tel. 73-607, it's open every day 1400-1600, closed Sat. June to Aug.; admission $1 pp. For bus info to Stoke, ask at the PRO. **Isel House,** an impressive two-story wood and stone house built around 1886, is also chock-a-block with priceless antiques, surrounded by 12 acres

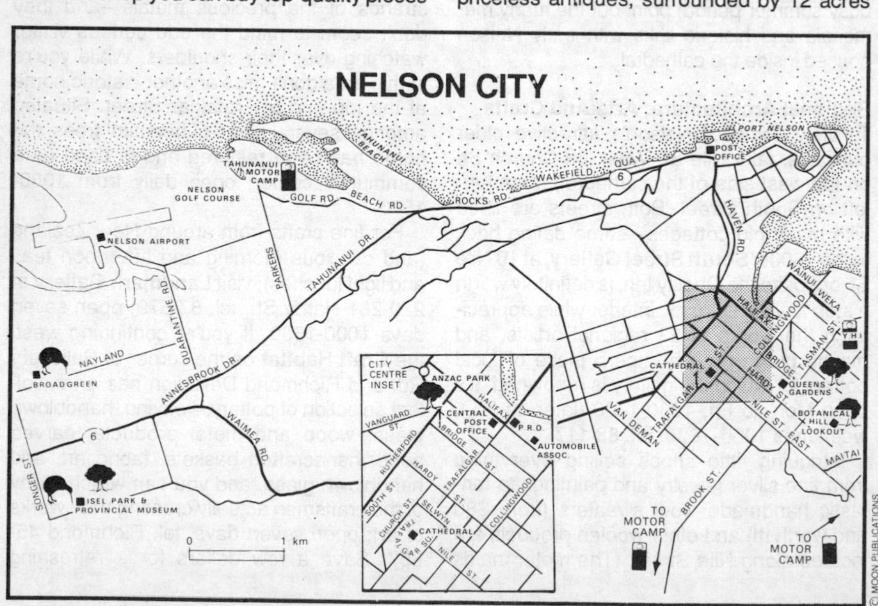

of woods. On Main Rd., Stoke, open weekends 1400-1600; admission adult 50 cents, child 10 cents.

Provincial Museum

While you're visiting Isel House, don't miss a visit to Nelson's fascinating Provincial Museum (at the rear) which features early Nelson history: displays of Maori carvings and artifacts found in the district, and objects and curios originally brought over by English settlers. The museum is set amongst the attractive gardens and grounds of **Isel Park,** where many of the trees have stood for more than a century, in the western Nelson suburb of Stoke. It's open Tues. to Fri. from 1000-1600, and Sat., Sun., and public holidays from 1400-1700; free admission weekdays (donations welcome), 50 cents pp weekends, and varying admission fees for special exhibitions.

Pottery Outlets

The Nelson area is known throughout N.Z. for its fine, varied clays, excellent raw materials, large community of talented, creative potters, and a vast number of outlets. Many of the clay and glaze materials (ground from naturally occurring minerals) used by potters throughout N.Z. come from around here. You can spend days visiting all the pottery shops throughout the area. To find out where they're located, pick up the free brochure *Tourist Guide to Nelson Potters* from the PRO, along with a number of other brochures on spinning, weaving, jewelry making, and other local crafts. For a huge pottery exhibition by Nelson's leading potters, visit **Clayworks Gallery** at 123 Bridge St. in Nelson; open weekdays 0900-1730, later Fri. nights, and Sat. mornings. Also don't miss **South Street Gallery** at 10 Nile St. and **Nelson Community Potters Incorporated** at 136 Rutherford Street. If you're leaving Nelson but continuing north, you'll also be continually tempted to part with your money at many small roadside stalls, snazzy shops, and isolated potters' retreats, along with many other arts and crafts outlets.

Beaches

The closest, **Tahunanui Beach** (also called Tahuna Beach), is five km west of city center, one of the safest and most popular beaches in the region. The back beach is also the site of unique car racing on the sand, an annual event at New Year. To get there from the city center take Haven Rd. west to Port Nelson and follow Rocks Rd. (Hwy. 6 south) along the waterfront, or catch the suburban bus (runs every hour) from Bridge Street. This pleasant route is especially colorful around Christmas when striking *pohutukawa* trees are a mass of scarlet flowers. Don't miss the incredible Aotearoa ("Land of the Long White Cloud") **wall mural** (a Nelson Provincial Arts Council Mural Project) on the right side of Rocks Rd. as you follow the waterfront toward the beach. The enormous **Tahuna**

stunning wall mural at the waterfront

Beach Holiday Park motor camp (turn off Rocks Rd. onto Beach Rd.) is within walking distance from the beach (see p. 355).

If you don't mind a 27-km drive west toward Motueka, you'll be rewarded with about 12 km of soft golden sand, dunes, pine trees, safe swimming, and good surfcasting at **Rabbit Island.** Take Hwy. 6 south out of Nelson, go through Richmond following signs to Motueka (Hwy. 60), and turn right at Pea Viner Corner. For more beautiful sandy beaches and less and less people, continue north to Golden Bay.

Scenic Drive

If you have your own transportation, watch for the white arrows on blue AA signs scattered around the city. This scenic circuit (start at any point) takes willing participants on a 27-km drive to Nelson's lookouts, scenic and historic spots, and general places of interest. (For bicycle hire, see the assorted hostel managers.) If you'd rather do a commercial tour, contact the PRO for details—many local operators offer coach, mini-bus, and taxi tours at varying prices to just about anywhere you want to go.

SHORT WALKS

The many good walks of varying distances around the city and throughout the suburbs are described in a series of free pamphlets put out by the Nelson City Council at the PRO. One of the best known and most scenic is the 20-minute (OW) **Centre Of N.Z.** track which gradually zig-zags up Botanical Hill (148 meters) to a lookout and monument marking the first trig station in Nelson. Start at the Botanical Reserve on Milton St. (east of downtown). **The Grampians,** another popular hike to a lookout, provides excellent views of the city and surrounding area, but note that the steep climb takes about 1½ hours OW. If you're still in an energetic mood once you've reached the top, continue south over the hilltops for about two km to Flaxmoor (390 meters), which can also be reached by footpath from Waimea Road. The first section of the Grampian foot track starts at the top (south) end of Collingwood St. in the city—take something refreshing to drink. The **Maitai River Walkway** starts at the bridge near the PRO and meanders along the river (past some good swimming holes) taking about four hours RT—take a picnic lunch and enjoy!

For an easy walk following the historic line of New Zealand's first railway, try the 9.5-km **Dun Mountain Walkway.** It starts on Tantragee Rd. (left off Brook St. in the suburb of The Brook, five km south of city center), finishes one km from the starting point on Brook St., and takes about three hours RT. One of the most scénic walks in the Nelson region is the **Dun Mountain Track** which passes through native bush to Third House and the summit. The track starts at Brook St. Reservoir Motor Camp (contact the caretaker before setting out), or from the Maitai Valley.

ACCOMMODATION

Hostels

Spacious **Nelson YHA Hostel** is housed in an attractive old building—one of Nelson's original homesteads—with spacious grounds. Despite the old-fashioned exterior, it's equipped with all the mod cons and provides plenty of room to spread out, and you can hire all the gear you need to do the Abel Tasman Track from the hostel shop; $12 pp per night. At 42 Weka St., tel. 88-817. If you're coming into Nelson from Blenheim, Picton, or Havelock via Hwy. 6, turn off at "The Wood" sign, continue to the YHA sign on the corner of Weka and Milton sts. and turn right (altogether a 10-minute walk from the main highway). From city center it's about a 15-minute walk east—take Trafalgar St. north, cross the river bridge, turn right at Wainui St. which becomes Weka St., and continue to the east end.

Tasman Towers at 10 Weka St., tel. 87-950, has equipment hire, bus pickup connections for the Abel Tasman Track (and plenty of info on the park), an equipped kitchen, eating area, comfy living room, excellent notice board, off-road parking; share and double rooms from $14 pp. **Pavlova House,** three km from town at 328 Brook St., tel. 89-

Brook Motor Camp

906, has budget accommodation starting at $13 per night (you can make reservations). It's a fun place to stay—a casual farm hostel surrounded by hills and fields, with a small river, BBQ area, and organic peach tree in the back yard—always humming with activity and people from around the world. Enjoy a piece of pavlova (specialty of the house) and a cup of tea on arrival with the entertaining kiwi owners, Cedric and Isabel Hockey. Faci-lities include a fully equipped kitchen, laundry, comfy living room, free use of bikes, storage, and pickup service, detailed Abel Tasman track info (every night they do a half-hour lecture on things you most want to know about the park), and a free RT bus service into town in the evenings.

Hostels (or private houses taking in guests) seem to come and go each year. Ask fellow travelers for their recommendations, and call in at the PRO for a list of registered hostels.

Motor Camps

No motor camps are in the center of town, and if you arrive during holiday periods (especially Christmas), finding central lodging may be difficult, unless you can afford one of the zillion motel rooms. The largest motor camp is **Tahuna Beach Holiday Park,** five km from city center—but if literally hundreds of people in close proximity to one another causes you any degree of claustrophobia, you may find the 400 tentsites, 600 caravan sites, plus cabins a problem! It's adjacent to a sandy beach, has a shop (open daily 0800-1900), TV theatrette, and the usual facilities. Tent and caravan sites are $13 d; two-, three-, and four-star cabins range from $22-60 d, and motel units (equipped for wheelchairs) are $60 d. The motor camp is located at Tahunanui Beach, tel. 85-159; follow the road west along the waterfront (Hwy. 6) to Tahunanui, turn off Rocks Rd. onto Beach Road.

The closest caravan sites and cabins to city center are found at **Nelson Cabins and Caravan Park,** 230 Vanguard St., tel. 81-445. Communal facilities and TV lounge. No tentsites. Caravan sites are $12.50 d, cabins start at $29 d, tourist flats from $39 d.

Peaceful **Maitai River Motor Camp** on Maitai Valley Rd. (a 5.5-km scenic drive from downtown) lies along the Maitai River, tel. 87-729. You can get there via Nelson Shuttle Service from the PRO, tel. 521-151. There's a swimming hole across from the picnic ground, good brown trout fishing, a golf course nearby, and bathroom, kitchen, and laundry facilities. Plenty of grassy tentsites ($7 s, $10 d) and caravan sites ($8.50 s, $15 d) lie among shady trees (complete with opossums!), and there are on-site caravans with gas stoves and fridges ($15 per night plus $6 per adult, $3 per child; provide all your own gear) and some cabins (ask for current rates). The camp is usually full between Dec. 26 and Jan. 10—book ahead if you can.

Brook Reservoir Motor Camp on Brook St., tel. 80-399, also has a scenic location about five km from town (reached by the same shuttle service as Maitai), with a brook running through the grounds, swimming pool, picnic area, trampolines, shop, and the usual communal facilities. Tentsites from $6 s, $10 d, caravan sites $7.50 s, $12 d. Fully equipped cabins (some with bunks, some with double beds) with cooking facilities range from $26-32 d (more in peak periods).

Guesthouses And Motels

If you feel like being pampered while staying in a beautifully restored old home, or breakfast is your favorite meal of the day, head directly for **California House** at 29 Collingwood St., tel. (54) 84-173. It's open Sept. through May, closed in winter. Built in 1893, this elegant colonial home has five spacious guest rooms, modern facilities, English oak paneling, kauri fireplaces, 24 original stained-glass windows, teddy bears everywhere, and a well-kept garden. Fully restored by hospitable Carol Glen (transplanted from guess where), each room is distinctly individual. The comfy parlor is well stocked with reading material on Nelson, New Zealand, and California, and although there are no cooking facilities, you can help yourself to coffee, tea, sherry, and biscuits. The breakfast menu features fresh fruit and cream, baked goodies, pancakes, blintzes, or omelettes—sumptuous and different each morning (forget all notions of a diet!). From $60 s B&B, $80-100 d B&B plus GST. Book as far ahead as possible (essential from Christmas to 15 Jan.) but if you haven't booked, just show up, cross your fingers, and see if there's room.

Mrs. Devlin's **Palm Grove Guest House** is an attractive old house with six sunny guest rooms, TV room, garden, coffee- and tea-making facilities but no guest use of the kitchen or laundry; $25 pp includes a hearty breakfast with homemade goodies; at 52 Cambria St., tel. 84-645. For more B&B guesthouses, private hotels, and motels, go to the PRO. Many motels are along Golf Rd. in the Tahunanui Beach area, most within walking distance from the beach.

FOOD AND ENTERTAINMENT

Nelson has a lot of cafes and restaurants—take a short stroll around town and you're bound to see plenty of places that'll lure you back later for a snack or meal. If you have a particular fancy, drop by the PRO and ask for a recommendation.

Light Meals

The rustic **Bridge Coffee House** at 123 Bridge St. (between Collingwood and Trafalgar sts.) is a great spot for morning and afternoon teas, *doner* kebabs, falafels, salads, pita-bread sandwiches, and a good self-serve salad bar. Everything is freshly prepared, wholesome, and delicious; open seven days from 0930-1600. **The Hole In The Wall** at 2 Buxton Square (between Bridge, Trafalgar, and Hardy sts.; walk through from Buxton Carpark) is another good place to go for homebaked morning and afternoon teas and lunches—filled croissants, soups, salads, and desserts at reasonable prices. Or try the excellent **Landmark Gallery** at the top end of Hardy Street.

Nelson Feasteries

At 142 Hardy St., trendy **City Lights Cafe** features seafood, steaks, salads, and nightly specials in an attractive, informal, and justifiably crowded atmosphere. Entrees are $8.50-10, dinners $16-20, desserts $5-8.50; open Mon. to Sat. from 1730 to late. Very popular with locals, it pays to book ahead at tel. 88-999. **Chez Eelco Coffee House** at 296 Trafalgar St. (tel. 87-595) draws a good local crowd, offering all kinds of salads, a variety of omelettes for around $9, salads for $12, various steaks with salad for $17. Try the house specialty—a plate of tasty Marlborough Mussels with salad. Desserts start at $5. They're open every day from 0800-2300, Sun. to 2100, and you can sit outside at the sidewalk tables and watch the world go by. For tasty Indian food in a non-smoking atmosphere, everyone suggests **Samadhi In-**

dian Vegetarian Restaurant at 30 Washington Rd., tel. 69-551. It's a BYO, open Mon. to Sat. from 1800. Mains range from $9-15 and come with vegies, yogurt, cucumber salad, and more.

For a substantial lunch or dinner, head for **The Swordsman Steakhouse** at 256 Trafalgar Street. The smorgasbord lunch is $10 pp, smorgasbord with steak is $14 pp, and appetizers start at around $5. Seafood and steak dishes start at $12, or you can visit the salad bar for $9.50 pp. The local **Cobb & Co.** licensed restaurant, part of Wakatu Hotel on the corner of Bridge and Collingwood sts., has filling main courses ranging from $11-18 (the pepper steak for $12 is really good). All mains come with french fries and salad bar or vegetables, desserts are $6, and if you have a smaller appetite you can get half portions for half price. It's open daily from 0730- 2200.

The Hitching Post serves good pizza and steaks and has a salad bar; reasonable prices, fun atmosphere, and outdoor eating on the patio in warm weather (have a go on the giant backgammon board in the open-air courtyard). Mains average $8-15, desserts from $1.50. At 145 Bridge St., tel. 87-374; open Mon. to Thurs. 0800-2100, Fri. 0800-2130, Sat. 1700-2130, and Sun. in summer. If you're in the mood to eat (and eat, and eat), head for **Figpeckers Restaurant** at 137 Bridge St., tel. 89-891. Here you can tuck in to a substantial lunch (soup, bread, casseroles, salads, dessert, tea or coffee) for $10 Mon. to Fri. from 1130-1400, and an equally substantial four-course dinner for $15 pp Mon. to Sat. from 1730. If you don't mind a short drive to Stoke (about 16 km south of Nelson) and it's Jan. or Feb., enjoy lunch or dinner in an outdoor orchard setting at **Robinson Brothers** on Main Rd.; open seven days, tel. 75-259. Savor BBQ'd steak or lamb, and a variety of salads, fruit, and wines (imported and local wines available for tasting).

Takeaways

On your way to Tahunanui Beach? Grab good Chinese takeaway from **The Wok** at 16 Muritai St. (behind Beach Road). Beef, chicken, pork, and seafood dishes range from $8-14. Open Tues. to Sun. 1600-2200. For fast food to go, discover **Washington Valley Takeaways** at 28 Washington Valley, tel. 83-582. They serve the "best fish in town," along with hamburgers, hot dogs, hot chips, fish kebabs, and a variety of other fast foods; open Mon. to Fri. 1130-1430, every day from 1630 till late.

Port Nelson

SERVICES

Urgent

For emergency **ambulance, police,** or **fire brigade,** call 111. **Nelson Public Hospital** is on Waimea Rd. (main entrance on Kawai St.), tel. 88-299. For the name of a local **doctor,** call the hospital at the above number or tel. 82-304, Mon. to Friday. If you need a doctor or pharmacy on weekends, refer to the back page of the Fri. newspaper where they're listed. The **urgent pharmacy** is at 54 Bridge St., tel. 84-291. If you need the **police** in the Nelson or Richmond area, call 88-309; in the Motueka area, call 85-800.

General

Late-night shopping is on Fri. until 2000. **Bank** hours are 0900-1630, but the **Canterbury Savings Bank** (branches in Nelson, Stoke, and Richmond) has extended hours on Fri. nights (till 2030). The **chief p.o.** is on Trafalgar St.; the postal section is open Mon. to Thurs. 0800-1730 and Fri. 0800-2000, and the savings bank section is open Mon. to Thurs. 0900-1600 and Fri. 0900-2000. Nelson's main **public library** is on Hardy St., tel. 84-691 (branches at Stoke, Tahunanui, and Richmond); open Mon. to Thurs. 0930-1730 and 1900-2000, Fri. 0930-2100. The main local newspaper is the *Nelson Evening Mail.* Nelson has no public laundromat, however **Master Valet** drycleaners on Collingwood St. offers a laundry service—take your clothes in by 1000 and they'll be ready by late afternoon. **Restrooms** can be found at the cathedral steps on Trafalgar Square, at Buxton Car Park, Millers Acre Car Park, Montgomery Car Park, and the Tahunanui playground.

INFORMATION

The main source of information is the **PRO** on the corner of Trafalgar and Halifax sts., tel. 82-303 or 82-304; open seven days from 0830-1730. It's also a booking and transportation center so you can get everthing you need in the one location. Collect a city map (10 cents), *Nelson Provincial Visitor's Guide* and *Welcome to Nelson* pamphlets, and various tourist newspapers before you hit the pavement, and check out the outside notice boards. Stick up a notice if you're trying to catch a ride to a particular destination or looking for people to share car rental costs.

If you want track info on the State Forests, stop in at the **Dept. of Conservation** in the Munro State Building on Bridge St., or call 81-175; they're open Mon. to Fri. 0800-1630. For excellent **Dept. of Survey and Lands** maps, drop by their office, also in the Munro State Building, tel. 81-579; open Mon. to Fri. from 0800-1600.

TRANSPORTATION

Getting There

From Picton there are two ways to reach Nelson by car. The most scenic route, Queen Charlotte Drive, winds steeply over bush-

Nelson waterfront

covered hills giving unsurpassed views of Queen Charlotte, Kenepuru, and Pelorus Sounds on the way to Havelock, then passes by mighty rivers, forest parks, and scenic reserves between Havelock and Nelson. Keep in mind that the road between Picton and Havelock takes longer than it looks on the map—it's twisty and narrow in places, and you need both a reliable car and driver (sometimes a difficult combo to find when you're hitchhiking!). The other route, Hwy. 1 south to the bustling town of Blenheim then Hwy. 6 west to Nelson, is longer but faster. When you're in Blenheim, stop at the PRO downtown (tel. 84-480), and at the Dept. of Conservation office also downtown (open weekdays 0830-1600) for info on the northern State Forest Parks and Nelson Lakes.

Nelson is also easily reached by bus from Picton (**Newmans Coach Lines** offices are on High St. and at the Picton Ferry Terminal and **Connections** office is at Port Nelson, tel. 68-650) and Blenheim (**Newmans Coach Lines,** Grove Rd.), by air via **Air New Zealand.**

Local Bus Service

Nelson Suburban Bus Co. at the lower end of Bridge St. provides local service covering the city center, Port Nelson, Tahunanui, Bishopdale, Stoke, Richmond, and Wakefield, and a variety of local bus tours. For schedules and bus stops, drop by the office or call Nelson 83-290 or Richmond 7095. To get out to the airport or the various motor camps on the outskirts of town, contact **Nelson Shuttle Service** at tel. 521-151 for all the details, or call in at the PRO.

Long-distance Bus Service

Make your first stop the PRO in Millers Carpark for all on-going transportation information. If you're continuing northwest, **Newmans Coachlines** services Motueka and Golden Bay; open daily at 220 Hardy St., call 88-369 for daily schedules and prices. They also provide daily service southwest to the west coast, southeast to Christchurch, and east to Picton and Blenheim, along with local bus tours. **Delta Coachlines** provides services to Abel Tasman Park, and to the west coast via St. Arnaud (Nelson Lakes National Park), departing from Skyline travel, tel. 80-285. **Skyline Travel** on Achilles Ave. runs a daily passenger and freight service between Nelson and Motueka, and bus tours; call 80-285 for current schedules—they run the Nelson-Motueka route more often during the busy summer period. Skyline Travel also services Kaiteriteri, Marahau, Takaka, and Totaranui. **Wadsworths Motors** runs a passenger and freight bus service to Lake Rotoiti on Mon., Wed., and Fri.; for more info call in at the Jarvis Home Decorating Centre at 28 Bridge St., or tel. 81-462.

If you're heading for the west coast and on to Queenstown, don't have your own transportation, and are in a hurry to see as much as you can, the **Magic Bus** is one of the best ways to do it. Catch either a Newmans bus from Nelson (or a Delta coach from Picton) to Greymouth and continue on the Magic Bus (Tues., Thurs., and Sat.—double-check the current timetable) from there. The company accepts Newmans bus passes. The **West Coast Express** bus service also runs to Queenstown via the west coast, starting from Nelson; get all the details at the PRO.

Air

Nelson Airport is located about eight km west of downtown; it's staffed 0630-2100 and for flight arrivals and departures. The **Nelson Shuttle** bus connects the airport with the PRO downtown; $5 s, $9 pp if there are two or more. For the schedule call 521-151, or the PRO at tel. 82-304. To get to the airport by car from city center, take Rutherford St. south which becomes Waimea Rd. and continue to the suburb of Wakatu. At Hays Corner where Waimea Rd. meets Annesbrook Dr. (Hwy. 6 south), turn right onto Annesbrook, then make a left on Quarantine Rd. and follow the signs to the terminal. The alternate (scenic) route from the city is via Hwy. 6 south (Wakefield Quay, then Rocks Rd.) along the waterfront, then Tahunanui Dr. which becomes Annesbrook Dr., and right on Quarantine Road. A taxi to the airport is about $8 OW.

Air New Zealand flies out of Nelson to

Trafalgar street—looking toward the Cathedral

most major destinations on both islands. The Air New Zealand office is on the corner of Trafalgar and Halifax sts., tel. 82-329, open Mon. to Fri. 0830-1700; for reservations call 80-189. **Mount Cook Airlines** (tel. 69-300) and **Air Nelson** (tel. 76-066) at the airport also offer regular scheduled flights to a variety of destinations. For **scenic flights** of varying duration (30-55 minutes for $35-60), call in at **Nelson Aero Club** at the airport, tel. 79-643.

Cars, Bicycles, Taxis

Quite a few car rental agencies are scattered around town. Check out the yellow pages and call them all for price comparisons—the smaller companies are often cheaper but have more restrictions on drop-off points, etc. The main agencies are **Avis** at 143 Trafalgar St., tel. 83-789; **Budget** at 27 Halifax St., tel. 80-169; **Hertz** at 31 Hardy St., tel. 82-239; **National** at Dayman Motors Ltd., 205 Bridge St., tel. 69-232; and **Thrifty** on Haven Road.

If you want to hire a **bicycle,** call the various hostels around town and compare rates. At **Greg Graine Cycles,** 101 Bridge St. (tel. 83-877), a standard bicycle rents for $6 a day, a 10-speed for $14 a day, and tandems from $15-20 a day. They also rent touring bikes with panniers, racks, etc., and have trained cycle mechanics on hand. For a taxi, call **Nelson Taxis** at 28 Bridge St., tel. 88-225.

THE REMOTE NORTHWEST

Traveling from Nelson to the South Island's remote northwest is a worthwhile adventure if you enjoy the great outdoors and have plenty of time. It's best seen at a leisurely pace by car or bicycle, but if you're relying on public transportation, Newmans Coachlines runs daily from Nelson and Motueka as far north as Takaka, and a connecting bus runs to Collingwood and the Heaphy Track. There's all kinds of scenery to appreciate—undulating valleys where hops, tobacco, apples, nectarines, and kiwifruit grow in abundance, a "marble mountain" riddled with underground caves and sinkholes, rugged ranges, crystal-clear springs, golden-sand beaches, and spectacular coastal views. Waterfowl such as black swans, ducks, and Canada geese are drawn in great numbers to the more isolated areas along **Golden Bay,** and oystercatchers and godwits flock to the sandy shores of remote **Farewell Spit** in the far north. The farther north you go, the less people and the more wildlife you see.

Abel Tasman National Park, one of the area's major attractions (80 km northwest of Nelson), lures people of all ages and fitness levels—hiking tracks of varying lengths and difficulties meander through the park. In summer **Totaranui,** the only coastal spot accessible by road in the far northern section of the park, rapidly fills with sun-seeking campers who grab their section of the beach and get away from it all! If you plan on visiting Abel Tasman National Park, pick up as much info as you can from the PRO and Dept. of Conservation in Nelson before you head northwest—you pass the south and west park entrances before you reach the town of Takaka where Park HQ is located. Otherwise stop at the Dept. of Conservation office in Motueka—you can also get all the info you need here. Hitching to Abel Tasman National Park is most difficult—and it's just as hard to get out again. If you don't have your own transportation, consider seeing the park coastline by sea kayak with **Ocean River Adventure Co.** based in Motueka (tel. 88-823; see below). Another good reason to venture even farther north to **Collingwood** is to hike the well-known 70-km **Heaphy Track.**

NELSON AND THE NORTHWEST

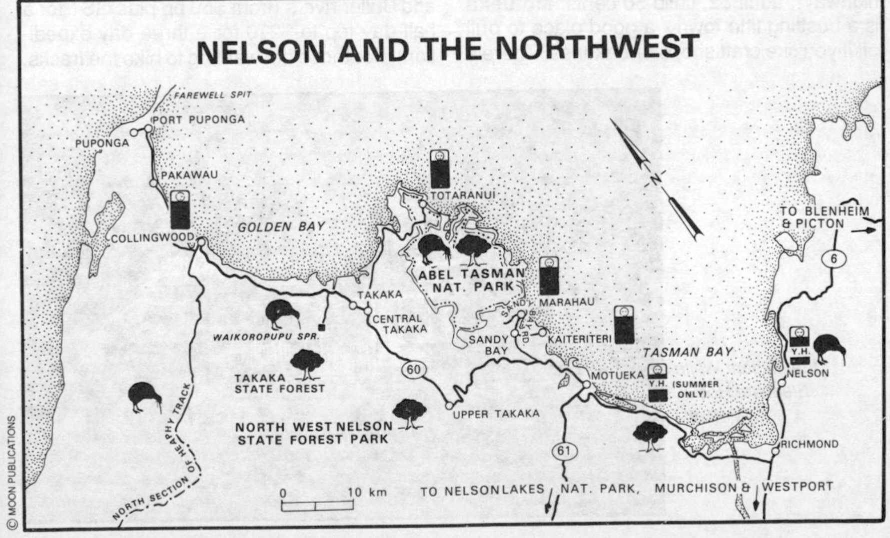

Usually walked from east to west, the head of the track is reached by road 35 km southwest of Collingwood or by plane from Nelson or Motueka (see p. 369).

NELSON TO ABEL TASMAN NATIONAL PARK

Take Hwy. 6 south out of Nelson and after going through Richmond, swing west on Hwy. 60. This scenic road along Tasman Bay passes pottery shops and weaving sheds, deer farms, and apple orchards (excellent apples in March). If staying at a dress-optional holiday resort sounds appealing, look out for the sign to **Mapua Leisure Park** on Toru St., Mapua, tel. 666. It's about a half-hour drive from Nelson, 15 minutes to Motueka. Aside from swimming, fishing, tennis, golf, and many other recreational activities, the camp has tent and caravan sites from $8 per night, on-site caravans and chalets from $39 d, and tourist flats starting at $50 d. Bookings are necessary for January. If nudity offends you, give this place a miss!

About eight km south of Motueka you can see the **Moutere tame eels** being fed at 1000-1200 and 1300-1600, on Wilsons Rd., Moutere Valley (look for the AA sign on the highway); adult $2, child 50 cents. **Motueka** is a bustling litte town—a good place to pull off if you like craft shops or bakeries. There's a summer-only YH, and Motueka is the last place of any size to pick up camping supplies before you continue north. Make your first stop the **Museum, Art Gallery, and Information Centre,** housed in the 1913 red-brick building on High St. (the main road), tel. 87-660; open weekdays Sept. to Jan. from 0930-1700, the rest of the year from 1030-1430 (museum admission $1). The staff can book you on one of many local tours—take a cruise, stagger through a winery (or four), visit local orchards, go on a horticultural tour (very popular), or scream down a river on a raft—and they have the latest rundown on Abel Tasman National Park. For all the details on hiking and hunting possibilities in the park, and other nearby Forest Parks, visit the Dept. of Conservation office at 1-7 King Edward St. (off High St.), tel. 89-117; open year-round weekdays 0800-1630, and weekends too during the peak summer period.

Another reason to stop in Motueka is to find out the latest offerings of **Ocean River Adventure Co.** The staff specialize in **sea kayaking** rentals (from $30 per day including RT transport from Motueka to the park, equipment, and instruction) and kayak tours of the Abel Tasman National Park coastline, and **white-water rafting trips** down the Gowan and Buller rivers (from $50 pp plus GST for a half-day trip to $270 for a three-day expedition). For those not wanting to hike the tracks,

the elegant White Elephant Hostel, Motueka

view from Takaka Hill

sea kayaking is the way to go! You can also rent kayaks from **Abel Tasman Kayaks** on Harvey Rd., Marahau (tel. 78-022) or **Park Cafe** at the Marahau Car Park; from $6 an hour to $26 a day, guided trips for $25-35. If you end up staying over in Motueka, consider a bed at the **White Elephant**—excellent budget accommodation in a big old mansion set on spacious grounds. The rooms (bunks and doubles) are large, spacious, and cheerful. Facilities include a fully equipped kitchen, laundry, drying room, free luggage storage, bicycle rental ($3 half day or $5 a day), sunny veranda, BBQ, and an orchard at the back where you can pick your own fruit. Dorm beds are $13 pp, individual rooms are $15 pp. Located at 55 Whakarewa St. (off High St., opposite the high school), tel. 86-208. For lunch or dinner ($7.50-15), try **Gothic Gourmet** restaurant on High St., downtown. For a quick sandwich, go across the road to the **Eaterie.**

After going through **Riwaka,** Hwy. 60 passes the turn-off east to the beach resort of **Kaiteriteri** (one of the best swimming beaches in the Nelson region, with a popular motor camp nearby), and the road that runs northeast to **Sandy Bay** (another good swimming beach) and **Marahau,** the southern entrance to Abel Tasman National Park (and the start of both the Coastal and Inland Tracks).

Highway 60 continues up **Takaka Hill** (made of marble with four major caves, the locals call this speleologist's delight "Marble Mountain") toward **Takaka** where **Abel Tasman National Park HQ** is located. You can take a tour of the **Ngarua Caves** of Marble Mountain from Sept. to June for adult $5.50, child $1.50, tel. 88-093 or 89-805. The western entrance to the park is the 12-km gravel Canaan Rd. that leads to **Canaan**. It turns right off Hwy. 60 before the summit of Takaka Hill, but if you don't already know where you're headed, continue to the summit for splendid views of North-West Nelson State Forest Park and on down to Upper Takaka passing the "Rat Trap" Hotel. Continue to **Takaka** where the **PRO** is easy to find on the left side of Commercial St. as you enter town from the south; pick up complete info on **Golden Bay** farther north, and maps of Park tracks. For a detailed map of the Park (essential for hikers and backcountry explorers) and the latest track and camping info, visit the **Dept. of Survey and Lands** office farther along Commercial St. (on the left side just beyond the carpark), or continue along Hwy. 60 to Park HQ.

ABEL TASMAN NATIONAL PARK

The Land And Wildlife

Abel Tasman National Park (22,139 hectares) is the smallest national park in New Zealand. Its highest point, **Mt. Evans,** is only 1,134 meters. The eastern boundary of this steep and rugged coastal park extends from **Separation Point** (which separates Tasman and Golden bays) in the north to **Sandy Bay** in the south, and includes all the islands and reefs up to 2.5 km out to sea. Its western boundary includes Mt. Evans and Murray's Peak (1,101 meters), both in the **Pikikiruna Range.** No roads run through the Park, but three main access roads lead to **Marahau** in the south, **Canaan** in the west, and **Wainui Inlet, Totaranui,** and **Awaroa Inlet** in the north. The only way to get into the interior and to most of the main attractions is on foot via the many tracks that lead off the main access roads.

Despite its small size and remote location, the Park attracts outdoor enthusiasts by the masses—in fact, the tracks in summer are often overcrowded and there is the danger that this park may be spoiled by its great popularity. The overall impression is one of dense beech forest, golden sand, and azure waters, but adventurous hikers can also enjoy sculptured granite gorges and marble outcrops, icy waterfalls and polished swimming holes, impressive cave systems and an enormous vertical shaft, pockets of rainforest, isolated beaches, and lush native bush alive with birds. Many seabirds make their home in the Park—shags, gannets, blue penguins, terns, oyster-catchers, herons, and stilts, and you can often catch sight of seals or the occasional dolphin frolicking not far offshore. The Park is not known for its great hunting (or fishing), though if you do plan on hunting the few deer, pigs, goats, and opossums present, a permit is required. No hunting is allowed from mid-Dec. to the end of Jan. because of the high number of hikers in the backcountry.

History

The stretch of coastline along Abel Tasman National Park has quite a history. Maori may have been living along the shores of Tasman Bay as early as the 13th C. (the earliest carbon-dated site shows occupation around A.D. 1540)—you can still see sites of some of their ancient settlements. In 1642 Dutch explorer Abel Tasman first spotted the shoreline that officially became the eastern boundary of the Park exactly 300 years later. In 1827 the French explorer D'Urville sailed along the western shores of Tasman Bay naming many of the landmarks, and after his detailed exploration, European settlement began in earnest.

Farmers moved into the Totaranui area, successfully clearing the bush, farming the land, and becoming self-sufficient. Shipbuilding from local timber began in the Awaroa Inlet area, and to many of the bays and inlets came hordes of farmers, loggers, shipbuilders, fishermen, and quarrymen. The entire coastal area was modified, became quite settled, and a few small areas (Totaranui, some of Awaroa, and Bark Bay) took on an almost English-countryside appearance. However, during the Depression in the early 1900s even the most prosperous farmers eventually found they could no longer afford to run their properties. Logging and shipbuilding also ceased, and the residents sadly abandoned their homes and farms. Today the coast shows little sign of past occupation and activities, and the bush grows down to water's edge in most places. Evidence of one of the most flourishing settlements of the recent past can best be seen in the Totaranui area.

SIGHTS AND HIKES

By Sea

If you want a good introduction to Abel Tasman National Park without hiking the tracks or driving all the way to Totaranui, take a 6½-hour **cruise** on MVs *Matangi, Ponui,* or

Waingaro, which run daily in summer from Kaiteriteri. Cruise along Tasman Bay, stop at a couple of the most scenic bays, and hear a bit of local lore; $30 RT. Take your own lunch; tea and coffee are provided. For more info, the current rates, and the seasonal schedule, call John or Lynette Wilson at tel. 87-801 Motueka. They also run a daily water-taxi service to Totaranui, dropping hikers off at Tonga, and Bark, Torrent, and Tinline Bays; $13-25 pp OW depending on your destination. Their four-day guided walks in the Park include three nights' accommodation in a private lodge and all meals for adult $485, child $465; call the cruise number above for more details.

Another alternative and extremely popular way to discover the beauty of the Abel Tasman coastline is by sea kayak. Contact **Ocean River Adventure Co.** in Motueka, tel. 88-823, to rent your own sea kayak (from $26 per day including RT transport from Motueka to the park, equipment, and instruction), or take a tour of the coastline with their experienced staff. If you haven't prearranged your kayak, you may still be able to rent one at the Marahau carpark. The company also provides exhilarating **white-water rafting trips** down the Gowan and Buller rivers (from $50 pp plus GST for a half-day trip to $270 for a three-day expedition).

Short Walks

Take any of the access roads to Park boundaries for a variety of short walks to scenic spots or lookouts. (Don't forget insect repellent!) If you're coming from the south, turn northeast off Hwy. 60 to Sandy Bay and continue along Sandy Bay Rd. to Marahau. **Tinline Walk** starts from the coastal track, about two km from Marahau carpark, and loops through groves of beech, kahikatea, pukatea, rimu, and other native trees; about 30 minutes RT. If you're feeling a little more energetic, follow the tracks to beautiful **Coquille Bay** (about 45 minutes from Marahau carpark), **Apple Tree Bay** (1½ hours), or take the Coastal Track to **Torrent Bay** (about four hours OW), one of the most scenic bays in the Park. From Torrent Bay, two other short walks lead to **Cleopatra's Pool** and **Cascade Falls,** and you can stay overnight in the eight-bunk Torrent Bay Hut or the 26-bunk Anchorage Hut (small charge, take your sleeping bag, cooking equipment, and supplies).

A geologically fascinating area to explore on foot is Canaan, a haven for cavers and potholers. Take Hwy. 60 to Takaka Hill, turn off on Canaan Rd. and continue almost to the end. The winding road passes amazing granite and marble rock outcrops and ends at rocky Canaan basin. Look out for the track marker to the left leading to **Harwood's Hole,** an incredible marble-walled vertical shaft 50 meters wide and 200 meters deep that leads to one of the most impressive cave systems in the area. The track to Harwood's Hole is an easy 45 minutes through beech forest, but be careful around the edge of the shaft as the ground is very unstable—a fall into this hole would definitely end your vacation! From the carpark at the end of Canaan Rd. are several other short walks, or you can join the inland track system to either Wainui or Marahau.

Totaranui at the northern end is perhaps the most popular holiday resort along Tasman Bay and the most accessible area of the Park by car, but note that the last 20 km of road is narrow, winding, and loose gravel—it can be treacherous for those towing caravans. Totaranui's ample camping ground (see "Accommodation" below), golden beach, bush-covered headlands and hills, hiking tracks, and ranger station (guided walks in summer), draw the multitudes, particularly in the summer. To get there take Hwy. 60 to Takaka (stop at Park HQ for maps and camping info), then take the coastal road that goes through Pohara, Tarakohe, Wainui Inlet, and on to Totaranui (about 33 km from Takaka). From Totaranui a short 45-minute walk north (OW) takes you to golden **Anapai Beach,** or if you want to make it an overnighter, continue on for another two to three spectacular hours to **Whariwharangi Bay** and hut. Another popular short walk is the **Waiharakeke Track.** It starts on Awaroa Rd. about one km south of the Totaranui turnoff and runs down to Waiharakeke Beach, taking about 1½ hours to pass through valleys, fern-filled gullies, and crystal-clear streams to end at yet another beautiful beach. What a life!

Tracks And Huts
Before starting out along any of the tracks you need to purchase a **Facilities Use Pass** for adult $4, child $2 which must be attached to your backpack and clearly visible—you also get useful track information with the pass. Backcountry hut tickets are $4 per night for camping, $4 a night for basic huts, $8 for intermediate huts, and $12 a night for fully serviced huts. Buy the tickets at any Dept. of Conservation office (Nelson, Motueka, and Takaka), PROs, YHs, campgrounds, from some of the transportation companies in the Nelson region, or at the Marahau Cafe at the start of the track.

The two main track systems—Inland Track and Coastal Track—both connect at Wainui Bay in the north and at Marahau in the south. Park rangers suggest that all hikers fill in the intention book prior to leaving on any of the longer tracks, and take plenty of insect repellent. The **Inland Track** starts at Marahau, takes three days, and finishes at Wainui Inlet. It averages four hours between each of the four huts along the route (small charge payable to park rangers, hut wardens, or local Survey and Lands offices). The huts have mattresses, wood stoves, limited cooking facilities, and fresh water, but to be on the safe side, take your own sleeping bag, stove, and supplies. Side tracks lead off to the Canaan area and Takaka.

The popular **Coastal Track** also starts at Marahau and finishes at Wainui Inlet, takes two to three days, with four huts four hours apart; this track also gives access to numerous excellent camping areas, some with toilets and fireplaces. Before you set out, check tide times for crossing the Awaroa and Wainui Bay inlets—posted at the end of main roads to the Park, at Totaranui, and at all coastal huts. Awaroa and Wainui Bay inlets can only be crossed on foot two hours either side of low tide; Torrent and Bark Bay inlets have high-tide as well as low-tide tracks. Before you set out on either the Inland or Coastal Tracks, get a detailed map.

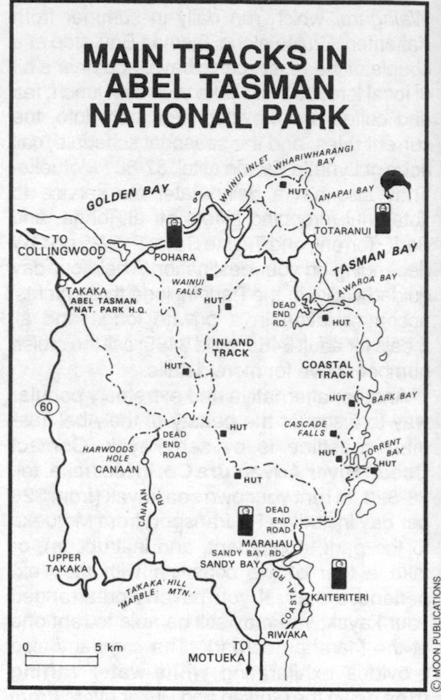

PRACTICALITIES

Accommodation
Aside from backcountry huts and campsites, within Park boundaries is the beachside **Totaranui Beach Camping Ground** with plenty of grassy tent and caravan sites (no powered sites), toilets, and fresh water; adult $5, child $2 payable to Dept. of Conservation offices at Totaranui or Takaka. Very popular, it's usually booked solid between 20 Dec. and 31 Jan. (the only period when bookings are accepted). If you're there then and haven't already booked, check with the Takaka office (tel. 58-026) or Totaranui office (tel. Motueka 88-083) before you head out. Also look out for Camp Full signs placed along the main public access roads.

The next closest motor camp to the northern section of Abel Tasman is at **Pohara,** along with several motels at Pohara, Clifton,

Tata Beach, and Takaka. **Pohara Beach Camp,** on yet another beautiful beach (along Golden Bay, not Tasman Bay), has sheltered swimming and sunbathing along with the usual facilities. Tent sites from $7 pp; caravan sites are $8 s, $14 d; cabins from $22-31 d, off-season rates available. Located at RD 1, Pohara (10 km northeast of Takaka on the way to the Park), tel. 59-500. A summer **YH** is set up in Golden Bay High School on Meihana St. in Takaka (usually in Dec. and Jan. only), tel. 59-067; $11 pp.

At the southern end of the Park, the closest motor camps are at Marahau and Kaiteriteri. **Marahau Beach Camp,** the nearest, provides communal facilities, and tent and caravan sites for $13 d, on-site caravans from $18-24 d, cabins from $25 d, and a self-contained flat for $35 d. Located on RD 2 at Marahau, 18 km north of Motueka, tel. 78-176. **Kaiteriteri Motor Camp** is adjacent to Kaiteriteri Beach (one of the most popular beaches on Tasman Bay) and has a store, tearooms, an 18-hole mini-golf course, and trampolines, along with the usual. Tent and caravan sites are $13 d. The resident caretaker can be reached at tel. 78-010 Motueka.

At Motueka (about 20 km from the Park), the **Motueka YHA Summer Hostel** is only open in Dec. and Jan. (call and check the opening and closing dates before you head there); $11 pp. Located in the local Motueka High School on Whakarewa St. (off High St. a couple of blocks from the p.o.—look for the Swan Hotel on the corner), tel. 88-962 (send advance bookings to 133 Thorp St., Motueka). Budget accommodation can also be found at the **YMCA Hostel** on High St. South. At the northern end of town **Fearson's Bush Motor Camp** provides communal facilities and tent and caravan sites for $6.50 pp, and cabins for $19 d; on Fearson St., tel. 87-189. At the southern end of town is **Motueka Beach Reserve Camp;** for those of you with boats in tow, it has a launching ramp. Tent and caravan sites $5 pp, off-season rates available. Located at Port Motueka, caretaker tel. 87-169. For cabins and flats with cooking facilities (no camping), try **Vineyard Tourist Flats** at 328 High St., Motueka, tel. 88-550. Cabins start at $32 d; tourist units with private shower and cooking facilities are $44 d. Motueka also has a variety of motels and hotels.

Food

No tearooms, restaurants, or shops (or petrol stations for that matter) are within Abel Tasman National Park. If you're heading into the south or southwest end, stock up in Motueka; if you're heading for Totaranui in the north, stock up in Takaka (insect repellent, suntan lotion, fuel for your camp stove and car, food, and other necessities). Motueka, the last town of any size in the north, naturally has the most places to eat. Try one of the mouth-wateringly good bakeries on the main street, the **Eaterie** on High St. for delicious pick-your-own-filling sandwiches, or for a sit-down lunch or dinner the **Gothic Gourmet** restaurant (in the pink church) also on High St.—tasty fare and reasonable prices ($7-14). For a surprisingly large number of places, also head for Takaka. **Telegraph Hotel** on the main street presents quick bistro meals in the lounge bar from 1130-1330 and 1800-1930. Try their steaks, mussels, or chicken, with chips, salad, and vegies for around $9, fish and chips for $7, or be daring and try their "peas, pie, and pud" of the day for $6. The hotel restaurant (more pricey and dressy) is open for dinner only from 1830-2000. **Junction Hotel** farther along the street has quick meals at the bar from 1800-1900. For delicious home-baked goodies and main meals (more expensive than the pubs), try the **Wholemeal Trading Company,** also on the main street but up a small alleyway—look for flower pots hanging outside the street entrance. Takaka also has a variety of cafes and takeaways, but if you're on a tight budget, you'll probably get more pleasure out of stocking up on dried and canned goods and cooking up a concoction on your own unspoiled beach under the stars.

Information

The main sources of info are **Abel Tasman National Park HQ** at 1 Commercial St., Takaka (open Mon. to Fri. 0900-1700), and the

Dept. of Conservation office (complete with display rooms) at 1-7 King Edward St. (off High St.) in Motueka, tel. 89-117 (open year-round weekdays 0800-1630, and weekends during the peak summer period). For an after-hours emergency, call the Chief Ranger at tel. 59-544 Takaka, the Takaka Ranger at tel. 59-644, the Marahau Ranger at tel. 78-110 Motueka, or the Totaranui Ranger at tel. 88-083 Motueka. Correspondence should be sent to the Chief Ranger, Survey and Lands Dept., Box 53, Takaka. You can also get Park info from the **PR/Survey and Lands Office** on the main street in Takaka, and the **PRO** in Nelson.

Transportation

To get to the end of the three main access roads into Abel Tasman National Park you really need your own transportation—or plenty of patience if you're traveling by thumb. However, you can catch a **Newmans Coachlines** bus from Nelson (or Motueka) daily as far north as Takaka, where bus and taxi operators run on-demand services (expensive) to Totaranui—call both **Bickley Motors** (135 Commercial St.), tel. 58- 095, and **Golden Bay Taxis** (114 Commercial St.), tel. 59-573, and compare prices and availability. From farther north, **Collingwood Passenger & Freight Services** (Collingwood P.O., tel. 48-188) also services the Park (from Nelson to Motueka $7.50, to Takaka $16, to Collingwood $20); from Takaka to Totaranui is $48 RT or $8 per head for more than six people, from Collingwood to the Heaphy Track is $50 per trip for up to five people. In summer **Newmans, Skyline Travel** (tel. 80- 285), and **Abel Tasman National Park Enterprises** run daily services between Nelson and Kaiteriteri or Marahau. To get to Marahau from Motueka call **Hickmott Motors,** tel. 87-040 Motueka, and **Motueka Taxis,** tel. 87-900 Motueka, both on High St., or **Skyline Travel** at tel. 88-850; $15 OW.

If you're staying at Kaiteriteri, a **water taxi** is a fun way to get to Totaranui (adult $22, child $11 OW), or to some of the beautiful beaches such as Tonga ($15 OW), and bays such as Bark, Torrent, and Tinline ($12-14 OW), that can otherwise only be reached by hiking along the Coastal Track. Call John or Lynette Wilson (Green Tree Rd., Riwaka) at tel. 87-801 Motueka for the seasonal schedule. The same family also operates an enjoyable scenic cruise along the park coastline, charter cruises, and four-day guided walks in Abel Tasman National Park (see p. 365).

CONTINUING NORTH

Waikoropupu Springs

Continue along Hwy. 60 north of Takaka and look out for a sign on the left at Waitapu Bridge to Waikoropupu (or "Pupu") Springs. This natural jumbo-sized freshwater spring pumps out an incredible 1,197,000 liters of icy-cold, crystal-clear water a day, the largest freshwater spring in Australasia (if not "the world!"). It's really worth the time to drive the three-km gravel road and take the short track (about 15 minutes) through this amazing scenic reserve. Take either the Fish Creek Springs route or the one that passes the remains of some goldworking claims from the 1800s. At the end of the track is a large multi-colored pool, calm around the edge but turbulent in the middle where water (about 11 degrees C) gushes and bubbles to the surface at a rate of 14 cubic meters a second! Local oldtimers claim the vent is so deep that divers have been unable to find the bottom of the pool, but the main vent, actually only eight meters down, is visited regularly by divers. In summer a few enthusiastic swimmers brave the cold waters, not seeming to mind the "unknown depth" or turbulence in the middle. A fascinating diagram and display near the pool gives you the run-down on the what, where, and why of the springs—don't miss the striking underwater photographs taken by adventurous divers.

Collingwood

Twenty-nine km from Takaka and the northernmost town of any size (Pakawau and Port Puponga farther north are mainly remote vacation spots), Collingwood has a motor camp, lodge, tavern, tearooms, p.o., hospital, small museum, and a number of vacation homes.

Surrounded by mountains and water, with few people but lots of birdlife, Collingwood has a distinct appeal in all kinds of weather—guaranteed to bring out the photographer in you! Catch a **Collingwood Passenger & Freight Services** bus from the T.N.L. Depot at 98 Commercial St., Takaka, tel. 48-188.

From Collingwood you can take a bus up the 26-km **Farewell Spit** in the far north with **Collingwood Safari Tours** for adult $29, child $18, but it's expensive for what you see. It runs daily from mid-Dec. to Feb., and every Wed. throughout the year, depending on tides (times change daily); for bookings call 48-257, after hours call 48-160. Alternatively, for only $15 pp take a five-hour tour of the lonely north with the **Royal Mail Van,** "but don't take your kids, they'll drive you nuts" said a mother of three!

Collingwood Motor Camp is located on the south side of town right along the water's edge—pull in a fish without leaving your tent-flap! It has tennis courts and a boat ramp along with communal facilities. Great tent-sites on a grassy area along the water's edge are $9 d, caravan sites are $11 d; cabins range from $14-28 d depending on the facilities. However, if the weather looks ominous (even *slightly* so), fork out for one of their reasonably priced cabins—frequent high winds and a sudden heavy downpour can turn the tent area into a miniature lake strewn with large branches at any time of year, and as any pessimistic camper knows, it's most likely to happen in the middle of the night! Located on William St., tel. 48-149/027.

Farewell Spit

If you have your own wheels, driving north to the end of the road is most worthwhile for scenery buffs, wildlife enthusiasts, and bird-watchers. The lonely road takes you through wild rugged scenery along the edge of Golden Bay chock-a-block with black swans, Canada geese, ducks, and shore birds, to Pakawau (motor camp, store, and petrol pump) and Port Puponga. All along the road there are few homes, buildings, or signs of human life—local kids attend correspondence school, receiving their daily lessons

black swan

via the Royal Mail Van. Continue northwest to Puponga and the end of the road, passing **Oldman Rock,** an exposed and weathered cliff "face," to the carpark; a trail (25 minutes OW) leads steeply up and over grassy hills and sand dunes to **Wharariki Beach** where you can view the off-shore seal colony of Archway Island through binoculars (largest number of seals are seen in winter). Be prepared with insect repellent and, again, if the weather looks ominous, appropriate raingear. The 26 km of sand dunes and quicksand that make up Farewell Spit is one of the country's most important wading-bird habitats, protected as a nature reserve by restricted access. You can only reach **Farewell Spit Lighthouse** via Collingwood Safari Tours (see above) but you can freely walk for 2.5 km along the inner beach at the base of the Spit or four km along the outer beach; fishermen must obtain a permit from a Dept. of Conservation office to fish from the outer beach.

THE HEAPHY TRACK

One of the most popular (and free) walking tracks in the country, the Heaphy Track passes through the vast and rugged wilderness of **North-West Nelson Forest Park.** The route can be done in either direction, but most hikers start in the east at Brown Hut (about

35 km south of Collingwood), walk toward the coast, and finish at the Kohaihai Shelter (15 km north of Karamea) and campground (tentsites, water, toilets). Swimming is not advised along the coastal section, but it's fine in the lagoons and the Heaphy River, and the Karamea offers good trout fishing (the lower Karamea is open year-round, the upper section is closed in winter).

On this 74-km hike you can expect to cross rivers by swingbridge and ford shallow streams, pass through forests, open tussockland, the **Gouland Downs Scenic Reserve** (a wildlife refuge), and finish up walking along a wild, surf-pounded West Coast beach. The track takes at least four days, five to six days if you "stop and smell the flowers"; seven well-equipped huts (with gas) and five shelters (no bunks or facilities) are situated at regular intervals; adult $8, child $4. The huts can be crowded at any time of year but they're most crowded in summer despite the rule of staying no longer than two nights. To be on the safe side take your own tent, stove, cooking gear and utensils—camping is permitted around the huts if they're full.

Be Prepared

The track is in a high rainfall area; pack for rain and soggy ground. The warm summer months are the most popular time to do the track, but unless you have a good supply of insect repellent you can be eaten alive by swarms of tiny pesky sandflies. Many prefer to do the track in winter when the frosts keep the sandflies and crowds away. The weather can suddenly turn nasty along the track at any time of year, even in mid-summer. Take wool clothing, essential wind- and waterproof gear, and a spare pair of tennis or sandshoes; wear comfortable sturdy hiking boots (tough terrain). Carry enough food to comfortably last at least five days, water is readily available along the track, and whatever you do, don't forget that insect repellent! Before you set out, leave your intended date of arrival with the Dept. of Conservation or reliable friends, and try to find a couple of accompanying hikers (safety in numbers) or at least a person with backcountry knowledge—the track passes through some rugged wilderness. The Dept. of Conservation puts out the most detailed Map of Heaphy Track (offices in larger towns). A free brochure on the Heaphy Track is also available at all the northern PROs but the map is only a rough guide. For more info on North-West Nelson State Forest Park and the Heaphy Track, stop by any Dept. of Conservation office (the closest are in Collingwood, Takaka, Motueka, and Nelson; open weekdays 0800-1630), and if you plan on hunting or rock-hounding in the park, you must first obtain a permit.

Transport

Getting to and from the track is relatively easy but moderately expensive by public transportation. From Nelson: catch a **Newmans Coach Lines** bus from the PRO in Nelson (tel. 88-369) to Takaka—it can also be caught at Motueka. At Takaka, catch a connecting **Collingwood Passenger & Freight Service** bus departing from the T.N.L. Depot at 98 Commercial St. (tel. 48-188 Takaka) to Collingwood. From Tasman St. in Collingwood, catch the bus to Brown Hut at the head of the track; $50 per trip for up to five people, or $10 a head for more than five passengers. From Westport (on the west coast): catch a **Cunningham Coaches** bus departing from Palmerston St. (tel. 7177 Westport) to Karamea ($11 OW), then a taxi to the track ($25 OW). Phones are located at Brown Hut and the Kohaihai Shelter; local calls for transportation from the track are free. If you have a car waiting at one end and you don't plan on doing the track in both directions *(and* you have oodles of money or at least five friends to share the cost!) you can charter a small plane from Nelson or Westport and fly directly to the Heaphy Track, then walk out, but expect to pay at least $90 pp OW for the luxury.

NELSON LAKES NATIONAL PARK

INTRODUCTION

Nelson Lakes National Park, a mountainous area with many peaks over 2,000 meters high, lush beech forests and bush-fringed lakes, lies inland at the northern end of the mighty **Southern Alps.** Located off Hwy. 63, approximately 104 km from Nelson and 158 km from the west coast town of Westport, this Park is a good place to head if you're looking for a rugged wilderness experience.

The Park can only be truly appreciated on foot. Due to the rough terrain no roads run through, but you can still reach a couple of scenic spots by car—the town of St. Arnaud, the two main lakes, and **Rotoiti Lookout** at the end of Mt. Robert Road. Short tracks put the day tripper close to plenty of scenic variety, long and more difficult tracks challenge the serious hiker, and tricky routes cross high mountain passes (where the weather is notorious for rapid and unexpected deterioration) providing an adrenalin rush for the high-country backpacker and climber. The Park also has its own unique skifield where you have to "climb to ski": quiet, uncommercial **Mt. Robert Skifield** can only be reached on foot via a two-hour track from the carpark, somehow turning a day's skiing into a virginal one-of-a-kind experience and successfully keeping the hordes and the less energetic at bay. Peaceful and secluded **Lake Rotoroa** is known for good trout fishing; the more visited **Lake Rotoiti** is a mecca for trout fishing, sailing, and boating.

The Land

This large wilderness Park (101,000 hectares) is sandwiched between Lake Rotoroa and Lake Rotoiti in the north and northeast, the lofty **St. Arnaud Range** on the eastern boundary, the **Spenser Mountains** in the south, and **Ella Range** in the west. Also running through the Park are the **Mahanga, Franklin,** and **Travers Ranges,** along with several major rivers and their catchment areas—the **Travers River** flowing into Lake Rotoiti, and the **Sabine** and **D'Urville Rivers** flowing into Lake Rotoroa.

The great Alpine Fault runs right through the northern section of the park (welcome to earthquake country), crossing the northern end of Lake Rotoiti, **Speargrass Valley,** and the southern end of Lake Rotoroa. The movement of land along the Alpine Fault plus glacial erosion are the two main factors in the formation of the spectacular scenery. Mighty rugged mountains and alpine tarns lie on the southeast side of the fault, and lower forest-covered ranges, ridges and valleys, deep river canyons, and two glacially formed lakes lie on the northwest side.

Flora And Fauna

Lush beech forests are Nelson Lakes National Park's trademark. All four beech species found throughout New Zealand are here: red and silver beech thrive in the lower areas, hard beech only around Rotoroa, a mixture of silver and mountain beech farther up, and

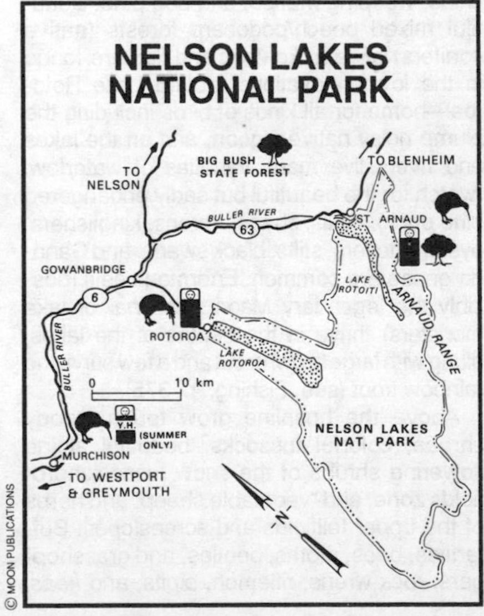

mountain beech in the high altitude areas (also in lowland low-nutrient soil areas). These trees form a dense dark canopy and the types of plants found on the forest floor depend on the amount of light that filters through. The high humidity "twilight zone" of the forest floor brings to life an amazingly luxurious assortment of mosses, lichens, ferns, liverworts, fungi, and tree litter, amongst which all kinds of insects, skinks, and geckos are found. On a stroll through the bush you're most likely to see fantails, tomtits, robins, grey warblers, riflemen, silvereyes, parakeets, white-bibbed tuis, bellbirds, and *kaka,* and mice, rats, stoats, and Australian opossums from the lower altitudes up to the bushline.

Apart from the beech forests, there are *kanuka/manuka* forests surviving on the edge of the Park in areas of poor soils and harsh climate, where broad-winged moths (their caterpillars have a great "twig" disguise), stick insects, *manuka* beetles, robins, and brown creepers hang out. Also scattered throughout are bogs where the insect-eating sundews thrive, along with several varieties of mosses, red tussocks, blue swamp orchids, weeping *matipo,* and bog pine. Beautiful mixed beech/podocarp forests (native conifers) of *rata, kowhai,* and flax are found in the lower elevations around Lake Rotoroa—home for all kinds of birds including the plump noisy native pigeon, and on the lakes and rivers live many varieties of waterfowl (watch for the beautiful but sadly endangered blue duck). Gulls, shags, herons, kingfishers, oystercatchers, stilts, black swans, and Canada geese are common. Enormous eels (possibly the legendary Maori *"taniwha"* or lake monsters) thrive in the depths of the lakes, along with large brown trout and a few surviving rainbow trout (see "Fishing," p. 375).

Above the bushline grow tough woody shrubs, colorful tussocks, beautiful alpine flowering shrubs of the snow tussock/herbfields zone, and "vegetable sheep" and herbs of the upper fellfields and screeslopes. Butterflies, bees, moths, beetles, and grasshoppers, rock wrens, riflemen, pipits, and *keas,* along with many other birds can be seen in the upper alpine areas. Large numbers of hares also live in the higher reaches, but only small herds of chamois and the occasional red deer can nowadays be seen—considered pests (causing extensive grazing, destruction of native forest, and erosion), both have been drastically reduced by selective culling in the last 20 years, and the Park continues to encourage their eradication (a hunting permit from HQ or Rotoroa Ranger Station is required).

THINGS TO DO ON FOOT

Walks Around Lake Rotoiti

Lake Rotoiti is the most visited area in Nelson Lakes National Park; go to Park HQ in St. Arnaud for pamphlets on all the walks and activities in the area. The lake is popular with sailors, powerboaters, water-skiers, and anglers. Several short tracks start near HQ and take up to two hours RT, and longer tracks link to form a circular route around the lake (at least six hours RT). For a short but rocky walk to a viewpoint 127 meters above Lake Rotoiti, take the **Black Hill Track** (1½ hours RT) which starts at Rotoiti Lodge. It crosses a *roche moutonnee* or volcanic rock intrusion (where large lizards like to hang out in the sun) and scrublands. If you're not feeling too energetic but enjoy lake views and all kinds of trees, try the easy (two-hour RT) **Peninsula Nature Walk** which starts at the western end of the beach at **Kerr Bay** and goes around to **West Bay.** The trees and shrubs along the track have been labeled, and short paths lead off the track to lookouts with views of the lake and the mountains.

Pinchgut Track (1½ hours OW) starts at the end of Mt. Robert Rd. and climbs through beech forest to the alpine herbfields and the skifield (great mountain views). For a longer hike (altogether five hours RT) returning along a different route, walk up via Pinchgut Track and return along three-hour **Paddy's Track.** It crosses the open face of Mt. Robert, and ends at the helicopter landing pad at Robert Road. **Lake Head Track** (three hours OW)

mallards waiting for a handout at Lake Rotoiti

starts at the eastern side of Kerr Bay and heads down the eastern side of the lake to the far end, passing countless bays that are likely to lure you off the beaten track and, in summer, into the water. If you plan on going all the way around the lake, ford Travers River near Lake Head Hut (only possible when the water is low enough) or walk from Lake Head Hut up the valley for at least another hour to the bridge. Return along the western side of the lake via **Lakeside Track.** This track starts in the corner of the lake, west of Coldwater Hut, passes a great view of **Whiskey Falls** en route, and eventually joins **Paddy's Track** to end on Robert Road. Total track time around the lake is about six hours but it can easily take much longer if you stop to admire the scenery or take a dip or two. If you have the time, stay overnight in one of two comfortable huts at the south end of the lake and make the round-trip an enjoyable and relaxed two-day adventure.

Getting a taste of the rugged St. Arnaud Range is possible from Lake Rotoiti via well-marked **St. Arnaud Track** (five hours RT). It starts at the eastern shore of Kerr Bay, climbs through beech forest, and comes out at 1,372-meter-high **Parachute Rocks.** From the top of the range you can see both sides of the divide—allow an entire day for this trip as you'll stop many times to absorb the magnificent scenery along the way.

Walks Around Lake Rotoroa

Peaceful Lake Rotoroa is larger, deeper, and less developed than Lake Rotoiti. No power boats or water-skiers (or anything noisy) are permitted on the lake—sailboats and windsurfers are fine. Head first for the Rotoroa Ranger Station for maps, hiking and hut info, and weather forecasts. If you feel like taking a stroll, try the 10-minute **Flower Walk** starting 100 meters from the lake foreshore (on the eastern side of the Gowan River)—great views of Lake Rotoroa. The **Short Loop Track** is another walk in the same area (20 minutes RT); it runs along the lake via Lakeside Track and back to the carpark. To get to the beginning turn left (looking toward the lake) on the road just past the Accommodation House, walk to the end of the road, and continue a short distance along **Porika Track** to the signpost where Loop Track branches off to the right. **Porika Lookout Track** climbs slowly along a ridge to a lookout with excellent views of the lake and the Travers, Ella, and Mahanga ranges, returning down the hydro track; about three hours RT.

One of the most beautiful "woodsy" walks in the area is the two-hour **Braeburn Walk.**

Start from Braeburn Rd. just down from the ranger station and head south on the western side of the lake. Passing through green arches of beech/podocarp forest full of bellbirds and a wonderland of ferns, the track gradually climbs to a softly cascading waterfall, drops down to the creek, and returns along an old hydro path to Braeburn Road. The area's longest walk (six hours OW), along the eastern side of Lake Rotoroa via **Lakeside Track,** takes you to the far end where the Sabine River enters. Fairly rough going, the Sabine Hut awaits you at the end. You need sturdy boots, warm wind- and waterproof clothing, your own stove (the hut has an open fireplace), and a tent in peak periods as the huts are more than likely to be full. There are no tracks along the western side of Lake Rotoroa.

Hiking Tracks

The many long tracks here range from wilderness hikes in river valleys to challenging tracks crossing high alpine passes, and climbing routes to test the most serious mountaineer. The main river valleys are the **Travers, Sabine, D'Urville,** and **Matakitaki,** with huts and campsites at regular intervals. The most popular tracks link the lakes, valleys, and passes to form a circular route. Twenty-five huts and a number of shelters are scattered throughout the Park, along with many excellent campsites. All the huts have fresh water nearby, and most have a stove or open fireplace (a few have no source of heat at all). During peak periods many huts may be full—it's best to take your own tent, stove, and cooking equipment whether you plan on staying in the huts or not, and extra food in case you're delayed by the weather. Get detailed info on the major tracks, conditions, huts, weather, and maps at Park HQ in St. Arnaud or Rotoroa Ranger Station at Lake Rotoroa.

peaceful Lake Rotoiti

The weather is notorious for changing rapidly, and in many of the low-lying areas it's hard to see bad weather coming—the elements are just suddenly upon you! Rain, snow, avalanches, high winds, disorienting mists and fogs, flooded rivers, and, yes, even fine sunny days—Nelson Lakes National Park gets it all! If you notice high wispy clouds coming from the north followed by a gray haze—expect rain, or snow higher up. The best way to tackle the weather is to hit the tracks prepared for everything; warm clothing, a wool hat and gloves are essential items no matter the season.

Skiing

Some fine downhill and cross-country skiing takes place within Park boundaries at the small, quiet **Mt. Robert Skifield** developed by the Nelson Ski Club. Providing beginners with gentle slopes and more advanced skiers with steep slopes and fairly long vertical drops, the season is generally June to Sept. depending on snow conditions (usually driest and most compact from July to mid-Sept.). There are several rope tows and ski-hire facilities, and instruction is also available. Cross-country skiers head for the popular area along **Robert Ridge.**

The unique thing about skiing here is the long walk to the skifield. The avid skier starts at the carpark at the end of Mt. Robert Rd. and follows **Pinchgut Track** all the way up, crossing to the Second Basin (altogether about two hours OW), carrying all gear and necessities;

the other alternative is to fork out for an expensive helicopter ride! This keeps the crowds away and adds to the club atmosphere of this beautiful skifield. Two lodges in the basin provide a limited amount of accommodation, but bookings must be made in advance for all weekends, and Aug. and September. Contact the Nelson Ski Club, Box 344, Nelson.

Rainbow Skifield, commercially operated with all facilities, is located on the east side of the St. Arnaud Range, just outside Park boundaries. Well signposted off Hwy. 63, the road to this skifield follows the Wairau River, then branches off to the right following Six Mile Creek—and you can drive to this one!

Fishing

Brown trout are the most commonly caught fish in the lakes and rivers of Nelson Lakes National Park. Rainbow trout are also caught in Lake Rotoroa and the Sabine River, but are less common and no longer being restocked. The most successful angling rivers are the Travers, Sabine, D'Urville, Matakitaki, Buller, and Gowan. The trout season changes year to year but in the rivers it's usually from the first of Oct. to the end of April (11 months a year in the lakes), and a fishing permit ($43 per adult for the whole season, child under 12 free) from Park HQ, Rotoroa Ranger Station, or local sports stores is required. You can use flies, lures, or bait to catch "the big one" and go anywhere you want if you're shore fishing; if you're lucky enough to be fishing from a boat, you can fish anywhere other than the areas marked by white poles along sides of river mouths and outlets. The trout share their underwater homes with monstrously large eels (just in case you were thinking of going diving!). If you're interested in guided fishing trips, call St. Arnaud 36-808 for prices, or call David Moate at tel. 36-887.

PRACTICALITIES

Accommodation

Three camping areas lie within Park boundaries, along with a large number of huts (stoves or open fireplaces, and fresh water) and shelters situated at regular intervals along the hiking tracks. At Lake Rotoiti are two well-established camping areas: **Nelson Lakes National Park Camp Ground** at West Bay has communal bathroom, and cooking and laundry facilities, but in winter the water is turned off and only one toilet and shower are left operating; from $5 pp for tent and caravan sites, apply to the Chief Ranger, c/o St. Arnaud Post Office. The **Kerr Bay Campground** adjacent to Park HQ at Kerr Bay provides a shelter with cold water taps, power points, an open fireplace, toilets, and cold-water basins; same rates as above. The Dept. of Conservation operates **Rotoiti Lodge,** bunk accommodation only for school groups, youth groups, workshops, and conferences.

The Yellow House in St. Arnaud is a comfortable, laid-back, and inexpensive place to stay, only a 10-minute walk from Lake Rotoiti, providing basic accommodation (bunk room and separate rooms) and communal facilities at $13-17 pp per night, no bookings accepted. **Red Deer Lodge** opposite Park HQ is a private hunting lodge with bunk accommodation for hunters; for more info apply at the N.Z. Deerstalkers Association in Nelson.

If you're looking for comfort and style, **Alpine Lodge Rotoiti** at St. Arnaud (tel. 36-869) provides a TV and video lounge, ski room and drying room, kitchen and tea-making facilities, ski store, and all meals (mains $12-19) in the large restaurant, and runs various specialized tours (including fishing) and transportation to the skifield; attractive rooms from $75-100 s or d. There's also a backpackers lodge with cooking facilities; from $12 pp per night. Eight km from Lake Rotoiti is a renovated 1880s cob (mud) hotel called the **Tophouse** where you can savor a home-cooked dinner, stay the night, have breakfast, and enjoy the hospitality of the Nicholls family and their animals (dog, cats, and angora-cross goats) for only $40 pp per night. Or just drop in for a Tophouse Tea ($3) and check out this charming hotel (note the bullet holes in the ceiling above the veranda)! Call ahead for reservations (it's the closest accommodation to Rainbow Ski Field) at tel. 36-848 St. Arnaud, and ask Mike if he's been hare shooting lately! To get there from St. Arnaud, take Hwy. 63 east and look for the road north signposted "Tophouse Historic Hotel" (it's also a backroad to Nelson). Then follow Tophouse Road.

On the Lake Rotoroa foreshore the **Rotoroa Campground** has more limited facilities than the two Rotoiti campgrounds but still provides a shelter, open fireplace, and toilets; $2 per site, ask at the Rotoroa Ranger Station. The **YMCA** on Gowan Valley Rd. about three km from the lake provides bunk accommodation (provide your own sleeping bag) and the usual facilities for $6 pp—inquire at the Rotoroa Ranger Station. The historic, recently renovated **Lake Rotoroa Tourist Lodge** on the edge of Lake Rotoroa has 10 deluxe suites ($250 s, $200 pp d) and a restaurant; make reservations at tel. Matiri 39-121.

The next closest town to the Park is **Murchison,** quiet, picturesque, and surrounded by mountains, 63 km west of St. Arnaud on Hwy. 6 (see "Murchison," p. 378). **Murchison Summer YH** is open from 1 Dec. to the end of March (check other hostel notice boards for current dates); $9 pp. It's located in Aorangi Hall in The Domain—turn off the main road (Waller St.) onto Milton St., turn left on Hampden St.—it's just inside the gateway. Attractive **Riverview Motor Camp and Cabins** is on Chalgrave St. next to the Buller River, just under two km north of downtown Murchison, tel. 39-315. Flat grassy tent and caravan sites are $7 pp—pay in the honesty box. Spacious comfortable cabins are $13 s, $22 d, tourist flats start at $33 s or d, and there's a large living room with TV and pool table as well as the usual communal facilities. In the evening enjoy a slide show featuring white-water rafting excitement on the Gowan, Buller, and Karamea rivers, then sign up with Mike for one of his **Go West Rafting** trips; one-hour to several-day heli-rafting adventures range from $27.50-270 pp (10% discount for YH members). For more details call 39-315, or call the Murchison Information and Adventure Centre at tel. 39-350. The other option is to stay at **Collis' Cabins** on Fairfax St., tel. 39-248: communal bathroom and kitchen, budget accommodation from $11 pp, standard cabins starting at $12 pp, B&B from $20 pp, self-contained cottages from $36 s, $46 d. Units at **Mataki Motel** on Hotham St., tel. 39-088, start at $52 d, and **Murchison Motels and Rentals,** tel. 39- 026, offers units for $45 d.

Food And Entertainment

There's not a large variety of food stores or places to eat in St. Arnaud—it's cheapest to stock up before you reach the Park and cook for yourself. **Lake Rotoiti Service Centre,** open every day, sells groceries, hot drinks, tasty tearoom fare, and petrol, and provides postal services (weekdays), and in the ski season, serves hot meals by the open fire. If you need a bit of dietary pampering, head for the **Alpine Lodge** bar, lounge, and restaurant in St. Arnaud (steak and salad meals), or at Rotoroa, the expensive **Lake Rotoroa Lodge** restaurant (check prices before you order!). Murchison, the closest town west of the Park, has several reasonable places to eat—two tearooms, one on the main street and one on Fairfax St. (better selection, salad bar, hot food, sandwiches, and cakes—also a general store), and takeaways. At **Stables Restaurant** in the **Commercial Tavern,** tuck in to large, tasty, bistro fare (chops, fish, steak) for $9-13; on Wallace St., Murchison, open seven days. Also see "Murchison," p. 378.

Entertainment-wise the Park is quiet—it's hard to muster the energy required to party after a hard day's hiking, climbing, or skiing! Meet your neighbors and make your own entertainment, take in one of the Park's guided walks or activities, sail a boat across Lake Rotoiti in summer, take a water taxi to a remote camping spot, or settle down for an apres-ski drink by an open fire in winter.

Information

The two sources are **Nelson Lakes National Park HQ (Lake Rotoiti Visitor Centre)** in St. Arnaud and **Lake Rotoroa Ranger Station** at Rotoroa. The Visitor Centre (tel. 36-806 St. Arnaud) is open weekdays 0800-1200 and 1300-1700, weekends 0800-1700, for info on tracks, huts, maps, permits, and weather forecasts. For an after-hours emergency, contact

Nelson Lakes National Park headquarters

the Duty Ranger (posted on Park HQ door). Lake Rotoroa Ranger Station (tel. 39-369 Murchison) is open on a casual basis for general Park info; the amiable ranger is also an excellent source of info on local rafting and fishing.

Transportation
If you're coming by car from the far northwest, take Hwy. 60 through Motueka and turn south on Hwy. 61. Eventually Hwy. 61 joins Hwy. 6 at Kohatu where you continue south toward Murchison and Westport. Coming from Nelson, take main Hwy. 6 south. To get to Lake Rotoiti, St. Arnaud, and Park HQ, turn east off Hwy. 6 at Kawatiri Junction and follow Hwy. 63 to St. Arnaud (63 continues on to Blenheim). To go to Lake Rotoroa instead, take Hwy. 6 a little farther south and turn east at Gowanbridge—the road ends at Rotoroa.

To St. Arnaud by public transportation from Nelson, catch a **Wadsworth Motors** bus leaving Montgomery carpark on Mon., Wed., and Fri. afternoons (about four hours, $8.50 pp OW; no service public holidays). The bus for Nelson departs from the St. Arnaud Store for the return trip also on Mon., Wed., and Fridays. For further info, call 34-248 Tapawera. Alternatively **Newmans Coachlines** buses stop at Gowanbridge, but you have to hitchhike, walk, or take a taxi the 11 km to Lake Rotoroa. **Nelson Lakes Service Car** (the St. Arnaud taxi service) operates a daily service between Nelson (Skyline Travel, Achilles Ave., tel. 80-285), St. Arnaud (Lake Rotoiti Service Centre, tel. 36-854), and Murchison (Murchison Auto Care, Waller St., tel. 13); $11 pp OW Nelson to St. Arnaud. For the latest schedule call 36-858 St. Arnaud.

To get to the park from Picton or Blenheim, take Hwy. 1 to Blenheim, then Hwy. 63 west to St. Arnaud. **Delta Coachlines** runs a daily service RT from Picton (departing the ferry terminal) to Greymouth (Revingtons Hotel), stopping at Blenheim, St. Arnaud, Kawatiri Junction, Murchison, Inangahua Junction, and Reefton; about $20 pp OW from Picton to St. Arnaud, $32 pp St. Arnaud to Greymouth. For more info call 81-408 Blenheim, or call in at 53 Grove Rd., Blenheim.

Water taxis operate on both Lake Rotoiti and Lake Rotoroa providing hikers, fishing enthusiasts, and campers with an alternate way to explore the lakes and their foreshores, or a shortcut to hiking tracks at the far ends of the two lakes.

BULLER GORGE, MURCHISON TO WESTPORT

Flowing from Lake Rotoiti to Westport and out into the Tasman Sea, deep, swift **Buller River** churns westward for more than 75 km through scrublands, meadows, and gravel flats, carving its way through rugged bush-clad mountains via the wild and beautiful Buller Gorge. About eight km southwest of Murchison, the emerald-green Buller pours between steep cliffs and the forested canyon of Upper Buller Gorge. At Inangahua Junction the Inangahua River joins forces with the Buller, then at Berlins, a historic goldmining settlement, the water rushes turbulently through the even more magnificent Lower Buller Gorge. The gorge has had quite a colorful past—it's been the scene of major earthquakes, mighty landslides and floods, goldmining rushes (thousands lived along the banks in the late 19th C.), and has been a formidable obstacle for early explorers, coach drivers, and road and bridge builders.

Nowadays Hwy. 6 parallels this mighty river all the way to Westport (less than a four-hour drive from Nelson Lakes National Park), crossing the century-old **Iron Bridge** (which replaced a punt that used to be the only way for coaches and horses to cross the river), and passing by beautiful scenic reserves where you can still fossick for gold, abandoned settlements and relics from goldmining days, short tracks to waterfalls and rapids, excellent camping spots, and a couple of small towns. Aren't you glad you came this way?!

Murchison

This attractive town is a popular spot for travelers to break the 232-km trip from Nelson to Westport. Old-style houses, a peaceful atmosphere, temperatures high in summer and mild in winter, and surrounding lush meadows backed by striking mountains give Murchison a definite appeal. Also, some fine trout-fishing rivers are within a half-hour drive of the town—ask locals for the current hot spots. Despite its unruffled appearance, the town is in an area of active faults and has an exciting geological history. On 13 June 1929, "a dense fog enveloped the town...the church bell tolled, buildings were hurled from their foundations, and it was impossible to keep to one's feet." The earthquake, with its epicenter close to Murchison, tore the town apart, blocked rivers and roads by slips, and destroyed all telephone communications. It took 21 months to reopen the main road south. Hodgsons General Merchants Store was totally demolished in the earthquake, rebuilt on the same site, and is open for business to this day! For more intriguing facts check out the **Murchison District Museum.** It's open most days in the afternoon or by arrangement (get the key at the petrol station); admission is free but donations are welcome.

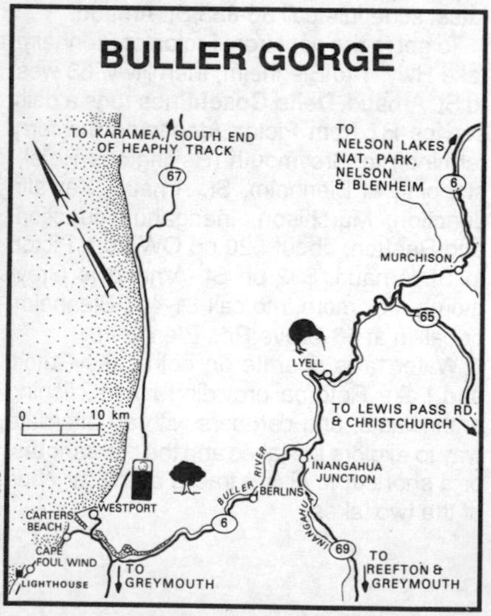

Make your first stop the **Information and Adventure Centre** on the highway (tel. 39-350) where eager volunteers arm you with info on local rafting, horseriding and trekking, fishing, and pig-hunting opportunities, and suggest scenic sights, walks, and drives; open in summer weekdays 0900-1700 and Sat. 0900-1200, in winter at variable hours. If you enjoy viewing or buying hand-slabbed stoneware and unique paintings, don't miss a visit to the studio of well-known N.Z. artist Dawn Blikshavn on Fairfax St., tel. 39-210. Or take a step back in time at **Newton Livery,** originally a "hotel" and well-known stopover built in 1899, about 17 km south of town on the Westport road. At this horse-powered farm the skills and knowledge of the horse-drawn era have been preserved—all the work is still accomplished with horsepower only; visitors welcome. **Rafting** enthusiasts should stop at Riverview Domain Camp and ask for Mike, or call 39-315 or 39-043. He runs exciting white-water rafting adventures on the Buller, Gowan, and Karamea rivers. For places to stay and eat in Murchison, see "Accommodation" and "Food" under "Nelson Lakes National Park," p. 375-376. Not far south of Murchison, Hwy. 65 branches south leading to Lewis Pass Rd. (Hwy. 7) which takes you to the east coast and Christchurch.

Lyell

Lyell, in the Upper Buller Gorge, was a busy gold- and quartz-mining town of 3,000 people in the late 19th C., but today all that remains is the original cemetery, reached by a beautiful track. Where the thriving town once stood is now a historic reserve: read about Lyell's colorful history on the display board, camp for free, or take a walk along **Lyell Walkway** (1½ hours RT). Ten minutes from the trailhead is the fascinating original Lyell cemetery, overgrown and disguised in the bush. The graves, dating from 1870 to 1900, have old-fashioned iron fences around them and trees growing out of their centers. The gravestones tell vivid stories of the difficult lives of the gold dredgers. Don't wander off the main track as numerous minor tracks lead to old claims, open shafts, and abandoned equipment that could be hazardous. For another perfect camping spot, head across the road from the reserve and down to the river to the small grassy flat suitable for tents.

Between Lyell and Westport the road passes through some of the most magnificent gorge scenery. At the small settlement of Inangahua Junction, Hwy. 6 crosses the Inangahua River and continues to Westport; Hwy. 69 branches off south—a more direct route to Greymouth, or to the Lewis Pass Rd. (Hwy. 7) to Christchurch.

Westport

Westport is a fairly large town, bustling with activity on weekdays but pretty dead on weekends and public holidays—not the best time to arrive! It also has some attractive beaches (though some are known for dangerous rips—look for warning signs before you take the plunge). Don't miss **Coaltown Museum** (coal- and goldmining displays) and historic **Cape Foulwind.** For a scenic hike, take the **Cape Foulwind Walkway** up to the top of the cliffs and look down on the local **seal colony,** or continue on to Cape Foulwind Lighthouse. If you don't have a lot of time and plan on seeing the entire west coast, continue farther south before you stop—much more to see as you continue down Hwy. 6. For more info on Westport's attractions and places to stay, see "The West Coast," p. 409.

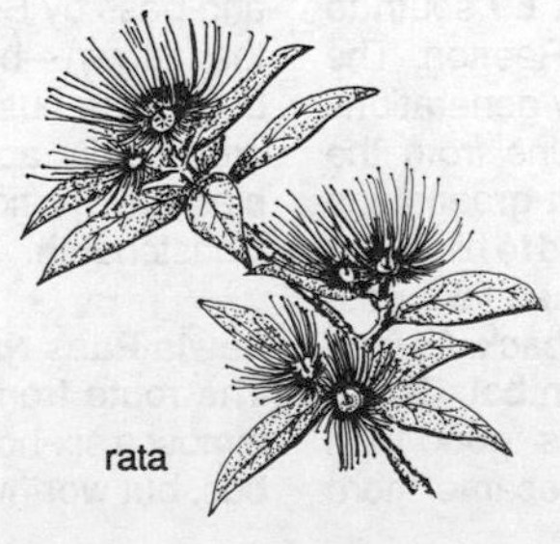

rata

CENTRAL
LEWIS PASS

Scenic Highway

Highway 7, commonly called the Lewis Pass Highway, is the northernmost route linking the west coast with the Canterbury Plains and east coast city of Christchurch (also see "Arthur's Pass," p. 399), re-discovered by Europeans in 1861. Starting at Greymouth, the highway winds through the mountains of the South Island's Main Divide via scenic Lewis Pass. From Westport take Hwy. 6 east to Inangahua Junction, then Hwy. 69 south to meet Lewis Pass Highway at Reefton. The pass (865 meters) was used by generations of Maori to cross the mountains from the Canterbury coast to west coast greenstone country—the Ngaitahu tribe used to hike over the pass, gather greenstone, then take prisoners to carry the precious rock back. As food supplies ran low around **Cannibal Gorge** (the original Maori name means "good feed of human flesh"), the slaves became more useful as fresh meat! Let your imagination run wild at this unique gorge by taking the short 50-minute RT track starting at the Lewis Pass picnic area (see below), which runs along the first section of the Ada Pass-St. James Walkway to Cannibal Gorge Bridge.

Both **Newmans Coachlines** and **InterCity** buses run between Nelson and Christchurch, and Westport and Christchurch, via Lewis Pass. The buses stop at Springs Junction, and pass by Boyle River where you can flag them down—be on the roadside half an hour before the bus is due as the times of arrival are usually approximate. Both bus companies have offices in Nelson, Westport, and Christchurch.

Lewis Pass National Reserve

The route from Westport to Christchurch is almost a six-hour drive by car, even longer by bus, but worthwhile if you have some time to stop and explore the wild, rugged, South Island interior with its high mountain peaks, fast-flowing rivers, forests, and tranquil lakes. Lewis Pass National Reserve (the most scenic stretch of the road, about halfway) starts east of Springs Junction and ends just north of the point where the highway crosses Boyle River. Although you can "ooh" and "aah" at the scenery from a car or bus, the reserve is an excellent place to pull off the road for a picnic, perfect campsite, spot of trout fishing in an icy cold stream, or large variety of hikes amongst mountain scenery. Tracks range from the short 10-minute **Waterfall Nature Walk** to the three- to five-day hike along the **St. James Walkway** (pamphlets available), and during the summer the rangers lead walks through the reserve. If you're doing any of the longer hikes, be prepared for sudden rain or snow storms and take extra food. Get detailed info, pamphlets, and maps at the **Ranger Station and Visitor Centre** at Springs Junction; tel. Maruia 873. Also at Springs Junction are a motel, shop, tearooms, restaurant, and service station.

Maruia Springs

This tiny settlement, about 17 km east of Springs Junction, is a great place to stop for a hike, then a swim in the **Maruia Springs Motor Inn's** thermal mineral pools (open 0800-1800; small charge for non-guests). Another good reason to stop is to eat in the hotel restaurant/bar—healthy meals and casual surroundings. Breakfast is available 0800-0930, lunch 1200-1400, and dinner 1800-2000—steak with fries, salad, and fresh veggies costs around $10, or pick from a variety of grilled meals at $9 a plate. Shoot some nine-ball while you wait. Hotel rooms (some with private pools) are $50 s, $65 d, with free use of the mineral pools, and non-powered camping sites are also available (tel. Maruia 840).

HANMER SPRINGS

This resort, 135 km northwest of Christchurch and 10 km north of Hwy. 7, is serviced by **InterCity** from the west coast and Christchurch (the local depot is on Conical Hill Rd., Hanmer Springs, tel. 7205). A popular getaway for those who enjoy soaking in thermal pools, hiking in exotic forests, fishing, or skiing at the local **Mount St. Patrick Skifield** (ski tow and all facilities during ski season), the resort attracts large numbers of New Zealanders and tourists year-round. The hot springs that feed **Hanmer Springs Thermal Pools Complex** on Amuri Rd. are saline and alkaline, and the nine pools vary in temperature from 36-40 degrees C. The complex (tel. 7239) is open seven days 1000-2000; adult $2.50, child $1; swimsuit, towel, and safe deposit hire $1.50. **Hanmer State Forest Park,** one of New Zealand's oldest government-owned exotic forests, covers 16,844 hectares of land near the town; the most widely grown tree is the *Pinus radiata.* Many good tracks allow you to amble through the different types of forest to panoramic lookouts. For more info, pamphlets, and maps of the park, stop by the **Information Centre,** open most days between 0900-1700 on Jollies Pass Rd., about one km from Hanmer Springs Post Office. Inquiries and bookings for jetboating, rafting, 4WD trips, trail riding, and skiing can be made at **Stage Post Gift Shop** in the Conical Hill Road Shopping Centre.

Practicalities

It's not too difficult to find a place to stay in Hanmer Springs—take your choice from a number of hotels and motels, tourist flats and cabins, and several good motor camps. The town also has restaurants, coffee shops, and takeaways. The **AA (Central) Tourist Park** is three km from the township at Jacks Pass, tel. 7112. Communal facilities, TV and game room. Tent and caravan sites start at $13 d, cabins from $30 d, and tourist flats from $44 d for members, slightly more per night for non-members. **Mountain View Holiday Park** on the outskirts of Hanmer (tel. 7113) has communal facilities, a squash court, TV and recreation room, and milk available daily. Tent and caravan sites are $15 d, cabins from $29-35 d, and tourist flats from $42-49 d. If you're looking for cabin accommodation, try

Hanmer Bridge Village, Hanmer (six km from town), tel. 7111. The units, $33 d, have their own kitchen-living room with cooking facilities but shared bathroom and laundry facilities, and a shop sells staples. Tourist flats are $44 d, and on-site caravans are $27.50 d.

CHRISTCHURCH

"THE MOST ENGLISH CITY OUTSIDE ENGLAND"

Largest city in the South Island, capital of the province of Canterbury, and third largest city in N.Z. (population 299,000), Christchurch conjures up vivid images of typical English charm—striking Gothic architecture and fine stone buildings, lush green parks and flower-filled gardens, grassy banks and drooping willow trees along the meandering Avon River, the "Wizard" of Cathedral Square, and droves of Christ's College schoolboys in black-and-white uniforms and straw boaters cycling home at the end of the day.

Christchurch Cathedral

Spreading out from the city in all directions lie the flat, patchwork-neat fields of the **Canterbury Plains,** the orderly design broken only by rivers and streams, and lakes and coastal marshes in the southwest, a favorite hangout for waterfowl hunters. The untamed hills and ragged coast of the **Banks Peninsula** lie due south, and the eastern perimeter of the city is bordered by the South Pacific Ocean.

Christchurch was founded in 1850 by the Canterbury Association as a planned Church of England settlement. The first group of settlers successfully started a typically "English" community in the new land—a look and feeling that Christchurch has always retained. This gives the city its unique charm and atmosphere—one that needs to be felt to be appreciated. Its flat terrain is ideal for walking and cycling, and an excellent public transportation network makes exploring its special nooks and crannies a snap. The central city area bustles with activity, but a short hop from Cathedral Square and you're strolling along a beautiful river with quacking ducks the only sound. Then several blocks later, you're passing house after house with spectacular, very "English" flower gardens— it's hard to believe you're still in the center of a city! Although the large international airport has made Christchurch the principal gateway to the scenic wonders of the South Island (or "Mainland" according to South Islanders!), the city itself is a N.Z. attraction that shouldn't be missed!

CENTRAL CITY SIGHTS

Cathedral Square

This large, flat, pedestrian-only plaza with its trees, flower-filled planters, pigeons, and striking Cathedral, is in the heart of the city. It's a great place to soak up some of Christchurch's unique atmosphere, sit and people-

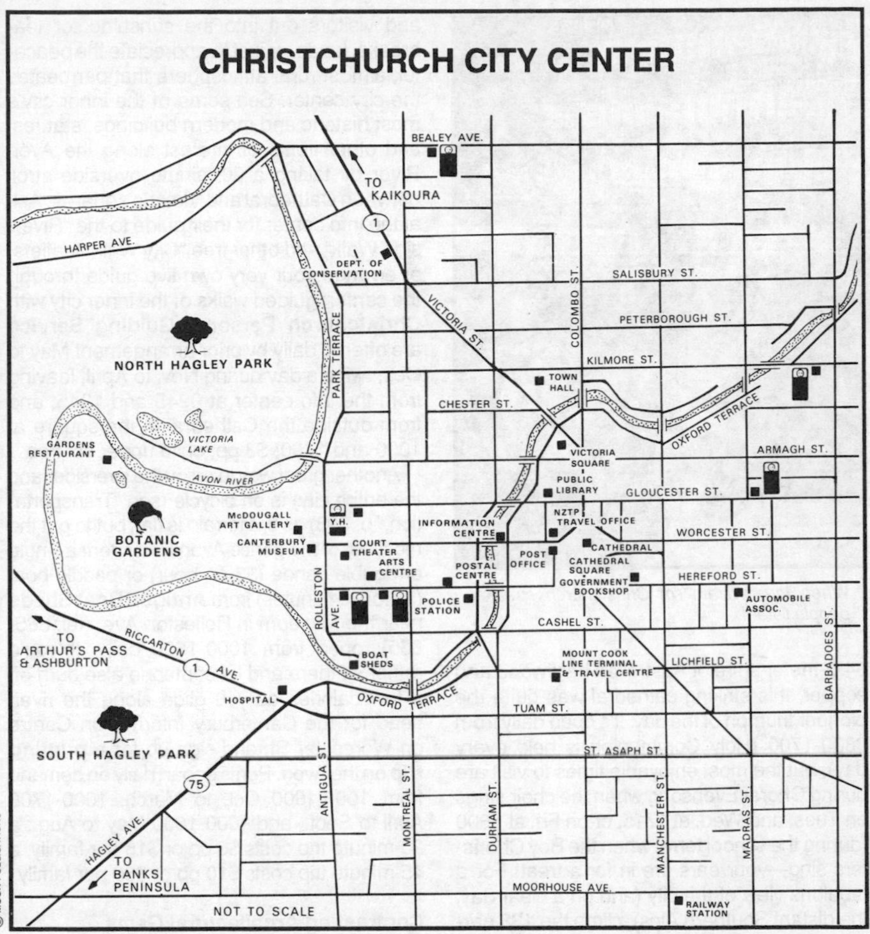

watch, make sightseeing plans, meet friends, and listen to the well-known orator and self-proclaimed **"Wizard" of Christchurch** in action! Dressed in eye-catching garb and propped on a stepladder, the Wizard usually speaks on weekdays at 1300 in front of the Cathedral, informing, humoring, annoying, and plain-out manipulating his daily audience. Grab a quick takeaway lunch and a piece of ground in front of the Cathedral (stand at the back of the crowd if you don't want to be picked on!) and settle back for some free entertainment. Afterward you can buy his upside-down "New World Map" poster or T-shirts (humorous and inexpensive Christchurch souvenirs) at the **Canterbury Information Centre,** corner of Worcester St. and Oxford Terrace (a block west of the Square—the first place to head for info, maps, brochures, and bus timetables).

Christchurch Cathedral is the centerpiece and dominant feature of Cathedral Square. Completed in 1904 and built of stone from local Canterbury quarries topped by a

When the "Wizard" of Christchurch speaks, people listen!

64.5-meter spire of Australian hardwood and copper, this striking cathedral was quite the pioneer triumph of the day. It's open daily from 0800-1700 (Holy Communion is held every day), but the most enjoyable times to visit are during Choral Evensong when the choir sings on Tues. and Wed. at 1715, or on Fri. at 1600 (during the school term) when the Boy Choristers sing—your ears are in for a treat! For a fabulous view of the city (and on a clear day, the distant Southern Alps), climb the 133 narrow stone steps up through the bell chamber to the balconies at the top of the tower; open weekdays and Sat. 0900-1600, Sun. 1300-1630, admission adult $1, child 50 cents.

The Avon River

Gently meandering through the city and particularly noticeable in the city center, the Avon River is one of the main attractions that gives Christchurch its appeal. Grassy daisy-dotted banks, weeping willows and old oak trees, ducks and trout, and small ornate bridges linking the main streets lure office workers and visitors out into the sunshine for tea-breaks, lunch, or just to appreciate the peaceful, almost rural atmosphere that permeates the city center. See some of the inner city's most historic and modern buildings, statues, and other items of interest along the Avon River by taking a 90-minute riverside stroll between Cathedral and Victoria squares. Ask at the info center for their guide to the "Riverside Walk" and other free "City Walk" leaflets, or arrange your very own live guide through the center: guided walks of the inner city with **Christchurch Personal Guiding Service** are offered daily by prior arrangement May to Oct., twice a day during Nov. to April, leaving from the info center at 0945 and 1345, and from outside the Cathedral in the square at 1000 and 1400; $8 pp, child under six free.

Another great way to enjoy the riverside (and the entire city) is on bicycle (see "Transportation," p. 398) as the terrain is flat; but to get the most out of the gentle Avon River, rent a single or double canoe ($3 an hour) or paddle boat ($3 for 30 minutes) from **Antigua Boat Sheds** near the Museum in Rolleston Ave. (tel. 665-885); open from 1000-1600 daily. If you'd rather sit there and let someone else burn off a few calories as you glide along the river, head for the Canterbury Information Centre on Worcester St. and sign up for a **punting trip** on the Avon. Punts depart daily on demand from 1000-1800 Oct. to March, 1000-1700 April to Sept., and 1000-1600 May to Aug.; a 20-minute trip costs $5 pp or $15 per family, a 45-minute trip costs $10 pp or $30 per family.

Contrasting Architectural Gems

The Provincial Council Buildings (or Provincial Chambers) beside the Avon River on the corner of Durham and Armagh sts. are another example of Christchurch's fine Gothic architecture. Until 1876 each province governed itself; built between 1859 and 1865, these were the main government buildings for Canterbury province. Today the last remaining provincial buildings in N.Z., they're sources of both historic and architectural interest. Guided tours of the entire buildings are offered every Sun. at 1400 for $1 pp, and the Stone Chamber is open Mon. to Fri. from

0900-1600 (call 799-760 to check times). From Cathedral Square walk north two blocks along Colombo St., turn left at Armagh St. and walk another block then over the river.

In direct contrast, don't miss the modern **Town Hall** on the banks of the Avon River on Kilmore Street. Completed in 1972, it's recognized as one of the finest town halls in the country with its eye-pleasing combination of glass, marble, and still and moving water. You can stroll through weekdays from 0900-1700 or weekends and public holidays from 1000-1700, or take one of the daily guided tours between 1100 and 1500 for adult $1.50, child 70 cents. From the Provincial Buildings on Armagh St. walk north along the river, passing the attractive **floral clock artwork** on Victoria St. (corner of Chester St. beside the Victoria Square Amphitheatre), until you come to the town hall building.

The Arts Centre

Formerly the University of Canterbury, the attractive old neo-Gothic buildings at the west end of Worcester St. have become a large cultural and community center, providing entertainment to suit just about everyone. It's the kind of place where you can quickly lose an entire day amidst intriguing daytime entertainment and a variety of shops, eating up a storm at **Le Cafe Concert Coffee Shop** (open seven days 1000-1600—great espresso!), **Dux de Lux Vegetarian Cafe,** and **Jambalaya Restaurant.** There's also plenty of evening entertainment here, all in one relatively small area. The Arts Centre Information Office is in the clock tower on Worcester St. (near Rolleston Ave.), open for general inquiries and bookings Mon. to Fri. 0830-1700, tel. 660-988/989.

During the day, stroll in and out of the many crafts, music, book, and wooden toy shops, and watch the potters, cane and stained-glass workers and candlemakers creating their works of art. The **Ginko Gallery** exhibits and sells prints and has a large supply of N.Z. artists' prints and drawings for sale; open Tues. to Fri. 0900-1530 and Sat. 0900-1300, tel. 660-989. On Sat. between 1000-1600 (and Sun. 1000-1600 Oct. to March), an **Arts, Crafts and Antiques Market** is held at the Centre with all kinds of stalls, buskers (singers, dancers, mime artists, etc.), and entertainment. In the evenings and on weekends, take in a performance at the **Court Theatre, Southern Ballet Theatre, Free Theatre,** or **Academy Cinema**—check here or at the Canterbury Information Centre for what's playing. To get to the Arts Centre from Cathedral Square, walk four blocks west along Worcester St. toward the Botanic Gardens; it's on the left.

Canterbury Museum

This unusual museum features an exceptional mounted bird display (one of the best in the Southern Hemisphere), Oriental art, furniture and fashions throughout the ages, early Maori culture during the Moa Hunting era, a reconstruction of a colonial Christchurch street from the 19th C., and the fabulous Hall of Antarctic Discovery (pioneer polar explorer Robert Scott visited Christchurch in 1901 and 1910 on his Antarctic expeditions—see his statue standing on the banks of the river opposite the info center). Attend a stargazing screening in the Planetarium on Sun. at 1500 (tickets available from 1400 at the foyer desk), and have a light meal or snack in the museum Coffee Bar off Garden Court; open 1030-1600. The Museum is open daily from 1000-1630 (free admission), located on Rolleston Ave. at the entrance to the Botanic Gardens, tel. 668-379. From the Arts Center walk to the west end of Worcester St. and turn right at Rolleston Avenue.

Airplane buffs should find their way out to Wigram on the south side of the city to feast their eyes and let their spirits soar at the **RNZ Air Force Museum.** It's on Main South Rd., tel. 482-049, ext. 636, open Mon. to Sat. 1000-1630, Sun. 1300-1600; admission is $7, child $2, family $15, and worth every cent for flying enthusiasts. Aside from extensive displays featuring the history of N.Z. aviation, watch a movie on the same in the small theater, then wander at will around a large number of beautifully displayed aircraft spanning the age of aviation. Allow two hours if you like reading all the details. Access to the

Begonia House in the Botanic Gardens

museum is from the main highway south (to Timaru), near the Springs Rd. turnoff.

Art Galleries

Robert McDougall Art Gallery, next to Canterbury Museum, is the region's major art museum, featuring regularly changing exhibitions and a large permanent display of paintings, drawings, sculpture, ceramics, and prints from artists around the world. It's free, open daily from 1000-1630; guided tours available on weekends at 1430, tel. 650-914; located on Rolleston Ave. by the Botanic Gardens.

The **CSA Gallery** at 66 Gloucester St., tel. 667-261, exhibits art and crafts for sale by N.Z. artists: painting, sculpture, prints, photography, weaving, ceramics, woodware, batik, glassmaking, jewelry, etc., changed every two weeks. The Selling Gallery has paintings, prints, and weavings for sale; open Mon. to Sat. 1000-1630, Sun. 1400-1630, admission $1. To get there from the north end of Cathedral Square, walk west along Gloucester St. and cross the river. For more info on local art galleries, ask for the *Art In Christchurch* brochure at the info center.

Parks And Gardens

One hectare in every eight in Christchurch is a public park, reserve, or recreation ground. Lush greenery and gardens abound everywhere you go, always well maintained and usually chock-a-block with flowers—hence the well-deserved title "Garden City." Christchurchians must surely have more green thumbs concentrated in their area than in the rest of the country! One of the best places to appreciate this profusion of vegetation within easy walking distance of the central city is the **Botanic Gardens;** open 0800 to dusk (a bell is rung at closing time). Stroll through grounds bordered by the gently meandering Avon River, through the rose, rock, and azalea gardens, past an area full of N.Z. native plants, and into all the individual show houses (open daily 1000-1600) featuring tropical, flowering, and alpine plants, cacti and succulents, ferns, and spectacular orchids. Seasonal displays feature the most beautiful flowering trees, daffodils, azaleas, rhododendrons, and bedding plants.

Finish your walk off with morning or afternoon tea or a delicious smorgasbord lunch in the restaurant/tea kiosk on the grounds (see "Food," p. 393); open daily from 1000-1630, smorgasbord 1200-1400, tel. 665-076. Guided tours are available on the "Toast Rack" electric vehicle which operates (only in fine weather) from 1100-1600, departing from outside the tea kiosk. To get to the Botanic Gardens from Cathedral Square, walk west along either Worcester St. or Hereford St.—the main entrance is off Rolleston Ave. close to Christ's College, and the Museum and Art Gallery.

Hagley Park, the enormous park that borders the Botanic Gardens to the north, south, and west, has kilometers of excellent walking, jogging, and cycling tracks, and is a venue for all kinds of organized sports. The park covers an area of about 180 hectares of woods and playing fields (separated from the Botanic Gardens by the Avon River, but bridges allow access), and is divided into two main north and south sections by Riccarton Avenue. If you want a bit of exercise or enjoy watching other people sweat, this is the place! Entrance from the inner city to North Hagley Park is from Rolleston Ave. and to South Hagley Park from Hagley or Riccarton avenues.

Sightseeing Tours

If you only have time to take in some highlights, check at the Canterbury Information Centre and NZTP Travel Office for tour brochures. Better still, ask one of the friendly personnel for suggestions to suit your timeframe and budget. For a guided walking tour in and around the city starting at $8 pp, call **Personal Guiding Service** at tel. 668-243, visit the kiosk in Cathedral Square (open in summer Mon. to Sat. 0930-1430), or book through the Information Centre. If you provide a vehicle, they provide a guide to show you around for $20 per car per half day, $40 per day. Guided city walks are also offered at $8 for two hours; book through the info center at tel. 799-629.

The most reasonably priced local tours, **Red Bus Scenic Tours,** are run by the Christchurch Transport Board. Their two-hour "City And Suburbs Tour" runs from 1 Oct. to the end of May and departs from Cathedral Square; adult $12, child $6. Their three-hour "Hills And Harbour Tour" (including launch trip) also departs from Cathedral Square; adult $15, child $7.50. Red Bus Tours also runs tours to **Orana Park,** a wildlife reserve (open daily 1000-1700, admission adult $7, child $3); tour adult $18, child $9, including admission. Buy tickets on the bus, or book at the kiosk in the Square (tel. 794-600) or at the info center. **Gray Line** does two popular three-hour tours departing daily from the Canterbury Information Centre: "Christchurch Roundabout" for adult $22, child $11, and "Christchurch Highlights" for adult $20, child $10. Their terminal is at 40 Lichfield St., tel. 799-120.

Another really enjoyable way to appreciate Christchurch is from the air. Take a 25-minute scenic flight over the city and harbor for $55 pp, see Akaroa on the one-hour flight for $95 pp, or fly farther afield to view the beauty of the Alps from $250 pp, depending on flight time. For more details, call the Canterbury Information Centre.

OUT-OF-TOWN SIGHTS

Northern Summit Road

For great views of the seaside suburb of Sumner, Lyttelton Harbour Estuary, the Seaward Kaikoura Range to the north, Christ-church City, checkerboard Canterbury Plains, and the distant snowcapped Southern Alps, take the 45-km scenic Northern Summit Rd. circuit. From city center, follow High St. east onto Ferry Rd. heading along the old main road to Lyttelton. Go through Sumner and up Evans Pass, but instead of continuing along the main road down into Lyttelton, turn right (south) onto spectacular Summit Road. Be sure to stop at the **Bridle Path,** the route early colonists took from Lyttelton Harbour over the steep hills to the flat, grassy Canterbury Plains and Christchurch. You can also walk the three-km Bridle Path (90 minutes OW) from the city to Lyttelton—catch a Lyttelton no. 28 bus from city center to the tunnel administration building, Heathcote, getting off at the intersection of Port Hills and Bridle Path roads. Return from Lyttelton township by catching the city bus at Norwich Quay. If you're in **Lyttelton** during the afternoon, the 40-minute scenic **launch cruise** on Lyttelton Harbour (a drowned volcanic crater) is well worthwhile, departing daily at 1450; for the current price, tel. Lyttelton 28-8368.

To return to the city from Summit Rd., turn right at the **"Sign of the Kiwi"** on Dyers Pass Rd. and continue down through Victoria Park with its impressive rock gardens to the **"Sign of the Takahe,"** a fine Gothic building and a great place to stop for morning or afternoon tea or a smorgasbord lunch (see "Food" below). From here continue through the attractive suburb of Cashmere via Dyers Pass Rd. or Hackthorne Rd. onto Colombo St., which leads back to Cathedral Square.

Red Bus Scenic Tours covers a similar route on the "Hills And Harbour Tour" (see "Sightseeing Tours" above), offering outstanding views and a stop at the "Sign of the Takahe" for afternoon tea. **InterCity** does a day trip from Christchurch to the "Eastern Bays," covering 102 km of the Northern and Southern Summit road (see below) with excellent harbor views for $19 pp RT (take your lunch and a camera). Another excellent and less organized way to see the northern bays is via the local mail-delivery service (arrange at the train station through InterCity) and bus; $28 pp. Take your own food and drink.

Southern Summit Road

Take Colombo St. south from city center, then Dyers Pass Rd. toward Governor's Bay, and at Summit Rd. turn right. This beautiful 52-km (RT) hilltop road gives spectacular views of Lyttelton Harbour, Governor's Bay, the Canterbury Plains and distant Southern Alps, Lake Ellesmere to the south, and the southern coastline. At Gebbies Pass Rd. turn right down to Motukarara, and turn right again on Hwy. 75 to Tai Tapu and Halswell to return to the city. If you want to explore Banks Peninsula and visit the quaint French township of Akaroa (see below) before returning to the city, turn left on Hwy. 75 and continue to the end.

BANKS PENINSULA

The remnant of two huge volcanos attached to the mainland by a gravel plain, rugged Banks Peninsula lies immediately southeast of Christchurch. Trails over craggy peaks, through deep valleys and forest remnants (most take about a day and are best done in summer), good swimming at sandy beaches along the sharply indented coastline, small towns nestled in striking crater harbors, and an overall island-getaway atmosphere make the peninsula an ideal place for a day trip from Christchurch—though you might find yourself staying longer!

Akaroa

This picturesque seaside town on Akaroa Harbour has a colonial village appearance with its late-Victorian architecture, quaint cottages, narrow streets, cosmopolitan shops, and French street signs and place names. The original Akaroa colonists came over from France in 1840 on the *Comte de Paris.* Once a whaling settlement, Akaroa is now recognized for its plentiful commercial, sport, and recreational fishing. Stroll around town soaking up the atmosphere, dangle a fishing line from the wharf, take a launch ride on the harbor, visit the local museum, or sample sole, grouper, *terakihi,* crayfish, or *gurnard* fresh off the fishing boats and cooked to perfection. Or take a two-hour cruise on Akaroa Harbour with **Canterbury Cat Cruises** (tel. Akaroa 7641 for bookings) for adult $16.50, child $5.50. Cruises depart daily at 1330 from the main wharf on Beach Road. For more info on what to see and do, visit the **Information Centre** on the waterfront road opposite the main wharf and Britomart Reserve; open daily during the holidays.

Get to Akaroa by car (a 90-minute drive from the city) by following the scenic Southern Summit Rd. (see above) to the end, turn right on Gebbies Pass Rd., then left on Hwy. 75 which leads to Akaroa. **InterCity** runs an eight-hour "day excursion" from Christchurch, departing the city at 0830 Mon. to Fri., at 0900 on weekends. Another more luxurious way to see the Banks Peninsula is to take **Town and Country Tours'** "Akaroa And Banks Peninsula Tour." This circular tour of the peninsula is in a comfortable mini-coach with full commentary, and includes stops for morning tea, a short bush walk, and lunch in Akaroa. Departing the Clarendon Hotel in Worcester St. daily at 0930 (10% discount for YHA members).

Okains Bay

If you have your own transportation, another secluded getaway is this small township on the northeast side of the peninsula, 83 km from Christchurch but only 19 km from Akaroa. Here you'll find a sandy beach, safe swimming, boating, fishing, large caves to explore

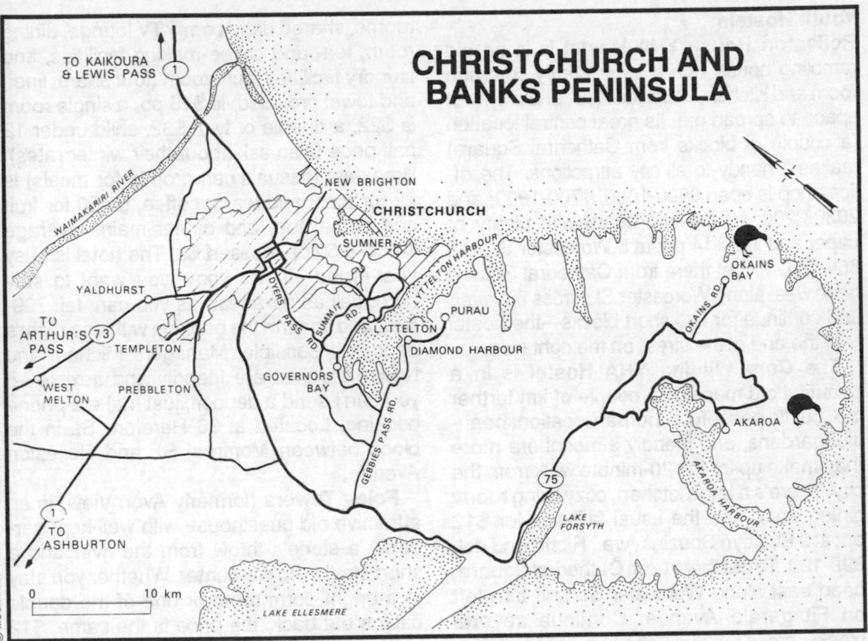

around the bay, great views, scenic walks, a museum featuring colonial and Maori culture (open daily from 1000-1700, call Okains Bay 485 if closed), and a small Domain campground. By car take Hwy. 75 toward Akaroa, but at Hilltop take the Summit Rd. (sealed) instead of the lower road down to Akaroa, and eventually turn left on Okains Road.

BEACHES

Christchurch has lots of sandy swimming beaches but the tidal currents can be dangerous—it's safest to swim in the patrolled areas between flags, and with friends. The closest beach, **New Brighton,** is eight km east, reached by a no. 5 city bus. **North Beach** is 10 km east (no. 19 bus), **South Brighton** is also 10 km east (no. 5S bus), and **Sumner** is 11 km southeast (no. 3 bus). **Lyttelton Harbour** has a number of scenic beaches, and **Corsair Beach,** a 15-minute walk from Lyttelton, has excellent swimming. If getting to the beach is part of the fun, consider taking a short 15-minute launch ride from Lyttelton across Lyttelton Harbour to Diamond Harbour and its beach (refreshments available). The launch crosses the harbor several times a day (less frequently on weekends and public holidays—note return times!). You can also take a refreshing 40-minute **harbor cruise** from Lyttelton at 1430 (tel. 28-8368).

ACCOMMODATION

Christchurch has YHA hostels (two), private hostels, budget hotels, B&B guesthouses, and plenty of comfortable motels and top-of-the-line hotels. If your first choice is full (the best fill quickly in holiday periods, though there's a fairly rapid turnover), most managers are willing to recommend their competition without any heavy-duty arm-twisting! Looking for a motel (from $50 d and up) or hotel ($100 d and up)? Head for the NZTP Travel Office (they do bookings) or the Canterbury Information Centre for suggestions, availability, and prices.

Youth Hostels

Rolleston House YHA Hostel is in an old rambling house with a large comfy common room and kitchen, usual facilities, and plenty of space to spread out. Its great central location (a couple of blocks from Cathedral Square) makes it handy to all city attractions. The office/shop is open 0800-1000, 1700-1900, and 2030-2200; hit the info board with plenty of paper and ink! $14 pp; at 5 Worcester St., tel. 666-564. To get there from Cathedral Square head west along Worcester St., cross the river, and continue for two short blocks—the hostel is at the end of the street on the right side.

The **Cora Wilding YHA Hostel** is in a beautiful old mansion a couple of km farther out, but its peaceful suburban location, beautiful gardens, and friendly atmosphere more than make up for the 20-minute walk from the city. There's a large kitchen, cozy living room/dining area, and the usual facilities for $12 pp; at 9 Eveleyn Couzins Ave., Richmond, tel. 899-199. To get there from Cathedral Square, head east along Worcester St. and turn left on Fitzgerald Avenue. Continue several blocks, cross the river, and turn right on River Road. Follow the river, then turn left on Evelyn Couzins Avenue. Or catch a no. 10 bus at the BNZ on Worcester St.—there's one every 15 minutes or so.

YMCA Hostel

This hostel is down the right side of the Y activities center (saunas, spa, squash courts, circuit training, fitness studio—non-members welcome) at 12 Hereford St. at the west end, tel. 660-689. If the hostel has spare beds (residents tend to stay here on a long-term basis) it's $19.80 pp, breakast extra, with dinner $24.20 pp, or $98 per week full board. There are no restrictions on length of stay and no curfew. Morning and afternoon teas, takeaway lunches, and health foods are available at the activities center cafe, open Mon. to Fri. 0830-2000 and Sat. 0830-1600, closed Sunday.

Private Hotels And Hostels

The Hereford Private Hotel, only a couple of short blocks from Cathedral Square opposite the Arts Centre, provides bright little rooms, shared bath, comfy TV lounge, dining room, tea- and coffee-making facilities, and laundry facilities; bunkroom (four share, linen and towel provided) is $15 pp, a single room is $22, a double or twin $32, child under 12 half price (also ask about their winter rates). Breakfast (casuals can drop in for meals) is $2 for toast and tea or coffee, $4.50 for fruit and cereal too, and dinner mains average $4.50-8.50 pp, dessert $3. The hotel is busy year-round—if you know you want to stay here, call as far ahead as you can, tel. 799-536, and confirm the booking with one night's deposit if possible. Managers Michael and Ngaire Hughes are friendly and flexible—if you can't send a deposit, just make a phone booking. Located at 36 Hereford St. in the block between Montreal St. and Rolleston Avenue.

Foley Towers (formerly Avon View) is an attractive old guesthouse with well-kept gardens, a stone's throw from the river and a short stroll from city center. Whether you stay in a bright dorm room or one of the double cabins out back, the price is the same, $12 pp if you share ($11 second night), $13 pp d ($12 second night), with dining room and comfy guest lounge, shared facilities, luggage lockers, sunny yard, and limited off-street parking. It's located at 208 Kilmore St. ("just downstream from downtown"), tel. 669-720. To get there from Cathedral Square, head north along Colombo St., cross the river, turn right on Kilmore St. and continue for a couple of blocks.

Latimer Hostel is a couple of short blocks east of Cathedral Square: fully equipped kitchen, TV lounge, table tennis and pool room, shared facilities, free baggage storage, a lock-up bike shed, and a combination lock so you can come and go at any hour. A bunk bed in the large "sleeping bag room" is $10.50 pp (supply your own bag). The individual rooms are brighter and more comfortable at $20 s, $28 d or twin, $29 d which includes linen and blankets. Long-term rates are also available. The hostel is at 268 Madras St., tel. 798-429. To get there from Cathedral Square, walk east along Worcester St. (it joins Madras St.), or catch a ride on an InterCity bus from any of the inner city transport bus depots or the railway station.

The **Backpacker's Hostel** at 70 Bealey Ave., tel. 666-760, is an excellent place to stay. Friendly, clean, bright sunny rooms, kitchen, lounge, laundry, courtyard and gazebo, and BBQs in summer—what more could you ask? From $12 pp share, $13 pp d or twin, linen hire available. Free city pick-up, and pick-up and drop-off at the railway station on request.

Motor Camps

The closest motor camp to city center is **Addington Showground Camp,** three km southwest of Cathedral Square and a short walk from South Hagley Park—but note that it's closed during showtime (agricultural shows early in Nov.) for two weeks. Communal bathroom, dining room, kitchen, and laundry; tentsites $5.50 pp, caravan sites $8.40 s, $12.60 d (reduced weekly rates off-season). Cabins start at $10 pp, $26-42 d. Located at 47-51 Whiteleigh Ave., off Lincoln Rd., tel. 389-770. To get there from Cathedral Square, take Colombo St. south, turn right (west) on Moorhouse Ave., left on Lincoln Rd., and right on Whiteleigh Avenue.

Amber Park is five km west of city center but has no tentsites—only caravan sites (from $7.50 pp), and units with basic cooking facilities and private bath from $40-44 d per night, plus a TV lounge and recreation room, and the usual facilities. Located at 308 Blenheim Rd. (Hwy. 1 south), tel. 483-327. **Meadow Park Motor Camp,** about five km from the city center but off the main highway heading north, has the usual, but also a spa, swimming pool, trampolines, BBQ, takeaway food bar, and tandem bicycles for hire. Tentsites are $7.50 s or $14 d, caravan sites $15 d; standard cabins and units range from $27-38 d. Located at 39 Meadow St., off the main road (Hwy. 1 north) near the junction of Cranford St., tel. 529-176.

If you're looking for supremely comfortable self-contained cottages, ask about the "Cosy Kiwi" accommodation offered by **Pineacres Holiday Park** on the main north road, about 10 minutes' drive north of the city near Kaiapoi, tel. 27-7421. The cottages are $60 d with bedding supplied, $50 d without. The park also has tentsites at $5 pp, caravan sites $7 pp, on-site caravans $25 d, cabins $12 pp, tourist flats $45 d, and a modern kitchen, laundry facilities, large TV lounge and games room, store, swimming pool, and a licensed restaurant on the premises (lunch from $4, dinner from $13). Backpackers can also share the lodge, which has its own kitchen, bathroom, and living room, for only $12 pp (doubles, and rooms with many single beds).

Getting a little farther out, **Russley Park Motor Camp** is opposite Riccarton Racecourse on South Hwy. 73 in the western suburb of Riccarton. Spa (charge), TV and recreation room, trampoline, pool table, communal facilities; tentsites $14 d, caravan sites $15 d, on-site caravans $26-30 d, chalets from $30 d. Located at 372 Yaldhurst Rd., tel. 427-021. If you don't mind being 10 km from city center and prefer to be closer to the ocean, try **South New Brighton Park** on the east side. Communal facilities; sites $8 s, $15 d, on-site caravans $15 per night. Located on Halsey St. off Estuary Rd., tel. 889-844. Get bus info and a timetable at the bus kiosk in Cathedral Square.

If you're approaching from the north, consider staying at Spencerville, 14 km north of Christchurch on the east coast. **Spencer Park Holiday Camp** lies adjacent to a sandy beach and has a recreation hall, TV room, spa, trampoline, mini-golf, and a wildlife park! Grassy tent and caravan sites amongst the trees are $7 pp; cabins are $26 d, flats are $35 d. Located at Spencer Park on Heyders Rd. (turn east at Belfast), Spencerville, tel. 298-721. If you're approaching from the south, you might stay at Prebbleton, 12 km southwest of city center (about a 15-minute drive along the motorway into the city). **Prebbleton Holiday Park** has a quiet atmosphere, friendly owners, swimming pool, trampoline, TV and game room, and the usual. Tentsites are $8 s, $12 d, caravan sites $10 s, $14 d; furnished cabins and spacious tourist flats from $16-21 s, $22-28 d. Before you leave, pick up handy tourist literature from the office. Located at 18 Blakes Rd., Prebbleton (watch for the AA sign pointing to the motor camp on Hwy. 1 at Templeton), tel. 497-861.

Bed And Breakfast
Christchurch also has its share of guesthouses offering B&B. Ask at the info centers for all the current listings. One that you may want to try is **Turret House** at 435 Durham St., tel. 653-900—a five-minute walk from downtown. In one of the city's large old homes (built in 1885) the owners provide spacious elegant rooms, most with private bath, and a Continental breakfast for $56 s, $72-106 d or twin, including GST. Get to know the other guests at the evening wine and cheese get-together or at breakfast, or relish complete privacy—whichever you choose.

Motels
There are so many fine motels in the Christchurch area that picking one becomes more of a problem than you'd think! The **Best Western** motel chain is always reliable and the rooms are usually spacious and well equipped for the price. **Colonial Inn Motel** provides particularly comfortable units with sunny bed-living rooms, tea-making facilities, refrigerator, TV, plenty of space to stretch out, and a community spa. Rooms start at $66 s, $84 d, breakfast is available. Located at 43 Papanui Rd., Merivale, tel. 559-139. For a top-class hotel, try **Noahs** on the corner of Worcester and Oxford Terrace, tel. 794-700. Rooms start at $193 s, $226 d or twin. Call in at the info center or NZTP Travel Office for complete motel listings.

FOOD

Restaurant Guides
If you have a particular kind of food in mind, the free *Scenic South* tourist newspaper has an entire page of dining suggestions categorized ethnically. Also grab a free *Christchurch Tourist Times*, which itemizes restaurants and gives you a rough idea of prices. Both papers can be found at numerous tourist spots around town, and at the NZTP Travel Office and Canterbury Information Centre. Another handy magazine crammed with cafe and restaurant advertisements (no prices) is *Christchurch Dining and Restaurant Guide* put out by The Press. It's updated every six months, available at the info center.

Brunch
The best places to head for breakfast or an early lunch are the cafes and tearooms amply scattered throughout the city, though you're not likely to find many places serving English- or American-style bacon and eggs, or pancakes. For that you generally need to be staying in a hotel or serviced motel, some of which serve breakfast to walk-ins, such as **The Hereford Private Hotel** (Continental only, see above). Also try the Pancake Palace (see below). **Cheers Cafe** serves a variety of delicious breakfasts for around $6—try the specialty croissant with bacon, mushrooms, and cheese—along with filled rolls, sandwiches, quiche and salad, desserts, etc. Lunches average $5-7. It's at 196 Hereford St. (near Manchester), tel. 63-431, open Mon. to Fri. 0730-1500.

In Cathedral Square are a number of takeaway food stands offering a large variety of foods that cater to just about everyone's taste—good-value lunches on the run. The **YMCA Cafe** at the Activities Centre has reasonably priced morning and afternoon teas, health foods, light lunches, and takeaways. It's open Mon. to Fri. from 0830-2000, Sat. 0830-1600, closed Sun., at 12 Hereford Street. A restaurant with an "arty" atmosphere (a place to see Christchurch trendies) is the licensed **Dux Deluxe Gourmet Vegetarian Cafe** in the Arts Centre. A good place for a wholesome lunch, expect to pay around $9 pp (more expensive at dinner). Also in the Arts Centre is the **Jambalaya Restaurant** serving authentic Louisiana/Cajun meals. Lunch averages $8 pp, dinner $20 for a main course, and you can expect live musical entertainment on Thurs., Fri., and Sat. nights. **Soup Plus** specializes in soups, pate, and quiche, and has a BYO license; open for lunch Mon. to Fri. 1130-1430, and dinner Thurs. to Sat. from 1700-2200; lunch is about $5, dinner $8-10 pp.

The Sign of the Takahe boasts fine food and a magnificent view.

For beautiful park surroundings, luscious Devonshire teas, or a delicious smorgasbord lunch, head straight for **The Gardens Restaurant And Tea Kiosk** in the center of the Botanic Gardens, tel. 65-076. It's open daily 1000-1630, 1200-1400 for the smorgasbord lunch; $9.80. If you're participating in the N.Z. custom of taking morning and afternoon tea, or you're in the mood for splurging on a mouth-watering smorgasbord lunch (1200-1400 daily), drive out to the **Sign of the Takahe** roadhouse (looks like a castle) on scenic Summit Rd., Cashmere (see "Out-Of-Town Sights" above for directions), and soak up some historic atmosphere and magnificent views while you eat! Dinner, however, is an expensive affair (expect to pay $25 for a main course), and reservations are essential at tel. 342-052—get on your best gear for this one!

Dinner

One of the best places to go for plenty of good tucker, a large salad bar, and reasonable prices, is the **Wagon Wheel Restaurant** on Papanui Rd. (northwest of city center, across from Derby St.), tel. 556-159. It's not a fancy restaurant—self-serve—but the main courses are large and the price includes unlimited trips to the salad bar. Get steak, seafood, chicken, lamb chops, or deep-fried oysters with fries and fresh vegies for an average of $10. Delectable desserts from the dessert cart average $4—half portions for half price, and you can help yourself to as much coffee as you can handle. Drinks are available from the adjoining bar; open Sun. to Thurs. 1700-2100, Fri. and Sat. 1700-2200. If you're hankering for American-style pancakes with maple syrup, a large breakfast, or a bit of spicy Mexican food, head for **Pancake Palace** at 633 Colombo St., between Tuam and Lichfield sts., tel. 794-324. Breakfast $2.50-8.50, lunch crepes are $5.50, light meals and salads are $6, daily specials are $9-10, dinner $10-14, and there's a great salad bar. Open Mon. to Fri. from 0700, weekends from 0800 till late, and it has as a BYO license.

For good roast meats with all the trimmings and delectable desserts, stop in at the ever-so-popular **Oxford tavern and restaurant** on Oxford Terrace. You can savor a very filling tasty meal for only $10 at dinner (lunchtime smorgasbords are $11 pp) in relaxed pleasant surroundings. It's also easy to meet Christchurch residents here. Two good old **Cobb & Co. Restaurants** are in the city area: one on the southwest side at the **Bush Inn,** 364 Riccarton Rd., Upper Riccarton, tel. 487-175, and one on the north side at the **Caledonian Hotel,** 101 Caledonian Rd., St. Albans, tel. 666-034; lunch $6-14, dinner $9-18, good salad bars. **The Jail Restaurant** opposite the library at 106 Gloucester St., tel. 666-641, whips up steaks, fish, chicken, and great salads; $10-18 for a main course. Open Mon. to Thurs. 1700-2100, Sat. 1700-2230; it has a BYO license. **Britas** is another popular steakhouse in the Gloucester Arcade on Gloucester St., tel. 666-553. Along with meat dishes, omelettes go for around $9.50; open for lunch 1200-1400 and dinner 1700-2100 (later on weekends).

Dux Deluxe Gourmet Vegetarian Cafe in the Arts Centre is open for lunch and dinners, has a friendly atmosphere, and main courses average $17, desserts $5. It's fully licensed, and some nights (usually weekends) a live band plays for a small cover charge.

Town Hall Restaurant on the corner of Kilmore and Victoria sts., tel. 666-651, is another popular place to go. It offers a tasty smorgasbord at lunch 1200-1400 for $18.75 pp, a Sun. lunch menu for $20 pp, à la carte dishes from $13. Expect to pay about $33 pp at dinner. It's open Mon. to Fri. 1200-1400 and seven days a week from 1730 till late. A band plays every Fri. and Sat. night.

Desserts, Desserts!
Those with a sweet tooth shouldn't miss a stop at **Strawberry Fare Dessert Restaurant** at 114 Peterborough St., tel. 654-897. Delectable treats such as "Death By Chocolate" that go straight to the thighs range from $8.50-12.50. Just reading the menu is a mouth-watering affair. However, the owners also serve breakfasts (croissants, waffles, and baked goodies) for $4-9, and savory dishes throughout the day—try their salmon and filo parcel for $10.50, chicken and avocado basket for $10, or share a cheese plate for $8.50 before diving into dessert! They're open year-round, seven days, 0700-2400.

ENTERTAINMENT

To find out what's on around the city, call in at the Canterbury Information Centre or NZTP Travel Office, where you can pick up all the free tourist guides and ask locals where the best action is. Daily newspapers have an entertainment page with all the cinema and theater listings, along with the venues for live bands and cabarets, music recitals, etc. Also pick up the free *Christchurch and Canterbury Visitors' Guide*, which has an extensive "What's on in Canterbury" section covering art, music, theater, sports, and special events.

Arts Centre
For theater, ballet, cinema, jazz and folk music concerts, head straight for the **Arts Centre of Christchurch** at the west end of Worcester Street. The **Information Office** in the Clock Tower (close to Rolleston Ave.) is the place to make general inquiries and bookings, or call 660-988/989; open Mon. to Fri. 0830-1700. Theater performances ranging from classical Shakespeare to modern playwrights with special emphasis on N.Z. plays are put on in the **Court Theatre** continuously throughout the year—enjoy dramas, comedies, tragedies, and farces for around $16 pp; theatre bar and coffee bar in the foyer are open before and after all performances and during intermission. For details see the back of the daily newspapers; book at tel. 666-992. The **Free Theatre,** made up of an experimental group of Canterbury University teachers and students, also presents a series of performances during the year (enter from Rolleston Avenue).

The **Southern Ballet Company** performs programs throughout the year at the Arts Centre, along with numerous individual recitals, and the **Banks Peninsula Folk Club** holds folk music concerts every Sunday. For retrospective movies, award-winning classics, and foreign films, head for the Arts Centre **Academy Cinema.** If you get hungry during all this entertainment, there are two good restaurants (see "Food" above), as well as the **Common Room Bar,** and the **Coffee Shop.** Listen to live jazz on Thurs. to Sun evenings from 1930 at the Coffee Shop while you munch on food ranging from sandwiches to pancakes; open seven days from 1030-1600, Thurs. to Sun. from 1930; by the Information Office.

Others
Music recitals happen regularly in the **Town Hall** (the booking office is open weekdays 0900-1700, Sat. 1000-1700, tel. 654-431; enter from Kilmore St.), and bands can be found in hotels and bars throughout the city almost every night of the week and always on weekends (the better the band, the larger the cover charge). Scan the papers, listen to the radio for advertisements, or check the info centers to find out current venues and prices. Two of the favorite hot spots are the **Palladium Nite Club** on Chancery Lane (off Gloucester St., opposite the library) which provides live entertainment, top music, a spectacular lasar lightshow, cocktails, dining, and dancing; and the **Firehouse Nightclub** at 293 Colombo St., tel. 39-208, open Wed. to Sun., providing live bands most nights, cocktails, and light suppers.

In summer the Canterbury Promotions Council arranges all kinds of **"Summertimes"** happenings—such as picnics in the park, country fairs, special exhibitions, kite days, international days, lunchtime entertainment in Cathedral Square, rock and jazz concerts in North Hagley Park, and if you're in Christchurch on New Year's Eve, don't miss all the fun and craziness of **Mardi Gras** in Cathedral Square.

SERVICES

Urgent

For emergency **police, fire,** or **ambulance,** call 111. **Christchurch Hospital** is on Riccarton Ave. and Oxford Terrace, west of city center and south of the Botanic Gardens, tel. 640-460. The city **police station** is on the corner of Hereford St. and Cambridge Terrace, tel. 793-999. For **emergency medical service,** call St. John Ambulance, tel. 669-133. The **urgent pharmacy** is at 15 New Regent St., tel. 664-439. At the **Medical Centre** in High St. Mall, 163 High St., tel. 660-237, visitors can get same-day appointments if necessary. For a dentist call 799-586, after hours call 661-866. If you need referral to a doctor, call the hospital above or the Canterbury Information Centre (Mon. to Fri. 0830-1700, weekends 0900-1600) at tel. 799-629.

General

Shopping hours are generally 0900-1730 Mon. to Fri., and Sat. from 0930-1230, closed Sunday. Late-night shopping (to 2100) in the central city area, Edgeware, Northlands, Papanui, Rangiora, and Sydenham is on Fri. night; in Barrington Park, Bishopdale, Hornby, Kaiapoi, Linwood, Lyttelton, Merivale, Riccarton, and Shirley, it's on Thurs. night; and in the coastal suburb of New Brighton, the shops are open from 0900-2100 on Sat. but closed all day Mondays. For **duty-free shopping,** head for the Duty-Free Shop on Colombo St. near Gloucester St., or the airport duty-free shop which opens two hours before each international departure. The **chief p.o.** is on the southwest side of Cathedral Square, open Mon. to Thurs. 0800-1730, Fri. 0800-2030, and Sat. from 0830-1100 for postal and telephone services only. **Trading banks** are generally open Mon. to Fri. from 1000-1630 (foreign transactions close at 1500), but a few stay open longer on late-shopping nights. The **public library** is on the corner of Gloucester and Oxford Terrace, tel. 796-914; open weekdays 1000-2100, Sat. 1000-1600, and Sun. 1300-1800.

INFORMATION

Sources

The two main sources of information are the **NZTP Travel Office**, Government Life Building, Cathedral Square (no. 11), tel. 794-900, and the **Canterbury Information Centre** at 75 Worcester St. (corner of Oxford Terrace), tel. 799-629. The NZTP Travel Office, open weekdays 0830-1700, Sat. 0900-1200, offers valuable info, advice, and brochures on N.Z. in general. They book local accommodations (small fee) and entertainment, sell tickets for local sightseeing attractions and entertainment, and make arrangements for national tours and accommodations, rental vehicles, special-interest vacations, and overseas travel.

The Canterbury Information Centre is open weekdays 0830-1700, weekends and public holidays 0900-1600 (extended hours in summer). They specialize in Christchurch. If asked, they willingly recommend budget places to stay, eat, and be entertained. Maps of varying sizes and detail (from $1.80), special-interest brochures (e.g., *Akaroa, Lyttelton And Christchurch, Historic Buildings, Landmarks, and Sights),* postcards, and "Wizard" souvenir posters and T-shirts are available. Christchurch has established sister-city relationships with Christchurch, Dorset (England), Adelaide (South Australia), Seattle, Washington (USA), Kurashiki (Japan), and Gansu Province (People's Republic of China)—the Centre particularly encourages people from these cities to come in and sign their special Sister-City Visitors' Book.

A third **Information Services** office is located in the main terminal building at Christchurch Airport, open daily 0800-2000, Sat. 0800-1900. The staff do bookings for all sights and accommodations, but not for flights. For park and forest info, hiking trail info, and detailed maps, visit the **Dept. of Conservation** office at 133 Victoria St., tel. 799-758; open regular hours Mon. to Friday.

General

If you need **interpreter service,** tel. 799-629. To find out if anything's going on in the local parks, call the **Parks and Recreation Dept.** of Christchurch City Council, tel. 791-660. The latest **weather forecast** can be heard at tel. 582-899. For general info on N.Z., head for the central **public library** on Cambridge Terrace or the **Government Bookshop** at 159 Hereford St., open Mon. to Fri. 0900-1700 (late on Fri.) and Sat. 0930-1230.

Outdoor Recreation

For "everything you want to know about out-of-the-city outdoor activities," along with friendly help and advice, call in at the **Outdoor Recreation Centre** in the Arts Centre at 28 Worcester St., tel. 799-395. The office is open Mon. to Fri. 0900-1600, and in summer on Sat. 1000-1300. Many of the brochures, pamphlets, and maps are free, as is first-hand advice on all kinds of commercial operations: white-water rafting, climbing, sailing, skiing, hiking, renting or buying equipment, instruction courses, and guides. The friendly staff also organize guided trips and evening lecture/slide shows on outdoor recreation events. If by chance they don't have the particular info you need, they'll find out who does—it's a great service! The Centre is open Mon. to Fri. 1000-1600.

Another place chock-a-block with outdoor info as well as general hostel info is the **YHA of New Zealand HQ,** also located in the Arts Centre at 28 Worcester St., tel. 799-970; open Mon. to Fri. 0830-1700. Here you can become a member of the association (pick up the handy *Come Hosteling* booklet), and don't miss the fantastic notice boards—a budget traveler's clearinghouse.

TRANSPORTATION

Getting There

Getting to Christchurch is easy. An excellent highway network leads to and from the city, it's well serviced by major coach companies and by rail from Picton in the north, Greymouth in the west, and Invercargill and Dunedin in the south, and it has a bustling national and international airport.

From the north: to get to Christchurch by car from Picton and Blenheim, take Hwy. 1 south down the east coast. Alternatively, take a Newmans Coachlines or InterCity coach, or catch the daily Picton to Christchurch train that leaves Picton in the afternoon (about six hours). From the west coast: from Westport by car, follow Hwy. 7 through Lewis Pass; by bus, take a Newmans Coachlines or InterCity coach. From Greymouth: take Hwy. 73 through Arthur's Pass, catch an InterCity coach, or the daily Greymouth-to-Christchurch TransAlpine Express train that leaves Greymouth in the afternoon. From the south: take Hwy. 1 north up the east coast, or catch a Newmans Coachlines, InterCity, or Mount Cook Line (H & H) bus, or the daily (except Sun.) *Southerner* train from Invercargill and Dunedin. From Mt. Cook in the southwest and Timaru, Christchurch is serviced by Mt. Cook Landline coaches.

Airport

Christchurch Airport is 10 km northwest of Cathedral Square. The easy 15-minute route to the airport through leafy suburbs with glimpses of beautiful gardens through hedges and white picket fences is well serviced by airport-city buses and taxis. International arrivals are in one building; international departures leave from the adjoining Domestic Terminal. Within the terminal are a bank (open Mon. to Fri. 0830-1600 and for all international flights), p.o. (open Mon. to Fri. 0830-1700), variety of gift and souvenir shops, bookshop, duty-free shopping (open two hours before every international departure), florist, beauty parlor, cafeteria (good selection, high prices), licensed restaurant, bars, major car rental agencies, left-luggage lockers, and an Information Services center, open Mon. to Fri. 0800-2000, Sat. 0800-1900, and Sun. 0800-2000.

When you first arrive at the airport, collect one of the small free *Christchurch and Canterbury* pamphlets—in small stands all over the place, packed with handy info for the "just arrived"—then stop at the **Information Services** center for orientation and a free city map. Luggage can be stored in the small **left-luggage lockers** for up to 24 hours; the large lockers are $1.50.

The cheapest way to get from the airport to city center (the bus stops outside the Avon Theatre on Worcester St., a stone's throw from Cathedral Square) is by the no. 24 **Airport Bus** from the bus shelter outside the Domestic Terminal; $1.05 (off-peak) OW, $2.10 (peak—before 0900 and between 1600 and 1800), departing every half-hour until 1800 on weekdays, then about once an hour in the evenings, on weekends, and public holidays. **Pacific Tourways Airport Bus Shuttle** (a blue-and-white mini-coach) also runs a service from the Domestic Terminal to the city via the main city hotels. It leaves about once an hour 0830 to 1730 and costs $5 pp or $12 per family; book at tel. 857-881. Or just take a **taxi,** about $15 OW weekdays, more on weekends: tel. 799-799 or 795-795, 24 hours. If you're driving from the airport (short-term car parking at the airport is about 60 cents an hour), take Memorial Ave. all the way onto Fendalton Rd., at the park turn left onto Harper Ave., then straight onto Bealey Avenue. Almost straight away turn right on Victoria St., then right on Colombo St. and you're there. The route in the opposite direction to the airport is well signposted.

The **Automobile Association office** is on Hereford St. by Madras Street. **Air New Zealand** is at 156 Armagh St.; **Ansett New Zealand** is at 776 Colombo St.; **Qantas** is in the C.M.L. Building in Cathedral Square; **Mount Cook Airlines** is at 91 Worcester Street.

Getting Around By Bus

Christchurch Transport Board has made traveling around Christchurch blissfully easy—the bright red buses (called "big reds") seem to go everywhere you want to go, from wherever you are, regularly! In addition, the red **Information Kiosk** in Cathedral Square is an invaluable source of transportation info. The kiosk, open seven days a week and public holidays, is manned by some of Christchurch's most patient and helpful people! If you're not in the Cathedral Square area and need bus info, just call 794-600, day or night. The cheapest time of day to use the bus system is during off-peak hours: from 0900-1600 and after 1800 Mon. to Fri., and at all times on weekends and public holidays, reducing the normal adult fare by 50 percent.

Sightseeing By Bus

You can also do the "City and Suburbs" (adult $12, child $6), "Hills and Harbour" (adult $15, child $7.50), and "Orana Park Wildlife Reserve" (adult $18, child $9, including admission) with **Red Bus Scenic Tours;** book at the kiosk (see above), at the Canterbury Information Centre, or buy your tickets on the bus. If you like to walk, pick up the *Buses Can Take You Walking!* brochure (50 cents)—it suggests walks in and around Christchurch that are accessible by bus from both ends or one, along with a map showing all the suggested walk locations—and *The Bus About Booklet* ($1), also available at the bus kiosk.

Gray Line on Lichfield St. does two popular trips, departing daily from the Canterbury Information Centre: "Christchurch Roundabout" (adult $22, child $11) and "Christchurch Highlights" (adult $20, child $10); for more info, call 799-120 (see "Sightseeing Tours," p. 387). If you'd rather get to a destination and see it on your own, consider taking an **InterCity** day excursion to Akaroa ($19) or the Eastern Bays ($28), or farther afield to Hanmer and Arthur's Pass—pick up a *Day Excursions from Christchurch* brochure, or call 799-020.

By Bike

One of the most enjoyable and fun ways to discover the flat terrain and lush beauty of Christchurch is on a bicycle—and many roads have special cycling lanes. You can rent all kinds of bikes (city and touring maps provided) from **Christchurch Rent-A-Bike** at Avon Carpark Building, 139 Gloucester St. (opposite the Coachman Inn), tel. 664-409, after hours 296-631. They have leisure bikes, five-speed sports bikes, ten-speed touring bikes with carrier bags and water bottles, tandems, triplettes, trishaw, and electropeds to choose from, and everything can be rented by the hour ($2-5), day ($7-20), or week ($35-80), plus insurance for $1 per day. Bicycles can also be hired from **Discount Cycles** at 81A Riccarton Rd., tel. 485-811 ($3 delivery charge). The **Christchurch Recreational Cycling Club** has regular Sunday rides departing from Victoria Square at 0945 throughout the year; for more info call 887-795.

If you're looking for a tad more speed (and are at least 20 years old with a current motorcycle license), hire a motorbike from **Motorbike Hire (NZ)** at the Airport Service Station on Memorial Ave., tel. 588-270, after hours tel. 555-764. Their single seat and two-seat Yamahas can be rented on a sightseeing rate with unlimited km (50 or 100 cc), or a touring rate with unlimited km (SR 250 cc, XS 400 cc, or XJ 650 cc) and by the day or week.

From Christchurch

Christchurch **Railway Station,** the **InterCity Travel Centre** office for both train and coach transportation, is on Moorhouse Ave., about seven blocks south of city center. For train and coach info, current timetables, and prices call in at the ticket sales office, open weekdays 0700-1830, Sat. 0700-1330, Sun. 0700-1830, tel. 799-020. One of the most spectacular train rides in New Zealand is on the **TranzAlpine Express** (panoramic windows, on-board commentary) from Christchurch to Greymouth through Arthur's Pass; $44 OW. If you're short on time, take the Greymouth Day Excursion for only $59 RT (or $66 pp RT which includes Devonshire tea and a half-hour mini-bus tour of Greymouth), or the Arthur's Pass Day Excursion for only $37 pp RT. If you'd rather head north by train, take the **Coastal Pacific Express** to Kaikoura, Blenheim, and Picton ($45 OW); day-excursion fares are $29 RT to Kaikoura, $56 RT to Blenheim. Heading south? Expect to pay $38 OW to Dunedin or $60 OW to Invercargill, by coach or train.

InterCity coach fares: to Queenstown $63 OW; Mt. Cook $41 OW; Dunedin $38 OW; Invercargill $60 OW; Greymouth $42 OW; Nelson $56 OW (connects with Newmans coach at Blenheim); Picton $43 OW; and to Wellington (including ferry, purchase at least one day ahead of departure) $54 OW.

Newmans Coach Lines is at 347 Moorhouse Ave. across from the railway station, tel. 795-641. **Mount Cook Line Coach Terminal and Travel Centre** is at 40 Lichfield St. (south of city center), tel. 799-120—it's the terminal for Mount Cook Line, Starliner, and Gray Line, open weekdays 0715-1730, tel. 482-099 or 790-690 (evening number for reservations only). Other terminals are located at 91 Worcester St. (open weekdays 0830-1700), and at 47 Riccarton Rd. (head office; open weekdays 0830-1700).

For info on tours and transportation to Methven (28 km from the Mt. Hutt skifield), call in at **Value Tours** at 174 St. Asaph St., tel. 650-249. For daily transportation from Christchurch and Methven to the Mt. Hutt Skifield, call **Skiers Express** at tel. 448-806 (24-hour reservation number). The fare from Christchurch is adult $27 RT, student or child $23 RT; from Methven $17 pp RT.

Hitching Out

If you're heading north, catch the Kaiapoi or Rangiora bus (the bus stop is in the Square to the right of the Cathedral) and get off at Styx Bridge. Going south, catch a no. 8 or no. 22 bus (left of the Cathedral) to Hornby or Templeton. Going west, catch a no. 8 bus (left of the Cathedral) to Russley Road. If you want to take advantage of all-day Sat. shopping (to 2100) at the coastal suburb of New Brighton, take the no. 5 bus from the Square to Brighton.

ARTHUR'S PASS

Arthur's Pass Road is the highest and most spectacular highway across the Southern Alps—the only crossing over the rugged Main Divide between Lewis Pass in the north and Haast Pass in the south. The 160-km sealed and well-maintained Hwy. 73 (fine for cars and motorhomes, not recommended for caravans) connects the town of Springfield on the western outskirts of Christchurch with the old goldmining town of Kumara in Westland, linking the east and west coasts of the South Island. Apart from passing through a variety of awesome landscapes just to get to the other side, many people travel this route to explore, hike, climb, and ski the mountains of magnificent Arthur's Pass National Park which surrounds the highway about 150 km west of Christchurch, 100 km east of Greymouth. Both **InterCity** train (TranzAlpine Express) and coach services connect Christchurch to Greymouth via this highway with a stop at the town of Arthur's Pass.

From Christchurch

From Christchurch the road traverses the fertile flatland of the Canterbury Plains, then climbs steeply up to the stark and desolate landscape of **Porter's Pass** (945 meters), a popular tobogganists' playground in winter, and **Lake Lyndon,** a good birdwatching spot in summer and natural skating rink in the frigid cold of July and August. From here the road passes through the lunar landscape of **Castle Hill** where the background mountains of the **Craigieburn Range** to the west are steep and impressive (with good winter skiing), while the hills closest to the road are round, smooth, and dotted by weirdly shaped limestone formations (some with overhangings covered in Maori charcoal drawings that are thought to be 500 years old). The scenery changes dramatically as the road enters the mountain beech-covered hills of **Craigieburn Forest Park** (stop at the Visitor Centre for track and general info), then changes yet again as you enter bare eroded hills, passing **Lake Pearson** (known for its great brown and rainbow trout fishing, birdlife, and mountain reflections) and **Lake Grasmere** (more good trout fishing). Early runholders burnt off much of the natural forest in this high country in order to clear the hills for grazing. The resulting lack of natural cover accelerated mass erosion of the hilltops and enormous shingle slides that continue today.

The scenery along Hwy. 73 gets even more spectacular. The hills give way to tall craggy mountains covered in trees almost to the tops (and snow in winter) as the road curves around the northern end of the Craigieburn Range following the mighty Waimakariri River into **Arthur's Pass National Park.** As you

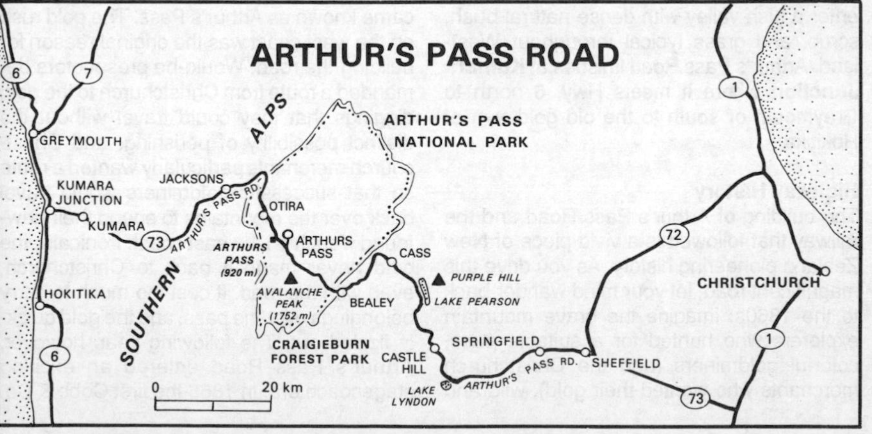

Castle Hill Basin along Arthur's Pass Road

drive through the Park, more incredible snow-capped mountains loom above, in front, and beyond, beckoning alpine explorers and nature lovers to pull off the road and stay for a while! Picnic shelters, camping spots, and walking tracks are clearly signposted as you follow the Waimakariri River into **Bealey,** then the Bealey River into the township of **Arthur's Pass.** The highway continues through the Bealey Valley to cross Arthur's Pass where rugged mountains covered in natural bush flank the roadway. Crossing the Otira River, the road takes you through the old railway town of **Otira,** and then the scenery subtly changes yet again as the road joins the Taramakau River. Descending steeply, you soon leave the tall mountains behind and enter a lush valley with dense natural bush, scrub, and grass typical throughout Westland. Arthur's Pass Road finishes at **Kumara Junction** where it meets Hwy. 6 north to Greymouth or south to the old goldtown of Hokitika.

Highway History

The building of Arthur's Pass Road and the railway that followed is a vivid piece of New Zealand pioneering history. As you drive this magnificent road, let your mind wander back to the 1860s: imagine the brave mountain explorers who hunted for a suitable pass, colorful goldminers (and the Christchurch merchants who wanted their gold), wild and crazy stagecoach drivers, highly skilled road engineers, and 1,000 courageous men who blasted their way through Otira Gorge in the winter of 1865, with picks, shovels, road drills, and bare hands, to bring the road into reality. Poor food and little shelter forced many to quit, and some even died before the road was completed. Similar hardships were suffered by the men who went on to build the railroad through Arthur's Pass.

Arthur Dobson was the first European explorer-surveyor to cross the pass in 1864—Kaiapohia Maori used this route (one of several) when they traveled to Westland for *pounamu* (or greenstone). Though at first it was considered far too difficult for building a road, when no better pass was found it became known as Arthur's Pass. The gold rush on the west coast was the original reason for building the road. Would-be prospectors demanded a route from Christchurch to the gold diggings that they could travel without the distinct possibility of perishing, and Christchurch merchants particularly wanted a route so that successful goldminers would travel back over the mountains to spend their newfound wealth on the east coast. Ironically, the gold never made it back to Christchurch, even with the road. It cost too much to carry belongings over the pass, and the gold quickly fizzled out. The following year, however, Arthur's Pass Road entered an exciting stagecoach era. In 1866 the first Cobb & Co.

stagecoach carrying passengers made the treacherous 170-mile, 36-hour journey over Arthur's Pass (prior to this crossing, mail had been carried over the pass by coach, pack horse, foot, and boat to Hokitika, taking about 4½ days). From then on, crossing the pass by stagecoach and overcoming its many dangers became the "in" thing for the wealthy and adventurous men and women "globetrotters" of the times.

Railroad History

At the same time, some amazing engineering feats were being accomplished as the railroad inched its way from both the east and the west toward the historic underground **Otira Tunnel.** Through the use of airdrills and explosives, the two ends of the railroad finally joined in the 8.5-km tunnel in 1918, and the first train thundered through in 1923. Stagecoaching quickly lost its popularity with the completion of the railroad. Today you can still see the original Cobb & Co. Seddon Coach that ran between Arthur's Pass and the Otira railheads in the 1890s until the tunnel opened; it's on display in the Visitors Centre in the town of Arthur's Pass. While you're there, ask to view the outstanding audiovisual on the history of the road—it brings the rest of your journey across the pass to life! Nowadays the road has regained its popularity as a major coast-to-coast route and as a spectacular access road to the mountain delights of Arthur's Pass National Park.

ARTHUR'S PASS NATIONAL PARK

The Land

Straddling the Southern Alps in the center of the South Island, 100,000-hectare Arthur's Pass National Park is the fourth largest national park in the country, noted for its sharp scenic contrasts and alpine flora. It's a paradise for avid alpine explorers, climbers, skiers, hikers, and naturalists, luring them toward its rugged snow-capped mountain peaks (many over 2,000 meters high) and glaciers (only the northernmost glaciers of the South Island remain), its steep ridges and deep gorges, sheer black cliffs and silver ribbon waterfalls, dense beech forest, bush-covered hills full of birds, flower-filled valleys, and rushing rivers with their wide beds of gravel. Situated at the southern end of the major earthquake zone, Arthur's Pass National Park ranges in altitude from 245 meters in the Taramakau River Valley to the highest peak, Mt. Murchison, at 2,400 meters. At first uplifted by enormous pressures within the earth, the mountainous landscape has obviously been glacially carved, deeply eroded by rivers carrying enormous loads of gravel and shingle, and weathered by an often harsh and unsettled alpine climate.

First impressions can be misleading as you cruise through the low valley floors craning your neck upward. From the highway the "mountains" appear to be steep forest-covered hills with snow-capped peaks behind them, but a full half of the Park landscape consists of towering mountains—17 named peaks over 2,000 meters high. The forces that continuously mold the landscape are visible and awesome—mighty rivers in flood tossing huge boulders as though they were pebbles, earthquake-triggered rock falls and landslides careening down cliff faces, and with the heavy snowfalls of winter, avalanches crashing down the mountainsides to line the valleys below. However, discovering the Park backcountry is safe if you have a good map and keep on the tracks, follow basic safety rules, and have enough food and warm clothing to suit all kinds of weather. One of the Park's best features is the easy accessibility from Hwy. 73 to scenic lookouts, short walking trails, longer hiking tracks, and a multitude of spectacular sights for the more energetic. The scenery can be enjoyed from the car, bus, or train, or on foot from deep within the wilderness—but before you venture out to off-the-road attractions, pick up a detailed map and track brochures, a weather forecast, and general info from the Visitor Centre in Arthur's Pass township.

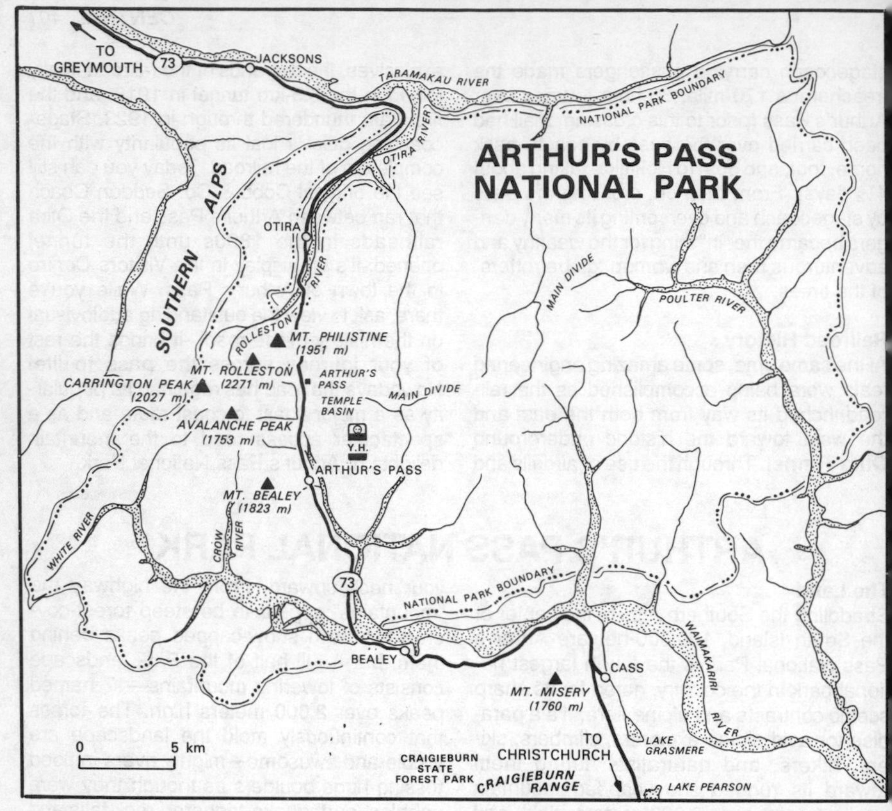

Climate

Wet and windy weather generally hits the Park from the northwest, dumping the highest amounts of rainfall on the western side of the pass. Though the Park is known for long periods of wet and unsettled weather, the rain tends to come in several heavy bursts rather than a continuous miserable drizzle, and you can hit extended periods of beautiful weather if you're lucky! The Otira area has the highest rainfall (around 4,500 mm per year), but it's quickly followed by the central area around Arthur's Pass at 4,000 mm (rain from dense low clouds descends on the pass approximately 160 days per year), Cass on the east side of the Waimakariri River at 1,300 mm, and the Craigieburn Ranges to the southeast at 1,000 mm. The weather comes in unpredictable cycles. The northwesterlies bring the bad weather, often heralded by cirrus clouds (strong winds high in the sky), hog's-back clouds (expect rain in a day or so), or a halo around the sun (ice particles in the air). These are eventually replaced by southerlies which bring a period of fine weather until the next northwesterlies arrive. In winter the Park turns into a white pristine wonderland, with bitterly cold winds from the west and heavy frosts in the shady valleys until Oct. and Nov. when the snow starts to melt off (the ski season is generally June to Sept.); however, around the town of Arthur's Pass the snow doesn't generally stick to the ground for long.

Flora And Fauna

The flora here is particularly interesting to naturalists: the range in altitude and difference in rainfall from the wetter west to the drier east is apparent in the large diversity of plantlife. On the western flood plains, podocarp forests of *matai, miro, rimu, kahikatea,* and *kamahi* are found, clothed in tree ferns and clematis, mosses, and fungi, and as you climb higher, *rata* and mountain *totara* become more abundant. Every couple of years in mid-summer, the slopes of Otira Gorge are totally covered in the scarlet flowers of the *rata*—a sight for sore eyes! The eastern forests are made up of beech trees, some covered in parasitic mistletoe, and wild orchids can be seen on the forest floor. The river gravel beds of the eastern side are home to mat daisies and a variety of ferns, mingling with the prickly shrub *matagouri* in the valley grasslands. The timberline ends abruptly, giving way to subalpine scrub. Up in the rocky alpine areas grows the beautiful white and yellow edelweiss, in the herb fields the anisotomes, alpine daisies, violets, gentians, snowberries, mosses and lichens, and in the alpine bogs, fascinating insect-eating sundews. The subalpine and alpine flowers are best appreciated in their summertime bloom between mid-Nov. and late February.

Many kinds of birds can be seen and heard throughout the Park. In the river beds and valley flats you'll often see pairs of striking black and white-headed paradise ducks, and banded dotterels, pipits, oyster-catchers, black-fronted terns and Canada geese. The *tui, morepork* (owl), shining cuckoo, yellowhead, and parakeet are seen in the bush, though the first two are more likely to be seen on the western side of the Park than the east. The cheeky *kea* resides in the upper forests and high in the mountaintops in summer, and the rock wren is also seen in the higher altitudes. Even the nocturnal great spotted kiwi can be seen in the bush if you have a keen eye and ear and don't mind hunting for it in the middle of the night! The Park is also home to extra-large dragonflies and grasshoppers, lots of moths and a few butterflies, and unfortunately, pesky sandflies (go armed with insect repellent). Small numbers of red deer and chamois, and brush-tail opossums (all considered pests) are found in the Park; however, hunting (encouraged but you must

rata

have a permit from Park HQ) has kept their numbers at low levels. Hunters have to be willing to work hard to get a deer.

HIKING

Short Walks

Most of the well-marked short trails cover a wide range of scenery, flora, and fauna, and are classified as half-day walks (one to four hours RT), or full-day walks (five to eight hours RT). For any of the nature walks, pick up the appropriate booklets at the Visitor Centre for lots of interesting info on the flora, fauna, and trails in general, and collect a Day Walks brochure which has a brief map showing all the short walks. Remember the weather can change rapidly in this alpine area—be prepared.

One of the most spectacular sights in the Park, worth seeing under any weather conditions at any time of year, is at the end of the short **Devils Punchbowl** trail. The track starts on the east side of Hwy. 73, half a km north of the Visitor Centre, and takes you to the Devils Punchbowl waterfall. These impressive falls plummet down a narrow gorge into a large rock basin more than 50 meters below (avoid clambering on the rocks around the falls). Several nature walks also start from the main highway—**Bridal Veil Nature Walk** (one hour RT) starts to the left after crossing the Bealey footbridge and takes you through beech forest to the Bridal Veil Lookout for views of Arthur's Pass village and the Bealey Valley. **Dobson Nature Walk** is a great track to take if you enjoy subalpine and alpine flowers. It starts on Hwy. 73 opposite the Dobson Memorial and takes about 30 minutes for the short loop track, or about two hours for the longer track which finishes at the Otira Valley carpark—booklet available at the Visitor Centre. **Cockayne Nature Walk** takes you through a diverse area of typical west coast plants and flowers following Kellys Creek. It starts on Hwy. 73 at Kellys Creek, north of Otira.

For fabulous mountain views, walk north from the village along Hwy. 73 to the **Top Of The Pass.** This four-km walk along the main road passes through mountain beech forest into the subalpine zone for some great scenery (don't forget your camera!). Another recommended short walk takes you along the Bealey River Valley for an hour or so until you reach the gorge where avalanche debris thunders down from Mt. Rolleston in the winter—don't go beyond this point unless you're experienced, and keep in mind that the valley can be hit by snow avalanches in both winter and spring. The track starts on Hwy. 73 opposite Jacks Hut, three km north of the village.

Longer Walks

If you're into photography, the **Temple Basin** track is for you! It wanders up the bluffs through subalpine scrub to the alpine grasslands of Temple Basin (the popular Park skifield open from June to Sept.) for spectacular views of Mts. Rolleston, Philistine, Barron, Phipps Peak, and many other snow-capped beauties; allow a full day for the entire route. To get to the start of the track, take Hwy. 73 north from Arthur's Pass town for five km to the carpark at Upper Twin Creek. Another good track to appreciate distinctly different vegetation zones is the **Carroll Hut** track. It's a fairly heavy-going uphill climb through *rata* and *kamahi* forest and subalpine scrub, onto tussock grasslands that surround the hut, but it's worth the effort. Again allow a full day. The track starts at Kelly's Creek, north of Otira (by Cockayne Nature Walk). Several other full-day walks take you to the top of **Avalanche Peak** and **Mt. Aicken,** up **Mt. Bealey,** and **Mts. Cassidy** and **Blimit** via the steep and rocky **Cons Track.** Another enjoyable day track takes you over old moraine to the scree-filled head of the **Otira Valley.** For more detailed info on these longer walks, call in at the Visitor Centre in Arthur's Pass township.

Backpacking

Arthur's Pass National Park is a popular mid-South Island area for serious hikers, providing many backcountry tracks with a great variety of scenery to appreciate along the way to the next hut. Eleven major tramping routes are described in a set of guide notes available at the Visitor Centre. Before setting off on any of the backcountry hikes, leave details of your proposed route and expected time of return with someone or on intention cards at the Visitor Centre—cancel the cards at the end of your trip. Huts have been situated along all the Park's major trails, some in radio contact with HQ. Most have a source of heat, but take your own stove and fuel for cooking. A list of the huts and their facilities is given in the *Park Handbook* along with a brief outline of basic backcountry safety procedures. Hut fees must be paid in advance—puchase hut tickets and collect maps and route guides at the Visitor Centre before you set off into the backcountry. If you'd like to hike and explore the wilderness with other people or want more specialized info, contact the Christchurch Tramping Club or the Canterbury University Tramping Club (ask for contacts at the Visitor Centre).

CLIMBING

The Park offers a full range of climbs from easy to challenging on rock, snow, and ice. The most popular climbing areas are the peaks along Hwy. 73, the headwaters of the Waimakariri River (many incline routes on the western flanks of Mt. Rolleston), and the headwaters of the Mingha, Deception, and White rivers. Although much of the rock is rotten, solid slabs are found at The Temple and Speight buttresses. Many experienced climbers come to the Park specifically in winter when some of the climbs become just as exciting and potentially dangerous as those found in the Mt. Cook region farther south. Climbs up the Otira face of Mt. Rolleston or the Crow Face are dangerous in sudden storms, so many snow or ice climbs are restricted. Potential hazards to climbers (and Park users in general) include stonefalls, snow avalanches, unexpected bad weather, and flooded rivers. Get more climbing info at the Visitor Centre; for possible climbing partners and more specialized info, contact the Canterbury Mountaineering Club or the Canterbury Westland section of the N.Z. Alpine Club (ask at the Visitor Centre for contacts).

SKIING

Temple Basin on the Main Divide is the Park's own skifield, providing winter enthusiasts and downhill skiers with spectacular views of mounts Rolleston and Philistine, the Avalanche and Bealey valleys, over Otira Gorge to the Kelly Range, and the distant deep-blue Westland hills—that is if you're willing to hike up to the skifield. Add to the views some excellent downhill slopes (a narrow and steep main run between Mt. Temple and Mt. Cassidy and nursery slopes on Mt. Cassidy), three rope tows (highest goes up to 1,800 meters on Temple Col), and a season generally running from June to September. The main hazard here is the possibility of avalanches after heavy snowfalls or rainfalls. Ski patrols protect the main fields, but skiers intent on trying the steeper alpine runs or leaving the main Temple Basin area should check with the ski patrol first for their own safety. To get to the skifield, leave your car at the Temple Basin carpark beside the main highway (a gravel road to the Bluffs, about halfway, is only suitable for 4WD vehicles), then walk the well-graded foot track (an hour or so depending on track conditions and your level of fitness) the rest of the way—sturdy footwear is essential. During the ski season you can get your skis and pack carried from the main road up to the basin by Goods Lift.

ACCOMMODATION AND FOOD

Camping And Park Huts

There are no special camping facilities, but the **Klondyke Corner, Hawdon River, Andrews Stream,** and **Kellys Creek** areas signposted along the main highway have day shelters, toilets, and fresh water, and you can picnic or put up a tent for free in any of these spots. (There's also a public day shelter in Arthur's Pass township.) Huts have been strategically placed along the major hiking tracks throughout the Park, and the Carrington, Casey, Goat Pass, Hawdon, and Locke Stream huts have radio contact with Park HQ. They provide bunks and heat—you provide everything else. No bookings are accepted; it's first-come, first-served. Hut fee tickets must be purchased at the Visitor Centre before you set off along the hiking trails. Each hut has a visitors book where it's advisable to enter your name, intended route, and dates of arrival and departure for your safety.

Youth Hostel

Sir Arthur Dudley Dobson Memorial YH (named after the "Arthur" of Arthur's Pass) can accommodate 39 people in two dorms (locked during the day) and extra room out the back, but during the summer months, particularly Jan., the hostel fills up quickly. Along with the usual communal facilities are a large day room/living area (left open in bad weather) and a relaxed atmosphere; $12 pp. If you'd like to play a game of squash (similar to racquetball), ask the warden—games cost $1.20 pp per half hour plus 50 cents for the lights, $2.50 for racquet hire. Be sure to check out the info board in the day room where there's plenty of general and Park info along with an intriguing chart of "Walks for Non-Walkers." The hostel is on Hwy. 73 in the center of Arthur's Pass village, tel. 89-230. The bus stops in the village on the main road north of the hostel and the train station is only a short stroll south—use the subway and turn right on the main road, continuing over the bridge to the concrete brick building on the right side. (The closest other YHs are in Greymouth and Christchurch.) There's also the Backpackers hostel in the village, tel. 89-258, providing accommodation for $13 pp.

If you don't have a tent and the hostel is full, try the Visitor Centre—they can sometimes help you to locate accommodation in private cottages. The ski clubs can also occasionally help with winter accommodation if they have room in their club lodges.

Motor Camps

The closest well-equipped motor camps or campgrounds to Arthur's Pass are in Greymouth, Hokitika, and Christchurch (see those chapters for more details).

Motel And Hotel

Alpine Motel is located on the main highway at Arthur's Pass, tel. 89-233, providing units with cooking facilities, private bath, and TV from $44 d. The **Chalet Restaurant** at the west end of the village serves morning and afternoon teas, lunch, and dinner, but also advertises B&B for $60 double. The **Otira Hotel** in Otira (on the northwest side of the Park) provides rooms from $22 s, $28 d; tel. OTI-802.

Food And Entertainment

It's best to stock up on supplies in Christchurch or Greymouth, find a place with cooking facilities, and whip up your own culinary delight. If you're not in a whipping mood, however, try the **Store and Tearooms** in Arthur's Pass village, open seven days a week, or the more expensive licensed **Chalet Restaurant** at the west end of the village, serving a.m. and p.m. teas, moderately priced lunch from 1130-1400, and dinner from 1800-1945 (bookings advisable—and get out your good duds).

If you're not already tuckered out from a long day in the great outdoors and fancy a quick game of squash to finish you off, get the rundown and hire racquets from the warden at the YH. Guided walks and illustrated talks may be given by rangers during vacation periods—find out what's on at the Visitor Centre. Otira, 14.5 km west of the Park, has a licensed hotel on the main highway, and for entertainment, a heated indoor public swimming pool.

INFORMATION

The main source of info on Arthur's Pass National Park is the **Park Visitor Centre** in Arthur's Pass village on the main highway—an essential first stop before any further exploration. Park HQ is also here, along with a large room crammed with fascinating displays on the geology, flora, fauna, history, climate, and legends of the Park. Read about the discovery of gold in Westland, the resulting construction of the road and railway over Arthur's Pass, the colorful coaching era, and see the original Seddon Coach on display—request to see the vivid audiovisual on building the road. Don't miss the extraordinarily beautiful panels by John Herbison along the walls of the display room and the wall hanging by Helen Young in the entrance room.

Detailed maps of the Park are available for $7.70, and you can pick up pamphlets describing all aspects of all Park activities. The Visitor Centre is open seven days 0800-1700, tel. 89-211, and the amiable staff is one of the most helpful around. During vacation periods, the rangers offer guided walks in the Park and illustrated talks in the lecture hall.

TRANSPORTATION

Access to Arthur's Pass National Park is easy by car, bus, or train. Highway 73 runs right through the Park, giving good access to the mountains. **InterCity** runs coaches daily Mon. to Sat. to the Park from Christchurch in the east and Greymouth and Hokitika on the west coast, stopping in the center of Arthur's Pass village. **InterCity** operates the TranzAlpine Express train (see spectacular scenery not accessible by road) daily to the Park from Christchurch and Greymouth, stopping at Otira (14.5 km west of Arthur's Pass village) and Arthur's Pass village—the station is a short stroll through the subway and right up the main highway to the center of town.

WEST

THE WEST COAST

A MOUNTAIN AND SEA SANDWICH

The magnificent West Coast of the South Island is really something to see! Although it has the unfortunate reputation for having rainy weather, dull skies, and an abundant summer population of bloodthirsty sandflies, it also has extended periods of blue skies and sunshine (particularly in winter)—all you need is a bit of luck, and insect repellent smothering on all exposed areas of your body! Well-maintained Hwy. 6 runs down this narrow strip of land squeezed between the Tasman Sea and the Southern Alps, giving the closest lowland views of the Main Divide and good access to both coastal and mountain activities. Visit the coalmining and fishing center of Westport in the north, wild and rugged surf beaches, a seal colony at Tauranga Bay, the amazing Punakaiki Pancake Rocks, the West Coast commercial center of Greymouth, and the historic goldmining town of Hokitika (a good place to browse for greenstone carvings and jewelry). Stop along the highway for a spot of trout fishing in one of several major rivers, or take a photography break at one of the many small lakes that reflect distant snowcapped peaks in their mirror-still waters, then push on south to the lush rainforests and mighty glaciers of rugged Westland National Park.

The best way to see the West Coast is by car or bicycle (you'll want to stop many times along the way), but you can also get your share of scenic delights from the bus. Getting to and traveling along the West Coast by public transportation (or thumb) is no problem. Westport and Hokitika airports are serviced by Air New Zealand, trains and buses run between Christchurch and Greymouth, buses connect Nelson in the north with Greymouth and Hokitika, and several bus companies cover all the main West Coast roads.

WESTPORT

Gold, Coal, And Other Rocks

New Zealand's largest coal-exporting town lies at the mouth of the mighty Buller River at the northern end of the West Coast. In the late 19th C. goldmining was an important industry on the Buller between Berlins and Lyell, bringing masses of people to the coast, but the coal industry was what really put Westport on the map. Along with coalmining (and export to Japan), the town is nowadays known for its timber industries, farming, good surf and river fishing (check out all the fishing boats at the wharf), 18-hole golf course, and opportunities to go rafting, caving, abseiling, horse trekking, you name it! The main attractions are the Coaltown Museum on Queen St. featuring the history of the coalmining industry, good surf beaches, historic Cape Foulwind, and the Tauranga Bay seal colony (see below). If you're going to be in Westport in Jan., don't miss the annual **Whitebait Festival**—aside from arts and crafts displays and a triathlon, the main event is a fish-filleting competition which draws quite a crowd.

First Stop

Make your first stop the excellent **Buller Information Centre** on Brougham St. (off Palmerston, the main drag) which features photographic displays on the Buller District, has racks of free brochures up for grabs, and enthusiastic staff who fill you in on all the local attractions and book tours, trips, and accommodations; open Mon. to Sat. 0900-1700, Sun. varied hours, tel. 6658. If it's closed when you hit town, check the map in the window for quick orientation.

For the latest info and maps on the Heaphy Track (starting at Karamea, about 100 scenic km north of Westport), Karamea Forest walks, regional forests, and Honeycomb Hill Caves (one of Karamea's main attractions), visit the **Westport Dept. of Conservation office** in the Government Buildings on Palmerston St., tel. 7869; open weekdays 0800-1630. (The **Karamea Dept. of Conservation office** is open weekdays 0800-1630 and weekends

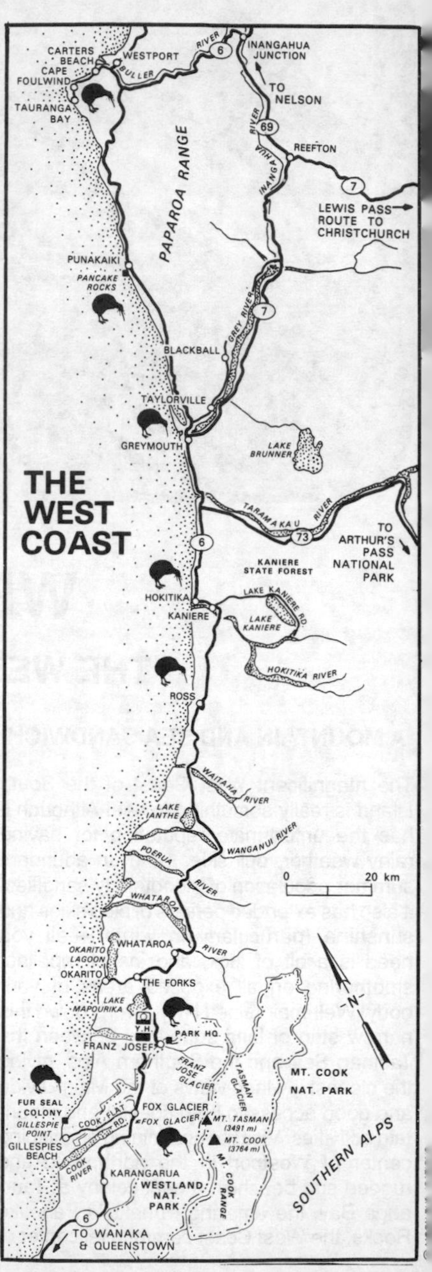

during peak summer months, tel. 852.) The **Automobile Association office** is at Seal Colony Tourist Park, Carters Beach, tel. 8002.

Sights

Coaltown, a museum and "living piece of the past," is a popular Westport attraction. Inside you'll find room after room of historic displays, all kinds of coalmining equipment, a film on the coalmining industry (shown every 30 minutes), and a room where special effects give the feeling of being underground in a coalmine. Also see the colonial and maritime wings and the goldmining exhibition. One of the rooms features a wagon from the famous Denniston Incline which, after completion in 1880, allowed coal to be lowered in wagons down a very steep hill by gravity—dropping 518 meters over a distance of two km in only 4½ minutes! The miners and inhabitants of the hill also used the wagons as their only form of transportation down to the railway (what a ride!) in the early years. Coaltown is located on Queen St. South (tel. 8204), open daily (varying hours), adult $4, child $2.

The Great Outdoors

For all sorts of outdoor adventures, including popular "underworld rafting" ($40 pp; allow four hours), contact **Norwest Adventures Ltd.** at tel. 8922 or 6686. **Buller Adventure Tours** also offers abundant outdoor activities in the area—jetboating, rafting (their one-day heli-raft Karamea trip for $99 pp is particularly popular), canoeing, horseback riding, goldpanning (no guarantees!), etc., starting at $30 pp; for all the details call in at their base on Buller Gorge Rd. (Hwy. 6), tel. 7286, or book at the Buller Information Centre.

Practicalities

Hotels, motels, and two motor camps provide accommodation, but if you're short of time and want to see as much of the West Coast as possible, continue south to Greymouth, Hokitika, or the glaciers for an overnight break—there's even more to see and do farther south. Looking for a place to pitch your tent or park your van? Do you want a comfortable cabin in town? **Seal Colony Tourist Park,** tel. 8002, six km south of town across the road from seemingly endless sandy Carters Beach, has tentsites for $13 d, caravan sites $14 d, spacious cabins $27-30 d, modern amenity blocks, and a recreation room. **Howard Park Holiday Camp,** tel. 7043, on Domett St., has tentsites for $12 d, caravan sites $13.50 d, share A-frame chalets $11 pp, mod cons, and living room with TV. Or try **Dale's Hostel** at 56 Russell St.; $10 pp includes breakfast.

The best and most unusual place in town for breakfast, morning or afternoon tea, lunch, or dinner is **Mandala Coffee House** on Palmerston St., tel. 7931. The owners created just about everything in the cafe—including the parquet floor, stained-glass lamps, and furniture—and the food is delicious, filling, and reasonable in price (dinner is a little more expensive, with main courses averaging $16). At the back is a small craft gallery and shop, worth visiting whether you eat there or not. **Black & White Hotel** on Palmerston St. serves good inexpensive bar meals—roasts are around $8 a plate. Another restaurant locally recommended is **Cristy's** at 18 Wakefield St., tel. 7640; open from 1830.

To continue south to Greymouth by bus, **Newmans Coach Lines** runs daily services Mon. to Sat., departing Westport at 1400, stopping for tea at Punakaiki Blowholes. For more info and bookings stop by the office on Palmerston St., tel. 7709. **Cunningham Coaches** runs a daily service from Karamea to Christchurch via Westport, Reefton, and Springs Junction, and return. Book at the Palmerston St. office, tel. 7177.

Cape Foulwind

If you have your own transportation, a ride out to **Carters Beach** (five km south of Westport) is a worthwhile sidetrack for a stroll along a sandy beach or a safe plunge in the surf. Then continue to the **Cape Foulwind Walkway** and the **Tauranga Bay Seal Colony** (another 10 km). To get there take Hwy. 6 south out of town, cross the Buller River Bridge, then turn right following Carters Beach and seal colony signs.

Cape Foulwind (named by Capt. Cook during a fierce storm in 1770) is a rocky promontory of granite bluffs covered in forests, wild grassy downs, and swampy streams and bogs. The walkway starts at the end of Cape Foulwind Rd. (a continuation of Carters Beach Rd.), runs south over the Cape's granite bluffs and undulating pasture, passes the Tauranga Bay Seal Colony, and finishes at the north end of sandy Tauranga Beach (the Maori word *Tauranga* means "Sheltered Anchorage") where a carpark, toilet, and interpretive display are located at the north end of Tauranga Bay Road. The easy four-km walk (wear light shoes) takes just over an hour OW, and can be done in either direction. From the top of the cliffs you get great coastal views and a peek at the Tauranga Bay Seal Colony. The fully protected *Arctocephalus fosterii* seal lives and breeds on the rocky shores around southern N.Z. and on subantarctic islands, and this colony is their northernmost breeding colony—don't climb down and disturb them. One of the best times to visit is around Jan. when you can sit at the top of the cliffs and watch the young seals frolic on the rocks, swim gracefully in the ocean, playfully catch waves, or bask with their parents directly below. Tauranga Beach is also an appealing place to walk or catch some sun, but resist the urge to catch a wave—the surf can be dangerous for swimming (look for the posted warning signs in summer or ask the locals about recent conditions).

PAPAROA NATIONAL PARK

Formed on Nov. 5, 1987, Paparoa National Park, New Zealand's 12th national park, lies about 57 km south of Westport. Here you can explore spectacular limestone cliffs, several rivers, steep bare-rock canyons, magical creeks that disappear underground, hills clad in lush ever-so-green ferns and nikau palms, numerous underground cave systems, and the Paparoa Range. The Pancake Rocks and the blowholes at Punakaiki (used to be Punakaiki Reserve) are the most well-known features; however, there is much to see inland. Some of its lush scenic beauty can be seen by driving along the coastal highway, but those who have escaped the beaten track claim the best way to appreciate the park is to walk the inland tracks or climb to the top of the range for spectacular views in all directions.

The Paparoa Range is not geologically connected with the Southern Alps. It began as an accumulation of Tertiary sand-, mud-, and limestone under the ocean that was uplifted, weathered, eroded, then reinvaded by the sea. Uplifted again, and eroded by wind, rain, snow, and ice, rivers slashed their way westward to the sea creating deep limestone (karst) gorges and canyons clothed in trees and ferns. Underground drainage in this limestone region is the most unique feature of the park—it is this, along with the dissolving action of rainwater on limestone—that sets the karst landscape apart.

The flora and fauna in the park are varied and diverse. If you explore a lot of the region you'll hike through towering forests of *rimu,*

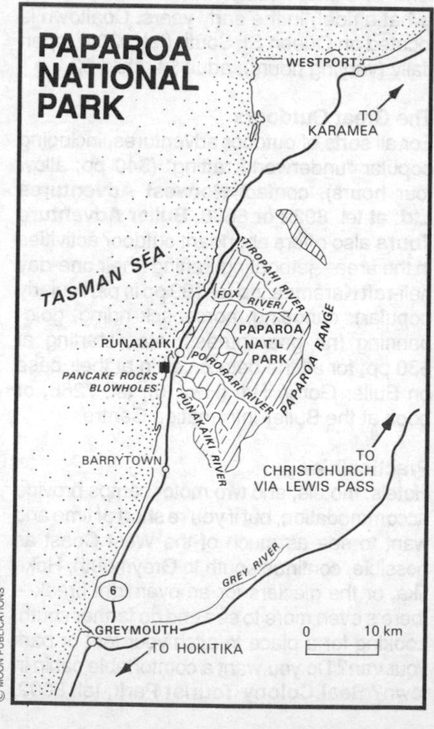

totara, rata, redbeech, *kamahi, quintinia, toro, horopito,* and lancewood. On the forest floor and steep banks along the coastal highway is an incredible conglomeration of ferns, mosses, lichens, and fungi. As you'd expect, all sorts of birds thrive in this green wonderland—bellbirds, fantails, *tuis, kakas, keas,* South Island robins, wood pigeons, parakeets, blue ducks, and native falcons, along with great spotted kiwis and the only breeding colony of Westland black petrels in the world. Bats, introduced animals, and of course, insects, also hide out in the lush park greenery.

The Road To Punakaiki

Highway 6 south follows the coastline through a smattering of old gold and coal towns backed by the Paparoa Range, passing through the first coastal section of the park—a lush, bright-green, fern- and nikau palm-filled strip. Pull off at signposted lookouts for some of the most stunning coastal views, or wander off along one of the walking tracks signposted from the highway. The scenery along **Truman Track** reputedly provides appreciative hikers with plenty of eye-opening camera action. The next major stop along the highway—the best-known and most-seen highlight of the park—is amazing **Pancake Rocks** and **Punakaiki Blow Holes**—a not-to-be-missed natural wonder. Made up of layer upon layer of limestone and mudstone, the much-photographed cliffs look like an enormous stack of wafer-thin rock pancakes. To see them take **Dolomite Point Walk,** a 15-minute (RT) stroll from the main highway through a wonderland of tree ferns, nikau palms, and northern *rata* to the clifftops. On the way you pass deep surge pools full of waving seaweed and mighty blowholes that in stormy weather boom and roar with the breaking of large waves—often unexpectedly blasting torrents of water skyward to soak startled onlookers with spray! The whole area is reputedly at its best in a westerly gale.

Pancake Rocks

Tracks

Ask at the info center for the brochure on "Walks and Tracks." It covers the equipment you'll need, and safety tips to make the park an enjoyable experience. It also outlines the short **Dolomite Point Walk, Truman Track,** and **Woodpecker Bay Track,** the trails to **Punakaiki, Teonumata Caverns,** and **Fox River Caves,** and the longer hiking tracks, **Tiropahi River Track, Pororari River Track,** and **Punakaiki/Pororari Track.** The 25-km three-day **Inland Pack Track** (you need hiking experience for this one) meanders along the historic inland road, built to avoid the rugged Te Miko Coast, through spectacular limestone canyons where deep crystal-clear river pools beckon (take care; the rivers can rise quickly), and past entrances to underground cave systems. If you only have time to see a little of the track, go up the Punakaiki or Fox rivers to walk the beginning or end sections. Before setting off along any of the longer tracks, get all the details and a weather forecast from the Visitor Centre at Punakaiki.

Guided Adventures

For those who enjoy exploring the unknown with local experts, **Paparoa Wilderness Guides** runs a large number of guided trips to suit all activity levels in and around the park. Their half-day walks start at $45 for up to three people, one-day walks $90 for up to three people, and extended treks at $155 pp per day. Prices include the use of tents, cooking utensils and cutlery, and food. For the complete rundown, call Barrytown (027-21) 826. They're based on Hwy. 6, five km south of Punakaiki.

Practicalities

Across the road from the walkway to Pancake Rocks is the **Paparoa National Park Visitor Centre** (open daily 0800-1700) which features photographic displays of the area's geology and history, and an audiovisual display. Rangers provide info and maps on the park, including brochures on coastal walks to nearby caves and the most intriguing rock formations in the immediate area. In summer they hold illustrated talks at the center and run scheduled guided walks of varying lengths. A variety of free pamphlets and brochures are available. **Pancake Tearooms,** a craft center, souvenir shop, **Nikau Palms Cafe,** toilets, and petrol facilities are next to the info center.

The modern **Punakaiki Camping Ground,** run by the Dept. of Lands and Survey (along Owen St., off the highway one km north of the Visitor Centre) is near the mouth of the Pororari River. Tentsites are adult $6 pp, child $3, caravan sites $13.50 d, the bunkroom is $10 pp per night, and cabins are $22 s or d, or $24 with cooking facilities. It's very popular in vacation periods—book ahead at Barrytown tel. (027-21) 894, or write to Camping Ground Manager, Punakaiki Camping Ground, Dept. of Conservation, Private Bag, Greymouth.

GREYMOUTH

Sights

Between Punakaiki and Greymouth, Hwy. 6 winds in and out of coastal native bush, passing tall cliffs and gray sandy beaches, and in summer the landscape is sprinkled with colorful wild flowers. Situated at the mouth of the Grey River and originally developed as a port in the 1860s after the discovery of gold, Greymouth grew into the largest town on the West Coast and the main port and commercial center for local coalmining and sawmilling industries. The town is known for good fishing in the Grey River system, and its many parks and native reserves; take a bushwalk up the hill (near The Gap) through **King Domain** for good views—the track starts on Mount St. near the railway station. **Shantytown,** a historical reconstruction of a West Coast gold settlement of the 1880s, is the best-known Greymouth attraction (admission $4). Wander through the old town with its bank and gold-buying office, store, jail, church, hotel, craft shops, printing shop, stables, and station. Take a quick ride on the steam train to the Chinese goldworkings, see how goldminers

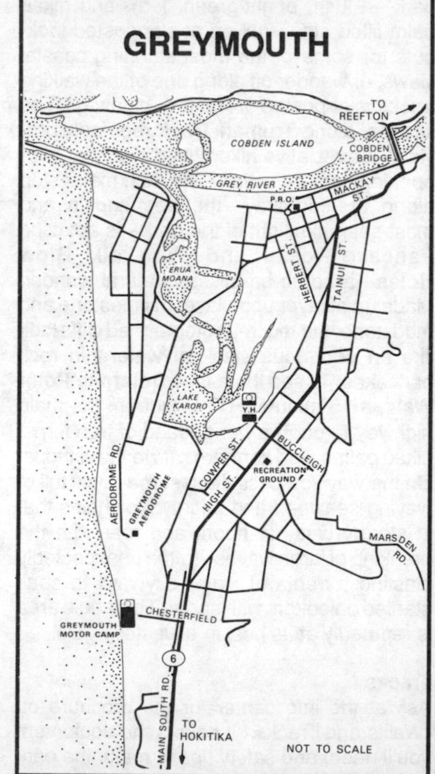

sluiced and panned for gold, or try your own hand at a bit of panning (extra charge). Tearooms serve the usual. Off the main highway at Paroa on the road to Marsden, about 10 km south of Greymouth, Shantytown is open daily from 0830-1700. If you don't have transportation, call Greymouth Taxi at tel. 7078.

About 15 km beyond the entrance to Shantytown (a gravel road) is the start of the one-km **Woods Creek Walkway,** a 45-minute RT track through virgin *rimu* forest that takes you past old goldmine tunnels, shafts (take a flashlight), and other evidence of past goldmining activities. Another local attraction is a no-longer-working old coal mine being restored at Rewanui (10 km along Coast Rd.) by the Preservation Society; it's open 0900-1730, adult $2, child $1—get all the details at the information center.

For hiking, fishing, swimming, and goldmining, head northeast to the Blackball area (see "Accommodation" below). To see local greenstone craftsmen, and for more info on the entire area, visit the friendly staff at the **Information Centre** based in the theater building (movies shown nightly); open Mon. to Fri. 0900-1700.

Accommodation

Plenty of places to stay in Greymouth range from the YHA hostel and motor camps to B&B guest houses, motels, and plush hotels; the info center has the complete list. The large, well-equipped **Kainga-ra YHA Hostel** overlooks a small stream and outdoor sports complex; it's $11 pp, at the south end of town on Cowper St., tel. 4951; from Tainui St. (the main street) continue south onto High St., turn right at Buccleigh St. by the DB Hotel and then onto Cowper Street. The closest motor camp to the city center is **Greymouth Seaside Motor Camp** on Chesterfield St. (off the main south highway, about 2.5 km south of Greymouth city center), tel. 6618. It's next to the beach, has a spa pool, TV room, a shop on the premises selling basic necessities, communal facilities, and a licensed restaurant and takeaways within walking distance. Tentsites are $7 s, $13 d, caravan sites $14 d, on-site caravans $28 d, cabins $28-32 d, and flats $45 d. The next closest, **Rapahoe Motor Camp,** is 11 km north of Greymouth, next to a good swimming beach in a small town surrounded by sea and mountains. Tentsites are $5 pp, caravan sites are $2 per night plus $5 pp, and cabins are $15-20 d. Located on the main coast road at Rapahoe, tel. 7337.

For a unique place to stay where you'll find home-cooked meals, backcountry character, and a casual atmosphere, head for the small, partially abandoned coal town of Blackball (a 20-minute drive northeast of Greymouth, it has a store, p.o., hotel, and two pubs). Here the **Blackball Hilton** provides hassle-free budget accommodation in a ramshackle two-story building built in 1909 (note the "Hilton" emblazened in gold on the old front door). It appears quiet enough at first but is locally known for its raging past! The coalminers used to drink, rant and rave, and party well into the wee hours in this hotel until the mines closed and the miners left in 1968. Renovated, it now offers plenty of individual rooms and dorms (provide your own sleeping bag or linen), TV lounge, old bar with a huge fireplace, and a sauna and spa. Shared bathrooms (getting hot water can be a problem) and cooking facilities, but breakfast and dinner are available—a hearty breakfast is $6 pp and dinner is $10 pp. No guest laundry facilities but if you're desperate you might be able to use the hotel washing machine with a bit of arm twisting. Dorm beds start at $12 pp, single room $17.50, double room $30. It's located on Hart St. (the main road) in Blackball, tel. 705 Ngahere—it's wise to call ahead to see if they have room before making the trek out. They'll collect you from Greymouth if there are at least two needing a ride, and the West Coast Express coach stops here twice a week depositing a large number of young backpackers.

Coming from the north, the road to Blackball turns east off Hwy. 6 before crossing the Grey River entering Greymouth; follow the sign to Taylorville. You wind along the Grey River through beautiful river and mountain scenery; the area is known for bush walking, lots of hiking tracks (pick up brochures and maps at the info center), mines, skiing, excellent trout fishing, and swimming.

the Blackball Hilton

Food And Entertainment

Many tearooms and coffee bars around town serve snacks and light meals, but if you're looking for something more substantial, try the **Raceway Carvery Restaurant** bistro in the Union Hotel on Herbert St., tel. 4013, open seven days a week; main courses start at $9 pp. Locally recommended **Cafe Collage** serves seafood crepes, steak, chicken, and spaghetti dishes for around $15-22 and has a BYO license. Upstairs at 115 Mackay St. (near the station), it's open from 1800 daily except Tuesday. For tasty takeaways try **Maywave Takeaways** on Albert St., tel. 5548.

For entertainment, head to any of the hotel bars, the discos at **Railway Hotel** on Fri. and Sat. nights and the **Golden Eagle Hotel** on Thurs., Fri., and Sat. nights, or movies at the **Regent Theatre,** tel. 5101. If you don't mind a bit of a splurge, take a short scenic flight over the goldmines and greenstone rivers of the West Coast with the Greymouth Aeroclub, Aerodrome Rd.; tel. 80-407.

Services

The **p.o.** is on Tainui St., tel. 80-123. The **public library** is at Mackay and Albert sts., open Mon. to Fri. from 1000. **Grey Hospital** is on High St., tel. 5039. For the **weekend doctor** and **pharmacy** on duty, see Friday's *Evening Star* newspaper or call the hospital. The **police station** is on the corner of Guinness and Tarapuhi sts., tel. 80-336.

Information

For general info and more on what to see and do in the area, all the West Coast reading material you could wish for, and a tour and accommodation booking service, go to the **West Coast Information Centre** in the foyer of the Regent Theatre on the corner of Mackay and Herbert sts., tel. 5101; open weekdays 0900-1700. There are plenty of pamphlets on the local area and the entire South Island—pick up the handy *Scenicland* pamphlet.

Transportation

InterCity runs a bus tour of Greymouth for $4 pp from the Railway Station, departing at 1230 each day (meeting the TranzAlpine Express train from Christchurch). InterCity provides buses in all directions (to Franz Josef $22 pp OW, to Fox Glacier $24 pp), and trains east to Christchurch (the TranzAlpine Express Day Excursion through superb scenery is $45 OW, $63 RT, departing daily at 1325; book ahead) from Greymouth Railway Station on Mackay St. near Cobden Bridge, tel. 4199. Ask at the Info Centre for more local and long-distance transportation information.

Newman's Coach Lines departs from Herbert St. (tel. 7078) north for Westport, Murchison, Nelson, Motueka, Takaka, Picton, and Blenheim.

West Coast Express runs a bus service from Greymouth to Queenstown in six days, stopping at all the highlights along the West Coast en route for $75 OW, or from Greymouth to Nelson with free transportation to the start of the Abel Tasman Track or Picton. **Magic Bus** also runs a West Coast to Queenstown service, stopping two nights at the glaciers, departing Greymouth Tues., Thurs., and Sat. for $75 OW. (From Nelson or Picton via either service it's $99 OW to Queenstown.) If you want to stay longer at the glaciers you just continue two days later. Book at Newmans, or at Greymouth Seaside Holiday Park, tel. 6618.

The **Air New Zealand Centre** is on Mackay St. (House of Travel), tel. 4479. **Air Nelson** flies out of Hokitika and Westport airports. For a taxi, call **Greymouth Taxis** on Herbert St. at tel. 7078—a 24-hour service.

HOKITIKA

The colorful goldtown of Hokitika lies beside the Tasman Sea at the mouth of the Hokitika River. Founded in 1864, Hokitika rapidly mushroomed into the large bustling "Capital of the Goldfields" when gold was discovered in the area a few weeks later. Hundreds of miners flocked to the West Coast from Australia (they called it the "Australian Invasion") and from other parts of the world, and by the end of 1866 up to 50,000 people were living at the various gold diggings in the area (the town itself had around 6,000 residents during the peak goldrush period). The rivermouth became a busy though treacherous port—many vessels were shipwrecked on the beach but beachcombers, salvagers, and refloating outfits made out like bandits! Hokitika became a conglomeration of banks, bars, and hotels—more than 100 hotels were hastily built, most of them on Revell Street. The last real West Coast goldrush occurred in 1867 in the Westport area, and by then more than 1.3 million ounces of gold had been removed. The majority of miners had left for the new goldfields on the Coromandel Peninsula by 1895, but gold remained a major industry along the Coast for many years. The last gold dredge on the Hokitika River was dismantled in 1952 and the port was closed in 1954, but plenty of old goldworkings, pieces of abandoned equipment, and other

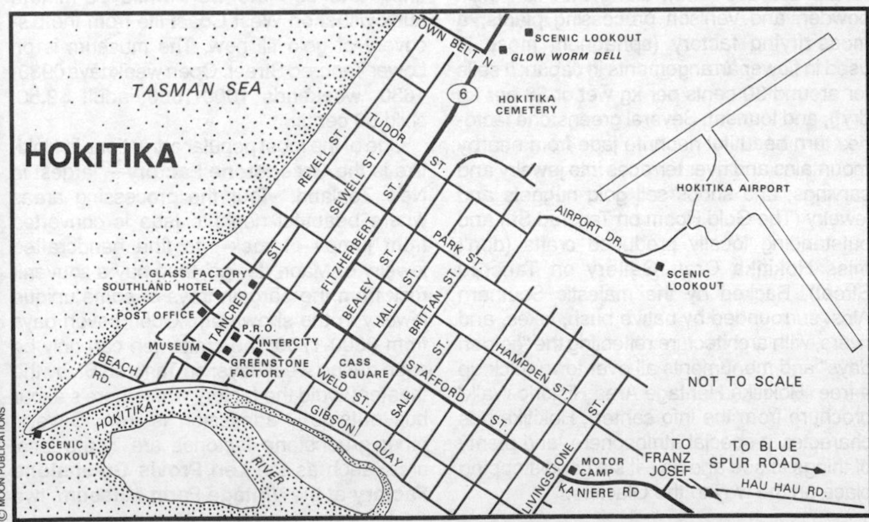

downtown Hokitika

relics can be seen in the surrounding district, and of course there's still gold in the local rivers and hills! Gold remains a major industry on the West Coast—locals say there are 100 or so mines still currently producing the metal dreams are made of. Many pamphlets showing all the places of goldmining interest are available at the PRO.

Nowadays farming is the most important industry in Hokitika (dairy farming on the alluvial flats, sheep and cattle raising on the less productive land), along with fish, milk powder, and venison processing plants, a moss-drying factory (sphagnum moss is used in flower arrangements in Japan; it sells for around 30 cents per kg wet or $8 per kg dry!), and tourism. Several greenstone factories turn beautiful nephrite jade from nearby mountains and river terraces into jewelry and carvings, and shops sell gold nuggets and jewelry (The Gold Room on Tancred St.) and outstanding locally produced crafts (don't miss Hokitika Craft Gallery on Tancred Street). Backed by the majestic Southern Alps, surrounded by native bush, lakes, and rivers, with architecture reflecting the "golden days" and monuments all over town (pick up a free "Hokitika Heritage Area Historic Walk" brochure from the info center), Hokitika has character, a special atmosphere, and plenty of things to see and do—it's a good stopping place on the way to the Glaciers.

Sights

If you're interested in finding out more about the goldrush days, don't miss the **West Coast Historical Museum**, devoted to "Westland's turbulent beginnings." It features displays of old photos and sketches from the goldmining era, a comprehensive collection of goldmining equipment, hall of pioneers, and an original stagecoach. Don't miss the Maori artifacts and native birds—some of which are extremely rare and possibly extinct, and see the worthwhile 20-minute audiovisual on West Coast life from the discovery of gold till now. The museum is on Lower Tancred Street. Open weekdays 0930-1630, weekends 1000-1600; adult $2.50, child 60 cents.

One of the most popular attractions in Hokitika is the **Greenstone Factory**—"largest in New Zealand." Tour the processing areas where beautiful nephrite jade is converted from lumps of rock into fine handcrafted jewelry of Maori design, then buy a souvenir rock from the bargain trays or some unique jewelry in the showroom. Open seven days from 0800-1700, the craftsmen can only be seen during weekdays; on Tancred St. by the theater (avoid the factory when there's a tour bus outside!), admission is free. Several other greenstone factories are in the local area, such as the **Len Provis Greenstone Factory** at the **Vintage Farm Museum,** two km east of town on Blue Spur Rd. (a continuation of Hampden Street).

Views
For a great view of Hokitika, distant mountains, Hokitika River, and the Tasman Sea, take a walk along the sandy driftwood-strewn beach to the south end or along Gibson Quay by the river to the scenic **rivermouth viewpoint.** The view from here is particularly magnificent at sunset and the weathered remains of an old pier, huge boulders and rocks, and silhouetted fishermen make fascinating photo subjects. The rivermouth also seems to be a popular place for anglers to congregate for some serious salmon fishing and some not-so-serious tale telling! For an even grander panoramic view, head for the **Plane Table Lookout** on the road to the airport (north of town). A pointer and map indicate all the mountain peaks you can see, along with their heights. For fabulous coastal views, head up to the **Seaview Lookout** and historic kauri lighthouse built in 1879; drive north on Fitzherbert St. and turn up the hill toward Seaview Hospital—the lookout is inside the cemetery on the right.

Another free sight well worth seeing on the north side of town is the **Glowworm Dell,** beside the main road at the north town boundary—after dark you'll see thousands of tiny lights scattered over the 14-meter banks (take a flashlight to see the path and don't make any noise—noise and bright lights disturb the glowworms and their lights go out!). Even if you don't have a flashlight you can easily feel your way up the path in the dark (take someone to hold onto if you're easily spooked)—and keep going, it's more spectacular the farther you go.

Out Of Town
If you have your own transportation, head east out of town along Blue Spur Rd. (a continuation of Hampden St. and Hau Hau Rd.) where several attractions are found. After about two km, you come to the **Vintage Farm Museum and Greenstone Factory**

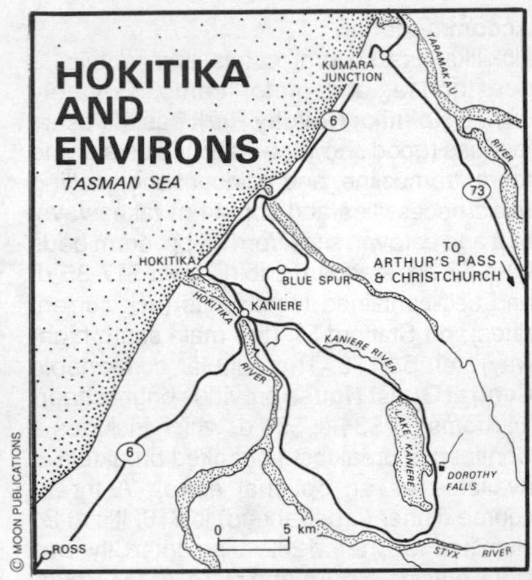

(free), then continue on to the **Blue Spur New Zealand Forest Look-Out**—at the Forest Service Notice Board turn right and continue for about four km.

So many tracks lead to old goldworkings and abandoned mining equipment, skirt rivers, and reach waterfalls and lakes that the best thing to do is stop at the **Lake Kaniere Reserve** information building (plenty of maps and photos; not staffed) where the river exits the lake and see all that's available. This lake (pronounced "Canary") and the surrounding area is known for its one-stop recreation. The reserve (brochure available at PRO) is about 18 km east of town (no public transportation). Choose from short or long tracks in the forest-clad hills around the lake, see sparkling Dorothy Falls, or hike along the **Kaniere Water Race Walkway** to hydroelectric power stations (four km OW, arrange own transportation at other end). There's good swimming and fishing in the lake, and campsites at Hans Bay or Geologist Creek. To get there take the main highway south to Kaniere township, then continue straight ahead onto Lake Kaniere Rd. (instead of the main road right over the Hokitika River). Continue to the Landing, where there's an info kiosk, mountain peak indicator board, and toilets.

Accommodation

Hokitika has several hotels and motels, a guesthouse, and motor camp. Privately owned **Hokitika Holiday Park** has the usual facilities (good showers—aah!), plus a game room, trampoline, and adjacent shop selling basic necessities and some hot takeaways; tent and caravan sites from $6 pp, dorm beds from $7 pp, standard cabins from $17-35 d, and self-contained motel units (ask current rates); on Stafford St. (the main south highway), tel. 58-172. The popular comfortable **Central Guest House** provides bright cheerful rooms for $34 s, $54 d, which includes a Continental breakfast (a cooked breakfast is available as an optional extra). A three-course dinner (order ahead) is $16. It's at 20 Hamilton St., tel. 1232. The InterCity bus stops outside. **Southland Hotel** at 111 Revell St., tel. 58-344, has really comfortable rooms, many with Tasman views, starting at $80 a night, or $90 with a private spa. Their budget rooms above the pub start at $40 a night; shared bath facilities.

remains of the old pier at the mouth of the Hokitika River

Food And Entertainment

There's not a large variety of restaurants in Hokitika, but many tearooms and coffee lounges serve the usual, as do plenty of takeaway bars. It's relatively easy to eat well on a tight budget in Hokitika—most of the eating houses are on Revell, Weld, and Sewell streets. For great sandwiches, head for **The Gold Strike Sandwich Bar** next to the Info Centre in the Regent Theatre building on Weld St. and sink your teeth into a wild venison or pork sandwich. They also have all the normal sandwiches (from $3-4.50), a variety of creamy ice creams, "American milkshakes," fruit juices, and coffee.

If you're in the mood for pizza ($8-15), spaghetti ($12.50), steak ($16), pastries and other baked delicacies, or dessert (the "Bananahana" is large enough for two), you'll discover half of Hokitika's population in the small **El Jabels,** in the New World Mall on Revell Street. And for a delicious selection of salads from a salad bar, pies, quiche, pastries, and desserts, go to **P.R.'s** on Tancred St.; open daily 0600-1630. For more of a splurge and excellent sunset sea views through picture windows, try **Tasman View Restaurant** at the Southland Hotel on Revell St. (open for dinner from 1800-2100, $15-23 for a main course; lunch served in the hotel bar), or sample some French cuisine at **Chez Pierre** on Sewell St., opposite the post office.

For entertainment, movies are occasionally shown at the **Regent Theatre,** games of "housie" (bingo) are played all over town, there are squash courts and a heated swimming pool, but for the money, nothing beats a sunset stroll along the beach to the rivermouth! Trout and salmon fishing are popular in the Hokitika region—get your license and free fishing info (ask for the detailed leaflet on trout fishing in the Westland Region) from the **Westland Sports Depot** on Weld St., tel. 481. If you're feeling a little more adventurous

Ross cemetery

and prosperous, try a scenic flight over the glaciers or Mt. Cook from Hokitika Airport with **Westland Transport.**

Services And Information

For a **doctor** call 58-110, 58-409, or 56-407; for the **hospital** call 58-445; for **police** call 111. The **Information Office** is at 23 Weld St., tel. 58-101; ask for hospitable Heather Cowie. **The Dept. of Conservation** takes up an entire building on Sewell St. and is open regular office hours; go here for detailed maps and info on Westland National Park and other national parks throughout the country.

Transportation

The area's major airport is two km north of Hokitika, serviced by **Air Nelson** from Christchurch three times a day, and by **Trans Alpine** daily from Christchurch (one of the most scenic 35-minute flights imaginable). A bus runs between **House of Travel** on Revell St. (tel. 58-134) and the airport, departing 25 minutes before each flight. A taxi to the airport is $4 OW. **InterCity** (Sewell St., tel. 58-233) runs coaches north and south; book at the Railway Station or at White's Agency on the corner of Hamilton and Tancred sts. near the station (bus stops outside Central Guest House). For a taxi, call **Gold Band Taxis** at tel. 58-437. For rental cars, call **Avis** at tel. 58-347, or **Hertz** at tel. 58-031.

FROM HOKITIKA TO THE GLACIERS

Between Hokitika and the glaciers (about 140 km), the main highway passes many small lakes, accessible tracks, a few small settlements that once bustled with goldmining activity, and mighty rivers where you can reel in brown and rainbow trout and the occasional salmon when the water is clear (many of the rivers are cloudy with glacial run-off). Farther south, the road runs by a saltwater forest, swampy areas of marshes and lagoons covered in waterfowl, then lush green paddocks backed by dark-blue mountains. As you get nearer to the town of Franz Josef on the northern boundary of Westland National Park, magnificent snowcapped peaks loom into view.

Ross

This small but typical West Coast goldtown, 30 km south of Hokitika, has a colorful goldmining history (kept alive in the local museum), walkways of historic interest, and several tourist attractions. Services include two licensed hotels (good bar lunches and dinners at the Empire Hotel), a motel, motor camp, and a variety of tearooms. Jones Creek Flat (behind Ross), a stable and productive goldfield in the early 1870s, was where New Zealand's largest gold nugget

This attractive fellow points the way to the Ross Goldfields.

was found in 1907—nicknamed "the Honourable Roddy" after the local mayor.

The first place to go for info on local walks is the **Ross Historic Goldfields Visitor Centre** (in a beautifully restored miner's cottage—look out for the tin man pointing the way) at the trailhead of the **Ross Historic Goldfields Walkway.** There are two loop tracks. The **Water Race Walk** is two km (steep in parts—at least 1½ hours RT) starting at the Visitor Centre. It takes you through an old cemetery where gravestones vividly describe the hard times and tragic accidents of the 1870s (allow extra time for intriguing reading!), to lookouts for good views of Ross, and past old coalmine workings along the disused water race. The **Jones Flat** loop (1½ hours RT) also starts at the Visitor Centre and winds through regenerating forest along old elevator claim tailings—passing the site of the famous "Roddy nugget."

Ross Furs is another local attraction. Watch furriers make coats, hats, and all sorts of useful things from super-soft opossum fur in the factory workroom, then buy whatever grabs your fancy; it's on the main street of town, closed Sunday.

Okarito

The Okarito shoreline was the first bit of N.Z. to be seen by Abel Tasman in 1642. During the goldrush era of the 1870s, the quiet settlement of Okarito flourished into a boomtown supporting 2,000 people, two banks, and many hotels and stores. Today it's again a peaceful settlement on a typically wild West Coast beach. Several walks starting here take you to panoramic views of the mountains, forests, and coastline for the energetic (pick up the free *Okarito Walks* brochure at the Forest Service office in Hokitika or at Park HQ in Franz Josef). You'll find good bird- and wildlife-watching at Okarito Lagoon and South Okarito Forest, surf-fishing and whitebaiting (seasonal), and goldmining from the beach or panning in nearby rivers.

There's also a **YHA Shelter Hostel** here; it's only $5 pp as there's no electricity (just candlelight, and an open fire for cooking). Buy all your food and supplies and get cash before you head for Okarito—the one shop is only open three days a week for about two hours, and there are no banks. To get to Okarito, turn west off the main highway to The Forks (an old goldmining center), then continue for about 13 km along the gravel road. If you're traveling by bus, ask the driver to let you out at The Forks turnoff (tell him your destination before he loads your luggage).

Lake Mapourika

About eight km north of Franz Josef, beautiful bush-fringed Lake Mapourika is the largest lake in Westland National Park, separated from the main sector of the Park by a short stretch of highway. Dark brown from rainwater filtered through the surrounding forest, the lake provides superb reflections, an abundance of birdlife, excellent salmon and trout fishing (get your license at the Franz Josef Store or Park HQ), warm swimming, and boating. There are plenty of shady picnic spots, and a free campground with fresh water and toilets at McDonalds Creek at the north end of the lake.

WESTLAND NATIONAL PARK

GREENERY AND GLACIERS

Westland National Park was established in 1960, centered around Franz Josef Glacier and Fox Glacier, the two largest glaciers, and the Copland/Karangarua Valleys; in 1982 the coastal landforms and rainforests of Okarito and Waikukupa were added. Highway 6 travels briefly along the northeast boundary of the Park, passing through the towns of **Franz Josef** and **Fox Glacier,** the two tourist centers in the area and main sources of Park information.

Backed by the magnificent mountain peaks of the Southern Alps, Westland National Park covers a rugged 70-km-long, 117,547-hectare area of high mountains and glaciers, lakes and waterfalls, hot springs, coastal lagoons, and icy, gray-blue rivers that tumble down through dense forest to the Tasman Sea. The land rises from sea level to peaks more than 3,000 meters high, providing incredible scenery, a diverse range of habitats, plenty of birds and wildlife, and all kinds of recreational possibilities for the masses of "swivelheads" (a coloquial term for tourists) that visit this popular stretch of the West Coast each year. Glacier excursions, mountain hikes, forest and beach walks, fishing, mountaineering, ice-climbing, flightseeing, alpine ski-touring, and ski mountaineering are just some of the activities available, and for the less adventurous or those in a hurry, some of the most striking glacier and bush scenery can still be appreciated from the road or at the end of short tracks. The most popular features of the Park are the stunning Franz Josef and Fox glaciers, both flanked by forests and backed by towering snow-covered peaks, yet easily reached by road and tracks, or by ski-plane or helicopter.

The Land

Thirty-km-wide Westland National Park, squeezed between the coast and the Main Divide, rises from Gillespies Beach and Okarito at sea level to the 3,498-meter summit of Mt. Tasman (second highest peak in New Zealand). The landscape is dominated by the Park's two largest glaciers (out of 60), Franz Josef Glacier and Fox Glacier, both of which descend about 11 km from 3,000-meter-high permanent snowfields to dense rainforest only 300 meters above sea level—the only glaciers in the world that descend directly into lowland rainforest.

In the last ice age, 14,000 years ago, even the lowland areas were totally covered in ice. Today, most of the terrain above 1,500 meters is still permanent ice and snow, with high peaks and ridges of frost-shattered rocks where up to 10,000 mm of rain and snow fall per year. The lowland moraines and river valleys are now clothed in alpine grasslands and herbfields, shrublands, and dense coniferous rainforest. Lakes and coastal lagoons nestle in glacially formed hollows, and the entire landscape is riddled with wide gravel beds and mighty glacier-fed rivers.

The Franz Josef and Fox glaciers cover a combined area of over 4,000 hectares—an ever-changing landscape of ice and rock. From high in the sky each glacier is a mass of deep blue cracks and fluffy blue-white peaks—"just like pale-blue meringue" claimed one enthusiastic visitor just back from a helicopter ride! A glacier is formed by fresh snow falling on the upper néneveé or snowfield (up to 300 meters deep), squeez-

Franz Josef Glacier

ing out air from underlying layers to create firn or soft ice; when most of the air is forced out, dense blue ice is formed. The enormous mass of ice moves downward with the force of gravity (up to five meters a day in Westland), creating great pressures deep within the ice as it's crushed against the underlying terrain, cracking into ravines and crevasses up to 100 meters deep as it spills slowly downward. You can hear its movement at the terminal face—cracking and creaking ice, and rushing glacial melt-off. The glaciers are always either advancing or retreating—the terminal face retreats if the melt rate (due to warm rain) exceeds the ice-replacement rate, and advances if ice replacement (due to heavier snowfalls or colder temperatures than normal) exceeds melt rate. Both glaciers have retreated dramatically over the last 50 years (during the last major glacial advance they swept all the way out to the sea), with small advances occurring periodically (since 1984 there's been a one-km advance which Park rangers predict will continue for a few more years) even though the overall trend is retreat. They are still spectacular sights well worth seeing today.

Climate

The weather is as varied as the terrain in this area. Westland ("Wetland" to visitors who whiz through the area in search of blue-sky "been-there" snapshots) has the reputation for dull gray skies and rainy days (and accompanying ferocious sandflies) in summer, but the winters are clear and cold and the scenery is dramatic. Be prepared for a downpour and cool temperatures even in the middle of summer and you'll be ready to make the most of your surroundings; if you're doing any of the hikes in the Park, get an up-to-date weather forecast from the Franz Josef or Fox visitor centers before you set off into the wilderness. The average yearly rainfall on the coast is about 3,000 mm; at the townships of Franz Josef and Fox Glacier and at the foot of the mountains, it can be as much as 5,000 mm per year; and up to 10,000 mm of rain and snow are expected above the 1,500-meter level each year.

Flora And Fauna

One of the most fascinating things about Westland National Park flora is the way the bare rock surfaces left behind by retreating glaciers are rapidly invaded through a process called "plant succession." In the early years after glacial retreat, windblown grasses and mat plants colonize the bare surfaces, and within 20 years, various shrubs such as *tutu* and native broom that fix nitrogen from the air to form soil have established themselves. Within the next 500 years, dense young forests of *rata* and *kamahi* trees spring up, and within 1,000 years, *rimu* and *miro* trees are well established, forming the canopy of a lush podocarp rainforest. The luxuriant rainforest you drive through on the way to the glaciers also contains *kahikatea, matai,* and *totara* trees, an assortment of small shrubs, and beautiful ferns of all sizes (best appreciated on some of the short walks). Above the *rata* and *kamahi* forests, shrublands and alpine grasslands cover the slopes. Alpine herbs such as edelweiss, buttercups, and hebe grow in the higher reaches of the Park, but only lichens survive on the highest rock areas below the snowline. Altogether about 600 species of plants and ferns inhabit the Park.

Native birds, such as the *tui,* kiwi, bellbird, pigeon, fantail, tomtit, robin, and parakeet (ears become rapidly accustomed to ever-present rapturous birdsongs), and oystercatchers and caspian terns can be seen in abundance, along with a number of godwits and the occasional crested grebe in the lake areas, wetlands, and coastal lagoons. White herons are prominent during their breeding season, Oct. to February. All kinds of insects creep around in the undergrowth including termites, *wetas,* and *huhu* grubs that feed on fallen trees. Opossums, red deer, chamois, and Himalayan thar live in the Park, and large numbers of fur seals haul ashore at Waikowhai Bluff near Gillespies Beach, west of Fox Glacier, during the winter months (see p. 430).

fantail

FRANZ JOSEF AREA

HIKES

Walks On The Way To The Glacier

Before you head along the Glacier Access road for your first glimpse of Franz Josef Glacier, stop by **Westland National Park Visitor Centre and HQ** (off the west side of the main highway in town) and collect the *Franz Josef Glacier Valley Guide.* It has a map showing local attractions, describes some of the short walking tracks, and contains general info on many of the natural features of the glacial valley and glacier itself. Also collect the many brochures on short walks in the area. The Centre has all sorts of fascinating displays, a stunning photograph/art gallery, all the reading material and maps you could possibly need, friendly staff, and indigenous arts, crafts, pottery, and photographs for sale in the lobby. Don't miss the 25-minute audiovisual on the history of the Park; it runs on the hour from 0900-1600; admission adult $2.50, child free. It's open daily from Christmas to the end of Jan. 0800-2030, Jan. to Feb. daily 0800-1830. The rest of the year it's open Mon. to Fri. 0800-1700, weekends 0800-1200 and 1300-1700.

To get to the glacier from the Visitor Centre (six km), head south along Hwy. 6 for about 400 meters, then turn left after the bridge onto the Glacier Access road. Continue for five km along this road through lush rainforest to a carpark and picnic shelter to get your first views. Many tracks of varying lengths branch off the Glacier Access road—look for the signs. The **Lake Wombat Track** is an easy-to-moderate fern-lined trail through *rimu* forest to a small glacial lake where you'll hear all kinds of songbirds and see plenty of waterfowl; 30 minutes OW. The more strenuous **Alex Knob Track** branches off the Lake Wombat Track, climbing steadily through subalpine scrub to alpine grasslands and herbfields for fantastic glacier, mountain, forest, and coastal views. It takes about four hours to climb up, three hours to come down, and you need to take food, water, raincoat, warm clothes, and a flashlight. Sign the intentions register at the Visitor Centre before doing any of the longer tracks—be sure to sign out again when you return.

The **Roberts Point Track** is reached via a 20-minute walk along the Douglas Track to Douglas Bridge. It climbs up the east bank of the Waiho Valley, crossing slippery rock and side streams to a lookout high above the glacier where you get incredible long-distance views. Classified as a moderate-to-hard forest track, it takes about three hours OW, returning via the same route (don't take a shortcut down from Roberts Point to the glacier track—very unsafe); wear sturdy footwear, and take a raincoat and some energy food.

The **Douglas Walk,** an easy forest walk over glacial landforms formed by advances of the Franz Josef Glacier between 1600 and 1750, starts on the Glacier Valley road. It takes five minutes to Peters Pool (a kettle lake), and about 45 minutes to complete the walk, finishing at a point farther back along the Glacier road—altogether an hour RT to the original starting point. If you don't have enough time to hike all the way to the glacier, take the short 10-minute climb up **Sentinel Rock** (four km along Glacier Access road) for impressive glacier views and many examples of plants that have progressively colonized this huge rock. Keep to the track.

Franz Josef Glacier Valley Walk

The most popular hike in the area leads to the terminal face of Franz Josef Glacier. Taking about one hour from the carpark at the end of the Glacier Access road (flat and easy at first, more strenuous as you approach the viewpoints), the route crosses riverbed gravel and several small streams, passes impressive waterfalls that cascade down steep glacially carved cliffs, then climbs up and over enormous boulders for great views of the glacier and the Waiho Valley. Stick closely to the marked track, watch out for possible rockfalls, and resist the urge to venture onto the ice without an experienced glacier guide—the front wall of the glacier is unstable. To be most comfortable, wear sturdy footwear, take a warm jacket for rest stops (it gets nippy as you approach the ice), and plenty of insect repellent in summer. The Park provides a program of guided walks during the summer vacation period.

Short Walks Around Franz Josef

The **Terrace Walk** starts opposite HQ off Hwy. 6. It's an easy 50-minute RT forest walk, zigzagging up the terrace behind Franz Josef to the sluice face (from which a considerable

Franz Josef Glacier from the Waiho River Bridge

Glacier helicopter heading off for glacier views

amount of gold was taken), passing old gold-mining relics and finishing on Cowan St. behind Franz Josef village. A 20-minute side-track also leads off the main track to scenic Tatare Gorge where clear water gushes down between enormous boulders. The **Canavans Knob Rainforest Walk** is another short walk/climb for good views. The 20-minute (OW) track starts on Hwy. 6, two km south of Franz Josef, where the highway makes a sharp left turn.

ACTIVITIES

Guided Glacier Tours

The THC Franz Josef Hotel offers guided **Franz Josef Glacier Walks** depending on prevailing ice conditions. Experienced glacier guides run the four-hour tours, departing the hotel at 0930 and 1400 daily (be there by 0900 or 1330 and take a raincoat if the weather looks at all doubtful); adult $24, child $12. Boots, socks, and transportation to the glacier are included. Call Trips 'n Tramps at tel. 719. If the ice is stable, they supply you with special boots and poles—and before you fully comprehend what's going on, you're in a line of courageous people scrambling up and down ice pinnacles and jumping crevasses (a guaranteed adrenalin rush, not recommended for chickens), with no turning back! **Rata Grove Motel** also runs scenic tours to the glacier; tel. 741.

Flightseeing

Several companies based in Franz Josef and Fox Glacier operate a variety of flightseeing glacier experiences, weather permitting, by ski-plane or helicopter. Seeing the glaciers and mountain peaks from the air is unforgettable in fine weather, and although it's expensive, it's worth every cent. But before parting with your cash, shop around for different prices and rides (scenic flights, snow landings, heli-hikes etc.). Book yourself on an early-morning flight (it's worth waiting an extra day to accomplish this)—the skies are most likely to be clear early, rapidly clouding over as the day progresses.

Glacier Helicopters has a variety of stunning flights ranging from 10 minutes for adult $45 pp to 40 minutes for adult $140 pp. For the most fun, take the 20-minute "Snow Landing Scenic Flight" for $70 adult pp—fly up the glacier to land amongst spectacular mountain peaks, leave your mark in the ice or frolic in fresh virgin snow, get a spectacular photograph of Mounts Tasman and Cook, then suck in your breath for close-up views of ice peaks and crevasses as the helicopter literally skims the glacier on the way back down. For info, stop by the office on the main road or call 755 Franz Josef/803 Fox Glacier. **Mount Cook Line** does ski-plane adventures from $94.50-241 pp adult; Franz Josef tel. 714, or Fox Glacier tel. 812. **The Helicopter Line** also provides similar flights at similar prices; tel. 767 Franz Josef.

Horseriding, Rafting, Or Fishing

A more sedate way to appreciate the magnificent scenery of the Park is via horseback. Hire a "quiet" horse for a half-day or full-day trip from **Waiho Stables** at Franz Josef (they also give lessons in English-style riding); tel. 747. Take to the water on a rafting trip down an icy-cold glacial river (wetsuits provided!) for only $10-25 pp. Get all the details at **Cottage Crafts** on the main road. For info and current prices on **guided river or lake fishing trips** by the hour or the day, call 721. Westland Guiding Service also specializes in local hunting, fishing, and **tramping safaris**—for more info and current prices, call 750.

White Heron Sanctuary

If you're visiting the West Coast in Dec. or Jan., consider a tour to a unique white heron *(kotoku)* bird sanctuary. For $55 pp, **White Heron Sanctuary Tours** provides minibus transportation from Franz Josef and an exciting 40-minute jetboat ride on the small Waitangi-Taona River. From here you take a short bush walk along a boardwalk to view the herons nesting—allow three hours from Franz Josef, two hours from Whataroa. If you can provide your own transportation to the jetboat starting point, it's only $45 pp. Rates include park admission. Book through Fern Grove Souvenirs in Franz Josef, tel. 731 or 744, or call the company direct at Whataroa, tel. 34-144 or 34-060.

ACCOMMODATION

Hostel

The new, fully equipped **Franz Josef YHA hostel,** backed by beautiful bush (two good tracks), is centrally located only a five-minute walk from Westland National Park HQ; $12 pp. At 2-4 Cron St., Franz Josef. It gets crowded in the height of summer—book ahead for Dec. to Feb., tel. 754.

Motor Camp

There's nothing quite like climbing out of your tent to the sound of a rushing river and a stunning view of Franz Josef Glacier (but be armed with insect repellent—the sandflies are ferocious in summer!). Renovated **Franz Josef Holiday Park** offers the above, and more: the kitchen and living area (with TV), and the indoor swimming pool are particularly good places to meet fellow travelers; the bathroom facilities are clean, spacious, with plenty of hot water, disabled facilities, and a baby's bathroom; and there are a barrage of coin-operated washing machines and driers. Tentsites are $6 pp, caravan sites are $14 d, shared dormitory-style cabins are $8 pp, standard cabins are $20 d, the roomy deluxe cabins are $14 pp, and tourist cabins with

You can expect glacier views from Franz Josef Holiday Park.

cooking facilities are $33 d. Or stay in the warm comfortable lodge which has shared bathroom facilities, a kitchen, and large living area; $32 d. Located next to the main road, one km south of Franz Josef, tel. 766.

The next closest motor camp is two km off the main highway at The Forks, 16 km north of Franz Josef. **The Forks Motor Camp** (tel. WAA 351) has tentsites for $5 pp, caravan sites for $7 pp, and several units that each sleep two to six people (call for current rates).

Guesthouses, Motels, And Hotels

Callery Lodge, tel. 738, offers a single room for $25, a double for $39-50 (some have shared bathrooms, others private). Continental breakfast available. Apart from the YH and motor camps, you're out of the budget category and into a motel room for the night. The many motels in Franz Josef all have rooms starting at around $66 d—refer to your *AA South Island Guide* for listings and current rates. **Glacier Gateway Motor Lodge** on the main road next to the motor camp provides rooms with cooking facilities for $66-77 d in peak season (off-season reductions), tel. 766. **Glacier View Motel,** also on the main highway, 2.5 km north of Franz Josef, tel. 705, has a game room and shop; $66-74 d with private cooking facilities; breakfast available. If you feel like splurging, stay at the impressive **THC Franz Josef Hotel,** tel. 719, one km north of town, where the rooms start at a mere $72-99 d!

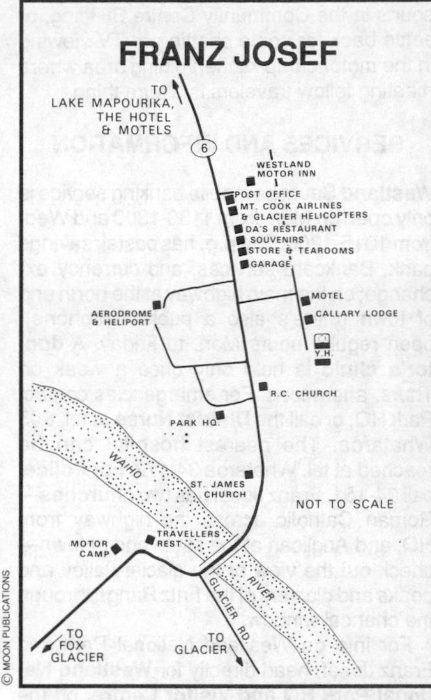

FOOD AND ENTERTAINMENT

To find out where to eat and go for entertainment, just take a stroll through the village—it's small enough that you can easily *see* what's happening! **Glacier Store and Tearooms** on the main road next to the souvenir shops serves the usual tasty tearoom fare (quite a selection; go an hour before closing and the sandwiches are only 20 cents each!), and sells groceries, dairy foods, fruit and vegies, and clothing; open seven days. **D.A.'s Restaurant,** on the other side of the souvenir shop, serves tearoom fare and light meals ($7-8), main dishes such as steak, pork, lamb, venison, fish, and salads for $11.50-16, desserts, and good espresso coffee. Open seven days from 1030-2130. The licensed family restaurant and bar at **Westland Motor Inn** attracts those going out for a dressy occasion as well as casual diners; in summer you can tuck in to a Sunday smorgasbord from 1730-2030 for adult $17, child $9 (reservations essential at tel. 728). The **THC Franz Josef** also serves all meals in the licensed á la carte restaurant—expensive and dressy.

The best source of entertainment is the **Park HQ and Visitor Centre** where rangers put on good slide shows and humorous talks on the Park at 2030 each evening during vacation periods (free; see the schedule on the main door), visitor programs (guided walks) in summer, and an excellent 25-minute audiovisual on the hour (see "Information" below). Otherwise, stop off for a drink, have an energetic game of squash at the public courts in the Community Centre Building, or settle back for some chatting or TV viewing in the motor camp kitchen/dining area where meeting fellow travelers is a sure thing.

SERVICES AND INFORMATION

Westland Savings mobile banking service is only open on Mon. from 1130-1300 and Wed. from 1015-1200. The **p.o.** has postal, savings bank, Bankcard services, and currency exchange; on the main highway at the north end of town (there's also a public telephone), open regular hours Mon. to Friday. A **doctor's clinic** is held only once a week on Thurs. afternoons. For emergencies contact Park HQ, or call the **District Nurse** at tel. 805 Whataroa. The nearest **hospital** can be reached at tel. Whataroa 34-172. For **Police,** call 34-151. Franz Josef has two **churches**—Roman Catholic across the highway from HQ, and Anglican at the south end of town—check out the view of the glacier valley and peaks and glaciers of the Fritz Range through the chancel window.

For info on Westland National Park and Franz Josef, head directly for **Westland National Park HQ and Visitor Centre,** off the main highway at the south end of town, tel. 727. Containing all kinds of intriguing displays, intricate models of glaciers, reams of info on the natural and human history of the Park (lectures are held in the evenings during summer, and the audiovisual shown on the hour is really worth seeing), the Centre is open weekdays 0800-1700, weekends 0800-1200 and 1300-1600, with longer hours during the peak summer period. During vacation periods the rangers give guided nature walks (free) throughout the Park—ask what's happening at the reception desk. Also at the desk buy detailed maps, Park handbooks, pamphlets, postcards, and many brochures (small charge) on local walks.

TRANSPORTATION

Getting There

To get to Franz Josef catch the **InterCity** bus from Hokitika Mon., Wed., Fri., and Sun. mornings or Mon. to Sat. afternoons; from Christchurch Mon. to Sat. mornings; from Queenstown daily; and from Wanaka Mon. to Saturdays.

Ongoing

From Franz Josef, **InterCity** buses depart Mon. to Sat. for Hokitika and Christchurch, for Wanaka and Queenstown, and for Greymouth and Westport from Ferngrove Souvenirs on Main Rd.; an extra bus leaves in the afternoons on Mon., Wed., Fri., and Sun. for Hokitika. Another bus connects Franz Josef to Fox Glacier (at least once a day). Check out the current timetables and fares on the noticeboard in the alley between Ferngrove Souvenirs and Glacier Store and Tearooms. Book your seat in Ferngrove Souvenirs.

Local

There's no local bus service—but you can get a **taxi** or **Glacier Car Tour** by calling tel. 721, go on a **Rata Grove Vintage Car Tour,** tel. 741, or hire a 10-speed **bicycle,** tel. 757. **Glacier Motors,** a full-service petrol station, is also the local **Avis** rental car agent, open seven days, tel. 725.

FOX GLACIER AREA

ACTIVITIES

Hikes On The Way To The Glacier

To get to the glacier from Fox Glacier village, take the main highway south about two km, then turn left just before the bridge over the Fox River onto the Glacier Access road. Continue for about five km to the carpark at the end of the road where the track to the glacier terminal starts. If you want to do some good hikes before you reach the glacier, watch for the sign on the right to **Glacier View Road, River Walk Viewpoint,** 2.5 km along the road. The 30-minute (OW) track takes you over a long, narrow suspension bridge (built in 1929) that literally sways in the breeze (great views of the rushing, icy-cold Fox River far below), and on through *kamahi* forest to meet the south end of **Glacier View Road.** The 40-minute (OW) **Chalet Lookout Track** starts here—till 1930 the main glacier access track, nowadays it only gives views of the terminal face and lower icefall. For even better views of the Fox Glacier, branch off Chalet Lookout Walk and take the **Cone Rock Track** which climbs steeply through forest and up an ice-scraped rock (remnant of a *roche moutonnee),* to eventually rejoin the Chalet Lookout Walk just before Chalet Lookout (two hours up, 40 minutes down via Chalet Lookout Walk)—the energetic are well rewarded with the view!

Fox Glacier

Continuing along the main route to the Fox Glacier takes you through green tunnels of overhanging *rata* and *kamahi* trees covered in ferns and mosses, along the icy Fox River passing huge potholes in the moraine filled with turquoise water, areas of quicksand (warnings posted), and towering vertical rock cliffs, and eventually ends at a large gravel carpark from where an easy 20-minute (OW) track leads over river gravels to the **terminal ice.** Wear comfortable shoes, keep on the marked track, watch out for rockfalls, and resist the urge to venture onto the ice—unsafe without a glacier guide.

Another special feature of this landscape are the *keas*—unique, dull-green birds with red underwings and large powerful beaks. Not the least bit afraid of mere mortals, they in fact seem to enjoy terrorizing us at times—swooping out of nowhere to land on the car or bicycle with a thud. They grab bread from your fingers with little encouragement and pose obligingly for photographs, but take particular pleasure in ripping holes in bicycle seats and shredding windshield wipers! They also have a reputation for sliding down the tin rooves of mountain huts during the night, and removing shoelaces from boots left outside—such friendly little critters!

Alternate ways to see the Fox Glacier up close are to take a 2½- to three-hour guided hike on the ice (year-round, leaves twice a day at 0930 and 1400; adult $24 pp, hostelers and motor campers $22, child $12), a day-hike for $35 pp (offered on demand if at least six are interested), or a heli-hike during Oct. to June (on demand, minimum three; $89 pp) with **Alpine Guides (Westland),** tel. 825. Boots, socks, parkas, and transportation are

kea

included in the price, and the tours depart from opposite the Fox Hotel (a courtesy bus calls at the motor camp). They do overnight fly-in walk-out trips to Chancellor Hut, just above the main icefall (good level of fitness required), all meals provided; $275 pp (minimum three). A variety of guiding services are also available on request, and they run a mountaineering school; tel. Fox 825. Mountain bikes can be hired for $3 an hour, $12.50 per half-day, or $20 a day, and they have all the equipment you need to hike the Copland Pass Track—crampons, ice-axes, packs, etc., for $5.50 per item per day plus a deposit (refundable at Mt. Cook or Fox). For a healthy snack or meal and home-baked goods, try the **Hobnail Coffee Shop** in the Alpine Guides building; open daily 0800-1600.

Other Local Hikes

If you enjoy glowworms, take a short nighttime walk along the track to the **Glowworm Grotto** which starts on the main highway just south of the village. Another short and easy loop track, the **Minnehaha Walk,** also starts on the main highway just south of the village. This 20-minute RT track follows the Minnehaha Stream through typical Westland rainforest chock-a-block with beautiful ferns—it's a good walk to keep in mind for a wet day, and if done at night (take a flashlight), thousands of tiny glowworms light up the rainforest. The rougher **Ngai Tahu Track** (60 minutes RT) branches off the Minnehaha Track to climb beside a waterfall through ferns and *rimu* forest to a kettle swamp at the top of the ridge. Easy **Moraine Walk** starts on Glacier View Rd. (1.5 km from the start), taking 40 minutes RT to meander through impressive tree ferns and *rata* forest, showing the effect of glacial advances during the 17th and 18th centuries (another one to keep in mind for wet days). Three km south from Fox Glacier village just beyond Thirsty Creek is the four-hour (OW) track to **Mount Fox.** The track climbs steeply through native bush to a viewpoint at 1,022 meters, then up to alpine grasslands and Mt. Fox at 1,337 meters (follow the snowpoles) to give impressive views of the Alps, glacier, and coast; wear sturdy shoes, take warm clothing, food and water, and leave your intentions in the book in the Fox Glacier Visitor Centre.

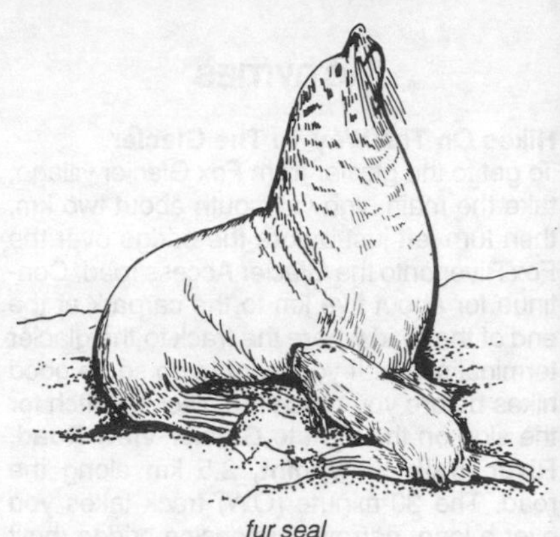

fur seal

Lakes, Beaches, And Seals

If you have your own transportation, a good day trip from Fox Glacier village is to take Cook Flat Rd. to beautiful Lake Matheson (a two-hour hike from Fox Glacier village) and on to the historic coastal settlement of Gillespies Beach (about 20 km from Fox Glacier). **Lake Matheson** is renowned for outstanding reflections (on a calm day) of 3,764-meter Mt. Cook and 3,498-meter Mt. Tasman, and for the beautiful forest walk around the lake. The best reflections are early in the morning before the wind stirs up the surface. The road to Lake Matheson branches off Cook Flat Rd., then a sturdy boardwalk takes you through the forest to the lake (40 minutes RT from the carpark) and around it (1½ hours RT from the carpark); the best views are from the far end. An alternate track leads up to the ancient glacial **Lake Gault** (a farther 1½-hour climb OW) and hydro-power scheme.

Cook Flat Rd. finishes at the settlement of **Gillespies Beach** where they sand-sluiced for gold (more than 600 people once mined this area) in goldrush days. A track starts at the bridge near the lagoon mouth. Follow an early miners' track through a cliff tunnel and down to the beach (20 minutes OW), or take a sidetrack at the tunnel for a 10-minute climb to a trig for superb views. One of the best 1½-hour (OW) walks is along Gillespies Beach to the **fur seal colony** at the north end, returning through beautiful Waikukupa State Forest. You can get near the seals, but don't disturb them or get between the seals and the sea. Park rangers guide walks from Fox Glacier village to Gillespies Beach during vacation periods—ask for dates and times at the Visitor Centre.

Flightseeing

The same kind of ski-plane or helicopter tours you can get at Franz Josef are offered at Fox Glacier township. For more info, stop by the **Mount Cook Airlines** office on the main highway, tel. 812, or call **Glacier Helicopters,** tel. 803 (also see p. 425). **Alpine Adventures,** based in the Alpine Guides' building, provides helicopter glacier flights starting at $45 pp for a 10-minute flight over Fox Glacier. For more info call 825 and ask for Russell.

Skiing

In winter (July to Nov.), **Alpine Guides (Westland)** sponsors a variety of skiing adventures (downhill and cross-country) on the Fox and Tasman glaciers, in conjunction with Mount Cook Airlines and Glacier Helicopters. You provide your own skis and boots (or rent them), clothing, and food; they provide safety equipment and many years of experience. A good level of fitness and stamina is required (they accept only strong intermediate skiers), with a minimum of three people. Prices start at $325 pp per day which includes guiding, air and ground transport, lunch, and safety equipment; tel. Fox Glacier 825.

The Copland Valley Track

The 47-km Copland Valley Track is a popular and challenging route for fit and experienced hikers and mountaineers, or for the less experienced with an alpine guide—it is not to be taken lightly or attempted in ordinary hiking gear. Generally walked from east to west (starting in Mt. Cook National Park) as it's safer, it can also be done from the Westland National Park end—the track starts on Hwy. 6 at the signpost 100 meters north of the Karangarua Bridge (26 km south of Fox Glacier). It passes hot pools and a hut at **Welcome Flat** (20 km or a six-hour hike from the highway), continues on to the **Douglas Rock** hut (10 km, three hours), crosses the tricky **Copland Pass** (14 km, at least an eight-hour climb) in Mount Cook National Park, and finishes at Mount Cook village. The Copland Pass, 2,150 meters, is notorious for bad weather and sudden dense fog, has tricky glacier and rock sections where you need experience and appropriate alpine climbing equipment, and above 1,400 meters the track is only lightly defined (many have lost their way in unexpected bad weather—read the hikers' descriptions of the track and conditions at Mt. Cook National Park HQ!). If you're seriously thinking about doing it, get the complete rundown at the Westland National Park Visitor Centre in Fox Glacier and from **Alpine Guides (Westland)** at Fox Glacier, tel. 825...or wait and do it from the east end of the track. Hut fees should be paid at either of the Westland National Park centers or at Mount Cook Park HQ. If you need a guide, it's cheaper to start at Mt. Cook village because you reach the Pass more quickly when traveling east to west. Experienced alpine guides and all the necessary equipment can be hired reasonably in Mount Cook village (see p. 441 and 444).

ACCOMMODATION

Budget

There's no YH in Fox Glacier, but **Golden Glacier Motor Inn** is an associate YH. It provides four-bunk rooms for $12.50 pp, a few double rooms for $15.50 pp, family units for $12.50 pp, private bathroom facilities with each room, TV and in-house video, game room, kitchen and laundry facilities, and a bar and licensed restaurant on the premises in the Backpacker Hostel. It's opposite Alpine Guides on the main highway.

Ivory Towers on Sullivans Rd., tel. 838, is a relaxed, laid-back, budget place to stay—a great spot to meet fellow travelers. Steve and

Lisa, the popular managers, make everyone feel at home. In several small separate houses, each with two or three dorm rooms, a central living area, equipped kitchen, and bathroom, a bed costs $12.50-15 pp per night. Check out the informative noticeboard in the office if you want to know everything about the area—or ask Steve. He also rents out bikes for $5 a day.

The only other budget accommodation in the village is the **Fox Glacier Motor Park,** 400 meters down the road to Lake Matheson (great views), tel. Fox 821. Communal facilities, and a camp store. Tentsites are $13 d, caravan sites $14.50 d, bunkhouse accommodation $9.50 pp (summer only), cabins from $23 d, and tourist flats from $41 double.

Motels

Several motels and two hotels (expensive) are in Fox Glacier and the surrounding area. The closest most reasonable motel is **Alpine View Motel,** tel. 821, on the grounds of Fox Glacier Motor Camp. **Golden Glacier Motor Inn,** tel. 847, on the main highway has rooms with TV and kitchenettes starting at $55 d. Rooms with private bath, TV, tea- and coffee-making facilities, and the use of the pool room, BBQ and bar, and dining facilities in the Garden Restaurant are $72 d per night. **Pinegrove Motel** has reasonable rates, but is 36 km south of Fox Glacier (tel. Fox 898). Rooms (cooking facilities) are $50 d, cabins with shared kitchen and bath start at $20 d, and there are a few caravan sites at $14 d.

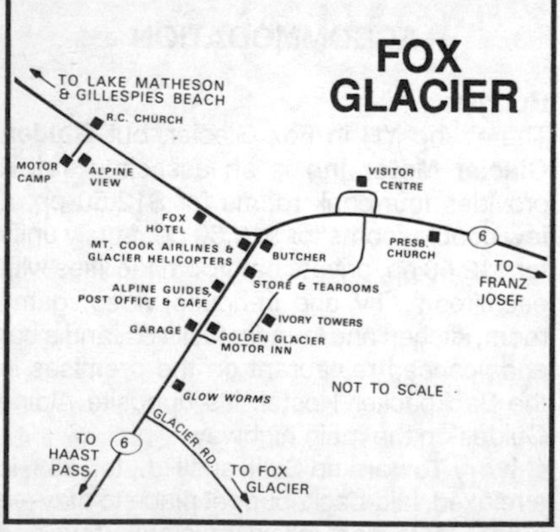

FOOD AND ENTERTAINMENT

It's best to rely on cooking for and entertaining yourself, but if you're not in the mood for that, try the **Hobnail Cafe,** part of the Alpine Guides complex, where you can tuck in to very good lunches and a.m. and p.m. teas (irresistable home-baked goods) daily 0800-1700. **Fox Glacier Tearooms and Restaurant** on the main road serves tearoom-type fare, tel. 829. Buy your meat at **Sullivans Butchery,** and groceries and produce at the **Fox Glacier Store,** tel. 829. If you're craving a good meal and don't mind parting with some cash, try the restaurant at **Fox Glacier Hotel,** tel. 839, or at the **Golden Glacier Motor Inn** (meals from $7-17; tel. 847).

For evening entertainment during vacation periods, take in the informal slide show and lecture on Westland National Park at the Visitor Centre—see the schedule on the door for times and topics, or ask at the reception desk. The only other forms of entertainment are getting to know fellow travelers, or dropping in for a quick one at one of the fancier hotels.

SERVICES AND INFORMATION

The **p.o.** (and public telephone) is on the main highway, open regular hours Mon. to Fri. for the usual postal and banking services. Mobile **Westland Savings Bank** is only open on Mon. from 1430-1600 and Wed. from 0800-1000. A **doctor's clinic** is held once a week, tel. 836; for emergencies 24 hours a day, call the District Nurse at tel. 816.

For info on the Park and the village, visit **Westland National Park Visitor Centre,** tel. 807, off the main highway at the north end of town. It has a great natural history display featuring the glaciers, lowland rainforests, and wildlife, a lecture hall where slide shows and talks are presented in the evenings, reading material, Park publications for sale, and has a variety of brochures on local walks and activities. The reception desk is open year-round from 0800-1700 seven days, but the building is open till late during vacation periods for slide show presentations.

TRANSPORTATION

The **InterCity** bus runs from Hokitika to the Fox Glacier Hotel Mon., Wed., Fri., or Sun., and from Queenstown and Wanaka Mon. to Saturday. From Christchurch, the InterCity bus runs to Hokitika and Fox Glacier Mon. to Saturday.

InterCity buses depart Fox Glacier Hotel for Hokitika and Christchurch and for Wanaka and Queenstown Mon. to Sat., and for Hokitika Mon., Wed., Fri., and Sun. in the afternoon.

There's no local transportation, but **Milner Motors** on the main highway offers **bicycle hire** and full petrol station services; tel. 823, after hours tel. 827.

THE GLACIERS TO MOUNT COOK

COASTAL SECTION

Copland Valley Track

Twenty-six km south of Fox Glacier, Hwy. 6 runs past the west entrance to the Copland Valley Track—look for the sign 100 meters before Karangarua Bridge. Many people hike the first or first two sections of this track; considerable experience and appropriate alpine equipment are needed to continue over Copland Pass (2,150 meters) to Mount Cook Village (three huts along the route). February and March are the best months to hike it—only attempt it if you really know what you're doing or have a guide. The huts at Welcome Flat and Douglas Rock have gas cooking, a wood stove, and a limited number of utensils (best to take your own); small charge per night—pay at either of the Westland National Park Visitor Centres or at Mt. Cook National Park HQ.

The first 20-km section from the main highway to Welcome Flat takes about six hours, starting at the marker on the opposite side of Rough Creek (sign the intentions book there)—if the water's high, a 25-minute walk upstream brings you to a wire crossing. The track wanders through bird-filled bush, crossing several small streams before emerging at Welcome Flat. The natural **hot springs** just beyond Welcome Flat hut are particularly popular with weary hikers—soak your tired muscles in the soothing 60-degree C water, but remember to keep your head out to avoid contracting amoebic meningitis (a real threat in any hot springs).

The second 10-km section starts at Welcome Flat, wanders through rivers, grasslands, and low forest, climbing gradually to cross several open slips and a suspension bridge before emerging at Douglas Rock hut; about three hours. The tricky 14-km alpine climb from Douglas Rock to Hooker Hut ($13 pp) in Mt. Cook National Park takes about eight hours, followed by an easier four- to five-hour walk down the Hooker Valley to end at The Hermitage in Mount Cook Village—for details, a map, and weather forecasts, contact Westland or Mt. Cook national park HQ (also see p. 440).

Lake Paringa

Between the mighty Karangarua River and Lake Paringa, Hwy. 6 moseys along the coast through lush tree ferns and forest in almost every shade of green imaginable, passing rugged headlands, desolate pebble beaches covered in driftwood, and the odd lonely farm hacked out of the bush. Surrounded by ferns and forest (in what seems like the middle of nowhere), Lake Paringa is deceptively tranquil, but teeming with brown trout, rainbow trout, and quinnat salmon—an angler's paradise. The lake used to be at the end of the road prior to the opening of the Haast route, yet despite the traffic that nowadays whizzes through, it's still a quiet spot for outdoorspeople. Campsites are found just off the road halfway around the lake, and the **Lakeside Motel** on the main highway at the north end of the lake (tel. Fox Glacier 894) has handy facilities for anglers. The friendly owners

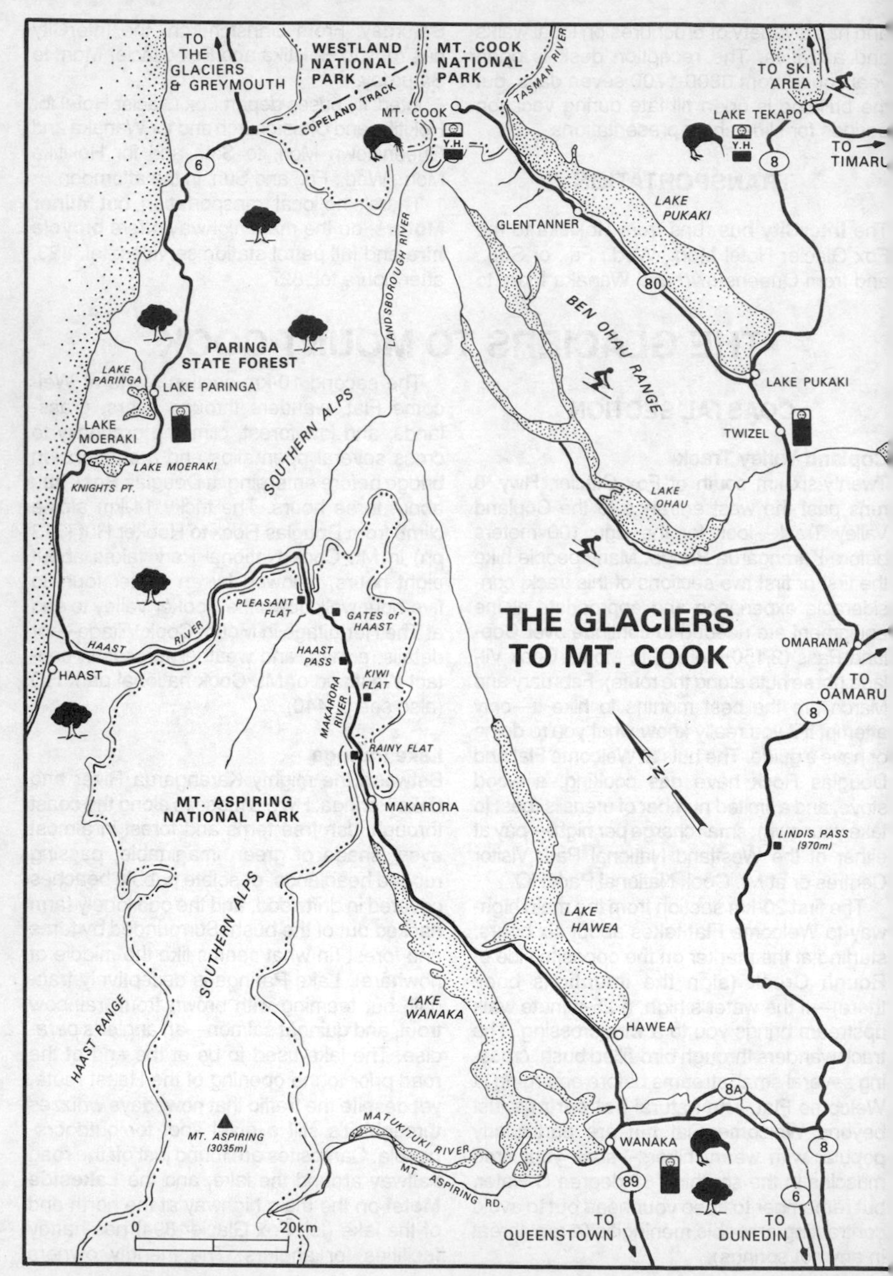
THE GLACIERS TO MT. COOK
TO THE GLACIERS & GREYMOUTH
WESTLAND NATIONAL PARK
MT. COOK NATIONAL PARK
COPELAND TRACK
MT. COOK
Y.H.
TASMAN RIVER
TO SKI AREA
LAKE TEKAPO
Y.H.
TO TIMARU
8
6
LAKE PUKAKI
GLENTANNER
LANDSBOROUGH RIVER
80
BEN OHAU RANGE
PARINGA STATE FOREST
LAKE PARINGA
LAKE PARINGA
LAKE PUKAKI
SOUTHERN ALPS
LAKE MOERAKI
LAKE MOERAKI
TWIZEL
KNIGHTS PT.
LAKE OHAU
PLEASANT FLAT
GATES of HAAST
HAAST RIVER
HAAST PASS
KIWI FLAT
OMARAMA
HAAST
TO OAMARU
MAKARORA RIVER
8
RAINY FLAT
N
MT. ASPIRING NATIONAL PARK
MAKARORA
LINDIS PASS (970m)
LAKE HAWEA
SOUTHERN ALPS
HAAST RANGE
LAKE WANAKA
HAWEA
8A
MT. ASPIRING (3035m)
MATUKITUKI RIVER
WANAKA
8
MT. ASPIRING RD.
89
6
0
20km
TO QUEENSTOWN
TO DUNEDIN

make you feel right at home whether you're a motel guest or just stopping at the adjoining restaurant for a light meal or tantalizing Devonshire Tea. Boats are also available for guests to sample the excellent fishing.

Lake Moeraki

Lake Moeraki is another beautiful lake known for its distinct glacier-blue color and good fishing. Take the easy 40-minute OW bushwalk along **Munro's Track** to the coast where you'll find sandy beaches interspersed with rocky headlands; the track starts near the lake outlet. A number of pleasing campsites found around the lake are free!

Knights Point And Ship Creek

Just southwest of Lake Moeraki is the headland of Knights Point, fringed by golden-sand beaches and rocky bays where seals can be seen frolicking and fishing in the surf. About five km south of Knights Point, 100 meters downstream from the traffic bridge lies the remains of a ship partially buried in the sand which can be seen at low tide. It's believed to be the *Schomberg of Aberdeen,* largest wooden ship ever launched from Britain, which foundered off the shores of Tasmania in 1885 and disappeared.

Haast

This town, at the west end of Haast Pass Rd., has a hotel, restaurant, pub, and petrol station—stock up here before you continue south. The **DB Haast Hotel** near Haast Bridge on the main road (tel. 827/828) provides rooms from $65 s, $70 d, all meals available. **Haast Motor Camp,** 14.5 km south of Haast at **Okuru** (tel. Haast 860; the coastal scenery along this road is worth the drive) has tentsites for $12 d, caravan sites for $13 d, bunkrooms for $8 pp, cabins for $16-22 d, and one self-contained cabin for $30 d. Supply your own linen. An access road leads from Okuru to the remote northwest boundary of Mt. Aspiring National Park. Continue south of Okuru toward Jackson Bay for sandy beaches and coastal views on one side of the road and dense bush and swampy areas backed by magnificent, steep, tree-covered mountains on the other.

HAAST PASS ROAD

From Haast To Wanaka

Haast Pass Rd. (Hwy. 6) from Haast to Wanaka is a 146-km route of great beauty. In less than three hours the scenery changes from lush West Coast greenery to the snow-capped peaks and deep river gorges of Mt. Aspiring National Park, the Gates of Haast and Haast Pass (563 meters), mighty lakes with sparkling blue-green water, and open space for as far as you can see. It's best not to drive it at night (you'll miss all the scenery) or when you're in a hurry—most sections of the road are sealed but some stretches are "metal" (gravel), and there are many one-lane bridges and some narrow stretches with sharp corners and steep drop-offs where it's almost inevitable you'll meet a large semi-trailer around a blind turn—"a terrible, terrible road" said a man from New York City as he frantically pawed through his luggage for tranquilizers! However, if you take time to enjoy the magnificent scenery, stopping at viewpoints and walking along the short tracks to waterfalls, you'll live to tell the tale—even without drugs!

The highway, only completed in 1965, follows the crystal-clear, turquoise Haast River which is joined by the large Landsborough River; then the road crosses a bridge with fantastic mountain views before passing **Pleasant Flat** where there's a day shelter and picnic spots. From Pleasant Flat to **Rainy Flat,** Hwy. 6 winds through a small northeast section of **Mount Aspiring National Park** (see below). Continue to **Thunder Creek Falls** and take the short forest track—here the water drops an impressive 30 meters from a small notch in the rock. About two km farther along the road at the Gates of Haast bridge, the Haast River roars down a gorge full of enormous schist boulders—another sight to see! **Haast Pass** is the lowest on the Main Divide at 563 meters, and from here to **Makarora Gorge** is some of the best scenery along the entire route. Rivers meander like silver ribbons in and out of dense bush and hills, through large flats covered in woolly "gorse scrubbers" or "grass cutters" (sheep) for as far as the eye can see.

One of the Mt. Aspiring National Park **ranger stations** is located at the small town of **Makarora** (Park HQ is at Wanaka), open weekdays 0800-1700 and weekends during summer holidays. **Haast Pass Tourist Service** on the main highway, made up of a shop and tearooms (closed in summer at 1900), and a swimming pool, sells petrol, and offers tent and caravan sites for $5.50 pp, cabins for $30 d, and motel units starting at $55 d. The Magic Bus and InterCity buses stop here. Scenic flights are offered over Mt. Aspiring, Mt. Cook, or Milford Sound, wilderness "fly-ins" and joy rides, and a 50-km, 1½-hour jetboat trip up the nearby Wilkin River into Mt. Aspiring National Park ($35 pp)—ask for more info at the shop or tel. Wanaka 33U. They also offer a special one-day wilderness excursion they call the "Siberia Experience," which includes a 25-minute flight over Mt. Aspiring National Park, a landing in the Siberia Valley, then a three-hour bush walk along a marked track to a jetboat for an exciting return trip to Makarora; $90 pp (minimum four). For more info call Wanaka 8372.

MAKARORA TO WANAKA

The road from Makarora to Wanaka emerges from closed-in Haast Pass to a landscape of wide open spaces and water, water, water as it first runs along the eastern shores of shimmering bright-blue **Lake Wanaka,** one of the largest southern lakes. Along with good trout fishing, the lakeshores also provide many ideal spots for free camping, and generally a good supply of driftwood for campfires; make sure you have an adequate supply of insect repellent before you make camp—in summer, thousands of sandflies alight on your tent in the early hours and attack with passion as soon as you climb out!

The highway crosses The Neck (between Lake Wanaka and Lake Hawea), then parallels the hilly western shores of equally beautiful **Lake Hawea,** also known for its excellent trout and land-locked salmon fishing, down to its southern shores and the small town of **Hawea.** The **Visitor Information Centre** is open daily 1000-1400, extended hours in summer. After crossing emerald-green **Clutha River** south of Hawea, Hwy. 6 swings east toward Oamaru and Dunedin, or west for a very short distance to the attractive tourist town of **Wanaka** (see p. 468). If you're heading north for Mount Cook National Park, take Hwy. 6 east for a short distance, turn onto Hwy. 8A (a shortcut), then take Hwy. 8 north to Twizel. If you're heading for Queenstown, go to Wanaka and take the mountain road south (gravel, steep and twisty, but fabulous views—a masochistic bicycle-rider's dream), or continue along the unexciting sealed roundabout route, Hwy. 6 south, which also goes to Queenstown.

WANAKA TO MOUNT COOK

Highway 8 then Hwy. 80 to Mt. Cook (211 km) via the Mackenzie Basin (the only route, dead-ending at Mt. Cook Village) takes about four hours by car, but the last section is best seen in the early morning before the clouds obscure the mountains. For scenery at its best, take Hwy. 8 north through the bleak tussock-covered hills of 971-meter **Lindis Pass** during the afternoon, through the small town of **Omarama** passing the access road to commercial **Lake Ohau Skifield** (16 km north of Omarama, 106 km from Mount Cook Village but the nearest commercial skifield), and on toward Twizel in the late afternoon/ early evening. Stop for the night about four km south of Twizel at enormous **Ruataniwha Motor Camp,** tel. 613, off the main highway along the shores of Lake Ruataniwha; tent and caravan sites from $6 pp, cabins from $10 pp. It's not a particularly scenic area unless you're into flat tussock-covered land, man-made dams, hydroelectric power plants, and high tension lines, but the scenery to the north is worth seeing in daylight. The Canterbury Rowing Championships, held on **Lake Ruataniwha** around Feb. each year, attract a large crowd; at this time the motor camp gets fairly full despite its great size. You can also camp for free anywhere in the Mackenzie Hydro Park area, but avoid camping near the

Canterbury Rowing Championships at Lake Ruataniwha

Tekapo, Pukaki, and Ohau rivers as they're used for power generation and the water levels can rise extremely rapidly with little warning.

Twizel And Beyond

Originally built as construction housing for the Upper Waitaki Hydro-Power Development Scheme, Twizel has since grown into the second largest town in the area. The scheme involves the Waitaki, Benmore, and Aviemore dams, lakes Tekapo, Pukaki, and Ohau (linked by canals to provide water for power stations), and lakes Ruataniwha and Benmore (largest earth dam and man-made lake in the country). For detailed info on the hydropower scheme and all the local attractions, visit the **Twizel Information Office,** Wairepo Rd., tel. 497; open daily 0900-1700. If you're continuing to Mt. Cook and doing your own cooking, Twizel is a good place to stock up on food—prices at the store and restaurants in isolated Mount Cook Village are inflated. **Mackenzie Mini Tours** runs a trip to Mt. Cook in summer departing at 0800 from the major hotels; $11 OW, $20 RT. For more details call Twizel 677.

At Lake Pukaki, north of Twizel, Hwy. 8 turns east toward Lake Tekapo and Timaru; Hwy. 80 continues north beneath the **Ben Ohau Range** and along the west shores of **Lake Pukaki,** a glacier-formed lake fed by the Tasman Glacier and Tasman River and main storage lake for the Upper Waitaki power scheme. The water is a striking milky-turquoise color due to "rock flour" (ground from the mountains by the moving glacier) in suspension. On a clear day Mt. Cook towers above calm Lake Pukaki even though the mountain is many km away—the best reflections are from the east side.

Glentanner

This small settlement lies about 40 km north of Lake Pukaki township on the shores of Lake Pukaki: **Glentanner Sheep Station, Glentanner Park Motor Camp and Store,** and an airport. The mountain scenery here is fantastic and the Glentanner residents take best advantage of it with a variety of scenic trips by 4WD vehicle, plane, helicopter, on foot or horseback, along with accommodations to suit all budgets (see "Activities" and "Accommodation" below). Continue along the road surrounded by snow-capped mountains, glaciers, rolling hills, flat grasslands, river valleys, and meandering milky-blue streams, to the ultimate in grandeur and scenery, Mt. Cook National Park.

MOUNT COOK NATIONAL PARK

This park, one of the South Island's major tourist attractions, preserves a spectacular alpine area of great beauty—well worth the 60-km trip off the beaten track by road (or air). With its snow-capped mountains, glaciers, river valleys, and incredibly fresh air, Mount Cook National Park is a popular playground for climbers, hikers, photographers, and skiers who catch skiplanes up to the top of glaciers for unforgettable experiences in the Southern Alps.

Before you continue into the world of Mt. Cook, it's important to grasp the various meanings of "Mt. Cook" as seen on maps and in various sightseeing brochures—there's Mt. Cook the mountain, Mt. Cook the village (sometimes just referred to as The Hermitage after the well-known long-standing hotel), Mt. Cook National Park, Mt. Cook Station (as in ranch), and Mount Cook Line (bus and plane transportation)!

The Land

The beautiful Maori word for the "High Mountain to the West" was *Aoraki,* name of the first-born son of Raki, the sky father. Towering above the surrounding snow-capped mountains and glaciers at 3,764 meters, majestic Mt. Cook has a perfect pyramid shape when viewed from the south that's both impressive and easily recognized. The mountain was given its European name by Capt. Stokes who sailed down the West Coast in the survey ship *Acheron* in 1851—naming the mountain in honor of the great English navigator and explorer.

Mt. Cook National Park, officially established in 1953 covering 70,013 hectares of the **Southern Alps,** is a long narrow area of rugged snow-covered mountains and glaciers, 65 km long and only 20 km across at its widest point. Along the Main Divide on its west border lies Westland National Park, stretching down from its tall mountain peaks and glaciers to the Tasman Sea. Within the Park, the land ranges from river flats at 750 meters to 140 peaks over 2,100 meters high, including 22 peaks that soar to more than 3,050 meters. New Zealand's three tallest mountains, Mt. Cook at 3,764 meters in the **Mt. Cook Range**, Mt. Tasman at 3,498 meters and Mt. Dampier at 3,440 meters in the Main Divide, all lie within a short distance of one another. Due to the high rugged terrain, more than one-third of the entire Park is covered in permanent snow and ice, and huge glaciers are another natural attraction. The gigantic **Tasman Glacier,** 27 km long

southern aspect of Mount Cook

and up to three km wide, is one of the world's largest glaciers outside the polar regions, and one of the most easily seen (definitely the most photographed)—view it from Hwy. 80 as you enter the Park. The other major glaciers, **Mueller, Hooker, Godley,** and **Murchison,** can also be seen if you're willing to drive or cycle to viewing points or hike the various tracks within the Park.

Mt. Cook National Park is not, however, completely made up of mountain peaks. Several large valleys occupied by glaciers and rivers separate the mountain ranges: the Godley Glacier, River, and tributaries in the northeast, and the Tasman Glacier, River, and tributaries in the southwest divide the Park into two main sections. The only road access is Hwy. 80 which runs up to Mt. Cook Village in the southwest, and Ball Hut Rd. from near the village up the west side of the Tasman Glacier as far as Husky Flat. The road is closed to vehicles beyond Husky Flat, but you can continue on foot for another 50-60 minutes to reach the old Ball Hut site. Short tracks give further access to many of the major natural attractions, and of course adventurous well-equipped mountaineers can discover it all!

Climate

The climate here is varied and unpredictable. In summer, long hot periods of near-drought conditions with temperatures as high as 30 degrees C can be experienced; in July, sudden snowfalls of up to one meter can stick to the ground for as long as a month. In winter the air temperature can get as low as minus eight degrees C during colder years, but in general, the dry cold and clear days make hiking around the Village (snow can restrict hiking mid-June to mid-Aug.) and skiing on the glaciers enjoyable experiences. Winter climbing is risky because of abundant snow and frequent avalanches. On average, Mt. Cook Village expects snow on the ground for about 21 days during winter; the average yearly rainfall is 4,081 mm, with up to 8,000 mm of rain and snow falling in higher altitudes.

If you're climbing or hiking in the Park, keep an eye out for cirrus clouds racing across the sky, followed by rapid cloud build-up—early warning signs of heavy rain, often accompanied by strong winds from the northwest (which can rapidly rise to gale force) and snow at low levels. Be more than adequately prepared for severe weather with warm waterproof clothing whenever you're out in the wilderness, and get a weather forecast before you set off.

Flora

Renowned for its variety in alpine flowers, this area literally springs to life in summer (mid-Nov. to the end of Feb.) when flowering plants put on their best show. Most of the alpine flowers are white, blending in with the snow and ice of their harsh environment—the most striking is the **Mt. Cook lily,** largest ranunculus in the world. It has pure white petals, a yellow center, and shiny saucer-shaped leaves, and although it's called a lily, it's actually an oversized buttercup. In December the mountain daisies put on a terrific display in the alpine scrub and grasslands—there are 58 endemic species. More than 300 species of native plants have been identified within Park boundaries, ranging from tiny ferns, herbs, mosses, and grasses to shrubs and trees; many are found within a short distance of HQ. Only a small area of what was once a large silver beech forest remains at **Governor's Bush** behind Mount Cook Village—in this grove you can also see mountain totara, mountain three-finger, broadleaf, and the occasional lancewood; a booklet identifying the trees and plants is available at HQ (also see "Short Walks" below).

Fauna

Birds are everywhere, about 40 species all told: riverbed birds such as black-backed gulls, pied oystercatchers, paradise ducks, and banded dotterels; bush birds such as native pigeons, tomtits, fantails, riflemen, grey warblers, and moreporks; and alpine birds such as New Zealand falcons (rare), rock wrens (also rare), pipits, and *keas* or alpine parrots (cheekiest and most familiar). Dull green in color with scarlet underwings and a black heavy-duty beak, the *kea* has a reputation for unlacing boots, tearing holes in bicycle seats, and sliding down tin rooves just for fun—hold on to your food when they're hanging around. Don't feed the *kea*—this encourages their menacing antics, in turn causing many problems for park staff and local residents. If you enjoy identifying birds, ask at the reception desk in HQ for a copy of the bird checklist. Also within the Park you can find large dragonflies, grasshoppers, a variety of moths and butterflies, alpine weta (locally called the Mt. Cook flea), and pesky sandflies, along with chamois and Himalayan tahr—liberated near Mt. Cook in the early 1900s, tahr numbers have been drastically reduced by control operations and trophy hunters; now only small numbers are left.

ACTIVITIES

Short Walks

Though the Park has many short walks around the Village and along the surrounding valleys to excellent viewpoints and other scenic attractions, it does not provide much in the way of major hiking tracks (the "Copland Pass Track" is an alpine pass, not a hiking track, and should not be attempted by the inexperienced). Due to the rugged alpine terrain, the Park is much more satisfying for serious climbers and experienced mountaineers than for hikers. However, the "short walks" are the only way to grasp a little of the Park's natural beauty, ranging from a 10-minute bush walk by the Village to a 4½-hour OW hike through the Hooker Valley for magnificent views of Mt. Cook and the Hooker Glacier. Pick up the handy *Easy Walks* brochure at HQ; it contains a map of the Village and brief descriptions and approximate times of each walk. Many of the walks also have individual brochures which aid in identifying native plants and items of natural history along each route.

Copland Pass Track

The Copland Pass Track is the most popular alpine hiking route in the Mt. Cook area. It involves crossing rugged terrain and a true alpine pass at 2,148 meters exposed to sudden changes in weather and snow conditions; high winds, rain or snow, and poor visibility are common. The track starts at Hooker Hut at the end of the four- to five-hour Hooker Valley Track from Mt. Cook Village, crosses the Pass (marked only by cairns), then descends through Westland National Park to end on Hwy. 6, 26 km south of Fox Glacier township (see p. 431). Three huts are located along the route; Hooker Hut ($13 pp) in this park, Douglas Rock ($8) and Welcome Flat ($8) huts in Westland National Park—pay at Park HQ or at one of the Westland Visitor Centres. The pass should only be attempted by experienced mountaineers with the necessary alpine equipment (ice axes, crampons, rope) or by those willing to hire a guide. **Alpine Guides** based in Mt. Cook Village have most of the necessary equipment for rent at $5.50 pp per day (provide your own rope, warm clothes, sleeping bag, and extra food); they also supply experienced guides for the crossing (basic technical equipment included) at $380 for one person, $230 pp for two, $190 pp for three. The office and shop is open seven days 0800-1700, tel. 834.

Mountaineering

The first attempt to climb Mt. Cook was in 1882, but it wasn't until 1894 that the summit was finally conquered by Clark, Fyfe, and Graham. This alpine region is considered one of the best mountaineering areas in the world, offering all levels of climbing possibilities amongst tall peaks of varing difficulty. High-altitude huts equipped with radios, stoves, cooking and eating utensils, and some blankets have been located throughout the Park—get more info and pay overnight fees ($12 pp) at HQ, and before attempting any climb, be sure to first notify Park personnel and sign out on leaving the area. **Alpine Guides** (see above) provide guided mountaineering services in summer, private instruction, and a School of Mountaineering, and they also hire out most of the mountain climbing equipment you'd need. If you'd like to read up on the climbing routes in the area, get your hands on the latest edition of *The Mount Cook Guidebook* by Hugh Logan.

Skiing

The usual season for both downhill and cross-country runs from July to early Nov., depending on conditions. Skiing in the Park is for many a unique experience, but it's also guaranteed to blow your budget unless you've made specific allowances! No commercial skifields or lifts are within the Park, so you ski ungroomed, untracked snow between towering peaks on glaciers; skiplanes are the only form of transportation. Much of the downhill skiing takes place on the long gentle slopes of the Tasman Glacier. The runs are 10-12 km long, "longest runs in the Southern Hemisphere," taking one to two hours each—surrounded by some of the most spectacular scenery imaginable, it's an exhilarating experience (for intermediate and advanced skiers). Guides from Alpine Guides patrol the runs. The Tasman hut, standing on a rock outcrop at the head of the glacier, is used as a base for ski-touring and climbing activities in the immediate area.

Advanced skiers can find challenging areas on the Tasman Glacier with a guide, but occasionally prefer the more difficult runs down the Murchison and Mannering glaciers. Heli-ski adventures are very popular, skiing virgin snow and the major valley runs of the Ben Ohau Range, south of Mt. Cook (outside the Park) on the western shores of Lake Pukaki. **Alpine Guides,** tel. 831, beside the p.o. in Mt. Cook Village, can make arrangements for just about anything you can dream up. Mount Cook National Park HQ is another source of skiing info and up-to-the-minute weather forecasts.

Nordic or cross-country skiing is mostly done on the Hooker and Tasman river flats when there's enough snow (a few skiers head for the glaciers); rent your equipment from Alpine Guides. Lake Tekapo, northeast of Mt. Cook Village, is another very popular area for nordic skiing—for more info contact **Alpine Recreation Canterbury**, Lake Tekapo, tel. 736.

If the cost of transportation up to the glaciers is out of your budget, the nearest commercial skifield with a T-bar and platter lift is at Lake Ohau (overlooking the lake), southwest of Twizel, a 94-km drive from Mt. Cook (just over an hour). The next closest commercial skifield is at Lake Tekapo (east of Mt. Cook), a family downhill area with a chairlift and platter lift, known for some of the best weather and snow records of any New Zealand skifield; a 90-minute drive from Mt. Cook.

Flightseeing

All kinds of flightseeing experiences are available by skiplane or helicopter from Mt. Cook—most similar to those at Franz Josef and Fox Glacier, and just as expensive. However, it's the only way to really see this area, so splurge if you haven't already! **The Helicopter Line's** variety of flights ranges from a 20-minute scenic for $88.50 pp to a 45-minute cruise around Mt. Cook, the major peaks, and a snow landing for $206 pp, departing from the heli-pad at Glentanner Park. For more info and reservations, call Mt. Cook 855 or Lake Tekapo 836. **Mount Cook Line** offers a variety of scenic flights with or without snow landings ranging from a 30-minute flight with ski landing for $121 pp to a 55-minute flight to see both sides of the Main Divide and a landing for $241 pp; tel. Mt. Cook 848 or 849. **Air Safaris** features "The Grand Traverse" from Glentanner Park and from Lake Tekapo, a 45-minute flight for $95 pp; tel. Mt. Cook 855 or Lake Tekapo 880. The activities desk in the foyer of The Hermitage Hotel in Mt. Cook Village makes reservations for many of the flightseeing tours and has all the latest brochures and current prices, tel. 809.

From Mount Cook airport you can go on a variety of flightseeing adventures.

Scenic Tours

Glentanner Tours & Safaris at Glentanner Park (about 20 km south of Mt. Cook Village) has all kinds of fun tours available: **farm tours** of Glentanner Station (a high-country sheep station) for $18.50 pp (minimum four), two-hour **4WD excursions** through some superb scenery for $26.50 pp (minimum four), **motorcycle trail ride tours** or trail bikes for hire at $40 per hour, **horse riding** on Glentanner Station at $27 per hour or half-day treks for $76 pp, and guided **fishing safaris** for brown or rainbow trout, or salmon (Oct. to April). Transportation from Mt. Cook Village to Glentanner Park is not included in these prices; by van it's $5 OW. Stop by Glentanner Park Store, tel. Mt. Cook 855, or drop by the Activities Desk in The Hermitage Hotel foyer, Mt. Cook Village, tel. 809. The Hermitage also offers **bus trips** up the Tasman Valley.

Scenic Drive And Hike

If you have your own transportation, head out of Mt. Cook Village onto Hwy. 80 and turn left on Ball Hut Rd. (the second road to the left after leaving the village, signposted "Tasman Valley Rd."). This long gravel road (rental cars are not insured for this road!) takes you along the western banks of the mighty Tasman River, passing beech forest, Wakefield Falls, walking tracks, and picnic spots, and continues beside the Tasman Glacier to Husky Flat. At the carpark and sign to **Blue Lakes** lookout (about halfway to Husky Flat), take the short, easy walking track to the right. After 15 minutes the uphill track gives you good views of the four colorful Blue Lakes (you can also take a track directly to the lakes—the fourth is particularly popular for swimming and sunbathing in summer). Glacier View Track branches off Blue Lakes Track and continues to the top of the moraine wall for tremendous views of the entire terminal area of the Tasman Glacier, Mt. Cook, and Mt. Tasman—it's well worth the short walk; don't forget your camera!

MOUNT COOK VILLAGE

You can't get lost in Mt. Cook Village (it's small!), but the quickest way to orient yourself to your surroundings is to drive to the end of the road. Depending on which route you take, you'll either end up at The Hermitage Hotel, where you can fight your way through the bus tours and collect a free map and brochures from the Activities Desk in the main foyer, or you'll reach Mt. Cook National Park HQ.

Campsites

Though not a lot of budget accommodation, plenty of beds for motel/hotel people are found in Mt. Cook Village. The **White Horse Hill Campground** run by the Park is located at White Horse Hill Picnic Area (no formal facilities) in the Hooker Valley, about 1.8 km from the village. It has running water and flush toilets in summer, a rainwater tank, pit toilets in winter (a shower is available at the Public Shelter in the village), and plenty of space for tents on a grassy hillside; $3 pp per night (self-registration). Note that the campground is exposed to prevailing inclement weather conditions and the normally dry creekbed can become a raging torrent during a storm—if you leave your tent there during the day, be sure it's well staked and not close to the creek! Head out of the village on Hwy. 80 and take the first road to the left. The closest commercial campground with facilities is at Glentanner Park, 20 km south of the village (see below).

Youth Hostel

The relatively new, very popular **Mount Cook YHA Hostel,** close to HQ and all amenities, is open all day, has excellent facilities including a sauna, and costs $14 pp per night. Book ahead if you can, at Mt. Cook tel. 820. It's on the corner of Bowen and Kitchener drives.

Motor Camp

The closest motor camp, **Glentanner Park** on the shores of Lake Pukaki, has great views in all directions. Along with communal facilities, BBQ, a camp store (open 0730-1800), and tearooms (close at 1600), they arrange all kinds of sightseeing and action tours (see "Scenic Tours" under "Activities" above). Tent and caravan sites are $6 pp, on-site caravans are $12 pp (minimum $24 per night), and cabins are $15 pp. Linen is available for hire at $5 per set. The motor camp is located on Hwy. 80, 20 km south of Mt. Cook Village, tel. 855. It's possible to hitchhike from here to Mt. Cook Village, but traffic is slow—try and flag down a bus! Alternatively catch a ride with the van that connects the two destinations for $5 OW (minimum four).

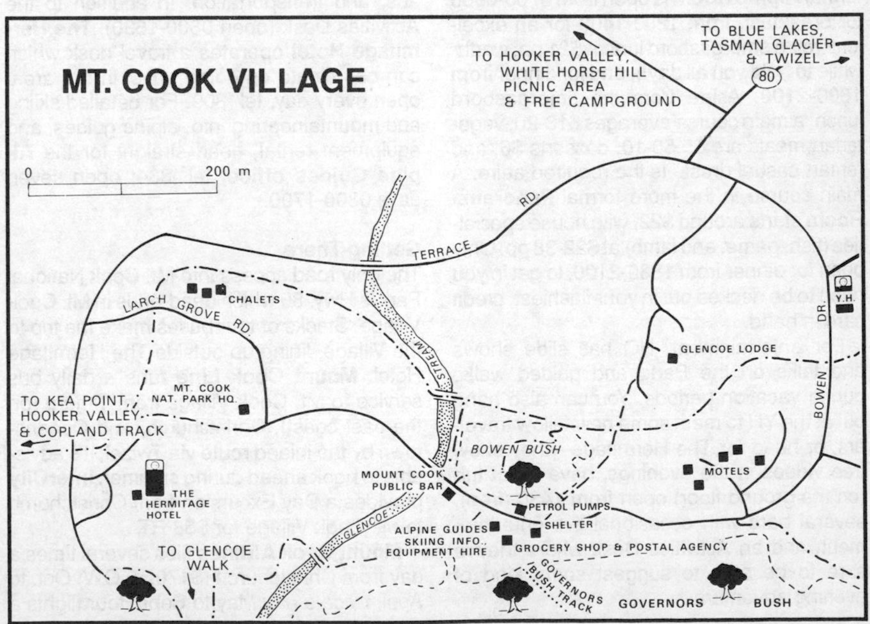

Motel/Hotel

The THC Hermitage Hotel has a variety of accommodations: motel rooms, lodge rooms, comfortable chalets, and deluxe hotel suites with breathtaking views. A **Mount Cook Chalet** with cooking facilities is $82.50 s or d; a standard room in **Glencoe Lodge** is $154 s, $165 d, which includes breakfast; and premium rooms in **The Hermitage** are $204 s or d, suites from $275, and all meals are available and extra. For more info, call The Hermitage at Mt. Cook, tel. 809.

Food And Entertainment

By far the cheapest way to eat at Mt. Cook Village is to cook your own. The one **food store,** open seven days 0900-1730, sells groceries and basic supplies at slightly inflated prices. The only other places to eat are within The Hermitage Hotel complex. Most reasonable is the **Coffee Shop** by the Games Room, open from 0930-1730 (later in summer) serving tearoom-type fare and light meals. Of the two main restaurants, the less formal **Alpine Room** is open from 0700-0900 for breakfast, from 1200-1400 for an excellent-value smorgasbord lunch ($21 pp; worthwhile to hold you all day!), and for dinner from 1800-2100. Aside from the smorgasbord lunch, a main course averages $13-20, vegetarian meals are $5.50-10, desserts $6, and "smart casual dress" is the required attire. A main course in the more formal **Panorama Room** starts around $22, with house specialties (fish, game, and lamb) at $22-38 pp. Only open for dinner from 1830-2100, to get in you need to be decked out in your flashiest, credit card in hand.

For entertainment, HQ has slide shows and talks on the Park, and guided walks during vacation periods. You can also hang out at the YH to meet some new fellow travelers, or head for The Hermitage—they show free videos in the evenings, have a hot tub (on the ground floor) open from 1430 (free), several bars with occasional live entertainment, and an Activities Desk where they're sure to be able to suggest some kind of evening adventure.

Services And Information

Within Mt. Cook Village you'll find a p.o. (open regular hours, weekdays), a shop selling groceries and supplies (open seven days a week), and petrol, and the Alpine Guides office and store (rental and sales, info on climbing instruction, and guide services, open seven days). Travelers cheques can be exchanged at The Hermitage Hotel. Phones are located at the p.o., calling box, and at The Hermitage reception desk. For emergency **fire** call 888, for **first aid** call 809 or go to Park HQ between the hours of 0800-1700.

The main source of info on the entire area is **Mount Cook National Park HQ,** open seven days 0800-1700, tel. 819. In case of emergency, contact the duty ranger; the tel. number is posted in the front window. All kinds of interesting displays represent a complete record of the Park from its creation to modern-day tourism, mountaineering, and skiing activities. Headquarters also has some handy info boards where you can find climbing partners, lost or found items, "want to buy" ads, and transportation. In addition to the Activities Desk (open 0800-1630), **The Hermitage Hotel** operates a travel desk which can coordinate on-going travel in the area; open every day, tel. 809. For detailed skiing and mountaineering info, alpine guides, and equipment rental, head straight for the **Alpine Guides office,** tel. 834; open seven days 0800-1700.

Getting There

The only road access into Mt. Cook National Park is Hwy. 80 which dead-ends in Mt. Cook Village. Stacks of tour buses make the trip to the Village, lining up outside The Hermitage Hotel. **Mount Cook Line** runs a daily bus service to Mt. Cook Village from Timaru (on the east coast), Christchurch, and Queenstown by the inland route via Twizel; it's advisable to book ahead during summer. **InterCity** provides a Day Excursion from Christchurch to Mt. Cook Village for $58 RT.

Mount Cook Airlines flies several times a day from Christchurch ($170.50 OW) Oct. to April, twice a day May to Sept.; four flights a day from Queenstown ($114.40 OW) Oct. to April, three flights May to Sept. (and air service from Dunedin via Queenstown for $135 OW). **Ansett New Zealand** flies from Christchurch and Queenstown to Glentanner Park airport; $76 OW from Christchurch, $69 OW from Queenstown, dependent on availability. Charter flights (very expensive) are also available, timed for a day's skiing. To catch a bus from The Hermitage to Mt. Cook Airport costs $5 OW unless you're going on a scenic flight when the fare is included. **Newmans Air** flies into Glentanner Airport from Christchurch, Wanaka, Queenstown, and Te Anau. For flight info, call Mt. Cook 855.

Local

Check out the info boards at Park HQ and the YH where people often advertise various forms of transportation—some do the Copland Track and need their cars or bikes brought around to Westland National Park (usually to Fox Glacier or Franz Josef) for free; others have room in a shared car; others are looking for traveling/cycling partners, etc. Motorcycles (and horses) are available by the hour or day from Glentanner Park. Skiplanes and helicopters fly you up to the glaciers for skiing adventures, flightseeing, and charters if, in a rash moment, you decide to throw your money completely to the wind! Get the complete rundown from the Activities Desk or the YH. For a taxi, call the Activities Desk or the YH.

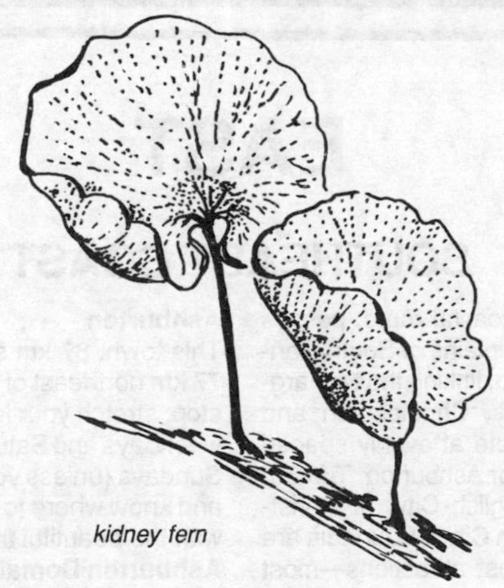

kidney fern

EAST

SOUTHEAST COAST

Highway 1, the main coastal route, passes through the agricultural plains of South Canterbury and North Otago, linking the two largest South Island cities, Christchurch and Dunedin. Along the route at evenly spaced intervals are the cities of Ashburton, Timaru, and Oamaru. The "English City" of Christchurch and the "Scottish City" of Dunedin are the two main east coast attractions—most visitors whiz down the stretch of road between them (about five hours by car) without many stops. However, keen fishing enthusiasts should explore the area in more detail, dangling their rods in the **Rakaia River** (good salmon fishing at **Rakaia Huts** and **Rakaia Rivermouth,** and waterfowl hunting in winter), the **Rangitata** and **Waitaki rivers,** and the many minor rivers and streams that riddle the plains—all well known in local fishing circles; get appropriate licenses from large sporting stores in each area.

Ashburton

This town, 87 km south of Christchurch and 77 km northeast of Timaru, is a good place to stop, stretch your legs, and grab a bite to eat weekdays and Saturday mornings, but not on Sundays (unless you're familiar with the area and know where to go)—it's very quiet. Along with the beautiful trees, gardens, and lake of **Ashburton Domain** (on the other side of the railway, off West St. between Willis St. and Walnut Ave.), trees and impeccable gardens are found all over the city. The locals take particular pride in their "green" downtown square (Baring Square east) with its ornamental tree garden, flower display, and refurbished **town clock** in a specially designed tower. A great number of the historic buildings and churches are made of brick—Ashburton once had a thriving ceramics industry. **Ashburton Information Centre** is on East St. (the main street) and the corner of Burnett St., near the clock square, tel. 81- 064; open Mon. to Fri. 0900-1630, Sat. and Sun. 1000-1600. Friendly staff will fill you in on all the things to do in the city and farther afield, including several walkways easily accessible to the public, and the best places to stay and eat.

Salmon and sea-run trout thrive in **Ashburton River** just south of the city, and many anglers make Ashburton their base while they fish the Rakaia River to the north and the Rangitata River to the south. If you like to hike, fish, and camp out, walk the 19-km **Ashburton Walkway** which runs along the east side of Ashburton River to the river mouth and beach at Hakatere. A free camping area with toilets (the river is the only source of water) is halfway along the walkway; pre-arrange a return ride (no public transportation at the coastal end) or be prepared to walk the same route back to town.

Mount Cook To The East Coast

Several routes go back to the east coast once Hwy. 80 from Mt. Cook rejoins Hwy. 8. If you're continuing south to Dunedin, the most direct route is Hwy. 8 to Omarama, then Hwy. 83 along the Waitaki River to Hwy. 1 south and Oamaru. If you're going north to Christchurch, take Hwy. 8 to Lake Tekapo (see below), Fairlie, and Timaru (serviced by Mount Cook Line and InterCity buses); or use the slightly shorter route, Hwy. 8 to Fairlie then Hwy. 79 to Geraldine. Both routes join Hwy. 1, taking about the same time from Fairlie.

Beautiful **Lake Tekapo,** always a deep milky-blue from "rock flour" in suspension, is a striking spot to camp, fish, water-ski, and hike in summer, and to ice-skate and ski in winter. The commercial **Round Hill Skifield** is about 35 km north of town on the east side of the lake; a bus runs there daily in winter. For info on nordic, telemark, or alpine ski tours (weekend or week-long tours), contact **Alpine Recreation Canterbury Ltd.** at tel. Lake Tekapo 736. In town, the simple **Church of the Good Shepherd,** a memorial to pioneer runholders of the Mackenzie, stands on the lakeshore east of the outlet—the view from its east window is best in the early morning or late afternoon when the light is just right.

Jetboat enthusiasts should make **Irishman Creek,** the original home of the world-renowned **Hamilton jet boat,** a definite stop. Displays feature jetboats past and present. Visit the original 1938 workshop with its pre-war engineering equipment, photos, and exhibits, the 1927 powerhouse which now generates power for the homestead, workshop, and shearers' quarters, the attractive homestead, and the dam which was built in 1930. Walkways provide views of the property,

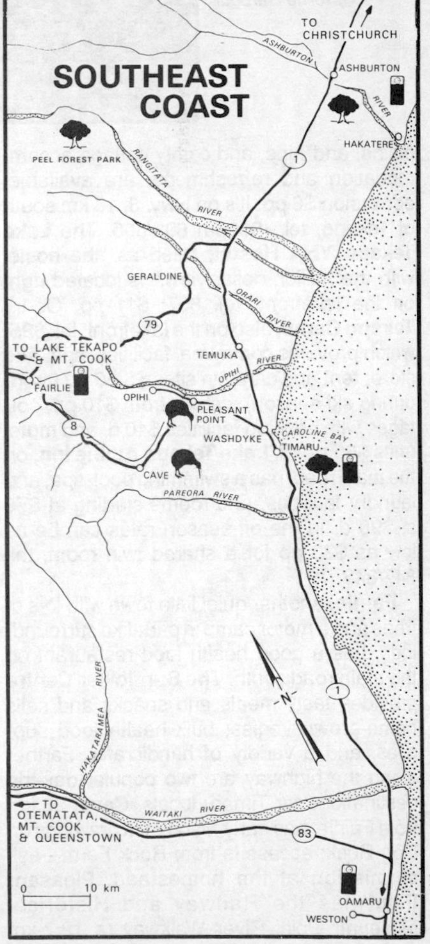

fishing boat in Caroline Harbour

plains, and Alps, and comfy cottage accommodation and refreshments are available; admission $6 pp. It's on Hwy. 8, 16 km south of Tekapo, tel. (05056) 603/605. The **Lake Tekapo YHA Hostel,** billed as "the hostel with the million-dollar view," is located right on the lakefront, tel. 857; $11 pp. Or try **Tekapo Camp,** also on the lakefront, tel. 825, which provides communal facilities, spa, and store; tent and caravan sites $6.50 pp (more during ski season), cabins from $10 pp, cottages with cooking facilities $40 d, and motel units $65 s or d. **Lake Tekapo Alpine Inn,** on the main road, has a swimming pool, spa, and laundry facilities, and rooms starting at $76 s, $90 d. In the off-season rates can be as low as $20 pp for a shared twin room, tel. 847/848.

Fairlie, another quiet little town with lots of trees and a motor camp in park-like surroundings, has a good health food restaurant on the main road south. **The Sunflower Centre** provides tasty meals and snacks and sells home-grown vegies, bulk health food supplies, and a variety of handicrafts. Farther along the highway are two popular day-trip destinations for Timaru locals. **Cave,** 28 km from Fairlie, has early Maori rock drawings on Dog Rock; access is from Rock Farm—ask permission at the homestead. **Pleasant Point** has the Railway and Historical Museum, Opihi River Walkway (a 12.7-km easy walk taking about 2½ hours OW; access from Arowhenua Rd. just south of the Hwy. 1 road bridge over the river), Pioneer Park, and Hanging Rock Bridge (about 11 km northwest)—a natural limestone bluff overhanging the Opihi River with good swimming holes and trout fishing.

TIMARU

Located on the east coast at the south end of the Canterbury Plains along an artificially developed harbor, Timaru has become one of the country's busiest ports. Prior to and during the building of the port (beginning in 1877), ships were frequently wrecked as they tried to get as close to shore as possible in order to transfer cargo through the surf by small boat. Timaru's many local industries include a tannery, brewery, and textiles and milling companies (many give free tours—get more details at the PRO), many "green spots" scattered throughout the city, and an interesting mixture of modern and traditional architecture (the Landing Service Building, built in 1870, is the oldest of its kind in the Southern Hemisphere). Timaru also produced the famous racehorse, Phar Lap, that won all the major races in Australia and the U.S. in the late 1920s and early '30s (a statue of Phar Lap stands in the paddock at Washdyke where he was born)—just one of the events of the past that makes Timaru the self-proclaimed "Home of Champions!"

Sights

Timaru's most popular attraction, **Caroline Bay,** is a sandy beach with safe swimming, an aviary, mini golf, tennis courts, picnic spots, and a roller-skating rink along the seafront. A large Christmas carnival is held there every year (see below). At the **port** at the south end of Caroline Bay you can watch the loading and discharge of the largest roll-on roll-off vessels in the world, and an all-weather mechanical conveyor system. Apart from serving a thriving local fishing industry, the port operates the largest bulk storage handling facilities in New Zealand. This is also where live sheep are exported to Arabia. If you have your own transportation, pick up a map from the info center and take the one-hour scenic drive starting from upper Sophia Street.

All kinds of local Maori artifacts and items relating to the settlement and development of the South Canterbury region are on display at **South Canterbury Museum,** along with

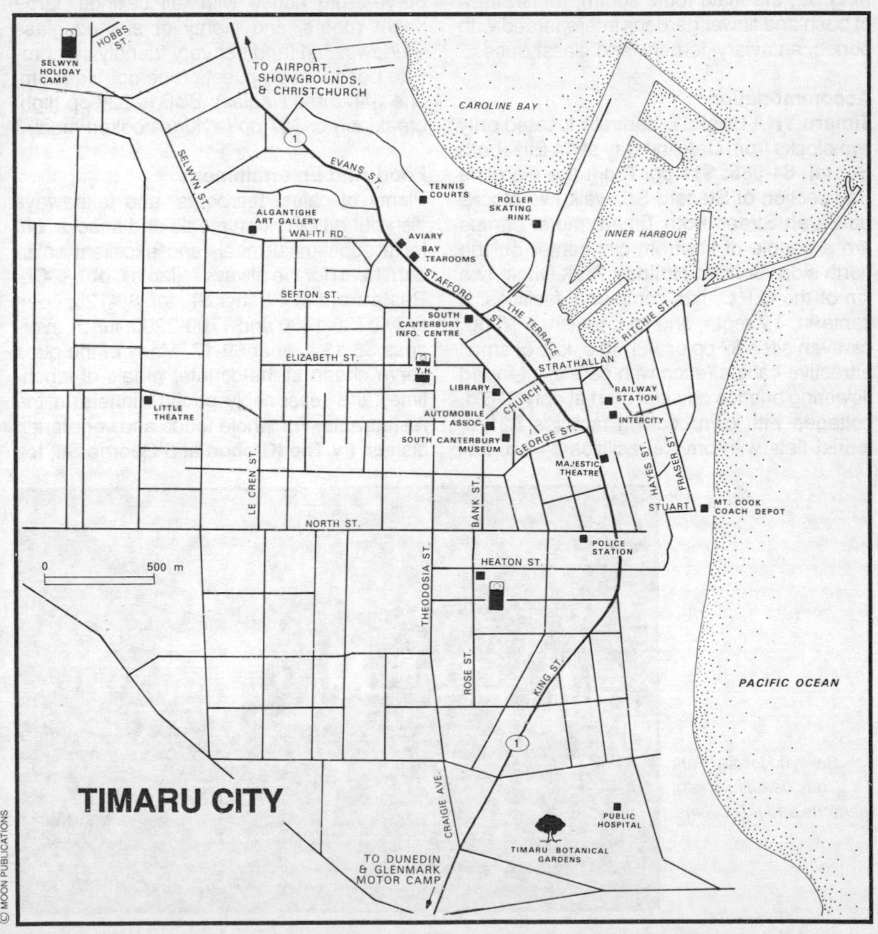

photographs showing the step-by-step building of Timaru's artificial harbor, and info on Maori rock drawings in the district; on Perth St., open Tues. to Fri. and Sun. 1330-1630. The **Aigantighe Gardens and Art Gallery** at 49 Wai-iti Rd. has collections of select N.Z. and British paintings, and English and continental china; open Tues to Fri. 1100-1630 and weekends 1400-1630, admission by donation. After absorbing all the local culture, relax in the greenery around the art gallery, or head for Timaru's **Botanical Gardens** on the south side of the city (entrance on Queen St., off King St., the main route south), a lush area of bush and flower gardens interspersed with ponds, an aviary, fernery, and glasshouses.

Accommodation

Timaru YHA Hostel is centrally located only two blocks from Caroline Bay at 14 Elizabeth St., tel. 84-685; $11 pp. From the Caroline Bay section of Stafford St., walk two blocks up Sarah Street. Both Timaru motor camps are a couple of km from city center on the north side. **Selwyn Holiday Park** within two km of the C.P.O. has communal facilities, a canteen, TV room, and spa; tentsites $5 pp, caravan sites $7 pp or $11.50 d, lots of small attractive cabins (each with carefully tended flowering bushes outside) start at only $16 d, cottages with own cooking facilities $21 d, tourist flats with private facilities $44 d. Located on Selwyn St., tel. 47-690; from the north end of town at Evans St. (the main road) turn right on Hobbs St., then left on Selwyn Street. **Glenmark Motor Camp** on Beaconsfield Rd. at the south end of Timaru, tel. 43-682, has the usual facilities, TV lounge, camp shop, and a swimming pool. Tentsites are $10 d, caravan sites the same plus $2 per night, and on-site caravans and cabins from $25 d.

Timaru has a bed and breakfast guesthouse, and plenty of more expensive motels and hotels—ask at the info center for listings. **Jan's Place** at 4A Rose St., tel. 84-589, is an 80-year-old house with tall ceilings, large bright rooms, and plenty of stained glass windows. Jan (and her very friendly cat) provide beds for five guests (one double room, one with three singles); B&B is $23 pp (light breakfast) or $27 pp (a huge cooked meal).

Food And Entertainment

Plenty of cafes, tearooms, and takeaways dish out quick cheap meals and snacks, but for a substantial meal (and excellent salad bar), head for the always reliable **Cobb & Co. Restaurant** at 4 Latter St., tel. 88-125; open daily 0730-1430 and 1700-2200, lunch averages $6-15, dinner $9-17. Many of the pubs serve cheap at-the-counter meals at lunchtime, and reasonably priced dinners in the restaurants. For whole foods and vegetarian dishes, try **The Kitchen** at 5 George St., tel.

Selwyn Holiday Park has beautifully kept gardens and tidy cabins.

84-344. It's fully licensed, and has live entertainment on the weekends; open Mon. and Tues. 0830-1630, Wed. to Sun. 0830-1830, till late on weekends. Several Chinese restaurants are along Stafford St. (along with many takeaways, open late)—check out the prices before you sit.

The largest crowd-pleasing event in Timaru is the **Caroline Bay Christmas Carnival** which starts on Boxing Day (day after Christmas) and lasts about three weeks over the peak vacation period. Talent, beauty, and other contests, side shows, and continuous evening entertainment keep the crowds happy, and they whoop it up with a fireworks display and enormous bonfire on New Year's Eve. The carnival attracts masses of people from all over N.Z. and the city quickly fills to its limits—if you're planning on being there, book well ahead! During the rest of the year, entertainment takes the form of drinking at the pubs where they often have bands on weekends, going to the movies (listings in the daily newspaper), or taking in a play at the **Little Theatre** on Church St., tel. 88-540. Late-night entertainment (2100-0300) can be found at the **Old Mill Licensed Nightclub** on North St., tel. 88-540. Rollerskating fanatics can rent skates for $1.50, pay $1.50 admission, and then skate to their little hearts' content at the **S.C.R.S.C. Roller Skating Rink** on weekends between 1345 and 1545.

Services And Information

For a **doctor** call 43-089; find out where the on-duty **urgent pharmacy** is by looking in the weekend newspaper; for **ambulance, police, fire** call 111. The **Laundrette** at 57 Sophia St. is open six days a week. For a city map and general info, drop by the **Aorangi Public Relations Office** on the corner of Stafford and Sefton sts., tel. 86-163; open Mon. to Fri. 0830-1700, and during Carnival time every day 0830-1700.

Getting There And Around

InterCity provides buses to Timaru from Dunedin, Christchurch, and Fairlie, and daily (except Sun.) train services from Christchurch to Invercargill stopping at Timaru. Get more info at the railway station on Station St., tel. 47-199. **Mount Cook Line** provides bus service to Timaru from Mount Cook, Christchurch, and Queenstown; office on Fraser St., tel. 83-159. **Newmans Coach Lines** runs buses from Christchurch and Dunedin, stopping at the Grosvenor Hotel on Cains Terrace. **Timaru Airport,** about 10 km north of town, can only be reached by taxi—call **Timaru Taxis** at tel. 43-063. **Air New Zealand** flies from most major centers to Timaru; the agent in Timaru is AA Travel, corner of Church and Bank sts., tel. 84-189. **Timaru Travel** on Stafford St. also does airline bookings.

The **Automobile Association** is on the corner of Church and Bank streets. **Maori Hill Service Station** at 43 Evans St. has 24-hour petrol service. **Avis** is at Dey Motors on Barnard St., tel. 86-240; **Dominion Budget,** Hwy. 1 at Washdyke (north of the city), tel. 82-010; **Hertz,** 56 Theodosia St., tel. 45-199.

OAMARU

Sights

Creamy-white stone buildings, wide treelined streets named after the rivers of Great Britain, and well-kept gardens give a distinctive air to Oamaru, main town of North Otago and commercial center for the inland sheepfarming, cash-cropping, and limestone-quarrying areas. The city is also a popular base for anglers fishing for quinnat salmon in the Waitaki River just north of town. **Oamaru stone,** a white granular limestone, has been used for many of New Zealand's most important buildings, including the customhouse in Wellington and the town halls in both Auckland and Dunedin; Weston, five km west of Oamaru, is the limestone industry center. Stroll around town to see some of Oamaru's most attractive stone buildings—the courthouse, National Bank, post office on South Thames St., the Garden of Memories, and the Centennial Memorial Buildings—and stop at the Athenaeum on Thames St. to visit the small **North Otago Museum** inside. Displays cover the geology and natural history, Maori and early European settlement of

North Otago, and features the extraction and uses of Oamaru stone; open weekdays 1300-1630 (later on Fri.) and weekend afternoons during summer; free.

Gardening enthusiasts will kick themselves if they don't make time to visit **Oamaru Public Gardens** which date back to 1876! Amongst all the spectacular floral displays are fountains, statues, a summerhouse, Japanese Red Bridge, an aviary and peacock house, and display and cactus houses; main entrance on Severn Street. Or tour the gardens in style—in a wagon pulled by Robbie, the Clydesdale horse—for adult $2.50, child $1.50; rides run four days a week (see the noticeboard at the entrance) from 1330-1530. If you're into geology, walk through from Warren St. to the geological reserves of **Target Gully Shell Pit** and **Hutchinsons Quarry** where "pillow lava" and sub-fossil remains of extinct birds, fossils, and shell deposits have been found. For good views of Oamaru, the coastline, and the inland mountains, head for **Lookout Point** at the east end of Tamar Street.

Coast Walk

For an enjoyable 40-minute (OW) walk (particularly flowerful in summer), take the **Graves Walkway** along a boulder-strewn beach dominated by sheer cliffs. A lighthouse sits atop the cliffs and "pillow lava" is found along the base. The track starts at the end of Waterfront Rd. (south end of the harbor), but can only be hiked during low tide (look for little blue penguins that often huddle in cliff-face cavities close to the northern access). The second section of the walkway climbs over Cape Wanbrow to beautiful orange-sand and boulder-strewn **Bushy Beach.** Great numbers of seabirds frequent the area, along with a variety of coastal vegetation and sealife on the benches and platforms protected from the pounding surf. At the far end of the beach is a yellow-eyed penguin breeding colony—the northernmost breeding colony in New Zealand. Don't be caught by the tide—once it covers the rock shelves, it quickly reaches the beach, cutting off access.

Accommodation

If you're in Oamaru in summer, stay at the comfortable **Red Kettle YHA Hostel,** with swimming pool across the road; $11 pp. It's generally open from Oct. to April/May, at the corner of Reed and Cross sts., tel. 47-348.

MOERAKI

Thirty-eight km south of Oamaru just south of Hampden, Hwy. 1 passes a short gravel road that leads to the unique **Moeraki Boulders Scenic Reserve.** Take a 300-meter walk to the north along sandy Moeraki Beach and you come to what at first looks like a group of extra-large turtles washed up on the sand. On closer inspection you find a great number of round, perfectly smooth, gray boulders of varying sizes (up to four meters round) with a cracked design, scattered haphazardly along the sand and sticking out of the cliffs almost as if they're being "born"—some have split apart into several gigantic pieces. Made of carbonate of lime, silica, alumina, and peroxide of iron, the boulders were formed by chemistry on the sea floor about 60 million years ago through the slow accumulation of lime salts around a small core; the cracks are filled with yellow calcite crystals. They "appear" from the beach and cliffs behind as the mudstone in which they reside is eroded away by the sea. According to Maori legend, the boulders were food baskets and water casks from one of the great canoes from Hawaiiki wrecked off Shag Point at the south end of Katiki Beach. These magnificent boulders were once found all over the beaches in this area (volcanic boulders lie on **Katiki Beach** a few km to the south, but they're older and smaller); sadly, most have been carried off as souvenirs—only the largest and heaviest boulders remain, and the area is now protected as a scientific reserve.

For a delicious snack, morning or afternoon tea, or light lunch, stop at **The Boulders** boulder-shaped restaurant and gift shop (signposted from the main road) and enjoy magnificent views of the beach as you munch and browse; open daily 0800-1830.

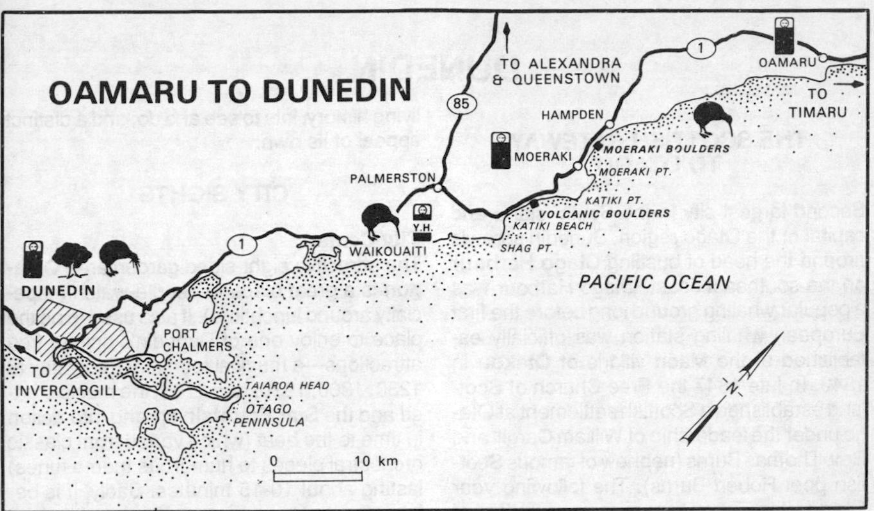

Practicalities

Continuing along Hwy. 1 south, you pass the road to the tiny picturesque fishing village of **Moeraki** ("Sleepy Sky") where you can often buy fish fresh off the fishing boats which usually come in around 1200-1300. Stay at the **Moeraki Resort Motor Camp** right on the beach. For an enjoyable walk in fresh sea air, good coastal views, and the possible added bonus of seeing seals and penguins, walk out to the end of **Shag Point** at the south end of Katiki Beach. More boulders lie just north of Shag Point.

Continuing South

Waikouaiti Beach, originally intended as the place for Otago's major settlement (now Dunedin), is a good place to enjoy some R & R before or after hitting the big city. This small town has a beautiful white-sand beach with safe swimming, surfing, and beachcombing, a good museum, and a wildlife refuge with walkway across the lagoon. **Waikouaiti Motor Camp** is in Waikouaiti Domain, also on Beach St. next to the beach, tel. 757-366. Communal facilities; tentsites $4.50 pp, caravan sites $8 s or $12.50 d, and on-site caravans $18 d per night plus camp charges (off-peak reductions available).

DUNEDIN

THE SCOTTISH GATEWAY TO OTAGO

Second largest city in the South Island and capital of the Otago region, Dunedin sprawls around the head of bustling **Otago Harbour** on the southeast coast. Otago Harbour was a popular whaling ground long before the first European whaling station was officially established at the Maori village of **Otakou** in 1840. In late 1847 the Free Church of Scotland established a Scottish settlement at Otago under the leadership of William Cargill and Rev. Thomas Burns (nephew of famous Scottish poet Robert Burns). The following year **Otago** (the European mispronunciation of "Otakou") was chosen as the official name for the settlement, and "New Edinburgh" as the name for the new town—the latter greatly criticized for its lack of originality and replaced by the old Celtic name for Edinburgh, Dun Edin (Edin on the Hill). The discovery of gold in Otago in 1861 brought numerous gold diggers, along with bankers, hoteliers, and great wealth to Dunedin, and within a couple of years, public works and enterprises had flourished to the extent that the city became the commercial and industrial heart of the country. It was the first city in N.Z. to set up a freezing works and send frozen meat to England in 1882, the first city to use kerosene lighting, the first place in the country to use a cable tramway, the successful developer of a hydroelectric works (which prompted the government to further develop hydroelectric power throughout the country), along with many other "firsts."

With its well-planned city center, hilly suburbs and harbor views, Victorian-style stone buildings decorated with spires and turrets, stately homes, historic statues and memorials, albatross and penguin colonies, and well-kept parks and flower gardens, the self-proclaimed "Rhododendron City of the South Island" and "Gateway to Otago" has plenty of living history, lots to see and do, and a distinct appeal of its own.

CITY SIGHTS

City Center

The attractive eight-sided garden area **Octagon** is a great place to people-watch (especially around lunchtime). It also used to be the place to enjoy one of Dunedin's unique free attractions—a musical fountain! Every day at 1230, 1800, 1930, and 2130, the music started and the **Star Fountain** sprang into action in time to the beat (which varied from classic orchestral pieces to humorous theme tunes) lasting about 10-15 minutes. Sadly, it is being relocated to the corner of Anzac Ave. and Castle St., near the railway station. If it's in action, it's best appreciated in the dark when you get the full effect of the colored lights and water designs as the fountain prances and dances to tunes like "Return of the Pink Panther."

Situated around the Octagon, you'll find the **Visitor Information Centre and PRO, civic centre offices, Regent Theatre,** and **St. Paul's Cathedral,** and one block back, the **town hall, public library,** and **post office.** The **NZTP Travel Office** is on Princes St., two blocks away on the south side of the Octagon.

Otago Early Settlers Museum

Crowded with all sorts of fascinating and unusual displays covering the life of early settlers, this museum has photos, costumes, furniture, antique medical and dental instruments (which look like great instruments of torture!), portrait gallery, goldmining exhibit, pioneer cottage and blacksmith's shop, penny farthing bicycle, horse-drawn vehicles, tram, a display devoted to "the forgotten sex and early feminists of New Zealand," and much, much more—it's the kind of place where you can easily lose several hours. Also, the excellent reference library and Re-

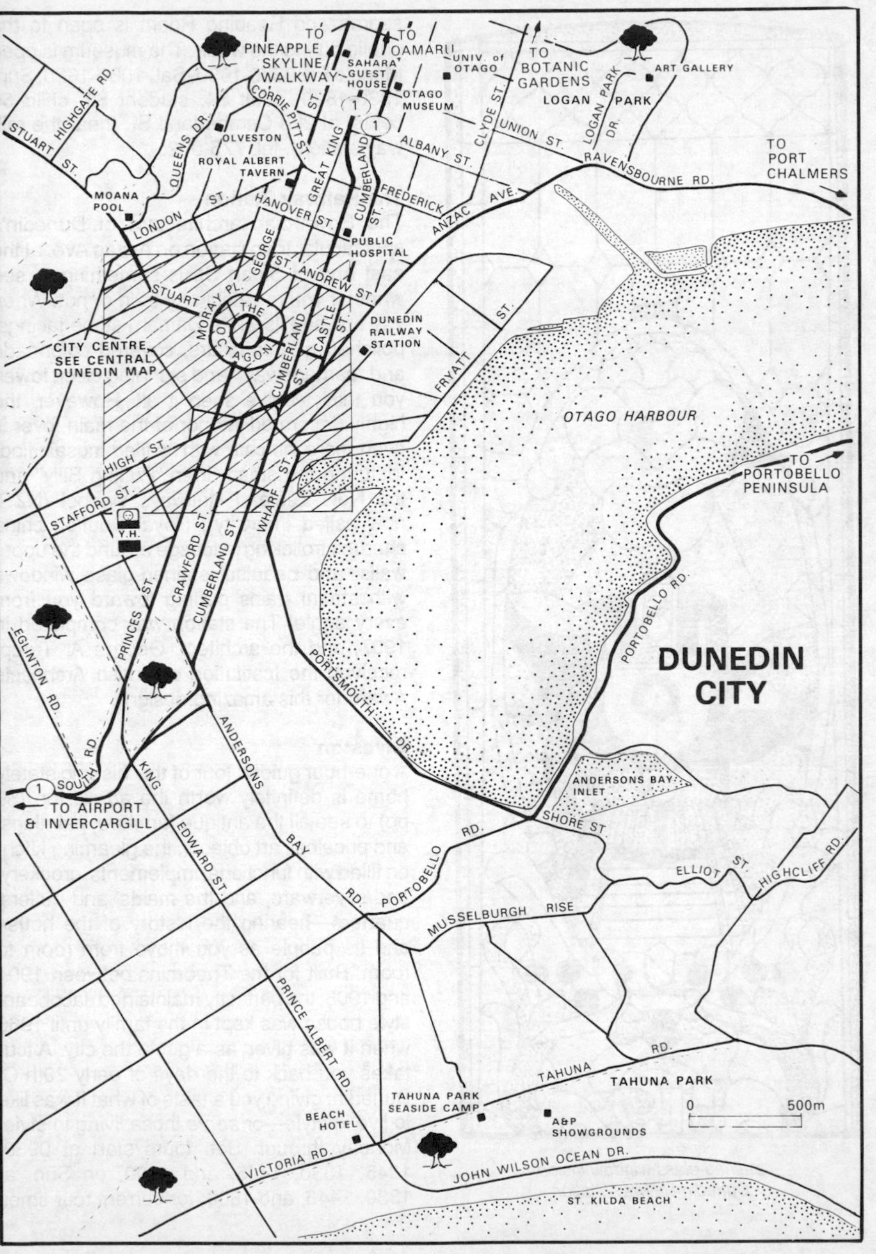
DUNEDIN CITY
TO OAMARU
TO BOTANIC GARDENS
PINEAPPLE SKYLINE WALKWAY
SAHARA GUEST HOUSE
UNIV. of OTAGO
OTAGO MUSEUM
ART GALLERY
LOGAN PARK
LOGAN PARK DR.
HIGHGATE RD.
STUART ST.
QUEENS DR.
CORRIE PITT ST.
GREAT KING ST.
CUMBERLAND ST.
CLYDE ST.
UNION ST.
ALBANY ST.
OLVESTON
ROYAL ALBERT TAVERN
RAVENSBOURNE RD.
TO PORT CHALMERS
MOANA POOL
LONDON ST.
HANOVER ST.
FREDERICK ST.
ANZAC AVE.
PUBLIC HOSPITAL
GEORGE ST.
ST. ANDREW ST.
STUART ST.
MORAY PL.
THE OCTAGON
CASTLE ST.
DUNEDIN RAILWAY STATION
FRYATT ST.
CITY CENTRE, SEE CENTRAL DUNEDIN MAP
OTAGO HARBOUR
HIGH ST.
WHARF ST.
STAFFORD ST.
Y.H.
CRAWFORD ST.
CUMBERLAND ST.
PRINCES ST.
TO PORTOBELLO PENINSULA
PORTOBELLO RD.
EGLINTON RD.
PORTSMOUTH DR.
ANDERSONS BAY RD.
SOUTH RD.
KING EDWARD ST.
TO AIRPORT & INVERCARGILL
ANDERSONS BAY INLET
SHORE ST.
PORTOBELLO RD.
ELLIOT ST.
HIGHCLIFF RD.
MUSSELBURGH RISE
PRINCE ALBERT RD.
TAHUNA RD.
TAHUNA PARK
TAHUNA PARK SEASIDE CAMP
BEACH HOTEL
A&P SHOWGROUNDS
0
500m
VICTORIA RD.
JOHN WILSON OCEAN DR.
ST. KILDA BEACH

stained-glass window inside Dunedin Railway Station

search and Reading Room is open to the public during the week. The museum is open Mon. to Fri. 0830-1630, Sat. 1030-1630, Sun. 1330-1630; adult $4, student $3, child 50 cents; at 220 Cumberland St. (near the railway station), tel. 775-052.

The Railway Station

The Edwardian architecture of Dunedin's spectacular train station on Anzac Ave. at the east end of Stuart St. is something to see whether you're catching a train or not. When you first see its white Oamaru stone facings, polished granite pillars, covered colonnade and "carriageway," and stunning clock tower, you think you've seen it all. However, the highly decorated interior of the main foyer is even more intricate with its tiled mosaic floor featuring the steam train "Puffing Billy" and the New Zealand Railways symbol (NZR; now called InterCity), Royal Doulton china cherubs frolicking in foliage around the upper walls, and beautiful stained-glass windows with steam trains puffing toward you from every angle! The station was completed in 1907, and the architect, George A. Troup, received the Institution of British Architects Award for this amazing design.

Olveston

A one-hour guided tour of this historic stately home is definitely worth the admission ($6 pp) to see all the antique furniture, paintings, and priceless art objects, the gleaming kitchen filled with functional implements, crockery, and silverware, and the maids' and butlers' quarters—hearing the history of the house and its people as you move from room to room. Built for the Theomins between 1904 and 1906, the perfectly maintained Jacobean-style house was kept in the family until 1966 when it was given as a gift to the city. A tour takes you back to the days of early 20th C. Dunedin, giving you a taste of what it was like to live in style—or *serve* those living in style. Monday through Sat. tours start at 0930, 1045, 1330, 1445, and 1600, on Sun. at 1330, 1445, and 1600; for current tour times and a reservation (find out which tours to avoid—tour buses always stop at Olveston), call 773-320; 42 Royal Terrace, a 20-minute uphill walk from city center. If you'd rather see Olveston as part of an organized tour of Dunedin sights, call Newtons Tours at tel. 52-199 or book at the Visitor Centre or NZTP Travel Office.

Otago Museum
Museum freaks can spend hours wandering around enormous Otago Museum with its outstanding collection of Polynesiana (largest collection in N.Z.), halls on Melanesia, the Maori culture, furniture and ceramics, lions and primates, cameras, coins and medals, birds, small animals, marinelife, world civiliza-

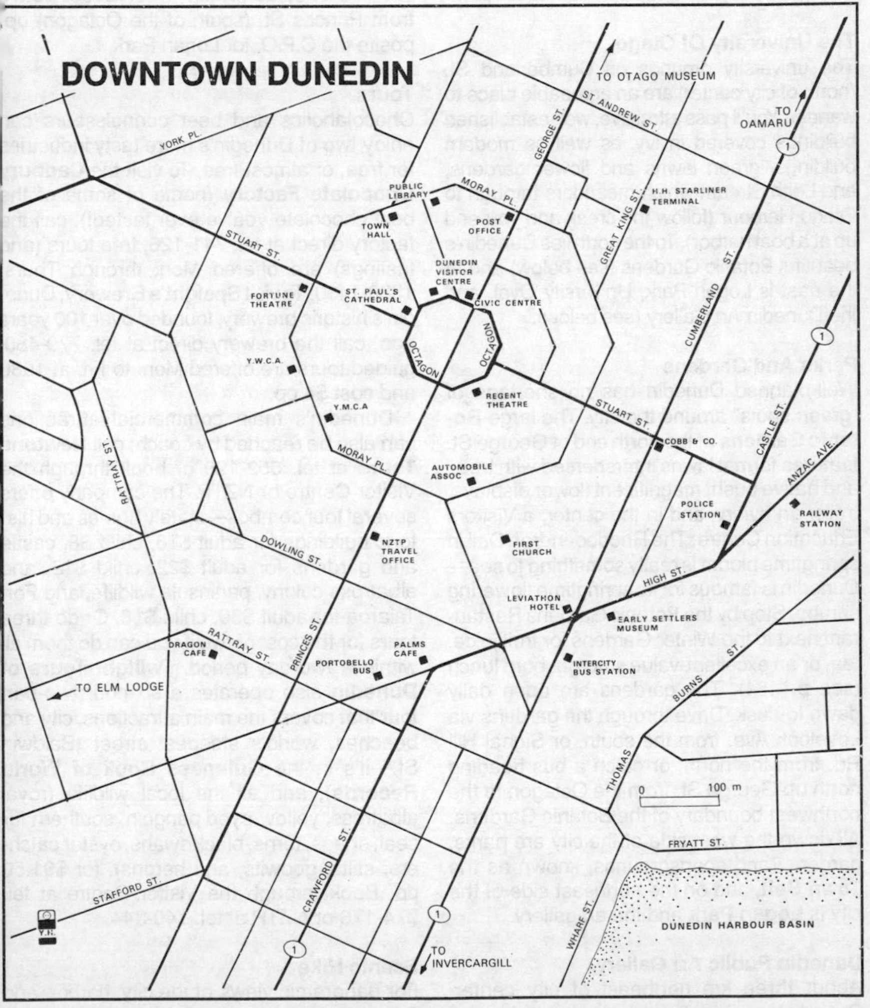

tions, and a maritime hall. It's open weekdays from 1000-1700 and weekends 1400-1700; free. If you only have an hour or so to explore, pick up the handy An Hour Of Your Time brochure in the entrance hall—it directs you to all the highlights. On Great King St. across from the University, less than two km north of the city; buses run from the Octagon along George St. to one block from the museum.

The University Of Otago

The university grounds off Cumberland St. (north of city center) are an agreeable place to wander. You'll pass attractive, well-established buildings covered in ivy, as well as modern buildings, green lawns and flower gardens, and Leith Stream which meanders through to Otago Harbour (follow the creek and you end up at a boat harbor). To the north lies Dunedin's beautiful Botanic Gardens (see below) and to the east is Logan Park, University Oval, and the Dunedin Art Gallery (see below).

Parks And Gardens

Well-planned Dunedin has no shortage of "green spots" around the city. The large **Botanic Gardens** at the north end of George St. features formal lawns interspersed with trees and native bush, magnificent flower displays, trails, an aviary, and in the center, a Visitors Education Centre. The Rhododendron Dell in springtime bloom is really something to see—Dunedin is famous for its springtime flowering shrubs. Stop by the Botanic Gardens Restaurant next to the Winter Gardens for fruit juice, tea, or an excellent-value smorgasbord lunch (see p. 464). The gardens are open daily dawn to dusk. Drive through the gardens via Lovelock Ave. from the south, or Signal Hill Rd. from the north, or catch a bus heading north up George St. from the Octagon to the northwest boundary of the Botanic Gardens. All down the west side of the city are parks, gardens, and sportsgrounds, known as the **Town Belt,** and on the northeast side of the city is **Logan Park** and the art gallery.

Dunedin Public Art Gallery

About three km northeast of city center, Dunedin's main art gallery is situated in Logan Park at the end of tree-lined Logan Park Drive. Founded in 1884, the gallery has two claims to fame—first, it's the oldest art gallery in N.Z., containing an extensive collection of foreign paintings and one of the most important N.Z. collections; second, it holds the only Monet in the country. The gallery is open weekdays 1000-1630, weekends 1400-1700, tel. 778-770; admission free. Buses leave from Princes St. (south of the Octagon) opposite the C.P.O. for Logan Park.

Tours

Chocolaholics and beer connoisseurs can enjoy two of Dunedin's more tasty industries for free, or almost free. To visit the **Cadbury Chocolate Factory** (home of some of the best chocolate you've ever tasted!), call the factory direct at tel. 741-126; free tours (and tastings) are offered Mon. through Thurs. 1330-1430. To visit **Speight's Brewery**, Dunedin's historic brewery, founded over 100 years ago, call the brewery direct at tel. 779-480; guided tours are offered Mon. to Fri. at 1030 and cost $4 pp.

Dunedin's main commercial attractions can also be reached by coach; call **Newtons Tours** at tel. 552-199 or book through the Visitor Centre or NZTP. The company offers several tour combos—stately homes and historic buildings for adult $16, child $8, castle and gardens for adult $22, child $12, and albatross colony, peninsula wildlife, and Fort Taiaroa for adult $30, child $18. Or do three tours for the cost of two if you can do them all within a two-day period. **Twilight Tours of Dunedin** also operates a six-hour two-part tour that covers the main attractions, city and beaches, world's steepest street (Baldwin St.—it's in the **Guinness Book of World Records**), and all the local wildlife (royal albatross, yellow-eyed penguin, southern fur seal, shags, terns, black swans, oyster catchers, stilts, godwits, and herons), for $91.50 pp. Book through the Visitor Centre at tel. 774-176 or NZTP at tel. 740-344.

Scenic Hike

For panoramic views of the city, harbor, and Otago Peninsula, consider hiking the five-km

OW **Pineapple Skyline Walkway.** The track starts at the carpark off Flagstaff Whare Flat Rd., takes about two hours (going downhill toward the city), and finishes at the end of Booth Rd. in the northern Dunedin suburb of Glenleith; it can be walked in either direction, depending on whether you want to go uphill or down. For info on public transportation to the track, call in at the Civic Centre offices at the Octagon. Several other hiking tracks are also in the area—get more info at the PRO. If you're in Dunedin in summer you may find the center manned by students—great sources of hiking (and entertainment) info.

Scenic Drive

If you have your own car, follow the one-hour "Golden Arrow Scenic Drive" which starts at the C.P.O. on Princes St. (look for the signs with a golden arrow on a green background); a free brochure with map and descriptions is available at the PRO. The drive takes you around the city and immediate vicinity to lookout points providing panoramic views of the city, harbor, and Peninsula, passing parks and several city attractions such as the Moana Swimming Pool complex (see p. 466) and Olveston, to name but a few.

OTAGO PENINSULA SIGHTS

Several of the area's best attractions (four out of "Dunedin's Top Five") are located along the narrow scenic Otago Peninsula, northeast of city center. Apart from the few commercial attractions, the Peninsula is an enjoyable place to tootle around for a day—for views, spectacular beaches and towering cliffs, farmland separated by century-old stone walls, and birdwatching. Along the Otago Harbour waterfront are large flocks of wading birds, oystercatchers, bar-tailed godwits, and shags. At **Taiaroa Head** (the northeastern tip), the albatross colony (see note below before you head out there; bookings are essential) and a beach full of yellow-eyed penguins are two Dunedin sights that shouldn't be missed. Pick up the excellent *Otago Peninsula* guide for 80 cents from the Visitor Centre ahead of time. It lists *everything* there is to see and do—and more—on the entire peninsula. Two main roads run along the Peninsula: the high Highcliff Rd. (good views) and the low Portobello Rd. along the waterfront (a birdwatcher's delight)—both join at the small settlement of **Portobello** (pub, gen-

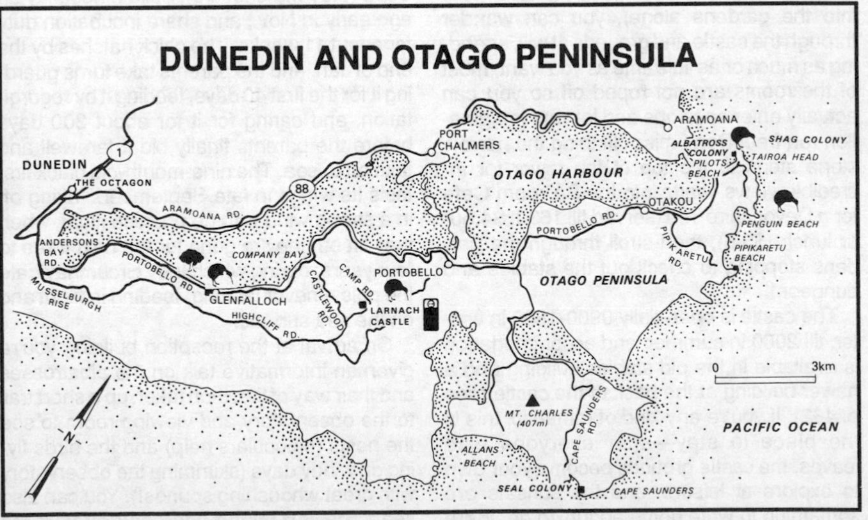

eral store and hot takeaway foods, and public telephone). Other than these, the Peninsula is relatively uncommercialized—buy your lunch, drinks, and munchies in the city before you venture up the Peninsula.

To get the most out of the Peninsula by car, take the high route first, and after visiting Taiaroa Heads, return to the city by the low route. To get to the Peninsula from city center, take Hwy. 1 south and turn left on Andersons Bay Rd. which becomes Portobello Road. Buses to Portobello depart from lower High St. (near Dowling St.) in the city, Mon. to Fri. (frequently) and Sat. (considerably less frequently); for times, call 779-238.

Larnach Castle

If you've always wondered what it would be like to live in a genuine castle, wonder no longer! Built in the early 1870s by extravagant banker, businessman, and politician William Larnach, Larnach Castle sits in 35 acres of bush and gardens, only 13 km from Dunedin city center—a grand and extravagant stone mansion built along Scottish baronial lines, filled with original marble, Venetian glass, plaster, and woodcarvings collected by Larnach from all over the world. Once you pay the adult $8, child $3.50 entrance fee (less into the gardens alone), you can wander through the castle and grounds at will, spending as much or as little time as you want; most of the rooms are not roped off so you can actually enter each one and let your imagination run free! Don't miss climbing the narrow stone steps to the top of the tower for incredible views, waltz into the Ballroom Cafe for a Devonshire Tea (served till 1630; $4.50) or lunch ($5-6), then stroll through the gardens stopping to check out the stables and dungeon!

The castle is open daily 0900-1800 in winter, till 2000 in summer, and accommodation is available in the old stables building and a newer building at the back of the castle (see p. 462). If you're any kind of romantic, this is the place to stay—after everyone else leaves, the castle grounds become your own to explore at leisure, and the sunsets are something to write home about! To get there by car from Highcliff Rd., turn left on Camp Rd. following the signs to the castle. To get there from Portobello Rd., turn right on Castlewood Rd., then left on Camp Road. By public transportation, catch the Portobello bus from Lower High St. (opposite Queens Gardens) to Company Bay (it runs Mon. to Sat.), then hike the four very steep km up Castlewood Rd. to the castle. Newtons Tours (tel. 52-199) and Twilight Tours of Dunedin (book through the Visitor Centre or NZTP) include Larnach Castle on their itinerary.

Royal Albatross Colony

The Royal Albatross Colony at **Taiaroa Head** is a unique sight—the only colony in the world found on inhabited mainland where albatrosses nest so close to civilization; open Nov. to September. It can be a unique experience if you're lucky enough to be there when the birds are flying (they need winds of at least 15-20 knots to take off but can land with very little wind). The all-white birds with black wings at Taiaroa are Great Albatrosses—true sea birds; with wingspans of more than three meters, these large bulky birds waddle ungainly on land but are magnificent fliers. The parent albatrosses arrive at the colony late in Sept. (they mate for life), build a nest, lay an egg early in Nov., and share incubation duty for about 11 weeks. The chick hatches by the end of Jan. and the parents take turns guarding it for the first 40 days, feeding it by regurgitation, and caring for it for about 300 days before the parents finally bid it farewell and take off to sea. The nine-month-old chick first tests its wings in late September. Taking off in a strong wind with no practice flight, when they lift off, they're gone for the next three to four years, during which they circumnavigate the pole—never landing, feeding in flight and on the sea surface!

On arrival at the reception building you're given an informative talk on the albatrosses and their way of life, then taken up a short trail to the observatory and viewing room to see the nests (binoculars help) and the birds flying on windy days (skimming the observatory with great whooshing sounds!). You can also see a **Stewart Island shag colony** from the ɒbservatory—their nests look like bunches of ïny volcanoes splattered over the rocks. **Pi-ots Beach** just below the headland is a ɒopular place for **fur seals**—you can walk lown to it for close-up views. The best time o visit Taiaroa Heads is late afternoon on a vindy day when the albatrosses are most kely to be flying, when the shags return to eed their chicks, and when the seals like to nang out on the beach.

Before heading out for the colony, you must irst buy a ticket (adult $8, child $6) from the Visitor Centre in the Octagon (tel. 774-176), hen visit the colony at the specified date and ime (try for late afternoon)—the colony has estricted access so that the birds are not listurbed. The only easy way to get to the Albatross Colony is by private transportation hitchhiking is almost impossible); the alter-nate way is to catch the Portobello bus from Lower High St. opposite Queens Gardens to Portobello (it runs Mon. to Sat.), then hike the nine km or so to the headland, or take a Newtons Tour which includes the colony in some summer itineraries.

Penguin Place

Another attraction for nature lovers is Penguin Place, a penguin and seal colony at Taiaroa Head. A short walk from the carpark takes you to Penguin Bay where you can watch yellow-eyed and little blue penguins climbing out of the surf and up to their nests, and seals basking on a rocky islet just offshore. The penguins are usually out at sea until at least 1700, so the best time to go is late after-noon/early evening. Again you really need your own transportation to get out there—the turn-off to the colony is about 1.6 km before the Heads; stop at the sign of the penguin to get the key to a locked gate, then continue about three km to the carpark at the end of the road—or catch a Newtons Tour, tel. 52-199. Entrance fee is adult $3, child 60 cents. (Another seal colony is found at Cape Saun-ders, on the southeast side of the Peninsula.)

Glenfalloch Woodlands Gardens

Are you a gardening nut, particularly into azaleas, rhododendrons, or fuchsias? Enjoy hand-feeding peacocks and all kinds of semi-tame birds? Then these 60-year-old gardens with their pioneer homestead, eight km from the city, are more than worth the admission fee of $2.50 pp. The grounds are spectacular in spring; in summer they're noted for colorful fuchsia displays. Take some of the short walks through the trees passing a stream and beau-tiful woodland gardens. The Chalet provides light lunches and teas seven days from 1000-1630 (closed in winter), and pottery is made and sold in the Potters Cottage, open 1300-1600. Glenfalloch, open seven days during daylight hours, is off Portobello Rd., and can be easily reached by the Portobello bus (it runs Mon. to Sat.). It's also one of Newtons Tours' (tel. 52-199) destinations.

ACCOMMODATION

Hostels

Stafford Gables YHA Hostel is a large Tu-dor-style building in a handy central location on the south side of the Octagon. It has all the usual plus many extras (reading room, music room, etc.), and the office (open all day) sells staples; $14 pp, at 71 Stafford St., tel. 741-919. Take Princes St. south from the Octagon, turn right on Stafford St., and walk two blocks.

Elm Lodge, a private hostel (no smoking) run by friendly Shirley Gilchrist, is excellent backpacker accommodation providing bright cheerful rooms (dorm, single, or double) with views of Otago Harbour, an equipped kitchen, comfy living room with TV, well-kept garden, and BBQ area—all the comforts of a home away from home, close to city center; $13 pp dorm, $15 pp s or d. It's at 74 Elm Row, tel. 741-872.

The **YWCA Kinnaird House,** centrally located, predominantly houses university students—both sexes, singles and couples. It usually has plenty of spare rooms for casuals during vacation periods, and while university is in session if booked a week ahead. The rooms are small but bright, have shared bath, and the dining room (open to the public) has a blackboard menu; lunch $3.50 pp, dinner $6.60 pp. B&B is $22 s or $30 d, backpacker's rate is $11 per night s or twin (does not include breakfast); at 97 Moray Place, tel. 776-781.

The **YMCA Residential Flats** are just across the street from Kinnaird House. They house university students in shared flats: living room, bathroom, kitchen; the complex has a communal game room and laundry. Usually only three or four beds are available for casuals in single or shared rooms at $12 pp without linen, $15 pp with linen (no meals); sometimes rooms with twin beds are available for couples. It's generally on a first-come first-served basis, but if you book a week ahead, they may be able to hold a bed. From Nov. to the end of Jan. there's plenty of room. Centrally located at 54 Moray Place, tel. 779-555.

Motor Camps

Three motor camps are within a reasonable distance of city center. **Tahuna Park Seaside Camp** is about five km out, but within earshot of the surf on adjacent St. Kilda Beach. The usual facilities, plus TV lounge, and pool room; tentsites $6.50 pp, caravan sites $13.50 d, cabins $22-40 d. Located in the A & P Showgrounds in Tahuna Park, St. Kilda (south of the city center), tel. 54-690. Take the St. Kilda bus from the Princes St. side of the Octagon and ask for the motor camp—buses run about every 20 minutes weekdays in both directions, less frequently weekends.

Aaron Lodge Motor Camp on the west side of the city is similar, and all meals are available in the adjacent restaurant; tent and caravan sites (mostly concrete) are $13 d (plus $1.50 for power), on-site caravans are $24 per night, cabins are $24-27. Motel units are also available. Located at 162 Kaikorai Valley Rd., tel. 64-725; take Stewart St. west from the Octagon and follow it uphill until it becomes Kaikorai Valley Road. Pass the 24-hour petrol station at the top of the hill, and Kentucky Fried; the motor camp is a little farther on the right. Buses from the Octagon run up Stewart St. to Wakari—get off at Highgate Road.

Leith Valley Touring Park at 103 Malvern St., tel. 741-936, has landscaped grounds bordered by a stream, only a few minutes from downtown. Tent and caravan sites are $7 pp, on-site caravans are $12 plus camp charges. Thirteen km on the north side of Dunedin is **Farmlands Camper Caravan Park,** about a 15-minute drive up Hwy. 1 followed by a short drive along Waitati Valley Rd., tel. 822-730. If you like animals, you're gonna love this place with its pet rabbits, ducks, chickens, peacocks, ponies, donkey, lamb, Banana the dog, and other assorted farm critters running and hopping around! Modern bathroom, kitchen, and laundry facilities, a large comfortable TV/recreation room with open fireplace, a shop, BBQ area, all sorts of activities to keep children content, and hospitable managers, John and Jan Leslie, to boot! Powered campsites are adult $7, child $4 (stay five nights and the sixth is free), on-site caravans are $18 s, $26 d, $28 triple.

Larnach Castle Lodge

The most fun place to stay when you're in Dunedin is at Larnach Castle on Otago Peninsula, 13 km out. You not only get to stay in the stables or colonial farm building, but the beautiful 35-acre grounds become almost your own private garden. There are no tentsites (no outside facilities) but a couple of campervan power points are available for the self-contained van at $18 d. **Stable Stay,** four-berth bunk rooms (in a coach house built in 1870) with shared bath, kitchen with dining

Be "King of the Castle" at Larnach Castle Lodge.

area and TV, and laundry, are only $20 s, $30 d ($6.50 extra for bedding and towel)—an outstanding bargain! **Larnach Lodge** rooms with shared bath are $48 s or d; rooms with private bath are $69 s or d, shared kitchen and laundry available. Continental breakfasts ($7.80) and cooked breakfasts ($12.50) are extra, and teas and light lunches are available in the Castle ballroom, but the ideal situation is to take food and cook it yourself in the microwave. Dinner is also available in the Castle Dining Room for Lodge guests; $37 pp. For more info and bookings call 761-302, or just turn up. For transportation and Castle info, see "Larnach Castle" above.

Private Hotels And Guesthouses

For a full listing of Dunedin B&Bs, and homestay and farmstay accommodations, visit the **Visitor Centre**. The **Wharf Hotel** is basically a pub and bottle shop with rooms upstairs (and a special window so that the barmaid can see if anyone uninvited tries to go up!). Dinner available, communal facilities. All rooms are $30 pp B&B, $38 pp for dinner, B&B. Centrally located at 25 Fryatt St. (by the wharf), tel. 771-233. The **Sahara Guest House** has a TV lounge, tea- and coffee-making facilities, laundry, and dinner available in the adjacent Sahara Restaurant; from $35 s B&B, $56 d B&B. Located at 619 George St. near Otago Museum, tel. 776-662.

The Leviathon Hotel has regular hotel rooms at $62.50 s, $67.50 d (reduced rates during "winter specials"), but they also have some very small single rooms (left over from redecorating) that they don't advertise for $39.50 s. These rooms are bright, have private bath, TV, etc.—but you have to specifically ask for them. The hotel has lounge rooms, bars, and a game room, and a large, old-fashioned, formal dining room where all the tables have starched white tablecloths, fancy red serviettes, and gleaming silverware (casual diners welcome); breakfast starts around $7 pp Continental, $11 pp cooked, dinner from $25 pp. Central location, opposite the Otago Early Settlers Museum; on the corner of High and Cumberland sts., tel. 773-160.

The Beach Hotel in the southern suburb of St. Kilda has a guest TV lounge, bar, and bottleshop, meals available in the adjacent restaurant, and the rooms have private bathroom facilities; $35 s, $48 d, breakfast extra at $5-7.50 pp. It's located one park from the beach, on the corner of Prince Albert and Victoria rds., St. Kilda, tel. 54-642. Take a St. Kilda bus from the Princes St. side of the Octagon and get off at the south end of Prince Albert Road.

If you're in search of a full facility hotel, complete with 24-hour cafe, hairdresser, souvenir shop, etc., try the **Southern Cross Hotel** at 118 High St., tel. 770-752; rooms are $120-140 s or d.

FOOD

Light Meals

Before treading the streets in search of a bite to eat, pick up a current copy of *Dunedin Dining Guide,* free from the Visitor Centre. In this you'll find listings of a large variety of restaurants, some with sample menus and prices, and a number of the trendiest entertainment spots. Around the Octagon and along the main streets radiating in all directions are all kinds of cafes, tearooms, sandwich bars, and restaurants—take your choice! For a quick tasty takeaway, head for the **Khmer Satay-away** stand in the Octagon where you can choose from a french roll filled with spicy meat, salad, and peanut sauce or stir fries for only $2-4.50, or try the **Spud McKellers Baked Potatoes** stand.

Potpourri vegetarian restaurant serves a large variety of health foods, fresh salads, light meals, and desserts (from $7 for lunch or dinner) weekdays 0900-2000, Sat. 1000-1400; at 97 Lower Stuart St. (east side of the Octagon). For "the finest coffee in Dunedin" and light meals around $5 pp, go to **Stewart's Coffee House** in the Lower Octagon, Mon. to Thurs. 0900-1700, to 1800 on Fri.—the aroma of freshly roasted coffee beans will set your nose a-tingling! For teas, a delicious smorgasbord lunch (from $8.50 pp), and a variety of baked goodies (from $1.80 a slice), head out to the **Botanic Gardens Restaurant,** open daily 1000-1600.

All kinds of diners serving light meals at cheap prices are situated along Lower Rattray St., and many fish and chips shops sell blue and red cod, lemon fish, orange roughy, or deep-sea perch. **The Dragon Cafe** at no. 175 has a good Chinese menu with dishes from $7 (tasty food and plenty of it), an English menu with main courses ranging from $6-10, and desserts for $3. If you're hankering for something hot and spicy, ask for a bowl of their chile sauce with your main course—it's guaranteed to satisfy that craving! Open Tues. to Sun. from 1130-2100 on Lower Rattray St. (south of the Octagon). For a lunch, light dinner, or Sun. brunch, try **Palms Cafe,** a highly recommended local hangout. Main courses from a blackboard menu (changed daily), such as lamb, chicken, or vegetarian mains and salad, average $12, desserts are $4.50, and they have a large variety of herbal teas. Open Mon. to Fri. 1200-1400 and Wed. to Mon. 1800-2100; at 84 High St., between Rattray and Dowling streets.

Several of the large retail stores have restaurants (closed Sun.), serving teas, snacks, and light meals: **DEKA, Arthur Barnetts,** and **Farmers Trading Co.** on George St., and **D.I.C.** on Princes Street.

More Substantial Meals

For excellent steaks, lamb chops, chicken, or fish at around $8 a plate in comfortable surroundings, head for the **London Lounge** above the Royal Albert Tavern, on the corner of London Rd. and George Street. It's open Mon. to Sat. 1200-2200, closed Sundays. Downstairs in the **Royal Albert Tavern** you can get a counter lunch—steak, lamb chops, eggs and chips, for around $5 during lunch hours only. The Dunedin **Cobb & Co. Restaurant** adjoins the Lawcourts Establishment Hotel at 53-65 Lower Stuart St., open seven days a week from 0730-2300; mains average $13 pp. **Mornington Tavern** in the suburb of Mornington has excellent bistro meals—hamburgers, steak sandwiches, fish, chicken, or steak, ranging from $5-15 (dinners

average $12 pp). Lunch is served Mon. to Sat. 1200-1400, dinners after 1700 (good live bands on the weekends); on Mailer St. (main street of Mornington), a couple of uphill km southwest of the Octagon—take Princes St. south, turn right on High St., then at the end turn right on Mailer St., or catch the Kenmure bus from the Octagon or High Street.

Foxy's Cafe and bar is a popular place to go between 1800-0100 if you feel like a dinner-time splurge and live entertainment (Thurs. to Sat. nights). It has a BYO license, and live bands (find out if you like the band by standing in the street below and listening). Main courses such as steak, curry, and lasagne average $15 a plate, but expect to pay more before you leave (take your credit card)—and people dress up for this one. It's on George St. (in the 300 block on the right side) up a narrow flight of stairs above the Robbie Burns Hotel—hard to find if you're cruising down the street unless you look up at the second level. Other local recommendations include **Governors** on George St., open weekdays 1200-2400 and even later on weekends; **Los Gatos** at 199 Stuart St. (good Mexican food; $9-14 mains); and **Smorgys** on the corner of Bath and Stewart sts. where the food is good value (mains averages $5).

Thyme Out on Stafford St. is always packed with locals enjoying a blackboard menu that features innovative International cuisine. It's only open for dinner (book ahead); mains are $12-20. For great views and fresh seafood, try **Harbour Lights** at McAndrew Bay. Dunedin has plenty more flashy restaurants; ask at the PRO for recommendations. If you're in search of food at an odd hour of the night or early morning, head for the **Southern Cross Hotel Deli-Cafe** on High St., open 24 hours for snacks and teas.

ENTERTAINMENT

The best sources of entertainment info are the *Otago Daily Times* which has a full listing of restaurants and an entertainment guide on the back (daily except Sun.), and the free *Midweek Weekender* (comes out on Wed. and Sun.). Also go to the **Visitor Centre** in the Octagon, and the **NZTP Travel Office** on Princes Street. The free *Dunedin Dining Guide,* available at the Visotor Centre, also lists some of the most fashionable spots around the city for live entertainment.

Live

The **Regent Theatre** in the Octagon presents a wide variety of local and visiting performers, plays, ballet, and grand opera. At the **Town Hall** on Moray Place you can attend performances by three local opera companies, and local acting groups, and various musical events. Go to the **Fortune Theatre** on Upper Moray Place for professional theater—see the back of the daily newspaper for details or call the box office at tel. 778-323. There are also the **Globe, Playhouse,** and **Allen Hall** theaters to check out. At **Castle Theatre** on Castle St. (off Albany St.) you can participate in the always-fun Theatresports for $5 or $7.

Bands playing rock 'n roll, disco, top 20s, etc. can be heard all around Dunedin in the pubs and hotels—just follow your ears on weekends. For listings of all the current band locations, skim the back pages of the *Otago Daily Times* on Fri. and Saturday. At the height of summer, the city springs to life with **Dunedin Festival Week.** All kinds of organized free entertainment and special events happen throughout the city—pick up a free Dunedin Festival newspaper to see what's on and where. All the **movie theaters** show current feature films; see the local newspapers.

Action

The best way to appreciate the beauty of Otago Harbour is by boat, and a three-hour cruise with **Otago Harbour Cruises** on the MV *Monarch* lets you explore the harbor attractions and hear about some of its marinelife, folklore, and history; refreshments provided. Departing from Dunedin Harbour Basin, the cruise costs $22 pp, and special charter fishing, diving, and sightseeing cruises can also be arranged (call the operators direct at tel. 774-215). For cruise timetables and bookings, call the Visitor Centre at tel. 774-176. For some jetboating, white-water rafting, or 4WD safari action, call **Silverpeaks Tours** at Mosgiel 6167.

The **Otago Excursion Train Trust** runs special trips during vacation periods. Pass through the rugged **Taieri Gorge** or around the cliffs near **Purakanui** and **Seacliff** (other destinations on request) in veteran trains with refurbished carriages that have retained their original character. The five-hour afternoon trips or 4½-hour evening trips with stops for photography are adult $35, student or YHA member $25. They also run dinner trips which include a three-course meal; for more info, trip dates, and bookings, call in at the NZTP Travel Office, Regent Theatre, or call 710-476 or 740-399.

Moana Swimming Pool (near Olveston) offers heated olympic-size, diving, and spa pools, waterslides, sun terrace, and restaurant with panoramic views. General admission is $1.20 adult, 60 cents child—and you can stay all day if you want to. Add $3 per adult, $2.50 per child for a half hour of flying down the waterslides. Open daily, hours vary seasonally—call 743-573; located on upper Stewart St., about one km from the city center. If skating grabs your fancy, head for **Skate Inn** at 538 Kaikorai Valley Rd., tel. 30-400. It's open every day for several sessions (check daily paper for hours); daytime admission $2.50 pp, nighttime $3 pp, Sat. night $3.70 pp. Skate hire is $1.30. **Hereweka Pony Treks** operates out of Portobello on the Otago Peninsula, offering one-hour horse-rides daily at 1430, half-day treks (with morning tea) or all-day treks (with lunch) daily at 1000, weather permitting. Call for current rates. Prior arrangement at tel. 780-844 is necessary.

godwits along Otago Harbour

SERVICES

For **emergency** and **telephone services**, see the telephone directory at the p.o. or dial the operator. The central **police station** is on lower High St. (near Stuart St.). Dunedin's **public hospital** is on Great King St., three blocks north of city center.

Most of the inner-city **trading banks** are around the Octagon and along George and Princes sts., generally open Mon. to Fri. 1000-1600. The central city p.o.s are on Princes St. between Water and Liverpool sts., and on George St. on the north side of the Octagon. City **shopping hours** are generally Mon. to Fri. 0900-1700 with many remaining open till 2100 on Friday. **Tumble Inn Laundrette** is open Mon. to Fri. from 0800 and Sat. 1200-1400 for coin-operated washing and drying, or you can have your laundry done for you; at 116 Stuart St., tel. 771-219.

INFORMATION

Dunedin Visitor Centre is on the north side of the Octagon, tel. 774-176/177, open weekdays 0830-1730 and weekends 0900-1700 (extended summer hours). The staff happily provide sightseeing info, city maps, accommodation and restaurant suggestions, hire out ten-speeds, mountain bikes, and mopeds through Little Rainbow Bikes, and book everything but airline reservations. Don't miss the 30-minute big-screen "Images of Otago" slide show and film put on in the center every hour, on the hour, from 1000-2100; adult $4, senior or student $3, child $2, and worth it! It's a great way to discover Dunedin and the Otago region, past and present, and whets the appetite to go off and explore more.

The **NZTP Travel Office,** open Mon. to Fri. 0830-1700, has general Dunedin info, books for many of the main attractions (such as the albatross colony) and local sightseeing tours, and arranges on-going transportation; at 131 Princes St., tel. 740-344. The **Automobile Association** has a general info service, free maps, and emergency breakdown service for members at 450 Moray Place, tel. 775-945. The central **public library** is also on Moray Place.

TRANSPORTATION

Getting There

Getting to Dunedin is easy from just about anywhere. The main coastal Hwy. 1 runs straight through the city center. **InterCity** operates rail service on the *Southerner* between Christchurch, Dunedin, and Invercargill daily except Sun., and bus services from Christchurch, Queenstown, and Wanaka (from Te Anau and Milford Nov. to April only) to Dunedin. **Newmans Coachlines** also operates services from Christchurch to Dunedin. **Dunedin Airport** (south of the city) is serviced by **Air New Zealand, Mount Cook Airlines,** and several other small aircraft companies, and a coach service connects the airport with the city center; $8 OW (go to the Visitor Centre to find out departure points).

Getting Around

Dunedin is a large and hilly city. If you don't have a car or bike (bike hire available through the Dunedin Visitor Centre, tel. 774-176), the best way to get around is by Dunedin City Transport buses which leave from a variety of stops around the Octagon and Princes St.—pick up an *Official Timetables* book (small charge) from the Civic Centre office or info center, or call 772-224 for more information.

Buses to Portobello on Otago Peninsula leave from outside the Air New Zealand office on Princes St., or Center City New World on Cumberland St., Mon. to Fri. (frequently) and on Sat. (less frequently); for times and fares, call 779-238. **Newtons Coachways** provides a variety of sightseeing tours covering Dunedin City and Otago Peninsula. For tour info, call in at the NZTP Travel Office, Visitor Centre, or call Newtons Coachways at tel. 52-199. For a taxi to the airport or a variety of sightseeing tours (up to five people), call **Dunedin Taxis** at tel. 777-777.

Long Distance

By car, the quickest and most interesting route to Wanaka and Queenstown is Hwy. 1 south from Dunedin to Clarksville Junction, then Hwy. 8 to Cromwell (passing good fishing rivers, and many 1860s goldmining sites of **Otago Goldfields Park**—detailed brochure and map available from Dept. of Conservation offices in Dunedin, Alexandra, Wanaka, and Queenstown), then either Hwy. 6 north to Wanaka or Hwy. 6 south to Queenstown; to Invercargill, take Hwy. 1 all the way; to Te Anau and Milford, take Hwy. 1 to Gore, then Hwy. 94 to Lumsden and Manapouri.

By bus, **InterCity** buses run from Dunedin to Wanaka and Queenstown via Roxburgh and Cromwell (the most direct route) or via Ranfurley (Hwy. 85); also to Invercargill, Te Anau, and Milford; the terminal is on Cumberland St. (near High St.). **Newmans Coachlines** operates a bus service north to Christchurch; the terminal is at the lower end of St. Andrew St., tel. 773-476. The **Mount Cook Landline Terminal** is on Great King Street.

By train, the **railway station** is at the bottom end of Stuart St.—the main foyer booking office is open 0900-1715; the *Southerner* connects Christchurch, Dunedin, and Invercargill daily except Sunday.

By air, **Dunedin Airport** is about 20 km south of city center. Get there via **Ritchies Coach Lines,** departing from the Southern Cross Hotel at 118 High St. and from the Octagon. It takes about 40 minutes OW; adult $8 pp, child $4. For departure times from the city, call 779-238; the bus departs the airport 15 minutes after each Air New Zealand arrival. **Air New Zealand** flies out of Dunedin to all major destinations in the country, **Ansett** flies to Christchurch and Auckland; **Mount Cook Airlines** flies to Alexandra and Queenstown. For info and reservations, contact Air New Zealand in John Wickliffe House, The Exchange, tel. 775-769/749.

SOUTHWEST

WANAKA

Encircled by mountains and nestled at the southern end of the crystal-clear, bright-blue waters of Lake Wanaka, this small resort town has the perfect combination of year-round wonderful weather and beautiful scenery. Initially developed to service the goldmining industry of the Cardrona and vicinity, Wanaka (a corruption of the Maori word "Oanaka," the name of a chief who went there to fish) became a commercial center for surrounding farms when the color ran out. Nowadays it's also a recreational center with a large variety of outdoor pursuits in both summer and winter.

If kicking back in the sunshine on a lakeshore beach or trying a new sport is your definition of fun, there's lots to do here in the great outdoors department. Though Wanaka is a smaller, more sedate version of tourist-oriented Queenstown (a two-hour drive southwest), hordes of vacationing New Zealanders and a good number of tourists are attracted to Wanaka in summer for the beaches, boating, waterskiing, trout fishing, and hiking and mountaineering in nearby Mt. Aspiring National Park (the town is packed in Dec. and Jan.). In winter they come to ice-skate on Diamond Lake, ski down the groomed slopes of Treble Cone or Cardrona, or heli-ski in the spectacular Harris Mountains to the southwest. No shortage of action here!

THINGS TO DO

A Gigantic Puzzle
The first place you notice as you approach Wanaka on the main highway is **The Greatest Maze On Earth and Puzzle Centre,** two

km from town. Want to tell someone to "get lost?!" Do it subtly by stopping at this popular local attraction—a 1.5-km, three-dimensional maze of wooden passages and under- and overbridges that can tease you from 30 minutes to several hours. At the adjoining puzzle center, all kinds of puzzles are demonstrated and you're encouraged to try them out yourself (and of course, buy them). Mini-golf, croquet, and Devonshire teas round off the entertainment. Open daily from 0830-1730 (later in summer), admission to the maze is $4.20 adult, $2.10 child; tel. 7489.

On The Lake

Take a short stroll along the lakefront to shop for all the ways you can view the lake: cruise boats, high-speed hovercraft, and paraflights high above the lake surface are just a few. Several options are offered by **Wanaka Lake Services** aboard the MV *Ena-De,* ranging from a one-hour scenic cruise for $14 pp to a four-hour cruise to Pigeon Island. (including a 1½-hour stop on the island) for $25 pp (summer only). They also hire fast runabouts, outboard dinghies, aquabikes, rowboats, and canoes, and have bicycles and tandems for hire. For more info, call 7495 (24 hours). The exciting **Wanaka Hovercraft** departs from the lakeside hoverpad at 1030 and 1500 daily (double-check times) on a one-hour high-speed cruise of the lake for $45 pp, or 15-minute economy voyages that depart regularly from 0830-1700 for $15 pp. Call 7495 for more info, to pre-book voyages (not necessary), or to get a free minibus lift to the hoverpad.

Another stimulating way to enjoy the lake *and* the Clutha River is onboard the ***Riverjet*** with always-entertaining operator Grant Edgar. Ask him to do a "Hamilton Spin!" The fun 50-minute trip (minimum four) departs daily at 1100, 1330, and 1500, and on demand; a steal of a deal for only $35 pp. For another adrenalin rush (in summer), consider a paraflight on the ***Aspiring Fun Jet*** from the waterfront. Attached to a parachute you're towed by a fast jetboat, soaring high above the lake, then splash-landing in the water; $24 pp—they claim anyone from age five to 84 can do it—and have! For bookings call 8647. Guided **trout fishing** is also offered by Wanaka Lake Services. Troll or fly-fish for the big one with friendly guide Paul Miller for $55 an hour, $200 per half-day, or $350 per full day.

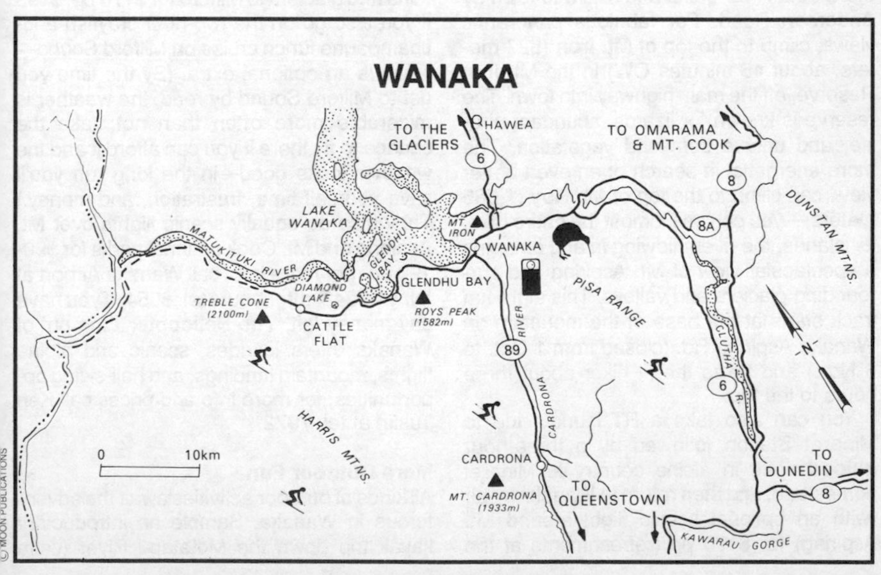

You'll see plenty of lizards in Mt. Iron Reserve.

Short Walks And Hikes

A variety of tracks and walkways around town range from a short stroll near the THC Hotel along **Bullock Creek** (the hatchery stream) to a 30-minute (OW) walk to **Waterfall Creek** (southwest shore of the lake) starting on the left side of Roys Bay and following the shoreline around to the creek. **Eely Point Walk** starts just past the jetty and follows the shoreline around the right side of the lake to Eely Point (20 minutes OW)—for a longer walk (a couple of hours) continue around the lake to the Clutha River outlet and return to town by Anderson Road. For fabulous panoramic views, climb to the top of **Mt. Iron** (527 meters, about 45 minutes OW) in the Mt. Iron Reserve, off the main highway into town. The reserve is known for lizards, abundant birdlife, and unique semi-arid vegetation. The more energetic, in search of an even better view, can climb to the top of **Mt. Roy** (1,585 meters)—you can see almost the entire lake, its islands, the rivers flowing in and out, plus a spectacular view of Mt. Aspiring and surrounding glaciers and valleys. This eight-km track starts at the base of the mountain on Wanaka Aspiring Rd. (closed from 1 Oct. to 6 Nov.) and takes the fit hiker about three hours to the top.

You can also take a RT launch ride to Minaret Station followed by a three-hour **guided walk** in alpine country to Minaret homestead, and then return to Wanaka by air (with an optional scenic flight around Mt. Aspiring) for $170 pp (refreshments at the homestead included). Book at tel. 7495. For long hikes through spectacular scenery or some serious climbing and mountaineering, head for **Mt. Aspiring National Park.** Access is at the end of Wanaka Aspiring Rd. (sealed at first, then gravel)—a minibus makes the 100-km RT from Wanaka to Raspberry Flat in the West Matukituki River Valley several days a week during summer and daily during the peak Christmas period. The road ends on the fringe of the Park; to Matukituki Station is $8, Aspiring Station $10, Cameron Flat $12, road end $15 pp (or $80 for one to six people). A scenic return trip is $20. For more details call Matuki Services, 15 Norman Terrace, tel. 7135. Before heading into the Park backcountry, call in at **Park HQ** in Wanaka for detailed maps and information (see "Information" below, and "Mt. Aspiring National Park," p. 476).

From The Air

Aspiring Air based at Wanaka Airport (about 10 km east of town) provides some reasonably priced flights, including short scenic flights over the local area for $45 pp and a spectacular flight over snow-capped mountains and glaciers to Milford for $170 pp, $195 if you also go on the two-hour crayfish-and-champagne lunch cruise on Milford Sound—lunch is an optional extra. (By the time you get to Milford Sound by road, the weather is miserable more often than not; take the chance to fly there if you can afford it and the weather looks good—in the long run you'll save yourself time, frustration, and money.) They also do equally scenic flights over Mt. Aspiring and Mt. Cook national parks for $90-190 pp. For more info, call Wanaka Airport at tel. 44-7943, after hours tel. 8054. If you have any money left, **The Helicopter Line** out of Wanaka offers joyrides, scenic and alpine flights, mountain landings, and heli-skiing opportunities; for more info and prices call Ken Tustin at tel. 7972.

More Outdoor Fun

All kinds of outdoor activities await the adventurous in Wanaka. Sample an introductory kayak trip down the Motatapu River (calm water and rapids), or go for a more challenging kayak trip down the Hawea or Matukituki rivers—previous kayaking experience required (tel. 7564). **Explorer Tours Wanaka** provides opportunities to try all sorts of guided outdoor adventures—horse trekking (a four-hour trip includes two hours of riding and a picnic lunch or evening BBQ; adult $49, child $35), a visit to Criffel Deer Park (adult $35, child $25), high country farm tours (from adult $39-55, child $29-40), flightseeing (from adult $36, child $25), "wilderness adventures" which include a scenic flight, bush walk, and jetboat ride ($195 pp), and on-demand transportation to Cardrona Ski Area. For arrangements call 8130 or book through Wanaka Lake Services at tel. 7495.

Fishing

Before you try to find your own special fishing spot, pick up the excellent $2 guide to about 20 fishing spots on the Upper Clutha River—it covers the area from the outlet to the Lindis River junction, with maps and details on how to get there; put out by the Upper Clutha Angling Club, it will save you time. Lakes Wanaka and Hawea and tributaries boast great rainbow and brown trout fishing, plus landlocked quinnat salmon. Trout and salmon are also abundant in the Clutha and Hawea rivers (fishability and ease of access to the Hawea River depends on the manipulation of water levels for hydroelectricity), Makarora, Wilkin, Young, Hunter, Matukituki, Motatapu, and Lindis rivers, and Timaru Creek. The maximum bag is three fish per day from any river flowing into lakes Hawea, Wanaka, and Wakatipu, and a southern lakes fishing license is required, available at sporting goods stores and at Wanaka Lake Services on the waterfront.

Wanaka Fishing Safaris fish the Wanaka, Hawea, Makarora, and Clutha areas in river or lake boats, tel. 7236. If you want to hire one of "Wanaka's longest established professional fishing guides" with a six-meter launch, wet and dry fly, spinning, and trolling gear supplied, call Paul Miller or Mark Napper at tel. 7495 or 8130.

SKIING

Skifields

Two commercial skifields lie within easy distance of Wanaka—Treble Cone Ski Area (20 km southwest) off Wanaka Aspiring Rd., and Cardrona Ski Area (33 km south) off Hwy. 89. Seventy-four-hectare **Treble Cone Ski Area** in Mount Aspiring National Park has open uncrowded slopes to suit beginner to expert (best for intermediate to advanced), basins of powder and groomed slopes, tremendous views, and a warm sunny season generally lasting from mid-June to the end of Sept. (peak skiing mid-July to mid-Sept.). You'll find chairlifts, T-bars, and learners' lifts, on-field ski hire, ski school and professional ski patrol, a good cafe, access by private (road toll $5) or public transportation (daily at 0830 from the Ski Centre in Wanaka, or from the foot of the toll road). Open daily from 0900-1600; half-day adult $30, child $15; full-day adult $40, child $20; ski hire adult $25, child $15. Heli-skiing is also available on the mountain through Alpine Helicopters. For more info call the skifield office at tel. 7443, or drop by the Ski Centre on Ardmore St. (opposite the p.o.) in Wanaka, tel. 7401.

Cardrona Ski Area is on the southeast slopes of Mt. Cardrona (higher than Treble Cone). Opened in 1980, it has modern facilities, wide and varied terrain of intermediate steepness (three basins and a vertical skiing drop of 390 meters—during peak season 665 meters), a learners' area, chairlifts (two quad, one double), rope tows, learners' grip tows, hut, two cafeterias, and a ski school with 35 international instructors. The base facilities are halfway up the skifield at car park level. The season is from late June to Oct., with peak skiing from July to Sept.; half-day adult $28, child $13; full day adult $40, child $20; ski hire adult $22, child $15. Regular scheduled bus services run from Wanaka, Queenstown, and the toll gate (toll $8). For more info on the ski area call 7341 or 7411. The Pisa Range opposite offers opportunities for superb ski touring or heli-skiing.

Heli-skiing

For an unforgettable experience, try guided backcountry heli-skiing in the Harris, Richardson, and Buchanan mountains with **Harris Mountains Heliskiing.** Experienced guides cater to small groups of skiers of all abilities—but strong intermediate skiers experienced in all snow types get the most out of it. Heli-skiing adventures start at $340 pp for four scenic heli-flights, three runs, and guide service. They also do a range of alpine ski-touring trips Sept. to Nov., Nordic cross-country trips, and sponsor the **New Zealand Powder 8's Contest** held annually (around Aug./Sept.) in the Harris Mountains—the premier powder-skiing event in the Southern Hemisphere. Contact Paul Scaife or the Wanaka Booking Centre at tel. 7277. Or write for the current *Harris Mountains Hand Book* (Wanaka Booking Centre, P.O. Box 177, Wanaka) which contains all the info you need, prices, and a handy "ability questionnaire" which lets you know if you've got what it takes!

Alpine Helicopters operates heli-skiing trips, heli-lifts, and heli-taxis in the Southern Lakes ski region, covering Wanaka's Treble Cone and Cardrona skifields, and Queenstown's Coronet Peak Skifield; call Wanaka 7221 or Queenstown 1452.

General Skiing Information

The **Ski Centre** on Ardmore St., tel. 7401, opposite the p.o. is the local ski info center, also offering ski hire and repairs. For daily snow reports listen to Otago Radio, Otago Radio Central, and 4ZB, and both TV channels; the office issues written reports as soon as conditions are assessed accurately. Or call Treble Cone or Cardrona ski areas direct.

ACCOMMODATION

Hostel

Wanaka YHA Hostel has the usual facilities, a drying room, and luggage storage available, and the manager has mountain bikes for hire. Only a five-minute walk from the lake, this hostel is popular year-round; $12 pp. At 181 Upton St., tel. 7405; from the main highway into town, veer left on Brownston St., then left on MacDougal St. and right on Upton Street.

Motor Camps

The closest motor camp to town is **Wanaka Motor Park,** 1.2 km from the post office. It has good showers, a kitchen, TV room, laundry facilities and a drying room, a spa, and a boat and caravan park; tentsites $6.60 pp, caravan sites $7 pp, backpacker share cabins from $9 pp (Sept. to mid-Dec., and Feb. to the end of June), cabins from $25 s or d, tourist flats $48 s or d. Reservations are essential for all sites and cabins from Dec. 20

Swoosh down Twin Falls run with an experienced Harris Mts. Heli-skiing guide.

Wanaka Motor Inn

to mid-Jan., and on weekends during the ski season for cabins. Located on Brownston St., tel. 7883; office hours 0800-2100. The next closest is **Pleasant Lodge Holiday Park,** three km west of town. TV and game room, swimming pool, indoor spa, BBQ facilities, and shop; tent and caravan sites $12 d, cabins from $17 d. Located on Mt. Aspiring Rd., tel. 7360. **Penrith Park** is four km from town, on the lakeshore at Beacon Point; tentsites $12 d, caravan sites $14 d, cabins from $24, tourist flats $40-48, lodge rooms from $30 s or d. On Beacon Point Rd. (off Lakeside Rd. heading for the Clutha outlet), tel. 7009.

If you have your own transportation and don't mind being 13 km out of town, head for the popular **Glendhu Bay Camp** on the lakeside at beautiful Glendhu Bay, renowned for magnificent views of Mt. Aspiring and attracting large numbers of swimmers, water-skiers, and boaters. Communal facilities (coin-operated showers), large kitchen, drying room, shop selling all the basics, and canoe rental from $3 an hour; tentsites $5.50 pp, caravan sites $6 pp, cabins from $24 s or d. Reservations necessary over Christmas. On Treble Cone Rd., tel. 7243.

Lodges, Guesthouses, And Inns

McThriftys, 51 Brownston St., has bunks with shared bath and kitchen, dining room and TV room; $39 s or d. At **Brook Vale Manor Motel** just down the road, studio units (one double bed and one single bed with separate bath and kitchen) are $58 per night, one-bedroom units are $60 per night; kitchen facilities, color TV, spa pool, and guest laundry; at 35 Brownston St., tel. 8333.

Several private guesthouses around town provide B&B accommodation from $25 pp—ask at the Booking Centre for all the current listings and rates. At **Creekside Bed and Breakfast** you get a self-contained room with its own entrance (at the back of the owners' house), TV, private bathroom, and cooking facilities; rates are $25 s, $30 s with breakfast, $40 d, $50 d with breakfast, and off-season rates are also available; at 84 Helwick St., tel. 7834. At **Country Lane Bed and Breakfast** the room rate of $33 s, $55 d or twin includes breakfast; 28 Dungarvon St., tel. 8040. Sue and Dick Williman, friendly owners of **Rippon Lea,** provide you with a large room, bathroom, tea- and coffee-making facilities, and a Continental breakfast for $25 pp (stay six nights and the seventh is free)—they're also a fund of info on Mt. Aspiring National Park, and run the Matuki Bus Service from Wanaka to the park.

Wanaka Motor Inn on Mt. Aspiring Rd., tel. 8216, has bright, spacious, timber rooms with private bath, balcony, tea- and coffee-making facilities, and a toaster. Some have a spa bath, some have lake and mountain views.

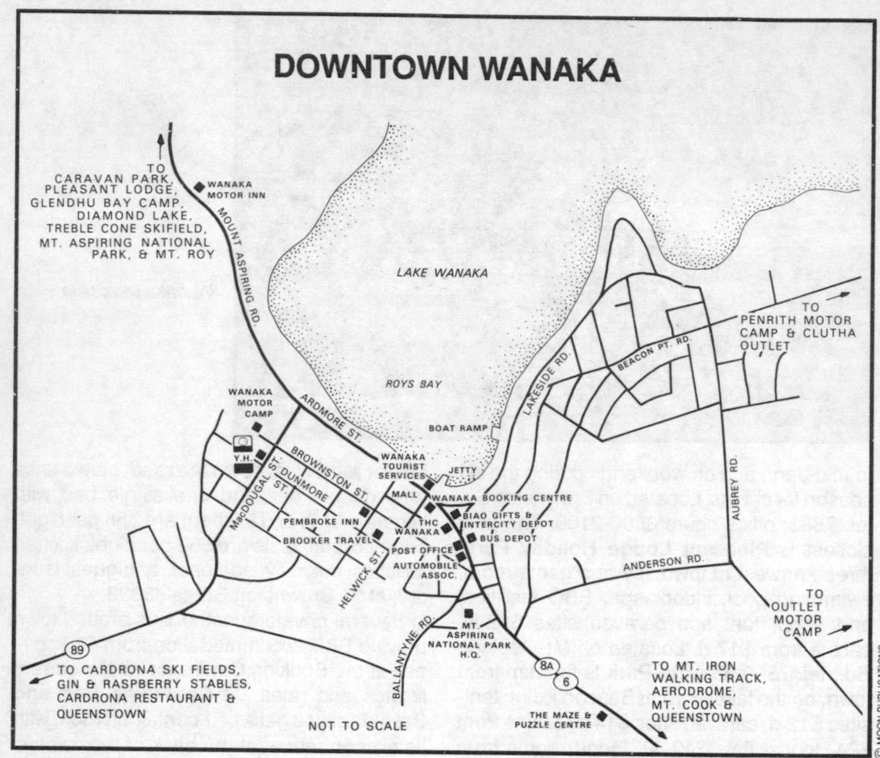

There's also laundry facilities, and a good in-house restaurant offering three-course meals for $22 pp (reservations necessary during peak periods); a studio ranges from $70-88 d, a superior unit from $101-127 (depending on the season). **Pembroke Inn** has rooms with private facilities and family units, and all meals ($10.50-13) are available in the adjacent restaurant; from $54 s, $65 d (rates vary season to season). At 94 Brownston St., tel. 7296.

FOOD AND ENTERTAINMENT

Wanaka is not renowned for its variety of budget restaurants or lively entertainment—if you're looking for these, head two hours south to Queenstown. However, there are enough choices to keep most visitors happy.

Pembroke Village Mall off Ardmore St. has several food shops and a good cafe—**The Vege Pot** sells fresh fruit and vegies at good prices, the **Dough Bin** has a large variety of delicious baked goods, and **Judy's Coffee Shop** has tasty tearoom fare, breakfast from $5, and lunch specials for $6. **The Snack Shack** caters to fast-food lovers. If you're in the mood for sandwiches, pies, and pastries, **Kingsway Tearooms** on Helwick St. has a large selection. **Aspiring Takeaways** serves hamburgers every day from 0800-2100, and sells groceries and campers' provisions.

First Cafe on Ardmore St. is one of the places to go for casual meals varying in price from $3.50 for soup to $15 for a main, open 1800-2200. **Freshwater Cafe** is particularly popular. The dishes are delectable, but the servings are small. Expect to pay around $7.50-12.50 for a main, plus more for inevitable extras, and see if you can resist the specialty desserts! It's in Pembroke Mall; open from 1100, dinner from 1830-2100. For more substantial dishes ($18-24), head for **Ripples Restaurant,** a local favorite with a BYO license. Also in the Mall, it's open 1830-2200, tel. 7413. Delicious Greek, Indian, and Mexican dishes are served at **Te Kano Cafe** at 63 Brownston St., tel. 7208. At dinner (from 1830) appetizers start at $5, mains are all $16 each, and desserts average $5. It's open until "everyone finally leaves" (late!), and has a BYO license.

Capriccio is another local favorite for Italian cuisine and a friendly casual atmosphere, however you don't have to be a pasta appreciater to enjoy this restaurant—they also whip up chicken, pork, steak, lamb, and seafood dishes (mains from $15-21.50), and desserts with an Italian flavor ($6.25-11). It's fully licensed, open from 1800; above the BNZ on Ardmore St., tel. 8579. The **Storehouse Restaurant** next to Wanaka Hotel is known for its good, inexpensive, bistro meals. **Pembroke Inn** on Brownston St. has a licensed restaurant with both a la carte and "travelers menu" meals ($12-26 a plate). Or if you feel like splurging ($12-30), head for the Pembroke Room in the **THC Wanaka Hotel** on Ardmore St. (also has several bars). The THC bistro is highly recommended by locals, and very reasonable at only $12.50 pp.

If you have your own transportation, drive 25 km south along Highway 89 to the **Cardrona Restaurant** in Cardrona. It used to be the old Cardrona Hotel, built in the mid-1860s during the Otago goldrush. The rustic, slightly decrepit exterior has been deliberately left looking that way, but the interior has been beautifully restored. Have a drink at the original brass bar, eat inside surrounded by items from the goldrush days, or enjoy your meal outside in the garden. Main courses are $18, desserts are $5. Open Tues. to Sat. for dinner, call 8153 for reservations; located on Hwy. 89, the most direct route to Queenstown.

For entertainment, see if there's anything happening at the **Mt. Aspiring National Park HQ** (talks, slides, guided walks, etc.), or if you're feeling energetic, have a game of tennis on Warren St., squash on Upton St., or a round of golf at the 18-hole **Wanaka Golf Club** (visitors welcome). Otherwise you may have to resort to bars for entertainment.

OTHER PRACTICALITIES

Shopping And Services

If you want to take home some high-quality N.Z. wool products and have been shopping around, look no further! The small **Perendale Wool Shop** on Helwick St. (opposite the police station) has an enormous selection of sweaters ($80-180), wool booties, scarves, and pillow covers, sheepskin booties, and sheepskin or suede coats and hats. Everything is generally less expensive than you'd find elsewhere—a buyer's delight! They also ship anywhere in the world.

Local **banks** are open Mon. to Fri. from 0900-1630; **petrol stations** are open every day from 0800-1900; the **pharmacy** on Helwick St. is open seven days from 0830-2000. **Wanaka P.O.** is on Ardmore St., open weekdays regular hours. For **police** call 7272; to report a **fire** or get an **ambulance** call 111; for a **doctor** call 7811.

Information

Wanaka Tourist Services at the lakefront is the first place to go for info on the local scene, on-the-lake activities, and bookings, and the entertaining operators have a wide assortment of brochures and pamphlets covering everything you need to know to enjoy your stay in Wanaka; open daily. **Wanaka Booking Centre** on Ardmore St. opposite the waterfront is another source of info on all the local attractions, skifields, heli-skiing, and accommodations. Pick up a free *Wanaka & Districts* info sheet and map, and all the brochures and pamphlets you can carry. They book local (and Queenstown) attractions, and accommodations, tel. 7277; open daily 0900-1800, in Dec., Jan., July, and Aug. 0800-2000. **Mt. Aspiring National Park HQ** on the corner of Ballantyne and Main (Ardmore St.) is open daily 0800-1700 from mid-Dec. to mid-

Jan., on weekdays only from 0800-1700 the rest of the year. Inside are all kinds of displays on the Park, local geomorphology, geology, vegetation, mounted birds, and history, and an audiovisual on birdlife. Buy a detailed map, collect brochures, and pick the staff's brains before you head for the Park. Also leave your intentions and date of return, and sign out when you get back. For ski info, see "Skiing" above.

Transportation

Getting to and from Wanaka is easy by car or bus, and hitchhiking isn't too bad as there's a high volume of traffic. From the West Coast take Hwy. 6 south via Haast Pass; from Queenstown, Hwy. 6 north or Hwy. 89 (the more direct and scenic gravel route over the Crown Range); from Dunedin, Hwy. 1 south then Hwy. 8 east.

The **InterCity bus depot** is on Ardmore St. by Biao Gifts, tel. 7885. **InterCity** runs bus services Mon. to Fri. (and Sat. during the peak vacation period) from Wanaka to Franz Josef and Fox Glacier, Queenstown, Dunedin, Mount Cook, and Christchurch. **Mount Cook Landline** also operates services to Queenstown ($20 OW), Dunedin ($39 OW), Mt. Cook ($41 OW), and Christchurch ($63 OW); book through Brooker Travel on Dunmore St. (also the local agent for Air New Zealand, Mt. Cook Airline, Ansett, Pacifica Air, Aspiring Air, and Avis and Thrifty rental cars).

To get to Mount Aspiring National Park from Wanaka, contact Matuki Services, 15 Norman Terrace, at tel. 7135. Their minibus service runs to Raspberry Flat in the West Matukituki River Valley, leaving for the 100-km RT several days a week during summer and daily during the peak Christmas period. The road ends on the fringe of the Park; to Matukituki Station is $8, Aspiring Station $10, Cameron Flat $12, road end $15 pp (or $80 for up to six people). A scenic return trip is $20. Book through the Wanaka Booking Centre on Ardmore St., tel. 7277.

MOUNT ASPIRING NATIONAL PARK

INTRODUCTION

The Land

Second largest national park in N.Z. at 161 km long and 32 km wide, it covers 287,311 hectares of the southern end of the Main Divide. In the center of this alpine park, spectacular **Mount Aspiring** (3,027 meters), a pyramid-shaped peak of snow and ice that the Maori called *Tititea* or "Upright Glistening Mountain" towers above a sea of mighty peaks and more than 50 named glaciers that they called *Titiraurangi* or "Land of Many Peaks Piercing the Clouds." Along the northern boundary are Mt. Brewster and the roaring blue-green Haast River, along the south boundary the Hollyford Valley and Fiordland National Park. Three main valleys allow easy access into the Park on foot (see below). This is an area of rugged snow-capped mountains, glaciers, and hanging valleys, with wide rushing rivers and open grassy flats—a wild and untouched paradise for backcountry hikers, mountaineers, climbers, photographers, and bird lovers.

Climate

Conditions in the mountains change quickly—this area's unpredictable weather is predictable! The drier eastern side of the Park generally receives about 1,270 mm of rain, the western side about 5,080 mm, and sudden snow storms can bring snow down to low levels at any time of year (even mid-summer). Savage storms can suddenly occur—no joking matter when you can't get out of their way in a hurry (and no one else can get in). As usual, be prepared for all kinds of weather when you're in backcountry areas, and take extra food in case you have to wait out a storm. Ask staff at the ranger stations in Makarora and Glenorchy or Park HQ in Wanaka about the seasonal weather in each region, and get a current weather forecast.

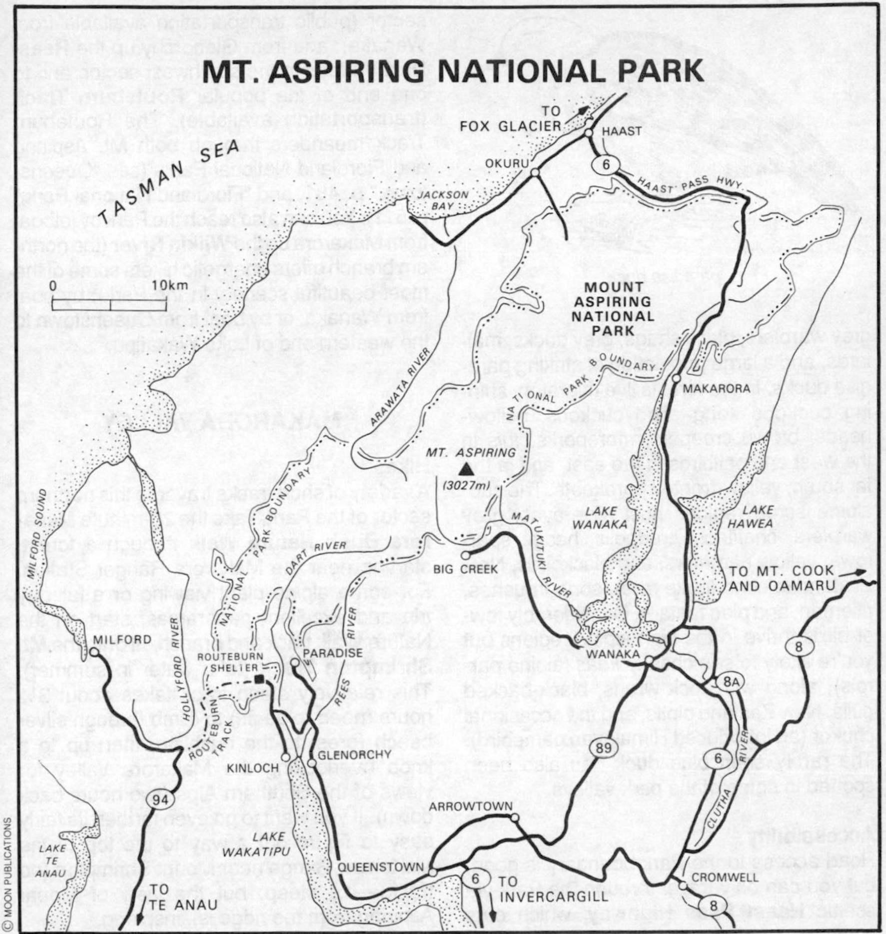

Flora And Fauna

Vegetation varies from dense forest (predominantly silver beech with *rimu, matai, miro,* and *kahikatea* at lower levels on the wetter side west of the Divide and red and mountain beech in the south), to alpine scrublands (snow totara, alpine daisies, heaths, hebes, celery pine, Great Mountain buttercups, mountain flax) and tussock grasslands. Introduced deer, chamois, goats, and hares have destroyed much of the natural vegetation and many of the beautiful alpine plants, but some can still be found on steep bluffs and isolated ridges. Since deer numbers have been greatly reduced by helicopter hunting, the alpine flora has been regenerating.

The Park is known for its abundant birdlife. On the valley floors are riverbed inhabitants such as migratory black-backed and black-billed gulls, black-fronted terns, South Island pied oystercatchers, banded dotterels, and spur-winged plovers. You also see skylarks, pipits, song thrushes, blackbirds, chaffinchs, redpolls, yellow hammers, and silvereye,

paradise duck

grey warblers, black shags, grey ducks, mallards, and a large population of striking paradise ducks. In the forests live migratory shining cuckoos, long-tailed cuckoos, yellowheads, brown creepers, moreporks, *tuis* in the west and bellbirds in the east, and in the far south, yellow-fronted parakeets. The subalpine scrub regions host silvereyes, grey warblers, chaffinchs, redpolls, hedge sparrows, yellow hammers, and blackbirds, New Zealand falcons (quite rare), song thrushes, riflemen, and pied fantails. Considerably fewer birds thrive in the high alpine regions but you're likely to see cheeky *keas* (alpine parrots), along with rock wrens, black-backed gulls, New Zealand pipits, and the occasional chukor (an introduced Himalayan gamebird). The rarely seen blue duck has also been spotted in some of the park valleys.

Accessibility

Road access to the Park boundary is good, but you can only travel *through* the Park via scenic **Haast Pass Highway,** which cuts across a small section in the northeast to Makarora and one of the ranger stations (see p. 435). To take best advantage of the scenery and walking tracks here, you really need your own transportation.

The other three access roads are mostly unsealed: from the Haast-Jackson Bay Highway (south of Haast) up the Arawata and Waiatoto Valleys to the remote northwest boundary (you need to be well equipped, experienced in river crossings, and have your own transportation); from Wanaka up the scenic **Matukituki Valley** to the central east sector (public transportation available from Wanaka); and from Glenorchy up the **Rees-Dart Valleys** in the southwest sector, and to one end of the popular **Routeburn Track** (transportation available). The Routeburn Track meanders through both Mt. Aspiring and Fiordland National Parks (see "Queenstown," p. 481, and "Fiordland National Park," p. 511). You can also reach the Park by jetboat from Makarora up the **Wilkin River** (the northern branch offers energetic hikers some of the most beautiful scenery in the Park), by boat from Wanaka, or by boat from Queenstown to the western end of Lake Wakatipu.

MAKARORA VALLEY

Hikes

A variety of short tracks traverse this northern sector of the Park. Take the 20-minute **Makarora Bush Nature Walk** through a forest, starting near the Makarora Ranger Station. For some alpine plant viewing or a full-day trip and excellent panoramas, start on the Nature Walk track and branch off onto the **Mt. Shrimpton Track** (take water in summer). This relatively steep track takes about 3½ hours (need to be fit!) to climb through silver beech forest to the bushline, then up to a knob overlooking the Makarora Valley for views of the Southern Alps (two hours back down). If you want to go even farther, its fairly easy to figure out a way to the top of the McKerrow Range near Mount Shrimpton (no track)—it's steep, but the view of Mount Aspiring from the ridge is...inspiring.

The one-hour (RT) **Cameron Creek Gorge** track starts at the Cameron Flat Picnic area (11 km north of Makarora) and leads to a spectacular waterfall. Longer hiking tracks lead along the Blue, Young, and Wilkin rivers (brochures at the ranger station) with huts (charge) at regular intervals. To get to the **Blue River Access** swingbridge, take the short 15-minute track from the carpark on the main road (nine km north of Makarora) down to the Makarora River; from here a 1½-hour walk takes you to the first open river flats. If you prefer a shorter walk, drop directly down from the swingbridge to the riverbed where the Blue River emerges from a gorge to form the beautiful deep **Blue Pool** (good trout fishing).

Another popular walk is on the 1½-hour (OW) **Bridle Track** from the top of Haast Pass to Davis Flat, following sections of the old Bridle Track, the original link between Otago and Westland. The Makarora, Wilkin, and Young rivers have good brown and rainbow trout fishing, and red deer and chamois are hunted within the Makarora catchments. For exciting jetboat trips up the Wilkin River or spectacular scenic flights, drop by the Haast Pass Tourist Service in Makarora for more details.

Accommodation And Food

Stay at the **Haast Pass Tourist Service** complex on the main highway, Makarora, tel. 33-U Wanaka. It has a swimming pool, tearooms, deerpark, shop, petrol, and postal facilities, jetboat rides and scenic flights available, along with tent and caravan sites, cabins, and motel rooms (see Haast Pass, p. 436).

Information

Get Park maps and info from the **Makarora Ranger Station,** off the main highway, tel. 33-S Wanaka; open weekdays 0800-1700, and weekends during summer.

MATUKITUKI VALLEY

Hikes

Wanaka Aspiring Rd. leads from Wanaka past Glendhu Bay (stunning views of the south face of Mt. Aspiring) for 47 km to **Cameron Flat**—the start of a trail up the east branch of the Matukituki River to Glacier Burn, Junction Flat, and Aspiring Flats (be careful crossing the east branch). The easy two-hour (OW) **Glacier Burn Walk** starts at the flats and climbs through beech forests to a saddle with excellent views of peaks and hanging glaciers, and at the head of the valley are impressive bluffs, waterfalls, and lots of birdlife. The two- to three-hour **East Matukituki to Junction Flat Walk** starts at Mt. Aspiring Station, enters the forest, and follows the river to Junction Flat where the Kitchener Stream joins the Matukituki (good trout fishing).

Another 6.5 km along the road beyond Cameron Flat following the west branch of the Matukituki River, you come to the carpark at **Big Creek** and the start of a trail—note that the road from Cameron Creek should only be attempted by car in dry weather as it can quickly flood by rain or river. The **West Matukituki to Aspiring Hut Walk** is an easy 2½-hour (OW) hike, leading up the valley along river flats (a popular river-bird habitat), crossing creeks on the way to Aspiring Hut. Using the hut as a base you can also do many scenic day hikes in this area. Easy and more difficult walks are possible beyond Aspiring Hut (keep an eye on the weather); several climbing routes of varying difficulty beyond Pearl Flat require proper equipment and experience. For a beautiful alpine valley hike and outstanding scenery at the end, sidetrack off the Matukituki Valley Track on the **Rob Roy Stream Walk.** Cross the Matukituki River on the swingbridge, follow the track up past the gorge at the stream mouth and through lush fern-filled forest to the valley head where you can see the south face of Rob Roy (2,606 meters) and its glacier, sheer bluffs, and waterfalls; two to three hours OW.

Accommodation And Food

Park huts (charge) are located along some hiking tracks. The nearest town is Wanaka, with lots of beds, board, and all the regular services (see p. 472).

Information And Transportation

Info on this central sector of the Park is available at **Park HQ** on the corner of Ballantyne and Main, Wanaka, tel. (02943) 7660. In summer, talks are held in the evenings—ask for the current schedule, and see the short, interesting audiovisual on the Park. To get up the Matukituki Valley from Wanaka, take your own transportation to Big Creek carpark, or catch the Matuki Services' minibus to Raspberry Flat that leaves Wanaka several days a week during summer, daily during the peak Christmas period. To get to Matukituki Station is $8 pp, to Aspiring Station $10, Cameron Flat $12, Road End $15, or take a scenic return trip for $20. For the current schedule, call in at the Wanaka Booking Centre on Ardmore St., tel. 7277, or call Matuki Services, 15 Norman Terrace, at tel. 7135.

DART AND REES VALLEYS

Hikes

The Dart and Rees valleys in the south sector of Mount Aspiring National Park provide easy to difficult hikes. The most popular longer hikes in the south sector are the two-day **Rees Valley to Dart Hut** and **Dart Valley to Dart Hut** tracks (many combine the two tracks to make a good RT through forest and open country with spectacular mountain and valley views), and the well-known three-day **Routeburn Track** which passes through some of the most spectacular scenery in both Mt. Aspiring and Fiordland National Parks (inaccessible in winter; see "Queenstown," p. 481, and "Fiordland National Park," p. 511).

Accommodation And Food

Park huts (charge) are found at regular intervals along hiking tracks. The small town of Glenorchy is the nearest place to the Park—with a grocery shop, p.o., garage, ranger station, and motor camp, lodge, and hotel (it has a good restaurant). For food, either eat at the hotel or cook your own. Queenstown (see p. 496) is about 53 km from Glenorchy.

Information

The Glenorchy Ranger Station is open weekdays 0800-1700, tel. Glenorchy (0294) 29937. In summer, guided walks depart from the Glenorchy Information Centre, and evening talks are held in the Centre at 2000—ask for the current schedule. The next closest info center is in Queenstown. For invaluable hiking and climbing info, pick up a copy of *Moir's Guide Book (Northern Section)* published by the N.Z. Alpine Club.

TRANSPORTATION

To get to the Park by car, take Glenorchy Rd. from Queenstown to Glenorchy, then Paradise Road. If you want to hike up the Rees Valley, turn right on Rees Valley Rd. and follow it to the end; to hike up the Dart Valley, take Paradise Rd. over Rees River, turn right, and follow it to the end. To get into the Park and the start of the Routeburn Track, take Paradise Rd. over the Rees River, turn left, continue along the Hillocks Rd., cross the Dart River, turn right on Routeburn Rd. and follow it to the end.

Buses service the Routeburn Track from Queenstown, passing the Rees and Dart Valley turnoffs every Mon. and Fri. from April to mid-Nov. and almost every day during summer. (The Routeburn Track is inaccessible in winter.) The Dart Valley to Paradise is also serviced by buses. From the head of the lake, bus service runs down the western side of Lake Wakatipu to Kinloch and the Greenstone Valley where the popular Caples and Greenstone hiking tracks start (see p. 492). Call in at any of the many booking centers in Queenstown to find out which bus companies are currently servicing the tracks (it's very competetive—companies come and go), and see the "Queenstown" chapter for more transportation info. **Taxis** also service the various tracks—from Glenorchy Motor Camp, tel. (0294) 29939, from Glenorchy Motors, tel. (0294) 29913, and from Queenstown.

QUEENSTOWN

Queenstown nestles along the edge of Queenstown Bay on the northeast shore of **Lake Wakatipu** facing the bare, craggy **Remarkables** range. Beautiful Lake Wakatipu is the second largest of the southern glacial lakes (behind Lake Te Anau) at 77 km long and almost five km wide. Although several rivers feed it (the Rees and Dart are largest), only the Kawarau River drains this always-blue, crystal-clear lake. With a colorful history steeped in gold, outstanding scenery in all directions, and modern-day notoriety as a center for jetboating, white-water rafting, fishing, backcountry hiking, downhill skiing, and bungy jumping, Queenstown is the most popular and attractive resort in the South Island.

From all over the world backpackers to businesspeople congregate in this cosmopolitan melting pot, and although tourism is the main industry, the resort has somehow managed to retain a friendly, small-town atmosphere. Its drawbacks? Irresistible outdoor adventures and heavy-duty nighttime partying require a healthy number of travelers cheques on hand (or an understanding credit card company at home)—come here for a couple of days and, time and budget permitting, you're more than likely to stay a couple of weeks!

Accommodations range from motor camps, a YH, and a number of budget backpacker lodges to motels and the ultimate in luxurious top-class hotels. Quick cafes and a great variety of restaurants keep you happily eating out day after day; nightclubs and pubs with live entertainment abound. The narrow streets are lined with alluring shops selling wool sweaters, sheepskin and suede coats, and all kinds of souvenirs. To complete the picture and remove any last doubts, Queenstown is easily reached by private or public transportation from anywhere in the South Island. Go for it!

SIGHTS

Around Town

The best way to appreciate the Queenstown atmosphere is on foot. Start at the waterfront-

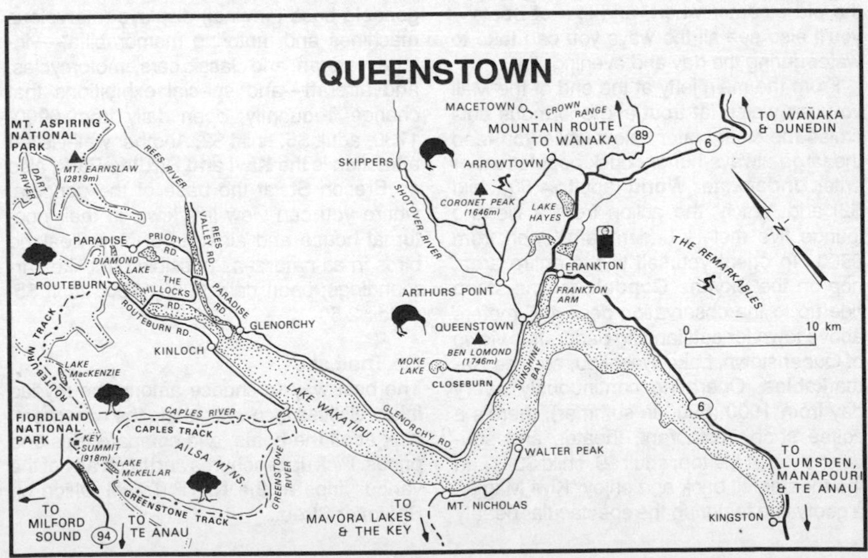

Queenstown Bay waterfront

end of the pedestrian-only **Mall** in the center of town—a great place to people-watch, listen to accents, and meet fellow travelers. Walk east along Marine Parade into **Government Tourist Gardens** (colorful any time but spectacular in autumn) and follow the walkway around the point. Walk back through town and stroll in the other direction along the Queenstown Bay waterfront, passing jetties, the old steamer wharf, and lots of boats—you'll also see all the ways you can take to water during the day and evening.

From the main jetty at the end of the Mall you can watch fat trout and enormous eels cruise the clear water below while you feed the large always-hungry duck population, or enter **Underwater World** (adult $4.50, child $2) and "catch" the action from a viewing lounge five meters underneath; open from 0900. To orient yourself to the entire area, hop on the **Skyline Gondola** for the steep ride up to the observation deck 445 meters above town for outstanding panoramic views of Queenstown, Lake Wakatipu, and the Remarkables. Operating continuously every day from 1000 (0900 in summer), there's a coffee shop, restaurant, theater, and souvenir shop at the top; adult $9, child $3 RT. In the theater, sit back and enjoy "Kiwi Magic," a goofy film featuring the spectacular beauty of New Zealand, with more than a splash of Kiwi humor; adult $5, child $3. For spectacular sunset views, live entertainment, and a huge meal, take the gondola up in the evening for the "New Zealand Carvery Buffet"; adult $35, child $17.50 includes the gondola ride (see p. 497) and live entertainment.

The popular **Queenstown Motor Museum** on Brecon St. (near the bottom of the gondola base terminal) displays "marvelous machines and motoring memorabilia"—vintage, veteran, and classic cars, motorcycles, and aircraft—and special exhibitions that change frequently; open daily from 0900-1730, adult $5, child $2. Another well-visited attraction is the **Kiwi and Birdlife Park,** also on Brecon St. at the base of the gondola, where you can view live kiwis in their nocturnal house and all sorts of New Zealand birds in as-natural-as-possible park-like surroundings; open daily 0900-1700, adult $5, child $2.50.

On The Lake

The best way to choose among the myriad lake activities is to walk along the waterfront, look at all the boats, and compare trips and prices. Pick up brochures and book any of the various trips at the NZTP Travel Office on Shotover Street.

One of the most leisurely ways to appreciate Lake Wakatipu from Aug. to June is on the historic vintage steamship, TSS *Earnslaw,* a Queenstown landmark. Known as "The Lady of the Lake," since 1912 she's carried supplies and stock to shoreside farms, and in recent times, taken visitors on tours. She departs daily at 1230 on a one-hour **lunch cruise** around Queenstown Bay and up Frankton Arm for adult $19.50, child $9.75; daily at 1400 on a 2½-hour **lake cruise** for excellent views of the lake head and a visit to Mt. Nicholas Sheep Station on the far side for adult $30.50, child $10; and from 26 Dec. to 31 March, she departs at 1800 for a 90-minute **evening cruise** with the option of dining aboard for adult $20, child $9. Buy tickets at Fiordland Travel, Steamer Wharf, or at Queenstown travel agents.

Another enjoyable way to take to the water, feel the wind in your hair, and perhaps learn a thing or two about sailing is onboard the ***City of Dunedin,*** New Zealand's only Round-The-World schooner that took part in the 27,000-mile, single-handed "Round The World" race in 1982. She sails daily from her berth at the Water Taxi Jetty, opposite the Parkroyal Hotel, tel. 28-665; adult $29, child $15. in summer **Queenstown Yacht Charters** does a 1½-hour yacht cruise, departing daily at 1000, 1200, 1400, and 1600 for $18 pp.

If speed is more your style, try a 30-minute air-cushioned cruise around the lake on the **hydrofoil,** departing daily every hour on the half-hour from 1000-1600 for adult $18, child $9; or catch the 20-minute mini-cruise to see area highlights, departing twice a day for adult $10, child $7.50. Another local attraction is most easily reached by boat—cross the lake by high-speed launch to **Walter Peak Station,** a high-country sheep and cattle station, for sheepdog displays, sheep-shearing and woolspinning demos, and viewing of the only fold of Highland Cattle in the country; daily at 0930 and 1400, adult $30, child $15. The evening departure (1715, returning at 2030) allows you to tuck in to the "Great Kiwi Carvery" at Colonels Restaurant. Book at Walter Peak Resort Office, 37 Shotover St., tel. 28-416, after hours tel. 28-101.

For a short thrilling parasailing ride (attached to a parachute you soar high above the lake behind a jetboat—it's like flying without wings) contact **Queenstown Paraflights** at the Queenstown Mall Jetty, or book through Danes Shotover Rafts on the corner of Shotover and Camp sts., or call 29-667; the 10-minute flight costs $35 pp, a one-hour jetboat river trip plus paraflight is $66.

Do-it-yourselfers can hire **U-Drive Jet Boats, jetbikes, hobiecats** or **windsurfers** (including wetsuits), or go for a fast jetboat

Queenstown and the Remarkables from the top of the gondola

ride, all from Frankton Beach; catch the courtesy coach at 1000, 1200, and 1400. If a persistent urge to land a rainbow or brown trout necessitates hiring a fishing boat, equipment, and guide, you can find all you need at varying prices along the Queenstown waterfront. Get the current guide rates and a tourist fishing license at the NZTP Travel Office, or book through Mount Cook Travel Centre, open seven days a week—in summer from 0800-1900, in winter from 0800-1800.

Scenic Drive

Magnificent scenery abounds in all directions from Queenstown, but for an interesting scenic 50-km RT drive, head north out of Queenstown along Arthur's Point Rd. to **Arthur's Point** for splendid views of the Shotover River. **Arthur's Point Pub** is a fun place to stop for a drink or a meal (see "Food" below), a bit of goldmining history, and evening entertainment—it does a booming business with the apres-ski crowd in winter.

Continue along Malaghan Rd. to **Arrowtown** which began as Fox's Rush, a wild and unruly goldmining settlement when gold was discovered in the Arrow River in 1862. A memorial marks the "golden" spot, an 800-meter walk upstream from the present township. The river was soon famous as one of the richest alluvial goldfields in the world, attracting hordes of miners from everywhere.

Today you can still appreciate the original goldmining character by strolling along the tree-lined streets of miners' cottages, viewing the fine collection of pioneer relics in the **Lake District Museum** (open 0900-1700, adult $2, child 50 cents), the old jail, churches dating back to 1873, memorials, and the historic Chinatown site at the west end of town (part of **Otago Goldfields Park**). Shops sell everything from goldpanning equipment to sheepskin coats; cafes and restaurants cater to Arrowtown's modern-day industry—tourism. Catch an original London double-decker bus from the top of Queenstown Mall to Arrowtown (adult $16, child $8 RT; book at any of the booking agents), or take a Gray Line tour—see "Tours" below. If you have your own transportation, don't miss visiting the sensual **Flower Barn** on Speargrass Flat Rd. (Lake Hayes), just outside Arrowtown (ask locals for directions or call 21-411); open daily 0930-1700 except Friday. It's the place to go for home-grown dried flowers, and more dried flowers, and even more dried flowers—in bunches, soaps and perfumes, as decorations, adornments, and as gifts for all occasions. It's a pleasure to wander through—your eyes and nose will thank you! You can also sample a Devonshire Tea in the large country garden, or stay for B&B with the friendly owners in their attractive comfortable home, Speargrass Lodge (see "Accommodation" below).

For an enjoyable hike from Arrowtown, consider walking 13 km up the Arrow River (about 27 river crossings) to the old ghost town of **Macetown.** There's not much left, but the remaining buildings and machinery of a once-thriving gold town are protected as part of Otago Goldfields Park. For more info on local walks and historic sites, stop at the Dept. of Survey and Lands Information Centre on Ballarat St., Queenstown. From Arrowtown continue along the road to Arrow Junction and Hwy. 6, then return south to Queenstown.

Slip Slidin' Away

One view that really shouldn't be missed is the breathtaking panorama from the top of **Coronet Peak,** Queenstown's downhill skiing mountain and resort (see "Skiing" below). In summer it's a popular lookout and launching place for hang gliders. Get to the summit by bus and chairlift (adult $9, child $4.50), then whiz down (Oct. to March) on the **Coronet Peak Alpine Slide.** This involves hopping on a toboggan for a 600-meter twisty stainless-steel slide down the mountain; open daily 0900-1600, weather permitting, one ride adult $4, child $3.50, five rides adult $16, child $13.50. If you need transportation to the run (a 25-minute drive from town), a van leaves Queenstown at 0900, 1000, 1200, and 1330.

Tours

If you don't have your own transportation in Queenstown, no problem! **Gray Line,** tel.

For an exhilarating ride, jetboat the Shotover River!

27-146/650, has tours to suit all age groups, time schedules, and budgets—for the complete rundown, departure points, and bookings, call in at the Mount Cook Travel Centre on Rees St. or at the NZTP Travel Office on Shotover Street. One of the most thrilling tours, **Skippers Canyon,** takes you along a tortuously narrow road high above a spectacular sheer-walled canyon (New Zealand's "Grand Canyon") while you hear the history of goldmining in the Shotover River, world's second richest gold-bearing river; 3½ hours, adult $43, child $21.50, tea provided. The 90-minute **Cattledrome Show Tour** is popular (similar to Rotorua's live sheep show) and good for a giggle or two. Take in a live cattle stage show and try your hand at milking if the urge overcomes you; departs daily at 0900 and 1400 (double-check times in July and Aug.), $15 adult, $7.50 child. (If you have your own transportation, the Cattledrome is a 15-minute drive along Arthur's Point Dr. from Queenstown and admission is only $6 adult, $3 child.) Or combine the Cattledrome with a stop at **Arrowtown** (see above), allowing time to browse through the historic town museum and shops. Catch the red double-decker bus from the top of the Mall.

ACTIVITIES

Jetboating

Jetboat tours from Queenstown combine power, maneuverability in just inches of water, and skilled drivers to provide a thrilling ride through impressive river and canyon scenery. If you haven't already been on a jetboat, this is the place! Jetboats are operated on the wide, tree-lined, swift-flowing **Upper Kawarau River,** the turbulent and exciting **Shotover River** with its narrow rocky gorge and incredible scenery, and the **Lower Shotover River** with its wide shingle riverbeds, tree-lined narrow sections, and varied terrain.

Most trips last from 30 minutes to an hour or so, some leave from Queenstown Bay while others provide courtesy transportation to launch sites, and they range from adult $35-60 pp, child $18-30. The one-hour **Shotover Jet** trip gives you one of the biggest adrenalin rushes for your money, departing every half hour and including a ride to the launch site for adult $49.50, child $24. If you can afford to spend more, consider one of the concoctions—a jetboat ride and helicopter flight, or a jetboat ride, white-water rafting trip, and helicopter flight. Just about anything can be arranged—for $55-145 pp! To decide which of the quickie tours suits you best, call in at the Mount Cook Travel Centre at the bottom of the Mall, the NZTP Travel Office, or the various booking centers downtown that advertise jetboat trips.

However, if you're looking for a combination of wind-whipping-through-your-hair excitement, outrageously beautiful lake, river, and mountain scenery (aptly described by Neil as a "scenic orgasm!"), a small friendly group, and have about five hours to experience all this fun, look no further. Call Neil Ross at tel. 29-667 (after 2000) or Danes Shotover Rafts booking office at tel. 27-318 and reserve a seat on the **Dart River Jetboat**

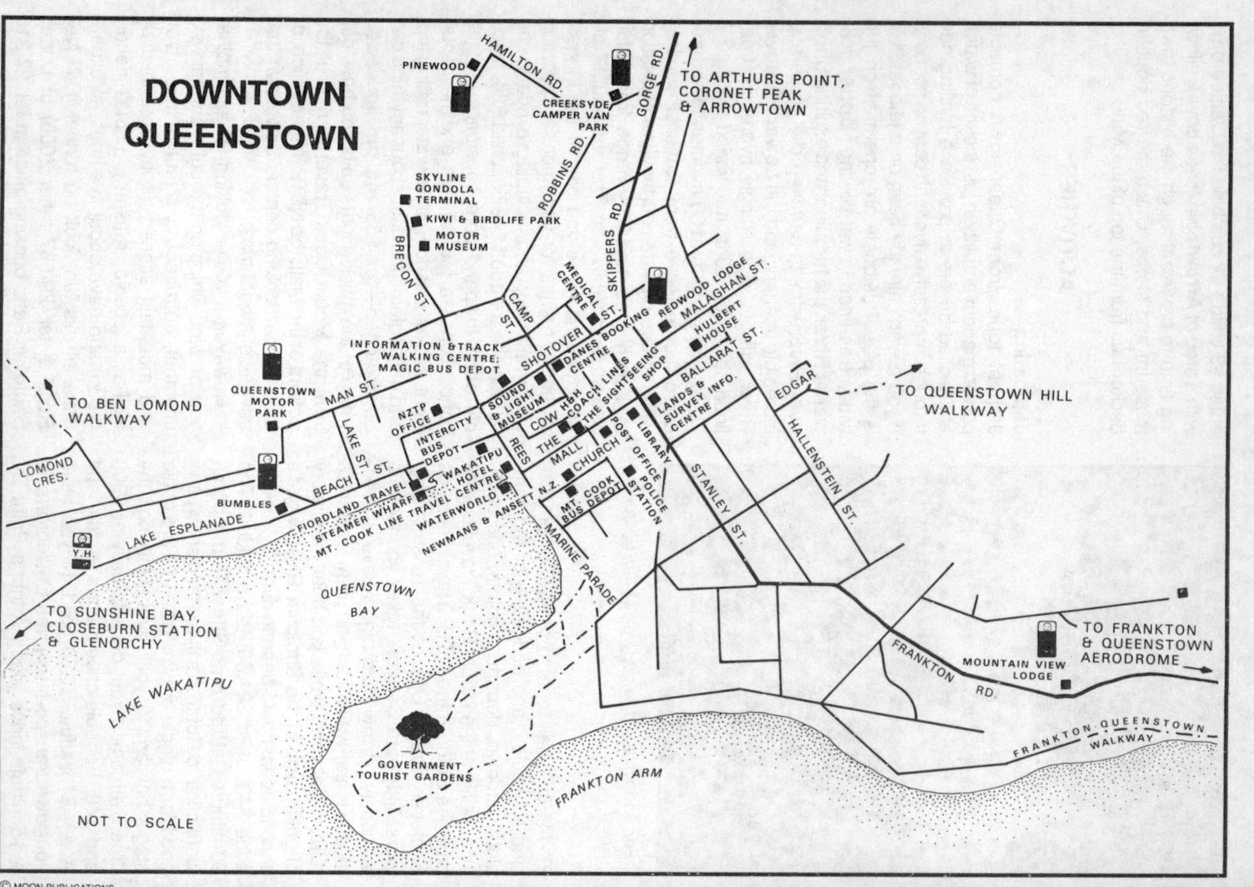
DOWNTOWN QUEENSTOWN
PINEWOOD
HAMILTON RD.
CREEKSYDE CAMPER VAN PARK
GORGE RD.
TO ARTHURS POINT, CORONET PEAK & ARROWTOWN
ROBBINS RD.
SKIPPERS RD.
SKYLINE GONDOLA TERMINAL
KIWI & BIRDLIFE PARK
MOTOR MUSEUM
BRECON ST.
CAMP ST.
MEDICAL CENTRE
REDWOOD LODGE
MALAGHAN ST.
HULBERT HOUSE
BALLARAT ST.
INFORMATION & TRACK WALKING CENTRE; MAGIC BUS DEPOT
SHOTOVER ST.
DANES BOOKING CENTRE
H&H COACH LINES
THE SIGHTSEEING SHOP
LANDS & SURVEY INFO. CENTRE
QUEENSTOWN MOTOR PARK
MAN ST.
TO BEN LOMOND WALKWAY
NZTP OFFICE
SOUND & LIGHT MUSEUM
COW
INTERCITY BUS DEPOT
THE MALL
REES
CHURCH
POST OFFICE
LIBRARY
EDGAR
TO QUEENSTOWN HILL WALKWAY
HALLENSTEIN ST.
STANLEY ST.
LOMOND CRES.
LAKE ST.
BEACH ST.
WAKATIPU HOTEL
TRAVEL CENTRE
N.Z.
MT. COOK BUS DEPOT
POLICE STATION
BUMBLES
FIORDLAND TRAVEL
STEAMER WHARF
MT. COOK LINE
WATERWORLD
NEWMANS & ANSETT
Y.H.
LAKE ESPLANADE
MARINE PARADE
QUEENSTOWN BAY
TO SUNSHINE BAY, CLOSEBURN STATION & GLENORCHY
LAKE WAKATIPU
GOVERNMENT TOURIST GARDENS
FRANKTON ARM
FRANKTON RD.
MOUNTAIN VIEW LODGE
TO FRANKTON & QUEENSTOWN AERODROME
FRANKTON QUEENSTOWN WALKWAY
NOT TO SCALE

Safari. The first 40 minutes is a scenic drive along Lake Wakatipu to the village of Glenorchy where you then board a jetboat and the real adventure begins. Whizzing across the lake then up the Dart River the boat performs for the next two hours or more in both deep and surprisingly shallow water with ease, climbing almost 500 feet in altitude.

During the trip you can expect to see lots of birdlife, silver-ribbon waterfalls snaking down cliffs, rapids, narrow canyons where the water is mirror still, turquoise, and crystal clear, and towering snow-capped mountains year-round. Neil, your entertaining first-class driver, is a barrel of laughs—and he knows the river and surrounding landscape better than the back of his hand. If you want to stop to take photos (a camera and/or video camera are essentials on this trip), go for a swim, or stretch your legs on the riverbank, no problem! At the end of the trip Neil does soak-to-the-skin "Hamilton spins" for a last burst of adrenalin, and then you recover and relive the excitement over a cup of tea and a snack (on the morning trip) or beer at the pub (afternoon trip) at Glenorchy before heading back to Queenstown. All this costs only $88 pp; lifejackets, windbreakers, and warm woolly hats are provided.

White-water Rafting

Queenstown is the self-proclaimed "Rafting Capital of New Zealand." Rivers are numerically graded from one (easy) to six (unraftable)—in the Queenstown area it's more than likely that, even if you're a total beginner, you'll be rafting a grade four/five river. Trips are on the **Kawarau River** with 15 km of large-volume water and four thundering rapids, and the **Lower Canyon** of the **Shotover River** with 17 km of grade four-plus roaring rapids, twisting and churning through spectacular rugged scenery to end by shooting 170 meters through the completely dark, narrow-walled Oxenbridge goldminers tunnel and down a waterfall—this trip takes guts and is the most popular! Most rafting trips generally take 3½ to 4½ hours and range from $55-75 pp; all companies provide helmets, lifejackets, and wetsuits (a necessity—the water is icy!), and you need to wear a swimsuit, wool socks and sandshoes or tennis shoes (some companies provide rubber booties), and a lightweight waterproof jacket. Forget the camera unless it's waterproof and floats. Combination rafting, helicopter, and jetboat trips are also available; from $50-110 pp. **Danes Shotover Rafts, Kawarau Raft Expeditions,** and **Kiwi Discovery** all give discount rafting rates to YHA members. **Danes** also does exciting heli-rafting combo trips (from $110 pp), and weekend trips on the Landsborough River (on the west coast; from $500, food and tent included). For more info and bookings, call in at the numerous booking centers advertising rafting, the Mount Cook Travel Centre, or the NZTP Travel Office.

Skiing

Coronet Peak Ski Area has excellent skiing (night skiing on weekends from 1800-2200) from July to Oct., on-field rentals and modern facilities (restaurant/cafe, takeaways, ski shop, service center), and magnificent panoramic scenery. "The Peak's" large, hilly, commercial field sports suitable runs for beginners through experienced skiers, along with chairlifts, pomas, rope tows, and ski instructors from around the world. The ski season at Queenstown is considered low season, so accommodations in town are very reasonable. Go during the week to avoid the long weekend lines for the chairlifts. Half-day skiing is adult $30, child $16, full-day adult $40, child $21, ski rental (full set) from adult $24, child $17. Get more info at the Mount Cook Travel Centre on Rees Street.

To get to Coronet Peak by car, take Arthur's Point Rd. north out of Queenstown for about eight km, then turn up Skippers Rd. following signs to the skifield—it's another eight km or so of sealed road to the carpark. The field is also easily reached by public transportation—**Mount Cook Line** buses go daily throughout the season from the Church St. Terminal, departing Queenstown 0800-1100 (0800 for main hotel pickup); for more info, stop by the Mt. Cook Travel Centre on Rees Street.

The **Remarkables Ski Area,** 24 km from Queenstown, is also run by Mount Cook Line,

and suitable for beginners through advanced. Lifts include two quads and one double chair and several learner tows, and there's an International ski school. Lift tickets are interchangeable with Coronet Peak (same prices). The season is from June to Oct. with peak skiing conditions from July to September. The base amenities building has a large self-service restaurant. For the latest **heli-skiing** info contact **Southern Lakes Heliski** through Great Sights Booking Centre on Shotover St., or call 26-222 or 23-012. You could be skiing the Remarkables Range and Coronet Peak, the Thomson Mountains (Mount Nicholas), or the Richardson Mountains, depending on snow conditions. Groups are graded according to ability and matched with suitable terrain. The season is from June to October. Also contact **Harris Mountains Heli-Skiing** on Shotover St. at tel. 26-722 for their variety of heli-skiing options and current prices.

Places to shop for ski equipment and/or hire: **Bill Lacheny Sports** (clothing, equipment for skiing, tramping, and climbing) in the Mall, tel. 28-438; **Brown's Ski Hire** on Shotover St.; **Kiwi Discovery** on Shotover St.; **Queenstown Sports** on Rees Street.

Bungy Jumping

Bungy jumping is the latest outdoor activity to provide thousands of people with the adrenalin rush of a lifetime. And once they've "jumped," many come back for more! If *you* relish the idea of diving off a 91-meter canyon-spanning bridge, 43 meters above a river, free-falling on the end of an elastic rope, then plunging into icy water before rocketing back toward the bridge for another fall (or two, or three, until momentum subsides), *and* surviving to tell the tale, Queenstown is the place to get your thrills.

It all happens at the Kawarau Suspension Bridge spanning the beautiful Kawarau River, about 23 km from Queenstown. You can choose from a wet jump (expect to be dipped in the river to your waist) or dry jump (you get close to the surface of the river, but stay dry). After working out how much rope is needed, experienced operators wrap your ankles with a towel and then the incredibly springy rope (similar to the rope used by mountain climbers). You're helped out onto a small platform and told to look straight ahead as you dive off, and then a large crowd of not-so-brave onlookers enthusiastically does a community countdown to encourage you to take the plunge! Afterward you're scooped into a boat, released from the life-saving rope, and taken to shore to walk the trail to the top for your designer bungy-jumper T-shirt (you have to jump to get one). Bungy jumping is also a spectator sport. It's almost as much fun to go out to the bridge to watch and listen to the blood-curdling screams, swear words, and shocked silences that occur as the daredevils take the plunge.

The crowd awaits the next bungy jumper to leap off Kawarau Suspension Bridge.

The jump costs $88, the shirt is "free," but jump in your birthday suit and you pay nothing! Book through Danes Shotover Rafts on the corner of Shotover and Camp sts., tel. 27-318 (ask to see the video of this new sport). Or just drive out there and take a place in the long, long line. If you need transportation, a van runs out to the bridge every afternoon, and on demand, from Danes; $10 RT.

Horseriding

Several outfits host guided horseriding amidst some of the most beautiful scenery. Moonlight Stables' treks are for experienced or inexperienced riders through the Shotover and Moonlight valleys. A 2¾-hour trek departs daily at 0930 and 1400; $39 pp includes tea. They also offer full-day treks from Oct. to April. For more info call 28-892 (transportation is available), or book through the Mount Cook Travel Centre, tel. 28-620. **Hillandale Rides'** guided trips through Wakatipu farmland with magnificent mountain views suit the more experienced rider. Coats, riding hats, and transportation are available. The three-hour rides depart daily at 0930 and 1400; $40 pp. Book at the Mount Cook Travel Centre or the NZTP Travel Office.

Flightseeing

Mount Cook Line flights from Queenstown Airport (northeast of town, near Frankton) range from a 10-minute "Buy A Plane" flight (up to five people; apply for current price) and "Wakatipu Highlights" flight for adult $67, child $50, to a "Magnificent Milford" flight for adult $189, child $142 RT which includes a boat ride on Milford Sound. Or you can take a Grey Line coach to Milford, see part of the Sound by boat, then fly back for $200 pp. Fantastic one-way flights to Milford Sound over some of the most awesome mountain, glacier, lake, and river scenery you're ever likely to see are $110 pp and take about 30 minutes; they leave daily. Book at the Mount Cook Travel Centre downtown, or call 27-650. A free shuttle is provided between the travel center and the airport.

Milford Sound Scenic Flights offer a variety of flights from Queenstown to Milford Sound, ranging from a 35-minute OW flight for adult $110, child $82, to a 4½-hour RT flight and cruise for adult $186, child $105. Inquire about off-peak savers and make bookings at tel. 23-065. **Air Fiordland** also provides a number of scenic options—from an 80-minute "Milford Overhead" flight for $120 to a "Mount Cook Experience" for $210. Make reservations at the Air Fiordland desk at the airport, or call 23-404.

The Helicopter Line flights from the helipad by the airport range from the short "Queenstown Hill" flight for $55 pp to the "Grand Circle" flight for $193 pp. They also run combo flights. Try the excellent "Heli Super Jet" flight for two bursts of adrenalin—a short helicopter flight (as close as you can come to heli-aerobatics!) followed by an exciting jetboat ride, then the return flight; $69 pp. For more info and reservations, drop by the Queenstown Information Centre on the corner of Shotover and Camp sts., tel. 27-820, or the airport, tel. 23-034.

HIKING

Local Short Walks

Before you set out on any walks in the Queenstown area, be sure to go to the **Dept. of Conservation Visitors Information Centre** first (see p. 499). A 4.5-km hike up **Queenstown Hill** is a great way to absorb the scenery as you steadily climb to a 902-meter vantage point; views of **Ben Lomond** peak, the Skyline Restaurant and Gondola, Queenstown, and much of Lake Wakatipu. From the summit you can see **Coronet Peak,** the **Crown Range, Lake Hayes, Frankton Arm Peninsula,** and the bare craggy **Remarkables Range.** The track starts and finishes at the east end of Edgar St. and takes about three hours RT—wear sturdy shoes and take a jacket for the summit.

The five-km **Frankton-Queenstown Walkway** wanders along the Frankton Arm shoreline of Lake Wakatipu, with views of the Remarkables and **Cecil and Walter Peaks** on the far side of the lake, and **Peninsula Hill.** The 1½ hour walk starts at the east end of Peninsula St. in Queenstown, passing a harbor bustling with boating activity and the fronts of private properties before reaching the north end of Frankton Recreation Reserve on the lakefront (return by bus).

Ben Lomond Walkway is a good 10-km climb through forest and grassland to the 1,746-meter summit of Ben Lomond (snowy in winter). From here you can see **Mt. Cook** in the distant northeast, **Mt. Aspiring** and **Mt. Earnslaw** to the north, the **Remarkables** and **Lake Wakatipu** to the southeast, **Arrow Flats** and **Lake Hayes** to the east, and **Moke Creek** and gorge and **Moonlight Creek** to the north. The track starts and finishes on Lomond Terrace (west end of Queenstown) via Skyline access road and takes about seven hours RT; wear sturdy shoes and take a warm jacket for the summit—the weather can change very quickly. On the return trip you can take the sidetrack to the Skyline (signposted) and catch the gondola down for half price.

Rees And Dart Tracks

The Rees and Dart valleys at the head of Lake Wakatipu are the main hiking routes into the southern sector of Mt. Aspiring National Park. They provide a variety of short walks, longer hikes, and a five- to six-day RT hike from one valley to the other (more challenging than the popular Routeburn Track, see p. 492). They also give access to difficult climbing routes only suitable for experienced climbers—the season is from early Nov. to mid-April; for guides or mountaineering instruction, call Mountain Ventures at tel. 29-603 or 26-345. Huts with wood fires are located at regular intervals along the Rees Dart Track; $8-12 pp, payable at the ranger station in Glenorchy or any Dept. of Conservation office. Maps and info are available at the Information and Track Walking Centre (37 Shotover St., tel. 27-878), or the Dept. of Conservation Visitors Information Centre (corner of Stanley and Ballarat sts., tel. 28-464), or the Mt. Aspiring National Park ranger station in Glenorchy.

To get to the valleys by car, take the waterfront road from Queenstown west to Glenorchy and on to the head of the lake where the Rees and Dart rivers enter. Magic Bus provides daily coach service to the Dart, leaving Queenstown at 1800 to arrive at Glenorchy at 1900 ($10 OW). The next day, it leaves Glenorchy at 0900, arriving at the Rees at 0930 ($10 OW). Magic Bus also sells discounted overnight packages that include transportation to the tracks and accommodation at Glenorchy Holiday Park for $25-44, depending on your destination. Book at the Information and Track Walking Centre, 37 Shotover St., or call 27-880. InterCity runs a daily bus service (by arrangement) from Queenstown to Glenorchy, and on to the start of the Rees and Dart tracks, departing Queenstown at 0815. Service to the Rees departs Glenorchy at 0915, arriving at the Rees at 0945. Service to the Dart departs Glenorchy at 1430, arriving at the Dart at 1500. Make a booking at the InterCity Travel Centre, Steamer Wharf, tel. 27-420. Taxis are available from Glenorchy, and they also offer a car pickup/drop-off service for any of the tracks.

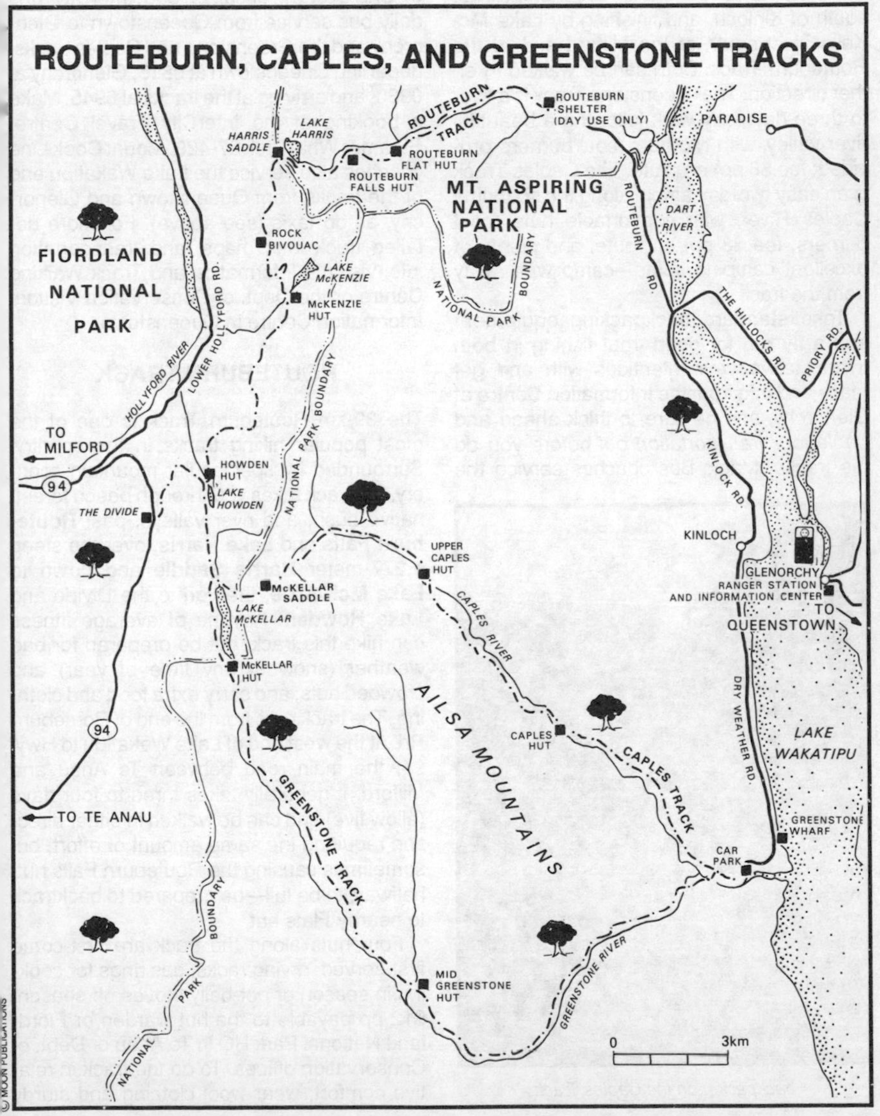

Caples And Greenstone Tracks

The Caples and Greenstone valleys, southwest of Queenstown on the other side of Lake Wakatipu, have good trails along each river. The tracks interconnect at both ends, starting at the carpark at the end of Greenstone Rd., south of Kinloch, and finishing by Lake McKellar, just south of the Milford end of the Routeburn Track. Both can be walked in either direction. The Greenstone Track is a two- to three-day easy walk following a beautiful river valley, with two huts (coal burners provided; fee $8 pp) en route. The Caples Track is an easy two-day amble along the sparkling Caples River, with comfortable huts (coal burners; fee $8 pp) en route, and plenty of excellent camping spots—camp well away from the track.

Take standard backpacking equipment and a fly rod for good trout fishing in both rivers; leave your intentions with and get maps and info from the Information Centre at Glenorchy, and be sure to think ahead and *book your transportation out* before you do the tracks. Magic Bus coaches service the tracks. They leave Queenstown at 1800 and arrive at Glenorchy at 1900, then the next day leave Glenorchy at 0900 and arrive at the tracks at 0915 ($20 OW); for bookings visit the Information and Track Walking Centre at 37 Shotover St., or call 27-880. InterCity runs daily bus service from Queenstown to Glenorchy and the Greenstone and Caples tracks, departing Queenstown at 0815, Glenorchy at 0930, and arriving at the tracks at 0945. Make a booking at the InterCity Travel Centre, Steamer Wharf, tel. 27-420. Mount Cook Line coaches also service the Lake Wakatipu end of the tracks from Queenstown and Glenorchy, as do taxis (see above). For more detailed track info, maps, and transportation info, visit the Information and Track Walking Centre or the Dept. of Conservation Visitors Information Centre in Queenstown.

backpacker on the Caples Track

ROUTEBURN TRACK

The 39-km Routeburn Track is one of the most popular hiking tracks in the country. Surrounded by spectacular mountain scenery, the track takes you through beech forest, native bush, and river valleys, past **Routeburn Falls** and **Lake Harris,** over the steep 1,277-meter **Harris Saddle** and down to **Lake McKenzie,** then on to the Divide and **Lake Howden.** Anyone of average fitness can hike this track, but be prepared for bad weather (snow at any time of year) and crowded huts, and carry extra food and clothing. The track runs from the end of Routeburn Rd. at the west end of Lake Wakatipu to Hwy. 94, the main road between Te Anau and Milford. It generally takes three to four days (allow five) and can be walked in either direction requiring the same amount of effort, but sometimes causing the Routeburn Falls hut, halfway, to be full—be prepared to backtrack to nearby Flats hut.

Four huts along the track are first-come first-served: drying racks, gas rings for cooking in season or pot-belly stoves off season; $12 pp payable to the hut warden or Fiordland National Park HQ in Te Anau or Dept. of Conservation offices. To do the track in relative comfort, wear wool clothing and sturdy hiking boots, take a waterproof coat, strong insect repellent, sleeping bag, cooking and eating equipment, and five days' supply of food. Get maps and detailed info on the track at the ranger station in Glenorchy, or at the Information and Track Walking Centre or Dept. of Conservation Visitors Information Centre in Queenstown. **Routeburn Walk Ltd.** sponsors four-day guided walks Nov. through April (from adult $484, child $418, supplies included), but pre-booking is essential. For more info, visit the NZTP Travel Office in Queenstown.

Getting There

If you don't have your own transportation, get to the start of the track from Queenstown by coach or taxi. Avoid hitchhiking—it can be tediously slow. Magic Bus operates coaches daily Nov. to May from Queenstown to Glenorchy ($10 OW) and the Routeburn ($18 OW), departing Queenstown at 0800, Glenorchy at 0900, arriving at the Routeburn at 0930; get more info and book at the Information and Track Walking Centre, 37 Shotover St., or call 27-880. InterCity runs daily coach service to Glenorchy ($12 OW) and the Routeburn ($18 OW), departing Queenstown at 0815, Glenorchy at 0915, arriving at the Routeburn at 0945. Make a booking at the InterCity Travel Centre, Steamer Wharf, tel. 27-420. The other alternative is to take a taxi from Queenstown to Glenorchy (five people can share the fare) or all the way to the Routeburn. Glenorchy Taxis also services the tracks and offers a pickup/drop-off car service. If you plan on continuing to either Milford or Te Anau when you reach the other end of the track, it's best to get bus timetables and prebook a place on a Magic Bus or an InterCity coach at the Queenstown depots (see "Transportation" below) before leaving—otherwise you're in for a long wait at the other end! Many keen hikers also combine the Routeburn Track with either the Caples or Greenstone tracks to complete three sides of a circular route and see an incredible variety of scenery. But if you're reliant on public transportation, it's easier to do the Caples or Greenstone tracks first and then the Routeburn.

ACCOMMODATION

Budget

The large, modern **Queenstown YHA Hostel** is only a short walk along the lakeshore from downtown, with stunning lake and mountain views. In summer an overflow hostel provides 100 extra beds ($14 pp) so there's plenty of room! At 80 Lake Esplanade, tel. 28-413. To get there from downtown, head for the lakefront and follow it around to the west (toward Glenorchy) onto Beach Street. This becomes Lake Esplanade.

One of the most popular places with backpackers and those on a budget is **Bumbles,** a fun always-crowded hostel with its own restaurant, do-it-yourself cooking facilities, token-operated laundry, and laid-back atmosphere. Dorms are $13 pp, shared twin or double rooms are $15 pp. At the restaurant you can get good meals for $7 or less; a vegetarian dish might cost you $6-6.50, a roast lamb dinner $7! As Bumbles is packed during peak season and holidays, it's best to reserve a bed four days ahead if you can at tel. 26-298. It's on the corner of Lake Esplanade and Brunswick St., a hop, skip, and jump from the lake and a one-minute walk from downtown. **Redwood Lodge** is also popular, providing all the usual facilities and dorm beds for $12 pp, twin, double, or triple rooms for $18 pp or $25 pp B&B. It's at 8 Malaghan St., tel. 29-116. **Pinewood** also offers budget accommodation; you can get a dorm bed for $12 pp, a twin or double room for $14 pp, and along with the usual communal facilities there's a store. It's at 48 Hamilton Rd., tel. 28-273.

If you're spending time exploring the shores of Lake Wakatipu or walking any of the major hiking tracks, consider taking a scenic 40-minute drive out to Glenorchy at the head of the lake to stay at the **Outdoor Activity Lodge,** tel. 29-968; a courtesy coach ride can be arranged for lodge guests. In this attractive very comfortable lodge are bunk rooms for $15 pp, single or double rooms for $25 pp, and rooms with private facilities for $27.50 pp, a large lounge with fireplace, laundry and drying facilities, restaurant, and store. The owner also arranges fly-fishing trips for $200 per day, boat fishing at $40 an hour, half-day horse trekking trips for $35 pp, and jetboat trips up the Dart River for $85 pp (see "Jetboating," p. 485), and can arrange transportation to all the walking tracks.

Motor Camps

Queenstown Motor Park and Motel, one km uphill from downtown, is a large motor camp with many rules and regulations to keep the crowd in order. Aside from the usual communal bathroom, kitchen, and laundry facilities, there's also a fully stocked shop on the premises. Tentsites are $6.30 pp, caravan sites are $7.20 pp. Tourist units start at $27.50 s or d, lodges (each with a toilet and shower) are $32.20 s or d, flats (with fully equipped cooking facilities) are $39.60 s or d, and motel units start at $49.50 s or d. Tariffs go up in June each year; discounts available for more than two-night stays. Located at the west end of Man St., tel. 27-252; from the Mall facing the lake, turn right on Rees St., left on Beach St., right on Lake St., then left on Man Street.

Mountain View Lodge Holiday Park is 1.25 km east of downtown but well worth the uphill walk or drive. The Lodge is primarily a motel, restaurant, and tourist attraction (the reception area is the well-known "Bottle House"), but the camping area is up the hill and disguised from the road by trees. The lower camping area is for tentsites at $6 pp (fabulous lake views through the trees, but the ground can get soggy after a short burst of rain); the upper area for tent or caravan sites is also $6 pp. All sites have the use of communal bath, kitchen/dining area, and laundry facilities, and the motel TV room, bar, and restaurant (main courses starting around $12). Also see "Hotels and Motels." Milk is available daily from the reception office. The Lodge is on Frankton Rd. (the main road east out of town), just past Suburb St., tel. 28-246.

If you're traveling by campervan and are looking for a powered site with water and waste disposal and even TV and phone connections, try **Creeksyde Camper Van Park.** The sites have been developed around a central building which has modern bathrooms (private ones also available), kitchen, and laundry, and a spacious lounge with TV and video. Milk, bread, and daily newspapers are available at the office. It costs $18 per van per night (up to two people), $9 per extra adult, $5 per child, or $28 per night for two adults and three or more children. There's also a cottage; for shared facilities but private rooms it's $10 pp, or you can take the entire cottage for $30 s or d plus $10 each extra adult. Creeksyde is on Robins Rd. (off Gorge Rd.), tel. 29-447.

Frankton Motor Camp is about five km from Queenstown at the end of Stewart St., Frankton, tel. 27-247. Communal bath (free showers), kitchen, and laundry facilities; tentsites are $5 pp, caravan sites are $5.50 pp, self-contained flats from $30.80 s or d, tourist lodges from $28 s or d, and a self-contained cottage from $41.10. From the main highway at Frankton turn right on Yewlett Crescent, then right on Stewart St. and continue to the end. **Queenstown Holiday Park** is at Arthur's Point (about five km north of town along Arthur's Point Rd.), tel. 29-306. Communal facilities, large TV room with pool table, trampoline, swimming pool, and camp store; tent and caravan sites $7.50 pp, cabins from $30 d.

Eight km from town on Glenorchy Rd. is the rather unique mountain retreat **Closeburn Alpine Park,** tel. 29-474 or 26-073. Aside from wooded tentsites with great views for $6.50 per night, the owners provide campervan sites for $11 d, or $13 d with private en suite bathroom units, and attractive, cozy, mountain lodge accommodation (bunks; provide your own sleeping bag or linen) with cooking facilities for $11 pp—or rent the entire chalet for $55 per night. If you continue to Glenorchy, you'll find the usual communal facilities at **Glenorchy Holiday Park,** plus a camp store, storage for hikers doing the tracks, transportation to the tracks, and guided sightseeing tours. Tentsites are $5 pp, caravan sites are $6 pp, cabins are $12 pp, lodge beds are $12 pp, and self-contained lakeside cottages are $40 d per night plus

$10 each extra adult. They also offer transport/accommodation packages for hikers doing the Routeburn, Greenstone/Caples, Rees/Dart tracks; get more info and the current rates at the Information and Track Walking Centre at 37 Shotover St. in Queenstown.

Bed And Breakfasts

Striking **Hulbert House,** a historic home built in 1889 and restored to its former glory by hospitable owner Ted Sturt, is now run as a luxury B&B guesthouse. The large rooms with private facilities are spacious and comfortable (the best have fantastic lake and mountain views), and range from $80-110 s, $110-130 d plus GST, which includes a delicious Continental breakfast. Several small bunk rooms (provide own sleeping bag or linen) at the back of the house have their own individual entrances and the use of a shower and toilet, though no kitchen or laundry facilities; $10 plus GST pp. A small cottage on the grounds is available for hire to couples. Breakfast for $10 is also available on request if the main house is not full. Located at 68 Ballarat St., tel. 28-767; walk up the Mall away from the lake and continue straight up the hill for several blocks.

Hulbert House

If you're looking for a more modern B&B in a peaceful country setting, or looking for an expert ski guide *and* a place to lay your head, call friendly owners Jenny and Denis Jenkins at **Speargrass Lodge.** Set in a large meadow surrounded by landscaped gardens next to the Flower Barn (also owned by Jenny and Denis; see "Sights"), this spacious lodge provides accommodation for 10 guests in four comfortable rooms (three with en suite), a lounge with open fireplace, dining and game rooms, and the added bonus of delightful company in the evenings; $50 pp per night ($300 pp per week) plus GST includes a sumptuous breakfast, and a packed lunch is available for $15, dinner for $20. It's on Speargrass Flat Rd. (between Queenstown and Arrowtown, just past Lake Hayes), tel. 21-411; if you're coming from Arrowtown follow the signs to the Flower Barn.

Hotels And Motels

You can get anything you want in Queenstown—from reasonable motel rooms (on the sparse side!) to luxurious first-class International-standard hotel units overlooking the lake. Pick your price range and go from there. Bookings can be made through the NZTP Travel Office on Shotover Street. One of the most reasonable, **Mountain View Lodge,** provides mini motel units with private bath for $24 s, $36 d, units with tea- and coffee-making facilities, fridge, and TV for $60, and units with cooking facilities for $75. A licensed restaurant serves breakfast (0630-0900) and dinner (1800-2030; mains from $12) on the premises (also see "Motor Camps" above). Located on Frankton Rd., tel. 28-246.

Another motel that is recommended by travelers is **The Goldfields,** 41 Frankton Rd. at Dublin St., tel. 27-211; comfortable at $74

Speargrass Lodge—a delightful home away from home for bed and breakfast.

d. If you don't mind a 40-minute scenic drive to the head of the lake, try the **Glenorchy Hotel** at Glenorchy. It provides seven recently renovated cheerful rooms with old-fashioned decor, gorgeous views, and private facilities, a TV room, bar, and Caples Restaurant (mains $14-24, Sun.-night specials for $10) which receives great raves from *everyone* who has eaten there—ask the locals where to eat and they all say this hotel! Before you drive out there, call 29-902 to see if they have a room available; $30 s, $50 d. The owners can also arrange a variety of sightseeing and jetboating trips.

Health Retreat

If you want to be close to Queenstown's action but stay in a beautiful secluded spot, head for **Bush Creek Health Retreat.** Stay in the large comfortable house on three acres, surrounded by flower, herb, and vegie gardens, with the constant sound of rushing water from a stream and several waterfalls that cascade naturally through the garden into the swimming pool. The friendly owner, Ileen Mutch, does iridology (eye) analysis, nutritional counseling, and reflex massage, sells herbal remedies, and is known for nutritious breakfasts included in the $30 pp plus GST room rate. Located 1.25 km from downtown on Bowen St., tel. 29-260; take Skippers Rd. toward Arthur's Point which becomes Gorge Rd., then turn left at Bowen St. and follow it to the end.

FOOD

Quick Bites

Rees Cafe is in the Rees Place Arcade, serving tasty finger foods—sandwiches, pies, sausage rolls, pizza, quiche, spaghetti on a muffin, a variety of pastries, cakes, and desserts (from $7 for two for brunch)—and delicious cappuccino. It's on Rees St. opposite the Mount Cook Travel Centre; open weekdays 0930-1630. **Habebes Lebanese Takeaways** in Wakatipu Arcade off Rees St. has excellent kebabs (meat- and salad-filled rolls) for $5.50 and $7.50, and an assortment of Lebanese delicacies—all tasty, all reasonable in price. This is a great spot to hit when you need a quick filling lunch to take on an excursion. **The Gourmet Express Restaurant and Coffee Shop,** one of the few restaurants open on Sun. mornings in Queenstown, is the place to go if you're hankering for an American-style breakfast. Breakfasts (from 0700-1200) start at $3.25, lunches and dinners range from $4-11 (good salad bar), and desserts are around $3; it's open seven days 0700-2100 in the Bay Centre, a small shopping arcade off Shotover Street. For reasonably priced takeaway Chinese or Mexican meals, or a good hamburger, go to the food mall on the lower floor of **O'Connells Pavilion** on the corner of Rees and Shotover streets. Tables and chairs are provided, but it's usually really crowded and hard to find a vacated spot to enjoy your meal—take it away!

Restaurants

One of the best places in town is **Avanti** in the Mall. Again, it's so popular with locals *and* visitors alike that you can't just walk in and get a table, but the wait is usually worthwhile! Typically Italian fare and seafood dishes (fresh from the sea on Wed.) are the specialties, though if you take a look at the desserts you may beg to differ! Expect to pay around $5-8 for a main course at lunch, $10-12.50 at dinner, and only $11 for their daily three-course dinner special. It also has a relaxed jovial atmosphere and the service is excellent. **The Stonewall Cafe** just across the Mall from Avanti is another busy spot. It's open daily from 1800-2200, serving lots of fish, oysters, etc., with specials around $8.50, mains ranging from $9-16. Sit in- or outside.

Westy's serves lunch on weekdays 1200-1400—sandwiches, vegie pasties, braised beef and prawns, omelettes, and Indonesian chicken dishes, and it has a BYO license. Dinners—all kinds of interesting vegetarian and meat dishes—are pricey, $15-30 a plate; open Mon. to Sat. from 1830-2130 (longer in summer), along an arcade in the Mall. **Cobb & Co. Restaurant** in the Mountaineer Establishment on the corner of Rees and Beach sts. offers the usual—from $8-15 for a small steak or light meal, slightly more at dinner (half portions are available), and desserts for around $5.

The very small **Cow Restaurant** on Cow Lane (off Beach St.) has undoubtedly the best pizza and spaghetti in town, an open fireplace that's very appealing when the evenings get chilly, good music, and a jovial laid-back atmosphere as everyone waits around the fire for their turn to sit and tuck in. A large variety of pizza sizes and combinations range from $8-18, various spaghetti dishes are $7.50-11.50, and there are crisp green salads, homemade soup, garlic bread, and desserts to complete your meal. It's open seven days a week from 1200-1400 and 1730-2230, has a BYO license (the bottle shop in Cow Lane has a great selection of cold wines and beers), and it's very popular with the locals—expect to wait for a table, or go in early (1730!), put down your name, and return later.

Licensed **Saguaro's Restaurant** on Shotover St. is the place for spicy Mexican food, margaritas or sangria by the glass or carafe, and special coffee drinks. Lunch specials are $8, Mexican dinners start around $14, steak dinners average $16, and desserts go up to $6. **Roaring Megs** is another hot spot with the locals, serving fine N.Z. cuisine seven nights. Soup starts at $5, appetizers $7-11, and main courses range from $15 for vegetarian to $22 for fresh salmon. BYO license. At 57 Shotover St. it's open from 1830; reservations are essential at tel. 29-676, and dress up. Another restaurant highly recommended by Queenstonians is **Upstairs-Downstairs** restaurant at 66 Shotover St., tel. 28-290. Enjoy the attractive old-fashioned decor and authentic German cuisine or a variety of steak dishes, the specialties of the house; expect to pay $15-18 for a main course.

For a delicious bistro meal in a 129-year-old stone building, a drink at the cozy bar or a game of pool, head out to the **Arthur's Point Pub and Restaurant** at Arthur's Point (about five km north of town). The pub was originally financed by Arthur Thomas with the gold he mined from the nearby Shotover River. Appetizers start at around $5, main courses are $9-12. Open Mon. to Thurs. 1200-2100, Fri. and Sat. 1200-2200, it gets especially busy during the ski season as it's on the main route back to Queenstown from the local ski resort.

If $35 pp doesn't sound too much for an all-inclusive evening of entertainment (a steal of a deal in Queenstown), head for the licensed **Skyline Restaurant** at the top of the gondola on Brecon St., tel. 27-860 (make reservations). For $35 per adult, $17.50 per child you get an exciting gondola ride up and down the mountain, the "New Zealand Carvery Buffet" (all you can eat), live entertainment, and fantastic views of Queenstown and its reflections twinkling in the lake far below. It's open from 1800 and is probably Queenstown's best restaurant deal when you're really hungry! You can also attend a showing of the 3D movie "Kiwi Magic" for adult $5, child $3 in the Skyline Showscan Theatre at the top; shown on the hour between 1100 and 2100. Buy tickets at the theater, the lower terminal of the gondola, or at The Copter Shop on Shotover Street.

ENTERTAINMENT

To find out what's on, pick up the free *Mountain Scene* newspaper and the various pamphlets on Queenstown available at the NZTP Travel Office and travel centers around town. Also, the friendly young staff at many of the booking centers around town always know where the best action is found! Queenstown really hops at night—in summer (the peak period) and during the winter ski season, bands play in pubs and nightclubs around town almost every night, particularly on weekends—just follow your ears. **Eichardt's Tavern** at the bottom of the Mall on the lakefront is one of the most popular places to meet people. Country and western, jazz, and rock 'n roll bands play every Sat. night in summer and regularly throughout the year, there are several bars (one with a big-screen TV), and no dress restrictions. **Diggins Bar** in the Mountaineer Establishment on Beach St. is another place for live music, as is the **Skyline Restaurant** at the top of the gondola. If you have your own transportation or don't mind taking a taxi, try **Arthur's Point Pub** at Arthur's Point. It's the hot spot for meeting locals and a popular apres-ski bar in winter.

Penthouse Nightclub above Eichardt's Tavern at the bottom of the Mall has live bands most summer nights, and live entertainment and disco nights during the ski season. Open 2130-0300; the cover charge varies according to the band (disco nights are cheaper), and you need to be neatly dressed to get in. **The Dolphin Club** at 54 Shotover St., tel. 29-692, is known for its great music, cheap drinks, free admission, and relaxed dress code—"come as you are." It's open from 2100-0300.

Relax after a rugged day of outdoor activities in a private pulsating hot spa under the stars at **Alpine Village Spas,** Alpine Village on Frankton Rd.; for reservations and prices, call 27-795. Between 26 Dec. and 1 April, cruise Lake Wakatipu on the TSS *Earnslaw* while you enjoy a buffet dinner, or during Christmas, catch the "Night Owl Cruise" departing at 2100 from the Steamer Wharf; reservations and tickets from Fiordland Travel at the wharf. In winter, there's **evening skiing** at Coronet Peak on Fri. and Sat. nights from 1800-2200, and other nights subject to demand. If you're planning on doing any of the well-known hiking tracks in Mt. Aspiring or Fiordland national parks, check out what's happening at the **Dept. of Conservation Visitors Information Centre** on the corner of Ballarat and Stanley sts., tel. 28-464; throughout summer they put on free slide shows, talks, guided walks, and overnight trips.

SERVICES

Emergency

For an **ambulance** call the operator or 23-033; **police** (Camp St.), tel. 27-900; **Frankton Hospital,** tel. 23-053; the **medical centre** (Shotover St. and the corner of Stanley), tel. 27-301—the pharmacy next door is open weekdays 0900-1730; **urgent chemist,** tel. 28-443; **urgent doctor,** tel. 27-302; **urgent dentist,** tel. 28-045/23-319/28-840. **Wilkinson's Pharmacy** in the Mall is open seven days a week, tel. 27-313; most pharmacies in Queenstown are open daily 0900-1800 and 1900-2100.

General

The **p.o.** is on Camp St. near the top of the Mall. **Queenstown Library** is on Stanley St., tel. 27-668. **Alpine Laundrette,** corner of Shotover and Stanley sts., is open daily 0730-2100. **Shopping hours** are generally weekdays 0900-1730 and 1930-2100, weekends 0930-1200 and 1930-2100. A shopper's delight, Queenstown has an incredible variety of shops and small boutiques selling handcrafted articles such as sheepskin, wool, leather and suede goods, local pottery, greenstone jewelry, and Maori woodcarvings; major credit cards and travelers cheques are accepted in most places.

Outdoor Equipment Specialists

The friendly staff of **Alp Sports** are billed as outdoor and adventure specialists—and they are! They can outfit you for climbing, backpacking, canoeing, and skiing, and they have all sorts of equipment hire; open Mon. to Fri. 0900-1800 and Sat. 0900-1300. **Queenstown Sports** on Rees St., tel. 29-305, also has sports equipment for rent along with backpacker supplies.

INFORMATION

For info on Queenstown attractions and accommodations, and general info on New Zealand, visit the **NZTP Travel Office** on Shotover St.; open Mon. to Fri. 0830-1700, and Sat. 0830-1230. Pick up free tourist newspapers and various pamphlets on Queenstown, and book just about everything. For info on Mt. Aspiring and Fiordland national parks, regional hiking track info (the Rees, Dart, Routeburn, Caples, Greenstone, and Milford tracks), detailed maps and some sound advice, visit the **Dept. of Conservation Visitors Information Centre** on Ballarat St. at Stanley, tel. 27-933; open Mon. to Fri. 0900-1630.

Booking Agents

At all the booking offices in Queenstown (they seem to be on every street and more spring up every year!) you can pick up sightseeing and general info, and book tours for all the local sights, tours, and outdoor adventures. **Mount Cook Travel Centre** is on Rees St., tel. 27-650; open seven days. **Great Sights Track Walking Information Centre,** 37 Shotover St., tel. 27-878, has info on all the local walks and hiking tracks, transportation to the tracks, sample menus from local restaurants, budget accommodation suggestions, and a service directory. **Fiordland Travel** is at Steamer Wharf on the lakefront, tel. 27-500. **Kiwi Discovery** is on Camp St., specializing in skiing and adventure activities, tel. 27-340. The **Sightseeing Centre** is at the top of the Mall, tel. 29-803; open seven days. **Shotover Shop and Bookings** on Rees St. is also open daily. **Danes Shotover Rafts** is on the corner of Shotover and Camp sts., tel. 27-318.

TRANSPORTATION

Getting There

Getting to Queenstown is a snap by private or public transportation. **Mount Cook Landlines** operates daily coach services from Christchurch via lakes Tekapo and Pukaki, and from Mt. Cook, Milford, and Te Anau. **InterCity** runs daily buses from Fox Glacier (Mon. to Sat.), Wanaka, Christchurch, Dunedin, Invercargill, Milford, and Te Anau. **Mount Cook Airline,** tel. 27-593/650, flies daily to the Queenstown Aerodrome (nine km east, at Frankton; get there by **Prestige Airporter Shuttle,** tel. 29-803, for $5 OW, or by taxi, tel. 27-888, for $12 OW) from Auckland, Rotorua, Taupo, Wellington, Christchurch, Dunedin, Milford Sound, Mount Cook, Nelson, Te Anau, and Wanaka. **Ansett New Zealand** flies several times a day from Auckland. They can be reached at the airport, tel. 23-010.

Local

The best way to explore Queenstown is on foot; a coach tour is another way. A regular bus service runs between Queenstown and Frankton, and bicycles and rental cars are readily available. To get to Arrowtown catch the red double-decker bus from the top of the Mall; adult $16, child $8 RT includes full commentary. **Queenstown Bike Hire** at 23 Beach St., tel. 26-039, is open daily till dark; they hire single-speed bicycles (from $4 an hour), tandems (from $8 an hour), triples (from $12 an hour), BMXs (from $5 an hour), five-speeds (from $5 an hour), 10-speeds (from $6 an hour), 10- and 12-speed mountain bikes (from $6 an hour), 18-speed mountain bikes (from $11 for two hours), and scooters (from $20 for two hours which includes insurance, petrol, and unlimited kms). You can also hire mountain bikes and/or go on a guided trip with **Kawarau Rafts Shop** at 37 Shotover St., tel. 29-792.

The main car rental agencies are **Avis** at 16 Beach St., tel. 27-280; **Budget** at 41 Shotover St., tel. 29-274; **Hertz** on Church St., tel. 28-418; and **Letz,** corner of Shotover and Camp sts., tel. 27-465 (Letz also rents scooters for $15 an hour, $30 per half-day, or $45 a day, plus $5 insurance). For a **taxi** call 27-888. For transportation to the start of the Routeburn, Rees, Dart, Caples, and Greenstone tracks, or a large variety of local sightseeing tours, call **Magic Bus, InterCity,** or the **Mount Cook Travel Centre** and compare prices and schedules.

On-going

To find out schedules and current prices, and book on-going transportation, call in at the offices listed below or at the NZTP Travel Office. If you're continuing south to Te Anau and Milford, ask about the current package deals—some companies offer excursion rates which include a RT coach ride to Milford with optional cruise on Milford Sound (lunch available on board)—a good timesaver when you consider that it's more often than not raining in Milford and you may want to leave as soon as you've "cruised the Sound." **Magic Bus** does a scenic "day-tripper" to Milford for $85 from Queenstown, launch ride on the Sound (and free ice cream on the return trip!) included, departing from the Track Walking Information Centre on Shotover Street. The Magic Bus drivers are a fun bunch—cracking jokes, giving an interesting commentary on highlights along the route, and playing music to keep you entertained the whole trip. They bring new meaning to long-distance coach travel! Magic Bus also runs the popular West Coast route from Queenstown to Picton or Nelson, stopping two nights at the glaciers en route, for only $99.

The **InterCity** office is on Beach St. near the Steamer Wharf. Apart from regular long-distance service, they run daily "day excursions" from Queenstown to Te Anau and Milford, departing at 0730 and returning at 2300 for $79 pp. If you're continuing south anyway, catch the cheaper day excursion rates from Te Anau to Milford RT. The InterCity OW fare from Queenstown to Christchurch is $47, to Dunedin $29.50, Franz Josef $52, Invercargill $20.25, Mt. Cook $31, Te Anau $20, and Wanaka $16. The **Mount Cook Landline** coach terminal (where buses depart daily for Coronet Peak, the airport, Milford Sound, Mt. Cook, and Christchurch) is on Church St., tel. 27-653. The Mount Cook Travel Centre (sightseeing and airline reservations) is on Rees St., tel. 27-650.

CONTINUING SOUTH

There are three ways to get to Fiordland from Queenstown: by Magic Bus to the head of Lake Wakatipu, then by foot via the three- to four-day Routeburn Track; by road (Magic Bus or InterCity coach) to Te Anau or Milford; or by air from Mount Cook to Te Anau or Milford Sound. If you have your own transportation, take the main road northeast out of Queenstown to Frankton, then Hwy. 6 south between the Remarkables and Lake Wakatipu, passing the access road to **Remarkables Ski Resort.** Continue down to the little village of **Kingston** at the south end of the lake where you can take an enjoyable 14-km "flight" (Oct. or Nov. to March, April, or May, depending on numbers; check at tel. 0225-8816) to Fairlight on the well-loved old steam train ***Kingston Flyer.*** Pullman green carriages with original wood interiors, black metal and polished brass engine, plume of black smoke, shrill whistle, and staff in period costume take you back to the days of the early 1900s when the *Flyer* first ran between Kingston and Gore. Leaving daily at 1000, go RT (1¼ hours; adult $15, child $6), or connect with regular train services at Fairlight (adult $12 OW, child $5). If you want to ride up front in the engine, buy a VIP pass for $25 OW, $35 RT. Continuing down Hwy. 6 you come to **Lumsden**—an angler's paradise with five trout-filled rivers (so rumor has it) criss-crossing the countryside within a relatively short distance of town. Just before Lumsden, Hwy. 94 branches west to Te Anau, Manapouri, and Fiordland National Park, and east to Gore.

Along the highway to Fiordland are several attractions: the small **Matuku Engine Museum, Bee Bazaar** (open by request; call

The Kingston Flyer runs daily "flights" between Kingston and Gore in summer.

6256 or 6404), and craft studio signposted off the main street of **Mossburn,** and access roads to several large forests north and south of the highway where there's good hiking, climbing, and fishing. **Mararoa River, Mavora Lakes,** and upper **Oretei River** in **Snowden State Forest** provide excellent dry fly-fishing (limit four fish a day, get your license at Te Anau), campsites (toilets and fresh water) at the south end of South Mavora Lake, and a long easy hike around the lakes following the Mararoa River into the Greenstone Valley (see p. 492); the Snowdon Forest access road branches north off Hwy. 94 at the Key. Between the Key and Te Anau the highway passes through a bleak yet dramatic "wilderness reserve" established to preserve a unique area of bog pine; as you approach Te Anau, well-stocked deer farms with the standard two-meter-high wire fences line the road.

At Hillside the highway branches in two directions—southwest to **Manapouri,** a small settlement on the edge of Lake Manapouri and starting point for some impressive Doubtful Sound attractions, or north to the town of **Te Anau,** "Gateway to Fiordland"—the place to stay if you plan to hike the Milford Track or explore Milford Sound. If you have time to spare for a short scenic drive, take Ramparts Rd. which runs between the roads to Te Anau and Manapouri after the highway splits at Hillside (see map).

FIORDLAND

The vast remote Fiordland region in the southwest corner of the South Island is made up of **Fiordland National Park,** largest national park in the country, and the towns of Te Anau and Manapouri which lie just outside the Park boundary (the Park Visitor Centre is in Te Anau). In a country that has spectacular scenery from top to bottom, Fiordland is one of the most majestic areas—the kind of place where you constantly hear the words "breathtaking," "spectacular," "awesome," and "magnificent." Though dull skies or endless days of rain and drizzle can be expected, keep in mind that the scenery is at its most dramatic after heavy rain! It's a remote area of deep dark fiords and magnificent waterfalls, rugged mountains covered in dense beech forest, large lakes and rivers, and three small settlements that cater to visitors.

If you can spend at least a couple of days in Fiordland, start at Manapouri and see Doubtful Sound, continue north to Te Anau and visit the local attractions and Park HQ, then travel the impressive road to Milford

Sound (take lots of film) starting as early in the morning as possible. The best time to visit Fiordland is June to Aug. when the weather is clear—in summer, be prepared for sandflies (if you think they're bad elsewhere you ain't seen nothin' yet), rain, and more rain—Fiordland is one of the wettest places on Earth!

MANAPOURI

The small settlement of Manapouri, 19 km south of Te Anau, nestles at the mouth of the Waiau River on the shores of Lake Manapouri (corruption of "Manawapouri" or "Lake of the Sorrowing Heart"), second deepest lake in the country at 443 meters and aptly described as "New Zealand's most beautiful lake." In the late 1960s and early '70s the lake was the subject of a large-scale conservation battle when the government proposed a plan to raise the lake level 12 meters for a hydroelectric scheme—which would have inadvertently destroyed its natural beauty. More than a quarter-million concerned New Zealanders (a lot of people when you consider the total population) signed a petition opposing the destruction of the lake, and the incoming Labour Government in 1972 pledged that the lake would be left alone—the power station at West Arm was lowered an impressive 213 meters underground instead!

machine hall in the Lake Manapouri Power Station

Backed by the the snow-capped **Keppler Mountains** with crystal-clear waters dotted with forest-covered islands, the lake *is* beautiful, and has excellent brown and rainbow trout fishing, boating, and swimming. Organized cruises and charter boats cross the lake, and a number of short bush walks are close to town (on the other side of the river) in adjacent Fiordland National Park. Even on gloomy days when the sky, lake, and bush become ominously dark and mist shrouds the mountains, the area has a beauty that has to be seen to be appreciated!

ACTIVITIES

Lake Tours

Fiordland Travel, tel. 602, on the riverfront at Pearl Harbour offers cruises, guided tours (discount packages), and coach service to Te Anau (where Fiordland Travel is based) to connect with cruises on the lake there; the office is open every day. Winter is the best time of year for clear views and little rain, but the busiest time for tours is spring and summer. The most popular tour takes you by high-speed launch to West Arm at the far end of the lake to visit the **Lake Manapouri Underground Power Station**—an impressive hydroelectric power station and engineering feat 213 meters underground, built over a 10-year period to provide power for the Comalco aluminium smelter at Bluff (south of Invercargill). After crossing the lake to the West Arm wharf, you're driven by coach down an eerie two-km spiral tunnel into the heart of a mountain for views of the machine hall carved

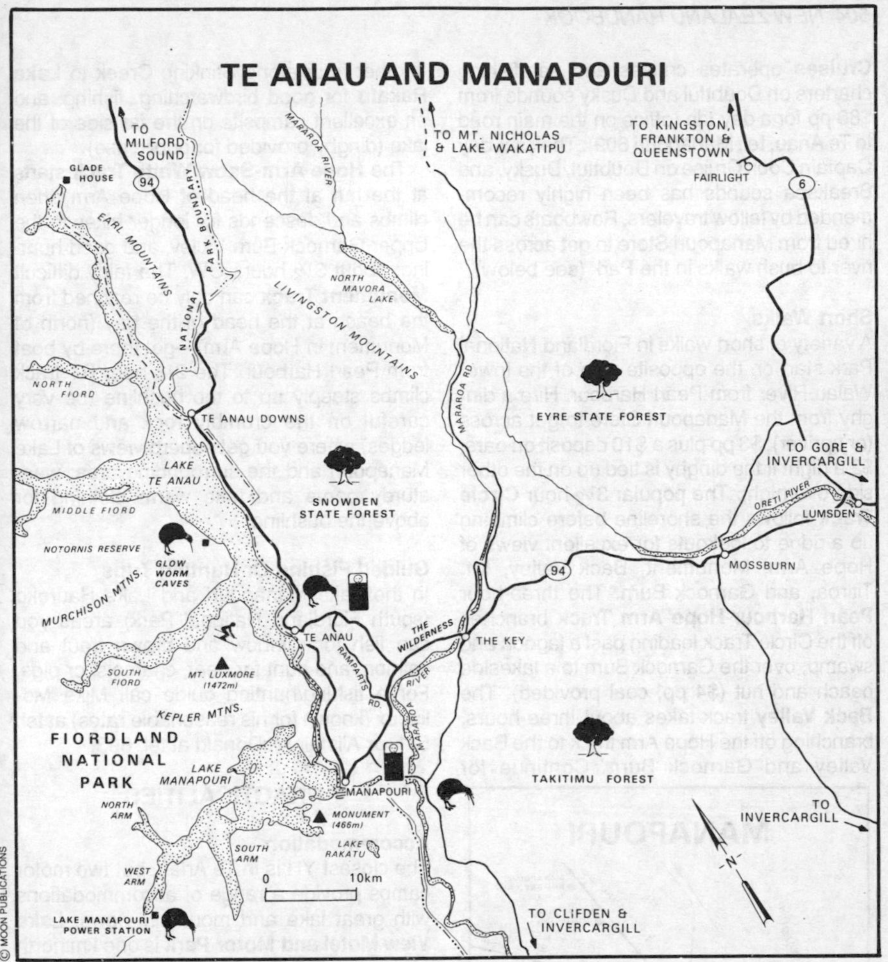

out of solid granite rock. A guide gives a lighthearted but detailed commentary on power production, the seven turbine-driven generators, and the 10-km tailrace tunnel which takes the water all the way to Deep Cove. The tours depart twice a day, allow about four hours; adult $35, child $9 (discounts available).

The very popular **Doubtful Sound** triple trip combines a visit to the power station with a coach tour over **Wilmot Pass** to **Deep Cove,** followed by a cruise on the remote, magnificent Hall Arm of Doubtful Sound (actually a glacier-formed fiord, misnamed by Capt. Cook). Geographical center of Fiordland National Park, the still waters of the fiord (broken only by penguins, dolphins, and the occasional crayfishing boat), fantastic reflections, sheer 1,500-meter mountain walls, hanging valleys, and tumbling waterfalls combine to make a lasting impression. Allow a day, take your own lunch or buy one of the box lunches available for about $5; adult $92.50, child $42.50 (discounts available).

Fiordland Travel also takes special groups and parties (hikers, fishermen, hunters, etc.) to any point on Lake Manapouri. **Fiordland**

Cruises operates cruises and sea-fishing charters on Doubtful and Dusky sounds from $80 pp for a day trip (office on the main road to Te Anau, tel. Manapouri 609). Their six-day Captain Cook Cruise on Doubtful, Dusky, and Breaksea sounds has been highly recommended by fellow travelers. Rowboats can be hired from Manapouri Store to get across the river to bush walks in the Park (see below).

Short Walks

A variety of short walks in Fiordland National Park start on the opposite side of the lower Waiau River from Pearl Harbour. Hire a dinghy from the Manapouri Store to get across (or upriver); $3 pp plus a $10 deposit on oars, $2 a night if the dinghy is tied up on the other side overnight. The popular 3½-hour **Circle Track** follows the shoreline before climbing up a ridge to lookouts for excellent views of Hope Arm, Monument, Back Valley, Mt. Titiroa, and Garnock Burn. The three-hour **Pearl Harbour-Hope Arm Track** branches off the Circle Track leading past a lagoon and swamp, over the Garnock Burn to a lakeside beach and hut ($4 pp, coal provided). The **Back Valley** track takes about three hours, branching off the Hope Arm track to the Back Valley and Garnock Burn. Continue for another hour along Stinking Creek to **Lake Rakatu** for good birdwatching, fishing, and an excellent campsite on the far side of the lake (dinghy provided for public use).

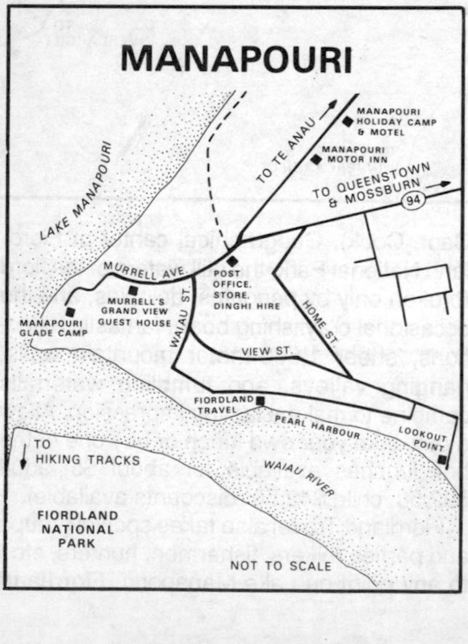

The **Hope Arm-Snow White Track** starts at the hut at the head of Hope Arm, then climbs and descends for longer hikes in the Upper Garnock Burn Valley, and good hunting; about 3½ hours OW. The fairly difficult **Monument Track** can only be reached from the beach at the head of the bay (north of Monument in Hope Arm)—get there by boat from Pearl Harbour. The 2½-hour RT track climbs steeply up to the bushline (be very careful on the crumbly rock and narrow ledges) where you get superb views of Lake Manapouri and the surrounding area; wear sturdy boots and take warm clothing for above the bushline.

Guided Fishing Or Hunting Trips

In the Lake Manapouri and Lake Hauroko (south Fiordland National Park) areas you can fish for rainbow and brown trout and salmon, and hunt for deer, chamois, or pigs. For a fishing/hunting guide call Mike Molineux (known for his reasonable rates) at tel. 511, or Alistair McDonald at tel. 893.

PRACTICALITIES

Accommodation

The closest YH is in Te Anau, but two motor camps provide a range of accommodations with great lake and mountain views. **Lake View Motel and Motor Park** is one km north of the p.o. on the main road to Te Anau. Situated along the lakefront, it has a sauna and spa pool, game room, two very creative playgrounds, communal facilities, and hospitable owners. In the shop you can buy all the basics. Tentsites are $14 d, caravan sites are $16 d in a large grassy area with plenty of shade trees. Cabins, some with double beds, are $13 s (be prepared to share) or $26 d (have it to yourself), very comfortable tourist cabins with cooking facilities (one has an outrageous lake view) are $33-35 d, a tourist flat with cooking facilities and TV is $55 d, and motel units are $65 d; located on Te Anau Rd.,

Murrell's Grand View Guest House

tel. 624. **Manapouri Glade Motor Park and Motel,** tel. 623, next to the river and lake, has a spa, TV, and trampoline. Caravan sites are $15 d, cabins are $24 d, the on-site caravan is $30 d, and motel units are $55 d.

The 100-year-old **Murrell's Grand View Guest House** is the most comfortable in Manapouri. The old rambling house boasts wide verandas, recently renovated homey rooms, mountain views, flower gardens, productive orchard and vegie garden (they're practically self-sufficient), and a deer pen with semi-tame deer (ask the owners to call in the deer—it's a delightful experience to be able to admire these gentle creatures close up). It's a stone's throw from the beach and only a short stroll from the store and post office. Friendly Jack and Klaske Murrell are the third generation of Murrells to run the guesthouse, and if you want to know anything about the local area, talk to Jack! Four rooms share two bathrooms, two rooms have private facilities; $46 s, $85 d B&B. A three-course dinner using home-grown vegies, fruit, and jams ("Grandmother's menu") is available for guests; $23 pp. Located on Murrell Ave. (look for the sign and the tall hedges across the road from the store), tel. 642.

Food And Entertainment

Manapouri is a quiet little settlement catering to outdoor pursuits and relaxation. The closest town of any size with a number of cafes and restaurants is Te Anau (19 km north)—but for a large variety in restaurants and exciting nightlife, you have to go back to Queenstown. The **Manapouri Store and P.O.** on the main road has all the basics, plus postal service, free maps of local walks, souvenirs, fishing equipment, petrol, and dinghy hire; open Mon. to Sat. from 0900-1730, Sun. 1400-1730. The only place to eat in Manapouri is the **DB Manapouri Motor Inn** on the main road to Te Anau, which has a tavern, bistro, and family bar (the only source of evening entertainment).

Services And Transportation

For medical aid, head for the **Te Anau Medical Centre** on Bligh St., tel. 7007; open by appointment Mon. to Fri., on weekends and public holidays for emergencies only. The main source of local **sightseeing info** and **coach service** to Te Anau is **Fiordland Travel Centre** at Pearl Harbour, open every day. The Manapouri-Te Anau bus departs twice a day. For a taxi, call **Murrell's Fiordland Car Tours** at tel. 642.

TE ANAU

THE CENTER OF FIORDLAND

Te Anau, commercial center of Fiordland, base for Fiordland National Park HQ, and year-round resort (the main industries are tourism and deer farming for venison), lies on the southeast shore of Lake Te Anau facing the rugged, glacier-carved mountains of Fiordland National Park. Lake Te Anau (61 km) is one of the longest lakes in the country, popular with trout and salmon fishermen. The word "Te Anau" is a shortened version of the original Maori word "Te Ana-au" or "Caves of Rushing Waters." The caves are on the other side of the lake—rediscovered relatively recently, they've become one of the most visited local attractions. Centrally located with a range of accommodations to suit all budgets, Te Anau is a good base for exploring the many natural attractions of the Park, and Milford Sound is less than a three-hour drive through magnificent scenery.

SIGHTS

Around The Lake

Start at **Fiordland Travel Centre** on the lakefront for cruise and tour information and tickets, brochures and maps (tel. 7416). Be sure to ask about the various discount packages and current "specials" before you hop on a boat. A cruise across Lake Te Anau to the 15,000-year-old "living" limestone caverns of **Te Ana-Au Caves** is one of the best cruises for the price; adult $25.50, child $9. The 2½-hour trip departs several times a day. If you've dabbled with the idea of someday doing the Milford Track (you have to book a year ahead through the THC Hotel and obtain the required $59.50 permit—or pay dearly for a guided hike) and want to get one step closer, take the **Glade House Tour** to Glade House, the track's starting point (see p. 518). The MV *Tawera* departs from Te Anau Downs, cruises to the northern end of the lake and allows time for exploring the Glade House area, for adult $32, child $9; catch an InterCity bus from Te Anau depot on Milford Rd. to Te Anau Downs (27 km north, additional cost). You can also book one of the cruises on Milford Sound (ask about Milford Sound-Doubtful Sound combined trip packages) at the Travel Centre—a good idea if you're traveling by bus or air and need a cruise that coincides with transportation schedules; if you're not on a tight schedule, buy your ticket at Milford Sound—there's plenty to see while you wait for a boat.

Another way to enjoy Lake Te Anau is onboard the *Manuska,* a 36-foot gaff ketch operated by **Sinbad Cruises**—highly recommended by fellow travelers. Choose from several daytime cruise options or an overnight trip with skipper/owner/boatbuilder Murray Cardno who "really knows his lake, mountains, and forests." For more info and bookings wander down to the Main Wharf where it's moored, or call 7106. A quiet, scenic raft trip (about 1½ hours), an exciting jetboat trip (also 1½ hours), or a combination are offered by **Rapid Travel** on the Waiau River bordering Fiordland National Park—get current prices (the trips range from $25-55 pp) and book through Fiordland Travel Centre or Mount Cook Line. Rapid Travel also provides water-taxi service to anywhere on Lake Te Anau (handy for hikers and hunters) and fishing charters (from $55 an hour, gear supplied). If you're traveling south to Manapouri, Fiordland Travel Centre operates bus transportation to coincide with Lake Manapouri cruises for $7 OW, and books a variety of scenic flights over the Park and fiords.

Around Town

For close-up views of rainbow, brown, and native trout, visit the **Te Anau Underground Trout Observatory** on Te Anau Rd., almost opposite HQ. You can feed them (food supplied free), get good "underwater" photographs, and stay in the observatory as long as you want. It's open seven days from dawn to 2145; entry is by two 50-cent (pp) coins in

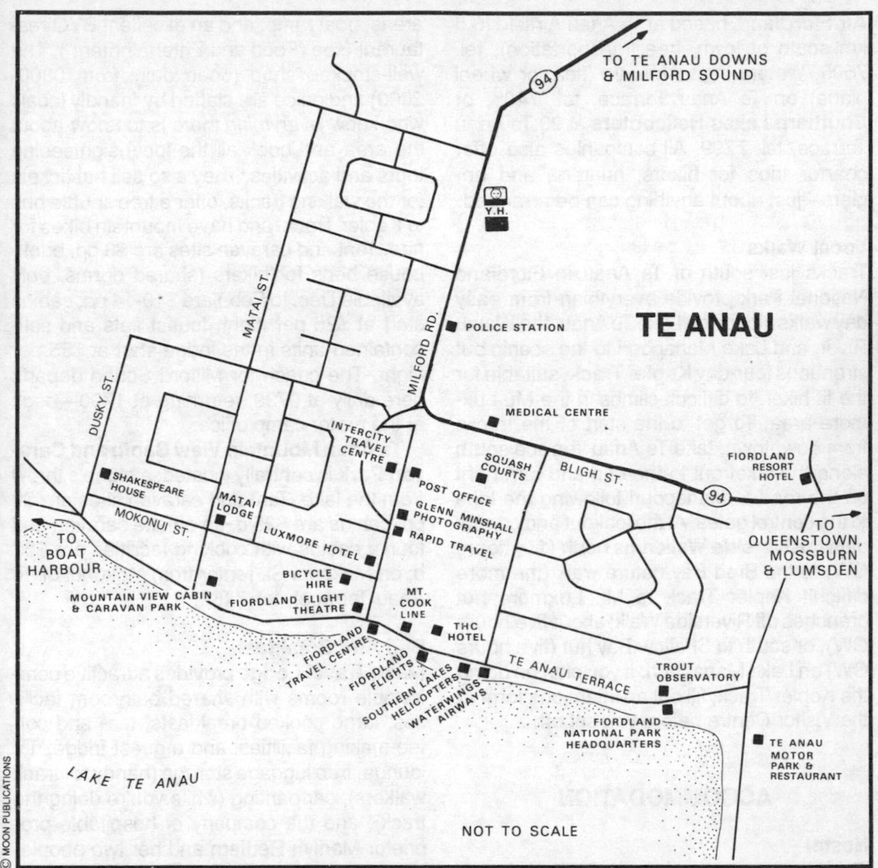

the turnstile. Other cheap entertainment (a place to keep in mind for a miserably wet day or early evening) is the **Milford Track and Milford Sound Audiovisual Theatre** in Glenn Minshall Photography on Milford Rd., tel. 7648. Relax in comfort while you watch a 20-minute slide show (six synchronized projectors on a giant screen in stereo) featuring the beauty of Fiordland National Park (a must if you're doing the Milford Track); open daily 0900-2100 in summer, 1000-2000 in winter, adult $3, child $2, family concessions.

Another must-see is the excellent **Te Anau Wildlife Centre** just south of Te Anau on the highway between Te Anau and Manapouri. Allow an hour to wander from one enclosure to the next to see some of New Zealand's most colorful and intriguing birds in park-like surroundings—including takahe (there are only about 150 of these rare flightless birds left in the wild), wekas, parakeets, aviary birds, waterfowl, and fish. Open dawn to dusk; admission is free.

Scenic Flights

Several companies in the area let you appreciate the bird's-eye view of Fiordland—by plane, float plane, or helicopter; the flights start at about $35 pp for 10 minutes and go all the way up! For brochures and prices call

Air Fiordland, based at Te Anau Airfield (6.5 km south of town, free transportation), tel. 7505, **Waterwings Airways** (float or wheel plane) on Te Anau Terrace, tel. 7405, or **Southern Lakes Helicopters** at 90 Te Anau Terrace, tel. 7799. All companies also offer charter trips for hikers, hunters, and anglers—just about anything can be arranged.

Local Walks

Tracks just south of Te Anau in Fiordland National Park provide everything from easy day walks alongside Lake Te Anau, the Waiau River, and Lake Manapouri to the scenic but strenuous four-day **Kepler Track,** suitable for the fit hiker, to difficult climbs in the Mt. Luxmore area. To get to the start of the tracks from downtown, take Te Anau Terrace south along the lakefront to the end and turn right on the road to Manapouri following the lake to the control gates. At the lookout and control gates, **Riverside Walk** runs north (1½ hours OW) to the Brod Bay nature walk (the more difficult Kepler Track to Mt. Luxmore hut branches off Riverside Walk; about five hours OW), or south to Shallow Bay hut (five hours OW) on Lake Manapouri. If you plan on doing the Kepler Track, fill out an intentions form at the Visitor Centre before you set off.

ACCOMMODATION

Hostel

The modern, well-equipped **Te Anau YHA Hostel** is on the main highway heading toward Milford Sound, 1.5 km from the lakefront. Storage facilities for hikers are available; $12 pp. Located on Milford Rd., four blocks from the lakefront, tel. 7847.

Motor Parks

If you're coming into Te Anau from Lumsden (Hwy. 94), large **Te Anau Motor Park,** tel. 7457 or 7965, is on Manapouri Rd. (first road to the left). It lies amongst plenty of trees in a beautiful lakeside setting, one km from downtown. Within the grounds are mini tennis courts, a sauna, volleyball court, TV, BBQ areas, boat ramp, and an excellent BYO restaurant (see "Food and Entertainment"). The well-stocked shop (open daily from 0800-2000) and office are staffed by friendly locals who know *everything* there is to know about the area and book all the local sightseeing tours and activities. They also sell hut tickets for the walking tracks, offer a free shuttle bus to Kepler Track, and have mountain bikes for hire. Tent and caravan sites are $8 pp, bunkhouse beds for hikers (shared dorms, only available Dec. to Feb.) are $10-14 pp, cabins start at $25 per night, tourist flats and self-contained units in the lodge start at $55 per night. The coach for Milford Sound departs here daily at 0730, returning at 1700—book at the motor camp office.

Te Anau Mountain View Cabin and Caravan Park is centrally located, a stone's throw from the lake. Tent and caravan sites are $8 pp, cabins are $25 d, an on-site caravan and tourist cabins with cooking facilities are $33 d; on Mokonui St. (enter from Mokonui or Te Anau Terrace), tel. 7462.

Bed And Breakfast

Matai Travel Lodge provides attractive comfortable rooms with shared bathroom facilities, large cooked breakfasts, tea- and coffee-making facilities, and a guest fridge, TV lounge, free luggage storage (handy for track walkers), car parking (while you're doing the track), and the company of hospitable proprietor Marilyn Redfern and her two people-loving cats; $38.50 s B&B, $58 d B&B, $78 triple B&B (reduced rates in winter—May through Sept./Oct.). Located at 42 Mokonui St. on the corner of Matai St., tel. 7360.

Shakespeare House has comfy rooms (some with private toilet and shower, others with private showers), an appealing breakfast room, and a great glassed-in porch that stretches along the front of all the rooms. Amiable owners, the Shakespeares, are bound to make your stay enjoyable; the house may be closed in winter—check ahead. The rates are $50 s B&B, $65-69 d B&B, and two budget rooms are $38.50 s or $50 twin; located at 10 Dusky St., tel. 7349.

Motels And Hotels

Te Anau also has plenty of motel and hotel rooms at the usual high prices—though it's worthwhile checking them out in winter for off-season reductions. **Fiordland Resort Hotel** offers excellent accommodations at prices to suit everyone from backpackers on a budget to those looking for comfort at no matter the cost! Facilities include a TV, pool, spa, TV room, kitchen, and laundry. Backpacker rooms each have three beds and a private bathroom for $10 pp ($13 pp with linen supplied), more comfy rooms with private baths and linen provided are $28.50 d, kitchen units are $51.50 d, and deluxe rooms with private bathrooms and kitchens are $71.50 d. As you enter Te Anau from Queenstown, the hotel is on the right side of the main highway (becomes Bligh St.), tel. 7511. **Luxmore Motor Lodge** on Milford Rd., tel. 7526, has all the modern facilities you'd expect, plus a coffee shop and several restaurants. Rooms start at $89 s, $71-99 d. The **THC Te Anau Resort Hotel** on Te Anau Terrace has lake views, several bars and restaurants, a pool and BBQ area, and rooms ranging from $130-300 plus GST per night.

OTHER PRACTICALITIES

Food And Entertainment

Te Anau has plenty of places to stay but lacks much of a selection when it comes to eating out on a budget. Your best bet is to buy some food and cook it yourself in the hostel or one of the motor camp kitchens. For fresh bread, cream and fruit buns, sponges, pastries, fruit tarts, pies, tacos, hot dogs, sandwiches, and filled rolls, try **The Upper Crust Bakery** in Luxmore Mall (off Mokonui St.); open daily 0730-2100.

Along the main streets downtown are several coffee shops, tearooms, and takeaways. One of the best is **Bailey's Restaurant and Coffee Shop** on Milford Rd., next to Luxmore Motor Lodge. It has a large selection of typical tearoom fare, light meals for around $7-10, and more substantial meals (steak, chicken, lamb, or fish with chips and salad) for $12-16. Mouthwatering desserts are $4-5.50. It's open daily 0700-2100, the staff are jovial, and this is the place where the Magic Bus stops to treat everyone to a free ice cream!

Another great place to eat is the BYO restaurant at **Te Anau Motor Park.** Aside from an excellent salad bar ($8.50 as a main order), the large variety of tasty dishes featuring New Zealand specialties range from $6.50-12.50, but you'll want to save room for one of the many delectable homemade desserts for $3.50 apiece; open daily from 0700 for breakfast, from 1800-2130 for dinner.

Two local suggestions include **Ming Garden Chinese Restaurant** where dinner for two is around $45, and **Keplers** (menu posted in the window), both on Milford Road. **Vacation Inn,** the Gallery, is open from 1800-2030 for meals at reasonable prices—good salad bar. For more ritzy dining at higher prices, head for the **THC Te Anau Hotel** on Te Anau Terrace (the family bar and bistro has good food at economy prices and a casual atmosphere), **Fiordland Motor Lodge** on Te Anau Highway, and **Luxmore Motor Lodge** on Milford Rd. (both have licensed restaurants).

For entertainment, the 20-minute **Milford Track Audiovisual Theatre** in the photography shop on Milford Rd. (see "Around Town" under "Sights") consists of spectacular slides of Fiordland; open 0900-2100, adult $3, child $2. For squash court bookings and prices, call **Fiordland Squash Club** at tel. 7461; equipment hire available. As a last resort, all the large hotels have public bars!

Services And Information

The **Te Anau Medical Centre** is on Bligh St., tel. 7007; make an appointment Mon. to Fri., open weekends and public holidays for emergencies. The **police station, p.o.,** and **bank** are all on Milford Road. For unusual designer wool sweaters and a large variety of "bush shirts" (a must for hikers), visit **Fiordland House** in the small shopping center on the corner of Milford Rd. and Te Anau Terrace.

Fiordland National Park Visitor Centre is on the lakefront at the east end of Te Anau Terrace; open daily from 0800-1700, tel. 7521 (after hours tel. 7397). For local **sightseeing info** and bookings, go to **Fiordland**

Travel Centre (tel. 7416, reservations tel. 7419), **Fiordland Flights** (tel. 7799), and **Mount Cook Line** (tel. 7516), all located along the lakefront on Te Anau Terrace; open every day.

Transportation

Getting in and out of Te Anau is no problem by public transportation, though hitchhiking might take you just short of forever! Bus services to and from Te Anau leave from the **InterCity** depot on Milford Rd., tel. 7559; ask about their RT day excursions to Milford Sound from Te Anau for $32 pp RT, $59 pp including a cruise (from Queenstown $95 RT). The InterCity bus to Manapouri leaves at 1100 daily (except Sun. in winter) for $7 OW; to Queenstown it's $26 OW, to Dunedin $42 OW. **Mount Cook Line** also runs coach service once a day to Milford Sound, tel. 7516; $55 from Te Anau ($95 from Queenstown).

Air services to and from Te Anau are operated by **Mount Cook Air Line.** Their office is on Te Anau Terrace, tel. 7516, open every day from 0830-1730 for airline, domestic travel (including InterCity), car rental, and local sightseeing reservations—it's also the place to go for general ongoing travel information. **Te Anau Airfield** is 6.5 km south of town. For single or tandem **bicycle hire** (bicycles $4 an hour, tandems $8 an hour), head for **Li'l Golf** (golf $4) around the corner from DCR Motors. For a **taxi,** call 7530.

FIORDLAND NATIONAL PARK

The Land

Fiordland National Park covers a remote area of more than 1.2 million hectares of forest-covered mountains, pristine fiords, lakes, enormous waterfalls, and rivers in the southwest corner of the South Island. It's the largest national park in the country (and one of the largest in the world), stretching from Martin's Bay and the Hollyford Valley in the north to Te Wae Wae Bay in the south, from the large lakes Te Anau and Manapouri in the east to 14 fiords along the heavily serrated western coastline. The rocks of Fiordland are among the most ancient in the country, and the mountains you see today were uplifted during the past 15 million years then carved into sheer valleys, large hollows, and fiords up to 40 km inland, during several periods of glaciation—the last ending only 14,000 years ago. After the ice melted, the sea flooded the coastal valleys and the inland hollows forming the mighty lakes of Te Anau and Manapouri, and lakes Monowai, Hauroko (deepest known lake in N.Z. at 462 meters), Poteriteri, and Hakapoua. In recent times the ice and snow have been largely replaced by an enormous amount of rain (in this area the people speak meters instead of millimeters!); however, after a heavy downpour the scenery is at its best.

The Park is a vast region of unspoiled wilderness—with areas not yet fully explored. The scenery can only be accurately described with superlatives—the deepest lake, finest walk, highest rainfall, second highest waterfall in the world, etc. Due to the remote rugged terrain, access is limited. Hikers, hunters, and anglers (with pioneer spirit in their blood) take boats to the far sides of lakes Te Anau and Manapouri to enter the Park; the only road access is Hwy. 94 (Milford Rd.) which runs from Te Anau town through the northern section of the Park to Milford Sound. If you're not able to get into the Park on foot, the next best ways to appreciate this magnificent landscape are by boat from Milford Sound, or by air from Te Anau or Milford Sound.

Climate

The climate ranges from mild to severe at any time of year. It's generally warm (but never hot) in the lower altitudes where snow is seldom seen and the rainfall is about 1,200 mm a year (Te Anau), but the entire west coast is battered by gale-force winds (the "Roaring Forties") and some of the heaviest rainfall in N.Z., receiving over 8,000 mm a year (up to 250 mm was recorded in one 24-hour period!); Milford Sound annually receives more than 7,200 mm. The coldest months (and best time to visit if you're hoping for drier weather) are May to Aug.—frost can be experienced east of the ranges, the road to Milford is usually open, but the high country beyond the Hollyford Valley is subject to heavy snowfalls and avalanches. The warmest months are Nov. to Feb. when much of the heaviest rainfall is experienced and the sandflies come out in force. Stop first at the Park Visitor Centre in Te Anau or Tuatapere Visitor Centre (in the south) for current weather forecasts, and make sure you're suitably equipped—Fiordland weather should never be taken lightly.

History

The Fiordland coast has a colorful history and is steeped in legend. Over many centuries the early Maori made seasonal visits here to fish, hunt, and collect greenstone, evidenced by old Maori campsites discovered in coastal rock shelters. Captain Cook first sailed along the coast in 1770, but was unable to land. He returned in 1773 and sailed the *Resolution* into Dusky Sound, accurately charting it and describing all the wildlife. From 1792 on, the Fiordland coast went through an intense period of mammal exploitation. Droves of Australian and American sealers slaughtered the N.Z. fur seal almost to extinction, and whaling lasted from 1829 (when land at inappropri-

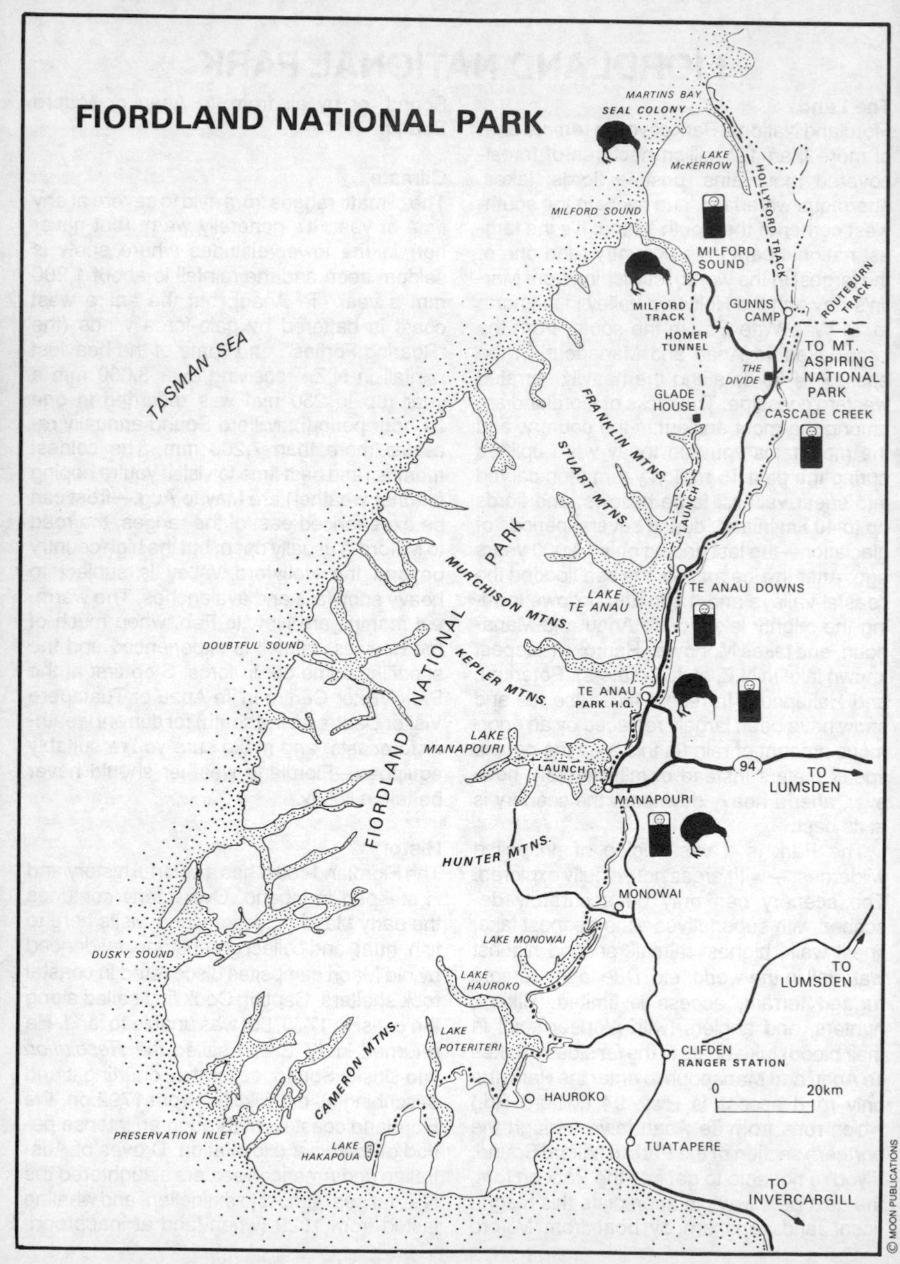
FIORDLAND NATIONAL PARK
MARTINS BAY
SEAL COLONY
LAKE McKERROW
HOLLYFORD TRACK
MILFORD SOUND
MILFORD SOUND
MILFORD TRACK
GUNNS CAMP
ROUTEBURN TRACK
HOMER TUNNEL
TO MT. ASPIRING NATIONAL PARK
THE DIVIDE
GLADE HOUSE
CASCADE CREEK
TASMAN SEA
FRANKLIN MTNS.
STUART MTNS.
LAUNCH
FIORDLAND NATIONAL PARK
MURCHISON MTNS.
TE ANAU DOWNS
LAKE TE ANAU
KEPLER MTNS.
DOUBTFUL SOUND
TE ANAU PARK H.Q.
LAKE MANAPOURI
LAUNCH
94
TO LUMSDEN
MANAPOURI
HUNTER MTNS.
MONOWAI
LAKE MONOWAI
DUSKY SOUND
LAKE HAUROKO
TO LUMSDEN
LAKE POTERITERI
CLIFDEN RANGER STATION
CAMERON MTNS.
HAUROKO
0
20km
PRESERVATION INLET
LAKE HAKAPOUA
TUATAPERE
TO INVERCARGILL
© MOON PUBLICATIONS

ately named Preservation Inlet in the south was bought from the Maori for a whaling station) to 1838.

During the mid- to late-1800s and early 1900s, pioneer explorers, surveyors, and gold prospectors set out to conquer this virgin wilderness, many of them naming the mountains, passes, and lakes they were the first to see. Quintin MacKinnon discovered the pass over which the famous **Milford Track** (see p. 518) crosses, and W. H. Homer found the Homer Saddle in 1889, proposing the tunnel (see "Te Anau To Milford" below) that took 14 years to complete, and which nowadays allows visitors to explore a small section of the Park by road. In the 1890s a brief gold rush again brought people to Preservation Inlet to mine or work the sawmill, but the gold ran out quickly, the township was abandoned, and the land was reclaimed by the forest. The Fiordland coast is now shared by seals, seabirds, and cray fishermen, and the Park is the realm of today's pioneering mountaineers, hikers, hunters, and anglers.

Flora And Fauna

Due to the high rainfall, just about everywhere you look you see flowing water and lush greenery. Rich, dark-green beech forest with a luxurlant understorey of prolific ferns, shrubs, mosses, and lichens carpets the landscape. Throughout much of Fiordland, the forest clings precariously to steep rock faces, roots entwined in a thin spongy pad of peat and moss that retains the heavy rainfall and allows understorey plants to thrive. Red, silver, and mountain beech are the three dominant species in the forest, with the podocarps—*rimu, miro,* Hall's *totara* scattered through the lowland forest, and *matai* and *kahikatea* found in swampier areas. In late spring and early summer the high slopes come alive with flowering alpine shrubs, daisies and buttercups, and other alpine herbs. Above treeline the land is dotted with small mountain lakes (tarns) and bogs surrounded by deep peat, white-flowered donatia, and alpine grasses.

A large variety of insects live in Fiordland—the sandflies are worst and most ferocious. These tiny black insects (they hatch in running water) inflict painful bites that swell and itch and cause great discomfort when your sleeping bag warms up at night! They're most annoying in calm weather and around dusk, and insect repellent is at times more of a "must have" for the outdoor enthusiast than food. (Mosquitoes are there, though not noticeable in comparison.) All kinds of native cicadas are found in the Park, along with night-flying moths, stoneflies and beetles, and some butterflies.

takahe

A great variety of both native and introduced birds thrive here—ask at HQ for the pamphlet "Fiordland Birds And Where To Find Them." The most unique aspect of local birdlife is the four kinds of flightless birds. The nocturnal South Island brown kiwi, *weka,* and *kakapo* (a large, nocturnal, yellow-green ground parrot on the brink of extinction), and the *takahe* (a large blue and iridescent green bird with scarlet bill and feet, one of New Zealand's rarest birds) all live in Fiordland National Park. You can see a mounted *kakapo* and *takahe* at the Visitor Centre in Te Anau. The Murchison and Stuart Mountains, west of Lake Te Anau, where most of the few remaining *takahe* survive, have been designated as a refuge, with no public access, to ensure that the birds survive in their natural habitat. Another rare bird found in the Park is the southern crested grebe. Along the fiords live great numbers of penguins, the Fiordland crested penguin the most predominant, and N.Z. seals are commonly seen. Stoats, red deer, chamois, pigs, and wapiti (or elk—the Fiordland herd is unique to the Southern Hemisphere) are also found throughout the Park.

SIGHTS

If you're an energetic type or camera nut, magnificent sights await discovery throughout the Park, and some of the best scenery in the country awaits you along the four major hiking tracks in the region—the Milford, Hollyford, Kepler, or Routeburn tracks (see p. 518). For the sightseer, various cruises operate on lakes Manapouri and Te Anau (see previous chapter) and launches run the length of Milford Sound; flightseeing companies offer a variety of scenic flights from Te Anau, Lower Hollyford Valley, and Milford Sound; and the scenic 119-km highway to Milford is the best way to get a taste of the Park if you're traveling by car or bus. For info and maps, stop at the **Visitor Centre** on Te Anau Terrace, Te Anau, tel. 7921; open daily from 0800-1700.

TE ANAU TO MILFORD

Set Off Early

Highway 94 north, or Milford Rd., is best seen by bicycle or car—viewpoints or short tracks are bound to lure you off the road at regular intervals. **Milford Sound Adventure Tours** offers a unique bicycle tour—ride all the uphill stretches by coach and the downhill stretches on a sturdy mountain bike, traveling to Milford Sound for a launch ride and then along the Hollyford Valley; $60 pp. For more info call Vaughn Campbell in Te Anau at tel. 7227. **Magic Bus** and **InterCity** operate daily coach excursions along Milford Rd., departing Te Anau in the morning and returning late in the afternoon (there's only one lodge providing budget accommodation and the THC Hotel at Milford).

Stock up on film and insect repellent, and set off as early in the morning as possible—the mountains cloud up and disappear as the day progresses, and in summer it's a case of beating the bad weather; allow at least 2½ hours without side trips. In winter the road may occasionally be closed due to various inclemencies—get current road conditions from the Visitor Centre or check the sign on the outskirts of Te Anau before continuing.

Places To Stop

Te Anau Downs, 27 km north of Te Anau, is the launch departure point for hikers doing the Milford Track, and location of the **Best Western Te Anau Downs Motor Lodge** (tel. 7811; economy rooms start at $62 d, fight your way through the bus tours), restaurant, shop, and petrol station. **Mirror Lakes** farther on are worth a stop; a short wooden plank walkway runs through a forest alive with bellbirds, along several small lakes that mirror all that's around them on a still day. Continuing along the highway you pass many picnic spots and a couple of camping areas with toilets and fresh water. The busy **Cascade Creek Campground** (shown on maps as the last campground, 74 km from Te Anau) is next to a large lodge, motel, and tearooms, but if you continue to beautiful **Lake Gunn,** you can camp in a nicer, more private area (no facilities) surrounded by trees along the edge of the lake—wake up to Fiordland songbirds and fabulous mountain reflections, and catch a trout for breakfast. For the best views of the lake and the Livingstone Mountains, take an early morning hike along the short **Black Lake Track** that runs along the west side of the lake at the south end.

At **The Divide,** lowest east-west pass in the Southern Alps (531 meters), the popular Routeburn, Caples, and Greenstone tracks lead overland to Lake Wakatipu, and not much farther along the highway, Hollyford Valley Rd. leads off the highway to **Gunn's Camp**—a campground with cabins, a small store and petrol station, and excellent **early settlers museum.** At the end of the road starts the Hollyford Track to Martins Bay. From Hollyford Rd. to Homer Tunnel, Milford Rd. passes through some of the most magnificent scenery to be found! The 1.2-km **Homer Tunnel** is another local feat of engineering (built on and off between 1935 and

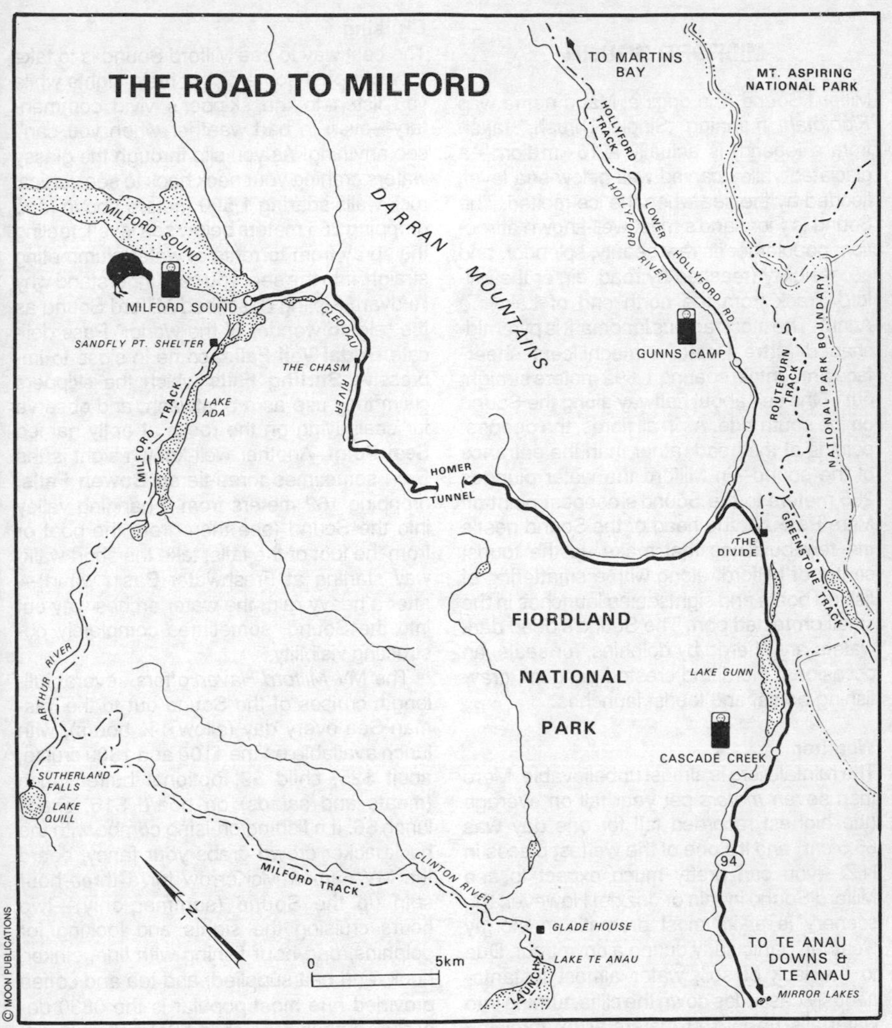

1954) descending at a grade of one in ten through a mountain to the **Cleddau Portal** on the other side—drive through it with care as it can get foggy and icy inside. Cross the Cleddau River, then look out for a track leading to the **Chasm,** a sight that shouldn't be missed; a 10-minute walk takes you to two fascinating view points. From the Chasm to Milford, the road descends steeply through the **Cleddau Valley** between sheer rock walls that become endless waterfalls after a good rain. After several river crossings you pass **Milford Sound Airport** and the road ends abruptly at the **THC Milford Resort Hotel.**

MILFORD SOUND

Milford Sound (the original Maori name was *Piopiotahi* meaning "Single Thrush," taken from a legend) is actually a 16-km fiord—a glaciated valley carved well below sea level, flooded by the sea when the ice melted. The Sound is Fiordland's most well-known attraction, popular for its raw beauty, splendor, and accessibility (reached by road, air, or the Milford Track from the north end of Lake Te Anau). The most famous landmark is pyramid-shaped **Mitre Peak,** a magnificent sheer-faced mountain soaring 1,692 meters straight out of the sea about halfway along the Sound on the south side. As in all fiords, the deepest point is at the head rather than the entrance of the sound—in Milford the water plunges 265 meters to the Sound's deepest point off Mitre Peak. At the head of the Sound nestle the few buildings that make up the tourist center of Milford, along with a smattering of fishing boats and sightseeing launches in the small protected port. The Sound's deep dark waters are shared by dolphins, fur seals, an occasional Fiordland crested penguin, cray-fishing boats, and tourist launches.

Weather

The rainfall here is almost unbelievable. More than seven *meters* per year fall on average (the highest recorded fall for one day was 65.5 cm) and it's one of the wettest places in N.Z.—you can pretty much expect to see Milford Sound in rain or drizzle! However, the scenery is at its most dramatic in stormy weather, particularly during a downpour. Due to the lack of soil, water almost instantaneously cascades down the cliffs, turning into waterfalls up to 100 meters wide, throwing plumes of spray high into the air. The clouds cover the mountain tops, the mist comes down, and you swear the waterfalls are falling straight out of the sky. The Sound also has distinct moods that change with the weather—it can be serenely beautiful on a sunny day when the reflections are mirror-perfect (in winter), mysteriously shrouded in low clouds and mist, or downright spectacular in the rain.

Cruising

The best way to see Milford Sound is to take a cruise past some of the main sights while you listen to the skipper's vivid commentary—even in bad weather when you can't see anything! As you slip through the glassy waters craning your neck back to see vertical rock walls soaring 1,500 meters above (and dropping 265 meters below sea level), feeling the spray from torrents of water plummeting straight into the sea, you can understand why Rudyard Kipling described Milford Sound as the "eighth wonder of the world." Pass delicate **Bridal Veil Falls,** come in close to impressive **Stirling Falls** which the skippers claim they use as a boatwash, and observe fur seals lying on the rocks at aptly named **Seal Point.** Another well-known sight is the two-, sometimes three-tiered **Bowen Falls,** dropping 162 meters from a hanging valley into the Sound (see them from the boat or from the foot of the falls; take the short walkway starting at Freshwater Basin wharf)—after a heavy rain, the water arches way out into the Sound, sometimes completely obstructing visibility.

The MV *Milford Haven* offers several full-length cruises of the Sound out to the Tasman Sea every day (allow 1¾ hours), with lunch available on the 1100 and 1300 cruise; adult $25, child $9, optional buffet lunch (meats and salads) on board $15, snack lunch $6. If a fishing/cruising combo with the backpacker crowd grabs your fancy, board the MV James McKerrow for a three-hour spin up the Sound (summer only)—two hours cruising the sights and looking for dolphins, one hour fishing with line, sinker, hook, and bait supplied, and tea and coffee provided (the most popular is the 0830 departure); adult $25, child $9; book at Fiordland Travel in Te Anau or buy tickets at the wharf. **Red Boats** (run by the THC) also offers a 1¾-hour cruise, about nine km to the head of the Sound, for adult $25, child $9; (the 1030 cruise is the longest and often the least crowded); buy tickets in the hotel lobby. For any cruise, take a warm waterproof jacket, even in mid-summer.

Get a great view of Mitre Peak from Milford Sound Airport.

Flightseeing
If the weather is fine and you can afford an unforgettable three-dimensional experience, head for any booking agent or the booth in the THC Milford lobby where the staff arrange regular **Mount Cook Airline** flights from Milford (tel. 8088) to Te Anau (tel. 7516) and Queenstown (tel. 27-650)—the 30-minute flight between Queenstown and Milford is one of the most spectacular in the country—and worth every cent of the $110 OW fare! The staff also make bookings for spectacular scenic flights over Milford Sound and environs by plane (from $35-86 pp), floatplane, and helicopter. Flights vary widely in duration and price, starting at adult $39, child $29 for a 10-minute flight over the mouth of the Sound. Scenic flights are also available from Martins Bay at the end of the Hollyford Valley Track; for more info call Hollyford Tourist & Travel Co., Invercargill, tel. 44300. **Milford Sound Scenic Flights** and **Waterwings** also provide scenic flight service; contact local booking agents or call in at the THC Milford. **Southern Lakes Helicopters** offers scenic flights starting at $61 pp for the 13-minute Mitre Peak flight; book at the THC or call 7167/7067.

Short Walks
Several short walks from Milford provide excellent views of the Sound. **Bowen Falls Walk** starts at the rock face by the jetties in Freshwater Basin, follows the shoreline, and comes out at the first view of the falls (which provide the hotel with water and drive a small hydroelectric plant); about 30 minutes, take a waterproof jacket. **Look-out Track** starts at the west end of the hotel and leads up a steep flight of steps to a lookout for magnificent views of the Sound (five minutes); for the more experienced, continue up the steep ridge for another hour or so to two more viewpoints. The track then descends to the road that leads to the tourist boat jetties.

Practicalities
The **THC Milford Hotel** provides accommodation (rooms start at $143 s or d), a licensed restaurant and bar, souvenir shop, and sightseeing cruise and flight offices. The staff can also arrange charter fishing trips and helicopter scenic flights. The **Lobster Pot Restaurant** serves a Continental breakfast for $9.90, a cooked breakfast for $16.50, and lunch for around $21. At dinner choose from vegetarian, lamb, pork, steak, and venison dishes, and fresh-from-the-sound seafood specialties for $12-27 a main course. Milford also has garage facilities and petrol.

Back about one km from the hotel (off the main road down a short road) is **Milford Lodge** providing budget hostel-type accommodation (twins, doubles, triples, quads, and dorms), communal bath and cooking facilities, a guest lounge with cozy open fireplace, sauna, shop with tramping supplies, and a restaurant where you can get hearty budget meals ($8 mains, $2-3 desserts); $15 pp on a share basis. Camp and van sites are also available from $5 pp.

The most reasonably priced place to eat is Milford Lodge (open only in summer). No regularly scheduled entertainment happens in Milford—it's strictly make your own! The friendly **Magic Bus** crowd departs from the boat wharf, the public bar, and Milford Lodge for Te Anau and Queenstown. The **InterCity** coach leaves daily from outside the hotel for Te Anau (schedule in hotel lobby). **Gray Line** runs coach tours for $95 from Queenstown and $55 from Te Anau to Milford, including a cruise on the sound. **Great Sights** also has a "Milford Daytripper" tour; $99 from Queenstown, including a cruise on the sound.

MAJOR HIKING TRACKS

Fiordland National Park is probably the best place in N.Z. for hikers. More than 500 km of developed tracks of varying standards and difficulty criss-cross the Park, with huts (fees payable to hut wardens, Park Visitor Centre in Te Anau, or Tuatapere Ranger Station) at regular intervals. The four major hiking tracks—Milford, Hollyford, Routeburn, and Kepler—can be walked independently (you're called an "independent walker"), staying in basic huts where you provide everything yourself, or done with a guided group staying in more comfortable huts with bedding, food, and hot showers in some. Info sheets on most tracks and detailed maps are available at the Park Visitor Centre and Tuatapere Ranger Station. Notify the Visitor Centre of your hiking intentions and be sure to sign out on your return, be adequately prepared for high rainfall and bad weather, and check transportation schedules before you set out on any of the three main hiking tracks—hitchhiking is terrible along Milford Road. Magic Bus and InterCity operate daily coaches but seats have to be booked ahead of time. Mount Cook and Waterwings fly in to Milford from Queenstown and Te Anau. Waterwings' floatplanes also service the Milford Track.

Milford Track

Often referred to as "the finest walk in the world," the Milford Track starts at the north end of Lake Te Anau; take a bus from Te Anau to Te Anau Downs then a boat to Glade House (see "Te Anau"). Hikers here follow in the footsteps of the earliest pioneers, passing through river valleys surrounded by magnificent mountain scenery, up and over 1,073-meter **Mackinnon Pass,** with a sidetrack to breathtaking **Sutherland Falls** which plunge 580 meters in three cascades—highest waterfall in N.Z. and fourth highest in the world. The track finishes at **Sandfly Point** on Milford Sound, where clouds of hungry sandflies descend on hikers awaiting the launch to Milford.

The track is 54 km long, takes four days, requires good fitness (rough terrain), and is so popular that it's usually booked out up to one year ahead—call the Milford Track office in the THC Te Anau Hotel (tel. 7411) or the Park Visitor Centre for all the details. Independent walkers need a $59.50 permit from the THC Te Anau Hotel to do the track; this includes hut fees and the launch ride at the end. You need to pre-arrange transportation connections and book your seat in advance. Expect to pay $125.50 pp for the track permit and transportation to and from the track; accommodation and meals extra. Guided walks are operated by the **Tourist Hotel Corporation of N.Z.** and **Freedom Holidays**—pick up brochures at most info centers. **Waterwings'** floatplanes fly hikers to Glade House for $288.75 (charter rate; up to four can share), or you can be collected at the end of the track at Sandfly Point and fly back over the track for $536.25 (up to four). They also offer daily flights from Milford Sound to Te Anau and Queenstown, overflying Milford Track, for $108 pp.

Hollyford Track

The Hollyford Track is another popular walk through the longest valley in Fiordland (80 km

ground fern

from the sheer jagged **Darran Mountains** to coastal sand dunes and a colony of protected fur seals), with spectacular scenery along the upper section and good fishing and hunting along the Lower Hollyford. The track begins at the end of Lower Hollyford Rd. (which branches off Milford Rd. about 100 km from Te Anau); Magic Bus and InterCity coaches drop off and pick up hikers here but seats have to be pre-booked. Expect to walk the nine km along the road to the start of the track (one Magic Bus a day, Nov. to May, goes to the start of the track; reserve a seat ahead of time)—hitchhiking is virtually nonexistent. If you hike all the way to Martins Bay, the track takes up to 10 days RT, with five huts along the way and more huts along side tracks—stock up on supplies at Gunn's Camp. If you only have time to do half the track, catch a jetboat back from Martins Bay to the south end of **Lake McKerrow;** book through Hollyford Tours (see below) before you set out. If you want to do the track as a guided walk, contact **Hollyford Tourist & Travel Co.** in Invercargill, tel. 4300 (24 hours). They offer four-day walk in/fly out tours or five-day walk in/walk out tours which include transportation to the start of the track, accommodation, meals, and jetboat ride.

Routeburn Track

The magnificent three- to four-day Routeburn Track is 39 km long and passes through high mountain scenery in both Fiordland and Mount Aspiring national parks. It runs between the Divide on Milford Rd. and Routeburn Rd. at the north end of Lake Wakatipu, with huts at regular intervals. An alpine pass has to be crossed, the weather can be severe, and it can snow at any time of year. It can be done by independent walkers, or as a guided tour with **Routeburn Walk Ltd.** of Queenstown, tel. 27-100. Get more info and a detailed map at Fiordland Park Visitor Centre in Te Anau, Mt. Aspiring Park HQ in Wanaka, or at the NZTP Travel Office or Dept. of Conservation Visitor Information Centre in Queenstown (see p. 499).

Kepler Track

This circular 67-km track is the latest to be constructed in the Park. Starting between Te Anau and Manapouri at the Lake Te Anau Control Gates (a 4.6-km, 45-minute walk from the Te Anau Visitor Centre), it meanders along the Waiau River and Lake Te Anau, then up past limestone cliffs to the bushline for panoramic views. From the Mt. Luxmore Hut the track climbs through stunning alpine scenery, wanders through beech and podocarp forest, along Lake Manapouri, then back along the Upper Waiau River to the original starting point. It's a four-day walk suitable for hikers with above-average fitness, though everyone can enjoy *some* sections of the track; access has been provided for those wishing to fish or hunt (appropriate licenses required) and climb. In summer take water for the alpine section (it can be very dry), and be prepared in winter for snow and adverse weather conditions that can close the alpine stretch. Serviced huts equipped with mattresses, water, flush toilets, heating, and gas cooking and lighting are found at regular intervals along the track; pay hut fees to hut wardens (not present from late April to early Nov.) or at the Park Visitor Centre. Camping is allowed only at Dock, Brod, and Shallow bays. Before setting out on the track, call in at the Park Visitor Centre (tel. 7921) to find out track and weather conditions, and collect the handy brochure giving a brief description of the track's geology, history, flora and fauna, scenery between huts, and map (buy a detailed map if you're doing the track). For your safety, don't forget to complete an Intentions Form before you set out (and remember to sign out again on your return), and sign the visitor book in each hut. **Waterwings** flies hikers over the Kepler Track then drops them off by the track at either Shallow Bay, Lake Manapouri, or Brods Bay, Lake Te Anau for $49 pp (minimum three). For reservations call 7405 or 7566.

CLIMBING, FISHING, AND HUNTING

The best rock climbing in the Park is on the hard granite of the **Darran Mountains** (near Homer Tunnel) where you find 2,746-meter **Mt. Tutoko**—highest peak in Fiordland. The Darrans are easily reached from Milford Rd. and the Homer huts are a favorite gathering spot for keen mountaineers during the summer—some tantalizing unexplored areas still await discovery. Before you set off to conquer the mountains, call in at the Visitor Centre for info, maps, and weather forecasts, and leave your intentions.

Excellent fishing for brown and rainbow trout is found in all the main lakes and rivers, with particularly large trout lurking in remote **Lake McKerrow;** the season runs from 1 Nov. to 31 May in most of the rivers, open all year in the main lakes—the Eglinton River is reserved for fly-fishing only. Pick up your Southern Lakes fishing license at Te Anau Sports Centre, Te Anau Visitor Centre, or Te Anau Motor Park.

Red deer, wapiti (elk), opossums, goats, chamois, and hares are found in the Park, and because of the damage they inflict on native vegetation, hunting is encouraged; get details on recreational and trophy shooting, maps, and a hunting or trapping permit from the Te Anau Visitor Centre or Tuatapere Visitor Centre.

SOUTH AND STEWART ISLAND

THE SOUTH

Southland, southernmost area of the South Island, is a landscape of hills, lush sheep pastures, plains liberally criss-crossed by trout-filled rivers, large forest parks, and a wild, rugged coastline. Intensive farming is practiced on the plains stretching from the Waiau River in the west to the provincial border in the east—this productive and obviously prosperous region produces more than six million lambs a year, 36 million kg of wool, two million bushels of wheat, 6,000 tonnes of potatoes, and 5,000 tonnes of cheese! The bulk of the region's wealth comes from more than eight million sheep, though the dairy factories, small seed producers, timber mills, fertilizer, cement, and freezer works, paper mlll, coalmine, and aluminium smelter are all major contributors.

The main economic and industrial center of Southland is **Invercargill,** the country's eighth largest city and departure point for traveling across Foveaux Strait to **Stewart Island. Bluff,** 27 km south of Invercargill, is the region's chief port and harbor, and southernmost point of the South Island. In the remote southeast lies the unspoiled scenic region of the **Catlins.** The central Southland town of **Gore** is the region's second largest town—its location near many of the best trout rivers makes it an excellent place to kick back and get into some real fishing.

From Te Anau To Invercargill

If you don't have much time, take direct Hwy. 6 south from Lumsden. But if you're agriculturally minded, have your own transportation, and enjoy scenic sidetracks off the main tourist drag, meander east along Hwy. 94 crossing fertile plains and sheep country to Gore. (Want some good sheep photographs? This is the area to find your subjects in all their woolly glory.) To the north of Gore along Hwy. 90 lies more beautiful countryside and the **Blue Mountains,** known for good deer hunting; if you continue north to the intersection of Hwy. 8 and drive east, the road wanders through several picturesque old gold towns. Return to Gore by Hwy. 1 south (this circular route takes about three hours).

The regional urban center of **Gore** (66 km northeast of Invercargill) lies on the banks of the **Mataura River,** reputedly one of the best brown trout rivers "in the world." Wide streets, attractive old-style architecture (dominated downtown by a five-story cereal and flour mill—one of the largest "in the country"), and many parks and gardens give Gore its appeal. The locals are friendly (this is not a tourist town), quite willing to stop and talk to a visitor. Anglers flock from afar to dangle their lines in the Mataura River and its myriad streams, and to explore the fishing possibilities of the **Mimihau, Pomahaka, Oreti,** and **Waikaia rivers** in the surrounding region; get your hot tips and a license at any sporting store downtown. About five km west of Gore lies a hilly scenic reserve, **Croydon Bush,** where you can view a large range of native flora, while wandering at will along tracks through grassland, forest, and valleys crammed with lush ferns. Formal **Dolamore Park** with its contrasting lawns and flower gardens lies next to the reserve, and camping (limited facilities) is permitted within the grounds; contact the caretaker at the kiosk.

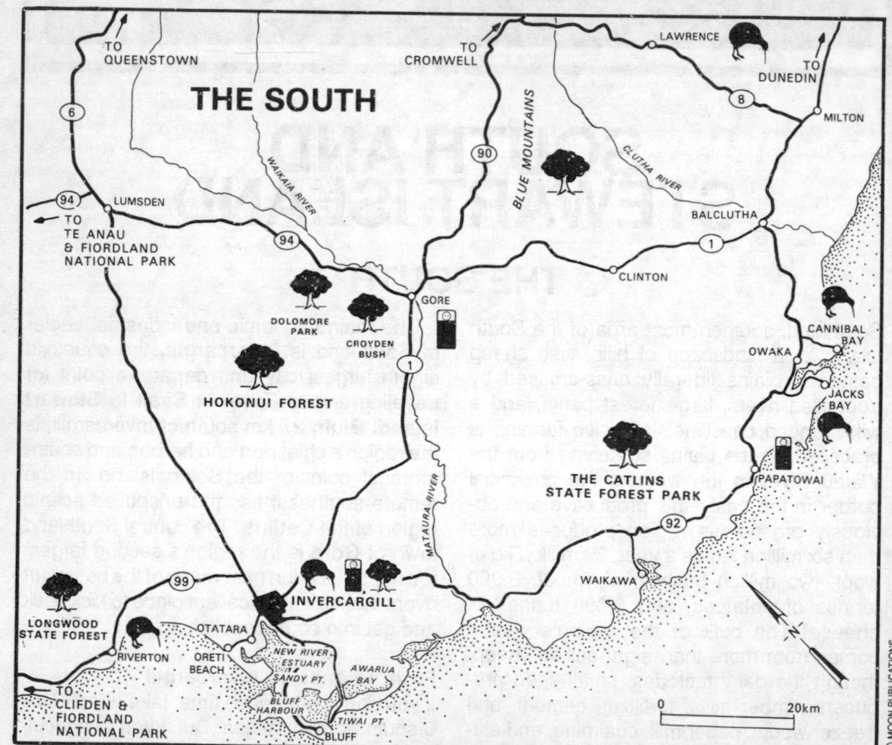

one of the highlights in Gore—an enormous brown trout!

Gore Camping Ground, tel. 84-919, is on the main road south, off Broughton St., one km from Gore P.O.; communal facilities, tentsites $6 pp, caravan sites $8 s, $14 d, cabins $15 s, $25 d.

If you have some extra time to explore, another alternate and worthwhile route from Te Anau to Invercargill is the sealed "Southern Scenic Route," passing gentle rural scenery (heaps of sheeps!), access roads to beautiful **Lake Monowai** and **Lake Hauroko,** lakeside huts, and walking tracks in Fiordland National Park, the small township of **Tuatapere** (info center on the main road), and several small coastal towns. Pick up the "Southern Scenic Route" brochure (lists attractions along the route) from info centers and Dept. of Conservation offices.

From Dunedin To Invercargill

The direct route is Hwy. 1 south via Gore—but if you have plenty of time and like to get off the beaten track, take the coastal route (Hwy. 92) from Balclutha through the remote, beautiful **Catlins Region** on your way to Invercargill (add two hours). Meander through the nine podocarp-hardwood forests that make up **Catlins Forest Park,** getting tempting glimpses of isolated sandy beaches and rugged coastal scenery; sidetracks to the coast are worthwhile (especially **Cannibal Bay** north of Owaka and **Jack's Bay** south of Owaka). Birds abound in the Catlins, the rivers provide all types of trout fishing and whitebaiting in season (get your license at local sportshops), and sea-fishing for blue cod is popular along the coast. Historic, scenic, and recreational reserves line the road—most providing short scenic nature walks, lookouts, campgrounds (limited facilities) or picnic areas, and toilets and fresh water. **Papatowai Motor Camp** has tent and caravan sites and the usual facilities at Papatowai, 30 km south of Owaka on Hwy. 92; caretaker, tel. Balclutha 58-063, reserves ranger, tel. 58-341. The nearest store (petrol available) is two km away at McLennan.

Before you explore this area, stop at the **Catlins Information Centre** on the corner of Campbell and Ryley sts., Owaka, tel. 58-341, or the **Dept. of Conservation Information Centre** on Don St., Invercargill, tel. 44-589—there's so much to see in this relatively small area that it's best to get the entire run-down beforehand. The Dept. of Conservation puts out excellent pamphlets, *Walks and Tracks in the Catlins, Catlins Birds, Catlins Trout Fishing,* and *Southern Solitude* (info about the Catlins region), along with a handy list of accommodations and *The Catlins—Guidebook to the Catlins and Surrounding Districts* by Rhys Buckingham and John Hall-Jones (lots of color photos, maps, and places of interest); all available at the Dept. of Conservation Information Centre in Invercargill.

INVERCARGILL

SIGHTS

Invercargill, "Capital City of the Friendly South," is a well-planned city originally settled by Scottish people, with wide tree-lined streets named after Scottish rivers, many beautiful parks and reserves (the acreage of parks per population is highest in N.Z.), and plenty of reasonable places to stay, though it's not the place to come for titillating tourist attractions or exciting nightlife! The main attraction is nearby Stewart Island, 24 km across Foveaux Strait.

Places To Walk

Eighty-hectare **Queens Park** on Queens Dr. is a peaceful green spot in the central city, the perfect place to while away some time, especially on the weekend when everything closes. Wander past perfect lawns under all kinds of native and exotic trees, visit the large aviary, statuary, gardens, and duck ponds, and if you're feeling energetic, follow the fitness trail. Beautiful lawns, gardens, and native bush are also found in **Anderson Park** around the **Art Gallery,** eight km north of city center. Before Invercargill was built, the entire area was natural bush—see how it used to be in **Waihopai Scenic Reserve,** 34 hectares on the city's northern outskirts, with a 2.8-km walk along the Waihopai River (starts on Hwy. 6 at Gladstone Terrace and finishes on Racecourse Rd.; one hour OW), and 120-hectare **Seaward Bush** southeast of Invercargill.

Sandy Point Reserve, west of the city along **New River Estuary,** is another good area for short bushwalks with views of the estuary, Invercargill, and several protected beaches. Get info and brochures on walking tracks around the city and the region at the Dept. of Conservation Information Centre in the State Insurance Building, Don St., tel. 44-589. **Oreti Beach,** 9.5 km west of the city along the shores of Foveaux Strait, is a long sweep of sand excellent for walking; on a clear day, you can see Stewart Island. The water is also warmer here than along many South Island beaches thanks to a warm current from Australia.

Southland Museum And Art Gallery

Located near the entrance to Queens Park, the museum features items from the province's early days, a collection of Maori artifacts, and a fascinating "tuatarium," the only place in the country where you can see live *tuataras* in a closely simulated native environment. The *tuatara* looks like a lizard but is actually the only surviving species of the *Rhynchocephalia* group of reptiles, once widespread but now only found on about 30 islands off the northeast coast of the North Island and Cook Strait (they're featured on the N.Z. five-cent coin). Described as New Zealand's "living fossils," the *tuatara's* lifespan is not known for sure but it's believed that they live to be at least 100 years old. The museum is open Mon. to Fri. 1000-1630, Sat. 1300-1700, Sun. and holidays 1400-1700. Also in Queens Park is the Astronomical Observatory, open Wed. evenings 1900-2100 April through September.

tuatara

City Bus Tour

A good way to see the sights and get an impression of the city and environs is by the **H & H Travel Lines** City Bus Tour, departing weekdays at 1315 from the depot on the

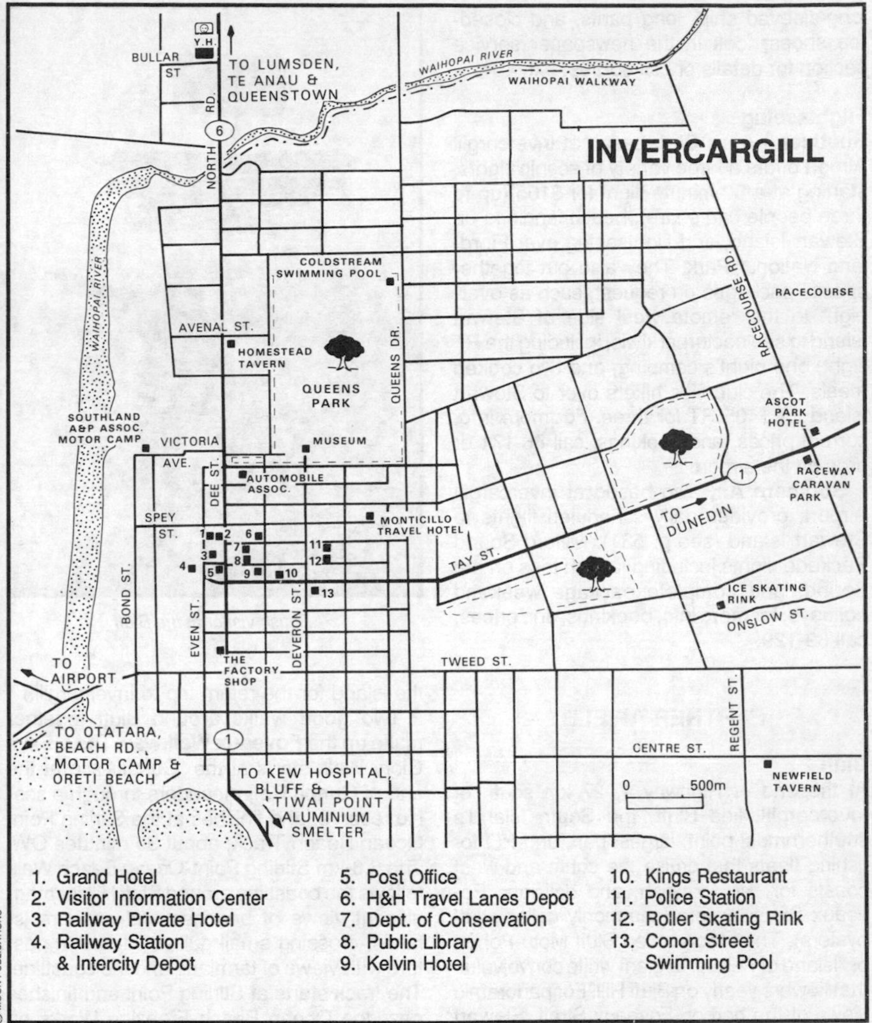

corner of Don and Kelvin streets. It covers (with commentary) the central city and open country, airport, Oreti Beach with views of Stewart Island, elegant Otatara homes secluded in native bush, incredible grounds of Ascot Park Hotel, racecourse, Queens Park, art gallery, and other parks and gardens; about two hours, $14.50 pp.

Tiwai Aluminium Smelter

The Aluminium Smelter at Tiwai Point, 26 km south of the city, is the largest smelter in the Southern Hemisphere, eighth largest in the world, and a vital part of Southland economy. Free tours are offered on Tues. and Thurs. at 1400 but you need to book ahead, have your own transportation out there, and wear a long-sleeved shirt, long pants, and closed-toe shoes; look in the newspaper service section for details or call 85-999, ext. 491.

Flightseeing

Southland Aero Club based at Invercargill Airport offers a large variety of scenic flights, starting at a 30-minute flight for $105 (up to three people can share), beach landings on Stewart Island, and flightseeing over Fiordland National Park. They also put together special packages on request, such as overnight to the remote west side of Stewart Island to see nocturnal kiwis, including the RT flight, one night's camping, and two cooked meals. The club flies hikers over to Stewart Island for $405 RT for three. For more info, current prices, and bookings, call 86-171 or drop by the airport.

Southern Air, also based at Invercargill Airport, provides daily scheduled flights to Stewart Island (see p. 531), Milford Sound Package flights including launch trips on the Sound, and complete package weekend holidays; for more info, bookings, and prices, call 89-129.

British visitor at the Bluff

FARTHER AFIELD

Bluff

At the end of Highway 1, 27 km south of Invercargill, lies Bluff, the South Island's southernmost point, largest port, and HQ for fishing fleets that cruise the south and west coasts for fish, crayfish, and delicious Foveaux Strait oysters (commonly called Bluff oysters). The Maori called Bluff Motu-Pohue or "Island of Pohue," a giant white convolvulus that flowers yearly on Bluff Hill. For panoramic views of the harbor, Foveaux Strait, Stewart Island, and the Tiwai Point Aluminium Smelter, head up to the top of **Bluff Hill** (265 meters) to the lookout—particularly enjoyable in the evening when the waters far below are dotted with fishing boats on their way home. **(H & H** provides bus transportation between Invercargill and Bluff; the 0815 bus from Invercargill connects with the 0900 ferry to Stewart Island, and the 1620 bus meets the 1615 ferry from the island for the return trip to Invercargill.)

Two good walks around Bluff together make up the **Foveaux Walkway.** The 1.5-km Glory Walk starts at the "Gunpit" site at the end of Gunpit Rd., meanders through a scenic reserve, and finishes at the Stirling Point Ocean Beach Track; about 30 minutes OW. The 6.6-km Stirling Point-Ocean Beach Walk follows the coastline around Bluff Hill for magnificent views of beaches and offshore islands, crossing small gullies into open pasture with views of farmland and the coastline. The track starts at Stirling Point and finishes near the Ocean Beach Freezing Works on the main highway; about 2½ hours OW, take a windbreaker, something to drink, and wear sturdy shoes. An H & H bus stop is located at the Ocean Beach end of the track.

Riverton

Historic Riverton, oldest settlement in the south and once the base of sealers and whalers, is situated at the mouth of the Aparima

Riverton

River, 38 km west of Invercargill. A popular marine resort, it has safe sandy beaches and good fishing. The small **Early Settlers Museum** displays items from pioneer days (Riverton is serviced by H & H bus from Invercargill). Nearby **Riverton Rocks** is a seaside resort with safe beaches, and farther west along the main highway, **Longwood Forest Park** has a variety of tracks and good fishing. Continuing along Hwy. 99 you come to **Clifden,** base of Fiordland National Park Ranger Station, and access to **Fiordland National Park.**

ACCOMMODATION

Hostel

Invercargill YH is modern and comfy, one km north of the city boundary on the main highway to Te Anau—a 40-minute walk or short bus ride from the stop opposite the railway station to the suburb of Waikiwi; $12 pp. Located at 122 North Rd., Waikiwi, tel. 59-344.

Motor Camps

Invercargill has several motor camps. The most central is **Southland A & P Association Caravan Park,** one km north of city center, next to a track where greyhounds are trained some mornings (free entertainment!) and raced two evenings a month. The camp has communal facilities, a TV lounge, and the office shop sells staples; tentsites in the large grassy camping area are $6 pp, caravan sites $8, comfortable on-site caravans from $25 d (definitely worth the extra bucks when it's raining!), and cabins $24 d. Located on Victoria Ave. off Dee St. (the main highway north), tel. 88-787. **Coachmans Inn Caravan Park,** just over four km east on the main highway to Dunedin, is also next to a racecourse; tentsites are $5.50 a night, caravan sites $15 d, campervans $15 d, cabins $20 d. Located at 705 Tay St., tel. 76-046.

Beach Road Motor Camp is on the road to Oreti Beach (and the airport), eight km from city center but close to the beach, tel. 330-400. Tentsites $5 pp, caravan sites $7 pp, cabins $12 pp, tourist flats $35 d.

Private Hotels

Montecillo Travel Hotel is an attractive 1895 house. The rooms are in a modern wing, but the dining room and TV lounge in the original building are appealingly old-fashioned. Laundry facilities are available. Bed and breakfast is $41 s, $68 d, rooms with private facilities are $59 s, $72 d, and a three-course dinner is available for $19 pp. Motel rooms are more expensive. Located at 240 Spey St., tel. 82-503. **Gerrard's Private Railway Hotel,** opposite the railway station and bus stops, has bright rooms, bath facilities but no kitchen or laundry, and a good restaurant (mains from

$18-21.50). Budget rooms are $36 s, $48.50 d B&B, standard rooms are $46 s, $66 d B&B, and rooms with private facilities are $63 s, $68 d. Located on the corner of Esk and Leven sts., tel. 83-406.

FOOD

Light Meals

Oyster lovers *must* sample Foveaux oysters—the region's delicacy. Try the fresh fish takeaway shop on Dee St. for oysters in season (March and April), fresh blue cod, and cooked mutton birds (another delicacy with a unique taste that you'll either love or hate), tel. 86-266. If you can't get them fresh, buy canned oysters in the local shops. **Joy's Gourmet Kitchen** and the **Lunch Box** are both on Dee St., open weekdays only—good food at reasonable prices. **Geone's Cafe** on Don St. is a good place for brunch, serving excellent filled rolls, all sorts of hot meat pies and tasty snacks, cream cakes, and good coffee. **The Sponge Kitchen** next door sells delicious baked goods, and next to that, upstairs, is **Tillermans Health Food Restaurant.** Sit in an airy room surrounded by elegant antique furniture while you munch on sandwiches and mixed salads, the hot dish of the day, or fresh fruit salad, starting around $4 pp. They're open weekdays 1200-1400 and 1700-1900, late on Fri. nights, at 16 Don Street.

Dinners

The best place in town for seafood is **Kings Restaurant** on Tay St. (go through the takeaway fish shop to the back; if you're on a tight budget, get takeaway). Meals average $10.50-13 and the portions are enormous. In March and April savor oysters fresh from the sea. Many hotels and taverns around town serve meals seven days a week. The **Grand Hotel** at 76 Dee St., tel. 88-059, puts on a good bistro Mon. to Fri. from 1200-1330 and 1600-1830 in the Prince of Wales Bar. **Newfield Tavern** on Centre St. also has a bistro bar Thurs., Fri., and Sat. nights. **Knight's Family Restaurant** serves sandwiches or main meals from $9-15, and desserts for $4; on Don St., open all day every day. **The Homestead** on the corner of Avenal and Dee sts. is a popular family restaurant and bar. The local **Pizza Hut** restaurant is on the corner of Dee and Fox sts., open daily from 1150. If you don't mind constant TV in the background, **Moa's Restaurant** at 142 Dee St. serves grills, salads, and fresh fish from $7; open late all week. If you feel like splurging on a fabulous seafood smorgasbord, call up the **Ascot Park Motor Hotel,** tel. 76-195, to check the price of the Sunday Family Day Smorgasbord (1800-2100); lunch averages $18, dinner $22; located at the corner of Racecourse Rd. and Tay St. (worth a trip just to admire the grounds).

Fast Food And Takeaways

As you drive into Invercargill from the north on North Rd. (it becomes Dee St.), the road is lined with all sorts of food stores and milkbars open seven days a week, and **Kentucky Fried Chicken, Pizza Hut, California-Style Chicken, Homestead Restaurant and Bar,** a Chinese restaurant, etcetera.

ENTERTAINMENT

Invercargill is not the most exciting place in N.Z. for evening entertainment—unless you enjoy drinking in the many hotel bars around town, or attending the "trots" (horse races) or greyhound races at various local racecourses (see the newspaper for dates and times). All the hotels and bottle stores in the city are operated by Invercargill Licensing Trust, a local authority founded in 1944 when liquor licensing was re-established after 38 years of prohibition, with members elected by the community; all profits are used to remodel the hotels or for community projects. The city has one movie theater, the **Civic Theatre** where opera is regularly performed, the modern **State Insurance Theatre** for drama and chamber music recitals, rollerskating at **Roller City,** 144 Esk St., tel. 88-50, and **10-Pin Bowling** on the corner of Kelvin and Leet sts., tel. 44-944.

If you feel like a good workout, an aerobics class, or enjoying a sauna, head for **Golds**

Gym at 34 Leet St., tel. 89-387. Invercargill has two public swimming pool complexes—**Central Pools** on Conon St. and **Queens Park Pool** in Queens Park, with several sessions daily. In summer (usually around Feb.) the city springs to life for the annual **Invercargill Summer Festival.** Parades, competitions, races, a rodeo, gymkhanas, and live music happen all over town for about a week straight. Your best sources of current entertainment info are the local newspaper, *The Southland Times,* and the info center (see below).

SERVICES AND INFORMATION

In an **emergency,** dial the operator at tel. 111. The **police station** is on Dee St. in the center of town, tel. 44-039. **Southland Hospital** is on Kew Rd. in Kew, a suburb south of city center, tel. 81-949. The **Chief P.O.** is on Dee St., tel. 48-889; open Mon. to Thurs. 0900-1700, till 2000 on Friday. **Invercargill Public Library** is on Don St., tel. 84-183. If you're looking for beautiful, high-quality sheepskin products, head for the **Hide Shop** on Esk St. or **Yours Naturally** in Pall Mall Arcade off Dee St., but if you don't mind the odd flaw, go to the **Factory Shop** on Dee St. which sells seconds in Knight sheepskin products (guarantee removed—check for major flaws)—you may find a real bargain.

For info on Invercargill, Southland in general, and Stewart Island, call in at the **Southland Promotions PRO and Visitors Information Centre,** 82 Dee St., tel. 86-090; open Mon. to Fri. 0900-1730 and from Dec. to mid-Feb. on weekends from 0900-1200 (after hours try the answering service at tel. 84-538). For info on Fiordland National Park, all the Southland forest parks, reserves, hiking trails, and outdoor activities, stop by the **Dept. of Conservation Visitor Centre** in the State Insurance Building—largest building on Don St., tel 88-075; they have a library of pamphlets and brochures and sell books and topographical maps.

TRANSPORTATION

Getting There

Major hwys. 1 and 6 both terminate in Invercargill center. The **Automobile Association HQ** is at 47-51 Gala St., tel. 89-033. The main car rental agencies are **Avis** at 109 Spey St., tel. 87-019; **Hertz** on the corner of Don and Kelvin sts., tel. 82-837; and **Budget Rent-A-Car** at 157 Clyde St., tel. 87-012/011.

The city is well serviced by public transportation. **InterCity** rail services connect Christchurch and Dunedin with Invercargill, terminating at the **railway station** on Levin Street. **InterCity** road services provides regular bus

Invercargill

services from Te Anau and Manapouri, Queenstown and Lumsden, Dunedin and Gore to Invercargill, terminating at the **Inter-City Depot** on Levin St., tel. 81-939; open Mon. to Fri. 0745-1800, Sat. 0745-1045, and Sun. 1200-1300 and 1600-1800. **Mount Cook Landlines** operates daily Starliner service from Picton ($99 OW; book in advance for a discount), Christchurch ($60 OW), and Dunedin ($28 OW), from Queenstown ($28 OW), Te Anau ($28 OW), and Wanaka ($51 OW). The **Mount Cook Line Travel Centre** is on the corner of Kelvin and Don sts., tel. 82-419. **Air New Zealand** (the Travel Centre is at 46 Esk St., tel. 44-737) flies into Invercargill Airport from all major centers in New Zealand, and **Southern Air** operates daily scheduled flights to Stewart Island (see "To Stewart Island" below).

Local Transportation
The main way of getting around Invercargill is by **H & H** bus. Their regularly scheduled bus services go to outlying areas, the airport, and various attractions (see "Sights"). Drop by the terminal on the corner of Don and Kelvin sts. for current schedules and prices, or call 82-419. The main departure point for city buses is the p.o. area on Dee Street. For a **taxi,** call 86-079.

By Air
The airport is 2.5 km from city center (about $5.50 OW by taxi). H & H buses leave the airport 10 minutes after each Air New Zealand arrival and leave the city 30 minutes prior to each departure; adult $3 OW, child $1.50. The **Air New Zealand office** is at 46 Esk St.; for reservations call 44-737, for flight arrivals and departures call 82-459. **Southern Air,** based at the airport, provides daily service to Stewart Island and package flights to Milford Sound; for more info, call 89-129. **Southland Aero Club,** also based at the airport, does local scenic flights, package flights to Milford Sound, and package flights and day excursions to Stewart Island (see "Sights"); the office is open seven days, tel. 86-171.

To Stewart Island
There are two ways to get to the island—by a 20-minute flight or a 2½-hour ferry crossing (can be rough). If you can afford the time and expense, ferry one way and fly the other for a broader experience. **Southern Air** has summer and winter timetables, with daily 20-minute flights to Stewart Island throughout the year—more frequent service during summer; adult $57 OW, child $28.50. With a Student ID card or YHA Hostel card the price is only $28.50 OW standby, a Golden Age ticket is $44.50 OW, and a Twosome ticket (two adults RT) is $199 (check current prices). A courtesy bus transports you from the Stewart Island Airport into Oban. Make reservations through any Air New Zealand office, travel agent, or call Southern Air collect at tel. 89-129. **Southland Aero Club** also runs a variety of flightseeing trips to Stewart Island; for details and costs call 86-171.

The alternative and less expensive way to get to the island is by **Stewart Island Charter Services** ferry from Bluff. This small ferry makes the crossing daily in peak periods, weather permitting; $34.50 adult, $17.25 child OW—also ask the price of their day excursion ticket, usually a little cheaper. H & H buses connect with the ferry; timetables and booking info available at Invercargill PRO or call H & H at tel. 82-419. If you have student ID or a YH card you can travel by ferry to the island on standby for $19.30 (standby can be difficult to get during Christmas, Easter, and school holidays). For more info call **Stewart Island Charter Services** at tel. Invercargill 77-031, Bluff 8377 or 8376.

STEWART ISLAND

Stewart Island is the third and most southerly of New Zealand's main islands, separated from the South Island by shallow, 24-km **Foveaux Strait.** Called *Rakiura* or "Land of the Glowing Skies" by the Maori, it became known as Stewart Island after William Stewart, an officer on the ship *Pegasus,* visited and charted Paterson Inlet in 1809. This peaceful secluded island's appeal lies in its virtually untouched bushland, well-maintained tracks, and lack of population. It's known for lingering twilights—a "heavenly glow" (in summer it's light until 2200), and spectacular sunsets. **Oban,** the only settlement, home of professional fishermen, vacationers, and island devotees, lies nestled along the protected shores of Halfmoon Bay on the east side of the island; it's reached from the mainland by boat or plane.

A thriving fishing industry (blue cod, crayfish, *paua)* and three fish processing factories support most of the population; deer hunting and tourism bring an increasing number of visitors to the island each year. Going to Stewart Island is like taking a giant step back in time—the locals depend on rainfall for water, some depend on individual generators for electricity, and there are few roads. It's not the place to go for lively evening entertainment—residents and visitors alike tend to go to bed early so they can make the most of the daylight for outdoor activities. Go there to revel in scenery and solitude, to hike through bush and along endless sandy beaches, and to cruise remote inlet waters.

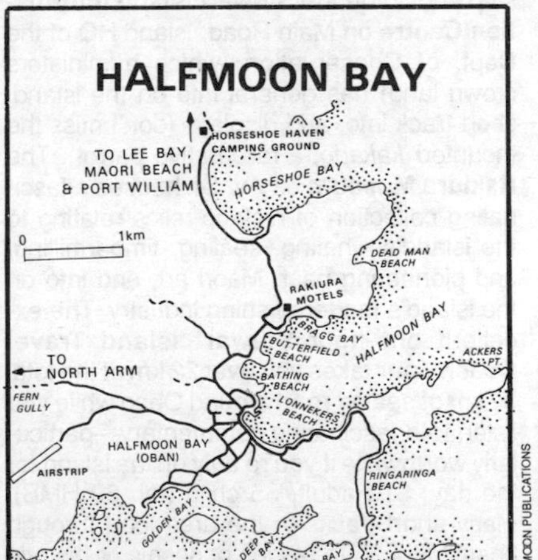

The Land

Including Ruapuke and outlying islands, Stewart Island County covers an area of 1,746 square km. The island, almost triangular in shape, stretches about 65 km from north to south, 40 km from east to west, and its deeply indented coastline is about 755 km. It lies between 46 and 47 degrees south latitude—probably the closest point that most people ever get to Antarctica. Most of the island is mountainous and hard to penetrate, with short, sheer gullies and steep ridge systems, but it's fringed with bays and sandy beaches. In the north the rugged highlands rise to 979-meter **Mt. Anglem,** highest peak on the island. **Paterson Inlet,** the main inlet with an average width of four km, has three main arms and an indented coastline, and extends 16 km westward across the central portion of the island, almost dividing it in two. Of the total 174,600 hectares of forest and bush, about 82% is designated as State Forest, Nature Reserve to protect native flora and fauna, Maori land, or Scenic Reserve.

Climate

Stewart Island has mild temperatures throughout the year, and relatively high rainfall ranging from 1,500 mm in coastal areas (such as Oban) to 5,000 mm in the high country. Frosts are rare, but snow lies on the highest peak, Mt. Anglem, for short periods. Westerly gales are common (cold from the southwest, warm from the northwest), and low clouds occur frequently—even though there can be fairly long periods without rain (the islanders welcome rain as they depend on it for their water supply). The locals are

Halfmoon Bay

only too willing to admit that the weather is for the most part unpredictable, and it's quite possible to experience four seasons in a single day! Go prepared for everything and you'll be comfortable.

Flora And Fauna

The high rainfall, mild winter, and fertile soil have resulted in dense forest and native bush. Though the vegetation has been modified by deer and opossum, it remains a unique forested wilderness of native *rimu, miro, totara,* ferns, mosses, scented native orchids (30 species), and a wealth of native plants. Stewart Island is a bird sanctuary to several rare birds and many seldom seen on the mainland. *Kakas,* parakeets, Stewart Island robins, fernbirds, dotterels, Stewart Island brown kiwis, and the almost extinct *kakapo* (a flightless nocturnal parrot found only here and in Fiordland), and pied shags, Stewart Island shags, and yellow-eyed penguins are all found on the island. The forest abounds with bush birds—*tuis,* bellbirds, pigeons, parakeets, cuckoos, *kakas,* brown creepers, fantails, tomtits, grey warblers, and finches. Along the shores you find oystercatchers, herons, black-billed gulls, Hookers sea lions, blue penguins, and fur seals. Muttonbirds or sooty shearwaters breed on the offshore islands and islets, the largest breeding ground of muttonbirds in N.Z. (descendants of Rakiura Maori have sole rights to the April capture of young muttonbirds). White-tailed deer, red deer, opossums, and long-tailed bats are found here, short-tailed bats are found only on the offshore islands.

SIGHTS

Around Oban

If you're only able to spend a day on Stewart Island (not long enough), you'll find lots of things to do in and around Oban. Your first stop should be the **Stewart Island Information Centre** on Main Road. Island HQ of the Dept. of Conservation (which administers crown land) has general info on the island, short track info, and displays (don't miss the mounted *kakapo,* a rare native parrot). The **Rakiura Museum** on Ayr St. houses a fascinating collection of historic relics relating to the island's whaling, sealing, timbermilling, and pioneering past, Maori art, and info on the island's modern fishing industry. The excellent one-hour **Stewart Island Travel Coach Tour** takes you over 22 km of the total 32 km of sealed road around Oban while you listen to a fascinating commentary—particularly worthwhile if you're only on the island for the day; $10 adult, $5 child (tel. 69 HMB). Many short tracks in the area lead through beautiful bush to places of scenic or historic interest, and to lookouts with spectacular views. Don't miss the view from **Observation Rock,** particularly splendid at sunset. Short launch rides are also available from Halfmoon Bay to cruise Paterson Inlet viewing its small bush-covered islands; boat trips and tours are advertised at the info center—see the notice board for details.

Farther Afield

If you're on the island for at least a couple of days, walk the many several-hour tracks (such as the 1½-hour track to **Horseshoe Bay),** search for shells along beautiful beaches, or if you're a well-equipped hiker, head off into the backcountry along well-maintained tracks (see below). Take a launch ride to isolated areas of the island totally inaccessible on foot, or to the island's newest industry, salmon farming, historical whaling sites, and beautiful **Ulva Island** in Paterson Inlet. Extended seafaring trips and fishing charters are also available; get all the options at the Information Centre.

HIKING AND HUNTING

Short Walks

Find out where all Stewart Island's tracks lead by picking up *Stewart Island Day Track and General Information* at the info center ($5.50). It's packed with useful information, and has directions and descriptions for all the day tracks close to Oban.

Hiking Tracks

Well-maintained tracks take you into some of New Zealand's most beautiful bush. As long as you can hike with a pack for at least four hours non-stop, you're fit enough to do the tracks on Stewart Island. Tracks in the northern sector of the island are especially intended for experienced hikers and sportsmen, winding along the picturesque shoreline and deep into the dense interior. The most popular walking track, the **North-West Circuit,** meanders along the northern coast of the island, taking seven to 10 days to complete—add several extra days if you sidetrack to Mason Bay on the west coast. Shorter tracks lead to Port William, Bungaree, and

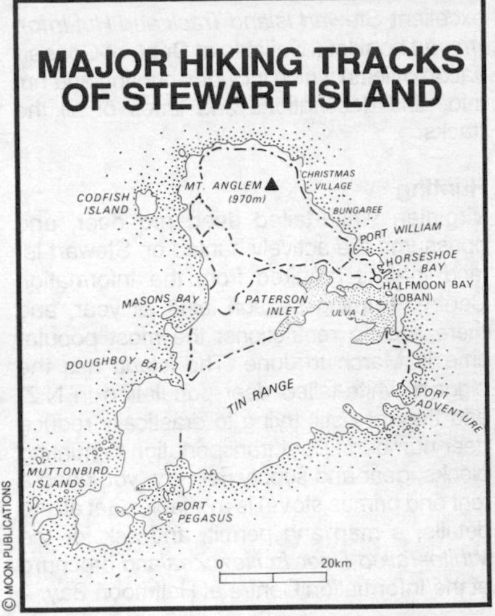

Christmas Village. The latest to be developed is the **Link Track** which takes three days.

A particularly good campground for tents only is at Apple Bridge on Fern Gully Track, North Arm; basic facilities. Huts with camp ovens and billies have been established along all the major tracks at regular intervals (always carry your own stove), but you can only spend a maximum of two nights per hut. In summer it's a good idea to take a tent and stove as the huts can be crowded, plus extra food in case you're delayed by weather. Wear waterproof hiking boots, shorts (your legs stay wet most of the time), and a bushshirt, and take a water- and windproof coat and warm dry clothes for when you stop. The wind is the worst problem you're likely to face when you're already wet.

Visitors are warned never to hike alone and not to wander off the tracks, even to avoid a mud hole—you can't get into trouble if you stay on the track, but even some of the most experienced hikers have wound up lost in the dense Stewart Island bush by trying to take shortcuts. Respect the rivers and keep an eye on the weather. Before setting out, you're required to sign the intentions book in the info center, and must sign out afterward. Buy the excellent *Stewart Island Track and Hut Information* booklet (available at Dept. of Conservation offices) which includes hunting and hut info, and descriptions and times of all the tracks.

Hunting

Virginian white-tailed deer, red deer, and opossums are actively hunted on Stewart Island; permit required from the Information Centre. Hunting season lasts all year, and there are no restrictions; the most popular time is March to June. The island has the biggest white-tailed deer population in N.Z. and they are still trying to drastically reduce deer numbers. Boat transportation to hunting blocks, gear and supply delivery (you need a tent and primus stove) is available. Get all the details, a map and permit, and ask for the *White-Tailed Deer In New Zealand* brochure at the Information Centre at Halfmoon Bay.

PRACTICALITIES

Oban is the principal settlement, nestled along the sandy shores of Halfmoon Bay. Most of the island's 460 residents live at Halfmoon Bay (half the residences are permanently occupied, the rest are holiday cottages), and the 50-boat fishing fleet is anchored here. A variety of short tracks start in Oban, and several beautiful beaches are within walking distance of town.

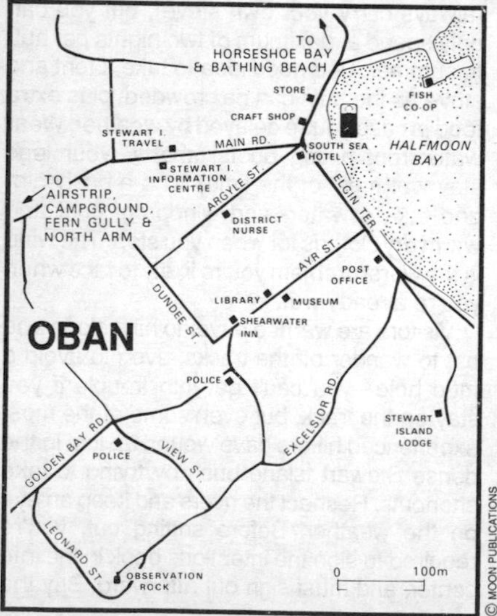

Accommodation

Free camping is permitted at a couple of locations—a particularly nice campground is at the end of the popular North Circuit Track by a huge old apple tree; toilets and fresh water provided. Ask for other free campground locations at the Information Centre. The info center has a list of those currently offering budget accommodation. **Horseshoe Haven** lies along a sheltered bay and gray sandy beach in a bush setting, at the start of the Northern Loop Track. It's a couple of km from town, but the tranquil setting makes the walk worthwhile. Excellent facilities are provided, including a large equipped kitchen, hot showers, laundry, dinghy and canoe hire, and a camp store where you can buy fresh fish, pre-packed frozen meats, general groceries, bread, and milk; tentsites from $6 pp, dormitory beds $12 pp, cabins $35 per night. Book early for peak periods at tel. 391-466. **Shearwater Inn** has communal bathroom and kitchen (fully equipped) facilities, dining room meals (breakfast $9, lunch $12, and dinner $14), and shared rooms for $12 per night if you're a YH member (own bag; linen hire available), single rooms for $26, double rooms for $21 pp, and group share rooms for $18 pp with linen and towels supplied; tel. 391- 114. **Ferndale Caravan Park** boasts luxury caravan accommodation at $55 d, tel. 391-176. Rooms at **Rakiura Motel** are $77 d (less in low season), tel. 391-096. Rooms in the licensed 100-year-old **South Sea Hotel** start at $50 s, $75 d, and all meals are available (breakfast $9, lunch $13, dinner $24 plus GST; book ahead for dinner by 1600), tel. 391-059. If price is no problem and you're looking for accommodation with the personal touch, contact the people at **Stewart Island Lodge,** tel. 391-085. Room and board (only eight guests at a time) plus extras such as launch trips are included in one flat rate, and you're treated like family—find out

South Sea Hotel on the shores of Halfmoon Bay

current prices at the info center or Stewart Island Travel.

Food And Entertainment

If you like fresh fish, living on Stewart Island is a culinary delight. The residents live off the sea, and although a thousand sheep graze the backcountry and deer are widespread, crayfish and blue cod are the main sources of income and diet. At **Anchor Merchants General Store** (only store on the island, tel. 391-069) you can buy just about everything you need, but as supplies are sent over from the mainland by ferry or plane, prices tend to be high; open Mon. to Fri. 0900-1730, weekends and holidays 1000-1200. Stock up on primus stove fuel and pressurized gas on the mainland. The **tearooms** next to Stewart Island Travel serve snacks, tea and coffee, tel. 391-269. **South Sea Hotel** provides large, delicious meals for guests and casuals with fresh blue cod (the specialty) almost always on the menu; breakfast is available for $9, lunch from $13, and dinner starts at around $24 pp plus GST, but you must book ahead by 1600 at tel. 391-059 (best to double-check prices beforehand).

Evening entertainment is strictly make-your-own—try a short walk up to Observation Rock for a lingering Stewart Island sunset, a stroll along the beach for shells, or a drink and chat with the locals in South Sea Hotel. In Jan. the Dept. of Conservation puts on slide shows and talks on the island at the Information Centre, and offers guided walks and launch rides.

Services

A **district nurse** provides medical services; clinics are held on Argyle St. (near the info center) several times a week and the hours vary; tel. 391-098. A doctor comes over from the mainland once a month. The only banking services are at the **P.O. Savings Bank** at Halfmoon Bay, open regular business hours weekdays. (Credit cards are accepted for some services in Oban but cash is preferred.) The **library** on Ayr St. is open Wed. 1400-1500 and Fri. 1100-1200. **The Fernery,** a waterfront shop crammed with beautiful things, has an emphasis on the natural history of Stewart Island. It's the place to buy living ferns, souvenirs, cards, books, delicate silk scarves, dressing gowns, and prints—all with a fern theme. **Stewart Island Travel** sells souvenirs and provides local sightseeing tours, tel. 391-269.

Information

The **Stewart Island Visitor Information Centre** has general info on the island, listings of budget accommodations, a list of launch operators willing to run you to remote areas, fishing and hunting charters and permits, interesting displays, and booklets on short walks and the major backcountry tracks. Also get info on all the scenic reserves, and a detailed Dept. of Conservation map of the island here ($5.50). Ron Tindal knows the island like the back of his hand, and the friendly staff are also a fund of information. Excess baggage can be left at the center for free, and passports and valuables can be left in the safe. The center is open daily, but check hours before you hit the trails at tel. 391-130.

Getting There And Around

Prior bookings for the ferry ride or plane flight to Stewart Island are essential. The island is serviced by the **Stewart Island Charter Services** ferry daily during peak periods, weather permitting, from Bluff (about a 2½-hour trip); for info, current timetable, and reservations, contact Invercargill PRO or any travel agent, or Stewart Island Charter Services at tel. Bluff 37-8376 or Invercargill 77-031. The fares are adult $34.50 OW, child $17.25 OW. (On the island, Stewart Island Travel provides scenic tours of the island and taxi service.) **H & H** coaches, tel. 82-419, leave from the Invercargill depot to connect with ferry departures and arrivals at Bluff, and minibuses meet ferry arrivals at Stewart Island. The Strait is very shallow and can become extremely rough at a moment's notice. The ferry makes crossings weather permitting, but it can still get uncomfortably rough. If you're susceptible to seasickness, take drugs!

The alternate way to reach the island is by a 20-minute **Southern Air** flight. Scheduled flights are made several times a day, seven days a week; report at Invercargill Airport 30 minutes before departure. Fares adult $57 OW, child $28.50 OW, "Twosome" (two or more adults) $99 pp RT, senior $44.50 OW, student or YH standby $28.50 OW. For info and reservations, call Invercargill 89-129, or Stewart Island Travel at tel. 391-269.

BOOKLIST

All the books listed can be bought at major bookstores throughout New Zealand, or at Government Bookshops in Auckland, Hamilton, Wellington (two locations), Christchurch, and Dunedin, or found in major libraries throughout the country, unless otherwise noted.

HISTORY

Best, Elsdon. *Polynesian Voyagers.* Dominion Museum Monograph No. 5. A.R. Shearer, Government Printer, New Zealand, 1975, 54 pages. A compact history of the Polynesian deep-sea navigators, explorers, and colonizers—the Maori voyage from their ancient homeland, Hawaiiki, to Aotearoa, New Zealand.

Buck, Sir Peter. *The Coming of the Maori.* Whitcoulls Publishers, New Zealand, 1950, 574 pages. Maori ethnology; the exciting adventures of early Polynesian Pacific navigators.

Howard, Basil. *Rakiura.* A.H. and A.W. Reed, New Zealand. The history of Stewart Island.

Pope, Diana and Jeremy. Mobil New Zealand Travel Guides: *North Island* and *South Island.* A.H. and A.W. Reed Ltd., New Zealand, (North) 1981, 266 pages, (South) 1983, 362 pages. Detailed geographic travel guides to the North and South islands, with emphasis on local history.

Reed, A.H. *Historic Bay of Islands.* A.H. and A.W. Reed, New Zealand, 1960, 48 pages. Beautifully illustrated history of the Bay of Islands in an easy-to-read format.

GEOGRAPHY

Egmont National Park Handbook. Edited by J.S. Tullett. The Egmont National Park Board, New Plymouth, New Zealand, 1980, 114 pages. The hlstory, volcanology, weather, vegetation and, flora and fauna of the Park, with sections on mountaineering and tramping, skiing, tracks and routes, and photography.

Gage, Maxwell. *Legends in the Rocks.* Whitcoulls Publishers, New Zealand, 1980, 426 pages. A comprehensive, illustrated, layman's guide to the geology of New Zealand.

Land of the Mist. The Story of Urewera National Park. The Dept. of Lands and Survey, New Zealand, 1983, 111 pages. The natural and human history of the Park, along with recreational opportunities, Maori legends, and Maori place names and their meanings.

A Microtone Colour Book. *Fiordland National Park.* Bascands Limited, Christchurch, New Zealand, 1976, 32 pages. A pictorial guide to the Park briefly covering local history, geography, flora and fauna, the main sights, and hiking, mountaineering, hunting, fishing, launch rides, and flightseeing.

A Microtone Colour Book. *Nelson Lakes National Park.* Bascands Limited, Christchurch, New Zealand, 1976, 32 pages. A pictorial guide to the Park covering the geography, flora and fauna, climate, sports and recreation.

The New Zealand Automobile Association. *AA Book of New Zealand National Parks.* Lansdowne Press, New Zealand, 1983, 176 pages. Another good souvenir book on New Zealand's national parks loaded with recreational information and color photographs.

Potton, Craig. *The Story of Nelson Lakes National Park.* Dept. of Lands and Survey and Cobb/Horwood Publications, New Zealand, 1984, 160 pages. An illustrated geography, flora and fauna, geology, and history of the Park, with comprehensive sections on outdoor activities—tramping, mountaineering, fishing, skiing, and hunting.

Reader's Digest. *Wild New Zealand.* Reader's Digest Services Pty. Ltd., New Zealand, 1981, 320 pages. A detailed guide to the less inhabited, off-the-beaten-track areas of the country, packed with geographical information and spectacular photography. Much more than a coffee-table book—an invaluable New Zealand souvenir.

The Restless Land. The Story of Tongariro National Park. The Dept. of Lands and Survey, New Zealand, 1981, 112 pages. The geography, history, flora and fauna, climate, and myths and legends of the Park, along with sections on skiing, climbing, huts, and services.

FLORA AND FAUNA

O'Brien, C. *AA Book of New Zealand Wildlife.* Lansdowne Press, 1982, 161 pages. A complete guide to New Zealand's native and introduced animals packed with color photographs.

Poole, A.L., and Adams, N.M. *Trees and Shrubs of New Zealand.* P.D. Hasselberg, Government Printer, 1980, 400 pages. A complete coverage of all the native trees and shrubs in the country, with illustrations.

Soper, M.F. *Birds of New Zealand and the Outlying Islands.* Whitcoulls Publishers, New Zealand, 1984. All you want to know about N.Z. birds, and more.

Turbott, E.G. *Buller's Birds of New Zealand.* Whitcoulls Publishers, New Zealand, 1967, 280 pages. New Zealand's native birds in color.

Yerex, David. *The Farming of Deer.* Agricultural Promotion Associates Ltd., Wellington, 1982, 176 pages. A comprehensive book covering world trends and the modern techniques of deer farming in New Zealand.

THE GREAT OUTDOORS

DuFresne, Jim. *Tramping in New Zealand.* Lonely Planet, Australia, 1982, 167 pages. An easy-to-read backpacking guide to all the major hiking tracks in the country.

Forrester, Rex. *Trout Fishing in New Zealand.* Whitcoulls Publishers, New Zealand, 1979, 208 pages. Find out how, when, and where to catch New Zealand's fighting trout, then learn how to smoke them.

Gould, Peter. *The Complete Taupo Fishing Guide.* William Collins Publishers Ltd., Auckland, New Zealand, 1983, 240 pages. A detailed guide to all the major fishing spots in the Taupo area, with advice on what to use, weather, fishing etiquette, and entertaining fishing yarns.

Harris, L.H. *A Hunting Guide to Introduced Wild Animals of New Zealand.* A.R. Shearer, Government Printer, Wellington, New Zealand, 1973, 112 pages. Descriptions of game animals and the regions they inhabit, along with photographs, maps, and safety tips.

The New Zealand Automobile Association. *AA Book of the New Zealand Countryside.* Lansdowne Press, 1982, 191 pages. Loaded with interesting facts about all the places you'll see along the major roads throughout the country, with plenty of color photographs—a good souvenir book.

The New Zealand Automobile Association (Auckland) Inc. *AA Book of New Zealand Walkways.* Lansdowne Press, 1983, 207 pages. "Written to encourage people of all ages and shapes to go for a walk," this book is packed with handy information, maps, and photographs.

New Zealand's Walkways. New Zealand Walkway Commission, c/o Dept. of Lands and Survey, Wellington, 1984, 63 pages. An invaluable guide to all designated New Zealand Walkways throughout the North and South islands, with track lengths, locations, and classifications.

Peat, Neville. *Detours: A journey through small-town New Zealand.* Whitcoulls Publishers, New Zealand, 1982, 250 pages. An entertaining tale of discovery as the author rides his 10-speed bicycle from the top of the North Island to the bottom of the South.

Ringer, J.B. *The Healing Guide to Cycle Touring in the North Island, New Zealand.* Produced by *Southern Cyclist* magazine and the Bicycle Association of New Zealand, 1983, 127 pages. An in-depth guide to major highway routes, alternative routes, connecting roads, and scenic routes of tourist interest, plus terrain, surface, traffic, road conditions, and location of accommodations along each route. Also see the companion volume, *Cycle Touring in the South Island, New Zealand,* by Helen Crabb, Canterbury Cyclists Association, 1982.

Shutt, Peter. *Fishing in the Central South Island.* Published by Peter Shutt, Timaru, 1983, 48 pages. A well-written guide to trout and salmon fishing in southern Canterbury, loaded with handy tips and detailed information for major rivers, lakes, and less-fished locations.

Smith, Rodney. *A Guide to the Skifields of New Zealand.* A.H. and A.W. Reed Ltd., 1981, 130 pages. A guide to most of New Zealand's commercial and club skifields, with terrain and run descriptions, facilities, suitability for beginner or pro, how to get to each field, and brief accommodation, food, and entertainment information.

Temple, Philip. *Shell Guides to the Great New Zealand Walking Tracks* series. Whitcoulls Publishers, New Zealand. Pocket-sized guides to the major tracks of both North and South islands, including track history, detailed descriptions, information, advice, and maps.

Turner, Brian (editor). *The Guide to Trout Fishing in Otago.* Otago Acclimatisation Society, Dunedin, New Zealand, 1984, 103 pages. A guide to all the main fishing rivers and lakes of Otago.

BOOKS OF GENERAL INTEREST

Auckland Regional Authority. *Auckland Regional Transport Guide.* Auckland Regional Authority, 1984, 98 pages. An invaluable guide to getting into, around, and out of Auckland by public transportation, taxi, bicycle, tourist and charter services, disabled services, and where to get more information. Buy it at The Bus Place, 131 Hobson St., Auckland.

Bowden, Beth. *Parliament And The People.* P.D. Hasselberg, Government Printer, 1984, 64 pages. Written primarily for children and for visitors to Parliament, this illustrated book describes New Zealand's constitution and explains its development.

Diamond, John T., and Hayward, Bruce W. *The Maori History and Legends of the Waitakere Ranges.* Lodestar Press, Auckland, New Zealand, 1979, 48 pages. Covers the history, archaeology, and local Maori folktales and legends of the Waitakere Ranges, west of Auckland.

Diners Restaurant Guide compiled by Assoc. Parnell Publishing Co. Ltd., Auckland, on behalf of Diners Club (NZ) Ltd., 1983, 286 pages. A guide to restaurants accepting the Diners Club card throughout New Zealand (no prices). Ask for it at PROs in major cities. (Also pick up the free tourist papers available at PROs throughout the country which generally have dining and entertainment sections.)

Gallen, Rodney, and North, Allan. *Waikaremoana. A Brief History of the Lakes of the Urewera National Park.* Te Urewera National Parks Board, 1977, 64 pages. A souvenir booklet of Waikaremoana, Wairaumoana, and Waikareiti, covering the history of the lakes, the people, and the land.

Ihimaera, Witi. *Maori.* A.R. Shearer, Government Printer, Wellington, New Zealand, 1975, 45 pages. A brief historical insight into the Maori from Hawaiiki to modern-day New Zealand.

Jungowska, Maria. *Livingston's Auckland Explorer.* David Livingston of Scarab Publishing, 1984, 193 pages. A handy pocket-sized book packed with everything a traveler could want to know about Auckland, with maps.

Leland Jr., Louis S. *A Personal Kiwi-Yankee Dictionary.* Pelican Publishing Company, U.S.A., 1984, 115 pages. An entertaining pocket-sized guide to the English language and colloquial New Zealandisms written specifically for Americans.

The New Zealand Automobile Association. *AA Outdoor Guide, North Island; AA Accommodation and Camping Guide, South Island;* and *AA Accommodation Directory North Island.* AA Association, 1987. Updated yearly, free to automobile association members on proof of membership (N.Z. or overseas) at any of the AA offices throughout the country, these invaluable guides to New Zealand's campgrounds, motorcamps, motels, and hotels are worth their weight in gold.

The New Zealand Automobile Association. *AA Road Atlas of New Zealand.* Lansdowne Press, 1983, 156 pages. A hard-cover invaluable companion for the driver on New Zealand roads.

New Zealand Tourist and Publicity Dept. *New Zealand Accommodation Guide.* NZTP, Wellington. A guide to motel/hotel accommodation, farm-style/home-style accommodation, and sporting lodges throughout the country, with prices. Updated yearly, free from any NZTP office throughout New Zealand.

Viggers, Elizabeth. *Around And About Wellington.* Northland School Association, Wellington, New Zealand, 1983, 93 pages, plus maps. A good guide to the many sights and hikes around New Zealand's capital city.

Youth Hostel Association. *1987 YHA Handbook.* Free on joining the association, this pocket-sized handbook tells you where all the YHA hostels throughout New Zealand are located, local sights, outdoor recreational information, services and discounts available to members. Can also be purchased at most YHs and at the YHA HQ in Christchurch.

INDEX

Italicized page numbers indicate information in captions, call-outs, charts, or maps. **Bold-faced** page numbers provide the primary reference to a given topic.

photo by Louise Foote

ABOUT THE AUTHOR

Born in Scotland, raised in England, high school, college, and nursing training in Australia interspersed with a variety of travel experiences, Jane King feels she has roots all over the world! She met American husband-to-be on vacation in New Zealand, and after many trips back and forth to the U.S., Canada, New Zealand, and a year backpacking through Europe, finally tied the knot with Bruce and settled in Chico, California. After working as a registered nurse in both Australia and the U.S., Jane now devotes her time to revising her two travel guides, *New Zealand Handbook* and *British Columbia Handbook,* and exploring more of the world with Bruce and baby daughter, Rachael. Her passions include flying airplanes, cross-country skiing, camping, the occasional white-river rafting adventure, taking photographs, spoiling her pets, and making the most of the great outdoors.

ABOUT THE ILLUSTRATORS

Louise Foote lives in Chico, California, with her youngest daughter, Julia. When she's not working in the backcountry as an archaeologist/cartographer for the Forest Service, Louise turns her creative hand to illustrating. She has contributed illustrations to many Moon books. See the Illustration Credits at the front of this book for the page numbers where her work is featured.

Diana Lasich Harper received a degree in art from San Jose State University, California, lived in Hawaii for four years, then moved to Japan for two years where she studied wood block and textile painting. Today she lives in San Francisco with her husband Peter, a writer, and has contributed illustrations to several Moon books. See Illustration Credits.

Carolyn Tolley lives in a rural community near Chico with her husband and two sons. She received a degree in art from the University of California at Davis, and worked as an elementary school teacher prior to raising her family. She continues to pursue a career in art, particularly drawing, calligraphy, graphics, and illustration. See Illustration Credits.

Bruce King farms a variety of crops and runs a custom hay business in Orland, California, and lives with his wife, daughter, two dogs, and a cat, in Chico. In his spare time he likes to travel, take photographs, fly airplanes, and go camping, fishing, and duck hunting. See Photo Credits for page numbers

If you are interested in contacting any of the above artists, please do so through Moon Publications, Chico, California.

Moon Handbooks—The Ideal Traveling Companions

Open a Moon Handbook and you're opening your eyes and heart to the world. Thoughtful, sensitive, and provocative, Moon Handbooks encourage an intimate understanding of a region, from its rich culture and history to essential practicalities. Fun to read and packed with valuable information on accommodations, dining, recreation, plus indispensable travel tips, detailed maps, charts, illustrations, photos, glossaries, and indexes, Moon Handbooks are ideal traveling companions: informative, entertaining, and highly practical.

TO ORDER BY PHONE: (800) 345-5473 • Monday-Friday • 9 a.m.-5 p.m. PST

The Pacific/Asia Series

BALI HANDBOOK by Bill Dalton
Detailed travel information on the most famous island in the world. 12 color pages, 29 b/w photos, 68 illustrations, 42 maps, 7 charts, glossary, booklist, index. 428 pages. **$12.95**

INDONESIA HANDBOOK by Bill Dalton
This one-volume encyclopedia explores island by island the many facets of this sprawling, kaleidoscopic island nation. 30 b/w photos, 143 illustrations, 250 maps, 17 charts, booklist, extensive Indonesian vocabulary, index. 1,050 pages. **$17.95**

SOUTH KOREA HANDBOOK by Robert Nilsen
Whether you're visiting on business or searching for adventure, *South Korea Handbook* is an invaluable companion. 8 color pages, 78 b/w photos, 93 illustrations, 109 maps, 10 charts, Korean glossary with useful notes on speaking and reading the language, booklist, index. 548 pages. **$14.95**

SOUTHEAST ASIA HANDBOOK by Carl Parkes
Helps the enlightened traveler explore with wide eyes and an open mind to discover the real Southeast Asia. 16 color pages, 75 b/w photos, 11 illustrations, 169 maps, 140 charts, vocabularies and suggested reading, index. 873 pages. **$16.95**

HAWAII HANDBOOK by J.D. Bisignani
Winner of the 1989 Hawaii Visitors Bureau's Best Guide Book Award and the Grand Award for Excellence in Travel Journalism, this guide takes you beyond the glitz and high-priced hype and leads you to a genuine Hawaiian experience. 12 color pages, 86 b/w photos, 132 illustrations, 86 maps, 44 graphs and charts, Hawaiian and pidgin glossaries, appendix, booklist, index. 879 pages. **$15.95**

KAUAI HANDBOOK by J.D. Bisignani
Kauai Handbook is the perfect antidote to the workaday world. 8 color pages, 36 b/w photos, 48 illustrations, 19 maps, 10 tables and charts, Hawaiian and pidgin glossaries, booklist, index. 236 pages. **$9.95**

MAUI HANDBOOK: Including Molokai and Lanai by J.D. Bisignani
"No fool-'round" advice on accommodations, eateries, and recreation, plus a comprehensive introduction to island ways, geography, and history. 8 color pages, 60 b/w photos, 72 illustrations, 34 maps, 19 charts, booklist, glossary, index. 350 pages. **$10.95**

OAHU HANDBOOK by J.D. Bisignani
A handy guide to Honolulu, renowned surfing beaches, and Oahu's countless other diversions. Color and b/w photos, illustrations, 18 maps, charts, booklist, glossary, index. 354 pages. **$11.95**

BIG ISLAND OF HAWAII HANDBOOK by J.D. Bisignani
An entertaining yet informative text packed with insider tips on accommodations, dining, sports and outdoor activities, natural attractions, and must-see sights. Color and b/w photos, illustrations, 20 maps, charts, booklist, glossary, index. 347 pages. **$11.95**

SOUTH PACIFIC HANDBOOK by David Stanley
The original comprehensive guide to the 16 territories in the South Pacific. 20 color pages, 195 b/w photos, 121 illustrations, 35 charts, 138 maps, booklist, glossary, index. 740 pages. **$15.95**

MICRONESIA HANDBOOK:
Guide to the Caroline, Gilbert, Mariana, and Marshall Islands by David Stanley
Micronesia Handbook guides you on a real Pacific adventure all your own. 8 color pages, 77 b/w photos, 68 illustrations, 69 maps, 18 tables and charts, index. 287 pages. **$9.95**

FIJI ISLANDS HANDBOOK by David Stanley
The first and still the best source of information on travel around this 322-island archipelago. 8 color pages, 35 b/w photos, 78 illustrations, 26 maps, 3 charts, Fijian glossary, booklist, index. 198 pages. **$8.95**

TAHITI-POLYNESIA HANDBOOK by David Stanley
All five French-Polynesian archipelagoes are covered in this comprehensive guide by Oceania's best-known travel writer. 12 color pages, 45 b/w photos, 64 illustrations, 33 maps, 7 charts, booklist, glossary, index. 225 pages. **$9.95**

NEW ZEALAND HANDBOOK by Jane King
Introduces you to the people, places, history, and culture of this extraordinary land. 8 color pages, 99 b/w photos, 146 illustrations, 82 maps, booklist, index. 546 pages. **$14.95**

BLUEPRINT FOR PARADISE: How to Live on a Tropic Island by Ross Norgrove
This one-of-a-kind guide has everything you need to know about moving to and living comfortably on a tropical island. 8 color pages, 40 b/w photos, 3 maps, 14 charts, appendices, index. 212 pages. **$14.95**

The Americas Series

NORTHERN CALIFORNIA HANDBOOK by Kim Weir
An outstanding companion for imaginative travel in the territory north of the Tehachapis. 12 color pages, b/w photos, 69 maps, illustrations, booklist, index. 759 pages. **$16.95**

NEVADA HANDBOOK by Deke Castleman
Nevada Handbook puts the Silver State into perspective and makes it manageable and affordable. 34 b/w photos, 43 illustrations, 37 maps, 17 charts, booklist, index. 301 pages. **$10.95**

NEW MEXICO HANDBOOK by Stephen Metzger
A close-up and complete look at every aspect of this wondrous state. 8 color pages, 85 b/w photos, 63 illustrations, 50 maps, 10 charts, booklist, index. 350 pages. **$11.95**

TEXAS HANDBOOK by Joe Cummings
Seasoned travel writer Joe Cummings brings an insider's perspective to his home state. 12 color pages, b/w photos, maps, illustrations, charts, booklist, index. 483 pages. **$11.95**

ARIZONA TRAVELER'S HANDBOOK by Bill Weir
This meticulously researched guide contains everything necessary to make Arizona accessible and enjoyable. 8 color pages, 194 b/w photos, 74 illustrations, 53 maps, 6 charts, booklist, index. 505 pages. **$13.95**

UTAH HANDBOOK by Bill Weir
Weir gives you all the carefully researched facts and background to make your visit a success. 8 color pages, 102 b/w photos, 61 illustrations, 30 maps, 9 charts, booklist, index. 450 pages. **$11.95**

ALASKA-YUKON HANDBOOK by Deke Castleman, Don Pitcher, and David Stanley
The inside story, with plenty of well-seasoned advice to help you cover more miles on less money. 8 color pages, 26 b/w photos, 92 illustrations, 90 maps, 6 charts, booklist, glossary, index. 384 pages. **$11.95**

WASHINGTON HANDBOOK by Dianne J. Boulerice Lyons
Covers sights, shopping, services, transportation, and outdoor recreation, with complete listings for restaurants and accommodations. 8 color pages, 92 b/w photos, 24 illustrations, 81 maps, 8 charts, booklist, index. 400 pages. **$12.95**

OREGON HANDBOOK by Stuart Warren and Ted Long Ishikawa
Brimming with travel practicalities and insider views on Oregon's history, culture, arts, and activities. Color and b/w photos, illustrations, 28 maps, charts, booklist, index. Approx. 400 pages. **$12.95**

BRITISH COLUMBIA HANDBOOK by Jane King
With an emphasis on outdoor adventures, this guide covers mainland British Columbia, Vancouver Island, the Queen Charlotte Islands, and the Canadian Rockies. 8 color pages, 56 b/w photos, 45 illustrations, 66 maps, 4 charts, booklist, index. 381 pages. **$11.95**

GUIDE TO CATALINA and California's Channel Islands by Chicki Mallan
A complete guide to these remarkable islands, from the windy solitude of the Channel Islands National Marine Sanctuary to bustling Avalon. 8 color pages, 105 b/w photos, 65 illustrations, 40 maps, 32 charts, booklist, index. 262 pages. **$9.95**

YUCATAN HANDBOOK by Chicki Mallan
All the information you'll need to guide you into every corner of this exotic land. 8 color pages, 154 b/w photos, 55 illustrations, 57 maps, 70 charts, appendix, booklist, Mayan and Spanish glossaries, index. 391 pages. **$12.95**

CANCUN HANDBOOK and Mexico's Caribbean Coast by Chicki Mallan
Covers the city's luxury scene as well as more modest attractions, plus many side trips to unspoiled beaches and Mayan ruins. Color and b/w photos, illustrations, over 30 maps, Spanish glossary, booklist, index. 257 pages. **$9.95**

BELIZE HANDBOOK by Chicki Mallan
Complete with detailed maps, practical information, and an overview of the area's flamboyant history, culture, and geographical features, *Belize Handbook* is the only comprehensive guide of its kind to this spectacular region. Color and b/w photos, illustrations, maps, booklist, index. 212 pages. **$11.95**

The International Series

EGYPT HANDBOOK by Kathy Hansen
An invaluable resource for intelligent travel in Egypt. 8 color pages, 20 b/w photos, 150 illustrations, 80 detailed maps and plans to museums and archaeological sites, Arabic glossary, booklist, index. 510 pages. **$14.95**

PAKISTAN HANDBOOK by Isobel Shaw
For armchair travelers and trekkers alike, the most detailed and authoritative guide to Pakistan ever published. 28 color pages, 86 maps, appendices, Urdu glossary, booklist, index. 478 pages. **$15.95**

IMPORTANT ORDERING INFORMATION

TO ORDER BY PHONE: (800) 345-5473 · Monday-Friday · 9 a.m.-5 p.m. PST

PRICES: All prices are subject to change. We always ship the most current edition. We will let you know if there is a price increase on the book you ordered.

SHIPPING & HANDLING OPTIONS:

1) Domestic UPS or USPS 1st class (allow 10 working days for delivery): $3.50 for the 1st item, 50 cents for each additional item.

Exceptions:

- **Moonbelt** shipping is $1.50 for one, 50 cents for each additional belt.
- Add $2.00 for same-day handling.

2) UPS 2nd Day Air or Printed Airmail requires a special quote.
3) International Surface Bookrate (8-12 weeks delivery): $3.00 for the 1st item, $1.00 for each additional item.

FOREIGN ORDERS: All orders which originate outside the U.S.A. must be paid for with either an International Money Order or a check in U.S. currency drawn on a major U.S. bank based in the U.S.A.

TELEPHONE ORDERS: We accept Visa or MasterCard payments. Minimum order is US$15.00. Call in your order: 1 (800) 345-5473. 9 a.m.-5 p.m. Pacific Standard Time.

MOONBELTS. A new concept in moneybelts. Made of heavy-duty Cordura nylon, the Moonbelt offers maximum protection for your money and important papers. This pouch, designed for all-weather comfort, slips under your shirt or waistband, rendering it virtually undetectable and inaccessible to pickpockets. Many thoughtful features: 1-inch-wide nylon webbing, heavy-duty zipper, and a 1-inch high-test quick-release buckle. No more fumbling around for the strap or repeated adjustments, this handy plastic buckle opens and closes with a touch, but won't come undone until you want it to. Accommodates traveler's checks, passport, cash, photos. Size 5 x 9 inches. Available in black only. **$8.95**

ORDER FORM

FOR FASTER SERVICE ORDER BY PHONE: (800) 345-5473 · 9 a.m.-5 p.m. PST
(See important ordering information on preceding page)

Name:______________________________ Date:______________

Street:______________________________

City:______________________________

State or Country:______________________ Zip Code:__________

Daytime Phone:______________________________

Quantity	Title	Price

Taxable Total	
Sales Tax (6.25%) for California Residents	
Shipping & Handling	
TOTAL	

Ship to: ☐ address above ☐ other______________________________

____

____

Make checks payable to:
Moon Publications, Inc., 722 Wall Street, Chico, California 95928, U.S.A.
We Accept Visa and MasterCard
To Order: Call in your Visa or MasterCard number, or send a written order with your Visa or MasterCard number and expiration date clearly written.

Card Number: ☐ **Visa** ☐ **MasterCard**

☐☐☐☐ ☐☐☐☐ ☐☐☐☐ ☐☐☐☐

expiration date:______________________________

Exact Name on Card: ☐ same as above

☐ other______________________________

signature______________________________

WHERE TO BUY THIS BOOK

Bookstores and Libraries:
Moon Publications handbooks are sold worldwide. Please write Sales Manager Donna Galassi for a list of wholesalers and distributors in your area that stock our travel handbooks.

Travelers:
We would like to have Moon Publications handbooks available throughout the world. Please ask your bookstore to write or call us for ordering information. If your bookstore will not order our guides for you, please write or call for a free catalog.

MOON PUBLICATIONS, INC.
722 WALL STREET
CHICO, CA 95928 U.S.A.
tel: (800) 345-5473
fax: (916) 345-6751

THE METRIC SYSTEM

Since this book is used by people from all around the world, the metric system is employed throughout. Here are the equivalents:

1 inch	=	2.54 centimeters (cm)
1 foot	=	.304 meters (m)
1 mile	=	1.6093 kilometers (km)
1 km	=	.6214 miles
1 fathom	=	1.8288 m
1 chain	=	20.1168 m
1 furlong	=	201.168
1 acre	=	.4047 hectares (ha)
1 sq km	=	100 ha
1 sq mile	=	59 sq km
1 ounce	=	28.35 grams
1 pound	=	.4536 kilograms (kg)
1 short ton	=	.90718 metric ton
1 short ton	=	2000 pounds
1 long ton	=	1.016 metric tons
1 long ton	=	2240 pounds
1 metric ton	=	1000 kg
1 quart	=	.94635 liters
1 US gallon	=	3.7854 liters
1 Imperial gallon	=	4.5459 liters
1 nautical mile	=	1.852 km

To avoid confusion, all clock times follow the 24-hour airline timetable system, i.e., 0100 is 1:00 a.m., 1300 is 1:00 p.m., 2330 is 11:30 p.m. From noon to midnight, merely add 12 onto regular time to derive airline time.

To compute centigrade temperatures, subtract 32 from Fahrenheit and divide by 1.8. To go the other way, multiply centigrade by 1.8 and add 32.

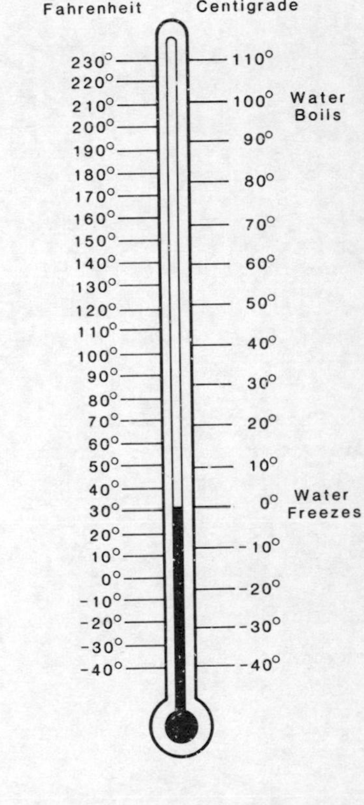

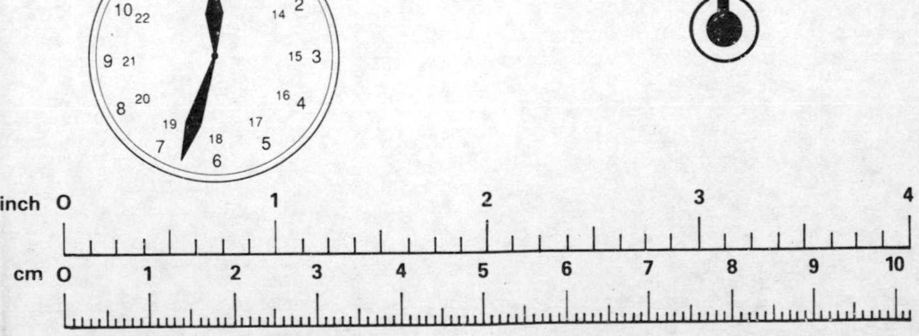